Psychology of Women and Gender

Psychology of Women and Gender

Miriam Liss
UNIVERSITY OF MARY WASHINGTON

Kate Richmond
MUHLENBERG COLLEGE

Mindy J. Erchull
UNIVERSITY OF MARY WASHINGTON

We used a feminist, collaborative process in which all authors contributed equally to this book.

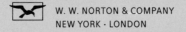
W. W. NORTON & COMPANY
NEW YORK · LONDON

W. W. NORTON & COMPANY has been independent since its founding in 1923, when Wiliam Warder Norton and Mary D. Herter Norton first published lectures delivered at the People's Institute, the adult education division of New York City's Cooper Union. The firm soon expanded its program beyond the Institute, publishing books by celebrated academics from America and abroad. By midcentury, the two major pillars of Norton's publishing program—trade books and college texts—were firmly established. In the 1950s, the Norton family transferred control of the company to its employees, and today—with a staff of four hundred and a comparable number of trade, college, and professional titles published each year—W. W. Norton & Company stands as the largest and oldest publishing house owned wholly by its employees.

Editor: Ken Barton
Project Editor: Linda Feldman
Editorial Assistant: Katie Pak
Manuscript Editor: Alice Vigliani
Managing Editor, College: Marian Johnson
Managing Editor, College Digital Media: Kim Yi
Production Manager: Eric Pier-Hocking
Media Editor: Kaitlin Coats
Associate Media Editor: Tori Reuter
Media Project Editor: Danielle Belfiore
Digital Production: Danielle Lehmann
Marketing Manager: Ashley Sherwood
Book Designer: Lissi Sigillo
Design Director: Rubina Yeh
Photo Editor: Stephanie Romeo
Photo Researcher: Donna Ranieri
Director of College Permissions: Megan Schindel
Permissions Associate: Patricia Wong
Composition: Graphic World
Manufacturing: LSC Crawfordsville

ISBN 978-0-393-66713-4 (pbk.)

W. W. Norton & Company, Inc., 500 Fifth Avenue, New York, N.Y. 10110
W. W. Norton & Company, Ltd., Castle House, 15 Carlisle Street, London W1D 3BS
wwnorton.com
1 2 3 4 5 6 7 8 9 0

To our mothers and grandmothers—thank you for raising us
to be the type of women who would write this book

and to the students—past, present, and future—who inspired us
to take on this project

brief contents

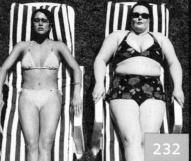
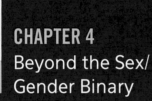

contents

author bios

Miriam Liss, a professor of psychological science at the University of Mary Washington, is a clinical psychologist who has been recognized for both her teaching and her research. She received the State Council for Higher Education for Virginia (SCHEV) Outstanding Faculty Award in 2015. She has published widely in an extensive range of fields within the psychology of women, including feminist identity, the objectification and sexualization of women, the division of labor, and motherhood. She is co-author of *Balancing the Big Stuff: Finding Happiness in Work, Family, and Life*.

Kate Richmond, an associate professor of psychology and the director of women's and gender studies at Muhlenberg College, is a clinical psychologist. She has published widely in the areas of multicultural psychology, men and masculinity, transgender health, feminism, and trauma. She has received multiple awards for excellence in teaching, including the Paul C. Empie Memorial Award for Excellence in Teaching, and has given invited talks both nationally and internationally. In addition to teaching, she maintains a private practice in which she specializes in the treatment of trauma and concerns related to gender.

Mindy J. Erchull, a professor of psychological science at the University of Mary Washington, is a social psychologist and a Fellow of both the American Psychological Association (APA) and the Association for Psychological Science. She has been recognized as an emerging leader for women in psychology by the Committee for Women in Psychology of the APA. She has also been recognized as an outstanding teacher though her receipt of the Mary Roth Walsh Teaching the Psychology of Women Award from the Society for the Psychology of Women. She has published widely under the umbrella of the psychology of women and gender with work addressing feminist identity, the objectification and sexualization of women, division of labor and parenting, and menstruation and other women's health issues.

preface

Some years ago, our affiliation with one another began with pairs of professional connections. Our relationships developed through conversations about overlapping research and teaching interests, and feminist process was often part of our conversations. We recognized that it wasn't always easy to live our feminist ideals in today's fast-paced, goal-directed world, yet we continued to strive for a more relational and equitable process for ourselves and for our students. Those conversations, over time, led to friendships. It was from this place of friendship that we thought hard and deep about the challenges facing the fields we love—psychology and women's and gender studies.

In particular, we found ourselves recounting conversations with both students and colleagues about a need for a contemporary psychology of women and gender textbook. As instructors, we knew our classes were exciting and transformative, yet the available books didn't match the experience in our classes. We were frustrated with the slow pace of revision in a field that is quickly evolving and that centers on current topics and timely social justice issues. Material we felt critical to teach wasn't in the books available to us, so we had to supplement with many outside readings. Our students were frustrated because they felt the books were covering topics related to the experiences of their parents and grandparents rather than their own experiences—their feminisms weren't part of the books. They also expressed frustration with the predominant focus on the experience of straight, White, cisgender, able-bodied, economically privileged women. None of us planned to be textbook authors, but the three of us realized that together we could create something bigger than any one of us could do on our own. We believed that our friendships with one another and our feminist process could result in an up-to-date book that would fill a gap in the field.

We started our process with several distinctive goals. One important shift in this field has been a move toward intersectionality in both research and theory, and it was important to us that our book reflect an intersectional perspective. This was not an easy task, since so much of the field is built on theory and research that takes a singular, less dynamic approach. Much of the published data disproportionately come from White, cisgender, heterosexual, able-bodied, well-educated, financially privileged researchers and participants. The truth is that our field has been largely shaped by the experiences of privileged women, so a goal of ours was to help students understand how systems of power influence the type of science that gets created on the basis of such data. We explicitly drew attention to these inequities and asked students to grapple with the challenges of applying an intersectional approach when conducting research, interpreting others' research, and participating in activism. The field still has work to do in this domain, and we hope our book motivates students to think in more intersectional and inclusive ways. We sought to present the important contributions of feminist research while also providing guidance to allow students to interrogate the hidden, biased assumptions in that research—and in all types of research, for that matter. We wanted students to continually revisit intersectionality and to learn that gender never operates in isolation, so we integrated questions and activities to help students identify the limitations of a one-dimensional approach to studying the psychology of women and gender. In some ways, this meant that gender was not at the center of every topic discussed, since we assumed that social identities mutually shape one another. We also worked to integrate the experiences of marginalized women through every section. When there were gaps in the research, we drew attention to them.

It was also very important to us that our book be interdisciplinary but grounded in science and feminist theory. We've integrated into the text recent research findings from economics, political science, demography, medicine, sociology, and anthropology while still highlighting psychological science as the core of this field. Moreover, it was important to us that we not make a lot of assumptions about student experience and/or knowledge. We found that many other texts assumed students had a background in women's and gender studies, psychological research, or both. However, the nature of the field of psychology of women and gender means that classes are often interdisciplinary and cross-listed. Students come to these courses with varied backgrounds, which can cause experiences of confusion in the first weeks. Given this, in the first few chapters, we explain the scientific method, the diversity of feminism, the need to complicate the way we think about sex and gender, and the importance of considering power and privilege. We also didn't assume that students would enter the class with similar levels of knowledge about women's sexual and reproductive health, so we integrated some foundational coverage into relevant chapters.

We also sought to write a textbook that would reflect both the latest research and the current issues directly affecting the lives of girls and women today. Because of this, our book covers a variety of topics that receive limited or no coverage in other textbooks in this field. These include (but are not limited to):

- comprehensive coverage of objectification theory and self-sexualization
- extensive coverage of the experience of transgender and non-binary individuals, including psychological, economic, and legal challenges
- the Me Too movement

- the pressures of intensive parenting
- the glass cliff and glass escalator
- female friendships
- the experiences and challenges of women with disabilities
- the psychological consequences of miscarriage and stillbirth
- current controversies about sexual consent
- the role of men as allies in the feminist movement.

Unique Features

Another important aspect was to ensure that students understand how it's possible to approach many key topics in several different ways. Research is often contradictory, or findings differ according to which aspects of social identity are considered. Depending on the perspective one takes, something might seem either beneficial or problematic. This reflects the nature of feminism and science—everyone doesn't agree.

While these underlying tensions are integrated throughout the text, we also highlight one example in each chapter in an **Empowering or Oppressing?** feature. For example, in one chapter we explore sex work and question whether it can be empowering for women or if it's oppressing. In another, we ask students to consider the research about single-sex education and whether these types of educational settings are empowering or oppressing for girls and women. There's no single answer in these features; these are complex, multi-faceted topics with data that aren't clear cut, so the issues are actively debated. The features can serve as critical thinking exercises for students, but they could also be used to prompt in-class discussion, inspire journal entries or reaction papers, or serve as topics for formal debate. Our goal was for students to understand that there's not a single "truth" being presented in this book. Rather, we sought to highlight the research that's been done, the research that's needed, and the many open questions that are still ripe for exploration.

We also placed priority on incorporating features to encourage critical thinking, so that students can practice how to effectively evaluate, research, and develop strategies for addressing complicated problems. We begin each chapter with one or more real-world examples of events or individuals connected to the material covered in that chapter, and we integrate more contemporary examples throughout the text. Sometimes these examples are worked into the body of the chapters, but at other times they're highlighted in **Spotlight On** features. For example, we shine a spotlight on topics such as the Me Too movement, cyberbullying, and pinkwashing. We also have **Your Turn** and **Try It for Yourself** features in every chapter. In these, students are asked to further reflect on an issue raised in the chapter. They're also often asked to talk to others or engage in an activity as part of exploring the given topic. Further questions appear at the end of each chapter in a **Think About It** section. Like the Empowering or Oppressing? features, these features can also serve as prompts for discussion, journaling, reflection papers, and the like. Each chapter ends with a list of online resources that students can visit to learn more about topics covered in the chapter and to spark further exploration.

We recognize that classes in the psychology of women and gender take many forms, vary in size, and are taught at the 200, 300, and 400 level. Given this diversity, we sought to use a readable style that would be approachable for a wide array of students and varying class formats. For students in more traditional, lecture-based classes with assessment done using tests, we integrated preliminary **SQ3R prompts** in the form of questions at the start of sections within the chapters. At the start of the book, we included an Introduction that seeks to help students understand this study method and the features found throughout the book. Each chapter contains bolded **key terms** that draw additional attention to key ideas and theories, and stand-alone definitions of each key term are included in a **glossary**. Each chapter also ends with bulleted **chapter summaries** to help students assess their degree of understanding.

This book has truly been a labor of love for us. We set out to create the text we wanted to teach with and our students wanted to read. It became so much more. It led us to learn about both the history of the field and contemporary areas of focus. It helped us reflect on our own teaching and why we made the choices we did. It also strengthened our relationships with one another—an important feminist process that is never lost on us.

Instructor Support

As teachers, we know how important support materials can be when choosing a text—particularly when it involves leaving a familiar text to adopt a new one. Therefore, we want to highlight the ancillary materials available for this text. Depending on the nature of your class and teaching style, different resources are likely of interest to you. In fact, the package of available resources offers something for everyone. For example, teachers of large lecture courses may be particularly interested in the test bank, lecture slides, and in-class activities. Those who teach writing-intensive, discussion-based courses may also be interested in the in-class activities as well as the discussion topics. Teachers of asynchronous online courses may be interested in discussion topics and lecture and art slides.

- A **test bank** offers over 1,000 multiple-choice and short-answer questions.

- There are **PowerPoint slides** that can be used for or adapted for use in lectures. These provide an overview of the major sections of each chapter and incorporate key art and figures from the text. They also include active learning elements; some of these are drawn from those included in the text, and others are from the supplementary activities and discussion topics that are also available for instructors.
- Easily downloadable resources include **lecture slides, sample syllabi, discussion topics**, and **in-class activities**. Some of these resources are pulled from those embedded throughout the chapters. Others were authored specifically for this guide. Some of these activities integrate material from the *Psychology's Feminist Voices* website (https://www.feministvoices.com/). The sample syllabi offer examples for larger lecture-based classes, smaller discussion-based classes, and online courses; all the examples include a schedule and sample assignments that work with the structure of this text.
- Separate **art slides** are also available. These include all images and tables from the text so you can integrate them into your own course materials as desired.
- Given concerns about cost and accessibility, many students and instructors prefer digital texts. Therefore, this book can also be accessed as an **ebook**. The ebook provides students access to the entire book and allows them to search, highlight, bookmark, and take notes while reading.

Acknowledgements

In publication, we often talk about a "first author" who holds primary responsibility for the project and the product it generates. Someone's name had to come first, but there is no first author for this book—it has been a true collaboration. We each brought training and research expertise from different areas to this project. Our book is strong, in large part, because of our collaboration. Chapters are not a product of one author's work with small edits suggested by the other co-authors. Rather, we each wrote material for every chapter and provided guidance, feedback, and editing at all stages. This enabled us to bring our unique expertise and to add depth to our coverage. As a result, the writing and editing process may have taken longer than would have been the case with "primary" authors of distinct sections, but we believe our book couldn't have existed without this fully integrated collaboration on all aspects of the project, and none of us could have accomplished this without the others.

This book would also not exist without the support of the talented and dedicated staff at Norton. We'd like to thank our editor, Ken Barton, for his belief in this book from the time he first read our book proposal. His excitement about the project was a large part of why we decided to publish with Norton, and his enthusiasm hasn't waned through the sometimes challenging process of arriving at a final book. We'd also like to thank his editorial assistants, Eve Sanoussi and Katie Pak, for helping us track the myriad moving pieces involved in all phases of this project; as well as Victoria Reuter, for her vision for and management of the instructor support materials. We also need to acknowledge the many other people at Norton who have worked to bring this book and its support materials to fruition. This project wouldn't have been possible without the contributions of Katilin Coats, Linda Feldman, Marian Johnson, Eric Pier-Hocking, Donna Ranieri, Stephanie Romeo, Megan Schindel, Ashley Sherwood, Lissi Sigillo, Allison Nicole Smith, Scott Sugarman, Patricia Wong, Alex Trivilino, Rubina Yeh, and Kim Yi. Last, but certainly not least, we want to offer sincere and deep gratitude to our developmental editor, Alice Vigliani. Alice worked tirelessly to help us solidify our collective voice while making the text as strong as possible. She helped us work to achieve our vision and became our cheerleader when we felt overwhelmed. She made it clear that she believed in this book, and that helped us reignite our passion when exhaustion took over in the final phases of the marathon that drafting this book has been.

This book would also not exist without the support and encouragement of many other people. When we began thinking about writing a textbook, Joan Chrisler was the first person we reached out to. She encouraged us to take on this project, helped us understand what was involved in proposing a book to publishers, and provided feedback about our initial book proposal. Her support and feminist mentorship have been invaluable. Similarly, the encouragement provided by Chris Kilmartin and Ronald Levant helped us feel more confident in taking on a project of this magnitude while balancing heavy teaching loads. In particular, Chris's own experience as a textbook author helped us understand important concerns around securing permissions, art budgets, and indexing. Isis Settles is yet another person who provided support and encouragement throughout the writing of this book. Her excitement about the text fed our own, and her willingness to provide feedback, both formal and informal, helped us arrive at a more inclusive final product. We'd also like to thank Janine Chi, Mel Ferrara, Abbie Goldberg, Bill Keller, Lizbeth Kim, Heather MacArthur, A. Lanethea Mathews-Schultz, Kaitlin McCormick-Huhn, Brian Mello, Kenneth Michniewicz, Jefferson Pooley, Jeff Rudski, Mark Sciutto, Stephanie Shields, Stephanie Sinno, Susan Stryker, Anne Tamar-Mattis, Leonore Tiefer, Sari van Anders, and Connie Wolfe for sharing their expertise with us. Thank you also to Laura Brown and Alicia Hupprich for providing their personal accounts for inclusion in the book.

We must also acknowledge the support of our schools—the University of Mary Washington and Muhlenberg College. We each, at various points during the writing of this book, received support in the form of funding and course releases through grant, fellowship, and sabbatical programs. Our schools' belief in our ability to succeed with a project of this magnitude meant a great deal.

We are also endlessly thankful for the understanding and support we received from our departmental colleagues. Sometimes this took the form of leaving us alone when we shut our doors to write, at other times it involved sharing their expertise with us, and at still other times it involved reminding us about how far we had come and how close the finish line was. We also benefited from the assistance of many student research assistants throughout the course of this project, and would like to thank each of them for their contributions:

Christine Abraham	Elizabeth Katriel
Christina Amaral	Stephanie King
Madeline Beasley	Sarah Merlo
Megan Blosser	Michelle Milligan
Courtney Bramen	Laura Morris
Marissa Cassens	Sabina Muccigrosso
Angela Elcan	Emma Olson
Rachel Gallagher	Joann Shehani Peiris
Mattie Goad	Ashlyn Runk
Jenna Gray	Grace Sterling
Kristine Harner	Lauren Tolsen
Katherine Hatton	Alexis Zollo

We also recognize that this book wouldn't be as strong as it is without the important feedback received from reviewers. Given this, we want to acknowledge the following people for their contributions:

Veanne Anderson, *Indiana State University*
Germine Awad, *University of Texas, Austin*
Stacey-Ann Baugh, *Trinity Washington University*
Theresa Botts, *Eastern Kentucky University*
Thomas Bradbury, *UCLA*
Britney Brinkman, *Chatham University*
Adrienne Carter-Sowell, *Texas A&M University*
Joan Chrisler, *Connecticut College*
Malissa Clark, *University of Georgia*
Lilia Cortina, *University of Michigan*
Lisa Diamond, *University of Utah*
Renee Engeln, *Northwestern University*
Oliva Espin, *San Diego State University*

Breanne Fahs, *Arizona State University*

Cordelia Fine, *University of Melbourne*

Pamela Flint, *University of North Texas*

Linda Gallahan, *Portland State University*

Linda Hoke-Sinex, *Indiana State University*

Carol R. Huckaby, *Albertus Magnus College*

Daphna Joel, *Tel-Aviv University*

Benjamin Karney, *UCLA*

Jennifer Katz, *SUNY Geneseo*

Sabra Katz-Wise, *Harvard University*

Nicole Knickmeyer, *Austin Peay State University*

Shenan Kroupa, *Purdue University, Indianapolis*

Elizabeth Kudadjie-Gyamfi, *Long Island University*

Emily Leskinen, *Carthage College*

Phoebe Lin, *Framingham State University*

Kathi Miner, *Texas A&M University*

Katharine Oh, *Cleveland State University*

Carmen Poulin, *University of New Brunswick*

Laura Ramsey, *Bridgewater State University*

Desdamona Rios, *University of Houston, Clear Lake*

Lisa Rubin, *The New School*

Wanda Ruffin, *Hood College*

Alex Rutherford, *York University*

Nazish Salahuddin, *University of Maryland*

Rakhshanda Saleem, *University of Massachusetts, Boston*

Isis Settles, *University of Michigan*

Andrew Smiler, *Wake Forest College*

Christine Smith, *University of Wisconsin, Green Bay*

Jonathan Weaver, *Michigan State University*

Grace White, *University of Central Florida*

Catina Williams, *Southwestern Illinois College*

Barbara Winstead, *Old Dominion University*

Finally, while professional support is important, it is often the personal support that makes it possible for us to take on and succeed with challenging tasks. Such is the case for this book.

Miriam Liss:

I would like to start by thanking Mindy and Kate, my co-authors. Working with them has been such a joy, and I am so honored that they included me in their process. I would also like to thank my mother, Barbara Liss, who raised me as a single mother and provided inspiration about what it meant to be a strong feminist woman throughout my life until her death two years ago. Jeffrey Hutterer was like a father to me and also provided encouragement and fascinating psychological discussions throughout my childhood. I would also like to thank my early feminist mentors—particularly my undergraduate mentor and role model, Jill Morawski. Thanks also to my graduate mentors, Deborah Fein and Marianne Barton, who never failed to believe in and encourage me—even when my areas of interest diverged from theirs. I also want to acknowledge and thank Mary Crawford, who reignited my passion for feminist research and profoundly influenced the course of my graduate career.

I send much love and thanks to my husband, Julian Kilmartin. He has supported me, encouraged me, and cooked me delicious dinners. I cannot count the number of times he has taken on the brunt of the parenting so that I could work on this book—often, late into the night. To my sister-in-law Deirdre Kilmartin—thank you for your encouragement, reviews of early chapter drafts, great discussions about feminism, and unwavering support throughout this entire process. Finally, to my children, Daniel and Emily—I love you both so much, and I look forward to years of engaging conversations about the issues in this book as you grow and mature.

Kate Richmond:

krichmond@muhlenberg.edu

Thank you to my psychology of women teachers, Kathy Harring, Patrice DiQuinzio, and Lenore Walker, who introduced me to this field and nurtured my love for feminist psychology. Thank you also to Ronald Levant, who has been the most prevailing influence on my career and development as a feminist scholar, and to Alan Tjeltveit, who nurtured my intellectual skills early in my academic career. Thank you to Laura Edelman for believing in and supporting my career at Muhlenberg College. To Mindy and Miriam, I have grown so much through our friendship and collaboration. I love how our personalities, intellect, and creative tendencies mesh so well. Thank you to the members of the SCI-Graterford Think Tank for advancing my knowledge on progressive pedagogies. I'd also like to thank Brenda Larimer for her administrative support, Sherri Young for organizing writing boot camps, and Jen Jarson and Jessica Denke for sharing their expertise in library science. Thank you to Feine Coffee for keeping me caffeinated and providing the perfect venue to write.

To my colleague and friend Linda Bips, who started this book journey with me but did not see it finish, your legacy and wisdom live on through this work. Thank you to my sisters, Amy Tufano, Becky Duffy, and Julie Richmond, whom I lean on every day and whose friendship shows me the real power of sisterhood. Thank you to my dad, Dan Richmond, who taught me how to be a community leader and fostered my passion for social justice. Thank you to my mom, Maryjane Richmond, who spent countless hours at our kitchen table teaching me how to write and instilling in me a love of learning. Mom, you are my greatest role model. Thank you also to my daughter, Jessica Jara, who teaches me to live in the moment and to confront every challenge, even the ones mentioned in this book, with resiliency and fierceness. And, finally, to my husband, Steve Jara—you are the foundation for which all of this is possible. Your unwavering love gives me courage and confidence. In every way, I am grateful for you. Green Eggs and Ham.

Mindy Erchull:
merchull@umw.edu

I want to offer a personal thanks to Joan Chrisler. You've been my advisor and mentor since before classes began during my first year of college. You introduced me to the field of psychology of women, and this book is possible because of all you taught me about the field, about writing, and about collaboration. I'd also like to thank my graduate mentor, Leona Aiken, for helping me forge my own path toward teaching when others sought to guide me in a different direction, and Nancy Russo for furthering my feminist and multicultural training. Thanks also to Sheila Heffernon for teaching me to have confidence in my abilities, that the risks were worth it, and that hard work and dedication make a difference. I also want to thank both Kate and Miriam. We have created a collaboration that is truly more than the sum of its parts. You are true friends, and I look forward to collaborating with both of you for many years to come.

Of course, none of this would have been possible without the tremendous support I've received throughout my life from my mother, Wilma Erchull. You made tremendous sacrifices so that I could have a top-notch education, and your support and encouragement allowed me to fully benefit from those opportunities. You also allowed me to become engaged in social justice work at a young age—after all, how many parents would sign a permission slip so their 15-year-old daughter could go march on Washington? Thank you for having faith in me and for respecting my need to speak up and speak out. My partner, Dave Marciniak, has also been a key source of support and encouragement throughout this process. You made it possible for me to take writing retreats and spend weekends revising drafts and evenings reading page proofs. Your life had to change so that I could take on this project. Thank you for making sure I had clean clothes to wear and food to eat—I truly don't know where I'd be without you.

Psychology of Women and Gender

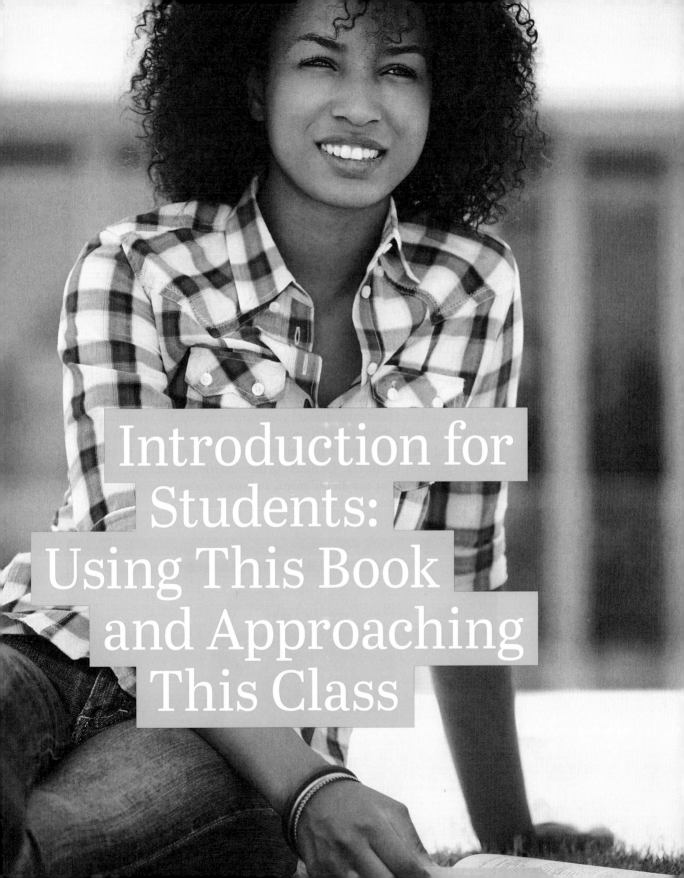

Introduction for Students: Using This Book and Approaching This Class

When we decided to write this textbook, we were excited! From our years of studying and teaching Psychology of Women and Gender, we know that it's not a typical class. Some students tell us that the content is transformative. It uncovers many social realities that often are not discussed, like body shame and menstruation, and can provide direction about ways to address everyday challenges such as confronting sexism and racism.

As you'll see throughout the semester, the field of psychology of women is evolving quickly, and no matter what your gender identity is, there are many opportunities for you to add to and challenge existing ways of thinking. There's an urgent need to address the psychological concerns of girls and women as well as a need for sophisticated ideas and people committed to pursuing research to promote well-being. This course will provide you with tools to identify, understand, and address those needs, even when faced with conflict and tension.

Unique Aspects of This Course

Before we get started, here are some tips that might be useful as you read this book and engage with some of the politically or emotionally charged material that may challenge (and even change) your current beliefs. We recommend that you read through the Table of Contents and your instructor's syllabus first, considering what topics might stir emotion in you—and keeping in mind that this will probably be the case for others in the class too. By anticipating charged material, you won't be caught off guard, and you can also come up with strategies to deal with reading and discussing controversial topics.

It's helpful to think about your goals for this course before you begin it. There's potential for you to broaden your current perspectives if you stay open to introspection, reflection, and critical thinking. A helpful tip is to use the mantra "seek to understand." Although it can be difficult to do, over time we've learned that suspending initial judgment first can leave room for intellectual growth and curiosity. You might try asking yourself questions like these: "What's interesting about this topic?" "What are some features about it that I want to know more about?" and "Under what conditions, and for whom, might this topic be most relevant?"

It will help to check in with your emotions too. When you begin reading, writing, and discussing the material, you might ask: "Am I feeling excited, guilty, or angry? Do I feel attacked or threatened?" Being aware of your emotions lets you delve deeper into your thinking about a topic. After all, emotions communicate important information—they let you know when you've hit a nerve that may need some attention. When emotions are high, it's helpful to stop and reflect on them a bit more—for example: "What thoughts lead me to feel this strongly?" and/or "What are my assumptions and belief systems, and how does this material conflict with them?" During this process, it will help to be kind and compassionate toward yourself because this type of learning can be emotionally draining. You can freewrite about the topic or, if you feel ready, talk to close friends or classmates. Doing this allows you to work through your thoughts and reactions to the material with a supportive person. Educational researchers believe that learning occurs when students feel emotionally connected to the material (Immordino-Yang, 2016), so emotions are an important step in learning—especially in a course like this one.

Once you're immersed in this class, you may be motivated to apply the information you're learning to your own life. In each chapter, you'll find two types of boxes that will help you do just that: *Your Turn* and *Try It for Yourself*. In the *Your Turn* boxes, we ask you to reflect on content and connect it to your own experiences and perspectives. In the *Try It for Yourself* boxes, in addition to asking you to reflect, we ask you to do an activity related to the topic. This will help you reflect critically on the course material while giving you practice in applying the research and theory from the book to your personal experience.

You may also want to share this information with others or take a stand on a particular issue. Although we'll address this topic in Chapter 14, we hope you'll use the theories and research in this book to spark conversations with friends and family members throughout the semester. Any of the material in the chapters may spark these conversations, but the *Spotlight On* boxes included throughout the book may be particularly likely to inspire them. In these features, we delve a bit more deeply into one topic or event than we're typically able to do in the main chapter text. However, as we've mentioned, the material in this course can be controversial, so we advise the "plant a seed" approach. In other words, it's a good strategy to first introduce a new theory or research study and then give the person some time to think about it before getting into a full discussion. You may find that you'll need to revisit the topic again as a way to fully understand different (and often conflicting) perspectives.

TABLE 1 The SQ3R Study Method

Step	Description
Survey (or **S**can)	Look through the chapter, focusing on headings, subheadings, and bold words. Get a big-picture view of the chapter.
Question	After the initial survey, develop questions for each section and sub-section to help guide your reading. These can later serve as study prompts.
Read	Try to answer your questions as you read, and add new questions (and the answers to them) as they develop from your reading. As you read, take notes in your own words, both as answers to your questions and as stand-alone pieces of information you'll want to review later.
Recite (or **R**etrieve)	Test your knowledge by asking yourself the questions you developed and trying to give thorough answers without looking at your notes or the book. If you identify material you can't recite, work back through the first three steps for that content in order to become more familiar with it.
Review	Review your notes each time you finish a section as well as at the end of a chapter to make sure you feel your answers (and other notes) are thorough and clear. Continue to review by returning to the Recite step periodically as you move into new material so you don't lose track of what you've already covered.

The SQ3R Method

We've tried to structure this book in an accessible way and have integrated features into each chapter that will help you connect with the material, identify key ideas, assess your understanding, and formulate new ideas. By actively working with this book on a regular basis and reviewing material more than once, you'll be in the best position to really comprehend, retain, and, ultimately, apply the information in productive ways (Taraban, Rynearson, & Kerr, 2000).

We've organized the chapters with a study system called the *SQ3R method*. SQ3R stands for Survey, Question, Read, Recite, Review (see Table 1; Artis, 2008; Robinson, 1941). Research shows that this method helps students better understand course material and retain it for a longer period (Carlston, 2011; McDaniel, Howard, & Einstein, 2009). It may seem to take a lot of time and effort when you start to use this method, but before long it will feel automatic. In the long run, it can save you time (and stress).

Survey

As we mentioned before, it's helpful to review certain material before you begin reading. This may seem counterintuitive, but it does help to survey or scan in order to get a big-picture view. One way to start is by looking at headings. Within each chapter, headings in larger type indicate the start of distinct main sections, and headings in smaller type indicate sub-sections. In addition to using these headings in the body of each chapter, we've listed the main headings in outline format at the start of the chapter. This is handy for making an initial survey before you flip through the chapter to look at the headings in the context of images, boxes, and other material. Each chapter also includes bold key terms. Some of these may be new to you, so looking at them during your survey can help you become familiar with them. Once you understand the organization, you can make informed choices about how to break the chapter into manageable chunks to work through in more detail.

Question

As you survey each chapter, it's a good idea to write down your own questions for each section or sub-section. For example, when you see the heading *The SQ3R Method* in this introduction, you might ask: "What's the SQ3R method? What do those letters stand for? How can I use this method?" To get you started, we provide overarching questions for major sections of each chapter underneath the headings to serve as a starting point for thinking about that chunk of material. In order to maximize your learning, we recommend that you develop your own sub-questions that will help you explore, and eventually review, the material in greater detail.

Initially, your questions can be fact-based ones for which you'll find answers in the text. A next step will be to ask how what you're learning connects with your own life and the lives of the people you know. As we discussed earlier, you'll more readily remember information when you connect ideas to things that are personally meaningful for and relevant to you (Symons & Johnson, 1997). For example, when reading about how women are perceived as leaders, you might try asking yourself why men are more frequently associated with leadership than women. In addition to this fact-based question, you might also ask yourself whether you've ever been particularly judgmental about a woman in a leadership role. It may even help to start with some questions that relate to your own experiences—for example, "Why do many of my female friends focus on the way they look?" or "How do my professional goals connect with my gender?" This type of questioning is good for identifying topics that might be emotionally charged. It also keeps you actively engaged and helps you begin to apply the course material to your own life.

Read

This is probably the portion of the SQ3R method you're most familiar with, but the trick is to stay involved as you read. It will help to keep in mind the questions you jotted down in the Q step and try to answer them. If you come up with new questions as you read, we suggest adding them to the list and trying to answer those as well. Also, it's important to read everything—even figure captions and boxes, because they provide key details. Equally important is taking notes as you read. Some of your notes will probably be in the form of answers to your questions, but others may be specific facts or terms that strike you as important or that you'll want to review later. Notes are most effective if you put things in your own words rather than just transcribing what we've written.

As you read, you'll find that we continue to ask questions to get you to think deeply about the material. For example, in the middle of a section, we may ask about your own experiences with a topic. Also, many of the boxes end with questions. These are all designed to get you thinking about the material at a deeper level. Sometimes the questions reflect a point of tension within the field—a place where researchers and/or theorists don't all agree. Most of these questions don't have a single correct answer. For example, in each chapter we ask you to consider whether something—such as single-sex education, participating in sex work, or modern Disney princesses—is empowering or oppressing for girls and women. Scholars have different opinions on these issues, and we present arguments from multiple perspectives. Our goal for these *Empowering or Oppressing* boxes is not for you to choose a definitive answer but, rather, to reflect on what you believe and why—in other words, to focus on forming your own opinion and being able to justify it with sound data.

As you'll soon learn, psychologists study gender in various ways. Therefore, we hope you'll flex your intellectual muscles and think critically about the content you read in this book. This will involve considering the purpose of particular points, their relevance to the field, and any limitations or biases. In what ways might you expand or refine an idea or topic? Is there enough evidence for a particular idea, or is additional research needed? Can you connect ideas from one topic area to another topic area? Is there enough information to evaluate claims that you see in the text? Thinking critically will help you produce new ideas and design original strategies to address complex questions—not only those that come up in this book and course, but also those that arise elsewhere in your life.

Recite

The second R stands for "recite," but it can also stand for "retrieve," because it's about testing your knowledge. You might think this is something you only do after you've finished reading—maybe even just in the lead-up to a test. While it's a good idea to do it at these times, it's also helpful to try to retrieve information from your memory as you read. Let's say you asked yourself the question "What does SQ3R stand for?" and, in reading this section, were able to answer it: survey, question, read, recite, review. Once you have that answer, you could take a minute to ask the question again and then tell yourself the answer—but without looking at the book or your notes. If you're alone, you might recite the question and answer out loud. If you're not, doing it in your head will work just as well. Then it's important to write down the answer in your own words.

A key component of this strategy is that it makes you retrieve the information from your memory rather than copying it from the book. Doing this will help you figure out where you might still be confused or have missing information. If you can't put it in your own words clearly, you'll know there's still a bit more work to do before you can truly answer your question.

The questions embedded in the text don't just help you engage with the material; they also help during the Recite phase. For example, when we ask you to reflect on your own beliefs, instead of simply stating them it's a good idea to try to connect them to the research and theories we've presented in that section. Making this connection will involve thinking about *why* you hold that particular belief and, at the same time, why others might have different beliefs and what evidence supports their points of view. This is one more way to assess your understanding of material as you work through the text. If you have trouble answering these questions in ways that integrate material from the course, then it probably would be a good idea to spend more time on that section.

There's also a list of key terms at the end of every chapter. We want you to be able to describe them in your own words after you finish the chapter without looking again at the text, the Glossary, or your notes. If you find you need to use these sources as a reference, this helps you identify where to do more review.

In addition to traditional ways of reciting this material, talking about it with others in informal settings can be helpful. For example, students have told us they often talk about the content of their Psychology of Women and Gender course outside of the classroom, with friends and family members. We encourage you to do the same because it will also help you recite the information in your own words. Sharing information with others not only helps you study but also provides an opportunity to clarify other people's possible misperceptions by mentioning specific research findings.

Review

The final step in the SQ3R method is to review—each time you reach the end of a section, as well as the end of a chapter. As you look over your questions and your answers, if anything is unclear, this is a good time to go back and flesh that out, add information to your notes, and so on. If you feel there's a key topic covered that isn't reflected in your questions and answers, adding in a new question will help you to cover the material more comprehensively. Much of the reviewing step will be based on your own notes, but you can also use the questions embedded throughout each chapter. There's also a bulleted summary of key ideas at the end of each chapter, organized by main section headings. Although the bullet points are useful for organizing your studying, they can't serve as your only source for review because they aren't comprehensive. Nevertheless, if we've highlighted a key idea and it doesn't show up in your notes or get much attention in them, this indicates an area of the chapter that you would benefit from reviewing.

You'll then continue to review material over time as you practice testing yourself (Reciting) to see what you're able to retrieve. Writing questions on one side of an index card and answers on the other is an easy way to do this because it allows you to check how well you were able to retrieve that information. This method lets you test yourself along the way to (a) see what you know and identify what you need to spend more time on, and (b) continue interacting with the material even if you're also working through another chapter. Testing yourself on each chapter is one of the best ways to make sure that you've retained the material being taught.

Things to Keep in Mind

The key to the SQ3R method is being actively involved while you're reading and learning. This means that it's best to work with the material over time, in small chunks, and return to it repeatedly. Research shows that people more readily remember things with spaced studying, even though they may think they do better when studying everything at one time (Kornell & Bjork, 2008). In other words, if you read three chapters the weekend before a test, there will probably be a lot you won't remember when you sit down for the test and even more you won't remember the week after the test. Instead, interacting with small chunks of material on a regular basis will strengthen your memory for the material while also deepening your understanding of it.

Rather than binge-reading lots of material at one time or studying that material just in the few days before a test, it's a good idea to set some time aside every day, or every other day if that works better for you, to work on a subset of a chapter using the SQ3R method. After you work through the section that's new to you, it helps to spend some time reviewing the material you covered on prior days to assess your understanding and identify areas of the text you might need to revisit. If you find it hard to retrieve the answers to questions, that's a sign to revisit that material and work through the SQ3R steps with it again to better cement your understanding.

In general, people tend to overestimate what they actually know (Callender, Franco-Watkins, & Roberts, 2016; Dunlosky & Rawson, 2012). We all assume we'll remember most of what we read in textbooks and hear in class. But in reality, we often remember far less than we think we will. The best strategy to avoid this pitfall is by working with the material multiple times over an extended period in an actively engaged way. This will help you more thoroughly process the course content and will improve your ability to recall it from memory later.

Conclusion

This book covers content that affects everyone, regardless of gender identification. Our goal is not to have you agree with any particular idea or perspective. Rather, we want you to use research and critical thinking to find your unique voice. This material came alive for us when we first studied it, and we wish the same for you. After the semester is over and final grades are turned in, it's not uncommon for students to continue to think about the ideas raised in this class. The issues we discuss will continue to be important in your life as you graduate, plan or continue a career, develop relationships, possibly have children, and grow old. We see this course as only the beginning of a lifetime of thinking about issues facing women and girls—and, ultimately, all of society.

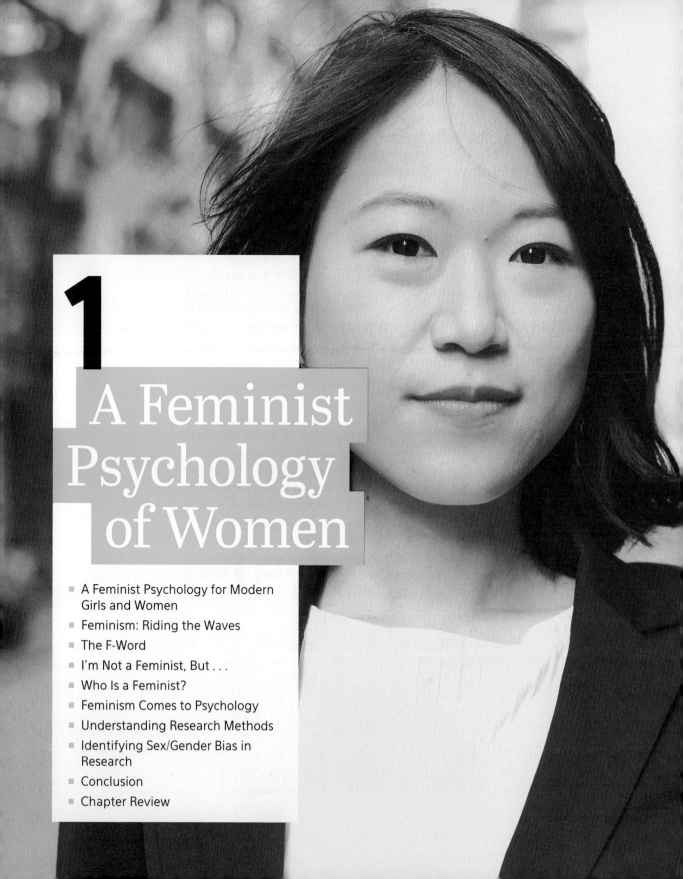

1

A Feminist Psychology of Women

EVERY YEAR, the Super Bowl draws one of the largest audiences of any event in the world. A little over half of the 100 million people who watch actually prefer the commercials to the football game (Russo, 2015). In many ways, the Super Bowl ads in 2015 should have been considered a victory for girls and women. Commercials that typically would showcase motherhood actually featured fathers doing housework and taking care of children. Female comedians were hilarious in ads that normally would spotlight men. One Proctor & Gamble commercial—which didn't even mention the Always menstrual products it was selling—focused on girls and sports. Female and male adults and a young boy were asked to run, throw, and fight "like a girl." In response, each person enacted a similar bouncy motion. The message was clear: to them, running like a girl was weak—almost silly. However, when pre-adolescent girls were asked the same question, they responded differently because they were simply being asked to run, throw, and fight as they normally would. They ran hard and fast, and they threw a ball with their full bodies. The screen then displayed this statement: "A girl's confidence plummets during puberty." The commercial ended with a woman explaining that young girls shouldn't listen when they're put down for doing something "like a girl." The last screenshot directed viewers to "rewrite the rules."

KEEP PLAYING #LIKEAGIRL

Rewrite the Rules
always

The "Like a Girl" advertising campaign encouraged girls to "rewrite the rules." What does it mean to "rewrite the rules," and who has the power to do this?

Almost immediately, social media exploded. Women posted the Always commercial on Facebook, and the #likeagirl hashtag began trending on Twitter, surging YouTube viewership to over 80 million worldwide (Vagianos, 2015). Salon.com declared it "positively feminist" (Williams, 2015, para. 1), and *Huffington Post* congratulated Proctor & Gamble for being "groundbreaking" and "inspiring" (Berman, 2015, para. 1). Certainly, the messaging appeared to be positive, but was the ad truly a victory for girls and women?

This commercial brought up many complicated issues that aren't easy to resolve. On a positive note, it acknowledged that unfair societal beliefs and expectations probably contribute to decreased self-esteem among girls during adolescence. However, the message about how viewers could address this was too simplistic. According to the commercial, girls should ignore sexist messages and "rewrite the rules" to maintain their self-esteem. But what does it mean to "rewrite the rules," and who has the power to do this? Further, why should the burden of societal change fall on the shoulders of pre-adolescent girls?

The commercial didn't offer realistic solutions. Although viewers might have felt good at the end of it, the message didn't help them take steps toward social change. The phenomenon in advertising that generates a strong emotional response—one that *feels* empowering—but that doesn't offer solutions has been called empowertising (Zeisler, 2014). In this case, although the ad took a positive step to address adolescent female athletes (and the biased expectations they face), it probably didn't create widespread change. For example, it didn't call for changing policies on sex segregation in sports. It also didn't question why female professional athletes are paid less than their male counterparts. But the ad did succeed in raising an issue—and it's one that forms one of the bases of this textbook about the psychology of women and gender: In society today, how can girls and women deal with many unequitable social realities that might contribute to their low confidence and decreased psychological well-being?

This chapter will introduce you to the field of psychology of women and to feminism. We begin by identifying several contemporary issues related to girls and women, and then we explore the history of feminism and several types of feminism. Next, we focus on what it means to consider oneself a feminist and the psychological and social implications of identifying as a feminist. Then, we explain how feminism has influenced the field of psychology. Finally, we describe the research process and give you tools for evaluating research and identifying how a scientific study can have a hidden bias against girls and women.

A Feminist Psychology for Modern Girls and Women

What is feminist psychology, and why is it important?

Psychology of women is a subfield of psychology that focuses on the lives and experiences of girls and women. It emerged and grew alongside many of the political and social movements connected to feminism (Rutherford & Granek, 2010). Although **feminism** has been defined in many ways, we like author and social activist bell hooks' version: "Simply put, feminism is a movement to end sexism, sexist exploitation, and oppression" (hooks, 2000, p. 26). As we'll soon discuss, there are multiple feminist perspectives, but all feminisms share the goal of ending sex bias and the unequal treatment of girls and women (Enns & Forrest, 2005).

Some psychologists use the term **feminist psychology** to signal when psychological research and theory are explicitly informed by feminism and to distinguish them from more general work about girls and women (Parlee, 1975; Rutherford & Granek, 2010). Feminist psychology argues that psychological research is never value-neutral or objective (Crawford & Kimmel, 1999; Teo, 2015). As a result, feminist psychologists make their theoretical positions explicit so as to create transparency and genuine equity, fairness, and respect among people (Stewart & Dottolo, 2006). Feminist psychologists are also particularly attentive to issues of **oppression**—the ways in which certain people experience degradation because of political, economic, or social realities (e.g., poverty, homelessness, lack of access to health care). Feminist psychologists believe that by addressing oppression, both through research and in the practice of psychology, everyone's well-being will improve.

As you begin to read this book, you'll notice that girls' and women's roles in society are complicated. Within the last few decades, girls and women have made substantial strides in creating more opportunities for themselves. Consider, for example, that in 1970 only 14% of U.S. women graduated from college and only

What comes to mind when you think of feminism—just one single, clear definition? In actuality, there are multiple feminist perspectives, though they all share the goal of ending sex bias and the unequal treatment of girls and women.

38% of U.S. women worked outside the home (Chronicle of Higher Education, 2015; Cohn, Livingston, & Wang, 2014). Compare the statistics from 2010, when 36% of U.S. women graduated from college and 59% worked outside the home (Chronicle of Higher Education, 2015; Cohn et al., 2014). There is even progress in men's involvement. In 2014, during an address to the United Nations, British actress and UN Women's Goodwill Ambassador Emma Watson kick-started the popular #heforshe campaign in which she asked men to join the fight for gender equity and to recognize that gender stereotypes are harmful for men as well as for women. The campaign's popularity clearly indicated that some boys and men are also ready to re-define masculinity in order to create societal change.

We might look at this progress, wipe our brows, and think, "Phew . . . thank goodness discrimination against women is over. The world is finally changing, and girls and women have all they need in order to live productive and happy lives." Well . . . not so fast. While some things have changed for the better, there's still a long way to go. If we aren't careful, this "half-changed world" might cause us to unquestioningly accept some gains without examining *whom* these gains benefit and *if* they actually provide equity (Orenstein, 2000, p. 11). It could also keep us from recognizing some of the harmful, at times even life-threatening, situations that certain girls and women still face. Consider these statistics:

- In the United States, women are the fastest-growing group who are incarcerated (Swavola, Riley, & Subramanian, 2016). They are disproportionately women of color and/or poor, and they are typically survivors of violence. Nearly 80% of women who are incarcerated are mothers, and most are single mothers (Swavola et al., 2016).
- The prevalence of eating disorders has been increasing since 1950 (Hudson, Hiripi, Pope, & Kessler, 2007). In a survey of *Esquire* magazine readers, over half of female respondents age 18 to 25 said they would prefer to be "run over by a truck" than to be fat, and two thirds of these women said they would rather be described as mean or stupid than fat (Carroll, 1994, p. 58; Maine, 2000).
- Transgender women of color are the victims of 61% of all lesbian, gay, bisexual, transgender, and queer (LGBTQ) murders in the United States (Waters, 2017). They are highly vulnerable to hate crimes and more likely than other victims to experience police violence, discrimination, threats, and intimidation.
- In the United States, women are paid 80% of what men are paid (National Women's Law Center, 2017). This pay gap occurs in almost every occupation, increases with age, and is worse for women of color. Single mothers, women of color, and elderly women living alone are especially vulnerable to poverty.

- Every day, 39,000 girls worldwide are forced into child marriage, resulting in early pregnancy, social isolation, disruption of school, and increased risk of domestic violence (UNICEF, 2013).
- The United States is the only industrialized nation in the world that does not require employers to offer paid maternity leave, resulting in 51% of U.S. mothers without any paid leave (Chatterji & Markowitz, 2004). These women are more likely than other new mothers to develop depression, fatigue, and anxiety.
- In 2017, only 19% of representatives in the U.S. Congress were women, and of them, only 32% were women of color (Center for American Women and Politics, n.d.). There was only one representative who was an out lesbian, and only one openly bisexual representative who was a woman.
- In the past half-century, only 38% of the world's nations have had a female head of government for at least one year (Geiger & Kent, 2017). In 2017, eight female leaders were the first in their country: Chile, Estonia, Germany, Liberia, Lithuania, Marshall Islands, Mauritius, and Nepal.

These statistics remind us that the psychological well-being of girls and women is still at risk. In the past, societal bias against women was much more direct. For example, employers were free to ask female job applicants about their marital status and childbearing plans, and women weren't allowed, among other things, to apply for credit or file a sexual harassment lawsuit (Chrisler et al., 2013). Examples like these are usually easy to spot. It's much more difficult to notice subtle incidents. For example, Facebook chief operating officer Sheryl Sandberg has observed that, in the workplace, women are often expected to do low-value tasks such as setting up meetings, serving as note-taker, or planning office parties (Grant & Sandberg, 2015). The cumulative effect can be costly since women spend more time doing mundane tasks that don't typically result in high-profile recognition or financial bonuses within a company. Because such subtle experiences are more common than the obvious ones, a course like Psychology of Women and Gender is even more necessary now than in the past.

This book and course will help you develop critical thinking skills that will allow you to see how gender biases shape women's psychology. Exactly *how* equity can be achieved is a difficult question—one that we'll wrestle with throughout the course. For example, let's consider the word **empowerment**, which refers to the capacity to attain power. It's a buzzword these days, but it isn't always well defined and applied (Archibald & Wilson, 2011). In the feminist view, far too often the idea of empowerment has been manipulated to sell products. Companies selling everything from Barely There push-up bras to Lean Cuisine microwavable meals have featured themes of female empowerment to market their products. However, this consumer-based approach generally doesn't lead to substantial changes in the lives of girls and women. When women hear that they can make strides by wearing fashionable clothing, doing their nails, and eating diet foods, the message may help a company's bottom line, but it doesn't translate into meaningful change for all girls and women. Although some may benefit because they already have adequate purchasing power, many who can't afford the so-called empowering products will be left behind.

The word *empowerment* is also often used to discuss the achievements of individual women, usually those who succeed in predominantly male domains. When the capacity to gain power is only used in this way, it limits the potential for larger-scale change. For example, a woman may feel powerful when she receives a promotion in a predominantly male law firm, or a girl may think she's empowered when she strikes out a male batter during a baseball game. Although these are excellent accomplishments, they're often isolated from the experiences of other women. In other words, some women will succeed in predominantly male domains, but most women will not.

With such a focus on the individual, there is little expectation that the system will change, and this realization places a huge burden on individual girls and women. The saying "the personal is political" was a rallying cry during the women's movement in the 1960s and 1970s (Collins, 2009). It means that the personal lives of girls and women are interconnected with larger social systems. A girl who thinks she's fat and ugly may feel alone with her worries, but her thoughts are driven by countless messages—from peers, parents, the media, and more—that girls should conform to specific ideals of beauty. A mother who struggles to manage her work hours, get dinner on the table, and find appropriate child care may think that these are her problems alone, but they should be understood within a social context in which (a) the availability of child care is inadequate, (b) inflexible work hours are the norm, (c) women are primarily responsible for household management, and (d) women are paid less than men. As these examples show, individual women's struggles are part of a larger social struggle for all women. Therefore, even today what seems personal is actually political.

For this reason, feminist psychologists believe that research focusing on both the individual and the culture in which that individual lives is important (Fine & Roberts, 1999). Power doesn't only exist within an individual; it also exists in relationship with other people and larger social structures. If we don't focus on the entire picture, we risk having a shallow, and ultimately problematic, approach to advancing psychological well-being for all people. Therefore, feminist psychologists are attentive to many different disciplinary perspectives (e.g., history, sociology, political science, religion, economics, etc.) in order to conduct sophisticated research and well-rounded practice.

your turn

Reflect on a time when you felt empowered. Was the feeling based on an individual accomplishment or a collective accomplishment? What does power mean to you? Now ask five other people who differ from you on some dimension (e.g., gender, age, race, ethnic background, sexual orientation). What similarities and differences among people's perspectives do you notice?

Feminism: Riding the Waves

What are the "waves" of the feminist movement, and what characterizes each one?

In order to understand the present, it's important to understand the past. Therefore, we can say that an understanding of the history of the feminist movement is key to understanding feminist psychology today (see the timeline on pp. 20–21). Some scholars view the history of the feminist movement as progressing through a series of waves—or enhanced periods of activism. Others claim that activism is ongoing, flowing more like a river. In the sections below, we'll review the waves of feminism and examine critiques of the wave metaphor.

The First Wave

Historians think that the *first wave* of feminism in the United States formally began in 1848 at the Seneca Falls Convention when over 200 women and 40 men (including the famous Black abolitionist Frederick Douglass) met to create a list of priorities for advancing women's rights (Rampton, 2015). There were many priorities because women had few rights in the 19th century. For example, they didn't have legal authority over their children, and they weren't allowed to own land, keep their wages, or refuse to have sex with their husbands. The top priority, though, was gaining women's right to vote—something that didn't happen until 1920, when the 19th Amendment was passed. At the time, feminist activists thought that winning the right to vote would end the unequal treatment of women in the United States—especially since they were making other legal gains too. For example, they were granted shared guardianship of their children and were allowed to file for divorce. Some even felt that little remained to be done, but in retrospect there was still a significant need for change.

The Second Wave

Winning the right to vote and other legal rights didn't end discrimination against women, so a *second wave* emerged in the 1960s. Second wave feminists were primarily interested in changing the day-to-day lives of women, including creating more equitable access to the paid labor force and re-defining a woman's role as wife and mother (Rampton, 2015). This was also around the time when the civil rights movement began and the sexual revolution was in full swing.

Timeline of Key Events for Feminism in the United States

1848

The Seneca Falls Convention, the first U.S. women's rights convention, is held in New York.

1851

Sojurner Truth gives her famous "Ain't I a Woman" speech in which she critiques the idea that opposition to women's suffrage was grounded in a desire to protect women by highlighting that no one was trying to protect her—a Black woman—from physical or emotional pain.

1920

Ratification of 19th Amendment to the U.S. Constitution gives women the right to vote.

1923

The Equal Rights Amendment (ERA), originally drafted by Alice Paul and Crystal Eastman, is first introduced in Congress.

1925

American Indian suffrage, which grants citizenship to all Native Americans born in the United States, is passed by an act of Congress.

1952

Christine Jorgensen is the first American whose sex reassignment surgery becomes public.

1964

Title VII of the Civil Rights Act is enacted, prohibiting employment discrimination on the basis of race, color, religion, national origin, or sex.

1969

Transgender and gender non-conforming people are some of the first to resist arrest at the Stonewall Inn in New York, an event credited with igniting the modern LGBTQ rights movement.

1972

Title IX is enacted, prohibiting sex discrimination in all aspects of education programs that receive federal support.

1972

The ERA is passed by both houses of Congress, after being re-introduced in 1971, and is submitted to the states for ratification. It has not yet been ratified by 38 states as required to amend the Constitution.

1973

The U.S. Supreme Court decision in *Roe v. Wade* declares it legal for a woman to terminate an early pregnancy.

1974

The Combahee River Collective, a Black feminist lesbian organization that emphasizes the need to understand interlocking aspects of oppression, holds its first meeting.

1978

The Pregnancy Discrimination Act bans employment discrimination against pregnant women.

1990

The Americans with Disabilities Act prohibits discrimination against individuals with disabilities in all areas of public life.

1994

The Violence against Women Act funds services for victims of rape and domestic violence.

2006

Thousands of Latinx immigrants and others boycott work, school, and shopping as part of the Day without Immigrants to highlight the contributions immigrants make to the economy.

2009

The Lilly Ledbetter Fair Pay Restoration Act allows employees, usually women, to file pay discrimination complaints within 180 days of their last paycheck.

2013

Restriction of same-sex marriage is deemed unconstitutional by the Supreme Court decision in *United States v. Windsor*.

2017

The Women's March on Washington, the largest single-day protest in U.S. history, is held. It has sparked some renewed interest in the ERA, with Nevada becoming the 36th state to ratify it.

Historians believe the second wave gained momentum following protests at the Miss America pageant in 1968 and 1969 (Rampton, 2015). A group called the Redstockings staged a counter-pageant while marching around a "freedom trash can" filled with items that they saw as symbols of female oppression (Gibson, 2011, p. 3). These included high heels, makeup, and bras. The stereotype of the bra-burning feminist comes from this event, although it's a myth that the protesters set the trash can on fire (Gibson, 2011). The protesters were particularly frustrated by the ways in which they felt women were being confined by unrealistic standards of beauty.

The Third Wave

Following the second wave, there was again some complacency and a sense that, because many women had entered the workforce, there was no more work to be done. But again, a lot still needed to be done, especially within the feminist movement itself. The *third wave* of feminism began in the mid-1990s and is best described as a struggle to change mainstream ideas of feminism by rejecting the idea that everyone's experience of being a woman is the same (Rampton, 2015). Third wave feminism emerged in reaction to previous feminist movements that largely ignored diversity among women and primarily focused on the interests of White, wealthy, heterosexual, educated women from Western parts of the world.

Black feminists critiqued the lack of diversity in the feminist movement and introduced the importance of **intersectionality** (Crenshaw, 1993). This framework describes the ways in which different types of oppression (e.g., racism, classism, homophobia, transphobia, ableism, sexism) are interconnected and, therefore, cannot be examined separately (Crenshaw, 1993). Although we'll explore this concept in more detail in Chapter 2, it's important to remember that, in this view, no woman is *just* a woman. She also has an age, a cultural identity, a race ethnicity, a religion, and many other social identity characteristics. Because these other aspects of her identity influence how she experiences being a woman, there can be no universal experience of womanhood.

Among feminists, one contentious aspect of third wave feminism is the revival of feminine aesthetics (e.g., lipstick, high heels) and raunch culture (i.e., female sexualization). Many women associated with the first two waves would have considered these things as evidence of oppression by a male-dominated society, but many third wave feminists have reclaimed them as a means of female empowerment (Rampton, 2015). We'll revisit this tension in Chapter 7 because it continues to be a source of debate among feminists. Another important feature of third wave feminism is use of the Internet to build social connections and political movements (Rampton, 2015).

A Fourth Wave?

Although the wave metaphor is often used to describe aspects of women's history, it has been criticized. A wave suggests that there are direct connections between movements and that activism peaks at certain points and retracts at others (Nicholson, 2013). In fact, feminists have been active even when there has been no definable wave. Some would say we're currently in a retraction between waves; others claim we're in a fourth wave characterized by more sophisticated use of social media to promote activism (e.g., tweets, memes). Still others reject the notion of waves altogether and say that the fight for equity is a constant and continual process.

your turn

Do you feel that there is a need for a feminist movement? If so, what do you think are the most pressing priorities feminism should address? What is the best way to make gains on those priorities? Talk to four other people with different social backgrounds. What are their thoughts on this? How do their thoughts align with yours? Where do their perspectives differ from one another?

The F-Word

What are seven major feminist perspectives, and what is the key focus within each perspective?

What does it mean to be feminist? This question has been with us for over a century. In 1913, journalist Rebecca West captured some of the ambivalence associated with feminism when she said, "I, myself, have never been able to find out what feminism is: I only know that people call me a feminist whenever I express sentiments that differentiate me from a doormat" (Vandiver, 2010, p. 1).

A common misperception is that feminists are all the same. In fact, feminists think in many different ways, and sometimes these thoughts even conflict with those of other feminists (Enns, 2004). For example, some feminists believe that, in order to achieve gender equality, women and men should be treated in exactly the same way; others argue that women and men should be valued for their differences. As we introduce you to many prominent feminist perspectives, we'll also introduce key terms that we'll use throughout the book.

Liberal Feminism

Supreme Court Justice Ruth Bader Ginsburg has been quoted as saying:

> If I could choose an amendment to add to the Constitution, it would be the Equal Rights Amendment. I think we have achieved that through legislation, but

that can be repealed, it can be altered. So, I would like my granddaughters, when they pick up the Constitution, to see the notion—that women and men are persons of equal stature—I'd like to see that as a basic principle of our society. (Schwab, 2014, p. 1)

This quote exemplifies **liberal feminism**, a form of feminism that focuses on the similarities between women and men and on using government policies to eliminate barriers that keep women from achieving their potential. The Equal Rights Amendment (ERA), which would have guaranteed that civil rights may not be denied on the basis of a person's sex, has not been ratified in the United States. Furthermore, despite some renewed recent interest, it has not received significant attention since 1982, when the deadline for states to ratify it expired.

Contemporary liberal feminists have moved away from championing the ERA and are more interested in changing laws and policies that give men (and members of other privileged groups) more resources and advantages than women (and members of less privileged groups). Such **structural inequalities** exist within organizations, institutions, and governments. For example, as mentioned previously, employers in the United States are not required to offer paid maternity leave. Because women who give birth will, at a minimum, leave the workforce for childbirth and recovery, liberal feminists argue that this policy disproportionately harms women through lost wages and possible opportunities for promotion. The outcome is vastly different for women who receive financial support following the birth of a child, as in countries such as Norway and Sweden. Additionally, within the United States, prior to the Affordable Care Act (ACA), only 62% of plans in the private market covered maternity care, another core policy concern of liberal feminists (Frankie-Ruta, 2013; Rosenthal, 2013).

Another component of liberal feminism is a focus on equal education and the belief that, at their core, women and men are more similar than different. According to liberal feminists, when girls and women have access to equal educational opportunities, they will develop and behave similarly to men (Enns, 2004). Contemporary liberal feminists are especially interested in making sure that girls and women have access to resources that help them compete in the global economy. Psychologists who hold a liberal feminist perspective tend to believe that even when research finds differences between women and men, they're generally the result of girls' and boys' different experiences rather than innate biological differences. This is a topic we'll explore in Chapter 3.

In the United States, most people hold liberal feminist attitudes even if they don't identify as feminists (Liss & Erchull, 2010). For example, most U.S. students agree that women and men should have equal rights and opportunities, a central tenet of liberal feminists.

Radical Feminism

In contrast to liberal feminism, **radical feminism** claims that it's naïve to think that women and men can become equal through attaining legal rights. Therefore, radical feminists advocate for separatism. They believe that the unjust treatment of women is the most fundamental and widespread form of oppression (Donovan, 2006). In this view, changing laws and policies isn't enough because gender biases are embedded in all aspects of everyday interactions. **Patriarchy**, a social system in which men hold positions of authority and power, is so normative that, according to radical feminism, most people see men's authority as natural and inevitable.

Radical feminists argue that, in order to achieve equity, women must develop new ways of thinking separate from **androcentric**, or male-centered, ways of thinking. Some radical feminists have advocated for cultural separatism as a way to achieve this goal. For instance, counselors at some domestic violence shelters refuse refuge for male survivors because their presence might undermine the safety of the women-only space (Haaken & Yragui, 2003).

One type of radical feminism is **lesbian feminism**, which focuses on sexuality and reproduction as a central place of oppression (Enns, 2004). A significant contribution of radical feminism is the concept of **compulsory heterosexuality**, the idea that sexual preferences are formed through the social ideal of heterosexuality. In other words, according to radical feminists, sexuality is learned, and the dominant message is that heterosexual romantic love is ideal. Girls and women, therefore, learn to prioritize the sexual desires of men, and the ultimate sign of success for a girl is to marry a man. For example, consider that almost every Disney Princess story ends in a marriage between a woman and a man. We'll revisit this idea in Chapters 5 and 7.

Socialist Feminism

Another perspective, **socialist feminism**, links gender oppression with capitalism, an economic system in

spotlight on . . .

The Michigan Womyn's Music Festival

The Michigan Womyn's Music Festival was a womyn-only music festival founded in 1976 on the principles of radical feminism. Use of the word *womyn* (instead of *women*) symbolized the festival's separatist underpinnings—the word *wo-men*, after all, according to radical feminists, implies that woman is a subset of man. From 1976 to 2015, the music festival drew between 3,000 and 10,000 womyn annually for five days of music, workshops, dancing, camping, and community building. The campground was built, staffed, and taken down exclusively by womyn. For years, attendees shared that the festival was a place for restoration and safety.

The concert was explicitly separatist, so attendance was limited to "womyn-born-womyn." In 1991, several transgender individuals sought admission but were turned away. Tension grew as organizers stood by their strict policy to include only those designated F at birth while many in the LGBTQ community called on the festival to change its policy.

In August 2015, the 40th festival was the last one. In discussing the festival's end, founder Lisa Vogel said, "We have known in our hearts for some years that the life cycle of the Festival was coming to a time of closure" (Ring, 2015, para. 3). The ending of the festival's life cycle did indeed signal a change in feminism. Some credit the rise of third wave feminism for promoting a different understanding of how to be equitable and inclusive in feminist spaces.

which power is constructed through work and production (Enns, 2004). In the United States, there is a perception that economic mobility is easily attainable through hard work. This view is called the **myth of meritocracy** because it suggests that merit is primarily responsible for accumulating wealth. However, contemporary research shows a widening gap between the upper-middle class and everyone else that appears to be more about inherited wealth than merit (Reeves, 2017). In one study, researchers found that since 1980, U.S. workers who are not upper-middle class are less likely than before to move up the social ladder (Carr & Wiemers, 2016). It appears that those at the top are more effective at passing down their status and wealth to their children, and this tendency reduces social mobility for everyone else (Reeves, 2017).

According to socialist feminists, merit alone is not responsible for accumulating wealth. Other factors, such as class, gender, and race, not only influence the accumulation of wealth but also affect the perceived value of what a person does.

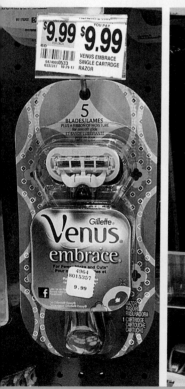

On average, girls and women spend $1,400 more each year than men when buying the same products because the "women's" version usually costs more. This pricing practice is referred to as the pink tax.

For example, socialist feminists have claimed that in capitalist societies men are primarily defined as workers and women are primarily defined as caregivers (Bianchi, Sayer, Milkie, & Robinson, 2012; Fillo, Simpson, Rholes, & Kohn, 2015). Such an arrangement means that women provide *free* labor by taking on the vast majority of domestic and caretaking responsibilities. Socialist feminists are particularly concerned with the second shift, a term that refers to the free labor performed at home in addition to paid labor in the workforce (Hochschild, 1989). According to socialist feminists, changing the way work is organized by encouraging men's increased involvement in child rearing would promote greater equality (Reid, 1993; Saris & Johnston-Robledo, 2000).

Socialist feminists are also concerned about how living as a girl or a woman is more expensive than it is for boys and men. The term *pink tax* refers to the additional cost of a product because it is marketed to women. It's estimated that, on average, girls and women spend $1,400 more each year than men when buying the same products (Duesterhaus, Grauerholz, Weichsel, & Guittar, 2011). Products such as razors, toothbrushes, and even pens cost more if they appear feminine. This practice is outlawed in California, New York City, and Miami-Dade County in

Florida, but it is perfectly legal elsewhere (Duesterhaus et al., 2011; Fried, 2016). Further, girls and women spend more money on items that men don't have to buy (e.g., makeup, bras, tampons). According to a poll by *Huffington Post* and *YouGov*, women in the United States spend over $426 billion on beauty products every year (Adams, 2013). This financial burden is particularly problematic when also considering that women, in general, are paid less than men (American Association of University Women, 2017). It appears that this cost is a necessary investment because research shows that women who wear makeup, for example, are seen as more reliable, capable, and trustworthy in the workplace than women who don't (Etcoff et al, 2011).

Cultural Feminism

Cultural feminism is a perspective that focuses on the differences between women and men and views women's inequality as related to a lack of value placed on the unique experiences, perspectives, and qualities of women (Donovan, 2006). Underlying cultural feminism is a belief in **gender essentialism**, the idea that women and men are fundamentally different because of deep and unchanging properties that are generally due to biology or genetics. For example, cultural feminists view girls and women as having certain innate characteristics, such as intuition and emotionality, that are complementary to the characteristics of boys and men, such as competitiveness and being analytical. As a result, unlike the liberal feminist focus on similarity, cultural feminists focus on difference. However, even while valuing difference, they also value equity. They would like to see women use their feminine characteristics to advance gender equity, and they argue for a societal shift in which traditionally feminine characteristics, such as being caring and nurturing, carry more value.

A contemporary example of cultural feminism is the rise of mompreneurs. In 2014, women-owned businesses increased by 45%, compared to just a 9% increase among all businesses (Weeks, 2015). Many of these businesses focus on traditionally feminine skills, such as cooking and crafting. According to cultural feminists, these businesses promote the valuing of women's unique capabilities and are successful because women are disproportionately more talented in these areas than men.

Women of Color Feminism

Women of color feminism sees women's inequality as deeply linked to *White supremacy*, a form of racism in which White people are considered superior to people of color (Enns, 2004). In fact, women of color feminism developed because previous types of feminism had ignored the concerns of racial

Cultural Feminism

There is a debate over whether taking a cultural feminist perspective is truly empowering for women. In other words, does the valuing of traditionally feminine activities promote equity between women and men? Before we discuss the debate, take a moment to explore your own beliefs. What do you think about activities that are traditionally associated with women (e.g., domestic work, child care)? Do you think our society values these activities? Why or why not?

Those who argue that cultural feminism is positive claim that girls and women are superior in areas that require empathy, care, and compassion. They're especially critical of the ways in which female empowerment has been linked to success in traditionally masculine domains. They prefer to see women achieve power from success in traditionally female domains. In other words, they aren't interested in seeing women become more masculine. Instead, they argue that female empowerment occurs when women honor their feminine side. For example, some proponents claim that women are powerful when they birth and breastfeed their children (McCarter-Spaulding, 2008). In fact, attachment parenting—a practice that includes co-sleeping, baby-wearing, and breastfeeding on demand—has been referred to as "cultural feminist theory in practice" (Bobel, 2008, p. 116).

However, others argue that cultural feminism cannot promote equity because it encourages women to maintain traditional and restrictive roles. According to these opponents, it's unreasonable to expect all women to have talents in traditionally feminine domains. Further, work associated with femininity is often less "valuable," carrying no monetary gain. For example, within the United States, childbirth and breastfeeding are not paid forms of labor. In France, in contrast, women are given incentives to have children and to breastfeed them (Bryant, 2008). For example, women are offered tax breaks, child and healthcare benefits, paid leave, subsidized daycare, housekeeping services, and even cash payments.

What are your thoughts on this debate? Do you think a cultural feminist perspective is empowering or oppressing? Why or why not? Can you see both sides of the argument? Would certain aspects of society need to change in order to promote a cultural feminist perspective? What are they, and whom would they benefit most?

When you see pictures like this one, do you tend to think that the women in them are feminists? Why or why not? Cultural feminists seek to reclaim and enhance the value of traditionally feminine activities and roles, so it's quite possible that women such as the one pictured here could identify as feminists.

minority women. For example, previous types hadn't considered the diversity among women and, instead, reflected **ethnocentrism**—the tendency to judge other groups according to the values of one's own group. Some White women went so far as to compare their experiences of oppression with those of ethnic minority individuals in the United States, a claim that minimized the social realities of women of color. The resulting tension sparked anger and frustration among women of color, motivating them to separate from White feminists and develop different goals for achieving equality.

One influential group of Black feminist lesbian activists, the Combahee River Collective, took up the task of defining a feminism that prioritized the lives of women of color. Named after the Combahee River Raid of 1863, which was led by Harriet Tubman and resulted in the freeing of hundreds of slaves, the Collective articulated a need to address all racial, gender, sexual, and class oppressions (Napikoski, 2017). In 1982, the group issued the Combahee River Collective Statement, which is credited as recognizing the often-overlooked contributions of women of color, including Harriet Tubman, and ushering in a focus on intersectionality.

Three queer Black women—Alicia Garza, Patrisse Cullors, and Opal Tometi—organized around the hashtag #blacklivesmatter, spurring a national movement against the systematic oppression of Black people and those who are part of other marginalized communities.

Women of color feminism is more likely to address concerns that have been of lesser focus for other types of feminisms—such as affirmative action, access to affordable housing, and prison reform. In fact, contemporary women of color feminists continue to advocate for social justice initiatives that do not only benefit girls and women. For example, in response to the murder of Black teenager Trayvon Martin, three queer Black women—Alicia Garza, Patrisse Cullors, and Opal Tometi—created the hashtag #blacklivesmatter (Garza, 2014), which spurred a national movement. Garza described it as "a call to action for Black people and a response to the anti-Black racism that permeates our society" (Garza, 2014, para. 1). In talking about the origin, she affirmed the movement's commitment to "the lives of Black queer and trans folks, disabled folks, Black-undocumented folks, folks with records, women and all Black lives along the gender spectrum" (Garza, 2014, para. 11). Black Lives Matter advances a broad and integrated expression of activism.

Queer Feminism

Queer feminism claims that inequality is related to the ways in which the categories of woman and man have been constructed, studied, and used to organize society. The focus of queer feminists is not to ensure that women are equal to men, but to question what is considered female and male in the first place. Queer feminism critiques the concept of **heternormativity**, the idea that people fall into a binary (something made up of only two parts) of two distinct sex categories—either F or M; that those categories have aligning gender roles (female or male); and that sexual desires are most naturally linked to the other sex. Queer feminists argue that sex, gender, and sexual orientation are not always aligned in a predictable way (Sullivan, 2003). For example, some people have a **cisgender identity**, meaning that their gender identification matches the sex they were assigned at birth, but other people may identify as **transgender**, reflecting a gender identity (woman, man, or other gendered identity labels) and/or a gender expression (feminine, masculine, or other gendered expressive labels) that doesn't conform to societal expectations for the sex they were assigned at birth.

Queer feminism is particularly interested in gender performances—how people express gender through their actions (Butler, 1990). For example, the clothes we put on every day, the hairstyles we favor, and the way we sit all communicate gender. Actor and television host RuPaul distills queer theory in the following quote: "We're born naked, and the rest is drag" (RuPaul, 1995, p. 11). Queer feminists believe that, over time, gendered behaviors become so much a part of daily life that they seem to be core parts of who we are, but in fact, they're simply behaviors that have the potential to change.

Post-colonial/Transnational Feminism

Post-colonial/transnational feminism connects women's inequality to the legacy of colonialism and critiques the belief that women in Western countries are the most liberated in the world (Else-Quest & Grabe, 2012). According to post-colonial feminists, a problematic dynamic occurs when women in Western countries think that women in non-Western countries are oppressed and need Western women to save them (Mohanty, 2003). An example of this occurred when some Western feminist women, mainly in European countries, called for a ban on the hijab, a headscarf worn primarily by Muslim women (Weaver, 2017). These Western women saw the hijab as a symbol of male dominance and female subservience. But, by suggesting a ban, they weren't seeing that they were imposing their own belief system on another group of women, and they weren't recognizing that the hijab often serves as a political statement against colonialism. A similarly problematic dynamic would occur if non-Western women were to call for a ban on bikinis, claiming they're a symbol of male dominance and female subservience in Western countries. These examples could be said to represent how all women struggle with patriarchy and how its manifestations can vary by context (Harcourt, 2012). We'll return to this topic in Chapter 6.

A particular type of post-colonial feminism, known as **third world feminism**, claims that feminism should not focus on commonalities among women (Herr, 2013); instead, it should address issues from multiple perspectives and not assume one unified position. This outlook promotes a wider view of feminism that respects the distinct, but interconnected, lives of girls and women. Third world feminists have been especially critical of organizations that attempt to apply a liberal feminist perspective in other places in the world. These feminists argue that it's inappropriate for women from powerful countries, like the United States, to come into an area and start planning ways to end gender discrimination there without acknowledging how local women have already theorized and organized as part of that particular community.

See Table 1.1 for a summary of the main characteristics of the seven types of feminist theory discussed in this section. The Sample Survey Item column shows statements that feminists in each category would agree with.

TABLE 1.1 Feminist Perspectives

Feminist Theory	Description	Sample Survey Item
Liberal feminism	Focuses on gaining equal rights and prioritizes changing laws and promoting education.	The government is responsible for making sure that all women receive an equal chance at education and employment.
Radical feminism	Focuses on transforming women's thinking since women are conditioned to prioritize men and to deem heterosexuality as a social ideal.	Pornography exploits female sexuality and degrades all women.
Socialist feminism	Highlights the ways in which money and capitalism are interconnected with gender inequities.	Making women economically dependent on men is capitalism's subtle way of encouraging heterosexual relationships.
Cultural feminism	Perceives gender inequity as being related to a lack of appreciation for women's unique feminine qualities.	Traditional notions of romantic love should be replaced with ideas based on feminine values of kindness and concern for all people.
Women of color feminism	Connects gender inequity to other structures of oppression, especially, but not limited to, racism.	Racism and sexism make double the oppression of women in the work environment.
Queer feminism	Calls for the elimination of binary gender categories since they are at the core of gender inequality.	Traditional definitions of feminism that solely focus on achieving equity between women and men contribute to oppression because they exclude people with non-binary gender identities.
Post-colonial/ transnational feminism	Connects women's inequity to the continued legacy of colonialism.	It is important to build coalitions, rather than assuming one unified voice of sisterhood.

Note. Sample survey items for queer feminism and post-colonial/transnational feminism were written by the authors. The other items are all drawn from the Feminist Perspective Scale (Henley et al., 1998).

The Power of Feminist Theory

Each of these perspectives has made lasting contributions to feminism, and they seek to provide a framework for understanding gender inequities. In this effort, theory aims to provide an explanation for *why* women experience inequities. Understanding theory is critical for consciousness raising, a form of activism that tries to promote awareness through knowledge. Many women experience discrimination or find themselves in situations that make them uncomfortable, but they often lack the language to talk about how they feel or to understand that their experiences are part of a larger problem. As a result, they may unnecessarily blame themselves. Understanding feminist perspectives and the fact that personal struggles often represent larger sociopolitical problems can give women a sense that they aren't alone. It can also help to explain the basis for certain inequalities. In this way, theory can have multiple benefits (hooks, 1994).

Understanding feminist perspectives can also help people identify the best ways to make changes for the better. Feminist theory provides the tools to discuss society's problems and ways to deal with them. This can lead to social change that is truly empowering for everyone. However, many people don't understand the diversity of feminist thought, they reject feminism entirely, or they think there's no longer any need for it. This is largely because they don't understand what feminism is.

your turn

What does the word *feminism* mean to you? Would you call yourself a feminist? Why or why not? Are women the only ones who can be feminists? Why or why not? Ask your friends, your relatives, and your professors whether they call themselves feminists and what they think of feminism. Is there a particular school of feminist thought that appeals to you? Is there a particular school of feminist thought that appeals to others in your life? If so, explain why.

I'm Not a Feminist, But . . .

What is post-feminism, and how is it related to not identifying as a feminist?

In her book *Modern Misogyny,* psychologist Kristin Anderson (2015) explains that we are living in an era of post-feminism, which began in the 1990s and evolved following the 9/11 attacks. A defining feature of **post-feminism** is the idea that the women's movement has reached its goals and, therefore, feminism is no longer needed. Feminists disagree with this belief. In fact, two of the goals of this book are to show (a) how gender inequities shape all aspects of the psychological development of girls and women and (b) how addressing inequities has the potential to improve everyone's lives.

In this post-feminist era, stereotypes about feminists are widely disseminated as a way to stigmatize women who speak out against sexism. As a result, a goal of the post-feminist era is to convince girls and women that identifying with feminism is problematic—and this leads to tremendous confusion about what it means to be a feminist (Anderson, Kanner, & Elsayegh, 2009). Susan Faludi (1992) coined the term *backlash* to explain how negative stereotypes generally develop when women begin to make social gains. From Fauldi's perspective, negative stereotypes prevent women from organizing as an activist group because they are less likely to self-identify as feminists when they're aware of such stereotypes.

There are no shortages of negative stereotypes about feminists. They've been called bra-burners and man-haters; they've been described as hairy, selfish, unattractive, angry, tense, and egotistical (Alexander & Ryan, 1997; Hall & Rodriguez, 2003; Liss, Hoffner, & Crawford, 2000; Rudman & Fairchild, 2007). Surprisingly, even when women believe in some aspects of feminism, they assume that the typical feminist is more radical than they are (Liss et al., 2000). This happens because negative beliefs influence a woman's decision to identify as a feminist (Alexander & Ryan, 1997). In one research study, for example, women who read a paragraph expressing negative stereotypes about feminists were twice as likely *not* to identify as feminist as compared to women who read a paragraph expressing positive stereotypes (Roy, Weibust, & Miller, 2007).

Who Is a Feminist?

What are the similarities and differences among self-identified feminists, non-labelers, womanists, and pro-feminists?

The backlash against feminists has an effect. Although many girls and women believe in feminist ideals, it is less common for girls and women to identify as feminists (Liss, O'Connor, Morosky, & Crawford, 2001). In a survey of female college students, 75% endorsed some beliefs consistent with feminism, but only 11% actually labeled themselves as feminists (Liss, Crawford, & Popp, 2004). In a more recent study, researchers found that 28% of female college students identified as feminists (Fitz, Zucker, & Bay-Cheng, 2012). Many took the "I'm not a feminist, but . . ." stance. This isn't surprising because self-identified feminists have to willingly take on a stigmatized identity. A woman who has some pro-feminist attitudes but who doesn't identify as a feminist is often called a non-labeler.

There are so many non-labelers that comedians have started to poke fun at the concept. Although comedian Aziz Ansari is not the perfect representative of feminism—a topic we'll return to in Chapter 12—he has offered what is perhaps the perfect analogy: "If you believe that men and women have equal rights, if someone asks if you're a feminist, you have to say yes because that is how words work. You can't be like, 'Oh yeah I'm a doctor that primarily does diseases of the skin.' Oh, so you're a dermatologist? 'Oh no, that's way too aggressive of a word! No no, not at all not at all'" (Gupta, 2014, para. 4).

The important distinguishing factor between women who self-label as feminists and those who are non-labelers is that feminists are aware that gender inequities still exist (Liss & Erchull, 2010). Non-labelers generally think that women are already empowered and that no more work is necessary because women have achieved equity. In contrast, feminists see work that still needs to be done. This discrepancy has important social implications because without addressing sexism it's unlikely that social systems will change (Anderson, 2015; Taylor & Whittier, 1992). The very act of calling oneself a feminist in front of other people is considered a form of activism because it undermines stereotypes of feminism. If only a few people stand up against sexism, there won't be enough critical mass to draw attention and promote change. Women who call themselves feminists understand this. They are willing to commit to causes larger than themselves (Yoder, Tobias, & Snell, 2011) and are more likely to confront sexism (Burn, Aboud, & Moyles, 2000; Yoder et al., 2011). Women who identify as feminists are also less likely to believe negative stereotypes about feminists, and they're more likely to hold positive views about feminists (Liss et al., 2001).

It isn't surprising, then, that people who are exposed to feminism—either because they have feminist relatives or because they've taken a women's studies course—are more likely to identify as feminists (Bargad & Hyde, 1991; Nelson et al., 2008; Zucker, 2004). Having a sexual minority identity is also associated with a higher likelihood of identifying as a feminist (Friedman & Ayres, 2013; Leaper & Arias, 2011; Lottes & Kuriloff, 1994). Further, experiencing overt sexism leads women to understand oppression, which results in a greater likelihood of identifying as a feminist (Leaper & Arias, 2011; Reid & Purcell, 2004).

Notably, some women choose not to identify as feminists because of bias within the women's movement. As we've discussed, the early feminist movement ignored and thereby perpetuated discrimination among large groups of women, including women of color, sexual minority women, trans and gender non-conforming women, and non-Western women. In response, for example, activist and writer Alice Walker (1983) coined the term **womanist**, an identity label that stems from the experiences of Black women and other women of color. The term encompasses feminism, but it also differs because it doesn't prioritize sexism over other forms of oppression (e.g., racism; Phillips, 2006).

There is evidence that women of color are more likely to identify with womanist beliefs rather than those associated with different types of feminism (Boisnier, 2003). Several researchers have found that, among women of color, holding womanist beliefs was associated with higher self-esteem (Ossana, Helms, & Leonard, 1992; Poindexter-Cameron & Robinson, 1997). Inspired by their womanist sisters, Latinx feminists coined the term **mujerista** (from the Spanish word *mujer*, meaning "woman"; Isasi-Diaz, 1992, 1996). Similar to womanists, mujeristas are critical of the marginalization of women of color by

White feminists and instead support a type of feminism that prioritizes the lives of Latinx[*] women. Mujeristas especially act toward the decolonization of all people (Anzaldúa, 2007; Isasi-Diaz, 1992). Taken together, womanism and mujerismo offer a way for psychologists to understand how women of color might identify with feminism that takes a distinctive intersectional approach (Comaz-Diaz, 2008; Holiday, 2010).

Current Issues Related to Feminist Identification

How does racism play a role in whether or not a person will identify as a feminist? What are the unique issues connected to men and feminist identification?

Although contemporary feminist thought includes the concept of intersectionality, much work remains to address discrimination *within* feminism (Phillips, 2006). For example, in 2015, the actress Patricia Arquette ignited tremendous criticism for saying in her Academy Award acceptance speech, "It's time for all the women in America and all the men that love women, and all the gay people, and all the people of color that we've all fought for to fight for us now" (Marcotte, 2015, para. 3). The statement didn't go over well because it sounded like she was saying that until now White women had fought for gay people and people of color, and now it was time for them to fight for White women. Arquette later admitted that she should have chosen her words more carefully. Another major critique has been launched against feminist Lena Dunham for showcasing almost no women of color in her popular HBO show *Girls*—despite the fact that it's supposedly set in New York, a highly diverse city. Because of incidents like these, some women of color prefer not to use the feminist label at all.

There is also evidence that the experience of racism influences feminist identity (Cole, 2009). While White feminists can focus on countering sexism, women of

---

Authors' note: Latinx is a gender neutral term used as an alternative to *Latina* or *Latino*. Because of its inclusivity, we will use *Latinx* throughout the book.

color worry about racism as well. To demonstrate this, researchers found that Black feminists place a high value on wearing feminine clothing, but White feminists did not (Cole & Zucker, 2007). The researchers proposed that Black women strategically attend to physical appearance to combat racist stereotypes of Black women being sexually promiscuous, aggressive, and bad mothers. This dynamic was evident when former first lady Michelle Obama was criticized by some White feminists for calling herself Mom-in-Chief and focusing her activism on traditionally feminine domains. A White woman who's worried about sexism may try not to be too domestic in the White House because that would activate sexist stereotypes. However, because a woman of color has to worry about racism too, Michelle Obama may have focused on domestic tasks so she wouldn't activate racist stereotypes of Black women being overly domineering. This is another example of how feminist identification can vary among girls and women depending on other aspects of their other social identities.

There is also debate over whether boys and men can label themselves as feminists. Many do identify as feminists, but some prefer the label *pro-feminist*, a term that incorporates feminism but also expresses interest in working alongside girls and women for social action and change. Pro-feminist men use the term to signal that they aren't speaking on behalf of women but, instead, see themselves as allies. Pro-feminist men recognize social inequities, and compared to men who don't identify as feminists, they're more likely to report incidents of gender bias and less likely to use sexist language (Hyers, 2007; Swim, Mallett, & Stangor, 2004). Perhaps most interestingly, research shows that when men confront instances of sexism, they are more likely to be believed and experience fewer personal costs than women who confront those instances (Eliezer & Major, 2012; Rasinski & Czopp, 2010). These findings underscore the vital role that boys and men can play when they become engaged in the feminist movement, regardless of how they refer to themselves. We'll revisit this topic in Chapter 14.

Although there's less research on understanding how men become feminists, the growing interest in examining men's roles within the context of unequal gender relationships has given rise to an entire academic field: men's studies. Although men continue to be less likely than women to recognize sexism, some men—particularly those who've been exposed to positive portrayals of feminism—report a great deal of support for feminism and subsequently engage in feminist activism (Flood, 2011; Swim, Hyers, Cohen, & Ferguson, 2001).

try it for yourself

Spend some time thinking about what it means to be a feminist man. Visit the website feministvoices.com, and search for social psychologist Peter Hegarty. Listen to his interview about the problems of taking on a feminist identity as a man. Do you agree or disagree with him? Explain your response. Then ask three men to describe their thoughts about feminism. Would they consider themselves feminists? Why or why not? Did you find any men who explicitly identified as feminists? Was this task easy or hard? How did you feel talking about this topic with men?

Advantages of Feminist Identification

What benefits are associated with feminist identification?

Although the discussion of the negative stereotypes about feminists may suggest otherwise, there are many benefits to identifying as a feminist. For example, some research has shown that feminists are perceived as intelligent, knowledgeable, productive, career-oriented, and active (Rudman & Fairchild, 2007; Twenge & Zucker, 1999). These positive beliefs influence girls' and women's decision to identify as feminists (Roy, Weibust, & Miller, 2007). Also, women who identify as feminists report better psychological well-being, experience less body shame, and have increased sexual satisfaction compared to those who do not (Hurt et al., 2007; Rudman & Phelan, 2007; Saunders & Kashubeck-West, 2006). Feminism helps women to develop relationships across difference—among White girls and women, having a feminist identity is associated with taking an anti-racist stance (Banks, Murray, Brown, & Hammond, 2014; Rosette & Tost, 2013). Additionally, feminism has helped to build positive relationships between heterosexual women and sexual minority women, and between able-bodied women and women with disabilities (LaMantia, Wagner, & Bohecker, 2015; Wehbi, 2010). Further, feminism has helped to cultivate relationships across national boundaries (Norsworthy & Khuankaew, 2013). Some feminist activists that we've worked with refer to these advantages as "having a good dose of Vitamin F."

Even among non-labelers, there is evidence that endorsement of feminist values has psychological benefits; however, more research is needed in this area (Saunders & Kashubeck-West, 2006). For example, psychologist Oksana Yakushko (2007) explored the psychological well-being of mostly White, U.S. women and found that those who endorsed feminist beliefs reported a greater sense of independence and purpose than those who did not. They were also more open to new experiences. In a different study of mostly White women, those who endorsed feminist attitudes reported greater self-confidence about their sexuality and a greater inclination to have sex based on their own desires and motivations as compared to women who didn't endorse feminist beliefs (Schick, Zucker, & Bay-Cheng, 2008). Greater endorsement of feminist beliefs has also been linked to high self-esteem, self-efficacy, and academic achievement (Eisele & Stake, 2008; Fischer & Good, 1994; Valenzuela, 1993).

Recent literature describes how men benefit from feminism as well. There are many psychological costs of conforming to traditional norms of masculinity, and feminist identification gives men the freedom to reject these rigid expectations (Kilmartin & Smiler, 2015). When asked about identifying as a feminist, actor Joseph Gordon-Levitt said, "What [feminism] means to me is that you don't let your gender define who you are—you can be who you want to be. . . . I'm a believer that if everyone has a fair chance to be what they want to be and do what they want to do, it's better for everyone. It benefits society as a whole" (Stern, 2014, para. 12). Men's roles have stayed relatively stable despite the dramatic changes in girls' and women's roles over the last 50 years (Levant, 2014). Organizations such as the Society for the Psychological Study of Men and Masculinity, and scholarly journals such as *Psychology of Men and Masculinity*, explore masculinity from a feminist psychological perspective.

Feminism Comes to Psychology

What were experiences within the field of psychology like for women from the late 19th century through the mid-20th century?

Now that you have a better understanding of what feminism is and isn't, let's explore how feminism has influenced psychology. Much like the women's movement, discussed earlier in this chapter, it took many years for feminism to transform the field of psychology. Throughout the history of American psychology, many individual women have worked toward change, and coalitions of women have collaborated to end discriminatory practices within the field. There have been some dramatic moments. Historians confirm that without feminist activism, the field of psychology would be very different from what it is today (Rutherford & Granek, 2010).

In the Beginning

At the end of the 19th century, corresponding with the first wave of feminism, a select group of women were entering the field of psychology for the first time. It's hard to imagine the world in which these first-generation female psychologists worked. Most female applicants were denied entrance into graduate programs, but some women—mostly wealthy and White—found ways to study psychology (Rutherford & Granek, 2010). For example, in 1890, with the help of her father and the president of Wellesley College, Mary Whiton Calkins petitioned Harvard University to let her sit in on psychology lectures. Although she completed all the courses required for a PhD and later became the first female president of the American Psychological Association (APA), she was never awarded her degree, either in her lifetime or after her death. It wasn't until 1894 that Margaret Floy Washburn became the first woman to receive a PhD in psychology—from Cornell University. Helen Thompson-Woolley, who earned her PhD from the University of Chicago in 1900, published the first dissertation that examined sex/gender differences.

These women were pioneers who strategically used the scientific method to challenge prevailing sexism. Most of their research focused on disputing *biological determinism*, the belief that the differences between women and men are biologically fixed. In the early 20th century, female psychologists conducted studies exploring how cultural expectations influence the perceived differences between women and men. These early psychologists were resisting biased ideas, and although they didn't realize it at the time, they were facing a feminist predicament that continues today—a topic we'll explore in more detail in Chapter 3.

Early 20th Century

In the early 20th century, more diverse women began to study psychology. In 1933, Inez Beverly Prosser became the first Black woman to earn a doctorate in psychology. However, it wasn't until 1962 that Martha Bernal became the first Latinx woman to earn a PhD in psychology in the United States. She also self-identified as a lesbian.

Women of color faced double (and sometimes triple) discrimination connected to their multiple minority status. One such well-known Black female psychologist, Mamie Phipps Clark, was awarded her PhD in 1944. At the time, she was the only Black student pursuing a PhD in psychology at Columbia University. As just one of the challenges she faced, her academic advisor believed in racial segregation. Moreover, she subsequently couldn't find a job because most job descriptions were for men only. This barrier, however, didn't stop her desire to make a difference in the field of psychology. She observed that young Black children were disproportionately affected by poverty and had limited access to quality psychological assessment and treatments. When she realized that existing clinics weren't going to extend services to poor Black children from Harlem in New York City, she started the Northside Center for Child Development in a one-room basement apartment. More than 70 years later, the center now provides services to more than 3,600 children and families each year.

Dr. Mamie Phipps Clark started the Northside Center for Child Development in a one-room basement apartment. More than 70 years later, the center now provides services to more than 3,600 children and families each year.

Moreover, Dr. Clark's research was critical to the historic Supreme Court decision in *Brown v. Board of Education* (1954). With her husband, psychologist Kenneth Clark, she published several studies showing how Black children were affected by racism. In the famous doll study, children were shown two dolls: one White and one Black (Clark & Clark, 1947). They were given a series of instructions: "Show me the doll that is the nice doll," "Show me the doll that looks bad," "Show me the doll that you like best." The Black children consistently showed a preference for the White doll, which, according to the Clarks, was evidence of internalized racism. This conclusion helped persuade the Supreme Court to rule against segregation in U.S. public schools.

Although there have been critiques of both the methodology and the interpretation of results from the Clarks' studies, the doll experiment was the first time social science served as evidence in a Supreme Court case. Today it is standard practice to rely on psychological research in court hearings. Interestingly, most psychology students don't know that the doll study was based on Mamie Clark's master's thesis. Although it's a famous case, and one studied by many psychology students, it's Kenneth Clark who generally gets credit for its influence. In many ways, Mamie Clark used her training to fight against social injustice, even when she herself was facing discrimination.

Mid-20th Century

What factors contributed to, and signaled the formation of, a specific discipline of psychology of women?

Although many women were working to undermine sexism in psychology, it wasn't until the 1960s that the field psychology of women emerged. This corresponded with an upswing in civil rights activism in the United States and other parts of the world. In 1963, author and activist Betty Friedan published *The Feminine Mystique*, in which she identified Sigmund Freud and the entire field of psychology as being partially responsible for women's oppression (Eagly, Eaton, Rose, Riger, & McHugh, 2012; Friedan, 1963). Before the 1960s and 1970s, psychological research was almost "womanless" (Crawford & Marecek, 1989, p. 147). Most studies didn't include girls or women, and when they were included, the research questions and methods were based on biased assumptions. When women were found to be different from men on various measures, the results were generally interpreted as indicating that women were inferior to men (Shields, 1975, 2007; Rutherford & Granek, 2010). Such differences were interpreted as arising from innate, generally biological, factors.

This practice was critiqued in psychologist Naomi Weisstein's (1968/1992) publication "Psychology Constructs the Female; or, The Fantasy Life of the Male Psychologist (With Some Attention to the Fantasies of His Friends the Male Biologist, and the Male Anthropologist)." Psychologist Carolyn Wood Sherif (1979) would later refer to Weisstein's publication as a "feminist shot that ricocheted down the halls between psychology laboratories and clinics, hitting its target dead-center" (p. 58). By effectively using experimental research to show how social expectations influence psychological research and practice, Weisstein revealed a glaring bias. She argued that the second-class status of women was responsible for many of the psychological effects observed in women. In other words, until that point, psychologists hadn't considered how discrimination against women influenced their studies about women.

Further, the clinical practice of psychology often involved sexist practices in which clinicians abused their power over clients. Feminist psychologist Rachel Hare-Mustin recounted attending a session at an American Psychological Association convention in the early 1970s where four male clinical psychologists debated the merits of having sex with their clients (Hare-Mustin, 2017). She was shocked. Because of subsequent feminist activism, the APA revised its Ethical Standards to prohibit sexual contact between a therapist and a client. Today clients seek disciplinary action against psychologists concerning sexual misconduct in therapy (Pope, 1993). The fact that the public understands the damaging effects of therapists' sexual exploitation is a direct result of activism among feminist psychologists.

It may be hard to imagine now, but until 1969, female psychologists were excluded from participating in much of the field. For example, job descriptions were organized by sex, and few women held high-ranking positions. Psychologist Nancy Henley, reflecting on this time, spoke of how women's role in research was even called out with different practices related to referencing: "in the reference lists, men's names were listed with initials only. Women's names had to have their first name so you could see they were women" (Henley, 2005, p. 5). Such discrimination was frustrating for the women who had spent years in school working to become psychologists, but a tipping point occurred in the late 1960s. Angered by the APA's overt sexism and lack of female leadership, several psychologists formed an alternative organization, the Association for Women in Psychology (AWP). In 1970, ten AWP members stormed a Town Hall meeting of the APA, presenting a list of 52 resolutions that they thought could address sexism within psychology. They demanded immediate action. This famous activist moment, referred to as the Storming of Council, was a catalyst for change within the field of psychology.

From 1969 to 1973, women spent many hours organizing and petitioning the APA to approve the formation of a division that solely focused on women. When Division 35 of the APA, the Society for the Psychology of Women, was finally formed, its mission was "to foster and nurture the growth of a feminist psychology of women and to create a knowledge base relevant to women's lives" (Mednick & Urbanski, 1991, p. 652).

With an increased focus on girls and women, feminist psychologists turned their attention to developing college courses and textbooks. This move not only provided academic legitimacy but also helped to build feminist consciousness on college campuses (Unger, 2010). With many more psychology students discussing concerns that disproportionately affected girls and women, a renewed commitment to feminism blossomed. Another sign that the psychology of women was flourishing was the development of specialized journals, including *Sex Roles* (1975), *Psychology of Women Quarterly* (1976), *Women & Therapy* (1982), and *Feminism & Psychology* (1991). These journals have helped to disseminate research to colleges and universities throughout the world and are critical to the production and sharing of gender research. Indeed, much of the research reviewed in this book was conducted by feminist psychologists using the scientific method to better understand the experiences of girls and women.

Late 20th Century into the 21st Century

How have feminists challenged the way that knowledge is produced and interpreted?

As feminist psychologists were developing organizations, academic programs, courses, and journals to enhance knowledge and scientific credibility, another competing movement arose in the late 20th century. Probably due to Weisstein's publication and a broader feminist critique of science that was happening in the early 1980s, feminist psychologists began to critique the scientific method and its philosophical underpinnings. In particular, they questioned the assumption of **positivism**, the idea that science is progressive and cumulative and that it relies on objectivity, neutrality, and rationality. In other words, feminist psychologists were calling attention to the ways scientists bring their own perspectives into what they study (Keller, 1987). This may be less obvious when the scientists are in powerful and privileged positions—their truth can simply look like *the truth* (Fine, 1994). However, according to critics, the positivist claim that scientists have access to a detached and objective truth reflects power and an inherently masculine approach.

Feminist psychologists also critiqued the positivist view that science could discover universal psychological truths. Instead, they proposed that it was possible for multiple truths to exist. This viewpoint was shared by scholars involved in the *multicultural movement* within psychology that began in the 1960s and 1970s. The movement sought greater diversity and inclusion in the discipline of psychology, including in psychological research. As multiculturalism and feminism became influential perspectives within psychology, feminist psychologists began to develop **feminist epistemologies**, or new ways to critique and produce methods of creating knowledge that attempt to address biases against certain groups of people, including girls and women. We'll focus on these ideas in more detail in the next section of this chapter.

Understanding Research Methods

What are the key elements of the research process that you need to know in order to critique research presented in this book?

The field of psychology relies on a scientific approach, and becoming familiar with how psychological research is conducted can help you be a more critical consumer of it. Moreover, as we just discussed, the history of using the scientific method to study girls and women has not always been bias-free. One goal of this book is to help you develop skills in uncovering hidden gender biases and appreciating the complexities associated with conducting psychological research.

One complexity involves how we define what it means to be a woman. You may like to rely on biological definitions. However, as we'll explore in Chapter 4, not everyone with a vagina, for example, considers themself a woman, and not all people who consider themselves women have a vagina. Furthermore, not all people who consider themselves women act or dress in ways that one might expect a woman to act. Researchers have clarified that it's possible to refer to someone's sex or gender, and that these are not necessarily the same thing. The APA publication manual instructs authors to use *sex* for biology and anatomy and *gender* for attitudes and roles associated with a biological sex (American Psychological Association [APA], 2009), yet there's still a tendency to confuse sex and gender (Smith, Johnston-Robledo, McHugh & Chrisler, 2010). It's not always clear, for example, when a researcher is referring to biology, psychology, or both, when studying girls and women. Furthermore, as we'll discuss in Chapter 4, the idea that there are only two sexes and two genders is an oversimplification of reality.

Because defining *woman* isn't always clear, research about sex and gender can be controversial. Problems come up when observations are interpreted through an oversimplified lens, which, especially when conveyed in the popular press, can be demeaning to everyone. For this reason, feminist psychologists have called for a more socially responsible approach to psychological research, one that doesn't shy away from a complicated exploration of sex and gender (Fine & Roberts, 1999).

Doing Research

Because we're constantly surrounded by sex and gender, ideas for research can come from everyday interactions. For example, let's say you're planning a day at the beach during a family vacation, and you notice a distinct difference

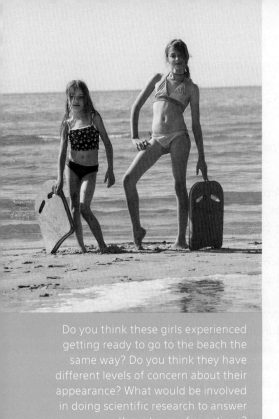

Do you think these girls experienced getting ready to go to the beach the same way? Do you think they have different levels of concern about their appearance? What would be involved in doing scientific research to answer these types of questions?

between two of your cousins. Your 6-year-old cousin excitedly puts on her bathing suit and grabs her Frisbee. Your 13-year-old cousin, in contrast, spends over an hour trying on different bathing suits, standing in front of the mirror, and evaluating her body. Although there are probably lots of explanations for this, you think their ages might explain their different behaviors. This is a *theory*, or a proposed explanation for why certain things occur. Initially, theories can come from personal observations or from previously established concepts. They are then refined through the process of collecting data and drawing conclusions based on that data. Let's explore how.

First, a theory will lead to a scientific question that can produce a testable *hypothesis*, or prediction. In our example, your hypothesis might be: "As a girl *ages*, her *body anxiety* increases." Each of the italicized words or phrases in the hypothesis is a *variable*, and variables can be measured in many different ways. For example, to measure body anxiety you might use direct *observation* by recording behaviors that reflect body anxiety—such as by noting how many times a girl examines her body in a mirror. As another option, you might use a *survey* to ask participants to report their beliefs, attitudes, and behaviors related to body anxiety. Although the conceptual definition of body anxiety is the same, the measurement, or *operationalization*, of it can vary quite a bit. And data can change depending on how the researcher decides to operationalize a variable. For example, the 13-year-old may not want to admit she's anxious, but as a researcher you might observe her frequently checking herself in the mirror. This measurement decision could affect the results, since anxiety might be lower if operationalized through self-report and higher if operationalized through observation.

Returning to our example, the research process requires expanding your investigation beyond your cousins and collecting data from a larger sample of girls of different ages. A common method is to recruit girls you already know, referred to as a *convenience sample*. You might ask fellow classmates or post a message about your study on Twitter. Of course, this might mean that all the people in your sample share similar characteristics because they all have something in common: their relationship to you! It's more challenging to recruit participants you don't know, and for this reason, it might be necessary to offer an incentive for participating in your study. This type of recruitment takes longer and requires more resources—like money to pay for the incentives.

Once data are collected, more often than not you'll use statistics to make interpretations about the data. Most psychological research relies on *quantitative methods*, an approach that attempts to represent variables with numbers. For example, body anxiety could be represented numerically as the score on a self-report measure so that higher numbers signify higher levels of body anxiety. Let's say that a group of 6-year-olds averages a score of 15 and a group of 13-year-olds averages a score of 25. When psychologists use statistics to examine this difference, they're interested in evaluating *statistical significance*. Statistical significance suggests that if body anxiety was not actually related to age, finding a difference this large (15 vs. 25) by chance would be unusual. How unusual this would be is often indicated as probability, or a p-value, and results are typically considered statistically significant if $p < .05$. This level of statistical significance means that there's a probability (p) of less than 5% that the results of the study are due to chance.

If you were to find statistically significant differences in body anxiety among girls of different ages, you could have confidence in assuming that development is related to body anxiety. If the results were not statistically significant, however (i.e., $p > .05$), you might have to revise your original theory: Maybe body anxiety is related to general levels of anxiety, rather than age. In other words, maybe your 13-year-old cousin is just a more anxious person than your 6-year-old cousin. With this revised hypothesis, the scientific process can begin again. However, this time, you might reconsider your study's design, as design decisions can also play a role in non-significant findings.

When researchers don't find statistical significance, it can be frustrating because they have to start the process over again and typically don't submit the original findings to an academic journal for publication. In general, academic journals only publish studies that show statistically significant findings. This means that most published psychology research reflects a preference for finding differences, rather than similarities, between groups—including gender differences, a topic we'll focus on in Chapter 3.

When researchers do find statistical significance, however, they can write up the findings in a report and submit it to an academic journal for *peer review*. During the peer-review process, experts in the field review the research and determine if it meets a rigorous standard for publication. If the reviewers and the journal editor decide that the research is of high value, it will be published. Such research then has the potential to influence people, policies, and social structures.

In our example, you might submit your report to a journal that focuses on gender, such as *Psychology of Women Quarterly* or *Sex Roles*. By doing this, you know that the reviewers are other scientists with expertise in gender. Once the research is published, a media outlet might feature the study in a magazine or on a morning talk show. The study might also influence curriculum decisions in middle schools, high schools, or after-school programs.

Experiments versus Correlational Research

What are the key differences between experimental and correlational designs?

If you have already taken a statistics or research methods course, you may have noticed that the above example isn't an experiment. Instead, it would be considered a correlational design. In a *correlational design*, relationships between variables are examined—in this case, the relationship between age and body anxiety. One of the most important tenets of psychology is that *correlation does not imply causation*. In other words, even if variables are related, it doesn't mean that one caused the other. For example, if umbrella sales go up when grass grows, it doesn't mean that selling umbrellas causes grass to grow or that growing grass causes increased umbrella sales. In this case, they're both caused by another variable: rain. However, in an *experiment*, the researcher manipulates a variable in order to investigate whether changes in that variable (the *independent variable*) cause a change in another variable (the *dependent variable*).

A critical component of experiments is *random assignment*—the process of assigning participants to conditions in a way that guarantees all participants have an equal chance of being in any group. Returning to our example, you couldn't randomly assign people to different age conditions because people already have an age. In other words, you couldn't randomly assign people to the 6-year-old condition or the 13-year-old condition because the people in those groups already exist as 6-year-olds or 13-year-olds. Therefore, even if you were to find a difference between 6-year-olds and 13-year-olds, you couldn't conclusively say that age *causes* the change in body anxiety. You could, however, design an experiment that explores another variable that might affect the development of body anxiety. For example, you could randomly assign girls to two conditions. In the manipulated condition, sometimes referred to as the experimental group, you could tell the girls that boys are watching them. In the control condition, the group you're comparing the effects of the manipulation against, you could tell the girls to simply enjoy one another's company. If you were to find that body anxiety is statistically significantly higher in the manipulated condition, then you could confidently state that the anticipation of being watched by boys caused the increase in the girls' body anxiety. Because all participants had an equal chance of being in either condition, you likely eliminated other factors that might have influenced the outcome. However, it's important to note that many variables cannot be randomly assigned, including sex and gender. Therefore, the ability to use psychological research to make causal statements about the role of sex or gender is limited.

try it for yourself

In what ways have your views on any topic been influenced by reports about scientific findings? How often have you questioned the results of a scientific study presented in the news or through social media? Have you noticed bias in the way science is reported? Why or why not? Ask three people if they would question a scientific finding presented in the popular press. Now find a news story summarizing a research study, locate the original research report, and compare the two. Is the summary in the news story accurate? Is it complete? What are the differences between the way the journalist framed the results and the way the scientists did?

Identifying Sex/Gender Bias in Research

The field of psychology has produced many studies with relevance to people's lives, and results found using the scientific method have tremendous economic, political, and social influence (Hare-Mustin & Merecek, 1990). As you may recall, Mamie and Kenneth Clark's research was one factor that contributed to school segregation being deemed unconstitutional. Given that psychological research is socially influential, it's important to understand the various ways in which research can be biased—and, specifically, biased against women. Many people take research results that they read in the media at face value, assuming that if something is published it must be "true." However, much research, even when it's published in peer-reviewed journals or summarized in popular magazines, contains hidden bias against girls and women. This section will give you the tools to be a critical consumer of that research and to be able to identify sources of potential bias.

Who Is the Researcher?

How does the identity of the researcher contribute to bias?

Many factors influence the research process, including who actually does the research. The phrase "the myth of the impartial researcher" refers to a common misperception—drawn from positivism—that people who conduct research are value-neutral and thoroughly objective. As discussed earlier, all psychological theories start from personal observations or previously established theories (i.e., concepts based on a previous researcher's work, perhaps based on their own observations). Therefore, if science is primarily conducted by one group of people, it results in a narrow range of possible theories. Most senior authors of peer-reviewed publications are White, upper-class men who are senior professors at top research universities (Cundiff, 2012; Eagly & Riger, 2014). Although it is certainly valuable to develop theories that stem from the life experiences of White, upper-class men, it becomes a problem when that is the predominant worldview represented in psychological research.

As an example, Freud, the founder of psychoanalysis, said that a key component of women's psychological development is their experience of penis envy (Freud, 1905/1949b). In the 1930s, Karen Horney, a psychoanalyst, criticized Freud's inability to consider a woman's perspective and called for a more woman-centered approach (Westkott, 1986). Astonishingly, Freud later responded to her critique by saying, "We shall not be very greatly surprised if a woman analyst, who has not been sufficiently convinced of the intensity of her own wish for a penis, also fails to attach the proper importance to that factor in her patients" (Freud, 1940/1949a, p. 107). How fascinating that Freud was accusing someone else of bias! This example demonstrates the limitations of having only one type of person conduct research.

In 1988, several feminist psychologists published "Guidelines for Avoiding Sexism in Psychological Research" (Denmark, Russo, Frieze, & Sechzer, 1988). They noted many examples of how the predominance of White male researchers caused a bias in what is studied and how questions are asked. For example, they noted that leadership had traditionally been understood as dominance and that topics relating to White men (e.g., television and aggression) were seen as more important than topics relating to women or people with other marginalized identities (e.g., pregnancy and menopause).

What Is the Research Question?

How do research questions themselves contribute to bias?

Who the researcher is will influence not only the formation of theories but also the specific research questions asked. In discussing research about sex differences, for example, psychologist Rhoda Unger (1979) argued that the very decision to study *differences* between women and men reinforced the status quo rather than allowing the discovery of anything new. It's intriguing to consider how different the entire field might be if we changed the question to ask "How are women and men *similar*?" As another example, you might consider what would happen if we asked women to describe their experience of menstrual *joy* instead of menstrual *discomfort*.

There are also hidden assumptions in research questions. Let's imagine, for example, a group of researchers exploring the effects of daycare on child development, with a specific interest in maternal working status. Their research question might be "Should mothers be employed out of the home early in their child's life?" This question doesn't include fathers, so the hidden assumption here is that mothers, not fathers, are the ideal caretakers, and that researchers should question a mother's, but not a father's, employment status during their child's early years. How different do you suppose the findings would be if the researchers explored "Should mothers *or fathers* be employed out of the home early in their child's life?"?

Who Are the Research Participants?

How does the identity of research participants contribute to bias?

Another area of potential bias is choice of participants. Psychological research has a long history of using male participants and then generalizing results to all humans (Eagly & Riger, 2014). For example, Carol Gilligan criticized fellow psychologist Lawrence Kohlberg because his theory of moral development was entirely based on interviews with wealthy, White boys and men (Gilligan, 1982). Kohlberg (1969) argued that children move through a fixed set of stages in which morality shifts from focusing on avoiding punishment, to focusing on following the rules or being "good," to focusing at the highest stage on abstract ideals of individual rights and autonomy. In response, Gilligan argued that Kohlberg's highest stage of development, based on individual autonomy, reflected an androcentric view and didn't include the communal and care ethic often observed in girls and women. Gilligan was especially critical of the way Kohlberg used data collected from boys and men to explain *human* development. According to Gilligan, it was unreasonable to apply findings based on boys and men to girls and women.

Psychological research continues to be guilty of this tendency, which undermines *generalizability*, or the ability to use findings from a given study to explain phenomena that occur in the general population. Even today, the titles of studies rarely indicate when participants are exclusively men or exclusively White (Cundiff, 2012). Yet when participants deviate from the White male norm, researchers not only provide a rationale for their decision but also often signal it in the title of their article (Cundiff, 2012).

Recently, the number of female participants has substantially increased—probably due to their over-representation in psychology undergraduate participant pools, a source of convenience samples for many psychologists (Cundiff, 2012). As a result, most of what we know about human behavior is now based on a very specific type of woman. She's likely an undergraduate student at a large university who is enrolled in an Introduction to Psychology course. Such *sampling bias* overlooks the experiences of all other people. If you think back to other psychology courses you've taken, it might be interesting to recall how often your textbooks indicated *who* was included in the samples used in the studies described. If you knew that a study sample was based only on undergraduate women, would that change your perception of the results?

Sampling bias is also a challenge *within* the field of psychology of women. In its early stages, feminist research didn't fully address the diversity among women. Instead, it focused primarily on the experiences of White, well-educated, middle-class, heterosexual women who were disproportionality members of Western, industrialized, rich, democratic societies (Henrich, Heine, & Norenzayan, 2010). Within a field that was supposedly trying to undo bias, feminist researchers' sole focus on such privileged women actually replicated power hierarchies. It's easy to see how this can happen. When researchers use convenience samples, they tend to get a group of participants who resemble them or the students at their college or university. When research, even feminist research, is predominantly done by White women at predominantly White institutions, this can lead to systematic sampling bias that over-represents the concerns of White, well-educated women. For example, body anxiety centering on concerns about thinness is well researched within the feminist community. However, this research area might reflect concerns that are particularly important to White women, an issue we'll revisit in Chapter 6.

Bias also exists in the ways demographic questions are asked—such as when marginalized women are clumped into one social identity category. The term **LGBTQ** (lesbian, gay, bisexual, transgender, and queer) places all sexual minority individuals into one category, ignoring differences among them. For example, there is tremendous diversity among bisexual women, but this will be overlooked if researchers don't study bisexuality separately from other sexual-minority identities. Notice, too, that the term places all people who are sexual minorities in contrast with people who are heterosexual. In other words, all other people are being compared to heterosexual people. This reinforces the idea that some people are the norm against which all others should be compared—which creates a bias within research.

How Are the Variables Measured?

How does the operationalization of variables contribute to bias?

Another potential source of bias involves the way variables are measured. Recalling the example from above, body anxiety could be measured in many different ways, and decisions about how to operationalize a variable could be a source of bias. Let's take something as seemingly straightforward as aggression. In the past, researchers have measured aggression in mostly overt ways (e.g., physical and verbal assaults; Brown, 2005). By doing this, their data showed that boys were more aggressive than girls. However, when researchers began to measure relational aggression (e.g., gossiping and socially isolating other girls), a different picture emerged: Girls were aggressive too (Crick & Grotpeter, 1995).

Ideally, consumers of psychological science should be informed about how variables are defined, although this information is rarely included in popular press summaries of research. The lack of information makes it hard to evaluate research claims because doing so requires tracking down the original article. How often have you looked for the original article of a study you read about on social media? It can be difficult to find the time to do this, and costly too, because academic journals generally aren't free to the public. For example, in 2017 it cost $36 to purchase access to an individual article published in *Psychology of Women Quarterly* and $106 per year to subscribe to the journal as a whole. If you're a student at a college or a university, you can probably access articles for free through your school's library system—a privilege that not everyone has.

How Are the Data Analyzed?

How does the method used to analyze data contribute to bias?

Most psychological research relies on quantitative methods. As we've discussed, the reliance on statistics also perpetuates bias since the design of many statistics is to look for differences within a sample. Although quantitative research is the most widely used methodology among psychologists, some feminist scholars have advocated the use of another methodology. *Qualitative methods* produce descriptive data, with little attention to statistics. Qualitative researchers often rely on interviews, diaries, observations, and archival data. In these cases, data analysis involves identifying themes or patterns in participants' responses in order to understand how participants interpret various aspects of their lives. Since themes emerge from the data, researchers are, theoretically, less likely to control or manipulate variables and are more flexible in making design changes alongside their study participants. In this approach, researchers and participants can develop close relationships, which is very different from the detached relationships usually associated with quantitative methods.

Feminist researchers are critical of the rigid separation of researchers from study participants, suggesting that it reflects power and control (Rutherford & Granek, 2010). In labs, researchers are considered experts who manipulate situations in order to study outcomes. This hierarchy may be problematic for collecting accurate data. However, qualitative methods offer an exciting alternative to the detached aspect of quantitative methods. One such qualitative method, participatory action research (PAR), includes participants in the decision process during every stage of the research (Yost & Chmielewski, 2013). For example, participants might use cameras to document their day-to-day experiences and then collaborate with the researcher about how to use this information to develop research questions and to design a study.

To minimize bias, researchers should be attentive to all aspects of the scientific method. What areas of research do you think are most vulnerable to bias?

Despite their appeal, qualitative articles are far less likely than quantitative ones to appear in psychology journals. In a review of all psychology journals listed with the academic database PsycINFO from 1960 to 2009, only 8.7% of articles were qualitative (Eagly et al., 2012). Interestingly, most of these articles were written and published outside of the United States (e.g., in Canada, Australia, the United Kingdom), and there was a 26.2% increase in qualitative methods in journal articles that focused on gender (Eagly et. al., 2012). So does research need to be qualitative to be considered feminist? Not at all! Feminist researchers use both qualitative and quantitative methods. However, no matter what methods feminist researchers use, they pay attention to how their own experiences and perspectives influence the questions they ask and the results they find.

How Do Researchers Write about Their Results?

How does the way researchers write about their work contribute to bias?

Bias is also evident in the language used to present research. One concern is use of the generic *man* or *he* to describe humans. This usage is problematic because it both includes and excludes women (Smith et al., 2010). As we'll discuss in Chapter 2, the generic *he* also excludes people who use pronouns that aren't gender specific (e.g., *they/them/their*). Because of this, the APA publication manual advises against using generic pronouns (APA, 2009). Language can also reflect more subtle biases—for example, use of words that have masculine connotations (e.g., *penetrate, dominate*) or descriptions of sex-related differences in ways that are demeaning toward women (e.g., *submissive*). Even in writing this textbook, we came across an instance of our own bias. A reviewer of an early draft pointed out that we were consistently putting men first when we made a statement about "men and women." In a textbook about women, she said, please start with women. These subtle biases might seem unimportant, but the cumulative effect suggests that men should be prioritized. In fact, in a review of psychological studies, male participants' results were disproportionately presented before those of female participants (Miller, Taylor, & Buck, 1991).

Where Are the Results Published?

How does the place where research is published contribute to bias?

You might recall that when describing the hypothetical body anxiety study earlier, we suggested submitting the research article to a journal that focuses on gender. This would ensure that the reviewers had previous knowledge about sex and gender. Although doing this makes a lot of sense, the drawback of always doing this is that research about sex and gender would then only appear in specialized journals. For example, in a review of the literature in 2012, researchers found that 89% of articles published about sex and gender appeared exclusively in *Psychology of Women Quarterly* or *Sex Roles* (Eagly et al., 2012). This means that journals specializing in other aspects of psychology will be less likely than specialized publications to include feminist perspectives.

Further, according to feminist psychologist Stephanie Riger (1992), feminist research shouldn't simply be used for the production of knowledge; it should also be used for social action and social justice. If research is only published in academic journals, it will only reach a small subset of the population that would benefit from it. Feminist researchers prefer to "give research away." Examples include sharing results on social media or through e-mail, and using results in formal conversations with policy makers and legislative bodies that often overlook the psychological needs of marginalized individuals. These efforts are in distinct contrast to the role of detached and objective researcher. Indeed, feminist researchers become advocates as they share their findings and continue to ask questions in hopes of finding answers that can increase equity.

Another way to give research away is to talk about research findings in the popular press. Unfortunately, the popular press tends to simplify the findings of psychological research, particularly those that confirm popularly held stereotypes (O'Connor & Joffe, 2014). Television and social media predominantly feature stories that exaggerate the differences between women and men (Fine 2010; O'Connor & Joffe, 2014). They also generally ignore the diversity among women and often reinforce the idea that everyone can be clearly labeled as either a woman or a man (Golden, 2004). This probably happens because short, simple stories are more likely to be read, which ultimately increases revenue for the media outlets (O'Connor & Joffe, 2014).

Minimizing Bias in Feminist Research

What are key ways psychologists minimize bias in feminist research?

Because the foundation of psychology relies on conducting studies, feminist psychologists have worked to transform inherent biases in both the content and the methods of psychological research (Eagly & Riger, 2014). From their perspective, science is not counter to feminism because it has value in generating reliable information about women's lives. While there is no one type of feminist research, two characteristics tie contemporary feminist researchers together:

- *They are aware of power dynamics inherent in research.* A core belief is that no research method is free of bias and that, therefore, it is essential to carefully consider potential problems at every stage of the research process (Crawford & Kimmel, 1999; Rutherford & Granek, 2010; Unger, 1983). For example, feminist researchers reject the myth of the impartial researcher and avoid making overly simplistic interpretations of their research results. Ironically, feminist researchers have commonly been criticized because they often explicitly acknowledge their biases. In reality, all research is biased, and feminists are just being honest.

■ *They consider intersectionality.* In addition to attending to gender, feminist researchers take into account intersectionality (Cole, 2009; Rutherford & Granek, 2010). In order to ensure that psychological research addresses intersectionality, psychologist Elizabeth Cole (2009) proposed three questions that researchers should ask:

1. *Who is included within this category?* For example, at most universities, if student samples are used, then the experiences of predominantly White and middle-class women are likely to be taken for the experiences of all women. This practice should be avoided.
2. *What role does inequality play?* Due to historical and institutional forces, some social groups have more power than others, and these power differences can shape behavior and experiences. We will address this more in Chapter 2.
3. *Where are the similarities?* Even if people are from different social groups, they may have shared experiences or concerns. For example, people of diverse social identities may all be concerned with violence in their community, although their concerns may express themselves in different ways.

Table 1.2 shows how these questions can inform each stage of the research process.

TABLE 1.2 Questions to Encourage Intersectionality throughout the Research Process

	Question		
	Who is included within this category?	**What role does inequality play?**	**Where are the similarities?**
Research question	Attends to diversity within social categories.	Background research and theory generation attends to social and historical contexts of inequality.	May be exploratory rather than explicitly focusing on similarities.
Participant recruitment	Focuses on underrepresented groups.	Social categories mark groups with unequal access to power and resources.	Diverse groups connected by similar relationships to social and institutional power are included.
Measurement of variables	Measures used are developed from the perspective of the group(s) being studied.	Differences are conceptualized as coming from structural inequalities rather than from individual-level differences.	Social categories are understood in terms of both individual and institutional practices rather than just as characteristics of individuals.
Analysis of data	Attends to diversity within a group—analyses may occur separately for each group studied.	Statistical tests should explore both similarities and differences.	Attention is not just placed on differences.
Interpretation of results	No group's findings are assumed to represent a universal experience.	Differences are interpreted in the context of structural inequalities.	Attention is paid to variations across groups even when similarities are identified.

Note. Adapted from Cole (2009).

In practice, every methodological choice has advantages and limitations. The goal is to constantly reflect on research decisions in order to minimize bias. No method can be completely neutral or objective. Therefore, it's important to read every psychological study with a degree of caution.

Conclusion

As we conclude this chapter, we hope you're developing more questions than answers. You are now in the process of sharpening your critical thinking skills as they relate to psychology. This book has drawn on the most up-to-date research in the psychology of women and gender, but the field is quickly changing. New approaches are urgently needed to address many gendered social and psychological realities. As you continue reading, you might ask yourself how these theories and studies can help you tackle some of the most complicated and controversial topics.

Chapter Review

SUMMARY

A Feminist Psychology for Modern Girls and Women

- Psychology of women is a subfield in psychology that focuses on the lives and experiences of girls and women. It arose alongside the political and social movements connected to feminism.

- Feminism is the movement to end sexism, sexist exploitation, and oppression.

- Feminist psychology includes research and practice that is explicitly informed by feminism.

Feminism: Riding the Waves

- Historians believe the first wave of feminism began in 1848, and it is most associated with the movement for women to gain the right to vote.

- The second wave began in the 1960s and focused on improving women's day-to-day lives, including having more equitable access to paid work and redefining the roles of wife and mother.

- The third wave began in the mid-1990s as a movement to change dominant ideas within feminism, including the notion that there is one universal experience of womanhood.

- Some feminist scholars say we're currently in a retraction between waves; others claim we're in a fourth wave characterized by more sophisticated use of social media to promote activism.

The F-Word

- There are many feminist perspectives, including liberal, radical, socialist, cultural, women of color, queer, and post-colonial/transnational.

- Despite diversity and occasional conflict within feminist perspectives, all feminisms share the goal of ending sexist exploitation and oppression.

I'm Not a Feminist, But . . .

- Some people claim we are living in a post-feminist era, characterized by the idea that the women's movement has achieved its goals and, therefore, feminism is no longer needed.
- Negative stereotypes about feminists contribute to some people not identifying with feminism, which makes them less active in addressing social inequities.

Who Is a Feminist?

- Although many women endorse some feminist beliefs, fewer are willing to identify as feminists.
- Some women prefer the term *womanist* or *mujerista* (compared to *feminist*) because it acknowledges racism and other forms of discrimination along with sexism.
- Some men prefer the term *pro-feminist*, a label that incorporates feminism but also expresses an interest in working alongside girls and women for social change.
- Men who identify as feminists are less likely to use sexist language and are more likely to recognize social inequities and confront instances of sex bias than men who don't identify as feminists.
- Women who identify as feminists reap the greatest psychological gains and are more likely than those who don't identify as feminists to engage in activism, which promotes social change.

Feminism Comes to Psychology

- Most early research by female psychologists aimed to dispute biological determinism.

- In the early 20th century, many women of color faced double discrimination because of their multiple minority status.
- Psychology of women became an academic field in the 1960s and the 1970s, corresponding with a surge in civil rights activism.
- In the early 1980s, feminist psychologists began to critique the scientific method—particularly assumptions that science is progressive and cumulative; that it relies on objectivity, neutrality, and rationality; and that it can discover universal truths.

Understanding Research Methods

- The field of psychology relies on the scientific method, and the history of its use to study girls and women has not been bias-free.
- The scientific method begins with a theory, which leads to a hypothesis, which becomes refined through the process of collecting data and drawing conclusions based on those data.
- In a correlational research design, relationships between variables are examined. In an experiment, the researcher manipulates a variable to investigate whether changes in one variable cause a change in another variable, providing the ability to make causal conclusions.

Identifying Sex/Gender Bias in Research

- To minimize bias in research, feminist psychologists pay attention to every stage of the process—including researcher and participant identities, research questions, operationalization of variables, data analyses, publication of results, and media attention. When people evaluate research, it's important for them to consider these factors too.
- Feminist researchers are unified through their awareness of power dynamics and consideration of intersectionality.

KEY TERMS

psychology of women (p. 15)
feminism (p. 15)
feminist psychology (p. 15)

oppression (p. 15)
empowerment (p. 17)
intersectionality (p. 22)

liberal feminism (p. 24)

structural inequalities (p. 24)

radical feminism (p. 25)

patriarchy (p. 25)

androcentric (p. 25)

lesbian feminism (p. 25)

compulsory heterosexuality (p. 25)

socialist feminism (p. 25)

myth of meritocracy (p. 26)

cultural feminism (p. 27)

gender essentialism (p. 27)

women of color feminism (p. 27)

ethnocentrism (p. 29)

queer feminism (p. 29)

heternormativity (p. 30)

cisgender identity (p. 30)

transgender (p. 30)

post-colonial/transnational feminism (p. 30)

third world feminism (p. 31)

post-feminism (p. 32)

womanist (p. 34)

mujerista (p. 34)

positivism (p. 42)

feminist epistemologies (p. 42)

LGBTQ (p. 50)

THINK ABOUT IT

1. What are the limits of and opportunities for the concept of empowerment? Does it offer girls and women an opportunity to make change in the world?

2. Think about a current issue facing women in your community. How would each of the different feminist theories think about and address it?

3. Imagine you're having a conversation with a friend who isn't familiar with feminism. How would you explain feminism to that person? Given the research on feminist identification, what is the value in identifying as a feminist?

4. In what ways are current political and academic climates similar to those experienced by feminist psychologists in the past? In what ways are they different?

5. Using PsycINFO, find a peer-reviewed research article that discusses an issue related to the psychology of girls and women. Applying the three questions of intersectionality, in what ways does the article address intersectionality? If it doesn't, how could it be improved to better address intersectionality?

ONLINE RESOURCES

- **AMENA-Psy** — resources provided by the American Arab, Middle Eastern, and North African Psychological Association, with attention toward intersectionality and post-colonial psychology: amenapsy.org

- **Feminist.com** — activist resources: feminist.com

- **Feministing** — an online community of feminist activists and bloggers by and for young feminists: feministing.com

- **Psychology's Feminist Voices** — firsthand accounts of feminist psychologists who were instrumental in creating and sustaining feminist psychology: feministvoices.com

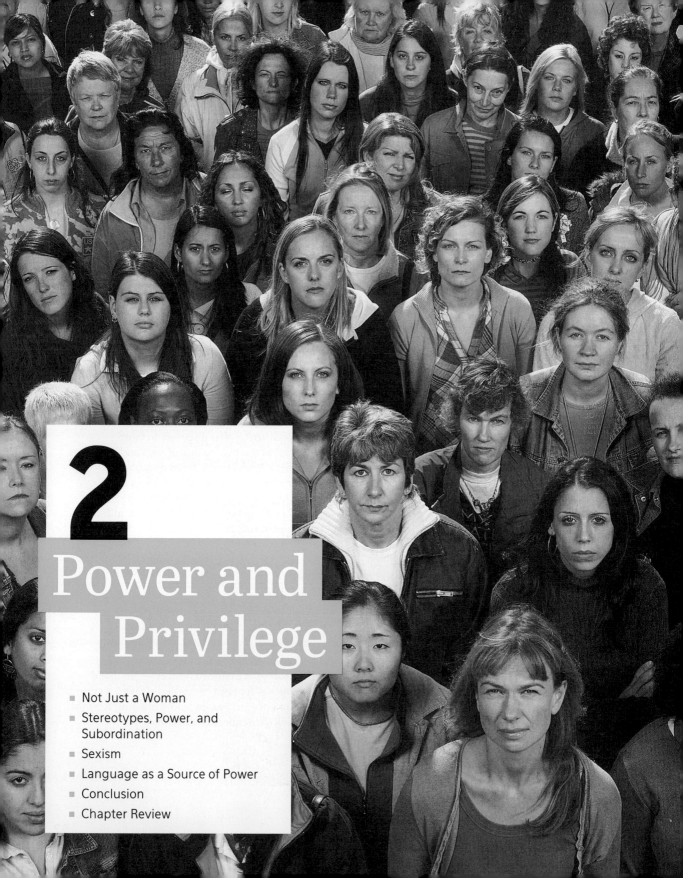

2

Power and Privilege

- Not Just a Woman
- Stereotypes, Power, and Subordination
- Sexism
- Language as a Source of Power
- Conclusion
- Chapter Review

AT SIX YEARS OF AGE, Sophie Cruz appeared small, but her voice was gigantic when she addressed the 500,000-plus people who gathered for the Women's March in Washington, D.C., in January 2017. In both Spanish and English, she called on people to "fight with love, faith and courage so that our families will not be destroyed" (Blay, 2017, para. 3). Sophie spoke about the urgency of immigration reform, one of the many social issues elevated at the Women's March. Along with 2.6 million people worldwide, Sophie showed up to demand recognition for a series of principles uniting women that were outlined on the march's official website (Rogers, 2016). These principles included ending violence and advocating for reproductive freedoms, LGBTQIA rights, workers' rights, civil rights, disability rights, women's rights, immigrant rights, and environmental justice ("Our mission," n.d.). Sophie was the youngest speaker that day, showing that involvement in feminist activism can occur at any age.

For some, this march was a great success—a resurgence of feminist activism. The *New York Times* reported that it was the largest single-day demonstration in U.S. history (Chenoweth & Pressman, 2017). Many sister marches took place on the same day, with at least 261 solidarity marches occurring outside of the United States, from Antarctica to Zimbabwe. The momentum was undeniable, but critics raised concerns about the march's inclusivity and messaging (Tolentino, 2017). Since these criticisms started at the origin of the march, it is helpful to understand its evolution.

The Women's March started as a grassroots initiative when Teresa Shook, a retired attorney and grandmother, created a Facebook event suggesting that

Sophie Cruz was the youngest person to address the 500,000-plus people who gathered for the Women's March in Washington, D.C., in January 2017.

friends rally in Washington, D.C., against what she saw as the biased and inflammatory rhetoric that occurred during the 2016 U.S. presidential campaign. Her message went viral, and overnight more than 10,000 people agreed to attend. Shook wanted to call the event a Million Woman March, a name originally claimed by a famous Black women's unity march held in Philadelphia in 1997. As interest in Shook's event grew, however, contentious conversations began (Stockman, 2017). Author Mariella Mosthof (2017) reported that many women of color felt White women's use of this name was inappropriate and an example of appropriation, especially given the concern that the rally would primarily focus on issues that affected White women. This concern was related to the fact that the march's initial leadership consisted of White women (Desmond-Harris, 2017; Ramanathan, 2017). Racial tensions especially flared up on social media when some White women became defensive and angry after being "asked to check their privilege" (Stockman, 2017, para. 15). Eventually, the name was changed to the Women's March, and the planning became more sophisticated when three experienced and well-respected female community leaders of color—Tamika Mallory, Carmen Perez, and Linda Sarsour—joined as co-chairs.

Others were angered by the predominant use of genitalia imagery (Goins-Phillips, 2017). On the day of the march, many participants wore pink "pussy" hats. While this seemed fun and empowering to some of the participants, the use of genitalia as a political symbol seemed exclusionary to other participants, especially to transgender women. Some also felt that emphasizing women's genitalia to symbolize women's rights was objectifying rather than a symbol of empowerment (Perlmutter, 2017).

Figuring out the best way to mobilize women in order to combat oppression is challenging and complex. Much of the complexity is due to the fact that sources of inequality are not simply based on gender; they're also based on race, socioeconomic status, religion, age, and a multitude of other variables. Without paying careful attention to how systems of power and oppression work, there is a problematic tendency to replicate exclusionary and oppressive practices. The organizers of the march wanted to make clear that "women's rights" meant those of *all* girls and women of *all* backgrounds. This was an important goal, but it led to conflict when the effort to balance the interests and needs of many diverse women became a source of tension among would-be participants.

Conflict like this is an inevitable part of organizing women from a variety of backgrounds with different levels of power and representation. Yet anti-feminist critics used the within-group conflict as evidence that the march lacked a unified or justifiable message (Christie, 2017; Dalmia, 2017; May, 2017; Van Laar, 2017).

In particular, critics felt that a focus on so many principles spread feminism too thin, making it politically useless. Brittany Cooper, a professor of Women's & Gender Studies and Africana Studies, disagreed. She said, "When we organize under the banner of shared womanhood, acknowledging all these moving parts makes our collective work not weaker but stronger" (Desmond-Harris, 2017, para. 49).

Anti-feminist critics also wondered why women were marching at all. They felt that the rally promoted a false sense of victimhood on the part of women who were looking for a reason to be angry (Christie, 2017). From the critics' perspective, it was inappropriate for women participating in the march to claim disenfranchisement because, as the critics saw it, the only thing that would stop a woman from achieving empowerment is her own inabilities. As we discussed in Chapter 1, this position is consistent with post-feminism ideas.

The conflicts surrounding the march demonstrate some of the critical issues facing contemporary feminism. Many dynamics are involved, as well as dozens of urgent social concerns. In 1984, the feminist writer and activist Audre Lorde said, "There is no such thing as a single-issue struggle because we do not live single-issue lives" (Lorde, 2007, p. 138). As a result, figuring out how to be inclusive and attentive to many different issues, while staying unified enough to actually get something done, continues to be one of the most pressing challenges for feminists.

In this chapter, we'll explore what it means to say that some people have more power than others. First, we'll examine women's varied social identities and how they're connected to larger social systems that give some women more access to power than other women—and, in general, give men more power than women. We'll also explore how these power dynamics are often difficult to see. We'll then consider how certain stereotypical assumptions contribute to maintaining power dynamics among groups of people. Finally, we'll explore how power relates to sexism and how sexism is sometimes so subtle that it blends into normal parts of daily life.

Not Just a Woman

What are women's varied social characteristics, how do they influence an individual woman's experience, and how do they connect to the matrix of domination?

A woman is not just a woman. Her identity also includes a race/ethnicity, social class, sexual orientation, religion, nationality, and age as well as a variety of other characteristics. These categories form a **social identity**, a person's sense of self, which is based on that individual's affiliations with different social groups (Tajfel & Turner, 1979). As individuals, our social identity is deeply personal because it ultimately determines how we experience and express ourselves (Shields, 2008). At the same time, our social identity is connected to other people. For example, we derive positive feelings of self-worth and belonging when a member of our group succeeds, and we worry that poor behavior on the part of a fellow group member might reflect poorly on us (Cohen & Garcia, 2005; Sellers, Rowley, Chavous, Shelton, & Smith, 1997). Additionally, how we perceive ourselves and how others perceive us isn't necessarily fixed—it can vary across time and from situation to situation. For example, Evelyn Alsultany, director of Arab and Muslim American Studies at the University of Michigan, reports that she is perceived to be Latinx in some U.S. contexts, Arab in some other places, and not adequately Arab, Latinx, or American in other places (Alsultany, 2002).

Social Identity

One way to think about social identity is through a model developed by psychologist Pamela Hayes (2001) called the ADDRESSING model (see Table 2.1). She outlined 10 social characteristic variables with initial letters that spell the

TABLE 2.1 The ADDRESSING Model for Exploring Social Identity with Examples from the United States

Social Characteristic	Power	Less Power
Age	Adults	Children, adolescents, elders
Developmental disability	Neurotypical individuals	Neurodivergent individuals
Disability status (acquired)	People without a disability	People with acquired physical/ cognitive/ psychological disability
Religion	Christians	Jews, Muslims, atheists, other non-Christians
Ethnicity	European Americans	People of color
Social class	Middle-class and educated people	Poor and working-class people
Sexual orientation	Heterosexual people	People with sexual minority identities
Indigenous background	Non-native people	Native peoples
National origin	U.S.-born people	Immigrants and refugees
Gender	Men	Female, transgender, non-binary, and intersex people

Note. Content adapted from Hayes (2001).

word addressing, and noted that these characteristics are linked to power. This situation reflects **social stratification**, or the idea that people are ranked in a hierarchy such that some people and groups have more power and status than others. In contemporary society, being White, male, able-bodied, heterosexual, well educated, and middle-aged are all social categories that are deemed powerful.

In Chapter 1, we discussed intersectionality, a concept that describes the ways in which different types of oppression (e.g., racism, classism, homophobia, transphobia, ableism, sexism) are interconnected and cannot be examined as separate entities (Crenshaw, 1993). When an intersectional framework is applied to social identity, it's best to think of the social characteristics outlined in the ADDRESSING model as a cake, rather than as a beaded necklace (Bowleg, 2013; Ferber & O'Reilly Herrera, 2013; Ken, 2010; Spelman, 1990). In the beaded necklace analogy, individual social characteristics (e.g., race, gender, religion) are seen as different-colored beads strung together to make up a single piece of jewelry (Spelman, 1990). This analogy is problematic because any bead can be removed or added as a separate entity without changing the substance of another bead (Ferber & O'Reilly Herrera, 2013). In the cake analogy, each social characteristic is seen as an ingredient in a cake (Ken, 2010). For example, gender could be sugar, and religion could be eggs. Once the cake is baked, the result is something fundamentally different from any and all of its ingredients (Bowleg, 2013). Each ingredient changes form and interacts with the others during the process of baking, with the result that, say, the sugar can no longer be separated from the eggs. The whole is greater than the sum of the parts, but the parts also change in relation to one another. In this way, the cake analogy is a better depiction of social identity. It's not truly possible to study gender in isolation because it's only one part of the overall cake (Ken, 2010).

your turn

Using the characteristics in the ADDRESSING model, how do you understand your social identity? In what ways do these characteristics inform one another to make your social identity unique? On which characteristics do you have power, and on which do you have less power? Which of these characteristics do you routinely think of as part of your identity, and which ones are not typically included in how you define yourself?

Research provides support for the notion that individuals perceive inextricable links among their various social characteristics (Chun, Lipsitz, & Shin, 2013; Harnois, 2015; Juan, Syed, & Azmitia, 2016). For example, in one study of 89 Black women, all participants rated the combination of a Black-woman identity as more important than a singular identity of race (Black) or gender (woman; Settles, 2006). Therefore, for these participants, race and gender couldn't be separated, resulting in a unique racialized gendered identity. In another study, researchers found that across three biracial subgroups of women and men (Latinx-White, Asian-White, and Black-White), socioeconomic status, religion, and gender determined how participants defined their racial identity (Davenport, 2016). For example, those who were upper class and had a Jewish religious affiliation were likely to identify as White, whereas those affiliated with religions that are usually associated with racial minorities were likely to claim a minority identification. Women, however, were more likely to identify as multi-racial than were their male counterparts. Overall, then, how people see themselves on one dimension (e.g., race) may be affected by their status on another (e.g., class, religion, gender).

Our different identity characteristics can also influence how others see us. In a study conducted in the United Kingdom, researchers found that South Asian Muslim women were less likely to receive employment than their similarly credentialed White Christian female counterparts (Tariq & Syed, 2017). This finding suggests that the combination of race, religion, and gender influenced and changed another social characteristic—class (because class is connected to social mobility and income, which are affected by employment status). Class intersected with other social characteristics in another study comparing working-class and upper-middle-class Chinese immigrant women (Zhou, 2000). After immigrating to the United States, participants reported a shift in gender roles within the family, but this outcome was based on class. Upper-middle-class participants experienced a decline in their power to make financial decisions for the family, and working-class participants reported increased power because they had begun to financially contribute to their families.

The various aspects of women's social identities are intertwined and complex. No two women's experiences are the same because access to power varies. According to an intersectional perspective, it's not enough to examine bias based on sex/gender without also considering the ways other forms of oppression contribute to any given situation (Cole, 2009; Gunnarsson, 2017). The idea that each system of bias (e.g., racism, homophobia, sexism) interconnects with and stems from the same system of social stratification is known as the **matrix of domination** (Collins, 1990). From this perspective, it's impossible to eradicate sexism without also ending other interconnecting oppressions (e.g., racism, classism). Therefore, many feminist scholars argue that developing the capacity to work together—even with tensions and conflicts like those experienced during the planning of the Women's March—is the best approach for undoing the overall structure of oppressive forces.

Power Hierarchies

What are the mechanisms by which those with a dominant status maintain their power, and why is this often difficult to see?

As discussed in Chapter 1, there is a widely held perception that merit often accounts for why some people have more than others. However, life's playing field isn't level, and some people have advantages simply because of aspects of their identity. **Privilege** is a term that describes the social, economic, and/or political advantages that people enjoy simply because they're part of a certain

TABLE 2.2 Characteristics Associated with Members of Dominant and Subordinate Groups

Dominant Group	Subordinate Group
Have access to power and resources	Have reduced access to power and resources
Establish norms and standards	Are perceived as less than or deviant from dominant norms and standards
Have limited awareness of or knowledge about subordinate groups	Have increased awareness of and knowledge about dominant groups
Are believed to be competent and credible—given the benefit of the doubt	Are viewed suspiciously—not given the benefit of the doubt
Create "truth" or "reality"	Have their truth and experiences dismissed and/or invalidated
Are seen as individuals	Are seen as representing a group
Have a sense of belonging	Feel invisible or hyper-visible

Note. Content adapted from Goodman (2011).

group, rather than because of anything they did or failed to do (Johnson, 2006; McIntosh, 1989). Privilege results in tangible benefits—such as increased security and money for housing, food, health care, and education—which almost always results in greater power (Case, 2013). Table 2.2 shows key characteristics associated with people who have either more privilege or less—that is, who are members of either dominant or subordinate groups.

Unearned Entitlements Privilege gives people *unearned entitlements*, or things of value that ideally should be provided to everyone but aren't (Johnson, 2006; McIntosh, 1989). Let's consider high school sports events. Boys' teams tend to have more fanfare and publicity than girl's teams. Girls' sporting events are less likely to have halftime performances, cheerleaders, or a stadium full of spectators (Dusenbery & Lee, 2012). Also, teams from wealthy school districts generally have more access to nicely fitting uniforms and transportation to games. In fact, even the ability to have a high school sports team is more likely in wealthier districts (Wong, 2015). In other words, some athletes enjoy additional perks simply because they live in a wealthy school district (mostly likely indicating that they were born into an upper-class or upper-middle-class family) or because they play on male sports teams. In this sense, the perks are an unearned entitlement because they aren't necessarily based on performance.

Another aspect of an unearned entitlement is that the characteristics of privileged groups are considered normal (or the default), and all others are compared to that group. For example, being male is considered the norm, and

In 2016, controversy erupted when an all-White team of directors and producers cast Zoe Saldana (left) to play Nina Simone (right) in the biopic about the singer. Although Saldana identifies as Black, some critics claimed that Saldana's features are much whiter and more anglicized than Simone's, and that Simone was being white-washed.

many institutions are organized around a male standard. As one feminist scholar pointed out, "Men's physiology defines most sports, their health needs define insurance coverage, their social needs define biographies, workplace patterns and career expectations . . . their image defines god, and their genitals define sex" (MacKinnon, 1989, p. 224). The same dynamic occurs with Whiteness. For example, as we'll discuss in Chapter 6, White beauty is considered the norm, and women are held to that standard, even when reaching it is impossible. When celebrities of color are featured in beauty magazines, they're often "whitewashed" or "anglicized" (Kite, 2012). And in theatrical contexts, lighter-skinned actresses are often given the parts of darker-skinned characters, although the reverse is rarely true. For example, the singer/songwriter Nina Simone was a dark-skinned Black woman who often spoke out about how she was mistreated due to her skin tone. However, when a movie was made about her life (*Nina*, 2016), an all-White team of directors and producers cast Zoe Saldana—a light-skinned actress with more typically European features—in the title role.

The idea that White is normative is also evident in what's considered an appropriate hairstyle. For example, companies such as Air France, Six Flags, and FedEx faced—and lost—lawsuits when they created policies that banned people of color from wearing their hair natural and/or in dreadlocks (Afro-Europe, 2012; Battle, 2017; Cukan, 2001; Gandy, 2017; Gearty, 2001; Gordon, 2006; Honey, 2017). The companies claimed that such hairstyles were not typical or appropriate for the workplace (Dossou, 2013). In one study, Black women reported more anxiety surrounding their hair and more pressure than White women to straighten their hair for work (Johnson, Godsil, MacFarlane, Tropp, & Goff, 2017). To combat such discrimination, many career women have posted pictures of their natural hair to the #naturalisprofessional campaign (Wells, 2016). Feminist scholars have identified that an unearned entitlement of White people is the ability to wear their hair as it grows and to have their hairstyle considered normal, professional, and appropriate. This is an entitlement that White women rarely think about. Black women, however, must spend time, money, and effort managing their hair if they want to more closely match the dominant norm. In fact, market research indicates that Black female consumers are the highest users of hair-care products, resulting in a $2.7 billion industry in the United States (Hare, 2016).

Invisibility As another consequence of dominant groups being considered normative, individuals with multiple marginalized social characteristics are often invisible (Purdie-Vaughns & Eiback, 2008). This is because their identity isn't considered prototypical in a particular social category (Purdie-Vaughns & Eibach, 2008). For example, in the category of race, the prototypical member is White, and in the category of gender, the prototypical member is male. As a result, Black women often go unnoticed or unheard because of their non-prototypical status in regard to race (Black) and gender (female). This is very evident in the fact that the contributions of White women are more readily associated with second wave feminist activism (Freedman, 2013) and in the fact that the contributions of Black men during the 1960s civil rights movement tend to overshadow those of Black women (hooks, 1989).

The tendency to render non-prototypical people less visible has been tested empirically. In one study, researchers provided White college students with a memory task and found that the participants were less likely to remember photos of Black women than those of White women or Black men (Sesko & Biernat, 2010). The same participants were also less likely to recall statements made by Black women than those made by White women or Black men. In another study, participants read about a pair of employees assigned to work together at a task in which they either succeeded or failed (Biernat & Sesko, 2013). Participants were then asked to rate the competence and deserved salary of each of the employees. Researchers found a pro-male bias in the White male–White female work pair, but not in the White male–Black female pair or the Black male–Black female pair. The researchers speculated that the Black women were buffered from the effects of gender bias by virtue of their non-prototypicality, or invisibility. These findings support the idea that both White women and Black men have the privilege of being seen as prototypical members of their groups (women and Black people, respectively), and that they are more likely than Black women to be noticed and remembered.

Conferred Dominance A second component of privilege is *conferred dominance*, in which one group (e.g., men) is socially assumed to have more authority or power over another group (e.g., women; Johnson, 2006). There are many ways in which men are considered more dominant and, therefore, more capable than women. One way this assumption plays out is in the expectation that men are more effective leaders than women or that men should be in charge and women should follow (Eagly & Sczesny, 2009; Ryan, Haslam, & Postmes, 2007; Schlehofer, Casad, Bligh, & Grotto, 2011). Another example occurs among people with disabilities, who are often treated as if they are much younger than their actual age or not capable because of their disability (Johnson, 2006). For example, in the 1988 Winter Paralympic Games, Diana Golden Brosnihan won a gold medal skiing on one leg with regular ski poles. Although she wanted to be admired for her athleticism and skill, in media reports her capacity to "overcome" her disability became the sole focus of her success (Litsky, 2001; Lorber & Moore, 2007).

Why don't people regularly challenge such expressions of privilege? This is because most people adhere to **legitimizing myths** (Chen & Tyler, 2001). These are attitudes, values, or beliefs that exist to justify social hierarchies. Many people tend to believe that certain things are "just true"—for example, that men are natural leaders and that women are naturally better at doing care work (Koenig, Eagly, Mitchell, & Ristikari, 2011). Many legitimizing myths about gender are based on assumptions about gender differences—a topic we'll explore in Chapter 3. Other legitimizing myths may involve race, class, or ability status. For example, some people believe that individuals with disabilities are less competent than those without disabilities or that people who speak English as a first language will be better representatives of an organization than those for whom English is not their first language (Cichy, Li, McMahon, & Rumrill, 2015; Lee & Rice, 2007).

The Invisibility of Privilege

Why is it often difficult to notice privilege, what does it mean to check your privilege, and how can having a subordinate status positively influence someone?

You may have heard the phrase "check your privilege," but you may not be entirely sure what that means or how you're supposed to do that. As was evident during the Women's March, there's often a lot of confusion about privilege, who has it, and how it works. It's also difficult to see when we have privilege. Indeed, privilege is often invisible to those experiencing it, even among people who are socially conscious and trying to address inequality (McIntosh, 1989; Wildman, 1996). This might have been the case for the White women who responded angrily and defensively in discussions about White privilege during the planning of the Women's March. White people probably don't spend a great deal of time contemplating their Whiteness and what it means to their position in society. Likewise, heterosexual people probably don't spend much time wondering if they're heterosexual and why they are, or wondering when or if they should come out as heterosexual to friends or family. In the same vein, a Christian student probably wouldn't notice that classes are cancelled for Christmas but not for Yom Kippur—but a Jewish student probably would.

Because most people have both subordinate and dominant identity characteristics, people can be in one or more privileged groups but still not think they have a great deal of status or power overall (Wise & Case, 2013). For example, if a White man is poor, not well educated, and under-employed, he may think he doesn't have much power or status in society. In this case, the social class dimension may be more noticeable to him than the race or gender dimensions. He still benefits from a great number of privileges associated with being White and male. For example, this man would probably be perceived as more competent than a similarly educated woman, especially within a masculinized setting like a blue-collar job (Eagly & Carli, 2003). He would also be less likely than a man of color in his social class to be pulled over by police or harassed while shopping (Brunson, 2007).

However, it can be difficult to notice the rewards associated with being in a dominant group because people generally don't notice when things are *not* happening to them. For example, the man described above may feel angry and put upon, especially when listening to upper-class people of color speaking about race or upper-class women speaking about feminism. In fact, he may resent people telling him that he's privileged because he's a White man, because he certainly does *not* feel privileged. The privileges he does have are invisible to him, and when people point them out, he may feel that he's being criticized. This is a major barrier for creating positive change because, rather than directing anger at the power structure that causes his feeling of subordination, he may engage in **scapegoating**. In other words, he may blame a person or a group for things that are not their fault. Even though his resentment may be directed toward women or ethnic minority individuals, the real source of his perceived low social status is the social stratification that makes his social class subordinate.

Individuals who have multiple social characteristics that are low in privilege face many challenges. However, there is evidence that they also develop unique perspectives (Fiske, 2010a). In a study that explored altruism among Black adults in an urban, economically distressed housing community, participants reported a heightened sense of responsibility toward their fellow community members (Mattis et al., 2008). Those with slightly more resources shared food, clothing, housing, or child care because they empathized with the challenges of others less well-off than them. In interviews with three Afro-Peruvian female leaders participating in the World Conference against Racism held in Durban, South Africa, in 2001, sociologist Sylvanna Falcón (2008) discovered that their approach to political action was unique because of their capacity to encompass race, gender, and nationality in their worldview. In other words, their multiple marginalized identities gave them unique insights and interpersonal skills to navigate between and among different social identity groups.

What might you discover if you "checked your privilege"? Recognizing privilege can be difficult, but feminists and other activists recommend that everyone consider their own privileged identities when thinking about the challenge of eradicating oppressive systems, including sexism. We'll return to these ideas in Chapter 14.

Stereotypes, Power, and Subordination

What are common gender stereotypes, and how do they vary based on women's other social characteristics?

The counter to privilege is subordination, and much like privilege, experiences of subordination are often difficult to notice. **Sexism**, or a bias based on the belief that men are superior to women, looks different today than it did in the past. In Chapter 1, we discussed the fact that sexism has changed forms over time and is now more difficult to see. This is one reason why many people think we live in a post-feminist era where the women's movement has achieved its goals and, therefore, feminism is no longer needed. But sexism still permeates all societies worldwide. It has been said that a fish doesn't know it's swimming in water. We can think of sexism as water, and all of us as fish. We don't notice sexism because it's all around us—we're swimming in it!

Sexism begins with stereotypes. A **stereotype** is a set of beliefs about the characteristics of a particular group that are generalized to all members of that group (Judd & Park, 1993). Since nothing can ever be true of all group members, stereotypes are inherently problematic, and they influence not only what we expect from people but also how we interact with them. Some stereotypes are based on **gender roles**, or the behaviors within a culture that are generally considered acceptable or desirable for a person based on that individual's actual or perceived gender. Feminist psychologists consider rigid gender role beliefs to be a source of control over girls and women because of the ways in which people are socialized to adhere to stereotypes.

Gender stereotype research has often focused on two major dimensions: communion and agency (Bakan, 1966; Fiske, Cuddy, Glick, & Xu, 2002). In the past, men were likely to be considered **agentic**—that is, assertive, dominant, competitive, and acting to get things done (Newport, 2001). In contrast, women were likely to be considered **communal**—that is, warm, friendly, concerned with others, and emotionally expressive. These traits were considered fundamental to what it meant to be a woman and a man. For example, when study participants were asked to list traits associated with the terms *feminine* and *masculine*, the vast majority of responses fell on the communal/agentic dimension (Deaux & Lewis, 1984). But these stereotypes don't strictly reflect today's reality. Other research has shown that women and men are equally assertive and agentic (Twenge, 1997, 2001; Twenge, Campbell, & Gentile, 2012). However, the association of men with agentic traits and women with communal traits continues to this day (Abele, & Wojciszke, 2014; Conway & Vartanian, 2000).

Traditionally, communal or feminine traits are considered "nice," but they don't confer power or status. Being seen as nice but incompetent is characteristic of other lower-status groups. For example, people over age 65 or people with disabilities are often seen as "nice" and "sweet," but they're considered less competent than younger or able-bodied and neurotypical people (Fiske, 2010b). In contrast, traditionally agentic or masculine traits confer a sense of competence and power. In fact, participants in one study described low-status people as having communal traits and high-status people as having agentic traits (Conway & Vartanian, 2000). Some scholars believe that boys are socialized to take on characteristics associated with masculinity (e.g., strength, ambition, restricted emotion, aggression) because these characteristics convey power and status, which ultimately maintain patriarchy (Levant & Richmond, 2016).

Although, in general, women are stereotyped as communal, there are within-group differences. In one study that examined the intersection of class and gender, primarily White midwestern college students described poor women in ways that matched both masculine (e.g., hardworking, responsible) and feminine (e.g., friendly, loving, family-oriented) stereotypes (Cozzarelli, Tagler, & Wilkinson, 2002). A similar finding emerged for lesbian women, who were stereotyped by undergraduate German students as having more masculine attributes than heterosexual women (Niedlich & Steffens, 2015). In contrast, transgender women were stereotyped by a sample of primarily White American university students as being communal and having a high degree of attentiveness to feminine appearance (e.g., wearing makeup and wigs; Gazzola & Morrison, 2014). In this regard, they were seen as stereotypically feminine in similar ways to cisgender women.

Racialized Sexist Stereotypes

What are some specific ways in which gender stereotypes can be impacted by racism?

Gender stereotypes can also be influenced by racial/ethnic identity. In one study, researchers asked primarily White college students to assess the communal and agentic characteristics of 20 people who were described differently in terms of gender (female, male), race (Black, White), and age (adolescent, young adult, middle-aged, young-old, and old-old; Andreoletti, Leszczynski & Disch, 2015). Responses showed that while gender stereotypes about agency and communion generally held up across the life span, they were more applicable to

White people than Black people. In particular, Black women were less likely to be perceived in traditional gender-stereotypic ways across the life span.

In another study, researchers asked American undergraduate students to generate attributes of different groupings of people based solely on race/ethnicity or gender (e.g., Asian Americans, Black Americans, Latinx Americans, Middle Eastern Americans, or White Americans; men or women), or by groupings based on race/ethnicity-by-gender pairings (e.g., Black men or Latinx women; Ghavami & Peplau, 2013). As shown in Table 2.3, the researchers found many stereotypes that differed by both race/ethnicity and gender as well as by the interaction of the two. In the race/ethnicity-by-gender condition, participants generated different and unique attributes that weren't generated when students worked with groupings focusing on only race or gender. For example, Middle Eastern *women* were described as family oriented, quiet, and housewives, but these attributes weren't offered when participants were asked about Middle Eastern people in general or Middle Eastern men. Attributes associated with ethnic groups when no gender was specified were more similar to those given for men than for women in each group. Also, when participants were asked to list attributes of women and men with no race/ethnicity specified, their descriptions were most similar to those provided for White women and White men as compared to ethnic minority women and ethnic minority men. Black women in particular, who were described as "loud, assertive, and having an attitude," were found to share few attributes with White women (p. 118).

The prominent stereotype of the *strong Black woman* (SBW) combines two central and overlapping concepts: caregiving (feminine) and strength (masculine; Donovan & West, 2015). This stereotype perpetuates the idea that Black women are tough, naturally strong, self-sacrificing, and communal (Collins, 2004; Wallace, 1990). In her description of the SBW stereotype, writer Tamara Winfrey Harris said, "We are the mothers who make a way out of no way. On TV, we are the no-nonsense police chiefs and judges. We are the First Ladies with the impressive biceps" (Winfrey Harris, 2014, p. 1).

Historians believe that the concept of the strong Black woman arose as a means to cope with the violence of slavery and that it has been passed down intergenerationally, particularly from mothers to daughters (Thomas & King, 2007). When Black women endorse the SBW stereotype, they see it as a positive way to promote pride (Abrams, Maxwell, Pope, & Belgrave, 2014; Romero, 2000). However, this stereotype emphasizes self-sacrifice, and in response, Black women

Inspired by a speech given by Michelle Obama, CaShawn Thompson created the hashtag #blackgirlmagic to celebrate the resiliency of Black girls and women. While many people found the hashtag empowering, others were concerned that this effort might reinforce the strong Black woman stereotype. What do you think?

TABLE 2.3 Attributes Associated with Women and Men of Different Racial/Ethnic Groups

Black People	Black Men	Black Women
Ghetto/unrefined	Athletic	Have an attitude
Criminals	Dark-skinned*	Loud
Athletic	Loud	Big butt*
Loud	Quick to anger*	Overweight*
Gangsters	Tall	Confident*
Middle Eastern People	**Middle Eastern Men**	**Middle Eastern Women**
Terrorists	Bearded	Quiet*
Dark-skinned	Dark-skinned	Religious
Oppress women	Terrorists	Covered*
Muslim	Sexist	Oppressed
Hairy	Speak English with accent	Conservative
Latinx People	**Latinx Men**	**Latinx Women**
Poor	Macho	Feisty*
Have many children	Poor	Curvy*
Illegal immigrants	Dark-skinned	Loud
Dark-skinned	Day laborers	Attractive
Uneducated	Promiscuous*	Good cooks*
White People	**White Men**	**White Women**
High status	Rich	Arrogant
Rich	Tall	Blond
Intelligent	Intelligent	Rich
Arrogant	Assertive*	Attractive
Privileged	Arrogant	Small build/petite
Asian American People	**Asian American Men**	**Asian American Women**
Intelligent	Intelligent	Intelligent
Bad drivers	Short	Quiet
Good at math	Nerdy	Short
Nerdy	Quiet	Bad drivers
Shy	Good at math	Shy

Note. Content drawn from Ghavami & Peplau (2013). Additional attributes are listed in the source. *Attributes participants used to describe only one gender are designated with an asterisk.

may de-prioritize self-care and be less willing to ask for help. In fact, endorsing the idea of constant resiliency in the face of serious hardship is associated with negative mental and physical health outcomes. For example, embracing the SBW stereotype has been related to depression, obesity, and cardiovascular disease among Black women (Donovan & West, 2015; Harrington, Crowther, & Shipherd, 2010; Watson & Hunter, 2015). In addition to the SBW stereotype, there is another, more pejorative stereotype of an angry Black woman, which depicts Black women as hostile, irrational, and overbearing (Ashley, 2014). This stereotype can serve to silence Black women who are afraid that if they express any negative emotion they will be characterized as an angry Black woman and, consequently, dismissed.

Other pervasive and influential stereotypes depict female sexuality in heteronormative and racialized ways. The historical image of the Jezebel—a hypersexual, aggressive, and uncaring Black woman—is another stereotype stemming from slavery when White men used it to justify their sexual abuse and rape of Black women (Brown, White-Johnson, Griffen-Fennell, 2013; Lack, 2015). Contemporary media examples of the Jezebel, like those often depicted in music videos, create a framework for how some Black girls and women internalize and subsequently think about Black female sexuality (Stephens & Phillips, 2003). In one study, for example, Black women who were primed with a three-minute video clip featuring the Jezebel stereotype, compared to participants who viewed a neutral clip, were likely to perceive a Black female job candidate as more sexual and to recommend she seek employment as a cocktail waitress or exotic dancer (Givens & Monahan, 2005).

your turn

Think of the images of women of color in the media. How do they fit the stereotypes described here? Do you think other representations are starting to show up as well? If so, what are they? What are the implications of having limited images of women of color?

The frequent representation of Asian women as submissive, sexy, and in need of rescuing stems from the china doll stereotype. One example is *Miss Saigon*, a highly successful Broadway musical, based on the Vietnam War, which has been criticized for its gendered racism (Mok, 1998). In a review of its 2017 revival, a theater critic noted that the lead Asian female character, Kim, has no story line, doesn't make her own decisions, and is continuously victimized (Teeman, 2017). In addition, the colonial constructs of the Native American princess and the squaw have remained influential in contemporary stereotypes of Native American women (Bird, 1999). Both were deemed highly sexual, but the princess was considered exotic and self-sacrificing, while the squaw was seen as a servant who had sex frequently and indiscriminately, often resulting in multiple pregnancies (Merskin, 2010). The tendency to see women of color as sexually promiscuous simultaneously reinforces racism and sexism and also perpetuates an image of White womanhood that is based on sexual purity (Stephens & Phillips, 2003). This can be considered an example of how stereotypes reinforce social stratification by setting different expectations for women based on their gender and race/ethnicity.

One reason stereotypes of women of color are problematic is that there are so few positive images of them in popular media (Rios & Stewart, 2016). For example, Black and Latinx women are often portrayed as criminals or villains (Rios & Stewart, 2016). One privilege of being a member of a dominant group is having a diverse array of representations of your group present in the media (Schug, Alt, Lu, Gosin, & Fay, 2017). Therefore, even though White women are often sexualized and stereotyped in the media, there are many more images of them, so any one stereotypical or sexualized image carries less weight. Women of color, women with disabilities, and LGBTQ women are less visible. Because the few images that exist are largely negative, people may develop discriminatory attitudes and behaviors based on that limited information (Rios & Stewart, 2016).

How Stereotypes Shape Behavior

How do stereotypes shape behavior in relation to both the self and others?

In addition to influencing how people are likely to view girls and women, gender stereotypes convey how they should behave. As we'll discuss in Chapter 5, children learn rules about gender very quickly, and they can apply rigid stereotypes to both themselves and others. Although adults are less rigid in their beliefs about gender, knowledge of gender stereotypes continues to affect the way people view themselves and how they choose to act. This is called *self-stereotyping*. In other words, individuals can act in ways that confirm stereotypes because that's how they think they're supposed to act. For example, if a woman believes that it's more important to be nice than academically successful, she may attempt to present herself as nice but not work as hard at presenting herself as intelligent. Alternatively, a man who is very caring and considerate may choose to present himself in a more dominant or assertive manner because he has internalized that masculine stereotype.

Of course, the more that people act in ways that confirm gender stereotypes the more the stereotypes continue. This reflects a circular process in which social expectations influence the performance of gender, which in turn influences social interactions. This is known as *doing gender* (West & Zimmerman, 1987). There is also tremendous pressure to adhere to traditional stereotypes. Many people notice and react when stereotypes are violated. When individuals violate gender stereotypes, they often experience some degree of social and economic penalties, known as **backlash effects** (Rudman, 1998; Rudman & Fairchild, 2004). For example, as we'll discuss in Chapter 10, when women in leadership positions act in traditionally masculine ways, they're more likely than other female leaders to be criticized and seen as unlikeable (Eagly & Carli, 2007). For this reason, stereotypes are quite resistant to change. Despite considerable advancement for women in all domains of public life, many people continue to hold the same beliefs about strong stereotypical differences between women and men that they did in the 1980s (Haines, Deaux, & LoFaro, 2016).

Sexism

What types of discrimination do women commonly experience, and why can it be challenging to know when this has happened?

Whereas stereotypes are beliefs about what members of social groups are like, **prejudice** is a negative attitude toward someone because of their actual or perceived membership in a certain social group. Sexism is a form of prejudice. Typically, when people think of sexism, they come up with examples of **overt sexism**, or unequal treatment of women that's easily identifiable and, therefore, easily documented. **Discrimination** is a form of prejudice that occurs when someone is treated unfairly because of actual or perceived membership in a social group that is less powerful than the dominant group. For example, not hiring a woman for a leadership position simply because she's female would be an example of sex discrimination. An example of overt sex discrimination would involve telling a woman during a job interview that the company doesn't like to hire young women because they tend to quit to have babies, and then not giving her the job. As a result of many anti-discrimination laws, including the Civil Rights Act of 1964 and the Pregnancy Discrimination Act of 1978, these types of practices are illegal in the United States.

Modern Sexism and Subtle Discrimination

Rather than overt sexism, it's now much more likely that girls and women will experience **modern sexism**, or gender bias that is communicated in subtle or indirect ways (Swim, Aikin, Hall, & Hunter, 1995). Modern sexism often leads to more subtle discrimination. For example, a woman might not get a job offer but not actually know that her gender played a role in the hiring decision. As we'll discuss in Chapter 10, it's not always easy to prove discrimination when this happens. One reason why modern sexism is so hard to notice and, therefore, change is that much of it is implicit. *Explicit bias* is conscious and deliberate. In contrast, *implicit bias* occurs outside of conscious awareness and can be unintentionally directed toward specific groups.

Because most people aren't aware of their implicit biases, psychologists have devised tests, such as the Implicit Association Test (IAT), to assess them. The IAT records the time it takes for a person to associate certain words or images with other words or images associated with different social groups. For example, participants might be asked to pair pictures of women and men with words relating to either career or family. If participants respond more quickly when pairing women with family and men with career (the stereotypical pairing) than when pairing women with career and men with family (the non-stereotypical paring), that is considered to be evidence of an implicit bias associating women with family and men with careers. Many studies using the IAT find that well-intentioned people may not know they have biased associations related to girls and women (Ebert, Steffens, & Kroth, 2014; Latu et al., 2011; Mascret & Cury, 2015; Simon & O'Brien, 2015). However, other researchers have qualified these findings because results can be different, especially for first-time users, if a test is taken multiple times, and IAT results don't consistently predict discriminatory behavior (Fiedler, Messner, & Bluemke, 2006; Mitchell & Tetlock, 2017; Rezaei, 2011).

Because modern sexist attitudes are often implicit, it can be hard to notice them. A central feature of modern sexism is the *denial of discrimination* (Ellemers & Barreto, 2009; Swim & Campbell, 2001). That is, if people assume that gender equality has been achieved, they're likely to see any failure of women to succeed as a result of women's own shortcomings rather than systematic disadvantage (Swim et al., 1995). People who hold modern sexist views are often resentful of demands for equality; they see these as coming from women who expect special treatment. As we mentioned earlier, some of the criticism directed at participants in the Women's March included many of these sentiments. However, denial of discrimination is considered sexist because it justifies not addressing gender inequalities and maintains the status quo while also blaming women for their lack of equality and social mobility (Becker & Swim, 2012; Hayes & Swim, 2013).

Modern sexism is viewed as harmful because it prevents social change and can have negative consequences. Women who experience modern sexism have been found to report greater anxiety and insecurity than women who don't report experiencing modern sexism, and they're also more likely to engage in self-defeating behaviors (Barreto & Ellemers, 2005; Ellemers & Barreto, 2009). Interestingly, some women also engage in *denial of personal discrimination* (Crosby, Iyer, Clayton, & Downing, 2003). They acknowledge that sexism exists, but they feel they don't *personally* experience it—at least, not often. Psychologists suggest that this may be a form of self-protection because it's difficult to accept that one is disadvantaged due to being a woman (Barreto & Ellemers, 2005; Ruggiero & Taylor, 1997). Such denial makes it less likely that women will engage in collective social action, which in turn maintains the status quo (Ellemers & Barreto, 2009; Wright, 2001).

try it for yourself

In 2011, researchers at Harvard University created the Project Implicit website: https://implicit.harvard.edu/implicit/. It offers a free opportunity for anyone to take Implicit Association Tests. Take a test that is specific to gender (you can take others as well). Are you surprised by the findings? What are the challenges in addressing implicit forms of sexism? Is it easier to address the more explicit forms of sexism? Why or why not? What approach might you take for each?

Microaggressions

Modern sexism and the resulting subtle gender discrimination can be so unobtrusive that they begin to seem like normal parts of life (Swim & Cohen, 1997), so there is often guesswork involved in deciding whether one is experiencing it. Let's consider a male boss telling a female employee, "You look nice today." Does he avoid making the same type of comment to male employees? He might be paying her a compliment, but he might also be cultivating a work environment in which female employees, but not male employees, are noticed for their appearance. **Gender microaggressions** are brief, everyday acts of sexism, whether intentional or unintentional, that demean and insult a person based on that individual's gender (Sue, 2010). These everyday acts are frequently perpetrated by people with good intentions who most likely don't see themselves as prejudiced (Sue, 2010; Swim & Cohen, 1997), an idea we'll revisit later in this chapter.

Microaggressions are often the result of stereotyping. For example, one study showed that Black women at predominantly White institutions experienced gendered racial microaggressions based on stereotypes such as those discussed above, including the Jezebel or the angry Black woman (Lewis, Mendenhall, Harwood, & Browne Huntt, 2016). In another study, researchers found that, compared to Latinx men, Latinx women experienced more microaggressions that were based on racialized gender stereotypes (Nadal, Mazzula, Rivera, & Fujii-Doe, 2014). Other microaggressions reported by women of color include feeling as though they were sexual objects and being treated as if they were a nanny instead of a mother (Nadal et al., 2015). Researchers have also found that people with disabilities frequently experienced microaggressions (Keller & Galgay, 2010). They were often infantilized (i.e., treated as children), patronized (e.g., praised for doing mundane tasks), and de-sexualized (e.g., punished for displaying sexual interest).

Other research shows that microaggressions may appear ambiguous or neutral (Cortina, Kabat-Farr, Magley, & Nelson, 2017). An example is *selective incivility*—the tendency to make rude, condescending, and ostracizing acts that violate norms of respect toward women and people of color (Cortina, 2008). Because acts of selective incivility (e.g., using a condescending tone, ignoring or interrupting a colleague) appear neutral, they aren't identified as sexist or racist acts (Cortina et al., 2017). They're attributed to the personality or carelessness of an individual instigator rather than seen as indicating a hostile climate. However, incivility is actually a covert manifestation of bias.

Identifying and Addressing Microaggressions Although the idea of subtle, unintended slights toward members of socially disempowered groups isn't new, this is a relatively new area of research. As a result, there are still inconsistencies in how microaggressions are operationalized, which make it hard to draw clear conclusions about outcomes and impacts (Lilienfeld, 2017). When we leave the lab and look to the real world, then, it's no surprise that microaggressions are hard to document and many people don't notice when they're taking place. The Everyday Sexism Project created #everydaysexism in order to more regularly document and promote awareness of gender microaggressions. With over 250,000 Twitter followers, there are postings made every day showing women's experiences with microaggressions. For example, one mother posted a picture of a sign in her son's classroom that listed all the children's names under the category of either Gorgeous Girls or Brilliant Boys. A waitress in her forties posted that while waiting on a table of businessmen she was referred to as a "good girl" for clearing the table. A college student explained that she was groped in a bar by a man who later apologized to her two male friends while simultaneously ignoring her.

Microaggressions can also be difficult to address. For example, if someone calls a woman "a girl" or inappropriately stares at her body, she has to decide whether it's better to ignore or confront it. This process can be stressful. First, she simultaneously has to discern the truth, protect herself from additional insults, and make a decision about whether to take action (Cadinu, Maass, Rosabianca, & Kiesner, 2005; Salvatore & Shelton, 2007; Sue, 2010). For a woman of color, the process can be more complex because she also has to take into account negative racialized stereotypes. For example, one Black woman described how a man at a club told her to "shake her booty." She wanted to tell him that he was being inappropriate but censored herself because she feared being labeled as an angry Black woman (Lewis, Mendenhall, Harwood, & Browne Huntt, 2016, p. 769).

your turn

Have you or anyone you know ever experienced incidents such as the ones we've described? If so, would you classify the experience as overt or modern sexism? How did you or your friend handle it? Can you think of a time when you inadvertently said or did something that you didn't intend to be offensive, but that was perceived as offensive? If so, how did you handle that situation? Would you handle a similar incident the same way in the future? Why or why not?

Women can have a hard time deciding whether to directly address microaggressions or if other strategies are more appropriate. Research shows that women are concerned about the consequences associated with responding to microaggressions, and it can be difficult to know what to say (Kahn, 2015; Sue & Capodilupo, 2008). For example, in one study, researchers found that Black women used a variety of strategies to deal with microaggressions based on their power in the situation (Lewis et al., 2016). If the perpetrator was a boss or professor, participants reported withdrawing in order to be self-protective. They deliberately did not address the incident because the power difference made it likely that they couldn't safely predict the outcome of the situation.

However, when microaggressions go unaddressed, there can be psychological costs, including decreased self-esteem and increased anger and frustration (Sue, 2010). In one study, researchers found that Asian American women who were exposed to microaggressions reported more negative mental and physical outcomes than their male counterparts who were more likely to be affected when they were exposed to more overt forms of discrimination (Hahm, Ozonoff, Gaumond, & Sue, 2010). This finding suggests that microaggresions motivated by both racism and sexism are likely to be particularly problematic because the person being targeted has to do additional work to determine if the attack is motivated by race, gender, or some combination of both. We'll return to this topic in Chapter 13.

Ambivalent Sexism: Hostility and Benevolence

What are hostile and benevolent sexism, and how do they work together to maintain gender hierarchies?

Another reason that it's often hard to see sexism is that it can be cloaked in a positive context. As we've discussed, stereotypes can include both positive and negative components, and the positive aspects can cloak the negative ones. For example, people don't usually go around saying, "I hate women. They're horrible." In fact, many sexist beliefs arise from the assumption that women (at least women who conform to traditional gender roles) are wonderful, virtuous, and warm. **Ambivalent sexism** is a term that describes the ways in which contemporary sexism includes two related but complementary components: hostility and benevolence (Glick & Fiske, 1997). **Hostile sexism** consists of negative and derogatory beliefs about girls and women. Examples of hostile sexist beliefs are that women are incompetent, unintelligent, or sexually manipulative. In contrast, **benevolent sexism** takes a positive spin, suggesting that girls and women should be treated differently than men because they are special and worthy of being cherished and in need of protection. Examples of benevolent sexist beliefs are that women are pure, maternal, or intuitive. One can say that benevolent sexism puts women on a pedestal and hostile sexism puts women in the gutter (Begun & Walls, 2015).

Hostile and benevolent sexism work together to create sexist environments (Glick & Fiske, 1997; Wood & Eagly, 2010). Hostile sexism operates by punishing women for challenging traditional gender expectations; benevolent sexism rewards women for maintaining the gender status quo. One tool for assessing people's endorsement of hostile and benevolent sexism is the Ambivalent Sexism Inventory (ASI; Glick & Fiske, 1997), and sample items for each type of sexism are shown in Table 2.4. Research with 15,000 women and men from

Benevolent sexism is based on the idea that women should be protected and cherished. Regardless of gender identity, it can be nice when people open doors for us or carry heavy objects, but benevolent sexism places women in a "less than" position in relation to men and has been shown to have detrimental effects on girls and women.

TABLE 2.4 Sample Items from the Ambivalent Sexism Inventory

Hostile Sexism	Benevolent Sexism
Many women are actually seeking special favors, such as hiring policies that favor them over men, under the guise of asking for "equality."	Women, as compared to men, tend to have a more refined sense of culture and good taste.
Most women interpret innocent remarks or acts as being sexist.	No matter how accomplished he is, a man is not truly complete as a person unless he has the love of a woman.
Most women fail to appreciate fully all that men do for them.	Every man ought to have a woman whom he adores.
Women seek to gain power by getting control over men.	A good woman should be set on a pedestal by her man.
Once a woman gets a man to commit to her, she usually tries to put him on a tight leash.	Men should be willing to sacrifice their own well-being in order to provide financially for the women in their lives.

Note. The entire Ambivalent Sexism Inventory is provided in Glick and Fiske (1997). Respondents are instructed to rate the extent to which they agree with each item using a 6-point scale ranging from *Strongly Disagree* to *Strongly Agree.*

19 countries using the ASI showed that levels of hostile and benevolent sexism can reliably predict the status of girls and women (Glick et al., 2000). In countries with high levels of both hostile and benevolent sexism, women were found to be less likely than men to hold high-ranking government positions, receive pay equity, or have equivalent levels of education to their male counterparts.

Benevolent sexism is based in **paternalistic chivalry**, the idea that women should be protected and cherished—at least, as long as they conform to traditional gender roles. It can be appealing for many women to be put on a pedestal, and the appeal of benevolent sexism is what makes it so insidious and hard to change. However, a pedestal is a tight place to stand, and being there traps women within a narrow range of what's acceptable. Also, hostile and benevolent sexism go hand in hand. In fact, people who hold negative beliefs about women (as evidenced by hostile sexism) tend to hold positive beliefs about women who conform to traditional gender expectations (as evidenced by benevolent sexism; Glick & Fiske, 2001). Given this relationship, it can be easy to switch between hostile and benevolent sexism. This occurs, for example, when a man who cherishes his girlfriend calls her a slut after they

your turn

Students frequently ask us, "What's wrong with chivalry? Isn't it nice for men to hold doors for women and pay for dinner?" The problem isn't the act of opening a door for someone else—it's the fact that it only involves men opening doors for women. After all, how common is it for a man to open a door and stand to the side so another man can enter? How do men react when a woman opens a door for them in this way? Were you raised in a family that valued chivalry? Was it framed as men needing to be chivalrous toward women or as human beings needing to be kind? Where do you think the line falls between chivalrous behavior reflecting sexism and acting out of kindness and concern for others?

break up. It also occurs in the cases of men who worship their mothers but are very hostile to sexual women—a phenomenon known as the *Madonna/whore complex* (Tanzer, 1985; Tavris & Wade, 1984). This phenomenon stems from the fact that some men see the women they care for and respect and the women they desire as being in mutually exclusive categories, so men will engage in both benevolent and hostile sexism—but toward different women (Tavris & Wade, 1984).

Although women are likely to reject hostile sexism, they often do endorse benevolent sexism (Glick & Fiske, 2001). In fact, one study has found that, in countries where men endorse high levels of hostile sexism, women are more likely to endorse benevolent sexism (Glick et al., 2000). This may, in part, be a self-protective response (Fischer, 2006). If a woman is in danger of being persecuted because she deviates from gender norms, it would be to her advantage to internalize the importance of staying within gender norms.

People appear to differentially apply benevolent sexism across groups of women. In one online study, researchers found that primarily White participants expressed more benevolent sexism toward White women than toward Black women (McMahon & Kahn, 2016). However, when Black women were described as chaste, the participants expressed more benevolent sexism toward them. As a result, the researchers concluded that when Black women conform to traditional expectations of femininity, a possible outcome would be experiencing benevolent sexism.

Negative Outcomes of Sexism It probably seems obvious how hostile sexism is detrimental. Studies show that those who more strongly endorse hostile sexism make less favorable attributions about career women and are less likely to believe a woman's claim about sexual harassment in the workplace (Carli, 2001; Heilman, Wallen, Fuchs, & Tamkins, 2004). Among men, hostile sexist attitudes are also associated with finding sexist jokes amusing rather than offensive, being more likely to minimize the seriousness of rape, and thinking that a woman is to blame for being raped if she was wearing revealing clothing or had too much to drink (Chapleau, Oawald, & Russell, 2007; Greenwood & Isbell, 2002; Yamawaki, 2007). In one study, hostile sexism was significantly associated with more negative evaluations of a female job candidate and with lower recommendations that she be employed as a manager (Masser & Abrams, 2004). Women and men high on hostile sexism were also likely to evaluate male candidates more favorably than female candidates.

It's often harder to see why benevolent sexism is detrimental, but it can impede women's advancement. Benevolent sexism assumes that women are in need of men's protection, an attitude that places women in a "less than" position in relation to men. Because many people see male protection as natural, and even beneficial, benevolent sexism is often not considered sexist. In fact, during the 1970s, the justification for not ratifying the Equal Rights Amendment (ERA) was based on benevolent sexist principles. Opponents of the ERA claimed that equality would actually disadvantage women because it would eliminate protections that had been put in place for women (Sue, 2010). More recently, politicians have used benevolent sexism to justify limiting military women's participation in active combat by suggesting that women are weaker than or not as capable as their male counterparts, which subsequently prevents advancement of women in the military (Choma, 2016).

Also, when women are exposed to benevolent sexism, they may show increased levels of stress. In one study, a racially diverse group of women was asked to complete a challenging problem-solving task prior to being exposed to a male researcher who made either a hostile, a benevolent, or a non-sexist comment (Salomon, Burgess, & Bosson, 2015). In the benevolent condition, he said, "Girls don't like the hard section, so I'm going to go ahead and get rid of it for you. I'm willing to sacrifice a little data, so I don't make another girl upset about how hard the last section is" (p. 472). Compared to women who weren't exposed to benevolent sexism, the women who were had increased cardiovascular activity that took longer to return to baseline. This outcome indicates that the women who were exposed to benevolent sexism experienced the stress of the problem-solving task for a longer period than was true for the women who were exposed to either the hostile sexist or the non-sexist comment. In another study, women who simply witnessed a benevolent sexist act (a man offering to pick up a box for another woman) felt more self-conscious about their bodies than those who didn't witness such an act (Shepherd et al., 2011). On the basis of these findings, one can say that even witnessing benevolent sexist acts has detrimental effects.

Benevolent sexism can even interfere with women's thinking. In one study researchers examined women's brains while completing a memory task after hearing a male researcher make a benevolent sexist statement, a hostile sexist statement, or a neutral statement (Dardenne et al., 2013). When the women were exposed to the benevolent sexist statement, the brain regions associated with stopping intrusive thoughts (e.g., bilateral, dorsolateral, prefrontal, and anterior cingulate cortex) reacted. This finding indicates that those in the benevolent sexism condition shifted attention from the task to block out intrusive thoughts. Since this wasn't true for

spotlight on . . .

Sexism and Violence

In 2014, a man killed two White women and four men of color and injured 14 others in Isla Vista, California. Following the attack, authorities uncovered a manifesto in which the attacker outlined his hatred for women and racial minority men (Magnoli, 2015).

The attack and the documents spurred a national discussion about **misogyny**, or hatred of girls and women. Some commentators saw this as reflecting a widespread problem of sexism in American culture (Hess, 2014). Other commentators, however, claimed that this was a singular act, more connected to mental illness and the problematic beliefs of a single individual. This perspective was mostly shared through Twitter via the hashtag #notallmen to claim that not *all* men are sexist. In reaction, #yesallwomen was created to offer the perspective that all women experience sexism.

The challenge is that both sides are right. Most people condemned the killings, including those who tweeted with #notallmen. They could see how harmful and unjustified these acts were and could rightly claim that not *all* men engage in overt violence. Those who posted with #yesallwomen, however, highlighted that the very fact that men can live without the threat of sexism is an example of male privilege. In this way, acts of sexism are not always overt, and privilege exists in day-to-day interactions that can appear to be harmless but, over time, can add up in potentially lethal ways (Sue, 2010).

those exposed to the hostile sexist statement or the neutral statement, benevolent sexism may well be particularly detrimental to women's performance.

Language as a Source of Power

What are different ways that language is used to maintain gender hierarchies?

Language is another area in which sexism can be overlooked. There are many patriarchal assumptions in language. When internalized, these messages can further reinforce sexist attitudes and behaviors (Swim, Mallett, & Stangor, 2004). Yet, in the same way that most people may not notice benevolent sexism or microaggressions, it's often the case that people don't notice the problematic messages in everyday conversations. Psychologists have identified biased language as a source of microaggressions (Nadal, 2013; Sue, 2010; Woodford, Howell, Kulick, & Silverschanz, 2013). Let's explore some of the subtle ways language reflects sexism.

People = Male Bias

Words like *humankind* and *freshman* have one thing in common—they use *man* to represent everyone. As we mentioned earlier, one component of privilege is that the privileged group is considered the norm. Accordingly, *man* is often used interchangeably with *human*, and this usage reinforces the idea that male characteristics and actions are representative of all humans. In fact, classic studies have shown that when participants receive no other information, they tend to associate the generic word *person* with a White, heterosexual, able-bodied, young man (Fiske, 1998; Stroessner, 1996). This tendency reflects the *people = male bias*. For example, when researchers asked a sample of primarily White college students to read passages in which an occupation was introduced with either a male-biased noun (e.g., *policeman*, *salesman*) or a gender-neutral noun (e.g., *police officer*, *sales person*), participants later recalled the gender-neutral noun in reference to a man (Hamilton, 1991). In another study, college students most frequently assumed that a generic person named "Chris" was a man, and White college students were more likely than students of color to label "Chris" as a White man (Merrit & Harrison, 2006).

Both women and men are likely to name men as examples of famous people they know and are likely to refer to God as male (Foster & Keating, 1992; Moyer, 1997). Moreover, when study participants were asked to describe the most typical person they know, men were mentioned more often than women

(Hamilton, 1991). The same study showed that participants were three times as likely to spontaneously describe a man, instead of a woman, after reading a gender-neutral description. In another study, when discussing attitudes toward sexual minority individuals, participants overwhelmingly referred to men (Haddock, Zanna, & Esses, 1993).

There is even an *animal = male bias* in which both children and adults are likely to refer to animals using a male pronoun (Lambdin, Greer, Jibotian, Wood, & Hamilton, 2003). This effect was even found when researchers shared a story with children about an animal that used a female pronoun. All the children later used a male pronoun to refer to the animal.

In addition to emphasizing the masculine, language has a strong cisgender bias, most notably in the use of pronouns. In English, there is no gender-neutral third person singular pronoun. Only the third person plural pronoun (*they*) is gender neutral. Since English pronouns are based on a binary (*he/she*), *he* often serves as the human generic (McHugh & Hambaugh, 2010). But such usage wasn't always standard. The singular use of *they* was much more common until 1850, when the British Parliament required that all official documents only use masculine pronouns (McCurdy, 2013). The change was made because, according to Parliament, men were simply superior to women. Although some grammar enthusiasts might argue otherwise, use of the generic *he* in English was the result of a sexist political decision. In this way, pronoun use can be seen to reflect social beliefs (McCurdy, 2013; Zimman, 2015).

Additionally, when language patterns change, social perceptions also change. For example, when feminists introduced the term *Ms.* as an alternative to terms that reflect women's marital status (*Miss* or *Mrs.*), it initially met significant resistance. Today, however, *Ms.* is commonly used to refer to women regardless of their marital status. This practice subsequently changed the way women are viewed— there is less focus today on marital status as their most important attribute.

The use of gender-neutral pronouns is gaining in popularity. In 2014, Facebook and the dating website OkCupid publicly announced they would provide non-binary pronoun options. In the same year, the University of Vermont became the first institution of higher education in the United States to offer students the option of registering with gender-neutral pronouns (see Table 2.5; Poon, 2015). Since then, several other institutions have also permitted gender-neutral pronouns, although K–12 schools have been more reluctant to do so. These decisions did come with challenges, though. The capacity to add gender-neutral options to the University of Vermont's information system took years of lobbying, a special task force, and $80,000 in software updates. And not everyone supports using resources in this way. In order for attitudes to change regarding the use of gender-neutral pronouns, scholars say that people will need to start introducing them more often in everyday language (Zimman, 2015). As with the *Ms.* movement, gender-neutral pronouns would probably become more commonplace if large groups of people began to use them on a regular basis.

TABLE 2.5 Possible Pronouns in Different Grammatical Forms

Pronoun (all singular)	Nominative (subject)	Objective (object)	Possessive determiner	Possessive pronoun	Reflexive
He	*He* smiled.	I called *him*.	*His* eyes gleam.	That is *his*.	He likes *himself*.
She	*She* smiled.	I called *her*.	*Her* eyes gleam.	That is *hers*.	She likes *herself*.
They*	*They* smiled.	I called *them*.	*Their* eyes gleam.	That is *theirs*.	They like *themselves*.
Ze	*Ze* smiled.	I called *zir*.	*Zir* eyes gleam.	That is *zirs*.	Ze likes *zirself*.
Xe	*Xe* smiled.	I called *xem*.	*Xyr* eyes gleam.	That is *xyrs*.	Xe likes *xemself*.

Note. Content drawn from Wikipedia. **They* is being used as a third-person singular noun.

Men Come First

In language, men come first. Shakespeare didn't title his play *Juliet and Romeo*. We don't refer to royalty as *queen and king*, and teachers generally don't address their classes as *girls and boys*. The tendency to name men before women is characteristic of a *binomial pair*, a two-word expression in which the word order is fixed and unchangeable (Hegarty, Watson, Fletcher, & McQueen, 2011). In fact, researchers have found that participants habitually named men first in heterosexual pairings, and among non-heterosexual couples, they attributed first-named partners with more stereotypically masculine qualities. Also, men's names tend to appear before women's names on the Internet (Wright & Hay, 2002). The common phrase "ladies and gentlemen" does break from this rule, but it's worth mentioning that the term *lady* isn't always perceived favorably. One study showed that people are more likely to associate the term *gentlemen* with greater competence and warmth than the term *lady*, which is associated with being cold and distant (Moely & Kreicker, 1984). Further, historically the concept of ladyhood was associated with White, upper-class, married women (Myers, 2010). As a result, it's possible to say that the term *lady* not only has elements of benevolent sexism, but it also prioritizes a particular social order that privileges some women over others.

If you review the words in Table 2.6, you'll notice a pattern of prioritizing men and viewing the male as the norm. *Unmarked words* tend to be used as the generic. For example, the unmarked word *lion* can describe a male or female lion. The word *lioness*, however, only refers to a female lion. The female version is a *marked word* and can't be used to describe a male. In this way, the female version is a deviation from the norm. Women may choose to call themselves *waiters*, *hosts*, or *actors*. But men would never call themselves *waitresses*, *hostesses*, or *actresses*. However, when unmarked terms are used, people generally assume that the person being referred to is male (McHugh & Hambaugh, 2010). Further, marked words can be seen as conveying a lower status, which can influence how girls and women think about themselves as well as how others behave toward them (McHugh & Hambaugh, 2010).

For example, even in writing this textbook, we discovered our own biases. One reviewer of our early work pointed out that we were consistently marking the race of people of color, but not doing the same for White people. As we mentioned in Chapter 1, we also found that our default was to say "men and women" rather than "women and men." It is important that we address these linguistic biases. They may seem subtle, but the cumulative effect shows a tendency to prioritize some types of people over others. These patterns revealed how easy it is to perpetuate the status quo.

Gender-fair language, which refers to all people with symmetrical linguistic forms, has been found to promote gender equality (Koeser & Sczesny, 2014). Instead of using male generics, gender-fair language aims to use more inclusive terms, like *they* (as singular use) instead of *he* or *first-year student* instead of *freshman*. Further, gender-fair language seeks to reduce stereotypes. Instead of saying, "Dear Mothers, please bake cookies for the bake sale," a gender-fair alternative would be: "Dear Parents, please bake cookies for the bake sale." Gender-fair language is less common in everyday language than gendered language is, but research shows that women are more likely to use gender-fair language than men (Koeser, Kuhn, & Sczesny, 2015). In another study, when men were made aware of sexist language, their use of gender-fair forms did increase, but they tended to return to

TABLE 2.6 Examples of Marked and Unmarked Language

Male/Unmarked	Female/Marked
author	*authoress*
waiter	*waitress*
host	*hostess*
headmaster	*headmistress*
landlord	*landlady*
actor	*actress*
hero	*heroine*
lion	*lioness*

sexist language when tired or distracted (Koeser & Sczesny, 2014; Koeser et al., 2015).

One example of a move toward gender-fair language is use of the word *Latinx*, meant to be a gender-neutral alternative to *Latina* and *Latino*. People who use *Latinx* are part of a linguistic movement seeking to reject gender binaries, be inclusive, and modify the language and traditions of Europeans that relate to people of Latin American descent (Love Ramirez & Blay, 2016). Critics, however, feel that the new word is disrespectful to the Spanish language, which is linguistically gendered. In Spanish, nouns are gendered—such as *guitar* being feminine and referred to with *la* instead of *el*—but there is evidence that this practice reinforces sexist beliefs. In one study, when bilingual high school students were randomly assigned to complete a survey addressing sexist attitudes in either English or a language with a grammatical gender (French or Spanish), students in the English condition expressed less sexist attitudes than those in the French or Spanish conditions (Wasserman & Weseley, 2009). Further, because language is used every day, the repetition can normalize these subtle forms of sexism.

Most people are not aware of the larger social effect of language, but research shows that using more gender-biased language and holding sexist beliefs are related (Prewitt-Freilino, Caswell, & Laakso, 2012; Wasserman & Weseley, 2009). In the years to come, as gender-fair language becomes more integrated into our daily lives, as has already happened with the use of *Ms.*, it will be interesting to see if research continues to show the same patterns related to marked and unmarked words, a people = male bias, and so on.

What's in a Name?

Names also reveal hidden biases. For example, some girls' names reflect aesthetics or femininity (e.g., *Bella*, *Lily*, *Jasmine*, *Grace*), and gendered patterns are even found among nicknames. When researchers analyzed 380 popular nicknames, they found that male nicknames—especially among peers—often implied strength, largeness, hardness, and maturity (e.g., *Champ*, *Digger*, *Stud*, *Maddog*; Phillips, 1990). In contrast, female nicknames were more associated with beauty, pleasantness, kindness, and goodness (e.g., *Angel*, *Babe*, *Munchkin*, *Honey*).

Women's subordinate status shows up again with the use of formal titles. In formal settings, the probability of being addressed by a professional title is greater for men than for women. It's likely that most faculty at your school are referred to as either *Professor* or *Doctor*. Have you ever heard instructors being addressed as *Mr.* or *Ms.* or *Mrs.*? It's likely that if you have, it was a female professor being addressed this way. One study showed that students were more likely to refer to male professors by a formal title than female professors (Takiff, Sanchez, & Stewart, 2001). However, when female professors were addressed by title, students perceived them as less accessible—a pattern that didn't hold for male professors. This is especially true for women of color, who are often referred to as *Ms.*, while their colleagues are referred to as *Doctor* or *Professor* (Berry, 2014). Being addressed as *Mrs.* is a major pet peeve of ours. Addressing a professor this way not only denies the status and recognition of being called *Dr.* or *Professor* that she earned—it also reflects an assumption that (a) she is married and (b) she changed her name when getting married.

Each year, about 90% of women in the United States who marry men will change their last name to their husband's last name (Goldin & Shim, 2004; Johnson & Scheuble, 1995). This practice originates from the traditional family structure in which, upon marriage, a woman became her husband's property (Suarez, 1996). The practice basically erases maternal lines over generations and can also erase many of the social networks that women develop prior to marriage. This happens because people can be difficult to find, even through social network searches, when they change their name unless you know their new last name.

Until the 1970s, in some states women were not permitted to vote unless they registered using their husband's last name (Goldin & Shim, 2004). The practice of taking a husband's name varies considerably by country. In Spain, Latin American nations, and China, women typically keep their birth name after marriage. In France, most women retain their birth name for legal documents and use their husband's name in social settings (Chapman & Ciment, 2015).

In the United States, changing one's name is time-consuming and expensive. Several Internet businesses, like *HitchSwitch.com* and *MissNowMrs.com*, have emerged to help manage the time and cost of ordering a new driver's license and passport, updating bank accounts, and changing other official documents (Urken, 2012). Despite the hassle, the practice appears to be popular, particularly among White women. In an analysis of wedding announcements published in the *New York Times* from 1982 to 2002, 71% of all women changed their names, while 29% chose to keep their birth name or hyphenate it (Hoffnung, 2006). However, only 39% of women of color changed their names. This finding is consistent with other research showing that women of color are less likely than White women to change their name following marriage (Twenge, 1997). Women's level of education can also be a factor (Gooding & Kreider, 2010; Hoffnung, 2006; Twenge, 1997). According to results from one study, women with a master's degree are nearly three times more likely to use their birth name than those without a bachelor's degree, and those with a doctorate are nearly 10 times more likely to do so (Gooding & Kreider, 2010).

The decision to take a spouse's name is far less common among non-heterosexual couples. In one study, lesbian and gay couples reported that they kept their own surnames in order to maintain their personal and professional identities, reject heterosexual customs, and avoid the cost and inconvenience of having to change their name (Clarke, Burns, & Burgoyne, 2008). Interestingly, within the United States, a husband who wishes to take his wife's last name (or a hyphenated version

Reclaiming Words

Can misogynistic words ever be used in ways that are empowering? **Reappropriation** occurs when a person or group of people from a subordinate group intentionally reclaims a slur that was previously used by a dominant group to oppress or stigmatize them (Galinsky et al., 2013). The ability to reclaim negative words has been hotly debated within feminist circles, and much like other feminist discussions, there is tremendous diversity in how people think about it.

For some feminists, words like *bitch* and *slut* are hateful terms that perpetuate denigration and rape culture. From their perspective, these words—and others that are generally considered even more offensive—are sexist, plain and simple. According to those who hold this perspective, it's important to advocate for the complete elimination of their use because such words cause harm, particularly when normalized as acceptable parts of everyday language (Hodge, 2012). Some scholars have even suggested that such words qualify as hate speech and should be taken as a literal threat, particularly when used by someone in a dominant position (Hom, 2008; Hornsby, 2001).

Despite this view, slurs *are* used by many women to build solidarity and to mobilize for political purposes. As an example of reappropriation, we can think of the enthusiasm around the pussy hats during the 2017 Women's March. Before that, in 2011, activists used the provocative title Slut Walk to describe their protest against the ways in which law enforcement routinely suggests that women invite rape by wearing revealing clothing. In *The Vagina Monologues*, one very popular monologue encourages the audience to repeat a word for women's genitalia that many find particularly offensive as a way to gain momentum and power.

There is also evidence that reappropriation can be successful under the right conditions (e.g., Croom, 2013; Galinsky et al., 2013). For example, in one experiment, participants were exposed to the term *slut* in different contexts (Gaucher, Hunt, & Sinclair, 2015). Women were less likely to endorse common rape myths after being exposed to the word in the context of a protest march (e.g., Slut Walk) than they were if they heard it on the street. Further, within the context of Slut Walk marches, the use of the word did not significantly lower women's feelings of empowerment, and women were more likely to refer to themselves and friends as sluts after participating in the event (Gaucher et al., 2015).

What are your thoughts about this debate? Is the use of slurs empowering or oppressing? Why or why not? Are there certain situations in which it may be politically beneficial to do so? Does it matter who uses the slurs? Are there ways in which other variables (e.g., racism or classism) might determine whether the use of a slur is empowering or oppressing?

SlutWalks began in 2011 in Toronto in response to a police officer telling a group of college women that, in order to prevent sexual assault, they shouldn't dress "like sluts." The comment sparked a worldwide campaign. Although many people supported the goal of ending rape culture, not everyone was comfortable with the name "SlutWalks."

of it) must obtain a court order (Slade, 2015). Only nine states do not require this: California, Georgia, Hawaii, Iowa, Louisiana, Massachusetts, New York, North Dakota, and Oregon. The fact that husbands, and not wives, are required to obtain court permission shows how the government continues to regulate gender relations in marriage.

Some individuals (usually women) have adopted the strategy of using their surname in some situations (e.g., professional settings) and their spouse's name in other settings (e.g., familial situations). This practice is known as **name shifting**. Among 600 married women who taught at a college or university or were married to university faculty, 12% were found to use name shifting (Scheuble & Johnson, 2005). Engaging in name shifting was related to working full-time, having a higher level of education, and being older. Researchers suggest that name shifting might reflect women's ambivalence in managing social pressures that create a conflict between personal identity and the role of wife and mother (Scheuble & Johnson, 2005). For example, when 222 college students were asked to rate women who took their husband's name, those who did were perceived as less agentic and more communal than women who kept their surnames or hyphenated their surname with their partner's name (Etaugh, Bridges, Cummings-Hill, & Cohen, 1999).

Last names have implications for children too. Even when women keep their last names, they are unlikely to pass that name along to their children. One study found that 90% of heterosexual women who kept their own name when they got married still gave their children their husband's surname (Johnson & Scheuble, 2002). It is worth considering this statistic in light of the fact that women, not men, carry and birth children. Another study showed that, as an alternative, women who kept their surname were more likely to include their birth surname in their child's name—for example, as a first or middle name (Liss & Erchull, 2013).

try it for yourself

If you're married, did you change your name? Why did you make the choice you did? If you're not married, have you considered your options in regard to surnames if you were to get married? What do you think you will do? Ask a diverse group of people these questions. What patterns do you see? Are men less likely to change or consider changing their surname? What do you think explains the patterns you observe?

Degrading Language

There are many slang words that degrade women (e.g., *bitch* and *slut*). The equivalent slang words for men aren't nearly as negative (e.g., *tool* and *stud*). Most notably, slang words that are used to describe women are disproportionally sexualized. One linguist found that North American English has no fewer than 220 words for a sexually promiscuous woman but only 20 for a sexually promiscuous man (Lei, 2006). People also seem to be more likely to spontaneously use sexual slang terms to describe women than men. When researchers asked college students to list slang words used to describe women and men,

50% of the terms used to describe women were sexual as compared to 23% for men (Grossman & Tucker, 1997). Studies also show that men are more likely to use slang and women are more likely to be targeted with slang words (Braun & Kitzinger, 2001; Grossman & Tucker, 1997). This is especially true when women deviate from traditional feminine behaviors. In one study, when women deviated from gender-typical behaviors, speakers were more likely to use animal references (e.g., *chick*, *bitch*) to express their disapproval (Nilsen, 1996). Also, girls and women are commonly referred to as food (e.g., *honey*), animals (e.g., *chick*), or children (e.g., *baby*; Hines, 1999).

When men deviate from gender-typical behaviors, they are often described in terms of female genitalia (Fair, 2011). Referring to someone by terms associated with male genitalia, while not nice, still conveys status and power, which is why men don't consider it as offensive as a homophobic slur (Saucier, Till, Miller, O'Dea, & Andres, 2015). Also, when someone does something courageously, it's common to say, "That took balls"—slang for a part of men's genitalia. Ironically, the gonads are actually very sensitive, and the uterus is the strongest muscle in the human body (Norton, 2010). So maybe people should start saying, "That took uterus!"

Talking Styles

How do talking styles, speech use, and interrupting reflect power differentials?

Another way in which we can see how language reflects men's higher status and power is by examining the different ways gender operates in conversation. It's a popular stereotype that women talk more than men, but numerous studies have debunked this myth (Cashdan, 1998; Mehl, Vazire, Ramirez-Esparza, Slatcher, & Pennebaker, 2007; Tannen, 1995). One study showed that men take up to 75% of talking time in a mixed-group setting (Karpowitz & Mendelberg, 2014). This is an example of how sexism can be overlooked since it's generally not noticeable when men take up conversational space, but it's *very* noticeable when women do it. The tendency for men to control most of a conversation is consistent with the *theory of communicator status*, which holds that individuals with higher status are perceived as having more credibility and expertise than those with lower status. This translates into more talking time for men and women's decreased ability to control conversations.

This theory has very real implications because talking time influences everything from whose thoughts get heard, to who gets to influence major decisions in meetings, to who gets opportunities for active learning in a classroom. For example, studies have shown that male students speak more frequently than female students in college classrooms and are more likely to be listened to by a professor (Basow, 2004; Litosseliti, 2013; Swann, 1992). In elementary school, boys raise their hands in more disruptive ways, which results in more teacher attention (Sadker & Sadker, 1994). Men appear to dominate media conversations too. In 2012, the OpEd Project determined that men wrote 80% of traditional opinion pieces, 67% of online opinion pieces, and 62% of college newspaper opinion pieces (Yaeger, n.d.). In social media, although girls and women make up 62% of Twitter users, men have been found to be re-tweeted almost twice as often as women (Bennett, 2012).

Another way men may exhibit control of conversations is through *mansplaining*. This term was coined to describe a man explaining something, typically to a woman, in a condescending way (Solnit, 2015). Some feminists have critiqued the term because it implies that the problem is only about men explaining things to women (Kelly, 2015). In reality, it's likely that people in positions of power often attempt to explain things to those in lower-status positions; this may have to do with many different characteristics that make up a person's social identity—including, but not limited to, gender (Bridges, 2017).

Tentative Speech   In her now-classic book *Language and Women's Place*, the feminist linguist Robin Lakoff (1975) was one of the first to offer an explanation for why men, rather than women, dominate talk time. Women, she said, are taught to be polite and to speak in ways that are unconfident and powerless. In particular, Lakoff proposed that women are more likely than men to use **tentative speech forms**, including hedges (e.g., *mostly*), hesitations (e.g., *um*), tag questions (e.g., *right?*), and intensifiers (e.g., *very*). For example, a woman may say "I . . . um . . . don't really like it" rather than "I don't like it," or "I just wanted to check the time, okay?" rather than "I'm checking the time."

Several studies have been done to examine women's and men's conversations in order to test the dominance model, and the results have been mixed. Overall, results do show a small difference, with women being somewhat more likely than men to use tentative speech (Reid, Keerie, & Palomares, 2003). However, linguists are concerned that these small findings have led to overgeneralizations about women. For example, most women in most contexts will not use tentative speech; however, when they do use tentative speech, people notice it, contributing to confirmation bias (Reid et al., 2003). In other words, people selectively attend to stereotypical behaviors and then conclude that certain behaviors are characteristic of the whole group. One sociolinguist has referred to this as the "naming and shaming" phenomenon (Liberman, 2007, para. 2).

Further, Lakoff's original claim that tentative speech reflects powerlessness may not be true. In fact, tentative speech may improve connection and increase power in certain social contexts. For example, in one study, women were more likely to use tentative styles of speaking in longer versus shorter conversations, in research labs versus other settings, and in groups versus dyads (Leaper & Robnett, 2011). Some researchers believe these findings reflect interpersonal sensitivity rather than a lack of assertiveness. Tentative speech has also been found to relate to some aspects of success, particularly among women. For example, successful female contestants on *Jeopardy* are more likely than contestants who aren't successful to use uptalk (also known as upspeak), a style of speech in which declarative sentences end with a rising intonation that is typically indicative of questions (Linneman, 2013). In high school settings, the "cool girls" are more likely to use tentative talk than the "nerd girls" (Bucholtz, 2001).

In fact, it appears that when women do use more direct styles of communication, they risk social punishment. There is no shortage of studies showing all the ways in which girls and women face a "damned if you do, damned if you don't" situation, known as a *double bind*. In other words, if girls and women speak in tentative ways, they're perceived as weak and inferior. However, if they speak up and act assertively, they're perceived as stepping out of line and, more often than not, experience backlash. The communication double bind happens in many settings and situations.

For example, in one study, researchers asked businesswomen and businessmen to evaluate the competence of chief executives who voiced their opinions (Brescoll, 2011). Male executives who spoke up were often rewarded with higher ratings of competence; however, the same behavior was punished in female executives. When female executives spoke with more frequency, both women and men punished them with lower ratings. We'll talk more about how the double bind affects women in work contexts in Chapter 10.

Policing women's language is a profitable social phenomenon. For example, in 2015 the app Just Not Sorry was marketed to women to help them develop "stronger voices" by warning them about their use of so-called undermining words, such as *sorry* and *just* (Cauterucci, 2015). As another example, women, but not men, have been critiqued for their use of vocal fry (an unnaturally low, creaky voice). The irony here is that many famous men—including Leonardo DeCaprio, Johnny Depp, and Bruce Willis—use vocal fry (Saxena, 2015). In fact, radio-show host Howard Stern criticized women about their use of vocal fry while he himself was using it. In her blog, *language: a feminist guide*, sociolinguist Debbie Cameron sarcastically described all the articles written in the *Economist* and the *Business Insider* aimed at coaching men on their use of language in business settings: "OK, people haven't been talking about that article—mainly because I made it up. No one writes articles telling men how they're damaging their career prospects by using the wrong words" (Cameron, 2015, para. 2). From her perspective, the critique of female voices is just another way to tell women to stop talking (Marcotte, 2015).

your turn

In 2015, *Fortune* magazine published a satirical essay in which famous quotes were rewritten as if women had said them (Addady, 2015). For example, U.S. president Ronald Reagan's Cold War challenge—"Mr. Gorbachev, tear down this wall!"—directed to Soviet leader Mikhail Gorbachev was rewritten this way: "I'm sorry, Mikhail, if I could? Didn't mean to cut you off there. Can we agree that this wall maybe isn't quite doing what it should be doing? Just looking at everything everyone's been saying, it seems like we could consider removing it. Possibly. I don't know, what does the room feel?" (Addady, 2015, para. 6).

The goal of the article was to showcase the double bind that women face with language. If a woman had actually said the original quote, she probably would have been perceived as aggressive, but the alternative wouldn't have been nearly as effective. Do you think this essay helps to point out power dynamics in language, or does it hurt and shame women? Explain your response.

Interrupting Another manifestation of power in language is that women are interrupted more than men. These interruptions can come from both men and women. In one study, when researchers transcribed the conversations of 20 women and men in pairs, they found that, in a three-minute conversation, women interrupted men just once, on average, but they interrupted other women 2.8 times (Hancock & Rubin, 2015). Men interrupted their male conversational partner twice, on average, and interrupted female partners 2.6 times. Also, a comprehensive review of 43 studies found that men were likely to interrupt women with the intent to assert dominance in the conversation, meaning that men were interrupting to take over the conversation (Anderson & Leaper, 1998). When women interrupted, it was because of increased enthusiasm or interest in the speaker's topic. Women were especially likely to do this in mixed groups as opposed to one-on-one conversations.

There have been four female U.S. Supreme Court justices. Pictured from left to right, they are Sonia Sotomayor, Elena Kagan, Sandra Day O'Connor, and Ruth Bader Ginsburg. It has been documented that women justices are interrupted far more often than their male colleagues.

The phenomenon of men interrupting women is getting increasing attention in the media. In 2017, the *New York Times* asked women to report on Facebook their experiences of being interrupted (Chira, 2017). There were hundreds of responses. One woman said, "I can't even count the number of times I've witnessed a woman being interrupted and talked over by a man, only to hear him later repeat the same ideas she was trying to put forward" (para. 8). Another reported, "My female boss told me she needed to allow each man to interrupt her four times before protesting in a meeting. If she protested more often, there were problems" (para. 9). Even women in very high-powered positions are interrupted more than men in the same positions. For example, between 2004 and 2015, the female U.S. Supreme Court justices were three times more likely to be interrupted than male justices (Jacobi & Schweers, 2017). Ruth Bader Ginsburg, Sonia Sotomayor, and Elena Kagan were each interrupted more than 100 times. However, only 4% of interruptions were *by* female justices. Clearly, women in positions of authority are likely to be interrupted—especially if they're in the minority, as the female justices are.

Body Language

How do people use body language to demonstrate their social status?

Language is not only spoken, and power is regularly performed in non-verbal ways (Hall, Coats, & LeBeau, 2005). Non-verbal communication is communication without words. It includes gestures, expressions, body posturing, eye contact, and physical appearance (Mast & Sczesny, 2010). Much like spoken communication, non-verbal cues reflect a social hierarchy (Hall et al., 2005). Many high-status people have been found to say whatever they want without concern for social approval, appear more relaxed, take up more space, and be likely to make eye contact when speaking as opposed to listening (Renninger, Wade, & Grammer, 2004; Tiedens & Fragale, 2003). They have also been found to be more likely than lower-status people to display non-verbal cues of disengagement (e.g., doodling, self-grooming) and less likely to show non-verbal cues of engagement (e.g., laughing, nodding, raised eyebrows; Kraus & Keltner, 2009).

Because of women's lower social status, psychologist Nancy Henley (1977) initially proposed that women are more likely to engage in low-status non-verbal behaviors whereas men are more likely to engage in high-status non-verbal behaviors. However, this theory hasn't received consistent research support since there is evidence that women in high-powered positions don't always engage in low-status non-verbal behaviors (Mast & Sczesny, 2010). In other words, much like other forms of communication, non-verbal communication and its relationship to gender and status are complicated.

In some ways, women have been found to be more likely than men to exhibit behaviors that reliably predict low status (Mast & Sczesny, 2010). In one study, girls and women were found to smile more, gaze more, exhibit more expressive gestures, self-touch more, speak with a softer voice, and maintain smaller interpersonal distance (Hall, Carter, & Horgan, 2000). The same study showed that men appeared to engage in behaviors that display dominance. This finding was indirectly supported in 2014 when the New York Metropolitan Transportation Authority released a series of public service ads targeted at men's tendency to engage in *manspreading*, a sitting style characterized by spreading the legs wide into a V-shaped slouch, effectively occupying two seats (Fitzsimmons, 2014). Moreover, the tendency to take up space isn't limited to public transportation. If you look around the next time you're sitting in class, you'll probably notice some degree of manspreading on the part of male students, while female students are likely to be sitting with legs crossed and body turned inward, a low-status position. In fact, some of our female students say they feel uncomfortable if they aren't sitting with their legs crossed. This practice might come from years of being told to cross their legs as a way to shield their genitals.

Smiling, in particular, seems to be something women do more than men (Hall, 2006). This tendency appears to come from a feeling of obligation rather than a display of authentic positive emotion (LaFrance, 2001). After all, women are taught to be "nice" and "sweet" rather than "strong." If you Google *men telling women to smile*, you'll find several hundred links suggesting that this phenomenon is a popular topic. Particularly when the request comes from a stranger, women report accommodating because of fear of retaliation (Glaser, 2014). Smile requests can be considered a form of street harassment that disproportionately

Have you noticed instances of manspreading as illustrated here? How do you think people would react had it been a woman sprawled across two seats?

affects women of color (Nielsen, 2000). In fact, artist Tatyana Fazlalizadeh unveiled a series of public art displays in 2013 entitled *Stop Telling Women to Smile* in order to draw attention to this problematic practice.

The practice of asking women to smile also can occur in high-profile situations. After winning her 21st Grand Slam tennis title, an exhausted Serena Williams was asked by a male reporter why she wasn't smiling (Capogna, 2015). Later Roger Federer, also a non-smiling, winning tennis player, wasn't asked to comment on his stoic appearance. Not surprisingly, the frequent request for girls and women to smile results in one of the largest gender differences in non-verbal behavior between women and men (Mast & Sczesny, 2010). A comprehensive review of several studies that explored smiling showed that girls and women smile 66% more than boys and men (Hall, 2006). Smiling is an excellent example of doing gender since it conforms to gender-role stereotypes that girls and women should be nurturing and communal (Bosak, Sczesny, & Eagly, 2008).

Conclusion

In 1993, author Octavia Butler said, "All struggles are essentially power struggles. Who will rule? Who will lead? Who will define, refine, confine, design?" (Butler, 1993, p. 94). This quote illustrates much of the current questioning both within feminism and within society as a whole. As we discussed in this chapter, power operates on many different levels. When people and institutions abuse power, there can be negative psychological and social implications. The ideal scenario is for people to learn how to share power, yet this is often difficult to do because so many aspects of privilege and power are unseen. Feminist psychologists aim to explore these unseen realities and make recommendations for more equitable ways to live.

Chapter Review

SUMMARY

Not Just a Woman

- Women have a wide variety of social identity characteristics that intersect in ways that can't be untangled and explored separately.

- Some social characteristics are associated with more power, while others are associated with less power. In contemporary society, being White, male, able-bodied, heterosexual, well educated, and middle-aged are all social categories that are deemed powerful.

- Power works through unearned entitlements and conferred dominance.

- Privilege is often invisible to those who have it.

- Because everyone has a mix of social identity characteristics, someone can be powerful on one dimension and subordinate on another, making it difficult to identify the source of one's oppression.

Stereotypes, Power, and Subordination

- Sexism can be difficult to see because it permeates society and is largely based on stereotypes.

- Women have traditionally been stereotyped as communal and men as agentic.

- Women of color face specific stereotypes such as the strong Black woman (SBW), the squaw, or the Asian china doll.

- Stereotypes influence people's behavior, and people can hold stereotypes about themselves.

Sexism

- Overt sexist discrimination is less common than it used to be. More subtle discrimination and microaggressions are now the norm.

- Microaggressions are not easily identifiable, and many people don't notice when they are taking place. For this reason, microaggressions are challenging to address when they occur.

- Sexism involves both positive and negative attitudes toward women.

- Benevolent sexism is generally aimed at women who conform to traditional gender roles. Hostile sexism is directed at women who fall outside them.

- When women are exposed to benevolent sexism, they show increased levels of stress and reduced task completion.

- The idea that not all men commit sexist acts has been countered by the fact that all women experience some form of sexist discrimination.

Language as a Source of Power

- The way in which we use language is an important form of sexism.

- Generic forms of language are usually assumed to be male.

- There are accepted, singular, gender-neutral pronouns gaining acceptance in the English language.

- Men are usually mentioned first (e.g., *boys and girls*).

- Unmarked language usually refers to men.

- Girls' names and nicknames are likely to represent beauty and kindness.

- The frequent practice of women changing their last name to their husband's name is based in patriarchal practices.

- Slang words for women's sexuality are more pejorative than slang for men's sexuality.

- Despite stereotypes to the contrary, men talk more than women.
- Women are more likely than men to engage in tentative speech consistent with subordinate status. Men are more likely to interrupt women, which is an expression of dominance.
- Mansplaining is another expression of dominance.
- Typical male body language demonstrates dominance.
- Women are often expected to smile, which can be a sign of having low status and wanting to please others.

KEY TERMS

social identity (p. 62)

social stratification (p. 63)

matrix of domination (p. 64)

privilege (p. 64)

legitimizing myths (p. 68)

scapegoating (p. 69)

sexism (p. 70)

stereotype (p. 70)

gender roles (p. 70)

agentic (p. 70)

communal (p. 70)

backlash effects (p. 75)

prejudice (p. 76)

overt sexism (p. 76)

discrimination (p. 76)

modern sexism (p. 76)

gender microaggressions (p. 78)

ambivalent sexism (p. 80)

hostile sexism (p. 80)

benevolent sexism (p. 80)

paternalistic chivalry (p. 81)

misogyny (p. 83)

gender-fair language (p. 87)

reappropriation (p. 90)

name shifting (p. 91)

tentative speech forms (p. 93)

THINK ABOUT IT

1. Imagine that you and a classmate are in a heated debate about gender and race issues. Your classmate says, "I don't know what the big deal is! I'm not sexist or racist. I've never been given any special privileges just because I'm a White man. In this country, if you work hard enough, you have just as good a shot as anyone else." Using the research from this chapter, how would you respond to your fellow student's comment?

2. What things would you recommend a friend consider when deciding about responding to a microaggression? What specific things could your friend say or do that might be effective?

3. How often do movies and books depict benevolent sexism? Think about ways in which you could rewrite them to eliminate sexism. Do you think they would be as popular? Why or why not?

4. In your next class, notice how the students sit and talk. Do the men take up more space than the women? If so, what types of things could you do to make the discussion and the use of the classroom more gender fair? What types of barriers might you encounter, and how might you address them?

ONLINE RESOURCES

- **Dr. Kim Case** – a website featuring links to Case's writing. A social psychologist and professor at the University of Houston, Clear Lake, she writes about intersectionality, feminism, critical race theory, and queer theory: drkimcase.com

- **Everyday Feminism** – resources about intersectional feminism for everyday life: everydayfeminism.com

- **Girls Inc.** – a website dedicated to equipping girls with the skills needed to navigate gender, economic, and social barriers so that they can grow up healthy, educated, and independent: girlsinc.org

- **Language: A Feminist Guide** – a feminist blog about language: debuk.wordpress.com

3
Similarities and Differences

IF YOU VISIT ALMOST ANY BOOKSTORE, you'll probably find books about sex/ gender differences. Many of these are for couples seeking relationship advice, and they typically describe women and men as totally different from each other. A famous book of this type was John Gray's *Men Are from Mars, Women Are from Venus*, an international best seller published in 1992. Gray (1992) imagines that "men are from Mars and women are from Venus" (p. 1) and then tells how they fell in love and moved to Earth, after which they forgot they were supposed to be different. When women and men in relationships think they're supposed to be similar, Gray says, the result is unmet expectations and relationship conflict. He believes the fundamental difference is that men experience fulfillment through success and accomplishment, and women experience it through sharing, relating, and feeling.

Another book, *Men Are Like Waffles, Women Are Like Spaghetti* (Farrel & Farrel, 2007), explains that men separate life into compartments like waffles and focus on one thing at a time (career, family, leisure). Women, in contrast, see all aspects of life as interrelated like pieces of spaghetti. They want to connect issues and talk things through. In *His Needs, Her Needs* (Harley, 2011), the author presents the contrasting needs of women and men. For example, she needs affection; he needs sexual fulfillment. She needs financial support; he needs peace, quiet, and domestic support. She needs intimate conversation; he needs recreational

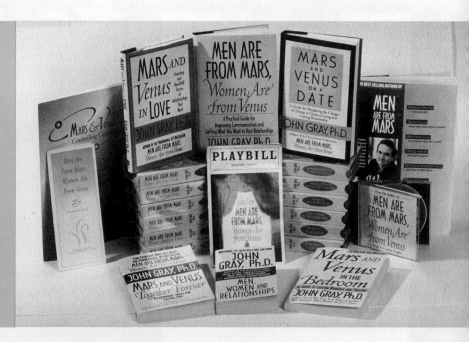

The prolific Mars and Venus series provides many examples of books that take an essentialist approach to gender differences.

companionship. The book aims to teach heterosexual couples how to meet the needs of their partner—needs that are completely different from their own.

In *Act Like a Lady, Think Like a Man* (2011), comedian Steve Harvey instructs women about what to expect from and how to attract men. He notes that women and men have different goals and needs: Men need to protect and provide for their women, and in exchange they want support, loyalty, and sex. Harvey warns women who are self-sufficient that "if you've got your own money, your own car, your own house, a Brinks alarm system, a pistol, and a guard dog, and you're practically shouting from the rooftops that you don't need a man to provide for you or protect you, then we will see no need to keep coming around" (Harvey, 2011, p. 182). So he advises women, even those with plenty of money, to let men pick up the check—and if they need their sink fixed, to "act like you haven't a clue what to do" and then tell him, "Baby, thank you so much for doing this for me—I don't know what I'd do without you" (p. 188).

All these books make assumptions about women and men being fundamentally different. But does this view reflect reality? In this chapter, we'll explore why the assumption of difference is so popular and how it has historically served to justify sexism. Then we'll consider how psychologists study the topic and explore the data on gender similarities and differences. Finally, using STEM fields (science, technology, engineering, and mathematics) as an example, we'll explore how sex/gender differences that start small can become magnified to lead to large differences in certain fields.

The Pervasiveness of Gender Essentialism

What is gender essentialism, and how has it historically served to justify women's subordinate social status?

All the advice in books like those mentioned previously rests on the pervasive assumption that there is something fundamentally different between women and men. The assumption is also that difference lies at the essence, or core, of the person and generally arises from biological or genetic factors. As we discussed in Chapter 1, this perspective is known as gender essentialism (Prentice & Miller, 2006). But what does this really mean?

It's easy to understand the idea of essential differences between groups by thinking about animals. We know that a dog is a dog and a cat is a cat because fundamental differences make up their essence—for example, dogs bark and cats meow; dogs leave their poop uncovered and cats do not. Because dogs and cats have different essences, knowing that an animal is a dog as opposed to a cat provides a lot of information about how it will behave. Gender essentialism makes the same assumptions about human gender. The idea is that because women and men have biological differences (a topic we'll complicate in Chapter 4), they must also have differences in behavior, attitudes, expectations, hopes, goals, talents, and skills (Dupre, 2016).

Gender essentialist assumptions have an intuitive appeal. However, data show that in most ways women and men are more similar than different (Hyde, 2005; Zell, Krizan, & Teeter, 2015). Despite this finding, the popular media typically take any difference—even a small one—and focus on it, creating a magnifying effect. Let's consider the following example. One group of researchers found a small gender difference in the left and right hemispheres of the brains of women and men, such that the two halves of women's brains were somewhat better able to communicate than the men's (Ingalhalikar et al., 2014). The researchers didn't link the brain difference with actual differences in behavior or abilities. However, the press release about the study suggested that this small difference explained why women and men have distinct sets of cognitive skills, such as better memory and social understanding in women and better spatial skills in men (Penn Medicine, 2013). Although, as we'll discuss below, other research has found small differences in some cognitive and social skills, this particular study didn't actually link the brain difference to any behavioral and cognitive differences.

But because gender essentialism quickly gains traction, in response to that press release, the popular press and blogosphere used the research findings to make statements expressing stereotyped views of women and men—usually reflecting the assumption that women are inferior to men (O'Connor & Joffe, 2014). This one article and press release generated at least 87 popular press articles, 162 blog posts, and 420 blog comments. Some were overtly sexist. One commenter said, "C'mon Ladies . . . let's face facts. Men invented piratically [*sic*] everything you use and enjoy. The Telephone, The Computer, The Jet Engine, The Train, the Motor Car, Etc Etc the list is endless. Without us, you would still be scratching around in caves so lets [*sic*] have no more of this nonsense and concentrate on your hand bags" (O'Connor & Joffe, 2014, p. 7). Housework wasn't mentioned in the research article or the press release, but another commenter noted that the article showed "Men are less likely to notice dust, which, women tell me, is a mix of fine particles that settle on furniture" (p. 6). As you can see, a very small finding snowballed into something bigger that could influence people's thoughts and help them justify sexist beliefs.

Using biology to make claims about gender essentialism has a long history, and generally these claims justify stereotypes of women's inferiority. Claiming that there are fixed, biologically based differences between women and men as a means to justify or reinforce gender stereotypes is called **neurosexism** (Fine 2010; Fine et al., 2013). In reality, though, neurosexist claims are not justified by scientific fact.

A Short History

Psychologist Stephanie Shields (1975, 2007) studied how gender differences have been understood historically and noted that in the 19th century many philosophers claimed that women were fundamentally inferior to men. As scientists sought explanations for why, one theory blamed women's reproductive capacities, arguing that menstruation consumed biological resources that could otherwise have "promoted further brain development" (Geddes & Thomson, 1890, as cited in Shields, 2007, p. 96). Other explanations focused on brain size (Shields, 1975). Scientists initially thought that men had larger brains than women (since their skulls were larger), which supposedly would justify women's inferiority. But when scientists subsequently measured brain weight as a ratio to body weight and found that women's brains are actually larger than men's, brain size lost favor as an area of research.

So much early scientific research was explicitly sexist that when women began to enter the field of psychology, they dedicated almost all their energies to debunking problematic stereotypes about women (Rutherford & Granek, 2010). Early feminist psychologists conducted studies showing that menstruation did not impair mental or motor abilities (Hollingsworth, 1914) and that women and men were actually more similar than different on most psychological traits (Thompson, 1903). The need to defend against sexism continued for so long that eventually feminist psychologists questioned the necessity of doing any research that focused on gender differences—whether to confirm or debunk those differences. The concern was that simply giving attention to the issue of similarities and differences makes them seem more important than they are. Instead, feminist psychologists turned to other areas in need of attention (e.g., rape, domestic violence, and pregnancy; Rutherford & Granek, 2010).

Distinguishing between Sex and Gender In 1979, psychologist Rhoda Unger boldly asserted that questions about sex differences, which seemed to dominate psychological research and the popular press, were "someone else's questions" (Rutherford & Granek, 2010, p. 29; Unger, 1979). To Unger,

your turn

Think about articles or books you've read that deal with sex or gender differences. What are the common themes? Are they derogatory to women or to men? If so, in what ways? Have you read any books or articles that focus on gender similarities? Do you think books about gender similarities—as opposed to differences— would be best sellers? Why or why not?

questions of difference maintained the status quo because they couldn't be disentangled from their history, which involved a false assumption of female inferiority. To move the conversation away from gender essentialism, she made a distinction between biological sex and the social construct of gender. In this view, biological sex is fixed, but how one behaves is a product of socialization and, therefore, should be considered gender. Unger's goal was to show that sexist socialization practices, rather than innate features, might account for observed differences (even small ones) between women and men. Unger also encouraged feminist psychologists to pursue research that focused more on social explanations than on biological ones.

Although it was productive to delineate sex and gender, in doing so, Unger opened the door to new challenges. First, separating sex and gender mistakenly suggests an exclusionary relationship between biology and psychology when, in fact, research shows that they're interdependent. It is impossible to attribute any one characteristic solely to biology or psychology (Unger & Crawford, 1993). When studying sex and gender, researchers remind us that "complex interactions are the rule, not the exception" (Unger & Crawford, 1993, p. 124). Unger's decision to separate these concepts was a strategic push, specific to the late 1970s, to move the field in a direction that focused less on biological essentialism.

As we discussed in Chapter 2, more contemporary feminist researchers move beyond defined categories of sex and gender and, instead, take intersectional approaches that recognize the fluidity and dynamic nature of identity categories (Rutherford & Granek, 2010). In other words, modern feminist psychologists acknowledge that it's impossible to distinguish between sex and gender, much like it's impossible to disentangle race from gender, because what we think of as part of our biology can be socially constructed (see Chapter 4). In practice, researchers use these terms inconsistently, and language choices vary over time and among academic journals (Unger & Crawford, 1993). For this reason, we will use the term *sex/gender* throughout this chapter to signify the interdependence of the two categories, a practice that is increasingly popular among contemporary feminist researchers (van Anders, 2015).

Sex/Gender Differences and Sexism Historically, sex/gender differences have served to justify sexism, and this practice continues today. However, the sexism is more subtle now than it used to be. Consider the books discussed above. Nowhere do they describe women as explicitly inferior; they simply describe women as different from men. For example, women are seen as good communicators who want intimacy and connection. These aren't negative descriptions; however, these attitudes are consistent with benevolent sexism. As we saw in Chapter 2, benevolent sexism is often a justification for gender inequality and can lead to hostile sexism when women step outside of the boundaries considered appropriate for their sex/gender.

In fact, research has shown that belief in sex/gender differences is related to both hostile and benevolent sexism (Zell, Strickhouser, Lane, & Teeter, 2016). In one study, men who believed in large sex/gender differences were more likely to endorse hostile sexism, and women who believed in large sex/gender differences were more likely to endorse benevolent sexism (Zell et al., 2016). Also, sexism increased among participants who read a paragraph about how women and men are different, while it decreased among those who read a paragraph about how they're similar. In light of these findings, it appears that believing that women and men are different is one current cause of sexism.

Because discussions about difference have historically been motivated by assumptions about women's inferiority, some feminist psychologists hesitate to discuss sex/gender difference at all (Rutherford & Granek, 2010). Nevertheless, it's important to understand what the science says. Some sex/gender differences do exist, but as this chapter will show, they're mostly small, and their causes are extremely complex. Explanations focusing only on biology or socialization are now considered to be overly simplistic. Instead, many important aspects of the lives of girls and women are best understood within a *biopsychosocial model* in which biological, psychological, and social factors all interact. Since popular culture is full of statements about gender essentialism and assumptions about neurosexism, it's critical to understand the history as well as the tensions associated with research in this area.

Perspectives on Similarities and Differences

What are some advantages and disadvantages of the similarities and the differences perspectives?

Because claims about sex/gender differences have been long linked to sexism, many feminist psychologists, especially liberal feminists, take a **similarities perspective**. This is the idea that women and men are more similar than different (Hyde, 2005). This view stems from the hope that if women and men are seen as more similar than different, then barriers that keep women from achieving in traditionally male-dominated domains would disappear (Eagly, 1995). For example, in 1903 psychologist Helen Thompson-Woolley tested motor skills among 25 female and 25 male White undergraduate students (Thompson, 1903). She then graphed the distributions of data from the female and male students demonstrating tremendous overlap and argued that the small difference found resulted from socialization practices rather than from heredity. Therefore, she argued that if women were given the same educational opportunities as men, those differences would likely disappear. Thompson-Woolley's work is an example of how focusing on a similarities perspective provided evidence to refute sexist ideas that girls and women shouldn't advance in academic and professional settings. More recently, feminist psychologist Janet Hyde (2005, 2014) has analyzed similarities and differences between women and men and strongly supports the similarities perspective. She notes that there are important costs to over-emphasizing difference. For example, a couples therapist who believes that women and men fundamentally cannot communicate may not be optimally effective (Hyde, 2014).

However, other feminist psychologists take a **differences perspective**. They view women and men as more different than similar and think people should appreciate and value women's unique experiences and attributes (Hare-Mustin & Marecek, 1988). Although those who take a differences perspective may appear to advocate for gender essentialism, this can be a strategic choice to help support social causes that uniquely affect large numbers of women. This practice is known as **strategic essentialism** (Spivak, 1990). The 2017 Women's March, discussed in Chapter 2, is an example of strategic essentialism because it was framed around how women are systemically disadvantaged compared to men.

try it for yourself

Take a piece of paper, and list all the ways in which you think women and men are different. Next ask five of your friends, of different genders, to come up with as many examples of differences between women and men as they can. Then list all the ways in which you think women and men are similar, and ask your friends to list similarities too. Which list was easier to generate? Do you advocate more of a similarities or a differences perspective? As for your friends, do their responses seem to relate to their gender identity?

Those who hold a differences perspective generally view women as a unified social group, despite the fact that women vary on numerous other social identity dimensions. Seeing women as unified and sharing a special quality of womanhood can be a way to mobilize for social activism (although, as discussed in Chapter 2, this approach can be controversial). Furthermore, the idea that women have unique qualities that should be valued is consistent with cultural feminism. In Chapter 1, you considered whether cultural feminism is empowering or oppressing, and the same issues are relevant in deciding whether a similarities or differences approach is helpful or harmful for girls and women.

According to the differences perspective, ignoring differences between women and men can be harmful, especially if knowledge gained from studying only men is applied to women. In clinical research, for example, if the symptoms of a heart attack typically differ in women and men, but if only men have been studied, then doctors may not recognize symptoms of a heart attack in women (Eagly & Wood, 2011). The differences perspective has also had some influence in modern science. In 2014, the U.S. National Institutes of Health (NIH) changed its policy for cell and animal research to require that all funded studies have a balanced number of female and male subjects (Clayton & Collins, 2014). Previously, most animal research had been done on males so that the female reproductive cycle wouldn't complicate the data.

Both perspectives can be useful, and both can be problematic. It could also be argued that questioning whether women and men are similar or different in the first place is overly simplistic and reinforces gender essentialism because it keeps the attention on difference (Shields, 2013). Therefore, it would be more useful to ask what factors increase or decrease similarities and differences.

Four Questions about Differences

What four questions should be asked when studying sex/gender differences?

It may seem easy to determine whether women and men are similar or different: Simply measure their scores on a given variable. In reality, it's much more complicated. For example, this line of research rarely takes into account the experiences or traits of transgender women and men. Contemporary scholars have suggested specific questions to guide researchers when investigating sex/gender differences (Joel & McCarthy, 2017). Without rigorous scrutiny, researchers may unknowingly propose simplistic models that risk over-emphasizing gender essentialism.

Does Everyone Show This Difference? As discussed in Chapter 2, much of the research in psychology does not incorporate an intersectional analysis, so research has often ignored other important factors that shape sex/gender. Therefore, a first question to ask is this: *Is the difference consistent, or does it change based on other aspects of one's social identity?*

Recent research shows that many sex/gender differences change when other intersecting variables—such as age, race, or socioeconomic status—are taken into account. For example, some sex/gender differences may only appear during certain developmental stages (Joel & McCarthy, 2017). For example, in one meta-analysis, researchers exploring aggression found that some differences were only true at certain ages (Archer, 2004). Specifically, while women reported engaging in more indirect aggression (e.g., socially isolating others) than men, these effects greatly varied by age. Women were more likely than men to participate in indirect aggression as children or adolescents, not as adults.

Other studies show that sex/gender differences disappear when race and/or ethnic background is taken into account. For example, a meta-analysis of almost 700 studies found that sex/gender differences in experiencing guilt were only true for White participants and not for Asian American, Black, or Latinx participants (Else-Quest, Higgins, Allison, & Morton, 2012). In a study based on hundreds of thousands of state assessments mandated by the No Child Left Behind Act, researchers found that the over-representation of boys at the highest levels of math achievement was only true for White students (Hyde, Lindberg, Linn, Ellis, & Williams, 2008). For Asian American students, the reverse was true. For example, at the 99th percentile of math achievement, White boys out-numbered White girls by a ratio of around 2:1. However, for Asian American students at this level of achievement, there were slightly more girls than boys, with 0.9 Asian American boys scoring at this level for every 1 Asian American girl (Hyde et al., 2008).

Social class also appears to influence research findings on sex/gender differences. In a study of spatial skills, researchers found that among middle- and upper-middle-class participants, boys did better than girls (Levine, Vasilyeva, Lourenco, Newcombe, & Huttenlocher, 2005). Among participants of lower socioeconomic status, however, no sex/gender differences were found. All of these findings illustrate how solely exploring differences between girls and boys without considering other identity variables can result, at best, in incomplete understanding.

As the influence of intersectionality becomes more mainstream, it's likely that research on sex/gender differences will become more nuanced. Because so much previous research has involved primarily White participants, an intersectional approach will also address ethnocentric tendencies in this line of research.

Does the Difference Change in Different Contexts? Much research on sex/gender differences hasn't accounted for the ways in which context may influence findings. So a second question to ask is: *Does the difference depend on context, or does it occur in any situation?*

Research suggests that a great number of gender differences can change, and even reverse, depending on the situation. In one study, researchers examined the density of neurons in the hippocampus of rats, a part of the brain involved with memory (Shors, Chua, & Falduto, 2001). When the rats had led peaceful, non-stressful lives, female rats had denser neurons than male rats. But when the rats had been exposed to even a short stressful experience, the sex/gender difference reversed: Males had denser neurons. In other words, the context seemed to matter quite a bit.

The same is true of helping behaviors. In studies where helping behavior was openly observed by others, men tended to help more than women did (Eagly & Crowly, 1986). However, when helping took place without anyone watching, there were no sex/gender differences. Men were also more likely to help women than to help men. These findings suggest that men may act in a brave or heroic manner because that's how they think they're supposed to act, especially in front of others.

Research has also suggested that differences in spatial skills may have a great deal to do with how researchers ask questions. In one study, researchers gave women and men a spatial perspective-taking task that involved viewing a diagram of a city from above and navigating from one location to another by writing "right" or "left" at every turn (Tarampi, Heydari, & Hegarty, 2016). In one condition, participants were given the start and stop points and were told

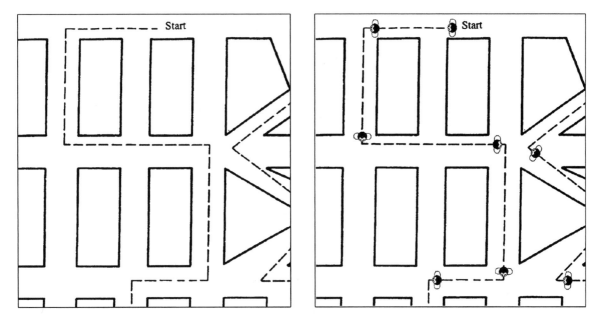

FIGURE 3.1 In the Tarampi et al. (2016) study, the map on the left was used for participants who were told that the study was exploring spatial ability. The map on the right, identical except for the inclusion of a human figure at each turn, was used for participants who were told that the study was exploring empathy. A sex/gender difference was found when participants thought it was a task of spatial ability but not when they thought the task was about empathy.

the task was a measure of spatial ability. Men did better than women. However, in another condition, the researchers showed the exact same map but drew a human figure that needed to be directed through the city (see Figure 3.1). Participants were told that it was a task of empathy rather than of spatial ability. Voilà—the sex/gender differences disappeared! The context in which participants encountered the task mattered. This suggests that differences in some spatial skills may have more to do with expectations about what women and men are supposed to be good at than actual cognitive differences.

Is the Difference Categorical or Dimensional? If a sex/gender difference is categorical (i.e., occurring in two distinct forms), then women and men can be treated as truly different groups or separate categories. So an important third question is this: *Is the difference categorical (women are one way, men are another way) or dimensional (any differences between women and men are a matter of degree)?*

Taxonomic analysis is a statistical technique for determining whether observed groups can be classified as categorical or dimensional (Carothers & Reis, 2013). If women and men are categorically different, then they're so different that they can be considered completely different groups (or classes or taxons). Accordingly, simply knowing that someone is a woman or a man would enable others to predict what that person is like on a given trait.

For example, dogs and cats are categorically different (they represent different taxons), and knowing that Puddles is a dog and Whiskers is a cat allows you to predict with near certainty that Puddles will bark and Whiskers will meow. This kind of assumption about women and men is found in the popular press books described previously (men = waffles and Mars; women = spaghetti and Venus), and it also underlies gender essentialism. In contrast, if the differences between women and men are dimensional, then any differences found are differences of degree with considerable overlap—and knowing that someone is a woman or a man wouldn't give much information about how that person would score on a given trait. Two species of dogs may have barks that, on average, differ in loudness, but knowing whether you have a Labrador or a Golden Retriever won't tell you with certainty how loud a given bark will be.

In one study, researchers used taxonomic analysis to determine whether the differences between women and men could better be described as categorical or dimensional (Carothers & Reis, 2013). The authors picked the most gender-stereotyped behaviors they could identify, such as enjoying taking a bath and using cosmetics (associated with women) and enjoying boxing and playing video games (associated with men). Not surprisingly, they found that interest in these activities was categorical (see Table 3.1). Therefore, if the researchers knew whether a participant liked using cosmetics more than playing video games, they could relatively accurately guess whether that person was a woman or a man. Of course, just because there were categorical differences doesn't mean that all women like to take baths and all men like to box. It simply means that, on average, this information does a good job predicting whether a person is a woman or a man.

However, on all other psychological variables studied, the differences between women and men were better described as dimensional than categorical (Carothers & Reis, 2013). Knowing that a participant was a woman or a man didn't even enable researchers to accurately predict whether that person was feminine or masculine. Empathy, interest in science, and comfort with casual sex were also found to be dimensional. This study suggests that women and men may, on average, be different, on these variables, but there is too much overlap between women's and men's scores to describe them as being in distinct categories.

What Is the Source of the Difference? Even if an observed sex/gender difference persists over time and across situations and is found to represent a categorical difference between women and men, it isn't clear what causes the difference. It could be based in biological factors, and biological differences may be rooted in different evolutionary pressures. However, differences may also be due to differential gender socialization, internalized stereotypes, or a complex combination of factors. To make things more complicated, differences may be related to an array of variables across various social identities. Often, many variables contribute to sex/gender differences. Therefore, a fourth question must be: *What is the source of the difference?*

TABLE 3.1 Categorical Sex/Gender Differences Identified in Carothers & Reis (2013)

Categorical Differences Found	Categorical Differences Not Found*
Men	sexual attitudes
enjoy playing golf	sexual behaviors
enjoy boxing	mate selectivity
enjoy construction	empathy
enjoy video games	perspective taking
enjoy watching pornography	importance of relationships
better at long jump, high jump, and javelin throw	masculinity
have wider shoulders	femininity
	importance of care
Women	interest in science
enjoy taking a bath	fear of success
enjoy talking on the phone	personality traits
enjoy scrapbooking	social support
enjoy watching talk shows	intimacy with friends
enjoy cosmetics (including hair and nail care)	intimacy with partners

Note. *For these variables, dimensional differences were found.

Four Explanations for Differences

What are four explanations for sex/gender differences? How are they distinct, and how may they overlap?

As we discussed previously, historically there has been tension between those who emphasize biological explanations and those who emphasize social and cultural explanations for sex/gender differences. Biological and evolutionary explanations have often served to justify sexism, so feminist psychologists have instead gravitated to social and cultural explanations. However, it's overly simplistic to assume that *anything* is either completely biological or completely sociocultural, as these factors often can't be clearly separated. Given this complexity, it's important to understand evolutionary, biological, and more social explanations for sex/gender differences. For any given trait or behavior, any or all of these explanations may apply.

Evolution The evolutionary perspective holds that differences between women and men stem from pressures for survival and reproduction throughout human evolutionary history (Buss & Schmitt, 2011). Of course, women and men faced many similar challenges to survival as humans evolved, so it's possible to expect that they should be quite similar. However, one evolutionary theory emphasizes the different pressures women and men faced in terms of mating and survival, leading them to develop different mating strategies to ensure their success (Buss, 1995; Buss & Schmitt, 1993). This **sexual strategies theory** argues that, as humans evolved, men impregnated as many women as possible in order to maximize the chance that some of their children would survive. As a result, according to this theory, even today men should be more invested in short-term mating strategies (e.g., hookups, flings) and have lower standards for short-term relationships. Women, in contrast, had greater maternal investment in each child in order to aid their survival (e.g., pregnancy, breastfeeding) and therefore preferred long-term, stable mates who would contribute resources to promote their children's survival. Evolutionary psychologists point to data that suggest, for example, that tall men have greater reproductive success (Nettle, 2002). They argue that this mate preference is due to an evolved tendency for women to select mates who could protect them. Of course, a preference for taller male partners may have nothing to do with protection. Being taller could have signaled better health, which could make someone a more desirable mate as one's children may then be more likely to be healthy.

The fact that women, due to gestation and lactation, are more invested in their offspring than men underlies the **differential parental investment theory**—an evolutionary explanation for why women are more invested in child care than men (Bjorklund & Shackelford, 1999). Another reason men may be less invested relates to the fact that early human men could never be 100% sure that a child was theirs, an idea known as **paternity uncertainty** (Goetz & Shakleford, 2009). Evolutionary psychologists also argue that paternity uncertainty helps explain why men developed aggression toward and control over women (Goetz, Shackelford, Romero, Kaighobadi, & Miner, 2008). Such tendencies ensured that the children the men were supporting hadn't been fathered by other men.

Although evolutionary theorists claim that women and men adapted to ensure survival, it's unclear what the best reproductive strategy actually was during humans' evolutionary past. For example, one might assume (as sexual strategies theory does) that men would maximize the likelihood of producing children by impregnating lots of women. However, if humans traveled in small bands in which many individuals were related, a man would probably do better by mating with and remaining monogamous to one of the women in his social group. In contrast to sexual strategies theory, **attachment fertility theory** focuses on how evolutionary forces may have selected for similarity in reproductive strategies (Miller & Fishkin, 1997). This theory suggests that survival was enhanced when women and men worked together to ensure the survival of their offspring.

Because human infants are dependent and vulnerable, this theory implies that it wouldn't be adaptive for men to impregnate women and then leave their offspring to potentially die. Instead, it was more adaptive for men to stay with their mating partner and help nurture infants to ensure offspring survival.

Evolutionary theorists are often criticized because, although attitudes and behaviors can be measured in the present, one can only make hypotheses about the evolutionary past (Ketelaar & Ellis, 2000). Also, while there are feminist approaches to evolutionary theory (e.g., attachment fertility theory) and evolutionary theorists who identify as feminists, evolutionary theories about gender have a long history of tension with feminism (Smith & Konik, 2011). For example, some evolutionary theorists have argued that rape was an adaptive strategy to help men impregnate fertile women (Thornhill & Palmer, 2000). Others have argued that domestic violence was a way for men to control women to make sure they weren't having affairs or having children with other men (Peters, Shakleford, & Buss, 2002). Critics have accused evolutionary theorists of insensitivity, victim blaming, and assuming that men can't control sexual urges (Rose, 2000). Of course, not all evolutionary psychologists view rape and domestic violence as adaptive traits. Furthermore, viewing sexual and domestic violence as having evolved to control women does not mean excusing or justifying these behaviors (Peters et al., 2002).

Biology Most research on biological explanations for sex/gender differences has focused on the brain and on hormones. In general, research on brain differences between women and men has yielded a complicated picture. Although some studies find small differences between the brains of women and men, the differences often disappear when other variables are taken into account.

A review of research found no compelling evidence for many beliefs—held by both the general public and scientists themselves—about differences between women's and men's brains (Wallentin, 2009). One belief is that women have a bigger corpus callosum, the band of fibers that connect the brain's hemispheres, and some have used this supposed difference to justify sex/gender stereotypes. For example, in the 1990s, a *Time* magazine article claimed that the fact that women's brain hemispheres talk to each other more than men's accounts for women's greater intuition (Gorman, 1992, as cited in Bishop & Wahlsten, 1997). However, a review of the literature reported no consistent difference across studies and called this belief a myth (Wallentin, 2009). The fact that studies finding non-significant sex/gender differences are less likely to be published than those that do find significant differences is a particular problem for brain research (Fine et al., 2013).

Even if a sex/gender difference in the brain is found, the difference doesn't necessarily lead to women and men acting differently. In 2009, a review of the literature concluded that "hundreds of sex differences have been found in the central nervous system, but only a handful can be clearly linked to sex differences in behavior . . . we do not know the functional consequences of most of the others" (de Vries & Södersten, 2009, p. 598). For example, in a study of women and men with similar scores on intelligence tests, there were some brain differences in what areas correlated with intelligence (Haier, Jung, Yeo, Head, & Alkire, 2005). But because the participants' intelligence levels were the same, this was an example of brain differences having no actual behavioral effect. In fact, researchers hypothesized that instead of causing sex/gender differences, observed brain variations might serve to compensate for other biological differences (e.g., hormonal levels), so that behavior is actually more similar than might be expected (deVries, 2004).

Another complication to biological theories is that while there may be small sex/gender differences in the brain, on average, that doesn't mean individual women and men have clearly gender-typed brains. In one study, researchers examined MRI scans of over 1,400 adults and identified the brain areas where the largest average differences between women and men occurred (Joel et al., 2015). Researchers then looked at each brain, one at a time, to see if women and men consistently had gender-typed brains. But instead of "female" or "male" brains, the researchers found a mosaic with a mix of female-typed and male-typed brain characteristics. Most participants had parts of the brain that were "female-typed," other parts "male-typed," and still other parts somewhere in between (see Figure 3.2).

Finally, even if there are brain differences between women and men, one can't assume that different brains *cause* different abilities or behaviors. In fact, research suggests that the reverse may be true. Brains demonstrate **plasticity**—that is, they have the ability to change to a certain degree in response to aspects of the environment and learning experiences. For example, taxi drivers develop larger-than-usual brain structures devoted to visual memory due to their experience with driving (Maguire et al., 2000), and musicians develop a larger-than-usual auditory cortex due to their greater need to process sound (Jäncke, Gaab, Wüstenberg, Scheich, & Heinze, 2001). So even if women and men do show brain differences, it may be the result of different experiences. In other words, biological explanations don't rule out social explanations. They can go hand in hand.

Biological explanations also focus on hormones' potential for shaping sex/gender differences. This research raises similar questions about whether biology is a cause of difference or a consequence of environmental factors. Although it's often assumed that stereotypically masculine behavior is caused by testosterone (van Anders, 2013), the data are complicated. Instead of masculinity per se, high testosterone appears to be linked to behaviors such as competitiveness, and low testosterone appears to be linked to nurturance. Moreover, these connections occur in both women and men. Testosterone levels also appear to be reactive to environmental situations. For example, a longitudinal study found that testosterone levels decreased in fathers and that men who did more child care had the largest decreases (Gettler, McDade, Feranil, & Kuzawa, 2011). In another study comparing fathers from two communities in Tanzania, those who were involved in daily child care had lower levels of testosterone than those who weren't (Muller, Marlowe, Bugumba, & Ellison, 2009).

Females   Males

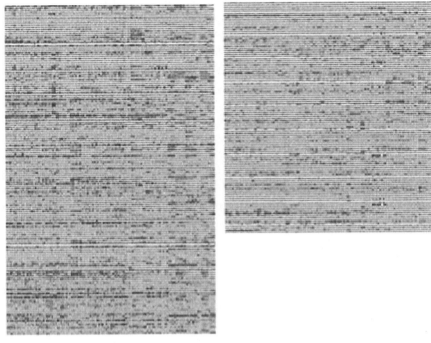

FIGURE 3.2 This illustration shows the human brain mosaic. Each horizontal line represents the brain of one participant (women on the left and men on the right); each column represents one brain region, and darker gray colors represent greater gray-matter volume. Each brain is a unique mosaic of features. While there are some sex/gender differences on average, each brain is unique and extremely variable. (From Joel et al., 2015)

Variations in testosterone levels appear to be linked to the ability to nurture. When young men were in a room with a fake baby that cried but couldn't be comforted, their testosterone levels went up (van Anders, Tolman, & Volling, 2012). But when they were able to comfort the baby, their testosterone levels went down. Testosterone levels are also linked to displays of power and aggression. In another study, when women were asked to act out firing someone (an act that demonstrates power), their testosterone levels went up (van Anders, Steiger, & Goldey, 2015). In general, men have higher testosterone levels than women (Mayo Clinic, n.d.). However, researchers hypothesize that the fact that women are socialized not to display aggression may be one reason for their lower testosterone (van Anders et al., 2015).

Social Role Theory Another theory, known as **social role theory** or **social structural theory**, emphasizes how gender roles are responses to, rather than causes of, different roles in society (Eagly & Wood, 1999, 2011). This theory holds that differences between women and men arise from the roles they've traditionally held rather than from biologically based differences. These roles, such as women being caretakers and men being breadwinners, may have their origins in biology. However, according to social role theory, cognitive and personality differences, such as women having nurturing qualities and men having better spatial skills, reflect adaptation to social roles. In other words, this theory argues that being a caregiver causes someone to be nurturing, not that being nurturing causes someone to be a caregiver.

It's important to note that this theory is not inconsistent with some of the biological research we've discussed. After all, hormone levels can change in response to social roles (e.g., they decrease during caregiving). Furthermore, due to plasticity, the very structure of the brain can change in response to the activities one engages in. Therefore, social role theory and biological theories can be seen as complementary rather than oppositional. Gendered behaviors shape the brain and endocrine system, which, in turn, influence gendered behaviors (Kaiser, Haller, Schmitz, & Nitsch, 2009).

Expectancy Role Value Theory Yet another theory, **expectancy role value theory**, also focuses on how environmental factors and gender socialization promote sex/gender differences. This theory centers on the notion that women and men have internalized stereotypes about how they're *supposed* to act (Eccles, 1994). As a result, men may have a difficult time assuming caretaking roles because doing so goes against their internalized beliefs that a man is supposed to be assertive and a powerful breadwinner (Croft, Schmader, & Block, 2015). According to this theory, people make decisions about what activities to pursue based on two factors: the expectation that doing the activity will lead to success, and the value that person puts on the activity (Eccles, 1994).

For example, if a woman is thinking about taking a challenging math class, she'll first consider whether she believes she can succeed in the class. She'll then consider whether the class is interesting and valuable to her. Even if she has the skills to successfully complete the class, she may think she doesn't. Also, she may not value math because she doesn't see it as something that "girls" do. Expectancy role value theory adds to the idea of social roles by noting that people make active choices about the kinds of activities they wish to pursue.

The four explanations are not mutually exclusive. Evolutionary forces can help shape social roles. Biological differences can be influenced by evolution but can also be a result of gendered environments. While arguments often present evolution and biology on one side and social roles and expectancy role value on the other side, this needn't be the case. The explanations can be complementary.

your turn

Think about the four explanations presented previously. Which one (or combination of them) do you think best explains some of the research on differences between women and men? Which one have you most heard other people use to explain differences? Why do you think some explanations are more appealing than others? These four don't reflect all possible explanations. What other explanations can you think of for why some differences are found between women and men?

Methods Used to Study Sex/Gender Similarities and Differences

What are some methods and statistics used in studying sex/gender similarities and differences?

Before reviewing data on sex/gender differences in cognitive skills, personality, and behavior, it's important to discuss commonly used research terminology and statistics. *Human sex difference* is an index term in PsychINFO, and there are over 79,000 peer-reviewed studies with this index term. Since the results of these studies may vary, it's useful to consider how researchers combine results from many studies to examine the big picture. This involves *meta-analysis*, a process that statistically combines results from a large number of studies. It's essentially a study of studies in which findings from existing studies serve as the data used in the new summary study. A meta-analysis has the potential of combining data from thousands of studies that look at millions of people. A more recent technique is *meta-synthesis*, which statistically combines the results of many meta-analyses (Zell et al., 2015).

Once again, it's important to note that the field of psychology has traditionally been, and continues to be, geared toward detecting and reporting difference. There are no index terms in PsychINFO about sex or gender similarities. However, if you search for "sex similarities" or "gender similarities" (putting quotation marks around the words), you'll find fewer than 500 results. Additionally, while researchers' statistical tools measure difference, there are no tools to measure similarity (Nelson, 2015). When a study looking for sex/gender differences doesn't find any, the findings are considered "non-significant" (e.g., no significant differences are found) and generally remain unpublished, leading to the *file drawer problem* (Rosenthal, 1979). In other words, studies that don't find differences are often filed away (in the metaphorical circular file, or trash bin). For this reason, the field is biased toward finding and explaining difference.

Although the file drawer problem is a challenge, it may not be insurmountable. A lot of published studies report scores for women and men separately, even when they weren't designed to explore sex/gender differences. These studies may find similarities between women and men but still get published because their main finding is about something else. Therefore, meta-analyses and meta-syntheses can be used with some level of confidence to determine the level of sex/gender difference. In fact, some meta-analyses account for the bias toward difference by reporting a fail-safe number, which represents how many non-significant and non-published results would need to exist for the findings that they report to be eliminated (Chaplin & Aldao, 2013). Other meta-analyses examine both published and unpublished studies, such as data sets from dissertations (see Else-Quest et al., 2012).

When data from many studies are combined in a meta-analysis or meta-synthesis, the results are generally presented in terms of an *effect size*, or a *d* statistic (Cohen, 1988). This number indicates how big or small a difference is. As Table 3.2 shows, an effect size of 0.1 (or less) is considered negligible, meaning any difference is essentially assumed not to exist. An effect size of 0.2 is considered small, 0.5 is considered medium, and 0.8 is considered to be a large difference between groups. It is also important to understand how to interpret the *d* statistic. It's a general convention to report effect sizes such that positive *d* scores reflect men scoring higher than women and negative *d* scores reflect women scoring higher than men. Although not all studies do this (Priess & Hyde, 2010), we'll use this convention when reporting effect sizes.

It's important to remember that even when a large effect is found to exist, this doesn't mean that women and men are two completely distinct groups. After all, taxonomic analysis has shown that women and men are not distinct groups on most variables (Carothers & Reis, 2013). To think about this in terms of effect sizes, consider that even with a large effect there would be a 69% overlap between women and men, as Table 3.2 shows. The overlap is even greater with smaller effects, and small effect size differences are the most common in sex/gender difference research. If the effect size is small, 92% of women and men would have similar scores—indicating a great deal of overlap.

Another statistic to consider is *variability*, or the degree to which the scores are spread out. Imagine a set of five scores with an average of 100. If the scores were 99, 100, 100, 100, and 101, there would be low variability. But if the scores were 50, 75, 100, 125, and 150, there would be greater variability. Men and women may have similar scores on average, but their scores may differ in variability—in other words, even though the groups don't differ on average, there may be more of one group who score very low and very high.

In her review of how assumptions about sex/gender difference have served to justify women's subordinate status, psychologist Stephanie Shields wrote in 1975: "The variability hypothesis is all but absent from contemporary psychological work, but if it ever again promises a viable justification for existing social values, it will be back as strongly as ever" (Shields, 1975, p. 751). Indeed, the variability hypothesis did come back. In 2005, Larry Summers, then president of Harvard University, spoke at a conference on diversifying the science and engineering workforce to address why there are proportionally fewer women than men in the sciences. He noted that "in the special case of science and engineering, there are issues of intrinsic aptitude, and particularly of the variability of aptitude" (Summers, 2005, para. 6). His comments caused a firestorm of controversy at the time—probably because they sounded very similar to statements made historically to justify claims about women's supposed inferiority.

TABLE 3.2 Common Effect Size Standards

Effect Size: *d*	Effect Size: Label	Percentage overlap between groups	What does it look like?
0.1	Negligible	96.01%	Cohen's d: 0.1
0.2	Small	92.03%	Cohen's d: 0.2
0.5	Medium	80.26%	Cohen's d: 0.5
0.8	Large	68.92%	Cohen's d: 0.8

The Big Picture

Overall, are women and men more similar or different, and what is the degree of overlap?

Researchers have reviewed data from many meta-analyses to gain an overall picture of the extent of sex/gender differences. In 2005, psychologist Janet Hyde reviewed 46 meta-analyses. She found that 30% of the effect sizes were negligible ($d < 0.1$) and 48% were small ($d = 0.11$ to 0.35). Therefore, 78% of sex/gender differences were either negligible or small. In 2015, researchers conducted an updated review using meta-synthesis of 106 meta-analyses with 386 different reported results (Zell et al., 2015). The total number of participants across all the studies reviewed was over 12 million. The meta-synthesis found an effect size for the overall difference between women and men of 0.21, a small effect. Overall, women and men were found to have a great deal in common—over 90% of women and men overlapped, but there was a small overall difference. When the authors of the meta-synthesis looked specifically at the 386 different meta-analytic results, they found, similar to Hyde (2005), that 85.5% of the effect sizes indicated either negligible or small differences.

Interestingly, the meta-synthesis authors also provided some support for the file drawer problem, in which only studies that find statistically significant sex/gender differences get published (Zell et al., 2015). When the authors incorporated results from both published and unpublished studies, there was a slightly smaller effect size ($d = 0.19$) than when using only published studies ($d = 0.24$).

Cognitive Variables

What are the main findings on similarities and differences in cognitive variables, and what role does culture play in these findings?

We'll now focus on sex/gender similarities and differences in general intelligence, mathematical ability, spatial skills, verbal ability, and academic achievement. Much of the data we discuss is based on large-scale studies or meta-analyses. As you'll see, the cognitive picture is complicated. In some domains, women have a slight advantage; in others, men do. In some domains, the interesting question is not who scores better on average but who has the greater variability. However, in all cases there is high overlap, and similarity is more the rule than difference. We'll also explore data relevant to the four questions above. For many cognitive skills, context matters, and the findings can change depending on how the question is asked and where or when the data are collected. Also, it's important to remember that finding a difference doesn't tell us the cause.

Differences may have biological or social causes—and most likely a combination of factors is in play.

General Intelligence

Women and men typically score similarly on tests of general intelligence. This is largely because IQ (intelligence quotient) tests are designed to be free of sex/gender bias. During test development, when women and men score consistently differently on an item, either it is removed or items are balanced so that there are no sex/gender differences overall (Halpern, 2006). In fact, one early intelligence test, the Stanford-Binet, showed a small advantage for women, but the items were subsequently revised so that women no longer outperformed men (Terman & Merrill, 1937). There are, however, some differences in specific domains included in IQ tests—memory, for example. Meta-analyses indicate that women consistently score better on memory tasks, with effect sizes in the small to moderate range ($d = -0.20$ to -0.56; Halpern & LaMay, 2000). Another component on which women consistently outperform men is processing speed, or the ability to maintain concentration and perform quickly while under pressure (Camarata & Woodcock, 2006).

There are also small sex/gender differences in variability on IQ tests. Men's scores generally have greater variability than women's. For example, researchers found more men than women at both the very top and the very bottom of the score distribution in a study with more than 80,000 participants from Scotland (Dreary, Thorpe, Wilson, Starr, & Whalley, 2003). However, a later analysis of this sample indicated that men had extremely variable scores at the low end of the distribution. At the high end, the variability was less extreme (Johnson, Carothers, & Deary, 2008).

Mathematical Ability

Because general intelligence tests are designed to be free of sex/gender bias, more attention has been given to differences between women and men on tests of specific cognitive abilities such as math skills, spatial skills, and verbal skills. The stereotype is that women excel in verbal skills and men excel in math skills. However, the data represent very complex findings. An effect size of -0.05 was found in a meta-analysis on math skills done in 1990 (Hyde, Fennema, & Lamon, 1990). This means that the difference in math skills was negligible—but in the direction of women having higher scores than men! However, there was some indication that at the highest levels of math skills, men did outperform women. For example, when only looking at highly selective samples, such as those who attended very selective colleges or those who were selected for study because they excelled at math, the effect size was larger, with men having higher scores than women (d = 0.54).

A more recent meta-analysis reviewed math achievement scores of almost a half million students across 69 nations (Else-Quest, Hyde, & Linn, 2010). Researchers found, on average, a very small male advantage in various domains of math skills (d < 0.15 for each skill). However, this small effect indicates large gender similarities. Also, there were extensive variations from nation to nation, and girls outperformed boys in some countries. Furthermore, in nations with greater gender equality (e.g., more women enrolled in schools, represented in the legislature, and holding high-level science and math positions), girls performed better on math tests, and the sex/gender difference often disappeared. Another study looked at almost 300,000 students in 40 countries who took identical, challenging math tests designed to be free of cultural bias (Guiso, Monte, Sapienza, & Zingales, 2008). This study confirmed that countries with the greatest level of gender equity, such as Iceland, Norway, and Sweden, show either similarities between women and men or a difference with a slight female advantage.

These two studies support the **gender stratification hypothesis**, the idea that differences found between women and men (especially on cognitive skills) relate to the level of gender equality in a country. Interestingly, countries that have smaller sex/gender gaps in mathematics—possibly because of social programs that promote the education of girls—also tend to have large sex/gender gaps in reading, with girls outperforming boys (Marks, 2008).

The international data have also challenged the idea of greater male variability. In one study, researchers found, based on data from the international math study described above, that in Iceland, Thailand, and Great Britain either as many or more girls scored in the top 99% of math tests as boys (Guiso et al., 2008). Other researchers have found in several nations, including Ireland, Tunisia, and the Czech Republic, that women and men are equally variable in their math performance (Machin & Pekkinarin, 2008).

Finally, the idea that men are over-represented at the upper levels of math performance may have been more applicable decades ago than it is today. For example, in one study, researchers reviewed data of mathematically gifted children—those who take and excel on the math portion of the Scholastic Aptitude Test (SAT) before they reach age 13 (Hyde & Mertz, 2009). In the early 1980s, boys doing this outnumbered girls by a ratio of 13:1, but by 2005, boys only outnumbered girls 2.8:1.

Spatial Skills

There are a wide variety of spatial skills, but mental rotation—the ability to imagine what an object would look like when rotated in three-dimensional space—has been the subject of much research. Mental rotation has consistently shown a male advantage, with generally large effect sizes ($d = 0.70$; Voyer, 2011). However, it's important to remember that even this large effect implies an approximately 72% overlap between groups. There are also data suggesting that men do particularly well on this task under time limits (Maeda & Yoon, 2013). Other spatial skills, though, don't show such a strong sex/gender difference. For example, imagining what a paper will look like when folded demonstrates a pattern of gender similarities (Miller & Halpern, 2014). If you look at the sample materials from the two tasks shown in Figure 3.3, can you explain why men reliably outperform women on one but not the other? Stumped? So are the researchers who found this outcome (Harris, Hirsh-Pasek, & Newcombe, 2013).

There are some spatial skills in which women have an advantage. As noted earlier, women generally outperform men on memory tasks. In line with this, spatial memory, or the ability to remember where an object was located, shows a small female advantage, although still a great deal of overlap ($d = -0.23$; Voyer, Postma, Brake, & Imperato-McGinley, 2007). Interestingly, this female advantage can disappear and even reverse when the objects are stereotypically masculine (e.g., a car or a train; Cherney & Ryalls, 1999; Voyer et al., 2007). In another study conducted in France, researchers showed girls and boys a

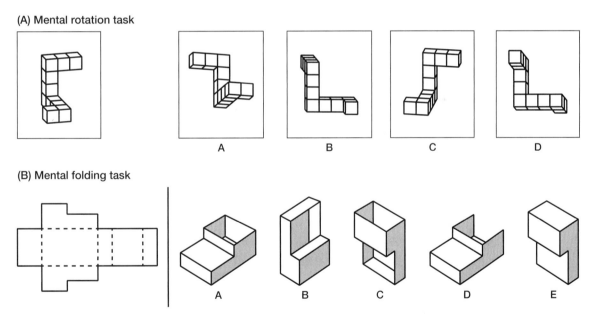

(A) Mental rotation task

(B) Mental folding task

FIGURE 3.3 For the example mental rotation task shown on top, participants are asked to imagine rotating the drawing on the left and to pick two of the four drawings on the right that match (Answers: B and C). For the example mental folding task shown on the bottom, participants are asked to imagine folding the drawing on the left along the dotted lines and to choose the folded shape on the right that would match (Answer: A). The mental rotation task shows a large sex/gender difference, while the mental folding task shows a very small one. The reason why there are large sex/gender differences for one but not the other remains a mystery. (After Miller & Halpern, 2014)

Single-Sex Education

Those who claim that single-sex education is better for girls generally offer two arguments (Pahlke, Hyde, & Allison, 2014). First, they argue that biological differences between girls and boys mean that they have different learning styles and should be educated in different ways. For example, Leonard Sax, author of *Why Gender Matters*, argues that boys respond better to energetic teachers who speak to them loudly and abruptly, but because this approach makes girls scared and nervous, they should be addressed in a kind, soft voice (Sax, 2007, as cited in Halpern et al., 2011).

The second argument is that girls do better if they aren't around boys, who may dominate the classroom or receive undue attention from the teacher. The underlying idea behind this "girl power" argument (Pahlke et al., 2014, p. 1043) is that a single-sex educational setting gives girls the freedom to excel in these domains without the sexism and discrimination that may occur in co-educational classrooms.

Do single-sex classrooms provide girls with a beneficial learning experience, or do they just promote gender stereotypes?

However, others have argued that girls and boys actually act in more gender-stereotypical ways in single-sex classes (Halpern et al., 2011). Critics claim that just as racial segregation failed to create racial equality, sex/gender segregation fails to create gender equality. They argue that the best way to eliminate sex/gender differences in educational outcomes is to allow girls and boys to work together on meaningful tasks and to train teachers to use the most effective methods to teach all people (Halpern et al., 2011).

One problem with research in this area is *selection effects*, that is, higher-achieving students are usually the ones placed in these kinds of educational settings in the first place. If they do better than those in co-ed settings, it's not clear whether this is due to single-sex education or the fact that they were high achieving to begin with. Results from a meta-analysis showed that, in the poorly designed studies that didn't control for selection effects, positive effects of single-sex education were found (Pahlke et al., 2014). But when only studies that controlled for selection effects were analyzed, there were negligible effects. Another recent study showed that when prior educational achievement was accounted for, high school girls did equally well in single- versus mixed-sex classrooms for math and science subjects, but they actually underperformed in single-sex classrooms in other subjects (Pennington, Kaye, Qureshi & Heim, 2018). However, when prior achievement was not considered, single-sex education appeared to result in better performance across all subjects.

What do you think? Is single-sex education empowering or oppressing? Can you think of circumstances in which you'd seek out single-sex educational opportunities for yourself, your children, and others you know? Would you avoid single-sex education? Explain your responses.

complicated object and then asked them to draw it from memory. The test's context made a big difference. Girls did better than boys when told it was a test of drawing skills, but boys did better than girls when told it was a test of geometry (Huguet & Régner, 2009).

Verbal Ability

Data show that women generally have higher verbal abilities than men, although the difference is relatively small, meaning that there is more similarity than difference ($d = -0.11$; Hyde & Linn, 1988). More recent data suggest a moderate female advantage in reading comprehension, which varies from nation to nation. For example, in 2009 when almost a half million students in 69 countries took a standardized reading assessment, there was a female advantage in reading comprehension both in the United States ($d = -0.26$) and internationally ($d = -0.42$; Reilly, 2012). A key component of this difference may have been that a much greater proportion of boys than girls scored very poorly on the test (4.5:1 boys to girls at the lowest levels of achievement). Girls also outperformed boys at the high end of the test 2.4:1, but the difference was not as large as at the low end.

Academic Achievement

Although most meta-analyses focus on achievement as measured through standardized tests, one meta-analysis of 350 studies from the period 1914–2011 examined sex/gender differences in grades across subjects from elementary school through college (Voyer & Voyer, 2014). Researchers found that girls got higher grades than boys across all subjects ($d = -0.23$), although the small effect indicates considerable overlap. The differences were largest for language-related courses and were near zero for math, but girls still had higher grades in math. There was also no effect of year of publication, indicating that the female advantage in grades is not a recent phenomenon. It's interesting that women get higher grades, even in math courses, all the way through college but are still extremely under-represented in STEM fields: science, technology, engineering, and mathematics. It's also interesting to consider why girls get better grades but boys have a slight advantage on standardized tests. It may be that girls are likely to be socialized to be attentive and polite in the classroom, behaviors that may positively impact their grades (Houtte, 2004; Zusman, Knox, & Lieberman, 2005).

In sum, the data on cognitive differences between women and men paint an overall picture of sex/gender similarity rather than difference. Although there are some small differences in various domains, they vary according to race, culture, and social class.

Personality, Beliefs, and Behavior

How similar or different are women and men in personality and behavioral variables, and what role does cultural context play in these patterns?

Many of the stereotyped sex/gender differences expressed in the books mentioned at the beginning of this chapter have to do with personality and behavior. Women supposedly want relationships, desire intimacy, and seek connection. Men supposedly want sex, are poor communicators, and are protective of their romantic partners. But in reality, how different or similar are women's and men's personalities? In this section, we'll explore sex/gender similarities and differences in personality and behavior. As we present the research, it will be useful to think back to the four questions discussed above. Many of the findings vary according to other aspects of social identity such as the race or age of the participant as well as the sociocultural setting. Also, a combination of biological, social, and psychological factors probably contributes to these patterns.

Personality Traits

Researchers generally view personality as varying on five major dimensions, known as the Big Five: openness to new experiences, conscientiousness, extraversion, agreeableness, and neuroticism (e.g., the tendency toward anxiety and depression; Costa, Terracciano, & McCrae, 2001). Each dimension has many sub-dimensions. In a meta-analysis, researchers found sex/gender differences on several of the dimensions as well as on particular sub-dimensions (Feingold, 1994). The largest effects were for men outscoring women on measures of assertiveness (a sub-dimension of extraversion; $d = 0.50$), although some studies indicated that this was more true on paper-and-pencil personality assessments than in behavioral observations. There was also a large effect for women outscoring men on tender-mindedness (a sub-dimension of agreeableness; $d = -.97$) and a small effect for anxiety (a sub-dimension of neuroticism; $d = -0.25$ to $-.28$). However, these differences still imply a great deal of similarity. Even the largest effect mentioned represents an overlap of approximately 62%. Also, these differences are consistent with sex/gender stereotypes. Being tender-minded is part of the feminine stereotype, and being assertive is part of the masculine stereotype.

More recently, researchers have reviewed studies that examined the Big Five internationally. Data from 26 countries and over 23,000 people were used to test for sex/gender differences (Costa et al., 2001). Researchers found results similar to those described above. Women tended to be more agreeable, neurotic, and open to feelings. Interestingly, this study found that sex/gender differences were magnified in the United States and Europe and were less strong in countries with more traditional gender roles, such as those in East Asia and Africa. For example, in Japan there was no difference between women and men in neuroticism, and in Zimbabwe and Black South Africa there were no differences in neuroticism or agreeableness.

The authors suggested that one explanation for these findings is that personality is typically measured through self-report, and how people report their personality may depend on whom they compare themselves to (Costa et al., 2001). In countries with cultures that are heavily sex/gender segregated, women may compare themselves to other women, and men may compare themselves to other men. In more egalitarian countries, women and men probably compare themselves to both women and men. For example, if you're a very agreeable woman in Zimbabwe but only compare yourself to other women who are just as agreeable as you are, you may rate yourself as less agreeable than you would if you compared yourself to the men in your community. This tendency would reduce or eliminate reported (but not actual) sex/gender differences.

Emotions

There are many stereotypes about gender and emotions. Women are generally perceived as "more emotional" than men—although the same level of emotion in a man is generally seen as passion or stress. For example, when researchers gave participants scenarios describing women and men in problematic, emotion-inducing experiences (e.g., having relationship problems, getting a bad medical diagnosis), women were described as "emotional" and men as "stressed" (Robinson & Johnson, 1997). Women are expected and encouraged to show traditionally feminine emotions such as sadness but aren't encouraged to show anger—an emotion associated with masculinity. When women do show anger, they're often punished—for example, with loss of status and influence (Brescoll & Uhlmann, 2008; Salerno & Peter-Hagene, 2015). Women and men have internalized these stereotypes, so when researchers ask participants to imagine their responses to hypothetical situations, gender differences are generally found (McCormick, MacArthur, Shields, & Dicicco, 2016). However, when asked to identify their emotional response close to the time when an actual event happened, gender differences are largely absent.

Also, there are differences in the expression of emotion—which isn't surprising, given that what people express is influenced by what they consider appropriate for their gender. For example, women tend to cry more than men, although this is actually more true in Western countries that are affluent and democratic (such as the United States) than in non-Western countries (van Hemert, van de Vijver, & Vingerhoets, 2011).

Gender similarities and differences in emotion are also not consistent across the life span. For example, research on emotional expression in children has shown almost no differences. A meta-analysis of studies on emotion expression in children showed that, overall, there were small sex/gender differences (Chaplin & Aldao, 2013). Girls, as compared to boys, did show somewhat more internalizing emotions, such as anxiety and sadness, and more positive emotions, such as happiness. Furthermore, boys showed somewhat more externalizing emotions, such as anger. However, all the effect sizes were less than 0.1, which puts them in the very small to negligible range. In other words, similarity was more the rule than difference—this represents a 96% overlap. When the researchers looked at whether sex/gender differences in emotions changed with age, they found no differences in emotions in infancy, and any differences were only seen starting in pre-school.

Sexuality

Although we'll talk more about sex and sexuality in Chapter 7, we'll mention here that many people think men want sex and have sex more than women do. In one meta-analytic review, researchers explored sex/gender differences in sexual behavior based on data from 730 studies published between 1993 and 2007 with almost 1.5 million participants (Petersen & Hyde, 2010). The researchers identified some differences in sexual behavior; for example, men reported masturbating more than women ($d = 0.53$), having more relaxed attitudes toward casual sex ($d = 0.45$), and having more sexual partners ($d = 0.36$). However, even the largest difference here represents over a 76% overlap between scores. Small or negligible differences, and consequently large similarities, were found for frequency of intercourse, sexual satisfaction, and attitudes toward extramarital affairs.

Interestingly, differences between women and men in studies on this topic may be exaggerated because when participants report their sexual behavior, they might over- or under-report in order to fit what they believe is expected of their sex/gender. In one study of predominately White participants, researchers tried to account for this phenomenon by asking randomly assigned participants to answer questions under one of three different conditions (Alexander & Fisher, 2003). In the bogus pipeline condition, participants were hooked up to what they thought was a lie detector and were told that the machine could identify lies, even if they wrote down their responses. (The device actually did nothing.) They were then left alone to answer the questions in private. In the anonymous condition, participants completed the survey privately and put their anonymous surveys in a locked box. In the exposure threat condition, they were told they would have to hand in their completed survey to a peer who would be able to see their responses.

Do you suppose the different conditions produced different results? Indeed, they did. For example, women reported more masturbation and use of pornography when they thought they were hooked up to a lie detector. In fact, their answers didn't differ from men's in that condition (Alexander & Fisher, 2003). Also, women reported having had more sexual partners when they thought they were connected to a lie detector than they did in the exposure threat condition (4.4 vs. 2.6). Men's results didn't change as much, and in fact, in the bogus pipeline condition, women actually reported having had somewhat more sexual partners than did men (men reported 4), although that difference wasn't statistically significant. In the exposure threat condition, women reported having had fewer sexual partners than men did (women: 2.6; men: 3.7). These results suggest that, particularly for research on sexual behavior, *how* researchers ask questions matters. As this study shows, women may be having much more sex than researchers might have thought; women have just been socialized not to admit it. Furthermore, the results of this study have been replicated in other research (Fisher, 2013). Moreover, the same approach has been used to show that when men think they're being monitored by a lie detector, they report the use of illegal sexual assault strategies 6.5 times more often than under standard testing conditions (Strang & Peterson, 2016).

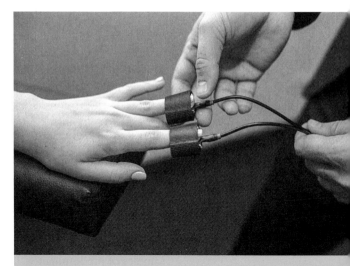

When participants believe they're answering questions about their sexual history while connected to a lie detector, they give responses that differ from those of participants who aren't connected. Why would thinking you're connected to a lie detector result in different reporting patterns than when completing an anonymous survey in which your responses can't be attributed to you personally?

Aggression

Earlier in this chapter, we reviewed how differences in the use of indirect aggression between women and men vary by age. There are also theories about men being more likely than women to use physical aggression. One meta-analytic review showed moderate sex/gender differences in physical aggression based on self-report data ($d = 0.59$) and observational studies ($d = 0.53$). Peer-report data reflected a larger difference ($d = 0.80$—although this still represents a 69% overlap; Archer, 2004). Men also showed greater verbal aggression, but the effects were smaller (e.g., $d = 0.19$ for self-reports). Researchers noted that while the majority of women and men were similar in level of aggression, some men were highly aggressive, and their data influenced the overall results. Therefore, while there is some support for men showing more physical aggression, much of this can be accounted for by a small number of particularly aggressive men.

Self-Esteem

There is a common stereotype that young women lose self-esteem as they reach adolescence. This is the basis of books such as *Reviving Ophelia* (Pipher, 2005), which point to a crisis in young women's self-esteem. However, the data don't support such extreme assumptions. Results from one meta-analysis indicate that men do have slightly higher global self-esteem than women ($d = 0.21$; Kling, Hyde, Showers, & Buswell, 1999). Moreover, they indicate that differences in self-esteem are small in pre-adolescents ($d = 0.16$), grow in middle school ($d = 0.22$) and high school ($d = 0.33$), and decrease again in college and through adulthood ($d = .18$ in college, $d = 0.10$ between ages 23 and 59, and $d = -0.03$ for participants over 60). However, even at the height of the difference, the effects are small, and more than 85% of women and men overlapped in their scores. This meta-analysis also showed that differences were not seen in research samples of predominantly Black participants.

In another meta-analysis, researchers exploring domain-specific self-esteem found a more nuanced relationship (Gentile et al., 2009). For example, men scored higher than women in appearance-based self-esteem ($d = 0.35$) and athletic self-esteem ($d = 0.41$)—although this indicates around a 84% overlap. Women, however, scored higher than men in moral/ethical self-esteem ($d = -0.38$), and there were no differences in family, social acceptance, or academic self-esteem.

Finally, when people hear that women have lower self-esteem than men, the assumption is that women should raise their self-esteem to match that of men. However, overly high self-esteem can be related to poor adjustment. In one study, college students with higher self-esteem reported drinking more alcohol than those with lower self-esteem (Sharp & Getz, 1996). Negative consequences are especially likely when people with high but unstable self-esteem feel threatened. Then they may engage in negative behaviors such as bullying, sexual experimentation, or drug or alcohol use in order to protect their self-esteem (Baumeister, Campbell, Krueger, & Vohs, 2003; Stake & Eisele, 2010). Therefore, even if adolescent girls have somewhat lower self-esteem than boys, this may actually not be a crisis at all.

Helping and Morality

If you picture someone you consider to be a hero, what do you see? Chances are you picture a man, perhaps pulling someone out of a burning building. Given this likelihood, one might think that men are generally more helpful than women. However, as discussed previously, one study showed that men were only more likely to help when they were being observed and when they were helping women (Eagly & Crowly, 1986). The type of help can also matter. Other research has shown that women were more likely than men to provide emotional support, and that both women and men would rather turn to

Both women and men engage in pro-social behavior, but context matters in terms of who is more likely to help and when.

a woman than a man for emotional support (Eagly, 2009). Women are even more likely than men to donate a kidney to a relative (58% of donors are women), and many report seeing such a donation as part of their family obligation (Eagly, 2009). So both women and men have the potential for pro-social behavior, but rates are related to context, not just sex/gender.

Some scholars have argued that women and men have fundamentally different senses of morality. In her book *In a Different Voice*, psychologist Carol Gilligan (1982) proposed that women base their judgments of morality on an **ethic of care**, thinking about how their actions will affect interpersonal relationships and the well-being of others. The ethic of care theoretically stands in contrast to men's **ethic of justice**, in which moral judgments are based on abstract principles of right and wrong. Gilligan's view, a perspective most aligned with cultural feminism, is that women and men are fundamentally different in their sense of morality. She argued that previous research had ignored women's care orientation and had considered the highest levels of morality as those based on a justice orientation. While her work is valued for pointing out that caring for others is an important aspect of morality, the data don't suggest that women and men differ much in their moral reasoning. In fact, studies have shown that both

your turn

Would a woman or a man be more likely to rescue a baby from a burning building? Who would be more likely to help an elderly person cross the street? Who would be more likely to comfort someone who's upset? As you consider these questions, do your answers change depending on the kind of help being given and to whom? If so, why might that be?

women and men use reasoning based on both justice and care when making moral judgments (Rothbart, Hanley, & Albert, 1986; Jaffee & Hyde, 2000).

Interests

Although sex/gender differences in intelligence and personality are small, differences in interests are larger. A popular way of classifying interests involves indicating whether a person is interested in people or things. One meta-analysis (Su, Rounds, & Armstrong, 2009) showed a large effect in which women were more interested in people and men were more interested in things ($d = 0.93$—a statistically large effect, but one that still represents over a 63% overlap in scores). For example, women were more interested in social tasks such as being involved in social causes, teaching, and helping others. Men were more interested in hands-on, practical tasks, including building and fixing things and working on cars. These interest differences tended to be stable across the life span starting around age 12 and have been found in research spanning many decades.

In sum, while there are some generally small differences in personality and behavior, most have a "now you see them; now you don't" quality. In other words, they're more likely to appear in situations where sex/gender stereotypes are activated. In everyday life, it's hard to disentangle the cause of a sex/gender difference because we live in a world where gender stereotypes are constantly activated. Therefore, even a small difference can become magnified as people internalize gender stereotypes and act in ways to confirm them.

The Case of STEM/EMCP

If, overall, sex/gender differences in intelligence and personality are relatively small, why do researchers find such large differences in certain fields? Let's look at STEM fields to explore how small sex/gender differences can become magnified to ultimately promote larger differences in women's and men's career choices. In particular, we'll look at engineering, math, computer science, and physics (EMCP fields), a subset of STEM that is particularly sex/gender imbalanced (Hyde, 2014). This is a controversial topic. Recently, a Google employee circulated a memo claiming that women don't hold leadership positions in tech companies because of biological differences, largely in personality (Bergen & Huet, 2017). This memo caused considerable controversy, and ultimately its author was fired. But the controversy highlights the need to understand the various factors that can influence women's participation in STEM/EMCP fields.

At the high school level, there are small sex/gender differences in math and science participation. For example, male students are more likely than female students to take calculus Advanced Placement exams (59% vs. 41%; National Science Board, 2014). In college, the difference gets larger. Between 2002 and 2007, men earned an average of 7,521 and women earned an average of 6,102 bachelor's degrees in math per year (Gillen & Tannenbaum, 2014). The numbers were lower for some women of color. Although Black, Latinx, and Native American women represent 16% of the U.S. population, they earn only 10% of the bachelor's degrees in STEM fields (Espinosa, 2011). Gender and racial disparities are greatest at the doctoral level, where men earned almost three times as many doctoral degrees in mathematics compared to women (2,341 vs. 788), and only 6% of those degrees were awarded to Black, Latinx, and Native American women.

As one moves up the ladder of success in math, the sex/gender discrepancies increase. For example, only 3% to 12% of the top 50 universities in the United States have female professors at the highest rank in math-intensive fields (Ceci, Williams, & Barnett, 2009). Overall, in 2010, women made up only 13% of people employed in engineering and 25% in math and computer science (National Science Board, 2014). Furthermore, in 2010, Black, Latinx, and Native American women held only 2.1% of STEM faculty positions (Hess, Gault, & Yi, 2013).

It's clear that something happens in women's progression toward careers in math and science. The fact that women aren't pursuing these careers at the same rates as men is particularly striking considering that girls get better grades in math than boys, even at the undergraduate level (Voyer & Voyer, 2014). Although all women experience academic and professional barriers in STEM/EMCP fields, the type and magnitude of those barriers depend on other aspects of social identities—for example, the challenges are greater for women of color (Williams, Phillips, & Hall, 2014). The following section reviews some of the research that explores these varied experiences. If you keep expectancy role value theory in mind as you read about those studies, you'll discover that the barriers keeping women from STEM/EMCP careers can affect not only their expectations for success but also the value they place on these careers.

Lowered Expectations

How do expectations relate to the performance of girls and women in STEM fields, and how can other aspects of their social identities interact with these expectations?

Although she is tremendously successful in her career, psychologist Maria Dolores Cimini recalls many times when people downplayed her skills, likely due to her visual impairment. In high school, when Cimini intended to apply to Ivy League colleges, her guidance counselor suggested she consider "a special school—not necessarily even a college or university" (Miller, 2013, para. 3). Now Cimini works to make sure that other students who have disabilities and show interest in STEM fields have a different experience (Miller, 2013). Her efforts couldn't be more timely. Research shows that both teachers and parents have lowered expectations about girls' math ability (Gunderson, Rameriz, Levine, & Beilock, 2012), and especially for girls with disabilities (Hammrich, Price, & Nourse, 2002). Much like Cimini, girls with disabilities are often advised to pursue academic tracks other than STEM (Faulkner, Crossland, & Stiff, 2013).

To complicate matters, a disproportionately large number of low-income and Black, Latinx, and Native American students are placed in special education programs (Hawley, Cardosa, & McMahon, 2013). Researchers speculate that some of these students have been misclassified because of racial bias in the referral and evaluation processes (Ferri, 2010; Sullivan & Artiles, 2011). When students are placed in special education tracks, because of either a documented disability or misclassification, their teachers often lack the knowledge base or experience to teach high-level math or science (Aron & Loprest, 2012; Faulkner et al., 2013; Moon, Todd, Morton, & Ivey, 2012). Such inequalities in early education probably prevent potentially qualified students from developing STEM/EMCP-related skills and interests (Hawley et al., 2013). These findings lead some scholars to conclude that recruitment and retention of under-represented minorities in STEM/EMCP fields won't change until biases found in middle and high school are addressed (Hawley et al., 2013).

Unfortunately, low expectations can lead to a **self-fulfilling prophesy**. This is the idea that expectations for how someone is going to behave, in either a positive or a negative way, influence that person's behavior so that the expectations are fulfilled, making the prophesy come true (Merton, 1948). For example, in one study of primarily White participants, parents who believed that boys were better at math than girls had lower expectations for how their daughters would perform in future math courses (Jacobs, 1991). When parents had lower expectations for their daughters, the daughters also had lower expectations for themselves and did less well in math courses. These expectations predicted achievement more accurately than the girls' actual grades in previous math classes. In another study with mostly White participants, seventh-grade girls, as compared to boys, perceived their teachers as having lower expectations for them in math (Wang, 2012). These expectations predicted how motivated the girls were about math and how well they expected to do in tenth grade. Furthermore, the expectations from seventh grade predicted whether the girls took challenging math courses in twelfth grade. Researchers have also found that Latinx and Black high school students perceive their science teachers as being particularly unsupportive (Aschbacher, Li, & Roth, 2010).

Expectations about math are somewhat different for individuals who are Asian American. A common stereotype is that Asian American people are hard-working, smart, and over-achieving. As reflected in this stereotype, they're thought of as a **model minority**, or the ideal example of a minority group. Although this perception may seem positive, research shows it has drawbacks (Suzuki, 2002). For example, when teachers treat Asian American students in differential ways, that behavior can create conflict with other students and perpetuate the stereotype that all Asian American people are good at math (Thompson, Kiang, & Witkow, 2016). Therefore, despite not facing low expectations around math and science, Asian Americans, particularly women, face different academic, professional, and social pressures (Thompson et al., 2016; Williams et al., 2014).

Low expectations appear to follow girls into their working environments in adulthood. Women in STEM/EMCP careers often have to provide more evidence of competence in order to be seen as credible (Eagly & Mladinic, 1994; Foschi, 2000). One study showed that over 75% of Black female scientists felt pressured to provide more evidence than was typical of other colleagues in order to prove competence to colleagues (Williams et al., 2014). The numbers were also high for other women: 65% of Latinx female scientists, 64% of Asian American female scientists, and 63% of White female scientists felt a need to prove their competence (Williams et al., 2014).

Stereotypes

What is stereotype threat, and how can it contribute to the experiences of girls and women in STEM?

There's a pervasive stereotype of a scientist as a White man in a lab coat working alone (Archer, Dewitt, & Osborne, 2015). It's an image that probably alienates many people who don't match this perception. For example, in one study, researchers found that many LGBT individuals working in STEM/EMCP fields weren't completely "out" to their colleagues, although those working in STEM/EMCP fields with better female representation reported a higher degree of openness (Yoder & Mattheis, 2016). Other research showed that transgender women were more likely to avoid male-dominated professions because of fear that the climate wouldn't be supportive (Brown et al., 2012).

Research also shows that STEM/EMCP colleagues interact with women on the basis of stereotypes, which are often racialized (Williams et al., 2014). One study

try it for yourself

Picture a scientist. What images come to mind? Do you see someone with a white coat working alone in a laboratory? Do you see someone working on a team with others? Do you see men? Do you see women? How do these internalized images of what constitutes a scientist and science affect your interest in science? Ask three of your friends these questions, and see if their answers are similar to or different from your own. Talk to people who are majoring in STEM/EMCP fields as well as those majoring in other fields. Are there differences in their responses?

showed that Latinx female scientists were more likely than White, Asian, or Black female scientists to experience backlash for expressing frustration in the workplace. Latinx female scientists reported that if they weren't deferential, colleagues perceived them as being angry or "too emotional" (Williams et al., 2014, p. 6). Black women, however, were given more latitude to act assertively—as long as they weren't seen as "angry Black women" (p. 6). Asian American women reported more pressure to conform to traditionally feminine roles, such as office mother or dutiful daughter. Research such as this indicated that many female scientists' experience of work has been influenced by racialized gender stereotypes.

Such stereotypes can interfere with performance. The term **stereotype threat** refers to the idea that when people think their social group does poorly on a certain task (or think that others believe this is true), their anxiety about confirming that stereotype can actually undermine their performance (Shapiro & Williams, 2012; Steele & Aronson, 1995). In a testing situation, stereotype threat likely interferes with performance because becoming self-conscious and having distracting, stressful thoughts about doing poorly can hijack attention and memory resources that are needed to do well on the test (Schmader, Johns, & Forbes, 2008). In the absence of an intervention, women generally come into math tests with internalized negative stereotypes about their math abilities. In fact, one meta-analysis showed that women had lower math self-confidence than men despite having similar math abilities (Else-Quest et al., 2010). Ironically, women's reduced self-confidence in math seems unjustified, given that the sex/gender differences in math achievement are small enough to be negligible (e.g., Hyde et al., 1990) and that women get better grades than men in math all the way through college (Voyer & Voyer, 2014).

One study showed that when women and men were told that performance on the math test they were taking typically showed large sex/gender differences, the differences in participants' actual test scores were very large (Spencer, Steele, & Quinn, 1999). But participants who were told that the same test typically *did not* show sex/gender differences had no differences in performance. In other words, thinking there was a sex/gender difference magnified it, and thinking there was no difference eliminated it. Because the idea that women are less skilled at math than men is pervasive, most women taking a math test are probably aware of it, and this perception may actually interfere with their performance.

In fact, simply having women write their sex/gender on a test can decrease their performance. In one study, researchers asked a diverse sample of girls and boys to record their sex/gender on a calculus Advanced Placement exam (Stricker & Ward, 2004). Although the effects were small and originally seen as non-significant, a re-analysis of the data indicated some important findings (Danaher &

Crandall, 2008). When researchers asked for sex/gender information *after* giving the test (i.e., participants took the test before the sex/gender stereotypes were activated), the sex/gender difference in test scores was reduced by 33% compared to when the researchers asked *before* giving the test. In fact, based on these data, Danaher and Crandall (2008) calculated that 4,700 additional girls could get college credit for calculus if sex/gender were regularly asked after the test!

As we discussed earlier, there are two contrasting stereotypes about math performance by Asian American women (Shih, Pittinsky, & Ambady, 1999). As women, they're stereotyped to have poor performance in math, but as Asian Americans, they're stereotyped to have good performance. In one study, researchers randomly assigned Asian American women to three groups. One group answered questions designed to make them think about their sex/gender (e.g., whether they lived on a co-ed or single-sex floor). Another group answered questions designed to make them think about their race or ethnic background (e.g., how many generations it had been since their family immigrated). For the control group, researchers asked questions unrelated to the women's social identities (e.g., whether participants liked the phone service provided by the university). All participants then took the same math test. Women who were prompted to think about their sex/gender performed worse than those in the control group, and women who were prompted to think about their race or ethnic background performed better. Therefore, internalized stereotypes can affect women's performance. Another study showed that more than half of Asian American female scientists surveyed felt the need to continuously prove their competence to colleagues, suggesting that the negative stereotype about women was probably more salient than the positive stereotype that Asian American people are good at math and science (Williams et al., 2014). It may be that the positive stereotype actually benefits Asian American men more than women.

Stereotypes interfere with the value women place on STEM/EMCP careers, and stereotype threat can interfere with their perception that they will succeed. However, it's important to note that while stereotype threat may be one factor affecting women's performance in math, it isn't the only one. A meta-analysis of data on stereotype threat specifically on math performance showed that the effects are generally small. It also showed that while stereotype threat may affect some women, it would be inaccurate to say that stereotype threat is the main cause of sex/gender differences in math (Stoet & Geary, 2012).

Goal Congruity

What is the goal congruity perspective, and how does it explain the low rates of participation by women in STEM fields?

Because White men generally dominate STEM/EMCP fields, their lifestyles and interests shape the norms around work. People in STEM/EMCP careers generally commit to long hours and almost constant availability, and this can contribute to assumptions about the ideal worker (Kachchaf, Ko, Hodari, & Ong, 2015). One Black woman in the last year of a post-doctoral position in mathematics noted that she had to work 12-hour days, six days a week, to meet the expectations and level of work of her advisor. She commented: "[Many] of the people are men without family, or with wives that don't do anything else" (Kachchaf et al., 2015, p. 181). This norm discourages people who might have different priorities from joining the field.

Also, many women want a career that meets their interests in working with people and their goals of caring for others (Diekman, Clark, Johnston, Brown, & Steinberg, 2011). This attitude reflects the **goal congruity perspective**, which holds that people want to engage in activities that meet their goals. Because most women value communal goals (e.g., caring for and feeling connected to others) and have internalized stereotypes about the type of work involved in STEM/EMCP fields, many may not value STEM/EMCP careers. For example, one study found that Native American women and men and White women who were majoring in STEM fields highly endorsed communal goals (Smith, Cech, Metz, Huntoon, & Moyer, 2014). In a follow-up study, Native American STEM students with particularly high communal goals (especially compared with White male STEM majors) had low motivation around their STEM major, perceived poor performance after one semester of college, and felt they didn't belong (Smith et al., 2014).

Both women and men tend to think that STEM/EMCP careers involve working alone in a lab without much interaction with others. In other words, STEM/EMCP is perceived as being more about working with things than with people. Yet this stereotype is largely untrue. Being a scientist can be extremely collaborative and often involves working on a team and mentoring others. In fact, one study investigated the goal congruity hypothesis by having participants respond to statements describing the life of a scientist as either independent (e.g., "Do data analysis . . . and troubleshoot any problems that come up by

Which of these two images best represents your idea of the life of a scientist? Is it the woman on the left working alone, or the group of people working together on the right? Most people think that being a scientist involves working alone, but the reality is that scientists spend a lot of time collaborating with others.

myself") or collaborative (e.g., "Mentor new members of my statistics group in doing data analysis"; Diekman et al., 2011, p. 910). When the work was described as independent, men were more interested in the career than women. When the work was described as collaborative, women were more interested than men.

The fact that women may not consider STEM/EMCP fields as valuable to them is reflected in research suggesting that it's not women's math scores, but their *language* scores, that predict whether they pursue careers in STEM/EMCP. One longitudinal study identified two groups of people with equally high math skills: those with high verbal abilities (mostly girls) and those with moderate verbal abilities (mostly boys; Wang, Eccles, & Kenny, 2013). While only 34% of those with both high math and verbal skills went into a STEM/EMCP field, 49% of those with high math but only moderate verbal abilities did so. Because girls with high math skills are also more likely than boys to have high verbal skills, they have more options. Given these greater options, girls may prefer to choose careers that they regard as valuable and in which they feel welcomed and comfortable.

Discrimination

In what ways do girls and women experience discrimination in STEM, and how can being a token exacerbate this?

Another factor that decreases women's expectations for and likely success in STEM/EMCP fields is discrimination. It can interfere with a woman's confidence that she will succeed in STEM/EMCP as well as the value she places on it. After all, why would she choose a field in which she'll probably experience discrimination? These attitudes are acquired early in a girl's academic career. For example, in high school, girls with physical disabilities may not have the same opportunities to engage with STEM/EMCP fields as able-bodied students (Lunsford, & Bargerhuff, 2006; Rankel, Amorosi, & Graybill, 2008). Labs may not be accessible for people using wheelchairs or other assistive devices, and research shows a tendency for teachers to ask visually impaired students to simply listen to summaries of experiments rather than being involved and analyzing data themselves (Rankel et al., 2008). When these factors are added to the sexism that girls already encounter in STEM/EMCP fields, it increases the barriers they face.

Discrimination also occurs among peers. In one study, researchers asked primarily Asian American and White biology students to nominate the strongest students in the class (Grunspan et al., 2016). Male students were nominated more frequently than female students, especially if they were outspoken. For example, in one class, an outspoken male student with a 3.6 GPA received 52 nominations while an outspoken female student with a 4.0 GPA received only 9 nominations. Male students were particularly likely to see other men as the stars of their class.

Discrimination may continue after students graduate from college. In one study, researchers sent identical applications with identical resumés for a position as a laboratory assistant to science faculty at large research institutions (Moss-Racusin, Dovidio, Brescoll, Graham, & Handelsman, 2012). The hiring faculty were randomly told that the application was from either a female student (Jennifer) or a male student (John). Both female and male faculty said John was more competent. They also expressed greater willingness to mentor him and said they would pay him $3,730 more than Jennifer per year (see Figure 3.4).

As we'll discuss in Chapter 10, workplace discrimination is very common, especially in fields where women are a minority. Since women are a minority in STEM/EMCP fields, the conditions there are ripe for workplace discrimination (Ceci et al., 2009). Results from a survey of approximately 1,300 scientists indicated that 53% of female respondents had personally experienced sex/gender bias during their careers (American Association for the Advancement of Science, 2010; see Shen, 2013, for a review). Only 2% of men reported the same. Further, racialized gender biases may prevent women of color from advancing in the field. In one study comparing White female scientists with female scientists of color, White women reported higher levels of influence in their departments

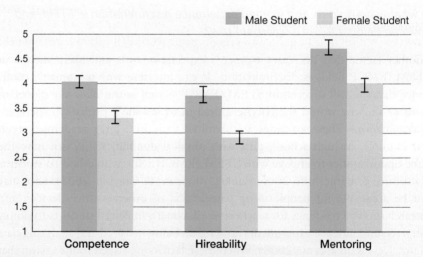

FIGURE 3.4 Scientists at research-intensive universities were randomly assigned to rate application materials from either a woman or a man for a laboratory assistant position. The only difference was the applicant's name. When the application was from a male student, scientists rated the applicant as more competent, were more likely to want to hire him, and were more likely to offer mentoring than if the application was from a female student. All questions were asked on a 1–7 scale where higher numbers represented higher perceptions of competence and greater likelihood that the participant would hire or mentor the applicant. Error bars represent Standard Errors. (After Moss-Racusin et al., 2012)

than did the women of color (Settles, Cortina, Stewart, & Malley, 2007). Another study showed that Latinx female scientists were far more likely than other groups of women to report that their colleagues expected them to manage the office, including making coffee and providing emotional support to colleagues and students (Williams et al., 2014). Given this atmosphere, women who enter STEM/EMCP fields may not remain in them.

It's also noteworthy that women working in STEM/EMCP fields are often one of very few women in their lab or division. A member of a socially marginalized group whose group makes up less than 15% of the workforce in a workplace setting is known as a **token** (Kanter, 1977; Yoder, 1994). When tokens are members of lower-status groups (e.g., women or Latinx), negative effects can occur. For example, tokens have increased visibility, so their work is more carefully scrutinized (Williams et al., 2014). In one study of STEM professors working at colleges and universities, 43% of women of color reported feeling under close scrutiny as compared with 33% of White women and 18% of White men (Hollenshead & Thomas, 2001).

When a woman is a token, she feels considerable pressure not to make mistakes because her work is viewed as representing that of all people like her. She may also feel socially isolated and likely to be seen in sex/gender-stereotyped ways—such as a temptress or a mother (King, Hebl, George, & Matusik, 2010). Race and ethnic background can exacerbate women's experience of tokenism. In one study, researchers found that Black and Asian American women reported tokenism more often than Latinx and White women (Williams et al., 2014). However, conditions do improve as more members of that group enter the field as a whole or in a given workplace. For example, as the number of women in a science department increased, women in that department felt more comfortable and were more likely to believe their department valued the advancement of women (Hillard, Schneider, Jackson, & LaHuis, 2014).

An excellent example of how discrimination can marginalize women in STEM/EMCP fields is found in the 2016 book and subsequent Oscar-nominated movie *Hidden Figures* (Shetterly, 2016). Both relate the stories of three women of color—Katherine Johnson, Dorothy Vaughan, and Mary Jackson—who conducted important mathematical analyses for NASA during the space program's early years. These women were systematically discriminated against, required to use a separate bathroom far from their work area, and had their work dismissed as unimportant. Their work was, in fact, vital to the success of the space program, but they didn't receive any public recognition for it until 2016.

In sum, sex/gender differences in abilities cannot sufficiently account for the disproportionately small number of women in STEM/EMCP fields. The situation is much more complicated. What starts as a negligible or small difference between girls and boys can develop into a large difference, especially considering how other structural pressures (e.g., racism) influence girls' and women's success in these fields.

Conclusion

Psychologists have a long history of exploring sex/gender differences, both to support and to disconfirm beliefs about innate, biological differences. The differences that have been identified seem to be the result of complex interactions between sociocultural variables and biology (Eagly, 1995; Hyde, 2005). Although the perception that women and men are "from different planets" is popular, women and men are actually more similar than different. While small differences do exist, they're often magnified in popular culture, and over-stating difference has served as a way to justify sexism. Therefore, education about the reality of relatively small sex/gender differences is key for reducing sex/gender prejudice. So the next time you hear a sexist joke or comment that reflects gender essentialism, you now know that spaceships truly aren't necessary—women and men are actually from the same planet!

Finally, it's worth reflecting on the fact that much research has been devoted to discussing and debating similarities and differences between women and men. However, feminist psychologists see this entire conversation as flawed. Asking "Are there differences between women and men?" keeps the focus on *whether* there are differences instead of explaining and contextualizing them (Shields, 2013). Furthermore, the question assumes one clear, singular identity of "woman" and "man." Instead, every woman (and man) is uniquely different as a result of a complex array of intersecting identities (McCormick et al., 2016; Shields, 2013). Many feminist psychologists would argue that instead of focusing on difference, it would be more useful to explore how psychological research can improve the lives of women—and, ultimately, of all people (Kitzinger, 1994; Rutherford & Granek, 2010).

Chapter Review

SUMMARY

The Pervasiveness of Gender Essentialism

- Gender essentialism is the idea that women and men are fundamentally different at their very core, or "essence," because of biological or genetic factors.

- Gender essentialist arguments are popular and have an intuitive appeal.

- Historically, sex/gender differences have been used as a way to justify sexism.

- Belief in gender essentialism is linked to hostile and benevolent sexism.

Perspectives on Similarities and Differences

- A similarities perspective emphasizes the ways in which women and men are similar and is aligned with liberal feminism. A differences perspective emphasizes the ways in which they are different and is aligned with cultural feminism.

- In order to understand sex/gender similarities and differences, one must ask: (a) Is the difference consistent, or does it change based other aspects of one's social identity? (b) Does the difference depend on context, or does it occur in any situation? (c) Is the difference categorical or dimensional? (d) What is the source of the difference?

- Evolutionary psychologists argue that differences stem from evolutionary pressures, especially different mating strategies and parental investment. Other psychologists emphasize sex/gender similarities based on similar evolutionary pressures.

- On average, there are some small biological differences between women's and men's brains, but these have not been clearly linked to behavioral differences.

- Men have higher levels of testosterone, but testosterone can vary based on one's experiences. Acting aggressively increases testosterone; acting in a nurturing way decreases it.

- Plasticity is the capacity for biological structures, such as the brain, to change in response to environmental factors and learning experiences.

- Social role theory emphasizes that sex/gender differences stem from the roles that women and men have traditionally held.

- Expectancy role value theory holds that differences stem from women and men valuing different activities and having different expectations for success.

Methods Used to Study Sex/Gender Similarities and Differences

- Because there is so much research on the topic, it is useful to look at the results of meta-analyses and meta-syntheses. These analyses use a statistic called an effect size to quantify difference.

- Because non-significant results are generally not published, published research tends to be biased toward studies that find difference.

- Psychologists are also interested in whether women and men differ in variability, reflected by whether there are greater differences on very low or very high scores.

- Meta-analyses and meta-syntheses generally find that women and men are more similar than different.

Cognitive Variables

- There are no differences on tests of general intelligence.

- There are no overall differences in mathematics skills, but men have greater variability.

- Men score better at mental rotation, and women score better on verbal tasks.
- Women tend to have higher academic achievement through college.
- All the differences found vary according to race, culture, and social class and are inconsistent from task to task.

Personality, Beliefs, and Behavior

- There are some differences in personality—women tend to be more agreeable, and men tend to be more assertive.
- Gender differences in emotion are consistent with internalized gender stereotypes and are more likely to be seen in self-report data than in behavioral data.
- Men self-report having more sexual partners and experiencing greater comfort with sex. However, the data depend on whether participants think they are being monitored for truth telling.
- Men are more likely than women to exhibit physical aggression; however, the data are skewed by small numbers of highly aggressive men, and most women and men show similar levels of aggression.
- Men have somewhat higher global self-esteem, but this varies depending on age as well as the type of self-esteem measured.

- Both women and men use reasoning based on ethics of justice and care when making moral judgments.
- Women are more interested in people, and men are more interested in things.
- Most of the above differences represent relatively small effect sizes and vary according to how questions are asked, the participants' age, and the participants' culture.

The Case of STEM/EMCP

- Research suggests that parents and teachers have lower expectations for girls than they do for boys in math and science, which influences girls' interest and performance.
- Lowered expectations can be a particular problem for girls with physical disabilities.
- People associate being good at science with being White and male.
- Stereotype threat may lower achievement in math and science for some women.
- Women may not be interested in STEM/EMCP careers because they see them as incompatible with communal goals. This interferes with the value women place on math and science.
- Women experience discrimination in math and science fields. This can be related to being a minority in these settings and being treated as tokens.

KEY TERMS

neurosexism (p. 105)

similarities perspective (p. 107)

differences perspective (p. 108)

strategic essentialism (p. 108)

sexual strategies theory (p. 114)

differential parental investment theory (p. 114)

paternity uncertainty (p. 114)

attachment fertility theory (p. 114)

plasticity (p. 116)

social role theory/social structural theory (p. 117)

expectancy role value theory (p. 118)

gender stratification hypothesis (p. 124)

ethic of care (p. 133)

ethic of justice (p. 133)

self-fulfilling prophesy (p. 136)

model minority (p. 137)

stereotype threat (p. 138)

goal congruity perspective (p. 140)

token (p. 143)

THINK ABOUT IT

1. Imagine you're conversing with a friend who is convinced that there are fundamental differences between women and men. Using research results from this chapter, explain how this perspective is more complicated than your friend might expect.

2. What are the benefits and drawbacks of conducting research on sex/gender differences? How would you advise psychologists to approach research in this area?

3. In explaining sex/gender similarities, can you use the same theories that have been proposed to explain sex/gender differences? If not, what other theories might explain sex/gender similarities? Why aren't we likely to discuss theories on sex/gender similarities?

4. Design a campus-wide campaign to address gender disparities in STEM fields. What types of information are important to include? What types of interventions do you believe will have the greatest influence?

ONLINE RESOURCES

- **Cordelia Fine** — a website featuring links to Fine's writing. A neuroscientist and professor of history and philosophy of science at the University of Melbourne, she writes about neurosexism and gender essentialism in the popular press: cordeliafine.com

- **Girl Start** — a blog dedicated to increasing girls' interest and engagement in STEM educational programming: girlstart.org

- **STEM Women** — a website created by women in STEM fields to encourage and promote gender equity in STEM fields: stemwomen.net

- **Van Anders Lab** — a website hosted by Dr. Sari van Anders at the University of Michigan, Ann Arbor, offering resources about social neuroendocrinology, feminist science, sexuality, gender/sex, and sexual diversity: www-personal.umich.edu/~smva/

4

Beyond the Sex/Gender Binary

THE COMPETITION WAS SET. Contestants would endure a series of intensive weight-lifting, gymnastics, and interval workouts in order to compete for the title of The 2014 Fittest Woman on Earth. Chloie Jonsson, a personal trainer, was no stranger to the Reebok CrossFit Games (Sieczkowski, 2014). She had competed before and was preparing again for the brutal test of strength, endurance, and toughness. This time, however, was different. Motivated by an anonymous tip, the competition organizers declared that all participants had to compete according to their sex as assigned at birth. Chloie, who had identified as female since adolescence, had received cross-sex hormone treatment, had undergone gender-affirmative surgery, and was now legally recognized by the state of California as a woman, could *not* compete in this year's competition. She was devastated. She would later sue for discrimination, but the games continued without her.

The requirement for elite female athletes to prove their *true* sex isn't new. Between 1968 and 1999, the International Olympic Committee (IOC) required that all female athletes, but not male athletes, undergo gender verification testing (Ha et al., 2014; Mitra, 2014). Such tests were deemed necessary after rumors emerged that some male athletes were masquerading as women in order to have a competitive advantage (Ha et al., 2014). Yet from the start of testing, there were problems. Because there is no scientific criterion for separating all women from all men, critics claimed the testing was both ethically and medically flawed

In 2009, Caster Semenya, a decorated track athlete from South Africa, was forced into the spotlight when she was disqualified from competing in the Olympics based on results from gender verification testing. After much controversy, she was cleared to compete again in 2010.

(Ha et al., 2014; Simpson et al., 2000). For example, between 1972 and 1984, 13 female athletes did not pass the gender verification tests (Elsas et al., 2000). These athletes didn't neatly fit into female or male categories. Instead, they were classified as **intersex**, a term that describes a wide variety of conditions in which a person's body isn't sex typical. Many of these elite female athletes, who had spent their entire lives training to compete in the Olympics, were encouraged to feign injury as an explanation for their non-participation in order to prevent public humiliation (Henne, 2014). The IOC eventually replaced its compulsory gender testing policy with a different system: Female athletes would only be tested in cases of "reasonable doubt" (Ha et al., 2014, p. 1036).

It didn't take long, however, for a new case to emerge. In 2009, after winning the 800-meter race as part of the World Championships in track and field, Caster Semenya, a South African runner, aroused suspicion because of her masculine appearance (Wiesemann, 2011). Although Semenya maintained that she was a woman and had been raised as a girl, she was forced to undergo gender verification testing. She was no stranger to having people question her sex—she regularly took coaches and teammates into the bathroom so they could inspect her genitals because people didn't believe she was female (Wieseman, 2011). But in 2009, in a blatant disregard for her privacy, the results from her medical evaluation—which included a gynecological exam, blood test, and chromosome test—were leaked to the international media (Levy, 2009). It turned out that she had *both* external female genitalia (vulva, labia) and internal male genitalia (undescended testes). She did not have ovaries or a uterus. Therefore, Semenya was disqualified from competing in the Olympics—a blow that not only crushed her Olympic dreams but also caused her to experience depression and an identity crisis (Wiesemann, 2011). South Africa would later file a human rights complaint with the United Nations stating that the testing violated international commitments on the protection and advancement of women's rights, including their right to privacy and their right to participate in sports (Dworkin, Swarr, & Cooky, 2013).

The fact that Semenya was a woman of color caused some people to point out that gender verification tests also reveal racialized assumptions about sex. In sports, people perceive the bodies of athletes of color differently than the bodies of White athletes, and this is especially the case for female athletes (Douglas, 2012; Withycombe, 2011). In particular, Black female athletes are associated with increased muscularity and are often depicted as being hyper-masculine (Schultz, 2005; Messner, 2002; Withycombe, 2011). As anthropologist and bioethicist

Katrina Karkazis (2008) stated, "[Semenya] did not conform to White, Western standards of what a woman should look like" (p. 2). The head of Athletics South Africa agreed with Karkazis's assessment. He said, "Who are White people to question the makeup of an African girl? I say this is racism, pure and simple" (Smith, 2009, para. 2). In fact, in mainstream, dominant society, expectations for the female body are based on White and/or Western cultural norms (Beauchamp & D'Harlingue, 2012). Women who don't fit such standards often struggle to reconcile these norms with their racial and national identities, and in the case of elite athletes, there is increased scrutiny on bodies that don't adhere to dominant ideas about feminine appearance (Karkazis & Fishman, 2017; Singh & McKleroy, 2011).

All these cases highlight the difficulty of labeling a person's sex. The **sex/gender binary**, or the idea that there are only two sexes, dictates that a person must be assigned a sex of either female (F) or male (M) that will align with a predictable gender. This standard is widely held despite significant medical and social evidence that some people cannot be classified in this way (Fausto-Sterling, 2000; Karkazis, 2008). In reading this textbook, by now you may have become comfortable with the idea that gender roles are complicated. There are plenty of women who act masculine and plenty of men who act feminine. Feminist psychologists have greatly contributed to critiquing the social construction of gender. To date, though, much less attention has been paid to how the understanding of bodies, and therefore biological sex, is also socially constructed (Fausto-Sterling, 2000). But as this chapter will show, sex and gender are deeply intertwined, making the sex/gender binary complicated too.

Biological processes don't always conform neatly with gendered expectations. Some women are flat-chested, and some men have large breasts. Some women are bald and grow hair on their chins, and some men don't grow beards. Despite these variations, most institutions in our society act as though every person can easily be identified as either a woman or a man. Prisons, sports teams, bathrooms, toy stores, and some religious organizations and schools use sex as a primary means of categorizing and separating people, as well as their interests and the physical spaces they use (McKenna & Kessler, 2000). Even the Oscars are divided into Best Actress and Best Actor categories. Because so many social structures are organized around expectations about our bodies, people tend to think that one's sex is an important and unchangeable fact of life. In reality, however, biology is not so clear-cut.

your turn

Many schools organize their sports teams by sex. Some feminist scholars have argued that, in addition to reinforcing the sex/gender binary, this perpetuates the myth that girls are less athletic than boys. How are sports organized at your school? What are your thoughts about organizing teams about something other than gender? Should schools consider organizing sports by other variables such as skill level, height, or motivation? Why or why not?

In this chapter, we'll explore the sex/gender binary and examine the various ways in which the categories of woman and man are defined and regulated within Western society. We'll consider important questions about who determines a person's sex and gender, what harm can come from others deciding a person's sex and gender, and what it means to identify and live outside of the sex/gender binary. As we consider these questions, we'll keep in mind that the answers have very real implications for how all of us think about who we are and how best to organize our lives.

Challenging Heteronormative Assumptions about Sex and Gender

What are common assumptions about how biological factors, gender identity, and sexual orientation relate to one another, and how have feminist scholars challenged these assumptions?

Figure 4.1 shows the traditional assumptions about how biological factors (including genes and hormones), gender identity, and sexual orientation relate to one another. This model has been dominant in White, Western culture and reflects an essentialist view. In this model, genetic differences tied to biological sex are seen as the core from which both gender identity and sexual orientation

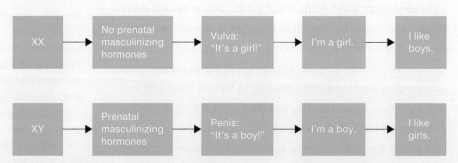

FIGURE 4.1 This diagram illustrates traditional assumptions about how biological factors (including genes and hormones), gender identity, and sexual orientation relate to one another. It reflects an overly simplistic essentialist view as genetic differences tied to sex are seen as the core from which both gender identity and sexual orientation develop.

develop. The model acknowledges only two genetic variations: XX (female) and XY (male). The chromosome pairs XX and XY lead to specific prenatal hormonal patterns that, in turn, lead to two different sets of easily identifiable external genitalia (e.g., XX chromosomes will yield a clearly identifiable vulva; XY chromosomes will yield an easily identifiable penis) and internal genitalia (e.g., XX will yield a uterus and ovaries). XX people believe "I'm a girl" and XY people believe "I'm a boy," and this self-identification then determines the individuals' gendered-aligned characteristics and behaviors (e.g., acting feminine, acting masculine). Finally, this model is heteronormative. It assumes that girls/women will be attracted to boys/men and boys/men will be attracted to girls/women—in other words, that people will have a heterosexual orientation. Although many people today realize that this linear model is no longer applicable, it still holds power in shaping assumptions. For example, most people are aware that not everyone is heterosexual, but they still tend to assume heterosexuality until they encounter evidence to the contrary.

Feminist scholars have challenged the assumptions in this model in many ways (Fausto-Sterling, 2000; Karkazis, 2008). First, they assert that at each step there are more than two options (e.g., more than two genetic possibilities, more than "I'm a girl" or "I'm a boy"). Second, the process, as depicted in Figure 4.1, can be disrupted because the sequence isn't necessarily linear and straightforward. The arrows in the diagram actually can cross over and change at any point throughout a person's life. Although, as noted above, these assumptions reflect White, Western norms, in many cultures such assumptions have long been challenged, and anatomical sex is not the primary factor in determining gender (Davis, 2015; Karkazis, 2008; Kessler, 2002; Nanda, 2014). In the West, however, individuals who don't fit the model are generally deemed "deviant" and "ill" (Karkazis, 2008). We will spend much of this chapter challenging the assumptions at each stage of this traditional model and exploring how their normative influence creates strain on people for whom this model doesn't apply.

Feminist scholars regard the sex/gender binary as overly simplistic and exclusionary (Karkazis, 2008; Springer, Mager Stellman, & Jordan-Young, 2012). They advocate approaching the concept of gender as having multiple dimensions that can interact in a variety of ways (Butler, 1990; Dean & Tate, 2017; van Anders, 2015). The metaphor of a *gender bundle* is useful because it suggests that aspects of sex/gender (e.g., gender assignment, gender identity, gender bodily expression) aren't necessarily ordered or connected in a meaningful way (Tate, Youssef, & Bettergarcia, 2014). Instead, they're all part of the personal and social understanding of gender. Later in the chapter, we'll present another multi-faceted model that considers sex, gender, and sexual/romantic attraction. Because of the complex interplay among these constructs, we'll use the term *sex/gender* throughout this chapter, much like we did in Chapter 3, as a way to make explicit that both sex (biology, evolution, medicalization) and gender (socialization, identity, politics) are interrelated and cannot be easily untangled (van Anders, 2015).

Transgender: An Umbrella Term

What are gender identity and gender expression, and in what diverse ways do transgender individuals identify?

A good way to start exploring the gender bundle is by examining the experiences of transgender individuals because they disrupt binary assumptions that one's sex assignment at birth corresponds with one's sense of being a woman or a man. Instead, gender identity can be seen as just one part of the gender bundle that may or may not be related to other parts of it. The term **gender identity** refers to one's understanding of oneself as gendered (e.g., as a girl, a boy, or as holding an identity that does not fit into the binary). It is based on a fundamental sense of belonging to a sex/gender category regardless of assignment at birth. As we saw in Chapter 1, the term *cisgender* describes individuals whose gender identity conforms to societal expectations for the sex they were assigned at birth: A cisgender person is someone who either was assigned F at birth and identifies as a girl/woman, or was assigned M at birth and identifies as a boy/man. In contrast, the term *transgender* describes individuals whose gender identity and/or **gender expression** do not conform to societal expectations for the sex they were assigned at birth.

Transgender is an umbrella term that encompasses a variety of self-labels and definitions (Gagné, Tewksbury, & McGaughey, 1997). It can include many types of people, including those who identify with binary identities (e.g., transwoman/transfeminine, transman/transmasculine) and non-binary identities (e.g., genderqueer, gender non-conforming). Individuals who identify with non-binary identities feel that their gender identity is either somewhere in between that of woman and man or not connected to the sex/gender binary altogether. Table 4.1 highlights some of the gender identities that often fall under the transgender umbrella. Although the actual number of transgender people is unknown, in 2016, researchers estimated that 0.6% of adults in the United States—about 1.4 million people—identified as transgender (Flores, Herman, Gates, & Brown, 2016).

Because the term *transgender* encompasses so many diverse types of people, there is variability among gender identities and expressions within the transgender community (Stryker, 2008). Some trans individuals want to

your turn

Why is it important to label gender? Imagine a world in which the sex/gender binary has been disrupted and a third gender or multiple forms of gender are accepted. What would need to change—think beyond bathrooms—and what would stay the same? Currently, people often ask about and group others by gender. If the current gender system were disrupted, in what situations would such groupings continue, and in what situations would they be a relic of the past?

TABLE 4.1 Gender Identities under the Transgender Umbrella

Identity Label	Definition
Genderqueer	An umbrella term for people whose gender identity is outside of, not included within, or beyond the binary of female and male.
Gender non-conforming	A term used to refer to individuals or communities who may not identify as transgender but who do not conform to traditional gender norms.
Transwoman, Transfeminine individual	A transgender individual who identifies as a woman and/or has a feminine gender expression.
Transman, Transmasculine individual	A transgender individual who identifies as a man and/or has a masculine gender expression.
Gender bender, Pangender, Polygender	Terms used to refer to individuals who are non-binary; they may identify with all genders.
Androgynous	A term used to refer to individuals who have complete gender neutrality; they may be people whose gender identity is both female and male or neither female nor male.
Two-spirited	The term comes from the traditions of some Native North American cultures to describe Native people who display characteristics of both male and female genders; this is often associated with having a third gender.

"go stealth" and live as clearly gender-categorized as possible rather than challenging binary assumptions about sex/gender (Lev, 2004). They prefer to conform to the dominant biological and socially ascribed gender expectations associated with their identity (Kessler & McKenna, 2000). For that reason, they might not identify as transgender, since they eventually become clearly recognizable as either women or men (Fassinger & Arseneau, 2007). Other individuals may identify in any number of other ways, some of which are presented in Table 4.1.

Some people believe that the presence of such diverse identities and labels causes confusion and division within mainstream society, yet labels can be helpful as well as harmful (Fincke, 2014). When sex/gender labels are imposed by others, they can be oppressive because they limit self-expression and dictate options, such as which public bathrooms people can use or what sports teams they can join (Galupo, Henise, & Mercer, 2016). When labels are self-directed, though, they provide a way to name experience, and self-labeling can have positive social and political implications (Fincke, 2014). Without a way to name their experience, transgender individuals can have difficulty finding one another for social support or for coalition building to gain political recognition.

Transgender Identity Development

What are some of the unique challenges that transgender individuals face in terms of gender identity development, and how does misgendering play a role in their experiences?

In 2014, at age 12, Zoey Luna was featured on a morning show, surrounded by her family and friends. Although Zoey was assigned M at birth, she began telling her mother she was a girl at a young age. Zoey described a painful reality: "Even kids that seem like good kids, they make fun of me" ("Born this way," 2014, para. 3). When asked what happens when she's treated "like a boy," Zoey said, "I always get upset, because I'm not a boy. I'm a girl. You know, like, I like the color pink. I scream like a girl. I act like a girl. I breathe like a girl. I'm not a boy!" Because Zoey's mother wants her to be true to herself and be happy, she whole-heartedly supports Zoey living as an openly transgender girl. Still, Zoey's mom is fearful about how society will treat her daughter. "It's scary," she says (para. 4).

Much like Zoey's experience, some transgender individuals begin to question their assigned sex early in life. Transgender children as young as two years of age may reveal dissatisfaction with their sex assignment through behaviors such as wanting to wear cross-gendered clothing or refusing to comb their hair in ways that are typically associated with their assigned sex (Cohen-Kettenis & Pfafflin, 2003). However, other trans people don't reveal gender dissatisfaction until later in life (Hunter, 2005). It's worth noting that people often ask transgender individuals

Zoey Luna, shown here at age 15, faced bullying and had to stand up to school officials for her right to self-identify her gender in school.

(and other LGBTQ* people) "How early did you know?" because mainstream society tends to grant more legitimacy to early awareness. In other words, a person who says, "I always felt this way" is considered more authentic than a person who says, "Since I turned 40, I began feeling this way." The fact that society privileges early and continual awareness can be considered another example of the power of essentialism—something is presumed to be more natural if it occurs early in life rather than later. However, research supports more fluidity and flexibility in gender, sex, and sexuality, and a realization about one's identity that happens later in life is no less valid than one that happens earlier (Diamond, 2008a).

Among transgender people, gender identity—not assigned sex—is generally closely aligned with gendered behaviors and attitudes (Endendijk, Beltz, McHale, Bryk, & Berenbaum, 2016; Olson, Key, & Eaton, 2015). For example, when Zoey says she screams "like a girl," you probably imagine a high-pitched scream because most people generally associate that type of scream with femininity. However, the gender roles we all enact and the gender expressions we present may or may not align with gender identity. For example, a cisgender woman may enact masculinity, a transwoman may be more androgynous than feminine in self-presentation, or a genderqueer individual may object to having behaviors labeled as feminine or masculine at all.

Although everyone develops a gender identity, for transgender individuals the process can be especially difficult. It often includes experiencing discrimination, stigma, and prejudice (Egan & Perry, 2001; Grant et al., 2011; Katz-Wise & Budge, 2015; Koken, Bimbi, & Parsons, 2009). Because mainstream society has very clear cisgender expectations, the process of developing a transgender identity takes time and can be highly stressful (Devor, 2004). In fact, psychologists have developed several models of transgender identity development (Gagne et al., 1997; Lev, 2004). The process typically starts with awareness (Barr, Budge, & Adelson, 2016; Devor, 2004; Lev, 2004). One study showed that among 65 primarily White transgender women between the ages of 24 and 68, personal awareness started with a doubtful feeling that their sex or gender was "wrong" and that it didn't "fit" (Gagne et al., 1997, p. 486). Other studies have shown that awareness came along with experiencing social disapproval (Gregor, Davidson, & Hingley-Jones, 2016; Katz-Wise & Budge, 2015). For example, in one study, transgender women of color reported experiencing harassment, violence, and sexual objectification when they expressed cross-gendered desires or engaged in cross-gendered behaviors (Koken et al., 2009; Lombardi, Wilchins, Priesing, & Malouf, 2001; Mallon & De Crescenzo, 2009). Those who were

*Authors' note: We generally use the acronym LGBTQ (Lesbian, Gay, Bisexual, Transgender, Queer) throughout this book. However, in this chapter we sometimes use variations of the acronym with fewer letters (i.e., LGBQ and LGB). We use LGBQ, leaving out the T, when we talk specifically about sexual orientation and want to keep gender identity distinct. We use LGB at one point in the chapter when talking about how organizations and social movements that are focused on the rights of gender and sexual minority individuals have, over time, expanded their focus and added in the T and Q.

raised in traditional, religious households experienced the highest levels of rejection (Koken et al., 2009). As a result, awareness of their identity came from a dynamic between their own desires and the social context in which they lived (Fassinger & Arseneau, 2007).

When guardians reject transgender children, the likelihood of school dropout, homelessness, substance use, incarceration, and engagement in sex work increases (Wilson et al., 2009). Parents who struggle with their children's gender identity may think that the atypical gender expression is temporary, which is one reason why parents may not be supportive (Rosenberg, 2002). In one study, researchers found that fathers were more likely than mothers to react negatively toward their transgender children (Grossman, D'Augelli, Jarrett Howell, & Hubbard, 2005). But even when parents are supportive of their children, the youngsters may face criticism from extended family, friends, and school personnel (Birnkrant & Przeworski, 2017). However, when adults are flexible in their attitudes toward young people's exploration of gender, it reduces anxiety and depression in transgender children (Ehrensaft, 2014).

Once transgender individuals discover that there's a name for their feelings and that there are others with similar feelings, they're able to develop a stronger sense of gender identity (Gagne et al., 1997). One transgender woman described the discovery this way: "The lightbulb went off and I went 'Wait a minute. This isn't really about clothes; it's about who I am'" (Katz-Wise & Budge, 2015, p. 162). Trans individuals who begin to feel "true to themselves" report a noticeable shift in their desire to show their gender and to experience validation in their identity from others (Katz-Wise & Budge, 2015, p. 159). At this point, they are ready to begin **gender transitioning**, the process of publicly demonstrating their gender identity in both appearance and behavior (Katz-Wise & Budge, 2015; Lev, 2004). Gender transitioning is a complex process that often unfolds over a long period and requires attention to many aspects of a person's life.

When a person publicly identifies as transgender, sometimes called a social transition, family members must redefine their relationship and their family structure (Zamboni, 2006). Some family members experience *ambiguous loss*, the sense that they have lost a family member either physically or psychologically, which leaves them grieving and searching for answers (Veldorale-Griffin & Darling, 2016). After all, even though they still have a child, sibling, or parent, for example, they no longer have a son, sister, or mother. This type of grief was evident on the reality TV show *I Am Cait*, featuring Caitlyn Jenner. When she disclosed her decision to transition, some of her children expressed anger and confusion (Bueno, 2015).

For trans individuals, one aspect of publicly identifying as transgender involves asking friends, family, and others to refer to them with a new pronoun and/or name. Trans individuals may use pronouns and names that are either consistent with the sex/gender binary (e.g., *she/her* or *he/him*) or outside of it (e.g., *they/them*). These requests are often met with confusion and apathy, and they are complied with inconsistently (Kacere, 2013). In one study, researchers found that while cisgender people may be able to temporarily focus on using a pronoun requested by a transgender person, these efforts can be easily disrupted when cisgender individuals are distracted (Friedman, 2014).

When interacting with trans individuals, many people routinely **misgender**, or use a pronoun that doesn't accurately reflect the trans person's gender identity (Ansara & Hegarty, 2014; Friedman, 2014, Gazzola & Morrison, 2014; McLemore, 2015). When trans people are misgendered through the incorrect use of pronouns or names, they can feel stigmatized (McLemore, 2015) and can experience depression and anxiety (Stets & Burke, 2005). In contrast, one study showed that having someone use a correct pronoun legitimized transgender participants' experience of themselves and created a sense of connection and belongingness (Bosson, Weaver, & Prewitt-Freilino, 2012). In another study, which focused on racially diverse transgender individuals, participants reported experiencing several positive emotions (e.g., happiness, hope, pride) when people used correct pronouns (Budge, Orovecz, & Thai, 2015). One transgender man said, "If my stepmom was sending me a card or talking to me, she would say 'he' or 'son.'. . . And the other day, she said, you're a really good man. And man, that just . . . I was flying high all night!" (p. 421). For this reason, one recommendation is that cisgender people indicate their pronouns when meeting someone new as a way to recognize that pronouns vary among people. In fact, we now have our students in all of our classes introduce themselves with their names and pronouns.

Medical Concerns

What are some of the diverse choices that transgender individuals can make regarding gender-affirming medical interventions?

Gender transitioning may involve some type of body modification, often referred to as a medical transition. This might include using cross-sex hormones, undergoing electrolysis for hair removal, or having surgeries (Lev, 2004). A common term used in transgender literature is *passing*, or the degree to which a person is perceived as their* gender—usually based on gender expression and

---

* *Authors' note:* We use the singular *they/them* here, and in other places throughout the book, in a conscious way. While there is not yet one universally preferred pronoun adopted by those who have non-binary gender identities, the singular *they* is currently the dominant option.

conformity to gender norms. Some scholars, however, prefer the term *recognition*, which focuses on the social context rather than the individual (Connell, 2009; Katz-Wise & Budge, 2015). Recognition also highlights the reality that transgender individuals must continuously prove the authenticity of their gender—something that cisgender people don't have to do because of cisgender privilege (Serano, 2007). Further, if the gender identity of a transgender person isn't clearly expressed through their appearance and behaviors, there is an increased risk of violence and discrimination, so body modification is often a necessary change in order to be safe (Mizock & Lewis, 2008). This can be a particular focus during adolescence, when puberty begins and it becomes difficult to modify physical characteristics without medical support (Lev, 2004). For example, transgender adolescents who don't pass are more likely than those who do pass to experience homelessness and have negative experiences in trying to access homeless shelters, many of which are gender segregated (Begun & Kattari, 2016).

One medical intervention that can be helpful for adolescents involves taking a hormone (GnRH agonist) at the beginning of puberty that postpones the onset of further pubertal changes. This gives adolescents (and their guardians) time to evaluate the risks and benefits of starting cross-sex hormone treatment, which typically begins around age 16. In one study, transgender adolescents who used GnRH at age 13, took cross-sex hormones at age 16, and underwent sex-reassignment surgery at age 20 had the same psychological outcomes as their cisgender peers in their 20s (de Vries et al., 2014). There are controversies around pubertal blockers, however. One concern is that not much is known about the long-term effects of delaying puberty; another is that pubertal blockers are very expensive and typically not covered by insurance, so this intervention often can only be accessed by people with financial privilege (Schagen, Cohen-Kettenis, Delemarre-van de Waal, & Hannema, 2016). Furthermore, legal guardians have to support their child's gender identity and must consent to (and pay for) gender-affirming treatments during childhood and adolescence. This requirement brings up questions about who has the right to make such decisions, an issue we'll explore later in this chapter.

Some individuals desire *sex reassignment surgery (SRS)*, the surgical procedures involved in changing one's sex (Lev, 2004). These procedures are now often called *gender-confirming surgery* or *gender-affirming surgery*. People who believe their bodies don't represent their sex and who have a strong desire for body modification have traditionally been referred to as *transsexual*. While some individuals still use this term to describe themselves, many others prefer the term *transgender* because *transsexual* seems dated and stigmatizing ("Glossary of terms—Transgender," n.d.; Zimman, 2016). An individual can be pre-operative, post-operative, or non-operative (Lev, 2004). For example, hormone treatment may be sufficient to reduce anxiety about being recognizable as a certain gender (Meyer et al., 2001). Regardless, because studies show high satisfaction following SRS, it is widely accepted as an affirming option (Klein & Gorzalka, 2009; Kuiper & Cohen-Kettenis, 1998; Rolle, Ceruti, Timpano, Falcone, & Frea, 2015; van der Sluis et al., 2016).

Some trans individuals choose not to have any medical treatment, or they may select some medical treatments but not others (Aguayo-Romero, Reisen, Zea, Bianchi, & Poppen; 2015; Fein, Salgado, Alvarez, & Estes, 2017). This is particularly true for those who are non-binary (Pinto & Moleiro, 2015). For example, a person assigned F at birth who identifies as genderqueer may choose to have top surgery (breast removal) but may never take cross-sex hormones. Other medical considerations might also come into play—for example, an older transgender woman may not be able to take estrogen because of cancer or cardiac risk. As a result, part of the gender identity development process for trans individuals is not simply understanding themselves as transgender, but also figuring out what they want their gender presentation to be and whether medical modifications may help affirm that choice.

Transitioning Obstacles

What obstacles may transgender people encounter as they transition?

Transitioning obstacles are impediments outside of a person's control that influence when and if they're able to transition (Katz-Wise & Budge, 2015). Money and time are notable obstacles. The Philadelphia Center for Transgender Surgery estimated that in 2015 the cost for male-to-female transitioning was $140,450 and the cost of female-to-male transitioning was $124,400 (Jackson, 2015). Insurance may cover some expenses (e.g., hormone therapy, a portion of surgery) but not others (e.g., facial electrolysis, breast augmentation). Moreover, 19% of transgender individuals are uninsured (dickey, Budge, Katz-Wise, & Garza, 2016). Despite it being a risky practice, some trans individuals seek hormones on unregulated markets, such as via the Internet, because of the high costs associated with body transitioning (Sanchez, Sanchez, & Danoff, 2009; Xavier et al., 2013). Getting hormones via the Internet is also a route some adolescents take when they have unsupportive guardians (Shield, 2007).

Transitioning obstacles can be related to other aspects of one's identity as well. In one study of racially diverse older transgender individuals, some participants reported that they had waited to transition because they feared being seen as mentally ill or losing family (Elder, 2016). One participant said, "Back in the 50s—when it was totally unacceptable to be transgender—one of the things they did was to tell you that you had to divorce your family, leave your friends, your job and everything. You had to disappear"

(p. 183). Others identified racism as an additional obstacle in transitioning. One participant shared that the doctor "only gave hormones to the White girls he thought would pass. Others he gave water shots instead of hormone shots" (p. 182). Religious beliefs can also influence decisions about gender transitioning. In Islamic traditions, for example, genital surgery disallows certain burial rituals, which can complicate family acceptance and reduce the likelihood that a transgender person will pursue certain types of surgeries (Lev, 2004; Teh, 2001).

Further, it can be difficult to find health-care providers. Insensitivity or hostility from the medical community was reported by 32% of transgender participants in one study (Xavier & Simmons, 2000), so this can contribute to trans individuals being less likely than cisgender individuals to seek medical support (Lombardi et al., 2001). Counselors and psychologists report lack of training on the unique needs of transgender clients; as a result, therapists may unknowingly hold anti-trans prejudice or engage in microaggressions during the counseling process (Nadal, Skolnik, & Wong, 2012). This issue is particularly important because psychologists often play a gatekeeper role for those seeking SRS, even though some view determining if a person is "fit" for surgery as an inappropriate role (Bockting, Robinson, Benner, & Scheltema, 2004). The issue also has the potential to create a pattern whereby clients feel they have to act as "perfect" candidates instead of using therapy in a more authentic way to address challenges they may be experiencing (Benson, 2013; Carroll, Gilroy, & Ryan, 2002).

Additionally, some feminist scholars, among others, have critiqued the current existence of a mental health diagnosis that classifies many transgender people as mentally ill. According to the *DSM-5*, the current edition of the American Psychiatric Association's list of diagnoses for mental disorders, *gender dysphoria* is characterized by a strong desire to be treated as the "other" gender or to want to change "one's sex characteristics" (American Psychiatric Association, 2013, p. 452). This psychiatric label can further stigmatize individuals who are already in need of empathy (Dresher, Cohen-Kettenis, & Winter, 2012). However, from a different perspective, a medical diagnosis makes it more likely that some insurance companies will cover gender-affirming treatments, which greatly increases access to them (Richmond, Carroll, & Demboske, 2010).

Transgender activist Michael Hughes took to Twitter in order to change public perception about the idea that people should be required to use the bathroom associated with their assigned sex at birth. Using the hashtag #wejustneedtopee and starting with the statement "Do I look like I belong in women's facilities?" he emphasized that trans people are not going into bathrooms to spy or to cause women harm.

Everyday Living

What is minority stress theory, and what unique stressors do transgender individuals experience?

Minority stress theory suggests that having a marginalized identity, such as being transgender, carries additional social stressors that can negatively affect mental and physical health outcomes (Hendricks & Testa, 2012; Meyer, 2003). Researchers have identified three particular stressors that impact transgender individuals. First, they are exposed to discrimination and prejudice. Second, they may internalize negative messages about transgender people, resulting in **internalized transphobia**. Third, it's estimated that over half of transgender individuals experience violence at one time in their lives (Kenagy, 2005; Lombardi et al., 2001; Stotzer, 2008), although the probability of experiencing a violent attack is related to younger age, racial minority status, and lower socioeconomic status (Lombardi et al., 2001). Given the negative effects of these stressors, transgender individuals' experiences with violence and discrimination may create a justifiably heightened fear of encountering future discrimination. This is known as **stigma awareness** (which can also be experienced by people with other marginalized identities). All three factors were associated with greater psychological distress in a large survey of racially diverse transgender individuals (Breslow et al., 2015). Transgender adults also experience significant barriers to obtaining employment, housing, and quality health care (Grant et al., 2011). Transgender people of color experience even worse outcomes, with Black trans people reporting the highest levels of discrimination (Grant et al., 2011; Saffin, 2011).

Transgender individuals also experience within-group stress. Although former LGB (lesbian, gay, bisexual) organizations began to "add the *T*" in the early 1990s in order to express inclusion of transgender individuals (and more recently a *Q* for queer), many trans people felt that this was a shallow gesture (Minter, 2006). Historically, the transgender experience has

spotlight on . . .

Legal Concerns

Transgender individuals face many legal concerns. For one, it is incredibly difficult to have sex designations changed on official documents. In the United States, many states require evidence of SRS, so many transgender individuals are unable to have their gender legally recognized (Grant et al., 2011).

Furthermore, 58% of transgender respondents in one study avoided going out in public because of lack of access to a safe bathroom, and 70% reported being denied entrance to or harassed while trying to use a bathroom that matched their gender identity (Herman, 2013). In 2016, North Carolina passed House Bill 2 (HB2), which banned transgender individuals from using bathrooms that didn't align with their sex assignment at birth—ostensibly to protect girls and women from transgender women (Scout, 2016). In reality, there is no documented case of a transwoman using a public bathroom to prey on girls or women, and transwomen are the ones likely to experience violence in bathrooms (Herman, 2013). Laws similar to HB2 have been proposed in Arizona, Maryland, Kentucky, and Florida. In response, transgender activists have posted selfies using the hashtag #wejustwanttopee to showcase how challenging it would be for a transgender man to enter a women's bathroom.

Over the past 30 years, activists have tried to pass LGBTQ non-discrimination laws. While there is no federal law to date that bans discrimination against transgender people, 18 states and many cities have passed laws that ban discrimination because of gender identity/expression.

What could you do to increase the support for transgender people? Think about small steps you can take. What changes to your campus would make the lives of trans students easier? For example, do all forms require a strictly F or M designation? Are there bathrooms that trans students can use comfortably? What on-campus housing options are there for students who identify as transgender or non-binary? Also, what advocacy groups exist on your campus or in your community? How could you become involved with their initiatives?

been minimized and ignored within the LGBQ movement (Stone, 2009). For example, Marsha Johnson and Sylvia Rivera, two transgender activists, are often forgotten for their role in the Stonewall uprising, one of the events widely considered to have ushered in the contemporary fight for LGBTQ rights in the United States. It began when members of the LGBTQ community retaliated against a police raid that took place on June 28, 1969, at the Stonewall Inn, a LGBTQ bar in New York City. Historians believe that Sylvia Rivera threw the first brick during the police raid and that Marsha Johnson threw a shot glass at the bar mirror (Duberman, 2013).

The level of support a transgender person feels from an LGBTQ group is dependent on the willingness of gay and lesbian members to divide resources among different priorities (Stone, 2009). Often, LGBTQ organizations support initiatives that favor White, upper-middle-class, able-bodied, lesbian and gay people who are legal residents within the United States. For example, the issue of gay marriage has been a priority for many LGBTQ organizations while other issues, such as job discrimination and fair housing, have gone relatively unaddressed (Alimahomed, 2010).

Resiliency

What contributes to the resiliency of transgender individuals?

Despite high levels of social discrimination, transgender people are quite resilient. In one study with participants who identified as Black, Multiracial, or White, researchers found that cultivating a strong sense of identity and self-worth, while also being conscious of oppression and connecting with a supportive community, was related to developing hope and resiliency (Singh, Hays, & Watson, 2011). Another study, focusing on transgender youth of color, showed that using media to affirm both gender and racial pride strengthened resiliency (Singh, 2013). As one Black transgender girl said, "There are more trans people on the media, but it's all adults and no kids. I think the documentary [*Transgeneration*] about trans youth in college was good because I can show my parents—'There are trans people who are *not* White'" (p. 697).

The degree to which a transgender person has social support is crucial for health and well-being. Transgender individuals who perceive strong social support and have satisfying friendships report positive mental health (Bockting, Miner, Swinburne Romine, Hamilton, & Coleman, 2013; Budge, Adelson,

& Howard, 2013; Meier, Pardo, Labuski, & Babcock, 2013). Connecting with an LGBTQ community also increases activism, another important resiliency strategy that has been shown to decrease stress, anxiety, and depression (Riggle & Mohr, 2015; Singh, 2013). In fact, many trans individuals engage in community-based activism in order to improve life for both themselves and others (Breslow et al., 2015). This involvement can provide a sense of agency, but particularly for women of color, activism is related to an increase in anti-transgender discrimination (Breslow et al., 2015; DeBlaere et al., 2014). It may be that individuals who experience discrimination may be more likely to engage in activism, or conversely, those who engage in activism may experience more discrimination.

In the past few years, certain transgender people have become well known (e.g., Laverne Cox, Janet Mock, Caitlyn Jenner, and Chaz Bono). The Amazon series *Transparent* has also been praised for bringing the discussion of trans people to the forefront. In this series, Maura, a transwoman, makes important decisions about transitioning, comes out to her family, and experiences discrimination—even within the feminist community (Zulch, 2015). Although feminist psychologists and many others see the growing representation of transgender individuals in popular culture as a significant step toward social acceptance, the success of the few who make it into the spotlight can overshadow the challenging day-to-day realties for most trans individuals, especially when their financial resources are limited.

Intersex activists have been at the forefront of creating awareness and change. Among many accomplishments, they have worked to reduce the use of stigmatizing language and labels. They have also influenced doctors and parents to exercise more caution before agreeing to genital surgery on children who are too young to consent for themselves.

Complicating Gender Assignment

According to the traditional linear model shown earlier in Figure 4.1, your gender identity should align with your sex assignment at birth. But transgender individuals, as we have noted, have gender identities that don't match their sex assignments at birth. As a society, we seem to care quite a bit about sex assignment. In fact, one of the first questions expectant parents are asked is "Are you having a girl or a boy?" The answer has very real implications for how society will perceive that person and how that person's life will be organized.

You might think the decision to assign someone as F or M at birth is relatively straightforward—a simple glance should do the trick. However, the process of determining sex at birth can be complicated. As we'll discuss below, there are several biological markers that medical providers use to guide decisions about sex assignments. These include genes, hormones, internal genitalia, and external genitalia. We'll next look at the main biological markers of sex (e.g., genes, hormones) and show how, for each of these markers, there is potential disruption of the sex/gender binary.

Genetics

What are Klinefelter and Turner's syndromes, and how do they make it harder to understand sex as a binary?

Non-invasive prenatal testing can determine the presence of sex chromosomes as early as 10 weeks after conception (Hall, Bostanci, & Wright, 2010). You may remember from biology class that people have 46 chromosomes: 22 matched pairs (called autosomes), and two sex chromosomes (XX or XY). There are exceptions to this rule, though. People with Down syndrome, for example, have 47 chromosomes due to an extra copy of chromosome 21. This is the result of *nondisjunction*, or the process whereby chromosomes fail to disconnect when a cell divides (Callahan, 2009). Nondisjunction can occur with sex chromosomes too. For example, a single sperm can have multiple X or Y chromosomes, and the Y chromosome can vary in size. And even after fertilization, sex chromosomes can be lost or gained (Callahan, 2009). Because of this variability, people can have any number of genetic variations in their sex chromosomes (e.g., XXX, XYY, XXXY, XXXXY). Below we'll discuss some of the more common genetic variations and how, for individuals with those variations, the concept of a sex/gender binary is harder to apply.

Klinefelter Syndrome Harry Fitch Klinefelter, a physician, was one of the first to explore variations in sex chromosomes (Diamond & Watson, 2004). After working with several men who had enlarged breasts, long arms, and small testes, Klinefelter initially thought he was observing men with hormone irregularities. Later he discovered that these men had 47 chromosomes. Each carried an extra X chromosome. This genetic type was labeled **Klinefelter syndrome (KS)**, and it includes any chromosomal type that has more than one X chromosome plus one or two Y chromosomes. Because of the presence of the Y chromosome, individuals with KS have a penis and are generally assigned M at birth. However, not all those with KS identify as male; some identify as intersex. Approximately 1 in 800 individuals assigned M at birth carry one or more extra X chromosomes (Grumbach, Hughes, & Conte, 2003).

Most boys and men with KS will never know they have an extra X chromosome (Bourke, Snow, Herlihy, Amor, & Metcalfe, 2014; Herlihy, Gillam, Halliday, & McLachlan, 2011). At birth, there's no sign of anything atypical, and they grow up living just like others assigned M at birth. There is tremendous variability in the effects of KS, and it appears that the number of X chromosomes matters: With each X chromosome, there's a greater potential for physical, cognitive, and emotional challenges (Cederlöf et al., 2014). Compared to boys and men without KS, almost all boys and men with KS have lower levels of testosterone, which makes it difficult to produce sperm—a condition known as *hypogonadism*.

Moreover, the medical community's typical description of men with KS has contributed to stigma (Lauerma, 2001). For example, some researchers have focused on an association between KS and increased criminality and severe mental illness. However, most individuals with KS lead typical lives. Despite this, one study in the United States showed that 45% to 70% of expectant parents who were surveyed indicated they would terminate a pregnancy if they received a prenatal diagnosis of KS (Girardin & Van Vliet, 2011).

Turner's Syndrome The second most common condition associated with an atypical genetic makeup is **Turner's syndrome (TS)**, or a chromosomal pattern of XO. A person with TS only has 45 chromosomes; this occurs when a sperm carrying an X chromosome fertilizes an egg with no X chromosome or when a chromosome becomes lost during fetal development. About 1 in 2,700 newborns has TS (Grumbach et al., 2003). Unlike KS, in which individuals have male-typical genitalia, children with TS have female-typical external genitalia, and although they have a uterus, they don't have ovaries. Infants born with TS are assigned F at birth, but some later identify as intersex (El Abd, Turk, & Hill, 1995).

The most common attribute among people with TS is that they are typically shorter than their peers (Gatta, Pertile, & Battistella, 2011). Without medical intervention, the average height for those with TS is 4 ft 8 in., so many

your turn

If you were to find out that you have a different set of sex chromosomes from what you originally thought, would that change the way you feel about yourself? In what ways would your life change or stay the same? Should this new knowledge change other people's opinion about you? Why or why not?

If you are someone for whom this has occurred, what was your experience like? What would you want someone to know about it?

children with TS take growth hormones (Catinari, Vass, & Heresco-Levy, 2006; Christopoulos, Deligeoroglou, Laggari, Christogiorgos, & Creatsas, 2008). Because individuals with TS don't have ovaries, they're unable to produce estrogen, and this condition prevents breast and pubic hair growth and menstruation (Christopoulos et al., 2008). In fact, without genetic testing at an early age, many individuals with TS don't know they have the condition until they fail to develop typically when they reach puberty. At that point, some girls with TS opt to use estrogen therapies to promote the development of female secondary sex characteristics. Infertility can be a source of stress for individuals with TS if they want to have children (Smith, 2015). Although some manage to carry an embryo provided by an egg donor, it's rare that a woman with TS can conceive, so many women chose adoption and/or surrogacy (Toft & Rehan, 2014).

Hormones

What are three conditions related to hormones that complicate the understanding of sex as a binary, and what happens for people with each condition?

Turner's syndrome and Klinefelter syndrome are two of many possible variations in genetics. However, even for individuals who have XX and XY chromosomes, the role of sex-specific hormones can be complex. For example, when hormones are altered prenatally during fetal development, the result can be a newborn with genitalia that don't appear to fit neatly into F and M categories. Before we discuss how that process happens, let's review the role of hormones in the typical development of a fetus.

For a little over a month after conception, a growing fetus has no internal or external sex organs. *Sex differentiation*, the process of developing sex-specific characteristics, begins during the sixth week of pregnancy. A pair of sex glands, referred to as *gonads*, then appear, which have the potential to become *ovaries* (which will produce eggs and female sex hormones) or *testes* (which will produce sperm and male sex hormones). Without the presence of a Y chromosome, the gonads become ovaries—female sex development is the default. Although the Y chromosome is much smaller and carries fewer genes than the X chromosome, it plays a critical role in sex development. The Y chromosome carries a sex-determining region that operates like a switch that can turn on other genes that are responsible for the development of testes. Once the testes are formed, additional hormones, known as *androgens*, shape the development of the typical male body. *Testosterone*, a specific androgen, promotes the growth of internal male reproductive organs, and *dihydrotestosterone*, a component of testosterone, promotes the growth of a penis and testicles. Testosterone converts into dihydrotesterone with the help of an enzyme called *5-alpha reductase*. We'll discuss this enzyme in more detail later because it can play an important role during puberty.

Androgen-Insensitivity Syndrome The production of testosterone isn't enough to form a penis and testicles. Testosterone must also be able to bind to specific molecules in order for typical male genitalia to develop. In other words, when testosterone is present but cannot connect with cell receptors, the developing tissue cannot use the testosterone to promote male genital growth. This condition is referred to as **androgen-insensitivity syndrome (AIS)**, and it occurs in about 1 in every 20,000 people (Saucier & Ehresman, 2010). Individuals with AIS have XY chromosomes, no female-typical internal organs, and active testes (Sobel & Imperato-McGinley, 2004). They also have typical male levels of testosterone, but because of the body's inability to process it, masculinization of the genitals and development of secondary sex characteristics don't occur (Saucier & Ehresman, 2010).

Individuals with complete androgen insensitivity (CAIS) have genitals that appear female and are typically assigned F at birth. Individuals with partial androgen insensitivity (PAIS) can present with "ambiguous" or partially masculinized genitalia and may be assigned either F or M at birth. Whether a person develops CAIS or PAIS depends on the degree to which that individual's body can utilize testosterone. Caster Semenya, the South African Olympic runner we discussed earlier, was presumed to have CAIS, and in her case, she was entirely unaware of it (Bowcott, 2009).

Congenital Adrenal Hyperplasia The inherited condition known as **congenital adrenal hyperplasia (CAH)** causes the adrenal glands to over-produce androgens. This impacts fetal genetic development and can also affect development later on. For example, the increase in androgens causes fetuses with XX chromosomes to develop varying degrees of male-typical genitalia. It can also cause the uterus, the fallopian tubes, and the vulva to develop differently. Classical CAH is typically detected right after birth, and it occurs in 1 in 15,000 births. When infants with XX chromosomes are born with classical CAH, their genitalia don't typically fit into the categories of F or M. In many cases, surgery is performed to change the appearance of genitalia to be more "typically" female. Non-classical CAH, also known as late-onset CAH, does not present with "ambiguous" genitalia and can occur at any time in a person's life. It's usually noticed in late childhood or early adolescence and is associated with early onset of puberty (Callahan, 2009). When CAH is diagnosed, medical interventions can stop the over-production of androgens.

Many studies have explored the effects of increased androgens on those with CAH assigned F at birth. Research has found that, compared to their siblings, these individuals were more likely to show behaviors associated with traditional masculinity (Berenbaum, 1999) and be more physically aggressive (Pasterski et al., 2011). In one study, researchers found that parents' doubts about the sex of the child influenced their child's gender role behavior, suggesting that both prenatal androgen exposure and parental socialization contribute to increased masculinity in CAH girls (Wong, Pasterski, Hindmarsh, Geffner, & Hines, 2013). Despite having some preferences for male-typical play, most individuals with CAH assigned F at birth do identify as female (Gooren, 2006). In a study of 250 individuals who were assigned F at birth and who also had CAH, 95% identified as a girl; 5% reported dissatisfaction with their sex assignment and preferred to be identified as a boy (Dessens, Slijper, & Drop, 2005).

As we've already discussed, there is great variability in the possible number and combinations of sex chromosomes, and CAH can occur in people with any combination. The effects of the condition do differ, however. For example, in those with XY chromosomes, the over-production of androgens can result in hyper-masculinization, such as a deeper-than-usual voice and well-developed muscles.

5-Alpha Reductase Deficiency In the early 1970s, physicians described a group of girls who, at puberty, began to develop phalluses much like penises (Callahan, 2009). They also began to speak with deep voices and grow facial hair. Although they were born with female genitalia and had been raised as girls, at puberty they underwent a complete physical change. Individuals with **5-alpha reductase deficiency** have XY chromosomes, but because they don't have sufficient 5-alpha reductase, they're unable to convert testosterone to dihydrotestosterone and, therefore, cannot masculinize their external genitalia in utero. These individuals are typically assigned F at birth.

There is very little research about individuals with this condition, including its prevalence. However, incidences seem to occur with more frequency in the Dominican Republic, Papua New Guinea, Turkey, and Egypt ("5-alpha reductase deficiency," 2017). Much is still not understood. For example, if there is no medical intervention, secondary sex characteristics typically associated with men (including a penis) usually develop at puberty, but it's not always clear when or if this will happen. For example, one study found that siblings who have 5-alpha reductase deficiency, have similar hormone and enzyme levels, and were raised in the same household don't always develop in the same way (Karkazis, 2008). One might develop male genitalia, and the other might not. Researchers have yet to determine the exact mechanism that leads to the physical changes. Parents of children with 5-alpha reductase deficiency report tremendous social isolation, and there is no consensus about what sex to assign those with this condition (Kessler, 2002).

Challenges of "Ambiguous" Genitalia

What does it mean for genitalia to be "ambiguous," and how do society at large and the medical community in particular react to such occurrences?

Sex assignments are generally made at birth by visually inspecting a newborn's external genitalia. This sounds fairly straightforward, but the actual process of labeling genitals is relatively arbitrary. Although most penises of newborns range between 2.8 and 4.5 cm in length, there is tremendous variability in how doctors determine if a penis is too small to be considered a penis but still too large to be a clitoris (Kessler, 2002). Doctors and nurses generally don't carry rulers; they report that they know a sex organ when they see it.

When an infant is born with "ambiguous" genitalia, clinicians and parents describe a shift from the happiness of delivering a new baby to worry. As one mother who had a child with CAH described, "The doctor delivered her, and the resident mumbled, 'You have a boy.' The doctor immediately turned around and shot the resident a look and said, 'Shh. We don't know yet.'" After some time, the doctors returned to inform this new mother that they weren't sure if she "had a boy or girl" (Karkazis, 2008, p. 184). She was stunned. In many cases, parents aren't aware that infants can be born with external genitalia that don't neatly fit into F or M categories (Gough, Weyman, Alderson, Butler, & Stoner, 2008; Zeiler & Wickstrom, 2009).

Using genitals (and other biological markers) to determine sex is the standard practice in Western cultures, but this is not true in all cultures (Nanda, 2014). In other words, nature doesn't decide where the category of "female" ends and "male" begins. Humans decide. Biological factors can be a starting point in determining sex, but behavioral factors can eventually become relevant in making sex/gender designations. For example, Native American and Polynesian cultures may determine sex through other means later in life, such as through a person's gendered occupation (Nanda, 2014).

There is also no medical consensus regarding what exact combination of bodily markers defines sex. For this reason, current standards of care, outlined by the American Pediatric Association, suggest that doctors or birth attendants consider genital configuration, reproductive potential, and likely psychological outcome when making a sex designation at birth (Lee, Houk, Ahmed, & Hughes, 2006). Further, the current standard of care outlines that children should be permitted to change their sex designation later in life if they want to. This recommendation prioritizes self-identification of sex, rather than a medical or legal classification. However, it can be difficult to legally change one's sex designation, and government officials often require additional gender verification testing (e.g., genetic testing) for a change to occur. In this way, sex assignment isn't simply a medical decision; it's also a legal and civil decision.

A child with "no sex" is in social and legal limbo. For example, the state of New York requires parents to complete a birth certificate, with an assigned sex, within 48 hours of delivery, so parents and health-care providers can be left scrambling to figure out options (Kessler, 2002). In one case, the parents completed two birth certificates and refused to sign either one until a sex assignment had been made. In situations like this, the presence of "ambiguous" genitalia turns a civil requirement to get a birth certificate into a medical emergency. In fact, in December 2016, New York City issued the first known birth certificate in the United States marked intersex rather than F or M to Sara Kelly Keenan at age 55 as a result of a court order (Segal, 2017). The idea that there can only be two legal sexes does not exist in every country, however. In Australia, Bangladesh, Denmark, Germany, India, Nepal, and New Zealand, individuals can legally register with a gender outside of the F/M binary (Macarow, 2015).

The term *"ambiguous" genitalia* is often used in medical literature. However, some scholars believe this wording doesn't just reinforce the idea of a binary—it actually depends on a binary (Davis, 2015; Karkazis, 2008). In other words, genitals can only be "ambiguous" if we assume that only two types of genitals are possible. There is actually tremendous variability in the appearance of genitals. Yet because most of us haven't seen the diversity among genitals, we assume that all bodies look the same. Some artists have undertaken projects to highlight the diversity of genitals and reduce stigma and shame. For example, Jamie McCartney created "The Great Wall of Vagina," which depicted hundreds of castes of vulvas. In describing his work, McCartney said, "Vulvas and labia are as different as faces, but many people, particularly women, don't seem to know that" (McCartney, n.d., para. 6). Another group of artists created a series of penis emojis to showcase the diversity in penis sizes and shapes (La Jeunesse, 2015).

To demonstrate how culture influences the way we label genitalia, the terminology used to describe individuals with "ambiguous" genitalia has changed over time. For example, at one time the term *hermaphrodite* was used to describe those with ambiguous genitalia and/or both ovarian and testicular tissue. Although some intersex individuals today like to reclaim *hermaphrodite* in reference to themselves, most now view the term as stigmatizing because it relies on a binary assumption of sex and falsely implies that a person is both female and male ("Is a person who is intersex," n.d.).

The term *intersex* is more widely used, but leaders in the medical community decided to replace *intersex* with **disorders of sex development (DSD)** in 2006. Although the new term was supposed to represent an "enlightened advancement" (Hughes, 2010, p. 161), some individuals with intersex conditions worry that the new language continues to stigmatize (Topp, 2012). They're concerned that the continued medical focus, as in the word *disorder*, reinforces the idea that there's something "wrong" with the bodies of intersexed individuals (Davis, 2015). Instead, they would prefer a questioning of why there is a binary notion of bodies at all. Some clinicians and researchers have begun to define the acronym DSD as "differences of sex development" rather than "disorders of sex development" to address the concern about stigma.

Medical Management Technologies advanced during the first half of the twentieth century, enabling doctors to intervene when intersex conditions were identified. Such interventions were aimed at "fixing" the bodies so they could more readily fit the binary model of sex (Karkazis, 2008). Although the majority of intersex conditions aren't life threatening, genital ambiguity is typically considered a medical emergency because of the potential for psychological trauma for the parents and, some argue, ultimately, the child (de Maria Arana, 2005; Nussbaum 2000; Warne et al., 2005). Medical providers often recommend early intervention, and research shows that many parents seek out medical intervention because of tremendous social pressure from family members and healthcare providers to "do something" (Lee, Houk, Ahmed, & Hughes, 2006; Roen, 2008, p. 47).

Often, medical procedures performed on intersex bodies are purely cosmetic and don't benefit (and can even harm) physical health. For example, although CAH is rare, if doctors are aware of an elevated risk (because of a family history), they may suggest using a steroid known as dexamethasone (DEX). When taken during pregnancy, it prevents the masculinization of female genitalia (Dreger, Feder, & Tamar-Mattis, 2012; Fausto-Sterling, 2000). Some research, however, has pointed to health risks for the child, including delayed motor development and impaired memory (Fausto-Sterling, 2000; Lajic, Nordenström, & Hirvikoski, 2011). Despite these risks, DEX remains a popular treatment because of fear and stigma associated with having a child with "ambiguous" genitalia (Dreger et al., 2012; Fausto-Sterling, 2000; Vos & Bruinse, 2010).

There are remarkable variations in what parents are told about the risks and benefits of early medical interventions, and many parents describe feeling isolated and anxious about having to make a major medical decision on behalf of their child (Karkazis, 2008). Decisions are often made during times when families are coping with confusion, fear, and grief (Leidolf, Curran, Scout, & Bradford, 2008). Further, the fact that parents are making decisions on behalf of their children can be considered ageism (Holmes, 2008).

Many parents are asked to contemplate "corrective" surgery for their newborns. *Genitoplasty* is any surgery on the genitals. Infants who are assigned F may undergo *clitoroplasty*, a type of surgery that reduces the size of the clitoris, and often have to undergo additional surgical procedures over the course of their lives (Kessler, 2002). In one study, 89% of clitoroplasty procedures were found to require additional surgical interventions, and 41% of participants reported poor cosmetic results (Creighton, Minto, & Steele, 2001). Surgery can also impair sexual function and pleasure (Creighton & Minto, 2001; Creighton, Minto, & Woodhouse, 2001). Among infants assigned M, *phalloplasty* may be used as a surgical procedure to increase the size of the penis and to relocate the placement of the urethral opening.

It's estimated that five surgical procedures are performed each day in an attempt to cosmetically match newborns to an assigned sex (Fausto-Sterling, 2000), yet there is no official protocol for how and when this type of surgery should happen. Although research on the outcomes of genital surgery is limited, some research shows that early surgical intervention was later associated with feelings of anxiety, betrayal, and helplessness—largely due to the child's inability to consent to irreversible surgical and hormonal treatments (Creighton & Liao, 2004).

Further, because the presence of "ambiguous" genitalia is rare, health-care providers are often extremely curious. The philosopher Michel Foucault (1973) referred to this as the **medical gaze**, a process of dehumanization that occurs when medical providers treat a person's body separate from that person's sense of self. For example, one woman with CAH described a room full of 30 people who, after watching a doctor examine her, each inserted their fingers into her vagina: "They didn't look me in the face or eyes. They'd come in and talk about me like I wasn't there" (Karkazis, 2008, p. 222).

Experiences like this can cause shame and depression, and many young adults with CAH struggle with suicidal thoughts because of constant medical surveillance (Kessler, 2002). As a result of this stress, there is also an increased risk for alcohol abuse (Engberg et al., 2015). Some individuals recall childhoods during which their condition was kept secret from them. For example, one woman with AIS reported that her parents and a doctor told her she was having "cancer removed" when, in fact, the doctor was removing her testes (Callahan, 2009, p. 107). For years afterward, the woman had baseless fears about cancer until, as an adult, she discovered the truth from her medical records. Understandably, adults who learn about their DSD later in life have considerable anger. Many adults report feeling as though their parents failed to protect them from pain, humiliation, and unnecessary surgical procedures (Karkazis, 2008).

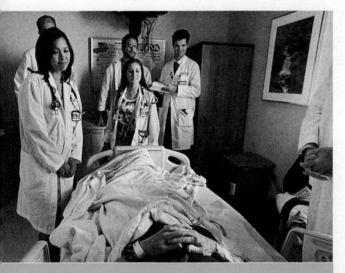

Many intersex and trans individuals experience the "medical gaze" while receiving health care. Have you ever experienced the medical gaze? Would having many health-care professionals staring at your body make you more cautious about seeking medical treatment?

Research shows that individuals with DSD have a clear preference for open communication about their condition (Alderson, Madill, & Balen, 2004; Davis, 2015). However, some medical providers continue to push for withholding information from children and adolescents because of a fear that such information would compromise a child's self-esteem and gender identity development (Kessler, 2002). When individuals do receive truthful information about their bodies and have the opportunity to openly talk about their experiences, however, their shame is notably reduced (Colapinto, 2000).

Despite this, some physicians argue that surgery prevents confusion in how a child develops a gender identity and an eventual sexual orientation (Karkazis, 2008). This belief stems from an older theory that if children undergo surgery early and subsequently are unambiguously girls or boys, then they will be treated as girls or boys, will grow up feeling like they're girls or boys, and ultimately will take on a heterosexual identity (Money, Hampson, & Hampson, 1955). Of course, this justification reflects the belief that the optimal form of development is to have a binary gender identity and to be heterosexual—assumptions that many, including feminist scholars, now reject.

Medical interventions, particularly surgery, remain common practice with intersex children today, but many organizations have issued formal statements against this practice. For example, in 2013 the United Nations explicitly condemned countries for failing to ban unnecessary surgery on children (United Nations, 2015), and in 2017 three former U.S. surgeons general wrote that they believed there was little evidence that genital surgery on infants was necessary and that additional evidence suggested it was actually harmful (Elders, Satcher, & Carmona, 2017). Also in 2017, Human Rights Watch and Inter-ACT released a 160-page review of the existing research and concluded that the practice should end because of no evidence of its effectiveness or safety (Human Rights Watch, 2017). Because such medical interventions are generally irreversible, critics are especially alarmed by the lack of informed consent from the individuals who are most affected—the infants themselves (Cull, 2002).

Advocacy groups have been at the forefront of creating change. In 1993, for example, intersex activist Cheryl Chase organized the first patient advocacy group, the Intersex Society of North America (now known as Accord Alliance). The goal was to advocate for improvements in the way patients are treated, more caution surrounding genital surgery, and the elimination of stigmatizing language and labels. In 2005, the group's advocacy resulted in a consensus statement, produced by medical professionals in the United States and the United Kingdom, regarding treatment protocols for people with intersex conditions (Lee et al., 2006). Although current recommendations favor delaying surgery and having more open and confidential communication with patients, there is no formal mechanism to ensure these protocols are followed. As a result, many intersex advocates are working to find ways to ensure compliance at health-care facilities. Furthermore, organizations like this tend to

your turn

If you had a child with "ambiguous" genitalia, would it be possible for you to raise that child without assigning a binary sex/gender? Why or why not? If you were that child, how might you feel about having your sex/gender chosen for you by your parents and/or health-care providers?

primarily consist of White, middle-class individuals and may overlook the needs of intersex individuals from other demographic groups (Davis, 2015).

Sexual Diversity

How do common views about sexual orientation reflect an assumption of a sex/gender binary, what are some less well-known sexual orientations, and what is heterosexism?

As we've mentioned, in the simple, linear model shown earlier in Figure 4.1, the traditional assumption is that sexual orientation will align with one's sex assignment and gender identity. However, sexual orientation is far more diverse and complicated. **Sexual orientation** is generally understood as an individual's predisposition toward sexual and/or romantic attraction for persons of the same sex/gender (homosexual) and/or the other sex/gender (heterosexual). There are, however, more than just these two sexual orientations (although Table 4.2 is not comprehensive, it defines sexual orientations that are not exclusive to

TABLE 4.2 Sexual Orientations beyond the Binary of Heterosexuality and Homosexuality

Orientation	Definition
Asexuality	A sexual orientation in which a person has low sexual attraction or no experience of sexual attraction.
Bisexuality	A sexual orientation characterized by having attraction to both women and men.
Demisexuality	A sexual orientation in which attraction occurs only when a person forms a strong emotional connection with another person.
Heteroflexible	This term refers to self-identified persons (either cis or trans) who are mostly attracted to cis- or transgender individuals of the other gender but who are occasionally attracted to other individuals (e.g., cis- or transgender individuals of the same gender; those who are genderqueer).
Pansexuality	A sexual orientation in which an individual is sexually and/or romantically attracted to all genders based on an individual's personality.
Queer	A sexual orientation in which an individual does not identify with any specific sexual orientation; also an umbrella term sometimes used for those who are not heterosexual and/or gender-binary.
Skoliosexuality	A sexual orientation in which a person experiences attraction toward non-binary-identified individuals.

Note. Definitions adapted from The Safe Space Network (http://safespacenetwork.tumblr.com/define)

either heterosexuality or homosexuality). Moreover, many people assume that others are heterosexual (at least until proven otherwise) and that it's more desirable to be heterosexual—a bias known as **heterosexism**. Like sexism and racism, heterosexism can manifest in many different ways. Examples include being harassed for showing public displays of affection with a romantic partner or having a lack of positive and accurate depictions of romance and relationships in movies or television.

Because sexual orientation is often conceived of as a binary, people who have non-binary identities can feel invisible (Scarlette-Callis, 2014). For example, individuals whose sexual orientation is **asexual**—that is, involving little or no little or no sexual attraction—report being ignored or discriminated against (Bogaert, 2006). There are also negative and incorrect beliefs about asexual people, including that they were sexually abused as children or that they use their orientation as an excuse for being single because they're unattractive (Bogaert, 2006). Some mental health professionals have linked asexuality with illness—a claim that has been significantly challenged in contemporary research (Bogaert, 2006; Prause & Graham, 2007). In fact, the Asexual Visibility and Education Network (AVEN) was formed as a way to combat inaccurate information that has the potential to stigmatize those with asexual identities. However, asexual individuals are still under-represented in research and are largely absent from advocacy groups (Pinto, 2014). Consider, for example, that the letter *A* is typically omitted in discussions of LGBTQ rights (Pinto, 2014). Even in this book, we as authors don't include *A* because most psychological research doesn't regularly identify participants with asexual orientations. Indeed, one of the dilemmas associated with the expanding LGBTQ acronym is that in attempting to be inclusive, it ignores unique differences and thereby alienates some groups of people (Bell, 2016).

Theories of Sexual Diversity

What is sexual configurations theory, and how are romantic and sexual attraction understood as part of sexual orientation?

Even among those who identify as gay, straight, or bisexual, there can be tremendous diversity. This is not a new idea. In the 1940s, the biologist and sexologist Alfred Kinsey developed the Kinsey Scale to illustrate how people fall on a continuous scale of sexual orientation ranging from same sex/gender attraction to other sex/gender attraction (Kinsey, Pomeroy, & Martin, 1948). However, this model has weaknesses, including the assumption of a sex/gender binary and the assumption that all people experience both sexual and romantic attraction (and that the two always align). While there's no perfect way to reflect the complexity of gender and sexual diversity, there are newer options, such as

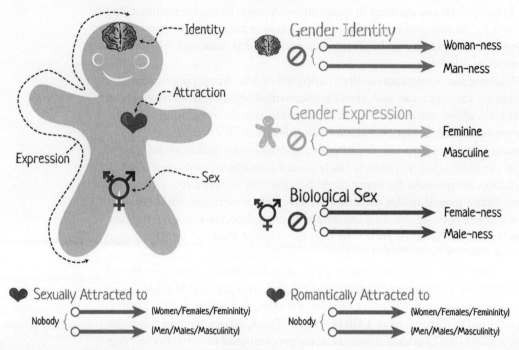

The Genderbread Person v3.2 by it's pronounced METROsexual.com

Identity

Attraction

Expression

Sex

Gender Identity

⊘ { Woman-ness

Man-ness

Gender Expression

⊘ { Feminine

Masculine

Biological Sex

⊘ { Female-ness

Male-ness

❤ Sexually Attracted to

Nobody { (Women/Females/Femininity)

(Men/Males/Masculinity)

❤ Romantically Attracted to

Nobody { (Women/Females/Femininity)

(Men/Males/Masculinity)

FIGURE 4.2 Author and activist Sam Killermann created the Genderbread Person in order to illustrate the complexity of sex/gender/sexual orientation. This diagram has been revised numerous times in response to feedback about how it could better represent the complexities of people's experiences with sex, gender, and sexual/romantic orientation.

the Genderbread Person (Killermann, 2015), to help conceptualize sex, gender identity, gender expression, and romantic and sexual attraction in more complex ways. The Genderbread Person diagram (see Figure 4.2) is one way to visually represent the gender bundle we talked about earlier in this chapter.

Feminist psychologist Sari van Anders (2015) has developed **sexual configurations theory (SCT)** to better account for the fact that sexuality is multi-faceted, socially situated, and dynamic. As is true with the Genderbread Person, SCT argues that an individual's sexuality must be understood along a variety of dimensions. For example, someone may have fantasies about people of one sex/gender but engage in sexual behaviors with those of another sex/gender. Although it's generally assumed that sexual orientation implies being attracted to someone's sex, rather than someone's gendered characteristics, that may not always be true. For example, if an individual is attracted to men, is that person attracted to penises or, instead, to masculine gender expression, like having facial hair or a short haircut? What about women who are attracted to feminine men? Are they just as heterosexual as women who are attracted to masculine men? Furthermore, sexual and romantic attraction and desire—as well as sexual orientation identity and sexual behavior—can be fluid and changeable over time, a characteristic known as *sexual fluidity* (Diamond, 2008b; Katz-Wise, 2014). In fact, some women have reported an abrupt change in sexuality in midlife, beginning to experience attraction to women after years of being attracted to men (Diamond, 2007).

Individuals may also make a distinction between romance and sex (Scherrer, 2008). Although having an asexual orientation means having little or no sexual desire, some asexual individuals do feel romantically attracted to others. Within this group, there are heteroromantics (romantic attraction to a different sex/gender), homoromantics (romantic attraction to the same sex/gender), biromantics (romantic attraction to more than one sex/gender), and panromantics (romantic attraction regardless of sex or gender). Finally, some people identify as **aromantic**, meaning that they experience little to no romantic attraction. Aromantic individuals still form relationships with others, but usually as friendships (Van Houdenhove, Gijs, T'Sjoen, & Enzlin, 2015). For some, this type of relationship may even develop into a long-term, non-romantic partnership. Also, while some aromantic individuals identify as asexual, others do experience sexual attraction.

Many non-Western cultures do not prioritize the gay/straight binary. In places such as Brazil, Thailand, Indonesia, Polynesia, and the Philippines, effeminate men are typically seen as gay or transgender men, but their male partners aren't considered to be gay or transgender (Nanda, 2014). In India (the sadhin) and in the Balkans (sworn virgins), some women assume a male social identity if they vow to lead a virginal life—a third gender option, and another that disrupts the gay/straight binary.

Gender Diversity and Sexual Orientation

How can gender identity complicate the way people identify their sexual orientation, and how can transitioning impact people's sexual orientation?

Gender diversity can complicate sexual orientation. Gender identity and sexual orientation identity are different, yet many people mistake transgender identities as an expression of sexual orientation rather than as an expression of gender identity (Mizock & Fleming, 2011). It's important to understand that whether one *feels* like a woman, like a man, or like someone who doesn't fit within a sex/gender binary isn't the same thing as whether one is *attracted to* women or men (or both or neither). Transgender individuals may use a wide range of sexual orientation identity labels (Katz-Wise, Reisner, White Hughto, & Keo-Meier, 2015). For example, a transwoman who is attracted to men may consider herself to be heterosexual (although she may have been considered a gay man before she transitioned), but she may choose to use other sexual orientation identities instead, such as queer. Moreover, gender-affirming medical treatments, such as cross-sex hormones, can affect sexual orientation (Katz-Wise et al., 2015; Meier et al., 2013; Reisner, Perkovich, & Mimiaga, 2010). In one study, 54% of transwomen participants reported being primarily attracted to women before they transitioned, and 9% reported being primarily attracted to men (Lawrence, 2005). After they transitioned, 25% reported being primarily sexually attracted to women, and 34% were primarily sexually attracted to men.

Sexuality shift stress, the stressors associated with changes in sexual orientation as a function of gender transitioning, can also influence intimate relationships (Mizock & Hopwood, 2016). In one study, partners of transgender individuals showed increased anxiety related to changes in the relationship following transition (Lenning & Buist, 2013). Transgender participants reported that both they and their significant others struggled with their identities during the gender transitioning process. They felt a sense of loss of the non-transgender partner's sexual identity and a rejection of their status as a couple from friends, family members, and co-workers. A person's sexual orientation may also change depending on the sexual orientation identity of the partner. As an example, we can consider a lesbian who marries a woman who, later in life, transitions to become a man. That woman may continue to consider herself a lesbian who happens to be married to a man. However, after her partner transitions, she may be perceived by others as being heterosexual. Some transgender women describe a double stigma when they go from being transgender/heterosexual to being woman/lesbian. As one woman described, "I went from one closet into another because I went from being trans to—now I'm a lesbian" (Mizock & Hopwood, 2016, p. 98).

Given that some people don't fall neatly into a binary, the idea that it's possible to easily label all people's sexual orientation becomes invalid (van Anders, 2015). Some individuals may be specifically attracted to people outside of the binary, while others may be attracted to people who fall within the binary as well as those who fall outside of it (Tate & Pearson, 2016). Because most labels reflect the sex/gender binary and don't take into account sexual fluidity, some people reject the idea that one's gender should determine how one's sexual orientation is labeled (Galupo, Davis, Grynkiewicz, & Mitchell, 2014; Lenning & Buist, 2013).

Regardless, labels appear to matter quite a bit, especially when dating. For example, intersex individuals face a unique dilemma in deciding when and how to bring up their intersex identity with a potential romantic/sexual partner. In an attempt to seek advice, one woman with AIS posted to a discussion board asking how she should approach the subject with a new male partner. "I look like a normal girl," she posted, "but my vaginal canal is considerably smaller than most women's" (Karkazis, 2008, p. 216). Although most people posted nuanced and compassionate responses, one person commented that it was unethical for the woman to withhold her condition from any potential partner. This is one reason why many individuals with intersex conditions report a lack of sexual confidence and sexual satisfaction (Fliegner et al., 2014).

Development of a Sexual Minority Identity

What is the process through which some women develop sexual minority identities, and how can this process be more complex for non-monosexual women?

How individuals come to define their own sexuality is complicated, and what it means to identify with a particular sexual orientation can vary from person to person. Many people are brought up in families where a heterosexual identity is assumed, so developing a sexual minority identity can be a process of struggle and difficulty. While the experiences of coming to identify as lesbian, bisexual, or pansexual (to name a few possible identities) may share some commonalities, they may also be quite different, particularly considering how other identity variables (e.g., religion, class, race) influence sexual orientation. One woman, for example, stated that "often, [she] felt compelled to speak [her]self into existence as a coherent, fixed, and finished subject—a lesbian and Muslim. That [she doesn't] comfortably or uniformly identify as a lesbian, and that being Muslim is a complicated set of religious and cultural processes, fell outside the purview of what was possible to speak" (Charania, 2005, p. 31). Because mainstream society expects that sexual orientation (and other social identities) will remain stable, it can be virtually impossible to experience social validation for more fluid and flexible identities.

Furthermore, as noted previously, sexual orientation can shift based on the person with whom one is partnered. One woman who identified as a lesbian but who fell in love with a man described how this fact complicated her sense of identity and how other people saw her: "I can't say I'm a lesbian dating a man. People just don't accept that, even though that's sort of what I feel like. . . . My feelings about women haven't really changed, it's just that I'm more open and accepting about my feelings for men, or at least to this man" (Diamond, 2007, p. 150). In a 10-year longitudinal study of lesbian and bisexual women, psychologist Lisa Diamond (2007) found that two thirds of women shifted their sense of identity over that period, and a quarter did so more than once. The changes included shifting from labeling as bisexual to labeling as lesbian, shifting from labeling as lesbian to labeling as bisexual, and shifting from labeling as lesbian or bisexual to rejecting labels altogether.

Early work on the development of a lesbian identity described a process in which women spent many years denying or blocking out their identity (Kitzinger, 1995). Despite feelings of romantic and sexual love for other women, many

Jamie Shupe (left, who uses the pronoun *they*) became the first person in the United States to legally have their gender recognized as non-binary. They are pictured here with their wife, Sandy. Jamie and Sandy married when Jamie identified as male, and Sandy was supportive when, after more than 20 years together, Jamie transitioned their gender identity—initially to a transgender woman, before publicly identifying as non-binary. How might Jamie's changing gender identity have influenced both spouses' perception of their own sexual orientation?

women denied these feelings through a variety of strategies—such as noting that their sexual attraction was a result of being "a good friend" or that any sexual acts were just experimentation. For example, one woman noted: "After Judy and I made love for the first time I got very scared that this meant I was a lesbian. I withdrew right away. I said, 'This doesn't mean I'm a lesbian'" (Kitzinger & Wilkinson, 1995, p. 99). Some women described having difficulty accepting the lesbian label because of internalized stereotypes and the belief that they couldn't possibly be lesbians because, for example, they had long hair, had children, or didn't know how to fix cars. But once they embraced the label, they felt a sense of exuberant rebirth. This was described variously as "an explosion of aliveness," "like waking up having been half asleep all my life," "like a conversion experience," and "like emerging from a chrysalis" (p. 100).

Consistent in accounts of lesbian identity development are the presence of intense, passionate friendships with other women during adolescence and early adulthood (Tate & Pearson, 2016). These friendships spark emotional and sexual feelings, but the extent of these feelings is generally kept secret. Many women who eventually identify as lesbians go through a period of dating or even having sexual relationships with men before they become comfortable with accepting a lesbian identity. Individuals who adopt a non-monosexual identity (e.g., bisexual, pansexual, queer) report a stage of sexual identity uncertainty; however, unlike lesbian women, they report that the uncertainty can continue after the adoption of an identity or that they choose to label themselves "unlabeled" (Diamond, 2008a, p. 6).

Some researchers theorize that this uncertainty stems from external pressures to adhere to the dominant binary of homosexual or heterosexual—in other words, to be **monosexual**, or sexually attracted to only one sex/gender (Alarie, & Gaudet, 2013). Stereotypes of people with non-monsexual identities are often derogatory and invalidating (Brewster & Moradi, 2010; Dyar, Feinstein, & London, 2015). One negative stereotype is that people who have non-monosexual identities are in a transitional stage—they're simply at the beginning of recognizing they're gay. Another negative stereotype is that non-monosexual individuals are promiscuous and incapable of maintaining a monogamous relationship. **Binegativity** is a social stigma directed specifically at bisexual people; it can come from people who identify as heterosexual as well as from those who identify as lesbian or gay (Yost & Thomas, 2012). Bisexual individuals are often viewed with suspicion by both the straight and the lesbian/gay communities because of unstated assumptions that bisexual people in either gay or straight relationships will become unsatisfied and, ultimately, cheat.

When non-monosexual individuals internalize negative stereotypes, they're unlikely to disclose their non-monosexual identity to others (Dyar, Feinstein, Schick, & Davila, 2017). Moreover, negative attitudes can build pressure to conform to dominant binary standards (Ross, Dobinson, & Eady, 2010). Because of this pressure, some bisexual individuals choose to describe their sexual identity differently depending on the gender of their partner (Mohr, Jackson, & Sheets, 2016). For example, a bisexual woman may identify as a lesbian when dating a woman or as heterosexual when dating a man. The varying self-presentation may be a strategy to ward off binegativity. In this sense, the decision to publicly label their sexuality is based on managing the negative attitudes of other people rather than their own desires (Dyar et al., 2017).

Negativity may be diminishing, however, as people in their 20s and 30s appear to be endorsing a greater diversity of sexual identities (Savin-Williams, 2005; Thompson & Morgan, 2008). Some college women, for example, describe their experiences as "mostly straight," "bicurious," and "questioning" (Morgan & Thompson, 2006). Many describe the excitement of making dating decisions based on factors like personality or emotional availability rather than gender (Diamond, 2008a; Scales Rostosky, Riggle, Pascale-Hague, & McCants, 2010). When girls and women with a non-monosexual identity reject binary notions of sexuality, they report higher sexual certainty and increased psychological well-being (Brewster & Moradi, 2010; Dyar, Lytle, London, & Levy, 2015).

Coming Out

What are the barriers to and benefits of coming out?

Coming out is a process by which LGBTQ individuals accept, appreciate, and inform themselves and others about their LGBTQ identity. Coming out is a lifelong process because there will always be someone new who doesn't know about one's identity. As a result, a LGBTQ person will continually have to

The Search for a "Gay Gene"

In 2011, Lady Gaga famously sang the lyrics "I was born this way." Her song illustrated a popular argument for securing LGBQ rights: If sexual orientation is biologically determined, people shouldn't be discriminated against because of an innate trait. This position counters an alternative argument that being gay is a choice, which some people consider immoral. The implication of arguments focused on choice is that discrimination is justified because gay people could voluntarily choose to stop behaving immorally. However, associating biology with gay rights and choice with discrimination over-simplifies a complicated situation. What if sexuality can't be reduced to either biology or a choice? Would that undermine arguments against discrimination? Some people worry that defining sexual orientation within a rigid nature/nurture debate could actually constrain freedoms and undermine the notion that sexuality is fluid and identities can shift throughout the life span.

In the early 1990s, a flurry of research studies explored the potential biological bases of sexual orientation. Some suggested that being gay ran in families (Bailey et al., 1999; Whitam, Diamond, & Martin, 1993) or that the size of certain parts of the brain (e.g., hypothalamus, amygdala, corpus callosum) could be related to the development of a gay identity (LeVay, 1991). Scientists later changed their approach and suggested that variations in prenatal hormone levels influence genetics, which, in turn, affect sexual orientation (Balthazart, 2012; Baroncini et al., 2010). Despite all the recent research on the human genome, no "gay gene" that reliably predicts minority sexual orientation has been identified. Like many other characteristics, sexual orientation may be both complicated and malleable. Our bodies, and thus our biology, change throughout our life span and in response to various social and environmental factors (Burri, Cherkas, Spector, & Rahman, 2011).

Even though there are no definitive research findings, citing the concept of a "gay gene" has been very effective as a political strategy. When political leaders suggest that having an LGBQ lifestyle is a "choice" and that people should stop choosing it, the alternative "born this way" argument seems very practical. This argument may, however, be harmful to LGBQ rights in other ways. In 2012, actress Cynthia Nixon came under fire for claiming that she chose to be a lesbian. She responded by saying, "Why can't it be a choice? Why is that any less legitimate?" (Witchel, 2012, para. 21). Others agree that the exclusive either/or debate reflects homophobia, since it suggests that LGBQ people "can't help themselves" and must prove their legitimacy through biological means. Another argument is that the search for biological proof relates to a time when being gay was considered an illness—after all, no one talks about a search for a "straight gene." In other words, scholars don't research what makes people heterosexual because that is deemed normal, which is an indication of heterosexism. One researcher fears that identifying a "gay gene" may lead to terminating pregnancies when the so-called gay gene is suspected in an effort to reduce the population of sexual minority individuals (Spector, 2014).

What do you think about this issue? Is the search for biological evidence of minority sexual orientation empowering or oppressing? In what ways are biological explanations more persuasive than other explanations for sexual behavior and/or sexual orientation identities? In what ways may you unknowingly give more credit to an argument because it is linked with essentialism?

decide when and how to share information about their sexual orientation and/or gender identity with others (Cohen & Savin-Williams, 1996; Hunter, 2007).

There are, however, real risks associated with coming out (Hunter, 2007). For example, in one study, coming out was related to greater likelihood of victimization, which was related to lower academic outcomes among rural LGBTQ individuals (Kosciw et al., 2015). The process of coming out can range from being easy to difficult depending on the individual's social context. Members of younger generations have come of age in a time when LGBTQ rights are more widespread, including the legal right for same-sex marriage. In one study, researchers showed that members of younger generations (people in their 20s and 30s) come out at a younger age than did members of older generations (people in their 50s and 60s; Grov, Bimbi, Nanín, & Parsons, 2006).

Religion has been identified as another factor contributing to difficulty in coming out. In a study of LGBTQ Filipino American individuals, participants described that the combination of being Filipino, gay, and Catholic couldn't be easily reconciled (Nadal & Corpus, 2013). They reported tremendous guilt, shame, and conflict with family members who perceived their LGBTQ identity as "morally wrong" (p. 169). Because of their multiple minority statuses, some individuals felt they had to "pick and choose" which identity was the most important (race, religion, sexual orientation, etc.)—a challenge that was psychologically draining (p. 172). The degree to which any given social identity is important to an individual varies by person and context, but it's clear that having multiple minority statuses complicates the process of coming out.

Overall, in terms of coming out, less is known about the experiences of bisexual women and lesbians of color (Greene, 2000; Moradi, DeBlaere, & Huang, 2010). The few studies that have been done suggest that lesbians of color may be more likely to conceal their identity in order to maintain family harmony (Bowleg, Huang, Brooks, Black, & Burkholder, 2003; Parks, Hughes, & Matthews, 2004; Ryan, 2003). There is also some evidence that people from racial/ethnic minority groups are more likely than White people to hold conservative views toward sexuality, which may influence a group member's decision to come out and limit the positive effects of being out (Herek & Gonzalez-Rivera, 2006). In one study, Latinx LGBQ adolescents were more likely to experience family rejection than their White counterparts, and this rejection was associated with depression and suicidality (Ryan, Huebner, Diaz, & Sanchez, 2009). In another study, Latinx lesbians were less likely to experience depression if they came out to a non-family member than if they came out to a family member (Aranda et al., 2015). Because level of familial support has been found to predict life satisfaction and well-being among poor Mexican American women, it's not surprising that they generally opt to conceal their sexual minority identities (Diaz & Bui, 2016).

Still other studies find that White LGBQ individuals experience the fewest barriers in coming out (Grov et al., 2006; Riley, 2010; Rosario, Schrimshaw, Hunter, & Levy-Warren, 2009). Black and Latinx lesbian and gay adolescents (between the ages of 14 and 21) reported disclosing their identity to fewer people than did White adolescents in one study (Rosario, Schrimshaw, & Hunter, 2004). Initially, Black youths also had lower levels of comfort with their sexual identity and participated in fewer activities with other gay/lesbian youths than White youths did. However, over time, Black youths showed a greater increase of positivity and in certainty toward their identity as compared to White and Latinx adolescents.

Individuals who are uncomfortable with their sexual orientation identity may have internalized feelings of negativity toward being LGBQ and wish that they didn't experience attraction to members of the same sex/gender. This phenomenon has several names, including **internalized homophobia** and **internalized biphobia**. Another name is **internalized heterosexism**, as the word *phobia* implies a fear that is generally not present in those who are uncomfortable with their own sexual orientation (Bregman, Malik, Page, Makynen, & Lindahl, 2013). Others have referred to the outlook as **internalized homonegativity**. Regardless of the term used, this set of attitudes has been widely studied and found to be related to depression, especially among older individuals who came of age at a time when variations in sexual orientation were less accepted (Newcomb & Mustanski, 2010).

Parental reaction to coming out is a key predictor of whether LGBTQ individuals accept their identities, and it is also a predictor of their emotional health. In one study, sexual minority youth discussing their experiences described a broad range of family reactions, from being vehemently disapproving to being extremely accepting and engaging in LGBTQ activism along with their children

These students are part of a LGBTQ affinity group at their school. These groups help students feel supported and contribute to developing a positive self-identity. What would it be like to go to a school where your sexual orientation and/or identity was never acknowledged—or was explicitly disapproved of? Alternatively, what would it be like to attend a school where you could find support from allies and others with shared identities?

(Higa et al., 2014). In another study, children who reported that their parents rejected their sexual orientation identity were more likely to have negative feelings about their sexual orientation identity, more likely to want to conceal it, and more fearful that others wouldn't accept them than those who reported parental acceptance (Bregman et al., 2013). Parental acceptance was also found to be related to higher self-esteem, greater perceptions of social support, and lower levels of depression and substance abuse, as well as fewer suicide attempts (Ryan, Russell, Huebner, Diaz, & Sanchez, 2010).

LGBTQ adolescents, especially adolescents of color, are also disproportionately incarcerated in the juvenile justice system (Hunt & Moodie-Mills, 2012). This is likely because many LGBTQ adolescents who are rejected by family members run away and experience homelessness, which can result in a higher incidence of drug and alcohol use (Birkett, Koenig, & Espelage, 2009; Garofalo, Deleon, Osmer, Doll, & Harper, 2006; Walls, Kane, & Wisneski, 2010). One study estimated that 40% of homeless people in the United States are LGBTQ youth (Majd, Marksamer, & Reyes, 2009).

Further, sexual minority individuals can experience a great deal of discrimination and bullying. Bullying can come from peers at school or within the community as well as in social or religious organizations. In one study, many youths described being called names, being told they were going to hell or being called out to "repent," and experiencing or witnessing physical harassment and violence (Higa et al., 2014). In all contexts, having people who were supportive or having other visible LGBTQ people who could be relied on helped to make a school or community environment more positive and welcoming.

On a more positive note, many LGBTQ individuals accept their identity and feel that it's central to who they are. A major component of feeling affirmed in one's identity, coming out has been associated with many positive outcomes, including higher self-esteem and lower levels of depression (Kosciw, Palmer, & Kull, 2015). Some may also think that being LGBQ is preferable to being heterosexual (Mohr & Kendra, 2011) or feel special and unique because they don't have a sexuality that fits within a narrow definition (Higa et al., 2014). Furthermore, some research suggests that when individuals have a positive racial/ethnic identity, they're more likely to have a positive LGBTQ identity (Singh, 2013).

Conclusion

We started this chapter questioning the dominant acceptance of essentialism and the traditional sex/gender binary—the assumed link from genes to bodies to identity to sexual

try it for yourself

Think about various communities that you're part of, such as your neighborhood, your school, or your religious community. What specific things could you do to create (or add to) an LGBTQ-affirming climate in each of these communities? What barriers would you face? Would they be different for different communities you're part of? Then ask a friend to also brainstorm ways to increase acceptance for sexual and gender diversity. Work together to develop a plan to implement at least one strategy by the end of this semester.

orientation. Throughout the chapter, we've shown that there are many facets in the gender bundle that influence people's bodies, identities, expressions, and orientations and that these don't always conform to a sex/gender binary. Nonetheless, mainstream society generally expects people to consistently identify and express themselves as either a woman or a man with a corresponding heterosexual orientation. These expectations are encountered in places such as health-care settings, school/work environments, and athletic competitions; they can even relate to obtaining legal recognition. People whose lives conform to mainstream assumptions about sex/gender binaries are often unaware that many individuals fall outside of these expectations. This lack of awareness reflects privilege, and it is yet another domain in which privilege needs to be acknowledged in order for change to occur.

Chapter Review

SUMMARY

Challenging Heteronormative Assumptions about Sex and Gender

- Many people assume, inaccurately, that there are only two sexes that directly correspond to two genders. This view reflects the sex/gender binary.

- Feminist scholars regard the sex/gender binary as overly simplistic and instead advocate for the concept of a gender bundle, in which aspects of sex/gender (e.g., gender assignment, gender identity, gender bodily expression) are all part of the personal and social understanding of gender.

Transgender: An Umbrella Term

- Gender identity and gender expression do not always conform to assigned sex.

- Transgender individuals identify their gender identity in diverse ways and may question their assigned sex at any point throughout the life span.

- Compared to cisgender individuals, gender identity development is more complicated for trans individuals since they often face stigma and prejudice from both loved ones and society at large.

- When trans individuals accept their identity, they typically opt to share their gender identity with others—a process known as gender transitioning, which can include medical interventions including hormones and surgery. Transitioning also involves redefining relationships with friends and family members, but cultural values, traditions, and prejudice can all be barriers to transitioning.

- Misgendering is a common experience among trans individuals.

Complicating Gender Assignment

- Not all cultures determine sex in the same way or focus on biological factors to do so (as is typical in the West).

- Many potential genetic variations in sex chromosomes can complicate identifying an individual's sex within a simple binary.
- Klinefelter syndrome (KS) occurs when those assigned M at birth have more than one X chromosome. Some individuals with KS identify as male while others identify as intersex, and there is great variability in the degree to which KS impacts their lives.
- Turner's syndrome (TS) occurs when those assigned F at birth have only a single X chromosome. While many individuals with TS identify as female, some identify as intersex. TS is most often associated with being of short stature and not developing secondary sex characteristics at puberty.
- Androgen-insensitivity syndrome (AIS) is a condition in which those with XY chromosomes don't have typical male genital development because of an inability for testosterone to connect with all cell receptors. Those with AIS are often assigned F at birth.
- Congenital adrenal hyperplasia (CAH) is a condition in which androgens are over-produced; in XX fetuses, this can lead to the development of male-typical genitalia. Infants with CAH can be assigned either F or M at birth, and most assigned F do identify as girls despite showing some behaviors traditionally associated with masculinity.
- 5-Alpha reductase deficiency is a condition in which individuals with XY chromosomes cannot process testosterone in a way that allows for the development of external genitalia in utero. While many individuals with this condition are assigned F at birth, they may develop male-typical secondary sex characteristics at puberty, although the mechanism through which this occurs is not yet understood.
- When infants cannot be easily classified as F or M because of "ambiguous genitalia," there can be complications with legal identity for birth certificates and other legal documents.

- Biomedical interventions, including genital surgery and hormone treatments, are common for children with intersex conditions. As this is often begun in infancy, the children generally have very little say in their treatments, and decisions about sex assignment are usually made by medical personnel.
- The United Nations, Human Rights Watch, and InterACT denounce medical interventions for intersex children. Advocacy groups such as Accord Alliance call for improvements in the way patients are treated, more caution surrounding genital surgery, and the elimination of stigmatizing language and labels.

Sexual Diversity
- There are many diverse sexual orientations, although those that don't reflect a sex/gender binary are less well known, and people with these identities can feel invisible.
- Sexual and romantic attraction don't always align, and not everyone experiences both.
- Sexual orientations can change throughout the life span for a variety of reasons.
- Women can struggle to accept their sexual minority identity, and it can be further complicated by other social identities.
- Non-monosexual individuals can face particular challenges because of binegativity from both the straight and the lesbian/gay communities.
- Coming out is an ongoing process, as there are always new people who could be told about one's gender and sexual minority identities. Coming out is associated with positive outcomes, but many individuals do not find acceptance from their families and communities.

KEY TERMS

intersex (p. 150)

sex/gender binary (p.151)

gender identity (p. 154)

gender expression (p. 154)

gender transitioning (p. 158)

misgender (p. 159)

minority stress theory (p. 163)

internalized transphobia (p. 163)

stigma awareness (p. 163)

Klinefelter syndrome (KS) (p. 167)

Turner's syndrome (TS) (p. 167)

androgen-insensitivity syndrome (AIS) (p. 169)

congenital adrenal hyperplasia (CAH) (p. 169)

5-alpha reductase deficiency (p. 170)

disorders of sex development (DSD) (p. 172)

medical gaze (p. 174)

sexual orientation (p. 176)

heterosexism (p. 177)

asexual (p. 177)

sexual configurations theory (SCT) (p. 178)

aromantic (p. 179)

monosexual (p. 183)

binegativity (p. 183)

coming out (p. 183)

internalized homophobia (p. 186)

internalized biphobia (p. 186)

internalized heterosexism (p. 186)

internalized homonegativity (p. 186)

THINK ABOUT IT

1. After reading this chapter, what recommendations would you make to organizations that are divided by sex/gender? Think about athletic teams, prisons, school dorms, bathrooms, and locker rooms. What barriers might you encounter when making your recommendations? How could you address them?

2. What are some drawbacks of having celebrities represent transgender concerns? In what ways could the concerns of trans and gender non-conforming people be more accurately represented in media? Given the research discussed in this chapter, what topics should be covered by the media?

3. What are the benefits and consequences of medical intervention for intersex individuals? Are there societal interventions that might help?

4. Design a high school affinity group that is supportive and inclusive of sexual diversity. What would you name your group, and what type of support services would you include? How might school personnel, parents, and students react to your new group?

ONLINE RESOURCES

- **Accord Alliance**—an organization that promotes comprehensive and integrated approaches to care that enhance the health and well-being of people and families affected by disorders of sex development (DSD): accordalliance.org

- **Autostraddle**—an online magazine and social network for lesbian, bisexual, and queer women (cis and trans) as well as non-binary people: autostraddle.com

- **Black Girl Dangerous**—a blog dedicated to amplifying the voices of queer and transgender people of color: bgdblog.org

- **National Center for Transgender Equality**—a website created by transgender activists to advance transgender equality: transequality.org

5

Gender
Socialization

- Marley Dias loves to read, but she noticed that none of the girls in the books her teachers assigned looked like her—they were almost all White, and she is Black (Anderson, 2016). So Marley decided to start collecting books about girls who look like her, with the goal of collecting 1,000 books. Her project, #1000blackgirlbooks, has exceeded its goal—she has collected over 4,000. Her quest points to a major problem in how girls of color are represented. At age 11, she was determined to resist invisibility.

- In 2011, a YouTube video of a 4-year-old White girl named Riley ranting about marketing in stores went viral (dbarry1917, 2011)—by 2017, it had been viewed over 5 million times. "Why do all the girls have to buy princesses?" she complained, standing in front of a toy aisle full of pink dolls. "Some girls like superheroes, some girls like princesses. Some boys like superheroes, some boys like princesses!" Her comments, along with other complaints, led Target, in 2015, to decide that it would no longer designate toy aisles by gender.

- In September 2015, Ms. Nwoye's fourth-grade class in Montgomery County, Maryland, posted a video entitled *The Lie* (Untitled Productions, 2016). In it, the 10-year-old students repeat lies that they've heard about people like themselves. One girl stands and says, "Muslims are terrorists." Another girl says, "Asian girls are not athletic." And another girl says, "I'm too pretty to be

At age 11, Marley Dias collected over 4,000 books to support her project #1000blackgirlbooks.

Togolese." The students wanted to open a conversation about the negative comments they heard about minority groups during the 2016 U.S. presidential campaign. Over 60,000 people have now watched their video, and it has gone viral internationally. One viewer said, "It was just powerful when 10-year-olds get the message and here we are adults, fighting and still trying to get the message" (George, 2016, para. 32).

■ In Pretoria, South Africa, administrators told Black girls at a prestigious high school that had been all White under apartheid to "fix" their hair or they wouldn't be allowed to attend school or sit for exams (Vilakazi, 2016). Zulaikha Patel, a 13-year-old girl, became the center of protests. She noted that she'd been told her whole life that her Afro wasn't natural, was exotic, and was unwanted. Ultimately, the protests succeeded after thousands of supporters started an online petition, and the codes about hair were suspended (Mahr, 2016).

These stories show how some young girls have reacted to socialization practices with resistance, but such stories are the exception rather than the rule. Most young girls passively absorb messages about gender, as well as other aspects of their social identities. These messages send information about how they're supposed to look and act throughout their entire lives and shape the way they perceive themselves and the world. In this chapter, we'll explore how gender socialization takes place, sources of socialization, how socialization practices affect girls and young women at various stages of development, and how other social identities intersect with gender socialization.

Theories of Gender Development

Children are constantly trying to figure out who they are and how they're supposed to act. Messages about gender play are influential in figuring that out. This process, known as **gender socialization**, occurs when individuals internalize the social expectations and attitudes associated with their perceived gender. Gender socialization is a very complex process—one that starts before we're born and lasts a lifetime. Because norms about gender change over time, it's challenging to study gender socialization. Psychologists have developed various theories, although, as you'll see, some are outdated and don't take an intersectional approach and/or consider many of the social and political changes that have altered gender expectations over the years.

FIGURE 5.1 Taking a moment to consider their options.

your turn

Before we review the dominant gender development theories in psychology, take some time to reflect on what you think gender is and how people develop it. What is your theory of gender development? Do you think we're born with gender, or is it learned—or both? In what ways do other aspects of one's social identity (e.g., sexual orientation, race/ethnicity, social class, ability status) influence gender development?

Psychoanalytic Theories

What are the main elements of the psychoanalytic theories of Freud, Horney, and Chodorow?

Psychoanalytic theories suggest that gender development (and personality in general) is controlled by unconscious forces—that is, forces that people aren't aware of (Freud, 1924/1961a, 1925/1961b; Person & Ovesey, 1983). All psychoanalytic theories consider early childhood to be the critical time in development. Yet psychoanalytic theory is controversial. Some scholars claim that psychoanalytic concepts have not been properly operationalized or systematically studied (Fonagy, 2003). Others disagree and report research support for the core tenets of psychoanalytic theory and practice (Corvin & Fitzgerald, 2000; Leichsenring, Rabung, & Leibing, 2004; Westen, 1999; Westen & Gabbard, 2002). Nevertheless, psychoanalytic theories have had a profoundly influential effect on many people's understanding of development and gender.

Sigmund Freud Most people associate psychoanalytic theories with Sigmund Freud, an Austrian neurologist who is considered the founding father of this perspective. Freud started with the assumption that there are only two sexes and that one's genitalia determine whether a person is a woman or a man (Freud, 1924/1961a, 1925/1961b; Person & Ovesley, 1983). In fact, in Freud's view, the genitalia (vaginas and penises) don't simply determine whether a person is a woman or a man but are also the root cause of many of the differences between women and men. Largely informed by the norms and values of the time in which he was writing, Freud proposed that being male and having a penis was superior to being female and having a vagina. Also, he proposed that both girls and boys realized the superiority of maleness. As a result, according to Freud, a driving force in the development of both girls and boys is that boys are protective of their penis while girls are jealous that they don't have one.

Early psychoanalytic theory assumed that children are raised in a traditional nuclear family that includes a father, a mother, and their biological children. Within the context of this traditional family, Freud theorized that young girls and boys develop in a similar way until approximately 3 years of age (Freud, 1924/1961a, 1925/1961b; Person & Ovesley, 1983). At this time, he claimed, boys develop an unconscious love for their mothers and a feeling of hostility toward their fathers. This is the **Oedipus complex**, named after the lead character in an ancient Greek play who unknowingly kills his father and marries his mother. Freud believed that a central part of a young boy's feelings at this time is fear that his father will cut off his penis—a fear known as **castration anxiety** (Freud, 1900/1999). According to Freud, hostility toward the father and fear of castration cause tremendous anxiety for the boy, and he eventually decides that, instead of getting rid of his father and marrying his mother, he would rather be like his father. As a result, he learns to identify with the masculine role model in his life and forms his sense of masculine gender identity.

The situation for girls is quite different, according to Freud. As soon as a girl realizes that she doesn't have a penis, she experiences **penis envy**, which she continues to have for the rest of her life (Freud, 1925/1961b). She becomes angry and hostile toward her mother because she blames her mother for her "inferior" anatomy. Instead, she becomes attached to her father—a process Freud's protégée Carl Jung called the **Electra complex**, based on another ancient Greek play in which Electra plots to murder her mother because her mother and stepfather have killed her father (Jung, 1915). According to Freud, the girl never fully resolves her complex because she's never able to get a penis, and so she resigns herself to the inferior status of femininity. Acknowledgment of this inferiority, Freud argued, results in women developing inherently feminine traits—including passivity, narcissism (an arrogant focus on the self), and masochism (the tendency to want to hurt oneself).

Karen Horney and Nancy Chodorow Freud's theories have been widely criticized as being sexist. A focus of this criticism is his insistence that the differences between girls and boys have to do with whether one has or doesn't have a penis and the assumption that the penis is inherently superior. However, over time, some feminist scholars have used Freud's fundamental concepts, particularly his idea of the unconscious, to help explain the perpetuation of men's power (Beardsworth, 2004; Mitchell, 1974).

Karen Horney (1932), a feminist critic of Freud, argued that power inequalities, not biology, cause the psychological differences observed in girls and women. According to Horney, girls don't envy having a penis simply because a penis is superior to a vagina. Instead, they envy what the penis represents—specifically, men's power and ability to have control over their own lives. Horney also stated that men experience **womb envy**—an envy of women's reproductive ability. In fact, she argued that one reason men try to dominate women is because of their fear and awe of women's reproductive capacities.

In the 1970s, during the second wave of the feminist movement, Nancy Chodorow (1978), a feminist sociologist and psychoanalyst, combined psychoanalytic theory and feminist perspectives. She emphasized how the social structure of the family (again assuming a traditional nuclear family) and the gendered division of labor influence the development of gender roles. According to Chodorow, most children develop a primary attachment to the mother because she is typically their primary caregiver and has a strong attachment to her children. Since the father is more likely to be engaged in work outside the home, he is both physically and emotionally distant. Because a girl will recognize that she is similar to her mother, Chodorow claimed, she will never fully disconnect from her mother. A boy, however, must shift from being bonded and intimate with his mother to seeing himself as different from her, thus developing a sense of himself as separate and autonomous. In Chodorow's view, this means that girls grow up to be women who are more comfortable with the role of caregiver and emotional intimacy than men. The fact that boys develop a sense of themselves as separate from others means that they're less likely to be intimately involved in caring for children than girls are. In this way, Chodorow argued, the cycle of the family reproduces itself.

Of course, since the 1970s, many people's ideas about what the "typical" family structure looks like has changed. Not all children are raised in a family with a mother and a father who are heterosexual and follow a traditional division of labor. More contemporary psychoanalytic theorists recognize that all children have the capacity for both feminine and masculine attributes and that gender develops from a dynamic relationship among biological, familial, and cultural factors (Dimen, 2005; Harris, 2005). Moreover, contemporary psychoanalytic theorists acknowledge that children, not just parents, influence how families enact gendered roles. For example, in one study, parents of gender-variant children reported that it was their child, not their own parenting style or familial configuration, that determined their child's gender identity (Ehrensaft, 2011). In such cases, children's gender simply "showed up," and parents had to respond—suggesting that a child can shape the family and familial roles much more than was described in the original conceptualization of psychoanalytic theory (Ehrensaft, 2011, 2014a).

Behavioral and Social Learning Theories

How do behavioral and social learning theories explain gender socialization?

Instead of focusing on unconscious forces, **behavioral theories** consider how aspects of the environment influence behavior. A behavioral approach uses learning theory to understand gender development. For example, the principles of **operant conditioning** suggest that gender develops when certain behaviors are reinforced, or rewarded, and other behaviors are punished. Therefore, according to these principles, gender development occurs when others reinforce behavior that conforms to gender norms and punish behaviors that do not.

The messages that parents send about what is and isn't appropriate are often subtle, and parents may not realize they're doing it. For example, a father may be wildly enthusiastic when his son wants to play football with him but give only a tolerant smile when his son wants to play dolls. Research suggests that children often receive messages that parents don't realize they're sending. In one study of an economically and racially diverse group of pre-school children, researchers asked them to sort toys into "girl toys" and "boy toys" and say whether their parents would approve or disapprove of them playing with the toys (Freeman, 2007, p. 357). The pre-schoolers were easily able to sort the toys and generally thought that their parents wouldn't approve of play that could be categorized as cross-gender. This was especially true of boys. For example, only 9% of the 5-year-old boys said their fathers would approve of them playing with "girl toys." But when the parents themselves were surveyed, they reported considerably more egalitarian attitudes than their children reported. While only 20% of girls said their mothers would approve of them playing with "boy toys," 100% of the mothers actually said they would approve. (Only three fathers participated in this study, so the researchers couldn't accurately assess fathers' approval.) These results suggest that even if parents don't realize what messages they're sending, children can be influenced by the subtle, indirect messages they receive. Also, boys' suspicion that their fathers would disapprove of them playing with "girl toys" might be based in reality. Other researchers have found that fathers, especially fathers of sons, were more likely than mothers to hold explicit attitudes about appropriate gendered behavior, such as refusing to buy a boy a doll or being upset if their son were to dress up in girls' clothing (Endendijk et al., 2013).

Parents also may not be aware of how their own gendered behaviors influence their children's gender socialization process. **Social learning theories** suggest that learning takes place in a social setting even when children aren't directly being reinforced or punished (Bandura, 1971). In particular, **observational learning** occurs when children learn from watching what others do (Bandura, 1971; Bussey & Bandura, 1999). In fact, psychologist Albert Bandura argued that observation is the quickest way for children to learn any new behavior (Bandura, 1971). He made this claim at a time when many children grew up in a traditional nuclear family, watching their mothers cook and clean while their fathers relaxed after work. Although this dynamic continues to be the norm in some families, it's also possible for observation to be a way of teaching gender non-conformity (Chesley, 2011). This has been found in families where the father stays home while the mother works outside of the home. It can also occur in families where both parents work but domestic roles aren't traditionally

Children often model what their parents do, whether it's gender conformity or gender non-conformity. What kinds of gendered behavior do you think you learned from your parents?

divided by gender. For example, in the home of one author of this book, her husband does the vacuuming. One day, when her son was playing house, he announced that he had to vacuum because that's something men do. Being a feminist, she considered this to be a parenting win!

It's important to note that even today our society continues to be androcentric, or male centered. As a result, it values traditionally masculine attributes (e.g., being strong and assertive) more than feminine ones (e.g., being caring and nurturing). Because masculinity is valued more and is associated with more power, masculine behaviors are more likely to receive positive reinforcement. In one study, researchers interviewed an economically and racially diverse group of parents and asked how they felt when their children showed behaviors that didn't conform to gender stereotypes (Kane, 2006). When girls didn't conform and acted tomboyish, parents generally responded in a positive light. One mother noted that her daughter "does a lot of things that a boy would do, and we encourage that" (p. 157). But when boys didn't conform to gender stereotypes, there was much more concern. One father noted: "I don't want him to be a sissy. . . . I want to see him strong, proud, not crying like a sissy" (p. 161). One aspect of this fear was parents' concern that their sons would be perceived as gay if they appeared to be too feminine.

A similar dynamic was seen when parents were asked what types of books their children preferred (Wagner, 2017). Parents stated that their daughters would enjoy books starring both female and male protagonists. However, they felt that their sons would only enjoy books starring male protagonists. In this way, parental attitudes can reinforce and encourage behaviors and interests unevenly. While masculine activities and traits are encouraged in both boys and girls, feminine traits and activities are only encouraged in girls. This further reinforces the idea that masculine characteristics are more valuable.

Cognitive Developmental Theories

How do cognitive developmental theories explain gender socialization?

Behavioral theories tend to emphasize how the environment shapes children's behaviors. But children aren't passive recipients of reinforcement and punishment. They're thinking beings who try to make sense of the world around them. Children are "gender detectives," constantly trying to figure out what being a girl or boy means for them (Martin & Ruble, 2004, p. 67). Cognitive approaches focus less on reinforcements and punishments and more on what children are thinking and assuming about their gender roles. According to psychologists, children engage in a process of **self-socialization** (Zosuls et al., 2009). In other words, they don't need parents to tell them how to behave; instead, they continually look for clues and figure it out themselves.

In *Delusions of Gender*, psychologist Cordelia Fine (2010) asks readers to imagine a world where right-handers and left-handers are separated and marked as much as girls and boys currently are. Can you imagine if left-handed babies were dressed in pink clothing and right-handed babies in blue clothing? What if only left-handed babies had bibs, pacifiers, and cribs decorated with flowers and fairies, while right-handed babies had these things decorated with trucks and footballs? In this imaginary world, children would almost certainly figure out that handedness is an important part of who they are, given the amount of attention paid to the distinction. And so it is with gender.

Children are smart. They quickly figure out that gender is one of the most important distinguishing variables for people (Horn, 2007; Martin et al., 2002). Very early on, children are able to distinguish between girl and boy. For example, infants can distinguish female and male voices by 6 months of age, and female and male faces or photographs by 9 to 10 months of age (Levy & Haaf, 1994; Quinn, Yah, Kuhn, Slater, & Pascalis, 2002). Babies also learn stereotypes about gender at very early ages. In one study, researchers found that children as young as 18 months associated male faces with stereotypically masculine items such as a fire hat, pants, and a hammer, as well as metaphorically masculine items such a bear and a fir tree (Eichstedt, Serbin, Poulin-Dubois, & Sen, 2002). In an earlier study, researchers found that by 26 months, children put pictures related to fire fighting and truck driving with a picture of a man and pictures of laundry, cooking, and sewing with a picture of a woman (Weinraub et al., 1984). Overall, these findings strongly suggest that babies figure out that gender is a very important social category and, in some cases, learn to distinguish on the basis of this category even before they can speak.

Cognitive developmental theories emphasize that children's understanding of gender goes through stages corresponding to the development of cognitive skills and that children are active participants in their attempt to understand and take on gender roles. In this view, after children learn to distinguish women from men and girls from boys, they learn to label people and things by gender. **Gender labeling**, or the ability to say whether someone is female or male, is often assessed by having young children sort photographs of girls, boys, women, and men into categories. This ability is generally achieved by 30 months (Fagot, Leinbach, & Hagan, 1986; Halim & Ruble, 2010) and, according to one study, may develop as early as 17 months (Zosuls et al., 2009). Children's ability to gender label is closely tied to their ability to label their own gender. When this occurs, children have gained a sense of gender identity, and this generally involves labeling oneself within a gender binary as a girl or a boy. Most children develop this skill between 2 and 3 years of age (Halim & Ruble, 2010; Ruble & Martin, 1998).

The very fact that psychologists have designed studies to explore when children are able to gender label and how children learn to stereotype by gender can be seen as supporting a gender binary. This is because such studies require participants to indicate if they are a girl or a boy, rather than offering a wider array of identity options (Fine, 2010). In this way, such research supports the binary both for participants' families as well as for those who later read about the research. The growing awareness of children who don't clearly label themselves as a girl or a boy has called into question the way in which psychologists research children's thinking about gender.

Recent work has shown that developing gender identity can be a tremendously stressful process for children who aren't cisgender because of the predominant view that there are only two genders (Cicero & Wesp, 2017; Devor, 2004). For intersex children, the stress can be almost intolerable. In fact, Accord Alliance, the largest organization in the United States dedicated to advocacy for intersex children, recommends that children have a gender assignment of either F or M at birth because it is so hard to live in U.S. society without a gender assignment (Consortium on the Management of Disorders of Sex Development, 2006). According to this view, even if parents and children reject rigid notions of gender, they would be better off choosing a gender assignment in order to make it easier for children to function in mainstream society. This shows how pervasive the gender binary is and how it influences the choices parents make as well as the ways researchers ask questions.

Once children have established a gender identity, they usually accept that identity and start acting in accordance with gender norms (Martin & Ruble, 2004). In order to figure out how to act, children develop a *gender schema*, or a network of assumptions about how people with different genders are supposed to think, feel, and act (Bem, 1983). **Gender schema theory** focuses on how children integrate this network of assumptions about gender with their understanding of themselves (Bem, 1983). Their schemas generally involve stereotypes about what it means to behave in accordance with socially acceptable gender-aligned behaviors. As we'll see, when these schemas first develop during the pre-school years, they can be quite rigid (Martin, Ruble, & Szkrybalo, 2002).

Most children develop a sense of **gender constancy**. This is the understanding that even if a change in physical appearance takes place, a girl will still be a girl and a boy will still be a boy. So even if a girl wears pants or cuts her hair short, she'll still be a girl. And even if a boy grows his hair long, wears a dress, or puts on nail polish (aspects of appearance typically associated with femininity and girl-ness), he'll still be a boy. Gender constancy generally occurs by the time children enter elementary school (Ruble et al., 2007). Once they realize they'll remain girls or boys no matter what they do, their gender schemas generally become more flexible. In other words, when children figure out that acting in a gender non-conforming way won't turn them into the other gender, they can become more comfortable with people acting in ways that don't reflect traditional gender norms (Halim, Ruble, & Amodio, 2011; Ruble et al., 2007).

Moving forward, it will be interesting to see how gender-diverse children might disrupt the traditional notion of gender constancy, especially because adults are supporting more flexibility in thinking about gender now than was true in the past (Blakemore, Berenbaum, & Liben, 2009). For example, some parents tell their children that "not all boys have penises" and "some girls have penises" (Rahilly, 2015, p. 356). One elementary school developed lessons aimed at reducing rigid thinking about gender by discussing princess boys and pregnant men (Ryan, Patraw, & Bednar, 2013). Children in this program subsequently developed less rigid thinking around gender. Moreover, parents of transgender children report different strategies in helping their children navigate the world and the expectations of others (Rahilly, 2015). For example, they let their children define their own gender (e.g., "boygir") and help them understand that while they, as parents, accept their children's gender expression, not everyone will be as accepting. Such flexibility has been shown to reduce anxiety and depression among gender-variant children (Ehrensaft, 2014b). This is one factor that has been shown to contribute to creating a more supportive environment for these children's exploration of their gender identity.

Social Construction Theories

How do social construction theories explain gender socialization?

Social construction theories are based on a **postmodern perspective**. This perspective suggests that knowledge isn't objective; rather, it is constructed and, therefore, can change as a function of time, place, or culture (Gergen, 2001). In this perspective, even very basic ideas that many people think are facts, such as there being only two genders (female and male), are only true in certain social situations (Beall, 1993). For example, India officially recognizes a third gender (hijras—people who were assigned male at birth and are officially recognized as a third sex), and the Navajo Nation recognizes five genders (women, men, hermaphrodites, masculine women, and feminine men; Thomas, 1997). In these cultures, children develop a gender identity accordingly, showing that the concept of gender can be affected by place.

According to **social construction theories**, cultural beliefs about gender exist to uphold particular social and economic systems and inequalities. These beliefs also inform people about how they're supposed to enact gender. For example, by defining masculinity as being dominant and aggressive and femininity as being submissive and nurturing, the gender socialization process in most societies all but guarantees that girls and women will continue to have a lower status than boys and men (Levant & Richmond, 2015). Also, social construction theories emphasize the concept of **doing gender** (i.e., performing or enacting behaviors associated with a specific gender in day-to-day life) rather than *having* a gender

(West & Zimmerman, 1987). In this way, all individuals have the capacity to perform femininity or masculinity, but in a patriarchal society, rewards are generally associated with conforming to traditional gender roles and negative consequences are associated with failure to conform (Levant & Richmond, 2015).

Sources of Gender Socialization

Messages about gender socialization surround us. Often, they're so pervasive that we may not even notice they're there. You may recall that we discussed in Chapter 2 that a fish doesn't notice the water it's swimming in. Sources of gender socialization surround us just as water surrounds that fish. Everything has the potential to contribute to gender socialization, but researchers have identified some major sources. In the following sections, we review the role of the media, toys, parents, peers, and schools in the gender socialization process. It's important to note, though, that research on this topic has largely assumed a gender binary. Little is known about the gender socialization of those with non-binary gender identities. However, some research does indicate that the gender socialization of transgender children typically aligns with their gender identity rather than with the sex they were assigned at birth (Olson, Key, & Eaton, 2015). When matched with cisgender children with the same gender identity, their preferences for peer groups, clothing, and toys have been found to be indistinguishable.

The Media

How do books, television, video games, and social media send messages about gender?

The media constitute a large portion of the water we all swim in, and messages about gender permeate it. There are many categories of media, but here we've chosen to focus on books, television shows, video games, and social media. Our discussion will illustrate how gendered assumptions surround us and can influence us as individuals as well as our understanding of gender as a whole.

Books When you were a child, did you love the stories of Winnie the Pooh? These are charming stories, but did you realize that all the characters, except for Kanga (the kangaroo mother), are male (Blakemore et al., 2009)? The over-representation of boys and men in children's books has been widely studied. For example, when researchers examined award-winning children's books from the 1940s to the 1960s, they found that for every female human character there were 11 male characters (Weitzman, Eifler, Hokada, & Ross, 1972). There were also a whopping 95 male animals for every female animal in these books. Of course, the books examined in this study were published a long time ago. A more recent study of award-winning and best-selling books from 1995 to 2001 found a less extreme gender bias in terms of numbers of girls and boys depicted, but for every book with a female main character there were still 1.8 books with a male main character (Hamilton, Anderson, Broaddus, & Young, 2006). However, disparities in animal representations haven't equalized. In a study of the last hundred years of children's books, researchers found a tendency toward greater equality in the representation of female and male human characters over time but persistent inequality in animal representation (McCabe, Fairchild, Grauerholz, Pescosolido, & Tope, 2011).

Many children's and young adult books lack diversity in other domains too. Early in this chapter, we talked about Marley Dias's difficulty in finding books about Black girls. She's correct that such books are hard to find, but that situation has been changing. For example, the Cooperative Children's Book Center at the University of Wisconsin, Madison, has been counting the number of children's books by and about people of color ("Publishing Statistics on Children's Books," n.d.). In 2016, 22% of children's books were about people of color. This is in contrast to 8.6% from 1994, when the Center started collecting data.

It's not just people of color that are underrepresented in children's books. For example, people with disabilities are almost never portrayed. In one study, researchers found that when they removed people with glasses or pirates with eye patches from the count of those with a disability, only 7% of the books represented individuals with disabilities (Koss, 2015). The majority of those were older people using a wheelchair or a cane. Even when books make an effort to represent diversity, they often do so in a limited way. For example, in an investigation of 68 LGBTQ-themed children's books, almost all characters were White, middle class, and adhering to traditional gender roles (Lester, 2014). In another analysis of LGBTQ-themed children's books, very few stories featured bisexual characters (Epstein, 2014).

Although girls and women are represented more frequently in books now than was true decades ago, they're still mostly shown in traditional roles. One analysis found that adult female characters were largely depicted indoors and working inside the home, while adult male characters were largely depicted outdoors or working outside the home (Hamilton et al., 2006). When women *were* shown working outside the home, they were portrayed in traditionally female jobs (e.g., teacher, flight attendant, librarian) ten times more frequently than in non-traditional jobs (e.g., police officer). In another study, researchers examined how parents were portrayed in children's books (Anderson & Hamilton, 2005). Mothers were much more likely than fathers to be shown as nurturers and as providing hands-on care and emotional support. If fathers were depicted at all, they were generally portrayed as ineffective or distant parents.

There are also differences in the way children are most commonly portrayed (Kortenhaus & Demarest, 1993; Tsao, 2008). Boys, in children's books, are generally go-getters. They use their intelligence to solve problems and overcome adversity. They're described with adjectives like *big*, *horrible*, and *fierce*. Girls, in contrast, are likely to appear in situations where things happen to them rather than in situations where they make things happen. They're often shown as silly and concerned mostly with their appearance, and they're described with adjectives such as *beautiful*, *frightened*, *sweet*, and *weak* (Turner-Bowker, 1996). In an analysis of coloring books published after 1972, boys and men were shown in more active roles such as running, climbing, and rescuing others, while girls and women were likely to be shown sitting or standing and not doing anything, or looking in the mirror (Fitzpatrick & McPherson, 2010). Male characters were also likely to be shown in strong and powerful contexts such as being adults or superheroes; female characters were likely to be shown as children. In another study, girls were 3.3 times more likely to be portrayed performing nurturing behaviors than were boys (Hamilton et al., 2006).

Not all books display girls and boys in such sexist ways. For example, a study of award-winning Australian children's books found little evidence of gender stereotyping (Kok & Findlay, 2006). However, most research finds that stereotyping continues, even if it's subtle. In one study, researchers evaluated books that have been praised as non-sexist (Diekman & Murnen, 2004). Although they showed girls as active go-getters, they failed to show boys with traditionally feminine traits, such as being nurturing and caring. Therefore, even if these books are seen as endorsing gender equality, their unequal portrayal of girls and boys likely promotes the idea that masculine traits are acceptable for girls (and women) but feminine traits are not acceptable for boys (and men). If the books were fully equitable, all characters would display a diverse array of traditionally feminine and masculine traits.

The messages that books convey are important. In one study of mostly White Australian third graders, when children read stories about protagonists with a gender that matched their own (e.g., girls read stories about girls), their self-esteem increased as compared to when they read about a character with a different gender (Ochman, 1996). This finding suggests that simply reading stories with characters that represent one's own gender can benefit self-esteem. In another study conducted in Australia, this one including both White and Aboriginal participants, researchers found that after children were exposed to a counter-stereotypic children's story—for example, about a little girl who gets a model plane and builds a runway for it—girls engaged in less stereotypical play (Green, Bigler, & Catherwood, 2004). However, it may be that non-stereotypical representations can only go so far. Other research suggests that, especially in children with very rigid gender schemas, there's a tendency to misremember information that they read in books in order to make what they've read consistent with the gender stereotypes they already hold (Abad & Pruden, 2013; Frawley, 2008).

Although there has been less research on gendered messages in young adult novels as compared to children's books, an examination of a few of the most popular young adult series shows that characters are often portrayed in stereotyped ways. The Harry Potter series, for example, has been criticized for showing boys having adventures while girls spend time being studious (Mayes-Elma, 2006). The series has also been criticized for a lack of diversity among the characters (Anne, 2015). Author J. K. Rowling confirmed Dumbledore's status as a gay male character only after the books were published, and other forms of diversity (e.g., religion and race) were never explicitly discussed in the series. When the actress Noma Dumezweni was cast to play Hermione in the London stage play *Harry Potter and the Cursed Child*, there was much controversy because many readers had assumed Hermione was White and objected to a Black actress playing the part (Schaub, 2015). The Twilight series has also been criticized—for glorifying the relationship between a controlling, powerful man and a passive, dependent woman (Silver, 2010).

In contrast, some young adult novels do subvert gender stereotypes. For example, Katniss in the Hunger Games series is a strong and powerful female protagonist (Scott & Dargis, 2012), and Tris from the Divergent series is also a strong character—she jumps on and off moving trains, faces her fears, and becomes a leader of a rebel faction (Bennett, 2014). Both the Hunger Games and the Divergent series have also been praised as promoting gender equality because, even though they star female heroes, they're marketed to both girls and boys (Bell, 2014). Of course, the protagonists in both books are conventionally attractive, heterosexual women whose love interests are central to the plots. Moreover, while Tris sacrifices herself for the cause at the end of the Divergent series, Katniss ends the Hunger Games series getting married—an outcome that can perpetuate the idea that heterosexual coupling should be an ultimate goal for young women.

Television, Movies, and Video Games According to a report from Common Sense Media (Common Sense, 2017), children under age 8 spend over two hours a day watching screens. While television accounts for almost an hour of that time, mobile devices account for an ever-increasing proportion— up from five minutes a day in 2011 to 48 minutes a day in 2017. Levels are even higher for tweens and teens, who spend approximately two hours a day watching television and up to nine hours a day consuming screen-based media once their time on phones, tablets, and computers is added in. This means that, for many hours a day, children are encountering messages about gender from these sources.

Television shows often convey sexist messages about gender. This can be especially true for cartoons. An analysis from the 1930s to the 1990s found that male cartoon characters appeared much more frequently than female characters (Thompson & Zerbinos, 1995). This practice was so widespread that in 1991 the term *Smurfette principle* was coined, in a *New York Times* article, to describe instances in which a single female character exists only in reference to the male characters in a book, movie, or television show (Politt, 1991).

Much like depictions in books, there is an over-representation of White, able-bodied, heterosexual television characters. An analysis of television shows popular with adolescents in 2015 found that Black characters made up approximately 15% of the total characters and women were less than 40% of the total characters. The proportion for Black characters matched that of the number of Black individuals in the U.S. population; but as women make up 50.8% of the U.S. population, female characters were underrepresented (Ellithorpe & Bleakley, 2016). In another analysis, researchers found that among television's most-watched shows from 1987 to 2009, Native American, Asian American, and Latinx characters were all under-represented (Tukachinsky, Mastro, & Yarchi, 2015).

Characters are also portrayed in stereotypical ways. When television's most-viewed shows between 1987 and 2009 were analyzed (Tukachinsky, Mastro, & Yarchi, 2015), it was found that these shows tended to depict Latinx characters as passionate and seductive and Black and Latinx characters as having a poor work ethic. Another, more recent study found that less than 1% of characters on the most-watched television shows have a disability, and 95% of these characters are played by able-bodied actors (Woodburn & Kopić, 2016). Often, the plot revolves around the character's perceived impairment rather than other important aspects of the person's life, like work or relationships.

As with books, male characters in television shows are more likely than female characters to (a) be shown as independent, assertive, and athletic and (b) have paid jobs as opposed to unpaid care-giving roles (Thompson & Zerbinos, 1995). Although this study was conducted over 20 years ago, more recent research reflects a similar pattern. For example, an analysis of tween television shows found that male characters outnumbered female characters 2:1 overall and outnumbered them 3:1 in the action/adventure genre (Gerding & Signorielli, 2014). Female characters were more likely than male characters to be conventionally attractive and more likely to be shown primping or paying attention to their appearance. However, there was no difference between female and male characters in terms of how good they were

your turn

Under-representation of women in the media has led feminists to adopt the *Bechdel test* to assess the presence of female characters in television shows and movies (Garber, 2015). The test gets its name from cartoonist Alison Bechdel, who featured this idea in a 1985 *Dykes to Watch Out For* strip. In order to pass the test, a show or movie must (a) include at least two female characters (b) who have at least one conversation (c) about something other than a man. In 2015, for example, all the Oscar Best Picture nominees were movies about men; only three of the eight films nominated passed the Bechdel test. The winner, *Birdman*, only passed because of a 30-second scene in which two women discussed theater before going on to discuss men. There was improvement in the 2016 and 2017 nominated films. Five of eight 2016 films passed the test (Whitmar, 2016), and seven of the nine 2017 films did (Radic, 2018).

Look at television shows you watch regularly. Also, review the last ten movies you watched. Do any of them pass the Bechdel test? How many? Do your findings motivate you to look differently at the media you consume?

with technology or whether they were likely to rescue others. In another study, researchers asked first and second graders what their favorite shows were and then analyzed the content of those shows (Aubrey & Harrison, 2004). Among these, male characters were more likely to be shown answering questions, showing ingenuity, and eating.

A similar pattern was found in a study of the portrayal of superheroes (Baker & Raney, 2007). There were many findings consistent with gender stereotypes—for example, male superheroes outnumbered female superheroes 2:1, and male superheroes were more likely to express anger while female superheroes were more likely to be emotional, excitable, and superficial. Female superheroes were also portrayed (once again) as concerned about their appearance, and they were highly sexualized. However, female superheroes were just as likely as male superheroes to demonstrate intelligence, bravery, dominance, and technical skills.

Of course, children aren't only exposed to gendered messages through television programming; they're also exposed to these messages in commercials. Research on stereotypes in commercials finds a similar pattern to research on programming. In one older study, researchers found that boys appeared more frequently than girls, took on more dominant roles, and were more active and aggressive (Browne, 1998). Girls were shown as shy, giggly, and silly, and less likely than boys to assert control or take action. In a more recent analysis of fashion advertisements directed at adolescent girls, researchers also found stereotypical racialized gender depictions, including the White beauty ideal, the hypersexual Black woman, and the technologically savvy East Asian woman (Sengupta, 2006).

Some data suggest that gender inequality in TV commercials may be decreasing, at least in some countries (Matthes, Prieler, & Adam, 2016). In the United Kingdom, for example, there was no difference in whether women or men did a voiceover, and women and men were equally likely to be shown at home. In the United States, women and men were equally likely to be shown at home and at work and were equally likely to be shown using electronic products. However, in other countries, such as Germany, some stereotypes were observed more frequently. Interestingly, even in countries known for high levels of gender equality, such as the Netherlands, women were more likely to be portrayed in home settings and in advertisements for beauty products while men were more likely to be portrayed in work settings.

Children also receive sexist messages from movies. For example, in this chapter's Empowering or Oppressing feature, we discuss how Disney movies have sent gendered messages in different ways over the years. Disney movies have also given priority to men in other ways. Linguists Carmen Fought and Karen Eisenhauer presented research at a conference in 2016 analyzing dialogue from Disney movies and reported that, in many, men dominated the vast majority of talk time (Guo, 2016). For example, men spoke 68% of the time in *The Little Mermaid* (which made sense because Ariel lost her voice), 71% of the time in *Beauty and the Beast*, and 90% of the time in *Aladdin*. Even in *Mulan* and *Pocahontas*, where the title characters were women, men spoke 76% and 77% of the time, respectively. It should be noted that even when Mulan was dressed as a man, her utterances counted as a woman speaking. Women do talk more than men in *Brave*, although men talk more in both *The Princess and the Frog* and *Frozen*—even with the latter being about two princesses. Furthermore, children learn racialized sexist stereotypes from these movies. Research has shown that Disney princesses of color (e.g., Jasmine and Pocahontas) are shown with less clothing and more sexual posturing than White Disney princesses (e.g., Belle and Ariel; Lacroix, 2004).

Children also absorb messages about gender from video games. In fact, these messages are just as problematic as those conveyed by television. For example, in an analysis of popular video games, researchers found that female characters were under-represented (Beasley & Standley, 2002). Only 14% of characters were women, and most appeared in one Olympic sports game that included a number of female athletes. There were more characters of an indeterminate gender than there were explicitly female characters. Women in video game magazines are increasingly portrayed as aggressive, but they're also generally shown as either scantily clad, sexualized, or objects of beauty (Beasley & Standley, 2002; Dill & Thill, 2007).

Media viewing has consequences. One study found that 4-year-olds who watched more television were likely to say that other people thought boys were better than girls (Halim, Ruble, & Tamis-LeMonda, 2013). In a longitudinal study, researchers found that children who watched television shows or movies with superheroes were more likely to engage in stereotypically masculine play, such as fighting or using weapons, in the future (Coyne, Linder, Rasmussen, Nelson, & Collier, 2014). Researchers also found that superhero exposure was related to physical aggression one year later, but it wasn't related to more pro-social behavior like helping or defending others—behavior that is also exhibited by superheroes (Coyne et al., 2017). In another study with young children, researchers found that exposure to Disney princesses was related to engaging in more female-stereotypic play (e.g., playing with dolls) a year later, even after controlling for initial levels of stereotypic play (Coyne, Linder, Rasmussen, Nelson, & Birkbeck, 2016).

The sexist portrayal of women in video games also has consequences. In one study, researchers found that men who played video games high in sexist content (e.g., *Grand Theft Auto*) were likely to have benevolent sexist attitudes (Stermer & Burkley, 2015). In a study of over 13,000 girls and boys, ages 11 to 19, in France, researchers found that video game exposure, but not television viewing, was related to increased sexism—for example, endorsing the idea that women's primary role is to have and raise children (Bègue, Sarda, Gentile, Bry, & Roché, 2017).

Social Media Children and adolescents today are coming of age in a rapidly changing media landscape, and social media and photo/video sharing are outpacing other forms of media (Lenhart, Purcell, Smith, & Zickuhr, 2010).

The Modern Disney Princess

The characteristics of the Disney princesses have evolved over the years (England, Descartes, & Collier-Meek, 2011). The older Disney princesses such as Snow White (1938) and Cinderella (1950) were conventionally feminine and passive. They demonstrated these values by doing submissive domestic tasks without complaint and waited to be saved by fairy godmothers, princes, or both. Those from the next generation of Disney princesses were a bit more empowered. Jasmine, from *Aladdin* (1992), could fight; Mulan (1998) dressed as a man and fought in the army; Belle, from *Beauty and the Beast* (1991), was intellectual and brave, although she tolerated violent behavior from the Beast. Ariel, from *The Little Mermaid* (1989), was also more assertive and independent. She enjoyed exploring and was rebellious toward her father. However, she chose to lose her voice for the sake of love and ultimately abandoned her family to keep her prince. Overall, while this generation of princesses showed agentic traits and often acted bravely, they generally, ultimately, settled down with a man. In this way, these movies sent a message that even though other pursuits might be useful, a woman's ultimate goal is to be attractive, find love, and marry a man.

A third generation of Disney princesses seems to send a different message. Princess Tiana, the first (and only) Black princess, from *The Princess and the Frog* (2009), enjoyed her career and was independent and agentic. In *Brave* (2013), Merida rejects her suitors, and the movie concludes with her regaining the love (and humanity) of her mother. In *Frozen* (2013), the "true love's kiss" that saves Anna from being frozen comes from her sister rather than from a man. In this way, these movies present a different message from those before them. The princesses are active and agentic, and marriage is not their only goal.

However, while there's an empowering aspect to the modern Disney princess, there's an oppressive one too. All these princesses are able-bodied, physically idealized, and sexualized. While Merida wasn't overly sexualized in

The way Disney princesses are depicted has changed over the years, but some critics have argued that they still send problematic messages to young girls.

the movie, the marketed doll changed her look to emphasize her sexuality. Elsa is highly sexualized, especially after she leaves Arendell. By the time Elsa has "let it go," she has gone from wearing a conservative dress to wearing a sexy, revealing dress, and walking with a "come-hither" swagger (Stevens, 2014, para. 6). These elements can all be considered oppressive aspects of the princess characters. But, in contrast, it's possible to see Elsa's embracing of her emotions and sexuality as empowering.

Overall, while the modern Disney princess is less gender stereotyped than the earlier ones—she's more active and assertive and might not need a man to be happy—these movies still convey gendered messages about beauty and sexuality. Do you think the modern Disney princess is empowered or oppressed? Are the images empowering or oppressing to young girls? To older women? To mothers? What would it take to have a truly empowered Disney princess?

Some girls take many selfies before deciding which one to post and spend a great deal of time worrying about how many likes and positive comments they get. However, despite its potential drawbacks, social media can foster connection with others. How do you think social media is affecting young women?

According to the Common Sense (2017) media report, children ages 8 to 12 spend about six hours a day consuming media on mobile devices, and those ages 13 to 18 spend about nine hours. Some 13-year-olds report that they check social media 100 times a day. Both girls and boys frequent the Internet at the same rate, but they appear to have different habits (Miller, Schweingruber, & Bradenburg, 2001). In general, girls are more active than boys on Facebook, Twitter, Instagram, and Pinterest (Women's Media Center, 2015). Since Instagram is a photo app, much of the commenting and liking revolves around how girls look. This pattern has the potential to increase young girls' anxiety about how they look and how others perceive them—a topic we'll return to in Chapter 6.

Social media also gives girls an opportunity to compare themselves to other people and, in that way, learn gender norms. In one study, researchers explored the social media use of a diverse group of eighth and ninth graders from schools with students of low to middle socioeconomic status (Nesi & Prinstein, 2015). The researchers found that girls were more likely to use social media than boys, spending a lot of time comparing themselves to and getting feedback from others. This comparing activity was related to increased levels of depression, especially in girls who were ranked by their peers as less popular than others.

However, social media can also help to combat gender stereotypes. For example, in one study, researchers found that girls were just as likely as boys to assume leadership positions online (Cassel, Huffaker, Tversky, & Ferriman, 2006). Another potential benefit of social media is the ability to form supportive communities. This was found to be particularly true for adolescents who are marginalized because of their sexual orientation, gender identity, race/ethnicity, or because they have a disability (Craig, McInroy, McCready, Di Cesare, & Pettaway, 2015). Additional research shows that for members of socially marginalized groups, online venues offer opportunities to build a supportive community and develop strategies to fight back against discrimination (Craig, McInroy, McCready, & Alaggia, 2015). For example, LGBTQ adolescents often use online media to digitally come out (Green, Bobrowicz, & Ang, 2015), and LGBTQ youth of color use social media to help integrate their racial identities and gender identities, which ultimately provides resilience (Singh, 2013). More research is needed to better understand how and when social media involvement can be supportive rather than detrimental.

Toys

What messages do toys send about gender socialization?

In 2015, as described early in this chapter, after pressure from girls like Riley and other consumers, Target stores stopped labeling toy aisles by gender. Despite this move, many of the toys sold there, and elsewhere, continue to be marketed specifically to girls or boys—for example, in pink or blue packaging with pictures of girls or boys on the boxes. In fact, research has found that color can influence a child's willingness to play with a toy. In one study, boys were more willing to play with a blue doll than a pink doll (Wong & Hines, 2015). The researchers theorized that if toys came in gender-neutral colors, there might be more gender-neutral play. However, other research suggests children have preferences that go beyond the color of toys. Specifically, girls preferred dolls and stuffed animals while boys preferred manipulative toys and action figures (Cherney & London, 2006).

Additional research suggests that many toys marketed to girls have different characteristics from those marketed to boys. Toys for girls are likely to involve domestic and nurturing tasks or emphasize physical attractiveness—for example, Easy-Bake Ovens, makeup, tea sets, and doll houses (Blakemore & Centers, 2005). Boys' toys, however, are likely to be violent or dangerous and to involve competition—for example, guns and other weapons, action figures, and footballs. Toys that enhance cognitive or physical skills were seen as either gender-neutral (e.g., LEGO) or moderately masculine (e.g., microscope, erector set, volcano creator, weather forecasting toy). Given the differing characteristics of certain toys, when girls play with those that are explicitly marketed toward them, they gain experience with traditional femininity—such as a focus on personal appearance and domesticity.

In another study, researchers examined toys that were marketed on a Disney website specifically for girls or boys, or to both girls and boys (Auster & Mansbach, 2012). Toys labeled "girls' toys" were likely to be pink and were

Toys are often separated into "girls" and "boys" categories in stores. Do you see any toys on the "girls" shelf that boys might want to play with? How about toys on the "boys" shelf that girls might want to play with? Where are gender-neutral toys placed? What are the consequences of labeling toys in this way?

mainly dolls, cosmetics, and jewelry. The "boys' toys" were more likely to have bold colors and be action toys, weapons, or building toys. Those listed in both the girls and boys categories were likely to resemble boys' toys, implying that girls might play with masculine toys but boys wouldn't be willing to play with girls' toys. In yet another study, researchers examined how girls and boys were portrayed in dolls, action figures, and other products (Halloween costumes and Valentine's Day cards) marketed to children (Murnen, Greenfield, Younger, & Boyd, 2016). Girls in these products were likely to appear in sexualized poses and wear decorative or revealing clothing. Boys were likely to be wearing functional clothing (e.g., a uniform) and were often portrayed with a weapon or some other sign of violence or aggression (e.g., hands in fists). The authors summarized their findings in the title of their article: "Boys Act and Girls Appear."

In response to these trends, some companies have been marketing engineering products toward girls. For example, LEGO Friends, or "pink" LEGO, are explicitly marketed for girls. However, LEGO Friends has been criticized because the scenes are often traditionally feminine (e.g., pet salons, horse stables, and bakeries) and because many of the sets come partially assembled, making them less challenging than comparable sets marketed to boys (Dockterman, 2014). LEGO Friends has also been criticized for having figures such as Stephanie and Olivia who are very slim, a striking deviation from the typically square, largely male, figures (Milmo, 2012). Other companies, too, are marketing engineering toys for girls. For example, GoldieBlox building sets feature a book that stars a female character solving a problem by building something (Causer, 2013). The instructions for building are embedded in a story, the idea being to capitalize on girls' verbal skills. Even though toys like these are changing the aisles that used to consist primarily of dolls and kitchen sets, their marketing still reflects problematic assumptions. These include the assumptions that girls have to be lured into playing with building toys by coloring them pink and purple, combining them with reading, and constructing traditionally feminine spaces.

Parents

How do parents send messages to their children about gendered expectations?

Most parents would probably say they want to treat their children similarly regardless of their gender identity, and a meta-analysis of 172 studies has suggested that in terms of love, warmth, and affection, the similarities do outweigh the differences (Lytton & Romney, 1991). However, one major difference was found in the way parents treated their children: Parents encouraged gender-typed activities and play. Even though this meta-analysis was conducted over 25 years ago, its findings are still relevant, as the following discussion will show.

One domain in which parents treat children differently is chores. In one study, researchers found that girls were expected to do feminine-type chores such as helping to care for younger siblings and cooking, while boys were generally expected to do masculine-type chores such as taking out the trash and mowing the lawn (Raley & Bianchi, 2006). In another study, researchers found that when mothers were under work stress, they tended to rely more on their daughters than their sons (Crouter, Head, Bumpus & McHale, 2001). This even happened when the daughter had an older brother. In terms of this division of household labor, it's important to emphasize that children learn through observation. Given that most mothers do more of the domestic labor than fathers, even if both parents work full-time outside of the home (Coltrane, 2000; a topic we'll return to in Chapter 8), children learn about who is responsible for certain chores even if the parents aren't explicitly teaching them (Sinno & Killen, 2009, 2011). This pattern is less likely to occur with children of LGBTQ parents. In fact, researchers have found that children of gay and lesbian parents tend to have more egalitarian views of gender relations—largely because they likely aren't witnessing a typically gendered division of household labor in their family (Fulcher, Sutfin, & Patterson, 2008).

Parents also shape children's emotional experiences in gendered ways. Although some parents may have explicit gendered rules about emotions (e.g., boys aren't allowed to cry), other parents may influence their children's emotional expressions in more subtle ways. In one study, researchers followed a group of children from age 4 to age 6 (Chaplin, Cole, & Zahn-Waxler, 2005). While observing play sessions between the children and both the mother and the father, the researchers noted the extent to which the parents paid attention to different kinds of emotion. They found that parents, especially fathers, paid more attention to submissive emotions, such as sadness and anxiety, in girls and to aggressive emotions, such as anger, in boys. In another study, researchers examined emotional expression among Native American, Black, and White families and found that mothers responded more favorably to girls who showed sadness than to boys who did so (Brown, Craig, & Halberstadt, 2015).

Additional data suggest that parents, especially fathers, treat girls and boys differently in terms of allowing them to take risks. In one study, researchers asked predominantly White, middle-class, pre-school children to walk on a catwalk 5 feet above the ground and observed the level of parental monitoring (Hagan & Kuebli, 2007). Fathers more closely monitored daughters than sons. Mothers monitored their sons and daughters equally. In another study, mothers of 11-month-old infants estimated how steep a slope their child could climb down (Mondschein, Adolph, & Tamis-LeMonda, 2000). They estimated correctly for their sons, but they underestimated their daughters' abilities considerably. Moreover, as children become older and more independent, parents may set different standards for what is appropriate and how independent the children are allowed to be (Bulcroft, Carmody, & Bulcroft, 1996). For example, parents across a range of ethnic groups were found to be less comfortable leaving their middle- to late-adolescent daughters at home alone than their sons.

In other studies, researchers have found that parental gender socialization patterns are related to social class, race, and religion. For example, in one study of Black parents, researchers found that both mothers and fathers expressed support for gender equality (Hill, 2002). However, those who were below middle-class status or who had recently reached middle-class status had more traditional gender socialization practices. Because religiosity was found to be related to social class in this study, the researchers theorized that religious beliefs may have influenced the parents' decision to socialize their children in more traditional ways. One mother who was college educated but had grown up in a poor family expected her daughter to be a warrior and to fight against racial injustice while also being a lady who sat and carried herself properly. One reason she emphasized ladylike behavior was fear that any display of loud or assertive behavior on the part of her daughter would trigger discrimination and feed into the negative stereotype of the angry Black woman.

LGBTQ parents tend to convey more gender-egalitarian messages to their children, possibly because they have more flexible attitudes toward gender themselves (Fulcher et al., 2008; Goldberg, 2007). One study showed that 2- to 4-year-old children with lesbian and gay parents engaged in much less gender-stereotyped play than children of heterosexual parents (Goldberg, Kashy, & Smith, 2012). In fact, similar gender flexibility was seen in children of both lesbian and heterosexual parents who held egalitarian attitudes and practiced an equal division of labor in the home (Fulcher et al., 2008). Parental attitudes were more strongly related to the children's beliefs about gender than their sexual orientation. These differences indicate that how gender is socialized differs from family to family and often reflects other aspects of the family's identity, beliefs, and values.

Peers

How does interaction with peers shape gender development?

One of the biggest factors associated with peer socialization is **gender segregation**. This is the tendency for children to segregate on the basis of actual or perceived gender identity (Fromberg, 1999; Martin, Eisenbud, & Rose, 1995). It starts in pre-school and continues throughout the life span. Generally, children only spend 10% of their time with peers who don't share their gender identity (Fabes, Martin, & Hanish, 2003; Martin et al., 2013). Given this tendency, gender segregation can be especially difficult for gender-variant children, who are often excluded, teased, and bullied (Berlan, Corliss, Field, Goodman, & Austin, 2010).

Girls and boys generally engage in different styles of play. Girls tend to play in groups of two or three, and their play is usually more cooperative than boys'

(Lever, 1976; Maccoby, 1998). Boys tend to play outdoors in larger groups and in more competitive games. Gender segregation may occur because of these gender-typed activities—for example, girls seeking out cooperative games such as make-believe, jump rope, or hand-clapping games, and boys choosing rough-and-tumble play or football games (Martin et al., 2013). In fact, girls and boys tend to seek out playmates of their own gender no matter what activities they're doing (Martin et al., 2013). These peer socialization groups have the potential to matter because the more time children spend with same-gender peers, the more gender-typed their behavior becomes (Martin & Fabes, 2001). This phenomenon is known as *dosage-dependent effects*.

Of course, girls and boys do sometimes enter each other's play areas, but this is often as a form of torment and teasing. They may accuse each other of having cooties, or they may play chasing games (Thorne, 1993; Thorne & Luria, 1986). This type of interaction has been called **borderwork** because it reinforces the invisible border between girls' spaces and boys' spaces. In order to more fully understand borderwork, one group of researchers observed children playing at a summer day camp over a nine-week period (McGuffey & Rich, 1999). They found that the most popular boys were allowed to break gender stereotypes, but those boys actively policed other girls and boys. Interestingly, the observations also showed that race and social class intersected with gender. The boys engaged in cross-race and cross-class play. The girls, however, only crossed racial or class lines when a boy threatened a girl or when a girl succeeded against a male competitor.

your turn

Who was popular in your school? What were some of the characteristics of popular students? Did this change from elementary to middle to high school? Was the students' popularity based on attributes that aligned with gender-specific characteristics? Were they financially secure? As you got older, were popular students more sexually active than unpopular students? What does all this say about characteristics that our society values?

An examination of the characteristics of children identified as "popular" reveals what other children consider valuable (Lease, Kennedy, & Axelrod, 2002). Popular girls and boys do share many of the same characteristics. For example, they both tend to be bright, socially skilled, and financially well off. But differences were found in terms of certain characteristics. For example, for girls, popularity was more associated with being physically attractive. Boys, in contrast, were more likely to have high status if they were athletic and seen as dominant.

Schools

How do schools promote gender socialization, and how does race influence this?

Research suggests that many teachers have different expectations for girls and boys in terms of both academic performance and behavior. For example, teachers are more likely to praise girls for being neat and tidy and to praise boys for academic

These girls' style of dress would violate the dress code in many schools. Do you think they have a right to dress the way they want, or do you feel that certain clothing is inappropriate for a school setting? What are the consequences of the policing of girls' bodies that often occurs when school dress codes are strictly enforced?

achievements (Skelton, Carrington, Hutchings, Read, & Hall, 2009). A theme in research on teacher attitudes is the tendency to see girls as succeeding through diligence and hard work but to see boys as being naturally intelligent (Skelton, 2006). So when boys don't achieve, it's considered to be a result of laziness or boredom and as a problem that needs teacher intervention.

These different patterns occur even when teachers say they treat children similarly. In one study, White third-grade teachers from the United States said they treated children equally (Garrahy, 2001). However, because boys were expected to be rambunctious, they were more likely to be allowed to talk out of turn, whereas when girls talked out of turn, they were more likely to be reprimanded.

One teacher reinforced gender stereotypes by letting the boys choose the research topic for the class. This led to the assignment of researching a sports hero, but the library only had books about female athletes who engaged in traditionally feminine sports (e.g., figure skating and gymnastics).

The term **hidden curriculum** refers to the ways the school environment indirectly teaches norms, beliefs, and values. In several studies, researchers have observed a hidden curriculum in terms of social roles related to gender, race, and class (Anyon, 2006; Hemmings, 2000; Langhout & Mitchell, 2008). Examples of the hidden curriculum include dress codes and disciplinary practices.

Schools tend to enforce dress codes more strictly for girls than for boys. Often, the enforcement is humiliating—girls are inspected, sometimes in front of others, and frequently sent home for violating the code. Schools often report enforcing dress codes because they don't want (male) students

try it for yourself

Did you have to follow a dress code in your middle or high school? If so, was it enforced differently for girls and for boys? What did you think of it? Ask a diverse group of your friends about their experiences with dress codes. Were their experiences similar to or different from yours? How do you suppose their gender, racial/ethnic background, social class, or sexual orientation affected the way they experienced school dress codes? How did aspects of your own social identity impact the way you experienced them?

to be "distracted" by girls wearing revealing clothing (Bates, 2015). But this practice teaches girls that it's their responsibility to protect themselves against harassment rather than the boys' responsibility not to harass.

Another example of the hidden curriculum is the disciplinary code (Langhout & Mitchell, 2008). There is evidence that Black girls are particularly likely to face discrimination in school, and this sets a norm about who are considered to be troublemakers. Black girls are, in fact, disproportionally disciplined more than Black boys, even though Black boys are suspended more than any other group. However, Black boys are only suspended three times more often than White boys (Crenshaw, Ocen, & Nanda, 2015). Black girls, in contrast, are suspended six times more often than White girls. Research suggests that bias and stereotypes play a role in these practices (Blake, Butler, Lewis, & Darensbourg, 2011; Skiba, Michael, Nardo, & Peterson, 2002). Black students are more likely than White students to be sent to the school office for behavioral infractions that are subjective, such as excessive talking and disrespect (Skiba et al., 2002). Although this research was initially done with boys, researchers in a subsequent study found that Black girls are also more likely to be sanctioned for subjective infractions, such as defiance (Blake et al., 2011). Black girls are also more likely to receive sanctions that take them out of the classroom and interrupt their learning. In contrast, White girls are most likely to be referred for truancy (e.g., not being in class). Moreover, Black girls with darker skin tones are more likely to be suspended than Black girls with lighter skin tones (Hannon, DeFina, & Bruch, 2013).

Some scholars believe Black girls are more likely to be punished because they're seen as disobedient and unruly, and teachers may punish them for acting in ways that challenge traditional ideas of femininity. For example, researchers have found that Black girls were more likely to be disciplined for inappropriate dress and inappropriate language than White and Latinx girls (Blake et al., 2011). In another study, researchers found that adults from various racial/ethnic backgrounds and different educational levels reported that compared to their White peers, Black girls needed less nurturance and protection because they were perceived as more independent and

spotlight on . . .

Transgender Students in the Classroom

Educators from organizations like QuERI (The Queering Education Research Institute) have reported an increase in calls from elementary school principals claiming that teachers are "freaking out" about "what to do" with transgender children in their classrooms (Payne & Smith, 2014, pp. 399 and 406). One area of concern is bathrooms. While some elementary schools have moved toward gender-neutral bathroom options, according to newspaper reports, the majority of schools have not (Goodyear, 2016). Although Title IX protects students' right to use the bathroom that aligns with their gender identity, there have been cases of parents challenging school districts, enraged about transgender students using bathrooms aligned with their gender identity rather than with the sex assigned at birth (Parks, 2016).

What responsibility does a school have to protect the rights of transgender students? Should gender-neutral bathrooms be more widely available? What would you do if you were the teacher of a transgender student?

more knowledgeable about adult topics (Epstein, Blake, & González, 2017). Black girls have also reported feeling that their academic achievements are unrecognized or unappreciated, possibly because these girls are seen as more self-reliant and less needy of positive feedback: "[G]irls who do well just kind of get overlooked. [T]here is rarely anything done to celebrate them or to encourage them to keep going" (Crenshaw et al., 2015, p. 32).

Because of the hidden curriculum, girls can experience school differently from boys, and this experience can depend on other aspects of their social identities. In one study, researchers examined the educational experiences of working- and middle-class White and Latinx high school girls who were successful in college-prep courses (Bettie, 2002). Both groups of students were aware that their social class set them apart from their wealthier peers, so they made deliberate decisions to use less makeup or to wear conservative clothing as a way to appear "nice" and "not hard" and, in this way, to display themselves as upwardly mobile (p. 419). Both groups also expressed ambivalence about surpassing their parents' academic ability. However, Latinx students also had to cope with peer distancing due to perceptions that they were "acting White" (p. 419).

Stages of Gender Development

Gender socialization starts early, even before birth. In this section, we'll discuss how gender socialization practices manifest during different developmental stages—from infancy to toddlerhood, and through childhood and adolescence. As you read this section, it will be helpful to think about the theories we reviewed in the first part of the chapter, as well as the various sources of gender socialization, to better understand how they influence children and adolescents at each stage of development.

It's a . . . BABY

How does gender socialization start before children are even born?

Parents and their doctors have used ultrasound to determine the sex of a fetus since the 1960s (Hvistendahl, 2012). It's now a routine part of obstetrical care for women in developed countries. Although ultrasound is a medical tool intended to help identify potential abnormalities, it's also regularly used to assign a sex to a developing fetus. There's not a great deal of data on what percentage of parents wish to know the sex of their unborn child. A 2004 study, however, found that 58% of both mothers and fathers getting prenatal ultrasounds planned to find out the sex of their child (Shipp et al., 2004). And in 2007, a Gallup poll found that 66% of pregnant women between the ages of 18 and 35 wanted to know the sex of their baby before giving birth (Carroll, 2007).

Unfortunately, in many cultures, identifying the sex of a fetus might be done in order to allow for decisions to selectively abort female children. In fact, since 1970, 163 million girls have been aborted by families who prefer sons (Hvistendahl, 2012). In China, where a one-child policy was in effect from 1979 to 2015, this resulted in a ratio of 121 boys for every girl. However, selective abortion for sex also happens in Western cultures, including the United States. The implications of this practice are serious. When boys outnumber girls in the population, there will be millions of men who will want wives but be unable to find them; and in places where this already has occurred, the gender imbalance has caused increased rates of sex trafficking (Hvistendahl, 2012).

Most parents are excited about the prospect of having a healthy baby no matter the sex of the child. However, a great deal of emphasis is still placed on finding out the sex. Recently, it has become trendy to host a "gender-reveal party," where expectant parents invite family and friends over to find out the sex of their unborn baby. One idea for these parties is to give the ultrasound results (without looking at them) to a local bakery with instructions to bake a cake or cupcakes with neutral-colored frosting on the outside and either pink or blue frosting on the inside. Once friends and family come over, the expectant parents cut into the cake or bite into the cupcake to find out if they're having a girl or a boy (DeLoach, n.d.). Other ways to do this include having a balloon or piñata filled with pink or blue confetti, or covering cans of Silly String that will reveal themselves to be pink or blue when sprayed (bumpreveal, 2017). The very fact that these parties exist highlights the early start of gender socialization—even the use of the phrase *gender reveal* in relation to finding out the baby's *sex* reflects a mainstream assumption that gender and sex are the same and that every baby will be clearly identifiable as a girl or a boy. As we discussed in Chapter 4, these are overly simplistic assumptions.

Even before babies are born, there are different expectations for girls and boys. In one study, parents were asked to recall what sex they had been hoping for when planning to have a child (Kane, 2009). Men tended to want a son to play sports with, and mothers wanted a son so their husbands would have a companion for activities. These responses reflect an assumption that girls can't play sports or enjoy the same activities as their fathers. Daughters were desired for other reasons. Mothers reported being excited to have a girl so they could dress her up, buy her dolls, and take her to dance classes. Mothers also assumed that daughters would provide a greater level of emotional intimacy and connection than sons would. This assumption is consistent with Chodorow's view that girls stay emotionally connected to their mothers while boys separate from them. It can be said that children are not born into a gender-neutral world; even before birth there are many assumptions about what they'll be like.

People tend to see an infant's sex as the most important piece of information about the newborn. One study showed that, more than 80% of the time, the first question asked by friends and family about infants was their sex (Karraker, Vogel, & Lake, 1995). For many people, this information influences how they perceive the infant and how they'll subsequently interact with the child. For example, as one early study showed, within the first 24 hours after being born, infant girls are more likely than infant boys to be described as little (Rubin, Provenzano, & Luria, 1974; also see Fausto-Sterling, Coll, & Lamarre, 2012). In another study, researchers interviewed mothers and fathers one day after the birth of their children. Newborn girls were rated as less strong, more delicate, and as having finer features than newborn boys, even though there was no observable difference in the features of the baby girls and boys (Karraker et al., 1995).

Evidence for the different treatment of girls and boys continues in analyses of cards that congratulate parents on the birth (Bridges, 1993; Willer, 2001). Cards acknowledging a baby girl are likely to use words like *sweet, precious,* and *dear.* Words on cards for a baby boy are more likely to include *bold, brave,* and *tough.* Cards acknowledging a boy are also likely to show sports equipment or a vehicle, and baby boys are generally pictured in more active positions than girls. Even the cards' emotional tones can differ. Cards about girls feature more expressions of love, while cards about boys have more expressions of joy and pride.

A famous series of studies from the 1970s and 1980s, known as the Baby X studies, found that people make very different assumptions about babies that they think are girls as opposed to those they think are boys (Seavey, Katz, & Zalk, 1975; Sidorowicz & Lunney, 1980). In these studies, participants were asked to interact with a baby in gender-neutral clothing who they were told was either a girl or a boy.

your turn

If you or your partner became pregnant, would you want to know your baby's sex before the actual birth? Why or why not? How do you think others would react if you told them you didn't want to know, or share with them, your baby's sex?

If you are a parent, what choices did you make in regard to learning of and sharing your baby's sex? What factors influenced your decisions?

How can knowing in advance influence the way you would or did interact with your infant? How might this knowledge change the way other people would interact with your baby, or even with you, before the actual birth?

In another condition, the participants weren't told the baby's sex and were asked to guess. The first study used a baby girl in all conditions (Seavey et al., 1975), and the second study used many different babies, both girls and boys (Sidorowicz & Lunney, 1980). In all cases, when participants thought the baby was a girl, they were likely to give them a doll; when they thought the baby was a boy, they were likely to give them a miniature football. When asked to guess the sex of the gender-neutral babies, they made guesses based on gender stereotypes. For example, a male participant interacting with a male baby said, "She is female and female infants smile more" (Sidorowicz & Lunney, 1980, p. 71). A female participant interacting with a male infant said, "She is a girl and girls are more satisfied and accepting" (p. 71). It didn't matter whether the baby was actually a girl or a boy. Evidently, the only thing that mattered in terms of the participants' responses was how the babies were labeled. These studies were conducted more than 30 years ago; do you think researchers would find similar results if the studies were repeated today?

The Pre-school Years

How do pre-school children show evidence of rigid gender schemas, and how is this related to cognitive development?

During the pre-school years, children transition from being babies who don't know about gender expression to being youngsters who are likely to express extremely rigid views about gender. This is an important time from the cognitive perspective because gender identity develops around age 2 (Halim & Ruble, 2010). At this age, children learn about the traditional stereotypes associated with each gender. For example, by age two and a half, many children say that dolls are for girls and trucks are for boys (Ruble, Martin, & Berembaum, 2006). As they become more cognitively sophisticated, the stereotypes they hold also become more sophisticated. For example, by 5 years of age they begin to associate personality traits with gender. They might say things like "girls are gentle" and "boys are adventurous" (Powlishta, Sen, Serbin, Poulin-Doubois, & Eichstedt, 2001), and they're likely to describe girls in terms of their appearance and boys in terms of their activity (Miller, Lurye, Zosuls, & Ruble, 2009).

The stereotypes that pre-school children incorporate into their gender schemas tend to be rigid and inflexible (Martin et al., 2002; Martin & Ruble, 2004; Trautner et al., 2005). If you've ever interacted with 4-year-olds, you may have noticed that they can act as gender police, saying, for example, that

Pre-schoolers can often act as gender police, monitoring and correcting gendered behavior.

only girls are allowed to like pink and only boys are allowed to like Spider-Man. Many children this age don't seem to understand that there can be individual differences and variation—that not all girls or boys like the same things or do the same activities. In one study, most 5- and 6-year-old participants were likely to say that various gender-typed activities are done *only* by girls or by boys rather than *mostly* by girls or by boys (Trautner et al., 2005). These activities included playing with dolls, cooking, knitting, being affectionate, and giving hugs (feminine stereotypes) as well as playing with toy models, playing with trucks, and playing soccer (masculine stereotypes). Other research has shown that gender-stereotyped play increases after children are able to cognitively understand gender categories, and these patterns are similar across a variety of racial/ethnic groups (Zosuls, Ruble, & Tamis-LeMonda, 2014).

Psychologists say that children at this age have **gender rigidity**, or strict gender typing, and a sense of inflexibility in terms of what girls and boys are supposed to do (Martin & Ruble, 2004). Gender rigidity is found in both cisgender and transgender children (Olson et al., 2015). For transgender children, the rigid guidelines for their own gendered behavior correspond to their gender identity rather than the sex assignment made at birth. Gender rigidity is also consistent across racial and ethnic groups. In one study, researchers followed Black, Mexican, and Dominican children from the ages of 3 to 5, studying appearance, play, and friend choices (Halim, Ruble, Tamis-LeMonda, & Shrout, 2013). The researchers found similar levels of gender rigidity that peaked between 3 and 4 years of age before decreasing in children of all three racial/ethnic groups. One area in which gender rigidity was apparent was friendship choice, as gender rigidly influences who children want to interact with. Another study of ethnically diverse 5-year-olds found that most had very stereotypical views of gender differences and weren't interested in cross-gender play or interaction; these findings were consistent across ethnic groups (Halim, Ruble, Tamis-LeMonda, Shrout, & Amodio, 2017).

The pre-school years are also a time when parents of transgender and gender non-conforming children have to decide if they'll reveal their child's identity to their child-care facility (Picket, 2015). From kindergarten to twelfth grade, schools are often hostile places for transgender students (Kosciw, Greytak, Palmer, & Boesen, 2014; Reisner et al., 2015). As mentioned in Chapter 4, the prevalence of school-related bullying and discrimination directed at gender-diverse children is well documented (Greytak, Kosciw, & Boesen, 2013; Grossman & D'Augelli, 2006; Grossman et al., 2009; Reisner et al., 2015). Unfortunately, these problems are also faced by families interacting with pre-schools and day-care facilities. In one study, teachers reported feeling fear and anxiety about having a transgender child in their class, and these feelings can limit the potential for flexibility in gender socialization in the classroom (Payne & Smith, 2014). One parent of a transgender child described the difficulty of informing her child's pre-school that despite being assigned F at birth, her child identified as a boy (Kleman, 2015). The pre-school staff respected that identification and were open to learning more about gender non-conformity, even taking an interest in the child's gender journey. When the family moved, however, it was harder to find a pre-school that would accept their son's decision. At one school, they were lectured about teaching their 4-year-old how to control unwanted urges, and another school informed them that it didn't have to follow gender discrimination laws because it was a private pre-school.

Middle Childhood

How do gender roles become more flexible (for girls) in elementary school?

In elementary school, many young girls go through a transition in the way they enact their gender identity. While extreme femininity and pink frilly dresses are the norm for many pre-school girls (Halim & Ruble, 2010), they're much less common in the elementary school years. Instead, quite a few young girls reject expressions of femininity and begin to identify as tomboys (Halim et al., 2011). In fact, retrospective research indicates that one half to two thirds of women recall being tomboys in childhood (Burn, O'Neil, & Nederend, 1996; Morgan, 1998). Other studies of elementary school age children reflect a similar picture, with approximately one third to one half identifying as tomboys (Halim et al., 2011; Martin & Dinella, 2012).

Several cognitive developments are associated with this shift from a rigid adherence to femininity to being a tomboy. One is that elementary school children become less rigid about stereotypes in general (Halim et al., 2011). Children at this age learn to distinguish between knowledge of a stereotype and belief that people always act or should act in accordance with that stereotype (Halim & Ruble, 2010). This is the same realization that Riley, the girl mentioned early in the chapter, had when she noted that not all girls like princesses and not all boys like superheroes. (Riley was only 4, so she was clearly precocious.) Furthermore, gender flexibility has been found to go hand in hand with gender constancy (Halim et al., 2011; Ruble et al., 2007). In other words, girls realize

spotlight on . . .

A Gender-Neutral Pre-school

In 1996, Sweden opened its first gender-neutral pre-school (Barry, 2018). Instead of participating in gender-specific activities, children were encouraged to play with one another and with all types of toys. Instead of gendered pronouns, teachers used the newly developed gender-neutral Swedish pronoun *hen*. Although there was some backlash about this (Tagliabue, 2012), the national pre-school curriculum in Sweden now requires teachers to actively counter traditional gender socialization. Pre-schools that, for example, encourage boys to dance and girls to yell can be found throughout Sweden (Barry, 2018). Further, the gender-neutral pronoun *hen* is now commonly used.

However, traditional gender socialization cannot be fully eliminated; it's difficult to counteract the hundreds of gender-specific messages children are exposed to outside of school. Research on such pre-schools has shown that children are more likely to play with peers of different genders and are less likely to endorse gender stereotypes than those in traditional pre-schools, but they still notice gender (Shutts, Kenward, Falk, Ivegran, & Fawcett, 2017). Though there are limits to what a school can do in terms of encouraging gender-neutral childhood experiences, do you think this is worth pursuing? Why or why not? Would you support a school like this in your community? Would you enroll your children?

they don't have to act feminine to still be a girl. They don't have to worry that acting like a boy will turn them into one. This allows a loosening of gender stereotypes as it combines with the cognitive realization that individual differences matter and not all girls or boys are alike.

Interestingly, it's only girls who loosen their gender stereotypes and rules about appropriate gendered behavior, and even this loosening has limits. Elementary school boys are often under enormous pressure to adhere to strict gender expressions (O'Neil & Luján, 2009), and homophobic slurs are usually used by peers to enforce this conformity (Horn, 2007; Phoenix, Frosh, & Pattman, 2003; Plummer, 2001). In a study of elementary school students in the United Kingdom, researchers found that gender-conforming boys and gender non-conforming girls were the most popular, indicating the valuing of masculine traits and the devaluing of feminine ones (Braun & Davidson, 2017). Gender non-conforming boys were considered the least popular.

According to one study, elementary school age children have begun to realize that masculinity conveys more status and power than femininity (Bigler, Arthur, Hughes, & Patterson, 2008). In other words, children have figured out that they live in an androcentric world. This realization reflects a developing sense of *public regard*, the awareness that other people might evaluate one's group positively or negatively (Ashmore, Deaux, & McLaughlin-Volpe, 2004). It's interesting that children reach this conclusion, because in their everyday experiences there are many instances in which girls perform better than boys. For example, girls often do better in school than boys (Voyer & Voyer, 2014). Nevertheless, children are continually exposed to media messages that masculinity is more valuable and important than femininity. Also, children begin to understand the concepts of sexism and gender discrimination. For example, as they learn more about the presidents of the United States, they may realize there has never been a female president. A 5-year-old might not think too much about this, but research suggests that by age 10 many children have noticed this phenomenon and report that it's because they think men don't want to vote for women (Bigler et al., 2008).

Given the findings mentioned above, the rise in tomboyism may reflect both the realization that men are more valued in our society, as well as the desire to access some of the advantages of masculinity (Carr, 1998). After all, tomboys generally have an increased social status—they're more likely than more traditionally feminine girls to be considered popular (Braun & Davidson, 2017; Reay, 2001). They also have other positive qualities demonstrating self-confidence, such as assertiveness and self-reliance (Burn et al., 1996). Further, in a study of women who recalled being tomboys, many noted that their mothers' lives didn't seem interesting or exciting (Carr, 1998). One commented, "Did I want to be like my mother? Absolutely not, because I thought she lived a pretty boring life" (p. 537). Others saw traditionally feminine activities, like playing jacks or worrying about appearance, as boring. Tomboys seemed to be doing something more useful and interesting.

However, being a tomboy may not only involve reject-ing femininity and embracing masculinity. It may also reflect an increased acceptance of gender flexibility. For example, in one study, researchers found that tomboys were more likely than more feminine girls to be comfortable with other people violating gender norms (Ahlqvist, Halim, Greulich, Lurye, & Ruble, 2013). In another study, tomboys were more likely to think that people should act the way they want—that girls don't have to act like girls, and boys don't have to act like boys (Martin & Dinella, 2012). Also, for chil-dren who are assigned F at birth but don't identify as a girl, being a tomboy can be a way to express a masculine identity. One study showed that among adult female-to-male trans-gender individuals, almost all had been tomboys in child-hood (Grossman, D'Augelli, Howell, & Hubbard, 2005).

Of course, not all girls turn to tomboyism when they notice women's lower status in society. In one study, 28% of elementary school age girls identified themselves as "in betweens," meaning that they didn't identify as tomboys but reported not being traditional girls either (Ahlqvist et al., 2013). Another study of a predominantly working-class and ethnically mixed third-grade classroom identified sev-eral sub-groups of girls, including "tomboys," "spice girls," "nice girls," and "girlie girls" (Reay, 2001). Interestingly, the social status of both the nice girls and the girlie girls, the two most feminine groups, was the lowest. The tomboys were accorded the highest social status, especially by the boys in the class.

Adolescence

What happens to gender socialization in adolescence?

Adolescence is a time when many children go through a process of **gender inten-sification**, in which girls and boys start to more rigidly enact their gender roles. For girls, this typically occurs when the signs of puberty signal, both to the girl and to society as a whole, that she's no longer a child and will begin to transition to adult gender roles (Galambos, Almeida, & Petersen, 1990; Hill & Lynch, 1983). During this period, the flexibility of gender roles from middle child-hood and the acceptance of tomboy behavior decreases, and there is an increase in traditionally feminine behavior (Carr, 2007). For example, most girls who engaged in tomboyism report that they stopped being tomboys around age 12 or 13 (Burn et al., 1996; Morgan, 1998). One of the most frequently mentioned reasons for this shift was pressure from peers (e.g., "Jr. high peers said I looked too much like a guy"), but former tomboys also noticed that their friends began to desire boys and decided that they should too (Burn et al., 1996, p. 424).

Girls who give up being tomboys in adolescence may do so for a good reason. As discussed above, in middle childhood, gender non-conforming girls are generally valued and considered popular (Braun & Davidson, 2017; Reay, 2001). However, in adolescence, they're more likely to experience peer victimization and exclusion (Bos & Sandfort, 2015; Smith & Juvonen, 2017; van Beusekom, Baams, Bos, Overbeek, & Sandfort, 2016). In one longitudinal study of ethnically diverse seventh and eighth graders, researchers found that the sense that one wasn't a typical girl or boy was related to problems a year later, such as getting into trouble at school, social anxiety, and complaints about physical illness (Smith & Juvonen, 2017). These problems were, however, largely due to experiences of peer victimization.

As children enter adolescence, being gender non-conforming becomes linked in the eyes of many peers to having a non-conforming sexual preference, whether or not that is actually the case. In a study of Dutch 11- to 16-year-olds, researchers found that gender non-conformity was related to psychological distress and social anxiety, and this was partially due to homophobic name calling (van Beusekom et al., 2016). These effects were worse for those who actually did experience same-sex attraction. While gender non-conforming girls and boys suffered in similar ways, gender non-conforming girls experienced somewhat lower levels of harassment than boys. This is another instance of femininity being seen as lower in value than masculinity. In another study, researchers found that both those who were gender non-conforming and those who experienced same-sex attraction had poor relationships with peers, but those who were both had the poorest relationships (Bos & Sandfort, 2015). Moreover, bullying of non-gender conforming and LGBTQ children is a significant problem. In 2014, a national school climate report identified U.S. schools as hostile environments for LGBTQ students, leading many students to avoid school activities or miss school entirely (Kosciw, Greytak, Palmer, & Boesen, 2014). Transgender youth experience particularly high levels of bullying. In one study, researchers called the bullying of transgender students pervasive, noting that over 80% had some negative interactions with peers (McGuire, Anderson, Toomey, & Russell, 2010).

The idea that adolescent girls lose their true selves in order to become more feminine gained traction in the 1990s when several movies, such as *Love and Basketball* and *She's All That*, showed a character transition from acting like a tomboy to behaving and dressing in a more traditionally feminine manner. The result was that she became happier and more popular. The book *Reviving Ophelia*, published in the same decade, painted a dire picture of many girls' transition into adolescence (Pipher, 1994). The author, therapist Mary Pipher, described how girls morphed from confident children into passive people-pleasers whose only goal is to attract men.

The girls featured in *Reviving Ophelia* were primarily White, but there's evidence that many girls of color face similar experiences (Chan, 2008; Denner & Dunbar, 2004). For example, several studies have found that adolescent Latinx girls feel pressure to conform to feminine cultural ideals such as family commitment, respect for authority, and restrictions on where they can go (DeLeón, 1996; Negy & Woods, 1992; Solis, 1995). They learn to sacrifice their needs in order to maintain the reputation and well-being of the family (Gil & Vazquez, 1996). In a more recent study, researchers found that Mexican American adolescent girls who had a strong sense of ethnic identity more strongly identified with the feminine values of being virtuous, chaste, and committed to the family (Sanchez, Vandewater, & Hamilton, 2017).

Additional research has suggested that gender intensification and the negative consequences associated with it may have been a bigger problem in the past than is true today. For example, researchers followed a group of adolescents from fifth grade to ninth grade and found no large increase in femininity or decrease in masculinity among the girls (Priess, Lindberg, & Hyde, 2009). Girls did endorse higher levels of femininity than boys in fifth grade, and both girls and boys rose slightly in femininity over the four years. However, girls didn't become particularly more feminine than boys during that time. In terms of masculine traits, there was no difference between the girls and boys. They consistently scored equally high in masculine traits from fifth to ninth grade. These findings suggest that while there's a perception that adolescent girls become passive and feminine and lose their assertiveness and independence, this pattern is not fully supported.

Of course, adolescence isn't completely smooth sailing for all young women. As they enter puberty and gain body fat, their body image concerns increase (Williams & Curie, 2000), a topic we'll cover in Chapter 6. Girls who reach puberty earlier than their peers may be especially at risk for negative consequences including depression, unplanned pregnancy, and delinquent behaviors (Hayward, Killen, Wilson & Hammer, 1997; Skoog & Stattin, 2014). This may be related to socializing with older peers and facing pressures to engage in activities that they're not emotionally ready for (Clemans, DeRose, Graber, Brooks-Gunn, 2010; Skoog & Stattin, 2014).

In addition to the risks associated with being an early-maturing girl, other risks are associated with the transition to adolescence. For example, it's a time when young women start to feel less confident about their skills in math and science and begin to see math as a male domain (Leedy, LaLonde, & Runk, 2003). This is true even though their performance in math and science classes remains equal to that of men through college (Voyer & Voyer, 2014).

Also, while sports participation is highly beneficial for young women, there is a decrease in sports participation and physical activity for young girls throughout

your turn

Did you reach puberty before your peers, around the same time as your peers, or after your peers? Do you think the timing of puberty affected your development? If yes, in what ways? If no, why not? How were the early- and late-maturing children whom you knew treated by their peers? How important was the timing of puberty to you (and your peers)?

Jesminder "Jess" Bhamra (played by Parminder Nagra) in the movie *Bend It Like Beckham*.

adolescence (Biddle, Whitehead, O'Donovan, & Nevill, 2005; Pate, Dowda, O'Neill, & Ward, 2007). Early-maturing girls are particularly likely to stop engaging in physical activity, which can worsen feelings of depression and low self-worth (Davison, Werder, Trost, Baker, & Birch, 2007). Maturing early may make young women feel uncomfortable about engaging in physical activity, especially if they have to wear uniforms that are revealing (e.g., short shorts or swimsuits). When girls start to develop breasts, they may find running to be awkward or embarrassing. All these factors may contribute to a decrease in sports participation around the time of puberty.

However, not all girls give up masculine activities such as sports when they hit puberty. An example of this is in the movie *Bend It Like Beckham* (2002), in which Jesminder (Jess) resists family pressure to embrace traditional femininity. Instead, she continues to play soccer. In fact, there are important advantages to maintaining some aspects of tomboyism, particularly engagement in sports. In one study, researchers found higher self-esteem in young women who continued to participate in sports in high school than those who didn't (Richman & Schaffer, 2000). In other studies, researchers found that, compared to those who don't engage in sports, young women who do play sports feel better about their bodies (Dishman et al., 2006) and are more likely to embrace other positive, masculine personality characteristics such as being self-confident, active, and independent (Richman & Schaffer, 2000).

As this section has shown, while there's pressure for girls to engage in gender intensification, the stereotype of the passive and silenced adolescent girl is outdated. Many girls continue to be active and independent as they mature. Yet there are some risks as young women develop, and an early maturation into puberty seems to intensify these risks.

Conclusion

Gender socialization doesn't end in adolescence, and gendered expectations continue throughout life. We'll explore these topics in later chapters that cover important life transitions—for example, Chapter 8 (Relationships), Chapter 9 (Reproduction and Mothering), Chapter 10 (Work), and Chapter 11 (Older Women).

Gender socialization is a complex process incorporating unconscious forces, cognitive schemas, and observational learning. This begins before birth and continues throughout our lives. As you learn about the gender socialization process, you may find that you notice ways in which messages about gender have shaped your own life and your understanding of yourself, for better or for worse. To a great extent, our understanding of ourselves is tied up with what we've learned is appropriate for our gender. However, while these messages are everywhere, they also can be resisted. For example, the young women introduced at the beginning of the chapter resisted socialization messages and managed to change their environments while doing so. As you begin to notice the omnipresence of gender socialization, can you also notice the big and small ways in which people resist it?

Chapter Review

SUMMARY

Theories of Gender Development

- Psychoanalytic theories focus on unconscious forces that shape gender socialization.

- Freud assumed that many gender differences are due to women's lack of and desire for a penis. His theories are criticized for sexism as well as lack of scientific validity and poor operationalization of constructs.

- Karen Horney proposed that women don't envy men's penises but rather their social power. She also proposed that men suffer from womb envy and are jealous of the ability to give birth.

- Nancy Chodorow hypothesized that gender differences stem from the fact that women do the majority of the caregiving, so girls are closer to their mothers and develop a sense of self that is more connected to others.

- Behavioral theories focus on how the environment shapes gender; they include reinforcement and observational learning.

- Cognitive developmental theories focus on how children create schemas about gender and self-socialize in order to fit into their internalized gender role.

- Social construction theories focus on how beliefs about gender are constructed and can vary according to time, place, or culture.

Sources of Gender Socialization

- Messages about gender are conveyed through books, television, movies, video games, and social media.

- In books, women are generally shown as working in the home, and girls are shown as passive responders to action. Even books touted as being non-sexist portray girls and boys unequally.

- In television shows, boys are more likely to be shown being active and solving problems while girls are more likely shown as physically attractive and spending time primping.

- In television and video games, female superheroes are strong and assertive, but they're also sexualized.

- Social media gives girls the opportunity to compare themselves to others and, as a result, learn gender norms.

- Girls of color are under-represented in all forms of media.

- Toys marketed to girls generally promote caretaking and domestic work, while toys marketed to boys generally promote activity and skill building.

- Parents treat children differently in terms of encouraging gender-typed play, encouraging more independence and risk taking in boys, encouraging emotional expression with girls more than boys, and expecting girls to do more chores around the house.

- Peers engage in gender-segregated play and borderwork designed to keep girls and boys separate. Peers can exclude, tease, and bully gender non-conforming children.

- A hidden curriculum in schools socializes girls to enact traditional forms of femininity. Black girls are subject to excessive disciplinary action and may feel that their needs and achievements are unrecognized.

Stages of Gender Development

- Gender socialization begins before birth, and assumptions about sex/gender can influence the way people treat babies.

- Pre-school is a time when children internalize rigid gender schemas and engage in gender policing.

- During middle childhood, many girls lose interest in the trappings of femininity and identify as tomboys. The loosening of gender rigidity is only true for girls; boys are penalized by peers for expressing femininity.

- Adolescent girls experience gender intensification. Although most adolescent girls successfully navigate this stage, the risks of negative outcomes are higher for those who hit puberty early.

KEY TERMS

gender socialization (p. 193)

psychoanalytic theories (p. 194)

Oedipus complex (p. 195)

castration anxiety (p. 195)

penis envy (p. 195)

Electra complex (p. 195)

womb envy (p. 196)

behavioral theories (p. 196)

operant conditioning (p. 197)

social learning theories (p. 197)

observational learning (p. 197)

self-socialization (p. 199)

cognitive developmental theories (p. 199)

gender labeling (p. 199)

gender schema theory (p. 200)

gender constancy (p. 200)

postmodern perspective (p. 201)

social construction theories (p. 201)

doing gender (p. 201)

gender segregation (p. 214)

borderwork (p. 215)

hidden curriculum (p. 216)

gender rigidity (p. 222)

gender intensification (p. 225)

THINK ABOUT IT

1. What are the advantages of and limits to the different theories about gender development? Think about your own gender socialization process. What gender theory best describes it? In what ways does the theory fit? In what ways does it not reflect your experiences?

2. Go to a store or website that sells children's toys and clothing. Are items organized by gender? Using the research on gender socialization, what are the benefits and costs of organizing products in this way?

3. Should schools address the hidden curriculum? If so, what specific recommendations would you make to ensure inclusivity?

4. Given the contradictory messages girls receive about gender, what advice would you give to an adolescent girl as she enters middle school?

ONLINE RESOURCES

- **Feminist Frequency** — conversations with feminist writers, activists, artists, and scholars working in media: feministfrequency.com

- **How to Be a Girl** — conversations with single mom Marlo Mack and her transgender daughter as they attempt to sort out just what it means to be a girl: howtobeagirlpodcast.com

- **Popaganda** — conversations about movies, books, and TV from a feminist perspective: bitchmedia.org/feminist-podcasts/popaganda

- **The Representation Project** — evaluates gender stereotypes in film and media: therepresentationproject.org

- **Rookie Mag** — a feminist alternative to traditional teen magazines written by girls for girls: rookiemag.com

6

Women's Bodies

IN 2004, DOVE, INC., launched its Campaign for Real Beauty, in which billboard, print, and television advertising featured images of "real" women. Many of the ads showed several women in a row wearing simple white underwear. Viewers, therefore, could see the women's diversity—their different sizes, different body shapes, different skin tones. On the surface, this campaign seemed progressive because it featured a diverse array of "real" women instead of traditional models. It certainly was a striking change from the usual portrayal of women in the media (e.g., young, thin, White). However, while many people praised the campaign as being empowering for women, it was also criticized and can be considered an example of empowertising (as discussed in Chapter 1).

One reason this ad campaign may have been empowering was that it prompted increased discussion about media portrayals of women and female beauty. The campaign, and the underlying idea that beauty isn't about any one specific look, received significant media attention with coverage on shows such as *Good Morning America*, *The View*, and *Ellen*. The fact that an array of body types not typically seen in advertising was at the heart of this campaign was compelling. Moreover, the ads didn't just show different bodies—the ads portrayed them positively. For example, a dark-skinned woman wasn't shown trying to lighten her skin, a woman with small breasts wasn't shown trying to increase

This billboard, pictured in New York City in 2005, features one of the iconic lineup images at the heart of Dove's Campaign for Real Beauty. What messages, both positive and negative, do ads like this send?

her cup size, and a curly-haired woman wasn't shown trying to straighten her hair. Many people would argue that, because of the positive portrayal of diverse bodies, the campaign was empowering to women.

Yet some elements generated a lot of criticism. First, while some of the ads showed women "who were wrinkled, freckled, pregnant, had stretch marks, or might be seen as fat" as compared to traditional media images of women (Johnston & Taylor, 2008, p. 942), the women in the ads still didn't reflect the average woman. For example, the women in the lineup ad wore U.S. clothing sizes 6–12. This is larger than the typical commercial model (size 4; Mears, 2011) but smaller than the average American woman (size 16/18; Christel & Dunn, 2016).

Also, the women in the ads generally didn't have tattoos, scars, or visible disabilities, and they had smooth skin and were mostly young. In this way, Dove seemed to be encouraging body positivity while featuring women who still largely conformed to traditional beauty standards. In fact, the original campaign was centered on advertising a line of "skin firming" products. So the ads indirectly said that women can be beautiful as long as they aren't too heavy, aren't disabled, have styled hair, and have firm skin (presumably because they've bought and used Dove products).

Of course, Dove is in business to sell products, and this campaign definitely helped its bottom line. Previously best known for its bar soap, the company raised its brand awareness and increased its market share largely as a result of this campaign (Jeffers, 2005). Ironically, Dove's parent company, Unilever, markets SlimFast, a diet supplement; the Axe product line, known for ads featuring sexualized images of women; and Fair & Lovely, a brand of skin-lightening products sold in many countries. Thus, while Dove was sending the message that women should accept their bodies, the parent company's other products send messages that women's bodies are unacceptable as they currently are. The Dove campaign represents some of the mixed messages women receive about their bodies.

In this chapter, we'll talk about the cultural focus on women's bodies. Women spend a great deal of time thinking about their bodies from the outside (how they look). This is largely because the female body is generally portrayed as something to be looked at. We'll discuss the messages girls and women receive about what is beautiful, and we'll explore the impact of accepting these views. One consequence

your turn

Do a quick image search on "Dove Campaign for Real Beauty." What do you think of it? Based on what you've read here, what aspects of it do you like, and why? Do any aspects of it trouble you? If so, which ones, and why? Ask at least three friends or family members to do the same image search. How do they react to this campaign? Do their responses vary by age? Do they vary by gender? Given the company's economic goals, can you think of any type of advertising campaign that wouldn't result in at least some of the criticisms you've read about here?

of girls and women spending a lot of time focusing on their bodies from the position of an observer is that they tend to pay less attention to what their bodies actually do. Therefore, we'll also discuss some of the functions of women's bodies (e.g., menstruation) and examine why these functions are often shrouded in secrecy. Finally, we'll explore some ways that girls and women can shift their focus away from how their bodies look to an appreciation for all of the things that their bodies can do.

Women's Bodies: From the Outside Looking In

What is objectification, and how is it related to self-objectification?

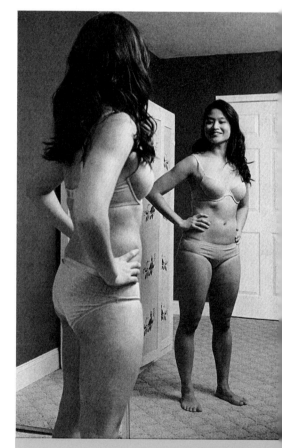

Women are often taught that how they look is one of the most important sources of information about themselves.

In many ways, society is obsessed with the appearance of women's bodies, and images of their bodies are constantly on display. As a result, girls and women can become preoccupied with their appearance, viewing their bodies as objects to be gazed at and enjoyed by others. When this happens, the internal qualities that make a girl or woman unique can get ignored, and instead, her body and appearance become the primary source of information about her (Bartky, 1990). This process is known as **objectification**—the viewing of a person as an object to be looked at rather than as a human being inhabiting a skin (Fredrickson & Roberts, 1997). Objectification is generally framed as the female body being an object gazed at by others. Those others are typically thought to be heterosexual men, and therefore the **male gaze** is central to the understanding of objectification. While men also experience objectification, it's a far more common experience for women, and the consequences of living in a culture of objectification are more severe for women (Calogero & Thompson, 2010). In fact, art critic John Berger (1972) summed up the dominance of the objectifying gaze toward women when he stated that "men look at women" and "women watch themselves being looked at" (p. 47). The gaze can occur in everyday interactions—for example, a man can be at a bar checking a woman out, or a woman can walk down the street, and a man may oogle her or catcall.

However, the gaze is more complicated than these examples of everyday interactions suggest. Media images of women, for example, often put the observer in the position of the gazer. The iconic lineup ad in Dove's Campaign for Real Beauty was primarily intended for viewing by women (the target market for Dove's products). Of course, these ads were also viewed by men, and some men even made critical comments about the women's bodies. Perhaps most prominently, film critic Richard Roeper said, in a *Chicago Sun-Times* editorial, "I find these Dove ads a little unsettling. If I want to see plump gals baring too much skin, I'll go to Taste of Chicago, OK? I'll walk down Michigan Avenue or go to Navy Pier. When we're talking women in their underwear on billboards outside my living room windows, give me the fantasy babes, please" (Roeper, 2005, p. 11). However, the ad wasn't primarily designed for men to look at women. Essentially, everyone who saw it was the gazer, seeing the women from behind the camera. Placing the "audience" in the role of the gazer isn't unique to this ad—or even to advertising in particular. Even decades ago, before the psychological study of objectification began, it was documented as a common strategy when displaying women's bodies in art (Berger, 1972), movies (Mulvey, 1975), and advertising (Goffman, 1979). More recent research has shown that not only does this pattern persist, but objectification has actually increased (Thompson, 2000).

Given the extent of attention on women's bodies, it isn't surprising that many women also gaze at and "check out" other women's bodies. This practice isn't simply about sexual desire. If that were true, only heterosexual men, lesbians, or others who are attracted to women would gaze at women's bodies. In fact, researchers find that women's bodies are examined and evaluated both by women and men and by people of all sexual orientations (Gervais, Holland, & Dodd, 2013; Strelan & Hargreaves, 2005). The Dove ads, however, were aimed at women—the consumers most likely to purchase Dove products. Female viewers were essentially invited to objectify the models, compare themselves to the models, find themselves lacking, and decide to buy a Dove product in order to remedy that situation.

Objectification theory addresses how living in a culture that objectifies women is harmful to women. According to psychologists Barbara Fredrickson and Tomi-Ann Roberts (1997), the developers of this theory, women "internalize an observer's perspective as a primary view of their physical selves" (p. 173). Essentially, they turn the objectifying gaze on themselves in order to evaluate the extent to which they conform to societal standards of beauty. When people do this, they're engaging in **self-objectification**. It can occur in many situations, and in certain contexts it's considered normal, expected, and even beneficial. For example, when trying on new clothes in a store, it's normal to consider how we look in them. In the moment when we look in the mirror and consider our appearance as another person would, we are self-objectifying.

However, some people spend an excessive amount of time thinking about how their bodies look. While playing tennis, they may wonder whether their arms are jiggling; when giving an oral presentation, they may wonder if their stomach looks too big. People who self-objectify on a regular basis are considered to be self-objectifiers. Frequent self-objectification can become very distracting, and as we'll see, even occasional self-objectification can have negative consequences for the mental health of young women (e.g., Moradi & Huang, 2008). We'll cover the consequences later in this chapter, but before doing so, we'll explore why the focus on beauty matters so much in the first place.

Beauty Matters

What is normative discontent, and what are some of the consequences of not conforming to society's version of attractiveness?

The objectifying gaze is not value neutral. It implies that there are good bodies and bad bodies, and that beauty matters. But inevitably, most women are unable to live up to society's standards of beauty. Dove stated that it launched its Campaign for Real Beauty after commissioning a study in which only 2% of female respondents selected the word *beautiful* to describe themselves (Etcoff, Orbach, Scott, & D'Agostino, 2004; see Table 6.1). Because of research findings like this, women have been described as living in a continual state of

TABLE 6.1 Adjectives Women Would Be Most Comfortable Using to Describe Their Appearance

Adjective	Endorsement Rate
natural	31%
average	25%
attractive	9%
feminine	8%
cute	7%
good-looking	7%
pretty	5%
beautiful	2%
sexy	1%
sophisticated	1%
stunning	1%
gorgeous	0%

Note. Data from Etcoff et al. (2004).

body dissatisfaction, meaning that they don't feel comfortable or satisfied with their physical appearance. Several studies have found that approximately half of girls and women are dissatisfied with their bodies, and most want to be thinner (Bearman, Presnell, Martinez, & Stice, 2006; Smolak, 2012; Tantleff-Dunn, Barnes, & Larose, 2011). In fact, a survey of over 9,000 women indicated that 89% of respondents were dissatisfied with their bodies in terms of weight, and 84% wanted to be thinner (Swami, Tran, Stieger, Voracek, & The YouBeauty. com Team, 2015).

Body dissatisfaction has the potential to be a lifelong issue for women, as it has been found in girls as young as 5 years of age (Dohnt & Tiggemann, 2005) and in women as old as 70 (Mangweth-Matzek et al., 2006). The phenomenon of girls and women being dissatisfied with their bodies has been referred to as a **normative discontent** (Rodin, Silberstein, & Streigel-Moore, 1984; Tantleff-Dunn et al., 2011), meaning that the normal state for girls and women with respect to their bodies is to feel unhappy or dissatisfied. Of course, normative discontent among women is essential to the bottom line of the multi-billion-dollar beauty industry. A huge part of that economic sector is driven by convincing women that they must be beautiful to be happy and by promoting standards of beauty that are almost impossible to achieve.

The popularity of the Dove campaign, and the fact that diet supplements, makeup, and other beauty products are multi-billion-dollar industries, reveal just how enormously beauty matters to girls and women in our society. However, it isn't simply an issue of vanity. In our society, girls and women are constantly evaluated by the extent to which they meet beauty standards. For example, research shows that people assume that those who are beautiful are also good (Dion, Berscheid, & Walster, 1972; Langlois et al., 2000). Moreover, many girls and women assume that their lives will be better if they more closely conform to beauty standards (Engeln-Maddox, 2006). There may be some truth to this assumption: In one study, researchers found that attractive children and adults were treated more positively by others than unattractive ones were (Langlois et al., 2000). Other studies have shown that women who don't conform to beauty ideals are often the targets of ridicule and shaming (e.g., Chrisler, 2012) and may have a more difficult time getting hired and promoted at work (Fiske, Bersoff, Borgida, Deaux, & Heilman, 1991).

Being overweight, in particular, can be problematic, as higher-weight individuals are more likely to face discrimination in many contexts, including education, health-care settings, employment, and relationships (e.g., Burmeister, Kiefner, Carels, & Musher-Eizenman, 2013; Carr & Friedman, 2005; Chen & Brown, 2005; Han, Norton, & Stearns, 2009). Women, more so than men, are likely to be targets of fat shaming (Chrisler, 2012). It's also important to recognize that fatness can be related to poverty (Rothblum, 2011). Whereas eating healthy meals and staying fit often involve spending a fair amount of money, high-caloric, processed foods with low nutritional value are cheap

(Drewnowski & Specter, 2004). A dollar can buy 1,200 calories of potato chips, for example, as compared to only 250 calories of vegetables or 170 calories of fresh fruit (Townsend, Grant, Monsivais, Keim, & Drewnowski, 2009). Gym memberships and workout videos are also costly, and even informal exercising requires time and a space to do it in.

Further, while poverty may cause fatness, there's evidence that the opposite may also be true (Ernsberger, 2009). In contemporary society, size discrimination is so great that fatness can actually lead to downward social mobility (Rothblum, 2011). In most places in the United States, for example, it is legal to discriminate based on weight. Law professor Paul Campos (2004) has argued that fat prejudice is just a modern way to discriminate without being openly sexist, racist, or classist. This type of discrimination perpetuates the *myth of transformation*—the widespread belief that weight loss will result in increased economic and interpersonal gains (Striegel-Moore & Franco, 2002).

Beyond norms of thinness, violations of any beauty norms can be problematic. In one study, when researchers showed participants a picture of a woman with leg and underarm hair, the participants rated her not only as less attractive but also as less intelligent, less happy, and less sociable than the same woman pictured without body hair (Basow & Braman, 1998). Women of color face the added expectation that they conform to White standards of beauty. For example, sociologist Patricia Hill Collins (1990) noted that Black women may encounter barriers in the workforce if they wear their hair "natural" (i.e., not straightened). We'll return to the topic of racialized standards of beauty in the next section.

To complicate matters, beauty is a double-edged sword because women can also be judged negatively if they seem too beautiful or focus too much on their appearance (Heilman & Stopeck, 1985; Vaillancourt & Sharma, 2011). In fact, women have been legally fired for being too beautiful. For example, a dental assistant in Iowa was fired because her boss felt she was attractive enough to be a threat to his marriage, as he was tempted to have an affair with her (Kimmel, 2013). When denying her appeal, the Iowa Supreme Court ruled that she

The Selfie

What is the potential effect of social media on young women's tendency to engage in self-objectification? For many individuals, a large part of interacting on Facebook, Instagram, and Twitter is the taking and posting of selfies. This practice illustrates how young women tend to view their bodies from an observer's perspective. Instead of wondering how they look or having to catch a glimpse of themselves in a mirror, they can take a selfie and immediately go from inhabiting their body to observing it. While there's not yet a lot of research on this topic, some studies indicate that higher levels of selfie posting are related to higher levels of body dissatisfaction and greater internalization of the thin ideal among girls (Cohen, Newton-John, & Slater, 2018; McLean, Paxton, Wertheim, & Masters, 2015). Moreover, body concerns are greater for those who edit their selfies before posting in an effort to "improve" their appearance. In contrast, other research has shown that high body satisfaction is actually related to selfie posting, in part so girls and women can show how satisfied they are with their appearance (Ridgway & Clayton, 2016).

No matter what your gender identification is, do you take selfies? How often, and in what situations? Do you ever edit your selfies? If so, in what ways—and why? If not, why not? How do you feel about selfies in general and yours in particular?

could "be lawfully terminated simply because the boss views the employee as an irresistible attraction" (para. 3).

So there are negative consequences for not conforming to beauty norms, but there are also negative consequences for conforming to those norms. This double bind means that some women are likely to spend a great deal of time thinking about how they look, evaluating their bodies, and feeling depressed if they decide their bodies don't live up to society's standards. Furthermore, to the extent that women spend time, money, and energy enhancing their beauty, they don't have that time, money, or energy to do other things.

Beauty Norms

What are some dominant beauty norms, and how does culture impact these norms?

What does it mean to be beautiful? The term means different things to different people and can differ across cultures and time frames. More generally, though, **beauty norms** are shared standards for attractiveness, whether implicitly or explicitly stated, that are held by members of a given social group. Sometimes these standards are taught explicitly by being stated outright—for example, young girls may be told to brush their hair before leaving the house. At other times, these standards are taught implicitly—they're never clearly stated, but girls figure them out from cues in their environment and from seeing how others behave. For example, girls might learn that straight hair is beautiful because they see other women using flat irons in a locker room (or that curly hair is beautiful because they see others using curling irons). Like other social norms, these standards convey information about what is accepted, expected, and valued, and these are generally well known and fairly uniform within a given group (Zones, 2000). Would you say, for example, that Beyoncé is an attractive woman? Some people may find her somewhat more or less appealing, but most would probably admit that she's beautiful.

Beautiful = Racialized

A serious limitation of research on beauty is that not all beauty norms have received equal attention. The vast majority of studies on body image and body satisfaction have used samples consisting primarily of White women and have been conducted mostly by White researchers (Striegel-Moore & Smolak, 2000). Therefore, the results may only reflect patterns among and concerns of White women. Many studies also use White women as a comparison group, which limits the ways in which researchers can understand beauty norms within groups of women who aren't White.

In fact, several studies have shown that White women are more dissatisfied with their bodies than Black women are (Grabe & Hyde, 2006; Kronenfeld, Reba-Harrelson, Von Holle, Reyes, & Bulik, 2010). One reason why Black women may report greater body satisfaction is that the norms most frequently investigated—particularly the norm of thinness (a topic we discuss below)—may be less central to their perception of beauty (Beauboeuf-Lafontant, 2003; Capodilupo, 2015; Hesse-Biber, Howling, Leavy, & Lovejoy, 2004; Hall, 1995b).

Given this consideration, researchers may not be focusing on the concerns of and beauty norms relevant for women or any other specific group. For example, one factor that contributes to body dissatisfaction among women experiencing homelessness is lack of consistent access to hygiene products (Mitchell, Ramsey, & Nelson, 2018). Women who have the privilege not to think about this, however, may never consider that this factor could contribute to body image.

Skin Color and Colorism Women of color may have different sources of dissatisfaction about their bodies that stem from a history of racism. In fact, there has been a long history of **colorism**, or preference for lighter skin, both within the United States as a whole and among the Black community itself (Kerr, 2005; 2006). For example, in an interview for *The New Yorker*, Nobel Prize–winning author Toni Morrison talked about the "paper bag test," something she encountered as a student at Howard University (Als, 2003). She explained that having skin "darker than the paper bag put you in one category, similar to the bag put you in another, and lighter was yet another and the most privileged category" (p. 68). Essentially, Morrison was saying, the closer one is to having "White" skin, the more privileged one is. In this context, both skin color and hair texture have been highlighted as aspects of appearance that may be particularly important for Black girls and women (Awad et al., 2015; Hall, 1995b; Hesse-Biber et al., 2004; Neal & Wilson, 1989). Several studies have shown that when women of color are satisfied with their skin color, they also tend to be satisfied with their bodies and have higher self-esteem (Falconer & Neville, 2000; Thompson & Keith, 2001).

In one study involving women of color, concern about the color of their skin was related to higher general levels of body shame (Buchanan, Fischer, Tokar, & Yoder, 2008). Likewise, Asian and Asian American women have also identified skin color as a beauty concern (Brady et al., 2017; Chen, Yarnal, Chick, & Jablonski, 2018; Hall, 1995a), and skin-whitening creams are popular—particularly in Asia (Karnani, 2007). Many Asian cultures have traditionally viewed light skin as a sign of femininity, purity, and upper-class status (Chen et al., 2018; Kawamura & Rice, 2009). This perspective has been linked to the fact that wealthier Asian women didn't have to work outside in agricultural and other labor-intensive jobs (Chen et al., 2018; Jones, 2013). So in addition to racism, the focus on light skin reflects classist views that have influenced beauty norms.

Hair Texture and Facial Features Black women's potential dissatisfaction with hair texture has also been related to a White beauty ideal of longer, straight or wavy hair rather than the very curly or kinky hair that's more common among Black women. The terms *good hair* and *bad hair* have been used to refer to the ease with which Black women can straighten and style their hair, and *good hair* more closely resembles the hair of White women (Bellinger, 2007; Robinson, 2011). After being dismayed by his Black daughter's desire to have straight hair, a White writer for *Sesame Street* wrote a song called "I Love My Hair" for a Muppet with an Afro and darker "skin" to sing (Darden, 2010).

Not all Black women who straighten their hair do so just to conform to White beauty norms—after all, everyone has opinions as to what styles best suit them (Hall, 1995b). Likewise, Black women who wear their hair "natural" often view this choice as making a statement about their political views and pride in their racial identity (Bellinger, 2007; Neal & Wilson, 1989), and others may do so to avoid daily styling and costly salon treatments (Okazawa-Rey, Robinson, & Ward, 1987; Robinson, 2011). In fact, this is big business—Black hair-care product sales were estimated to be $2.56 billion in 2016 (Easter, 2017).

Facial features have also been identified as another potential focus of dissatisfaction for women of color. In one study, researchers found that Chinese, Japanese, and Asian Indian college students reported greater dissatisfaction with their facial features, being particularly self-conscious about their eyes, as compared to White

Researchers studying body satisfaction have been less likely to study aspects of appearance that may be of concern to women of color (e.g., hair texture, skin tone) than aspects that concern White women. How could an intersectional framework address this gap?

college students (Mintz & Kashubeck, 1999). Larger and rounder eyes became the aesthetic ideal because they're associated with White people. Asian American women (and men) have reported that they've experienced discrimination because of their facial features (Kawamura & Rice, 2009; Root, 1990). Given this finding, it's no surprise that eyelid surgery has become the most common plastic surgery procedure selected by Asian American individuals (American Society of Plastic Surgeons, 2014). Further, rhinoplasties ("nose jobs") have increased in popularity among Latinx American and Asian American girls and women, although the procedures have been declining among Jewish American girls and women (Baker, 2012).

Beautiful = Able-Bodied

Research on beauty norms has reflected an able-bodied perspective. For example, women with chronic illnesses, those who have experienced serious injuries, and those with visible disabilities have unique concerns about their bodies that aren't captured in typical body image research. Although there hasn't been much research on the body image concerns of these groups of women, studies have generally shown that women with disabilities report dissatisfaction with their bodies (e.g., Mathias & Harcourt, 2014; Taleporos & McCabe, 2001; Wolman, Resnick, Harris, & Blum, 1994), as do women with visible scarring from burns (Connell, Coates, Doherty-Poirier, & Wood, 2013). Women with disabilities have also reported more negative attitudes about their bodies compared to women without disabilities (Cromer et al., 1990; Moin, Duvdevany, & Mazor, 2009; Wolman et al., 1994). However, other research has found no real differences in body image between women with and without disabilities (Ben-Tovim & Walker, 1995). Still other research has shown more complex relationships, reflecting a need for more research about the experience of people with different disabilities. For example, in one study, researchers found that poor body image was related to dissatisfaction with prosthetics among amputees (Murray & Fox, 2002).

Beautiful = Cisgender

For transgender and gender non-conforming individuals, body satisfaction may be tied to their perceived sense of congruence between body presentation and gender identity (Kozee, Tylka, & Bauerband, 2012). And there can be serious negative consequences for transwomen who don't pass as women. In a review of hate crimes against transgender people in the United States, researchers found that the vast majority of violence was perpetrated specifically against transgender women (Currah & Minter, 2000). Because the threat of violence is real, beauty norms can play a particularly important role in the lives of transwomen.

Yet not everyone can afford all the many things needed to conform to conventional beauty ideals. The financial resources and access to medical treatment that are necessary in order to meet these ideals aren't available to most transwomen because these individuals are among the poorest demographic group in the United States (Talusan, 2015). In fact, the popular media took up the economics of passing as a source of discussion following Caitlyn Jenner's glamorous debut on the front cover of the July 2015 issue of *Vanity Fair*. Meredith Talusan (2015), a writer and editor, made this observation: "If we accept Jenner because she fits our understanding of the gender binary, then we're celebrating not just her transition but her economic privilege" (p. 1). When media outlets selectively feature transwomen who not only meet, but exceed, beauty ideals, this practice sets an impossible standard for most transwomen.

During the 17th century, the Flemish artist Peter Paul Rubens depicted idealized female beauty through his paintings of voluptuous women, like those in this work titled *The Three Graces*. Do you consider the three women depicted here to be beauties? Why or why not? Why might others have a different view from yours?

Beautiful = Symmetrical

One characteristic frequently linked to perceived attractiveness is facial symmetry. A symmetrical face has features that are the same size and shape and in the same location on each side of the face—with the right and left sides essentially being mirror images. But most people don't have symmetrical faces. One eyebrow might be higher than the other, a nose may lean slightly to the left, or one corner of the mouth may pull a bit higher than the other. Researchers who study facial symmetry often use computer programs to generate images of faces that are symmetrical and then ask participants to rate the attractiveness of various faces that differ in the degree of symmetry. Using techniques like this, many studies have found that symmetrical faces are consistently rated as more attractive (e.g., Fink, Neave, Manning, & Grammer, 2006; Grammer & Thornhill, 1994; Jones, DeBruine, & Little, 2007; Rhodes, 2006). Investigators aren't sure why this effect occurs, however. Some have suggested that evolutionary preferences for selecting a potential mate underlie this preference (Grammer, Fink, Møller, & Thornhill, 2003). Symmetrical faces may signal good health and good genes, and one study showed that individuals with symmetrical faces were perceived as being healthier than those with less symmetrical faces (Fink et al., 2006).

Beautiful = Thin

While facial symmetry is a beauty standard that's relatively consistent across cultures and through time (Rhodes, 2006), the standard of thinness shows much more cultural variation.

The Barbie doll may be viewed as a representation of an ideal woman's body. However, these pictures show a Barbie doll next to a doll that reflects the measurements of an average 19-year-old girl—the age Barbie is supposed to be. Barbie is taller and has longer legs and a longer neck than the average 19-year-old. If she were scaled up to human size, her bust would be 4 inches larger and her waist would be 13 inches smaller than that of the average girl.

For many centuries, heavy women were considered beautiful. This is evident, for example, in art from ancient Greece, the Renaissance, and the 17th century—the time when Rubens painted highly sexualized pictures of heavy women (Polivy, Garner, & Garfinkel, 1986). In fact, being heavy was considered a sign of wealth, status, and sexuality (Polivy et al., 1986). However, standards have changed, so now thinness is considered a sign of beauty for women (Calogero & Thompson, 2010). Furthermore, the gap between the body size of an average woman and that of a model has grown. In 1975, a female model weighed only 8% less than the average woman; now a model weighs 23% less (Ross, n.d.). Given the influence of advertising images, it's no surprise that many women are dissatisfied with their bodies and want to be thinner. Researchers have even found a desire to be thinner among girls just starting elementary school (Lowes & Tiggemann, 2003).

However, being thin isn't enough. Women—especially young, White women—are supposed to be thin with no obvious body fat, have well-defined but sleek muscle tone, and have voluptuous breasts (Calogero, Boroughs, & Thompson, 2007; Thompson & Tantleff, 1992). Each of these standards can be difficult, if not impossible, to achieve, but trying to meet all three adds additional challenge. After all, muscle adds bulk and can make the body appear less thin, and breasts are partly made of fat tissue. What are the implications of these beauty standards? In essence, girls and women are receiving a message that they should reduce their caloric intake to become thinner, increase their physical activity to become more muscular, and undergo surgery to have larger breasts—all in an effort to achieve an "ideal" body that (almost) no one has.

Beautiful = Hairless

A particular beauty norm that has received a lot of attention lately is that of women having little to no body hair below the neck. Actually, this isn't a new norm. Ads in the United States promoting products to help women remove body hair have been around since 1915 (Hope, 1982). By 1945, ads no longer had to focus on convincing women to remove leg and underarm hair; they just focused on the benefits of using a given product. Numerous studies have shown that most women in the United States, the United Kingdom, and Australia regularly remove body hair (Basow, 1991; Tiggemann & Hodgson, 2008; Tiggemann & Kenyon, 1998; Toerien, Wilkinson, & Choi, 2005), and younger women may be those most likely to do so (Toerien et al., 2005). However, hair removal isn't a universal norm. For example, there's less pressure for women to remove body hair in some European countries (Toerien et al., 2005). Also, while many feminists opt to remove body hair, there is evidence that feminists are less likely to remove it than women who don't identify as feminists (Basow, 1991).

More recently, the decision to remove some or all of one's pubic hair has become a topic of research as an ideal of hairless female genitalia has developed (McDougall, 2013). For example, in one study of women in Canada, 50% of respondents reported removing some pubic hair (e.g., at their bikini line), and 30% reported removing all pubic hair (Riddell, Varto, & Hodgson, 2010). Some women remove pubic hair because they view it as unattractive (Braun, Tricklebank, & Clarke, 2013; DeMaria & Berenson, 2013). However, all women are not equally likely to engage in this practice. Research has shown that older women are less likely than younger women to regularly remove pubic hair and that they remove less hair when doing so (DeMaria & Berenson, 2013; Herbenick, Schick, Reece, Sanders, & Fortenberry, 2010). Another study showed that White women were more likely than Black or Latinx women to report removing pubic hair, and this practice was more common among women with higher incomes (DeMaria & Berenson, 2013).

There are, of course, more beauty norms that we haven't specifically explored—such as having clear skin and straight teeth. Moreover, there's still much to learn about the beauty norms that are most relevant for different women, as well as the complex relationships that women can have with their bodies for a host of reasons. Regardless, it's clear that beauty norms do affect most women on a daily basis.

How We Learn about Beauty Norms

What is the tripartite model of social influence, and how does each component contribute to our understanding of beauty norms?

There is no one source from which people learn beauty norms. Instead, messages come from different sources at different points throughout the lifetime, and this information is combined to influence perceptions of norms. The **tripartite model of social influence** is based on the idea that the combination of parents, peers, and the media constitutes the key influence on body image (Keery, van den Berg, & Thompson, 2004; Shroff & Thompson, 2006). These three external factors influence whether we internalize beauty norms and judge ourselves against them.

Parents

Parents, particularly mothers, influence how girls and women feel about their bodies. For example, mothers' discomfort with their own bodies and weight has been related to decreased **body esteem**—the degree to which people view their bodies positively—among their daughters (McKinley, 1999; Smolak, Levine, & Schermer, 1999). How people feel about their bodies is also related to their relationships with their parents in general. Research with a racially and ethnically diverse sample has shown that feeling as though one doesn't communicate well with one's mother was related to higher levels of body dissatisfaction (Taniguchi & Aune, 2013). Problematic communication with fathers was also related to body dissatisfaction, but the relationship was stronger for poor communication with mothers.

Sometimes parents communicate with their children in ways that imply a criticism of their child's body. Encouragement to lose weight by both mothers and fathers has been shown to be related to a desire to be thinner (Thelan & Cormier, 1995), and girls have been found to receive more information about weight and dieting from their parents than boys do (Phares, Steinberg, & Thompson, 2004). Research has also shown that comments, criticism, and teasing from family about weight and appearance are linked to decreased body satisfaction among girls (Levine, Smolak, & Hayden, 1994; Neumark-Sztainer et al., 2010).

Parents can positively influence their children's body image, though. Research with a racially and ethnically

your turn

What sort of messages did your parents give you about weight and attractiveness? Did you get different messages from your mother and your father (or other key adult figures in your life)? Do you think your mother (or other key female figures in your life) is satisfied with her own appearance? Does this affect your view of yourself? If you have siblings with a gender identity that's different from yours, did they receive the same messages you did?

diverse sample of girls highlighted that having parents who didn't discuss their own weight-related concerns and who emphasized healthy eating and exercise for fitness rather than dieting was associated with high levels of body satisfaction (Kelly, Wall, Eisenberg, Story, & Neumark-Sztainer, 2005). However, other research has shown that peer influence is often more important among adolescents than parental influence (Sheldon, 2013).

Peers

Many girls and women compare their bodies to those of their peers, and when girls and women judge themselves as less attractive than those around them, they report greater body dissatisfaction (Bailey & Ricciardeli, 2010). Moreover, body dissatisfaction isn't limited to girls with low social status. In fact, in one study of adolescent girls, researchers found that popularity was actually associated with more negative attitudes toward eating and feeling more negatively about their bodies (Lieberman, Gauvin, Bukowski, & White, 2001). Beauty and appearance can be common topics of conversation among women as they share beauty tips and techniques as well as advice about products and services. Research shows that those who talk about appearance more frequently with friends are more concerned with beauty norms and are generally more dissatisfied with their bodies (Jones, 2001; Jones, Vigfusdottir, & Lee, 2004).

Often, the way girls and women talk to each other about their bodies involves negative body talk, or **fat talk**. Such talk usually occurs in informal conversations among friends in which one or more of the girls or women involved express dissatisfaction with their bodies, especially in terms of weight or body size/shape. For example, if two teenage girls are in a store dressing room, one who looks quite thin might say, "I look so fat in this shirt." The other girl might reply, "No you don't. You look great, but my thighs are so huge in these pants!" Research suggests that interactions like this happen frequently (Britton, Martz, Bazzini, Curtin, & LeaShomb, 2006; Garnett et al., 2014; Jones, Crowther, & Ciesla, 2014; Salk & Engeln-Maddox, 2011), that they happen across racial groups (Engeln-Maddox, Salk, & Miller, 2012; Katrevich, Register, & Aruguete, 2014), and that they happen regardless of body size (Salk & Engeln-Maddox, 2011). Moreover, fat talk doesn't just happen in person; it also occurs on social media (Lee, Taniguchi, Modica, & Park, 2013). In fact, talk like this is so normative that participants in one study thought a conversation was more realistic when it contained fat talk rather than positive body talk (Barwick, Bazzini, Martz, Rocheleau, & Curtin, 2012).

The purpose of fat talk appears to be to elicit a positive response from peers. After someone calls herself fat, the usual response is for someone else to contradict her and either give her a compliment or insult herself. But what is the consequence of fat talk? Does it boost self-esteem if it results in a compliment? The answer appears to be no; there's nothing positive about fat talk. In several studies, it has been associated with body dissatisfaction (Engeln-Maddox et al., 2012; Ousley, Cordero, & White, 2007; Salk & Engeln-Maddox, 2011), and it's possible that the fat talk causes the dissatisfaction, rather than the dissatisfaction causing the fat talk.

Even listening to fat talk can have detrimental effects. Researchers have found that hearing other women engage in fat talk leads to increased body dissatisfaction, even among those who felt good about their bodies in the first place (Corning, Bucchianeri, & Pick, 2014; Salk & Engeln-Maddox, 2012). In other words, if a girl were in a locker room next to two girls participating in fat talk, she would probably feel worse about herself as a result. Even though it increases body dissatisfaction, some women may enjoy participating in it because it invokes a friend telling them they aren't fat (Salk & Engeln-Maddox, 2011). For this and many other reasons, fat talk can be a difficult cycle to stop.

your turn

Do you engage in fat talk? If so, how frequently? Does it make you feel better or worse about yourself? Who do you engage in fat talk with? What do you do when you hear women initiate fat talk? If you do engage in fat talk, does reading about its negative consequences inspire you to stop?

Fat talk isn't the worst social interaction one can have about one's body, though. Explicitly negative interactions such as teasing, bullying, and making weight-related comments are all key ways that peers may influence perceptions of beauty norms. Peer teasing has repeatedly been found to relate to levels of body dissatisfaction, as well as to more serious problems such as eating disorders (Cash & Henry, 1995; Fabian & Thompson, 1989; Gleason, Alexander, & Somers, 2000; Menzel et al., 2010; Thompson, Cattarin, Fowler, & Fisher, 1995). We also know that the effects of negative comments about appearance don't just affect girls during childhood; these effects can persist into adulthood (McLaren, Kuh, Hardy, & Gauvin, 2004; Murray, Touyz, & Beumont, 1995; Paxton, Schutz, Wertheim, & Muir, 1999). Positive comments can also be problematic—at least when they occur in the context of weight loss (Lieberman et al., 2001). When a woman loses weight and receives compliments ("Wow, you look great, did you lose weight?"), this can set her up for continuing to feel bad about her body, especially if the weight loss isn't sustained, and to be increasingly concerned about how she looks.

The tripartite influence model has been extended to include the influence of romantic partners in addition to parents and peers. Women's reports that their romantic partners criticize their weight or pressure them to change their appearance are associated with feeling worse about their bodies (Befort et al., 2001), thinking they're supposed to look like models in magazines (Johnson, Edwards, & Gidycz, 2015), and having disordered eating behaviors (Eisenberg, Berge, & Neumark-Sztainer, 2013; Shomaker & Furman, 2009).

The Media

While parents and peers convey important information and feedback about beauty norms, the media's influence is unparalleled (Hardit & Hannum, 2012; Harrison, 2003; Shroff & Thompson, 2006). Female beauty, particularly thinness, has been a dominant theme in representations of women across all forms of media (Levine & Harrison, 2004). Most models and actresses are far thinner than the average American woman. Moreover, digital editing (e.g., photoshopping) is often used to "improve" a woman's appearance by smoothing out wrinkles, plumping up her breasts, shaving inches from her waist, and so on (Kilbourne, 1999). This is routine practice in advertisements, fashion spreads, magazine covers, and movie posters. The use of body doubles is also routine in movies. Given these practices, even beauty icons aren't meeting societal expectations of beauty and attractiveness.

The more we're exposed to media, the more the images we see seem realistic and believable. This effect is known as **cultivation theory** (Gerbner, Gross, Morgan, & Signorielli, 1994). For example, if girls and women constantly see images of thin, toned, young women with blemish-free skin, they're likely to believe that this is typical, and they'll desire this type of appearance themselves. Research shows that the more a woman is exposed to media images, the worse she feels about her body (Ferguson, 2013; Grabe, Ward, & Hyde, 2008). For example, women who watch more TV are more likely to perceive themselves as overweight, regardless of their actual weight (McCreary & Sadava, 1999). Other research has involved showing female participants images of women who conform to the thin ideal and then having the participants complete surveys or perform tasks. After seeing the thin ideal images, participants report more negative feelings about their own bodies and appearance (Dittmar, Halliwell, & Stirling, 2009; Yamamiya, Cash, Melnyk, Posavac, & Posavac, 2005). Women have also been found to eat less in the presence of others after being exposed to these images (Harrison, Taylor, & Marske, 2006).

Some of the most compelling data on the influence of media come from a field study done by Anne Becker, an anthropologist and psychiatrist, and her colleagues in Fiji in the 1990s (Becker, 2004; Becker, Burwell, Herzog, Hamburg, & Gilman, 2002). They surveyed Fijian girls during the first few weeks after television was introduced in 1995 and then collected data from another group of girls three years later. After being exposed to TV, Fijian girls had higher rates of disordered eating and an increased desire for thinness. (We'll return to the topic of disordered eating in Chapter 13.)

The media constitute one of the primary vehicles for the objectification of women. One extreme manifestation of objectification occurs when a woman's body is displayed literally as an object (e.g., like a bottle) or when only parts (usually sexualized parts) of the body are displayed. For example, in May 2017, Dove started packing body wash in a series of bottles that varied in shape to, theoretically, represent women's diverse bodies (Calfas, 2017). Researchers have

These pictures of Lupita Nyong'o (left) and Chadwick Boseman (right) were taken at the premiere of *Black Panther* in January 2018. Notice how the image of Nyong'o is framed from a distance, showing more of her body, while Boseman's picture is largely focused on his face. This pattern, demonstrating face-ism, is typical in shots of women and men.

systematically examined magazines and identified that women are more likely than men to be objectified by being shown in dismembered ways (e.g., just legs or breasts) rather than the full body or just the face (Conley & Ramsey, 2011).

A particular area of investigation has focused on **face-ism** in advertising. Initially, this term described a tendency to have greater facial prominence (i.e., a larger proportion of the image devoted to the face) in depictions of men, while body prominence is more typical for images of women (Archer, Iritani, Kimes, & Barrios, 1983). Subsequent research extended this idea to race, finding that White individuals are more likely to be portrayed with facial prominence as compared to Black individuals, and that Black women have the lowest rates of facial prominence (Zuckerman & Kieffer, 1994). Evidence of this practice hasn't been limited to photographs and print ads (e.g., Dodd, Harcar, Foerch, & Anderson, 1989; Sparks & Fehlner, 1986); men also have been found to receive greater facial prominence in television (Copeland, 1989). Even in political headshots (which are only supposed to show the face and shoulders), men's faces are more prominently displayed, while pictures of women focus more on their bodies (Konrath, & Schwartz, 2007; Konrath, Au, & Ramsey, 2012). Why does this matter? In some studies, facial prominence has been linked to higher ratings of competence, intelligence, ambition, and dominance (Archer et al., 1983; Schwarz & Kurz, 1989; Zuckerman, 1986; Zuckerman & Kieffer, 1994)—all positive, and masculine, traits that can be helpful in the professional world.

Invisibility Not all women are portrayed in the media in the same way or at the same rate. Many, such as fat women, old women, and women with disabilities, are largely missing from the media. However, when women who don't meet typical beauty norms are shown, it's often in a negative light.

When fat women are shown, they're often depicted in stereotypical, negative, and stigmatizing ways (e.g., eating, not exercising). In one study, researchers found that 72% of images of larger-bodied individuals were negative (Heuer, McClure, & Puhl, 2011). This is noteworthy because other research has shown that anti-fat attitudes increased when viewing these types of negative images (McClure, Puhl, & Heuer, 2011; Pearl, Puhl, & Brownell, 2012), and that research participants didn't want to be physically or socially close to individuals portrayed in this way (Pearl et al., 2012; Puhl, Luedicke, & Heuer, 2013). Moreover, stigmatization of fat and fatness is common in media, and it has been suggested that obesity is one of the contexts in which joking is "fair game" (Burmeister & Carels, 2014, p. 223).

Movies and television are full of jokes at the expense of fat people. For example, Burmeister and Carels (2014) used several movie clips in their study of the relationship between anti-fat attitudes and weight-related humor. One was from the 2007 movie *Norbit* in which a fat woman is depicted as gaining so much momentum on a water slide that she lands far away in a different pool and causes all the water to splash out. Not surprisingly, participants who found such clips funny were more likely to have disparaging attitudes toward higher-weight people.

Fat women are by no means the only women who are hard to find in the media. Individuals with disabilities are rarely portrayed (Darke, 2004; Riley, 2005). When they are, they're usually depicted in stereotypical ways that involve a focus on either impairment or courage (e.g., overcoming limits). Little research has focused specifically on the representation of women with disabilities (Meekosha & Dowse, 1997). Given the rarity of including women with disabilities in the media, no real attention has been paid to the way in which these women, and their bodies, may be objectified. Invisibility like this can, itself, become problematic. After all, many women with disabilities report greater body dissatisfaction than those without disabilities (Cromer et al., 1990; Moin et al., 2009; Wolman et al., 1994). The experience of almost never seeing someone who looks like oneself in the media may add to this dissatisfaction.

Older women are also under-represented in the media as compared to their presence in the population. In a study published in 2003, individuals over age 50 were found to make up 27% of the population, but only 18% of the characters in commercials appeared to be over age 50 (Ganahl, Prinsen, & Netzley, 2003). Moreover, since women live longer than men, they make up a larger percentage of the older population, yet men accounted for 66% of the representations of those over the age of 50. Other research has found that older women are dramatically under-represented in both prime-time television (Greenberg & Worrell, 2007; Kessler, Rakoczy, & Staudinger, 2004; Lauzen & Dozier, 2005a) and movies (Lauzen & Dozier, 2005b). Essentially, then, youth is itself a beauty norm for women. This, in turn, reflects a double standard for aging: Men become distinguished, and women just get old. (We'll return to these ideas in Chapter 11.)

Another study, one that compared rates of representation in women's magazines to population data, showed that White women were over-represented (73% in the Census vs. 91% in the magazines), while Black (12% vs. 6%) and Latinx (10% vs. 1%) women were under-represented (Covert & Dixon, 2008). In another study, researchers found similar issues with ads from *Cosmopolitan* and *Family Life* (Sanchez-Hucles, Hudgins, & Gamble, 2005). This study did find, however, that magazines targeting specific ethnic groups had a majority of ads featuring individuals from that group (e.g., 64% of ads in *Latin Girl* featured characters identified as Latinx). Studies of televisions ads have also shown that Black, Asian, Latinx, and Native American individuals are under-represented (Coltrane & Messineo, 2000; Mastro & Stern, 2003). Similar patterns of under-representation of women of color have been found in television shows, although there is evidence that rates are improving for Black women—but not for women who are members of other racial/ethnic groups (Greenberg & Worrell, 2007). Invisibility isn't only about numbers; it's also about how women are portrayed when they are present, and women of color are often portrayed in stereotypical, and sexualized, ways (Sanchez-Hucles et al., 2005). We'll return to these ideas in Chapter 7 when we explore the sexualization of women.

In 2014, the extent to which digital retouching can play a role when older women are shown in the media was apparent when Diane Keaton, then age 68, accepted an award on behalf of Woody Allen at the Golden Globes ceremony. In the next ad break, a L'Oréal ad featuring Keaton was shown. At the Golden Globes, she had visible wrinkles (as shown here), as one would expect for someone of this age; in the ad, however, her skin was completely smooth.

The Role of Internalization

What is internalization, why is it so important to consider in the context of beauty norms, and how can girls and women be protected from its negative effects?

Girls and women learn about beauty standards from their parents, peers, and objectified, unrealistic images of women in the media. But not everyone who is surrounded by these influences takes them fully to heart. Feminist psychologists, among others, think that if enough women, and men, ignore these beauty norms, the norms themselves will start to change. However, some women—particularly White, wealthy, able-bodied, thin, cisgender women—benefit from beauty norms. Many girls and women are likely to internalize them and pressure themselves to conform. **Internalization** is the process of taking on the standards and norms of dominant society as one's own and then striving to meet those standards (Thompson, Heinberg, Altabe, & Tantleff-Dunn, 1999). This is believed to be a key risk factor for body dissatisfaction and disordered eating (Thompson & Stice, 2001).

Through a process of **social comparison** (Festinger, 1954), women and girls may check their appearance against these standards, as well as against the actual appearance of others. Exposure to advertisements featuring the thin ideal has been related to engagement in social comparison, which, in turn, was related to body dissatisfaction and depression (Bessenoff, 2006). This was especially the case for women who felt their bodies didn't meet the thin ideal. These days, lots of social comparison happens on social media. For example, women who use Facebook have been found to compare their appearance to others, and doing so was related to body image concerns (Fardouly & Vartanian, 2015). In a qualitative study about experiences on Instagram, a girl from Singapore described her experiences this way: "If you've never gone out to see the world, you'll probably love yourself, because you don't look at others. But when you look at social media, you start comparing. You start comparing yourself to other girls, and you'll start to wonder why you're not looking like them" (Chua & Chang, 2016, p. 194).

Resisting Internalization

Some women do manage to resist social comparison and the internalization of appearance norms. For example, researchers have found lesbian women to be more satisfied with their bodies than heterosexual women (Morrison, Morrison, & Sager, 2004) and Black women more likely to have higher body satisfaction than White women

(Grabe & Hyde, 2006). One explanation may be that these groups of women have internalized a different set of norms about beauty—ones that they're better able to achieve. For example, Black women have been found to be less likely to internalize traditional beauty norms, particularly the thin ideal (Capodilupo, 2015; Evans & McConnell, 2003). The same has been found with lesbians (Beren, Hayden, Wilfley, & Striegel-Moore, 1997; Bergeron & Senn, 1998). In a study with Latinx women who either immigrated to or were born in the United States, those who immigrated endorsed a larger ideal body than those who were born here, indicating that they may have internalized a different beauty norm (Lopez, Blix, & Blix, 1995).

It's also been suggested that feminist women, as compared to non-feminist women, are less likely to accept traditional beauty norms (Brown, 1987), and research has shown some support for this. For example, one study with a predominantly White sample found that identifying as a feminist was related to rejection of the norm of thinness (Hurt et al., 2007). In another study with a majority White sample, researchers showed that Instagram use was unrelated to engaging in body surveillance for women who scored high on a measure of feminist attitudes (Feltman & Szymanski, 2017). However, greater Instagram use predicted greater body surveillance for women with low and moderate levels of feminist attitudes. At the same time, other research indicated that feminist women experience conflict because they recognize that they've internalized beauty norms (Rubin, Nemeroff, & Russo, 2004). In other words, feminists are more likely to be aware of the unrealistic nature of these norms as well as the negative influence of internalizing them, and feminists *want* to be immune to them. However, they see the benefits that society gives to those who are beautiful. As a result, many feminists struggle because they find themselves caring about beauty but feeling they should be able to rise above it.

Various media literacy programs are targeting adolescent girls to counteract the media's negative influences. These programs teach girls to critique media representations because, as discussed above, they reflect only a small percentage of the population and are often manipulated. Research has shown that media literacy programs can lead

spotlight on . . .

Health at Every Size

Health at Every Size (HAES) is a grassroots movement opposing fat oppression and fat stigma (Burgard, 2009). It focuses on the importance of healthy practices and self-acceptance rather than body size, shape, or weight. The premise is that eating well and being active are key to a healthy lifestyle, and these are things that someone of any size can do.

HAES focuses on the fact that weight is not the only, or even the most useful, indicator of health. While some studies have found that a higher weight is associated with negative health outcomes, the correlations aren't large, and data rarely show whether weight loss actually changes health outcomes (Bacon, 2008; Kasardo & McHugh, 2015). Moreover, other data show that people classified as overweight or moderately obese live at least as long as, and often longer than, people classified as being normal weight (Bacon & Aphramor, 2011). Given this, more people are advocating for fat/size acceptance, and some seek a shift in public health policy toward a HAES perspective (Bombak, 2014).

Daily goals reflecting the HAES perspective (Bacon, 2008) include

- Eat when hungry.
- Attend to how foods taste and make you feel.
- Choose foods that you like and that make you feel good.
- Honor your body's signals of fullness.
- Find an enjoyable way to move your body.
- Treat your body with love and respect.

How often do you meet these goals? How might adopting a HAES perspective change your relationship with your body?

to increased body satisfaction among both adolescent girls (Wilksch, Tiggemann, & Wade, 2006; Wilksch & Wade, 2009) and college-age women (Yamamiya et al., 2005). Another effective approach has involved asking young women to make statements against the thin ideal (e.g., by writing an essay or role-playing discouraging a peer from focusing on the thin ideal; Becker et al., 2010; Ciao, Latner, Brown, Ebneter, & Becker, 2015). In this approach, because the young women have to make statements that are inconsistent with their own internalization of the thin ideal, they must change either their statements or their feelings about the thin ideal. Because the statements are already out in the world and can't be undone, the young women change their attitudes. However, long-term follow-ups of these programs have not yet been undertaken, so researchers don't know how long the effects of these interventions last. More research on this topic is needed.

Consequences of Self-Objectification

What are the negative consequences of self-objectification, and through what process do these happen?

We have established that beauty norms are learned from parents, peers, and the media and that they're generally internalized so that women feel they must live up to those standards, even if they're unrealistic. But does this actually harm women? To better understand this, it might be useful to imagine yourself participating in the following study—the first experimental exploration of self-objectification. You arrive at the assigned time and think you're taking part in a study about consumer preferences. After evaluating a unisex cologne (to throw you off track about the real purpose of the study), you're asked to enter a dressing room with a full-length mirror in order to try on an article of clothing—either a swimsuit (a one-piece for women and swim trunks for men) or a V-neck sweater in your size. You're asked to wear it for 15 minutes before making your evaluation, and while you wait, you're asked to complete a math test. How do you think you would do on the test? Would the clothing you've put on impact your performance?

It turns out that for the predominantly White, female participants who took part in the study described above, the clothing did make a difference (Fredrickson, Roberts, Noll, Quinn, & Twenge, 1998). The women wearing swimsuits performed significantly worse than those in sweaters, but there was no such difference for men. The women also reported more negative feelings about their bodies while wearing the swimsuit as compared to the sweater. Wearing a swimsuit placed the female, but not the male, participants into a state of self-objectification, and their focus on their bodies distracted them, inhibiting their performance on the math test.

But men aren't immune from self-objectification. In a subsequent study in which male participants had to wear a Speedo rather than trunks, men and women of all ethnic groups were found to self-objectify when wearing a swimsuit (Hebl, King, & Lin, 2004). Those in swimsuits also performed worse on a math test than those who wore a sweater.

It doesn't take wearing a swimsuit to create a state of self-objectification, however. Countless events can have the same effect. We can offer two familiar examples. If someone makes a comment about your appearance right before you enter the classroom, you might start thinking about how your body looks instead of focusing on the classwork. And if you're wearing a form-fitting shirt, you might worry about visible fat rolls while you sit. In situations like these, some people self-objectify more than others.

In one study with a primarily White sample, participants were asked to unscramble sentences that either did or did not contain words related to objectification (e.g., *appearance*, *slender*, and *shapely* vs. *honesty*, *happy*, and *silly*; Roberts & Gettman, 2004). Just being exposed to these words was enough to change participants' self-reported levels of self-objectification. Overhearing fat talk has also been shown to induce self-objectification (Gapinski, Brownell, & LaFrance, 2003). In another study, predominantly White female participants who anticipated interacting with a man reported higher levels of self-objectification than those who anticipated interacting with a woman (Calogero, 2004).

Even though the human mind is able to multi-task, there's a limit to what it can focus on at any given moment (Pashler, 1994). When we think about our appearance, we're less able to focus on a math test, athletic performance, or an oral presentation, for example. Once we enter a state of self-objectification, the effects also tend to linger. For example, one study showed that after being in a bathing suit, women were still distracted by thoughts about their body even after they had put their regular clothing back on (Quinn, Kallen, & Cathey, 2006).

The studies mentioned above use experimental designs, randomly assigning participants into situations that produced a state of self-objectification or into a control group, but most of the research on self-objectification relies on correlational designs. This type of research typically uses surveys to assess the extent to which women report experiencing self-objectification on a daily basis. For example, researchers might ask them to report how much they value their bodies' appearance as compared to their bodies' function (e.g., what the body can do; Fredrickson et al., 1998). Women who report that they value being thin more than they value being physically coordinated, for example, would be considered higher in self-objectification.

Other studies assess the extent to which women report viewing their bodies from an observer's perspective and evaluating their physical appearance—a process that has been named **body surveillance** (McKinley & Hyde, 1996). Body surveillance is a behavioral manifestation of self-objectification. Women who report checking in on their appearance more frequently are considered to be higher on self-objectification. Research has shown that self-objectification is

try it for yourself

To what extent do you think you regularly engage in body surveillance? Try going for an entire day without looking in a mirror. (Yes, reflective surfaces count too—so do your best to avoid them.) How did it make you feel not to be able to use a mirror? Were you comfortable leaving the house and doing all your usual activities? Did you change what you were wearing or how you styled your hair because you couldn't easily evaluate your appearance? Were you tempted to "cheat" and look in a mirror? Did you actually make it through an entire day? Explain your responses.

related to a host of negative outcomes (Moradi & Huang, 2008; Tiggemann, 2011).

One commonly studied negative outcome of self-objectification is **body shame**. This is an ongoing experience of negative emotions as a result of judging one's body as undesirable. It can occur when people continually evaluate their appearance against the societal beauty norms that they've internalized (Fredrickson & Roberts, 1997; McKinley & Hyde, 1996; Moradi & Huang, 2008). Because few, if any, women can conform to these norms, when women engage in body surveillance and find their appearance lacking, they're likely to experience body shame. Highly valuing the thin ideal, for example, has been related to a greater likelihood of reporting body shame (Calogero & Thompson, 2009; Noll & Fredrickson, 1998). The feeling of shame can, in turn, relate to other negative outcomes, as we'll discuss below.

The Process of Self-Objectification

As shown in Figure 6.1, researchers believe that the process of self-objectification works in the following way. Exposure to objectification, through both personal experiences (e.g., people commenting on your body) and exposure to objectified women in the media, leads to the internalization of beauty norms and the belief that it's important to meet cultural standards of beauty. When this happens, it leads to self-objectification, or the placing of greater emphasis on the body's appearance as compared to its function. Self-objectification, in turn, leads to an increase in body surveillance. Once people think that being beautiful is more important than what one's body does, they view the body from the outside in, continually checking their appearance to make sure it lives up to society's standards of beauty. Greater surveillance almost inevitably leads to increased body shame because it's typically impossible to meet current beauty standards. Body shame is then believed to relate to a host of negative outcomes, ranging from decreased task performance

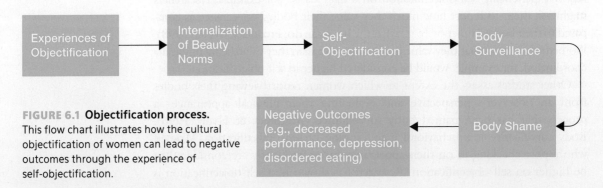

FIGURE 6.1 Objectification process. This flow chart illustrates how the cultural objectification of women can lead to negative outcomes through the experience of self-objectification.

(e.g., doing poorly on a math test: Fredrickson et al., 1998; Hebl et al., 2004) and self-esteem (Choma et al., 2010; Mercurio & Landry, 2008) to increased levels of depression (Szymanski & Henning, 2007; Tiggemann & Kuring, 2004) and disordered eating (Calogero, Davis, & Thompson, 2005; Tylka & Hill, 2004).

Intersectionality and Self-Objectification

How can social identity influence women's experience of self-objectification, and what are research limits in this area?

Women's experiences with self-objectification may be related to dealing with discrimination in terms of aspects of their social identities. For example, one study showed that among deaf women, struggles with deaf cultural identity predicted greater internalization of beauty norms, which was related to body surveillance, body shame, and disordered eating (Moradi & Rottenstein, 2007). A similar pattern has been found with lesbian and bisexual women. When these women internalize problematic messages about being a sexual minority, they're more likely to experience self-objectification (Brewster et al., 2014; Haines et al., 2008). Further, among transgender and gender non-conforming individuals, experiencing high levels of transphobia can be related to increases in body surveillance and compulsive exercise (Cox, 2015).

Among ethnic/racial minority women, there are mixed findings. In one study, researchers found that the relationship between body surveillance and body dissatisfaction was stronger among Asian and Latinx women than it was for White women (Frederick, Forbes, Grigorian, & Jarcho, 2007). However, in another study of Black and White adolescent girls, researchers found no differences in self-objectification (Harrison & Fredrickson, 2003). Engaging in surveillance related to skin tone may also be an important predictor of body shame, in addition to engagement in general body surveillance (Buchanan et al., 2008). That said, although there is some research on how race and ethnicity influence self-objectification, most studies have involved predominantly White samples (Moradi & Huang, 2008). When women of color are included, their experiences are typically compared to White women's. Furthermore, as with research on body satisfaction, research on self-objectification prioritizes concerns that are more typical of White women. For example, body shame is generally operationalized as shame about one's weight rather than including other aspects of appearance that may be more relevant for women of color (e.g., hair texture, eye shape). These patterns reflect research bias. The very nature of the questions being asked reflects the fact that most of the research is being done by and about White women. Research on self-objectification would benefit from a less Eurocentric approach. Using the intersectionality questions presented at the end of Chapter 1 to inform methodology would be a good first step.

Wearing a Hijab

The hijab is a head covering worn by some Muslim women. Although many variations of the hijab exist, varying in terms of the amount of the body concealed from view, the most common forms cover the hair or the hair and neck.

Some people have argued that the hijab, or other modesty requirements, is oppressing for women. Some opponents of the hijab see it as a means of controlling and limiting women's sexuality while also serving as a reminder that women are sexual objects, which is why they need to be hidden (Bakr, 2014; Hatem, 1988; Mernissi, 1987). Others, however, have indicated that wearing a hijab can be a means of protecting oneself from the male gaze and allowing women to assert themselves as individuals rather than as sexual objects by drawing their own and others' focus away from appearance (Ali, 2005; Droogsma, 2007; Noor, 2009; Ruby, 2006). Salma Yaqoob, a British Muslim activist, spoke in support of women's right to choose to wear a hijab by stating that "the aim of hijab is to de-emphasise sexuality in public interactions, whilst encouraging sexuality in private ones" (Yaqoob, 2004, para. 7). People who support the hijab argue that Western women are oppressed by social expectations that they display their bodies. These supporters would argue that the requirement to wear a bathing suit on a beach is more oppressive for women than the requirement to wear a hijab.

There's not much data on this topic to inform us on how it relates to women's relationships with their bodies. However, we can consider a few studies. In one, more than 500 Muslim women who lived in London completed a survey (Swami, Miah, Noorani, & Taylor, 2014). Those who wore the hijab reported less body dissatisfaction, had lower levels of internalization of beauty norms, and viewed appearance as less important than did women who didn't wear the hijab. Researchers also found that among Muslim women in the United States (Tolaymat & Moradi, 2011) and Australia (Mussap, 2009), hijab wearing was related to lower levels of self-objectification. Young Muslim women in the United States who wore the hijab were also less likely to have internalized the thin ideal (Dunkel, Davison, & Qurashi, 2010).

What do you think? Is wearing a hijab empowering or oppressing? Does it "allow women to claim the gaze and to become the ones who observe the world" (Afshar, 2000, p. 531), or does it serve as a constant visual reminder of women's status as sexual objects? Would your answer be the same or different if we were talking about the burqa, which covers the entire body and face (see cartoon at left), rather than the hijab, which covers much less of the body?

What we see as oppressive is influenced by our culture.

Other research has shown that self-objectification can change as people age (Augustus-Horvath & Tylka, 2009). It may start as early as 10 years of age and may be linked to peer sexual harassment that becomes particularly problematic around puberty (Lindberg, Grabe, & Hyde, 2007). Self-objectification also appears to rise throughout adolescence and peak around college age (McKinley, 1999). As women age, they appear to self-objectify less frequently, with the lowest levels of self-objectification occurring for the oldest women (in one study, up to 84 years old; Tiggemann & Lynch, 2001). It's not clear why self-objectification decreases as women age. It may be that when they're no longer the age of the majority of models they see in the media, they feel less pressure to conform to beauty standards. Alternatively, it may be that when women age, they become more concerned with what their bodies *can do* (e.g., be physically active) than with how their bodies *look*. This pattern may also reflect generational differences among women's body concerns. Nevertheless, research shows that no matter what age women are, self-objectification is still related to body shame, disordered eating, and depression (Grabe, Hyde, & Lindberg, 2007; Slater & Tiggemann, 2002; Tiggemann & Lynch, 2001).

Why Does Objectification Occur?

What psychological and economic processes likely contribute to objectification?

All this attention directed toward women's bodies is big business. As long as girls and women continue to experience self-objectification, companies can guarantee big payouts. For example, in 2016, more than $8.5 billion was spent on cosmetic surgical procedures and nearly $6.8 billion on non-surgical procedures, and approximately 91% of these procedures were performed on women (American Society for Aesthetic Plastic Surgery, 2016; see also Table 6.2). In the feminist classic *The Beauty Myth,* author Naomi Wolf (1991) argued that as long as women focus on their bodies, they would have less economic power and less time to focus on changing sexism in society. She argued that the obsession with female beauty is actually a political weapon against women's advancement. The stereotype of the ugly feminist is one example of this. In a more recent book, *Beauty Sick*, psychologist Renee Engeln (2017) argues that while young women are aware of the unrealistic nature of the images of women that surround them, they live in a "beauty-sick culture" (p. 8). She reinforces Wolf's message that the cultural focus on girls' and women's appearance gets in the way of them living happy lives and continues to limit their options and govern their actions.

Another interesting theory is that society is obsessed with managing the female body because of a fear of death. **Terror management theory** states that because humans fear death, anything that reminds us that we're mortal and

TABLE 6.2 Most Common Cosmetic Procedures among Women in the United States in 2016

Surgical Procedure	Number
Liposuction	369,323
Breast augmentation	310,444
Tummy tuck	173,536
Breast lift	161,412
Eyelid surgery	145,858
Non-Surgical Procedure	
Botox injections	4,144,605
Skin and lip filler injections	2,326,026
Laser/pulsed-light hair removal	910,224
Intense pulsed-light photorejuvenation	596,423
Chemical peel	574,141

Note. Data from American Society for Aesthetic Plastic Surgery (2016).

will die needs to be managed in a way that reduces our anxiety (Goldenberg, Pyszczynski, Greenberg, & Solomon, 2000). For example, the typical image of a model in a magazine is of someone young, beautiful, and hairless. She's almost more like a statue than a person, and a statue is immortal! Also, the female body has many more reminders of mortality than male bodies do. Female bodies can menstruate; they can lactate; they can give birth. These are signs that women are living beings who will eventually die. Given this context, some scholars claim that the objectification of women may be a cultural practice to help protect against mortality anxiety (Goldenberg & Roberts, 2004).

The female body has been described as the "monstrous feminine"— something with messy, undesirable processes that need to be managed through social and medical practices (Ussher, 2006, p. 1). As we've discussed, idealized and objectified images of women are the norm, not the exception. For example, in the Dove ad campaign discussed at the start of the chapter, the women in the ads show no body hair below the neck. And none appear to be leaking menstrual fluid or breast milk, despite the fact that many women experience such leaks at one time or another.

Some researchers have explored the concepts of fear of death and the monstrous feminine. In one study, half of the participants were primed to think about their mortality by describing their emotional response to thoughts of their own death (Grabe, Routledge, Cook, Andersen, & Arndt, 2005). Women who were asked to contemplate their death subsequently reported higher levels of self-objectification than those who did not. They were also more likely to report objectifying other women. Other research has explored self-objectification in the context of pregnancy, breastfeeding, and menstruation (Morris, Goldenberg, & Heflick, 2014). In this study, women, but not men, who were both encouraged to think about death and shown images of pregnant women were more likely to self-objectify. This effect also occurred when they were instructed to think about death and then asked if they had a tampon (as opposed to a pencil). Evidently, thinking about death and being reminded of the humanness of the body have the potential to make some women desire to separate themselves from their own humanness and view themselves more as an object. Objects, after all, are immortal.

Women's Bodies: From the Inside Out

Psychologist Stephen Franzoi (1995) suggested that there are two distinct ways of approaching our bodies. Sometimes we focus on our bodies as objects and attend primarily to our appearance. At other times, we focus on how our bodies function—what they can and can't do. As we've discussed throughout this chapter, appearance does matter, and there can be rewards for conforming to beauty norms and negative consequences when this isn't the case. As a result, women are likely to view their bodies as objects (i.e., self-objectify). However, what goes on inside our bodies is just as important—if not more so. Yet especially for women, much less attention is paid to how their bodies function or whether they're functioning well. As a result, some women don't have a clear sense of how their bodies work. For example, they may not fully understand the process of menstruation; they may not understand bodily cues, especially in regard to hunger; and they may exercise because of how it will make them *look* rather than how it will make them *feel*. These are examples of thinking about their bodies from the outside in, rather than from the inside out.

Menstruation

How does the menstrual cycle work at a biological level, and what are the cultural views of menstruation?

Let's look at menstruation, the shedding of the lining of the uterus (more commonly known as the period)—a process subsequently described in more detail.

Many people have negative attitudes toward menstruation (Beausang & Razor, 2000; Forbes, Adams-Curtis, White, & Holmgren, 2003), and men's attitudes tend to be more negative than women's (Brooks-Gunn & Ruble, 1986; Marván, Ramirez-Esparza, Cortes-Iniestra, & Chrisler, 2006). Menstruation is seen as messy, bothersome, and painful. Menstruating (or pre-menstrual) women are also seen as more emotional and, in some cases, less likeable and less competent than they are at other points in their menstrual cycle.

It's important to note that while menstruation is typically associated with women, not all women menstruate. For example, many women with Turner's syndrome (discussed in Chapter 4) don't menstruate; women who've had their uterus removed through a hysterectomy don't menstruate; and women with very low body weight or hormone imbalances may not menstruate. Moreover, not all menstruators are women—some transmen and people with non-binary gender identities menstruate as well. Transmen report mixed attitudes toward menstruation and generally favor using hormones to suppress it (Chrisler et al., 2016).

The Menstrual Cycle The menstrual cycle is an interaction between the female reproductive organs (see Figure 6.2) and the endocrine system, which regulates hormone production. At the start of a menstrual cycle, which lasts an

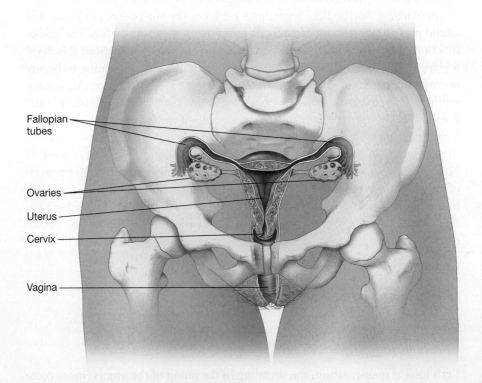

Fallopian tubes

Ovaries

Uterus

Cervix

Vagina

FIGURE 6.2 The female reproductive system.

average of 28 days, estrogen levels are low. This leads the *pituitary gland*, the master gland of the endocrine system, to produce *follicle-stimulating hormone (FSH)*. FSH then stimulates the follicles—sacs that hold eggs, or *ova* (singular, *ovum*)—in the ovaries to produce estrogen. *Estrogen* plays a key role in the development of the *endometrium*, the lining of the uterus. As estrogen levels rise throughout the menstrual cycle, *luteinizing hormone (LH)* released by the pituitary gland triggers *ovulation*, the release of an ovum from an ovarian follicle. This also stimulates the production of *progesterone* in the ovaries, as this hormone plays a role in the further thickening of the endometrium in preparation for the possibility of nourishing a fertilized egg.

When the ovarian follicle opens, the ovum moves into one of the fallopian tubes, which provide a pathway from the ovary to the uterus, or womb. Typically, one ovum from one ovary is released as part of each menstrual cycle. The follicle then develops into a *corpus luteum*, a structure that produces both estrogen and progesterone. If the ovum is fertilized by a sperm as it travels through the fallopian tube, the egg may implant itself in the endometrium and produce hormones that keep the corpus luteum active. The fetus that develops from this egg will then mature in the uterus. If the ovum isn't fertilized, the high progesterone levels lead to decreased production of LH and degeneration of the corpus luteum. The resulting drop in estrogen and progesterone levels causes the uterus to shed its lining, leading to a menstrual period. The menstrual flow moves from the uterus through the cervix into the vagina. From there, it flows out of the body unless it's absorbed internally by a product such as a tampon or collected internally in a device such as a menstrual cup.

Knowledge about Menstruation Many girls, and even some women, are relatively uninformed about menstruation and the menstrual cycle. Poor knowledge about menstruation has been found in both adolescent and teenage girls and may continue throughout adulthood (Lei, Knight, Llewellyn-Jones, & Abraham, 1987; White, 2013; Wood, Koch, & Mansfield, 2007). Mothers are usually the ones who tell their daughters about menstruation, although they often present it negatively with a focus on biology, hygiene, and physical discomfort (Costos, Ackerman, & Paradis, 2002; Koff & Rierdan, 1995a, 1995b; Lee, 2008).

However, mothers don't always discuss the topic with their daughters before **menarche**—the first menstrual period—so some girls may learn about it after being surprised or scared by their own first period (Cooper & Koch, 2007). The average age for menarche is 12 to 13 years (Coleman & Coleman, 2002), but some girls begin earlier (e.g., at 8 or 9 years) and others later (e.g., at 16 years). Because of this variation, some girls are first exposed to information about menstruation through (typically "girls-only") health education programs in school (Koff & Rierdan, 1995b), which may, in turn, prompt mothers to discuss the topic with daughters. Scholars have also pointed to the fact that girls may now act as their own sources of information about menstruation by searching the Internet (Stubbs, 2008).

Lack of knowledge and negative attitudes are associated with negative menarche experiences, but advance preparation and education are associated with more positive attitudes and experiences (Chang, Hayter, & Wu, 2010; Kieren & Morse, 1992; McPherson & Korfine, 2004; Rembeck & Gunnarsson, 2004; Rierdan & Koff, 1990; Teitelman, 2004). Hygiene related to menstruation is a key topic about which girls are provided information. Because of this, most girls are comfortable with the idea of using pads, and often tampons, to absorb menstrual fluid (Koff & Rierdan, 1995a, 1995b). Girls also report familiarity with the basic biology of menstruation and some of the structures that make up the female reproductive system (i.e., ovaries, fallopian tubes, uterus, cervix, and vagina).

Many girls have negative views about their menstrual education, however, and report confusion and misperceptions (Beausang & Razor, 2000). For example, they may not know exactly where the ovaries, fallopian tubes, and uterus are located or how they function in relation to one another (Koff & Rierdan, 1995a; Koff, Rierdan, & Stubbs, 1990). The fact that menstrual fluid is actually a mix of blood, other fluids such as cervical mucus and vaginal secretions, and tissue from the uterine lining may also be an area of confusion. So can ovulation and the hormonal cycles involved with the female reproductive system. As much education about menstruation happens informally, the lack of comfort and/or knowledge of those providing information may well contribute to confusion (Bennett & Harden, 2014; Erchull & Richmond, 2015). For girls who don't live with their mothers, finding accurate and timely information can be even more challenging, as they may not feel comfortable approaching their fathers or other adults for information (Kalman, 2003). Fathers may also be uncomfortable talking to their daughters about menstruation, particularly if they hold traditional beliefs about what should be involved in fathering (Erchull & Richmond, 2015).

When girls talk about menstruation, they often do so in surreptitious ways because they've learned it's something that should be kept secret. This can perpetuate shame as well as a lack of clear knowledge about menstruation.

Attitudes and Secrecy It's no surprise that many girls and women lack a clear understanding of the menstrual cycle since there is typically a great deal of secrecy surrounding menstruation and one's status as a menstruator. Also, there can be real social consequences for public reminders of one's status as a menstruator. For example, how might you react in the following situation? You're sitting in the library working on a class project. A woman at the table next to you stands up and grabs her purse. As she does, an unused, wrapped tampon falls out of her bag and onto the floor next to you. What would you think of her? Would seeing a tampon, and probably assuming that she's menstruating, affect your opinion of her? In a study, both female and male participants who experienced this event rated the woman as less likeable and less competent if they saw her drop a tampon as compared to a hair clip (Roberts, Goldenberg, Power, & Pyszczynski, 2002).

Because of concern about this type of negative reaction, it's easy for girls and women to think they need to conceal evidence of menstruation and avoid talking about it (White, 2013). Hiding menstruation from boys and men is of particular concern to girls (Jackson & Falmagne, 2013; Uskul, 2004). Although they learn not to talk about menstruation openly, research has indicated that they develop codes for talking about it (Fingerson, 2005, 2006; Kissling, 1996) and use online venues to share information and experiences (Polak, 2006). Although this practice can help girls feel empowered, it also serves to maintain taboos around open and public communication about menstruation.

In addition, advertisements for menstrual products often encourage secrecy (Berg & Coutts, 1994; Simes & Berg, 2001) and shame (Berg & Coutts, 1993; Havens & Swenson, 1988; Raftos, Jackson, & Mannix, 1998). This happens through the marketing of smaller products with quieter packaging so that the products are less noticeable to others and by installing a fear of having a visible menstrual fluid leak. Moreover, a content analysis of menstrual product ads noted that women weren't even pictured in 48% of the ads published between 1998 and 2009 (Erchull, 2013). Social media has also been involved in menstrual censorship: Instagram removed a photo of Rupi Kaur lying on a bed clothed with a visible menstrual leak that had also stained her sheets (Gray, 2015). This photo had been taken as part of her coursework and was posted on her own account, but it was repeatedly removed for violations of "community guidelines." In contrast, people routinely post pictures that show blood in other contexts (e.g., injuries), and those images are not removed as violations of these guidelines. Menstrual cycle activists and feminist psychologists, among others, argue that these practices reinforce the idea that women shouldn't draw attention to the fact that they menstruate.

Some women report negative experiences with menstruation. One that many women report is *premenstrual syndrome (PMS)*. PMS is a collection of physical (e.g., bloating) and psychological (e.g., moodiness)

spotlight on . . .

Menstrual Joy

Many people hold negative views about menstruation, so it may seem strange to think about its positive aspects. That, however, is just what the Menstrual Joy Questionnaire (MJQ) asks people to do (Chrisler, Johnston, Champagne, & Preston, 1994; Delaney, Lupton, & Toth, 1988). The MJQ was created as a cultural critique of a focus on the negative aspects of menstruation—best reflected in the persistent use of the Menstrual Distress Questionnaire (Moos, 1968) in menstrual cycle research (Delaney et al., 1988). Rather than asking about pain, bloating, and negative moods, the MJQ asks about increased sexual desire, concentration, and self-confidence, for example.

While the originators didn't intend for this to serve as a research tool, it has been used as such. Although it's not the best measure from a statistical standpoint (Heard, Chrisler, Kimes, & Siegel, 1999), the items have been shown to prime participants to focus on positive rather than negative aspects of menstruation (Aubeeluck & Maguire, 2002; Rose, Chrisler, & Couture, 2008).

Do you hold positive attitudes about menstruation? Why or why not? How might exposure to ideas like those in the Menstrual Joy Questionnaire influence your perspective? Talk to at least four friends, making sure they don't all have the same gender identity. Do they report positive views about menstruation? If they don't, challenge their thinking about this. Is this easy to do? Do some people take a more positive perspective than others?

experiences during the days before menstruation begins. PMS is not reported in all cultures, however, and this observation has led to the framing of PMS as a "culture-bound syndrome" related to Western expectations of menstruation and women's roles (Chrisler, 2008, p. 159; Ussher & Perz, 2013). In this view, it's largely the expectation that the pre-menstrual phase will be negative that shapes women's experience of it as negative. In fact, in one study, women were asked to rate the pleasantness of their mood on a day-to-day basis (McFarlane, Martin, & Williams, 1988). They were then asked to look back over the month and rate their moods. When measured daily, the participants' reported moods didn't fluctuate according to their menstrual cycle. However, when the participants were remembering, they felt as though they'd had a terrible mood right before and during their period and a better mood just after. Other researchers have found that women can and do identify positive pre-menstrual changes (King & Ussher, 2013). In other words, PMS may be more a stereotype than a reality.

As negative attitudes about menstruation and the pre-menstrual period persist, it's likely that menstruation will continue to be viewed with secrecy and shame. Researchers have found that negative attitudes, secrecy, and shame surrounding menstruation have been linked to the tendency to self-objectify (Grose & Grabe, 2014; Johnston-Robledo, Sheffield, Voigt, & Wilcox-Constantine, 2007; Roberts, 2004). However, when girls better understand their body processes, they can feel more comfortable with and positive about them.

Awareness of Body Cues

How does a focus on appearance influence awareness of body cues and eating behaviors?

Another consequence of the focus on appearance is the potential to lose a sense of how the body feels from the inside. To explore this issue, let's first consider when and how much we eat. Ideally, we would only eat when hungry and would stop when we feel satisfied (not "full," as many people experience after a traditional American Thanksgiving dinner). However, this isn't how many people in American society eat. Instead, people may eat at prescribed meal times because that's when others are eating or when their schedules allow time. Stopping when they're satisfied also doesn't always happen. They may eat past the point of satiation until feeling "stuffed" because they haven't realized that they're satisfied. At other times, they might hear an inner voice reminding them to "clean your plate" and not waste food. Or they might eat so fast that their brains don't have time to process signals of satiation coming from the stomach. The habit of focusing more on appearance than on what the body actually feels makes it difficult for many people to tell what their bodies actually need in a given situation.

For others, ignoring bodily cues may develop out of necessity. The reality is that many people, both globally and in the United States, are food insecure.

Although many individuals in the United States think of this as a problem that happens to other people in other places, 12% of households in the United States are estimated to experience food insecurity, and it's experienced by people in every county in the nation (Feeding America, 2017). There's also evidence that college students are particularly at risk for food insecurity (Blagg, Whitemore-Schanzenbach, Gundersen, & Ziliak, 2017). In a large study of college students, 48% reported food insecurity, and 22% reported having the most severe level of food insecurity (Dubick, Mathews, & Cady, 2016). People who don't have ready access to plentiful and nutritious food may purposely try to distance themselves from bodily cues of hunger in order to better focus on demands from school or work.

In general, a greater focus on bodily functions might lead to **intuitive eating** (also referred to as *mindful eating*). This approach involves eating based on physiological cues of hunger and satiation rather than situational or emotional cues (Tylka, 2006), and research with college women who predominantly identified as White showed that a focus on body function did predict intuitive eating (Avalos & Tylka, 2006). While the Health at Every Size (HAES) movement discussed earlier in this chapter is weight neutral, it does include a focus on eating in response to bodily cues. Moreover, research indicates that when people eat intuitively, they generally consume nutritious foods and are able to maintain their weight (Eneli, Crum, & Tylka, 2008).

In order to engage in intuitive eating, people have to be aware of their internal physiological signals. This is known as having **interoceptive awareness**. For example, does an uncomfortable feeling in the belly signal hunger or sadness? Numerous studies have shown that self-objectification is related to lower levels of interoceptive awareness (Ainley & Tsakiris, 2013; Myers & Crowther, 2008; Peat & Muehlenkamp, 2011; Tylka & Hill, 2004) and a decreased likelihood of reporting intuitive eating (Andrew, Tiggemann, & Clark, 2015). Of course, this line of research assumes that people have access to plentiful sources of food.

Motivation to Exercise

What are some motivations for exercising, and how are they related to positive and negative outcomes?

It would be rare to find someone who thinks that being physically active isn't a good practice. However, many people don't undertake physical activity solely for the benefits in terms of short- and long-term physical health, for the potential increase in energy levels that can result, or for the sense of satisfaction that can come from using one's body. Rather than these function-oriented motivations, girls and women often engage in exercise in order to "improve" their appearance (Laus, Braga Costa, & Almeida, 2013; McDonald & Thompson,

1992; Tiggemann & Williamson, 2000). Appearance-related, as compared to health-related, messages have also been found to be dominant on health and fitness magazine covers (Bazzini, Pepper, Swofford, & Cochran, 2015), and 20% of the content in these magazines is focused on appearance (Willis & Knobloch-Westerwick, 2014).

Those who do exercise have been found to report a more positive body image compared to those who don't (Hausenblas & Fallon, 2006). Research exploring more specific motivations for exercise among girls and women, however, shows a more complex picture. Appearance-focused motivations have been linked to negative feelings about the body, self-objectification, decreased self-esteem, and disordered eating (Cash, Novy, & Grant, 1994; de Bruin, Woertman, Bakker, & Oudejans, 2009; Gonçalves & Gomes, 2012; McDonald & Thompson, 1992; Mond, Hay, Rodgers, & Owen, 2006; Strelan, Mehaffey, & Tiggemann, 2003; Tiggemann & Williamson, 2000; Vinkers, Evers, Adriaanse, & de Ridder, 2012). Thus, while exercising is generally related to positive benefits, exercising with the goal of improving appearance is related to negative outcomes. In contrast, exercising for functional, rather than appearance-oriented, reasons has been found to be either unrelated to feelings about the body (Vinkers et al., 2012) or associated with more positive feelings about one's body and higher self-esteem (McDonald & Thompson, 1992; Strelan et al., 2003; Tiggemann & Williamson, 2000).

Because this research is correlational, one can't assume that exercising for appearance reasons increases body dissatisfaction; it could be that body dissatisfaction increases appearance-related motivations to exercise. Most likely, there's some of each going on. Regardless, engaging in any activity for external rather than internal reasons is harder to maintain over time (Rothman, Baldwin, Hertel, & Fuglestad, 2011). Interestingly, research has indicated that, among midlife women, appearance-oriented motives for exercising were related to decreased levels of physical activity (Segar, Spruijt-Metz, & Nolen-Hoeksema, 2006). Exercising can result in an improvement of what our bodies can do: They can lift more, stretch more, run more. It may also result in better conforming to societal standards of attractiveness. However, data suggest that in order to fully benefit from exercise, we should focus on what we can do rather than how we look.

Conclusion

Many girls and women experience their bodies as physical objects. Approaching their bodies as though they're observers means that they risk losing touch with what their bodies can do and what they feel like from within. Due to pervasive messages from the media, as well as the influence of parents and peers, many girls and women come to understand their value in terms of the extent to which their bodies conform to societal beauty standards. This can be a recipe for dissatisfaction and disappointment, as beauty norms are difficult to achieve, change over time, and are often incompatible with one another. Even if those norms can be met, it's typically only for a fleeting moment in time.

However, research shows that girls and women can undermine the power of objectification, largely by learning to be critical of beauty standards and resisting internalization of the messages that surround them. Also, as we'll see in Chapter 13, mental health vastly improves when girls and women focus on activities that help them to get in touch with their bodies from within and to approach their bodies (and all aspects of themselves) with a sense of kindness and self-compassion.

Chapter Review

SUMMARY

Women's Bodies: From the Outside Looking In

- Society typically focuses more on the physical appearance of girls and women than on what girls and women are like internally.

- Girls and women can internalize this objectifying perspective and focus primarily on how their bodies *look* rather than on what they *can do*.

Beauty Matters

- Women are rewarded for being attractive and can face negative consequences when they don't conform to beauty standards.

- Because few, if any, women can meet beauty standards, most women report body dissatisfaction.

Beauty Norms

- Society has specific standards for what is and is not considered attractive.

- Beauty norms for girls and women include, but are not limited to, having symmetrical features, being thin, and having little to no body hair.

- Specific beauty norms (e.g., skin tone, hair texture, being able-bodied) may be relevant for girls and women who identify as being part of specific groups (e.g., women of color, women with disabilities, transwomen).

How We Learn about Beauty Norms

- The tripartite model of social influence identifies parents, peers, and media as key factors influencing body image.

- Parents are a key source of information about beauty norms, and research has shown that mothers are particularly important.

- Peers, particularly same-gender peers, can provide key information about beauty norms and the extent to which girls and women do and do not meet them. Fat talk plays a major role in this process.

- The media may be the most important source of beauty norms. However, images of girls and women in the media rarely reflect typical individuals.

- Not all women are represented in the media at the same rates or at rates that reflect their actual presence in the population.

The Role of Internalization

- Beauty norms become problematic when they are internalized because they reflect largely unattainable standards.
- Some girls and women manage to resist certain beauty norms (e.g., Black women, lesbians, feminists).

Consequences of Self-Objectification

- Experiencing objectification leads to greater internalization of beauty norms, which leads to self-objectification and body surveillance.
- Body surveillance leads to body shame, which leads to other negative outcomes such as decreased performance, depression, and disordered eating.
- The process and effects of self-objectification may be somewhat different for different groups of women (e.g., lesbians, women of color, older women).

Why Does Objectification Occur?

- Objectification benefits a capitalist society, as it spurs spending on beauty products, procedures, and services.
- Objectification may also be a way of sanitizing and controlling the female body—perhaps to stave off thoughts of mortality.

Women's Bodies: From the Inside Out

- Because most girls and women are very focused on how their bodies look, they aren't as focused on or aware of how their bodies work and what they can do.
- Girls and women generally hold negative attitudes about menstruation and may have an incomplete understanding of how the menstrual cycle works.
- Norms of shame and secrecy surround menstruation.
- People who are not experiencing food insecurity typically eat in response to cues other than hunger (e.g., schedules or emotions).
- Girls' and women's engagement in physical activity is often motivated by appearance concerns rather than those related to improved physical functioning.

KEY TERMS

objectification (p. 235)

male gaze (p. 235)

objectification theory (p. 236)

self-objectification (p. 236)

body dissatisfaction (p. 238)

normative discontent (p. 238)

beauty norms (p. 240)

colorism (p. 241)

tripartite model of social influence (p. 247)

body esteem (p. 247)

fat talk (p. 248)

cultivation theory (p. 250)

face-ism (p. 251)

internalization (p. 254)

social comparison (p. 254)

body surveillance (p. 257)

body shame (p. 258)

terror management theory (p. 261)

menarche (p. 265)

intuitive eating (p. 269)

interoceptive awareness (p. 269)

THINK ABOUT IT

1. Go to a bookstore or library and examine images in magazines. How do the images align with beauty norms, and how do these norms relate to real women's experiences of their bodies? Using the research in this chapter, what types of recommendations would you make to magazine executives?

2. Compare the research on how people learn about beauty norms to your own experience. In what ways does the research reflect your experience? In what ways does it differ?

3. What advice would you give a friend to help her combat self-objectification based on the research in this chapter?

4. Go to your local drug or grocery store and examine the products related to menstruation. What types of things do you notice (e.g., color of box, images, wording, cost). Are there any gendered and stigmatizing themes? If so, how would you address them to make the products less stigmatizing?

ONLINE RESOURCES

- **Adios Barbie** — broadens concepts of body image to include race, gender, LGBTQ identify, dis/ability, age, and size: adiosbarbie.com

- **Bad Fat Broads** — conversations with fat women on diverse topics: badfatbroads.com

- **Health at Every Size** — Health at Every Size pledge and community: haescommunity.com

- **The Back Talk** — conversations, essays, and anecdotes from young women of color with a focus on body positivity: soundcloud.com /thebacktalk

- **The Body Is Not an Apology** — offers information on radical self-love for everybody and every body: thebodyisnotanapology.com

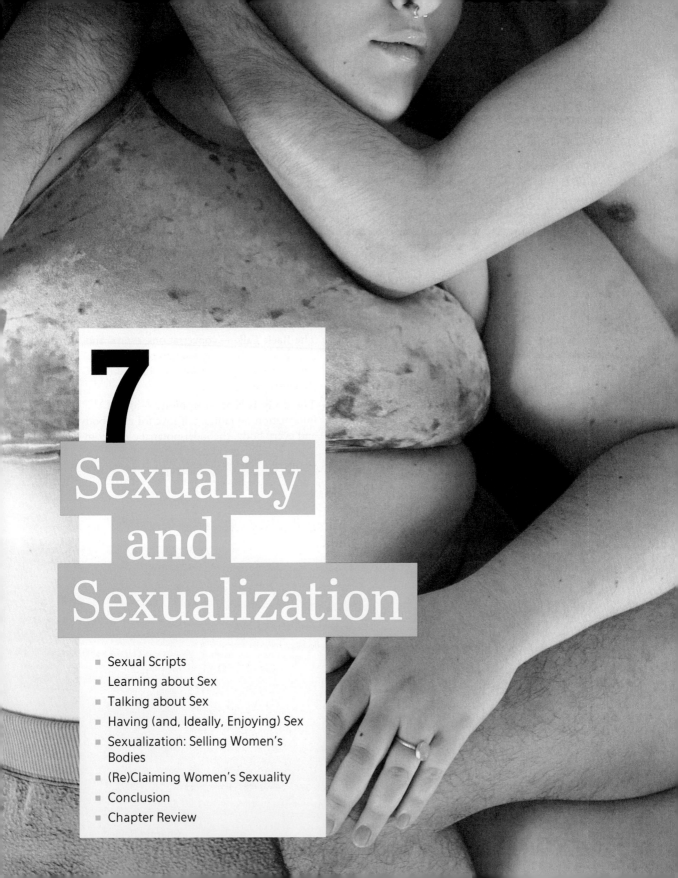

7
Sexuality and Sexualization

- Sexual Scripts
- Learning about Sex
- Talking about Sex
- Having (and, Ideally, Enjoying) Sex
- Sexualization: Selling Women's Bodies
- (Re)Claiming Women's Sexuality
- Conclusion
- Chapter Review

ON AUGUST 18, 2015, the U.S. Food and Drug Administration (FDA) formally approved Flibanserin (U.S. Food and Drug Administration, 2015). While drug approvals often receive some attention, this one drew significant media coverage because it was approved to treat low sexual desire in women. On the surface, this sounds like a wonderful thing. If women are experiencing sexual dysfunction, it should be taken seriously, and medical interventions have the potential to be beneficial. Also, the FDA approval could be seen as an indication that women's, not just men's, sexuality is understood as important. After all, the approval of Viagra, a drug to treat male sexual dysfunction, in 1998 quickly became "the topic of evening news programs, late-show comedy monologues, cocktail party conversations, online chat rooms and pillow talk in bedrooms everywhere" according to *The Washington Post* (Weeks, 1998, para. 1)—so why should the response to approval of a drug to treat female sexual dysfunction be any different?

Flibanserin, sold under the brand name Addyi, is the first FDA-approved drug for increasing women's sexual desire. The approval of this drug and its introduction to the market have been fraught with controversy.

As with other issues discussed in this book, not everything about Flibanserin is positive. First, although it's often referred to as the "female Viagra" (e.g., Goldschmidt, 2015), there are important differences. For example, Viagra is taken only when planning to have sex; Flibanserin must be taken daily. Also, unlike Viagra, Flibanserin doesn't treat a particular physiological issue that makes having sex challenging; instead, it increases overall levels of sexual desire by changing levels of neurotransmitters in the brain (it was initially developed as an antidepressant). Second, critics have argued that this drug (and the disorder it purports to treat) reflects an androcentric view of healthy or "normal" sexuality. Maybe women's sex drives are perfectly normal and just reflect the variation inherent in human beings—that is, some people want to have sex a lot, while others want it less frequently (New View Campaign, 2014). Do women really need to take what's basically an antidepressant if they don't want to have sex "enough," or is this just an example of a pharmaceutical company capitalizing on the medicalization of women's sexuality?

However, both women and men do experience sexual dysfunction, yet women's sexual dysfunction has received less medical and research attention

What do you think is a normal amount of sexual desire? Do you think "normal" varies among different groups of people (e.g., women, men, teens, the elderly)? Do you think a woman who has a lower level of sexual desire than her partner should take a drug like Flibanserin? Can you imagine a situation in which a woman would be pressured to take such a drug? Alternatively, how might taking such a drug be empowering for women?

than men's (at least, compared to the focus on erectile dysfunction). Sexual dysfunction can cause significant distress for individuals and be a source of stress within relationships. Given this context, is the approval of Flibanserin a good thing?

The different perspectives regarding the approval of Flibanserin remind us that women's sexuality is complex. What is considered normal, abnormal, desirable, and undesirable depends on whom you ask. It's critical to understand how sexuality shapes women's experiences, particularly because gender oppression often occurs through the regulation and control of female sexuality. In this chapter, we'll explore cultural assumptions and expectations surrounding sex and women's sexuality. We'll examine how people learn about and talk about sex, as well as the challenges they face when trying to do so. We'll discuss women's positive and negative experiences with both engaging and not engaging in sexual activity. We'll also explore the influence of our sexualized culture on women and perceptions of women's sexuality. In doing this, we'll be able to explore the ways in which culture shapes expectations about women's sexuality as well as women's experiences with sex and sexuality.

Sexual Scripts

What are sexual scripts, and what core messages are conveyed as part of the traditional sexual script?

Sexual scripts are descriptions of behaviors that reflect beliefs about what is "normal" sexual behavior in a given culture (Gagnon & Simon, 1973; Simon & Gagnon, 1986, 2003). We see such scripts in the behavior of those around us, but the media are a key source of these, and other, scripts. For example, in television shows we primarily see depictions of men as initiators of sexual activity (Kim et al., 2007). Because this is what's represented most commonly, people come to understand it as typical, and even expected. Although multiple sexual scripts exist, there's a single dominant sexual script in Western culture that comprises a number of interrelated assumptions. These assumptions, and the script as a whole, can have a powerful effect because they convey information about what counts as sex, how to act in the context of a sexual encounter, who can be sexual, and when one can engage in sexual activity. In this section, we'll discuss some of the key assumptions that combine to form the dominant sexual script.

Sex = Heterosexuality

One key assumption is that heterosexuality is the default sexual identity and that all other sexual identities are "other." This assumption is a core component of *compulsory heterosexuality*, the idea that the only "appropriate" or "normal" romantic and sexual behaviors are heterosexual (Rich, 1980). According to compulsory heterosexuality, learning to prioritize heterosexuality is a key part of gender role socialization. We can consider, as just two examples, that many Disney movies end with a princess marrying a prince, and that some parents jokingly refer to cross-gender friendships in children as "having a girlfriend/boyfriend." These examples show that assumptions about heterosexuality are interconnected with feminine and masculine social norms, and they contribute to gender oppression. Decades ago, the poet, writer, and radical feminist Adrienne Rich asserted that compulsory heterosexuality reinforces patriarchy because it teaches girls and women that, instead of attending to their own needs and desires, they should work to gain male attention. Therefore, girls and women may learn that they should attempt to gain power and status through male recognition, which would keep them from focusing on gaining power and status in other ways (a topic we'll return to later in this chapter). Seen in this way, heterosexuality isn't simply *just* about sexual behaviors or identities; it's also a set of powerful norms and gendered practices that could be adopted by anyone, regardless of sexual orientation.

Although compulsory heterosexuality was originally written about in 1980, it still remains the dominant script today. For example, popular media regularly convey messages that reinforce compulsory heterosexuality. In one study, researchers reviewed 51 hours of primetime television and coded instances of depictions that conformed to the dominant, heterosexual sexual script (Kim et al., 2007). The researchers identified depictions of women as sexual gatekeepers, men as initiators of relationships, and women as engaging in self-sexualization (all topics discussed in this chapter). Across these 51 hours of TV, the heterosexual script was portrayed 662 times. In contrast, non-heterosexual scripts are much harder to find or are presented in ways that signal deviance (Power, McNair, & Carr, 2009). For example, even though shows like *Glee* and *Degrassi* have been praised for their portrayal of gender and sexual diversity, the primary plots revolve around narratives of discrimination and assault motivated by hatred and ignorance (Sandercock, 2015).

Performative bisexuality (Fahs, 2009) has surfaced as one non-heterosexual script. In this script, heterosexual women make out and engage in sexual activities with other women for the enjoyment of men who are watching them. For example, in season 1 of the HBO series *Girls*, the characters Marnie and Jessa leave a bar with a man and go to his apartment. Marnie, who later in the scene says, "I'm not gay,"

The 2003 MTV Video Music Awards is often remembered as the awards show where pop icon Madonna kissed Britney Spears (picture here) as well as Christina Aguilera (not shown). Do you think such instances of performative bisexuality are harmless and fun, or do they send negative messages about how and when women should express desire for other women?

begins to kiss Jessa, who, after initial surprise, smiles knowingly and reinitiates the make-out session while the man watches. Because performative bisexuality usually revolves around the sexual pleasure of one or more men, even this script can be considered androcentric and primarily heteronormative. In fact, the co-opting of female homosexuality has been considered part of the modern heterosexual script by some researchers because it's about arousing men rather than women (Kim et al., 2007).

Sex = Prioritizing Men: Penetration and Orgasm

Because our society is androcentric, men's experiences tend to be central. That's just as true with sex as with other aspects of life. As a result, women's sexuality is often understood as non-normative, or at least undesirable, if their experiences differ from those of men. Thinking back to this chapter's opening story about the drug that treats low sex drive in women, it's possible to offer an alternative, non-androcentric perspective: Maybe it's not women who need treatment; maybe it's men who have overactive sex drives. How likely do you think it would be for the FDA to approve a drug designed to reduce sex drives in men? Probably not very likely, and while we're not advocating that this would be a good idea, it's hard to even contemplate because men's sexual desires and experiences are viewed as the norm.

To think about this in another way, how would you describe "sex"? A website aimed at parents who want to talk to their children about sex suggested: "When a man and a woman decide they want to do this [have sex], the man's penis goes inside the woman's vagina, and sperm comes out of the man's penis" (Gorney, 2018, para. 3). The *Encyclopedia Britannica* described it this way: "Sexual intercourse . . . [is a] reproductive act in which the male reproductive organ . . . enters the female reproductive tract. If the reproductive act is complete, sperm cells are passed from the male body into the female, in the process fertilizing the female egg and forming a new organism. . . . Sexual intercourse both culminates and terminates in orgasm, a process in which the male expels semen . . . into the female's vaginal canal" ("Sexual Intercourse," 2017, paras. 1 and 2).

Both descriptions are accurate, but they also both reflect heteronormative and androcentric assumptions: heteronormative because they assume sex only involves a woman and a man; androcentric because only male orgasm is addressed. However, some people engage in sex that doesn't include a woman and a man—according to one study, 8.7% of women and 8.2% of men (Twenge, Sherman, & Wells, 2016). The same study showed that more people report engaging in same-gender-partner sex than was true in the past (e.g., 3.6% of women and 4.5% of men reported this in the early 1990s). Also, some people engage in sex with more than one person at the same time. In one study of mostly White, heterosexual college students, researchers found that 13% of participants reported engaging in mixed-gender threesomes, and 64% of participants reported having interest in them (Thompson & Byers, 2017). These findings are another indication of the limits of normative explanations of sex, which are narrow and inaccurate.

Returning to the definitions given above, in both descriptions the woman is passive—the entire definition is about how the man puts his penis inside of her and sperm comes out. She basically just needs to be there. The sex act ends when the man ejaculates, not when the woman has an orgasm. In fact, according to the definitions above, even if the woman never has an orgasm, the sexual act would still be considered "complete" as long as the man ejaculates.

Sex = Men Always Want It and Initiate It, but Women Must Ward It Off

The heterosexual sexual script centers on the idea that men are frequently focused on sex and are likely to initiate sexual encounters, whereas women are supposed to ward off sexual attention from men and keep their "purity." When women do have sex, they're supposed to be more focused on their partner's pleasure than their own and be passive participants in sexual relationships. In popular culture, this script plays out, for example, in TV shows where men are typically portrayed as the ones seeking to have sex (with women; Kim et al., 2007). In contrast, women are less likely to be depicted trying to get and enjoy sex. Essentially, these scripts tell us that women are the recipients of sexual attention and important participants in men's sexual encounters, but they are not, in and of themselves, driven by sexual desires.

One way that compulsory heterosexuality contributes to the oppression of girls and women is by reinforcing beliefs that boys and men should prioritize their sexual desires and act on their sexual needs, and that hormones are the primary factor driving male sexual urges (Tolman, 2006). Girls and women, in contrast, are expected to manage male sexual urges by being the gatekeepers of sex. They should seek to please, but at the same time they should "wish and wait" for male attention (Kim et al., 2007, p. 146).

The reality is different, however. Women do think about sex, initiate sex, actively participate in sexual encounters, and enjoy sex (at least some women, some of the time). However, when women are described as desiring and initiating sex, they're generally punished and called sluts (Attwood, 2007). This perspective reflects the **sexual double standard (SDS)** by which women are judged more harshly than men for engaging in comparable sexual behaviors. Research findings about the existence and prevalence of the SDS have been mixed. While many people say that women and men *shouldn't* be judged differently for the same behaviors, they actually often are (Crawford & Popp, 2003). Although this attitude may no longer be true for having sex before marriage, it continues to apply for less common sexual behaviors, such as having a threesome (Sagebin Bordini, & Sperb, 2013). Furthermore, some women anticipate being judged negatively for sexual behaviors (Conley, Ziegler, & Moors, 2013), even when they themselves reject the double standard (Milhausen & Herold, 1999). Research has also indicated that men are more likely to endorse the SDS than are women (Sakaluk & Milhausen, 2012; Sprecher, Treger, & Sakaluk, 2013).

The SDS negatively impacts women in several ways. For example, in one study, researchers found that teen girls with many sexual partners were less likely to be accepted by their peers than were boys with many partners (Kreager & Staff, 2009). Other research indicated that predominantly White, college student participants were more likely to judge a woman who initiated a casual sex encounter as being less intelligent and less mentally healthy than a man who did the same thing (Conley et al., 2013). Sometimes, instead of these more subtle social judgments, women who are—or are perceived to be—more sexually active are explicitly targeted through **slut shaming**. This occurs when girls and women are criticized for their actual or presumed engagement in sexual behaviors, and it's particularly common among adolescents and young adults (Armstrong, Hamilton, Armstrong, & Seeley, 2014; Bamberg, 2004; Ringrose, Harvey, Gill, & Livingstone, 2013). Even wearing sexy clothing or dancing suggestively can result in receiving this label (Papp et al., 2015).

The heterosexual sexual script doesn't focus on women actively wanting, enjoying, and initiating sex, but if a woman doesn't want sex enough to please her partner, that's also considered problematic. Moreover, asexuality, which we first discussed in Chapter 4, is completely absent from these scripts. In recent years, there has been increased awareness of asexuality as a sexual orientation identity held by some people. There's not a great deal of research exploring asexuality to date, and researchers operationalize asexuality in different ways across studies. As a result, there are no consistent estimates of the rates of asexuality or asexual identification in the population. Estimates of prevalence range from less than 1% of the population to about 5.5% of the population either identifying as asexual or reporting attitudes and/or behavior consistent with asexuality (Van Houdenhove, Gijs, T'Sjoen, & Enzlin, 2014). However, lack of interest in sex or low sex drive is often pathologized as a disorder (Brotto & Yule, 2017)—a topic we'll return to later in this chapter—as evidenced by the FDA approval of Flibanserin. In this atmosphere, women can find themselves in a double bind: If they completely avoid sex, they're likely to be seen as prudish or frigid; but if they're highly sexual, they're likely to be seen as sluts.

Sex = Something for the Young, Beautiful, and Able-Bodied

When you think of people having sex, what do you imagine they look like? Do they conform to traditional standards of attractiveness? Are they young? Do they have visible disabilities? It's very possible that your answers reflect our culture's normative heterosexual script—and that's because sexual scripts not only tell us *how* we can be sexual, but also tell us who *isn't* supposed to be sexual. For example, popular media rarely show images of older people, particularly older women, being sexual (Gill, 2009), and the bodies of midlife women are often depicted as targets of humor rather than desire (Weitz, 2010). One exception is the hypersexual "cougar" who pursues sexual relationships with younger men (Montemurro & Siefken, 2014), and although this term reflects the fact that older women don't necessarily lack sexual desire, it's generally used in a derogatory way. Furthermore, women with physical and intellectual disabilities are often thought of as asexual (Milligan & Neufeldt, 2001). Even though some women with disabilities do, in fact, identify as asexual (Kim, 2011), this isn't true of all women who have disabilities. Regardless of the fact that many women, and men, with disabilities are sexually active, some people believe that this is inappropriate, particularly for those with intellectual disabilities (Cuskelly & Bryde, 2004).

The reality is that all women have the potential to be sexual, but sexual scripts limit our thinking about women's sexuality—and sexuality in general. By specifying what sex is supposed to involve and who is supposed to enjoy it, they increase the focus on some women's sexuality while ignoring that of others. Like so many topics we've already covered, it's not enough to change norms and scripts to a different set. Replacing one narrow perspective with another just shifts the problem and results in different people being marginalized rather than stopping marginalization. Broader education about sexuality and the diversity of attitudes and experiences would aid a shift away from a single dominant script and toward an array of equally viable, although different, scripts.

your turn

If you were to explain sex and sexuality to someone who was unfamiliar with the idea, what "rules" would be part of your explanation? Now imagine trying to explain sex to someone who doesn't understand gender—at least, not as a binary in the way it's typically discussed. Would these "rules" make as much sense? Would sex "look" different if we didn't focus on gender?

Learning about Sex

How do we learn about sex, and what is typically covered and not covered?

As we've discussed, cultural messages about sex and sexuality surround us and can influence both thinking and behavior. But how do we actually learn about sex? What do we learn? Most people learn about sex from a variety of sources, including parents and other family members, peers, and the media. Many also learn about sex as part of formalized school-based sex education programs. Information gleaned from these sources can vary, and the different sources are not equally influential on attitudes and behavior. Degree of knowledge and level of comfort of those providing information can also impact what is learned.

Parents

When you think about talking with parents about sex, you might imagine an awkward moment when a parental figure tries to have an intimate discussion about sexuality with a squirming adolescent; this is often referred to as "the talk." **Sexual socialization**—the process of learning about sexuality—actually begins far earlier than adolescence. It starts when parents (and others) talk to young children (e.g., pre-schoolers) about their body parts, romantic and sexual relationships, and so on (Martin & Luke, 2010). These conversations may result from a daughter's questions about why parts of her body are different from those of her brother, or from children asking where babies come from. Research has indicated, however, that parents are often uncomfortable about talking with

When you hear the phrase "the talk," what comes to mind? Who's involved in the conversation? What's covered? Did you receive "the talk"? Have you ever given it? If you have children or plan to have children, what have you said or would you say to them about sex and sexuality?

their kids about sex and aren't sure how much information to give, or when (Geasler, Dannison, & Edlund 1995; Stone, Ingham, & Gibbins 2013). Given this discomfort, many parents take the approach of answering questions when asked but not initiating discussions about sex and sexuality (Frankham, 2006). Of course, this approach results in less information being shared.

Regardless, children manage to absorb information that gives them insight into sex and sexuality. In fact, children learn not just from what they're explicitly taught; they also learn about the world by identifying what isn't discussed. In the context of sex and sexuality, silence or limited conversation about certain topics also teaches children about family and cultural attitudes (Dyson, 2016). For example, children might see two women kissing at the park and ask their mother why the women are doing that. If the mother brushes off the question or skirts the issue by saying that they must be friends, the children are, perhaps unintentionally, being told indirectly that it's not okay for two people of the same gender to be intimately involved (or, at least, not to indicate this with public displays of affection). In this way, heteronormativity is reinforced.

As children reach puberty, parents may wish to impart specific knowledge about sex and sexuality, or have their children engage in some type of formal or informal sexual education. According to numerous studies, mothers tend to be the primary providers of sex education in the home (DiIorio, Pluhar, & Belcher, 2003; Raffaelli, Bogenschneider, & Flood, 1998; Wisnieski, Sieving, & Garwick, 2015), but many remain uncomfortable and feel that they lack the necessary knowledge to be successful educators (Jaccard, Dittus, & Gordon, 2000; Orgocka, 2004; Walker, 2001; Wilson, Dalberth, Koo, & Gard, 2010). In one study that explored Latinx maternal and adolescent communications about sex, researchers found that daughters were resistant to talking about sex, which caused initial discomfort for their mothers (O'Sullivan, Meyer-Bahlberg, & Watkins, 2001). Over time, however, mothers can build open communication patterns (McKee & Karasz, 2006). This is important, because other research indicates that Latinx girls, in particular, are likely to make decisions about sexuality on the basis of familial conversations, especially those with their mothers (Denner & Coyle, 2007; Hovell, et al., 1994).

When parents do talk to children about sex, key themes that are generally communicated include girls' responsibility for avoiding and/or controlling sexual encounters and the consequences of sexual intercourse. Positive and pleasurable aspects of sex and sexuality are rarely part of these conversations (DiIorio et al., 2003). In a study examining Asian American girls' perception of their parents' communication style, all the girls reported that their parents relayed messages indirectly (Kim & Ward, 2007). Parents who were more acculturated to U.S. cultural norms and practices conveyed a message that premarital sex was acceptable; however, those parents who were more religious and who didn't speak English in the home leaned toward abstinence-based messages.

Peers

Many parents don't actually talk about sexuality with their children—at least, not a lot or in an ongoing way as children grow up (Warren, 1995; Wilson et al., 2010). As a result, broader social networks are often important sources of information about sexuality for young people: family members such as grandparents, aunts, and siblings, as well as family friends, parents of peers, and peers (George et al., 2013; Wisnieski et al., 2015). Peers, in particular, can be an important source of information. In several studies, girls and young women rank peers as a more important source of information about sex than their parents (Bleakley, Hennessy, Fishbein, & Jordan, 2009; Heisler, 2005; Sprecher, Harris, & Meyers, 2008). For example, Black and Latinx girls report learning sexual standards from observing and talking with their peers (O'Sullivan & Meyer-Bahlberg, 2003). In another study of Latinx young adults, researchers found that female peers helped to promote "smart sex," which included learning about contraceptive use and devising plans to avoid "players" and to manage their sexual reputations (Faulkner, 2003, p. 188).

The Media

The media constitute another important source of information about sex and sexuality for many young people (Bleakley et al., 2009; Sprecher et al., 2008; Ward, 2003) and, like peers, often rank as a more important source than parents (Sprecher et al., 2008). Being a major source of information about what constitutes acceptable sexual behaviors, the media contribute to the sexual scripts that people develop (Kim et al., 2007). In fact, it has been suggested that the media may serve as a "sexual super peer" (Brown, Halpern, & L'Engle, 2005, p. 421). Because movies, TV shows, magazines, and the Internet are readily accessible, the information they provide about sex can be particularly important, especially for early-maturing girls (Brown et al., 2005). Because these girls reach puberty earlier than their peers, they may feel isolated and unsure, and lack ready access to others with more information. The media may fill that role.

Why does it matter where girls learn about sex? As discussed above, the sexual script that dominates popular media reinforces heteronormativity and largely ignores the sexual desires of girls and women. Moreover, sexual risk-taking is higher among girls who report learning about sex primarily from the media and peers as opposed to parents or other important family figures (DiIorio et al., 2003; Hutchinson, Jemmott, Jemmott, Braverman, & Fong, 2003; Moore, Berkley-Patton, Bohn, Hawes, & Bowe-Thompson, 2015). Sexual risk-taking includes being less likely to engage in behaviors to minimize the risk of contracting sexually transmitted infections (STIs), as well as a higher likelihood of having sex without birth control to minimize the risk of unplanned pregnancy. While people might disagree about when it's appropriate for individuals to begin engaging in sexual activity, few would disagree that if one is having sex, it's better to have **safe sex** (frequently called safer sex—e.g., sex involving birth control, often condoms) in order to minimize the risk of STIs and pregnancy. Learning about sex from parents, as opposed to peers or the media, has also been linked to starting to engage in sexual behaviors at a later age (Bleakley et al., 2009; DiIorio et al., 2003). However, one study with racially diverse participants found that when parents relied on lecturing to provide information about sex, instead of allowing adolescents to express their own ideas and opinions, the adolescents were actually more likely to engage in sexual intercourse (Rogers, Ha, Stormshak, & Dishion, 2015).

Young people are also increasingly learning about sex through pornography, especially in the absence of clear information from parents or schools. One study showed that 93% of boys and 62% of girls had been exposed to pornography before the age of 17 (Sabina, Wolak, & Finkelhor, 2008), and another showed that 49% of boys had exposure to pornography before the age of 13 (Sun, Bridges, Johnson, & Ezzell, 2016). Young people may turn to pornography for a variety of reasons, including being curious, to learn about aspects of sex that were perceived to be taboo or kinky, and to explore their sexuality and sexual identity (Attwood, Smith, & Barker, 2018). However, pornography consumption has been linked to asking, and even pressuring, partners to engage in acts that have been seen in pornography as well as to decreased enjoyment of sex with a partner (Stanley et al., 2018; Sun et al., 2016).

your turn

How did you learn about sex? When do you remember first learning about sexual topics? Where did this information come from? Were you comfortable asking questions? Did you get the information you wanted to have when you wanted it? In an ideal world, what would your process of learning about sex have been like?

School-Based Sex Education

What are the different approaches to sex education in school, and what outcomes are associated with these different approaches?

Although some people believe that sex education should only happen at home (Jordan, Price, & Fitzgerald, 2000), a majority of both parents (Bleakley, Hennessy, & Fishbein, 2006; Jordan et al., 2000; McKay, Byers, Voyer, Humphreys, & Markham, 2014; Millner, Mulekar, & Turrens, 2015) and teens (Byers et al., 2003) favor sex education through schools. Most parents and teens also agree that sex education should begin by middle school (Bleakley et al., 2006; Byers at al., 2003; Jordan et al., 2000; McKay et al., 2014). However, there's considerable debate about what should be included in the instruction.

Types of Programs In the United States, an **abstinence-only sex education** approach (also known as abstinence-only-until-marriage) has been a commonly adopted one for decades. Whether this education is undertaken at home, through religious groups, or in schools, the approach focuses on teaching that abstaining until marriage is the only way to avoid pregnancy, STIs, and negative psychological consequences. School-based programs using this approach have received significant funding from the federal government (Planned Parenthood, 2012). These programs promote abstinence as the only morally correct choice and are often developed by religious organizations even though federally funded programs can't make direct references to religion. They also typically include no information about contraception or only indicate that contraception is not effective at preventing pregnancy and/or STI transmission. Only 2% of school-based programs used this abstinence-only approach in the 1980s, but 35% were using it by the late 1990s, and an additional 51% promoted abstinence as the preferred means of contraception—an approach discussed below (Lamb, 2010b).

Because many school-based sex education programs in the United States are fully or partially funded through money from the federal government, shifts in elected federal government officials can drastically change the funding priorities and, as a result, the prevalence of different types of sex education approaches. For example, in 2010 under the Obama administration, federal funding for abstinence-only programs was reduced by two-thirds, and funding was specifically established for the implementation of programs that included information on contraception (Planned Parenthood, 2012). Priorities shifted again after the 2016 federal elections resulting in Republican control of both houses of Congress as well as the White House. For example, President Trump's proposed 2019 budget included an allocation of $75 million for abstinence-based sex education programs (Richmond, 2018). At the same time this was presented, the U.S. Department of Health and Human Services defunded grants to support a number of sex education programs with a teen pregnancy prevention focus rather than an abstinence focus (Kodjak, 2018). As election cycles unfold and government representatives change, the state of funding for different types of programs will likely continue to fluctuate.

Regardless of fluctuating government funding priorities, a great deal of research has indicated widespread support for sex education that includes accurate information about contraception. For example, one survey using a nationally representative sample of U.S. adults found that only 36% of respondents supported abstinence-only programs, 50% specifically opposed them, and 82% supported programs including information about contraception in addition to abstinence (Bleakley et al., 2006). Studies focusing on specific areas of the country, including southern Alabama (Millner et al., 2015), Minnesota (Eisenberg, Bernat, Bearinger, & Resnick, 2009), California (Constantine, Jerman, & Huang, 2007), North Carolina (Ito et al., 2006), and Indiana (Yarber, Milhausen, Crosby, & Torabi, 2005), have found similar patterns—even when the states mandate abstinence-only sex education.

Sex education approaches that include information about contraception typically fall into two categories: abstinence-plus sex education and comprehensive sex education. As with abstinence-only approaches, both of these approaches can be used in either formal or informal educational contexts. **Abstinence-plus sex education** still promotes abstinence as the most effective way to prevent pregnancy and disease, but this approach also includes information about contraception and strategies for safer sex practices. **Comprehensive sex education** approaches cover abstinence as well, but not as the primary focus. Rather, abstinence is discussed as one of a number of ways to remove or reduce the risk for pregnancy and STIs along with other contraceptives. Another component of this approach is a focus on communication and interpersonal skills training. Also, sex and sexuality are framed as positive and healthy components of life.

The view of sex and sexuality as positive and healthy aspects of life reflects **sex positivity**. This perspective has been central to the development and implementation of comprehensive sex education programs. Sex positivity involves the idea that all sexual expression and behavior is healthy as long as it is practiced with explicit consent from all parties involved. Advocates of sex-positive education emphasize that it's possible to teach children about consent at very young ages. For example, very young children can be asked for their permission before being touched, hugged, or tickled and can be made to feel they have the right to say what they are and are not comfortable with. Both at school and at home, they can also be encouraged to feel comfortable with their bodies and to learn appropriate boundaries. For example, one sex-positive mother told her daughter, "We don't play with our vulvas at the table. Go wash your hands and finish your food" (Grover, 2014, para. 2).

Comparing Outcomes Given the different approaches to sex education, you might ask if one is better than another. A great deal of research has shown abstinence-only sex education programs to be ineffective in actually encouraging abstinence. For example, a review of more than 100 different program evaluations led to the conclusion that abstinence-only programs don't seem to delay initiation of sexual activity or reduce reported numbers of sexual partners (Kirby, 2007). In the same review, one surprising finding was that sex education programs that included information about contraception were related to delayed initiation of sex and decreased number of sexual partners. In other words, it appears that telling students about contraception, which some people may fear would encourage sexual activity, actually decreased it—although additional research is needed to understand why this happens.

This is a particularly important topic to consider in the United States because of the teen birth rate and rising STI rates. According to data from the World Bank (n.d.), despite consistently declining rates of teen births, the United States still has the highest rate of teen births as compared to other Western, industrialized countries (see Figure 7.1). Also, more than half of pregnancies in the nation are unintended, and these rates are higher for poor women (Guttmacher Institute, 2016). Additional data indicate that diagnoses of chlamydia, gonorrhea, and syphilis are increasing (Centers for Disease Control and Prevention, 2015).

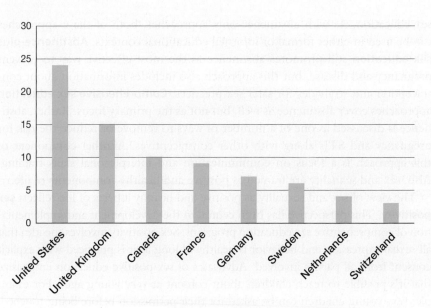

FIGURE 7.1 **Teen birth rate per 1,000 girls, ages 15 to 19, in 2016.**

Data from http://data.worldbank.org/indicator/SP.ADO.TFRT.

The Centers for Disease Control and Prevention (CDC) reports that the rates of HIV diagnoses among Black women are particularly high (Centers for Disease Control and Prevention, 2016).

Providing adolescents with information about how to prevent pregnancy and reduce the risk of contracting STIs is clearly a central component of successful sex education, but many people, including many feminists, argue that this is only part of what comprehensive sex education should include. As far back as 1988, psychologist Michelle Fine talked of the "missing discourse of desire" (Fine, 1988, p. 29), specifically female desire, in school-based sex education. In other words, sex education typically fails to talk about how pleasure and enjoyment are often part of sex. When they are mentioned or alluded to, it's almost always in terms of male, rather than female, desire. Often, sex education focuses only on the negative consequences of sexual activity (Allen, 2007; Bay-Cheng, 2003), and when pleasure is discussed, it's in the context of negative outcomes such as regretted sex and pregnancy, so pleasure gets associated with danger (Lamb, Lustig, & Graling 2013). Moreover, the bulk of the responsibility for avoiding negative consequences of sex is placed on girls (Allen, 2007; Bay-Cheng, 2003; Tolman, 2004). For example, teen pregnancy is often discussed in terms of girls getting pregnant (with no partner referenced) rather than boys impregnating girls.

School-based sex education has also been criticized for failing to provide information about many sex- and sexuality-related topics (Bay-Cheng, 2003; Fine & McClelland, 2006; Lamb, 2010b). For example, most programs only discuss intercourse involving a woman and a man or only briefly mention other sexual orientations or sexual activity involving same-gender partners. They typically assume that all participants are cisgender, and since some sex education programs are organized around gender-segregated groups, educational practices can further marginalize transgender individuals. The programs also don't typically discuss sexuality concerns that might be relevant for individuals with disabilities. One study showed that health-care providers, caregivers, and educators reported avoiding frank discussions about sexuality with people who have disabilities because of anxiety about the topic (Travers, Tincani, Whitby, & Boutot, 2014). Further, other studies have shown that, because of role confusion regarding who should initiate such conversations (e.g., health-care providers, family members, teachers), people with disabilities had less knowledge about important topics related to sex (e.g., STIs, safer sex practices, sexual rights) than the general population (Galea, Butler, Iacono, & Leighton, 2004; McCabe, 1999). In these various ways, individuals with disabilities may be particularly harmed by the limited information given in abstinence-only programs.

your turn

What were your experiences with school-based sex education? At what grade level(s) was it integrated into the school curriculum? Would you describe the focus as abstinence-only, abstinence-plus, or comprehensive? What, specifically, was covered? Search for information online about sex education in Sweden and the Netherlands—two countries with especially progressive programs. Based on what we've discussed, what you learn about the programs in Sweden and the Netherlands, and your own experiences, what approach would you take if you were going to design a school-based sex education program? What would and would not be included?

Concerns such as these have led some people to call for comprehensive sex education curricula that have an explicit social justice approach and are organized on a human rights framework (Berglas, Angulo-Olaiz, Jerman, Desai, & Constantine, 2014; Lamb 2010b). These programs would move beyond providing information about sex, sexuality, safety, and communication. They would also cover principles of and values associated with human rights and would include discussions and activities addressing equality and access. One suggested approach is to include a focus on sexual ethics to help teens examine their own moral positions on what they do and do not find acceptable (Lamb, 2010b). Such programs would also ask students to consider how their parents, peers, and the media affect their personal opinions. According to advocates of this approach, truly comprehensive sex education is complex and multifaceted and could serve to educate people not only about their own sexuality but also about the diverse array of beliefs, behaviors, and identities that constitute sexuality as a whole.

Talking about Sex

How do people typically talk about female anatomy, and what are the major components of women's genitalia?

Despite formal and informal sex education, many people are still uncomfortable talking about sex. The language we use (and don't use) provides information

What words and phrases were you taught for genital anatomy and for sexual acts? When did you add new terms to your vocabulary? What were they? Where, and from whom, did you learn them? Which terms do you prefer to use now?

Now step back from your own experiences and preferences. How many terms can you think of for male genitals? for female genitals? When you list them, does one group of terms seem more negative than the other? Why do some terms seem acceptable and others not?

about how we feel, what we approve of, and what we disapprove of. For example, in many families, genital anatomy is referred to as "private parts," penises are called "pee-pees," and vulvas and vaginas are referred to as "coochies" or "down there." In a study conducted in the early 1980s, researchers found that 40% of men and 29% of women were taught the correct anatomical names for male genitalia during childhood, and only 6% of women and 18% of men learned the correct names for female genitalia (Gartrell & Mosbacher, 1984). Twenty years later, a study of pre-school children similarly found that most participants used slang terms for sexual body parts (Thackeray & Readdick, 2003). More recent research has also found that mothers tend to use vague terms (e.g., "down there") when talking with girls (Martin, Baker, Torres, & Luke, 2011). This is all part of sexual socialization. While the language people use does change as they get older, people continue to use slang terms most of the time.

"Down There"

Because there's so much diversity in terms used, in this section we'll review what really is "down there," where these body parts are located, and how they work.

Women's external genitals are collectively referred to as the *vulva*; this includes hair, folds of skin, and the openings of the urethra and the vagina (see Figure 7.2). The *labia majora* are the outer lips of the vulva. Made up of fatty tissue covered in pubic hair, they begin next to the thigh and extend inward to surround the *labia minora* as well as the urethral and vaginal openings. The labia minora, sometimes referred to as the inner lips of the vulva, are hairless and sensitive folds of skin that extend from the clitoris past the urinary and vaginal openings.

We can't talk about female sexuality without talking about the *clitoris*, a highly sensitive genital structure that has the sole function of providing sexual pleasure. Actually, the clitoris isn't a single structure; rather, it's part of an interconnected network of internal and external structures collectively known as the *clitoral complex* (see Figure 7.3). The common use of the term *clitoris* refers to the *clitoral glans*—the head of the clitoris that contains a huge number of nerve endings, resulting in great sensitivity. However, the glans is really just the most visible part of the clitoral complex, as it may protrude from the *clitoral hood*, particularly when aroused. The glans is the tip of the *clitoral shaft*, which extends from the glans into the body under the clitoral hood. Most women achieve orgasm through direct or indirect stimulation of the clitoral

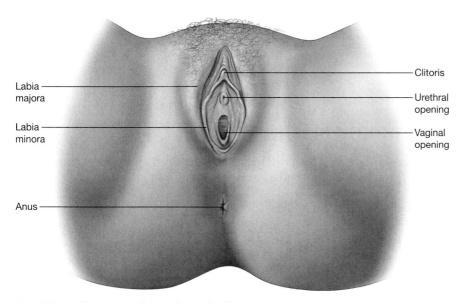

FIGURE 7.2 **The external female genitalia.**

Labia majora

Labia minora

Anus

Clitoris

Urethral opening

Vaginal opening

glans and shaft (e.g., through manual or oral stimulation, or through rubbing against a partner's pubic bone). When aroused, the clitoral shaft and glans become engorged with blood (similar to the way a penis becomes erect). Other portions of the clitoral complex also become enlarged due to increased blood flow during arousal. The *clitoral crura*, or the legs of the clitoris, extend from either side of the clitoral shaft where it meets the body, and just below the crura

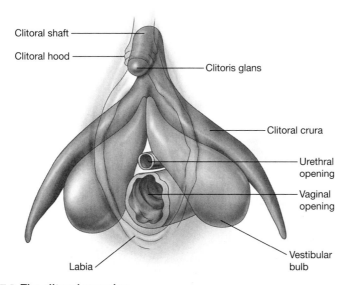

Clitoral shaft

Clitoral hood

Clitoris glans

Clitoral crura

Urethral opening

Vaginal opening

Labia

Vestibular bulb

FIGURE 7.3 **The clitoral complex.**

are *vestibular bulbs.* These structures surround the vagina, and they become more sensitive to touch, pressure, and vibration when swollen due to arousal. This can also play a role in women's orgasms, along with stimulation of the clitoral glans.

Contraception: Staying Safe

What types of birth control are available, how effective are they, and how do they relate to disease protection?

Responsibility for preventing unwanted pregnancy often falls to women. Part of the explanation for this may be that women are the ones who become pregnant, so most contraceptives are options they can employ. This responsibility may also fall to women because of the cultural expectations we've already discussed: Women's expected role is to be sexual gatekeepers while not being particularly interested in sex themselves. It is, however, important for all partners involved in sexual activity to also be involved in decision making around safety. Research has shown that even though cross-gender couples do share decision making about contraception, it often falls along gendered lines—with women being responsible for most forms of birth control and men solely for condom use (Fenell, 2011). Other research has shown that talking openly about contraception relates

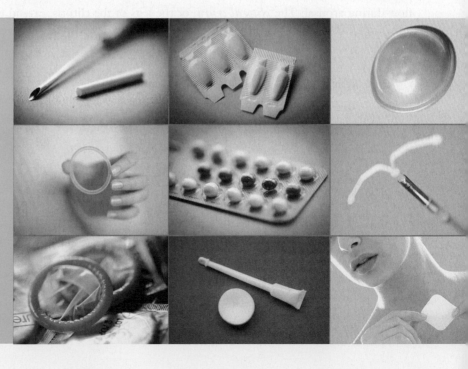

There are many contraception options available to women. Each has different benefits and risks, and not all are equally accessible because some are quite expensive and many require working with a health-care provider. What are some of the factors that you or women you know take into consideration when choosing contraceptives?

to an increased likelihood of actually using it (Manlove, Franzetta, 2007).

There are several types of contraceptives. Hormonal contraceptives include birth control pills, rings, patches, injections, implants, and intrauterine devices (IUDs). Barrier methods include female and male condoms, vaginal spermicides, diaphragms, and sponges. Fertility awareness methods involve some or all of the following: tracking menstrual cycles, tracking body temperature, and monitoring for changes in cervical mucus. There are also non-hormonal IUDs and sterilization (e.g., tubal ligation for women and vasectomy for men). Abstaining from penetrative sex or engaging in **outercourse** (i.e., forms of sexual activity that don't involve penile-vaginal penetration) are also contraceptive practices. Finally, women may make use of "emergency contraceptives" (e.g., Plan B) after a sexual encounter. The most commonly adopted forms of contraception are birth control pills (16% of women), female sterilization (15.5%), male condoms (9.4%), and long-acting reversible contraceptives (i.e., IUDs and implants; 7.2%), but rates of adoption do vary by age (Daniels, Daugherty, & Jones, 2014). For example, female sterilization is most commonly chosen by women age 35 and older.

Many factors can influence women's choice of contraceptive methods. For example, if one wants to have children in the future, reversibility may be a key factor. Access to contraceptives is also important to consider. Many forms of contraception require visits to health-care professionals and prescriptions; others can be purchased over the counter. Some, like male condoms and vasectomies, need cooperation from a partner. Cost is also a concern. For example, without insurance, hormonal implants cost around $800, and IUDs cost around $1,000, although these can be effective for years (Kosova, 2017). The annual cost of birth control pills is between $240 and $600, injections cost approximately $240 per year, and the birth control ring costs about $1,000 per year.

Contraceptive options also vary in effectiveness at preventing pregnancy, and the effectiveness of most methods is decreased with incorrect or inconsistent use (Trussel, 2011; see Table 7.1). Disease prevention is also a key

spotlight on . . .

The Dark Side of Birth Control

The availability of birth control benefits women who wish to control their reproduction. However, the origins of the wide availability of birth control go back to the *eugenics* movement in the United States during the late 19th and early 20th centuries. This movement focused on "improving" the human population by encouraging educated, "intelligent" people to have more children and discouraging "inferior" people from having children. In 1927, for example, the U.S. Supreme Court ruled in *Buck v. Bell* that states could force mandatory sterilization on women in institutions who were considered "feeble minded" (Diekema, 2003). However, many of those women had been institutionalized only because they were "promiscuous or had become pregnant out of wedlock" (Roberts, 1997, p. 69). Carrie Buck, the defendant in the case, was sterilized because she was poor and had a child without being married.

Black and Mexican American women also frequently experienced forced sterilization (Stern, 2005a, 2005b), and not just in the distant past. In 1965, 60% of Black women in one Mississippi county were sterilized without consent after they had children (Roberts, 1997). In 1975, a class action lawsuit against two Los Angeles hospitals resulted from the forced sterilization of Mexican American women (Stern, 2005b). It's estimated that 100,000 to 150,000 poor women were sterilized annually under federally funded programs during this time (Roberts, 1997).

Thus, while birth control can allow women autonomy over their bodies, it can also be a tool to control their sexuality and reproduction.

TABLE 7.1 Effectiveness Rates of Birth Control Methods

Method	Percentage of Women with Unintended Pregnancy within the First Year of Use	
	Correct and Consistent Use	Typical Use
Abstinence[a]	0%	0%
Outercourse[a]	0%	0%
Birth control pills	<1%	9%
Birth control patch	<1%	9%
Birth control vaginal ring	<1%	9%
Birth control shots	<1%	6%
Birth control implants	<1%	<1%
Hormonal IUD	<1%	<1%
Non-hormonal IUD	<1%	<1%
Male condoms	2%	18%
Female condoms	5%	21%
Vaginal spermicides	18%	28%
Diaphragms	6%	12%

Vaginal sponges
   women who have never given birth
   women who have given birth
	9%
	20%
		12%
		24%

Fertility awareness methods	<1% – 5% depending on method	24%
Sterilization	<1%	<1%
Withdrawal	4%	22%
No contraception	85%	85%

Source: Trussell, 2011; [a]https://www.plannedparenthood.org/learn/birth-control

concern, and abstinence, outercourse, and the use of female and male condoms are the primary options available to reduce the likelihood of disease transmission. Although women don't have worries about unintended pregnancy as a result of sexual activity with another woman, disease transmission is a concern, so some use dental dams, which are thin sheets of latex (originally intended for use by dentists during dental procedures) that can be stretched across the vulva to reduce risk.

Having (and, Ideally, Enjoying) Sex

What are common beliefs about having sex and the rates at which others are having sex?

Women can engage in sexual activity and have body parts that serve no purpose other than to provide sexual pleasure. However, as with all behavior, there's a great deal of variability in the experiences of individual people. Some women may choose not to engage in sexual activity at all, some become sexually active at young ages, and some wait to engage in some or all sexual activity until they're married or in a committed, long-term relationship.

Data from one nationally representative survey in the United States indicated that the average age of first intercourse was 15.5 years (Halpern & Haydon, 2012). Data from another nationally representative survey show that 55% of women reported having had sex by age 18 and 75% by age 20 (Abma & Martinez, 2017). However, there were differences depending on the race/ethnicity of respondents. Data from White respondents were consistent with the overall data. Latinx respondents reported a similar pattern of sexual activity by age 18 (55%) and a slightly higher rate by age 20 (79%), and Black respondents reported higher rates of having initiated sexual activity at both ages (62% and 82%, respectively). These surveys were largely focused on vaginal intercourse, but there are other ways that people can be sexually active. Rates of oral and anal sexual activity, for example, have been found to be lower than rates for vaginal sex among women (Halpern & Haydon, 2012).

The "First Time"

First times in many contexts receive a lot of attention—we can think about first steps, first days of school, and so on. First sexual experiences can, similarly, be very meaningful. The first sexual experience that many people focus on is the first time they experience vaginal-penile intercourse, often referred to as losing one's virginity. There is, however, great variability in how people define losing virginity. In one study of participants with diverse ethnicities and sexual orientations, although 100% indicated that vaginal-penile intercourse for the first time would constitute losing virginity, there was less agreement about whether other forms of sex would do so (Carpenter, 2001). For example, 28% of young women and men interviewed believed that engaging in oral sex with a partner of the other sex could constitute losing virginity, and 56% believed that engaging in anal sex could result in losing virginity. Recognizing that sexual activity can involve same-gender participants, 80% of those interviewed indicated that virginity could be lost with a same-gender partner, but 47% felt that the definitions for virginity loss would have to be different in this case. Other research has indicated that women have broader definitions of "having sex" than do men (Trotter & Alderson, 2007) and that lesbians have broader definitions than do heterosexual women and men (Horowitz & Spicer, 2013). Also, many LGBTQ participants in one study reported that the coming-out process is a more important rite of passage than losing virginity (Averett, Moore, & Price, 2014).

The focus on virginity can be considered a holdover from a patriarchal past where a woman's value was centered on her status as a sexually chaste woman. For example, in one early study, researchers found that Latinx women described holding on to their virginity as a sign of honor for their family (Gil & Vazquez, 1996). Other studies have shown that girls with strong religious ties also value virginity status (Bersamin, Walker, Waiters, Fisher, & Grube, 2005; Brewster & Tilman, 2008; Orgocka, 2004). For those holding these attitudes, the "loss" of one's virginity could be perceived as harming a woman and/or making her less valuable and desirable. Virginity can be perceived as a gift to give (typically from a woman to a man) or as a stigma to shed as soon as possible (Carpenter, 2002). Virginity loss can also be seen as simply part of the process of growing up.

TV shows aimed at teens typically use one of three sexual scripts when portraying virginity loss (Kelly, 2010). These are (a) an abstinence script, according to which virginity loss should be delayed, (b) an urgency script, in which virginity is a stigma that must be shed in order to gain and/or maintain status among peers, and (c) a management script, which portrays sexual behavior as inevitable and the managing of related risks as important. Teens do report being influenced by media narratives about virginity, and when they feel that their own virginity loss experience is "imperfect" in contrast to what they've seen in the media, they report higher levels of distress about their experience (Carpenter, 2009).

People have complex and diverse expectations about what their first sexual experiences will be like. First-time experiences vary, and women have a wide range of feelings afterward. What advice would you give to a young woman to prepare her for her first time having sex?

When researchers examine women's accounts of their own experiences of "virginity loss," a complex relationship emerges. In one study of young Black and White women and men, researchers found that women reported lower levels of satisfaction with their first experiences of vaginal intercourse than did men (Higgins, Trussell, Moore, & Davidson, 2010). This was particularly true of physical satisfaction. Psychological satisfaction wasn't always experienced, especially when sex occurred outside of the context of a committed relationship or involved feelings of guilt. In a study of young, Catholic, Filipina women, researchers found a mix of reactions to first vaginal sexual encounters (Delgado-Infante & Ofreneo, 2014). Those who saw their encounters as an outlet for self-expression were more likely to report experiencing pleasure—"It's fun. I enjoy it. I like it" (p. 402)—and that not having sex "would suppress one part of my, you know, expressing myself" (p. 401). However, those who viewed their first vaginal sexual encounters as "giving in" or getting "carried away" were more likely to report experiencing pain and feeling shame and a sense of loss. One woman summed this up: "You will feel ashamed to face them . . . you're afraid that they'll judge you even if you're good friends . . . there's always that fear that there's gonna be judgment passed and that people will look at you in a different light" (p. 400).

Researchers conducting a study of young people in the United Kingdom found that virginity loss was experienced differently by women and men. For men, it was about achieving status, but for women, it was more about managing loss (Holland, Ramazanoglu, Sharpe, & Thomson, 2010). One young man said, "It's the old saying, 'you enter the bed a boy and you leave it a man' or words to the effect. I felt the same, I didn't alter physically, but I felt different after that first time," and another said, "'Yes' I was saying to myself, 'now I am a man, I'm a man'" (p. 354). Women, in contrast, often reported that their experiences didn't match their expectations. One woman said, "I wasn't very happy about it afterwards. I mean he didn't force me or anything, you know. He said, and I agreed, but afterwards I sort of felt dirty. I think partly because I was so young, and I was infatuated with this person, and he turned out to be so ordinary" (p. 358). Others reported having made conscious choices about having sex but didn't report enjoying their experiences. One woman said, "I just wanted to get it over and done with. . . . I hated it. It's not great the first time. Never"; another said, "I've done it now, I can go and do it with someone I like" (p. 359).

Everyone's Doing It (or Not)

Even though the "first time" doesn't always live up to young women's expectations, many women continue to have and enjoy sex. Often, sexual encounters occur within the context of romantic relationships, but this isn't always the case. In fact, women's involvement in **casual sex**—sex outside of the context of a committed relationship—has been on the rise (Garcia, Reiber, Massey, & Merriwether, 2012). Casual sexual encounters are often described as "hooking up," and studies indicate that this is a common practice for both women and men. Between 72% and 85% of participants in various studies report having engaged in at least one hookup (e.g., Armstrong, England, & Fogarty, 2012; Currier, 2013; Lambert, Kahn, & Apple, 2003; Paul, McManus, & Hayes, 2000), with men reporting slightly higher rates of hooking up than do women (Bogle, 2008; Fielder & Carey, 2010; Paul et al., 2000).

It isn't clear what exactly constitutes a **hookup**, although most people agree that it involves sexual activity between two people with no expectation of commitment. In one study, participants described hookups as "anything from kissing to having sex" and as being "in the eye of the beholder," although some were adamant that hookups had to include vaginal-penile penetrative sex (Currier, 2013, p. 713). Moreover, some equated hooking up with a one-time encounter with a stranger or acquaintance; others identified hooking up as something they do multiple times with the same partner (e.g., a "friends with benefits" arrangement). This ambiguity isn't much different from the ambiguous definitions as to what constitutes sex or virginity loss discussed above. Moreover, it's important to recognize that hooking up doesn't only happen with heterosexual-identified individuals, although comparatively little attention has been paid to hooking up among LGBTQ individuals (Watson, Snapp, & Wang, 2017). It has, however, been suggested that hookups provide women the opportunity to explore same-gender attraction, often before explicitly identifying as bisexual, lesbian, or queer (Rupp, Taylor, Regev-Messalem, Fogarty, & England, 2014).

try it for yourself

How do you define sex? What about virginity and virginity loss? What about hooking up? Ask others you know how they define these terms. Where do you see overlap, and where do you see differences? Does age, gender, sexual orientation, or any other aspect of identity seem to influence people's definitions? Does anyone report that their definitions have changed over time?

People don't just have different understandings as to what sex is or what a hookup entails. There's also inconsistency in beliefs about who is engaging in sexual activity, how often, with how many partners, and in which contexts. In general, most people tend to think that everyone *else* is doing it more than they are. In one study of first-year, heterosexual-identified college students who primarily identified as White, women reported having had lower numbers of oral and vaginal sex partners than they believed was true for the typical female first-year college student (Zelin, Erchull, & Houston, 2015). Male first-year students similarly reported having fewer sexual intercourse partners than they thought the typical female or male college student did (see Table 7.2). Moreover, perceptions of others' behavior was a predictor of participants' own sexual behavior—in other words, those who thought "everyone is doing it" were more likely to do it themselves.

TABLE 7.2 Average Numbers of Sex Partners among First-Year, Heterosexual-Identified College Students

	Vaginal Sex	Give Oral Sex	Receive Oral Sex
Self: Women	1.87 partners	1.81 partners	1.49 partners
Women's perceptions of other women	2.71 partners	3.47 partners	2.24 partners
Men's perceptions of women	2.85 partners	3.57 partners	2.34 partners
Self: Men	2.37 partners	1.24 partners	2.76 partners
Men's perceptions of other men	3.13 partners	2.24 partners	3.75 partners

Note. Data are from Zelin et al. (2015). (No data were collected about women's perceptions of men's numbers of sexual partners.)

There is a perception that hooking up is commonplace and a key part of college social life (Currier, 2013) and that risky sexual encounters (e.g., unplanned encounters that often involve intoxication) are rampant (Holman & Sillars, 2012). However, one study has indicated that dating is actually more common than hooking up, especially for Latinx students (Eaton, Rose, Interligi, Fernandez, & McHugh, 2016). College students have been found to overestimate their peers' comfort with and participation in hookups (Lambert et al., 2003). In fact, persistent discrepancies between individuals' own beliefs and behaviors and the perceived beliefs and behaviors of their peers have been described as examples of **pluralistic ignorance** (Lambert et al., 2003). This occurs when people mistakenly think their own attitudes and behaviors are different from those of others. The misperception can lead to conforming to perceived social norms that don't reflect reality. In this case, thinking that everyone else is hooking up may lead people to engage in hookups themselves (Fielder, Walsh, Carey, & Carey, 2013; Holman & Sillers, 2012).

The influence of inaccurate perceptions is important because there may be costs associated with hooking up. This is particularly important because research has found hookups to be related to some negative outcomes, particularly for women. For example, engaging in hookups has been linked to psychological distress (Fielder & Carey, 2010), depression, and STIs (Fielder, Walsh, Carey, & Carey, 2014) among women. And while, on average, positive reactions are more likely to be reported than negative ones, many people do report regret about hookups (Garcia et al., 2012).

your turn

Do you think "everyone is doing it"? What exactly do you think people are doing? Is there pressure to hook up or engage in other types of casual sex? If you or anyone you know has engaged in hooking up, how did you/they feel afterward? Do you think pressures are the same or different for women who have sex with men and for women who have sex with people of other genders?

However, the way questions are asked and when participants are surveyed does seem to impact responses. Specifically, when researchers ask participants if they've *ever* experienced regret about a hookup, reported rates are higher than when participants are asked about either their typical hookup experience or their most recent hookup. Whether one feels positively or negatively about a hookup may depend on why one had it. In one study, researchers explored the role of motivations for hooking up in relation to outcomes (Vrangalova, 2015). When women hooked up because they wanted to, they didn't experience negative outcomes. However, when they hooked up because they were pressured or felt they had to because everyone else was doing it, they experienced lower self-esteem and increased depression and anxiety.

Enjoying Sex

What are women's experiences with masturbation and orgasm, and how do these compare to men's?

Women engage in sexual activity for many reasons, and pleasure is an important one. Whether engaging in sexual activity with a partner or alone, sex can feel good physically. Of course, not everyone reports the same degree of satisfaction with their sexual encounters, and not everyone defines sexual satisfaction in the same way.

Masturbation Although many women have conflicting feelings about sex, ideally it's supposed to be pleasurable. While pleasurable sexual activity can involve a partner, it doesn't have to. One other way to experience sexual pleasure is through masturbation. **Masturbation** involves stimulating oneself sexually, usually through touching one's genitals, to result in sexual pleasure. Meta-analyses have consistently shown that men are more likely to report masturbating than women, although there's inconsistency in the extent of this difference, as the effect sizes from these studies vary from large ($d = 0.96$; Oliver & Hyde, 1993) to moderate ($d = 0.60$; Petersen & Hyde, 2010). It's important to note, however, that many women do masturbate. In fact, in one nationally representative sample from the United States, 48% of teenage girls (as compared to 73% of teenage boys) reported having masturbated (Robbins et al., 2011). In another study, approximately 85% of women in their 20s (as compared to 94% of men this age) reported having masturbated (Herbenick et al., 2010b). Researchers found gender differences in masturbation to be smaller in countries with egalitarian gender attitudes (Petersen & Hyde, 2010), and meta-analyses have not found gender differences in attitudes toward masturbation—in other words both women and men find masturbation equally acceptable (Oliver & Hyde, 1993; Petersen & Hyde, 2010).

Why would women think masturbation is acceptable but be less likely than men to do it? It may be that women have lower sexual desire than men. It may also be that women are less familiar with their bodies and signs of their own sexual arousal than men are. It's difficult for a man to miss the fact that his penis is erect, but a woman may or may not know when she's aroused (Petersen & Hyde, 2011). Women may also be uncomfortable about masturbating because they've been taught that it's dirty or smelly "down there" (Fahs, 2014b). Internalization of sexual scripts can also play a role—after all, if cultural messages imply that sexual activity should prioritize men's pleasure, then what purpose would female masturbation serve?

Regardless of differing attitudes, masturbation is a sexual act with benefits and no known negative consequences. It can provide women with a greater understanding of their own anatomy and pattern of sexual response; it can also provide information about what they actually enjoy in sexual encounters (Coleman, 2002; McCormick, 1994).

Orgasm Many people regard orgasm as the ultimate sign of sexual pleasure. As discussed earlier in this chapter, men's orgasm is typically considered the marker for the end point of a sexual encounter. And men do report higher rates of orgasm when engaging in sexual activity with partners than women do (e.g., Garcia, Lloyd, Wallen, & Fisher, 2014; Herbenick et al., 2010a). Research with a large U.S. sample, for example, showed that women report having fewer orgasms than do men (Frederick, St. John, Garcia, & Lloyd, 2018). Heterosexual men were the respondents most likely to say they usually or always orgasmed when engaging in sexual activity (95%). Gay men (89%), bisexual men (88%), and lesbian women (86%) also reported fairly high rates. Bisexual women (66%) and heterosexual women (65%) reported the lowest rates of orgasm.

Although orgasm is a key component of sexual satisfaction, its presence or absence isn't the only reason a sexual encounter may or may not be deemed pleasurable. Experiencing emotional closeness, bonding, love, affection, and acceptance are also reasons women may enjoy sexual activity with a partner, even without an orgasm (Basson, 2000). Also, even when a traditional physiological orgasm cannot be experienced (e.g., as with some spinal cord injuries), women may still report having orgasms—although they may be different from orgasms experienced prior to the injury (Alexander & Rosen, 2008; Kettl et al., 1991; Komisaruk & Whipple, 2011; Tepper, Whipple, Richards, & Komisaruk, 2001).

A meta-analysis has shown that women report being somewhat less satisfied with their sexual encounters than men are (Petersen & Hyde, 2010). This may be largely due to expectations. For example, if women believe that satisfaction in sexual relationships results from pleasing one's partner sexually, they would likely report sexual satisfaction whether or not they orgasm. However, if women expect to have an orgasm, they'll be dissatisfied if they don't. Research has shown that both women and men feel that both they and their partner are entitled to sexual pleasure and orgasms within ongoing relationships (Armstrong et al., 2012). Interestingly, the joint entitlement to sexual pleasure didn't apply to short-term relationships as well as long-term ones. Although it was still expected that men would orgasm during a hookup, women were not viewed as being entitled to an orgasm within these casual sexual encounters. Given these findings, it shouldn't be surprising that women report greater sexual satisfaction in relationships as opposed to hookups. The researchers concluded that this is probably because sexual activity during ongoing relationships, rather than during hookups, is more likely to involve the types of genital stimulation that usually result in orgasm.

Not Enjoying Sex

What are some reasons women may not find sex enjoyable?

Although women do frequently experience sexual satisfaction in a variety of ways, that isn't always the case, and the lack of satisfaction is so distressing for some women that it reaches the level of dysfunction. Reported rates differ somewhat from study to study, but overall rates of sexual dysfunction are reported by approximately 40% of women sampled (Laumann, Paik, & Rosen, 1999; Shifren, Monz, Russo, Segreti, & Johannes, 2008). The levels of distress that women experience as a result of sexual dysfunction have also been found to vary, with rates ranging from approximately 20% to 60% depending on the study and the specific sexual problem reported (Hayes, Bennett, Fairley, & Dennerstein, 2006; Shifren et al., 2008). According to the 5th edition of the *Diagnostic and Statistical Manual of Mental Disorders* (*DSM-5*), types of sexual dysfunction among women fall into three categories: desire/arousal, orgasmic, and sexual pain disorders (American Psychiatric Association, 2013).

Types of Sexual Dysfunction We started this chapter with a discussion of the recently approved drug Flibanserin to treat low levels of sexual desire among women. In the medical community, this condition is known as *hypoactive sexual desire disorder*. It consists of a lack of interest in sexual activity or the complete absence of sexual desire, including thoughts and fantasies, prior to and/or during sexual experiences (Basson et al., 2004). Receiving a diagnosis depends on the perceptions of "normal" sexual desire held by both the individual reporting the (potential) dysfunction as well as their therapist or doctor. For example, individuals who identify as asexual wouldn't consider their low or absent levels of sexual desire to be dysfunctional—just different from levels experienced by others.

Dissatisfaction with levels of sexual desire may also reflect a *desire discrepancy* between oneself and a partner (Willoughby & Vitas, 2012). For example, if you want sex daily and your partner wants to have sex twice a month, you might well feel that your partner has an abnormally low sex drive—at least in comparison to you. Your partner may even internalize this idea and seek assistance from a doctor or therapist. If someone is distressed, there's nothing wrong with seeking help, but it's also possible that the problem may be with a partner's high sex drive or with a disconnect between the two partners' sex drives. Someone with a low sex drive isn't inherently abnormal or dysfunctional.

Sexual arousal disorder, in contrast, occurs when the desire for sex is normal but women have difficulty achieving or maintaining physiological sexual arousal (Berman, 2005). This is typically experienced as low levels of vaginal lubrication, but it can also include decreased engorgement and/or sensation in the clitoris and labia. These symptoms can cause pain during intercourse and difficulty achieving orgasm. Collectively, these experiences may result in a decreased desire to have sex—after all, if it hurts and doesn't result in physical pleasure, why do it?

Female orgasmic disorder is the absence, delay, or decreased intensity of orgasm after experiencing "sufficient" sexual stimulation and arousal (American Psychiatric Association, 2013; Basson et al., 2004; Walsh & Berman, 2004). Some women may never or rarely experience orgasm alone or with a partner. Other women are able to orgasm through masturbation but not when engaging in sexual activity with a partner. It's important to note, however, that women are most likely to report experiencing orgasm through manual stimulation (by oneself or a partner) or oral sex (Fugl-Meyer, Öberg, Lundberg, Lewin, & Fugl-Meyer, 2006; Hite, 2004; Richters, de Visser, Rissel, & Smith, 2006). Therefore, some orgasm difficulties may result from not receiving the stimulation that is "sufficient" enough to result in an orgasm.

Rather than discussing the fact that they didn't experience an orgasm or talking about how to increase the likelihood of this desired result in the future, many women opt to fake an orgasm. In this case, sex becomes about performance rather than pleasure. In fact, research indicates that two thirds to three quarters of women report having done this (Erchull & Liss, 2014; Landsburg, 2004; Muehlenhard & Shippee, 2010). Women may fake an orgasm for several reasons: because they want the sexual encounter to end, because they want to validate their partner's sexual skills, or because they want to appear "normal" (Fahs, 2011, 2014a; Muehlenhard & Shippee, 2010). While, in the moment, faking an orgasm may seem like a beneficial decision, it can be part of a vicious cycle and can exacerbate both sexual and relationship problems in the long run (Darling & Davdon, 1986). After all, if Partner A doesn't stimulate Partner B in a way that makes it likely for Partner B to orgasm, and that partner fakes an orgasm instead, this reinforces the sub-optimal sexual behavior. Since Partner A thinks Partner B was satisfied during a prior sexual encounter, they'll probably keep engaging in the same behaviors. Partner B will either have to keep faking orgasms or have a difficult conversation about what does and doesn't work and why they faked orgasms in the past.

Dyspareunia, or painful intercourse, is the third category for women's sexual dysfunction (American Psychiatric Association, 2013; Basson et al., 2004; Walsh & Berman, 2004). The specific experiences of pain (e.g., location, intensity, frequency) can differ, but individuals with this dysfunction all report pain during at least some instances of vaginal penetration. Arousal disorders resulting in decreased vaginal lubrication can contribute to pain during penetration. Commercially available lubes can help alleviate discomfort and make penetration more enjoyable. A particular sexual pain disorder that results from strong, involuntary spasms of vaginal muscles is *vaginismus*. This disorder can make penetration—even by a finger or a tampon—painful or, in some cases, impossible. Vaginismus is most common among those who have experienced sexual trauma or have strong fears about sexual intercourse.

Women's sexual dysfunctions haven't been well studied, as most research attention has been on male sexual dysfunctions (Berman, 2005; Walsh & Berman, 2004). Among studies that have been done, the focus has largely been on heterosexual women's experiences with and desire for vaginal intercourse. Little research exists on sexual dysfunction among women who have sex with women, although one study indicates similar levels of sexual desire and orgasm disorders, as well as lower levels of pain disorders, among lesbian women as compared to heterosexual women (Matthews, Hughes, & Tartaro, 2006). It's also important to note that women who seek treatment for these issues are likely to have insurance that makes it easier to obtain this type of care, a fact that reflects social privilege.

Body Concerns: The Mirror in the Bedroom Although many physiological and psychological factors can contribute to sexual dysfunction in women, body concerns are an underlying factor reported by many women (Sanchez & Kiefer, 2007). As we discussed in Chapter 6, body dissatisfaction is very common among women (Bearman, Presnell, Martinez, & Stice, 2006; Smolak, 2012; Tantleff-Dunn, Barnes, & Larose, 2011). When they're concentrating on how their bodies look rather than on how sex feels, it's hard to enjoy sex. In other words, these women worry about looking sexy rather than being sexual. Engaging in body surveillance during sex is typically called **body image self-consciousness**, or body image self-consciousness during physical intimacy (Sanchez & Kiefer, 2007; Steer & Tiggemann, 2008; Wiederman, 2000, 2001). Like general body surveillance, this often goes hand in hand with body shame (Claudat & Warren, 2014; Steer & Tiggemann, 2008). Body shame is also linked with sexual displeasure for transgender women, and body modification—in particular, gender-affirming surgery—has been found to significantly improve both body image and experiences of sexual pleasure (Sammons, 2010).

Women with body image self-consciousness also worry about how their partners perceive their appearance. **Cognitive distraction** occurs when a person shifts to a secondary focus, which then interferes with the ability to focus on the primary task, experience, or goal. In the context of sexual activity, this is often referred to as cognitive distraction during sex (Claudat & Warren, 2014; Dove & Wiederman, 2000; Meana & Nunnink, 2006). If a woman is worried about whether her partner is noticing a fat roll or a non-flat belly, for example, this concern takes up cognitive resources that might otherwise be focused on the actual sexual experience. Cognitive distraction is related to concerns about sexual performance, and it often reflects a desire to satisfy one's partner through one's appearance (Claudat & Warren, 2014; Dove & Wiederman, 2000; Meana & Nunnink, 2006). Cognitive distraction can result in **spectatoring**, or an "out-of-body" experience in which a woman's focus is on things other than the sexual encounter (Wiederman, 2001). Instead of thinking "That feels good" or "Wow—I'd like this even more if I shifted position," she might be thinking "I'd better suck in my belly before he notices it's not flat" or "I wonder if my breasts will look better if I'm on top." Essentially, women who engage in spectatoring reframe themselves as sexual objects existing for the pleasure of their partners rather than as active sexual beings focused on their own sexual enjoyment. Being focused on their partner's sexual experience rather than their own can result in women not receiving what they need to be sexually satisfied.

Wanting to please a partner sexually isn't a bad thing, and many people would argue that it's an important component of sexual relationships. However, being focused on appearance as the means to satisfy one's partner seems to be particularly problematic. In fact, a recent line of research with predominantly White and heterosexual-identified samples has begun to explore the effects of objectification by partners. This occurs when one partner focuses on the appearance rather than the innate characteristics of the other partner. In one study, women and men who reported objectifying their partners were found to be less satisfied in their relationships, and the men who objectified their partners were less sexually satisfied (Zurbriggen, Ramsey, & Jaworski, 2011). In another study, women who felt that their partners were primarily focused on how they looked had lower levels of relationship satisfaction (Ramsey, Marotta, & Hoyt, 2017). Yet another study linked feeling objectified by a partner to being less comfortable with one's sexuality as well as to feeling pressured and coerced sexually by the partner (Ramsey & Hoyt, 2015).

Given that many women are concerned about how they look sexually and what their partners think about how they look, women often focus on ways to alter their bodies. In a sexual context, women may remove body hair—especially pubic hair—because they think doing so will make them sexually desirable to their partners and/or will improve their sexual experiences (Braun, Tricklebank, & Clarke, 2013; Tiggemann & Hodgson, 2008). Some women even opt for more permanent forms of body modification through genital cosmetic surgery, including procedures to tighten the vagina (vaginal rejuvenation or vaginoplasty) and to alter the appearance of the labia, usually to make them smaller

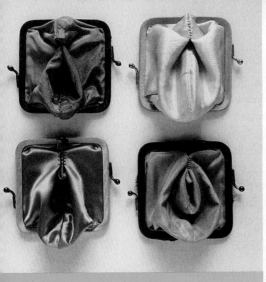

Many women report dissatisfaction with or concern about the appearance of their vulva. Because most women don't see many vulvas, some artists have undertaken projects to raise awareness about the diversity of vulvas. This portion of a work by Suzanna Scott uses artfully arranged linings from coin purses as proxies for vulvas.

and/or more symmetrical (labioplasty or labiaplasty; Braun, 2009, 2010). The desire to undergo these procedures often arises from beliefs that a "tight" vagina is more desirable than a "loose" vagina, that this can increase sexual pleasure for both women and men (Braun & Kitzinger, 2001), and that the appearance of one's labia is unattractive and abnormal (Braun, 2010; McDougall, 2013). However, just as with all other aspects of our bodies, there's great variation from individual to individual. Because most women see very few vulvas, they aren't aware of the diversity of appearance, and media images—often in porn—tend to show a relatively hairless vulva with small, symmetrical labia (McDougall, 2013). This issue has inspired art projects, books, and educational websites showing diverse images of vulvas.

Sexualization: Selling Women's Bodies

How does the sexualization of women manifest at both societal and personal levels?

So far, we've learned that women receive relatively little information about sex and sexuality, they're often expected to prioritize their partner's pleasure over their own, and they may not be enjoying their sexual experiences. While women aren't expected to be particularly focused on sex or be very sexual, they are typically encouraged to be sexy. Essentially, they're supposed to be sexual objects rather than active sexual beings, and many women internalize this idea. Another way of saying this is that women are sexualized. **Sexualization** occurs when sexuality is imposed on others, when people are regarded as sex objects, and/or when their value is reduced to their sexual appeal or sexual behavior (American Psychological Association Task Force on the Sexualization of Girls, 2007). Objectification is understood as one component of sexualization, and like objectification, sexualization is both ever-present and highly problematic.

As we saw in Chapter 6, commercial media objectify women's bodies in order to sell products. The same is true with sexualization. If you turn on the television or open a magazine, you're likely to quickly encounter a sexualized image of a woman (Gill, 2003). You may have heard that "sex sells." Research indicates, however, that people are actually less likely to remember products when the marketing is paired with sex (or violence; Bushman, 2005, 2007; Bushman & Bonacci, 2002). Given these findings, sex might be attracting attention, but it's not actually selling products. These types of sexualized ads could be understood as selling a limited view of women's sexuality, however.

On this page, you see a typical advertisement featuring a woman. Sexuality is a key aspect of this ad, as the nearly naked woman is shown on a bed with mussed sheets. But she's not active. She's lying passively in the middle of the bed, curled up in a pose indicating a lack of power. In some other ads, women are depicted in more sexually agentic ways. For example, they may beckon to men or look as though they are the ones seducing their (male) partners. Some people might consider a more active portrayal of women's sexuality to be empowering, but the woman's sexuality would still be serving to sell a product. Moreover, that type of ad conveys the idea that women can use their sexuality as a way to have power (often over men). Additionally, like ads in general, the women in most sexualized ads are typically thin, young, White, heterosexual, and lacking apparent disabilities. Such images convey a narrow view of sexuality and a narrow array of women who can enact it (Gill, 2009).

We do see (some) other women in media, but even then, the portrayals of sexuality are limited. For example, Black women are more likely to be portrayed as passively sexual rather than as actively expressing their sexuality (Gill, 2009). Black women are also often portrayed in hypersexual ways, in line with the Jezebel stereotype discussed in Chapter 2 (Bounds Littlefield, 2008; Watson, Robinson, Dispenza, & Nazari, 2012). Similarly, many Asian women are portrayed as hypersexualized, often in the context of being sex workers (Shimizu, 2007). The "hot lesbian" stereotype is a slightly different take on the sexualized (and sexual) woman (Gill, 2008, p. 49; Gill, 2009). This lesbian conforms to traditional (i.e., heterosexual) standards of beauty and is typically depicted as a target for male attention. She's usually portrayed touching or kissing another woman, but with the intent of sexually arousing men—in the show, the audience, or both. Arousing men is not, typically, a goal for lesbians. However, women enjoying sex without men isn't part of our culture's dominant sexual script (discussed earlier in this chapter). Essentially, we have performative lesbianism joining performative bisexuality.

Transgender women, in particular, are depicted in documentaries and movies with a high number of close-up shots of body parts. Even in shows that are trans-positive, like *Transamerica*, there's a tendency to highlight "fetishized, sexualized body parts" that reflect a narrow perspective on femininity—such as showing feet with high heels or hands with bright nail polish (Addams, 2009, para. 4). Further, when transgender celebrities are interviewed, questions often focus on

This ad shows a woman in a passively sexualized pose. How could it be redesigned to convey the woman's sexuality in an active or agentic way?

their genitals rather than on more meaningful aspects of their lives (Mock, 2014). For example, the trans actress Laverne Cox was asked by daytime talk show host Wendy Williams if she had breast implants and was later pushed by show host and news anchor Katie Couric to discuss her "private parts." Cox responded by saying, "I do feel there is a preoccupation with my private parts. The preoccupation with transition and surgery objectifies trans people. And then we don't get to really deal with the real lived experiences" (McDonough, 2014, para. 3).

Sex Work

Women's sexuality is more directly commoditized through sex work. **Sex work** is an umbrella term that refers to the exchange of sexual services, performances, or products for compensation (Gerassi, 2015; Weitzer, 2010). This can include in-person sexual interactions such as oral sex or sexual intercourse, often referred to as prostitution. It can also include pornography, stripping, webcam models, and the like. Although prostitution is legal in some parts of the world—most notably in much of Europe and South America, Canada, and Mexico (http://chartsbin.com/view/snb)—prostitution, and even legal forms of sex work, are widely considered to be immoral (Weitzer, 2007). As such, it's hard to know how many women, and men, are involved with sex work because it's not something most people talk about openly.

Sex work is big business. One study of the illegal commercial sex economy in just eight U.S. cities in 2007 estimated that it generated between $39.9 and $290 million (Dank et al., 2014). When the scope is broadened to include pornography, researchers identify a $10–$12 billion industry in the United States and a $97 billion industry worldwide (Morris, 2015). These estimates probably don't include stripping, webcam work, and myriad other forms of sex work. Moreover, the returns for women who engage in sex work aren't always equitable. In one study of Black and Latinx dancers, researchers found that Black and dark-skinned Latinx women received less money than White or lighter-skinned Latinx women for their erotic services (Brooks, 2010). This was attributed to marginalization due to patrons' racialized stereotypes of such women being hypersexual or aggressive.

Although some women do watch pornography (Hald, Seaman, & Linz, 2014) and visit strip clubs (Montemurro, Bloom, & Madell, 2003; Wosick-Correa & Joseph, 2008), this sort of sex work disproportionately provides sexual and entertainment services to men (Weitzer, 2010). As discussed in the Empowering or Oppressing feature, some women choose to engage in sex work, but for others it's a "choice" of last resort. For example, pervasive workplace discrimination can make sex work the most viable option for transgender women to support themselves (Nadal, Davidoff, & Fujii-Doe, 2014). In one study of 48 transgender women of color who were sex workers, researchers found that although there were multiple reasons for doing sex work, nearly all of them thought their gender identity, race/ethnicity, class, and appearance contributed to their involvement in the work (Sausa, Keatley, & Operario, 2007). Further, some women, both in the United States and worldwide, are forced into sex work through human trafficking, and often this begins when they are girls (Gerassi, 2015). We'll return to this topic in Chapter 12.

The fact that sex work is often illegal (and even when legal, is disapproved of) means that it's a very dangerous industry. For example, sex work can expose people to sexually transmitted diseases, drug use, and incarceration (Hoffman, 2014). Transgender women, in particular, report a high level of physical abuse from law enforcement as a result of working in the sex industry (Nadal et al., 2014). Racism also influences experiences with both sex work and violence. For example, Black sex workers report high levels of harassment from law enforcement (Porter & Bonilla, 2000; Raphael & Shapiro, 2004). According to one study, Black women in Brooklyn, New York, make up about one third of the total population, but 94% of charges on the offense of "loitering for the purposes of prostitution" were against Black women (Berlatsky, 2014).

Enjoying Sexualization and Self-Sexualization

Despite the negative aspects of a culture that sexualizes women and profits from their sexuality, some women report enjoying aspects of this and find empowerment through embracing their sexuality in public ways (Levy, 2005). For example, a woman may wear a push-up bra and high heels because it makes her feel sexy and powerful. Or she may put on a highly sexualized Halloween costume (e.g., sexy nurse, sexy cat) and, rather than feeling oppressed, see it as a fun, sexy, and empowered choice. Engaging in these types of behaviors is known as **self-sexualization**.

Some psychologists have questioned whether the perceived empowerment that women may associate with self-sexualization is as positive as it may seem on the surface (Lamb, 2010a; Peterson, 2010). After all, our culture conveys messages that sexualized behaviors are the norm for women and will lead to positive outcomes (Murnen & Smolak, 2012), including a sense of empowerment (Tolman, 2012). Given this, however, the underlying question is whether women engage in

A common trend among women's Halloween costumes is that they're designed to be "sexy"—sexy police officer, sexy nurse, sexy zombie. It's often hard to find women's costumes that aren't intentionally sexualized. Why might women want to wear these types of costumes? Why might they not?

Participation in Sex Work

Many people consider sex work to be oppressive for women (Weitzer, 2009). It's seen as promoting exploitation, violence, poverty, and drug use. Although this may be true for many sex workers, particularly those who participate in illegal prostitution, it's not the only experience sex workers have. Even in countries where prostitution is illegal, other legal forms of sex work exist that may involve fewer negative perceptions and consequences. For example, you might have heard people talk about "a friend who worked her way through college as a stripper." From this perspective, the choice to participate in sex work as a viable source of income and/or personal expression can be seen as empowered (Weitzer, 2009). Even though people who hold this perspective recognize that sex work isn't always empowering (because not all sex workers voluntarily engage in it), they claim it can be safe and empowering when women choose to engage in it and it is not criminalized.

Some aspects of sex work have gone mainstream. For example, well-known porn stars have written best-selling books, modeled in mainstream ads, launched fashion lines, and acted in mainstream movies. These are unusual examples, but some women do transition from sex work to other careers. Of course, that's not the case for all sex workers. Those who enter sex work through human trafficking (see Chapter 12) may be unable to buy their way out of servitude to those who paid their way into the United States and/or provide for their ongoing support (Gerassi, 2015). Even women who do sex work part-time while in school may face challenges, such as lacking employment experiences necessary to prepare for their planned careers (Sinacore, Jaghori, & Rezazadeh, 2015). These women also worry how the stigma of being in this industry, even where it's legal, may impact their lives long-term.

Although sex work may have the potential to be empowering and oppressing, research suggests that the oppression is greater when such work is criminalized. In these cases, women who experience violence or coercion can't seek assistance from law enforcement. However, decriminalization can make sex work safer for all involved. Research on the effects of decriminalization of sex work in New Zealand shows that condom use is high and sex workers feel able to impact their personal safety by choosing where, when, and with whom to work (Abel, Fitzgerald, Healy, & Taylor, 2010). In fact, the United Nations has called for the decriminalization of sex work so that the health and safety of sex workers can be protected (Godwin, 2012). Nevertheless, decriminalization wouldn't inherently eliminate the stigma for engaging in sex work (Abel et al., 2010).

Do you think sex work is empowering or oppressing? If it can be empowering, whom does this apply to, and what factors should be in place for this to be true? If it's oppressing, what can be done to help those who do engage in sex work—at least, those who don't want to? Do you think sex work should be decriminalized? Why or why not?

self-sexualization as a result of informed choices about how they want to express their sexuality, or just as a result of being taught that it's the *only* way women can be sexual.

Researchers have, in fact, found that some women do enjoy feeling sexy and being admired by others, particularly men (Liss, Erchull, & Ramsey, 2011). Studies also have shown that women do, at times, engage in self-sexualization (Nowatski & Morry, 2009; Smolak, Murnen, & Myers, 2014) and that when women feel attractive and embrace their sexuality, self-esteem can increase (Breines, Crocker, & Garcia, 2008; Helminiak, 1989). In fact, one way women can verify if they meet traditional standards of beauty is to receive sexualized attention from men, so they may actually enjoy this experience (Liss et al., 2011). For example, when a woman dresses in revealing clothing and then receives admiring stares from men, it may make her feel good about herself. Essentially, sexualized attention signals approval, so when it's received, it suggests to women that they're "looking good," and when it's not received, it can signal "hardly worth looking at." Earlier in this chapter, we presented the idea that compulsory heterosexuality helps maintain patriarchy by encouraging women to focus on gaining power through sexuality rather than through other means (Rich, 1980). Research has, in fact, demonstrated that some women do view female sexuality as a source of power (Erchull & Liss, 2013a). In this context, it has been suggested that women use their "erotic capital" to successfully compete in the male-dominated business world (Hakim, 2011, p. 1).

Despite the potential for boosting self-esteem under certain circumstances, there's also a negative side. As discussed earlier in this chapter and in Chapter 6, body focus can lead to self-consciousness, dissatisfaction, and shame. So looking sexy and "strutting your stuff" may feel empowering, but it may also make women self-conscious and ashamed—especially if their "stuff" doesn't live up to society's standards of beauty and sexiness. Also, research finds that consuming large amounts of sexualized media is associated with engaging in self-sexualization, and self-sexualization has been shown to predict negative feelings about one's sexuality and sexual experiences (Ward, Seabrook, Manago, & Reed, 2016; Ward, Seabrook, Grower, Giaccardi, & Lippman, 2018). So women may be engaging in these behaviors because they feel it's typical and expected rather than because they derive benefits from doing so. Moreover, several studies have shown that women who self-sexualize may be viewed as less competent than those who don't, particularly if they're being considered for high-status positions (Fasoli, Durante, Mari, Zogmaister, & Volpato, 2018; Glick, Larsen, Johnson, & Branstiter, 2005; Peluchette & Karl, 2013; Smith et al., 2018; Wookey, Graves, & Butler, 2009).

Although some people may consider using one's sexuality as a source of power, most women who embrace sexualization aren't doing so because of feminist values about disrupting patriarchy and valuing women's sexuality. In fact, research has shown that enjoying sexualized attention was related to holding traditional views about gender among women (Liss et al., 2011). This pattern was also found with women who self-identified as feminists (Erchull & Liss, 2013b). Even if courting and receiving sexualized attention is empowering, power in sexual domains may not transfer to power in other domains (Lamb, 2010a). For example, women who feel empowered through sexualization may not be more likely to negotiate for high salaries, seek promotions, clearly express their sexual desires, and so on. Furthermore, telling women they can gain a sense of empowerment by feeling sexy puts the focus on what individual women can do to feel empowered rather than on how people can collectively work to empower all women (Gill, 2012).

Sexualization and self-sexualization become especially problematic when they involve girls, and research confirms that sexuality is being increasingly imposed on ever-younger groups of girls (American Psychological Association Task Force on the Sexualization of Girls, 2007). For example, girls are more likely to be shown in sexualized clothing, like low-cut tops, in magazines now than in the past (Graff, Murnen, & Krause, 2013). One study of girls' clothing available on websites for major retailers in the United States showed that sexualization was a feature for nearly 30% of the options (Goodin, Van Denburg, Murnen, & Smolak, 2011). This included bikinis, push-up bras, and thong underwear (items associated with sexiness), as well as clothing printed with sexualizing writing (e.g., sweatpants with "cute butt" written on them). With these types of messages being directed at girls from an early age and these expectations being reinforced frequently—even by parents through the clothes they buy for their daughters—it's not surprising that many women embrace or internalize aspects of sexualization.

(Re)Claiming Women's Sexuality

What is sexual agency, and in what different ways are women working to claim their own sexuality?

Feminist psychologists want women to have a strong sense of **sexual agency**—that is, being comfortable with and in control of one's own sexuality. However, sexual agency, like empowerment, has often been co-opted to sell products—and this is not a new pattern. For example, in a 1994 ad for the Wonderbra, model Eva Herzigova displayed her breasts in a Wonderbra with the tag line "hello boys" ("Eva Herzigova: Wonderbra," 2014). Even though representations such as this challenge existing norms of women as passive recipients of sexual attention, they still place limits on women's sexuality. These representations are typically more about men's enjoyment (and selling products) than women's. Such ads generally portray women as choosing to be as sexually enticing as men want them to be; the ads don't represent true sexual agency (Bay-Cheng, 2015; Lerum & Dworkin, 2015). Instead, true sexual agency focuses on what a woman herself wants and doesn't want—not on what's most desirable for men (Tolman, Anderson, & Belmonte, 2015).

One way women can be sexually agentic is through **sexual assertiveness**, or the ability to ask for what one wants and to refuse what one doesn't want within a sexual encounter. This could involve a woman asking a partner to wear a condom or refusing to have sex when she isn't interested in doing so. It could also involve asking for sexual contact to include particular types of touch, particular positions, and so on. For example, researchers have found that sexual assertiveness predicts higher levels of sexual satisfaction among women (Hurlburt, 1991; Ménard & Offman, 2009). Of course, to be sexually assertive, women need to be *aware* of what they want and enjoy in sexual encounters. If, instead, they're focused primarily on their partner's sexual experience rather than their own, and are distracted because of body concerns, then having and maintaining such awareness can be difficult.

While individual women may focus on becoming more sexually assertive, it's also important to focus on the larger ways in which women can work together to reclaim control of their sexuality. In their daily lives, women can do this by questioning social norms and expectations and calling people out if they express surprise or disgust when women violate their expectations related to sex. For example, if someone mentions seeing a woman take the "walk of shame" on Sunday morning, others could challenge their thinking and ask how they know she isn't taking the "stride of pride."

Women can also engage in organized, collective action to draw attention to particular issues related to their sexuality. For example, as discussed in Chapter 2, some women have tried to reclaim the term *slut* and have engaged in SlutWalks in order to protest slut shaming and victim blaming. Others have worked to target the sexualization of girls in the media, and the SPARK movement (http://www.sparksummit.com/) brings girls together with adult activists so that they can, themselves, engage in activism (see Chapter 14). Changing social

spotlight on . . .

Sexual Communication

One reason why sexual satisfaction, and orgasm specifically, is more likely to occur in relationships, rather than in casual encounters, is that partners learn what pleases each other through repeated sexual activity. While observing one's partner (or partners) can contribute to this, open and honest communication, both during and outside of sexual activity, are important. However, it can be hard to ask for exactly what one wants—especially sexually, because of social norms related to discussion about sexual body parts and sexual behaviors. As a result, people are more likely to use indirect (e.g., "a little to the left") rather than direct (e.g., "please touch my clitoris") forms of communication (Harris, Monahan, & Hovick, 2014).

People can improve their communication skills outside of sexual activity. For example, try exchanging a massage with a friend (Hamkins & Schultz, 2007). Be specific about what feels good, and direct that person to give you as much pleasure as possible. Then switch places, and have your friend tell you what feels good. Is it easy or hard to ask for what you want? Are you more comfortable giving or receiving directions? How might this be easier or more difficult if the communication were about pleasure in a sexual encounter? Try extending this challenge and asking for what you want in different contexts over the next few days. When is this easier to do? Does your relationship to the person you're interacting with matter?

norms and practices doesn't happen quickly, and there continue to be different cultural expectations associated with women's sexuality compared to men's; but when people engage in both individual and collective efforts, change can happen.

Conclusion

As is true of all people, women can benefit from the freedom to express and enact their sexuality in ways with which they are comfortable. This is, however, hard to do in a culture that considers information about and discussions of sexuality to be taboo, while also prescribing which women can be sexual and in which ways, with whom, and when. The ways in which women experience their sexuality are constrained by our sexualized culture, which objectifies women and limits their options for sexual expression. The idea of the sexually agentic, empowered woman must be understood within these constraints, which influence both attitudes and behavior. That said, feminist psychologists and other sex-positive advocates seek to change norms surrounding sex and sexuality so that all people have a chance to experience and express their sexuality more freely.

Chapter Review

SUMMARY

Sexual Scripts

- Sexual scripts provide information about what is considered "normal" sexual behavior in a given culture.

- Heterosexual sexual scripts are dominant, and they contribute to compulsory heterosexuality. Non-heterosexual scripts tend to signal deviance.

- Sexual scripts center on men's experiences and pleasure, telling us that men desire and initiate sex, while women should be sexual gatekeepers. This reflects a sexual double standard, and there can be negative social consequences when women violate it.

- Sexual scripts imply that only thin, young, White, able-bodied, heterosexual individuals are sexual.

Learning about Sex

- Parents are a key source of sexual socialization, which begins in early childhood. Mothers tend to be the primary providers of sex education in the home, but they generally feel uncomfortable with this role and their own knowledge.

- Given the lack or inadequacy of information coming from parents, children often look to peers as a more important source of sex information.

- The media can serve as a "sexual super peer" and provide a great deal of information about sexual scripts. Porn has also been identified as a growing source of sexual information among adolescents and young adults.

- Sexual risk-taking is higher among those who primarily learn about sex through peers and the media.

- Abstinence-only sex education has been dominant in the United States, but these programs are not effective at increasing abstinence. Abstinence-plus and comprehensive sex education programs that include information about contraception and STIs are more effective.

- Sex education programs rarely talk about desire or pleasure, particularly female pleasure.

- Sex education programs can further disenfranchise non-heterosexual, transgender, and disabled students, as their concerns and experiences are rarely integrated.

Talking about Sex

- People typically use slang and euphemisms to refer to genitalia.

- Many people are unfamiliar with the anatomy of women's external genitalia.

- Most women achieve orgasm through stimulation of the clitoris, which is actually an interconnected series of structures.

- Women typically have primary responsibility for the use of contraception to prevent pregnancy. Although many types of contraception can be effective, some require visits to health-care providers, which can be a barrier to use. Cost is also a concern.

- Many forms of contraception do not protect against STIs.

Having (and, Ideally, Enjoying) Sex

- Most people believe that losing one's virginity involves having penile-vaginal sex; but people also recognize that, especially for individuals who didn't identify as heterosexual, other behaviors may constitute having sex for the first time.

- There is great variability in when and how women begin having sex, as well as how they feel about their experiences.

- Casual sex and hookups are one context in which people, particularly young adults, may engage in sexual activity.

- People typically believe that others are having more sex, and more sex outside of committed relationships, than they really are.

- Women are less likely to masturbate than men. However, masturbation can provide women with a better understanding of their own sexuality.

- Orgasms are not the only standard that women use to define a sexual encounter as satisfying. Satisfaction is typically higher when expectations are met—whether that constitutes having an orgasm or satisfying one's partner.

- Women can experience sexual dysfunction, but dysfunction is subjectively defined and often depends on the perceptions of partners as well as health-care providers.

- Body image concerns can contribute to sexual dysfunction for women. When women worry about how they look, they no longer focus on the sexual experience itself, and they may find it difficult to experience physical arousal and/or pleasure.

Sexualization: Selling Women's Bodies

- Women's bodies are routinely sexualized and commoditized.

- Some women participate in sex work—either through choice, or because of lack of other options, coercion, or force.

- Some women embrace sexualization and use their sexuality to gain male attention and/ or power. It's unclear whether this is actually empowering. Self-sexualization is connected to both positive and negative outcomes.

- Sexualization is particularly problematic when it involves young girls.

(Re)Claiming Women's Sexuality

- Women can develop strong sexual agency and learn to be sexually assertive so that they know and can make clear to others what they do and do not want.

KEY TERMS

sexual scripts (p. 276)

performative bisexuality (p. 277)

sexual double standard (SDS) (p. 280)

slut shaming (p. 280)

sexual socialization (p. 282)

safe sex (p. 285)

abstinence-only sex education (p. 285)

abstinence-plus sex education (p. 287)

comprehensive sex education (p. 287)

sex positivity (p. 287)

outercourse (p. 293)

casual sex (p. 298)

hookup (p. 298)

pluralistic ignorance (p. 299)

masturbation (p. 300)

body image self-consciousness (p. 304)

cognitive distraction (p. 304)

spectatoring (p. 305)

sexualization (p. 306)

sex work (p. 308)

self-sexualization (p. 309)

sexual agency (p. 312)

sexual assertiveness (p. 313)

THINK ABOUT IT

1. Given the limitations of dominant ideas about sexual scripts, devise a more inclusive definition of sex. Do you think most people would agree with this new version? Why or why not? If not, what could you do to convince them?

2. Compare the research findings on how people learn about sex to your own experience. In what ways does the research reflect your experience? In what ways does it differ?

3. Evaluate the merits of abstinence-plus and comprehensive sex education, and decide what option you think is best for students. How would you convince school personnel and parents that your option is worthy of school funding?

4. Imagine you're talking to a friend about research on self-sexualization. What would you say to your friend? Would you encourage or discourage self-sexualization?

ONLINE RESOURCES

- **Advocates for Youth** — access to sexual health information and resources for girls and young adults: advocatesforyouth.org

- **Guys We F**ked** — anti-slut-shaming and sex-positive conversations: soundcloud.com/ guyswefucked

- **Rewire** — commentary, analysis, and investigative reporting on issues related to sexual health: rewire.news

- **Scarleteen** — inclusive, comprehensive, and supportive information on sexuality and relationships for teenagers and emerging adults: scarleteen.com

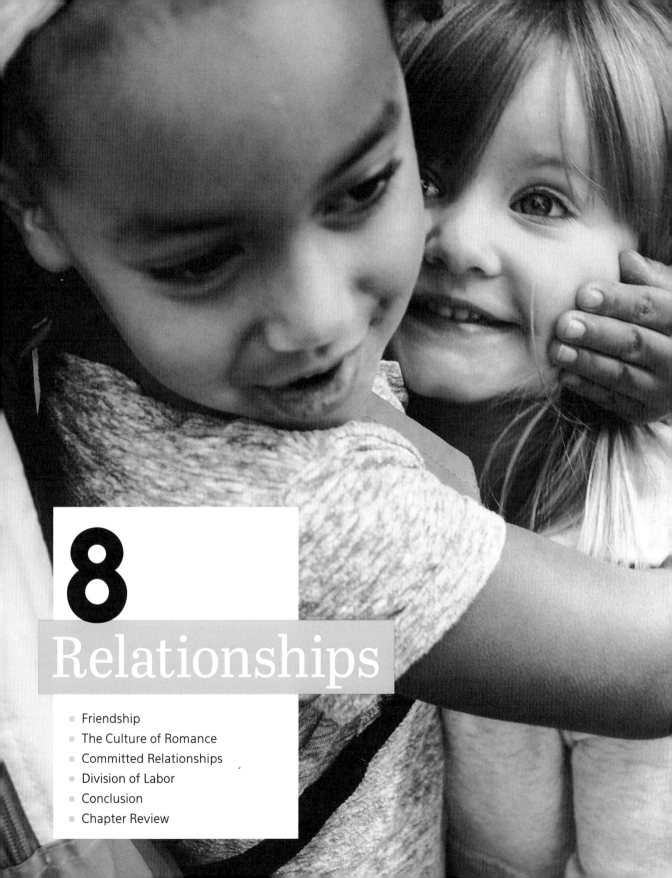

8

Relationships

Gayle King (left) and Oprah Winfrey (right) have maintained a close friendship for more than 40 years. What things make it possible to maintain a supportive friendship across a life span?

TELEVISION HOST AND MEDIA MOGUL OPRAH WINFREY has had a very high-profile and long-standing friendship with journalist Gayle King. They met in 1976 when working at the same local TV station in Baltimore, Maryland—Oprah was an anchor, and Gayle was a production assistant. Oprah has said, "We became friends, especially after a big snowstorm. When she couldn't go out, get home and didn't have enough clothes, I said, 'OK, you can have my underwear.' But then I added, 'And don't return it'" (staff writers, 2014, para. 4). Their friendship has withstood more than a snowstorm. It has stood the test of time—through new jobs, new romantic relationships, living in different parts of the country, and, of course, Oprah's fame. While not everyone is fortunate enough to have a best friend for 40 years, many people can relate, at least in general terms, to how Oprah describes their friendship: "She is . . . the mother I never had. She is . . . the sister everybody would want. She is the friend that everybody deserves. I don't know a better person" (Wallace, Thomson, & Sher, 2010, para. 2).

Friendships can be incredibly meaningful, and for many women they provide stability and a sense of connection. However, not everyone understands this type of close, intimate, non-romantic relationship. Rumors that Oprah and Gayle are, in fact, lovers have persisted for years (Nudd, 2010). Although neither identifies as lesbian or bisexual, some people assume there must be something more to their relationship than being close, platonic friends. Some people have a hard time understanding why those who are "merely" friends would choose to spend so much time together and maintain a relationship for so long. The public nature of the two women's friendship, in contrast to the more private nature of Oprah's relationship with her long-term romantic partner, Stedman Graham, may also play a role in this. The fact that Oprah and Stedman have never married has further ignited questions. Apparently, some people can't imagine being in a romantic relationship for 30 years without getting married.

In this chapter, we'll explore some of the relationships that women have throughout their lives, including friendship, dating, marriage, and other long-term relationships. We'll discuss how all these relationships play key roles in women's lives and can enrich them. We'll also talk about the challenges of relationships;

not all relationships are positive, and even positive ones can bring a lot of demands. Relationships also don't happen in a vacuum. They're influenced by cultural expectations and values, and these can shape what women look for in relationships and what they accept as typical and desirable.

Friendship

How do women benefit from friendships?

In 1980, the poet and radical feminist Adrienne Rich put forth a theory suggesting that close female friendships are threatening to patriarchy because they reduce women's focus on heterosexual relationships and might cause women to need less male attention (Rich, 1980). Indeed, Oprah and Gayle's friendship has often been mentioned as an explanation for why Oprah isn't married (Dries, 2014). The fact that the two are Black women may also play a role in their affection for each other. According to one study, there's a long tradition of Black women bonding together in a way that has been necessary for success in a White, male, heterosexual dominant society (Smith, 2000). Yet many factors influence the degree to which women can sustain friendships. When in school, girls are around other girls, and they can connect over common interests. As girls age, however, connecting can become more difficult (Stevens & Van Tilburg, 2011). For one thing, they stop meeting new potential girlfriends. Also, women may move to new locations (e.g., for school for employment), removing themselves from an existing network of female friends. Moreover, women's jobs, and commuting to them, can take up large amounts of time, reducing the time available for social activities. Finally, as Rich also suggested, when women enter into romantic relationships and start having children, there's less time to dedicate to female friendships.

A strong friendship network is something all people can benefit from throughout their lives. Research has shown that, among children, having friends is associated with being sociable, cooperative, and self-confident (Hartup, 1996), and a study of more than 25,000 adults showed that satisfaction with friendships predicted life satisfaction (Gillespie, Lever, Frederick, & Royce, 2015). Having a good friend offers a sense of connection and can even improve health and well-being (Marmot & Wilkinson, 2006). For example, in a study of predominantly White Americans, participants with larger friendship networks were shown to have lower levels of fibrinogen, a physiological marker for inflammation and cardiac disease (Kim, Benjamin, Fowler, & Christakis, 2016). Having supportive friendship networks is also related to engaging in positive health behaviors, such as higher likelihood of seeking preventive health care, as a study of low-income Black women showed (Pullen, Perry, & Oser, 2014).

Friendships can help improve academic achievement too. Studies have shown that, among adolescents, friendships can improve a sense of belonging and academic success (Juvonen, Espinoza, & Knifsend, 2012; Kingery, Erdley, & Marshall, 2011). In a study of Latinx adolescents, those who had the most friends, both by their own report and by their peers' reports about them, were the most likely to feel they belonged at school and, in turn, had improved academic achievement (Delgado, Ettekal, Simpkins, & Schaefer, 2016).

Friendships also buffer the effects of discrimination. For example, in one study, friendships among lesbians were shown to reduce their discomfort with their sexual identity (Stanley, 2002). Several other studies have shown that teens with disabilities use their close ties with one another to combat discrimination and ableism (Kennedy, 2009; Low, 1996; Salmon, 2013). Further, there is extensive research showing that friendships between different groups of people can reduce racial, religious, and sexual prejudice (Davies, Tropp, Aron, Pettigrew, & Wright, 2011; Pettigrew & Tropp, 2008; Turner & Feddes, 2011). For example, a study of college students showed that women with cross-racial/ethnic friendships were more likely to develop positive feelings toward racial/ethnic groups that are different from their own (Levin, van Laar, & Sidanius, 2003). Reducing prejudice through friendship can occur quickly. In one experiment, researchers paired heterosexual students with an instant messaging partner whom they believed to be gay or lesbian (Lytle & Levy, 2015). After only 45 minutes of interaction, the heterosexual undergraduates felt close to their talking partners and had more positive attitudes toward the LGBTQ community than they did at the start of the study.

your turn

What sorts of friendships do you have? Do they enrich your life? Do you have friendships across lines such as religion, sexual orientation, or racial/ethnic background? If not, why might that be? In what ways can such friendships help to reduce prejudice?

Social Support

What is social support, and how does gender relate to giving and receiving social support?

One key benefit of friendship is **social support**—a feeling of being cared for and having support and assistance from people around us, including family, friends, and romantic partners. This support can take many forms, but it's typically classified as informational, instrumental, or emotional support (Taylor, 2011). **Informational social support** involves others giving advice or ideas to help people find strategies or resources to better cope with life events. For example, a friend who offers you advice about how to search for a job in the semester before graduation based on her own experience the prior year is providing informational support. **Instrumental social support**, in contrast, involves others providing tangible assistance in terms of money, goods, or services. In this case, a friend who loans you money for pizza, gives you a #2 pencil for an exam, or drives you to the airport is providing tangible support. **Emotional social support** occurs when we feel nurtured and/or cared for by others. A friend who commiserates with you over a bad date or a poor grade is offering emotional support.

Social support has been consistently found to relate to increased physical and mental health. For example, social support has been linked to decreased psychological distress such as depression and anxiety, increased adherence to medical regimens, faster recovery after surgery, and increased longevity (see Taylor, 2011, for a review). These outcomes highlight the value of maintaining relationships with those who can provide support. However, the kind of support women report receiving can vary based on aspects of their social identities. For example, in one study, although White working-class and White middle-class women said that friends are people who can be counted on, the working-class women were more likely to seek out their friends for instrumental social support, and the middle-class women were more likely to report sharing leisure time rather than seeking particular types of support (Walker, 1994).

There's evidence that women both provide and draw on more social support than men, and some theorists have made evolutionary arguments to explain these patterns (Taylor et al., 2000). They propose that women evolved a **tend-and-befriend coping strategy**, which involves nurturing and protecting others in times of stress (i.e., tending) and developing social networks that facilitate these patterns (i.e., befriending). In light of this idea, it may not be surprising that research has shown same-gender friendships to be a key source of social support for women (Roy, Benenson, & Lilly, 2000). Moreover, social support and friendship are particularly important for women as they age. Although people of any age can feel lonely (Luhamann & Hawkey, 2016), older adults—especially those age 65 and above—are particularly at risk for loneliness (Luhamann & Hawkey, 2016; Stevens, Martina, & Westerhof, 2006; Stevens & Van Tilburg, 2011). After all, the longer we live, the more likely we are to see our friendship networks reduced through illness, mobility limitations, and death. In fact, social isolation and loneliness have been linked to increased death rates (Steptoe, Shankar, Demakakos, & Wardle, 2013).

One way to enhance social support, both in friendships and in romantic relationships, is through **active constructive responding**. This is a way to respond when someone shares good news, and it involves reacting enthusiastically (e.g., "I'm so excited for you") and asking follow-up questions to prolong the conversation and sense of excitement. How relationship partners respond to positive events has been found to be more predictive of well-being than how they respond to negative events (Gable, Gonzaga, & Strachman, 2006). Enthusiastic active responses (e.g., "That's so exciting, tell me more about it") provide better social support than passive ones (e.g., "That's nice"). Responses that either shift the focus (e.g., "Let me tell you what happened to *me* today") or undermine success (e.g., "Are you sure you're going to be able to handle the increased work?") are related to negative outcomes.

Additionally, certain kinds of emotional support in response to bad news can have negative consequences (Taylor et al., 2000). For example, emotional support can sometimes cross over into **co-rumination**, which involves extensively discussing problems and dwelling on negatives in conversation with another person (Rose, 2002). In giving a friend emotional support after she has a bad date, you may commiserate and remind her that there are other potential partners out there. If, however, this discussion devolves into a rehash of many other bad dates and even spills over into other negative aspects of life, it becomes co-rumination. In one study, pairs of female college students who identified as close friends were asked to discuss a problem chosen from a list as they normally would (Byrd-Craven, Geary, Rose, & Ponzi, 2008). After doing this, the women had increased levels of stress hormones as compared to those in a control group who were asked to design a recreation center.

Overall, although emotional support can make us feel cared for, it doesn't necessarily always help us reduce stress, and it can even lead to more stress for both parties in the conversation if it involves co-rumination. Despite these challenges, there are real benefits to both giving and receiving social support, as discussed earlier.

Identity and Friendships

How does social identity influence friendships, and how do assumptions about identity and friendship correspond to the realities of actual friendships?

If you think about your closest friends, it's likely that they share some of your social identity characteristics. Both classic and more recent research indicate that we tend to be friends, particularly close friends, with people who share our social identities and our interests (e.g., Kupersmidt, DeRosier, & Patterson, 1995; Vătămănescu, Andrei, & Pînzaru, 2018; Verbrugge, 1977). This occurs, in part, because we tend to spend more time with people who share our social identity characteristics—such as people with the same race or religion (McPherson, Smith-Lovin, & Cook, 2001). Although cross-identity friendships promote flexibility in thinking by offering new perspectives, research has shown that individuals with socially privileged identities (e.g., heterosexual, White) are less likely to form cross-identity friendships than individuals with socially marginalized identities (e.g. sexual minority, racial minority; Galupo 2009).

However, as communities become more diverse, people are, in fact, more likely to develop cross-group friendships (Smith, McPherson, & Smith-Lovin, 2014). Moreover, those who place less value on having similar lives as an important element of friendship are more likely to have friends with different social identity characteristics than themselves (Galupo & Gonzalez, 2013). There is variability in these patterns, though. For example, in one study, participants who self-identified as Asian American, Latinx, or multiracial were more likely to report cross-race friendships than were participants who identified as Black or White (Plummer, Stone, Powell, & Allison, 2016).

Much early research explored same- and cross-gender friendships, although this research was limited by assumptions of a gender binary. Women's friendships with other women have been described as following a face-to-face pattern in which interactions center around getting to know each other well and experiencing concern for each other (Ridgeway & Smith-Lovis, 1999; Walker, 1994). Men's friendships, in contrast, have been described as typically following a side-by-side pattern in which the men do something together. For example, women might sit in a coffee shop talking to each other about their lives, while men might play video games together. Because of these differences in how women and men interact with their friends, researchers have found that young men generally have larger friendship networks (i.e., more people they call friends) than do women, but that women tend to feel more intimately connected to their friends than do men (Claes, 1992).

These patterns appear to change when researchers consider other intersecting aspects of identity, however. For example, research with married, older adults has indicated that women in this population typically have larger social networks than do men (Ajrouch, Antonucci, & Janevic, 2001; Amato, Booth, Johnson, & Rogers, 2007). As another example, when sociologist Karen Walker (1994) interviewed people about their friendships, she found

Stereotypically, women's friendships with other women are defined by face-to-face interaction involving intimate sharing of emotions and providing a great deal of support to each other. In contrast, men's friendships with other men are expected to involve side-by-side interactions in which they engage in shared activities but don't focus on emotional connection.

that, in contrast to stereotypes, White, working-class men were more likely to socialize at home than through shared recreational activities. The men also were likely to talk about their feelings with their friends; in fact, 75% of the men interviewed reported doing this regardless of social class. White, middle-class women, in contrast, reported lower levels of emotional intimacy in their friendships because their lives were busy and demanding: "You don't have time to talk to people about anything but the essentials" (p. 259). It's unclear how other social identity variables such as age and sexual orientation may have contributed to these patterns, and this is an area for future research.

Friendships aren't always gender segregated, and as we've discussed previously, there are more than two gender identities. Most people, regardless of sexual orientation, have both same-gender and cross-gender friendships, although most people do tend to have more same-gender friends (Galupo, 2007; Lenton & Webber, 2006; Monsour, 2002). For example, participants in one study reported that, on average, just under 42% of their friends were of another gender and that 30% of their close friends were (Lenton & Webber, 2006). Also, people hold overlapping expectations for friendships with those of the same gender and other genders (Felmlee, Sweet, & Sinclair, 2012), but some small differences have been found as well. For example, women reported expecting emotional closeness in both types of friendships in one study with predominately Latinx and White participants, but they expected more companionship from same-gender than other-gender friends (Fuhrman, Flannagan, & Matamoros, 2009).

Despite the fact that both same- and cross-gender friendships are typical, a common cultural assumption is that women and men—at least, heterosexual women and men—can't be "just" friends because romantic and/or sexual attraction will get in the way. A quick Google search brings up an overwhelming number of links to popular press articles and blog posts considering this question, and the inevitability of sexual/romantic relationships among friends is a common plot point for TV shows and movies. Research shows that friends, regardless of sexual orientation, do sometimes flirt with each other, although not in the same overt ways that they do with romantic partners (Egland, Spitzberg, & Zormeier, 1996; Diamond, 2002; Weger & Emmett, 2009). In one study, 58% of heterosexual participants reported feeling physical attraction to a friend (Kaplan & Keys, 1997), and 51% of heterosexual-identified college students in another study reported being sexually active with a friend (Afifi & Faulkner, 2000). Among racially/ethnically

try it for yourself

Can people ever *just* be friends? In what ways do you think cross-gender friendships are the same as or different from same-gender friendships? How are platonic friendships the same as or different from romantic relationships? Talk to a number of people you know about their views on these topics. Try to talk to people with different gender identities, sexual orientations, ages, and so on. What themes emerge? What do people agree on? What do they disagree on? Do social identity variables seem to influence people's responses? Try asking if they think two lesbian women or gay men can "just" be friends. What themes do you see here?

diverse bisexual women, studies show that attraction and flirting behaviors in close friendships with other women helped women define a bisexual identity (Budnick, 2016; Diamond, 2002; Morgan & Thompson, 2007; Thompson, 2007). Other research, however, has indicated that some people work to keep friendships platonic in order to avoid complicating the relationship with sex (Diamond, 2002; Galupo, 2007; Messman, Canary, & Hause, 2000). Also, romantic attraction in friendships can change over the life of the friendship and can be influenced by whether the friends have romantic partners (Fuhrman et al., 2009; Reeder, 2000).

Enemies and Frenemies

What is relational aggression, how does it relate to gendered power dynamics, and what are the consequences of being a target of relational aggression and bullying?

"I don't even know what I did. But somehow, my friend—I guess I should call her my ex-friend—got it in her mind that I was talking to her boyfriend or something and then the next day at school the entire group ignored me. They conveniently didn't have an extra seat for me at the lunch table, and then at volleyball practice they would not even make eye contact with me" (Hinkelman, 2013, p. 36).

Friends help us feel connected, loved, and supported. At the same time, some people can make us doubt ourselves and feel disconnected. Usually, the people who do this aren't those we consider to be our friends. But relationships can be complicated, and sometimes our friends can also act like our enemies. While boys and men tend to engage in more physical aggression, girls and women are more likely to engage in indirect forms of aggression (Archer, 2004). These acts constitute **relational aggression**—that is, they involve damaging others' existing or potential relationships and/or social status. Making someone a social outcast, calling someone a slut, or drawing attention to the non-designer nature of a peer's clothes are examples of relational aggression. It's a way to bully others, and it's a common way for girls to bully other girls.

Relational aggression can be non-verbal or verbal and can be directly aimed at an individual or be done behind someone's back. Non-verbal interactions—such as glaring to show contempt, rolling eyes to be dismissive or show disgust, or turning away to exclude someone—are all ways of being relationally aggressive, and girls typically aggress against one another through such actions (Underwood, 2004). Generally, those who are socially powerful (e.g., popular) use these tools against those who are less powerful (Jeuken, Beersma, ten Velden, & Dijkstra, 2015). Relational aggression can also occur among

Not all relationships are positive. Bullying is common, and a typical way for girls to demonstrate aggression is through gossiping and social exclusion.

friends, and as illustrated in the above quote, sometimes friends can turn into enemies. In fact, researchers have suggested that the very intimacy and closeness that describe female same-gender friendships may actually make it easier to aggress in this way (Murray-Close, Ostrov, & Crick, 2007). Essentially, by knowing people better, it's easier to know what to target to hurt them, and some women explicitly report emotionally manipulating their same-gender friends (Abell, Brewer, Qualter, & Austin, 2016). Relational aggression is also one way of maintaining social position and status at the top of a friendship group, and those more concerned with popularity are more likely to use it (Adler & Adler, 1998; Duffy, Penn, Nesdale, & Zimmer-Gembeck, 2017; Dumas, Davis, & Ellis, 2017).

Psychologist Lyn Mikel Brown (2003) has argued that there are many reasons why girls tend to aggress against other girls and often do so through relational aggression. According to Brown, girls have less power than boys, so their only viable targets for aggression are other girls. This ultimately reinforces patriarchy by increasing conflict among girls, rather than directing their anger at the oppressive patriarchal system and those who contribute to it. Girls learn to behave in ways that conform to societal expectations of girls being "good," so they aggress in subtle ways that don't obviously violate the "good girl" expectation (Simmons, 2009). This maintains the status quo because when girls (and women) fight with each other about boys, beauty, and status, the indirect result is that they aren't addressing the cultural and structural forces that keep them in a position of decreased power.

It's important to note, however, that relational aggression (or physical aggression) can take the form of **identity-based bullying** when it's directed toward people who are actual or perceived members of a devalued social group because of that group membership (Brinkman, 2015). People who are likely to be targeted in this way include individuals with sexual minority identities (Cénat, Blais, Hébert, Lavoie, & Guerrier, 2015), individuals with disabilities (Rose, Simpson, & Moss, 2015), and transgender individuals (Kosciw, Greytak, Bartkiewicz, Boesen, & Palmer, 2012). For example, in a survey of 705 racially diverse transgender middle school and high school students, 75% reported being regularly verbally harassed, 32% reported being physically harassed, and 17% reported being physically assaulted (Kosciw et al., 2012). These results are notably higher than the reports of bullying in the general adolescent population, which was estimated to be 22% in 2015 (United States Department of Education, 2015).

Of course, people can be targeted for any reason—for example, for being poor; for being a member of a particular racial, ethnic, or religious group; for being overweight; or for being considered a slut. As we discussed in Chapter 7, the sexual double standard can result in girls and women being labeled as sluts for engaging in (or being perceived to have engaged in) sexual activity (Armstrong, Hamilton, Armstrong, & Seeley, 2014). Slut shaming seems to be an effective tool in the relational aggression toolbox, as research has shown that some people have less desire to be around those labeled as sluts and are more likely to marginalize them (Kraeger & Staff, 2009). Moreover, as discussed in Chapter 6, fat shaming is most likely to target women (Chrisler, 2012), and obesity is a stigmatized condition in the United States (Carr & Friedman, 2005).

Recognizing and reducing relational aggression is important because this type of aggression can have serious consequences. These include decreased success in school (Popp, Pegurero, Day, & Kahle, 2014) and increased psychological distress, such as depression and low self-esteem (Prinstein, Boergers, & Vernberg, 2001). Although most research has focused on these negative outcomes among children and adolescents, the consequences are potentially long-lasting. One study of primarily White college students, for example, showed that experiences of childhood teasing predicted social anxiety at the time of the study (Boulton, 2013).

It's also noteworthy that those who aggress have the potential to benefit from doing so, such as being perceived as more popular (Cillessen & Mayeux, 2004). For example, one study, which followed a largely White group of children from fourth through eighth grade, showed that girls who exhibited high levels of relational, but not physical, aggression had higher levels of peer acceptance and more friends by eighth grade (Ettekal & Ladd, 2015). Given these findings, efforts to reduce relational aggression should recognize that aspects of our society reward aggression and, therefore, should work to create a cultural shift whereby popularity and social status become related to kindness rather than aggression.

The Culture of Romance

What are common romantic beliefs, where do they come from, and how can they impact relationships?

When most people hear the word *relationship*, they probably don't think about friendship; instead, they probably think of romantic relationships. Love and affection, from short-term or long-term partners, can be wonderful. However, cultural beliefs about romance may create fairy-tale expectations. The psychotherapist Irvin Yalom (2013) famously claimed that he was "love's executioner" because he often challenged and changed many of his clients' unrealistic expectations about their romantic relationships.

We're not born with an understanding of romance. Rather, we learn about it from those around us. Through personal interactions and the media, we're exposed to messages about love and romance and are socialized to understand what it is—at least, within our particular cultural context. Yet if you were to ask 20 people, you'd probably get 20 different definitions of romance. Nevertheless, researchers have identified core romantic beliefs that predominate in the United States: that people have one true love, that love can happen at first sight, that love will allow couples to overcome obstacles, and that one's partner will be perfect (Sprecher & Metts, 1989). Although these ideas may seem outdated, idealized, and unrealistic, they also probably sound familiar, and more recent research indicates that they continue to be endorsed by study participants (Hefner & Wilson, 2013; Regan & Anguiano, 2010). Gender socialization can influence the way people view and understand romance. Researchers have found that romantic relationships are seen as central to femininity, along with being nice and investing in one's appearance, among other factors (Mahalik et al., 2005). However, they've also found that valuing relationships is *not* seen as a central part of masculinity, but that factors like taking risks and pursuing status, among others, are (Mahalik et al., 2003).

The media play an extremely important role in how we understand romance (Bachen & Illouz, 1996). One consistent message is that it involves a woman and a man, reinforcing the idea of compulsory heterosexuality (see Chapter 7). And these messages start young. In a study of financially successful G-rated movies from 1990 to 2005, only two had no heterosexual romantic references (Martin & Kazyak, 2009). Mary-Lou Galician (2004), a professor of journalism and communication, has extensively studied how the media affect beliefs about romance. Using the acronym PRESCRIPTION (as shown in Table 8.1), she has identified 12 stereotypical beliefs about romance that are perpetrated by the mass media.

TABLE 8.1 PRESCRIPTIONs about Romance Perpetuated by the Media

Belief	Example
Partner is predestined	Your ideal partner is out there.
Right away, you know	Love happens at first sight.
Expression not necessary	Your ideal partner will just know what you're thinking/feeling.
Sexual perfection	Sex with your soul mate is always easy and satisfying.
Centerfolds preferred	Women should look like models to attract their (male) partners.
Role of gender (or "real men")	Men should always be taller, more powerful, richer, and older than their (female) partners.
Into a prince (from beast)	Love can change a man into an ideal partner.
Pugilism = passion	Fighting is a sign of love and passion.
Totally opposite values	Love will overcome differences in values.
Incomplete without mate	Your ideal partner completes you and fulfills your needs.
Often, actors = roles	Actors are just like the characters they portray.
Not real/no effect	You're not affected by media portrayals of romance because you know they're not "real."

Note. Adapted from Galician (2004).

While people may believe that media portrayals of romance have no effect on public opinion because they're works of fiction, the opposite appears to be true. Research shows that those who consume more romantic media are also more likely to endorse unrealistic beliefs about relationships, including beliefs that partners should be able to read each other's minds and that romantic partners will be perfect (Haferkamp, 1999; Hefner & Wilson, 2013; Lippman, Ward, & Seabrook, 2014; Shapiro & Kroeger, 1991). Such expectations can influence people's actual relationships. In one study, researchers found that greater consumption of TV shows focusing on romantic relationships was related to decreased satisfaction in viewers' own romantic relationships as well as a greater tendency to report conflict in the relationships (Reizer & Hetsroni, 2014). Moreover, people, women especially, tend to believe that the way love is portrayed on television is realistic (Punyanunt-Carter, 2006). Of course, in romantic media, people rarely engage in unromantic behaviors that happen daily in real life—like flossing their teeth, blowing their noses, or going to the bathroom. As a result, in comparison to media images, one's own partner or relationship can seem quite imperfect.

your turn

What are your favorite movies and television shows? Which romantic themes do these show (if any)? Do any characters challenge the stereotypical themes of romance? What happens to these characters? How do you think the media you consume now, or consumed in the past, have influenced your views on love and romance?

Dating Scripts

What are common characteristics of dating scripts, and what does research say about online dating and hooking up?

The lessons about romance that we absorb from popular culture influence our beliefs about what should happen when people date, known as **dating scripts**. Like the sexual scripts discussed in Chapter 7, dating scripts are descriptions of supposedly "normal" behaviors in this context, and they are overwhelmingly heteronormative. Although dating and sexual scripts can overlap (since dating can involve sexual activity), dating scripts focus primarily on what happens before sexual contact.

An interesting exercise is to imagine how you would describe a date to someone who has no understanding of the practice. Maybe you'd talk about a man coming to a woman's home to pick her up for the date. Maybe he brings flowers. He probably takes the woman out to dinner, followed by some kind of shared activity such as watching a movie together. It's likely that you imagine the man driving, paying for dinner, selecting where they go, and so on. At the end of the evening when the man brings the woman home, he might kiss her. Despite its probable familiarity, does this script sound unrealistic or outdated—like something that belongs in a 1950s sitcom rather than in real life in the 21st century?

If you met someone who had never heard of dating, how would you describe it to that person? What would be key elements of your description, and what wouldn't be included?

Are Traditional Scripts Still Relevant? Despite claims of increasing egalitarianism in heterosexual dating practices, dating scripts still generally conform to traditional expectations (Laner & Ventrone, 2000). For example, psychologists Asia Eaton and Suzanna Rose (2011) reviewed all research on heterosexual dating published in the journal *Sex Roles* between 1975 and 2010. Although they identified some examples of behaviors that challenged this traditional script (e.g., women initiating dates) from more recent research, the traditional gender-typed script was found to remain largely unchallenged and unchanged. The researchers also reviewed popular dating advice books and found that the traditional script still dominates there as well. Men are portrayed as active and women as passive. For example, women are advised to get men to ask them out rather than doing the asking themselves and to let men feel like leaders in the relationship.

Research with lesbians has indicated that they don't typically adhere to traditional gender roles in dating (Klinkenberg & Rose, 1994; Rose & Zand, 2000), so the dominant dating scripts and the gendered culture of romance might not be as relevant to women who don't identify as heterosexual. However, sometimes LGBQ individuals model their dating practices after those in the dominant culture (Klinkenberg & Rose, 1994; Patterson, Ward, & Brown, 2013). When this occurs, LGBQ individuals may encounter legal, social, or practical barriers to demonstrating relationship seriousness (e.g., disclosing their relationship or their marriage). For example, in one study of mostly White, sexual minority women in their 20s (Patterson et al., 2013), researchers found that differing levels of outness between partners often slowed relationship progression (e.g., delaying the start of sexual activity) or caused relationship stress (e.g., pretending to just be friends in public).

Other research has shown more diversity of dating scripts among lesbian girls and women, including a romance script, a friendship script, and a sexually explicit script (Rose, Zand, & Cini, 1993). Of these, the romance script was identified as the one most likely to involve dating, although the dating phase may be short and a more serious relationship may evolve quickly. The friendship script involves becoming friends, then falling in love, and then establishing a committed relationship. The sexually explicit script focuses on sexuality and attraction, but there may be no intent of a future commitment—essentially, it reflects hooking up. In a subsequent study, the friendship script was identified as the most widely used script, and the sexually explicit script as the least popular one (Rose & Zand, 2000).

In a popular TED Talk, psychologist Danielle Sheypuk discussed how traditional dating scripts can make dating particularly challenging for people with disabilities (TEDx Talks, 2015). There's a widely held, stereotypical

your turn

Do you date? Do you know people who date? If so, what are the expectations around dating? Who does the asking? Who pays? Do traditional dating scripts (e.g., men ask and pay) still apply among you and your peers? Is hooking up the only alternative to traditional dating, or is there a more egalitarian dating script within your social circle?

assumption that women with disabilities do not, and should not, date (Howland & Rintala, 2001; Liddiard, 2018; Rintala et al., 1997). Because of this, many people believe that women with disabilities should be grateful for the attention of any partner or potential partner (Howland & Rintala, 2001; Liddiard, 2018). However, attention can be inappropriate or intrusive. For example, Sheypuk recalled a frequent experience on Tinder in which a potential male match would ask, "Can you have sex?" Sarcastically, she'd respond, "Yeah, can *you*?" Individuals with disabilities may have more difficulty finding and forming personal relationships that lead to intimacy because of social and environmental barriers such as lack of opportunity to find partners, although this situation is changing with the wider availability of online dating options (Mazur, 2017; Roth & Gillis, 2015; Saltes, 2013; Wada, Mortenson, & Hurd Clarke, 2016).

Online Dating and Hooking Up Regardless of ability status, online dating through websites and apps, as highlighted in the nearby Spotlight feature, has become common. However, online dating is fundamentally different from conventional, offline dating (Finkel, Eastwick, Karney, Reis, & Sprecher, 2012). First, there's more opportunity to select from a wide range of potential dating partners in online formats than offline. Second, people can have conversations with multiple potential partners before agreeing to meet face-to-face. This reduces the time needed to rule out poor fits and can enhance a sense of connection before meeting. Third, online dating, at least through websites, typically offers a mathematical algorithm to help match compatible people—something many sites use to promote their services over competitors' services.

Do these differences result in better dating outcomes? The research results are mixed. According to one study, online profiles often reduce people to two-dimensional displays of information (Heino, Ellison, & Gibbs, 2010). Also, although people initially like having access to a large number of potential partners, it can be exhausting to review hundreds of profiles and can actually result in decreased satisfaction with the date selected (D'Angelo & Toma, 2017; Wu & Chiou, 2009). Although the ability to communicate with a person before meeting up is a benefit, the time between initial online contact and face-to-face meeting is important (Whitty & Carr, 2006). One study showed that if people don't meet face-to-face after six weeks of communicating online, they're unlikely to have a satisfactory match (Ramirez & Zhang, 2007). Further, although mathematical algorithms eliminate potentially poor fits, they aren't effective in determining long-term relationship success (Finkel et al., 2012). This is because algorithms can't take into account the chemistry between two people, how they treat each other, or how people may change over time.

Some people have argued that dating, whether involving an online component or not, has largely been replaced by hooking up (Bogle, 2008; Glenn &

Marquardt, 2001). But as we saw in Chapter 7, hook-ups aren't as common as many people think (Lambert, Kahn, & Apple, 2003). Dating was also found to be a more prevalent script for women than hanging out or hooking up (Bradshaw, Kahn, & Saville, 2010). Young adults and Latinx students were particularly likely to report that their most recent romantic encounter was a date rather than hanging out or hooking up (Eaton & Rose, 2012; Eaton, Rose, Interligi, Fernandez, & McHugh, 2015).

Thus, dating, and the traditionally gendered dating script, remain prevalent. However, there is a negative side to this. Research with Latinx college students, for example, showed that hostile and benevolent sexist attitudes predicted greater endorsement of traditional dating scripts (Bermúdez, Sharp, & Taniguchi, 2015). For some women, however, the traditional dating script has advantages. For example, women who are undocumented immigrants are advantaged to be in roles where they aren't expected to pay or drive—actions that can be challenging for those who can't get a driver's license or find a job that provides a regular income (Pila, 2015). For most women, though, the traditional dating script doesn't carry the same benefits. Given this, feminist psychologists, among others, support the development of a more egalitarian script in which a woman can feel as comfortable as a man in both initiating a date and planning for and paying for an activity.

What Are People Looking For in Romantic Partners?

What patterns are there to characteristics that women desire in romantic partners?

What determines whom we fall in love with? According to cultural myths, there's one soul mate out there for each of us, and we'll fall in love with that person at first sight. That, however, is not how love works. Instead, we make choices and set priorities about what we're looking for in our partners. In Chapter 3, we explored sexual strategies theory (SST), which holds that women and

Spotlight on . . .

Online Dating

Dating websites, like PlentyofFish, eharmony, and OKCupid, have over 25 million users searching for potential partners (Finkel et al., 2012). There are also apps like Bumble, Grindr, and Tinder. Research shows that app users tend to be younger than website users, and although these apps are often thought of as facilitating hookups rather than dating, people use them for both purposes (Gatter & Hodkinson, 2016). Nearly 50 million people have tried online dating ("Online Dating Statistics," 2017), and 19% of Internet users in the United States were using dating apps or websites as of April 2017 ("Online Dating—Statistics & Facts," n.d.).

Online dating is especially helpful for those who are looking for partners with certain identities, interests, or characteristics—for example, people of a certain age (SeniorPeopleMeet), sexual orientation (GaySinglesOnline), religious orientation (JDate), race (BlackSingles), or ability status (DatingforDisabled). As one example, teens who identified as LGBTQ were shown to be more likely to find romantic partners online than were heterosexual-identified teens, in part because it was harder for them to meet potential partners in their daily lives (Korchmaros, Ybarra, & Mitchell, 2015).

Have you, or people you know, had experience with online dating? If so, what were those experiences like? What do you see as advantages and disadvantages of online dating? Will it ever replace meeting people in person? Why or why not?

men approach mating, and therefore relationships, differently in order to best ensure reproductive success (Buss & Schmitt, 1993). In addition to addressing how evolutionary pressure may have influenced mating practices, this theory addresses mating preferences. According to the theory, men are attracted to young, physically attractive partners because, in our evolutionary past, these partners had the best chance of producing healthy offspring (thereby carrying on the man's genetics). Women, in contrast, are attracted to slightly older partners who have status and access to resources because, in our evolutionary past, such partners were most likely to help both the woman and her offspring to survive (thereby carrying on the woman's genetics).

Research has shown support for some of these ideas. For example, even in extremely egalitarian Norway, men prefer partners younger than themselves, with the age gap widening as men age, and women show a stable preference for men slightly older than themselves (Grøntvedt & Kennair, 2013). Also, in a study of nearly 10,000 people from 37 cultures, women placed more value on social status than men, and men placed greater value on physical attractiveness (Shackelford, Schmitt, & Buss, 2005). Other research, however, has not shown support for SST (e.g., Pedersen, Putcha-Bhagavatula, & Miller, 2011). For example, a meta-analysis showed that physical attractiveness and earning potential both predicted positive romantic evaluations and that there were no significant gender differences (Eastwick, Luchies, Finkel, & Hunt, 2014). It's also possible that women's desire for men who are older and financially secure may have to do with the fact that women generally have less power and need financial security. One study showed that women and men in more egalitarian countries were more similar to each other in terms of what they wanted in a partner than those in less egalitarian countries (Eagly & Wood, 1999). Therefore, what might be seen as evolved gender differences might, today, actually be responses to social roles and differential access to power.

Research hasn't always taken into account the effect that the desired type of relationship might have on partner preferences. For example, what someone might desire in a partner for a one-night stand may be very different from what that person wants in a long-term partner. This idea has led researchers to begin exploring preferences for partner traits within specific types of relationships. Regardless of gender or sexual orientation, studies have shown that participants valued attractiveness when evaluating potential short-term partners and placed greater importance on similarity and characteristics like intelligence and honesty when considering potential long-term partners (Regan, Levin, Sprecher, Christopher, & Gate, 2000; Regan, Medina, & Joshi, 2001). Of course, not all women (or men) are looking for the same things in short- or long-term partners. For example, in a study of primarily White, heterosexual women, researchers found that some women seemed particularly concerned with how attractive their partners were, while others were more interested in partners who were personable, intelligent, and hard-working (Castro, Hattori, & de Araújo Lopes, 2015).

Given these findings, it has become increasingly apparent that, rather than making broad assumptions, researchers would do well to look more carefully at what different women want in partners. For example, one study showed that both Black women and men valued the income of a potential partner and seemed to desire an income that would allow the family greater upward social mobility (King & Allen, 2009). In contrast, in a study of primarily White female undergraduate and graduate students at a large university, researchers found a relationship between intelligence and partner preferences in terms of income and status (Stanik & Ellsworth, 2010). Those who scored higher on an IQ test were less interested in a potential partner's wealth and status. The authors suggested that these women may have been less concerned with partners' wealth because they felt confident in their own ability to financially support themselves and their families. Another study examined personal ads placed by Muslim individuals living in the United States, and the women's ads were particularly likely to emphasize seeking partners who were religious (Badahdah & Tiemann, 2005). A similar study of personal ads placed by lesbians showed that honesty was a particularly valued trait for partners (Smith, Konik, & Tuve, 2011).

Some women are concerned that they won't be able to find the partners they want because of expectations of gendered roles in a relationship. For example, in one study of heterosexual, Mexican American college students, women were concerned that their level of education would be seen as a threat to the masculinity of potential Mexican American partners (Gonzalez, 1988). More recent research showed that Latinx women thought having more education would make it harder to find a partner of the same race/ethnicity, but Latinx men didn't hold this perspective (Niemann, Romero, & Arbona, 2000). Concerns about finding a desirable partner can result in being either highly selective or not selective at all, and this mix of patterns was found in a qualitative study about the dating experiences of women with physical disabilities (Howland & Rintala, 2001). Some participants felt they couldn't be selective: "If some guy would show me affection, I kind of felt like I'd better grab him because I probably wouldn't get anyone else" (p. 53). Other participants reported being non-selective because they felt the need to prove that they were desirable. Those who reported being highly selective had more variability in their reasons for this pattern.

Committed Relationships

In 1985, psychologist Suzanna Rose asked, "Is romance dysfunctional?" (p. 250). She argued that because media portrayals of romance primarily address courtship, they don't provide information about maintaining long-term relationships.

Jealousy in Relationships

Jealousy within a relationship might seem to be a bad thing, signaling lack of trust between partners and/or lack of belief in one's own desirability as a partner. Yet media portrayals of jealousy often show it as a sign of passion and a signal of commitment to the relationship (Bonomi, Altenburger, & Walton, 2013; Collins & Carmody, 2011; Hayes, 2014). For example, in the love triangle at the center of the *Twilight* book and movie series, both Edward and Jacob display jealousy over Bella's involvement with the other, and this apparently demonstrates how deeply the men care for Bella. Some women may try to evoke jealousy in a partner through behaviors such as flirting with others (Brainerd, Hunter, Moore, & Thompson, 1996). This may make women feel powerful and in control of the relationship. It may also confirm the extent to which they are romantically and sexually desirable. After all, as discussed in Chapter 7, women often learn that a key source of power is their sexuality.

Jealousy, however, has a downside. It's sometimes viewed as an excuse for violence and other types of abuse in relationships (see Chapter 12), and jealousy-related violence is more likely to be classified as a sign of love than as abuse (Power, Koch, Kralik, & Jackson, 2006; Puente & Cohen, 2003; Vandello & Cohen, 2008). Jealousy can also be associated with controlling behaviors within relationships, which may be viewed as signals of love (Bonomi et al., 2013; Donovan & Hester, 2010; Hayes, 2014; Power et al., 2006). For example, teenagers in one study reported that telling a girlfriend how to dress is an indication that the boyfriend cares about her (Chung, 2005). Moreover, using words like *ownership* and *protector* to describe a relationship were seen to communicate intimacy. These types of controlling behaviors, referred to as **mate retention behaviors**, are tactics that may serve to keep a partner away from potential rivals and ensure the partner's fidelity (Buss, Shackelford, & McKibbin, 2008). Some mate retention behaviors may be interpreted as caring and romantic (e.g., giving a partner a ring to show that the partner is "taken"), but others are more easily identified as tactics of control (e.g., checking to see that a partner is where she said she would be).

There are potential dangers with believing jealousy is positive. In one study, heterosexual women who held pro-jealousy attitudes were more likely to report having sexist attitudes and desiring a man who endorsed violence and male dominance over women (Hartwell, Humphries, Erchull, & Liss, 2015). Other research showed that pro-jealousy attitudes were related to viewing mate retention behaviors as romantic, which, in turn, was related to experiencing violence in relationships (Papp, Liss, Erchull, Godfrey, & Waaland-Kreutzer, 2016).

Do you think jealousy from a partner can feel empowering? If so, when? And when does it cross the line to being problematic? Alternatively, is jealousy just a way of controlling and oppressing a partner? If so, how can we change attitudes about this and the way jealousy is represented in our culture?

In fact, for many people, the reality of long-term relationships is far from the "happily ever after" that ends most of the romantic scripts permeating popular culture. So what actually happens after the couple walks off into the sunset together? In this section, we'll talk about marriage, divorce, committed relationships outside of marriage, and power dynamics within relationships. Even though cultural messages about love, romance, and relationships can be problematic, there are also real benefits to being in committed relationships.

Marriage and the Wedding Industrial Complex

What are current trends related to marriage, and what cultural expectations surround weddings as well as the marriages that follow?

When most people think about long-term relationships and living "happily ever after," they usually think about marriage. Indeed, the vast majority of people marry at some point in their lives. Estimates are that 90% of women in the United States will marry at least once (Goldstein & Kenney, 2001). But not everyone is married. Data from the United States Census Bureau (n.d.) indicate that, in 2017, approximately 51% of women and 54% of men were married, 29% of women and 35% of men had never been married, 11% of women and 9% of men were divorced, and 9% of women and 3% of men were widowed. These rates vary by demographic group. For example, women who identified as Asian American were most likely to be married (62%), and women who identified as Black were least likely to be married (32%).

Marriage status also varies by age. On average, women and men in the United States get married (for the first time) at 27 and 29 years of age, respectively (U.S. Census Bureau, n.d.). These numbers show an increase from 1950, when women got married at age 20 and men at 23. Although the average age at first marriage varies from country to country, worldwide there's a trend for women to delay their first marriage (from age 22 to age 25 between the 1970s and the mid-2000s). The 2015 World Marriage Data from the United Nations indicate that men, on average, tend to be older than women when they marry, and this is true in all countries for which data were available. However, the size of the age difference varies. For example, in Egypt the gap is five years, as compared to a two-year gap in the United States.

Marriage, like romance, carries a lot of cultural expectations. In fact, for many people, marriage is synonymous with weddings (Auchmuty, 2012). Weddings have historically been associated with formalizing a commitment between a woman and a man. However, on June 26, 2015, this standard officially changed in the United States when the Supreme Court ruled that same-sex marriage was a legal right. Although it had already been legal in many states, there was a constant threat of changes in legal status, so the Court's decision signaled a significant

Weddings take many different forms, both in the United States and worldwide. When you call up a mental image of a wedding, what's part of it? In what ways is it similar to and different from the one pictured here?

shift not just in terms of marriage equality but also in terms of recognizing LGBQ individuals as a whole (Frost, Meyer & Hammack, 2014).

Technically, all it takes to get married in the United States is the nominal fee for a marriage license and then, usually, a nominal fee to an officiant. But weddings are rarely this simple. For many couples, regardless of sexual orientation, weddings are a link to tradition, and for those marrying within a religious context, tradition can involve religious beliefs and cultural practices. For example, Jewish couples may marry under a huppah, and the groom may break a glass with his foot at the end of the ceremony. Catholic couples may take Communion together as part of their wedding mass. Weddings are also often quite expensive. A survey by the wedding planning website The Knot showed that the average amount spent on a wedding in 2017 was $33,391 (Schweizer, 2018), and 45% of couples reported spending more than they had planned to (Schwahn, 2018). The wedding industry is big business, estimated at $72 billion in 2016 (Schmidt, 2017), and this has led people to label it as the wedding-industrial complex (Ferguson, 2017).

Weddings also often involve traditions and practices that have roots in traditional gender roles. For example, the practice of the father "giving away" his daughter to another man is important to many families, but it also reflects the patriarchal history of weddings and women's role as possessions—first of their fathers, and later of their husbands. Not everyone is comfortable with these types of traditional practices, however. One study showed that women are more likely than men to favor being pronounced "husband and wife" at the end of a wedding ceremony rather than the more traditional "man and wife" (Ogletree, 2010). Even religious officiants are sometimes uncomfortable with traditional practices. A minister in another study said, "I won't ask a question of the father: who gives this woman away? I won't do that because I think that's inappropriate because women aren't chattels to be passed around between the men folk" (Baker & Elizabeth, 2014, p. 402). Research does indicate, though, that those with more traditional attitudes toward gender are likely to want traditional, expensive weddings and support buying expensive engagement rings (Ogletree, 2010).

Regardless of the form a wedding takes, and no matter how memorable the celebration is, it is not itself representative of marriage. As one woman said, "There's the getting married and then there's *the day* of getting married, and all the stuff that goes with it—and I find that sort of thing is very separate" (Currie, 1993,

p. 420). Psychologist Les Parrott and marriage and family therapist Leslie Parrott (2015) have highlighted four myths of marriage that can be characterized as both harmful and widespread: (a) that individuals and their spouses have the same expectations within the marriage, (b) that positive aspects of the relationships will get better within marriage, (c) that negative aspects will disappear once marriage happens, and (d) that spouses will complete each other. In fact, these beliefs are hard to live up to. Any relationship that lasts for a significant period will involve some negative components, such as disagreements about money, stress due to illness, and so on. While these myths haven't received a great deal of research attention, one study showed that when such expectations don't match reality, those involved can experience dissatisfaction with their relationships as well as decreased personal well-being (Casad, Salazar, & Macina, 2014).

Benefits of Marriage

What benefits are associated with marriage?

There are many interpersonal benefits from marriage—at least, if the marriage is a healthy one (Robles, Slatcher, Trombello, & McGinn, 2014). Marriage offers a stable source of social support from one's partner. Regardless of sexual orientation, married individuals report a sense of shared commitment, emotional connection, and support (Ducharme & Kollar, 2012). In some ways, women partnered with women may be better off in this regard than women partnered with men. For example, one study showed that married lesbian women, compared to married heterosexual women, received more social support from their spouse and were better able to communicate with their partners about family matters (Brashier, Hughes, & Cook, 2013).

Research has also shown that, overall, married individuals earn more, on average, than those who are divorced, widowed, or never married (Waite, 1995). However, this is largely due to the fact that married *men* generally earn more than unmarried men, not that married women earn more than unmarried women. Married men benefit from having wives who do more at home (Chun & Lee, 2001; Dougherty, 2006). We'll discuss this topic later in the chapter. Since women generally earn less money than men (Institute for Women's Policy Research, 2017)—a topic we'll discuss in Chapter 10—they experience a greater financial boon with marriage since they have partners bringing greater income into the family. Moreover, other research shows that married individuals have better mental and physical health than those who aren't married (e.g., Guner,

Kulikova, & Llull, 2014; Wilson & Oswald, 2005). This may partially explain why both married women and men live longer (e.g., Kaplan & Kronick, 2006; Manzoli, Villari, Pirone, & Boccia, 2007), although some data do point to a slight additional benefit for men (e.g., Rendall, Weden, Favreault, & Waldron, 2011).

In the past, theorists suggested that men benefited considerably more from marriage than women and that there was actually a "his" marriage that contributed to well-being and a "hers" marriage that detracted from it (e.g., Bernard, 1972). Men, according to this argument, get a cook, a maid, and a therapist when they marry. Women, however, have to provide these services and receive insufficient emotional intimacy from their partners in return. Some subsequent research supported this idea and found that men were more satisfied in marriage than women (Fowers, 1991). However, although every couple is different, more recent work indicates that both women and men benefit from marriage (Waite & Gallagher, 2000).

In addition to the physical, psychological, and financial benefits discussed above, there are institutionalized benefits of marriage (Guillen, 2016). For example, in the United States, married partners receive tax benefits, and there are benefits associated with inheritance if a partner dies. Further, married partners can receive Social Security benefits accrued by their spouse. Typically, Social Security benefits are based on one's own lifetime earnings, but spouses can get 50% of their partner's benefits instead if that would entitle them to more than would be the case based on their own lifetime earnings. Employers may also offer benefits, such as medical insurance, for spouses. Moreover, spouses can visit their partner in the hospital because they are considered next of kin. The latter benefit was one reason the fight for marriage equality was so important to many LGBQ individuals.

Marriage equality is a recent change, so most research on marriage has focused on relationships between a woman and a man. However, both LGBQ and heterosexual individuals in long-term committed relationships have spoken of similar important components (Frost & Gola, 2015). These include commitment, communication, emotional connection, and support of each other. LGBQ individuals were also more likely to talk about stigma playing a role in their relationships. Heterosexual couples rarely need to conceal their relationships or fear discrimination because of their relationship status, but many partnered LGBQ individuals face these issues. More research on the benefits of legally sanctioned marriage for LGBQ individuals is needed, however.

Divorce

What are positive and negative outcomes of divorce for women?

There's a common saying that 50% of marriages end in divorce. In fact, a report written for the U.S. Department of Health and Human Services (DHHS) indicated that 48% of first marriages among women and 44% of first marriages among men end in divorce within 20 years (Copen, Daniels, Vespa, & Mosher, 2012). Divorce rates also reflect demographic characteristics. For example, marrying before age 25 and earning less than $25,000 per year have been identified as risk factors for divorce (Clarke-Stewart & Brentano, 2006). Data have also shown racial and ethnic differences in divorce rates: In the DHHS report, Asian American people were least likely and Black American people most likely to have a first marriage end in divorce, while those who identified as Latinx and White had rates in the middle (Copen et al., 2012).

Some researchers suggest that the divorce rate increased in the late 20th century, in part, because feminism and other social justice movements created a climate of greater opportunities for women (Stevenson & Wolfers, 2007). They

Many people experience divorce. Some consider it a bad thing and a signal of failure. In what ways could divorce be positive?

were, therefore, better able to support themselves and didn't need marriage to survive. Although divorce is generally thought of as a negative and undesirable life event, 64% of the women interviewed in one study spoke of positive consequences resulting from their divorces (Bevvino & Sharkin, 2003). In particular, they spoke of changes they made to themselves as well as divorce providing new opportunities for growth.

It can definitely be beneficial to leave a dysfunctional relationship, but there can also be negative consequences. When couples divorce, assuming both partners work, they lose access to one salary. For heterosexual women, this means losing access to their male partner's income, which is typically higher than their own. Several studies have indicated that divorce is a real financial threat for women (Hilton & Anderson, 2009; Smock, Manning, & Gupta, 1999). However, according to a different study, women's earning power has increased over time, so the financial consequences of divorce are smaller now than in the past (Tach & Eads, 2015). Nevertheless, other research shows that, despite increased earning power, most women still experience a financial decline after divorce (Gadalla, 2008). Moreover, income is only one financial benefit of marriage. Health insurance coverage from a partner's job is another, and women lose access to this after divorce, which can add to their economic decline (Lavelle & Smock, 2012). This may be one reason why women's physical health has been found to decline after divorce (Forste & Heaton, 2004; Prigerson, Maciejewski, & Rosenheck, 1999). Mental health, too, has been found to decline following divorce (Prigerson et al., 1999). Those who have divorced are more likely to report depression and low self-esteem (Symoens, Van de Velde, Colman, & Bracke, 2014) as well as lower feelings of competence (Symoens et al., 2014) and happiness (Forste & Heaton, 2004).

The reasons for divorce aren't particularly different from the reasons why other romantic relationships, or friendships, end. People's commitment to any given relationship is lower when they believe better potential alternatives are available, they aren't satisfied with the relationship, and they haven't invested a great deal in the relationship (Rusbult, 1983). One study showed that the most commonly reported causes for divorce were incompatibility and growing apart (Amato & Preveti, 2003). Another study identified poor communication and the inability to resolve conflict (Bevvino & Sharkin, 2003). Of course, larger issues can also lead to divorce, such as infidelity, abuse, and drug and alcohol use (Amato & Preveti, 2003; Bevvino & Sharkin, 2003). Other risk factors include experiencing stress, such as being unemployed, having experienced rape, and having unwanted children (Clarke-Stewart & Brentano, 2006).

Reasons for divorce in lesbian couples are similar to those in heterosexual couples. Like heterosexual relationships, lack of satisfaction with, investment in, and commitment to a relationship can contribute to its failure—as can a belief that better options are available (Beals, Impett, & Peplau, 2002). Social stigma, internalized heterosexism, and societal discrimination can also play a role in relationship conflict for lesbian couples; this and other factors unique to having a sexual minority identity may contribute to relationships ending (Barrantes, Eaton, Veldhuis, & Hughes, 2017; Beals et al., 2002).

Relationships Other Than Marriage

What other forms, beyond marriage, do women's committed romantic relationships take?

Not all long-term relationships happen within the context of marriage. Even if most people marry at some point in their lives, they may experience other long-term committed relationships. In fact, data indicate that an increase in cohabitation—that is, living together in a committed relationship without being married—is one reason the age for first marriages is increasing (Copen et al., 2012). Approximately 3% of women were cohabiting in 1992, and this figure rose to 11% by the time data were collected for the 2006–2010 National Survey of Family Growth (Copen et al., 2012). Cohabitation sometimes is a precursor to marriage, but not always. For example, one study showed that 68% of women's marriages were preceded by cohabitation with that partner (Kennedy & Bumpass, 2008). In another study, researchers found that, within three years of beginning to cohabit, approximately 40% of women married their partners, 32% continued to cohabit, and 27% ended the relationship (Copen, Daniels, & Mosher, 2013).

The transition to marriage may occur for a number of reasons. For some people, it's a way to formalize the relationship through a public commitment; for others, having or planning to have children may lead to the decision to marry;

and still others report having experienced social pressure to do so (Baker & Elizabeth, 2014). As discussed earlier, there are also legal and financial benefits associated with marriage. However, even when cohabitation transitions to marriage, for some couples the relationships that follow aren't perfect. Data from several studies indicate that a higher proportion of marriages that were preceded by cohabitation end in divorce than those in which couples did not first cohabit (Dempsey & De Vaus, 2004; Duncan, Barlow, & James, 2005; Lichter, Qian, & Mellot, 2006). However, this trend may be changing (Manning & Cohen, 2012; Reinhold, 2010). Some researchers suggest this may reflect the fact that it's becoming much more common for couples to cohabit before marriage (Hewitt & De Vaus, 2009). It may also reflect the fact that fewer cohabiting relationships are transitioning to marriage than in the past (Guzzo, 2014).

With or without cohabitation, not everyone marries, and this can be a conscious choice. For example, Carol Smart (1984), a feminist sociologist, called for the abandonment of marriage. Instead, she argued, we should "devise a system of rights, duties, or obligations which are not dependent on any form of 'coupledom' or marriage or quasi-marriage" (p. 146). She saw marriage as a broken, patriarchal system that couldn't be fixed and would continue to oppress women. Marriage hasn't gone away since the early 1980s when Smart made her argument. In fact, marriage is being embraced by more people. However, being married is no longer considered the only role for women—it has become a lifestyle choice (Auchmuty, 2012). This means that women can choose to engage in casual sexual relationships, date, cohabit, or remain single. Of course, there are still social pressures to marry (DePaulo & Morris, 2005), but they're less intense than in the past. Moreover, as we discussed in Chapter 4, some people may opt out of marriage and other forms of committed relationships because they identify as aromantic.

Consensually Non-Monogamous Relationships Some people prefer committed romantic relationships that are intentionally non-monogamous; these are referred to as **consensually non-monogamous (CNM) relationships**. One type of non-monogamous relationship is **polygamy**, which involves one husband having many wives—a practice that may be connected to religious belief or cultural practices. **Polyamorous** (often shortened to *poly*) **relationships**, in contrast, aren't tied to religious beliefs or to specific gender identities. Poly individuals may love and/or be sexually involved with multiple partners, and honesty and openness within relationships are considered essential (Haritaworn, Lin, & Klesse, 2006; McCullough & Hall, 2003). Other CNM relationships, such as swinging or open relationships, are more focused on sex with multiple partners rather than ongoing committed relationships with multiple partners.

There are very limited data on rates of consensual non-monogamy as opposed to non-monogamy more generally, which may involve cheating on a partner who believes the relationship is monogamous (Rubin, Moors, Matsick, Ziegler, &

Conley, 2014). Research specifically looking at CNM points to approximately 5% of people in the United States being in these types of relationships at any given time (Rubin et al., 2014). Research also indicates that women are slightly less likely to be involved in CNM relationships than are men (Rubin et al., 2014); but it has been argued that these relationships may actually be beneficial for women, as monogamy can be seen as a form of gender oppression (Ziegler, Matsick, Moors, Rubin, & Conley, 2014). After all, as we'll discuss next, women in traditional heterosexual monogamous relationships have less power, take on more domestic responsibilities, and generally have less agency over their lives.

Consensually non-monogamous relationships have received little research attention compared to romantic relationships between two people, but these types of relationships are of interest to a growing minority of people (Anapol, 1997; Barker, 2005). Some poly individuals believe that those who support monogamy are threatened by the different nature of polyamorous relationships (Barker, 2005), and these relationships are stigmatized (Conley, Moors, Matsick, & Ziegler, 2013). Those who engage in CNM are often perceived by others as being less happy in their relationships, less sexually satisfied, and even as less good citizens (Conley et al., 2013). Some people argue, however, that the relationships themselves aren't necessarily that different. Recent research, in fact, shows few differences in the quality of monogamous and consensually non-monogamous relationships (Conley, Matsick, Moors, & Ziegler, 2017). One participant in a study of polyamory said, "I don't think it's vastly different to monogamous relationships. Romantic relationships are always about the same kinds of things: fun, friendship, sex" (Barker, 2005, p. 82).

It has been argued that polyamory is largely the purview of White, middle-class, well-educated, able-bodied individuals, so more information is needed about CNM relationships among people with diverse social identities (Noël, 2006). One study, however, found that White individuals and people of color were equally likely to participate in monogamy and in CNM relationships, and LGBQ individuals were more likely than heterosexual individuals to participate in them (Rubin et al., 2014). Moreover, one group of researchers found that, despite stereotypes that gay men are those most interested in CNM relationships, sexual minority women and men have similar attitudes toward and desire to participate in such relationships (Moors, Rubin, Matsick, Ziegler, & Conley, 2014).

Power Dynamics in Relationships

What is the principle of least interest, and how does it relate to power and relationship satisfaction?

In traditional, monogamous, heterosexual relationships, dynamics of power are extremely important to consider. In Chapter 2, we discussed how men have more power than women and how their greater power and privilege can be difficult to see. Within heterosexual relationships, there are many manifestations of men's greater power, although couples may not be fully aware of how power dynamics shape their relationships. While some couples hold traditional values and think that men should lead the household, other couples value egalitarian relationships. Even in the latter case, though, men's greater power can find its way into relationships.

In the 1930s, sociologist Willard Waller (1938) described the **principle of least interest**, which states that the person who wants a relationship less has greater power within that relationship. You might have intuitively experienced this dynamic yourself; it's why people don't text back immediately after a date—they don't want to be perceived as too eager and, therefore, be placed in the less powerful position. Longitudinal studies exploring the balance of power over time between partners in heterosexual couples support the idea that the least emotionally invested partner is the one who has more power in the relationship (Felmlee, 1994; Sprecher & Felmlee, 1997; Sprecher, Schmeekle, & Felmlee, 2006). In contrast, couples with equal levels of emotional involvement were found to be more satisfied with their relationships, and their relationships tended to last over time (Sprecher & Felmlee, 1997; Sprecher et al., 2006). This dynamic isn't limited to heterosexual couples. Equality of power within lesbian relationships has also been found to relate to greater satisfaction with that relationship (Peplau, Padesky, & Hamilton, 1982), and power sharing continues to be seen as a relationship ideal for many lesbians (Kurdek, 1995; Peplau & Fingerhut, 2007; Reilly & Lynch, 1990).

The principle of least interest is related to gender because it's generally assumed that women are the ones who more strongly value relationships. For example, in one study of primarily White college students, researchers found that a typical woman was perceived as wanting both marriage and children more than a typical man (Erchull, Liss, Axelson, Staebell, & Askari, 2010). However, other data suggest that this belief may be incorrect. In the same study, when college students were asked about their own desire for marriage and children, female and male participants reported desiring them equally. Given these results, the researchers concluded that men may have power in relationships because it's assumed that they're less interested—even if this isn't actually the case.

Furthermore, the principle of least interest isn't the only source of power dynamics. In one study, researchers found that, among married lesbian couples with children who lived in states that legally restricted the rights of non-birth parents, the biological mothers tended to hold more power and the non-biological mothers tended to feel insecure (Butterfield & Padavic, 2014). One non-biological mother expressed: "Since the moment I looked into my daughter's eyes I have been overwhelmed, thinking how powerless I am. They could walk out of my life and there is nothing I can do. . . . I need constant reassurance from Karen. And it's starting to affect our relationship, which makes me worry even more" (p. 761).

Moreover, as we'll discuss next, the partner with the greater earning potential and status (most frequently the man in heterosexual couples) usually holds the most power. One consequence of power inequity within relationships is that the person with less power generally has to do more to maintain the relationship. This can play out in decisions about who does what around the house.

Division of Labor

What is the second shift, and what types of labor are women more likely to engage in than men?

Maintaining a house takes a lot of work. Chores, or household labor, include cooking, cleaning, laundry, shopping, household repairs, and yard work. However, not all household labor is the same. Some tasks, like cleaning up messes, doing laundry, shopping, cooking meals, and doing dishes, have to be done frequently on a regular schedule—often, every day; sometimes, multiple times per day. This kind of labor is called **routine labor**. It's also called **low-control labor** because the person doing it has little control over when and where it gets done (Coltrane, 2000). Other types of chores, such as taking out the trash or fixing things around the house, are considered **intermittent labor** because they're only done occasionally and there's usually some leeway as to when they need to get done. Dinner has to be on the table and the dishes cleaned up every night. However, the trash can

While men are doing more housework now than in the past, women still are doing a disproportionate amount of household labor. What factors contribute to the persistence of this pattern?

usually sit for an extra day without major consequences. Data consistently show that women do more work around the house—in particular, more low-control or routine tasks (Aassve, Fuochi, & Mencarini, 2014; Bianchi, Milkie, Sayer, & Robinson, 2000; Bianchi, Sayer, Milkie, & Robinson, 2012; Coltrane, 2000; Craig & Powell, 2018). This occurs even when women work outside of the home. The phenomenon of women coming home from their jobs and doing another round of work in the home has come to be known as the **second shift**, a term that gained popularity in the late 1980s (Hochschild & Machung, 1989).

However, to better understand the second shift, we need to look at more than gender. For example, research shows that Black men do more chores around the house than their White male counterparts (McLoyd, Cauce, Takeuchi, & Wilson, 2000). Also, in a study of low-income Mexican American families, men in families that identified as Mexican did more around the house than those who were more acculturated to American society (Coltrane, Parke, & Adams, 2004). Given the lack of connection to traditional gender roles within lesbian relationships, there tends to be greater equality in the division of labor among lesbian couples than among heterosexual couples (Downing & Goldberg, 2011; Goldberg & Perry-Jenkins, 2007; Kurdek, 2007).

Inequity in the division of labor has changed over time (Bianchi, Sayer, Milkie, & Robinson, 2012). As Table 8.2 shows, married women did 7.2 times the total housework of men and 16.6 times the routine housework in 1965. By 1998–1999, the division of housework was considerably more equitable; women were doing 1.4 times men's total housework and 2.5 times the routine housework. However, progress stalled after that. Data from 2009–2010 show that women actually did a greater proportion of the routine, core housework than they did in 1998–1999. Overall, while there has been some progress toward equality, it hasn't been fully achieved. Furthermore, while the statistics reported in Table 8.2 end at 2010, more recent data indicate that the trend continues. The U.S. Bureau of Labor Statistics (2016) reported that, in 2015, men spent an average of 1 hour and 25 minutes on housework while women averaged 2 hours and 15 minutes a day.

Inequality in the division of household labor becomes more pronounced when couples have children (Gjerdingen, & Center, 2005; Yavorsky, Kamp Dush, & Schoppe-Sullivan, 2015). One study of mostly White, high-income families in

TABLE 8.2 Ratio of Married Women's Time to Married Men's Time Spent on Housework, 1965–2010

	1965	1975	1985	1995	1998–1999	2003–2004	2009–2010
Total housework	7.2:1	3.9:1	2.1:1	1.9:1	1.4:1	1.8:1	1.7:1
Routine/core housework	16.6:1	12.3:1	4.6:1	4.3:1	2.5:1	4.2:1	3.4:1
Other housework*	1.2:1	0.6:1	0.6:1	0.5:1	0.5:1	0.6:1	0.6:1

Note. Data from Bianchi et al., 2012. *"Other housework" includes intermittent labor such as home repairs or financial planning.

which both adults worked full-time showed that women and men were doing equal levels of housework during the third trimester of pregnancy (Yavorsky, Kamp Dush, & Schoppe-Sullivan, 2015). When the baby came, both members of the couple returned to work at somewhat reduced hours, although women worked three hours a week less than men. However, women did considerably more work in the home. Including paid work, household work, and child care, women were working 77 hours a week compared to the men's 69 hours. The eight-hour weekly difference translates into women working one hour more than men every day. Interestingly, this study showed equality before children, when most other research has not (see Bianchi et al., 2012, for a review). The authors suggested that this may have reflected the men doing more because the wives were far along in their pregnancy.

In general, mothers report doing about twice as much child care as men (Bianchi et al., 2012; Fillo, Simpson, Rholes, & Kohn, 2015). According to the U.S. Bureau of Labor Statistics (n.d.), in 2016 mothers with children under age six spent 2.56 hours per day caring for children as their main activity, while fathers with children under age six spent 1.47 hours caring for them. Another study showed that, on non-workdays, fathers engaged in leisure activities 47% of the time while mothers did child care (Kamp Dush, Yavorsky, & Schoppe-Sullivan, 2018). Mothers, however, only did leisure activities 16% of the time while fathers engaged in child care. In lesbian couples, although there's generally more equality, one study found that inequality in the division of labor was related to who served as the child's biological mother, in part because biological mothers are more likely to engage in intensive parenting (Downing & Goldberg, 2011). We'll return to the topic of intensive parenting in Chapter 9.

Another aspect of the division of labor generally gets overlooked in research studies. Aside from tasks such as cleaning, cooking, doing dishes, and taking care of children, a great deal of planning and organizing is required, and this invisible work is sometimes called the *mental load*. For example, someone needs to ask: What will we have for dinner? Do the pets need to be taken to the vet? When was the last time the air conditioner filters were changed? Once children are added to the mix, the planning and organizing get more complicated: Who organizes the doctor's appointments? How about the playdates? Who enrolls children in extracurricular activities and summer camps? According to one study, although men do considerably more routine labor around the house now than they did 40 years ago, women still bear the vast majority of the mental load (Gager, 2008). When the women who participated were asked what they wished their husbands would do to make the division of labor more equitable, by far the most frequent response was that they wanted help with managing and organizing the household. Only a minority of participants whose husbands did very little around the house wanted more help with routine chores such as doing dishes. Women didn't want household helpers; they wanted co-leaders.

Women are also more likely to do **emotion work**. This encompasses tasks that make other people feel loved and cared for (Erickson, 2005), such as sending birthday cards to relatives, writing thank you cards for presents, and coordinating the purchase of gifts by various members of the household. Emotion work also occurs within the marriage relationship—for example, when the husband has a bad day and the wife helps him feel better (Pederson, 2017). Given the gendered association between femininity and caring for others, it's not surprising that women do the majority of this work, and research has suggested that both women and men who have more traditionally feminine traits are more likely to do emotion work (Erickson, 2005). Women are also more likely to suffer negative consequences if emotion work isn't done, especially if it involves reaching out to extended members of the family to make sure that their emotional needs are met. For example, if the family forgets to call an aunt on her birthday, the husband isn't usually blamed for the oversight (Erickson, 2005).

Why the Inequity?

What factors contribute to an inequitable division of labor?

There are a number of theories for why women do more chores around the house. The **relative resources theory** states that the person who brings more resources to the relationship gets to use those resources in order to avoid doing chores. In this view, couples view relationships as a **social exchange** between partners—that is, one person provides the bulk of the financial resources and the other does the bulk of the domestic labor (Lachance-Grzela & Bouchard, 2010; Mannino & Deutch, 2007). A related theory involves **time availability**. This theory holds that the person with the most available time should do a larger proportion of housework (Fuwa, 2004; Lachance-Grzela & Bouchard, 2010). Women who stay at home or work part-time, for example, have more time available at home. As we'll discuss in Chapter 10, women often reduce their work hours after having children. One factor in the decision to have the mother, rather than the father, work less is that men typically earn more than women (Stone, 2007), another topic we'll explore in Chapter 10. Another possibility is that some women who out-earn their spouses choose to reduce their work hours and spend more time on domestic chores in order to maintain the notion of the male breadwinner, which can be important to the identity of many men (Bertrand, Kamenica, & Pan, 2015). Of course, when women work less in order to spend more time with children, this reduces their future earning potential. As a result, women may have more time available to do household chores and child care, but at a cost to their own careers and future finances.

Data generally support the idea that the person with more time and fewer relative resources does the most household labor. For example, two studies found that women who are more highly educated and earn as much as their husbands do less housework (Cunningham, 2007; Kroska, 2004). Among lesbian couples, although there's typically a more egalitarian division of labor than among heterosexual couples, the member of the lesbian couple who earns more generally does fewer household chores (Goldberg, Smith, & Perry-Jenkins, 2012). When heterosexual couples were interviewed about this type of exchange, male respondents found it to be fair (Gager, 2008). One man said that even though both he and his wife worked full-time, it was fair that she did the bulk of the household labor because "I make twice as much money as she does" (p. 528). International data suggest that having more resources or more time available translates into less work only for women in countries with high levels of gender equality and female empowerment (Fuwa, 2004).

If women do more around the house because they earn less, then one might expect greater equity if the wife were to earn more than the husband. However, some data suggest that, when wives out-earn their husbands, the women actually do more housework (Brines, 1994; Greenstein, 2000). One study showed that earning more money was correlated with doing less housework up to the point at which a wife earned 51% of what her husband earned (Bittman, England, Sayer, Folbre, & Matheson, 2003). At that point, earning more was actually related to doing more housework. Although this finding may be counterintuitive, it has been hypothesized that wives who out-earn their husbands engage in **gender deviance neutralization** (Greenstein, 2000). In other words, because they're acting in a way that's gender atypical in one domain (i.e., out-earning their husbands), they overcompensate by acting in a stereotypically feminine way in another domain (i.e., doing more domestic labor). This behavior may also help husbands maintain their sense of masculinity, which may be threatened by a high-achieving wife (Atkinson & Boles, 1984; Bittman et al., 2003). The pattern may be particularly true in blue-collar families when husbands with particularly traditional attitudes about gender experience unemployment (Sullivan, 2011).

More recent research suggests that gender deviance neutralization may be less of an issue now than in the past (Van Bavel, Schwartz, & Esteve, 2018). For example, some research shows that when women have large salaries (not necessarily compared to their husbands'), they do less housework (Gupta, 2007; Sullivan, 2011). This may happen because women with high salaries outsource domestic labor. Also, according to another study, the dynamics appear to vary by racial group (McLoyd et al., 2000). This research showed that White and Latinx men do more work around the house when they're unemployed, but that Black men do more work around the house when they're employed.

Women also may do more work around the house than men because they're socialized to believe that these tasks are part of what it means to be a woman (Mahalik et al., 2005). The fact that routine, low-control chores (e.g., cooking, cleaning, laundry) are seen as part of the feminine role was supported in a study of lesbian couples—those who identified as more masculine did fewer routine chores (Civettini, 2016). As we saw in Chapter 5, women are socialized from an early age to play with domestic toys such as toy kitchens and dolls. Daughters are also asked to do more chores around the house than sons, especially when the mother is under stress (Crouter, Head, Bumpus & McHale, 2001). Gender ideology influences division of labor in more subtle ways. For example, women report feeling greater responsibility for housework, say that they enjoy it more, and often report higher standards for cleanliness than their husbands do (Poortman & Van der Lippe, 2009). Since girls do more chores from a young age, they're likely to enter a relationship with a greater sense of competence about how to do them (Alberts, Tracy, & Trethewey, 2011; Babcock & Laschever, 2003). Nevertheless, it's noteworthy that women may be more responsible for household chores because they're more likely to feel judged by others if they don't maintain a clean home (Liss & Schiffrin, 2014).

There is considerable variability in people's views of what constitutes an appropriate division of labor. Some endorse traditional norms according to which men are the breadwinners and women are in charge of the house-work, while others have more egalitarian beliefs and think that responsibilities should be shared (Lachance-Grzela & Bouchard, 2010). Egalitarian beliefs tend to increase over the life span and have been found to relate to greater education and women's employment (Fan & Marini, 2000), and these beliefs play an important role in

Not everything that's done around the house gets noticed or appreciated.

the division of labor. In one study, women with more egalitarian beliefs reported doing less work around the house, and men with egalitarian beliefs reported that their wives do less (Bianchi, Milkie, Sayer, & Robinson, 2000). Egalitarian beliefs about gender have also been found to influence how college students would like to divide labor when they're in committed relationships (Askari, Liss, Erchull, Staebell, & Axelson, 2010). Female participants with liberal feminist beliefs wanted to do less around the house, and male participants with these beliefs wanted to do more. However, these college women also expected that they would have to do more household work and child care than they would ideally like to, indicating an anticipation that desired equality wouldn't necessarily be achieved.

Research has also pointed to the importance of gender ideology on a national scale. In countries where people have egalitarian gender attitudes, women do less housework (Fuwa, 2004; Fuwa & Cohen, 2007). Furthermore, in more egalitarian countries, women's level of education and income more easily trans-lates into doing less housework (Fuwa, 2004). Additionally, countries that don't have discriminatory laws about the kind of work that women can do (e.g., pro-hibit women from heavy lifting or working at night) also have more egalitarian division of labor at home (Fuwa & Cohen, 2007). In fact, in countries where most people support gender equality, both women and men do less housework (Treas & Tai, 2016). The authors of this study suggest that this may occur because of a general decline in the standards of housekeeping in these countries and because people there generally appreciate housework less as an activity. A country's level of poverty also makes a difference; women do a particularly large amount of housework in countries that have substandard housing (Treas & Tai, 2016). This may occur because lower-quality houses require more work to maintain and may not have time-saving devices such as dishwashers.

Consequences of Inequity

What consequences does an inequitable division of labor have for relationships?

Inequality in the division of labor has negative consequences for relationships, especially when the inequality is perceived as unfair. Women with more liberal gender attitudes, greater income, and higher levels of education perceived an unequal division of labor as unfair in one study (Greenstein, 1996). Another study, which took an international perspective, showed that women are likely to see an unequal division of labor as unfair in countries with higher levels of gender equity as well as in countries where women spend more hours in the workforce overall (Jansen, Weber, Kraaykamp, & Verbakel, 2016). This may be due to social comparison, as women notice what other women around them are doing. Researchers in yet another study found that women who do more housework than those around them may feel it's unfair; however, if they're doing most of the housework and all the other women in their social networks are too, then they see what they do as fair (Nakamura & Akiyoshi, 2015). Gratitude is another important factor to consider because even if the division of labor is unequal, women are more likely to feel it's fair if they think their contributions matter and others are grateful for what they do (Kawamura & Brown, 2010). Of course, women are rarely thanked for doing routine chores such as laundry or dishes (have you ever said, "Gee, Mom, the laundry is so well washed today, thanks"?), and since women do more of these tasks, they may feel particularly unappreciated.

When women perceive the division of labor as unfair, marital satisfaction is lower (Claffey & Mickelson, 2009; Mikula, Riederer, & Bodi, 2012). This is likely because a sense of unfairness leads to marital conflict and arguments about who is doing which chores and what is and isn't fair (Mikula et al., 2012). A sense of unfairness has been found to especially relate to marital dissatisfaction in women who have egalitarian attitudes (Greenstein, 1996). Another study tracking mothers found that, after having children, women did more housework (Dew & Wilcox, 2011). This led to a sense of unfairness and, ultimately, to feeling dissatisfied in the marriage. Moreover, equality in the division of labor has been found to relate to relationship satisfaction among lesbian and gay couples

Stephen Marche (2013), the author of an opinion piece in the *New York Times*, suggested: "The solution to the gender divide in housework generally is just that simple: don't bother. Leave the stairs untidy. Don't fix the garden gate. Fail to repaint the peeling ceiling. Never make the bed. A clean house is the sign of a wasted life, truly. Hope is messy: Eventually we'll all be living in perfect egalitarian squalor" (para. 18–19). What are your thoughts on this? Would it really equalize the division of labor? What other consequences might result?

(Kurdek, 2007). In contrast, inequity—especially for those doing more of the routine, traditionally feminine chores—has been linked to lower satisfaction (Marecek, Finn, & Cardell, 1982). Inequity in the division of labor is also related to lower levels of sexual satisfaction. In one study, when mothers felt dissatisfied with the division of household labor when their children were 6 months old, they were likely to feel dissatisfied with their sex lives when their children were 12 months old (Maas, McDaniel, Feinberg, & Jones, 2018).

Achieving Equity in the Household

How can greater equity in household labor be achieved?

The research findings presented in this chapter suggest that there are good reasons for couples to strive for equality in the division of labor in the home. In fact, one study showed that couples who desired equality and actually were able to achieve it were the happiest (Crompton & Lyonette, 2005). These couples were even more satisfied than those who held traditional attitudes and maintained a traditional division of labor. There is no one particular way that couples achieve equality, however. For example, equality doesn't have to mean sharing each task 50-50; instead, couples can choose to specialize based on their desires and skills (Gager, 2008). Lesbian and gay couples don't necessarily divide up tasks 50-50, although they've been found to generally achieve greater levels of equality compared to heterosexual couples (Kurdek, 2007). However, they're less likely to have assumptions based on gender about who should be responsible for which tasks (Goldberg, 2013).

One thing that's clear from the research is that couples who are satisfied with their division of labor have open conversations about their expectations for who should do what around the house. Researchers in one study found that while the majority of women in their sample wanted to talk to their husbands about the inequity in their homes, only 13% actually did so (Mannino & Deutsch, 2007). However, those who did were often able to restructure the division of labor so that they were satisfied. Another study showed that open communication can help couples share the managing and organizing of tasks—they can discuss together items such as what to cook for the week, what repairs need to be done, and whether the children have received their flu shots (Otero, 2009). In this way, the managing and organizing of tasks can become a shared responsibility.

Conclusion

Although we haven't talked about all possible relationships in women's lives (we haven't considered siblings, cousins, grandparents, co-workers, etc.), it should be clear that relationships are a key part of women's lives. This is true throughout the life span. Friends, family, and romantic partners can all provide social support, but they can also tax women's resources, given the extent to which women are expected to provide support to others. While developing and maintaining relationships can be beneficial, it's also important for women to have a clear sense of themselves as individuals. For many, achieving a balance between connection and independence is a fundamental task of adult life.

Chapter Review

SUMMARY

Friendship

- Receiving social support is one way people benefit from friendships.

- Women provide more social support than do men, so same-gender friendships can be particularly important for women.

- We often share social identity characteristics with our friends, but cross-group friendships can help us better understand others.

- Stereotypes suggest that women engage in face-to-face friendships while men's friendships follow a side-by-side pattern, but there's actually a lot of individual variability, especially when other aspects of people's social identities are considered.

- Women tend to have both same-gender and cross-gender friendships, although many people believe that (heterosexual) men and women can't be just friends.

- Girls may engage in relational aggression against friends and acquaintances. This type of behavior can be a way to assert and/or gain power.
- Sometimes bullying is tied to the social identity of the target. There are long-lasting consequences for those who experience bullying.

The Culture of Romance
- Idealized and unrealistic beliefs about love and romance are common and are perpetuated through the media.
- Dating scripts continue to reflect traditional, gendered, heterosexual standards. These scripts don't well reflect the experiences of women who date other women.
- Online dating has risen in popularity. While some people have success connecting with long-term partners through these websites and apps, others do not.
- Dating hasn't been replaced by hooking up, and studies have shown that it's preferred by women, young adults, and Latinx students.
- Both women and men desire attractive and successful partners. The traits desired in short-term partners can differ from those desired in long-term partners.

Committed Relationships
- Ages for first marriage are rising.
- There are many cultural, and often gendered, expectations associated with weddings.
- Most people's expectations about marriage are unrealistic.
- Healthy marriages provide benefits in terms of social support, finances, and health. There are also legal and financial institutionalized benefits of marriage.
- Some women report positive consequences from their divorces. However, financial strain commonly increases for women after divorce.

- Cohabitation is becoming increasingly common.
- Some women purposely opt never to marry.
- Some women chose consensually non-monogamous relationships, such as polyamoury, rather than traditionally monogamous relationships with a single partner.
- Gendered power dynamics commonly play a role in heterosexual relationships, and the partner who is least invested in the relationship (usually assumed to be the man) typically has more power.
- Couples who are equally invested in their relationships tend to be more satisfied with their relationships.

Division of Labor
- Women do more household labor than do men in heterosexual relationships, and progress toward equity over the latter half of the 20th century has stalled.
- Women are also more likely than men to manage what needs to be done around the house and to engage in emotion work.
- Men's generally greater power within relationships contributes to inequity.
- Women are more likely to have been socialized to do household labor and are more likely to be viewed negatively if it's not done.
- There is greater equity in countries with more egalitarian gender attitudes, and individuals with more egalitarian beliefs are more likely to have an equitable division of labor in their relationships.
- Relationship and sexual satisfaction decrease when women perceive the division of labor as unfair.
- Open communication between partners can make achieving equity more likely.

KEY TERMS

social support (p. 320)

informational social support (p. 320)

instrumental social support (p. 321)

emotional social support (p. 321)

tend-and-befriend coping strategy (p. 321)

active constructive responding (p. 321)

co-rumination (p. 322)

relational aggression (p. 325)

identity-based bullying (p. 326)

cyberbullying (p. 327)

dating scripts (p. 330)

mate retention behaviors (p. 336)

consensually non-monogamous (CNM) relationships (p. 343)

polygamy (p. 343)

polyamorous (or poly) relationships (p. 343)

principle of least interest (p. 345)

routine labor (p. 346)

low-control labor (p. 346)

intermittent labor (p. 346)

second shift (p. 347)

emotion work (p. 348)

relative resources theory (p. 349)

social exchange (p. 349)

time availability (p. 349)

gender deviance neutralization (p. 350)

THINK ABOUT IT

1. Imagine that you've been asked to develop an anti-bullying campaign at a local high school. Using the research findings described in this chapter, what topics would you include? What potential barriers would you anticipate? How might you address them?

2. Google "Valentine's Day cards" and explore the different messages that are conveyed about romance. What themes emerge? Can you think of a way to write a card that doesn't include some of the more problematic messages associated with the romantic script?

3. What advice would you give to a friend who is setting up a dating profile? What theories would best help guide your advice? How would dominant dating scripts help or hinder the dating process?

4. As you learned in this chapter, progress toward equal distribution of household labor stalled around 1998–1999. Think about what might have caused that shift. What types of social and interpersonal things would need to change in order to increase and sustain gender equity in all households?

ONLINE RESOURCES

- **Call Your Girlfriend** — a podcast featuring the conversations of three unapologetic feminist friends: http://www.callyourgirlfriend.com/

- **Freedom to Marry** — contemporary and archival resources about the campaign to secure marriage equality for LGBTQ Americans: freedomtomarry.org

- **Role Reboot** — articles on sex, relationships, and family: rolereboot.org

- **Stop Bullying** — information regarding bullying and prevention strategies: stopbullying.gov

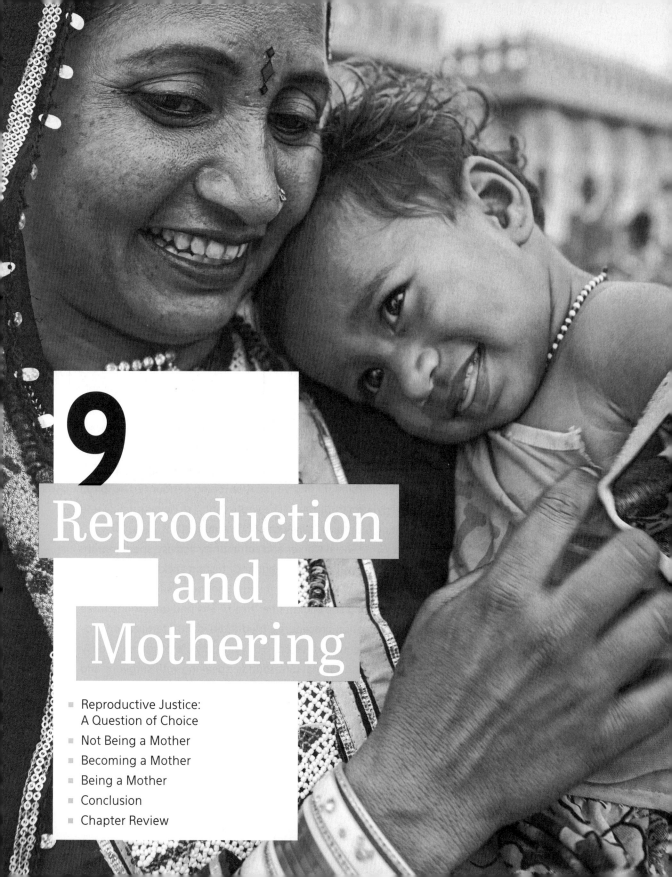

9

Reproduction and Mothering

There can be many rewards associated with mothering, but the transition to motherhood can be a complex and difficult process.

- In 2009, journalist Polly Vernon, a young White woman, wrote about not wanting children. She described the baby craziness around her and said she felt as though she was sober while everyone else was drunk. She'd never wanted children, and her life was fulfilled without them. She enjoyed being able to eat, sleep, read, binge watch HBO, and travel on her own schedule. But her article sparked anger and vitriol. After being denounced as "bitter, selfish, un-sisterly, unnatural, evil," she wrote that "I'm now routinely referred to as 'baby-hating journalist Polly Vernon'" (Vernon, 2009, para. 14).

- Casey Berna, a White social worker and community activist, spent months peeing on ovulation predictor and pregnancy testing sticks and charting her basal body temperature and cervical mucus. She then visited a reproductive endocrinologist fearing she couldn't be "fixed." She had undergone three intrauterine insemination procedures, tried three in vitro fertilization procedures, and had 34 embryos tested. "For years, my life consisted of daily hormone injections and vaginal ultrasounds, speaking with surgeons and geneticists, and fighting with insurance companies" (Berna, 2014, para. 8).

- Cherisse (last name not given), a Black paralegal, had an unwanted pregnancy. She made an appointment with an organization that she *thought* was a clinic that provided abortions, but it wasn't. The woman there tried to convince Cherisse to keep the baby and sent her home with a onesie and a rattle. She was inaccurately told, "If you have an abortion now, you'll rupture your uterus and won't be able to have children in the future" (Winter, 2013, para. 8). Since Cherisse didn't want to risk not having children in the future, she had her son, but she noted, "Those people weren't there after I lost my job and couldn't afford my COBRA, utilities, rent, food" (para. 8).

- Laura Browder, a Black college student who had recently moved, had a job interview at a Starbucks. Being new to the area and lacking child care, she brought her two young children to the mall and settled them at the food court while she had her interview 30 feet away, attempting to keep an eye on them throughout the interview. She was offered the job, but as she walked back to her children, she was arrested for child abandonment (Associated Press, 2015).

As these stories demonstrate, motherhood is a complicated topic. The decision about whether or not to become a mother may seem to be an individual one or one made just with a partner. However, many social expectations can influence how and if a woman becomes a mother. This chapter will explore how women make decisions about whether to become mothers. Not all women want to become mothers, and for other women, particularly those who don't fit traditional expectations of motherhood, the process of becoming a mother isn't easy. We'll also discuss the challenges associated with getting and staying pregnant, the changes in women's bodies and their sense of self during pregnancy, and the joys and strains associated with being a mother.

It is important to note that despite the use of female pronouns and the term *mother* throughout this chapter, not everyone who becomes pregnant and births a child is a woman. Transmen and non-binary individuals can also become pregnant and birth children.

Reproductive Justice: A Question of Choice?

How does the reproductive justice movement differ from approaches to motherhood that focus solely on the choices women make?

A lot of people frame the discussion of motherhood in terms of personal choice. Will a woman choose to become a mother or not? When will she start "trying"? Once she has a baby, will she choose to work or not? However, many women aren't able to make free choices about these topics. For example, if a woman decides she must have an abortion because she can't afford to have a child, this isn't really a choice. Some women may want to combine motherhood and work but can't due to lack of adequate child care. Other women may wish to stay at home with their children but can't due to financial constraints. In general, women with more power and privilege have more choices about their reproduction.

The **reproductive justice movement**, led by organizations supporting the health of indigenous women and women of color, acknowledges that many women experience interlocking sources of oppression that can limit their choices (Silliman, Fried, Ross, & Gutierrez, 2004). Essentially, women who are less privileged have fewer reproductive choices than do privileged women. For example, certain economic, social, and political forces limit many women's ability to freely make personal decisions about mothering. Those with more resources based on factors such as class, race, ethnicity, or immigration status have greater autonomy and choice in terms of their ability to have and raise children. This unequal situation is known as **stratified reproduction** (McCormack, 2005).

The reproductive justice movement acknowledges the inequalities of stratified reproduction and advocates for all women to be able to make informed choices about motherhood and to raise their children in environments that are safe and free of fear. The movement centers around four basic rights: (a) to have children, (b) to not have children, (c) to parent one's children in safe, healthy environments, and (d) to express one's sexual and gender identity free from oppression and fear (Silliman et al., 2004).

Not Being a Mother

Becoming a mother isn't the right choice for all women. Many can't make this choice due to social pressure, stigma, and lack of access to appropriate birth control or safe and legal abortions. Others choose not to have children for reasons such as career advancement and personal fulfillment outside the norm of traditional family life.

Voluntary Childlessness

What pressures are faced by women who don't want to have children? How does this pressure relate to the motherhood mandate?

The preference to be child-free appears to be on the rise (Gillespie, 2003). When women choose not to have children, that choice is sometimes called **voluntary childlessness**. Studies of birth rates don't generally separate voluntary childlessness from childlessness due to infertility or happenstance (e.g., not having a partner). Nevertheless, data do indicate that fewer women are having children now than in previous generations. According to one report, only 9% of women born in England and Wales in 1946 were childless, whereas for those born there in 1970, 17% have had no children ("The Rise of Childlessness," 2017). Research on women born in 1968 shows that 23% of those in Germany, 21% of those in Switzerland, and 20% of those in Italy and Finland are childless (Beaujouan, Sobotka, Brzozowska, & Zeman, 2017).

Childlessness may be rising in the United States too. According to U.S. Census data, the percentage of women ages 30 to 34 who were childless in 2006 was 26.2%, and by 2016 that number had risen to 30.8% ("Childlessness Rises," 2017). However, Pew Research Center data for 2016 show that older women were, overall, *more* likely to be mothers than a decade earlier: 86% of women ages 40 to 44 were mothers in 2016, compared to 80% in 2006 (Livingston, 2018). The fact that older women are now more likely to be mothers while at the same time younger women are *less* likely to be mothers indicates that women may be waiting longer to have their first child. The choices younger women will make about motherhood are still unclear, but there's evidence that millennials are less interested in having children than previous generations were. Stewart Friedman, a professor at the Wharton business school, interviewed Wharton graduates in 1992 and again in 2012. In 1992, 78% said they wanted children, but only 48% said so in 2012 (Friedman, 2013).

There are many reasons a woman may choose not to have children. In one study, 79% of childless women and 83% of childless men reported simply being happy without them (Debest & Mazuy, 2014). Other reasons include prioritizing other aspects of life, like career aspirations, and feeling that having children would compromise personal freedom (Debest & Mazuy, 2014; Park, 2005). One woman noted, "I would never say 'childless' because it implies missing something. No, it's 'child-free.' I'm free from that burden" (Peterson, 2015, p. 186). In 2015, the cost of raising a child between birth and age 17 in the United States was estimated to be $233,610; in this context, having a child can be a significant financial stressor (Lino, Kuczynski, Rodriquez, & Schap, 2017).

There are, however, strong pressures in our society to have children—something called the **motherhood mandate** (Russo, 1976). In 1949, feminist scholar Simone de Beauvoir asked "What is a woman?" (de Beauvoir, 1949, p. 3). She noted that many people equate womanhood with motherhood such that woman = mother = womb (de Beauvoir, 1949; Shapiro, 2014). Also, when women menstruate for the first time, they're often told they've "become a woman," indicating that womanhood reflects the ability to bear children. The motherhood mandate also operates in divorce cases, in which women become custodial parent five out of six times (Grall, 2011). Women who choose not to have children are often portrayed in the media as bitter career women or selfish individuals who don't care for others (Graham & Rich, 2014). Women without children are often asked who will care for them when they're older, and they're told they can't fully understand love until they have a child, they won't leave a legacy unless they have a child, and they'll ultimately change their minds about not wanting a child (Rupersburg, 2015).

There is some evidence that negative views toward voluntarily childless women are decreasing. In one study, 46% of participants agreed that childless people could lead fulfilling lives, and another 40% responded neutrally (Koropeckyj-Cox & Pendell, 2007). While not a ringing endorsement, those results show that negative attitudes toward child-free women aren't pervasive. Another study found that women, especially highly educated women, held more positive attitudes toward those who choose not to have children than did men (Merz & Liefbroer, 2012). The researchers suggested that well-educated young women in industrialized countries may be focusing more on personal fulfillment than on traditional family values and that they realize having children is time consuming and expensive.

Many people do think children are the key to happiness and that those without children lead sad, lonely lives (Hansen, 2012). However, the data tell a different story. One study showed that child-free people, rather than parents, have higher levels of life satisfaction in most countries (Hansen, 2012). The researcher speculated this may be because child-free individuals have been able to pursue life interests and career goals and have had more time and money for enjoyable activities such as travel. The same study found high marital satisfaction in child-free couples. According to other researchers, being child-free increases the time and energy couples have for each other, and they probably don't feel the need to stay together for the sake of the children (Pelton & Hertlein, 2011). Although some suggest that the child-free will be lonely in their old age and not have anyone to care for them, research suggests that older individuals without children may actually have less stress than those with children (McMullin, & Marshall, 1996; Shapiro, 2014). A study in Italy found that older people without children received support from friends and non-profit organizations and didn't lack social support (Albertini & Mencarini, 2014).

Some countries, however, are pro-natalist. In these countries, over 70% of the population say it's necessary for a woman to have a child (Tanaka & Johnson, 2014). Such countries include those in northern, western, and eastern Africa, south central and southeastern Asia, and other countries such as Russia, Slovenia, Hungary, and Estonia. Women in these countries without children can experience great stigma, lower life satisfaction, and greater distress than such women in countries with less emphasis on motherhood. This may occur because there's less access to social support beyond the family and there are fewer socially accepted roles for women outside of motherhood (Tanaka & Johnson, 2014). As a result, the "choice" to remain childless isn't one that all women can make. For example, as studies have confirmed, in many countries women don't have adequate access to birth control (Sedgh, Ashford, & Hussain, 2016), and marriage is seen as giving husbands the right to have sex anytime they please (Mugweni, Pearson, & Omar, 2012).

Abortion

How common is abortion, what are the social consequences of limiting abortion, and what are the psychological consequences of having an abortion?

If a woman becomes pregnant but doesn't feel she's able to birth and/or raise the child, she may consider having an abortion—the ending of a pregnancy by removing an embryo or a fetus. In 2011, half of pregnancies among U.S. women were unintended, and 4 in 10 unintended pregnancies were terminated by abortion (Guttmacher Institute, 2016). Most people who seek abortions are already mothers to at least one child—59% of U.S. women obtaining the procedure in 2014 were mothers (Guttmacher Institute, 2016). In one study of a diverse group of women in the United States, the most frequent reasons for having an abortion included desiring to continue with education, not being able to afford a baby, not wanting to be a single mother, and having relationship problems (Finer, Frohwirth, Dauphinee, Singh, & Moore, 2005). An earlier international study showed similar reasons (Bankole, Singh, & Haas, 1998).

The Complex Social and Political Aspects of Abortion Abortion is a politically charged topic. Although most U.S. adults hold nuanced views on the topic, there's a tendency to focus on two diametrically opposed sides. The terms *pro-life* (not supportive of legal access to abortion) and *pro-choice* (supportive of legal access to abortion) regularly frame discussions about abortion, and staunch positions are often the most heard. For example, in a study of 700,000 tweets about abortion, statements against abortion accounted for 61% of the tweets (Sharma, Saha, Ernala, Ghoshal, & De Choudhury, 2017). This may be a disproportionate number, considering that other data from 2017 showed that 25% of U.S. adults believed abortion should be legal in all cases, 33% believed it should be legal in most cases, 24% believed it should be illegal in most cases, and 16% believed it should be illegal in all cases; 3% did not know or have a response ("Public Opinion on Abortion," 2017).

Most people take a nuanced stance. Some argue that the term *pro-life* doesn't accurately reflect the views of the

try it for yourself

Do you think there's room in feminist movements for those who are anti-abortion? Why or why not? Talk to five people who identify as feminists. What are their views about this?

anti-abortion movement. A Catholic nun noted, "I do not believe that just because you're opposed to abortion, that that makes you pro-life. . . . In many cases, your morality is deeply lacking if all you want is a child born but not a child fed, not a child educated, not a child housed. . . . That's not pro-life. That's pro-birth. We need a much broader conversation on what the morality of pro-life is" (Salzillo, 2015, para. 2). Moreover, some pro-life feminists emphasize maternal health care and child care in addition to fetal rights (Chandler, 2018). This position has been controversial within certain feminist groups. For example, in 2017, organizers of the Women's March on Washington dropped an anti-abortion group as a partner and advocated for safe and legal abortions for all people as part of its platform (Stein, 2017).

Given the complex issues surrounding women's reasons for seeking abortions, exploration of the topic can benefit from considering the broader context in which women make decisions about becoming and staying pregnant. For example, as this chapter's first Spotlight feature shows, sometimes the fetus's health is the determining factor. In other cases, financial constraints and lack of support for the mother are key concerns (Finer et al., 2005). More research is needed to better understand the role contextual variables play in women's access to and decisions about abortion.

Alicia Hupprich learned, while pregnant, that her daughter would likely suffer and surely die shortly after birth. In the nearby Spotlight feature, Hupprich shares her story about the difficult choice she made.

One reason abortion is so politically charged involves the history of reproductive realities. In the United States, abortions were illegal between 1880 and 1973. During this time, millions of women had them done illegally, often known as *back-alley abortions*. The death toll from illegal abortions was high, although the development of antibiotics subsequently decreased the death rates (Gold, 2003). Risks were higher for poor and minority women, who often lacked access to physicians and used dangerous at-home methods. In the 1960s, 1 in 4 pregnancy-related deaths was due to illegal abortions for White women, but 1 in 2 was due to illegal abortions for women of color (Gold, 2003).

In 1973, the U.S. Supreme Court, in *Roe v. Wade,* declared abortion to be legal under the constitutional right of privacy. Since then, the number of women in the United States who have died because of abortions has fallen to almost zero. However, most states have passed significant restrictions on abortions—over 1,100 through 2017 (Nash, Gold, Mohammed, Ansari-Thomas, & Cappello, 2018). These include mandatory waiting periods, bans on later-term (generally, second-trimester) abortions, mandatory parental consent for minors, limits on the use of public funds for this type of medical procedure, mandatory invasive vaginal ultrasounds, and mandatory counseling.

Who Gets Abortions? In 2014, 19% of pregnancies in the United States ended in abortion. Based on these rates, it's estimated that 1 in 20 women will have the procedure by age 20, 1 in 5 by age 30, and 1 in 4 by age 45 ("Induced Abortion in the United States," 2018). Although these numbers may seem high, abortion rates in 2014 were the lowest in the United States since 1973, when the procedure became legal. This change may reflect increased accessibility of birth control and/or increasingly restrictive abortion laws.

Abortions are more common for poor women, who made up 49% of those having the procedure in 2014; an additional 26% had incomes at 100% to 199% of the poverty level ("Induced Abortion in the United States," 2018). Women of various religious affiliations have abortions—in 2014, 17% identified as mainline Protestant, 13% as evangelical Protestant, 24% as Catholic, and 46% as another affiliation or no affiliation. Both mothers and non-mothers have abortions—59% of those having abortions in 2014 were already mothers. Many reported using contraception when they got pregnant—24% reported using condoms, and 13% reported using hormonal birth control.

While many women worry about obtaining access to an abortion, others worry they'll be forced to have one. Specifically, some medical providers and social workers believe that women with disabilities should have an abortion if they become pregnant (Lipson & Rogers, 2000; Saxton, 2013; Strnadová, Bernoldová, Adamčíková, & Klusáček, 2017; Waxman, 1994). In one study, the majority of medical personnel interviewed stated that women with intellectual disabilities should seek an abortion (Strnadová, Bernoldová, Adamčíková, & Klusáček, 2017). In another study, women with physical disabilities reported encountering negative attitudes from reproductive health-care providers and, especially, the belief that they shouldn't be sexually active because they might become pregnant (Ahumuza, Matovu, Ddamulira, & Muhanguzi, 2014). Also, a legal guardian of an individual with a disability might seek a court-ordered abortion, particularly after a rape (Dhillon & Lefebvre, 2011). A major goal of the disability rights movement is to affirm the right to make reproductive decisions, regardless of one's ability status (Saxton, 2013).

Women in the United States generally have access to safe and legal abortions, although some states have multiple restrictions and few abortion centers. In other countries, many women don't have access to safe and legal abortions, but they have the procedure anyway. For example, an estimated 49% of the abortions performed globally in 2008 were unsafe, and countries with restrictive abortion laws generally had higher rates of abortion than those with less restrictive laws (Sedgh et al., 2012). The researchers speculate the findings reflect the fact that countries with restrictive abortion laws also don't provide access to effective contraception.

Mental Health Outcomes One factor in the abortion debate is whether the procedure negatively affects women's mental health. Some opponents assert that having an abortion leads to psychological problems, a condition they call **post-abortion syndrome** (Kelly, 2014). In fact, counselors at pregnancy centers generally tell women that having an abortion is likely to negatively influence their mental health (Dadlez & Andrew, 2010; Kelly, 2014). However, some scholars have argued that telling women they're likely to develop psychological problems after having an abortion can make them feel scared and ashamed, which may actually contribute to psychological distress (Dadlez & Andrews, 2010; Kelly, 2014).

Some studies do suggest that women who have abortions show signs of decreased mental health (e.g., Fergusson, Horwood, & Ridder, 2006; Reardon et al., 2003), but these studies have methodological flaws. Notably, they generally compare women who've had abortions to women who have carried *wanted* pregnancies to term. Further, women who've undergone abortions may have other, unrelated risk factors—lower socioeconomic status, less education, or a history of violence—compared with women who carry planned pregnancies to term (American Psychological Association, 2008; Steinberg, McCulloch, & Adler, 2014).

In a 2008 report, the American Psychological Association (2008) concluded that abortion did not result in negative mental health outcomes but that having an unplanned pregnancy is a significantly stressful life event. The APA noted that, among women who have an unplanned pregnancy, the mental health risks of a first-trimester abortion are no greater than the risks of carrying the pregnancy to term. When controlling for prior history of mental health problems, women who had an abortion were found to have no greater mental health risk than those who didn't (Steinberg et al., 2014). Another study indicated that the most frequent emotional response after abortion was relief, and most participants said they had benefited more than they were harmed (Major et al.,

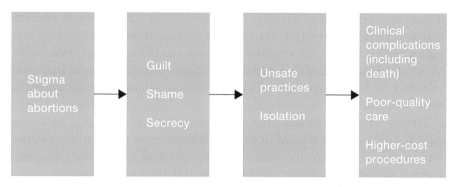

FIGURE 9.1 **The negative outcomes of abortion stigma.** Abortion stigma can negatively influence both the mental and the physical health of women. (After Kumar, Hessini, & Mitchell, 2009)

2000). In another research population, even among those who felt regret about having an abortion, 89% still thought it was the right choice (Rocca, Kimport, Gould, & Foster, 2013).

One can get a clearer sense of the psychological outcomes of abortion by comparing those who get abortions with those who wish to have them but don't get them. A longitudinal study followed women from throughout the United States for five years (Biggs, Upadhyay, McCulloch, & Foster, 2017). Some of these women were just under the gestational limits where abortions were allowed and received an abortion; others were just over the limits and were denied the procedure. After one year, those denied an abortion were more anxious and had lower self-esteem and lower life satisfaction. After five years, both groups were similar in terms of mental health. The researchers concluded that there's no justification in warning women about potentially negative psychological consequences of having an abortion. Nevertheless, 20 states include information about possible psychological responses in their mandatory abortion counseling, and as of 2018, eight of these states focus on how abortions will likely produce negative emotional responses ("An Overview of Abortion Laws," 2018).

The negative messages that women can encounter as they seek an abortion can cause extreme stress and make them hesitant to find social support. Participants in one study reported receiving messages that they were selfish and stupid for getting pregnant and seeking an abortion (Cockrill & Nack, 2013). They also reported resorting to secrecy and selective disclosure to avoid stigma. See Figure 9.1 for a flowchart of negative outcomes associated with stigma about abortions.

Abortion, although common, is rarely discussed. Most women think the procedure is rare and that they're deviant

your turn

What are your perspectives on abortion? Do you think there's stigma about having, or even talking about, abortions? If so, do you think the stigma should be reduced? How could this happen?

if they have one (Kumar, Hessini, & Mitchell, 2009). Reflecting an effort to counteract this misperception, the grassroots organization Exhale works to support women through their abortion experiences and to encourage them to talk about and reduce the stigma. Other movements include #shoutyourabortion and the 1 in 3 campaign, both of which provide an online space for women to share their stories.

Finally, although an unwanted pregnancy doesn't necessarily mean the child born is not then wanted or loved, a consideration of the effects of abortion must acknowledge the risks of raising children who weren't originally wanted. Research shows that children born to parents who say the pregnancy was unwanted are at greater risk for cognitive, emotional, and social problems (David, 2006; Russo, 2014), and a review of research on the effects of unintended pregnancy on children from 1981 through 2017 found considerable evidence for negative effects (Abajobir, Kisely, & Najman, 2017). These included high risk of child illness and infant mortality, lower birth weight and increased likelihood of stunted growth, less likelihood of vaccination, lower scores on skill development, fewer years of schooling, and increased risks of mental health problems and alcoholism.

Becoming a Mother

During the early years of sexual activity, young women usually worry more that they might accidentally get pregnant rather than that they might *not* get pregnant. Given this concern, a woman hoping to actually become a mother may imagine that, after some well-timed intercourse, she'll pee on a pregnancy-testing stick, celebrate, and nine months later enjoy the birth of a baby. However, becoming and staying pregnant can be challenging for some women.

Fertility

How can women learn to manage their fertility? What specific issues about fertility must be considered by lesbian women, transgender individuals, and women with disabilities?

According to one study, 95% of U.S. women either had children, planned to have children, or didn't have children but wished they did (Newport & Wilke, 2013). If a woman wants to become pregnant, it's useful for her to know something about her fertility. Individuals with childbearing capacities have monthly cycles in which they ovulate, and if they don't become pregnant, a menstrual period occurs approximately two weeks later. However, if they're trying to become pregnant, it's important to know when they're ovulating.

The body shows many signs of fertility, and women can usually predict fairly accurately when they're most fertile (Weschler, 2015). A woman's body temperature fluctuates throughout the month and rises about half a degree when she's ovulating, so she may track her *basal body temperature* (her temperature first thing in the morning) daily. However, the rise in body temperature happens after the egg is released—which can be too late unless intercourse quickly follows, as the egg must be fertilized within 24 hours of release. Also, as a woman approaches ovulation, her *cervical mucus* (vaginal secretions) becomes more plentiful, slippery, and translucent. When she's most fertile, these secretions resemble egg whites and can be stretched between two fingers (see Figure 9.2). Checking cervical mucus can be a good predictor of fertility, but women also can use ovulation predictor kits (Weschler, 2015).

Predicting ovulation is especially important for lesbian couples who may have limited donor sperm. One study found that vaginal insemination via syringe was the preferred method of conception for lesbian women, requiring a clear knowledge in timing fertility (Hayman, Wilkes, Halcomb, & Jackson, 2015). Moreover, as women with female partners think about conception and fertility, they must decide whether to use a sperm donor who is known or unknown to them, as well as the qualities desired in a donor. Some prefer an unknown donor because they don't want a third parent who might undermine the status of the co-parent who didn't bear the child; other couples prefer a known donor who could become part of the family as an uncle (Nordqvist, 2012). Another option is to have sperm donors who are willing to have their identities released when the children reach adulthood. Lesbian families who've chosen this option have generally felt comfortable with their adult children potentially contacting their sperm donors (Scheib, Riordan, & Rubin, 2003).

Transgender individuals who wish to have children need to consider how transitioning will affect fertility. Transwomen may

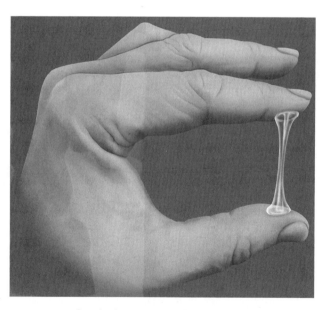

FIGURE 9.2 **Cervical mucus and fertility.** Vaginal secretions change one's menstrual cycle. A woman who wants to get pregnant may regularly check and record the consistency of her cervical mucus, by either examining her underwear, wiping the area with toilet paper before she urinates, or checking the consistency between two fingers (as shown here). When a woman is most fertile, the cervical mucus should stretch between two fingers like egg whites.

want to preserve their sperm or testicular tissue before starting hormonal or surgical treatment (De Roo, Tileman, T'Sjoen, & DeSutter, 2016). In contrast, though, some transwomen feel that freezing sperm conflicts with their core identity of being a woman (DeSutter, Kira, Verschoor, & Hotimsky, 2002). Transmen who haven't had gender-confirming surgery may become pregnant either accidentally or intentionally. Taking testosterone doesn't eliminate the capacity to have children. For transmen who wish to become pregnant, testosterone can be stopped, after which menstruation generally resumes three to six months later (Light, Obedin-Maliver, Sevelius, & Kerns, 2014). In one study of 41 pregnant transmen, about half the pregnancies were planned, and 88% were pregnant from eggs from their own ovaries (Light et al., 2014). For transmen, being pregnant and giving birth was considered the path to fatherhood, not motherhood: "Pregnancy and childbirth were very male experiences for me. When I birthed my children, I was born into fatherhood" (p. 4).

Women with physical disabilities can become pregnant, including women with spinal cord injury, cerebral palsy, multiple sclerosis, strokes, muscular dystrophy, rheumatoid arthritis, scoliosis, blindness, or deafness (Leavesley & Porter, 1982). However, people often perceive these women as being unable to

Pictured here while pregnant is Trystan Reese, a transman, with his husband, Biff Chaplow, and their adopted children in 2017.

have sex or to have children. Research has shown that some health-care providers hold negative attitudes toward those pregnancies (Lipson & Rogers, 2000). One woman's experience with spinal cord disability demonstrates frustration with the perception that women with disabilities can't or shouldn't get pregnant: "I got a lot of questions from women when I was pregnant. They realized then, of course, that I had intercourse. They were really surprised. I'd tell them, 'Of course people in wheelchairs make love'" (Leavesley & Porter, 1982, p. 418).

Infertility

How common is infertility, why do many women feel distressed by it, and what are common methods of treating infertility as well as ethical dilemmas associated with them?

Getting and staying pregnant doesn't always happen easily. **Infertility** is defined as an inability to become pregnant after 12 months of regular unprotected sexual intercourse. Approximately 1 in 10 women experience infertility over the course of their lives, but only half seek medical intervention (Cousineau & Dumar, 2007; Greil & McQuillan, 2004). However, this definition suggests that unprotected sexual intercourse is the only way to get pregnant—an assumption that excludes certain people and can make accessing treatment difficult for those whose experiences fall outside that definition.

Although infertility is often seen as a woman's problem, men can also experience it. In fact, the Mayo Clinic estimates that men are a contributing factor in about one third of cases (Mayo Clinic Staff, n.d.). However, women are more likely than men to initiate consultation and treatment (Fairweather-Schmidt, Leach, Butterworth, & Anstey, 2014). Age is a factor too. According to the American College of Obstetricians and Gynecologists (2014), women's fertility declines gradually beginning at age 32 and more rapidly after age 37. Those who delay childbearing are at increased risk of infertility, although many women don't realize this (Mac Dougall, Beyene, & Nachtigall, 2012). Male age can also increase the risk because older men produce sperm that are less mobile and have lower volume than the sperm of younger men (Kidd, Eskenazi, & Wyrobek, 2001). When couples seek treatment for infertility, they're more likely to be successful if the man is under 40, particularly if the female partner is younger (Dodge, Penzias, & Hacker, 2017). Furthermore, between 1973 and 2011, a significant decline in sperm counts (by around 50%–60%) occurred in men throughout North America, Europe, Australia, and New Zealand (Levine et al., 2017). The cause is unknown and potentially concerning. Nevertheless, most infertility research has focused on women, and concerns about one's "ticking biological clock" are almost always directed solely to women.

Research on the psychological impact of infertility generally focuses on those who have sought treatment, and results show that women can experience stress, grief, anger, shame, and anxiety (Cousineau & Dumar, 2007; Greil, 1997). One White woman who struggled with infertility stated, "There are times when I don't feel like a real woman. I wonder how I am ever going to feel that whole" (Letherby, 1999, p. 363). In another study, 32% of Black participants strongly believed that being a mother was central to being a woman and were particularly distressed about their infertility (Ceballo, Graham, & Hart, 2015). This distress connects to the motherhood mandate; women who internalize its message are particularly negatively affected if they experience infertility (McQuillan et al., 2012). Moreover, the negative social and psychological consequences are considerably higher in countries that are pro-natalist and that highly stigmatize non-mothers (Greil, McQuillan, & Slauson-Blevins, 2011; Rouchou, 2013).

Compassionate attitudes toward the self can help mitigate shame, self-blame, or other negative consequences of infertility (Raque-Bogan & Hoffman, 2015). In the long term, most people develop healthy coping strategies. One study showed that 75% of female participants who remained childless after infertility had no desire for a child ten years later and no longer felt an important part of their life was missing (Wischmann, Korge, Scherg, Strowitzki, & Verres, 2012). Other research showed that many women who are unable to conceive become **social mothers** through adopting, being a foster parent, or becoming a step-mother (McQuillan, Greil, White, & Jacob, 2003). These social mothers experience psychological well-being similar to that of biological mothers.

Treating Infertility Women who experience infertility, especially in industrialized nations, often seek treatment using **assisted reproductive technologies (ARTs)**. These include **intrauterine insemination (IUI)**, in which a concentration of washed sperm is injected into the uterus at the time of ovulation, and **in vitro fertilization (IVF)**. IVF involves stimulating egg production, extracting many eggs, fertilizing some of them outside of the body, and implanting one or more embryos in the uterus. About 10% of cases of IVF use donor eggs (Klitzman, 2016). Egg donors are generally young women who donate for a fee and are motivated by altruism and financial need (Kenney & McGowan, 2010). However, potential complications may damage the ovaries and endanger future fertility. Furthermore, there are questions as to whether the drugs that stimulate egg production are linked to uterine or other cancers (Klitzman, 2016).

An interesting application of IVF occurs with lesbian couples who wish to share biological motherhood of a single child (Zeiler & Malmquist, 2014). In the *ROPA (reception of oocytes from partners)* procedure, one woman supplies an egg, which is implanted into the other woman after fertilization by donor sperm. As a result, one woman is the genetic mother, and the other is the gestational mother. One study found that when lesbian mothers shared biological motherhood of a single child, it reduced potential feelings of jealousy among non-biological mothers (Pelka, 2009).

The use of ARTs is, however, extremely expensive. In 2014, a single cycle of IVF was estimated to cost around $12,000, plus an additional $5,000 in medications to stimulate ovulation (Uffalussy, 2014). In 2018, an article in the magazine *Self* profiled several couples who paid between $10,000 and $63,000 for IVF treatments; some insurance plans provided partial coverage, but others didn't (Bahadur, 2018). Success rates vary from 25% to 40% per cycle (Lintsen et al., 2005). These rates are based on numerous factors, including the parents' age (success rates decrease with age), whether they're smokers (which decreases

There are many ways for women to become mothers. Some women who are partnered with women opt to have one partner supply the egg and the other, using IVF, be the gestational mother. In this way, both women can have a biological connection to their child.

success rates), and whether the infertility is due to female or male factors (success rates are lower for male factor infertility).

Given the expense and the fact that it may take several trials to have a chance of success, ARTs aren't an option for women who don't have considerable financial resources. As a result, it's highly educated, White women who more frequently use infertility treatments (Chandra, Copen, & Stephen, 2014). Working-class and poor women are aware of ARTs but don't see them as something they're able to receive, so they may try interventions that involve vitamins and nutritional changes or pursue opportunities for social motherhood (Bell, 2009). Also, although low-income women generally don't seek treatment for infertility, several states mandate that health insurance cover at least some of the costs of fertility treatments, and certain agencies provide subsidies for low-income women (Haskins, 2015).

your turn

If you were to experience infertility, what would you do? Would you try assisted reproductive technologies (ARTs)? Would you consider adoption? What factors would you consider when making your decision? If you've had to make these choices, what factors played a role in your thought process? What challenges did you face?

Black women who experience infertility often face discrimination and racist assumptions about their alleged promiscuity and their income level (Ceballo et al., 2015). They're also more likely to experience infertility than White women because they're more prone to have *fibroids*, uterine growths that can affect fertility. However, Black and Latinx women are less likely to receive fertility treatments than White women, although this difference is partially accounted for by differences in social class (Greil, McQuillan, & Slauson-Blevins, 2011). Anecdotal reports by women of color seeking infertility treatments confirm that doctors are less likely to talk about fertility treatments with Black women; instead, doctors discuss birth control and sexually transmitted infections (Vega, 2014). The fact that access to infertility treatment varies by race and social class is an example of stratified reproduction.

Surrogacy, in which one woman becomes pregnant and delivers a child on behalf of another couple, is less common than other ARTs. In *traditional surrogacy*, the gestational mother's egg is combined with the father's sperm, making the surrogate the biological mother. In *gestational surrogacy*, the egg of the woman who intends to raise the child, or a donor's egg, is combined with the father's sperm through IVF, and the surrogate isn't the biological mother of the child. All cases raise ethical considerations. For example, some critics have likened surrogacy to prostitution because women sell the use of their body for money (van Niekerk & van Zyl, 2016). More positively, others see surrogacy as an altruistic act to help a woman who is unable to birth a child herself. A task force on ethics and law determined that surrogacy was ethically acceptable as a last resort for infertility treatment as long as surrogates were paid only for expenses and loss of possible income (Task Force on Ethics and Law, 2005).

Miscarriage and Stillbirth

How common are miscarriage and stillbirth, and how do women manage the loss?

Sometimes a pregnancy is lost. A **miscarriage** occurs when a pregnancy is lost before the 20th week. A **stillbirth** occurs when a fetus dies after the 20th week. Miscarriages are very common, occurring in 1 in 6 pregnancies (Radford & Hughes, 2015). Stillbirth is more rare, occurring in approximately 1% of pregnancies (Centers for Disease Control and Prevention, 2017). Because miscarriages are common, women often wait to announce their pregnancies until after the first trimester when the risk decreases (Murkoff & Mazel, 2008).

When a woman miscarries, pain and bleeding can occur, and surgery may be necessary to clear the uterus. Miscarriage can be a devastating loss, and women can experience grief, loss, guilt, emptiness, lack of control, fear, and a desire for closure (Radford & Hughes, 2015; Smith, Frost, Levitas, Bradley, & Garcia; 2006). One study found that many women who were distressed and overwhelmed immediately after a miscarriage felt considerably better after six weeks (Swanson, Connor, Jolley, Pettinato, & Wang, 2007). Other women continued to grieve and feel anxious and overwhelmed up to a year later. Anxiety is common after a miscarriage, and women may be afraid to attempt to get pregnant again.

Miscarriage may also negatively affect relationships. Approximately one third of married women in one study reported feeling more distant, emotionally or sexually, from their husbands after miscarriage (Swanson, Karmali, Powell, & Pulvermakher, 2003). These feelings stemmed from a reluctance to talk to their husbands about their loss and grief as well as from seeing sex as a reminder of their loss. Because miscarriage often occurs early in pregnancy, many women haven't told others they're pregnant, so they grieve in isolation.

The psychological devastation of a stillbirth is considerable (Hughes & Riches, 2003). Many full-term stillbirths occur in otherwise healthy, low-risk pregnancies, so it's usually shocking to learn about the death of an unborn infant (Campbell-Jackson & Horsch, 2014). Because of the late stage, women are generally encouraged to deliver the baby vaginally, which can be particularly overwhelming. Once the baby is born, mothers often rely on the guidance of health-care professionals to process how best to interact with their newborn (Kingdon, Givens, O'Donnell, & Turner, 2015). Women are encouraged to grieve, hold the child if they wish to, and perform whatever religious ceremony is appropriate (American College of Obstetricians and Gynecologists, 2009). A review of 23 studies found that women who saw and held their stillborn baby and collected memorabilia (e.g., pictures, baby blanket) were more likely to have positive mental health outcomes (Kingdon et al., 2015).

Reproductive Tourism

Because surrogacy costs can be prohibitive, and because surrogacy is outlawed in some U.S. states and Western European countries, individuals may engage in *reproductive tourism*, traveling to other countries to obtain reproductive treatments and, often, a lower-cost surrogate (Deonandan, Green, & van Beinum, 2012). Between 2002 and 2015, India was a common location for reproductive tourism (The Guardian, 2015). The cost of surrogacy there was approximately $30,000—about one third the cost in the United States. The surrogate received up to $8,000 of this money, although many received less.

The fact that wealthy women, or gay male couples, from one country pay poor women from another country to carry their children can be seen as exploitative

Some people use international surrogacy to have children, as the cost can be lower than in their home country. However, there are complicated concerns surrounding the use of other women's bodies for reproductive purposes. The woman shown here is resting at a temporary home for surrogate mothers in western India.

(Deonandan et al., 2012). However, poor women who engage in surrogacy to earn income may see this activity as making a free choice about the use of their bodies. Some feminists argue against the practice; others embrace it but advocate for it to be used in ways that benefit people's lives. However, the fact that people with more power pay people with less power to have their children raises complex concerns that cannot be ignored (Parks, 2010).

In one study, researchers determined that the demands of the parents who wanted the baby took priority over the health and safety of the surrogate (Tanderup, Reddy, Patel, & Nielsen, 2015). Furthermore, in order to maximize their reported success rate, doctors made decisions about how many embryos were implanted without fully disclosing the risks involved. One woman described signing the surrogacy contract: "They just told that like you have a drop of water, we will keep that and grow it by means of injection. You will have to keep it in your womb for nine months and then deliver the child. . . . No benefit, no risk was told" (p. 494).

In 2012, India banned gay couples and single people from seeking surrogates; in 2015, it banned all foreign couples from seeking surrogates (Sugden & Malhotra, 2015). Although some people applauded the decision, it was particularly devastating for couples who had started the process and paid considerable money, some of whom had eggs stored in Mumbai that they were attempting to retrieve. The decision was also questioned by some Indian surrogates who wanted to continue because they were comfortable, received three hot meals a day, and made more money than they would be able to otherwise. One surrogate who earned $1,797 when she delivered noted, "What my husband earned in four years, I managed to earn in the one year that I carried a child" (Kumar, 2015, para. 21). Overall, while many critics may see such women as being exploited by rich foreigners, the women themselves often see their decision as a free choice.

Do you think international surrogacy is empowering or oppressing for women? What policies could be put in place to make this practice more empowering?

A common theme among women experiencing stillbirth was a sense of over-whelming emptiness when they had to leave the hospital (Lindgren, Malm, & Radestad, 2013/2014). One woman said, "I think that was the worst thing of all, it was sick to leave your own baby, to leave it at the hospital. To return home empty handed. You just do not leave your baby" (p. 340). Since most people know that a woman is pregnant by 20 weeks, parents are in the uncomfortable position of having to tell friends and colleagues what happened. Many women grieve for up to two years or more, and the process of deciding to conceive again can be highly anxiety provoking (Hughes & Riches, 2003). Social support, especially from family members, can decrease depression and anxiety after a stillbirth (Cacciatore, Schnebly, & Froen, 2009).

Adoption

What are some of the psychological factors involved in adopting a child and placing a child for adoption?

One way to become a mother without biologically conceiving a child is through adoption. Some families adopt because of infertility; others do so regardless of fertility status. Research has shown that women considering adoption generally have attached great importance to being a mother and have been unsuccessful with medical interventions for infertility (Park & Hill, 2014). Aspects of social identity also affect attitudes and behaviors related to adoption. For example, one study showed that higher levels of religiosity were associated with believing that mothering adopted children would be as satisfying as birthing children, and Black women were more likely than White women to have actually taken steps toward adoption (Van Laningham, Scheuble, & Johnson, 2012). Other researchers have found that, compared to heterosexual couples, lesbian mothers felt less committed to having a biological child and perceived an easier transition from trying to conceive to adopting (Goldberg, Downing, & Richardson, 2009).

There are several routes to adoption (Child Welfare Information Gateway, 2015a). One involves public adoption—working with a state agency, fostering a child, and transitioning that relationship into an adoption. Public adoptions may take several years, particularly if parents place restrictions on the type of child they're willing to adopt. Uncertainty is often part of this process because a birth parent may also be seeking to reclaim the child. Children of any age can be available for public adoption, but newborns are rarely placed through this process. Public adoptions are typically not very expensive.

Families may also choose private adoption through an agency. In these cases, the birth mother (and sometimes the birth father) relies on an agency to place her child for adoption, and her level of involvement can vary depending on the agency. These adoptions can be expensive—in 2012–2013, the average cost was approximately $40,000 ("Comparing the Costs," n.d.). Instead of working through an agency, families may organize an independent adoption with a birth mother and her lawyer. Finally, families may consider international adoption.

In all public and agency-based private adoptions, as well as most international adoptions, prospective families undergo a home study by a social worker (Child Welfare Information Gateway, 2015b). This investigation typically includes parenting classes, background checks, examination of health and financial records, reference checks, submitting an autobiographical statement, an interview, and a home visit to assess the safety of the home and the neighborhood. All the scrutiny can be highly stressful for potential parents. One woman who'd been through several failed IVF cycles said: "Haven't I gone through enough already to prove that I deserve to be a parent?" (Davenport, 2010, para. 1).

Once a family adopts a child, the transition can be stressful (Goldberg, 2010). They may experience declines in relationship satisfaction and mental health as well as lingering legal complications (Goldberg, Moyer, Kinkler, & Richardson, 2012; Goldberg & Smith, 2011; South, Foli, & Lim, 2013). Post-adoptive depression is more likely if a mother's post-adoption realities don't meet her pre-adoption expectations (Foli, South, Lim, & Jarnecke, 2016). In one study done in the United Kingdom and Ireland, adoptive mothers reported feeling labeled as either "desperate" or "heroes," and many felt pressure to be perfect parents and felt stress when their children acted out (Weistra & Luke, 2017). Social support appears to reduce the stress associated with post-adoption transition, particularly when children had unexpected characteristics, such as behavioral concerns (Foli et al., 2016; Moyer & Goldberg, 2017).

Women who place their children for adoption can experience great loss. In one study, birth mothers' mental health improved over time, but 75% described their mental health as poor, very poor, or neutral (Brodzinsky & Smith, 2014). Because such research doesn't include a control group of women with unwanted pregnancies who didn't place their children for adoption, it doesn't clarify whether adoption, per se, is related to negative outcomes or whether the women would have had mental health difficulties anyway. Openness in the adoption process and contact between the birth mother and the adoptive child have been found to improve satisfaction and positive mental health for birth mothers (Ge et al., 2008).

Open communication can also benefit the adopted child. One study, focusing mainly on interracial adoptions, found that the ability to have contact with the birth parent predicted increased self-esteem and fewer behavior problems in adopted children (Brodzinsky, 2006). In another study, lesbian couples reported preference for open adoption, since it ensured that they wouldn't have to hide their sexual identity (Goldberg, Kinkler, Richardson, & Downing, 2011). They also were more likely than heterosexual couples to see birth parents as part of their extended family. Regardless of sexual orientation, couples who pursue open adoption often develop meaningful relationships with birth parents.

Mothering an adopted child, especially one whose race/ethnicity is different from one's own, presents joys and challenges. Children adopted into transracial families are generally psychologically well adjusted (Boivin & Hassan, 2015; Mohanty & Newhill, 2006). Such families do best if the adoptive parents neither deny nor overstate the differences between themselves and their child. However, children in transracial adoptions may experience discrimination that their family members do not. It's noteworthy that while White parents often adopt babies of different races or nationalities, parents of color rarely adopt White babies (Lee, 2003). One reason is that approximately one third of children in the foster system are Black, so Black families have a greater chance of adopting a same-race child (Dokoupil, 2009). Public reaction to the rarity of non-White families adopting White children was evident in the experience of one Black family—strangers would ask their White daughter if she was "okay" and even follow her to make sure she wasn't being kidnapped (Dokoupil, 2009). Unequal access in the adoption process is another example of stratified reproduction, and the negative reactions to Black families that adopt White babies reflect continued racism.

Pregnancy

How does pregnancy affect the body, women's view of their bodies, and the way women are treated by others?

Pregnancy can bring profound physical, social, and emotional changes. In early stages, approximately 85% of women experience **morning sickness**, which includes nausea and vomiting. Morning sickness is actually associated with lower miscarriage rates—in other words, it can be a sign of a healthy pregnancy (Flaxman & Sherman, 2000). It's usually triggered by the smell or taste of specific foods, including meats, some vegetables, cigarette smoke, and alcohol. Researchers hypothesize that morning sickness developed as an adaptive mechanism to keep women from ingesting potentially harmful substances while pregnant (Flaxman & Sherman, 2000). Although symptoms generally subside after the first 12 weeks, some women experience them throughout the pregnancy (Tiran, 2014). Morning sickness can be particularly stressful at work or in social settings, especially if the mother doesn't want to share that she's pregnant.

Pregnancy and Body Image One challenge is adjusting to body changes—particularly weight gain, since Western culture values the thin ideal. Some women, however, may feel liberated from that ideal and see their bodies as functioning to give life rather than as objects to be viewed and judged. Research reflects these contradictory perspectives. Some studies have shown that pregnant women are dissatisfied with their bodies (e.g., Skouteris, Carr, Wertheim, Paxton, & Duncombe, 2005; Strang & Sullivan, 1985)—especially early in the second trimester as they begin to gain weight but don't look obviously pregnant (Goodwin, Astbury, & McMeeken, 2000; Skouteris et al., 2005). However, other research has shown that pregnant women are more satisfied with their bodies than non-pregnant women are (Loth, Bauer, Wall, Berge, & Neumark-Sztainer, 2011).

Although pregnant women may feel less pressure to conform to the thin ideal, they can still experience pressure to remain physically fit. One study of a pregnancy-focused fitness magazine showed an emphasis on fitness before and during pregnancy in order to prepare the body for delivery and to facilitate weight loss afterward (Dworkin & Wachs, 2004). Following pregnancy, women were repeatedly encouraged to "get their body back." Media exposure to celebrities who've "gotten their bodies back" only weeks after delivery (ignoring the roles of chefs, personal trainers, and nannies) reinforces these unrealistic ideals. In fact, exposure to such celebrity images has been shown to decrease body satisfaction even among non-pregnant women (Hopper & Aubrey, 2016).

The fear of gaining weight during pregnancy and looking awkward ("Does my bump look big in this?") can detract from a woman's positive experience of pregnancy and lead to anxiety (Johnson, Burrows, & Williamson, 2004). Furthermore, body dissatisfaction during pregnancy can predict other negative psychological states, such as depression and a decreased commitment to mothering (Fuller-Tyszkiewicz, Skouteris, Watson, & Hill, 2012). In one study, women reported feeling better when they focused on what their bodies were doing rather than how their bodies looked, as well as when they received positive feedback about their appearance from partners (Watson, Broadbent, Skouteris, & Fuller-Tyszkiewicz, 2015). In contrast, other research showed that men's sexual interest in their partners decreases sharply during the third trimester (von Sydow, 1999). This lack of interest in sex can make pregnant women feel anxious and less comfortable with their bodies.

Pregnancy can be particularly disruptive to the body image of transmen. Being pregnant in a man's body isn't socially accepted, and pregnant men in one study reported being stigmatized and occasionally ridiculed (Light et al., 2014). Pregnancy can also increase gender dysphoria. One pregnant man noted, "Heavy time, having a baby, not passing as male, all the changes and a society telling me to just be happy" (p. 4).

How Pregnant Women Are Treated People treat women differently when they're pregnant—for example, with unwelcome belly touching. In one study, most participants reported that others routinely touched their bellies without permission—"You become public property and anyone can touch you" (Johnson et al., 2004, p. 365). Strangers also tend to talk to pregnant women and give unsolicited advice. In a project where Black women were asked to list acts of kindness that they wished would happen when they were pregnant, many said they wished strangers would stop talking to them and stop touching their bellies (Jones et al., 2010).

Pregnant women often experience benevolent sexism. Some people give up seats or help them carry boxes, and these gestures *can* be a welcome form of help (Jones et al., 2010). However, as discussed in Chapter 2, benevolent sexism is generally directed toward women who conform to gender roles. In one study, when women who appeared to be pregnant (but were actually wearing pregnancy prostheses) asked for help, they received responses such as smiling, nods, and over-helpfulness (Hebl, King, Glick, Singletary, & Kazama, 2007). But in the same study, when women who appeared to be pregnant applied for a job (a violation of traditional norms), people were generally rude to them. Other researchers have found that individuals holding benevolent sexist beliefs are more likely to stop a pregnant woman from engaging in a behavior that they deem risky (Sutton et al., 2011).

White, able-bodied, upper-middle-class women who are pregnant are generally treated with kindness and benevolent sexism, but pregnant, poor, single, Black, and teen mothers are generally negatively stereotyped. In one survey of mostly White and Asian undergraduate students, researchers found that a Black woman who was described as pregnant was seen as less likely to have the child's father involved and more likely to need public assistance than a White woman who was described as pregnant (Rosenthal & Lobel, 2016). Teen pregnancy is also often seen as a problem. Most people perceive teen mothers as deviant, and many social policies aim to decrease teen motherhood (Wilson & Huntington, 2006). However, research suggests that negative outcomes associated with being a teenage mother are almost entirely due to the increased likelihood of poverty rather than

Pregnancy and Alcohol

There are significant risks associated with alcohol consumption during pregnancy (Williams, Smith, & Committee on Substance Abuse, 2015). The American Academy of Pediatrics notes there is no known safe amount of alcohol consumption during pregnancy and recommends complete abstinence during pregnancy, yet in many parts of the world, consumption of small amounts after the first trimester is widely accepted (Shawe et al., 2015). And research has shown that although heavy alcohol consumption is related to low birth weight, pre-term birth, and childhood behavioral problems, the same patterns aren't found for children of mothers who engage in light drinking—less than one drink daily or one to two drinks weekly (Kelly et al., 2008; Patra et al., 2011).

In 2016, the U.S. Centers for Disease Control and Prevention (CDC) recommended that *all* sexually active women of child-bearing age refrain from any alcohol use unless they're using birth control (Centers for Disease Control, 2016b). Because this recommendation views any sexually active woman as potentially pregnant, feminist activists criticized it as patronizing and condescending. Writer Alexandra Petri (2016) quipped, "No alcohol for you, young women! The most important fact about you is not that you are people but that you might potentially contain people one day" (para. 15). Furthermore, although binge drinking and chronic alcohol use by men affect sperm and can contribute to fetal alcohol syndrome (Abel 2004; Ouko et al., 2009), the CDC recommendations didn't address male drinking.

your turn

Have you ever known anyone who was pregnant, or have you ever been pregnant yourself? How was that person (or you) treated? Take a moment to consider your own reactions to different kinds of pregnant women. Have you had a more favorable reaction if the woman was of a certain age, racial or ethnic group, or social class?

the teen being a poor parent (Morinis, Carson, & Quigley, 2013). Other research shows that teenagers report positive benefits when becoming a mother, including establishing themselves as responsible adults, securing a relationship with a partner, and creating an emotional connection with a baby (Boustani, Frazier, Hartley, Meinzer, & Hedemann, 2015; Solivan, Wallace, Kaplan, & Harville, 2015). These findings indicate that not all pregnant women and mothers are viewed positively, highlighting yet another example of reproductive stratification.

Childbirth

How do women's experiences in childbirth often differ from their expectations?

In the movies, a woman usually cries "The baby is coming!" and is rushed to the hospital. She briefly pushes and screams, and the baby pops out. In reality, though, childbirth can take a very long time. During labor, the cervix becomes dilated, widening to allow the mother to push the baby through. Before the baby can come out, the cervix must be dilated 10 cm, and this can take many hours—even several days—after contractions begin. Although it's generally recommended that labor proceed on its own, in some cases labor needs to be *induced*, or sped up through medical intervention.

Women may choose interventions to decrease their pain during labor and delivery. One common intervention is an *epidural*, which involves a healthcare provider administering anesthesia to the base of the spine with a needle. Although an epidural provides effective pain relief, it can disrupt the labor process and increase the likelihood that the woman will need additional intervention, including drugs, to speed her labor (Lothian, 2014). Also, if the baby's head doesn't have enough room to exit the vaginal opening, a provider may recommend an *episiotomy*, a cut between the vagina and the anus to create a larger opening for delivery (see Figure 9.3). Although an episiotomy may speed up delivery, it may increase pain compared to unassisted tearing. Furthermore, it can contribute to urinary or anal incontinence after childbirth, although stiches generally minimize this risk. As a third intervention, if labor isn't progressing or the baby is in breech position (i.e., with feet rather than head facing the vaginal opening), the woman may need a *cesarean section (C-section)*. During this procedure, the baby is delivered through incisions in the abdominal wall and uterus.

Advocates for healthy childbirth suggest that induced labor, epidurals, episiotomies, and cesareans are overused. For example, in 2015, 32% of women in the United States had cesarean births (Martin, Hamilton, Osterman, & Matthews, 2017), although other research finds that only approximately 10% of such births

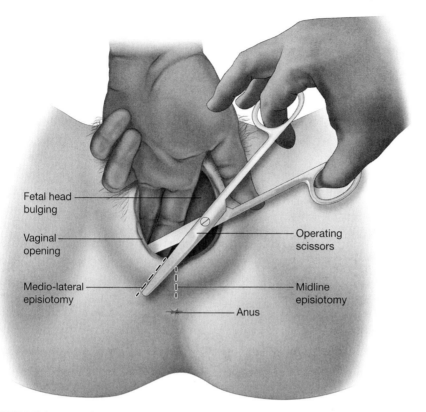

Fetal head
bulging

Vaginal
opening

Medio-lateral
episiotomy

Operating
scissors

Midline
episiotomy

Anus

FIGURE 9.3 In an episiotomy, a cut is made between the vaginal opening and the anus to widen the area for the baby's head to pass through during birth. Episiotomies are fairly common procedures, and the size of the cut varies by situation. Current guidelines, however, do not recommend them in every case.

are medically necessary (Ye, Betrán, Guerrero Vela, Souza, & Zhang, 2014). Pre-scheduled cesarean births are convenient for medical providers, and hospitals can charge higher fees for cesarean births as opposed to vaginal deliveries (Geirrson, 2016). An analysis by the World Health Organization concluded that nations with cesarean birth rates above 15% were performing many unnecessary cesarean births and were over-utilizing global resources (Gibbons et al., 2010).

Women in industrialized countries who are healthy and having no birth complications are routinely encouraged to select interventions such as labor induction, epidurals, and episiotomies (Declercq, Sakala, Corry, & Applebaum, 2007; Johanson, Newburn, & Macfarlane, 2002). One reason is that for many years practitioners operated under the belief that labor should progress by 1 cm an hour and that slower labor required speeding up through medical interventions. However, recommendations are shifting to acknowledge the fact that slower labors reflect natural variations and that doctors should have more patience (Caughey, Cahill, Guise, & Rouse, 2014). Practice, though, is often slow to catch up with recommendations.

Labor can be a very painful process. Although some women wish to experience labor without pain-reducing drugs, others choose interventions that involve pain medications, such as an epidural.

Moreover, many health-care providers worry about risk management and litigation in the context of childbirth (Healy, Humphreys, & Kennedy, 2016). In one study, Canadian providers expressed concern about litigation if something should go wrong during labor and delivery (Hall, Tomkinson, & Klein, 2012). They described how, in order to make a mother agree to a procedure she may not want, they might say, "You don't want your baby to die, do you?" even for non-urgent procedures (p. 582). Sometimes, providers intervene without a woman's knowledge or consent; 73% of participants in one study who received an episiotomy were given no choice in the decision (Declercq et al., 2007).

In response to concerns about women undergoing procedures without consent and without a true understanding of the risks and benefits, Lamaze International has issued six guidelines for a healthy birth (Mother's Advocate, 2009):

1. Let labor begin on its own, rather than through induction, to decrease risk of prematurity as well as risks of other medical interventions.
2. Walk, move around, and change positions during labor to promote pain relief.
3. Bring a loved one or a doula for support. A **doula** is a trained, paid professional who provides emotional and physical support before, during, and after birth.
4. Avoid interventions unless they're medically necessary, and medical professionals should acknowledge that labor can take a long time.
5. Try not to give birth on your back, and push only when your body tells you it's ready. Standing, squatting, or sitting takes advantage of gravity, but lying down may be convenient for a doctor who can easily see what's going on.
6. Keep mother and baby together, and let them experience immediate skin-to-skin contact.

Although these guidelines are useful, one study found that only 2% of participants experienced births that follow them (Declercq et al., 2007). For example, 39% of participants had babies taken away by staff for routine, non-emergency interventions (e.g., being cleaned and weighed) immediately after birth (Declercq et al., 2007; Ondeck, 2014). Also, immediate skin-to-skin contact was less common in public hospitals, where women of low socioeconomic status are more likely to give birth (Rowe-Murray & Fisher, 2002).

The World Health Organization (2018) recently issued guidelines, similar to those of Lamaze International, to improve women's childbirth experiences. These recommendations also caution against unnecessary interventions, such as episiotomies and induction if labor is proceeding slowly. Only time will tell if these recommendations become widely accepted and utilized.

How a woman feels during childbirth is important because that experience begins her assessment of her mothering ability (Reisz, Jacobvitz, & George, 2015). Those with positive birth experiences report self-confidence as well as a more positive view of their child. According to one study, a major factor in a woman perceiving her childbirth experience as positive involves her feelings of control (Green & Baston, 2003). Also, confidence going into labor can predict a positive birth experience, and one study found that Latinx and Black women had higher confidence going into labor than White women (Attanasio, McPherson, & Kozhimannil, 2014). The same study showed that shared decision making between the mother and her clinician predicted a positive birth experience. It's important to give women every possible opportunity to have a positive birth experience. This effort can, however, create pressure to have a "perfect birth," which can lead to distress and embarrassment when the experience doesn't live up to this unrealistic expectation (Pearson, 2014).

Maternal mortality is a global concern, and in some of the world's poorest areas, the lifetime risk of pregnancy-related death is 1 out of every 6 (Ronsmans, Graham, & Lancet, 2006). In the United States, maternal mortality appears to be increasing slightly. One study showed that between 2006 and 2010, pregnancy-related mortality rates were 16.0 deaths for every 100,000 live births—a slight increase from prior years in which data were collected (Creanga et al., 2015). This rate, however, varied across racial groups: 38.9 for Black women, 12.0 for White women, and 11.7 for Latinx women (Creanga et al., 2015). Reasons for pregnancy-related deaths were hemorrhage, hypertension, embolism, anesthesia complications, cardiovascular conditions, and infection. Thus, while it's important that medical interventions not be overused, it's also essential that women have access to safe labor and delivery services.

There's also evidence of differential infant mortality rates within the United States based on race/ethnicity. Black infants are more than twice as likely to die during childbirth than White infants—in 2015, 11.3 Black infants died per 1,000 live births compared to 4.9 White infants (Centers for Disease Control and Prevention, 2018). These rates are not linked to genetic differences (David & Collins, 2007) or maternal education (Schoendorf, Hogue, Kleinman, & Rowley, 1992). Researchers attribute these patterns partly to high levels of stress experienced by Black women, particularly institutional racism—including within the medical community (Giscombé & Lobel, 2005; Kramer & Hogue, 2009).

try it for yourself

Talk to someone who recently gave birth. What was her experience like? Did she receive medical intervention? If so, how did she feel about it? Did her birth experience align with her expectations? If you plan to have children, what kind of birth experience do you hope that you or your partner will have? If you have given birth, what was your experience like?

For example, one study showed that some medical professionals held false and racist beliefs about Black individuals, such as that they have thicker skin and feel less pain than White people (Hoffman, Trawalter, Axt, & Oliver, 2016). These racist assumptions and the higher rates of negative outcomes for Black women and their babies are another example of stratified reproduction.

Being a Mother

When a woman becomes a mother, she experiences a great deal of change. Many of the changes are positive, but there's also a lot of stress, including a sense of identity loss and the possibility of post-partum depression and anxiety.

Identity Changes

How does becoming a mother affect women psychologically?

First-time mothers experience a huge shift in identity. No longer defined solely as their own person, they're now someone's mother. And the process of becoming a mother involves many complicated emotions. Some women adjust easily, especially if being a mother was a role they'd valued throughout their lives. For example, in a study of identity change during the motherhood transition, one woman said: "Anyone who's had a positive pregnancy test, you're a mom. You love that child more than anything the moment you see that positive pregnancy test" (Laney, Hall, Anderson, & Willingham, 2015, p. 131). Other women don't feel instant love: "When he first came out I didn't have this 100 percent overwhelming feeling of, 'I love you, I will do anything for you'" (p. 132). Some mothers describe anxiety: "It was kinda scary really; this baby is just going to depend on me" (Cronin, 2003, p. 264).

Many women have reported a loss of identity because they have to give up their own needs in order to care for their child: "It almost feels like a loss of self at the beginning with the first child, just because newborns basically need you 24/7" (Laney et al., 2015, p. 132). This feeling can improve over time, though. One woman noted, "It makes me a better mom to find that balance [between doing things for myself and spending

Motherhood can be a time of profound identity shift for women. It's common for women to experience some sadness and anxiety as they adjust to their new role and the demands associated with parenting.

time with kids] because, if I only am focused on motherhood, the other part of you . . . can be lost and forgotten and you go, 'Wait, well, who am I?'" (p. 132). However, women who felt they were born to be mothers had difficulty figuring out how to define themselves as their children grew up. Transitioning to a mother identity is further complicated for women who don't give birth to their children. For example, lesbian co-mothers may struggle over how to identify themselves and what to call themselves and be called by their children (Dahl & Malterud, 2015).

Women who have a disability face unique changes. For many, the transition to motherhood is positive in that other people may see them not simply as a woman with a disability, but as a mother (Lawler, Begley, & Lalor, 2015). This can promote an increased sense of belonging and acceptance in a society that generally stigmatizes people with disabilities. However, women with disabilities often encounter stigma about their ability to mother, which can create anxiety or self-doubt. One woman who used a wheelchair described: "This woman [midwife] pulled my mother aside and said 'Your daughter is not fit to look after this baby, this baby is going to end up being taken away by social services,' after that I was always afraid that someone would ring social services" (Lawler et al., 2015, p. 7). Another woman, who was hard of hearing, noted: "The nurses were very judging . . . they were going around to all the other mothers in the ward saying 'How is she going to cope with the baby?'" (p. 7).

Much of the research on identity changes in motherhood is based in qualitative interviews because these changes are experienced on an individual basis. Nevertheless, some larger-scale research has been undertaken. A study of over 80,000 mothers from Norway showed that both self-esteem and relationship quality declined after having children (van Scheppingen, Denissen, Chung, Tambs, & Bleidorn, 2017). Relationship quality declined most precipitously after the birth of the child, especially the first child, while self-esteem increased immediately after childbirth but declined after the child was six months old. Whether these self-esteem changes are related to feelings of identity loss has yet to be carefully investigated. However, other research has shown that parents experience a greater sense that life is meaningful than do non-parents, and they experience joy while caring for their children (Nelson, Kushlev, English, Dunn, & Lyubomirsky, 2013). Interestingly, this research showed that fathers experienced more benefits related to parenthood than mothers.

Post-partum Depression and Anxiety

How common are post-partum depression and anxiety, and what forms can these disorders take?

The difficulty of caring for an infant is rarely discussed in public; instead, media images of women holding babies glorify motherhood as a time of pure joy and love. Yet women have identified a "conspiracy of silence" in which no one talks about the extreme difficulty of infant care, particularly in environments with few financial or structural supports (Mercer, 2004, p. 230). Most women, in fact, experience some negative feelings during the transition to motherhood. The **baby blues** occurs in 80% of women and involves crying, poor sleep, irritability, and anxiety. However, baby blues generally ends within 10 days after the birth.

Some women experience more significant difficulties after giving birth, including clinical levels of depression and anxiety. These combined difficulties are called post-partum mood disorders, an umbrella term that includes post-partum depression as well as post-partum anxiety. **Post-partum depression** involves symptoms including feelings of sadness, anxiety, exhaustion, guilt, worthlessness, and suicidal ideation. Post-partum depression occurs in 7% to 20% of women and is often undiagnosed and untreated (Gavin et al., 2005). Although post-partum depression is defined as beginning in the weeks after childbirth, in reality, depression often begins during pregnancy. However, pregnant women who are depressed receive accurate diagnoses less frequently than non-pregnant depressed women (Ko, Farr, Dietz, & Robbins, 2012).

Several factors can contribute to post-partum depression, especially a previous history of depression or anxiety, a perceived lack of social support, and stressful life events during pregnancy or early motherhood (Robertson, Grace, Wallington, & Stewart, 2004). Furthermore, after giving birth, a woman's progesterone and estrogen levels drastically decrease, which may contribute to both the baby blues and post-partum depression (O'Hara & McCabe, 2013). Research suggests that women who are particularly susceptible to hormone fluctuations may be more likely to develop post-partum depression even without a previous history of depression (Schiller, Meltzer-Brody, & Rubinow, 2015). Also, sleep deprivation in the early months of caring for an infant can trigger depression (Dørheim, Bondevik, Eberhard-Gran, & Bjorvatn, 2009).

Men, too, may feel depressed after the birth. One 23-year longitudinal study found heightened depression levels in men during the first five years after having children (Garfield et al., 2014). As noted earlier, the stresses of parenting young children are related to a decline in relationship satisfaction, which may contribute to this depression in men. Transmen who birth children may be particularly at risk for post-partum depression because of the lack of social support for their pregnancy (Light et al., 2014).

Although investigated less frequently than depression, anxiety is a common component of post-partum mood disorder (Belluck, 2016). In fact, one study showed that post-partum anxiety was actually more common than depression (Wenzel, Haugen, Jackson, & Robinson, 2003). **Post-partum anxiety** involves worry, a sense of dread, obsessive checking, difficulty sleeping, and other symptoms such as dizziness, nausea, and headaches. In a study of new mothers drawn from a large urban center, every mother reported fear that her child would be accidentally harmed (Fairbrother & Woody, 2008). Also, thoughts of intentionally harming the infant were unexpectedly common. When the infants were four weeks old, 49.5% of the sample had unwanted intrusive thoughts about intentionally harming their child. Such thoughts may be triggered by hearing the infants' crying; in fact, in a different study, 24% of new mothers reported thoughts of harm after being exposed to ten minutes of crying (Fairbrother, Barr, Pauwels, Brant, & Green, 2015). Mothers who have intrusive thoughts of harm don't usually act on these impulses, but they may withdraw from their infants and experience shame and guilt about their feelings. The shame can also contribute to post-partum depression. Moreover, mothers may not tell others about their symptoms because they fear judgment about being a bad mother. In this way, post-partum anxiety and depression are understood as interrelated.

Perhaps a key factor contributing to both post-partum depression and anxiety is the social pressure from media, family members, and peers about what it means to be a mother. Mothers generally expect they should feel nothing but happiness around their children, so if they experience negative emotions, they may worry that something is wrong with them (Held & Rutherford, 2012). Sensational media reports about women with post-partum depression who kill their children contribute to this dynamic (Martinez, Johnston-Robledo, Ulsh, & Chrisler, 2001). Moreover, social media provides an outlet through which mothers can compare themselves to others, and many women use it to communicate an identity of being a good mother (Bartels, 2015). Because people don't generally post images of screaming and crying children, most everyone's family looks happy and well behaved. As a result, some women can experience a sense of isolation about their mixed emotions and insecurities about parenting. Lately, however, some blogs and websites are becoming increasingly confessional, and mothers on these sites are sharing the challenges of parenting (Howorth, 2017).

Breastfeeding

What are the advantages of breastfeeding, and how do cultural views about breastfeeding affect women?

The American Academy of Pediatrics recommends exclusive breastfeeding for six months and continued for a year or as long as is comfortable for mother and child in combination with other foods (Eidelman et al., 2012). In developing countries, only 37% of children under six months are breastfed (Victora et al., 2016). Reasons for not breastfeeding include mothers' perceptions of fathers' attitudes, concerns about milk supply, and the need to return to work (Arora, McJunkin, Wehrer, & Kuhn, 2000). Women who are married, older, well educated, non-smokers, and of a higher socioeconomic status are more likely to breastfeed (Mathews, Leerkes, Lovelady, & Labban, 2014; Oakley, Renfrew, Kurinczuk, & Quigley, 2013). In the United States, 81% of infants born in

Breastfeeding has benefits for both mothers and infants. Consequently, women often feel a great deal of pressure to breastfeed. At the same time, however, many people still strongly disapprove of breastfeeding in public.

2013 were breastfed at birth, and 52% were still breastfeeding at six months (Centers for Disease Control, 2016a). The fact that women in positions of privilege are more likely to have the support necessary to breastfeed is an example of stratified reproduction.

The benefits of breastfeeding for children include decreased risk of infection and disease, decreased childhood obesity, decreased risk of attentional problems, and increased intelligence and cognitive outcomes (Bar, Milanaik, & Adesman, 2016; Victora et al., 2016). Benefits for the mother include decreased risk of breast cancer as well as possible decreases in risks for ovarian cancer and diabetes (Victora et al., 2016). Furthermore, women who exclusively breastfeed often don't ovulate, and exclusive breastfeeding has long been considered a form of birth control (Labbok et al., 1997). All research on breastfeeding is correlational rather than experimental, as it would be unethical to randomly assign some women to breastfeed and prevent others from doing so. Given this constraint, it's difficult to distinguish the benefits of breastfeeding from the benefits of being better educated, wealthier, and not smoking.

One barrier to breastfeeding is the fact that many women are embarrassed to breastfeed in public and risk being stigmatized for doing so. Research on attitudes toward public and private breastfeeding indicates that while breastfeeding is generally approved of in private, it's generally regarded negatively when done in public (Acker, 2009). In 2014, a woman in the United Kingdom was asked to leave a store for breastfeeding, spurring a mass protest of breastfeeding mothers (Newton, 2014). Analysis of the online response to this protest indicated that, although many posts supported a woman's right to breastfeed in public, 85% were unsupportive (Grant, 2016). Discomfort with breastfeeding often stems from the fact that Western society generally views breasts as having sexual, rather than functional, connotations. Furthermore, in one study, benevolent sexist beliefs were found to relate to disapproval of public breastfeeding, especially by men (Acker, 2009). Women who self-objectify may be especially concerned about breastfeeding because the appearance of their breasts might change (Johnston-Robledo & Fred, 2008; Johnston-Robledo, Wares, Fricker, & Pasek, 2007). Furthermore, respondents in one study saw breastfeeding women as less competent, especially in a work environment (Smith, Hawkinson, & Paull, 2011). Overall, then, while breastfeeding may benefit the health of the child and the mother, there can be real social costs.

From another perspective, "breast is best" may make women who cannot breastfeed feel inadequate. A study of lower-income women found that many respondents experienced pressure to breastfeed and thought everyone but them was an expert on caring for their children (Hoddinott & Pill, 2000). Moreover, not all birth mothers can breastfeed (e.g., women who have had mastectomies). Transmen who desire to "chestfeed" may or may not be able to do so, depending on whether they've had surgical mastectomies (Berger, Potter, Shutters, & Imborek, 2015). Some women can't produce enough milk and may choose to bottle-feed instead. Those who return to work must pump their breastmilk if they wish to continue breastfeeding, and unless a woman has a private office, there are rarely places to pump in the workplace except for public restrooms. Breastfeeding is difficult to learn and can be painful. It generally also puts all the responsibility for feeding onto the birth mother. Since newborns require feedings every two to three hours for several months, bottle feeding can be a way of involving both parents and giving birth mothers a period of welcome, uninterrupted sleep.

Clearly, women experience pressure from both directions in terms of breastfeeding. Those who breastfeed are often discriminated against and viewed as less competent. Those who don't breastfeed may feel guilty about their decision and may be viewed as less adequate.

Increased Gender Inequality

What changes occur in the family after women become mothers?

Another, possibly unanticipated, change is that gender roles tend to become more traditional after the birth. Although couples may plan on dividing child care somewhat equally, this is difficult to achieve. For example, one study showed that heterosexual women expected they would do 63% of the child care but ended up doing 73% (Biehle & Mickelson, 2012). Also, after the birth, both women and men in heterosexual couples were found to start holding more traditional beliefs about women being best suited to care for children (Katz-Wise, Preiss, & Hyde, 2010). The unequal division of labor can correspond to a greater sense of unfairness in the relationship and decreased relationship satisfaction for women (Biehle & Mickelson, 2012; Dew & Wilcox, 2011). However, when wives did more child care than men expected, men expressed greater marital satisfaction (Biehle & Michelson, 2012).

This pattern of inequity doesn't exist in all families. For example, there's considerable evidence that Black men spend more time taking care of children than men of other racial groups, particularly White men (McLoyd, Cauce, Takeuchi, & Wilson, 2000; Hossain & Roopnarine, 1993; Yogman, Garfield, & Committee on Psychosocial Aspects of Child and Family Health, 2016). One study of

If you don't yet have children, what are your expectations for the division of child care after you have children? If you have children and a partner, how have you and your partner handled dividing these responsibilities? If you identify as a woman, why might you do more child care than you expect? If you don't identify as a woman and anticipate having a female partner, why might you end up doing less child care than you expect? What might help you to avoid an unexpected slide toward inequality?

Black, heterosexual families showed that marital satisfaction was lower when men held traditional attitudes but higher when men participated equally in running the household (Stanik & Bryant, 2012). Studies of Asian American fathers have found that those who hold more egalitarian views are also more involved with child care (McLoyd et al., 2000). Another study showed that a mostly White sample of same-gender couples tended to share child care and housework more equitably than heterosexual couples (Goldberg, Smith, & Perry-Jenkins, 2012).

It's unclear why heterosexual women do more child care than they expect. It could be that fathers are unwilling to do as much as mothers would like. However, in one study, researchers found that, while college women and men ideally wanted an equitable division of labor, college men expected to do 47% of child care while college women expected to do 70% (Askari, Liss, Erchull, Staebell, & Axelson, 2010). The data show that the women were anticipating inequality but may also have been anticipating reality. That said, some of the inequity may result from **maternal gatekeeping**, in which mothers limit the extent of fathers' involvement in child care. For example, women may set high standards for parenting and assume that husbands are unable to meet them (Allen & Hawkins, 1999). Women may engage in this behavior because the mothering role provides an important source of identity and esteem that they don't want to have threatened (Gaunt, 2008).

The expectations that mothers are more engaged with their children than fathers continue as children grow. For example, parental involvement in schools is beneficial for children's outcomes, but research on such involvement focuses almost exclusively on mothers. One study whose title indicated it addressed parental involvement in schools actually was based on a sample that was 90% mothers (Barnard, 2004).

Mother Blaming

How are mothers, especially those outside of the mold of what is traditionally considered a "good mother," blamed for anything negative that happens to their children?

Mothers may feel compelled to take more responsibility for child care because they're generally considered responsible for how their children turn out. **Mother blaming**—the idea that mothers should be held responsible for the actions, health, behavior, and well-being of their children—is pervasive in

Western society (Allan, 2004; Jackson & Mannix, 2004). In one study, almost all mothers reported feeling it was their fault if their children misbehaved, acted against social norms, or became ill (Jackson & Mannix, 2004). Fathers were not interviewed.

The discipline of psychology itself has a history of blaming mothers. In one study, when researchers reviewed clinical psychology journals from the 1970s and 1980s, they found that mothers were blamed for 75 "problems," including agitation, arson, fetishism, homosexuality, incontinence, schizophrenia, school phobia, sibling jealousy, sleepwalking, transexualism, tantrums, timidity, and ulcerative colitis (Caplan & Hall-McCorquodale, 1985, p. 348). As one researcher pointed out, it was easier to blame mothers for their children's behavior than it was to look at the ways in which social policy and inadequate community services contribute to strain on families (Burrows, 2001).

Mothers who don't conform to expectations for being a "good mother" (e.g., White, heterosexual, married, middle class) are more likely to be blamed. Poor mothers, for example, are often blamed for their bad "choices" if they have low-birth-weight babies, but the health-care system's inadequacy is rarely challenged (Colker, 2015). In contrast, there's a notable lack of blame on wealthy women who have low-birth-weight babies due to carrying multiple fetuses as a result of IVF. Also, poor, Black women who are addicted to drugs have been arrested and prosecuted at higher rates than White women. One study showed that White and Black women had similar rates of drug use during pregnancy, but Black women were ten times more likely to be reported to government authorities (Roberts, 1997). In 2012, the *New York Daily News* reported that women in public hospitals mainly serving minority and low-income populations were being routinely tested for drugs, while women in private hospitals were only being tested if they were obviously intoxicated (Yaniv, 2012). Test results were turned over to child protective services, and family courts were seeing dozens of low-income mothers face neglect proceedings because of a positive marijuana screening.

Some people also perceive single mothers as neglectful, immature, irresponsible, promiscuous, insecure, pessimistic, making poor choices, and having mental health challenges (Haire & McGeorge, 2012). This attitude was evident in the case of the woman, mentioned at the start of this chapter, who was arrested for child abandonment after leaving her children in a food court while she attended a job interview nearby. Single fathers in a similar situation, however, are generally seen as struggling with a difficult situation rather than acting irresponsibly (Haire & McGeorge, 2012). Moreover, in the United States, mothers who don't speak English may be subject to mother blaming (Colker, 2015). If these women can't complete paperwork in English, they may be accused of not caring about their children's education.

Mothers of children with disabilities have a long history of being blamed and criticized (Colker, 2015). Psychologists once claimed that "refrigerator moms," or mothers who were cold and unattached, were the cause of autism (Kanner, 1949), and this idea was widely supported by medical providers until the 1970s. While mothers are generally no longer explicitly blamed for their child's disability, they continue to report being criticized no matter how they act. If they strongly advocate for their children, they're likely to be labeled as pushy; if they don't, they may be criticized for being passive or negligent (Colker, 2015). Furthermore, if they don't leave their jobs in order to care for their children full-time, they may face criticism for being under-involved. However, if they quit their jobs, they may have inadequate resources for their child. Similarly, if mothers choose to give their children medication, they may be accused of drugging them; if they don't, they may be accused of neglecting the children. In one study, mothers of children with autism spectrum disorder reported that they feel blamed for their children's cognitive and behavioral outcomes because they think they're expected to work tirelessly to promote the children's care and treatment (Courcy & des Rivières, 2017). Similarly, mothers whose children are sexually abused by their partners are generally shamed and blamed for not protecting their children and for making bad choices (McLaren, 2013). The shame can stop mothers from asking for and receiving help for their children.

Lesbian mothers can feel additional pressure because not everyone approves of children being raised in families without a cohabiting, married mother and father. However, over 30 years of research has indicated that, despite stigma, children from gay and lesbian families score just as high on measures of academic, emotional, and social outcomes as children of heterosexual parents (Perrin et al., 2013). Some of this research even suggests that children of lesbian parents have higher levels of emotional stability and resilience than children of heterosexual parents (Perrin et al., 2013). A different study showed that lesbian mothers had equally well-adjusted children and equally good relationships with their children as heterosexual mothers did (Golombok et al., 2003). However, lesbians hit their children less and played with their children more than did heterosexual mothers. Earlier, we presented research indicating that fathers psychologically benefit from parenting more than mothers do (Nelson et al., 2013). The culture of blaming mothers, but not fathers, when something goes wrong with children is one factor that likely contributes to this discrepancy.

Intensive Parenting

How have parenting norms changed in the last few decades to put increased pressure on mothers?

Pressures on mothers have increased in all domains. Today, women are expected to live up to the ideal of **intensive parenting** (Arendell, 2000; Hays, 1996)—they're expected to be fully immersed in the parenting experience, seek expert advice on how to parent, engage their children in cognitively stimulating activities to ensure optimal brain development, and feel fulfilled in their role as mothers. Furthermore, parents are supposed to monitor and supervise their children's actions and activities in a way that wasn't common a generation ago. Back then, young children were routinely told to "go play" and were allowed to walk independently to school. Today, though, a culture of fear and anxiety prevails (Warner, 2006), bombarding parents with messages about dangers and risks to their children. This culture continues even though crime has gone down since the 1990s, and most of us live in a safer world than the generation before us (McGill, 2016).

Intensive parenting began as a middle- to upper-middle-class phenomenon as parents attempted to "cultivate" their children's brain development and build up every possible talent or skill they may have (Ginsburg, 2007; Lareau, 2002). However, the idea that one must parent intensively has become more widely accepted as the "proper" mode of parenting (Arendell, 2000), despite evidence that children actually benefit from playing without adult supervision instead of always being scheduled into organized activities supervised by adults (Ginsburg, 2007). Lower-income mothers also feel the pressure to parent intensively, resulting in guilt because they cannot afford activities that they believe will promote achievement, such as enrichment lessons and extra classes (Romagnoli & Wall, 2012).

Feminist Mothering

What does it mean to be a feminist mother?

People often stereotype feminists as being anti-motherhood and anti-family. For example, feminists have been accused of destroying the family and of hating children (Dillaway & Pare, 2008; Faludi, 1991; Feder, 2006). More recently, a radio talk show host was quoted as saying, "I believe history will go back to this period of time and will look at feminism and say there was a time in which women lost the love of their children" (Steiger, 2013, para. 11). Although these false accusations reflect inaccurate stereotypes, feminists do report a lower desire to have children than non-feminists (Hartwell, Erchull, & Liss, 2014).

Feminists have had a conflicted relationship with mothering. A few decades ago, many second wave feminists saw motherhood as a source of oppression for women (Snitow, 1992; Umansky, 1996). However, around the same time, cultural feminists who emphasized women's special characteristics viewed motherhood as a source of women's enhanced empathy and strength (Ruddick, 1989). Today, many feminists recognize that Western society doesn't adequately value or compensate motherhood and care work in general

(Slaughter, 2015). Feminists also now work to support women during the birth process, discourage mother blaming, question intensive parenting, and promote policies that allow mothers to balance work and family (a topic we'll address in Chapter 10).

How does a feminist mother differ from a non-feminist mother? Just as there is no one type of feminist, there is no one type of feminist mother. Some research suggests that self-identified feminists endorse parenting practices that are more time consuming and involved than non-feminists do (Liss & Erchull, 2012). For example, **attachment parenting** focuses on meeting children's needs on their own schedule, such as by breastfeeding on demand, co-sleeping, and carrying infants and young children in wraps or slings (Green & Groves, 2008; Sears & Sears, 2003). Attachment parenting can be very time and labor intensive, and one might argue that if feminists were truly anti-child and anti-family, they probably wouldn't support such an intensive approach. However, women who identified as feminists were more likely to endorse attachment parenting practices than were non-feminists in one study (Liss & Erchull, 2012). In contrast, other feminists have expressed concern about attachment parenting, saying that being so continuously connected to one's children is oppressive for women (Jong, 2010).

Feminist mothering may be more difficult to enact than expected. For example, one study of heterosexual-identified women showed that feminist women who didn't yet have children anticipated that both they and their partner would equally share child care (Liss & Erchull, 2013). After all, gender equality, even in child care, is a central tenet in liberal feminism. Many also anticipated that they would reject patriarchal traditions of child naming and give their children a hyphenated name, their own last name, or a new shared last name taken by the entire family. However, the researchers found that feminist women who were already mothers actually did the majority of the child care and that most of them gave their children their husband's last name, even if they had kept their own last name for themselves.

Being a feminist mother does have advantages. First, feminist mothers challenge the culture of blame and anxiety surrounding motherhood (Warner, 2006). Second, women with liberal feminist attitudes have partners who are likely to more equally participate in child care (Kroska,

There are as many different types of feminist mothers as there are feminists. Shown here are a mother and her daughter participating in the Women's March in Washington, DC, in January 2017. Other feminist mothers might go fly fishing or bake cakes with their children.

2004; Stevens, Minnotte, Mannon, & Kiger, 2006). Third, feminist parenting has been linked to shared decision making in the family (Mack-Canty & Wright, 2004). One feminist father described feminist parenting as "a sense of cooperativeness and egalitarianism so that no single person is making decisions that overrules someone else" (Mack-Canty & Wright, 2004, p. 867). Fourth, parents who are feminists are more likely than non-feminists to raise their children to have a more flexible sense of gender roles, and these children have been found to feel empowered to challenge sexism and other sources of oppression (Mack-Canty & Wright, 2004). Finally, one study showed that having a feminist mother predicts identifying as a feminist when the child is older (Nelson et al., 2008).

To Work or Not to Work?

What makes the choice about whether or not to work challenging for mothers?

One of the most important decisions many mothers face after childbirth is whether to continue in the paid workforce. Acceptance and support of working mothers now represents the majority position in the United States. For example, only one third of survey respondents in 2012 thought that mothers of pre-school children shouldn't work, while more than half of survey respondents believed this in 1988 (Donnelly et al., 2016). Furthermore, for many families, the decision isn't a real choice; they simply need two incomes. In other cases, mothers can't work due to forces outside their control, such as a poor economy or a disability that precludes working. Despite the increased acceptance of working, women of different social classes may receive conflicting messages in terms of whether working is beneficial. Poor Black mothers may be stereotyped as welfare queens and encouraged to go back to work (Foster, 2008), while middle-class, White stay-at-home mothers are likely to be praised (Dillaway & Pare, 2008). Some people assume that maternal employment is bad for children, but research shows that, overall, children do just as well cognitively and emotionally—in some cases, slightly better—when their mothers work as when they stay at home (Goldberg, Prause, Lucas-Thompson, & Himsel, 2008).

In particular, girls whose mothers work can benefit because working mothers provide a positive role model (Goldberg et al., 2008). A meta-analysis indicated that maternal employment was related to higher levels of achievement and fewer problems with depression and anxiety in daughters (Lucas-Thompson, Goldberg, & Prause, 2010). However, this study did indicate small negative effects (on formal test scores) of maternal employment very early in children's lives (e.g., the first year), especially in White and middle-class families.

Such research results point to the importance of generous maternal leave policies (which we'll discuss in Chapter 10). However, one study with low-income Black and Latinx families found that when mothers worked during the first eight months of their children's lives, the children had enhanced social and emotional functioning at age seven, especially in Black families (Coley & Lombardi, 2013). Another advantage of maternal employment is that fathers are likely to spend more time with their children in families where mothers work (Hsin & Felfe, 2014).

In sum, the findings indicate that after children are one year old, maternal employment has beneficial effects. The effects in children under one year of age appear to vary and depend on the specific family situation.

Mothering as Children Grow Up

How do the challenges of mothering change as children grow?

The joys and challenges of mothering continue as children grow, and parents adjust not only their expectations for the children but also their own level of involvement. As children enter middle childhood and, especially, adolescence, they develop more independence from their parents, have more interactions with peers, and are expected to become more autonomous in terms of schoolwork (Steinberg & Silk, 2002).

Adolescence can bring particular challenges for mothers. One study suggests that *parenting* an adolescent is actually more difficult than *being* an adolescent (Steinberg, 2001). In fact, for parents, both life satisfaction and marital satisfaction have been found to decline when children are teenagers, and parent-child conflict continues to be a source of stress throughout a child's adolescence (Steinberg & Silk, 2002). In a study of mostly White, highly educated mothers, the ages 12 through 14 were identified as the most stressful period of parenting (Luthar & Ciciolla, 2016). This is when parents report the most negative feelings toward their children and the lowest levels of life satisfaction; however, mothers of daughters reported slightly higher levels of parenting satisfaction and felt closer to their child.

Parenting doesn't end when children reach late adolescence and young adulthood. Lately, there has been attention to the phenomenon of helicopter parenting—an intensive parenting style targeted at high-school-age and college-age students. One can think of it as intensive parenting for older children. Helicopter parenting has been shown to relate to depression and reduced satisfaction with life among college students (Schiffrin et al., 2014). Intense over-parenting of older children has also been linked to anxiety in parents as well as narcissism and poor coping skills in children (Segrin, Woszidlo, Givertz,

& Montgomery, 2013). Much of the literature on helicopter parenting takes a parent-blaming, particularly a mother-blaming, tone. However, it may be that these parents are responding to their children's needs in providing increased support. In fact, adult children who received intense amounts of emotional and financial support from their parents were more satisfied with their lives in one study (Fingerman et al., 2012). The parents, though, were less satisfied—probably because they were giving more support than they wished to. Overall, helicopter parenting appears to have negative effects on children when it's seen as intrusive and unwanted but more positive effects when supports are needed. However, over-parenting of adult children does not appear to be good for parents.

Conclusion

The transition to motherhood is a huge change in women's lives. It can be a source of both intense stress and intense joy. One source of stress is the dominant ideology that links womanhood with motherhood. Because of this, those who don't wish to or are unable to have children are marginalized. Further, the notion that women are natural mothers means that women are generally held responsible for the majority of child care, expected to engage in time-consuming and intensive parenting practices to maximize their children's outcomes, and are blamed when anything goes wrong with their children. Mothers who don't fit into dominant ideologies of motherhood are stigmatized. Although much of the discourse about motherhood focuses on choices that women are supposed to be making, the social pressures around motherhood mean that many of those choices are actually limited.

The reproductive justice framework introduced at the beginning of the chapter provides one way of conceptualizing what women need in order to have a healthy relationship with motherhood. They need to be able to choose if and when they will have children. They also need supports in order to raise their children in safe and peaceful environments. In Chapter 10, we will further discuss the supports women who have children do and do not receive as they try to combine having children with work roles. In Chapter 14, we'll re-visit some of what mothers and those who support a reproductive justice framework have done in order to advocate for themselves.

Chapter Review

SUMMARY

Reproductive Justice: A Question of Choice

- Many women who are less privileged have limited choices about whether and how to parent.
- The reproductive justice movement supports the ability of all women to be able to make informed choices about motherhood.

Not Being a Mother

- Most women feel pressure to have children, but some choose to be child-free and generally have high levels of life satisfaction.
- There are decreasing negative attitudes toward voluntary childlessness, except in pro-natalist countries.
- Most people have views about abortion that are nuanced and complex.
- Many women have abortions; most women who have abortions are already mothers and come from diverse backgrounds.
- Abortion is related to a range of emotions, but there is no evidence that having an abortion increases the risk for negative mental health outcomes more than bringing an unintended pregnancy to term.

Becoming a Mother

- Understanding their bodies' fertility signs can help women if they wish to become pregnant.
- Women who have difficulty conceiving can become distressed, especially if they value the role of motherhood as central to their identity.
- Assisted reproductive technologies can help women with fertility challenges become mothers. However, use of these techniques can bring up ethical and moral dilemmas.

- Miscarriage is very common, and many women suffer grief in isolation. Stillbirth, while rare, can be psychologically devastating.
- Adoption is a meaningful path to motherhood for many women, but private adoptions are expensive, and more affordable public adoptions rarely facilitate adoption of newborns.
- Women experience a range of feelings about their body while pregnant, and women can have body image concerns both during and after pregnancy.
- Pregnant women often experience unwanted touching and benevolent sexism.
- During childbirth, many women receive unnecessary medical interventions that may make them feel a lack of control over the birth experience.

Being a Mother

- Women may embrace the role of mother but may also feel a sense of identity loss.
- Post-partum depression and anxiety are common, but women are often ashamed to admit their feelings and seek treatment.
- Although breastfeeding is recommended for infants, there are inadequate social supports to help mothers breastfeed and negative attitudes toward breastfeeding in public.
- Those who are unable to breastfeed can experience social disapproval.
- Inequality in the division of household labor and child care increases after children arrive. This is often unanticipated and can lead to decreased marital satisfaction.

- Historically, mothers have been blamed for anything that goes wrong with their children, and poor, single, disabled, and teen mothers continue to be particularly blamed.

- Western society sets high expectations for the involvement of mothers in parenting their children. Feminists seek to support mothers, question mother blaming and intensive parenting, and seek to co-parent with their spouse if they have children.

- There is a double standard whereby White and middle-class women are encouraged to stay at home while poor women of color are encouraged to work. Maternal employment, at least after a child is one year old, is beneficial for children, especially daughters.

- As children develop, their needs change, and parents must adjust to these changes.

KEY TERMS

reproductive justice movement (p. 360)
stratified reproduction (p. 360)
voluntary childlessness (p. 360)
motherhood mandate (p. 361)
post-abortion syndrome (p. 366)
infertility (p. 371)
social mothers (p. 372)
assisted reproductive technologies (ARTs) (p. 372)
intrauterine insemination (IUI) (p. 372)
in vitro fertilization (IVF) (p. 372)
surrogacy (p. 374)

miscarriage (p. 375)
stillbirth (p. 375)
morning sickness (p. 379)
doula (p. 384)
baby blues (p. 388)
post-partum depression (p. 388)
post-partum anxiety (p. 388)
maternal gatekeeping (p. 392)
mother blaming (p. 392)
intensive parenting (p. 394)
attachment parenting (p. 396)

THINK ABOUT IT

1. In what ways has a focus on choice helped mothers, and in what ways has it harmed them? Using the tenets of reproductive justice, what is a better way to talk about motherhood?

2. What are the benefits and costs for women to have children? Based on the research, what things should women consider if they are contemplating having children?

3. Are there any places in your community where women can openly discuss abortion? If so, what helps to promote openness? Based on the research, what actions can you take to decrease stigma around abortion?

4. How do the dominant narratives of childbirth promote or undermine positive birthing experiences for women?

5. How would you address inequality in the division of household labor and child care?

ONLINE RESOURCES

- **Guttmacher Institute** — information regarding the reproductive choices of people of all genders: guttmacher.org

- **La Leche League International** — information and support for mothers who breastfeed: llli.org

- **MomsRising** — activism specific to mothering: momsrising.org

- **Planned Parenthood** — reproductive health care, sex education and information: plannedparenthood.org

- **Sister Song** — a women of color reproductive justice collective: sistersong.net

10
Work

ON A TYPICAL DAY, Machelle Diemart, a high school English teacher at Tulsa Memorial High School, wakes up at 4:30 a.m. and exercises for 30 minutes before heading to school (Covert, 2018). When she gets home at 4:00 p.m., she grades papers until 7:00. After dinner, she turns to lesson planning before going to bed. She also carves out time to teach online courses and classes at her synagogue just so she can "make close to what my husband makes, who's a manager at a Stanley Steemer" (para. 24). However, it wasn't the long hours or low salary that motivated her to join thousands of colleagues in a statewide strike. It was the school condition and her overall concern for the children in her classroom. She said, "The last three years have been horrendous. . . . My classes have 36 kids in them—so many that there aren't enough seats, especially since some chairs are broken" (para. 23). She uses her own money to buy pencils for her students.

It has been a long time since the United States has had massive teacher strikes, but in 2018, teachers walked out in West Virginia, Oklahoma, Kentucky, Colorado, and Arizona (Dastagir, 2018). These strikes indicate that some teachers are becoming fed up with their challenging working conditions and are demanding change. Their efforts seem to be successful. In West Virginia, for example, the teacher's union achieved all of its legislative goals, including pay raises and better funding for health insurance (McAlvey, 2018).

These teachers from Chicago, Illinois, are some of many nationwide who were protesting and striking in 2017 and 2018 in response to low pay and poor working conditions. Look into teacher salaries in your state, and compare them to other professions requiring similar levels of education. What patterns do you see?

Since three quarters of U.S. public school teachers are women (Tale, Goldring, & Spiegelman, 2017), it's not surprising that teachers are facing low wages and are working long hours (Bhattacharya, 2018). The fact that the kind of work that's mostly done by women is both undervalued and underpaid is one of many workplace barriers that women face. In this chapter, we'll explore this as well as other barriers to women's workplace equality. We'll discuss how women and men tend to cluster in different occupations, and we'll review the many explanations for the pervasive pay gap in which women—especially women of color—consistently make less than White men. We'll explore sources of gender discrimination in the workforce, the double bind that women face in evaluations of their leadership, and harassment at work. Finally, we'll discuss challenges that many women face when they combine working with caring for a family.

A Stalled Revolution?

Why do some researchers say that the gender revolution is stalled?

Since the 1970s, women have made great strides in the paid workforce. In 2016, women constituted 46.8% of the paid labor force, compared to 38% in 1970 (U.S. Department of Labor, n.d.). However, as Figure 10.1 shows, most of the gains occurred in the 1970s and 1980s, and women's participation in the labor force has remained at essentially the same level since then. Nevertheless, in terms of total participation in the workforce, women are within a few points of total equality.

Furthermore, most people today support the idea that women should work, and this support has increased since the 1970s. For example, in 1970, 51% of survey respondents indicated believing that it's better if a man achieves and a woman takes care of the family, but only 32% indicated this in the 2010s (Donnelly et al., 2016). Moreover, a Gallup poll released in 2017 showed that, globally, 73% of women and 71% of men felt that women should work outside of the home, but this varied widely by country (Farber, 2017).

However, overall employment rates and general attitudes about women and work tell only part of the story—in reality, equality has not been achieved. Some researchers have called the gender revolution stalled and uneven (England, 2010; Sullivan, Gershuny, & Robinson, 2018). For example, while women have increasingly entered the workforce, men have not been contributing to family life at the same rate as women (Goldscheider, Bernhardt, & Lappegård, 2015).

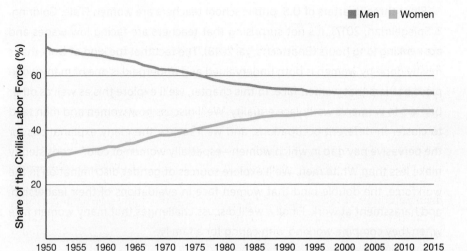

■ Men ■ Women

FIGURE 10.1 Percentages of workforce by gender. Participation in the workforce by women has been slowly converging with that of men over the past 70 years. However, presence in the workforce doesn't tell the full story. Gender inequality remains a problem in terms of salary, power, and status in the workforce.

Note. Data from the U.S. Department of Labor (*https://www.dol.gov/wb/stats/NEWSTATS/facts/women_lf .htm#one*).

Furthermore, as the teacher strikes demonstrate, care work (which is the kind of work that teachers do) continues to be largely done by women and is especially devalued and underpaid (England & Folbre, 1999).

Continued inequality in the workforce is evident from the top to the bottom of the income and status hierarchy. For example, at the top of the hierarchy, as of December 2017 only 25 women (5%) were CEOs of Fortune 500 companies (Wiener-Bronner, 2017), and only 22 of the 100 U.S. senators were women (United States Senate, n.d.). For another high-profile example, only 18% of all directors, producers, editors, and cinematographers of the 250 top-grossing films from 2017 were women (Women and Hollywood, n.d.).

While women are under-represented in high-status jobs, they are over-represented in low-status and low-pay jobs. As the teacher strikes indicated, many women struggle to get by from day to day. In 2016, 12.8% of all women in the United States lived in poverty, but only 9.3% of men did (Patrick, 2017). Other than Asian women, women of color had yet higher rates of poverty: 21.4% of Black women, 22.8% of Native American women, and 18.7% of Latinx women lived in poverty in 2016 (10.7% of Asian women did). Also, 30.7% of women with disabilities lived in poverty. So progress toward equality in work has been made, but gender inequality continues to harm women and their families.

The Pay Gap

How wide is the gender pay gap, and which groups of women are particularly affected by it?

It is widely known that men earn more than women overall. In 2016, women working full-time in the United States earned 80.5% of what men earned (Institute for Women's Policy Research, 2017b). In other words, if a man earned a dollar, a woman earned 80.5 cents. This is an improvement over the 59 cents that women earned for every dollar men did in 1974. However, most progress in this area occurred before 1990, so it's possible to say that the march toward financial equity has stalled. Moreover, overall numbers misrepresent variability in the pay gap. As Figure 10.2 shows, when the pay gap is broken down by race, it's evident that women of color experience a much wider gap, especially in comparison to White men's wages.

Further, women with disabilities earn about 73% less than women without disabilities and 19.2% less than men with disabilities (Jans & Stoddard, 1999; U.S. Department of Labor, 2015). This discrepancy contributes to the high rates of poverty among women with disabilities (Patrick, 2017). Statistics also show that women with disabilities are far more likely to experience involuntary unemployment (DeLoach, 1995; Smith, 2014; Wu & Eamon, 2011) and typically receive less money than men do through federal disability benefits programs (Ruffing, 2018). This is largely because, for those who worked prior to

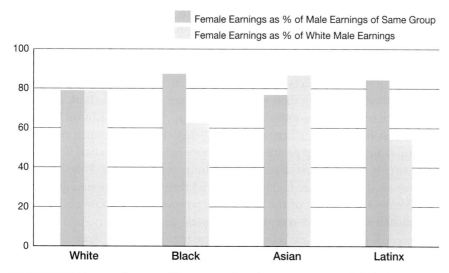

FIGURE 10.2 Pay gap by race. Women earn less than men across racial/ethnic groups. Women also earn less than men sharing their racial/ethnic identity. Black and Latinx women are particularly disadvantaged in terms of earnings, compared to those of White men.

Note. Data from the Institute for Women's Policy Research (2017b).

developing a disability that restricts ability to work, benefit amounts are calculated according to one's lifetime earnings, and women are more likely to have worked in jobs that pay lower wages. Women with disabilities are also less likely than men with disabilities to have had jobs at all, so their benefits are often through a separate program that provides less money.

The pay gap is particularly devastating for low-income women. Although men make up 53% of the workforce, women make up 62% of the people who earn minimum wage or lower (Krogstad, 2014). However, the minimum wage (which was $7.25 an hour as of 2018, although it's higher in some states) is insufficient to pay for the needs of a family. It has been estimated that, in the United States, a single mother with two children earning minimum wage would have to work 138 hours per week in order to make enough to meet her family's basic needs, including housing, food, child care, health care, and transportation (Glasmeier, 2016). That would mean working almost 20 hours every day, seven days a week!

Occupational Gender Segregation

What are the two forms of occupational gender segregation, and how do they relate to the pay gap?

One important reason for the pay gap is that women and men generally cluster in different jobs, and those dominated by women tend to be lower paying. The tendency for women and men to cluster in different professions is known as occupational gender segregation (Hegewisch & Hartmann, 2014). There are two types of occupational gender segregation, both of which contribute to the pay gap. **Horizontal occupational gender segregation** reflects the fact that men and women tend to cluster into different professions. **Vertical occupational gender segregation** reflects the fact that men tend to hold positions with higher status, authority, and pay than women within any given field. Both horizontal and vertical segregation contribute to the pay gap, but we'll focus on horizontal segregation here. Later, when we discuss issues that keep women from being promoted into leadership positions, we'll more fully discuss vertical segregation.

According to a report from the Institute for Women's Policy Research (2017a), women are more highly represented than men in low-paying jobs. For example, in 2016, some of the jobs where women considerably outnumbered men included secretaries, receptionists, nurses, and elementary/middle school teachers. All these jobs are relatively low paying. Men were more likely to be software engineers, managers, and executive officers. They were also more likely to hold blue-collar jobs such as auto mechanics, truck drivers, electricians, and carpenters. Women were three times more likely than men to hold jobs that had poverty-level wages. Further, when jobs require similar levels of education, those where men dominate tend to be higher paid. For example, teaching and software engineering require a similar amount of education, but the median weekly earning for male software engineers in 2016 was $1,863, while female teachers only earned $981. In 2016, janitors, who are mostly men, earned around $50 more per week than maids, who are mostly women, despite the fact that the educational requirements are very similar (Institute for Women's Policy Research, 2017a).

Research shows that the higher the number of women in a profession, the lower the salary of that profession (Cohen & Huffman, 2003; Hegewisch & Hartmann, 2014). This is the case across all skill levels, and although people tend to work a greater number of hours in male-dominated occupations, the differences are evident when looking just at hourly wages (Hegewisch & Hartmann, 2014). For example, women in low-skill, female-dominated occupations (where more than 75% of workers are women) earned 88% of the hourly wage of women working in low-skill, male-dominated occupations. The discrepancy was even more extreme for high-skill occupations; women in high-skill, female-dominated occupations earned 71% of what women in high-skill, male-dominated occupations earned. These findings show that women make more money if they work in traditionally male-dominated occupations. Men who work in female-dominated occupations experience a discrepancy as well. For example, men in high-skill, female-dominated occupations earned only 66% of what men in high-skill, masculine-dominated occupations earned.

The fact that female-dominated jobs tend to pay less is even evident within the same general profession. For example, one study found that civil service positions dominated by men were paid 30% more than civil service positions dominated by women (Cohen & Huffman, 2003). Likewise, managers of female-dominated industries were found to earn considerably less than managers of male-dominated industries (Cohen, Huffman, & Knauer, 2009).

Horizontal occupational gender segregation also intersects with race. In general, White and Asian women are more likely than Black and Latinx women to cluster in jobs that pay higher wages (del Río & Alonso-Villar, 2015; Mintz & Krymkowski, 2010). Further, although White men continue to dominate the most highly paid industries, White and Asian women have made the most progress over time. For Asian women, having a higher level of education tends to move them into occupations that pay more. However, for women of color from other groups, those with a college degree tend to remain clustered in occupations that generally pay less (del Río & Alonso-Villar, 2015).

Horizontal occupational gender segregation also intersects with other aspects of one's social identity, such as sexual orientation. LGBTQ individuals may avoid certain fields, such as education and health care, because they fear negative attitudes or prejudice (Chung, 1995). For example, some gay men avoid jobs in early education or remain closeted for fear that the "creepy pedophile" stereotype might harm their careers working with children (Artavia, 2013, p. 1). In one study, researchers found that LGBTQ participants were more likely than their heterosexual peers to work in the non-profit sector because they perceived this work environment to be less discriminatory than the private sector (Ng, Schweitzer, & Lyons, 2012). This finding aligns with other research showing that job candidates who mention previous experience with LGBTQ campus organizations faced discrimination during the hiring process in certain jobs (Tilcsik, 2011). Workplace environments that require gendered uniforms or job duties can be particularly challenging for transgender individuals (Grant et al., 2011).

Causes of Horizontal Occupational Gender Segregation and the Associated Pay Gap Several factors contribute to women and men clustering in different occupations. Women are more likely than men to choose work that involves caring for other people (England, Budig, & Folbre, 2002). Our society generally sees this work as a natural inclination for women, so it may be seen as less worthy of a high salary. In fact, research has shown that care work pays less than other kinds of work, even after accounting for education and experience (England et al., 2002). Women may pursue careers that involve care work for many reasons. For one thing, they may feel this work plays to their strengths in caring for others. As covered in Chapter 5, this can be due, in part, to gender socialization. For example, toys marketed to girls are likely to involve taking care of babies and working in a kitchen (Blakemore & Centers, 2005). Furthermore, as discussed in Chapter 3, there are many reasons why women are underrepresented in the highly paid STEM fields despite getting higher grades than men in math and science classes all the way through college (Voyer & Voyer, 2014).

Another reason why jobs typically held by men tend to pay more than those held by women has to do with the fact that pay rates for many jobs were set during a time when most employers assumed that women didn't need to earn income to support a family. For example, in 1930, the California Civil Service sent a memo to many companies instructing them to set wages for jobs dominated by women at a lower rate than jobs dominated by men (Kim, 1999). In 1936, when discussing whether to give clerical workers or janitors pay increases, another memo stated that "the clerical workers are more generally the younger single persons not having the same degree of family responsibility" and recommended only giving raises to the janitors (p. 54). In other words, it was assumed that (female) clerical workers were young and single or had a husband supporting them, so they didn't need high wages to support a family in the way (male) janitors did. Setting wages lower for a job held largely by women was perfectly legal and widely practiced before 1963, when the Equal Pay Act was passed (England, Allison, & Wu, 2007). Some sociologists and economists hold that these early discriminatory practices have had a continued effect on current wages since relative wages don't change a great deal over time (England et al., 2007).

Although the Equal Pay Act mandates equal salaries for equal work, it doesn't address horizontal occupational gender segregation and the fact that female-dominated jobs simply pay less. Some feminists want to resist the pay disadvantages associated with horizontal occupational gender segregation and advocate for **comparable worth**, arguing that jobs requiring the same education and skill and giving similar value should be paid the same (e.g., maids and janitors). A class action lawsuit against Washington State invoking comparable worth was filed in 1982 by those who were in jobs (such as education) that were more than 70% filled by women and were being paid less than comparable jobs in fields dominated by men (Mathews, 1985). The court in Washington State awarded the women $400 million in back pay. However, this decision was overturned by the U.S. 9th Circuit Court of Appeals, which held that the state could set rates based on market forces and didn't need to act to end pay discrimination. In another example, the City of Philadelphia was recently paying nurses less than gardeners even though one would be hard pressed to argue that taking care of plants requires more skill or is more important work than taking care of people (England, 2017).

The Effects of Decreasing Horizontal Occupational Gender Segregation

There is some evidence that horizontal occupational gender segregation is decreasing and that women are more fully integrating into all sectors of the economy. For example, between 1972 and 2012, women went from being 4% to 32% of lawyers, and from being 10% to 34% of physicians (Hegewisch & Hartmann, 2014). Even though women and men are moving toward greater integration within many occupations, this shift has been most clear for individuals with a four-year college degree rather than for those with less formal education (England, 2010). There has been considerably less integration in traditionally male-dominated, working-class positions such as construction, plumbing, and truck driving. Further, women of color continue to experience greater horizontal occupational gender segregation. One study showed that highly educated women of color are less likely to work in highly paid, male-dominated fields such as law than are highly educated White women (Alonso-Villar & Cotal, 2013). According to another study, highly educated Black women are more likely to work in management, sales, and the service sector, such as education or health care (Hardy & Jones-DeWeever, 2014).

However, a decrease in horizontal occupational gender segregation may not lead to equalization of salaries. In fact, a comprehensive analysis of 50 years of U.S. Census data revealed that the salaries and prestige of male-dominated professions tends to decrease as women move into them (Levanon, England, & Allison, 2009). For example, between 1950 and 2000, working in parks and being ticket agents changed from being predominantly male to predominately female professions, and salaries dropped by 57% and 43%, respectively. A similar pattern happened when women became designers in large numbers and wages fell 34% as well as when women became more likely to be biologists and wages fell 18% (Miller, 2016).

Horizontal occupational gender segregation isn't the only explanation for the pay gap. In fact, even when women and men work in exactly the same fields, men are typically paid more than women. This is true in both female- and male-dominated fields. For example, in 2016, female elementary school teachers earned 81% of what male elementary school teachers earned, female secretaries earned 85% of what male secretaries earned, and female nurses earned 90% of what male nurses earned (Institute for Women's Policy Research, 2017a). The relative percentages tend to be lower in male-dominated occupations. In 2016, female truck drivers earned 80% of what male truck drivers earned, and female managers earned 77% of what male managers earned. In one study, researchers examined the wage gap within the hospitality sector and noted that women were paid less than men in each domain—including food service, lodging, and recreation (Fleming, 2015). However, the discrepancy was the strongest for management: Female managers earned 26% less than their male counterparts. These differences remained even after accounting for other factors, such as education level and number of hours worked.

Salary Negotiation and the Double Bind

What are challenges women may face when negotiating a salary?

One reason women have lower salaries than men is that women's starting salaries tend to be lower. In many jobs, especially lower-wage jobs, starting salary isn't negotiable. However, for other jobs, especially professional jobs, starting salary is often negotiated. In one study, researchers found that undergraduate men expected their starting salaries to be $4,000 more than undergraduate women did (Hogue, DuBois, & Fox-Cardamone, 2010). They also expected their peak salary to be $33,000 more than women did. Expectations are important because expecting a high salary means that one is likely to negotiate for it. In another study, researchers found that those who negotiated received an annual salary $5,000 higher than those who didn't negotiate (Marks & Harold, 2011). Assuming a 5% increase in pay per year over a 40-year career, for example, a $5,000 difference in starting salary can translate to over a $600,000 difference in lifetime earnings (Marks & Harold, 2011). Furthermore, retirement benefits are often tied to salary, so a lower salary means less in retirement benefits.

Research on gender and negotiation has shown that, compared to men, women expect to make less, are less likely to ask for higher salaries, and are less confident in their negotiation abilities (Kolb, 2009). In one study, researchers found that male MBA students felt they were worth more than their female MBA peers and that they would prove their worth through the negotiation process (Barron, 2003). Women, in contrast, were more likely to be unsure of their

Women are less confident in their salary negotiating abilities, and this can contribute to them making less money than men. Increasing women's confidence in negotiating won't solve this problem, however. Women are actually penalized in ways that men are not if they assertively negotiate a salary—putting them in a double bind.

worth, felt they were only entitled to the same salary as their peers, and hoped to prove their worth through performance on the job.

It might seem that an easy strategy to address these imbalances would be for women to simply become more assertive, increase their sense of self-worth and entitlement, and negotiate like men. However, research has shown that women are more negatively evaluated than men if they negotiate assertively (Bowles, Babcock, & Lai, 2007). This finding can be explained through common gender schemas about what it means to be a woman: Women are supposed to care for others more than themselves, and they're not supposed to think about their own self-interest. In other words, women are supposed to exhibit communal and caring traits, and when they violate expectations they're perceived in a negative light (Kolb, 2009). In this context, women can find themselves in another double bind: There are social costs if they negotiate and financial ones if they don't.

The reality is that women don't have a skill deficit in terms of negotiating; in fact, they are excellent at negotiating for other people. In one study, researchers found that women were able to obtain higher starting salary offers than men were when asked to negotiate for someone else (Bowles, Babcock, & McGinn, 2005). When asked to negotiate for themselves, however, women received lower starting salary offers. The researchers suggested that women weren't seen as advocating for their own self-interest when negotiating on behalf of other people. Instead, they were seen as caring for others—which is consistent with the expected feminine gender role and, therefore, not evaluated negatively. For example, two other studies showed that female lawyers who were assertive on behalf of their clients were not rated negatively (Schneider, 2002; Tinsley, Cheldelin, Schneider, & Amanatullah, 2009). Also, when women acted

your turn

Have you ever negotiated a starting salary or a raise? If so, was it for a professional position? How about for babysitting or lawn mowing? No matter what the job, were you concerned about appearing self-interested? Have you ever noticed the double standard in how people respond to women and men who are negotiating?

assertively to advocate for a raise for their entire work team, they weren't perceived negatively (Tinsley et al., 2009).

Apparently, women are only negatively evaluated for negotiating when the negotiation is seen as self-serving and as violating feminine gender roles. Given these pressures, it's understandable that women end up with lower starting salaries. In this way, the pay gap can be partially explained by the fact that women are less likely to negotiate than men. Of course, for many women who work jobs that pay the minimum wage and cannot be negotiated, these challenges do not apply.

The Motherhood Wage Penalty

What happens to women's wages when they become mothers, and how does this relate to what happens to men's wages when they become fathers?

Some people dismiss the importance of the pay gap by noting that women make certain life choices (e.g., having children) that cause them to ultimately receive lower salaries. However, the pay gap begins too early for this argument to fully explain it. Data from the U.S. Department of Education showed that, averaged across all jobs, women were making 82% of what similarly educated men were making one year after college (Corbett & Hill, 2012). Another study done in Sweden found the wage gap immediately after college to be 12% (Carlsson, Reshid, & Rooth, 2015). Evidence suggests that this early career wage gap reflects horizontal occupational gender segregation, although it may also be influenced by other factors such as differences in salary negotiation (Carlsson et al., 2015).

However, the pay gap widens as women and men progress in their careers. Another study showed that, 10 years after graduation, women made 69% of their male counterparts' salaries (Dey & Hill, 2007). Researchers suggest that the widening pay gap as people's careers progress reflects women's increasing family responsibilities. In one study, women's increased family responsibilities, including motherhood, were found to influence women's decreased willingness to take on higher-status and higher-paying positions as well as their lower likelihood of being promoted within the jobs they held (Goldin, Kerr, Olivetti, & Barth, 2017).

Mothers do earn less than non-mothers; this phenomenon is known as the **motherhood wage penalty**. Research has shown that a mother's hourly wages go down 7.8% for each child she has; when education and experience are considered, the per-child wage penalty is 5% (Budig & England, 2001; Budig, Misra, & Boeckmann, 2012). Although mothers may work fewer hours than non-mothers, this wouldn't explain why these percentages reflect the fact that mothers earn lower wages *per hour* than non-mothers. In fact, one study showed that, for women under age 35, the pay gap between mothers and non-mothers was larger than the gap between women and men (Crittenden, 2001). The motherhood wage penalty varies internationally. For example, in the United Kingdom, the wage penalty for having two children is 25%, while it's only 15% in Germany (Grimshaw & Rubery, 2015). In developing countries, the motherhood wage penalty can be as high as 51%. Moreover, the motherhood wage penalty shows no sign of decreasing (Avellar & Smock, 2003), and it is likely one reason why so many women live in poverty. In other words, it most affects those who can least afford it.

There are many reasons why mothers may make less money than non-mothers. For one thing, there's evidence that employers discriminate against mothers—a topic we'll return to later in the chapter. It's also possible that mothers are unable to advance in their jobs because they're doing so much care work at home (Goldin et al., 2017). For example, they may not apply for a promotion that would involve a lot of travel or increased work hours. They also lose job experience if they take leave from work or switch to part-time work for a period (England, Bearak, Budig, & Hodges, 2016). In fact, research indicates that time away from the workforce explains a great deal of the motherhood wage penalty, especially among highly educated and high-achieving women (England et al., 2016).

While one could argue that these are choices that women make, their decisions must be understood within the context of the fact that women still do most of the housework and child care (see Chapters 8 and 9). In this way, the motherhood wage penalty and inequity in the division of labor reinforce each other. For example, women are more likely than men to reduce work hours because their salaries are often lower than their husbands', but one reason their salaries tend to be lower than their husbands' is that they've cut back at work (England et al., 2016; Goldin et al., 2017).

In contrast, fathers out-earn non-fathers by approximately 11%—although the pay bump for fathers is largest for White men and is nonexistent for Black men (Hodges & Budig, 2010). Researchers partially explain this pay bump by noting that fathers are more likely to be married than non-fathers and that, as we saw in Chapter 8, married men are paid more (Dougherty, 2006). There may be several reasons for mothers' and fathers' different experiences. First, research suggests that women are seen as warmer but less competent when they become mothers (Cuddy, Fiske, & Glick, 2004). However, when men become fathers, they're seen as warmer and more likeable as well as still perceived as competent. Furthermore, the fatherhood wage bonus only affects married, heterosexual men who live with their wives. This may reflect the fact that heterosexual men have internalized the provider role and increase their work hours or productivity in order to facilitate having wives who reduce their work hours in order to focus on caring for the children (Killewald, 2013).

Interestingly, lesbian women who become mothers do not experience a pay decrease; in fact, they experience a pay bonus of up to 20% (Baumle, 2009). This may reflect the perception that they probably have a wife at home to take care of family matters. Furthermore, lesbian couples are more likely to share household labor and child care with their partners in the transition to child care, so a lesbian mother would be less likely to be the sole family member changing work patterns in order to care for a new child (Goldberg & Perry-Jenkins, 2007).

Gender Discrimination at Work

Women don't usually reach the same level of achievement as men, even when they're in the same fields. As discussed earlier, this is known as vertical occupational gender segregation. As Figure 10.3 shows, it is especially the case for

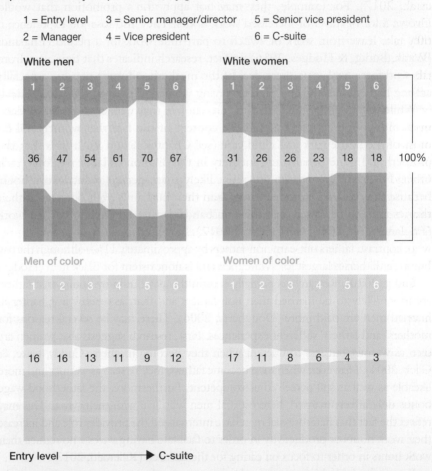

Representation by corporate role, by gender, and by race in 2017, % of employees

1 = Entry level   3 = Senior manager/director   5 = Senior vice president
2 = Manager   4 = Vice president   6 = C-suite

White men

1	2	3	4	5	6
36	47	54	61	70	67

White women

1	2	3	4	5	6
31	26	26	23	18	18	100%

Men of color

1	2	3	4	5	6
16	16	13	11	9	12

Women of color

1	2	3	4	5	6
17	11	8	6	4	3

Entry level ⎯⎯⎯⎯⎯⟶ C-suite

FIGURE 10.3 Women of color in the corporate pipeline. As women, especially women of color, move through the corporate pipeline, they find fewer opportunities for advancement than men do.

Note. Data for 2017 from *https://www.mckinsey.com/featured-insights/gender-equality/women-in-the-workplace-2017*

women of color. Numerous barriers make it challenging for some women to rise to the top of their profession and keep other women stuck at the bottom. Men also have some advantages when they seek to advance, especially if they do so in traditionally female-dominated professions.

The Glass Ceiling and the Sticky Floor

What are the glass ceiling and the sticky floor, and how do they impact women at work?

The invisible barrier that stops many women from rising to the highest levels of leadership has been called the **glass ceiling**. For example, in 2017 women in the United States made up 51% of the population and held 60% of college degrees, 60% of master's level degrees, 47% of law degrees, and 47% of medical degrees (Warner & Corley, 2017). However, even though they made up 44% of the labor force for S&P 500 companies, they filled only 20% of executive and senior officer positions, 20% of board seats, and 5% of CEO roles. In the law field, women accounted for 45% of associates but only 18% of equity partners. In the medical field, they represented 37% of physicians and surgeons but only 16% of medical school deans. Moreover, in 2016, 43% of the highest-earning companies in Silicon Valley had no women at all at the executive level (Warner & Corley, 2017). The glass ceiling is even more significant for women of color. Although these women represent around one third of the female workforce in the United States, they constitute only 3.9% of senior-level managers at Fortune 500 companies. Furthermore, as of 2017, after the departure of Ursula Burns, who had been CEO of Xerox, there were no Black women who were CEOs of Fortune 500 companies (Warner & Coley, 2017).

One could argue that these statistics should change as more and more women receive high levels of education and enter the workforce. However, women have been reaching higher levels of education than men for 30 years—they've received more bachelor's degrees than men since 1988, have earned more than one third of law degrees since 1980, and have outnumbered men in receiving business degrees since 2002 (Warner, 2015). The World Economic Forum (2017) found that, compared to other countries, the United States ranked first in gender equity in educational attainment but 19th in gender equity in economic participation and opportunity. These findings suggest that factors other than education are in play—there are invisible barriers that hold women back.

Some researchers argue that the glass ceiling analogy is inaccurate. They prefer to think of women's pursuit of leadership positions as navigating a labyrinth. In this view, some women do find their way out of the maze and achieve high levels of leadership, but many others find themselves stymied by the twists, turns, and obstacles (Eagly & Carli, 2007). Obstacles include the fact that men are seen as "natural" leaders and the fact that informal social networks and mentoring

Many metaphors are used to illustrate the barriers women face in the workforce, particularly as related to career advancement. Among these are the glass ceiling, the sticky floor, and the labyrinth. Which metaphors have you encountered before? If one or more is new to you, why do you think you haven't encountered them until now? Do any of them particularly speak to your own experiences?

for women are lacking. Another obstacle is the fact that, when women have male partners, their husbands' careers often come first. Moreover, women are expected to be helpful at work but aren't rewarded for their help, and women—especially mothers—can be targets of discrimination at work. These specific issues will be addressed later in this chapter.

Although the labyrinth metaphor acknowledges that not all women are constrained by barriers to advancement, the few women who do advance tend to be exceptional because of the difficulties the labyrinth imposes. Many of these women are tokens (as we discussed in Chapter 3), and their presence in visible, high-power positions can lead to false conclusions that equality has been achieved (Schmitt, Spoor, Danaher, & Branscombe, 2009).

The metaphors of the glass ceiling and the labyrinth that keep women from reaching the highest levels of success are only relevant for women in higher-status positions. Women at the lower end of the pay and status scale are likely to experience a **sticky floor**—that is, the tendency to remain at the bottom of an organizational hierarchy. The sticky floor also involves being in jobs with limited opportunities for advancement. Research has shown that men are more likely than women to be offered promotions from low-level positions and that the sticky floor is a problem for both White women and women of color (Yap & Konrad, 2009). Men tend to move up the ladder faster—for example, they're likely to be promoted to management in fast food and retail settings, while women are more often stuck on the sticky floor as cashiers and salespeople.

The Glass Escalator

How does the glass escalator advantage men at work, and what contributes to its existence?

While women face the glass ceiling and the sticky floor, some men are advantaged by the **glass escalator**. This term refers to the tendency for men to be promoted to leadership positions very rapidly when they work in traditionally female-dominated fields (Williams, 1992). For example, even though there are few male librarians, they represent a large proportion of library directors (Snyder & Green, 2008). Similarly, even though there are few male nurses, they're much more likely to be promoted to administrative positions than are female nurses. Male teachers are more likely to be promoted to school principal. In fact, even controlling for education and credentials, male elementary school teachers are three times more likely to be promoted to school principal than are female elementary school teachers (Cognard-Black, 2012). Moreover, the glass escalator mainly assists middle-class, heterosexual, White men without disabilities (Smith, 2012; Williams, 2013). In other words, being a token male results in benefits for men from socially advantaged groups. For example, White male nurses who participated in one study reported that they were often mistaken for doctors; in contrast, Black male nurses reported that they were often mistaken for janitors (Williams, 2013). Other research has demonstrated that men of color are half as likely to be promoted as White men and that men with disabilities are four times less likely to be promoted than men without disabilities (Woodhams, Lupton, & Cowling, 2015).

Some men in female-dominated professions may gravitate toward more masculine specializations in order to affirm their masculine identity. For example, a male nurse may gravitate toward administration because he sees it as a more "masculine" form of nursing, and he may feel uncomfortable in a stereotypically female-dominated profession or experience pushback about his career choice from friends and family members (Snyder & Green, 2008). However, another reason for the glass escalator may be that men are automatically seen as having leadership qualities, simply because they're men—a phenomenon we'll discuss below. At the same time, though, some scholars argue that the glass escalator is only applicable in jobs that have job security, consistent schedules, and the expectation that one can rise through an organization. Many men, such as those who work in low-wage jobs that don't have consistent

Leaning In

In 2013, Sheryl Sandberg, the chief operating officer of Facebook, wrote the book *Lean In* examining the difficulties women face at work. Sandberg attributed much of the leadership gap to women's low ambitions and their fear that being seen as ambitious might make them unlikeable. She encouraged women to choose partners who will support their careers, to focus on their jobs (e.g., to "lean in"), and not to think about eventually having to leave those jobs until they actually have children and face making that decision. At *leanin.org* women can create "lean in" circles to support one another as they climb the corporate ladder.

However, critics claimed that Sandberg's position only addressed the concerns of privileged White women and that this movement focused on individual women changing themselves rather than on changing broad social practices (hooks, 2013; Slaughter, 2012, 2015). Indeed, *Lean In* didn't discuss the problems of women in lower social classes who struggle to support a family with low wages, largely because traditionally feminine work is undervalued and underpaid. Nor did the book address other social problems such as inflexible work environments and the lack of affordable child care.

What do you think of the "lean in" movement? Is feminism advanced when privileged women break the glass ceiling and become corporate leaders? Is asking women to "lean in" the right solution to discrimination and injustice in the workplace? Is it part of the solution?

schedules or a clear way to be promoted through the ranks, don't benefit from glass escalators (Williams, 2013).

Why Men Are Seen as Leaders: The Double Bind Revisited

What double bind do women often encounter when seeking leadership roles, and how can negotiating this influence women's leadership style?

The traits that many people associate with leadership are agentic ones that are also associated with masculinity. This phenomenon has been conceptualized as a **"think manager–think male" bias** (Schein, 1973). In numerous research studies investigating this bias, participants are asked to rate the qualities of a leader or a manager and then to rate the qualities of both a typical woman and a typical man. Consistently, participants rate the qualities of a manager as being similar to those of a typical man. For example, both men and leaders are seen as ambitious, assertive, and dominant (Fischbach, Lichtenthaler, & Horstmann, 2015; Koenig, Eagly, Mitchell, & Ristikari, 2011; Sczesny, 2003). Women, but not leaders, are seen as possessing communal traits such as modesty, kindness, and intuitiveness. Other research suggests that these attitudes may be implicit—in other words, participants may unconsciously associate being male with being a leader but not report this association if they're asked directly (Latu et al., 2011). However, experimental research suggests that women and men are evaluated differently even when they act identically. For example, when participants listened to someone named "Eric" give advice about how to move a company forward, he was seen as a leader (McClean, Martin, Emich, & Woodruff, 2017). But when someone named "Erica" gave the same advice, she was not seen as a leader.

Because leadership is associated with masculinity, women face a difficult decision. If they act in traditionally masculine ways, they'll likely be seen as effective leaders. However since they violate norms of femininity when doing this, they won't be perceived as likeable. Here is another double bind: Be seen as a leader but unlikeable, or be likeable but not seen as a leader.

As we discussed in Chapter 5, girls learn what's expected of them as girls, and then as women, from a young age. This includes absorbing messages that they shouldn't be too assertive or aggressive. Those who are assertive are called bossy—a word that's not a compliment. Women in leadership positions who are seen as being too assertive are called a different, less flattering, b-word. Hillary Clinton's 2016 presidential campaign provides a good example. Because ambition is considered a masculine quality, the fact that Clinton was seeking the highest public office in the nation could certainly qualify her to be considered ambitious, which the popular press portrayed in a negative way (Tannen, 2016). In fact, in early 2016, if one googled *Bernie Sanders* (Clinton's rival for the Democratic nomination) or *Donald Trump* (the Republican nominee) and *ambition*, one could find positive articles about their ambitious policies. If one googled *Hillary Clinton* and *ambition*, negative articles about "naked," "ruthless," or "pathological" ambition would come up (para. 3). A similar dynamic played out when Australian voters elected their first female minister, Julia Gillard, in 2010. When her rise to power was described as reflecting her ambition, it was often expressed with disappointment, as though people had expected a woman in power to be a kinder and gentler leader than a man (Hall & Donaghue, 2013).

How do women negotiate this double bind? One solution is to combine feminine communal qualities with masculine agentic qualities. For example, it's been suggested that "a woman can finesse the double bind to some extent by combining assertive task behavior with kindness, niceness, and helpfulness" (Eagly & Carli, 2007, p. 164). In a study of women in upper management positions, researchers found that being both aggressive and empathic was related to self-perceived leadership success (Caliper Research and Development Department, 2014). Finding this balance can be tricky, but it's possible. It's another obstacle in the labyrinth that women face on the path to leadership.

Women often face a double bind in which they're either liked by others when they behave in traditionally feminine ways, or viewed as competent and respected leaders when they behave in traditionally masculine ways. Being both liked and respected, however, is a privilege usually only granted to men.

The irony of the negative perceptions of women as leaders is that research has suggested that women may actually be better leaders than men. A meta-analysis of 49 years of research revealed that women are rated as more effective than men in a variety of contexts (Paustian-Underdahl, Walker, & Woehr, 2014). This may occur because women are more likely to exhibit qualities of a **transformational leader** (Eagly, Johannesen-Schmidt, & van Engen, 2003)—someone who inspires others to focus on the mission of the organization and who stimulates optimism and excitement about the organization's future. Such leaders also focus on mentoring their followers and attending to their needs. Transformational leaders have a good understanding of their own emotions as well as those of others—a quality known as emotional intelligence. In fact, researchers have found that women generally have higher emotional intelligence than men, which may positively impact their leadership skills (Mandell & Pherwani, 2003). One reason that women may exhibit emotional intelligence and transformational leadership at work is that they have learned to navigate the tightrope of being both nice and competent.

Networking and Mentoring

How does access to mentors affect women at work, and what is the difference between a mentor and a sponsor?

People often say that it's not what you know, but who you know. In reality, it's harder for women than men to access informal social networks that lead to connections for getting ahead. Some groups of people, for example, have lunch or play golf together. In these settings, those involved engage in **networking**, in which they interact in order to make contacts to further their careers. One problem for women, though, is that a great deal of networking takes place in informal settings, some of which may be explicitly unfriendly to women. For example, a woman working in the financial sector noted, "There was a big social network there that revolved around men's sports and men's activities, and to be on the outside of that really impacted my ability to develop relationships with people" (Eagly & Carli, 2007, p. 145). Liz Featherstone (2004), an investigative journalist, interviewed Walmart employees and discovered that middle managers often met at strip clubs or Hooters, and one female executive was told she probably wouldn't advance because she didn't hunt or fish.

Women may also have a difficult time because the events central to networking, whether formal or informal, often take place after work hours or on weekends (Eagly & Carli, 2007). Men are better able to take advantage of these opportunities because, as discussed in Chapters 8 and 9, they're likely to have partners who take more responsibility for the household and children. In contrast, when women work, they're often still responsible for family life and, therefore, have less flexibility to attend informal social work events or to take advantage of other networking opportunities.

Sometimes, when a woman networks, she can find a mentor or a sponsor. A **mentor** is a person with more experience who can help and guide a person with less experience. A **sponsor** is someone who advocates for a person in order to help that individual get a job or a promotion. Mentors give support and encouragement directly, while sponsors say positive things about the individual when that person isn't present (Dufu, 2013). Finding a mentor isn't easy, and finding a sponsor can be even more difficult. For example, LGBTQ individuals report that lack of other visible LGBTQ workers makes it difficult to identify and connect with mentors (O'Ryan & McFarland, 2010; Parnell, Lease, & Green, 2012). When LGBTQ workers are able to find a mentor who also identifies as LGBTQ, they report higher work satisfaction and greater work advancement (Rumens, 2010).

Some organizations have formal mentoring arrangements, but a LinkedIn survey found that only 19% of women who responded had a mentor (Williams, 2011). Also, research has suggested that women don't benefit from formal mentoring programs as much as men do. A study of women and men who had received MBA degrees found that mentorship corresponded to a salary bump of $9,260 for men in their first post-MBA job, but having a mentor only corresponded to a bump of $661 in women's salaries (Carter & Silva, 2010). Two reasons for this discrepancy were identified. First, men's mentors were more likely to be at a senior level and, therefore, in a better position to advocate for their protégées. Second, men were more likely to have mentors who also acted as sponsors who actively advocated for them. There's a tendency for people in high-power positions to advocate for those who remind them of themselves when they were younger and whom they feel they have a lot in common with (Carter & Silva, 2010). Because there are fewer women in top positions, it's more likely that a high-powered mentor will be male. And even though a high-powered man may be willing to mentor a woman, he may be more comfortable sponsoring another man.

The problem of access to successful mentoring relationships is enhanced for women of color. Because the majority of people in power are not only men but also White men, women of color face a double challenge (Kay & Gorman, 2012). It's noteworthy that research in the field of law has found that formal mentoring arrangements do little to help people of color succeed (Kay & Gorman, 2012). In one study of female Latinx lawyers, researchers found that these women often felt ignored or left out socially due to their outsider status in the workplace (García-López , 2008). Equally important, though, is that when workers with racial/ethnic minority identities have a good relationship with a mentor, there are fewer negative effects if they also experience discrimination at the workplace (Ragins, Ehrhardt, Lyness, Murphy, & Capman, 2016). Being trained to mentor across difference is an important component in successfully mentoring diverse groups of women and is one goal of intersectional feminist psychologists (Chin, Desormeaux, & Sawyer, 2016).

Another way women can support women is through **amplification**. This occurs when one woman makes a comment in a meeting and another woman repeats the idea and gives credit to the original speaker (e.g., "I think Susan's point about XYZ was excellent, and we should consider moving forward in the direction she suggests"). This strategy became popular among female staffers in President Obama's administration (Eilperin, 2016). After the women began intentionally speaking in this way, President Obama began calling on women more frequently in meetings.

Unpaid Work at Work

What else are women expected to do at work other than their work?

In the office, women are often expected to go above and beyond in ways that aren't expected of men. As described in a *Washington Post* article, women are "expected to bring cupcakes for a colleague's birthday, order sandwiches for office lunches, and answer phones in the conference room, even if their job description is far up the ladder from such administrative tasks" (Williams, 2014, para. 5). Women aren't rewarded for these activities, which take time and attention away from tasks that may lead to greater rewards. After all, the person taking notes generally is not able to simultaneously concentrate on making a brilliant suggestion (Fletcher, 1998; Grant & Sandberg, 2015).

Moreover, since women are expected to be communal and act on behalf of others, these contributions to the work environment can simply "disappear" (Grant & Sandberg, 2015, para. 8). In one study, researchers had participants (a) read scenarios about either a female or a male employee who helped another employee or was asked for help but didn't help, or (b) read similar scenarios that gave no information about whether the employee helped or not (Heilman & Chen, 2005). The study participants then evaluated these employees. When male employees were described as helping, they were evaluated more favorably than male employees in scenarios where no information was given about helping. However, when female employees were described as helping, they were evaluated at the same level as women in scenarios where no information was given about helping. Conversely, female employees were rated less favorably when they were described as not helping, but male employees who didn't help were rated no differently from men for whom no information was given about helping. The researchers suggested that women are negatively evaluated for

not helping because helping is seen as part of the feminine role and not doing so violates a gender norm. Conversely, men are praised for helping because it's unexpected from them. Given this situation, how are women supposed to protect their work time without being perceived as unhelpful? One strategy is to frame their inability to help as reflecting a desire to help their team rather than themselves. For example, a woman in a consulting firm learned to say no to unreasonable requests by saying it would take her team past its breaking point (Grant & Sandberg, 2015).

The Glass Cliff

What often happens to women who are promoted into leadership positions?

As we have mentioned, some women overcome all the barriers described above and break through the glass ceiling. However, of those who do this, some may then face the **glass cliff**—that is, the tendency for women to be promoted to leadership positions precisely when a company is in a precarious position or at risk for failure. In fact, research has shown that women tend to be appointed to leadership positions during turbulent financial times, when the company is doing poorly, or when the company has recently experienced a big loss (Mulcahy & Linehan, 2014; Ryan & Haslam, 2005). Women and people of color are also more likely to be promoted in failing firms (Cook & Glass, 2014). An analysis of CEOs from Fortune 500 companies found that women were much more likely than men to be promoted to CEO when the company was at imminent risk of failure (Glass & Cook, 2016). When a company is on the road to disaster and picks a woman to lead it and then fails, the female leader is generally blamed. This occurs even though the problems plaguing the company existed before her appointment. The pattern can, however, lead to an incorrect perception that women are incompetent leaders.

There are many high-profile examples of the glass cliff. For example, Yahoo president and CEO Marissa Mayer was hired after the company lost significant market share to Google (Hass, 2012). In another case, two weeks after the appointment of General Motors' first female CEO, Mary Barra, the company recalled 1.6 million cars due to faulty ignition switches that had been linked to deaths (Covert, 2014b). Barra then spent her early days as CEO testifying in front of the U.S. Congress about mistakes made long before she was placed in charge. The glass cliff occurs outside of the corporate world as well. For example, Katie Couric was asked to be the first female anchor of the CBS Evening News when the broadcast was already in third place in the ratings (Covert, 2014b). Also, Julia Pierson, the first woman to lead the U.S. Secret Service, was hired in 2013 when the organization was in the midst of a high-profile scandal—some of its agents had been accused of hiring prostitutes, and uninvited guests had crashed a state dinner under the previous (male) director (Covert, 2014a). Pierson's leadership of the Secret Service was short lived; she resigned in 2014.

One may consider the phenomenon of the glass cliff to be a compliment to women. Maybe they're seen as particularly skillful at leading during precarious times. In fact, some researchers postulate that women are seen as ideal leaders in a crisis and have supplemented the "think manager–think male" stereotype with a "think crisis–think female" one (Ryan, Haslam, Hersby, & Bongiorno, 2011). Hiring a woman may be regarded as a sign that the company is going in a new direction, and women may be seen as interpersonally skilled and able to take the blame for failed companies (Ryan et al., 2011). Nonetheless, the glass cliff means that women are particularly likely to be promoted to leadership positions just before a company ultimately fails, and some women who do can find that their careers are destroyed.

Further, female CEOs face other barriers that men do not. For example, while male CEOs are also likely to be promoted to chief business officer (CBO), women are considerably less likely to get this kind of dual appointment (Glass & Cook, 2016). As a result, they're less likely to have the support of the board of directors and other senior personnel throughout the organization. Moreover, female CEOs are subject to greater levels of scrutiny than are male CEOs. In one study, women in executive positions described feeling they had to be perfect in every way because every move they made was evaluated (Glass & Cook, 2016). This included looking perfect and dressing accordingly. Many noted that a great deal of attention was paid to their clothing and weight, while no attention was given to the male executives' weight and appearance.

Another study showed that female CEOs were more likely than their male counterparts to come under scrutiny from activist shareholders (those who own more than 5% of the company) who wish to change aspects of the company (Gupta, Han, Mortal, Silveri, & Turban, 2018). Dealing with the demands of activist shareholders can be a source of stress for female CEOs and take up a great deal of their time. The researchers suggested that women come under fire from activist shareholders because these shareholders see women as less effective leaders than men and, therefore, feel compelled to provide unsolicited advice on how to run the company (Gupta, Mortal, & Turban, 2018). In all these ways, even women who break the glass ceiling or successfully navigate the labyrinth face barriers and discrimination.

Workplace Harassment

What are two types of workplace harassment, and how do they affect women in a variety of contexts?

To this point, we've talked about ways that women can be disadvantaged in the workplace, but many women also face explicit sexual harassment at work. There are two types of sexual harassment. **Quid pro quo harassment** occurs when a supervisor requests sexual favors in exchange for workplace benefits such as a raise or a promotion or to prevent negative events such as being fired or demoted. **Hostile work environment** occurs when the atmosphere at the workplace is hostile, intimidating, and/or offensive. Examples of hostile work environments include sexual comments and jokes, comments about women's bodies and clothing, unwanted touching, and sexual advances. Harassment can happen in any work setting and is surprisingly common. A nationally representative survey of women in the United States showed that 81% of participants had experienced some sort of sexual harassment in their lifetime and 38% had experienced it at work (Chatterjee, 2018). A survey of female union members from the United Kingdom showed that over 50% of participants had experienced sexual harassment at work (Trades Union Congress, 2016).

A report by the British trade group Trades Union Congress mentions one woman who anonymously reported on everydaysexism.com that she "used to work in a law firm. Whenever [she] won a case in court, [she] would be lambasted by a particular male colleague who would leer at [her] and make such inane comments as 'You only won because you're wearing a skirt', and 'Did you sleep with the judge then?'" (Trades Union Congress, 2016, p. 11). Despite experiences like this, harassment often goes unreported, and when it is reported, colleagues often minimize it. Another woman commented, "I went to HR about a sexist and flirty CEO. I was told to put up with it as I'm 'young and pretty and they're men, what do you expect?'" (p. 11).

Harassment at work can also be framed as attempted romance. A *New York Times* article by a professor of geobiology chronicled how women in science

Although the Me Too movement gained widespread recognition in 2017 as use of the #MeToo hashtag gained popularity, the movement actually was started in 2006 by Tarana Burke. She has been repeatedly recognized for her advocacy and activist work. Most prominently, she was named, along with other activists collectively called "the silence breakers," as *Time* magazine's 2017 Person of the Year and received the 2018 Ridenhour Courage Prize.

often receive unwanted romantic attention from male colleagues; she noted that this pattern has happened to many of her students (Jahren, 2016). These often start with an email in which the colleague references an altered state of mind ("'It's late and I can't sleep' or 'Maybe it's the three glasses of cognac'"; para. 7)—and then goes on to discuss his feelings of love for her, commenting on her "shiny eyes" or "sparkling hair" (para. 8) or calling her "incredibly attractive" or "adorably dorky" (para. 2). Recipients of emails like these are in an awkward position if the feelings aren't reciprocated because they often come from a supervisor or senior colleague with whom she has to interact regularly, which creates feelings of betrayal and social isolation. In this way, even in the guise of attempted romance, sexual harassment may be a factor that discourages women from pursuing careers in science.

Harassment and gender discrimination at work can be frequent but of low intensity, such as offensive remarks or jokes or mistaking female professionals for lower-level staff. For example, female Latinx lawyers reported, in one study, that other people often thought they were secretaries or custodial staff (García-López, 2008). Harassment can also be more intense but occur less frequently, such as sexual coercion or unwanted sexual attention. One might think that low-intensity but frequent harassment would have a less harmful effect than a single, more severe, incident of harassment. However, a meta-analysis indicated that low-intensity but high-frequency events have effects just as detrimental on job satisfaction, job performance, and mental health as more severe harassment does (Sojo, Wood, & Genat, 2016).

Targets of Harassment Research shows that women of color are more likely to be harassed at work than White women (Berdahl & Moore, 2006). For example, in a study of Black female firefighters, researchers found that these women experienced a great deal of harassment and hostility at work (Yoder & Aniakudo, 1996). Most of the women interviewed reported being called a wide variety of negative names, including "troublemaker," "bitch," "witch," "dyke," "rebel," and "militant" (p. 257). Another study suggested that Black women find sexual harassment by White men to be particularly disturbing, offensive, and frightening, and it is more strongly related to symptoms of trauma than sexual harassment from members of their own race (Woods, Buchanan, & Settles 2009).

Another group of workers who face harassment, but may not feel comfortable defining it as such or reporting it, are immigrants (Maldonado, 2006; Yakushko, 2009). Within the United States, a high number of working immigrants come from Latin American countries (53%), and they are more likely than U.S.-born citizens to be employed in physically demanding and low-paying jobs (Catanzarite, 2002; U.S. Census Bureau, 2004; Zavodny, 2015). Research suggests that immigrants who face harassment are unlikely to report it and are likely to question whether what they're experiencing actually counts as harassment (Welsh, Carr, MacQuarrie, & Huntley, 2006). This is largely because immigrant women are often socially isolated and are concerned about losing a job and resident status if they complain.

Workplace harassment can also be based on sexual orientation. One study showed that women who violated norms of femininity were likely to be labeled as lesbians, just as men who violated masculine norms are often called gay (Konik & Cortina, 2008). **Heterosexist harassment** involves expressing a negative view toward sexual minority identities (gay, lesbian, bisexual) whether or not the target of the harassment identifies as a sexual minority. Other research suggested that harassment based on gender and heterosexist harassment are strongly linked—both attempt to punish those who violate traditional gender norms (Konik & Cortina, 2008). Moreover, a review of the literature found that 27% to 43% of LGBTQ people have experienced workplace harassment or discrimination based on their sexual orientation (Sears & Mallory, 2011). Only one third of participants said they were "out" at work to all their co-workers, and 25% described not being out to anyone at work. Some of the documented incidents of harassment included calling individuals "homo," "pervert," or most commonly "fag," as well as instances of physical violence (p. 11).

Transgender individuals can experience even higher rates of workplace discrimination and harassment. In one review of the literature, between 52% and 78% of transgender individuals across various studies described such experiences based on their gender identity (Sears &

Mallory, 2011). As just one example, a transgender librarian in Oklahoma discovered a flier circulating that claimed that God wanted her to die. Other studies report higher numbers; for example, in a large national sample of 6,450 transgender individuals, 90% reported experiencing harassment at work (Grant et al., 2011). One explanation for such widespread discrimination is that transgender individuals are stigmatized as being mentally ill. In one study, participants were randomly assigned to review a description of a hypothetical job interview in which the applicant was either transgender or cisgender (Reed, Franks, & Scherr, 2015). Participants who reviewed the transgender applicant's interview were less likely to make a hiring recommendation than participants who viewed the cisgender applicant's interview. This decision was largely explained by the participants' inaccurate perception that the transgender applicant had a mental illness.

Currently, there is no federal law in the United States prohibiting workplace discrimination based on gender identity, and only some states, as well as over 200 cities and local towns, provide legal protection for transgender workers (American Civil Liberties Union, n.d.; Beyer, Weiss, & Wilchins, 2014). Although the U.S. Equal Employment Opportunity Commission (EEOC) recently ruled that workplace discrimination directed toward transgender individuals qualifies as sex discrimination (EEOC, n.d.), without an explicit federal law in place it's possible that the Supreme Court could reverse the EEOC ruling. Furthermore, in 2017, the U.S. Department of Justice released a memo stating that transgender individuals were not covered under sex discrimination laws (Moreau, 2017). As of the writing of this text, the EEOC is at odds with the Department of Justice, and it remains unclear how this will affect transgender individuals in the workforce.

Harassment and Hypermasculine Environments Harassment is likely to occur in environments that are traditionally masculine (Chamberlain, Crowley, Tope, & Hodson, 2008; Gruber, 1998). Further, those who harass are likely to hold hostile sexist attitudes and endorse hypermasculinity (Maass, Cadinu, & Galdi, 2013). The motivation for those who do the harassing can be sexual, but it can also be to assert power or feel more confident in their masculine gender identity (Maas et al., 2013). One study showed that women who were more masculine, rather than feminine, were more likely to be harassed. This was interpreted to mean that harassment is a way to put women who challenge men's power, or "uppity women," into their "place" (Berdahl, 2007, p. 425). Those who perpetrate harassment generally minimize what they're doing and see it as a form of fun and flirty banter. In fact, one study showed that endorsing the belief that harassment was simply fun banter was related to increased hostile sexism and increased intentions to commit sexual harassment in the future (Page, Pina, & Giner-Sorolla, 2016).

Computer coding is one example of a field with a hypermasculine culture that breeds a hostile environment for women. The industry is known for the predominance of "brogrammers"—that is, men who combine technology prowess with masculine, fraternity boy behavior and a desire to get rich quick (Kumar, 2014, p. 28). Although brogrammers may not recognize that they exclude others because they see themselves as "nerds" and, therefore, as socially excluded themselves (Tufekci, 2014), the brogramming culture can be very hostile toward women. For example, Ashe Dryden, a consultant about diversity in technology, said, "I've been a programmer for 13 years, and I've always been one of the only women and queer people in the room. I've been harassed; I've had people make suggestive comments to me; I've had people basically dismiss my expertise. I've gotten rape and death threats just for speaking out about this stuff" (Miller, 2014, para. 11).

Culture change is a necessary part of reducing workplace harassment. As society becomes less accepting of hostile work environments and those who contribute to them, toxic workplaces will become less common. While individuals may continue to engage in harassment, if the environments and organizations they find themselves in don't tolerate this behavior, harassment will decrease. In workplace environments that do not tolerate harassment it is the harasser, rather than the individual being harassed, that will experience negative consequences as a result of the harassment.

Balancing Work and Family

What is the difference between viewing work and family as being in conflict and viewing them as being mutually enriching?

Women in the workplace aren't just workers. They're often also spouses, children, and parents. Yet many women find it difficult to achieve work–life balance and can face obstacles when they try to do so. Combining work and family life can be beneficial. Research has

spotlight on . . .

Transgender Individuals Informing Workplace Discrimination

Some transgender people are uniquely positioned to observe gender discrimination in the workplace because they stay in the same job after they transition (Budge, Tebbe, & Howard, 2010). As a result, they can compare how they're regarded as both a woman and a man. Ben Barres, a biologist at Stanford University who spent most of his life living and working as Barbara Barres, noticed that people took him more seriously after he transitioned to a man. For example, a colleague who didn't know that Ben and Barbara were the same person commented: "Ben gave a great seminar today—but then his work is so much better than his sister's" (Nordell, 2014, para. 5).

In interviews with transgender men, sociologist Kristine Schilt (2010) noticed how much more respect they received after transitioning. Women who were considered aggressive became transmen who were respected for their take-charge attitudes. In contrast, transwomen started to experience gender discrimination. Joan Roughgarden, another biology professor at Stanford, lived much of her life as Jonathan Roughgarden. Since her transition, she has been accorded significantly less respect. "You get interrupted when you are talking, you can't command attention, but above all you can't frame the issues" (Vedantam, 2010, para. 32). Because Joan is in the same department as Ben, she can compare their situation: "Ben has migrated to the centre, while I have had to migrate to the periphery" (para. 32).

Parents can find it challenging to balance the demands of their job with the demands of their family—particularly as related to child care. Since women typically do more child care than men, this is an especially important issue for women. However, with the right structural supports, work can enhance family life, and family life can enhance one's experience at work.

shown that women who stayed in the workplace after they had children enjoyed greater physical and mental well-being than those who interrupted their careers, worked part-time, or stayed at home after having children (Frech & Damaske, 2012). This finding may seem counterintuitive because many people believe that mothers who work experience **work–family conflict**, which occurs when work interferes with family obligations or family life interferes with work. Although many women do experience work–family conflict, it isn't an inevitable consequence of combining work and family. Instead, some women experience benefits associated with being involved in multiple roles. **Role enhancement theory** states that when people are engaged in multiple roles (e.g., worker, mother, sister, friend), they actually find that they have more energy and their well-being is enhanced by being so involved and engaged (Castro & Gordon, 2012).

One way in which role enhancement occurs is through **work–family enrichment**, a two-way process in which what happens at work benefits family life and what happens in the family benefits work (Greenhaus & Powell, 2006). For example, the money earned at work can help provide opportunities for one's children. The social support received at work can help manage family stress; for example, if one's children have been difficult, telling a supportive colleague can reduce stress. Family life can also positively benefit work. Organizational or planning skills honed at home can be applied in the work setting, and patience learned at home can help if one is managing others at work (Ruderman, Ohlott, Panzer, & King, 2002). For example, a therapist reported that learning how to deal with her toddler's tantrums helped her also deal with tantrums from her adult clients (Liss & Schiffrin, 2014).

A Question of Choice?

How does framing work–family balance as depending on women's choices constrain the ways people can approach this topic?

People commonly think about work–family balance as involving choices that women make. The conversation is often framed around women's choice to stay in the workforce, opt out, or work part-time. However, as we've seen throughout this text, women don't make free and unconstrained choices. Their choices surrounding work–family balance are often limited by discrimination, inflexible work environments, and/or low pay that doesn't cover the cost of child care (Stephens & Levine, 2011; Stone, 2007). Furthermore, very few people discuss with the same level of attention the choices that *men* have to make about how to balance work and family.

When women's decisions about work are framed within the language of "choice," people are less likely to pay attention to sexist practices that constrain those choices. In one study, undergraduate students were shown posters about a book titled *Choosing to Leave: Women's Experiences away from the Workplace*, while others saw an almost identical poster about a book titled *Women at Home: Experiences away from the Workplace* that didn't mention choice (Stephens & Levine, 2011). Those who saw the poster about choices were significantly more likely to report believing that women and men have equal opportunities and that gender discrimination no longer exists. Interestingly, other research has shown that priming the idea of choice in other contexts decreases empathy toward members of marginalized groups, increases victim blaming, and decreases support for policies that increase the common good, such as reducing pollution (Savani, Stephens, & Markus, 2011).

Women's choices around work and family are constrained for many reasons that we'll discuss in detail in the following sections. First, women continue to be more responsible for household responsibilities and child care (Coltrane, 2010). Second, the workplace generally isn't designed for people who want to balance work and family (Blair-Loy, 2003). Further, mothers and caregivers experience discrimination within the workplace (Williams Manvell, & Bornstein, 2006). Finally, the lack of parental leave and inadequate child care makes it extremely difficult for many workers to combine their work and caregiving roles (Stone, 2007; Williams et al., 2006).

These constraints make balancing work and family difficult, especially in the United States. In fact, the United States ranks in the bottom eight of Organisation for Economic Co-operation and Development (OECD) countries in terms of work–life balance (OECD, n.d.-b). Countries that rank lower are Turkey, Mexico, Chile, Korea, Israel, Japan, and Australia (OECD, n.d.-b).

Women's Responsibility for Care

How does the fact that women do most of the care work make it difficult to balance work and family?

Theoretically, the ability to be actively involved in multiple roles and combine work and family should be an issue that both women and men face. After all, both women and men combine parenting and work roles. However, the

Having It All

Many young women have heard that they're supposed to try to "have it all" and seamlessly balance a successful career and a blissful family life. This may sound like an empowering message—women can (and should) be able to have both a fulfilling career and a family life. However, encouragement to "have it all" has made many chafe at the pressure it puts on women. In the *Huffington Post* article "Having it all kinda sucks," journalist Amy Westervelt (2016) noted sarcastically that "no woman (or man, for that matter) ever said, *hey, you know what would be great? If I could get up at 5 a.m., make breakfast for everyone, then get dressed (with heels, natch), drop my kids off at daycare, go to work for 10 hours, pick the kids up, come home, cook dinner, clean up, put the kids to bed, work in*

It can be hard to have it all when you're being told to go in four different directions at the same time.

bed 'til midnight so I don't get behind at work, then do it all again tomorrow on 5 hours sleep" (para. 26). It's possible that the goal to "have it all" has increased the extent to which women who work outside the home are overburdened and overwhelmed. In fact, some conservatives have blamed the feminist movement for putting too much pressure on women by telling them they're supposed to "have it all" and then failing to deliver (Szalai, 2014). In fact, after Anne-Marie Slaughter quit her job in the State Department to spend more time with her family, she famously wrote an article for *The Atlantic* noting that women actually could *not* have it all (Slaughter, 2012).

Have feminists let women down by selling them a bill of goods that they can't cash, or is there a greater need for feminism in order to finish the march for equality? As Gloria Steinem said, "The idea of having it all never meant doing it all. Men are parents too and actually women will never be equal outside the home until men are equal inside the home" (quoted in Fine, 2010, p. 89). As we have seen, gender equity has yet to be achieved. Although women have made strides in the workforce, as we saw in Chapters 8 and 9, men haven't taken responsibility at home in equal measure.

Instead of telling women they're supposed to have it all and admonishing them if they don't, perhaps it would be more empowering to change the narrative so that both women and men can have fulfilling careers and family lives. What do you think? Is it empowering or oppressing to encourage women to "have it all"? Moreover, why do you think people never talk about men "having it all"?

responsibility for family life often falls disproportionately on women. Worldwide, according to the latest available data from the Organisation for Economic Development and Co-operation, women spend 4.5 hours per day on unpaid work, including cooking, cleaning, and child care—double what men spend (OECD, n.d.-a). Men spend more time on paid work and in leisure activities. As discussed in Chapter 8, the practice of women coming home from their jobs and doing another round of work in the home is called the *second shift*.

Research indicates that patterns of domestic behavior can have intergenerational effects. For example, when fathers do more domestic work around the house, their daughters have been found to hold higher, and more nontraditional, career aspirations than daughters in families where fathers do less domestic work (Croft, Schmader, Block, & Baron, 2014). In other words, the daughters don't assume that having a family means they'll have to do all of the household work.

Another source of unpaid work for many women is caring for elder relatives. Adult daughters (as opposed to sons) are often primarily responsible for the care of their parents. For many women, elder-care responsibilities begin while they're still raising their children; this has led to the term **sandwich generation** to describe individuals, primarily women, whose work and hobbies need to fit between these two care-giving demands. For some women, elder-care responsibilities begin just as their children are becoming more independent, so these women may have had an opportunity to focus more fully on their careers if they didn't have to take on elder-care. Research has suggested that informal care provided to adult relatives greatly influences women's time available to devote to work. One study showed that women ages 55 to 67 who provided care to their parents reduced their work hours by almost half in order to do so (Johnson & Lo Sasso, 2006).

The fact that women have more responsibilities at home contributes to inequality at work. Many workplaces function under an outdated model in which an ideal worker is assumed to have no responsibilities at home because a partner (i.e., wife) takes responsibility for the home and children (Blair-Loy, 2003). Studies have, in fact, shown that having a stay-at-home spouse, which is more likely the case for men, is related to career success (Kirchmeyer, 2006; Schneer & Reitman, 2002). One executive noted how inequity in home life makes it easier for men than women to advance: "I saw that the older white, male partners who mentored the younger white, male associates were able to work long days and excel professionally precisely because their stay-at-home wives took care of everything else; I saw that virtually none of the female partners had a similar setup" (Filipovic, 2016, para. 13).

Having someone stay at home and take charge of domestic tasks is invaluable if one wants to reach the highest levels of success at work. In fact, in 2012, 7 out of 18 female CEOs of Fortune 500 companies had stay-at-home husbands

your turn

If you're married or in a long-term, committed relationship, how have you and your partner negotiated whose career is most important? (For example, who would move for the other person's career? Who, if anyone, would take time off from work if there were children to care for?) Was this the result of an explicit discussion, or is it a pattern that developed over time?

If you're not yet married or in another type of committed partnership, do you expect that your career or your partner's career would be most important? Why? Do you think your partner will have the same views or a different view?

When should partners have these types of discussions?

(Hymowicz, 2012). Others didn't have children or hired others to do the bulk of the child care. This points to the fact that it helps to have a full-time partner who takes responsibility for domestic labor in order to succeed at a demanding corporate job. The issue becomes even more challenging if women with male partners have children because, as we saw in Chapter 9, inequality in the home increases when children are born (Katz-Wise, Priess, & Hyde, 2010).

Inflexible Work Environments

How do inflexible work environments make it difficult to balance work and family?

A major barrier to women's ability to successfully combine work and family life is that the workplace isn't organized to facilitate it. In corporate environments, there's an expectation for long work hours done at the office in full sight of others and, often, an expectation for working more than 50 hours a week (Williams & Cooper, 2004). One study showed that the average worker in the United States put in 47 hours per week in 2014, and four in ten participants reported working more than 50 hours per week (Saad, 2014). In contrast, in the European Union, regulations limit the work week to 48 hours and provide at least four weeks of paid vacation annually.

Overwork can have negative consequences for both high- and low-income workers. For high-income workers subject to competitive pressure, long hours can be seen as a badge of honor and a sign of commitment to the workplace (Williams & Boushey, 2010). A worker from the Silicon Valley noted: "Guys try to out-macho each other. . . . There's a lot of see how many hours I can work, whether or not you have a kid. He's a real man; he works 90-hour weeks. He's a slacker; he works 50 hours a week" (Cooper, 2000, p. 382). One study interviewing workers at a consulting firm found that many men carved time out of their work day to meet family obligations, but they did so informally while still giving the impression of working long hours (Reid, 2015). Women, on the other hand, were more likely to ask for flexible work arrangements in a formal manner, and they were often penalized for this.

The expectation for long hours can drive women out of the workforce, even after they've invested considerable time and effort in their careers. A study of female Harvard graduates, many of whom delayed childbearing in order to focus on their careers, showed that those who worked in organizations that weren't family friendly were much more likely to leave the workforce than those who worked in more family friendly occupations (Herr & Wolfram, 2012).

This tendency was described in a *New York Times Magazine* article as *opting out* (Belkin, 2003), but it's only an option for those who have partners with sufficiently high incomes to support the family. Many women can't afford to stop working even if they'd like to. Moreover, sometimes women with very low wages cannot afford *to* work, given the high costs of child care.

Lower-income workers also put in long hours. Since minimum wage jobs don't pay enough to support a family, many low-income workers need multiple jobs in order to provide for their families (Williams & Boushey, 2010). Also, while higher-income workers may value flexibility such as the ability to work some hours from home or on their own schedule, lower-income workers often lack stability in work hours. Their hours may fluctuate from week to week, which means they're unable to organize child care in a stable and consistent manner. For example, although Starbucks claims to provide at least a week of notice for schedules, a reporter found that many workers interviewed reported being given less than a week and some were given only one day of notice (Kantor, 2014). In order to get a full-time schedule at Starbucks, workers must make themselves available for 70% of the hours the store is open—in other words, about 80 hours a week (Gross, 2008). Yet when the stores aren't busy, they may send workers home unpaid. Furthermore, work hours at retail stores are often late in the day and on weekends, when typical child-care centers aren't open (Kantor, 2014). This can cause problems for working mothers. For example, a woman who worked as a manager at Walmart was called to work on an inconsistent, as-needed basis. As a result, she had to have her mother move in with her in order to be able to work and care for her child. In fact, low-income workers often rely on a patchwork of care from family members, friends, and community organizations (Williams & Boushey, 2010).

Discrimination against Mothers

How does discrimination against mothers make it difficult to balance work and family?

Another barrier to work–family balance is explicit discrimination against mothers. This occurs not just in pay, as described previously, but in how mothers are perceived and evaluated. The discrimination that mothers experience in pay and promotion has been called the **maternal wall** (Crosby, Williams, & Biernat, 2004). Such discrimination is rarely obvious because, when employers make negative judgments about women who are mothers, they usually find other reasons to explain those judgments. For example, they may say that the woman is less committed to her job or a poor fit for the company (Richardson, 2013). Mothers also are likely to face higher standards than non-mothers.

In one study, in which participants evaluated applications that were identical except for parenthood status, mothers were judged more harshly than non-mothers (Correll, Benard, & Paik, 2007). For example, if the applicants were mothers, participants said they would have to receive a higher score on a management exam to be recommended for a job, and they would be allowed to miss fewer days of work before they would no longer be recommended. Fathers, in contrast, suffered no such penalties and were actually accorded some advantages. They were offered higher salaries than non-fathers, were seen as more committed than non-fathers, and were allowed to miss work significantly more often than non-fathers. One study of women in a law firm showed that more than half said they felt their co-workers treated them differently after they had children, and one fourth said they had been demoted, taken off of work assignments, or lost out on promotions after having children (Richardson, 2013).

Women can also experience discrimination while they are pregnant. The Pregnancy Discrimination Act of 1978 prohibits discrimination based on pregnancy and requires employers to treat pregnant women in a similar manner to a non-pregnant employee with a similar ability to work (Siegel, 2018). It does not, however, require that employers accommodate pregnant women by, for example, changing the job so they don't have to lift heavy objects, allowing for rest times, adjusting work stations for comfort, or allowing time off for pre-natal exams since these accommodations are not given to other workers. In one case that went to the U.S. Supreme Court, a UPS worker was told by her doctors that she was not able to lift more than 20 pounds, so she was fired because her job required her to lift up to 70 pounds. However, UPS gave other workers in different situations (e.g., those with disabilities or injuries) other jobs that involved lighter lifting. Although the district court ruled for UPS, the ruling was overturned when the Supreme Court ruled in favor of the UPS worker (Spiggle, 2015). It is also noteworthy that while the Pregnancy Discrimination Act does protect some women, it doesn't protect transgender men who become pregnant because the language of the act refers to "women" (Currah, 2008).

Women who become mothers are also often treated poorly at work when they return after giving birth. According to one report, a woman returned to work and faced consistent warnings not to get pregnant again as well as complaints when she had to take her child to medical appointments (Williams & Boushey, 2010). Eventually, her (female) supervisor asked her to find a pediatrician who had hours available after work. According to the same report, it's common for women to be passed over for promotions and to see men with considerably less experience get promoted ahead of them. Court records indicate that women from a variety of professions, including "a bank vice president, an attorney on a partner track, an assistant medical director, a hotel regional manager, and a national sales director," have been denied promotions or demoted because they are mothers (p. 58). One lawyer complained: "I had a baby, not a lobotomy" (p. 58).

Overall, across the income spectrum, discrimination against mothers and caregivers makes balancing work and family difficult, and not simply because of time spent out of the office. In her article on (not) having it all, Anne-Marie Slaughter (2012) pointed out that if co-workers left the office early in order to train for a marathon or observe a religious holiday, they were given more respect than someone who had to leave in order to care for a child.

Parental Leave

How do inadequate parental leave policies make it difficult to balance work and family?

Another reason it is difficult to balance work and family is that, in the United States, there are fewer social policies that support families than in other countries. One important example of this is the lack of paid leave for parents. As of 2015, the United States was the only industrialized country without a national policy to give paid parental leave (Livingston, 2016). In the United States, the decision whether or not to offer paid leave is left up to individual employers. In 2016, only 14% of civilian U.S. workers were offered paid family leave (Desilver, 2017); 88% had access to unpaid leave. Low-wage workers are the least likely to have access to paid leave (Adema, Clark, & Frey, 2015), and the lowest rates of leave are in the construction and leisure/hospitality sectors (Desilver, 2017). Data suggest that most Americans (82%) do, however, believe mothers should get paid leave after the birth or adoption of a child (Stepler, 2017).

The United States does have the Family Medical Leave Act (FMLA). This legislation provides 12 weeks of unpaid leave for the birth, adoption, or foster care placement of a child. It can also be used for personal illness or to care for a sick family member. However, many workers cannot afford leave without pay. Additionally, in order for FMLA to apply, the company must employ over 50 workers, and a person must have worked over 1,250 hours at the organization. Given these requirements, FMLA doesn't apply to approximately 40% of the workforce (Adema et al., 2015; Walsh, 2011).

Paid leave provides enormous benefits to mothers, children, businesses, and the economy. It increases women's ability to continue working, which allows them to provide for their families, stimulates economic growth, and saves businesses the costs of hiring and training new workers (Adema et al., 2015). Paid leave is extremely important for the mental and physical health of both mothers and children. Research has indicated that being in a job with little or no paid leave is related to increased depression in mothers and decreased ability to bond with their children (Aitken et al., 2015; Avendano, Berkman, Brugiavini, & Pasini, 2015; Chatterji & Markowitz, 2012). Paid leave has also been linked to a decrease in infant mortality (Tanaka, 2005), perhaps due to decreased maternal stress, as well as to positive physical and mental health in children.

When women return to work before their children are 12 weeks old, the babies are less likely to be breastfed, less likely to make it to their regular checkups at the pediatrician, and more likely to have behavioral problems (Berger, Hill, &

Waldfogel, 2005). In fact, women who must return to work early often have difficulty breastfeeding. In interviews with Human Rights Watch, women described inadequate support at work for pumping breast milk such that they pumped in "bathrooms, copy rooms, shared kitchens, bulk closets, a gymnasium, a phone booth, an equipment storage room, a photography studio, a mail truck, and an exam room" (Walsh, 2011, p. 55).

Fathers as well as mothers can benefit from paid leave. In contrast to the lack of paid paternity leave in the United States, most countries in the European Union have paid leave policies that are quite extensive—for example, 3 months paid paternity leave in Sweden, 90 paid days off in Iceland, 2 weeks paid leave in the United Kingdom, 15 paid days off in Spain, and 11 paid days off in France (Kelly, 2016). There is also paid leave in countries throughout Africa, Latin America, the Middle East, and Asia—for example, 4 days in Rwanda and Uganda, 5 days in Brazil and Chile, and 1 day in Saudi Arabia (International Labour Office, 2010).

Research in Sweden has indicated that when fathers take leave, they spend more time interacting with their children and have a better relationship with them (Haas & Hwang, 2008). In a different study, fathers in the United States who took at least two weeks off from work to help care for their infants were found to be more involved in all aspects of child care nine months later, including feeding, bathing, diapering, dressing, and getting up with the baby during the night (Nepomnyaschy & Waldfogel, 2007). This is important because fathers' involvement in child care has been found to relate to marital stability and happiness, including more satisfying sexual relationships (Carlson, Hanson, & Fitzroy, 2016; Kalmijn, 1999). It also benefits children as those with involved fathers are likely to develop faster as infants and to have greater well-being, higher cognitive skills, greater social competence, and fewer behavioral problems than those whose fathers are less involved (Amato & Rivera, 1999; Cabrera, Tamis-LeMonda, Bradley, Hofferth, & Lamb, 2000; Kim, Kang, Yee, Shim, & Chung, 2016). These effects are above and beyond those of other factors such as income and maternal involvement.

Fathers in the United States rarely have the opportunity to take leave. According to a national study of employers, only 14% of companies in the United States offer any leave for fathers (Matos & Galinsky, 2014). Moreover, men report being hesitant to use paternity leave because the practice is uncommon, so those who take it are very noticeable (Lieber, 2015). Yet when women take leave but men do not, women are penalized and perceived as less committed to their job.

It should be noted that some countries have extremely long maternal leave policies and that this may not be the best option if one hopes to achieve gender equality. For example, in Hungary, women are paid 70% of their wages for three years in order to take care of their children (Mandel & Semyonov, 2005; Weller, 2016). However, in countries like this with very long maternity leave, women earn considerably less money than men and are less likely to be

Many fathers take an active role in caring for their children. Workplace policies that facilitate fathers' involvement with child care make it easier for them to actively participate in day-to-day parenting tasks. These policies benefit fathers, mothers, and children—as well as the companies themselves.

in managerial positions. Also, explicit discrimination against mothers is evident in these countries. For example, a bank executive in Hungary said that "if you decide to have a baby, your job is over because no one will wait for you for three years" (Glass, & Fodor, 2011, p. 16). Overall, while providing some paid leave is important, extended leave that is only available to women isn't the optimal solution.

Child Care

How does the high cost of child care make it difficult to balance work and family?

Parents who work need child care. In the United States, 11 million children are in some sort of child care every week (Child Care Aware of America, 2017). Center-based child care is extremely expensive, although it varies tremendously from state to state. For example, a year of center-based care for an infant in 2016 was the most expensive in Massachusetts at $20,125 and was the least expensive in Mississippi at $5,178 (although this was still more than the average cost of a mortgage in Mississippi). In the Northeast and Midwest, child care was the highest family expense; in the West and the South, it was only exceeded by housing costs. To give a different perspective, the average annual cost of center-based care for an infant was higher than tuition and fees at a four-year public college in 28 states.

A single mother of an infant and school-age child described her financial situation: "Almost half of my paycheck goes to daycare. I pay $208 a week for my son and $25 a week for [my] daughter to go before and after school. Obviously I have to work but some days it really doesn't seem worth it. I love the daycare center they are in, they do an amazing job. But it's hard to live when daycare is almost $1,000 a month" (Child Care Aware of America, 2015, p. 31). For people living at or near the poverty line, center-based child care is truly unaffordable. For example, a Massachusetts resident living at the poverty line would have to pay 99% of her salary to put one infant in center-based care (Child Care Aware of America, 2017). Even for those who can afford child care, quality is an issue. One study showed that the most consistently poor-quality child care served areas where families were between poor and middle income, earning $15,000 to $40,000 a year (Williams & Boushey, 2010).

Child-care challenges are further complicated by the fact that about 20% of the U.S. workforce is on a non-standard schedule, such as working evenings or nights (Enchautegui, Johnson, & Gelatt, 2015). These are generally workers who receive low pay and few benefits. People on a non-standard work schedule have a particularly difficult time finding consistent child care. One divorced single mother with seven- and nine-year-old children relied on nine different adults, including her sister, a neighbor, and a grandmother, to watch her children while she was at work (Williams & Boushey, 2010).

There is some federal funding for child care in the United States. Child Care Development Block Grants (CCDBG) are given to states to subsidize child care for low-income families, and parents generally have to pay a portion of the child-care costs. These grants are given to approximately 1.5 million families, yet five times as many families are eligible but remain unfunded (Williams & Boushey, 2010). Funding for CCDBG hasn't gone up since 2002, despite states seeing higher demand. As a result, states have tried to stretch their dollars by offering lower reimbursement rates for providers, increasing the family contribution to the point that it becomes unaffordable for many families, or tightening the eligibility criteria so that fewer families are served.

The U.S. government does have other policies that can help parents alleviate the cost of child care. For example, there are tax breaks for child-care costs. However, this is no help to the many low-income Americans who don't pay federal taxes because their incomes are lower than the standard federal deductions. The effort to improve child care, as well as parental leave, has largely been taken up by individual states and corporations. We'll discuss some of these initiatives in Chapter 14.

One approach to child care that's available to wealthy women involves hiring other women to work as nannies. Highly educated women often hire female immigrants to care for children (Cortes & Pan, 2013). Only six states have legislation that protects the rights of domestic workers, so it's often the case that they are not provided a minimum wage or overtime pay, do not get health care coverage, and do not receive protection from harassment (Aviv, 2016). For example, one woman was paid $375 to care for two girls around the clock five days a week. As she described, "Mothers and daughters leave their families so they can do the type of 'women's work'—caring for the young, the elderly, and the infirm—that females in affluent countries no longer want to do or have time to do" (p. 3). This practice has led some scholars to note that immigrant women are often the ones helping wealthy women to "have it all" (Furtado, 2016). In fact, fertility rates of upper-class, U.S.-born women are higher in areas with a large population of female immigrants (Furtado, 2016). Thus, issues of work–family balance can exacerbate inequality between different groups of women. Social policies designed to improve the work lives of all women would help to alleviate these disparities.

Conclusion

In this chapter, we've explored barriers that keep women from fully achieving in the workplace. These barriers affect women across the income spectrum in different ways, but they are particularly devastating for low-income women who struggle to meet their families' needs. However, some people are advocating for change. There is increasing awareness of the importance of allowing women to thrive in the workplace and how this benefits them, their families, and their employers. The Me Too movement has shined a spotlight on the problem of sexual harassment and sexual assault in the workplace. By reading this chapter, you now have more tools to better understand these challenges as well as some ideas about how individuals and organizations can overcome them.

try it for yourself

Talk to a number of people who have children and work. Try to speak with people with different social identity characteristics, including gender identity, who work in a variety of occupations with different work expectations. Ask them how they balance work and family responsibilities. What barriers to work–family balance do they talk about? Do you notice any consistent themes? Do barriers cluster according to gender or type of employment (e.g., hourly, salaried, commission)? How do these people address the barriers? How does this activity influence your own thoughts about balancing work and family, now or in the future?

Chapter Review

SUMMARY

A Stalled Revolution?

- Although women have made great strides in the workplace, some researchers have called the progress toward gender equality stalled and uneven.

The Pay Gap

- Women, on average, are paid less than men, and women of color experience a larger pay gap. The pay gap is particularly devastating for low-income women.

- One explanation for the pay gap is that women tend to cluster in different occupations than do men, known as horizontal occupational gender segregation.

- Horizontal occupational gender segregation interacts with aspects of social identity, such as race and sexual orientation, in addition to gender.

- Women cluster in occupations involving care work, and these jobs have lower salaries than jobs with comparable training and education requirements.

- One cause of the pay gap is a history of discrimination that took place when the wages of many jobs were initially set.

- Women are generally paid less even in the same field as men, and when women move into traditionally male occupations, the pay tends to go down.

- Women are less likely than men to negotiate for higher starting salaries, and they are judged more negatively than men when they do.

- There is a significant wage penalty for women when they become mothers, but fathers generally receive a wage bump.

Gender Discrimination at Work

- Women are less represented in higher-power positions, and this is particularly true for women of color.

- Women in low-wage jobs are less likely to be promoted from the lowest levels than are men.

- Men who work in predominantly female-dominated fields are more likely to be promoted to management and leadership positions than are women.

- Leadership is seen as a masculine trait, but women who lead in traditionally masculine ways are generally disliked.

- Women have a harder time than men finding mentors and sponsors to help them advance in their careers. Networking often takes place in hypermasculine environments and during times when many women need to attend to family needs, limiting their ability to participate in networking events.

- Women are expected to be helpful around the workplace, and they are disliked if they don't help.

- Women are more likely than men to be promoted to positions of leadership at times when companies are at the edge of failure. Compared to men, female CEOs receive more unsolicited advice from activist shareholders about how to run the company.

- Workplace harassment is a common experience among women—especially for those who also have other devalued social identity characteristics such as race, sexual orientation, or immigration status. Workplace harassment is particularly problematic in masculine workplace environments.

Balancing Work and Family

- Although it's a common assumption that work and family will conflict, research suggests that people are enriched by engaging in multiple roles.

- People often consider work–family balance in the context of choices women make, but their choices are constrained in many ways. Focusing on choice obscures the role of gender discrimination.

- Work–family balance is difficult to achieve because of inequality in the division of labor at home. Care burdens increase further for women who also provide care for their aging parents.

- Inflexible work environments and expectations for long work hours make balancing work and family challenging. This is exacerbated for lower-income workers, who often have little say about when they work and little consistency in their schedules.

- There is widespread discrimination across the income spectrum against pregnant women, mothers, and family caregivers.

- The United States is the only industrialized country without a parental leave policy. Lack of parental leave has negative psychological consequences for both mothers and children. When fathers take leave, there are benefits for fathers, mothers, and children.

- In the United States, high-quality child care is extremely expensive and often difficult to find. High-income women often hire low-income and immigrant women to care for their children, so in these cases liberation for one group of women comes on the back of other groups of women.

KEY TERMS

horizontal occupational gender segregation (p. 408)
vertical occupational gender segregation (p. 408)
comparable worth (p. 411)
motherhood wage penalty (p. 414)
glass ceiling (p. 417)
sticky floor (p. 418)
glass escalator (p. 418)
"think manager–think male" bias (p. 420)
transformational leader (p. 422)
networking (p. 422)
mentor (p. 423)

sponsor (p. 423)
amplification (p. 424)
glass cliff (p. 425)
quid pro quo harassment (p. 427)
hostile work environment (p. 427)
heterosexist harassment (p. 429)
work–family conflict (p. 432)
role enhancement theory (p. 432)
work–family enrichment (p. 432)
sandwich generation (p. 435)
maternal wall (p. 437)

THINK ABOUT IT

1. Imagine you're advising a woman who is negotiating a salary for a new job. Based on the research, what things would you tell the woman to say? What would you advise her to avoid?

2. Using the research in this chapter, what specific actions can you do in your work environment to address inequalities?

3. Locate the sexual harassment policy at your school and/or workplace. How accessible is it? If it is hard to locate or unclear, what recommendations would you make to change that?

4. Imagine that a friend who has two small children decides to go back into the workforce. What types of stressors do you think she will encounter? What advice would you offer her?

ONLINE RESOURCES

- **Equal Rights Advocates** — information that protects and promotes economic and educational access and opportunities for women and girls: equalrights.org
- **Fairy God Boss** — advice about pay and workplace culture, with attention to gender equality in the workplace: fairygodboss.com
- **Girl Boss** — conversations with women who are leaders in the paid workforce: girlboss.com
- **National Women's Law Center** — policies and laws that help guide women and girls, with particular attention to women who face some of the toughest challenges: nwlc.org

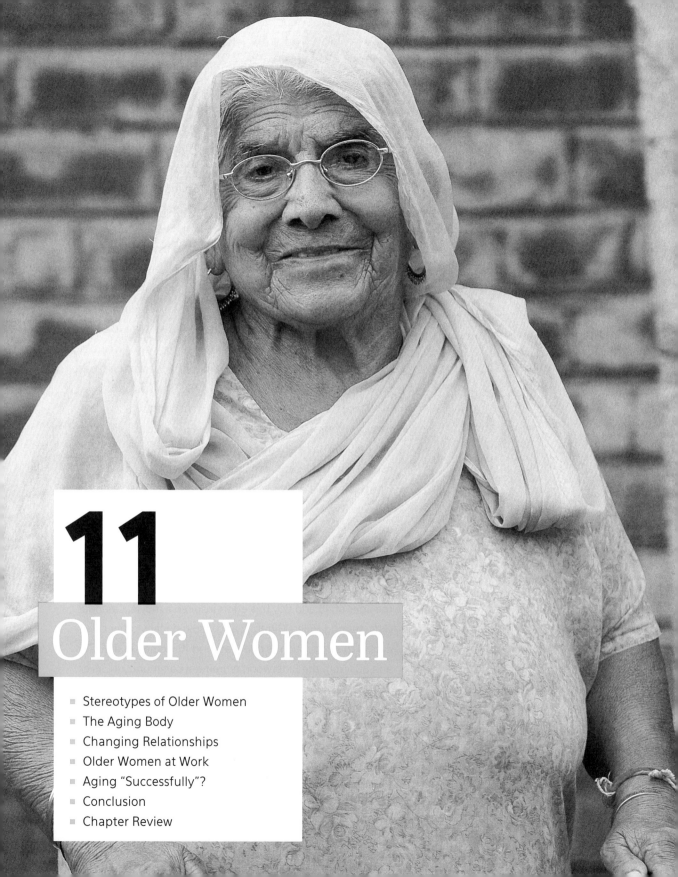

11
Older Women

- Oseola McCarty, a Black woman from Hattiesburg, Mississippi, retired at age 86 in 1995. Since dropping out of school in sixth grade, she had worked full-time as a "washerwoman" doing laundry for people to help support herself, her aunt, and her grandmother ("Oseola McCarty," n.d.). She had also saved some of her earnings, resulting in $280,000 in the bank when she retired. After setting aside enough to live on, she donated $150,000 to the University of Southern Mississippi to fund scholarships for students seeking the type of education she had been unable to pursue.
- At age 50, Carol Masheter, a White epidemiologist from Salt Lake City, Utah, began climbing mountains (Henetz, 2012). She did most of her training and climbing during her yearly three-week vacations. In 2012, the then 65-year-old, retired Masheter became the oldest woman to climb the tallest mountain on each of the seven continents—something she managed to do in a span of four years.
- In 2017, Alla Illyinichna Levushkina became the world's oldest working surgeon at age 89 (White, 2017). She has performed more than 10,000 surgeries and has had no fatalities. In Russia, where she lives, it's typical to retire in one's mid-fifties, but Levushkina can't imagine her life without her work. She still performs at least four surgeries per week.
- Pinup calendars with naked or nearly naked women are nothing new. However, in 1999, when the Rylestone Women's Institute in England made such a calendar as a fund-raiser for leukemia research in honor of a member's late husband, the women made waves (Hoge, 2000). That's because all the nude, but strategically blocked, models were between the ages of 45 and 60. This effort inspired a movie, *Calendar Girls*, starring Helen Mirren. It also inspired many other calendars in this vein, such as one featuring 16 women in their 70s and 80s from the Riderwood retirement community in Silver Spring, Maryland, to fund-raise for community residents who were struggling financially (Rosenwald, 2012).
- In 2016, LaDonna Brave Bull Allard, a member of the Standing Rock Sioux tribe in her 60s, founded the Sacred Stones camp on her property in North Dakota (Deerinwater, 2016; Merlan, 2016). This became the first of numerous camps for

Older women contribute to society in diverse ways. LaDonna Brave Bull Allard, pictured here, has worked as an activist to both preserve tribal lands and protect the Missouri River from the development of an oil pipeline. However, women such as this aren't usually the first to come to mind when people think of older women. Why do you suppose these women are viewed as the exception rather than the rule?

those calling themselves water protectors—people working to halt construction of the Dakota Access Pipeline to both preserve sacred lands and protect the Missouri River. Allard, who also identifies her name as Ta Maka Waste Win, meaning "Her Good Earth Woman," became a spokesperson for the water protectors at Standing Rock ("Standing Rock Sioux Historian," 2016). She spoke on their behalf at the United Nations (UN) in October 2016 to urge intervention since the proposed Dakota Access Pipeline violated treaties between the U.S. government and the Lakota people as well as the Declaration of the Rights of Indigenous Peoples adopted by the UN ("LaDonna Bravebull Allard Urges UN," 2016).

If you're like most people, the previous stories probably aren't the first that come to mind when you think of older women. Instead of active women working to make a difference in the world, you may think of frail women who can't care for themselves, or women in nursing homes living with dementia, or white-haired grandmothers rocking on a porch while knitting, or widows living alone in a small apartment struggling to pay the monthly bills. Those experiences are the reality for some older women, but they aren't the only ones. In this chapter, we'll explore both the assumptions about and the realities of being an older woman. We'll talk about appearance, health, relationships, and work. We'll touch on some of the stressors associated with being an older woman, and the ways in which older women are resilient and continue to make important contributions to their communities.

your turn

When you think of older women, what comes to mind? What do these women look like? How do they spend their time? What are their concerns? Now ask the same questions of others. Are there patterns to the responses based on the age or gender of those you talk with? How about sexual orientation or race/ethnicity?

Stereotypes of Older Women

When does someone go from being a woman to being an older woman? After all, we begin aging as soon as we're born, so each minute we're alive means we're now older than we were before. This isn't something we can pinpoint; it's often a matter of perspective. When you were 6 years old, people in their early 20s may have seemed old to you. However, most of our students in their early 20s don't feel old—some don't even feel like adults yet. When you're 20, people who are 40 or 50 may seem old. Many birthday cards associate both these milestone birthdays with being "over the hill," but people in their 40s and 50s may not see it this way. They're likely to be busy building their careers, raising children, and developing and/or maintaining romantic relationships. They may feel that being old will come with retirement in their late 60s. Do you notice a pattern here?

How Others Perceive Older Adults

What are the stereotypes of older adults, and how do they vary based on different aspects of people's social identities?

Regardless of the specific age at which "old" begins, it's common to expect different things from people as they grow older. Throughout this book, we've explored stereotypes of women and the way these stereotypes change when other aspects of women's social identities are considered. Older women constitute one more group for whom stereotypes abound. As with general stereotypes of women, stereotypes of older adults reflect a mix of positive and negative attributes (Levy & Macdonald, 2016). For example, older people are perceived as warm, caring, and communal, but they're also seen as as frail, forgetful, and less competent. Meta-analyses indicate that, overall, attitudes toward older adults are more negative than those toward younger adults (Kite & Johnson, 1988; Kite, Stockdale, Whitley, & Johnson, 2005). **Ageism** is prejudice related to a person's actual or perceived age, and the stereotypes given above reflect ageist views.

Do people judge older women and men in different ways? The answer appears to be yes. For example, a sample of predominantly White college students generally evaluated older adults positively and evaluated older women more positively than older men (Narayan, 2008). However, older women were rated more positively in traditionally feminine domains of having friends and participating in religious or leisure activities; older men were evaluated more positively in traditionally masculine domains related to competence and work. In another study whose participants ranged from 20 to 92 years old, older men, as compared to older women, were evaluated more positively in domains of finances and work (Kornadt, Voss, & Rothermund, 2013). These findings indicate that gendered expectations continue as people age.

Stereotypes become more complicated when other aspects of social identities, such as race or sexual orientation, are taken into consideration. For example, a sample of largely White undergraduates was asked to rate groups of people on traits related to agentic or communal orientations (Andreoletti, Leszczynski, & Disch, 2015). The groups were described as either Black or White, female or male, and between 15 and 95 years of age (e.g., Black 35-year-old women). When the researchers looked just at gender, women were perceived as more communal and men as more agentic. When looking just at race, White individuals were perceived as more communal and Black individuals as more aggressive,

competitive, and dominant. When looking just at age, older adults were generally seen as less agentic and more communal. A more complex picture emerged when the researchers considered how gender, race, and age interacted. For example, older Black and White women were evaluated differently. Specifically, older Black women were rated as similar in competitiveness to older Black and White men and as more competitive than older White women. Older White women were rated as more devoted to others than were older Black women.

Although little research has explored it, there's evidence that sexual orientation may also influence perceptions of older adults. In a study of college students who predominantly identified as heterosexual and White, older adults were, overall, perceived as being more frail but also more judicious (e.g., wise, mature, patient, and cautious) than younger adults, consistent with general aging stereotypes (Wright & Canetto, 2009). Moreover, heterosexual women and men were perceived as being traditionally feminine and masculine in line with gender stereotypes. Older lesbians, however, were perceived as more similar to heterosexual men than heterosexual women in terms of masculine/agentic traits such as being independent and being able to withstand pressure.

How Older Adults Perceive Themselves

What is stereotype embodiment theory, and how do stereotypes influence the way older adults see themselves?

Stereotypes don't just influence how others perceive older adults; they also influence how older adults see themselves and the choices they make.

Psychologist Becca Levy (2009) developed **stereotype embodiment theory** to describe this process. She argued that people learn age-related stereotypes at a young age and internalize them. As we grow older, these become self-stereotypes that influence the way we think and act, which in turn can affect our mental and our physical health. Researchers explore this by priming older participants to think about stereotypes of older adults (e.g., by showing them words associated with these stereotypes). For example, some participants will be shown words associated with negative stereotypes (e.g., *confused, dependent*), and others will be shown words associated with positive stereotypes (e.g., *accomplished, guidance*). In various studies, participants who were primed with negative stereotypes subsequently showed results ranging from worse handwriting (Levy, 2000) to heightened stress responses when solving puzzles (Levy, Hausdorff, Hencke, & Wei, 2000) to decreased performance on memory tests (Hess, Auman, Colcombe, & Rahhal, 2003).

The internalization of aging stereotypes is related to stereotype threat, an idea discussed in Chapter 3. Research has shown that stereotypes in domains that people particularly value, such as physical health and the capacity to independently care for oneself, seem to be those most likely to impact their thoughts and behavior (Bennett & Gaines, 2010). Given this, the influence of internalized stereotypes on older adults' health and well-being is of particular concern. Other research with older adult samples has indicated that they have worse outcomes in a variety of domains when they're exposed to or believe in ageist stereotypes. For example, endorsing ageist stereotypes has been shown to relate to lower levels of physical activity (Emile, Chalabaev, Stephan, Corrion, & d'Arripe-Longueville, 2014), and being exposed to ageist stereotypes has actually been shown to decrease the will to live (Levy, Ashman, & Dror, 2000; Marques, Lima, Abrams, & Swift, 2014). Believing in ageist stereotypes has also been related to decreased engagement in preventive health practices such as seeking regular medical care and taking prescribed medicines (Levy & Myers, 2004)—actions that can help improve and maintain health overall.

Nevertheless, other research shows that not everyone who might be considered "old" is affected by negative stereotypes about older people. In one study, many participants who held negative stereotypes about older people didn't actually self-identify as old, even at age 70 and above (Kornadt & Rothermund, 2012). If people don't view themselves as old, then negative stereotypes about aging will have a lesser effect on them. In fact, other researchers have found that when participants encountered negative stereotypes about aging, they were actually less likely to see themselves as old (Weiss & Lang, 2012). In a study on the conceptualization of aging among women from Québec (age 65 and older), most participants didn't identify as old, or did so only grudgingly (Quéniart & Charpentier, 2012). One 91-year-old woman said, "I think it [the label of old woman] best described some else, not me," and another said, "I told you my age [85], but I don't feel that age" (p. 992). This was largely due to their awareness of negative stereotypes of old women as being dependent, socially isolated, and fragile—characteristics they didn't associate with themselves. Rather, they saw themselves as aging well, maintaining physical and intellectual health as well as their independence.

Some women may also have a positive view of their own aging. For example, one study showed that older lesbians perceived the aging process as positive (Schope, 2005). This was attributed to the fact that the participants reported diverse social networks consisting of both younger and older friends. Also, older lesbian women reported feeling revered by younger lesbian women because of their wisdom and increased engagement in politics.

Overall, the findings just described suggest that people view "old" in different ways and that it may only be a state of mind. Apparently, age stereotypes don't have the same effect if one doesn't view oneself as old. No matter how old one may actually be in years, not seeing oneself as "old" means a lower likelihood of worrying about memory loss, physical frailty, or loss of independence.

The Aging Body

Many stereotypes about aging involve the body and how it changes as we get older. If you imagine an older woman, you may think of someone with gray hair and wrinkles. Perhaps you think of someone who uses an assistive device to help with mobility or who has other health concerns. It's true that bodies change as we age, in terms of both physical appearance and function. It's also true that eventually all of us will see our bodies fail—that's part of being human. Women, however, face added pressures related to their aging bodies because societal beauty standards are narrower and more harshly applied to women than to men.

Appearance

How do older women feel about their appearance, and what role does beauty work play in their lives?

Age stereotypes aren't just about how people act and what they can do. They're also about how people look. As we saw in Chapter 6, women in Western society are under particular pressure to conform to largely unachievable beauty ideals. Although appearance expectations and pressures to meet them do change as women grow older, they don't go away. This means that older women may have different concerns as compared to younger women. One reason is that beauty is typically equated with youth (Calasanti, & Slevin, 2001; Chrisler, 2007; Furman, 1997). So beautiful skin is smooth, not wrinkled; beautiful hair isn't gray; beautiful breasts are high and firm, not sagging. Even though women might be able to change their weight through dieting and exercise or their breast size through cosmetic surgery, they can't actually stop the aging process. Regardless of how they adjust their physical appearance, all women will get progressively further away from the beauty ideal as they age (Chrisler, 2011). As one woman put it when describing how society treats older women, "Well, you're old. You can't look good anyway" (Hurd Clarke & Griffin, 2008, pp. 660–661).

This attitude is reinforced by the fact that there are few images of older women in the media. As discussed in Chapter 6, older women are under-represented in the media—especially women of color (Coltrane & Messineo, 2000; Covert & Dixon, 2008; Mastro & Stern, 2003; Robinson, Callister, & Magoffin, 2009). Older lesbians are also rendered "invisible" within society (Rose & Hospital, 2015). When media portrayals of older women do occur in movies or television shows, the women are rarely in lead roles—especially not as sexually desirable romantic leads (Lauzen & Dozier, 2005a, 2005b). The few older women in TV shows and movies are typically portrayed in stereotypical, and sometimes explicitly negative, ways (Robinson et al., 2009). However, not all portrayals are negative. For example, Jennifer Lewis in the TV show *Blackish* and Meryl Streep in the movie *It's Complicated* play older women who are funny, intelligent, compassionate, multi-dimensional, and involved in love affairs. Still, the majority of positive images of older women are usually of affluent White women who conform to traditional standards of beauty (Lemish & Muhlbauer, 2012). Given this pattern, it's not surprising that a study of middle-aged women (ages 35 to 55) showed that greater media exposure through television viewing was related to body dissatisfaction and disordered eating (Slevec & Tiggemann, 2011).

In fact, many women report body dissatisfaction throughout their lives (Roy & Payette, 2012; Tiggemann & Lynch, 2001). In a study of women in Austria, fully 60% of participants ages 60 to 70 reported body dissatisfaction (Mangweth-Matzek et al., 2006). However, other research indicates that older women may be less worried about their appearance than younger women are. For example, in one study, researchers found that both older and younger women paid attention to their appearance at similar rates, but younger women felt worse about their bodies when they did so as compared to older women (Grippo & Hill, 2008). In another study of 20- to 84-year-old women in Australia, body dissatisfaction was shown to be stable across the lifespan, but self-objectification, body monitoring, appearance anxiety, and disordered eating all decreased with age (Tiggemann & Lynch, 2001). As covered in Chapter 6, self-objectification and body monitoring have been identified as cognitive distractions that can impair women's task performance (Fredrickson, Roberts,

Noll, Quinn, & Twenge, 1998; Hebl, King, & Lin, 2004). Thus, older women may be less likely to experience these negative consequences of feeling dissatisfied with their appearance.

Older women also have varying perspectives on attractiveness (Krekula, 2016). This research suggests that older women are sometimes influenced by youthful beauty standards, but they also draw on a different set of beauty norms related to age. Essentially, their comparison groups shift. Even though they may compare themselves to young women and media figures who represent cultural beauty ideals, they also compare themselves to other older women. This comparison with similar-age peers may help them maintain a positive self-image.

Beauty Work Because aging brings body- and appearance-related changes, it's common for women to feel increased pressure to engage in **beauty work**, or body modifications to conform to social norms of attractiveness. Beauty work isn't limited to older women, and it includes practices such as wearing makeup, shaving legs, and dying hair. It can also involve invasive procedures such as Botox injections or cosmetic surgery. Studies have shown that some women feel beauty work is necessary in order to hide the signs of aging and to "pass" as younger than one's chronological age (Hurd Clarke, Griffin, & Maliha, 2009; Winterich, 2007). This type of beauty work is known as **age concealment**. As a result, "anti-aging" products, such as skin creams, are popular. In 2015, Americans spent $281.6 billion on anti-aging products—a figure that's projected to reach $331.3 billion by 2020 (Elder, 2016).

It's often said that men become distinguished as they age, while women just get old (and become unattractive; Calasanti, & Slevin, 2001; Furman, 1997). The human body changes as it ages, and that's true regardless of gender identity, but women are generally perceived as "old" at earlier ages than men (Calasanti, 2005). Therefore, it may not be surprising that women, as compared to men, worry about looking young or younger (Halliwell & Dittmar, 2003). Women are also both expected to, and actually do, engage in age concealment more than men (Harris, 1994). Moreover, anti-aging products are largely marketed toward women (Smirnova, 2012), and when they are marketed to men, the focus generally shifts from appearance to body function (Calasanti, 2007). So, when anti-aging ads target men, they're more likely to promote products such as dietary supplements. Even in advertising for appearance-related products targeting men, a different tone usually prevails. For example, Touch of Gray hair dye marketed to men conveys the message that it's alright for men to have

INGREDIENTS: Aqua (Water), Vitis Vinifera (Grape) Seed Extract, Cyclomethicone, Glycerin, PEG-100 Stearate, Propylene Glycol, Prunus Armeniaca (Apricot) Kernel Oil, Butylene Glycol, Aesculus Hippocastanum (Horse Chestnut) Extract, Symphytum Officinale (Comfrey) Leaf Extract, Cucumis Sativus (Cucumber) Fruit Extract, Camellia Oleifera (Green Tea) Extract, Glycine Soja (Soybean) Oil, Glyceryl Distearate, Glyceryl Stearate, Dimethicone, Tocopheryl Acetate, Linoleic Acid, Cetyl Alcohol, Stearyl Alcohol, Alpha Lipoic Acid, Citrus Medica Limonum (Lemon) Peel Extract, Panax Ginseng (Ginseng) Root Extract, Cymbopogon Schoenanthus (Lemongrass) Extract, Rosa Canina (Dog Rose) Fruit Extract, Equisitum Hiemale (Horsetail) Extract, Chamomilla Recutita (Matricaria) Extract, Sodium Hyaluronate, Glyceryl Linoleate, Hydrolyzed Soy Protein, Retinyl Palmitate, Daucus Carota Sativa (Carrot) Root, Arginine, Superoxide Dismutase, Caffeine, Panthenol, Niacin, Phytonadione, Riboflavin, Folic Acid, Cyanocobalamin, Eucalyptus Globulus Leaf Oil, PEG-40 Stearate, Corn Starch Modified, Imidazolidinyl Urea, Methylparaben, Propylparaben, Tetrasodium EDTA, CI 14700 (Red 4), CI 19140 (Yellow 5), CI 15510 (Orange 4)

Re-Storation
DEEP REPAIR FACIAL SERUM

intensive anti-aging

Z. Bigatti

All beauty work takes time and money, and this expenditure increases when women engage in beauty work in an effort to conceal their age. If you compare the cost of "anti-aging" versus traditional moisturizers available at a local store, you're almost certain to find that the anti-aging versions cost more. Even more expensive products can be found at doctors' offices, spas, and premium retailers. The product pictured here retails for nearly $200 (for 1 ounce).

Go to a drug store or the health and beauty section of a big box store. Look at the products on the shelves as well as the advertising throughout the section and the product packaging. Are products aimed at women, at men, or at all people? Which products seem marketed explicitly toward older adults? Do you see any gender differences in these products? What about the products marketed as anti-aging? Are they for women, for men, or for everyone? Who is depicted in the ads or on the packaging? Do those people look "old"?

some gray (but not too much), as it shows that they have life experience. Can you imagine a similar product being marketed to women?

When women in research studies have been asked about their appearance-related body concerns, they've mentioned graying hair, wrinkles, sagging skin, facial hair, and weight gain (Hurd Clarke et al., 2009; Winterich, 2007). As noted previously, it's generally expected that most women will attempt to conceal their age, but they actually receive conflicting messages about whether or not they should. For example, primarily White participants of diverse ages judged older individuals described as using age concealment more negatively than those described as not engaging in such practices (Harris, 1994). However, women in another study reported receiving negative reactions if they didn't take steps to conceal their age (Hurd Clarke & Griffin, 2008). These women reported feeling that they were invisible, that others assumed they weren't knowledgeable or competent, and that it was challenging to keep or attract the interest of a sexual and/or romantic partner.

Overall, then, older women face a "damned if they do/damned if they don't" situation. Consequently, many try to conceal their age in subtle ways in order to achieve a "natural" look (Hurd Clarke & Griffin, 2007). Moreover, older women themselves often set and enforce appearance standards, as with "age-appropriate" dress (Hurd Clarke et al., 2009). Clothing identified as inappropriate included revealing items (e.g., low-rise jeans, short skirts), garments in bright or bold colors, and clothes that were "too fashionable" and youth oriented as opposed to those that were "classic" or "traditional" in style—and the older women who participated in the study made negative judgments about those whom they perceived as violating these standards (p. 715).

Women respond in various ways to the pressure for beauty work. A group of 46- to 71-year-old women, diverse in terms of race and sexual orientation, shared an array of perspectives (Winterich, 2007). One White lesbian woman said that when her hair began to gray, "students started to treat me differently . . . they started to talk to me like I was an old woman . . . I started dyeing my hair and that was the end of that" (p. 63). Other women embrace their gray hair. A Latinx lesbian said, "I worked for every single one! . . . Besides, I think it looks pretty cool," and a Black lesbian said, "I want to put that stuff to make the gray shine!" (p. 63).

One age-related change that most women find unacceptable is the growth of facial hair. Although a minority of women in one study reported experiencing this change, the majority of those who did engaged in practices to remove the unwanted hair (Winterich, 2007). As discussed in Chapter 4, people are often uncomfortable with the fact that sex/gender distinctions aren't as clear as they may have believed to be the case. The presence of facial hair is associated with masculine identity and violates norms of femininity in addition to youthful norms of attractiveness. As a result, facial hair as a body change associated with aging may be viewed as particularly problematic because it also disrupts assumptions of a strict and clear gender binary. One woman reported being asked "What are you?" as the presence of facial hair made her gender ambiguous (p. 65).

Some women may opt for more invasive beauty work in the form of surgical and non-surgical cosmetic procedures such as face and neck lifts, chemical peels, and Botox injections. In fact, in 2014, among those age 55 and older, the two most common cosmetic surgical procedures were eyelid surgery (which can address drooping eyelids) and facelifts (American Society of Plastic Surgeons [ASPS], 2014). A different report for the same year concurred that these were the most common procedures for those age 65 and older, but liposuction was slightly more common than eyelid surgery and facelifts among those ages 51 to 64 (American Society for Aesthetic Plastic Surgery [ASAPS], 2014). Botox (or other similar injections) and the injection of soft tissue fillers were the most common non-surgical procedures (ASAPS, 2014; ASPS, 2014).

These products and procedures can be considered empowering because they give women control, or the illusion of control, over the aging process. One study participant said, "You don't exactly cheat on Mother Nature, but you kind of, you know, get a handle on this particular ageing process" (Brooks, 2010, p. 245). However, other participants reported that anti-aging products and procedures can make them feel as if aging is their fault. These potential benefits and drawbacks associated with conforming to norms of beauty and sexiness are similar to the challenges younger women encounter if they engage in self-sexualization, as discussed in Chapter 7.

Some women may explicitly reject youth-oriented beauty norms typically associated with White and/or heterosexual women (Brooks, 2010; Winterich, 2007). Even if women don't do this, however, anti-aging products and procedures aren't accessible to everyone. They're rarely covered by health insurance, so the expense alone keeps many women from pursuing them. However, in one study with a predominantly White sample of midlife women, 81% of participants said they would undergo at least one cosmetic procedure if cost weren't an issue (Chrisler, Gorman, Serra, & Chapman, 2012). In fact, 38.5% of the women in this study had actually undergone some sort of procedure. Apparently, then, for some women the capacity to appear to be "aging gracefully" is directly connected to their ability to afford anti-aging products and procedures.

Older women may have mixed feelings about the results of no longer meeting traditional standards of beauty and sexiness. For some, the invisibility of older women in our culture may allow a reprieve from sexual objectification that they experienced in their younger years (Chrisler, Rossini, & Newton, 2015). This can be a relief. Other women, who had enjoyed receiving attention related to their appearance and may even have found it empowering, report that they miss the sexualized attention they received when they were younger (Chrisler, 2007).

Menopause

What is menopause, what are women's experiences of menopause like, and what role does medical intervention play in women's experience of menopause?

Menopause is the permanent end of menstrual periods, resulting from decreased hormone production in the ovaries. Typically, menopause occurs at around age 50; however, it can occur earlier (Laven, Visser, Uitterlinden, Vermeij, & Hoeijmakers, 2016; Shadyab et al., 2017). For example, if a woman has an *oophorectomy*, or removal of her ovaries, she will enter surgical menopause. This often occurs as part of a *hysterectomy*, or removal of the uterus—typically done to treat a disorder such as endometriosis (in which uterine tissue grows outside of the uterus) or a disease such as cancer. When the uterus is removed, menstruation stops. However, if the ovaries aren't removed at the same time, they continue to produce estrogen and other reproductive hormones, and menopause doesn't actually occur even if a woman can no longer menstruate. Early menopause can also occur for other reasons, including experiencing chemotherapy to treat cancer.

What most people refer to as menopause is better thought of as the menopausal transition, or perimenopause. **Perimenopause** is a term for the few years before and the 12 months after a woman's last menstrual cycle. Once a woman hasn't had a menstrual period for 12 months, she's considered postmenopausal, or in **postmenopause**. During perimenopause, many women experience body changes. These include changes in the length and regularity of the menstrual cycle, hot flashes, night sweats, and vaginal dryness. Although these changes occur to different degrees and for different periods of time for different women, irregular menstrual cycles and hot flashes typically occur over a period of a few years.

Although transgender and gender non-binary individuals who have ovaries can experience menopause, the vast majority of research about menopause focuses on cisgender women. This practice limits the understanding of menopause since people appear to classify their experiences based on their social identities. For example, in one study of women in the United States, researchers found that race/ethnicity influenced participants' attitudes toward menopause (Sommer et al., 1999). Black women held the most positive attitudes, followed by White, Latinx, and Asian American women. The researchers speculated that menopause represented a relatively minor stressor in comparison to the Black women's lifelong experiences of racism. Results from another study suggest that attitudes about menopause may influence the extent to which women notice body changes as well as how they respond to those changes (Ayers, Forshaw, &

Hunter, 2010). In other words, when women think menopause is something to be dreaded and feared, they may actually experience more severe symptoms.

Cultural context can also influence experiences of menopause. In one study, a sample of women in Canada and the United States reported more body changes than did a sample of women in Japan (Lock, 1994). Another study showed that country of residence was related to reports of body changes associated with menopause in samples of women from Lebanon, Morocco, Spain, and the United States (Obermeyer, Reher, & Saliba, 2007). Overall, body changes associated with menopause are found among women worldwide, and rates vary within every sample of women—with some reporting few changes and little to no distress, and others reporting much more (Obermeyer, 2000).

In a study of 50-year-old women and their mothers (all of whom identified as White), even though the participants' physical experiences were similar across generations, mothers generally viewed menopause as a natural stage of life while daughters regarded it as a medicalized experience of symptoms that needed to be treated and/or cured (Utz, 2011). One mother said, "Menopause just happened. We didn't do much about it" (p. 147); but one daughter said, "I will treat it [menopausal symptoms], or better yet, stop it before it ever starts" (p. 148), reflecting a more negative view—as if menopause were something to be delayed or avoided at all costs. This view was generally associated with a fear of aging and a discomfort with the body changes associated with menopause. In talking about their own experience with body changes, one daughter shared that she was "no longer able to lose weight, no matter how much I diet" (p. 148), and another said, "I began to notice skin changes, it just wasn't as tight as it used to be. . . . And weight gain, well, not really weight gain, my body just changed. It is a different shape now" (p. 147). Because the older women saw menopause as natural, it didn't bother them much. However, their daughters saw it is a medical issue and reported greater distress.

Hormones Menopause does contribute to changes in the body's physical appearance. As estrogen levels decline, collagen production decreases, so the skin loses elasticity and becomes thinner. Fat deposits are redistributed, which can make skin and breasts sag. As estrogen declines, testosterone in women's bodies can produce facial hair and a deepening voice. Vaginal tissues become thinner, and vaginal lubrication often decreases. The last two changes can contribute to some of the changes in women's sexual experiences as they age (discussed in Chapter 7). These changes may be particularly impactful for heterosexual women, as they're likely to define sex in terms of penile-vaginal penetration. In one study, heterosexual women described vaginal dryness as contributing to relationship problems because their male partners complained about the dryness impacting their own experience of sex (Winterich, 2003). In contrast, lesbian women reported that vaginal dryness (their own or their partner's) led to more communication about how to adapt their sexual activity so that both partners were satisfied.

For years, menopausal and postmenopausal hormone therapy (HT; also known as hormone replacement therapy, or HRT) was considered the best way to treat and prevent symptoms associated with menopause. In fact, in 1966 the gynecologist Robert Wilson published the book *Feminine Forever* promoting the use of HT to "cure" menopause, which was considered a hormone deficiency disease. The book contributed to large numbers of women being prescribed estrogen supplements, and later estrogen/progestin supplements. The shift to the latter occurred because a link between estrogen-only HT and endometrial cancer was identified in 1975 (Smith, Prentice, Thompson, & Hermann, 1975; Ziel & Finkle, 1975). Rates increased from approximately 1% of peri- and postmenopausal women using HT prior to 1980 to approximately 4.4% of women in the 1980s and 8.8% of women in the 1990s (Jewett, Gangnon, Trentham-Dietz, & Sprague, 2014). By the early 2000s, researchers and doctors alike were interested in HT as a preventive treatment for problems ranging from heart disease to osteoporosis to dementia.

However, the enthusiasm for HT ended abruptly when it became clear that this therapy actually increased, rather than decreased, the risk of many other diseases. In fact, in 2002, a large study of postmenopausal estrogen/progestin use was stopped 2.5 years early because the results indicated that taking HT was doing harm to the participants. Specifically, it was linked to increases in heart

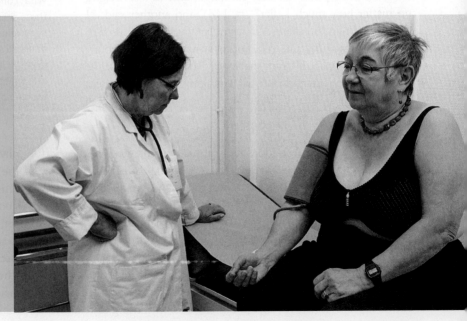

Even though people of all ages utilize health-care services, chronic illnesses increase as people age. Given this, older women are greater consumers of health-care services than younger women. Talk to an older woman you know, and ask about her experiences with the health-care system. Are they generally positive or negative? How can other social identity characteristics and financial resources influence older women's experiences with health-care providers?

disease, stroke, breast cancer, and pulmonary embolism—a blood clot in the lungs (Writing Group for the Women's Health Initiative Investigators, 2002). A related study of estrogen-only HT for women who'd had hysterectomies was stopped two years later because of the increased risk of stroke (Women's Health Initiative Steering Committee, 2004). Current medical recommendations for HT center on short-term use during perimenopause to address hot flashes and vaginal dryness (de Villiers et al., 2013). In line with changing recommendations, prescription rates have fallen substantially in recent years. For example, among women ages 45 to 64 in the United States, 13.5% were using HT in 1999, but only 2.7% were using it in 2010 (Jewett et al., 2014).

Physical Health

What physical health concerns disproportionately affect women or affect women and men differently?

One reason HT seemed to be a potential wonder drug was that researchers speculated it could help prevent diseases for which women are at increased risk. As Table 11.1 shows, heart disease and cancer are the two most common causes of death for women, followed by respiratory diseases (e.g., COPD, or coronary obstructive pulmonary disease), stroke, and Alzheimer's disease (Heron, 2016). The rates aren't the same for all women, however. For example, diabetes is among the most common causes of death for all groups of women other than White women.

TABLE 11.1 Most Common Causes of Death for Women in the United States

All Women	White	Black	Asian/ Pacific Islander	American Indian/Alaska Native	Hispanic (any race)
heart disease (22.3%)	heart disease (22.3%)	heart disease (23.2%)	cancer (27.3%)	cancer (17.4%)	cancer (22.6%)
cancer (21.6%)	cancer (21.4%)	cancer (22.5%)	heart disease (20%)	heart disease (16.8%)	heart disease (19.7%)
respiratory diseases (6%)	respiratory diseases (6.5%)	stroke (6.2%)	stroke (8.1%)	accidents (8.1%)	stroke (6%)
stroke (6%)	stroke (5.9%)	diabetes (4.6%)	Alzheimer's (3.9%)	liver disease (5.7%)	diabetes (4.7%)
Alzheimer's (5%)	Alzheimer's (5.3%)	respiratory diseases (3.2%)	diabetes (3.8%)	diabetes (5.4%)	accidents (4.5%)

Note. Data drawn from Heron (2016). Because the U.S. government collects data using the term *Hispanic*, we will report data throughout this chapter using this term.

For years, heart disease was considered a men's disease. Even today, this idea remains common—possibly because the disease tends to develop about 10 years later in women as compared to men (Finnegan et al., 2000; Maas & Appelman, 2010). Because the onset in women usually occurs after menopause, many researchers and health-care providers thought that estrogen might protect against heart disease (Writing Group for the Women's Health Initiative Investigators, 2002). In fact, this theory was a major contributor to the trend of prescribing long-term HT for postmenopausal women. However, as mentioned earlier, this view was incorrect.

Researchers have begun to view the potential roles of endogenous estrogen (produced within the body) and supplemental estrogen and testosterone in the development of heart disease as being even more complex than previously thought. For example, one study indicated that transwomen receiving estrogen supplements have a higher risk for heart disease than transmen (whose ovaries produce endogenous estrogen) receiving testosterone (Gooren, Wierckx, & Giltay, 2014). In fact, transgender individuals, both those who do and those who do not use supplemental hormones, have the potential to provide valuable and unique data about the influences of endogenous and supplemental hormones.

Regardless of why the onset occurs later, heart disease is now known to be common among women. Yet they're still less likely than men to receive proper diagnosis. For example, a study in Britain showed that women were significantly less likely to be correctly diagnosed with a heart attack than men (Wu et al., 2018). One explanation may be that women are less likely to have severe chest pain as a key symptom (Finnegan et al., 2000). They're more likely to experience pain in other parts of the body (e.g., jaw, neck, arm, back) as well as lightheadedness, breathlessness, and nausea. If women don't know they're having the symptoms of a heart attack, they're likely to delay seeking treatment. Moreover, if doctors don't recognize heart attack symptoms in women, then women probably won't receive proper treatment (Wu et al., 2018). In fact, research suggests that doctors often misdiagnose heart problems in women as anxiety, depression, stress, or panic, which can delay necessary treatment and, ultimately, lead to women having worse outcomes than men (Carnlöf, Iwarzon, Jensen-Urstad, Gadler, & Insulander, 2017)

In contrast to heart disease, many people do associate cancer—especially breast cancer—with women. Breast cancer is the most commonly diagnosed cancer among women (see Table 11.2; Centers for Disease Control and Prevention, n.d.), and it receives considerable attention and research funding from both public and private sources (Gander, 2014; Thompson, 2010). This occurs despite the fact that lung cancer is the leading cause of cancer death for women, except for Hispanic* women. Men can be, and are, diagnosed with breast cancer too—but at much lower rates than women (Giordano, Cohen, Buzdar, Perkins, & Hortobagyi, 2004).

---

*Authors' note: Because the U.S. government collects data using the term *Hispanic*, you will see us use this term at various points throughout this chapter in contrast to our typical use of the term *Latinx*.

Lung cancer and lung diseases like COPD (the third leading cause of death for women) are related to rates of smoking among women (U.S. Department of Health and Human Services, 2014). Risk for both heart disease and stroke (the latter is the fourth most common cause of death for women) is also increased by smoking, as is the risk for diabetes (one of the most common causes of death for all groups of women except White women). In fact, according to the U.S. Department of Health and Human Services (2014), women's risks for these diseases have increased dramatically over the past 50 years, and the pattern is linked to an increase in women's smoking rates over the same period. Nevertheless, lung cancer receives significantly less attention and research funding than other cancers (Gander, 2014; Thompson, 2010).

Why does this discrepancy occur? One explanation is that more groups lobby for allocating funds to research on certain diseases, including breast cancer. Such organizations, usually non-profits, can lobby for funding allocation while also raising their own funds, which can also be allocated to research. For example, in the United States, the Susan G. Komen Foundation is a well-known charity focusing on breast cancer. It is active in providing education and advocacy, raising funds, and

Having one or both breasts removed through mastectomy, as the woman pictured here did, can be challenging both medically and psychologically. However, many women find ways to reclaim their changed bodies. Some women get tattoos so they can focus on art and beauty rather than their surgical scars.

TABLE 11.2 Most Common Types of Cancer Diagnosed and Most Common Causes of Cancer Death among Women in the United States, 2014

	Most Common Cancer Diagnoses in Women					
Rank Order	All	White	Black	Asian/ Pacific Islander	American Indian/ Alaska Native	Hispanic (any race)
1	breast	breast	breast	breast	breast	breast
2	lung	lung	lung	lung	lung	colon
3	colon	colon	colon	colon	colon	lung
	Most Common Causes of Cancer Death in Women					
	All	White	Black	Asian/ Pacific Islander	American Indian/ Alaska Native	Hispanic (any race)
1	lung	lung	lung	lung	lung	breast
2	breast	breast	breast	breast	breast	lung
3	colon	colon	colon	colon	colon	colon

Note. Data drawn from Centers for Disease Control and Prevention (n.d.).

Breast Reconstruction Surgery

Although *lumpectomy* (removal of breast tissue from around a cancerous tumor), or breast-conserving surgery, is the more common surgical treatment for breast cancer today (62%), some women, particularly those with more advanced cancers, have *mastectomies* to remove the entire breast (38%; Mahmood et al., 2013). Any cancer treatment can affect body image, but breast surgery offers special challenges because breasts are often considered a uniquely feminine aspect of appearance and can be connected to women's gender identity. As one woman reported, "I would die without breasts; I could never live without breasts" (Fallbjörk, Salander, & Rasmussen, 2012, p. E45).

Slightly more than half of women who experience mastectomy undergo *breast reconstruction*, which involves creating a new breast with implants and/or other tissue from the body (Connors, Goodman, Myckatyn, Margenthaler, & Gehlert, 2016). Women may opt for reconstruction to better meet societal beauty standards, and one study showed that those who chose reconstruction had better body image following cancer treatment than those who didn't (Nano et al., 2005). Moreover, other studies show that women who have delayed as opposed to immediate reconstruction report more body concerns (Metcalfe et al., 2012) and that feeling uncomfortable about one's body after a mastectomy predicts seeking breast reconstruction later (Metcalfe et al., 2017). Given these findings, reconstruction may indeed help women feel better about themselves (Fallbjörk et al., 2012).

However, one could argue that breast reconstruction reinforces a narrow standard of beauty rather than promoting acceptance of bodies with differences. For example, instead of seeking reconstruction, some women opt for tattoos around their mastectomy scars to celebrate their lives and decorate their bodies (Conger, 2014). One woman summed up her comfort with her mastectomy (without reconstruction) in this way: "When you are older, imperfections count for less . . . you actually should have some rips in your sails when you get older" (Fallbjörk et al., 2012, p. E44).

Further, while breast surgeons strive to produce breasts that "will 'feel' like a natural breast," this "feeling" is from the perspective of an observer or sexual partner rather than the women themselves (Rabin, 2017, para. 7). One side effect of reconstruction is decreased sensation in the breast, so women's breast(s) go from being a source of pleasure for themselves to being a source of pleasure only for others.

Also, breast reconstruction isn't a choice that's available to all women. One study showed that older women and those without private health insurance are less likely to receive breast reconstruction, and Black women are 30% less likely to have reconstruction than White women (Connors et al., 2016). Although some of these differences may reflect different values, they're also indicative of systemic barriers, including financial ones, that influence and constrain women's options.

Ultimately, breast reconstruction is a personal choice that's connected to larger expectations about femininity. Overall, women who do and do not have reconstruction have no differences in quality of life (Sun et al., 2014). Do you think breast reconstruction is empowering or oppressing for women?

providing research funding. While one may argue that cancers that kill more women should get more research funding, it would be hard to find anyone who thinks that breast cancer research should be defunded—after all, funding research on all cancer is a good thing.

A number of years ago, while teaching a class, one of the authors of this book noticed a student's breast cancer–related shirt with a pink ribbon as part of the design and the slogan "save the ta-tas" printed on it. Well-intentioned T-shirts like this increase awareness about breast cancer, encourage breast self-exams and mammography to promote early detection, and help raise funds for research. However, the sexualized nature of the slogan and its placement over the wearer's breasts seemed to imply that the T-shirt campaign was about saving breasts rather than saving women's lives. This point may sum up why breast cancer, in particular, receives so much attention and funding. Breasts are a symbol of femininity and sexuality, are linked to standards of beauty, and are seen as a source of sexual pleasure—particularly for male partners.

Unlike breast cancer, many diseases that disproportionately affect women receive very little attention. For example, osteoporosis, osteoarthritis, and dementia all present significant risks. Osteoporosis is a disease of bone loss. Everyone loses bone density as they age, but for some people this happens at a greater and/or faster rate, resulting in osteoporosis. This is a particular concern for women, as estrogen plays a role in bone development and maintenance, and the decrease in estrogen at menopause is linked to decreased bone density, particularly for White women (U.S. Department of Health and Human Services, 2014). Many women who have osteoporosis don't know they have it, however. In one study, only 11% of women age 65 and older who were surveyed reported having osteoporosis, but testing indicated that 26% actually had the disease (U.S. Department of Health and Human Services, 2004). Consistent with these data, the Centers for Disease Control and Prevention estimate that 25% of women in the United States over age 65 have osteoporosis (Looker & Frenk, 2015). This is a concern because it contributes to fracture rates and, subsequently, hospitalizations and placement in nursing homes. Hip fractures, in particular, are associated with an increased risk of death in the initial year after the fracture occurs (U.S. Department of Health and Human Services, 2004).

While osteoporosis is a bone disease, osteoarthritis (OA) is a joint disease. It's a degenerative condition that occurs when cartilage in joints breaks down, so there's nothing left to cushion the movement of bones against one another. This can result in pain, stiffness, and swelling. It can occur in any joint, but the knees, hips, lower back, and fingers are among the most common sites. Anyone who lives long enough will eventually develop OA, and greater wear and tear on joints (e.g., due to physical labor or athletic activity) can be a contributing factor. OA is a leading cause of chronic pain and disability for both women and men (United States Bone and Joint Initiative, 2014). Although there's great variability in the experience of OA from person to person, the pain and physical limitations associated with it can interfere with individuals' ability to work and engage in preferred leisure activities. Because women generally live longer than men (see Table 11.3; Arias, Heron, & Xu, 2016), they have more opportunity to develop and live with OA, and research indicates that women are at higher risk (Srikanth et al., 2005).

Another disease that disproportionately affects women is Alzheimer's disease (Mazure & Swendsen, 2016). This is the most common form of dementia, and it involves progressive declines in cognitive abilities that typically begin with memory loss. Women are at 30% greater risk than men (Tejada-Vera, 2013), and while women's higher life expectancy can explain part of this, it doesn't explain the entire gap, particularly in people ages 60 to 80 (Viña & Lloret, 2010). Non-Hispanic White women appear to be at higher risk compared to non-Hispanic Black women and Hispanic women of all races (Tejada-Vera, 2013). Although some treatments seem to slow the progression of the disease in certain individuals, there is no cure, and women tend to live longer with Alzheimer's than do men (Mazure & Swendsen, 2016). As a result, women with dementia often live for extended periods in assisted living and long-term care facilities. It's noteworthy that women not only have the greater burden of living with this disease, but they also often serve as care providers for loved ones

TABLE 11.3 Life Expectancies in 2012 for Women and Men in the United States

	Women	Men
All	81.2 years	76.4 years
White	81.4 years	76.7 years
Black	78.4 years	72.3 years
Hispanic (all races)	84.3 years	79.3 years

Note. Data drawn from Arias et al. (2016).

who have Alzheimer's (Winblad et al., 2016). Wives make up a large proportion of these individuals, but daughters and daughters-in-law also frequently fill this role. As discussed later, caregiving, particularly in old age, can be challenging.

The Health-Care System

How can differing social identity characteristics, ageism, and other prejudices impact older women's experiences within the health-care system?

Even if a woman has no chronic illnesses such as high blood pressure, diabetes, or osteoarthritis, she'll almost certainly utilize health-care services at some point. Whether she has access to high-quality health care depends on where she lives and what type of health insurance, if any, she has. People's experiences with the health-care system are different depending on their social identity characteristics. There are, for example, significant racial disparities in access to adequate care. The American Medical Association (AMA) reviewed the existing research in 2002 and concluded that the evidence for racial disparities was overwhelming and unacceptable (Nelson, 2002). These disparities lead to higher death rates for cancer, diabetes, and heart disease among people with racial/ethnic minority identities. The AMA also concluded that, beyond economic factors, inequities stemmed from often-unacknowledged prejudice and discrimination on the part of medical providers, who tend to be disproportionately White. Recruiting more people of color into health-care fields can help address this issue, as can educating all providers about cultural issues and providing interpreters as necessary so that language proficiency doesn't become an additional barrier to treatment (Betancourt, Green, Carrillo, & Ananeh-Firempong, 2003).

Although these factors influence all people's experiences with the health-care system, older adults—and older women in particular—have unique challenges in navigating the system. As is true with race/ethnicity, health-care professionals bring their personal assumptions and biases into their interactions with patients, with the result that ageism plays a role in the care that many older adults receive (Chrisler, Barney, & Palatino, 2016; Nemmers, 2005). For those who also identify as belonging to other marginalized groups, this experience can be compounded by racism, heterosexism, transphobia, ableism, and other biases (Spring, 2015). For example, a transwoman who has long lived as a woman and is publicly recognized as such may find herself needing more health services as she ages. If she hasn't had genital surgery, she may have to "out" herself to providers. In doing so, she may experience an array of reactions ranging from surprise and discomfort, to misgendering, to humiliation and refusal to treat. Researchers have found that older LGBTQ adults often feel the need to "go back into the closet" because of fears of mistreatment by health-care providers (Bradford et al., 2016; Czaja et al., 2016; Gendron et al., 2013).

One challenge that older adults, and older women in particular, encounter is infantilization. Because of negative stereotypes about older adults being frail and experiencing cognitive decline, some people, including those within the health-care system, are likely to treat older adults as if they were children—for example, through elderspeak. **Elderspeak** involves simplified speech, a high pitch, and an exaggerated tone similar to baby-talk. Some people might think that addressing older women as "sweetie" and "dear" is an appropriate way to connect and doesn't belittle them (Leland, 2008), but those on the receiving end of elderspeak perceive it as a sign that the speakers see themselves as superior (O'Connor & St. Pierre, 2004).

There are real consequences to engaging in elderspeak. Research has shown that people perceive targets of elderspeak as less capable (Balsis & Carpenter, 2006), and those who are targets can experience it as a microaggression (Chrisler et al., 2016). Moreover, a growing body of research has linked the use of elderspeak by health-care providers to more aggressive and less cooperative behavior among those with dementia (Cunningham & Williams, 2007; Herman & Williams, 2009; Williams, Herman, Gajewski, & Wilson, 2009). Although much of the research on elderspeak has been done in medical contexts, elderspeak is used in all contexts.

Changing Relationships

Positive experiences with aging are related to having successful relationships and a sense of belonging. In Chapter 8, we examined the importance of friendships across the life span. Strong social ties with family members and friends are especially important predictors of positive mental and physical health among older adults (Cornwell & Waite, 2009). However, as women age, their relationships can change. As is true throughout our lives, changes can be positive or negative. Moreover, the same change can be experienced in varying ways by different people.

Romantic and Sexual Partners

In what ways may women's relationships with their partners change, and what are the impacts of these changes?

Among married women and men, older men have been shown to be more satisfied with their marriage than older women (Boerner, Jopp, Carr, Sosinsky, & Kim, 2014; Bulanda, 2011; Jackson, Miller, Oka, & Henry, 2014; Umberson & Williams, 2005). This is largely because men see their wives as nurturing and caring, and they report that their wives treat them better than the wives report about their husbands (Boerner et al., 2014). These findings may reflect the fact that the current cohort of older adults was raised at a time when women were more encouraged to be caring and nurturing than may be true of younger women today. It remains to be seen if these patterns will continue in future generations.

Sexuality Sex is often an important part of intimate relationships. Many older women desire and have sex; however, with the exception of the category of "cougars"—a term often perceived as derogatory since it implies a predatory approach to sexuality (Montemurro & Siefken, 2014)—advanced age is stereotypically associated with asexuality (Drummond et al., 2013; Fileborn et al., 2015). Even physicians don't generally talk about sexual health with older adults because they don't see it as a concern for this group of patients (Gott, Hinchliff, & Galena, 2004). Although rates of sexual activity do decrease with age, one study showed that the majority of women who were married or cohabiting remained sexually active, with rates ranging from 92% for those in their 40s to 44% for those age 80 and older (Thomas, Hess, & Thurston, 2015). Two of the most common reasons that older women provide for decreased sexual activity are their partners' poor health and the lack of a partner (McHugh & Interligi, 2015).

Moreover, research with older women indicates that they experience sexual desire and sex in diverse ways and that their conceptualizations of what constitutes a satisfying sexual encounter can change throughout their lives. In a study of Australian women ages 55 through 81 (all but one of whom identified as heterosexual), participants reported a wide range of attitudes about sex (Fileborn et al., 2015). Some reported that sex was "really important and it's a lot of fun achieving it too," while others expressed sentiments such as "We don't have it. It doesn't worry me" (p. 120). Among women not having, or not often having, penetrative sex, most still reported engaging in other types of sexual intimacy with their partners (e.g., cuddling) and/or masturbating in order to satisfy themselves sexually.

As discussed above, body changes associated with menopause include changes in vaginal lubrication and the thinning of the vaginal walls. These changes can make penetrative sex less comfortable and potentially less satisfying for women. However, one study indicated that poor or nonexistent communication between partners may also contribute to lack of sexual satisfaction in older women (Fileborn et al., 2015), and another showed that older women who talked about sex with their partners reported higher rates of sexual satisfaction (Thomas et al., 2015). The latter study also showed that those who enjoyed sex when they were younger were more likely to continue enjoying it as they got older.

Caregiving Another change to romantic relationships can occur if a partner becomes sick or develops a disability. The term **family caregiving** refers to the unpaid assistance provided to an older adult or an adult with chronic or disabling conditions, and women are those most likely to be caregivers (Brazil, Thabane, Foster, & Bédard, 2009; Strang, Koop, & Peden, 2002). In the United States, older adults receive care primarily through family caregiving

Caregiving is a common experience for women of all ages, but it's often part of changing relationships as partners age—particularly if one partner needs ongoing assistance and care. Although many couples adapt their relationship in response to their changing roles and abilities, caregiving can also serve as a source of stress.

(Taylor, Kuchibhatla, & Østbye, 2008). Overall, 60% of caregivers are women, and they typically dedicate more hours to care work than their male counterparts do (AARP Public Policy Institute, 2015). Among married couples, a spouse is the family member who provides most caregiving, accounting for 41% of all informal long-term care and 70% of short-term care (Schulz & Martire, 2004). Because LGBTQ older adults are less likely to have children and haven't always been permitted to marry, they're more likely to rely on friends to provide caregiving (Adelman, Gurevitch, Vries, & Blando, 2006; Croghan, Moone, & Olson, 2014; Czaja et al., 2016; de Vries, 2014; Shippy, Cantor, & Brennan, 2004; Shiu, Muraco, & Fredriksen-Goldsen, 2016).

Numerous studies have shown that the chronic stress associated with family caregiving is associated with increased levels of depression, fear, anxiety, and anger—especially among women (Bookwala & Schulz, 2000; Brazil, Bédard, Willison, & Hode, 2003; Strang et al., 2002). There is also an increased risk for loss of income, social isolation, and chronic illness (Cheung & Hocking, 2004; Pinquart & Sörensen, 2007). Because of the time demands and stress associated with providing care, caregivers are less likely to seek out positive experiences, social support, and opportunities to acquire or develop new skills (Mausbach et al., 2012). Long-term caregiving also has been shown to increase physical health risks, such as the likelihood of developing heart disease (Vitaliano, Young, & Zhang, 2004; von Känel et al., 2008). In one study that followed those caring for partners with dementia, researchers found that 24% of participants had an emergency room visit or a hospitalization within a six-month period (Schubert et al., 2008).

However, for many people, family caregiving is the only viable option. Other options, including hiring a caregiver or having a family member move to an assisted living facility, can be prohibitively expensive. For example, the median cost of an assisted living facility in the United States was $45,000 per year in 2017; in some states (e.g., Delaware, New Jersey, Massachusetts), the cost was over $65,000 per year (Heckler, 2017). The cost of hiring someone to help in the home varies, but according to *payscale.com* in 2018, an in-home caregiver makes a median of $23,893 ("Live-in Caregiver Salary," n.d.)—a salary that's barely above the poverty line but still out of reach for many families to afford.

Bereavement Because women have a higher life expectancy than men, most women with male partners will outlive them (DiGiacomo, Davidson, Byles, & Nolan, 2013). The death of a life partner is extremely stressful, and several studies show that almost half of all women over age 65 have lost their partner, with married women from lower socioeconomic backgrounds being the most likely to become widowed (Richardson et al., 2015; Zivin & Christakis, 2007). Following the death of a spouse, people are more likely to engage in high-risk behaviors, such as smoking and drinking (Wilcox et al., 2003; Zisook, Shuchter, & Mulvihill, 1990). They also tend to experience a decline in physical and mental health (Burns, Browning, & Kendig, 2015; Lee & Carr, 2007; Williams et al., 2011). In fact, a 48% increase in mortality risk occurs when people are widowed (Sullivan & Fenelon, 2014). This pattern, called the **widowhood effect**, is most pronounced immediately following the death, especially if the death was unexpected and if it results in a loss of financial resources (Manzoli, Villari, Pironec, & Boccia, 2007; Sullivan & Fenelon, 2014).

Bereavement is grief associated with losing a relative or a close friend through death. Although bereavement can occur at any time in a woman's life, it's most common in later life (Stahl & Schulz, 2014). In Chapter 8, we discussed social support, and such support can help in coping with grief (e.g., Jacobson, Lord, & Newman, 2017; Stroebe, Zech, Stroebe, & Abakoumkin, 2005). However, relationships may change when a loss occurs, and the change can affect support. For example, those in one's support network may also be experiencing grief related to the shared loss (Moss & Moss, 2014; Stroebe & Schut, 2015). Some people may also feel it's important to grieve on their own. In one study of Black and White widows, most of the women wanted to remain autonomous and independent and, therefore, didn't rely on family members to help process emotions (Moss & Moss, 2014). For example, they avoided discussing their sadness with their adult children because they thought the children wouldn't understand their experience.

The ability to openly mourn the loss of a partner is also related to bereavement experiences (Bristowe et al., 2018; Deevey, 2000; Ingham, Eccles, Armitage, & Murray, 2017). For example, one study showed that lesbian women who were unable to disclose the nature of their relationship with a deceased partner received less social support and experienced more prolonged feelings of grief as compared to those who could disclose (Bent & Magilvy, 2006). Older lesbian and bisexual women are vulnerable to experiencing **disenfranchised grief**, or the inability to openly grieve a loss because the loss isn't acknowledged by those around them. This type of grief occurs because, compared to those from younger generations, they're less likely to disclose their relationship status out of fear of economic insecurity, personal safety, familial and cultural relationships, and child custody issues (Beals & Peplau, 2001; Jenkins, Edmundson, Averett, & Yoon, 2014; Keppel, 2006; Whitman, Cormier, & Boyd, 2000). Further, inclusion in one's family or religious community may be contingent on keeping silent about one's sexual orientation (Hughes, 2009).

Following the death of a romantic partner, one difficult decision is whether to date or remarry. There appears to be a gender gap in late-life remarriage: Men are more likely to remarry than women (Livingston, 2014). There are several possible explanations for this. For example, because women generally outlive men, there are simply fewer potential partners for women who are interested in a male partner to find, so women may not end up in another marriage even if it's desired. Other research shows that older women tend to have strong social networks and receive support from their adult children (Antonucci, Akiyama, & Takahashi, 2004; Connidis, 2014), so they might not look to a new spouse for this. Also, as discussed in prior chapters, women do a larger proportion of caretaking and domestic labor than their male partners. Given this, older women may not be interested in taking on additional responsibilities like these that a new marriage might bring.

Finally, when women remarry, they risk losing or seeing a reduction in their Social Security or pension benefits (Brien, Dickert-Conlin, & Weaver, 2001). For example, if an older woman hasn't worked, or hasn't worked much, during her lifetime, she may depend on spousal Social Security benefits based on her late husband's earnings. If her new spouse's Social Security benefits are greater than hers, she will no longer be eligible to receive the ones from her late spouse. However, the potential new spouse's retirement income may not be enough to support both himself and the woman if she cannot retain the Social Security benefits derived from her late spouse's earnings. In fact, research has shown that higher income and lower worry about finances were significant predictors of widows remarrying (Moorman, Booth, & Fingerman, 2006).

Children and Grandchildren

What are the stereotypes about and the realities of older women's roles as mothers and grandmothers?

Mothers don't stop being mothers when they and their children get older, and many mothers subsequently become grandmothers. Changes in relationships between women and their children can add both beneficial and challenging aspects to older women's lives. Similarly, grandparenting can be very rewarding; but for some, it also brings significant caregiving responsibilities that women might not have expected to be taking on in their older years.

An Empty Nest The term *empty nest* became popular in the 1970s to describe the post-parental period—the time when children are grown and no longer live at home (Dennerstein, Dudley, & Guthrie, 2002). Because of changes in birth control that have allowed for smaller families, the post-parental period is now lasting longer than ever before (Bouchard, 2014). Among couples with children, nearly half of marriage is now spent after the children leave home (Vespa, Lewis, & Kreider, 2013), yet for many people the term *empty nest* still conjures an image of a sad and lonely mother (Sheriff & Weatherall, 2009).

This pessimistic view perpetuates an ageist and sexist understanding of life without children.

Overall, research shows that experiencing an empty nest is actually beneficial for most adults, and especially for women (Mitchell & Lovegreen, 2009; Schmidt, Murphy, Haq, Rubinow, & Danaceau, 2004). One explanation is the **role strain relief hypothesis**, which suggests that parents, particularly mothers, have an increase in well-being after children leave home because of a decrease in daily demands, time constraints, and work–family conflicts (Erickson, Martinengo, & Hill, 2010). In several studies, women reported that the post-parental period allowed for reconnection with partners, improved self-care, and increased freedom (Bouchard, 2014; Grover & Dang, 2013). Further, both women and men have been shown to experience increased marital and sexual satisfaction after their children leave home (Gorchoff, John, & Helson, 2008; Hagen & DeVries, 2004).

Although most women describe positive experiences post-parenting, some do report a sense of ambivalence (Dare, 2011). This is especially true for women with limited social relationships or roles outside of caretaking and for those who became parents earlier in life (Bouchard, 2014; Mitchell & Lovegreen, 2009). **Empty-nest syndrome** occurs when a person experiences depression, loneliness, identity crisis, or emotional distress after children leave the home (Mitchell & Lovegreen, 2009). Scholars suggest that such experiences may be connected to the **role loss hypothesis**, which proposes that parents, particularly mothers, will experience a decrease in well-being when their role as caregiver is no longer needed (Sheriff & Weatherall, 2009). The post-parental period may also present unique challenges for women with chronic illnesses and disabilities (Murphy, Roberts, & Herbeck, 2012). HIV-positive mothers, for example, have reported that their "mother role" was helpful in distracting them from their illness, so they had a particularly hard time adjusting when their children left home.

Of course, a lot has changed since the 1970s, when the idea of an empty nest became popular. Many mothers now work outside the home, which gives them a role beyond that of parent (Pew Research Center, 2013). Further, the process through which children leave home has become more dynamic (Sandberg-Thoma, Snyder, & Jang, 2015). For example, the term **launching phase** now refers to the period during which children are in the process of leaving the parental home; the oldest may have left, but younger children continue living with the parents (Hagen & DeVries, 2004). As a result, the nest doesn't empty at one point in time. Further, because of recent economic changes, the term *boomerang kids* has been coined to describe adult children who leave but then return home again (Sheriff & Weatherall, 2009). In one study, parents appeared to understand the economic pressures that contribute to this pattern and reported stronger familial bonds when their adult children returned home (Cherlin, Cumberworth, Morgan, & Wimer, 2013). Other studies show a more complex picture—the return of adult children contributed to conflict between parents, decline in marital satisfaction, and decreased sexual intimacy between parents (Bouchard, 2014; Lodge & Umberson, 2016).

Grandmothering New relationships and roles enhance women's lives as they age, and one of them—becoming a grandmother—can bring tremendous happiness and fulfillment (Shlomo, Taubman - Ben-Ari, Findler, Sivan, & Dolizki, 2010; Thiele & Whelan, 2008). Although becoming a grandmother is often viewed as a sign of aging, it can also enhance social status for older women (Armstrong, 2003). Grandmothers can act as caregivers, mentors, and teachers, and the practical and emotional support they provide has reciprocal benefits (Moore & Rosenthal, 2015). For example, a grandmother's involvement contributes to a grandchild's positive health and resilience (Barnett, Scaramella, Neppl, Ontai, & Conger, 2010; Greve & Bjorklund, 2009) while simultaneously improving the grandmother's mental and physical health (Grundy et al., 2012). Engagement with grandchildren has also been found to relate to overall life satisfaction among grandmothers (Moore & Rosenthal, 2015). Moreover, periodically visiting and providing caregiving can promote positive, affirming, and loving relationships with their adult children as well as their grandchildren (Armstrong, 2003).

Other research, however, shows that grandmothers who are very involved in child care experience greater levels of depression and health problems than their non-caregiving peers (Fuller-Thomson, & Minkler, 2000; Whitley, Lamis, & Kelley, 2016). This is most true for grandmothers who live with their

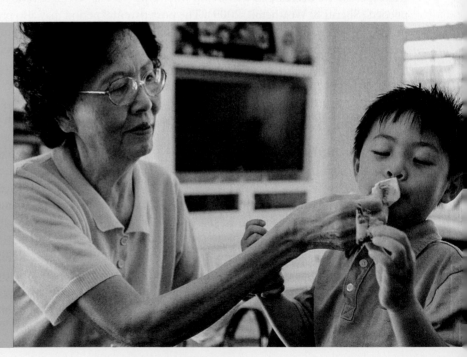

Many women look forward to grandmothering, and it can be a way to form and maintain rich, intergenerational relationships. However, some grandmothers also find themselves in the role of part-time or full-time caregivers for their grandchildren—something that may not have been part of their expectations for this role.

grandchildren, and especially for those who are primary caregivers. According to a report from the United States Census Bureau, nearly 4.6 million households (4%) included grandparents and grandchildren, and of these, 33% had no parent present (Ellis & Simmons, 2014). In 63% of these households, grandmothers reported being responsible for the care of their grandchildren. Multigenerational homes often occur when a teen or adult child has a baby or when a parent experiences health problems, divorce, or job loss (Musil & Ahmad, 2002; Pruchno & McKenney, 2002). These multigenerational households can be found nationwide and among families with diverse demographic profiles, but they're more common for those who live in the South, are of lower socioeconomic status, or identify as people of color (Ellis & Simmons, 2014).

Some grandparents assume a **custodial role** and become full-time, and often permanent, guardians of a grandchild. In 2006, for example, 2.6 million grandparents in the United States had legal custody of their grandchildren (Livingston & Parker, 2010). Because becoming a primary guardian often occurs as a result of unexpected stressors such substance abuse, incarceration, or death, grandparents may already have feelings of depression and anxiety when they take on this new role (Minkler & Roe, 1993; Standing, Musil, & Warner, 2007). Further, becoming a primary caregiver disrupts retirement plans, reduces social and leisure time, and creates financial strain, which further contributes to distress (Ludwig, Hattjar, Russell, & Winston, 2007). This role is especially demanding for grandparents who have chronic illnesses or physical disabilities (Marken, Pierce, & Baltisberger, 2010). Nevertheless, research shows that grandmothers with strong support systems report less depression and feel positive about their caregiving role (Doley, Bell, Watt, & Simpson, 2015; Gerard, Landry-Meyer, & Roe, 2006).

your turn

Do you know any children who were raised by their grandmothers? If so, how did this affect the grandmother's quality of life? How would you feel about being a primary caregiver to your own grandchild? How might the different circumstances that could contribute to this situation impact your feelings?

Older Women at Work

Despite a few high-profile women who continue to work into old age (e.g., Supreme Court Justice Ruth Bader Ginsburg), the media rarely portray older women working. However, despite their general invisibility as workers, they appear to be staying in the workforce longer than ever (Goldin & Katz, 2016). This upward trend is true for women in all age groups—even those over age 70. In fact, the gender gap for workplace participation among older workers is smaller now than the gender gap among younger workers. For example, among 60- to 64-year-olds during the period 2012–2014, fully 61% of men and 51% of women were working—a 10-point gender gap, compared to a 16-point gender gap among 30- to 40-year-olds (Goldin & Katz, 2016). These data indicate that, although women may leave the workforce during their mothering years, older women continue to vigorously participate in it. This may be a healthy sign of job engagement among older women, but it may also indicate that many women aren't financially able to retire. In fact, one study showed that some older women are working longer than in previous generations because they have more debt and cannot afford to retire (Lusardi & Mitchell, 2016).

Age Discrimination

In what ways do women experience workplace age discrimination, and how does this interact with other forms of discrimination they may experience?

Even though older women are participating in paid work more than ever, they still face job discrimination. In 2016, the *Harvard Business Review* profiled several women who experienced age discrimination at work (Rikleen, 2016). One was a 60-year-old who had worked for years in the insurance business. Despite outstanding performance evaluations, her situation became difficult when a new manager, 20 years younger than her, was hired. Suddenly, she was assigned the most difficult cases, and the manager was harsher on her than her younger colleagues. She received a bad performance review, was told she had 90 days to improve, and then was fired after only a few weeks. Another profile was of a 64-year-old bartender who had worked at a neighborhood bar for over a decade. When the bar was sold, the new owners told her she was too old for the job. They made fun of her age and gender in front of the other workers, and she was eventually fired.

Both women ultimately sued for age discrimination, something that's not easy to do. Although the Age Discrimination and Employment Act (ADEA) of 1967 makes it illegal to discriminate against older adults (defined as over age 40), discrimination can be difficult to prove. In 2009, the U.S. Supreme Court ruled that the burden of proof for age discrimination cases should fall on workers. Before this ruling, if age was just one of several factors, it was the employer's responsibility to prove that the worker was fired for a reason other than age. In other words, workers must now provide proof that age was the reason they were fired or demoted, and this type of clear-cut evidence is hard to come by.

Although age discrimination may be noticed when one is being fired or demoted, it's much harder to notice when being hired. After all, it's usually impossible to know why one isn't being offered a job. However, several studies have demonstrated that age discrimination can be a factor in hiring. The general design of such studies involves submitting resumés matched on experience and skills in response to job ads, varying only the applicant's age. Although people typically don't indicate their age on their resumé, it can be inferred from information such as the high school graduation date. In one study of female job applicants, those ages 35 to 45 got offered interviews 46% more frequently than those ages 50 to 62 (Lahey, 2008). Another study explored both the age and the gender of applicants and, again, showed age discrimination (Neumark, Burn, & Button, 2015). Older workers, especially those near retirement age (64 to 66), were called for interviews less often than younger workers, but the gap was much larger for women than for men. For example, for retail sales, the gap between older and younger workers was twice as large for women as it was for men. Older men were also called more often than older women for administrative jobs. The researchers were actually surprised at how little age discrimination was found for men.

Intersecting Factors There are many other reasons an older worker may be let go or encouraged to take early retirement. For example, because older workers who've been in a position or a company for a long time generally make more money, companies may be motivated to replace them with younger workers who can be paid less. In these cases, the employers could argue that their motivation is financial and not discriminatory due to age (Duncan, 2003). Furthermore, age isn't people's sole social identity characteristic, so age (and gender) need to be considered as part of the broader constellation of characteristics that constitute someone's social identity. For example, older workers are more likely than younger workers to have a disability. Just over 10% of people between 18 and 64 years of age in the United States have a

Older women can bring many years of personal and professional experience to their jobs. However, they also frequently face age discrimination—often in interaction with other forms of bias. What can be done to counteract this trend?

disability, but approximately 35% of those age 65 and older do (Kraus, Lauer, Coleman, & Houtenville, 2018). Of those adults with disabilities, only 36% were employed as compared to just over 76% of adults without disabilities. Given this context, ableism may interact with ageism. It may, similarly, be difficult to identify the source of discrimination for older women of color, given that they may experience discrimination along a number of dimensions (e.g., age, gender, race).

Research has identified several negative stereotypes about older workers that may contribute to workplace age discrimination. These include the stereotypes that older workers are less motivated, less willing to participate in training or career development, less willing to adapt to technology and change, less trusting, less healthy, and more likely to have work–family conflict due to greater interest in family and leisure activities than work (Ng & Feldman, 2012). However, when the researchers explored the reality of older workers' attitudes and behaviors, their meta-analysis showed no evidence to support most of these stereotypes. Older age was actually associated with being somewhat more motivated, being more interested in change at work, and having greater confidence about computer skills. No relationship was found between age and work–family conflict. Age was also not related to physical or psychological health overall, although greater age was associated with increased cholesterol levels. The only stereotype that received a small degree of support was that older workers were somewhat less interested in career development and training. Overall, these findings suggest that many of the reasons people discriminate against older workers are unfounded. In fact, other research has shown that job experience is a better predictor of job performance than age, and older individuals generally have more job experience than younger individuals do (Hardy, 2006).

Age discrimination may be particularly prevalent in periods of economic trouble when jobs are scarce. Under these circumstances, older workers can be de-valued because younger workers may perceive them as competing for resources (North & Fiske, 2016). For example, younger workers may feel that older workers should step aside and make room for younger generations. They may also think older workers are a burden on society or on the company through overuse of resources such as health care. Finally, younger workers may be irritated when older workers don't act their age and engage in activities that are associated with younger generations (e.g., use certain forms of social media or listen to certain types of music). In other words, when there's plenty of work to go around, there seems to be less bias toward older workers, but when younger workers are concerned about their own welfare, bias against older workers can occur.

your turn

What are your attitudes toward older workers? Do you think they bring valuable insights to the workplace, or should they move out of the way to make room for younger workers? Does the type of job you imagine older workers in influence your thoughts? Explain your responses.
Then ask friends and family about their attitudes toward older workers. Is there a general attitude of respect or competition?

While older workers may face unfounded discrimination in general, physical appearance is an especially relevant issue for older women. In one study, women across all age groups reported more discrimination at work based on physical appearance than did men, but this discrimination increased as women got older (Duncan & Loretto, 2004). In another study, a receptionist in her mid-fifties described her difficulty getting work: "On the telephone I can sound animated and I would often get called in for jobs, and then they would see me, and not that I looked bad, but I looked my age, and they instantly weren't interested" (Handy & Davy, 2007, p. 91). Consultants placing women in jobs often admitted that clients weren't interested in hiring older women because of physical appearance, especially for front-of-house receptionist positions: "They always want good looking at reception" (p. 93).

Older women experience discrimination based on both age and gender, but discrimination based on a combination of the two is especially hard to prove. Although age discrimination is illegal under the ADEA and gender discrimination is illegal under Title IX, no agency exists that can defend against a combination of gender and age discrimination, so older women who are discriminated against have little recourse. If a company shows that older men were retained, the women will have a difficult time proving that age discrimination took place (Spedale, Coupland, & Tempest, 2014). If younger women were retained, the older women will have a difficult time proving that gender discrimination took place.

Age and gender discrimination particularly affects women who are trying to re-enter the workforce (Hardy, 2006). As discussed earlier in this book, women are more likely than men to leave the workforce in order to care for children. These women then face a difficult situation when they attempt to return to work once their children are older. Similarly, women who weren't working might find themselves needing to find a job after a divorce or the death of a partner. Even among women who've maintained ongoing employment, smaller periods of unemployment may be especially detrimental for older women. For example, older women were particularly hard hit after the recession of 2007–2009. In one study, older women (over age 65) were more likely than older men to report long-term unemployment of more than six months (Monge-Naranjo & Faisal, 2015). Further, women over age 50 made up almost half of the long-term unemployed.

The situation becomes more complex when other aspects of social identity also play a role, as is the case for older women of color. Research typically focuses on a single type of discrimination (e.g., sexism) or sometimes a combination of two (e.g., sexism and ageism). Much more research is needed to understand the role of intersecting aspects of social identities as well as overlapping forms of discrimination. For example, future research would benefit from exploring the triple threat of ageism, sexism, and racism in the work environment. At the moment, in more general research on discrimination, older women of color have reported difficulties associated with a lifetime of discrimination and marginalization. For example, in a study of older Black lesbians and gay men, researchers found a common "uneasiness" among participants arising from their life-long experiences with stigma and stereotypical assumptions (Woody, 2014, p. 158). Participants reported often being the only person of color in their lesbian/gay circle of friends and being the only lesbian/gay person in their Black group of friends. This resulted in chronic feelings of being "othered" within both groups based on the participants' distinctiveness related to another aspect of social identity (p. 159).

Even though experiencing multiple sources of discrimination can enhance stress, other research does suggest a buffering effect by which someone experiencing additional discrimination can be less negatively affected by it than someone who has rarely experienced discrimination in the past (Raver & Nishii, 2010). For example, if someone has experienced bias related to race, they may be more prepared for the experience of bias in the future—even if it's related to a different aspect of their social identity (e.g., gender or age). They may also have developed coping strategies used for one type of discrimination, like reaching out to their support networks for emotional support and/or practical suggestions, which can be applied to the additional type of discrimination. Consistent with this idea, research has shown that White individuals are more negatively affected by age discrimination than Black individuals, presumably because the White individuals have had less need to develop coping mechanisms against discrimination (Foley & Lytle, 2015).

Retirement

What are women's positive and negative experiences of retirement?

Women face conflicting messages in deciding when to retire. On the one hand, society tells them they should be able to rest and focus on their relationships and leisure activities. On the other hand, there are a few high-profile media images of vibrant older women (e.g. the late poet Maya Angelou and Supreme Court Justice Sonia Sotomayor), which imply that older women should stay in the workforce and remain productive into late life (Lips & Hastings, 2012).

Women decide to retire for many reasons. Retirement may be a response to being phased out of work or feeling no longer valued. It can also reflect a positive desire to relax and enjoy leisure time. Further, women are more likely than men to retire due to the need to care for others, such as a spouse, a grandchild, or an older child (Duberley, Carmichael, & Szmigin, 2014). In a study conducted in Canada, researchers found that women age 55 and older who had to engage in intensive caregiving (more than 15 hours a week) were especially likely to be out of the labor market, be working part-time, or retire early (Jacobs, Laporte, Van Houtven, & Coyte, 2014).

Many women don't have a specific retirement moment at which they go from working full-time to not working at all. Instead, they may engage in part-time work, which can be essential if they cannot fully afford retirement. However, as discussed earlier, it can be difficult for older women to find work, so part-time work after retirement often involves a lower skill level and lower pay (Tavener, Vo, & Byles, 2015). Jobs obtained after retirement from another job are called **bridge work**, and these can serve as an important transition on the way to full retirement.

Affording Retirement A woman cannot enjoy a leisurely retirement unless she is well prepared financially. However, there's a great deal of evidence that older women don't financially plan for retirement as carefully as their male counterparts (e.g., Boisclair, Lusardi, & Michaud, 2017; Lusardi & Mitchell, 2008, 2011; Noone, Alpass, & Stephens, 2010). For one thing, women tend to be less informed than men about how to plan and save for retirement. Furthermore, they generally pick lower-risk investments with lower yields, which can negatively affect their long-term savings (Speelman, Clark-Murphy, & Gerrans, 2013). One study indicated that women who had a mother or a sister with breast cancer were less likely to plan for retirement than those with no family history of breast cancer (Zick, Mayer, & Smith, 2015). The researchers suggest that this pattern may be due, in part, to women not believing that they would live long enough to retire.

The Women's Institute for Secure Retirement (WISER) has identified risk factors that affect women as they plan for retirement (WISER, 2014). Financially, they're less secure than men. They tend to have less in savings, receive lower Social Security payments, and are less likely to hold a job covered by a pension. Moreover, because women have a longer life expectancy than men, they're at significant risk of outliving their assets. The latter risk factor is compounded by the fact that health-care costs can be extremely high—median health-care costs for older adults were estimated to range from $40,000 to $80,000 a year in 2014, depending on the level of care needed (WISER, 2014).

In one study of primarily White, retired women, participants reported that much of their stress derived from the fact that they hadn't planned for retirement appropriately (Price & Nesteruk, 2015). One woman noted, "My financial condition is a disaster. I have no savings. I was always working day and night and that is why I kept putting off saving for retirement. I think your study should [tell] women to get financial training in high school so they would know how to make good decisions about money when they are single retired women" (p. 427). The study participants also hadn't anticipated the level of caregiving they were doing during retirement. They were caring for their spouses, their adult children, their aging parents, and sometimes even their grandchildren.

try it for yourself

Have you given any thought to your retirement plans? What kind of lifestyle do you want to have when you retire? How do you plan on saving for retirement? Using one of the many online retirement calculators, estimate how much you'll need to save each year to have a "comfortable" retirement income. Talk to your parents and other working adults about how they saved or are saving for retirement. Are they comfortable with their choices? Why or why not?

In the United States, 10.6% of women over the age of 65 live in poverty, as compared to 7.6% of men (Patrick, 2017). These financial concerns are compounded for women of color. At 22.4%, 20.6%, and 19.8%, respectively, the poverty rates for Native American, Black, and Latinx women are more than double those of White women (8.2%). One factor causing these high poverty rates is the gender wage gap (discussed in Chapter 10), which translates into a retirement savings gap. For example, Black women earn $421,000 less than White men over the course of their careers and are less likely to be in jobs covered by pensions (WISER, n.d.). Another factor is the likelihood that women will outlive their male partners. One study of rural White Americans showed that becoming a widow greatly increased the risk of poverty, because of the loss of the husband's pension as well as his Social Security benefits (Gillen & Kim, 2009). Private retirement savings can pass to spouses or other surviving family members upon someone's death, but private pensions are often not available to spouses. While spouses are still eligible to receive a portion of their deceased spouse's full Social Security benefit, the reduction can be significant when still trying to pay the same housing costs, for example.

Joys and Challenges Even if a woman is financially able to retire, there are certain challenges stemming from retirement that she may not anticipate. For example, although work can be a source of stress, it can also be a source of social connections and provide a feeling of competence. In one study of primarily White women, researchers found that many were bored when they retired (Price & Nesteruk, 2015). One woman stated: "The one thing I did not plan for and that has caused me the most problem, is the lack of mental challenge" (p. 424). In fact, data from another study indicate that television viewing increases and physical activity decreases once people retire as compared to their pre-retirement levels (Barnett, van Sluijs, Ogilvie, & Wareham, 2014). Research shows that those who had been in more physically demanding jobs prior to retirement are the ones who experience larger decreases in activity level (Barnett et al., 2014; Berger, Der, Mutrie, & Hannah, 2005; Chung, Domino, Stearns, & Popkin, 2009). Their leisure activities, even when active in nature, couldn't compensate for the overall decrease in work-related activity.

To cope with the boredom that can come with retirement, many women engage in volunteer work or civic/community engagement, which can balance the loss of one's identity as a worker and can also help develop and maintain social connections (Tavener et al., 2015; van den Bogaard, Henkens, & Kalmijn, 2014). Another positive way to cope with the possible social isolation and lack of mental stimulation is to engage in new leisure activities (Liechty, Yarnal, & Kerstetter, 2012). **Leisure innovation**, or trying new leisure activities, has been identified as very important in having a successful retirement. One White woman said, "I want to experience everything. . . . I've never felt that way before, but as you get older, I think you kind of think, 'my time's running

out here.' I want to do everything!" (p. 397). Leisure innovation can promote a sense of autonomy, fulfillment, and new friends and connections.

Much of the research on women in retirement, like research on leisure innovation, focuses on White women. The experiences of women of color are largely studied in the context of increased risks of poverty (e.g., Sullivan & Meschede, 2016) rather than the joys they may also experience when they retire. However, one study on positive retirement experiences among women of color identified their role as caretakers, their participation in spiritual activities, and their status as keepers of the family history as beneficial aspects of aging and retirement (Nettles, 2016).

Another challenge of retirement is the changing relationship with one's spouse. Although many couples plan to retire at the same time in order to pursue leisure activities together (Blau, 1998; Loretto & Vickerstaff, 2013), retirement can put a strain on relationships. One woman reported: "It took a lot of attitude adjustment, patience, and love to deal with having my husband under my feet constantly" (Price & Nesteruk, 2015, p. 432). Another said: "I think that maybe we can get a bit on top of each other" (Loretto & Vickerstaff, 2013, p. 76).

Moreover, while men generally see retirement as a chance to pursue recreational activities, women more often see it as a break from juggling the demands of work and family life (Loretto & Vickerstaff, 2013). However, in some cases, the demands of caring for the home and other family members can actually intensify and exacerbate gender inequality in the home—as one study participant exclaimed, "Housewives never retire!" (Loretto & Vickerstaff, 2013, p. 77). Yet there's evidence of some men participating more in household labor after retirement. In one study that followed couples in Germany from ten years before to ten years after the husbands' retirement, the men's contribution to household labor doubled after retirement (Leopold & Skopek, 2015). Their activities included spending a little more time cooking, cleaning, and doing other traditionally feminine chores and considerably more time gardening and doing household repairs.

Health and Longevity Retirement may mean different things to different people depending on social and financial circumstances. A key question is whether retirement is good or bad for individuals' mental health and physical health. Would older women fare better if they continued to work? There is conflicting research on this subject. In one study of over 200,000 people in Australia, early retirement (before age 65) was related to psychological distress for both women and men, but retirement after age 65 was related to distress only for men (Vo et al., 2015). This may be because, as other research has shown, women have more social connections outside of work and are better able to stay engaged in the community (Byles et al., 2013). Retiring because of being laid off or needing to care for a family member has been specifically linked to increased psychological distress among retirees (Vo et al., 2015).

However, research indicates that retirement is not, overall, a negative experience. One study showed that retirement didn't decrease self-esteem or increase depression—instead, those who were depressed or had low self-esteem before retirement tended to experience the same problems after retirement (Reitzes, Mutran, & Fernandez, 1996). Another study indicated that decreases in self-esteem experienced in old age are accounted for by changes in both physical health and socioeconomic status (Orth, Trzesniewski, & Robins, 2010). Interestingly, additional research shows that retirement is actually linked to decreased antidepressant use (Oksanen et al., 2011) and is beneficial for mental health overall (see van der Heide, van Rijn, Robroek, Burdorf, & Proper, 2013, for a review).

Finally, there's evidence that one's health after retirement may be related to whether one expects retirement to be a positive or a negative experience. In one study, researchers followed more than 1,000 participants over age 50 for a period of 23 years (Ng, Allore, Monin & Levy, 2016). At the beginning of the study, they assessed participants' beliefs about whether retirement was associated with positive or negative mental health (e.g., hopeless or hopeful, meaningless or meaningful) as well as positive or negative physical health (e.g., sick or healthy, mobile or immobile). The researchers then followed the participants through their retirement years to determine how long they lived. Those whose general beliefs reflected positive stereotypes about physical health in retirement lived 4.5 years longer than those whose beliefs reflected negative stereotypes. Those with positive stereotypes about mental health in retirement lived 2.5 years longer than those with negative mental health stereotypes. These findings reflect stereotype embodiment, a topic discussed early in this chapter. In fact, most participants in this study had negative attitudes toward retirement: 76% were negative about physical health and 77% about mental health. The researchers noted that this negative perspective is consistent with persistent ageism seen in the media and in society overall. If one wants a happy and healthy retirement, it appears essential to have a positive attitude about what to expect.

Aging "Successfully"?

What is "successful aging," what are the problems with this perspective, and how can perspectives on aging be broadened to more positively frame aging and being old?

There is no right way or perfect way to age—there are as many experiences of aging as there are people. In the same way that there's no one path through childhood, college, parenthood, or work, there's no single path to the end of our lives. Nevertheless, researchers have attempted to define "successful aging" (Rowe & Kahn, 1987, 2015). The original approach was to focus on neutral and positive aspects of aging, as opposed to the typically negative focus on deficits and decline. In this way, *successful* aging was contrasted with *usual* aging.

However, as we saw in Chapter 1, researchers operationally define constructs in order to study them, and there is no single, agreed-upon operational definition of successful aging in the research literature. In fact, one review of the research identified 105 distinct operational definitions (Cosco, Prina, Perales, Stephan, & Brayne, 2014). Within these studies, researchers explored many potential aspects of successful aging, including physical health, emotional well-being, community engagement, and financial resources. Depending on the factors explored and the participants included, studies identified anywhere between less than 1% and more than 90% of people as aging "successfully."

Some researchers and theorists have questioned the idea that there's a successful way to age (for a review, see Martinson & Berridge, 2015). Certain critics believe that existing models are too narrow and focus on experiences that are more likely if one is White, physically healthy, and financially well off. Others call for greater consideration of each individual's perceptions of whether they are, in fact, successfully aging. Still others reject the entire idea of "successful aging" because it can be an additional burden for older adults, further marginalizing those with chronic illnesses, disabilities, or limited resources in other domains. In fact, one study showed that participants ages 42 to 61 blamed themselves for not aging "successfully" enough (Calasanti, 2016). Given these considerations, the notion that there's a particular way to age successfully can be a source of stress rather than a framework that helps people approach growing older in a positive manner.

Because of these problems with the framework of successful aging, some researchers have tried to re-frame work in this area by using more inclusive approaches. One proposed shift is to the concept of "harmonious aging," which focuses on balancing the challenges and opportunities that aging presents (Liang & Luo, 2012). Another approach, more common in Europe than North America, is "active aging," which involves being an active member of one's community—although this framework has also been criticized for focusing too much on employment-related activity (Foster & Walker, 2015). A third approach is a focus on "resilient aging," since resilience is something that everyone can develop and it acknowledges that one can have strength despite challenges or hardships (Harris, 2008). Another advantage of this model is that it can highlight the resilience of those within marginalized communities who have not been a key focus of research in this area (Wild, Wiles, & Allen, 2013).

In Chapter 6, when talking about beauty norms, we discussed the problems associated with replacing one narrow set of norms with another set, because doing so still involves establishing a standard that many people won't be able to meet. The same is true with aging. Focusing on individual choices that people make about aging won't be useful without also considering systemic factors that may influence the choices available to them (Katz & Calasanti, 2015). Ultimately, regardless of the language used, any "ideal" model of aging is inherently exclusionary. Instead of trying to identify how best to age, it has been suggested that the focus should be "on creating the conditions in which people can thrive, on their own terms, as they age" (Martinson & Berridge, 2015, p. 66).

Creating this type of social change will require more than replacing negative stereotypes of frail, dependent, older women with positive ones of active women. A broader focus will recognize that there are many ways to age successfully and be empowered (Chrisler et al., 2015). For example, a woman with decreased physical mobility because of osteoarthritis may still focus on her power to control her thoughts and emotions even if she has less control over her physical body. Similarly, a woman experiencing the onset of dementia may recognize that she still can choose the activities with which she fills her days and the people with whom she spends time. These women do live with limits—this is true of all people at all ages, but they can still be viewed as active, successful, and resilient by focusing on what they *are* doing rather than on what they *are not* doing.

Also, experiences, even challenging ones, from earlier in life can help during one's older years. For example, older women alive today lived through the civil rights and gay rights movements. They've generally experienced stereotypes and discrimination in different ways than younger women have (Harley & Teaster, 2016; Woody, 2014). These experiences can be a source of strength—as in developing coping skills and strong social networks (Witten, 2014). Of course, access to resources and social support can be key for older adults, and those in marginalized groups who lack such resources are particularly at risk (Bradford et al., 2016; Czaja et al., 2016). For example, one study showed that older transgender individuals who experienced stigma and victimization were particularly at risk for mental and physical difficulties (Fredriksen-Goldsen et al., 2014).

The Raging Grannies draw attention to themselves and their age by wearing clothes that are stereotypically associated with old women. They then violate those stereotypes by engaging in activism and education while wearing this attire—as is true of these women protesting in Detroit, Michigan, in 2016.

Regardless of their challenges, older adults can and do frequently contribute at both local and global levels. In particular, older women contribute to society by being part of the workforce, by serving in caregiving roles for family members, and by volunteering within their communities. In fact, in 2015, almost 25% of women age 65 and older in the United States volunteered (U.S. Department of Labor, 2016). Some older women chose to focus their energies on activism. For example, the Raging Grannies is an activist organization in Canada and the United States whose members dress in stereotypical "old lady" attire and raise awareness about social issues through song. One granny said, "I want to make a difference, I want to be a part of something bigger than me" (Hutchinson & Wexler, 2007, p. 103).

Conclusion

Research on stereotype embodiment demonstrates that our experience of aging has a lot to do with what we think will happen to us as we age. If we anticipate that getting older will be a depressing and lonely experience, it may come to pass. However, if we expect to still rock and rage through our golden years, that's more likely to happen. Women's experiences of aging are influenced by their own beliefs, societal stereotypes, and changing roles and relationships. There are also life challenges that are more common in older age, such as chronic health conditions and bereavement. There are, in fact, choices that we can make about how to approach aging, both as individuals and as a society, but there are also constraints on how aging can happen, on individual and societal levels. Much like other stages of development, the experience of aging isn't the same for everyone.

Chapter Review

SUMMARY

Stereotypes of Older Women

- People hold a mix of positive and negative stereotypes of older adults, but all are connected to ageist beliefs.
- Older women and men are judged differently, and this becomes more complex when looking at other intersecting social identity characteristics.
- Internalizing negative aging stereotypes can lead to poor outcomes for older adults.

The Aging Body

- Older women, like younger women, often report body dissatisfaction. Body changes associated with aging can be a cause of distress and dissatisfaction, and older women often report feeling invisible.
- Many older women feel pressure to engage in beauty work to conceal their age and conform to societal beauty norms. Others reject youth-oriented beauty norms typically associated with White and/or heterosexual women.
- While some experience menopause as a challenging medical event, other women view it as one of many transitions that happen throughout their lifetimes.
- Women's likelihood of developing chronic or terminal health conditions increases with age.
- Heart disease and cancer are the most common causes of death for women in the United States. Breast cancer receives a great deal of attention, but lung cancer causes the most cancer-related deaths among women each year. Osteoporosis, osteoarthritis, and dementia are health conditions that also present significant risks for women.

- More health concerns can mean greater use of health-care services, but disparities in access to high-quality care are related to factors such as social class, race/ethnicity, and language proficiency.
- Increased, age-related use of health-care services can be especially challenging for lesbian and transwomen, who may feel the need to hide their sexual and/or gender identities from health-care professionals.
- Infantilization from health-care providers is a common experience for older women.

Changing Relationships

- Many older women remain sexually active, although the ways in which they are sexual may change.
- Older women often serve as caregivers for partners or other family members with chronic or terminal health conditions, and this can lead to relationship strain and impact the women's own mental and physical health.
- Mental and physical health decline after losing a partner. This includes an increase in mortality risk, particularly for the period immediately following the death.
- Experiences with grief can be more complicated for women with female partners, as their relationship, and their grief, may not be publicly recognized.
- Some women experience an "empty nest" as challenging because they identified primarily as mothers, but others welcome the freedom that comes with reduced care-giving responsibilities.
- Being a grandmother is a welcome experience for many older women. For some, grandmothering involves being a primary caregiver.

Older Women at Work

- More older women are working now than in previous generations, and experiences of age discrimination are common. Younger adults may feel in competition with older adults for resources in the workplace.

- Because different laws address age, gender, and racial discrimination, it can be hard for women to prove discrimination based on a single cause since multiple social identity characteristics can play a role in their treatment.

- Women decide to retire at different times and for different reasons, ranging from the desire for leisure time to the need to become a full-time caregiver. Financial concerns may delay retirement for some, as they often have less money saved for retirement than is typical for men.

- Many women engage in volunteering and experiment with new leisure activities during retirement.

- Health in retirement is related to attitudes toward retirement.

Aging "Successfully"?

- Researchers have attempted to define and study "successful aging," but this perspective has been criticized for focusing on the experiences of privileged individuals and adding pressure to older adults rather than positively re-framing the idea of aging.

- Regardless of age-related challenges, older women can be empowered and politically active, and they frequently contribute to society at both local and global levels.

KEY TERMS

ageism (p. 450)

stereotype embodiment theory (p. 452)

beauty work (p. 455)

age concealment (p. 455)

menopause (p. 458)

perimenopause (p. 458)

postmenopause (p. 458)

pinkwashing (p. 465)

elderspeak (p. 468)

family caregiving (p. 469)

widowhood effect (p. 471)

bereavement (p. 471)

disenfranchised grief (p. 471)

role strain relief hypothesis (p. 473)

empty-nest syndrome (p. 473)

role loss hypothesis (p. 473)

launching phase (p. 473)

custodial role (p. 475)

bridge work (p. 481)

leisure innovation (p. 482)

THINK ABOUT IT

1. Go to a local store, explore magazines, and look for images of older women. What types of things do you notice? Are your observations consistent with the research presented in this chapter? If so, think of alternatives that might counter ageist and sexist stereotypes.

2. Do you think older women should be compensated for their caregiving work? If so, who should fund this? How much should women receive in compensation? What barriers do you think would prevent women from receiving compensation?

3. In what ways could our society's health-care system be improved to better provide for older women?

4. Imagine that you're advising someone about retirement. What should that person consider in planning for this transition? Who is more likely to have the resources to retire? What can be done to ensure that all people have an opportunity to retire?

ONLINE RESOURCES

- **American Association of Retired Persons (AARP)** — provides information and services to support and enhance the quality of life for people as they age: aarp.org

- **Raging Grannies International** — international network of older women who promote peace, justice, and social and economic equality through song and humor: raginggrannies.org

- **Women's Institute for a Secure Retirement (WISER)** — resources to improve the long-term security of all women: wiserwomen.org

- **WomensHealth.gov** — resources and information regarding top women's health issues: womenshealth.gov

12

Gender-Based Violence

RAZAN MOHAMMAD ABU-SALHA WASN'T SUPPOSED TO BE THERE. Her class let out early, so she decided to visit her newlywed sister, Yusor, and brother-in-law, Deah, at their condominium close to campus (Talbot, 2015). She hadn't been there long when an enraged neighbor knocked on the door. Within seconds, he took out a gun and repeatedly shot Deah. He then killed Razan and Yusor. An hour later, Craig Hicks turned himself in to police.

After the killings, two competing speculations about Hicks's motive emerged (Talbot, 2015). The first was that the shootings were related to a longstanding dispute over parking. The second was that they were triggered by hate. Hicks's anger had intensified when Yusor moved in with Deah. Yusor wore a hijab, and her father remembered Yusor worrying about Hicks's escalating anger. "Daddy," she'd said, "I think it is because of the way I look and the way I dress" (para. 31). Jack McDevitt, a criminologist, believes this was a **hate crime**, one that is motivated by bias. According to the FBI, anti-Muslim hate crimes in the United States multiplied after the terrorist attacks of September 11, and Muslim American women were more often attacked than their male counterparts (Abu-Ras & Suarez, 2009). Researchers believe that attackers more readily identify and target Muslim women who wear headscarves (Allen, 2015; Chakraborti & Zempi, 2012).

Pictured here are Deah Barakat, Yusor Abu-Salha, and Razan Abu-Salha. Some people argued that their murders were hate crimes, but the crimes weren't prosecuted as such. However, in the same year that these three young people were killed, the U.S. Department of Education did classify 860 criminal incidents that occurred on college campuses as hate crimes, using criteria developed by the FBI.

In this case, it's impossible to know if Hicks was responding to gender, religion, ethnicity, parking disputes, or some combination of all these factors. Thirty years ago, feminist sociologist Deborah King (1988) coined the term *multiple jeopardy* to describe the difficulty in identifying one factor as the most significant explanation for an oppressive act. Particularly when women have multiple marginalized social identity characteristics, their risk for violence increases (Collins, 2017; Creek & Dunn, 2014; Crenshaw, 1991). No one will ever know for sure, but Razan's friends believe her identity was connected to her murder (Talbot, 2015).

Ultimately, Hicks was charged with three counts of first-degree murder and discharging a firearm into a dwelling (Talbot, 2015). He wasn't charged with a hate crime because his motives weren't clearly identifiable. Nevertheless, this crime had the effect most often associated with hate crimes—it caused fear (Qualey, 2015). When violence occurs to a person with a marginalized identity, other people with a similar identity may experience fear and subsequently restrict their behavior to avoid becoming another target. In other words, one could think of the political and social goal of identity-based violence as putting people "back into their place" (Hodge, 2011, p. 12). Hate crime legislation acknowledges that some crimes have ripple effects beyond the individuals involved.

Crimes motivated by gender bias are technically classified as hate crimes. However, prosecutors rarely get hate crime convictions because it's difficult to prove beyond a reasonable doubt that gender bias was a motive for a crime against a woman (McPhail & DiNitto, 2005). Because of growing recognition that violence against girls and women isn't random but, rather, is bias-related, some feminists want prosecutors to more frequently seek hate crime convictions as a way to signify the seriousness of this issue (Lieberman & Freeman, 2017; Lynch, 2012; McPhail, 2002).

In almost every society, violence related to gender is both hidden and underreported. It's rarely identified as a social problem; rather, it's usually seen as the actions of a few bad people (Hodge, 2011). For this reason, it's challenging to stop. These types of violence happen across the lifespan, and the effects are deep and long-lasting, making it one of the most important areas feminist psychologists study. In this chapter, we'll examine specific types of violence, including childhood abuse, sexual assault, domestic violence, trafficking, and elder abuse. We'll also discuss the ways in which women can be resilient by working to end the culture of violence.

Gender-Based Violence

What is gender-based violence, and how can it be understood both individually and systemically?

Gender-based violence is a form of violence that is motivated by anger, hatred, or bias because of a person's gender. Gender-based violence occurs at both individual and structural levels. At the individual level, an attacker might threaten or use power against another person in order to inflict injury. *Structural violence* is subtler; it involves the systemic ways in which social structures hurt or otherwise disadvantage certain people (De Antoni & Munhós, 2016; Mukherjee et al., 2011). The ways in which sexism, racism, and prejudice against religious groups can cause harm are examples of structural violence. Because it's ingrained in a system, there's often no one person who can be held responsible (Saleem et al., 2016). Craig Hicks's actions are an example of violence at the individual level. However, the fact that his actions created widespread fear among other Muslim and female students exemplifies structural violence because those not specifically attacked became aware of an ever-present threat. For example, after the murder many Muslim students feared going out at night, and some reported walking together on campus during the day (Qualey, 2015; Talbot, 2015)

Decades ago, in writing about sexual assault, the feminist journalist Susan Brownmiller (1975) discussed how awareness of ever-present threat restricts personal freedom and can render those who are part of marginalized groups dependent on others for safety. As a result, girls and women may avoid wearing certain clothing or traveling alone at night (Hickman & Muehlenhard, 2006). In this way, gender-based violence acts as a source of power and control, whether or not a person has experienced a personal attack.

Violence against girls and women has become a public health crisis worldwide (UNICEF, 2014a). The United Nations reports that 1 in 3 women have experienced some form of physical and/or sexual violence during their lifetime (United Nations Statistics Division, 2015). Within the United States, 1 in 5 women (22.3%) have experienced severe physical violence (Centers for Disease Control and Prevention, 2016a). In 2015, men murdered more than 1,600 women, and the most commonly used weapon was a gun (Violence Policy Center, 2015). In 2016, the number of transgender women, particularly transgender women of color, who were murdered was the highest ever recorded within the United States (Human Rights Campaign, n.d.). These statistics are sobering, and behind each number is someone with a name and a story, like Razan.

try it for yourself

Some colleges and universities have implemented hate and bias policies to address crimes motivated by hate. Go to your student handbook or campus website, and search for any policy on hate and bias. Does your school have one? If so, what social identity characteristics does the policy include or exclude? Talk to fellow students, faculty, and staff. How many of them know about the policy or lack of policy? Do you think this type of policy would be helpful in deterring gender-based violence? Explain your response.

The United States has seen an overall drop in rates of violent crime in the last 30 years (Farrell, Tilley, & Tseloni, 2014). Since the 1990s, overall rates of crime—including homicide, theft, and burglary—have dropped by approximately half. There's no clear explanation for this. Better home and car security and decreased social acceptability of violence may be contributing factors (Farrell et al., 2014). However, not all the data are positive. Based on an analysis of rates of domestic violence and rape (which aren't always counted properly in crime statistics), crimes against women have actually increased since 2008, although crimes against men have continued to drop (Walby, Towers, & Francis, 2015). Thus, although overall crime has dropped, violence against women continues to be a significant problem within the United States.

Youth and Violence

Violence against children occurs in every region of the world (UNICEF, 2014a). Globally, approximately 40 million children are abused each year (UNICEF, 2014a). In the United States, child abuse referrals increased from 3.6 million in 2014 to 4 million in 2015, with the numbers of children involved increasing from 6.6 to 7.2 million (Children's Bureau, 2016). Moreover, 1,670 children died from abuse or neglect during the same period. Although all children are vulnerable to abuse, girls are especially susceptible (Allroggen, Rau, Ohlert, & Fegert, 2017; Finkelhor Turner, Hamby, & Ormrod, 2011). For example, child protective agencies receive more reports of childhood abuse toward girls than toward boys (Children's Bureau, 2016).

Types of Abuse

What types of abuse do children experience, and how is this abuse related to gender?

One type of abuse that children can experience is **physical abuse**, which is defined as acts of physical force intended to cause physical pain. This can include hitting, kicking, choking, burning, or biting a child. Many families believe that corporal punishment, or the use of physical force, is an acceptable way to discipline children (UNICEF, 2017). Studies from many countries worldwide suggest that 80% of children experience spanking, which is defined as open-handed hitting with intent to discipline (Gershoff & Grogan-Kaylor, 2016; UNICEF, 2017).

A recent meta-analysis showed that spanking was associated with children's increased aggression and antisocial behaviors, higher incidences of mental health concerns, lower self-esteem, lower cognitive abilities, and negative relationships with parents (Gershoff & Grogan-Kaylor, 2016). Sixteen countries have outlawed spanking by parents, and the American Academy of Pediatrics opposes it as a disciplinary technique (Fuller, 2009). As one scholar pointed out, the equivalent act among adults (e.g., one adult slapping another) would be considered a criminal offense (Finkelhor et al., 2011).

Another form of abuse is **psychological abuse**, a type of abuse in which perpetrators act in ways that cause fear, shame, isolation, or deprivation. Psychological abuse may include *verbal abuse*—speech that is denigrating or humiliating. It can also include *emotional abuse*—behaviors that aim to control or manipulate, such as withholding love, attention, or communication. This is also a component of neglect. While this type of abuse is believed to be common, specific rates are unclear since researchers use different operational definitions and psychological abuse rarely results in criminal abuse charges (Leeb, Paulozzi, Melanson, Simon, & Arias, 2008). However, psychological abuse can have severe consequences—for example, a higher lifetime risk for clinical depression (Infurna et al., 2016).

Children also can experience **childhood sexual abuse**, defined as any sexual activity between an adult and a minor. Girls are 2.5 times more likely to experience sexual abuse than adult women (World Health Organization, 2016). Whereas boys are more likely to be sexually abused by someone outside the family, girls are far more likely to be sexually abused by a family member or someone close to the family, such as a mother's boyfriend (Freyd, DePrince, & Gleaves, 2007). In many situations, a perpetrator first establishes a child's trust by spending time together or buying the child toys. After an assault, there may be a period when the perpetrator experiences remorse and promises not to victimize the child again. In this way, a cycle begins in which violent acts alternate

Fraidy Reiss (center) is the founder and executive director of Unchained At Last, an organization that is dedicated to ending childhood marriage in the United States. As a survivor of a forced marriage, Reiss is committed to advocating for girls and women through legislative action. What are the laws about marriage for people under the age of 18 where you live?

with loving behavior (Finkelhor et al., 2011). This cycle can be confusing to a child; it also makes it hard for the child to report the abuse and for other adults to believe that the perpetrator is actually causing harm (Firth, 2014).

In more extreme situations, childhood sexual abuse occurs within forced childhood marriage. According to UNICEF, over 700 million women living today were forced into childhood marriage, and 1 in 3 of those women was married before age 15 ("Child Marriage Database," 2018). Countries with the highest rates of child marriage are Niger (76%), the Central African Republic (68%), Chad (68%), and Mali (55%), but every country has childhood marriage, including the United States. Although 88% of countries set the minimum marriage age at 18, loopholes exist that make childhood marriage legal (e.g., parental consent, judicial approval). In the United States, 207,459 American children and adolescents were married between 2000 and 2015 (Tsui, Nolan, & Amico, 2017). Of them, 985 were 14 years old, 51 were 13 years old, and 6 were 12 years old—nearly all of them girls. Children who are forced into marriage are especially vulnerable to abuse, early pregnancy, and sexually transmitted infections (UNICEF, 2014b). In 2017, New Jersey became the first state in the nation to completely ban marriage before age 18 (Livio, 2017).

Another form of violence inflicted on girls is *female genital mutilation (FGM)*, a procedure typically performed on children that involves partial or total removal of external female genitalia for non-medical reasons (Jungari, 2016). Because a child cannot give consent, many people believe that FGM is a human rights violation. The practice can cause severe bleeding, infections, mental health distress, discomfort during sex, and reproductive health concerns, yet it continues because of cultural beliefs that FGM improves a girl's marital prospects and signifies that she's an adult (Vissandjée, Kantiébo, Levine, & N'Dejuru, 2003). The World Health Organization (2017) estimates that 125 million girls and women have undergone FGM, with most incidents occurring in African countries. Researchers also document that FGM is increasingly occurring among immigrant populations in Europe, the United States, and Canada (Goldberg et al., 2016).

Negative Outcomes and Resiliency

What are some outcomes of child abuse, what factors contribute to resiliency in the face of abuse, and how has the focus on individual resiliency been challenged?

Children and adolescents who experience abuse have high rates of depression and anxiety (Sachs-Ericsson, Sheffler, Stanley, Piazza, & Preacher, 2017). They may show delays in physical growth, experience sleep difficulties and chronic fatigue, have impaired immune function, and be medically classified as obese.

They also may act out aggressively or engage in self-destructive behaviors (Cooley-Quille, Boyd, Frantz, & Walsh, 2001). Moreover, the effects of childhood abuse can last a lifetime (Briggs, Thompson, Ostrowski, & Lekwauwa, 2011). Adults with histories of childhood abuse have shown higher incidences of many health problems, including irritable bowel syndrome, insomnia, fibromyalgia, infectious diseases, cardiovascular disease, and cancer (Springer, Sheridan, Kuo, & Carnes, 2007). They also have increased risk of developing psychiatric disorders and engaging in potentially harmful behaviors, such as substance use and risky sexual behaviors (Gallo, Munhoz, Loret de Mola, & Murray, 2018). They may have difficulty developing and maintaining stable and trusting relationships, which limits their support systems (Lassri, Luyten, Fonagy, & Shahar, 2018). This makes them more vulnerable to experiencing additional relational violence. In fact, the greatest factor that increases vulnerability to violence as an adult is having previously experienced violence as a child and/or adolescent (Dias, Sales, Mooren, Mota-Cardoso, & Kleber, 2017; Zamir, Szepsenwol, Englund, & Simpson, 2018).

Although the life-long risks of childhood abuse are clearly documented, some children grow up with no lasting effects of their childhood abuse (Cashmore & Shackel, 2013). This is known as **resiliency**, or the capacity to successfully adapt to trauma or stress, and it's associated with positive outcomes (Masten, 2014). A study of Latinx women showed that cultivating a belief in personal strength, developing a robust support group, and talking about childhood abuse were helpful in healing and becoming resilient (Ligiéro, Fassinger, McCauley, Moore, & Lyytinen, 2009). Likewise, a study of Native American women who experienced childhood sexual abuse showed that developing a sense of personal autonomy, social support, and connection to the cultural community provided some relief from negative effects in adulthood (Hobfoll et al., 2002). Resiliency appears to be an ongoing process that occurs over the course of a lifetime, with hope and optimism being key components (Bogar & Hulse-Killacky, 2006).

However, some scholars highlight that learning to cope with violence is ultimately limited and might shift too much responsibility onto survivors (Ungar, Ghazinour, & Richter, 2013). Especially when violence is ongoing (as is sometimes the case in childhood abuse) or is structural (as is the case with forced childhood marriage and/or female genital mutilation), a better approach may be to demand societal change. In fact, when Martin Luther King Jr. addressed psychologists at the American Psychological Association Convention in 1967, he famously said, "I am sure that there are some things in our world to which we should never be adjusted. There are some things concerning which we must always be maladjusted if we are to be people of good will"

try it for yourself

Google the term *resiliency*. After reading some of the links, list all the ways people are advised to develop adaptive coping strategies. How much of the advice is individually focused? How much is about changing systems of oppression like sexism, racism, classism, or homophobia? What messages are conveyed about whose responsibility it is to develop adaptive coping strategies and systems? How can people develop resiliency that considers the reality of abuse and violence?

("King's Challenge," 1999). In other words, even though resiliency in the face of violence is helpful for childhood survivors, society at large would benefit from efforts to end childhood violence itself.

From Objectification to Violence

How does the cultural acceptance of objectification of girls and women relate to violence against them?

As we discussed in Chapter 7, sexual objectification has negative effects on girls and women. It can undermine cognitive functioning as well as physical and mental health (American Psychological Association, 2007). It also contributes to violence and exploitation. In a review of over 100 empirical studies published between 1995 and 2015, psychologist L. Monique Ward (2016) identified that exposure to sexualized images in the media was associated with greater support for sexist beliefs and greater tolerance of sexual violence toward girls and women. Objectifying girls and women has been associated with having less empathy for girls and women, likely because objectification is related to dehumanization (Daniels & Zurbriggen, 2016; Holland & Haslam, 2016; Ward, Vandenbosch, & Eggermont, 2015). Among men, the reporting of higher levels of objectification of women has been associated with higher rates of minimizing violence, feeling entitled to sex, and endorsing coercion to control girls and women (Ward, 2016).

In one study, when primarily White girls and boys (ages 11–16) were exposed to sexually objectified images of female bodies, they reported stronger acceptance of sexual harassment (Strouse, Goodwin, & Roscoe, 1994). A more recent study showed that a racially diverse group of college men who readily associated women with words representing objects (e.g., *tool, device, thing*) or animals (e.g., *animals, paw, snout*), as measured by an implicit association test, were more willing to later expose women to sexually aggressive pictures (Rudman & Mescher, 2012).

Given that most media sexually objectify girls and women (American Psychological Association, 2007), the findings mentioned above are a serious cause for concern. Because Black and Latinx girls and women are more commonly portrayed in a sexualized manner than are White girls and women (Rivadeneyra & Ward, 2005), this may be an even greater problem for those who identify as or are perceived as part of these groups.

One source of sexual objectification is the adult entertainment industry—a $10 to $12 billion industry within the United States, with over 10,000 videos produced annually (Wosick, 2015). Much of the material produced within this industry depicts sexual themes with violence, dehumanization, and abuse. For example, researchers analyzing the content of the most popular pornographic videos found that 88.2% contained physical aggression and 48.7% contained verbal aggression (Bridges, Wosnitzer, Scharrer, Sun, & Liberman, 2010). Perpetrators were overwhelmingly male; targets were mostly female.

Moreover, under-age or nearly under-age actors are often portrayed in dehumanizing ways (Eberstadt & Layden, 2010; Foubert, Brosi, & Bannon, 2011). "Barely legal" pornography depicts adult women who are made to look youthful. Because the models are 18 years or older, this type of pornography is legal; however, there's evidence that viewing it affects adults' perceptions of children. One study showed that viewing "barely legal" pornography resulted in stronger associations between non-sexual images of children and words related to sex (Paul & Linz, 2008). Other studies have shown that consumption of online child pornography is on the rise, likely due to the normalization of girlhood sexualization as well as easy access through mobile devices (Steel, 2015; Wolak, Finkelhor, & Mitchell, 2012). A content analysis of packaging for 2,600 randomly selected, mainstream adult films produced from 1995 to 2007 found that 20% had references to young people/youth (Jensen, 2010). The increase in child pornography has also been linked to a growing illegal demand for sex with children and a steady increase in profits made in the child trafficking industry (Dank et al., 2014).

A Rape Culture

What is rape culture, and how common are sexual assault and rape in the United States?

The culture of objectification contributes to a *rape culture* in which sexual violence is normalized and perpetrators don't fear repercussions. Within the United States, rates of sexual abuse are high; yet rapists are rarely convicted (U.S. Department of Justice, 2016). Sexual violence is often dismissed, ignored, and deemed "no big deal." This is evidence of a rape culture. For example, in 2016, a California judge sentenced Brock Turner, a Stanford University student, to a mere six months in jail for his rape conviction. Critics believed the judge was influenced by the defendant's father, who complained that his son's life had been ruined for "20 minutes of action" (Stack, 2016, para 1). The judge claimed that a harsher punishment would have left a "severe impact" on Turner and, therefore, wasn't warranted (para. 4).

It is estimated that more than a third of women (37.1%) will experience some form of **sexual assault**, a general term that refers to different types of sexual abuse, including rape, attempted rape, unwanted sexual touching (e.g., groping, fondling), and/or sexual harassment (Smith et al., 2018). More specifically, **rape** is legally defined as "penetration, no matter how slight, of the vagina or anus with any body part or object, or oral penetration by a sex organ of another person, without the consent of the victim" (U.S. Department of Justice, 2012, para. 1). It's estimated that 1 in 5 women in the United States (20%) will be raped in her lifetime, with 81% of survivors reporting that the rape occurred before the age of 25 (Black et al., 2011; Smith et al., 2018). Most survivors are girls and women, and men are the primary perpetrators (Smith et al., 2018). Reflecting these numbers, women have a higher fear of rape than men, and women report fearing rape more than other forms of violent crime (Custers & Van den Bulck, 2013; Pryor & Hughes, 2016).

Rape Myths

What are common rape myths, and how do they correspond to the reality of rape?

A **rape myth** is a false belief about how and why rape occurs. Such myths perpetuate rape culture by inaccurately depicting reality, which then creates doubt and self-blame among survivors (Lonsway & Fitzgerald, 1994; Russell & Hand, 2017). Rape myths also reflect **victim blaming**, a type of blame that shifts responsibility away from the perpetrator and onto the survivor. Successfully combating rape requires accurately understanding rape threat and both recognizing and speaking out against misleading statements.

Myth: Women lie about being raped.
Reality: Women rarely lie about being raped; in fact, rape is extremely underreported.
Research suggests that only 0.05% to 7% of all reported rapes are unsubstantiated or false (Ferguson & Malouff, 2016; Lisak, Gardinier, Nicksa, & Cote, 2010; Lonsway, Archambault, & Lisak, 2009). In contrast, over 50% of women who experience an incident that meets the legal definition of rape won't actually label their experience as rape (Kahn, Jackson, Kully, Badger, & Halvorsen, 2003; LeMaire, Oswald, & Russell, 2016; Wilson & Miller, 2016). They may use a more benign label such as "bad sex" or "miscommunication" (Wilson & Miller, 2016, p. 1). These are examples of *unacknowledged rape*. Survivors are especially unlikely to acknowledge rape if they have a long-standing relationship with the perpetrator and if there was not much physical aggression used (Kahn et al., 2003).

Even when a woman acknowledges that she was raped, she's unlikely to report it. People are less likely to report sexual assault than other violent crimes (Chen & Ullman, 2010). One study of crime victims in the United States showed that only 38% of those who were raped reported the crime to police, in comparison to 47% of victims of other violent crimes and 62% of victims of aggravated assaults and robberies (Harrell, 2012). Reporting rates appear to be even lower among college students, with several studies finding that only 5% to 13% of rape survivors reported the crime to police (Demers et al., 2018; Wolitzky-Taylor et al., 2011). In another study, most mid-life and older women participants felt rape should be dealt with privately as opposed to being reported to authorities (Rennison & Rand, 2003). Rape survivors' reluctance to report may reflect their concerns about other people's reactions (Egan & Wilson, 2012). Fears of misbelief and retaliation also contribute to under-reporting (Cohn, Zinzow, Resnick, & Kilpatrick, 2013; Heath, Lynch, Fritch, McArthur, & Smith, 2011).

Myth: Rape is usually committed by a stranger or scary "other."
Reality: Rape is mostly committed by intimate partners or acquaintances.
In a large national study of female rape survivors, perpetrators were reported to be intimate partners (51.1%), acquaintances (40.8%), family members (12.5%), and strangers (13.8%; Black et al., 2011). Other studies corroborate this finding, showing that *acquaintance rape*—rape perpetrated by an intimate partner or someone known to the victim—is much more common than stranger rape (Clay-Warner & Burt, 2005; Fisher, Cullen, & Daigle, 2005). For example, one study showed that 10% to 20% of husbands or ex-husbands rape their partners (Herrera, Dahlblom, Dahlgren, & Kullgren, 2006).

Nevertheless, undergraduate students generally report that they think a "typical" rape includes physical aggression and is perpetrated by a stranger (Clark & Carroll, 2008). This is the *traditional rape script*. Although it doesn't describe the vast majority of rapes, the script is powerful because it shapes beliefs about what to classify as rape (Peterson & Muehlenhard, 2004). When an experience of rape doesn't match the traditional rape script, women are less likely to view it as rape and less likely to receive support (Weiss, 2009).

The traditional rape script has served to justify discrimination. In Chapter 4, we discussed House Bill 2 (HB2) from North Carolina that banned transgender individuals from using bathrooms that didn't align with their gender assignment at birth. Legislators claimed the ban was necessary to protect girls and women from male sexual predators who would claim to be transgender in order to enter women's bathrooms (Steinmetz, 2016). But several organizations dedicated to stopping violence against women asserted that the legislation perpetuated a rape myth in order to justify discrimination (National Task Force to End Sexual and Domestic Violence Against Women, 2016). Partially due to this effort, HB2 was repealed in 2017.

Understanding the history and politics of rape culture can shed more light on this myth. Over thirty years ago, feminist scholar Angela Davis (1981) discussed how the *myth of the Black rapist* uses rape threat to justify violence against Black boys and men. This particular myth perpetuates the idea that Black men are driven to assault White women, which unjustly increases fears of Black men (Dorr, 2004). For example, research participants see Black male perpetrators of sexual assault as more guilty than White perpetrators (Donovan, 2007; Foley, Evancic, Karnik, King, & Parks, 1995). In 2015, when 21-year-old Dylann Roof, a White man, murdered nine Black people at the Emanuel African Methodist Church in Charlestown, South Carolina, he repeatedly shouted, "You rape our women, and you're taking over our country, and you have to go" (Bouie, 2015, para. 1). His justification for committing murder was based on the myth of the Black rapist.

Feminist scholars also point to the ways in which media coverage and political rhetoric often portray men in the Global South and East (e.g., Africa, Latin America, Middle East, and parts of Asia) as sexually violent in comparison to North American and European White men (Khalid 2017; Nayak 2006; Sjoberg, 2013). Such portrayals reinforce racialized stereotypes (Nayak, 2006). Postcolonial scholars also warn that Western governments use images and rhetoric of violence against women in the Global South and East as a rationale for military action and restrictive immigration policies (Khalid 2017; Nayak, 2006).

Myth: Most survivors of rape actively fight off their attacker.
Reality: Many women who are raped are not able to fight back.
Most survivors of rape don't resist their attacker, especially if they know the attacker or are intoxicated (Ford, 2017; Porges & Pepe, 2015). In one study, 57% of women seeking treatment from a large hospital emergency room as a result of rape reported that they hadn't resisted (Carr et al., 2014). Many said they chose not to resist in order to reduce the risk of injury, and research does show that survivors who resist are more likely to be injured (Wong & Balemba, 2016). In other studies, survivors have reported being literally unable to resist because of **tonic immobility**, an involuntary "frozen" body response that occurs in high-fear situations (Marx, Forsyth, Gallup, Fusé, & Lexington, 2008; TeBockhorst, O'Halloran, & Nyline, 2015). This paralysis makes it impossible for a person to move or call out for help.

Women with a history of sexual assault are less likely to engage in assertive resistance behaviors (Gidycz, McNamara, & Edwards, 2006; Littleton & Decker, 2017). Studies have shown that when responding to scenarios, college women who had a history of sexual assault took longer to determine that a man's actions were sexually inappropriate and were less likely to assertively resist than college women without a history of sexual assault (Soler-Baillo, Marx, & Sloan, 2005; Stoner et al., 2007). Researchers speculate that survivors may be less physiologically reactive to danger, which would explain their slower resistance to a potential attack (Soler-Baillo et al., 2005).

Even though women's self-defense programs have been criticized for putting the responsibility for preventing rape on victims rather than assailants, several studies have shown that self-defense programs can help women resist sexual assault, build confidence, and reduce their belief in rape myths (Gidycz et al., 2006; Ullman, 2007). Especially when taught from a feminist perspective,

Self-defense programs, especially those taught from a feminist perspective, can help women gain confidence and feel stronger, and they've been shown to help women resist sexual assault and rape. However, they've also been criticized for putting the focus on women preventing assault, rather than on men not assaulting women.

self-defense programs can be effective (Gidycz & Dardis, 2014). In such programs, women are taught to accurately assess risk, acknowledge when they're in a risky situation, and respond quickly and assertively (Rozee & Koss, 2001). However, when the rape involves a romantic partner or an acquaintance, a woman's concern about rejecting the partner or being embarrassed may prevent her from identifying risk and actively resisting (Ullman, 2007).

Myth: Sex with someone who is incapacitated or drunk is not rape.
Reality: If someone is not able to give consent, sex with that person is rape.
When someone rapes a person who is intoxicated, unconscious, or asleep, *incapacitated rape* occurs. Women who experience incapacitated rape are most likely to blame themselves and are less likely to identify their experience as rape (Brown, Testa, & Messman-Moore, 2009; Walsh et al., 2016). People are also less likely to blame intoxicated male perpetrators than sober ones (Cameron & Stritzke, 2003; Finch & Munro, 2005). In some cases of incapacitated rape, the perpetrator even sleeps in the same bed with the rape survivor, suggesting that the perpetrator doesn't fear repercussions (Maurer, 2016).

College women, particularly those with a history of sexual abuse and who believe alcohol will enhance their sexual experiences, are especially at risk for incapacitated rape (Carey, Durney, Shepardson, & Carey, 2015b; Messman-Moore, Ward, & Zerubavel, 2013). One study showed that 15% of first-year college students reported attempted or completed incapacitated rape, and by their second year, 26% and 22% had experienced attempted and completed incapacitated rape, respectively (Carey et al., 2015a). Alcohol may increase vulnerability by altering a woman's ability to assess her risk and subsequently resist (Ford, 2017; Franklin, 2016; Sell, Turrisi, Scaglione, Hultgren, & Mallett, 2016). In fact, some college men have reported intentionally providing alcohol to women because of their intent to incapacitate and assault or rape them (Brennan et al., 2018).

Myth: *Girls and women are partially responsible for being raped if they wear revealing clothing, act in promiscuous ways, or make risky choices like being out alone or drinking at a party.*

Reality: *The only one responsible for rape is the rapist.*

In Chapter 7, we discussed how women are seen as sexual gatekeepers who are responsible for controlling men's (supposedly uncontrollable) sexual urges. When women fail to follow this expectation, they're blamed and punished (Farvid, Braun, & Rowney, 2017; Jozkowski, Marcantonio, & Hunt, 2017). *Rape threat,* or the ever-present fear of being raped, is something girls are warned about at a very young age (Gordon & Riger, 1989; Starkweather, 2007). They're taught "rules" to avoid rape, such as "Don't wear revealing clothes" or "Don't use your cell phone when walking alone" (Bedera & Nordmeyer, 2015). Studies show that women do restrict their behaviors, particularly at night, in order to prevent sexual assault and rape (Hickman & Muehlenhard, 2006; Yodanis, 2004). These restrictions even occur in cyberspace. Amnesty International found that 32% of women reported that they stopped using social media platforms (e.g., Twitter, Facebook) because of abuse and harassment, including explicit rape threats ("Amnesty International Reveals Alarming Impact," 2017).

Rape threat places the burden on women to prevent rape, and programs aimed at decreasing rape have been criticized for relying heavily on behavior change among girls and women (Bedera & Nordmeyer, 2015). An analysis of 40 college websites, for example, showed that tips about rape prevention were more often directed toward women (80%) than men (14%; Bedera & Nordmeyer, 2015). Of the 25 most common tips, 24 were directed at women (e.g., "Be aware of your surroundings," "Communicate sexual limits"), and only 1 was directed at men ("No means no"). Rules like these convey that it's women's responsibility to change their behaviors in order to stop rape. Moreover, many of the tips implied that a rapist would be a stranger ("Walk in well-traveled areas," "Avoid being alone," "Don't open doors unless you know who's there"). However, rapists are actually more likely to be partners or acquaintances (Black et al., 2011), so researchers have concluded that these tips may unnecessarily create a climate of vigilance and fear (Bedera & Nordmeyer, 2015). Even decades ago, feminist scholars identified rules about how to avoid rape as a problematic aspect of rape culture (Brownmiller, 1975; Riger & Gordon, 1981).

Myth: *Sexual force is a normal aspect of male sexuality.*
Reality: *There is no evidence that force is a normal aspect of male sexuality.*
The idea that "boys will be boys" embodies a stereotypical belief that men's sexual urges are out of control. When taken to the extreme, it normalizes the idea that any boy or man could be a rapist because his uncontrollable urges are a natural part of male biology (Smiler, 2008). Not only is this stereotype false (and offensive to men), but it has dangerous implications (Barnett, Hale, & Sligar, 2017). For example, 1 out of 5 women in one study excused their perpetrator's actions because they believed that male sexual aggression was natural or normal (Weiss, 2009).

Feminist scholars warn about the dangers of conflating sex and rape. Sex is about intimacy and connection; rape and assault are about violence (Bradshaw, Kahn, & Saville, 2010). Rape doesn't occur because a person is so turned on they can't control themself; it happens when someone feels entitled to degrade or harm others. Numerous studies have shown that men who have hostility toward women, a strong desire to be in control, anti-social traits, high consumption of pornography, and heavy alcohol use are more likely to rape (Francia et al., 2010; Murnen, Wright, & Kaluzny, 2002; Turchik, Garske, Probst, & Irvin, 2010). Most men don't rape, yet it does appear that many men have difficulty identifying and standing up to rape culture (Groth & Birnbaum, 2013).

Myth: *Rape only happens to heterosexual women.*
Reality: *Rape can happen to anyone.*
Between 3% and 8% of boys and men in the United States have experienced sexual assault (Coxell & King, 2010; Lowe & Rogers, 2017). Although the majority of assaults are perpetrated by other men, between 6% and 15% involve a female assailant (Fisher & Pina, 2013; Russell, Doan, & King, 2017). Many people don't believe a woman can rape a man, especially if the man is stronger or bigger than the woman (Javaid, 2016). Moreover, male sexual assault by a female perpetrator has often served comedic purposes (Carmon, 2010). The films *40 Days and 40 Nights* (from 2002) and *Wedding Crashers* (from 2005) depicted female-on-male rape as funny, and a *Saturday Night Live* sketch from 2015 poked fun at a female high school teacher who rapes a male high school student. The sketch went on to suggest that the crime was every teen boy's dream, a clear sign of victim blaming (Blay, 2016).

Sexual minority women may be at even greater risk for lifetime sexual victimization than heterosexual women (Coulter et al., 2017; Long, Ullman, Long, Mason, & Starzynski, 2007). In a review of research about sexual assault against sexual minority women and men, reports of sexual assault ranged from 11% to 53% across studies, with most incidents happening with a known male perpetrator (Ford & Soto-Marquez, 2016; Gurung et al., 2018). There's also a high likelihood of sexual assault among transgender individuals, with reports ranging from 14% to 54% (Coulter et al., 2017).

Myth: *Consent is clear-cut and can be readily understood.*
Reality: *The process of consent is not as simple as it may seem.*

A verbal *yes* or *no* is the clearest form of consent, yet most people negotiate sexual consent through a combination of verbal and non-verbal cues (Jozkowski, Sanders, Peterson, Dennis, & Reece, 2014; Marcantonio, Jozkowski, & Lo, 2018). Men are more likely to give permission for sexual activity in non-verbal ways and to rely on non-verbal cues for consent than women, who are more likely to give and rely on verbal strategies (Jozkowski & Peterson, 2013). Some people also say that getting consent can be awkward. One 16-year-old revealed his confusion: "What does this all mean . . . do [I] have to say 'yes' every 10 minutes?" (Medina, 2015, para. 4).

Complicating the issue is the fact that people sometimes agree to unwanted sexual acts (Muehlenhard, Humphreys, Jozkowski, & Peterson, 2016). This is known as **compliant sex** (Walker, 1997). As a result, researchers distinguish between *wanting sex* and *consenting to sex* (Peterson & Muehlenhard, 2007; also see Figure 12.1). Although heterosexual college women in the United States report engaging in compliant sex more than their male counterparts when in committed relationships, both women and men report consenting to unwanted sexual acts (Katz & Schneider, 2015; Sanchez, Fetterolf, & Rudman, 2012). This can occur because they don't want to hurt a partner's feelings or they feel obligated (Peterson & Muehlenhard, 2007).

Sometimes a person doesn't initially agree and is then coerced into consenting (Muehlenhard, 2011). This is a form of rape that's rarely acknowledged. The belief that women widely engage in **token resistance**, saying *no* to sex but really meaning *yes*, contributes to rape culture. When men believe that women demonstrate token resistance, they're less likely to report that a verbal *no* means refusing sex (Osman, 2003). Research has shown that men think women use token resistance more than they actually do (Emmers-Sommer, 2015).

The extent to which women do use token resistance is controversial. Original work in this area indicated that up to 39% of women reported saying *no* to sex when they meant *yes* (Muehlenhard & Miller, 1988). In subsequent research, women were asked to describe their experiences in more detail (Muehlenhard & Rodgers, 1998). This research showed that women often meant *no* when they said it but, subsequently, either changed their minds or were pressured to say *yes*. Moreover, women may have conflicting feelings about whether they

a. The Dominant Model: "Sex is either wanted and consensual or unwanted and nonconsensual."		
	Wanted	**Unwanted**
Consensual	Not rape	NOT POSSIBLE
Nonconsensual	NOT POSSIBLE	Rape

b. The Dominant Model: "Rape is unwanted nonconsensual sex."		
	Wanted	**Unwanted**
Consensual	Not rape	Not rape
Nonconsensual	Not rape	Rape

c. The New Model: "Wanting and consenting are distinct concepts; nonconsensual sex is rape."		
	Wanted	**Unwanted**
Consensual	Not rape	Not rape
Nonconsensual	Rape	Rape

FIGURE 12.1 A model for understanding rape and consent. Researchers have begun to differentiate between *wanting sex* and *consenting to sex*, as the two don't always align. This chart illustrates how the different combinations correspond to different ways of thinking about what is and isn't rape.

Note. Adapted from Peterson & Muehlenhard (2007).

want sex. For example, they may consent to sex but not actually want it—as can occur with compliant sex (Peterson & Muehlenhard, 2007). Given all these findings, feminists advocate that instead of looking for a lack of a *no*, people should initiate sex only when there's an enthusiastic *yes*. This is **affirmative consent**, which occurs when there is mutual, explicit, voluntary, active consent given before a sexual act. Affirmative consent cannot be elicited through coercion and can be withdrawn any time. Furthermore, a lack of resistance does not imply consent (Little, 2005).

Who Endorses Rape Myths? Not everyone endorses rape myths. In fact, several studies have shown that men as well as people who have higher degrees of sexual aggression and hostile attitudes toward women were more likely to endorse rape myths (Bhogal & Corbett, 2016; Hockett, Smith, Klausing, & Saucier, 2016; Stoll, Lilley, & Pinter, 2017). Endorsement of rape myths has also been linked to problematic drinking behaviors (Hayes, Abbott, & Cook, 2016), experiencing objectification as a woman (Papp & Erchull, 2017), having authoritarian personality traits (Begany & Milburn, 2002), and watching more television, particularly televised sports (Custers & McNallie, 2017; Kahlor & Eastin, 2011). Higher levels of sexism, racism, homophobia, ageism, classism, and religious intolerance have also been associated with rape myth acceptance among both women and men (Aosved & Long, 2006). All these findings suggest that rape myths are tied to the maintenance of other oppressive systems.

Additional research shows that greater endorsement of a **belief in a just world**—the belief that most people get what they deserve—is associated with greater endorsement of rape myths (Russell & Hand, 2017). When people hear about a rape, they can feel anxious because rape undermines their beliefs about a just world (Lerner, 1980). In order to restore their belief, they may distance themselves from the rape survivor or engage in victim blaming. Paradoxically, among women, the endorsement of rape myths may also provide an illusion of control (Hayes, Lorenz, & Bell, 2013). This can occur because women who endorse rape myths may be less fearful when hearing about a rape since they inaccurately perceive their own risk to be low (Papp & Erchull, 2017).

Rape myths often appear in media and social media coverage of actual rape cases. In one study, 65.4% of print articles about rape were found to include at least one rape myth (Franiuk, Seefelt, Cepress, & Vandello, 2008). In another study, 25.8% of comments on news stories were identified as victim blaming, and perpetrator support was found in comments on all but one of the articles analyzed (Zaleski, Gundersen, Baes, Estupinian, & Vergara, 2016). Rape myths commonly portrayed on television include the idea that victims' claims were false and that the victim did something to cause the rape (Cuklanz, 2000). Also, rape scenes are often depicted as precursors to romance. For example, the main romance in the *Blade Runner* movies starts with a rape; and in an early episode of *Buffy the Vampire Slayer*, Spike attempts to rape Buffy, only to later become one of the show's most beloved characters (Beck, 2018). Another study showed that rape myths—including the idea that victims could have done things to avoid rape and that when a victim said *no* she really meant *yes*—are a frequent component of sexual assault portrayals in comic books (Garland, Branch, & Grimes, 2016).

spotlight on . . .

Consent

When more people affirm to themselves and others that they have a right to start and stop a sexual activity at any time, coercion is less likely to occur. However, even an enthusiastic *yes* isn't as simple as it may seem. Communication scholar Kate Lockwood Harris (2018) explains that consent is often negotiated and that power and gender expectations influence how direct, verbal, and clear individuals can be.

In 2018, the website *babe* published an article describing an encounter between a woman and comedian Aziz Ansari (Way, n.d.). The woman described how Ansari ignored several verbal and non-verbal cues and pushed her to concede to a sexual encounter. She described the experience as "a violating night and a painful one" and "by far the worst experience with a man I've ever had," while Ansari "was surprised and concerned" that he had misread her cues of consent (paras. 44, 55, 57). Ansari is a self-proclaimed feminist, so this incident shows that even men who intend to treat women with respect can have difficulty interpreting consent. Given this, paying attention to a partner and becoming comfortable with conversations about what is and isn't wanted is a skill that can be valuable to everyone.

What factors make affirmative consent challenging? What are the potential barriers when interpreting *enthusiastic* consent? What could be done to improve communication about consent?

The Reality of Rape

Which groups of women are particularly at risk for experiencing rape and sexual assault?

Now that we've dispelled inaccurate myths, it's instructive to discuss the realities of rape and whom attackers most often target. Although some individuals are more vulnerable, not everyone who's "at risk" will experience sexual assault and/or rape. Also, regardless of risk, survivors are never responsible for their rape.

College Women Sexual assault and rape occur five times more frequently among college women than among non-college women (Fedina, Holmes, & Backes, 2018). During their first year of college, 1 in 7 women will experience incapacitated sexual assault or rape, and 1 in 10 will experience forcible sexual assault or rape (Carey, Durney, Shepardson, & Carey, 2015a). Between 5% and 9% of college women are raped in a given academic year (Testa, Hoffman, & Livingston, 2010).

One explanation for college women's higher risk for rape involves the social scene. College hookups typically occur in settings where men control the parties and there is heavy alcohol or drug use—factors that increase the likelihood of sexual assault or rape (Jozkowski & Wiersma-Mosley, 2017). Some research suggests that a hookup with an acquaintance or previous romantic partner involves a higher risk for being sexually assaulted (Flack et al., 2016; Gross, Winslett, Roberts, & Gohm, 2006), but other research indicates that a hookup with someone who is known by friends of the survivor, but not the survivor herself, is more risky (Ford, 2017).

At least 50% of collegiate assaults involve alcohol consumption, and hazardous drinking paired with casual sex increases the risk of rape (Abbey, Wegner, Woerner, Pegram, & Pierce, 2014; Messman-Moore, Ward, Zerubavel, Chandley, & Barton, 2015). Women with a sexual abuse history are more likely to engage in hazardous forms of drinking, particularly before sexual encounters, which contributes to their risk for re-victimization (Testa et al., 2010). Research has identified lower alcohol consumption as one reason for fewer rapes among undergraduate students at historically Black college or universities (HBCUs), where the rate was 9.7% compared to 13.7% among undergraduates at non-HBCUs (Krebs et al., 2011; Mohler-Kuo, Dowdall, Koss, & Wechsler, 2004). However, alcohol isn't the only factor that contributes to the likelihood of rape. Other factors, such as having rape-supportive beliefs, anti-social personality traits, and a history of sexual abuse and/or childhood adversity, may lead some men to drink heavily and then sexually assault (Porta, Mathiason, Lust, & Eisenberg, 2017; Zinzow & Thompson, 2015).

Women in the Military Women who serve in the military are also at risk. A Department of Defense report states that 23% to 30% of enlisted women report experiencing sexual assault during their military service (U.S. Department of Defense, 2016a). This is higher than the 20% lifetime rate of rape described previously. In fact, a woman who enlists is more likely to be raped by a fellow soldier than be killed by enemy fire (Harman et al., 2008). This phenomenon has been called the *invisible war* (Ziering, Barklow, & Dick, 2012).

One explanation for high rates of rape in the military is **cultural spillover theory**, which states that widespread cultural support for violence (e.g., the use of force in the military) leads to increased acceptability of violence in other aspects of life (e.g., rape of a comrade or civilian; Baron, Straus, & Jaffee, 1988; Rosen, 2007). Another explanation is that military service academies value characteristics associated with traditional masculinity (e.g., toughness, aggression, dominance, and power) and devalue characteristics associated with traditional femininity (Harway & Steel, 2015; Turchik & Wilson, 2010; Zurbriggen, 2010). Finally, incidences of rape in the military may be high due to lack of accountability. Researchers have found that individuals who report sexual assault in the military are 12 times more likely to be retaliated against than they are to see their offenders be convicted of a sex offense (Bergman, Langhout, Palmeiri, Cortina, & Fitzgerald, 2002).

Civilian women in military conflict zones are also at risk for rape and assault. We'll return to this topic later in the chapter.

Native American Women Within the United States, Native American women are between 2 and 3.5 times more likely to experience rape or sexual assault than are women of other racial/ethnic backgrounds (de Heer & Jones, 2017; Lehavot, Walters, & Simoni, 2010). In fact, in a study of Indigenous women within the United States, several participants reported not knowing anyone in their community who *hadn't* experienced sexual violence (Amnesty International, n.d.). Some scholars assert that the high rates of rape among Native Americans are connected to the history of colonization and genocide, which created a culture in which many White Americans don't respect Native Americans (LaPointe, 2008; Smith, 2013). According to the U.S. Department of Justice, in at least 86% of reported cases of rape or sexual assault against Indigenous women, survivors stated that the perpetrators were non-Native men (Perry, 2004). The same report states that this percentage is in stark contrast to non-Indigenous rape survivors, whose assailants are typically of the same race. Because of legal jurisdiction, tribes cannot arrest, investigate, or prosecute a non-Native person accused of rape, and this constraint creates a legal loophole that permits many rapes against Indigenous women to go unpunished (Joy, 2016).

Women with Disabilities Women with disabilities are at a higher risk for sexual abuse than women without disabilities (Horner-Johnson & Drum, 2006). In one study, 69% of deaf women reported having experienced one sexual assault, and 56% reported having experienced multiple types of sexual assaults, with most assaults being by a known male perpetrator (Smith & Pick, 2015). Other studies have shown that women with severe physical impairments experience the highest risk of sexual assault (Brownridge, 2006; Casteel, Martin, Smith, Gurka, & Kupper, 2008). Individuals with cognitive and emotional disabilities are also at risk for sexual exploitation and rape because perpetrators may perceive these women as being especially vulnerable (Khalifeh, Howard, Osborn, Moran & Johnson, 2013).

Aftermath of Sexual Assault

What are the psychological consequences associated with experiencing sexual assault?

Immediately following sexual assault, survivors may seek medical attention, typically through an emergency room. In this setting, a health-care provider can perform a forensic exam using a Sexual Assault Evidence Kit (SAEK), otherwise known as a rape kit. This container includes a checklist, materials, and instructions, along with envelopes and containers to package any specimens collected during a physical exam. A rape kit can be administered up to a week post-assault. When a survivor is a minor, the person performing the exam is a mandated reporter. Otherwise, survivors are not compelled to formally report the crime; however, any DNA evidence can become part of a national database that helps connect perpetrators to other crimes.

Most survivors experience negative psychological consequences immediately following an assault, including symptoms of post-traumatic stress disorder (PTSD), depression, and anxiety (Nickerson et al., 2013; Ullman, Townsend, Filipas, & Starzynski, 2007). However, most (but not all) survivors experience relief within a year (Hyland et al., 2016), with only 5% to 10% developing PTSD (Brewin, Andrews, & Valentine, 2000). Variables that make an individual especially prone to long-term negative effects include prior history of abuse, assault severity, having close ties with the perpetrator, engaging in more self-blame, and receiving negative reactions from other people (Dworkin, Ullman, Stappenbeck, Brill, & Kaysen, 2018; Peter-Hagene & Ullman, 2018). Further, individuals who use maladaptive coping strategies like avoidance and social withdrawal and who engage in self-destructive behavior after the assault typically have a slower recovery process (Frazier, Mortensen, & Steward, 2005; Ullman & Relyea, 2016).

Structural barriers also make recovery more challenging for some survivors (Loya, 2014; Tjaden & Thoennes, 2006). For example, there are fewer legal, medical, and social services available to women of color than to White women (Abbey, Jacques-Tiura, & Parkhill, 2010; Weist et al., 2014). Rural communities have limited medical care facilities that can offer forensic sexual assault exams (Logan, Evans, Stevenson, & Jordan, 2005), and in urban areas, overcrowded medical facilities can result in low-quality care (Campbell, Wasco, Ahrens, Sefl, & Barnes, 2001). Moreover, women of color and undocumented immigrants may hesitate to seek services because of their collective history of mistreatment by law officials and health-care providers (Sokoloff & Dupont, 2005). Also, since women of color face the compounded effects of racial and gender income inequalities, their financial ability to recover from a sexual assault or rape is limited (Loya, 2014). In one study, researchers estimated the medical costs of rape within the first 30 days to be $6,737, of which 14% ($943) was paid out-of-pocket by the survivor (Tennessee, Bradham, White, & Simpson, 2017). Another study determined that the lifetime cost of rape is $122,461 (Peterson, DeGue, Florence, & Lokey, 2017). These costs include expenses for medical and mental health treatment, legal advice, and lost productivity.

On a positive note, some survivors find that their experience with sexual assault was a catalyst for reorganizing their priorities, deepening their relationships, developing a heightened sense of meaning and spirituality, and/or

Often occurring on college campuses, Take Back the Night events typically consist of a protest walk followed by a vigil where survivors of sexual violence tell their stories. The first marches began in the 1970s in response to a rise in violent crimes against women. Does your school or community hold Take Back the Night marches?

Reporting Sexual Assault

t's impossible to address rape at individual or societal levels if survivors don't share their experiences with friends, family, and formal support systems (Ullman, 2010). When survivors do share their stories, they often challenge rape myths and strengthen a shared perception that rape is a major societal problem (Ullman, 2010). They also increase empathy and understanding among listeners. These are key factors in reducing rape. Speaking out also strengthens connections with other survivors, friends, and family members—a process that promotes healing and hope (Ahrens & Aldana, 2012). However, sharing highly personal details about sexual assault is a daunting task, and the research is mixed on whether telling others is helpful or harmful.

Some studies show positive effects for women who disclosed their rape (Milliken, Paul, Sasson, Porter, & Hasulube, 2016; Starzynski & Ullman, 2014). They were more likely to seek treatment for physical and emotional injuries and were less likely to blame themselves (Milliken et al., 2016). Another study revealed that survivors who actively sought help from friends and family members were more likely to receive positive than negative reactions (Ahrens, Campbell, Ternier-Thames, Wasco, & Sefl, 2007). However, in other research, those who received a negative response (e.g., blaming statements) reported increased self-blame, social withdrawal, reduced sexual assertiveness, and greater hostility and fear (Orchowski & Gidycz, 2015; Relyea & Ullman, 2015). Overall, disclosure

to a friend and/or family member has the potential to improve post-assault outcomes; however, this is contingent on receiving a supportive response.

What about formally reporting a rape? If the perpetrator is a current or former partner, there's a legitimate fear that reporting will cause an escalation of violence (Wolf, Ly, Hobart, & Kernic, 2003). Further, because some law enforcement personnel endorse rape myths, survivors may get a negative response (Cook & Lane, 2017; Parratt & Pina, 2017; Shaw, Campbell, Cain, & Feeney, 2017). Other research indicates that reports of rape by sex workers are rarely taken seriously and may place these rape survivors in greater danger of being charged and convicted of prostitution (Sherman et al., 2015; Sprankle, Bloomquist, Butcher, Gleason, & Schaefer, 2018). Survivors of prison sexual assault also are less likely to report victimization because of fear of retaliation and re-victimization (Fowler, Blackburn, Marquart, & Mullings, 2010). A similar fear exists among undocumented immigrants, who worry that their reports of rape will lead to deportation (Seyler, 2012).

Despite these problems, survivors are often encouraged to report their assaults so criminals can be prosecuted (Paul et al., 2013). However, most survivors aren't likely to receive justice. Arrests are made in only 38% of cases, only 18% result in convictions, and only 5% of convicted rapists go to prison (U.S. Department of Justice, 2016).

What do you think? It is empowering or oppressing to report rape?

improving personal resources and skills (Tedeschi & Calhoun, 2004). These survivors experience **post-traumatic growth**, a positive psychological change that can occur following a struggle with highly challenging life circumstances (Ulloa, Guzman, Salazar, & Cala, 2016). Individuals who experience such growth typically have strong support networks, rely on active and religious coping, and perceive greater control over their recovery. Another study showed that women of color, older women, and women with less education had greater post-traumatic growth (Grubaugh & Resick, 2007). Some researchers suggest this may be due to greater religious coping found among older women and women of color (Ahrens, Abeling, Ahmad, & Hinman, 2010).

Interpersonal Violence

What are the different types of intimate partner violence, and how do abuse and control manifest within abusive relationships?

In 2009, just days before the Grammy Awards, Rihanna and Chris Brown cancelled their performances after it was revealed that Brown had physically attacked Rihanna. Two female police officers had leaked photos showing Rihanna with a bloody nose, black eye, and split lip (Goldstein, 2009). Brown later pled guilty to felony assault and was sentenced to community service, probation, and counseling (Duke & Rowlands, 2009). Both Rihanna and Brown were reportedly overwhelmed by the extensive public attention that followed the assault. Years later, Rihanna disclosed that she felt punished "over and over again" (Robinson, 2015, para. 9). Her reaction wasn't surprising, given that media coverage reflected mixed messages about her culpability. Although most of the coverage stated that the assault was wrong, 53% of mainstream articles also included statements that the incident was romantic, erotic, normal, and partially Rihanna's fault (Rothman et al., 2012).

Domestic violence is defined as any abusive, violent, coercive, forceful, or threatening act by one member of a family or household toward another (World Health Organization, 2016). **Intimate partner violence (IPV)** is a particular form of domestic violence, involving violence by one member of an intimate couple against the other (Centers for Disease Control and Prevention, 2016b). It's a sub-type of domestic violence because it doesn't include elder or child abuse. IPV can occur in all types of relationship configurations (e.g., heterosexual, same-gender) and among married or dating couples. IPV perpetrators are more likely to target younger women, like Rihanna, than older women (Capaldi, Knoble, Shortt, & Kim, 2012; Kim, Laurent, Capaldi, & Feingold, 2008).

Before the 1970s, there was almost no public recognition of domestic violence (Circulating Now, 2015). Spousal abuse (and to a certain extent, child abuse) was considered an unfortunate, but understandable, custom. In the

United States, public opinion changed when three socially charged movements—women's liberation, women's health, and anti-rape—united and formed the battered women's movement (Jacquet, 2015). Activists wanted medical and legal systems to respond to domestic violence as a serious criminal offense rather than as a private matter between a wife and a husband. They worked to change public opinion and to create safe havens for women and children. Crisis hotlines became available, and the first women's shelter opened in 1973. Almost twenty years later, in 1994, the Violence Against Women Act (VAWA) provided the first comprehensive federal program to combat domestic violence. In a relatively short period, activists experienced considerable success.

However, cases such as that of Rihanna and Chris Brown indicate that much work remains to be done. Some people still think intimate partner violence can be deserved and is inevitable within some relationships (Rothman et al., 2012). Further, violence in romantic relationships among teenagers and young adults remains high. According to a national survey, as many as 1 in 10 high school students and 1 in 4 college students in the United States report being physically hurt by a romantic partner (Vagi, Olsen, Basile, & Vivolo-Kantor, 2015). Also, although early activist work focused on intimate partner violence between women and men, IPV occurs in same-gender relationships too (Hamby, 2009; Hassouneh & Glass, 2008).

Types of Intimate Partner Violence

There are three main types of IPV (Johnson, 2009). When conflict spontaneously escalates to violence and isn't severe, it's classified as *common couples violence* or *situational couple violence* (Johnson, 2009). This, the most frequent form of IPV, occurs when stress is high and a couple's normal coping strategies break down (Stark, 2010). Common couples violence is considered to be gender symmetrical, although some studies show that women report engaging in it more. For example, 17% to 48% of women and 10% to 39% of men have reported engaging in physical violence toward their partner (Hickman, Jaycox, & Aronoff, 2004; Luthra & Gidycz, 2006; Straus & Ramirez, 2004), and 60% to 83% of women and 55% to 80% of men have reported engaging in psychological abuse (Hickman et al., 2004). The fact that women generally report higher rates of violence than men is controversial (Anderson, 2013). Some researchers conclude that women are more willing to self-report, and others conclude that women have started to compete with men over dominant status as women gain status in broader society (Stark, 2010).

Violence that occurs with more regularity and that increases in severity over time constitutes *intimate terrorism*, also called *coercive controlling violence* (Jaffe, Johnston, Crooks, & Bala, 2008). It differs from common couples violence because perpetrators show clear patterns of emotionally abusive intimidation, domination, coercion, and control (Johnson, 1995, 2009; Johnson & Ferraro, 2000). When people, including researchers, use the term *IPV* to talk about domestic violence, they're usually talking about intimate terrorism (Johnson, 2011). The power and control wheel, depicted in Figure 12.2, shows some of the ways in which perpetrators maintain dominance and control, although not every relationship involves all of them (Pence & Paymar, 1993). Men are more likely to perpetrate intimate terrorism, and women are more likely to experience it (Johnson, 2009). Compared to common couples violence, survivors of intimate terrorism are more likely to reach out to police, hospitals, and women's shelters (Johnson, 2009). In some cases, control tactics can be so effective in

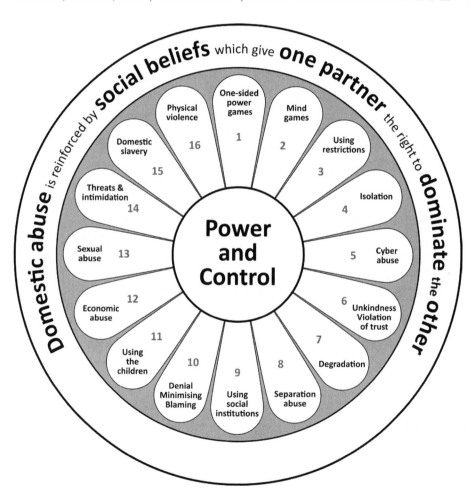

FIGURE 12.2 **Power and control wheel.** This diagram shows the different tactics an abuser can use to manipulate a partner. Sometimes these tactics are used in subtle ways and may be unrecognizable as manipulative until understood in the context of how they contribute to the cycle of violence.

Note. From www.speakoutloud.net © Clare Murphy Phd 2016

creating fear that physical violence might not occur at all (Johnson, 2009). This has led some people to advocate for the justice system to develop laws specific to coercive and controlling behaviors within intimate relationships, and to prosecute accordingly (Stark, 2007).

The third type of intimate partner violence is *violent resistance*, which occurs in response to violence from a partner (Pence & Dasgupta, 2006). In heterosexual relationships, women are the ones most likely to engage in violent resistance (Johnson, 2009). One large study of couples showed that women were more likely than men to be arrested with their partners, and police were more likely to mention self-defense in the arrests of women than men (Melton & Belknap, 2003). In another study, women arrested for IPV with their partners were less likely to have initiated the violence and were more likely to have called the police for help, have physical injuries, and need medical attention than men (Muftic´, Bouffard, & Bouffard, 2007). In the same study, women generally reported using violence in self-defense.

Intimate Terrorism The dynamics of intimate terrorism are complicated because relationships aren't usually violent initially (Keeling & Fisher, 2012). However, even at the beginning when partners report being satisfied and happy, there are predictable red flags. For example, one study of primarily White, heterosexual women who experienced intimate terrorism revealed a common pattern (Keeling & Fisher, 2012). Initially, their partners made them feel "like a princess," consistent with benevolent sexism (p. 1562). The *princess effect*, the tendency for a man to make his partner feel uniquely special, is a strategy to increase attachment and loyalty. Once loyalty was secured, participants reported that their partners initiated deep, intense conversations that required self-disclosing vulnerabilities, which were later used to control the women. Finally, the abusive men pushed for a significant commitment early in the relationship, leading to emotional dependency and social isolation. These tactics were employed before any violence took place, so when it did occur, it was hard for the women to leave the relationships.

Another study—this one of Asian, Pacific Islander, and Native Hawaiian queer women who experienced intimate terrorism—revealed that abuse was characterized by deep emotional intimacy combined with fear and pain, much like in heterosexual relationships (Kanuha, 2013). One woman shared, "I had never experienced a relationship that could be so loving and so hurtful" (p. 1182). Yet, unlike heterosexual couples, participants reported that the intimacy was intensified by the fact that they were in a relationship with someone similar to themselves. This contributed to their desire to stay in the relationship despite clear signs of abuse.

It's not surprising that many survivors describe their abusive relationships as mixed with intense love and violence. As we saw in Chapter 8, romance is often depicted within the context of jealousy, control, and aggression (Bonomi,

Altenburger, & Walton, 2013; Collins & Carmody, 2011). In fact, popular movies and books, such as the *Twilight* series, *Beauty & the Beast*, and *50 Shades of Grey,* have been criticized for conflating love with violence (Bonomi et al., 2013; Collins & Carmody, 2011; Olson, 2013). Such widespread endorsement of traditional romantic ideals creates a climate in which violence is normalized and sets the stage for intimate terrorism. Moreover, violence within the context of romanticized jealousy can be particularly problematic because it's often construed as a sign of love rather than danger (Puente & Cohen, 2003).

A complicating aspect is that the violence isn't constant. In many cases, a **cycle of abuse** consists of a tension-building stage, a violent episode, and a loving and contrition phase (Walker, 2017). The latter phase has been called a *honeymoon stage* because it's a time when perpetrators apologize and provide gifts, admiration, and attention. They may also promise to attend counseling, stop drinking, or seek spiritual guidance. These positive interactions strengthen the relationship and can convince the survivors that they're uniquely qualified to help the perpetrator reform or become a better person. When Rihanna reunited with Chris Brown in 2012, she told *Vanity Fair,* "Maybe I'm the person who's almost the guardian angel to him, to be there when he's not strong enough, when he's not understanding the world, when he just needs someone to encourage him in a positive way and say the right thing" (Robinson, 2015, para. 10). Believing that a perpetrator can change is called **learned hopefulness**, and it's one reason some survivors remain committed to an abusive relationship (LaViolette & Barnett, 2000).

Over time, these dynamics can have devastating effects. Abusers rely on many tactics to establish **coercive power**, a type of power that leads survivors to think they'll experience negative consequences if they don't comply with their abusers' demands (Felson, 2002). Lately, cell phone technology, drones, and social media have intensified abuse tactics. Perpetrators now can send threatening or insulting text messages, keep tabs on a partner, check a partner's browsing history and phone log, and post demeaning messages on social media sites (Dimond, Fiesler, & Bruckman, 2011). In one study of men arrested

Stranger Harassment

Stranger harassment (also called street harassment) is harassment of women in public places by men who are strangers (Davidson, Butchko, Robbins, Sherd, & Gervais, 2016). This can include catcalling, leers, winks, pinches, and remarks. It's difficult to address because it's nearly impossible to pursue legal justice against a stranger who disappears after an incident.

Stranger harassment happens frequently (Davidson et al., 2016; Fairchild, 2010). In a study of undergraduate women, 57% to 88% reported experiencing verbal street harassment, and 11% to 33% experienced sexual forms of street harassment (Davidson et al., 2016). Women also reported more public incivility (e.g., pushing in crowded spaces, cursing, yelling) than men did (Bastomski & Smith, 2017). Because such harassment reduces feelings of safety—especially at night or when alone—women, more than men, limit their use of public spaces (Macmillan, Nierobisz, & Welsh, 2000).

It's hard to know what to do when stranger harassment occurs. In one study, only 20% of women reported confronting harassers (Magley, 2002). Women were most likely to ignore or try to avoid harassers. However, in a study of college students, those who responded actively were less likely to feel sexually objectified than those who responded passively (Fairchild & Rudman, 2008).

In 2014, social worker and activist Feminista Jones launched #YouOkSis to encourage bystanders to intervene when witnessing stranger harassment. Anyone can go up to a girl or woman who looks uncomfortable and say, "Are you okay?" (Berlatsky, 2014, para. 13).

for IPV, 81% admitted to perpetrating at least one act of cyber abuse in the year prior to entering an intervention program (Brem et al., 2017). Technology has led to an increase of stalking, particularly among teens and young adults (Picard, 2007; Southworth, Finn, Dawson, Fraser, & Tucker, 2007).

Abusers also rely on *gaslighting*, a form of psychological abuse that involves manipulating victims into doubting their memory, perception, or sanity (Dutton, 2006). Gaslighting abusers respond to any conflict as if they've been victimized. This leads to one-sided arguments and may even cause the survivor to apologize or take responsibility for the abuser's behavior. This type of psychological abuse can lead to self-doubt, depression, anxiety, and low self-esteem (Afifi, Boman, Fleisher, & Sareen, 2009). Survivors may also feel shame and guilt, which can hinder their ability to end the relationship (Scheffer Lindgren & Renck, 2008). As one woman described, "He almost managed to persuade me that I'm nobody. Not worth a human life" (Walker, 2017 p. 71). In one study, over 20% of women living with abuse wouldn't tell anyone about their situation because of self-doubt, depression, and self-blame (Spangaro, Zwi, & Poulos, 2011).

Within lesbian battering relationships, tactics can be different. Compared to heterosexual perpetrators, lesbian perpetrators use emotional and psychological violence more often than other forms of violence (Badenes-Ribera, Bonilla-Campos, Frias-Navarro, Pons-Salvador, & Monterde-i-Bort, 2016; Matte & Lafontaine, 2011). Perpetrators might also use the threat of disclosing lesbian identity to instill fear. The double stigma of being outed as a lesbian and outed as abused is particularly distressing (Kanuha, 2013). Internalized heterosexism, discussed in Chapter 4, has been found to predict experiencing IPV, and abusers can use this to exploit and control a partner—for example, by threatening to "out" a partner who wishes to leave the relationship (Balsam & Szymanski, 2005). Other research, however, shows that the more out a person is, the most likely they are to experience IPV (Carvalho, Lewis, Derlega, Winstead, & Viggiano, 2011).

One result of frequent and ongoing abuse is *battered women's syndrome*, a type of post-traumatic stress disorder that includes disruption in interpersonal relationships, body image distortion, and sexual intimacy issues (Walker, 2017). Controversially, battered women's syndrome has been used as a defense for women who are prosecuted for killing their abusers. In these cases, the women resorted to extreme violence as a form of self-defense, an example of violent resistance.

Who's Involved in IPV?

What social identity characteristics are most common among those who experience and those who perpetrate IPV?

Using meta-analysis, researchers have found that women who were younger, had a low income, and had more children were at higher risk for IPV (Humphreys, 2007). In fact, women with children were three times more likely to experience

IPV than women without children. Other research has shown that incidents of IPV are the highest during pregnancy and right after the birth of a child, making it harder for women to mobilize and leave an abusive relationship (James, Brody, & Hamilton, 2013). Still other research suggests that bisexual women are more likely to experience IPV than are lesbian or heterosexual women; some researchers believe this is related to the high rates of early victimization among bisexual women contributing to vulnerability to abuse later in life (Goldberg & Meyer, 2013; Roberts, Austin, Corliss, Vandermorris, & Koenen, 2010). Transgender individuals also appear to be at higher risk. In one study, 31.1% of transgender participants, compared to 20.4% of cisgender participants, reported experiencing IPV (Langenderfer-Magruder, Whitfield, Walls, Kattari, & Ramos, 2016). In another study, 54% of transgender respondents had experienced IPV (James et al., 2016). Transgender individuals who were people of color, undocumented immigrants, people with disabilities, sex workers, and homeless individuals were those most likely to report IPV.

Perpetrators, regardless of gender or sexual orientation, also share similar qualities. They're likely to have witnessed interpersonal violence, to have experienced childhood abuse, to abuse substances, and to believe in traditional gender roles (Dardis, Dixon, Edwards, & Turchik, 2015). Women's perpetration of IPV is more strongly associated with depression, anger, and having experienced victimization, whereas men's is associated with lower socioeconomic status, low education levels, and anti-social personality characteristics (Dardis et al., 2015). Overall, researchers identify that men perpetrate more severe forms of violence and women report greater injury, fear, and psychological consequences (Swan, Gambone, Caldwell, Sullivan, & Snow, 2008; Tjaden & Thoennes, 2000). Regardless of ethnicity, race, or socioeconomic status, women are more likely than men to be injured or killed by IPV (Kelly & Johnson, 2008).

Challenges of Leaving Abusive Relationships

What factors play a role in whether women are able to successfully leave abusive relationships?

People who hear about instances of IPV may wonder, "Why doesn't she just leave?" Several factors make it challenging to do so. First, when a woman tries to leave, the likelihood of her abuser attacking her, and even killing her, increases (Campbell et al., 2003; Campbell, 2004; Dobash & Dobash, 2012; Halket, Gormley, Mello, Rosenthal, & Mirkin, 2014). Second, abusers may threaten to kidnap children if the relationship ends. One study found that 11% of children were actually kidnapped after a woman tried to leave an abusive male partner (Stahly, 2008). Third, women often don't tell others about the abusive situation for fear of losing their children if child protection agencies become aware of it (Rivett & Kelly, 2006; Robinson & Spilsbury, 2008).

Some perpetrators exert control because their partner is financially dependent or relies on them for health care or medical assistance (Cockram, 2003). For example, women with physical and mental disabilities have an increased risk for IPV, and researchers speculate that their vulnerability may be related to their financial dependence and decreased ability to fight back and/or leave (Brownridge, 2009; Plummer & Findley, 2012). Perpetrators also may withhold assistive devices, such as wheelchairs and hearing aids, or they may deny needed help, as in leaving a woman with mobility limitations in an uncomfortable position for long periods (Saxton et al., 2001). In a sample of predominantly well-educated women of color with physical disabilities, being younger, less mobile, more socially isolated, and more depressed were factors related to an increased likelihood of experiencing IPV (Nosek, Hughes, Taylor, & Taylor, 2006).

Housing instability and homelessness are also barriers for women who seek safety for themselves and their children (Clough, Draughon, Njie-Carr, Rollins, & Glass, 2014). As one woman said, "We left and I couldn't find a single place to sleep or anything and I went back. My two children said let's go, mommy, but, right then, I told them it was best for us to go back" (p. 7). Women who return to abusive relationships are likely to experience more extreme violence, which is one reason many psychologists suggest that women develop a detailed plan before leaving (Murray et al., 2015). In addition to securing financial resources and social support, women who contemplate leaving are encouraged to keep cash, a cell phone, copies of keys, important documents, and supplies for children or animals readily available (Campbell, 2002; Faver & Strand, 2003; Glass, Eden, Bloom, & Perrin, 2010; Murray et al., 2015).

Seeking support from a trained professional is one way in which survivors can get confidential help to deal with violence. Survivors can find someone to talk with about their experiences by reaching out to either local support organizations or national organizations like the Rape, Abuse & Incest National Network (rainn.org) and the National Domestic Violence Hotline (1-800-799-7233). Staff and volunteers at these organizations can also help survivors identify resources for additional support and long-term care.

For other women, stigma prevents seeking safety (Berg, 2014). One White woman said, "I was in a very wealthy marriage. And, my doctor-husband battered me constantly. I was ashamed and embarrassed. As a mental health professional, I felt I should have known better" (p. 144). In the United States, women are still often blamed for being abused (Meyer, 2016). In the case of Rihanna and Chris Brown, 46% of survey respondents stated that she was responsible for Brown's violence, and 52% said both partners were at fault (Nasaw, 2009).

As women contemplate leaving abusive relationships, they may rely on IPV programs that offer community outreach, case management, advocacy, health education, and support groups. However, within the United States, some programs have stringent policies that can make women feel unwelcome and overly scrutinized (Glenn & Goodman, 2015; Goodman & Epstein, 2008). Further, many shelters hire primarily White staff and are often located in predominantly White neighborhoods (Donnelly, Cook, Van Ausdale, & Foley, 2005). Researchers have speculated that one reason Black women are less likely to use shelters than White women is that they've experienced racial discrimination (Campbell et al., 2001). Moreover, IPV program staff may minimize the severity of violence within lesbian relationships and may have little to no training in working with LGBTQ survivors (Basow & Thompson, 2012; Brown & Groscup, 2009). This can significantly impair survivors' ability to seek formal resources for help and may even cause additional harm. Survivors can experience humiliation within IPV programs—particularly low-income single women of color, LGBTQ women, and women with severe mental illness (Koyama, 2006; Sokoloff & Dupont, 2005). However, a positive relationship with an IPV advocate has been found to be related to reduced symptoms of both depression and PTSD (Goodman, Banyard, Woulfe, Ash, & Mattern, 2016).

try it for yourself

Many people wonder why women don't leave abusive relationships. Ask three friends with diverse social identity characteristics about their thoughts on this issue. What kind of responses do you get? Now that you've learned more about factors that influence decisions to leave, what would you say to a friend who wonders why a person wouldn't "just leave" an abusive relationship?

Sex Trafficking

What is sex trafficking, and how is it similar to and different from IPV?

IPV sets the stage for even more dangerous relational situations. *Human trafficking* is a complex, worldwide problem. Although researchers characterize IPV and human trafficking differently, in some ways these two types of violence intersect. The Victims of Trafficking and Violence Protection Act (2000) defines **sex trafficking** as commercial sex induced by force, fraud, or coercion. Unlike individuals who voluntarily work in the sex industry, victims of sex trafficking are sold and traded against their will. IPV and sex trafficking often co-occur, with one study showing that 64% of female victims reported having been romantically involved with their pimp (Raphael & Ashley, 2008). Sex trafficking is the second largest criminal industry in the world, and it's the fastest growing, generating $99 billion annually (Human Rights First, 2016). Researchers have estimated that between 22% and 40% of adults working in the sex industry are in trafficking situations (Roe-Sepowitz, Hickle, Dahlstedt, & Gallagher, 2014).

Additionally, 1.2 million children are sold into the illegal sex trade internationally (UNICEF, 2014a). Any situation in which a person under age 18 performs a sex act in exchange for money constitutes childhood sex trafficking (Victims of Trafficking and Violence Protection Act, 2000). In the United States, childhood sex-trafficking victims are typically 12 to 14 years old, and children who run away or are kicked out of their homes are especially vulnerable (Mitchell, Finkelhor, & Wolak, 2013). Adult male customers often know the age of the children with whom they're having sex and, therefore, are knowingly raping children (Monto, 2004).

Similar to IPV, sex-trafficking relationships are based on unequal power dynamics and are characterized by secrecy, abuse, financial control, and fear (Roe-Sepowitz et al., 2014). One study showed that street-level sex workers experienced unpredictable violence as well as love and loyalty from their pimp/trafficker (Williamson & Cluse-Tolar, 2002). As is the case within IPV relationships, this confusing combination contributes to victims staying in trafficking relationships (Roe-Sepowitz et al., 2014).

Despite similarities, there are distinctions between IPV relationships and those that involve trafficking. For example, although IPV survivors may experience financial exploitation, it's more common for girls and women in trafficking situations to be used primarily for profit and revenue (Roe-Sepowitz et al., 2014; Williamson & Cluse-Tolar, 2002). Trafficking victims are forced to have sex with people outside of their primary relationship, with one study reporting that, on average, traffickers force women to have sex with 10 people per day (Raphael, Reichert, & Powers, 2010). Although many organizations and shelters focus on IPV survivors, trafficking survivors have fewer options. Only 13 states have organizations that specifically help trafficking survivors, and a mere handful of those offer long-term housing (Roe-Sepowitz et al., 2014).

Girls and women in sex-trafficking situations are often perceived, by both law enforcement and the general public, to be criminals rather than victims of a crime (Macias-Konstantopoulos & Bar-Halpern, 2016; Vanwesenbeeck, 2017). This has implications for when (and if) a trafficking victim tries to seek help. One study of primarily White undergraduate students showed that men, but not women, were likely to blame a victim of sex trafficking for being in that situation (Cunningham & Cromer, 2016). Men were also more accepting of human trafficking myths, such as the idea that victims gain wealth, enjoy having sex with multiple people, and either can't be raped or deserve to be raped (Cunningham & Cromer, 2016; Sullivan, 2007). These myths further justify the exploitation of women, increase violence against sex workers, and reduce the reporting of girls and women in trafficking situations (Farley, 2003).

Violence against Older Women

What unique issues are faced by older women who experience violence?

Women may experience violence at any point in their lives. Moreover, some women experience abuse as children, go on to experience it in their intimate relationships, and then experience it from their adult children or from a professional caretaker later in life (Hightower, 2004). In other words, gender-based violence has the potential to follow women through their lives, and as women age, the intersection of ageism and sexism impedes their ability to seek help (Crockett, Brandl, & Dabby, 2015).

Elderly women, like younger women, can be abused by their romantic partners (Lundy & Grossman, 2005). According to one study, current or former romantic partners committed 10% of violent victimization reported by individuals ages 50 to 64, and 6% of violent victimization reported by individuals ages 65 and older (Morgan & Mason, 2014). Another study showed that 9% of older adults have reported experiencing verbal mistreatment and 3.5% have reported experiencing financial abuse (Laumann, Leitsch & Waite, 2008). In this study, a spouse or romantic partner was identified as the perpetrator by 26% of participants.

Older women who experience IPV report more severe health consequences than younger women do, particularly if they've experienced additional trauma during their lifetime (Policastro & Finn, 2017). Abusers have been found to change their tactics with age, reducing physical violence and, instead, controlling finances and increasing verbal and psychological abuse (Stöckl & Penhale, 2015). In a study of older women who'd experienced violence throughout their lives, some reported that such non-physical abuse was harder to cope with than physical abuse (Dunlop, Rothman, Condon, Hebert, & Martinez, 2001).

Particularly when older women experience IPV in long-term committed relationships, they're likely to blame themselves and feel powerless and hopeless (Beaulaurier, Seff, & Newman, 2008). They're also more likely to stay in violent relationships because of financial vulnerabilities, lack of access to quality health care, and beliefs in traditional gender roles (Hightower, Smith, & Hightower, 2006; Rosay & Mulford, 2017). Older women who live in rural areas are the most at risk because of social isolation and the challenges associated with seeking help (Roberto, Brossoie, McPherson, Pulsifer, & Brown, 2013).

Elderly women also can be abused by family members or caretakers. **Elder abuse** is defined as a single or repeated act, occurring within the context of a trusting relationship, that causes harm to a person over the age of 60 (Hightower et al., 2006). In a large national study, more than 1 in 10 adults 70 years of age or older (14.0%) reported experiencing some form of elder abuse (Rosay & Mulford, 2017). Women are at higher risk than men (Zink, Fisher, Regan, & Pabst, 2005). Poor health and cognitive impairments can contribute to an individual's vulnerability, as do low educational attainment, substance abuse, and social isolation (Zink & Fisher, 2006). Immigrant seniors are especially at risk because of language barriers, small social networks, and increased dependency on others (Tam & Neysmith, 2006). Although elder abuse can be physical or sexual, most cases reported to adult protective services involve financial exploitation (50%), neglect (45%), and emotional abuse (45%; Teaster et al., 2007).

Elder abuse is often ignored as a crime because older research suggested that this type of abuse stemmed from caregiver stress (Zarit & Toseland, 1989).

The *caregiver stress model* assumed that the cumulative effects of being a caretaker resulted in abuse and neglect (Nerenberg, 2002). More recent research shows that elder abuse has more to do with the controlling characteristics of an abuser and with unequal power dynamics (Lundy & Grossman, 2005). However, because the caregiver stress model still holds sway, many social service agencies focus on reducing caregiver stress rather than assessing the power imbalances in relationships (Kilbane & Spira, 2010). The focus on the caretaker, without proper assessment of the dynamic between the caretaker and the elder, continues in many adult protective services and contributes to the minimization or ignoring of elder abuse (Kilbane & Spira, 2010).

Healing after Abuse

How do women heal from abuse, and what role can restorative justice play in their healing?

Even after years of abuse, some women do escape abusive situations and experience significant relief from depression and anxiety, but they also experience grief (Coolidge & Anderson, 2002). In one study of Filipino women who left abusive relationships, participants reported increased freedom, inner strength, and hope, although they also reported stress associated with the loss of a partner to help raise their children (Estrellado & Loh, 2016). In order to heal, women often transform their identity from "victim" to "survivor," an identity that signifies empowerment (Goodman & Epstein, 2008). Such healing occurs when a survivor realizes how individual experiences of violence are connected to a larger sociopolitical system in which few obstacles prevent men from using violence to control and dominate women. In Chapter 13, we'll discuss how feminist therapies can help women heal from violence and abuse.

Achieving Justice Scholars have noted that incarceration does not reduce repeat criminal offenses or lead to social change (Boots, Wareham, Bartula, & Canas, 2016; Will, Loper, & Jackson, 2016; Williams & Stransfield, 2017). Since many incarcerated individuals are themselves survivors, some researchers argue that prison might actually perpetuate a cycle of violence (Wolff, Shi, & Siegel, 2009). Further, the criminal justice system disproportionately punishes perpetrators who are people of color, those with mental illnesses, and the poor (The Sentencing Project, 2013; Walker, Spohn, & DeLone, 2012). Given this context, scholars have called for more progressive approaches to achieving justice (Boots et al., 2016; Karp & Frank, 2016; Zarling & Berta, 2017).

One such approach has been modeled on Indigenous peacemaking processes (Yazzie & Zion, 1996). Known as **restorative justice**, it focuses on rehabilitation through a process of facilitated meetings between perpetrators and survivors, with the goal of achieving reconciliation and commitment to peace. Restorative justice seeks to allow offenders to accept accountability for their actions, to restore community safety through collective action, and to address underlying issues that cause offenders to harm—such as poverty, living within a patriarchal environment, lack of education/work, and poor stress management (McAlinden, 2017).

Supporters of restorative justice believe that the traditional perpetrator/victim dichotomy doesn't acknowledge that many offenders are, themselves, victims and that cycles of trauma and abuse continue if communities don't attend to the suffering of all members (Daly & Stubbs, 2006). Critics, however, suggest that this approach may be too lenient and that it doesn't prioritize survivors' safety (van Wormer, 2009). For this reason, restorative justice meetings have very specific guidelines, particularly for crimes involving IPV and sexual abuse (Cameron, 2006). Successful models ensure that survivor and perpetrator meet face-to-face and that survivor safety is prioritized.

Research has found that restorative justice works better at reducing repeat offenses and reducing harm to survivors than jail time or other punitive models of justice (Sherman, Strang, Mayo-Wilson, Woods, & Ariel, 2015). In this study, victims who participated in restorative justice meetings reported reduced self-blame and desire for revenge compared to those who participated in conventional justice systems. Offenders who participated were more likely to admit they had breached a community moral standard and were more likely to apologize. A study of youth sexual violence showed that restorative justice conferences were a better option for survivors if the perpetrator admitted to the offense (Daly, 2002). However, scholars worry that apologies are notoriously part of the cycle of abuse, particularly among IPV situations, so a focus on this might be inappropriate. More research is needed to understand the effectiveness of using restorative justice among IPV survivors.

War and Violence

How do war and militarism contribute to women's experiences of violence, and in what ways do some feminists respond?

Worldwide, women and children account for almost 80% of war casualties as well as 80% of the 40 million people who are refugees (Kinkartz, 2015; United Nations, 2015). For women living in war zones, sexual assault and rape are estimated to be common, but actual numbers are unknown (Cook, Wilson, & Thomas, 2018; Simon, Nolan, & Ngo, 2013). One report released by the United Nations Development Fund for Women estimated that 59% to 94% of female civilians living in a war zone experience sexual assault and/or rape (Rehn & Sirleaf, 2002). Other research has confirmed that soldiers commonly rape civilians, and attackers are overwhelmingly male (Donohoe, 2013). Even after war ends, the risk can remain high, since UN peacekeeping forces and international police have been found to engage in sexual coercion and to accept bribes to facilitate sex trafficking (Higate, 2007; Hynes, 2004). Moreover, wartime crimes often go unpunished (Human Rights Watch, 2015).

Given these findings, the presence of U.S. military forces worldwide can be concerning. At the time of writing this chapter, U.S. military forces are deployed in 135 nations—roughly 70% of the countries on the planet (Turse, 2017). The proposed 2017 U.S. military budget was $582.7 billion (U.S. Department of Defense, 2016b). Since 2009, the United States has been engaged in multiple conflicts and wars that involve violent airstrikes and robotic technology (Carter, 2017).

These wars aren't always defensive—that is, they aren't occurring because a foreign government attacked the United States (Žarkov, 2016). In 2002, the U.S. national security strategy included the idea that preventive military action was justifiable in order to address potential future threats (The White House, 2002). This has been a controversial policy. Some scholars worry that preemptive military intervention might be an extension of **imperialism**, a practice that extends a country's power through either diplomacy or war, or both (Mohanty, Pratt, & Riley, 2008). Others see military action as necessary to ensure global safety. For example, in 2012, one U.S. national security goal was protecting the rights of girls and women (Pratt, 2013). Female empowerment (e.g., removing prohibitions on girls' education) was given as justification for U.S. military occupation in Afghanistan and Iraq. According to a recent survey, Americans are split over the use of preemptive military force: 12% believe it is *often* justified and 38% believe it is *sometimes* justified, while 28% believe it should *rarely* be used and 20% believe it should *never* be used (Tyson, 2017).

Some feminist and peace scholars are concerned with the proliferation of **militarism**—that is, the prioritization and justification of military values within both military and civilian life (Faludi, 2007; Sjoberg, 2013). These values include the belief that men are natural protectors and that both obedience to authority and the threat of physical force ensure safety (Enloe, 2016). In the United States, public spaces such as high schools, and public safety officers such as police forces, have become increasingly militarized (Abajian, 2016; Faludi, 2007). In this atmosphere, the proliferation of militarism can undermine feminist principles of equality and social justice (Enloe, 2016; Mayton, Peters, & Owens, 1999). For example, studies have shown that individuals who support militarism are more likely to value conformity than diversity and are less likely to endorse social and environmental justice (Bliss, Oh, & Williams, 2007;

your turn

Do you believe female empowerment can be achieved through military occupation and intervention? If so, how? If not, why not? Consider the various feminist philosophies covered in Chapter 1. Which ones are more likely to support military action and which ones are not?

Militarized vehicles like the one pictured here in Baltimore, Maryland, are being added to police resources in both urban and suburban settings. Additions such as these, along with an increase in military tactics in policing, have prompted a nationwide debate about the nature of law enforcement.

Mayton et al., 1999). According to feminist psychologist Eileen Zurbriggen (2010), sexual violence cannot be eliminated without significantly reducing or eliminating our nation's increasing emphasis on militarism.

Locally and internationally, *transnational feminists* work against militarism because they understand that girls and women bear the brunt of war more than others (Grabe, 2016). Some feminist scholars have called for Western women to challenge ongoing wars, especially the increased use of drone executions (Blanchard, 2011; Feigenbaum, 2015). In 2013, feminist international activist and Nobel Peace Prize recipient Malala Yousafzai (herself a survivor of violence) said, "Drone strikes are fueling terrorism. . . . Innocent victims are killed in these attacks, and they lead to resentment" (CNN Political Unit, 2013, para. 4). According to Yousafzai, as well as other feminists, an investment in education for children would be a better solution than increased violence through warfare.

Stopping a Culture of Violence

What can people do to stop rape culture and a broader culture of violence?

The types of violence discussed in this chapter and the high rates of occurrence are disturbing, but it's possible to address this widespread problem. Structural changes can make a large difference in the lives of girls and women. In general, when women have more power, violence is reduced. In an analysis of two very different countries (Nicaragua and Tanzania), researchers found a strikingly similar pattern in terms of women's status and violence (Grabe, Grose, & Dutt, 2015). When women owned land, they had access to more power and mobility, and this, in turn, was related to reduced violence. However, even small acts by individuals can have a ripple effect in creating awareness, resistance, and change.

Reimagining Gender

One way to address violence against girls and women is to have candid conversations with men about masculinity. Individuals, especially men, who believe in traditional gender roles are more accepting of violence toward women (Loveland & Raghavan, 2017; Seabrook, Ward, & Giaccardi, 2018; Willie, Khondkaryan, Callands, & Kershaw, 2018). Most boys and men are socialized to adopt traits of traditional masculinity, which include aggression, dominance, self-reliance, lack of emotional expression, homophobia, avoidance of femininity, and viewing sex as an accomplishment rather than a key part of an intimate relationship (Cuthbert, 2015; Levant, 2011; Levant & Richmond, 2008; Thompson & Bennett, 2017). In fact, in a meta-analysis, nearly all aspects of traditional masculinity were linked to sexual aggression (Murnen et al., 2002). Today, although not all boys and men conform to traditional notions of masculinity, they still experience pressure to adhere to these norms (Levant & Richmond, 2016). Offering boys and men an opportunity to discuss these pressures can change the way they think about and enact masculinity.

At an organizational level, higher incidences of violence occur when a group's identity is centralized around masculinity—as in the military, law enforcement, and professional athletics (Harway & Steel, 2015). Since many of these organizations value brotherhood and loyalty, an "us versus them" mentality can exacerbate sexism (Flood, 2011). One way to address this is to evaluate women's leadership roles and to promote their increased presence and power within such organizations (Harway & Steele, 2015).

See Something, Say Something

Violence can be prevented through a shared, community responsibility for creating a safe environment and a cultural intolerance of violence (Flood, 2015). For example, community members can hold religious and political leaders accountable for sending clear messages against violence toward girls and women and for creating a climate of respect (Bryant-Davis & Wong, 2013). Communities can also provide educational programs on identifying patterns of abuse so that everyone acquires the knowledge and skills to intervene if necessary (Flood, 2015).

In some ways, men are uniquely qualified to confront other men (Flood, 2015). They can encourage other men to talk about gender roles, dating norms, and issues relating to consent (Gidycz, Orchowski, & Berkowitz, 2011). Also, churches, community groups, and schools have sponsored programs that encourage men to talk to one another about how to stop violence enacted by others (Flood, 2015; Garrity, 2011). For example, the White Ribbon Campaign is a global movement of boys and men working to end violence against women and girls and to promote healthy relationships. Several studies have found that such programs are effective in changing men's attitudes and increasing their likelihood of intervening in potentially dangerous situations (Garrity, 2011; McMahon & Dick, 2011; Stewart, 2014). However, in other research, all-male groups were no more effective than mixed-gender groups in changing attitudes and increasing the likelihood of intervening (Anderson & Whiston, 2005).

Many colleges have encouraged **bystander intervention**—that is, intervening when people witness a problematic situation—with some success. In one study, students who received training in bystander intervention were less likely to be victims of violence, and men who participated were less likely to be perpetrators (Coker et al., 2015). Bystander intervention has also served to help young adults intervene in situations that may lead to dating violence—for example, by helping a friend who's in a controlling relationship realize that there may be red flags of violence (Storer, Casey, & Herrenkohl, 2016).

Becoming Media Literate

The media contribute to a culture of violence (Katz-Schiavone, Levenson, & Ackerman, 2008). Violence, especially toward girls and women, is a common theme in television shows (Gabrielli, Traore, Stoolmiller, Bergamini, & Sargent, 2016), movies (Bushman, Jamieson, Weitz, & Romer, 2013), video games (Hartmann, Krakowiak, & Tsay-Vogel, 2014), and music videos (Ward, Reed, Trinh, & Foust, 2014). In a large study across seven nations, researchers found that viewing violence contributed to aggression, even after controlling for other variables such as having experienced prior abuse (Anderson et al., 2017). Even brief exposure to violence can cause some people to become more aggressive and show less empathy and fewer helping behaviors (Anderson, Bushman, Donnerstein, Hummer, & Warburton, 2015). Exposure to violence increases aggressive thoughts, angry feelings, and physiological arousal such as increased heart rate (Bushman & Anderson, 2009). It also contributes to desensitization, and since violence is often rewarded in media portrayals, those outcomes reinforce the idea that violence is a winning strategy (Bushman, 2018).

Even the way the media talk about violence matters (Bohner, 2001). For example, media outlets often describe rape using the passive voice: "The woman was raped" instead of "The man raped the woman." A content analysis of over 1,500 U.S. newspaper articles indicated that writers more frequently used a passive (70%) than an active style (30%) to describe rape (Henley, Miller, & Beazley, 1995). The passive voice allows the perpetrator to be absent from the description, which suggests that the victim was somehow responsible for the rape (Bohner, 2001). In one study, female and male participants who read news reports that described rape in a passive way were more likely to believe that violence against women was acceptable, as compared to those who read the same report written in a more active style (Henley et al., 1995).

Research has shown that individuals can counteract some of the harmful effects caused by exposure to violence by critically evaluating media (Bergsma & Carney, 2008; Choma, Foster, & Radford, 2007). Other research confirms that becoming a critical consumer of media is a positive first step, but engaging in media activism is also necessary to truly counter problematic messages and strengthen feelings of empowerment among girls and women (Brinkman, Khan, Jedinak, & Vetere, 2015). Joining campaigns sponsored by the Women's Media Center and Women in Media and News is one way to begin engaging in media activism.

Thinking Globally, Acting Locally

Because war is ever-present, it's useful to reflect on how local policies affect global relationships. For example, in 1979 the United Nations adopted a resolution titled the Convention on the Elimination of All Forms of Discrimination against Women (CEDAW), which defines violence against women as a violation of human rights (United Nations, n.d.). Nations that accept CEDAW commit to incorporating principles of gender equality into their legal systems and to abolishing discriminatory laws. CEDAW also requires that countries establish funding for public institutions that can ensure effective protection of girls and women, and it affirms reproductive rights as a human right.

Although 185 countries have ratified CEDAW, at the time of writing this chapter, the United States is the only industrialized nation that has not ratified it. In 2002, the U.S. Senate Foreign Relations Committee recommended ratification, but the issue has never been brought to a vote because detractors believe it violates American sovereignty and too rigidly dictates a progressive view of gendered relations and reproductive rights. Grassroots organizations like the Women's Intercultural Network (WIN) are working to address this. WIN's campaign, Cities for CEDAW, encourages individual cities to pass ordinances to improve the lives of girls and women and reduce violence against them. Its website provides a "how to" organizational kit. As of July 2018, there are 31 U.S. cities, including San Francisco, Honolulu, and Pittsburg, that have adopted ordinances or affirmed resolutions for the principles of CEDAW ("Cities for CEDAW," n.d.).

Conclusion

Girls and women are at particular risk for violence throughout their lives, and many don't experience justice after surviving a violent act. Moreover, gender-based violence reflects larger social issues, such as women having less power than men and living in a culture of objectification. Experiencing violence can have long-term consequences in many domains—including those related to mental health, as we'll discuss in Chapter 13. However, it's possible to counter a culture of violence with activism. Each time one person speaks against rape culture, volunteers at a domestic violence shelter, or petitions local representatives to change policies, progress is made. If enough people start seriously addressing violence in our culture, coalitions can be built. To begin this process at any level, it takes only one person to speak out.

Chapter Review

SUMMARY

Gender-Based Violence

- Gender-based violence occurs at both individual and structural levels.

- Violence against girls and women has been described as a public health crisis.

Youth and Violence

- Childhood abuse can involve physical, psychological, and/or sexual abuse.

- Whereas boys are more likely to be sexually abused by someone outside of the family, girls are far more likely to be sexually abused by a family member or someone close to the family.

- Although childhood abuse can have both short- and long-term negative consequences, many survivors experience resiliency.

- When girls are objectified, they are dehumanized, and violence against them increases.

A Rape Culture

- There is evidence of a rape culture in the United States. Most survivors of sexual assault and rape are girls and women, and men are the primary perpetrators.

- Rape myths perpetuate rape culture by inaccurately depicting reality and creating doubt and self-blame among survivors. Rape myths are more strongly endorsed by men as well as by people who have higher degrees of sexual aggression and hostile attitudes toward women.

- Sexual assault and rape occur five times more frequently among college women than among non-college women. Women in the military, Indigenous women, and women with disabilities are also at higher risk for experiencing rape and sexual assault.

- Although survivors experience negative consequences immediately following an assault, most (but not all) will experience relief within a year. Some survivors report experiencing positive post-traumatic growth.

Interpersonal Violence

- IPV can occur in all types of relationship configurations (e.g., heterosexual, same-gender) and among married or dating couples. Three main types of IPV are common: couples violence, intimate terrorism, and violent resistance.

- The cycle of abuse consists of a tension-building stage, a violent episode, and a loving and contrition phase.

- Women who are younger, have a low income, and have more children are at higher risk for IPV.

- The most dangerous time for a woman is when she tries to leave an abusive relationship. Housing instability and homelessness are major barriers for women who seek safety for themselves and their children.

- Similar to IPV, sex-trafficking relationships are based on unequal power dynamics and are characterized by secrecy, abuse, financial control, and fear.

- Abusers change their tactics with age, reducing physical violence and, instead, controlling finances and increasing verbal and psychological abuse.

- Many incidents of elder abuse are perpetrated by caregivers.

- One technique that can increase healing after abuse and reduce the cycle of violence is to take a restorative justice approach.

War and Violence

- Women and girls account for the majority of casualties during war, and many women living in war zones are survivors of rape and sexual assault.

- Transnational feminists work to reduce militarism and end wars in order to improve the lives of girls and women.

Stopping a Culture of Violence

- Both systemic and individual changes can reduce gender-based violence.

- Challenging traditional masculinity can make a difference, and men are uniquely qualified to confront other men.

- Training in when and how to intervene can reduce violence.

- Becoming a critical consumer of media and engaging in media activism can help to undermine rape culture.

- People can participate in local programs connected to global initiatives designed to advance the status of girls and women while decreasing violence.

KEY TERMS

hate crime (p. 492)

gender-based violence (p. 494)

physical abuse (p. 495)

psychological abuse (p. 496)

childhood sexual abuse (p. 496)

resiliency (p. 498)

sexual assault (p. 500)

rape (p. 500)

rape myth (p. 501)

victim blaming (p. 501)

tonic immobility (p. 503)

compliant sex (p. 507)

token resistance (p. 507)

affirmative consent (p. 508)

belief in a just world (p. 509)

cultural spillover theory (p. 511)

post-traumatic growth (p. 515)

domestic violence (p. 515)

intimate partner violence (IPV) (p. 515)

stranger harassment (p. 519)

cycle of abuse (p. 519)

learned hopefulness (p. 519)

coercive power (p. 519)

sex trafficking (p. 523)

elder abuse (p. 525)

restorative justice (p. 526)

imperialism (p. 528)

militarism (p. 528)

bystander intervention (p. 531)

THINK ABOUT IT

1. Do you think hate crime legislation is helpful in deterring gender-based violence? If not, what type of policies do you think could deter and/or eliminate violence? Can you recommend a specific policy that could be implemented in your community now? Explain your response.

2. Using the research results discussed in this chapter, design an infographic as part of an anti-rape campaign in your community that would communicate important prevention information to the public.

3. Think about a few romantic novels and/or movies that you've seen or a romantic song that you know. What messages do they convey about control and jealousy? How could you rewrite them so that violent themes aren't part of the script? Do you think they would be as popular? Why or why not?

4. Have you ever witnessed behaviors that often precede violence against a woman (e.g., controlling behavior in a relationship, a friend hooking up while drunk, a peer joking about sexual conquests)? If so, did you or anyone else call out or intervene to stop the behavior? What would you do if you saw such a behavior now? Has this chapter changed your views about what you can do to stop violence? Explain your response.

5. How much do you know about U.S. involvement in military conflicts? What might you do to learn more to understand, and possibly reduce, the level of militarization? In what ways does war affect you, even if it seems distant and far away?

ONLINE RESOURCES

- **Battered Women Support Services** — education, advocacy, and support services to assist women who are in, or have been involved in, battering relationships: bwss.org

- **Code Pink** — a women-led organization aimed at ending U.S. wars and militarization: codepink.org

- **Hollaback!** — a website dedicated to creating space to understand harassment, engage in public conversations, and develop strategies to ensure equality in public spaces: ihollaback.org

- **INCITE!** — a website featuring a network of radical feminists of color working to end violence: incite-national.org

- **Rape, Abuse & Incest National Network (RAINN)** — an anti–sexual violence organization that provides resources and support for survivors: rainn.org

- **Survived and Punished** — resources for and information about survivors of domestic violence and/or sexual abuse whose survival actions resulted in incarceration: survivedandpunished.org

13

Mental Health

IN JULY 2015, Sandra Bland, a young Black woman, was on her way to a new job as a student ambassador for her alma mater, Prairie View A & M University in Texas, when she was pulled over for "failure to signal" (Yan, Sanchez, & Ford, 2015). Bland was angry and confronted the police officer. When he asked her to put out her cigarette, she responded, "I am in my car. Why do I have to put out my cigarette?" (para. 18). The officer then asked her to get out of the car, and when she refused, he threatened to pull her out. The officer told Bland she was under arrest, and they started to argue. He screamed at her: "Get out of the car! I will light you up! Get out! Now!" (para. 25). She refused, and after a struggle, he pulled out a stun gun. Bland then exited the car of her own accord, saying, "Wow, really, for a failure to signal? You're doing all of this for a failure to signal?" (para. 26). Their struggle continued, and video footage eventually showed the officer slam Bland's head on the ground. She told him that she had epilepsy. The officer replied, *Good!* (para. 30).

Bland was brought to jail and interviewed. She disclosed that she had a history of mental health concerns and a prior suicide attempt. However, there was no reason to think she'd been having mental health struggles right before the traffic stop because she was happy and excited about her new job. However, her experience of being pulled over, physically attacked, and put in jail was extremely upsetting. She told her sister that the officer had hurt her back and that she was afraid her arm was broken (Lai, Park, Buchanan, & Andrews, 2015). After she'd been in jail for three days, officials reported that Bland was found hanging in her cell. Although an autopsy report classified her death as a suicide, Bland's family insisted that police brutality was the cause (Sanburn, 2015). Her family filed a federal wrongful death lawsuit, which was settled for $1.9 million along with an agreement to change the way people are treated in the Waller County jail system (Lee, 2016).

This tragedy raised many unanswered questions. To what extent was the way the police officer handled this situation influenced by Bland's race? How could the officer have de-escalated the situation? To what extent did Bland's mental health history affect what happened? Clearly, the officer's response to a minor traffic violation was extreme and violent. In 2010, Black women in the United States were incarcerated at almost three times the rate of White women (Mauer, 2013). Given this statistic, Sandra Bland was probably more likely to be stopped for

Following the killing of several Black women, including Sandra Bland, the #sayhername movement and hashtag were developed to bring attention to police brutality and violence directed at Black women within the United States. This movement strives to reduce police brutality and anti-Black violence while also empowering and improving the quality of lives of those disproportionately targeted by police violence.

"failure to signal" than a White woman would (Epp & Maynard-Moody, 2014). Further, Bland didn't react in a traditionally feminine way. Instead of being apologetic and compliant, she was angry and showed it. This may have fueled the officer's rage, contributing to his aggression and his decision to transport her to jail. Once she was in custody, she was isolated and left to deal with the intensity of the situation alone. A subsequent state investigation found that guards had failed to do hourly checks and that many guards at the facility hadn't undergone state-required mental health training (Liebelson & Wing, 2015). So, if Bland was a suicide risk, the officers didn't perform the minimum mandated requirements to keep her safe.

Punishing a woman, particularly a Black woman, for displaying behaviors that aren't traditionally feminine isn't a new phenomenon. Historically, when women deviated from traditional femininity, they were seen as unruly and mentally unstable (Ussher, 2013). Moreover, Black women (and other women of color) who don't fit White, Western norms of femininity have frequently been viewed as threatening and criminalized (Gross, 2015). In many cases, Black women have attempted to protect themselves from domestic abuse only to be later punished for their acts of self-defense. In one case, a Black woman named Marissa Alexander spent three years in jail and two years under house arrest because she had fired what she identified as a warning shot toward her estranged, abusive husband; the jail time and house arrest were imposed despite the fact that the shot didn't harm Alexander's husband or anyone else (Hauser, 2017). Such systematic mistreatment of Black women decreases their reliance on asking police for help, which means less protection from additional violence. This dynamic can create stress and contribute to the development of many mental health concerns (Gross, 2015).

In contemporary America, women with mental health concerns are often incarcerated (Barlett & Hollins, 2018). Furthermore, many incarcerated women have been victims of violence, including physical and sexual abuse, before being arrested and incarcerated (DeHart, 2008; Green, Miranda, Daroowalla, & Siddique, 2005; Simpson, Yahner, & Dugan, 2008). For example, one study showed that between 85% and 90% of incarcerated women reported a history of domestic and sexual violence, compared to 22% nationally (Gross, 2015). Another study examined various types of interpersonal violence, such as childhood physical abuse, childhood sexual abuse, witnessing violence as a child, partner violence, sexual violence as an adult, and witnessing violence as an adult (Lynch et al., 2017). The researchers found that 92% of incarcerated women had experienced at least one form of interpersonal violence, 35% had experienced five or more types, and the average number of types of violence experienced by the women surveyed was over three.

Such trauma often leads to mental health problems, and these problems are very common in—and often exacerbated by—the prison system (Lynch et al., 2017; Yi, Turney, & Wildeman, 2017). In fact, the U.S. Bureau of Labor Statistics has reported that 73% of women in state prisons, 61% of women in federal prisons, and 75% of women in local jails had mental health problems (James & Glaze, 2006). One study of women from nine jails across several states showed that 67% had a mental disorder, such as major depression or bipolar disorder, and 83% had a substance use disorder (Green et al., 2016), Moreover, suicide in prison isn't rare. Between 2001 and 2014, research shows that 2,826 people committed suicide in U.S. state prisons (Noonan, 2016). The high rates of mental illness among women in prison also reflect lack of access to quality mental health treatment.

How we understand women's distress matters a great deal. When women enter the criminal justice system, they're often seen as "bad"; the stress and traumas they've experienced are often ignored. In other situations, women can also be labeled "sad" or "mad." They can be medicated, shocked, or hospitalized. In fact, there's a long history of women receiving such treatments without consent (Burstow, 2006; Chesler, 2005; Geller & Harris, 1984). Ideally, women who experience violence and mental distress can receive help to alleviate their suffering, but this doesn't always happen. And although mental health isn't just a concern for women, the interpretation and treatment of symptoms is a distinctly gendered phenomenon (Ussher, 2011).

In this chapter, we'll explore women's mental health. We'll discuss how women have historically been considered "mad" when they didn't conform to gender norms or were perceived as troublesome. We'll then look at the modern system of diagnosing mental illness in the United States, and we'll explore diagnoses that women receive more frequently than men. Finally, we'll discuss how feminist therapists bring an intersectional understanding of the ways in which systems of oppression (e.g., gender oppression, class oppression) can affect women's mental health.

Women and Madness: A Historical Perspective

Women have often been associated with madness (Chesler, 2005). They've frequently been labeled as mad if they don't conform to traditional standards of femininity. Ironically, it's also been argued that women are labeled as mad when they act in ways that are too feminine, and stereotypical aspects of femininity (e.g., passivity, dependence) have been associated with madness (Chesler, 2005). Moreover, women are often labeled as mad, sick, or ill when they respond in ways that actually may make sense within oppressive environments. Knowing the historical context in which these patterns developed will provide a better understanding of women's modern experiences.

The Beginnings

What factors contributed to historical categorizations of women as mentally ill?

Before modern science and medicine, there were many misattributions about how the body works and what causes particular illnesses. Madness was no exception. Some forms of madness were specifically tied to femininity, as they were believed to be a side effect of women's reproductive processes. Madness, particularly among women, has also been attributed to supernatural causes, and the label "mad" was often accompanied by other labels, such as being a witch.

The very first mental problem associated with women was **hysteria**. It was described by the ancient Egyptians, who believed it originated from the uterus wandering through the body (Tasca, Rapetti, Carta, & Fadda, 2012). Symptoms of hysteria were said to include seizures, fears, and a sense of suffocation. The ancient Greeks saw hysteria as being caused by a "sad" uterus that wanted to be linked to a man (Tasca, et al., 2012, p. 110). Symptoms included tremors and anxiety, and treatments included drinking wine and engaging in orgies or having vigorous sex with a male partner.

In the Middle Ages and into the 17th century, symptoms that had previously been attributed to the wandering uterus were considered to signal demonic possession (Chesler, 2005). During this time, non-conforming women, as well as women who experienced psychological symptoms, were labeled as witches. Many were probably midwives and healers, and some may have had property that the Church coveted (Chesler, 2005). Witches were regarded in opposition to the "good wife" because they spoke up against men, exhibited sexual desire, and sought revenge against enemies. One well-known example in which non-conforming women were targeted is the witchcraft accusations that occurred in New England during the 1690s, often referred to as the Salem witch trials.

Many witchcraft confessions were given under duress, but other women voluntarily confessed (Jackson, 1995). One woman who had suffered tremendously at the hands of her husband felt enormous guilt after he died. She decided that she must have killed him with her evil thoughts, so she confessed to being a witch. Other women who had negative feelings toward their children attributed these to the devil and also confessed to witchcraft. The persecution of witches during this period resulted in the deaths of tens of thousands of girls and women throughout Europe and North America.

Regulating Madness in the 19th Century

How was mental illness understood in the 19th century, and how were women with psychological problems treated differently from men?

As science and medicine advanced in the 19th century, approaches to madness increasingly involved a focus on medical treatment. Women, in particular, were viewed as vulnerable to mental illness, and many of the treatments used probably made their problems worse.

Hysteria and Women's Sexuality During the 19th century, hysteria was the most frequently diagnosed and treated condition in women, particularly wealthy White women (Ussher, 2011). It involved a wide variety of symptoms including seizures, fears, coughing, and paralysis. In fact, the diagnosis became so widespread that being considered hysterical became synonymous with being a woman. Hysteria was seen as a fundamental part of the female temperament. One French physician declared that "all women are hysterical and . . . every woman carries with her the seeds of hysteria" (Showalter, 1993, pp. 286–287). Women, and hysterics, were described as "difficult, narcissistic, impressionable, suggestible, egocentric and labile" (Smith-Rosenberg, 1986, p. 9). Essentially, hysteria was seen as an extreme version of what was considered to be traditional femininity. This view reinforced the connection between being a woman and being "mad."

Also, diagnoses of hysteria were often tied to women's sexuality; as mentioned previously, the ancient Greeks thought sexual activity would cure it (Tasca, et al., 2012). Although it's impossible to diagnose women from hundreds of years ago, some scholars have noted that the signs of hysteria overlap with signs of sexual frustration—including anxiety, irritability, nervousness, sensations of heaviness in the stomach, and erotic fantasy (Maines, 2001; Showalter, 1997). Because sex was defined as penile penetration, the clitoris wasn't well understood, and masturbation was discouraged, it wouldn't be surprising if many women at that time were sexually frustrated. However, women weren't supposed to have sexual desires—in fact, openly desiring sex or masturbating was seen as a sign of hysteria.

Nevertheless, the standard treatment for hysteria was genital massage to orgasm, called paroxysm at the time.

your turn

Although hysteria is no longer an official psychological label, the idea is still influential. For example, actress Amanda Bynes and singer Rihanna have both been described as hysterical ("Amanda Bynes—Serious Mental Issues," 2012; "Rihanna: Meltdown at the Grammys," 2016). Have you ever noticed that women who express strong emotions or behave erratically are called hysterical, or something similar? How do you think these labels influence the way people perceive these women and women in general?

A medical compendium published in 1653 and still in use during the 19th century advised: "We think it necessary to ask a midwife to assist so that she can massage the genitalia with one finger inside, using oil of lilies, musk root, crocus or [something] similar. And in this way the afflicted woman can be aroused to the paroxysm" (Maines, 2001, p. 1). This was a popular treatment that many women sought from their physicians. Eventually, vibrators were invented to alleviate the hand cramps of doctors and midwives who were tired of providing manual treatment (Maines, 2001). The water douche was also introduced, a treatment that could be given at a spa; it involved aiming a strong stream of water from a hose at a woman's genitals. Some women diagnosed with hysteria were probably sexually abused (Makari, 1998), so while these treatments may have been generally popular, certain women may have found genital stimulation reminiscent of sexual abuse.

Insane Asylums and Rest Cures Although women in the 19th century weren't burned at the stake as witches when they showed signs of "madness," treatments during that period were far from benign. Many women were involuntarily placed in insane asylums, where treatments could include beatings, prolonged periods in restraints, and being submerged in water. These women were often deemed hysterical because they acted in non-feminine ways, rejected their role as wives or mothers, and/or were sexually attracted to other women. Some were involuntarily hospitalized for "crimes" such as speaking their minds, becoming romantically involved with other women, dressing extravagantly, or disagreeing with their families' religious views (Geller & Harris, 1984).

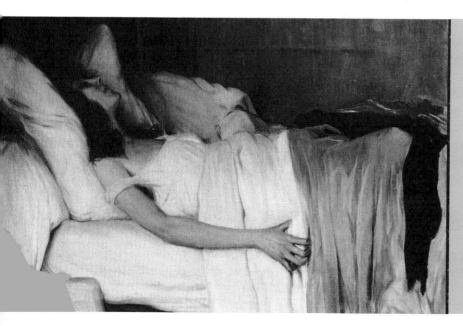

During the late 19th century, certain doctors prescribed rest cures to upper-class White women to treat symptoms of hysteria. Authors Virginia Woolf and Edith Wharton both experienced rest cures, during which they were allowed only limited time to be out of bed and to engage in intellectually stimulating activities such as reading or writing. These rest cures likely exacerbated symptoms and reinforced gender stereotypes about privileged women.

Particularly for wealthy White women, "cures" involved rest and inactivity. One such woman, Charlotte Perkins Gilman, suffered from boredom, exhaustion, and apathy in her unhappy marriage. She was prescribed a *rest cure* during which she was confined to bed, forbidden from writing or drawing, and only allowed two hours of intellectual stimulation a day. She wrote about the tortures of this "cure" in "The Yellow Wallpaper," a story about a young woman who is driven mad through isolation (Gilman, 1892/1997). Ironically, while wealthy White women were put to bed, doctors prescribed wealthy White men a "West cure" that involved adventures of cattle roping, hunting, horse riding, and male bonding (Stiles, n.d., p. 6). The different approaches to the same mental health condition reflected gendered stereotypes of the time.

Another "disease" that gained popularity during the 19th century was *drapetomania*. Derived from Greek words meaning "runaway slave" and "mad or crazy," it was a mental disorder that described an enslaved person who had a strong desire to escape slavery (Bynum, 2000). The "cure" was the presence of a "kind" slave master, who provided adequate living conditions and structured work environments. Much like the rest cure, drapetomania shows how political values can influence medical evaluation and treatment. These medical labels were often used to justify confining women, and members of other socially marginalized groups, to specific and oppressive roles within society.

The Freudian View Sigmund Freud's description of hysteria was profoundly influential. Early in his career, Freud found that when women discussed their symptoms—often under hypnosis—they recalled incidents of sexual trauma (Freud & Breuer, 1896/2004). Initially, he attributed their difficulties to having experienced sexual abuse, generally at the hands of family members. This was called *seduction theory*. However, Freud later abandoned this theory, largely due to public outcry, and soon began to relate women's hysterical symptoms to their unconscious sexual fantasies or their guilt about early childhood masturbation (Makari, 1998). Furthermore, Freud saw women's neuroses as stemming from penis envy, so in his view, improvement was dependent on women marrying, becoming mothers, and having male children. Many modern psychologists consider this shift in thinking to be a grave mistake in the history of psychoanalysis because it contributed to decades of clinicians ignoring women's actual experiences of abuse (Masson, 1984).

Madness in the 20th Century and Beyond

What developments in the 20th century shaped the way mental illness was understood, and what criticisms are leveled at existing diagnostic systems?

The early 20th century saw a precipitous decrease in the diagnoses of hysteria (Micale, 1993; Tasca et al., 2012). There are many proposed reasons for this decline. One hypothesis is that the symptoms of hysteria that were based in women's sexual frustration decreased as society became less sexually repressed; another is that what used to be called hysteria was re-labeled with other, more specific, diagnoses—for example, anxiety, depression, and anorexia (Micale, 1993).

Institutionalization, however, was frequent until the mid-20th century. Behaviors that resulted in involuntary hospitalization included getting pregnant out of wedlock, having affairs, being a lesbian, and generally being troublesome (Ussher, 2011). Many of these women were subjected to electroconvulsive therapy (ECT), sometimes referred to as electric shock treatment, in which electrical currents are applied to the brain. In early forms of the treatment, high doses of electricity were administered without anesthesia. Women received this treatment two to three times as often as men (Thompson, Weiner, & Myers, 1994). ECT is still sometimes used to treat severe depression, and in its current form, smaller doses of electricity and both anesthesia and muscle relaxants are used. However, ECT continues to have significant side effects for some patients, including memory loss (McLoughlin, Kolshus, & Jelovac, 2017). Although current guidelines only allow ECT to be given voluntarily, as recently as the early 21st century, women reported not fully understanding the risks and, sometimes, being given the treatment against their will (Burstow, 2006). One woman said, "All the therapy in the world is not going to erase the scars of being dragged into a room, having a band over your head and having your brain fried" (p. 381).

In the mid-20th century, there were almost half a million people in psychiatric hospitals throughout the United States, but this number rapidly decreased after **deinstitutionalization**—a mass release of people from psychiatric hospitals. For example, in 1955 there were 559,000 individuals in state-run hospitals but only 57,151 in 1998 (Lamb & Bachrach, 2001). Deinstitutionalization was largely a result of the increased use of psychiatric medications, but it was also motivated by both a concern for patients' rights and decreased federal funding for residential patient care (Yohanna, 2013). Although this shift had the advantage of allowing people who had been institutionalized to live independently, there was often inadequate support for those who still experienced psychological distress.

For example, although President Carter signed the Mental Health Systems Act in 1979 in order to expand community mental health services, this act was repealed in 1981 during the Reagan administration, and community mental health funding decreased (Pan, 2013). The mental hospital no longer became the place for treatment, and people who were unable to pay for treatment often went to homeless shelters and prisons (Dear & Wolch 2014; Kim, 2016). This legacy continues today.

"Mother's Little Helper" and the "Happy Pill" One reason mental health concerns were treated differently in the second half of the 20th century, particularly for White women with financial resources, was because of the rise of medications designed to treat psychological problems. While medication allowed many women who were distressed to obtain needed relief, there was a danger in over-use. In particular, Valium, a sedative that reduced symptoms of anxiety, was prescribed to millions of women—often middle- and upper-class White women who were unhappy with their roles in life (Herzberg, 2006). It's estimated that 20% of women in the United States during the 1970s had prescriptions for Valium and that 10% used it regularly. Valium, or "mother's little helper," was criticized early in the second wave feminist movement for making women accept their subordinate status rather than questioning their lot in life. Although concerns about the over-use of Valium are justified, the feminist concern about the drug was largely influenced by the fact that it was primarily affecting middle-class White women—the group most connected to second wave feminism (Herzberg, 2006). For example, the mental health of poor women of color didn't receive the same type of attention.

In 1987, the anti-depressant Prozac, the "happy pill," was introduced and quickly replaced Valium as the most frequently prescribed medication for women (Blum & Stracuzzi, 2004). Although anxiety was the most frequently diagnosed disorder when Valium was popular, depression became an increasingly common diagnosis with the rise of Prozac (Horwitz, 2010). Doctors were enthusiastic about Prozac because it had fewer side effects than earlier anti-depressants, and many women found needed relief through its use. Instead of having a sedating effect, the drug was seen as energizing because women who took it felt more productive. Instead of being prescribed to women to keep them happy with their domestic lives, it was prescribed to allow them to be "superwomen" and aid them in combining work and family demands. Marketing materials described the drug as making women more energetic, assertive, efficient, and ambitious—all qualities associated with traditional masculinity (Blum & Stracuzzi, 2004). Prozac, like Valium, was marketed primarily to middle- and upper-class White women.

Currently, anti-depressants are widely used and have helped many women to alleviate depression and decrease suicidal thoughts. Research indicates that 21.2% of women in their 40s and 50s, and 24.4% of women over age 60, take anti-depressants (Pratt, Brody, & Gu, 2017). In contrast, only 11.6% and 12.6% of men in these respective age groups take them. Anti-depressants continue to be more frequently used by White women than by Black, Latinx, and Asian American women (Alegria et al., 2008). For example, between 2011 and 2014, 21.4% of White women were prescribed anti-depressants, but only 4.6% of Asian women, 6.4% of Latinx women, and 7.9% of Black women received these prescriptions (Pratt et al., 2017). Although many people see medication as a critical therapeutic option that women benefit from, some critics believe that women's widespread use of medication as a treatment for mental illness supports the status quo because it doesn't address the social and political factors, such as poverty and abuse, that contribute to women's distress.

Diagnosis and Treatment The 20th century saw the rise of the formal discipline of psychiatry. Its purpose was to diagnose and treat mental disorders using the **medical model**. This model assumes that mental health concerns are the result of physical problems that can be treated through medical intervention. The first edition of the *Diagnostic and Statistical Manual of Mental Disorders* (*DSM*) was published in 1952 by the American Psychiatric Association, and currently the manual is in its fifth edition. The *DSM* promotes a disease model of mental illness that focuses on the presence or absence of specific symptoms enhanced by the use of seemingly objective checklists (Cosgrove & Wheeler, 2013). These checklists generally ask whether or not an individual is experiencing a symptom (e.g., sadness, hopelessness) but don't ask about the situations or contexts in which the symptom occurs—for example, after being yelled at by one's boss or before being hit by one's spouse.

Many people think of these diagnostic categories as real, physically identifiable, brain disorders that people either have or don't have. However, what is or isn't considered a mental illness continues to be a product of cultural context. For example, homosexuality used to be considered a mental illness, but it was removed from the *DSM* in 1973 (Kawa & Giordano, 2012). When mental illness is seen as a real disease within a person, it gains legitimacy, but social or environmental causes for the distress are generally minimized.

One concern about the current version of the *DSM* is that its authors have deep financial ties to the pharmaceutical industry (Cosgrove & Wheeler, 2013; Marecek & Gavey, 2013). In fact, 69% of the members of the entire American Psychiatric Association task force that wrote the *DSM-5* had ties to pharmacology, including receiving research funding from pharmaceutical companies, being paid to speak for them, or serving as paid consultants (Cosgrove & Krimsky, 2012). Another concern is that more people can be classified as having mental illnesses using the *DSM-5* than previous editions. For example, in the past, a diagnosis of major depression couldn't be made if a person had recently experienced the loss of a loved one. However, someone coping with grief from this type of loss can now be diagnosed with major depression and, consequently, be prescribed medication to alleviate its symptoms (Wakefield, 2016).

The ability to define what is normal and abnormal is very powerful because the mental health profession depends on the *DSM* for medical legitimacy and authority (Ali, Caplan, & Fagnant, 2010). For example, in order to cover the costs of treatment for a given

The *Diagnostic and Statistical Manual of Mental Disorders* (*DSM*) pictured here and the *International Classification of Diseases* (ICD) are the two tools clinicians typically use to diagnose mental illness. When are medical diagnoses helpful? When might they cause more harm than good?

mental health condition, insurance companies require a diagnostic code. The *DSM* is one of only two sources from which these can be drawn; the other is the *International Classification of Diseases* (*ICD*), developed by the World Health Organization. For many people, the ability to access care is entirely dependent on having health insurance coverage. In 2008, the Mental Health Parity and Addiction Equity Act expanded mental health care access by requiring insurance companies to cover mental health and substance abuse treatments. Then, in 2014, the Affordable Care Act enabled many more Americans to apply for mental health insurance coverage. Despite this, insurance companies are more likely to deny claims for mental health treatments than physical health treatments, and they reimburse mental health claims at lower rates than medical claims (National Alliance on Mental Illness, 2015). Nevertheless, without diagnoses, it's unlikely that insurance companies would be willing to cover any type of treatment at all.

However, feminist clinicians, among others, worry that reliance on the *DSM* means that mental health decisions are generally influenced by the small group of psychiatrists who developed the *DSM*—mostly wealthy, White, American men (Caplan, 1995; Cohen & Jacobs, 2007). One concern is that when men decide on the categories, they may view traits that have traditionally been associated with femininity (e.g., dependence, passivity, concern about appearance) as abnormal and as a sign of mental illness. As mentioned earlier, there's a long history of associating femininity with madness; the very definition of hysteria was linked to what was seen as feminine (Showalter, 1993).

In a now classic study, mental health professionals were presented with a list of adjectives and were asked to either identify if (1) a healthy adult (with gender unspecified), (2) a healthy man, or (3) a healthy woman would be very likely or not at all likely to have that trait (Broverman, Broverman, Clarkson, Rosenkrantz, & Vogel, 1970). Adjectives identified as describing a healthy man were generally the same as those identified as describing a healthy adult. However, a healthy woman was seen as exhibiting different traits. For example, a healthy woman, but not a healthy man or a healthy adult, was described as more likely to be very submissive, not at all independent, and not at all adventurous. Healthy women were also, in contrast to healthy men/adults, identified as having their feelings easily hurt, being very emotional, being very interested in their appearance, and disliking math and science a great deal. Of course, this study was done almost 50 years ago, and stereotypes about what's considered healthy in women have likely changed since then. Nevertheless, the study demonstrates that traditional femininity is defined in ways that could be considered unhealthy. When this view underlies a diagnostic code manual, the experiences of women who conform to traditional gender roles can be pathologized.

For example, the diagnosis of **dependent personality disorder (DPD)** is characterized by traits such as fear of disagreeing with others and difficulty in making everyday decisions without reassurance (American Psychiatric Association, 2013). Because social connectedness and passivity are associated with traditional femininity, a diagnosis like DPD can be seen as pathologizing femininity (Rivera, 2002). Moreover, there's no corresponding "independent personality disorder" characterized by traits such as refusing to ask for help even when help is needed (traits that are generally associated with men).

In addition to pathologizing aspects of femininity, the *DSM* classifies "atypical" gender preferences as disordered (Pillard, 2009). When individuals express a strong desire to be treated as a gender different from the one they were assigned at birth, a clinician may diagnose them with **gender dysphoria**. When the *DSM-5* was being developed, many activists called for the removal of any diagnoses associated with being transgender (Lev, 2006). Other clinicians worried that without a diagnosis, transgender people would have difficulty securing legal rights and accessing psychotherapy (Vance et al., 2010). Because psychotherapy is required before undergoing gender-affirming surgery, the lack of a billable diagnosis could also reduce health-care options for transgender individuals (Drescher, 2015). Gender dysphoria was ultimately included in *DSM-5*, but it remains controversial.

The Feminist Critique of Mental Illness It's undeniable that many women live with distress related to their mental health. However, the fact that symptoms are currently labeled as depression rather than hysteria or demonic possession reflects cultural context. Over 60 years ago, the philosopher Michel Foucault noted that it's necessary to understand how people interpret and give significance to their own experiences in order to understand mental illness (Foucault, 1954/1987). More recently, the psychologist Jane Ussher noted that "within medicalized discourse, women's negative emotions and reasonable responses to daily living or to family life are positioned as 'symptoms' worthy of a psychiatric diagnosis" (Ussher, 2011, p. 100). This observation doesn't simply reflect being diagnosed by others. People define their own experiences based on the options available to them within their cultural context. In the past, many women believed themselves to be possessed by a demon or to be suffering from hysteria; today, in contrast, many see their suffering as a sign of mental illness.

Modern psychiatry generally sees disorders as products of biological processes or irrational thinking patterns. Therefore, treatments generally focus on altering biological processes (through medication) and/or changing thinking patterns (through talk therapies). These treatments can be very effective, and they do represent important ways to relieve distress. However, a feminist approach to mental illness also seeks a more careful analysis of why a person is experiencing distress in the first place. Whether the distress is interpreted as depression, anxiety, an eating disorder, or some other condition, it is often a reasonable response to unacceptable or challenging life circumstances. Women

try it for yourself

Take a minute to consider your thoughts about the causes of mental illness. In what way does this inform your understanding of how mental illness should be perceived and treated? Now talk to peers and family members about this. How do they respond? Do they say different things if you ask them about mental illness in general versus women's experiences with mental illness in particular?

who are abused, harassed, sexualized, living in poverty, or stressed by balancing work and family demands may have legitimate reasons for their very real distress. However, if the focus of treatment is solely on changing the individual, then the broader structural causes of women's distress can be obscured. Further, when women themselves don't see the broader aspects of their oppression, they may blame themselves for their symptoms (Fischer & Holz, 2010; Klonoff, Landrine, & Campbell, 2000). In this way, a vicious cycle operates: Oppression contributes to mental distress, women blame themselves instead of oppressive systems, and the self-blame contributes to more mental distress.

Mental Health Diagnoses

As mentioned earlier, feminist psychologists have been critical of the *DSM*. However, given the necessity of diagnosis for insurance coverage, feminist psychologists do make use of this system. Also, diagnostic labels enable people to make meaning of their distress—the labels give them words to identify the pain they're feeling, and for that reason diagnoses can be empowering (Brown, 2004, 2006). However, rather than solely relying on a *DSM* checklist, feminist psychologists advocate for considering multiple forms of evidence and knowledge to understand a person's distress and dysfunction (Ballou, 1990; Eriksen & Kress, 2008). In other words, how we think about, and ultimately treat, mental health issues cannot stop with a diagnostic label. It's only one piece of a larger diagnostic picture that would also include the social context and how intersecting aspects of people's social identities shape their experiences.

Major Depression

What are the gender differences in depression, and what factors contribute to these differences?

Symptoms of **major depression** include depressed thinking such as feelings of sadness or emptiness, diminished pleasure in activities, negative thought patterns reflecting worthlessness or guilt, and physical symptoms such as fatigue, weight gain or loss, and excessive sleeping or insomnia (American Psychiatric Association, 2013). At any given time, approximately 8.1% of the U.S. population over age 12 has depression (Brody, Pratt, & Hughes, 2018). However, certain characteristics are more frequently associated with developing depression, and one of those is gender. Studies have shown that girls and women have higher rates of depression than do boys and men across all ages, ethnic/racial groups, and nationalities (Brody et al., 2018; World Health Organization, 2017). Other research has shown that approximately 19% of women and 12% of men have experienced depression over their lifetimes (Kessler, Petukhova, Sampson, Zaslavsky, & Wittchen, 2012; Silverstein et al. 2012).

Anyone can experience major depression at any time, but it is considerably more frequently diagnosed in women. There is no clear explanation for why women have a higher susceptibility toward depression, but social, cognitive, and biological factors all contribute.

There are many theories as to why women are more frequently diagnosed with depression than men. Overall, girls and women are more likely to seek treatment for mental health concerns than are men (Addis & Mahalik, 2003). This may be because men feel a conflict between their socially prescribed gender role to be seen as tough and their desire for help. Men may also anticipate being socially rejected if they seek help, especially if their social group values self-reliance. As a result, one reason for the different rates of depression diagnoses is that men may not admit they're depressed and ask for treatment (Addis & Mahalik, 2003). However, other studies have shown that Black and Latinx women have higher rates of depression than White women but are less likely to seek care (Centers for Disease Control and Prevention, 2010; Gonzalez et al., 2010). Most psychologists agree that differences in depression rates can't solely be explained by help-seeking behavior.

There's also some indication that men are less likely to remember previous incidents of depression than are women (Parker & Brotchie, 2010). In one study, participants were asked to discuss past and present experiences with depression every five years, and men were more likely to forget previous episodes while women were more likely to remember them (Wilhelm & Parker, 1994). This pattern was confirmed in more recent research (Wells & Horwood, 2004).

Another factor that contributes to depression is ability status; women may disproportionally have physical disorders that involve symptoms of depression (Feinstein, Magalhaes, Richard, Audet, & Moore, 2014; Klonoff & Landrine, 1996). For example, multiple sclerosis (MS) is an autoimmune disease that slows cognitive and motor abilities, and it's associated with fatigue and loss of energy and is disproportionately diagnosed in women (Whitacre et al., 1999). Approximately 50% of women diagnosed with MS are also diagnosed with depression (Siegert & Abernethy, 2005). This may be because many MS symptoms (e.g., fatigue and motor slowdown) are also symptoms of depression. Women are also more likely than men to be diagnosed with hypothyroidism, a disease that happens when the thyroid gland is underactive (Bauer, Glenn, Pilhatsch, Pfennig, & Whybrow, 2014). Symptoms of hypothyroidism include low energy, weight gain, and excessive sleeping. These are also symptoms of depression, and 64% of patients with hypothyroidism in one study also were diagnosed depression (Demartini et al., 2014). Whether these symptoms are actually caused by reduced thyroid functioning or by depression itself is unclear. Nevertheless, women who are experiencing symptoms of depression can benefit from a complete medical evaluation in order to determine whether a physical illness such as MS or hypothyroidism may be contributing to their symptoms.

Biological Explanations Some researchers have theorized that women experience more depression than men because of biological reasons. At certain times in their lives, women may have increased risk of depression due to hormonal factors; however, a clear link between hormones and depression has remained elusive. For example, although it's generally assumed that post-partum depression is caused by hormonal fluctuations, there has been no success in linking specific hormones post-partum and symptoms of depression (Blehar, 2006). Further, while some research suggests an increase in depression during perimenopause (Cohen, Soares, Vitonis, Otto, & Harlow, 2006; Freeman, Sammel, Lin, & Nelson, 2006), other research has shown that women generally have a sense of relief and well-being as they reach that life stage (Avis & McKinlay, 1991; Campbell, Dennerstein, Tacey, & Szoeke, 2017). Also, while some women may experience increased depression at certain times (e.g., pre-menstrually, post-partum, and at menopause), there's evidence that changes in women's roles, how women view themselves, and how others respond to them during these times can contribute to the experience of mood disturbance (Nolen-Hoeksema, 2001).

Some research indicates that the connection between hormones and depression may be more indirect than initially thought. For example, hormonal factors may influence women to be more biologically sensitive or reactive to negative stimuli in the environment (Parker & Brotchie, 2010). Specifically, there's some indication that higher testosterone levels may decrease the extent to which the body responds to stress, which may, in turn, decrease the risk of anxiety and depression (McHenry, Carrier, Hull, & Kabbaj, 2014). However, the data on this are unclear. While animal models have generally shown that higher levels of testosterone relate to decreased signs of anxiety or depression in male animals, this is less consistently found in female animals (McHenry et al., 2014). Overall, then, although hormonal factors may play an indirect role, psychologists generally believe that explanations about gender differences that rely solely on hormones are inadequate (Girgus & Yang, 2015; Hankin & Abramson, 2001; Nolen-Hoeksema, 2001; Ussher, 2010).

Cognitive Processes Other theories for women's higher rates of depression relate to how women think. One explanation is that women are more likely than men to obsessively mull over their problems or ruminate. **Rumination** involves thinking about what is making one upset and all of the causes and consequences of the situation. Although rumination may, in the moment, seem like productive problem solving, it's actually more like thinking similar thoughts over and over without making a plan to address the situation. Research does indicate that women tend to ruminate more than men, that rumination has more negative effects in women than in men, and that rumination may account for a portion of the gender differences in depression (Krause et al., 2018; Nolen-Hoeksema, 2012; Nolen-Hoeksema & Jackson, 2001). As we've discussed, girls are more likely than boys to be encouraged to display and talk about emotions such as sadness, so rumination may partially reflect gender socialization (Chaplin, Cole, & Zahn-Waxler, 2005; Fivush, Brotman, Buckner, & Goodman, 2000). Nevertheless, a meta-analysis exploring gender differences in rumination indicated a difference of 0.23, which is considered a small effect (Johnson & Whisman, 2013).

Women may also be predisposed to depression because they highly value relationships with others and may feel particularly distressed when those relationships aren't going well. This theory is consistent with Chodorow's (1978) idea that women are more likely than men to develop a sense of self within the context of relationships with others (see Chapter 5). This may lead to **self-silencing**, in which women both inhibit self-expression in order to please others and also sacrifice their own needs in order to maintain relationships (Jack & Dill, 1992).

Cultural differences can contribute to self-silencing too. For example, **marianismo**, a concept that underlies the gender socialization of Latinx girls and women,

We all withhold our thoughts from those around us from time to time. Women are particularly likely to engage in self-silencing, however, as they are socialized to attend to and please others. This tendency can contribute to developing depression. Regardless of your gender identity, how often do you silence yourself? What are the emotional costs of silencing your thoughts and emotions? Are there any benefits to doing so?

encourages self-sacrifice and the repression of anger. In one study, researchers found that women who adhered to marianismo showed consistently higher levels of depression regardless of age and marital status (Céspedes & Huey, 2008). In general, self-silencing is a risk factor for depression, and this has been found among women of diverse ethnic backgrounds (Grant, Jack, Fitzpatrick, & Ernst, 2011; Gratch, Bassett, & Attra, 1995). One study comparing Caribbean women who lived in the Caribbean with those who had immigrated to Canada showed that those who had immigrated were higher in both self-silencing and depression (Ali & Toner, 2001). This finding indicated that they may have felt they couldn't be their authentic selves in their new country.

In addition, pressures on Black women to project an aura of strength, to care for others selflessly, and to deprioritize their own needs can result in distress that may not be acknowledged or treated (Beauboef-Lafontant, 2007). Reflecting the cultural stereotype of the strong Black woman, one woman who experienced depression said: "No one ever knew there was anything wrong with me. *Not anyone*. I kept the façade up; I really did. [But in the process] I felt smothered" (p. 44). Research suggests that Black women who more strongly endorse this stereotype have higher levels of anxiety and depression and are less willing to seek treatment (Watson & Hunter, 2015).

Another theory involves beliefs about the body. As we saw in Chapter 6, body dissatisfaction is related to depression, and this pattern has been found across the life span (Muehlenkamp & Saris-Baglama, 2002; Paxton, Neumark-Sztainer, Hannan, & Eisenberg, 2006; Peat & Muehlenkamp, 2011; Szymanski & Henning, 2007). For example, one study of midlife women showed that those who were dissatisfied with their bodies were more likely to be depressed, and these results were similar for Black and White women (Jackson et al., 2014). Given these findings, seeing media images of unattainable beauty can contribute to women feeling dissatisfied with and shameful about their own bodies, which can lead to depression.

Doing Femininity Too Well Many of the previous explanations for depression have been criticized for conceptualizing it as a problem with the way women think (Ussher, 2010, 2011). In other words, if women are depressed because they ruminate, silence themselves, feel pressure to be strong, or feel shame about their bodies, then it's easy to assume that their thinking style should be changed. However, women are socialized to attend to their own emotional states and those of others (e.g., Chaplin et al., 2005; Fivush et al., 2000). Further, they're taught from a very young age that how they look is an important part of who they are and that they should conform to narrow standards of beauty (Fredrickson & Roberts, 1997; Moradi & Huang, 2008; Tatangelo, McCabe, Mellor, & Mealey, 2016). When women worry about maintaining relationships, put the needs of others before themselves, and focus on their appearance, they are "doing" femininity.

Even though women are encouraged to "do" femininity, there's a risk in doing it too well because conforming to traditional gender roles may be associated with poor mental health outcomes. Some studies have found that traditionally feminine traits are related to higher levels of depression (Brazelton, Green, & Gynther, 1996; Richmond, Levant, Smalley, & Cook, 2015; Tolman, 2002; Tolman, Impett, Tracy, & Michael, 2006; Tolman & Porche 2000). The fact that girls start to have higher rates of depression than boys at age 13 (Nolen-Hoeksema, 2001) has caused some researchers to hypothesize that gender intensification, discussed in Chapter 5, may influence the development of depression (Priess, Lindberg, & Hyde, 2009).

Indeed, some specific aspects of the traditional, feminine gender role have been linked to depression. For example, stay-at-home mothers have higher rates of depression than mothers who work either part-time or full-time, and this is particularly true for low-income mothers (Mendes, Saad, & McGeeney, 2012). Also, being a caregiver for a spouse or parent has been linked with stress and depression (Baumgerten et al., 1992; Penning & Wu, 2015), and as discussed in Chapter 11, the majority of caregivers are women. One factor that may contribute to the increased distress is that those in caregiver roles don't attend to their own needs (Tatangelo, McCabe, Macleod, & You, 2018). One wife caring for a spouse with dementia said, "It's a funny thing you don't think about your own needs. . . . I don't concentrate on my needs at all" (p. 10). In general, research suggests that having overly feminine traits that involve self-sacrifice and lack of self-care is related to increased levels of depression (Helgeson, 1994; Helgeson, Swanson, Ra, Randall, & Zhao, 2015). In contrast, having a mix of masculine and feminine traits has been linked to increased levels of well-being (Vafaei, Ahmed, Freire, Zunzunegui, & Guerra, 2016).

Discrimination Women also encounter a great deal of life stress that can contribute to depression. To start, many women grow up in sexist environments in which they learn that their needs should be secondary to others'. In one study, women were interviewed about sexism within their families, and a recurring theme was that they felt devalued as girls and as though their brothers were favored simply because they were boys (Atwood, 2001). These women also reported that their parents ignored or dismissed incidents when their brothers became abusive. The women were often teased about their weight by their parents or brothers, and they worried a lot about being fat. Many participants described taking on the role of the good girl, being extra pleasant and compliant in order to please their mothers. The women in this study were all depressed to some degree. They described a sense of powerlessness and felt they were entitled to less attention than others.

Mental health continues to be impacted as women encounter sexist environments outside the family. For example, sexual harassment at work has been consistently related to mental health problems such as anxiety and depression, as well as decreased psychological well-being (Cantisano, Domínguez, & Depolo, 2008; Gutek & Koss, 1993; Willness, Steel, & Lee, 2007). Another study showed that experiencing everyday sexism such as being objectified, being called a derogatory term (e.g., *bitch*), or being told a sexist joke was common for young women (occurring a few times a week) and was related to increased depression, anxiety, and anger (Swim, Hyers, Cohen, & Ferguson, 2001). In yet another study, chronic sexual harassment in college was found to relate to higher levels of depression, anxiety, and substance abuse (McGinley, Wolff, Rospenda, Liu, & Richman, 2016). In general, chronic experiences of sexism relate to women's higher rates of depression and other negative psychological symptoms (Klonoff et al., 2000).

Sexism isn't the only form of discrimination that can affect women's mental health. Depending on other aspects of their social identities, racism, homophobia, and discrimination based on gender identity are among other forms that can be harmful. Racism can negatively influence mental health for various reasons. First, it causes members of racial/ethnic minority groups to have fewer educational and job opportunities and an increased likelihood of living in poverty (Williams & Williams-Morris, 2000). Second, the experience of racial discrimination can be extremely distressing. A study of Latinx women found that those who encountered racist discrimination were more likely to experience depression as well as shame about their bodies (Velez, Campos, & Moradi, 2015). Another study showed that the experience of racist microaggressions, leading to feeling like a second-class citizen or feeling invalidated, related to higher levels of depression in an ethnically diverse group of largely female participants (Nadal, Griffin, Wong, Hamit, & Rasmus, 2014). Third, racist culture can lead racial/ethnic minority group members to internalize negative evaluations of themselves (Williams & Williams-Morris, 2000). One study of Black American and Caribbean women and men found that internalized racism was related to depression and other mental health problems (Mouzon & McLean, 2017). Discrimination can also affect access to treatment. In one study, psychologists were found to be less likely to offer therapy appointments when new clients called and were perceived to be Black or from a lower-class background (Kugelmass, 2016).

The combination of racism and sexism can be especially damaging. For example, Black women can be subject to comments that are both sexist and racist (e.g., comments about a woman's "sexy black ass"; Buchanan & Ormerod, 2002, p. 113). One study showed that Black women who experienced racialized sexual harassment had more symptoms of trauma and distress than those who experienced only gender discrimination, especially if the harassment was from a White man (Woods, Buchanan, & Settles, 2009).

Discrimination against members of gender and sexual minority groups also can have a significant negative impact. Several studies have shown that those in the LGBTQ community are twice as likely to experience depression as those who are not (D'Augelli, 2002; Gilman et al., 2001; Meyer, 2003). Stressors associated with being LGBQ, as well as the perceived stigma that others disapprove of one's sexual orientation, have been linked with depression (Lewis, Derlega, Griffin, & Krowinski, 2003). Individuals who are transgender or gender non-conforming also experience high rates of depression. Clinical levels of depression were found in 44% of transgender individuals participating in one study, and this outcome was strongly related to experiences of discrimination and stigma (Bockting, Miner, Swinburne-Romine, Hamilton, & Coleman, 2013).

Internalizing negative feelings about one's sexual orientation has been linked to depression and suicidal ideation in both lesbians and gay men (Igartua, Gill, & Montoro, 2009; McLaren, 2016). For women who hold both racial and sexual minority identities, discrimination and internalized negative feelings about the self can cause distress and decreased well-being. One study of women who identified as both Latinx and sexual minority group members showed that experiences of racial and heterosexist discrimination contributed to depression (Velez, Moradi & DeBlaere, 2015). Internalizing racism and heterosexism also contributed to depression and decreased life satisfaction and self-esteem.

Individuals with sexual minority identities are at increased risk for suicide too (Igartua et al., 2009). The riskiest time appears to be immediately after coming out to one's family, especially if the family's reaction isn't positive.

Bisexual women have been found to be at higher risk for suicidal thoughts than lesbian women (Shearer et al., 2016). The researchers speculate that this may occur because even though there has been increasing acceptance of lesbian women, there is less public acceptance of bisexuality.

An additional challenge for LGBTQ individuals is finding a therapist who is affirming and not discriminatory (American Psychological Association, 2012). A particular concern is that the therapist might support conversion therapy. **Conversion therapy**, or reparative therapy, seeks to change a client's sexual orientation from LGBQ to heterosexual (Haldeman, 2002). Research has consistently shown that conversion therapy has harmful effects, including increased depressive symptoms, suicidality, social isolation, and decreased feelings of self-worth (Flentje, Heck, & Cochran, 2013; Haldeman, 2002; Serovich et al., 2008; Shidlo & Schroeder, 2002). As a result, many mental health organizations, including the American Psychological Association, oppose the practice of conversion therapy. Yet in one recent survey of family therapists across the country, nearly 1 in 5 of those surveyed thought conversation therapy was ethical (McGeorge, Carlson, & Toomey, 2015). As of January 2018, 14 states as well as additional counties and districts have banned the practice for minors (Mallory, Brown, & Conron, 2018). It's estimated that 698,000 LGBQ people have gone through conversion therapy and that many more will experience it in those states that haven't banned the practice. Figure 13.1 indicates which states protect LGBQ youth from conversion therapy.

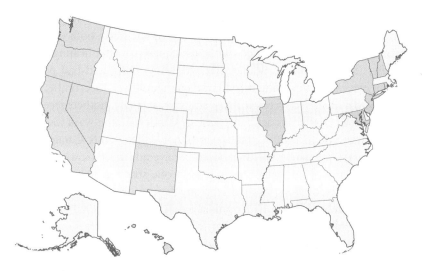

FIGURE 13.1 States that protect LGBQ youth from conversion therapy. Conversion therapy seeks to change the sexual orientation of those in the LGBQ community. As of 2018, these 14 states and the District of Columbia have banned this type of therapy for minors. Despite being identified as ineffective and harmful by organizations such as the American Psychological Association, conversion therapy is still legal in 36 states.

Note. Adapted from Human Rights Campaign website data, https://www.hrc.org/state-maps /conversion%20therapy.

Poverty In 2016, more than 16 million women in the United States (approximately 1 in 8) lived in poverty (Patrick, 2017). Women are 38% more likely to be living in poverty than are men. These rates are higher for women of color and women with disabilities than they are for White women without disabilities. Poverty rates are also higher for single mothers—almost 36% of single mothers live in poverty, and there are 13.2 million children living in poverty (Patrick, 2017). When including women who are at the brink of poverty, the numbers more than double (Shriver & Center for American Progress, 2014).

This high level of poverty has a significant effect on women's mental health. Some studies have found that rates of depression among poor women are approximately double that of the general population (Belle & Doucet, 2003; Brown, 2012). Other studies identify even higher rates. For example, 40% of poor, Black, single mothers in one study had symptoms consistent with clinical depression (Coiro, 2001). In a study of low-income White mothers, 54% reported feeling down, depressed, or hopeless during the previous 12 months (Goldhagen, Harbin, & Forry, 2013). In fact, poverty has been found to increase the risk of depression more than any chronic disease (Brown, 2012).

Women living in poverty can experience food insecurity, hazardous neighborhoods, over-crowded living situations, and homelessness (Goodman, Smyth, Borges & Singer, 2009; Siefert, Bowman, Heflin, Danziger, & Williams, 2000). Being a mother in poverty is particularly stressful. In one study, 69% of poor mothers felt as though raising children was too difficult or too much responsibility (Goldhagen et al., 2013). Also, poor women face a great deal of discrimination, especially if they receive public assistance (Belle & Doucet, 2003). In one study, both White women and women of color who received public assistance reported hearing comments from others in the community that they were lazy, slobs, and bad parents; the women of color reported being called racial epithets as well (Seccombe, James, & Walters, 1998). More recent research has shown that single mothers receiving welfare often perceive others as acting in rude or condescending ways toward them, such as talking to them as though they were stupid (Liegghio & Caragata, 2016).

Moreover, poor women are unlikely to receive adequate treatment for their depression. Fully 40% of welfare recipients in one study met the clinical cutoff for depression, but only 3% had received any form of treatment (Coiro, 2001). Barriers to treatment include being uninsured or under-insured, being unable to miss time from work, having transportation issues, experiencing long wait times for an appointment, having challenges arranging child care, and having internalized stigma about psychological disorders (Grote, Zuckoff, Swartz, Bledsoe, & Geibel, 2007). Poor women may also have a history of negative interactions with health-care providers and believe that a therapist would likely not understand them or their situation or be able to help them (Goodman, Pugach, Skolnik, & Smith, 2013). Some women do find that their therapists take a judging, rather than a helpful, approach. For example, one woman reported that a therapist called child protective services because she didn't have sufficient food in her pantry (Goodman et al., 2013). Another woman doubted that talk therapy could help: "Because talking may help, yes, but talking isn't going to provide me with food. Talking isn't going to get me a job" (p. 188).

Violence and Abuse As we saw in Chapter 12, violence is a major problem for women, and experiencing it is related to higher rates of depression. One older study suggested that up to 35% of the gender differences in depression rates could be accounted for by gender differences in childhood sexual abuse (Cutler & Nolen-Hoeksema, 1991). A more recent meta-analysis showed that childhood sexual abuse approximately doubled the likelihood that someone would experience major depression (Lindert et al., 2014). However, childhood sexual abuse is only one type of victimization. Another meta-analysis indicated that psychological abuse and neglect were particularly strong risk factors for depression (Infurna et al., 2016), and physical abuse has also been found to increase depression risk (Infurna et al., 2016; Lindert et al., 2014).

Violence in childhood is often inter-related and cumulative. Instead of assessing the impact of different forms of abuse separately, researchers have moved toward measuring how many negative childhood experiences one has had. These *adverse childhood experiences (ACES)* include physical abuse, sexual abuse, emotional abuse, neglect, loss of a parent, and witnessing violence. ACES tend to cluster—individuals who experience one form often experience multiple forms (Chapman et al., 2004). Also, the more ACES that one experiences, the greater the odds that one has depression.

Violence experienced in adulthood can also contribute to depression. One meta-analysis indicated that women who are depressed are 2.7 times more likely to have had a violent partner than those who aren't depressed (Trevillion, Oram, Feder, & Howard, 2012). Another study showed that women who experienced domestic violence while pregnant were three times more likely to develop post-partum depression than women who didn't experience domestic violence while pregnant (Howard, Oram, Galley, Trevillion, & Feder, 2013).

your turn

Have you or someone you know ever experienced depression? If so, what did you (or they) initially think was the reason for it? Has reading this chapter changed your thoughts about the causes of depression, both in general and for women in particular? How can women achieve positive mental health when living in a sexist culture? What can contribute to developing resilience, even in the face of oppression?

Anxiety

What are the gender differences in anxiety disorders, and what factors contribute to these differences?

Women have higher rates of almost all anxiety disorders than do men. Women are four times more likely to have **agoraphobia**, which is anxiety related to being outside of the home or in a public place (Bekker & van Mens-Verhulst, 2007). They're three times more likely than men to have **generalized anxiety disorder**, which involves chronic debilitating worry about many aspects of life. Women are two to three times more likely than men to have **panic disorder**, which involves panic attacks that appear unpredictably as well as fear about having such attacks; and they're twice as likely to have a **specific phobia**, or fear of a specific object or activity—such as spiders or hang gliding.

Reasons for women's higher rates of anxiety than men's are similar to those for their higher rates of depression. For one thing, women may find it more socially acceptable to discuss their anxiety and seek treatment (Beckker & van Mens-Verhulst, 2007). Furthermore, since men are more likely than women to use alcohol to self-medicate their anxiety (Bolton, Cox, Clara, & Sareen, 2006), men may be under-diagnosed because the substance use would mask their symptoms. Also, the life stress variables described previously—discrimination, violence, and poverty—contribute to women's higher rates of anxiety. Motherhood is also a tremendous source of anxiety. As we saw in Chapter 9, social pressures cause women to be anxious about what could happen to their children and about what they should be doing to maximize their children's chances of success (Warner, 2006).

A specific feminist analysis has been made about agoraphobia. This analysis holds that women's higher rates of agoraphobia are unsurprising given that their social domain has historically been in the home (Bekker, 1996; Callard, 2003). Women's agoraphobia can be seen as relating to their lack of autonomy and their traditional dependence on men (Bekker & van Mens-Verhulst, 2007).

Post-traumatic Stress Disorder (PTSD)

What factors make healing from trauma difficult, and how is this related to gender?

Although it was considered an anxiety disorder in previous editions of the *DSM*, **post-traumatic stress disorder (PTSD)** is included in a separate category of trauma-related disorders in the *DSM-5* (American Psychiatric Association, 2013). PTSD occurs after directly experiencing or witnessing a shocking or frightening event. Symptoms include re-experiencing the event through dreams or flashbacks, avoiding stimuli associated with the trauma, having a general sense of numbness, and experiencing physiological reactivity such as being easily startled or having insomnia. Traumas that can induce PTSD include war, sexual assault, natural disasters, and terrorism. Repeated experiences with microaggressions can also lead to the symptoms of traumatic stress (Bryant-Davis & Ocampo, 2005; Reisner et al., 2016; Torres & Taknint, 2015). For example, in one study, experiences of racial microaggression were related to symptoms of trauma among Latinx individuals (Torres & Taknint, 2015). In another study of transgender adults, everyday slights and discrimination were associated with PTSD symptoms, even after statistically accounting for prior trauma experiences (Reisner et al., 2016).

Not everyone who experiences trauma develops PTSD, though. For example, in one study, while most participants (78.2%) had experienced some sort of trauma in their lifetime, only 6.4% of women and 3.6% of men had current symptoms of PTSD (Frissa, Hatch, Gazard, Fear, & Hotopf, 2013). Some researchers note that the fact that women develop PTSD at higher rates than do men may be related to the different types of trauma that women and men experience (Tolin & Foa, 2006). For example, men are more likely to be exposed to war trauma, and women are more likely to experience trauma related to rape and sexual assault. But this doesn't account for all the differences. The researchers found that, even when women and men experienced the same trauma, women generally had higher PTSD rates than men. Another study supported this finding when looking specifically at combat trauma (Kline et al., 2013). These researchers noted that the pattern may reflect the fact that men have considerably more social support in the military than women do. For example, women and men serving in Iraq had similar levels of exposure to combat, but the men reported feeling more prepared and having a greater sense of cohesiveness with their unit. The researchers also suggested that other factors, such as sexual harassment and gender discrimination, may increase women's psychological distress in the military and, consequently, their susceptibility to PTSD.

The original conceptualization of PTSD involved experiencing one traumatic episode (Herman-Lewis, 1992), but researchers and clinicians have, more recently, identified a different set of trauma responses described by survivors who faced ongoing, prolonged interpersonal violence during childhood and adolescence (Courtois & Ford, 2009). In these cases, symptoms of **complex PTSD** include an inability to foster stable relationships, stress-related physical ailments, and difficulty maintaining boundaries and personal safety (Pearlman & Courtois, 2005). Although complex PTSD isn't in

Anxiety, Depression, and Social Media Use

Social media use can contribute to anxiety and depression. In a *New York Times* article, psychologist Leonard Sax asked readers to "imagine [a] girl sitting in her bedroom, alone. She's scrolling through other girls' Instagram and Snapchat feeds. She sees Sonya showing off her new bikini; Sonya looks awesome. She sees Madison at a party, having a blast. She sees Vanessa with her adorable new puppy. And she thinks: *I'm just sitting here in my bedroom, not doing anything. My life sucks.*" (Sax, 2016, para. 6). This scenario is probably an accurate reflection of reality. In one study, a female participant noted that "I feel like [Facebook] consumes you . . . you can't live your normal life because you see everyone else's. . . . it makes you think your life is not as fun or as exciting or interesting than other peoples'" (Fox & Moreland, 2015, p.172).

Fear of missing out (FOMO) has been found to relate to lower life satisfaction and less positive mood (Przybylski, Murayama, DeHaan, & Gladwell, 2013). Social media use also can lead to comparing one's real life with the curated lives of others, promoting envy and a sense of inadequacy (Appel, Gerlach, & Crusius, 2016).

How do you use social media? Do you experience fear of missing out or compare yourself to others? Do you think this contributes to experiencing symptoms of depression or anxiety?

the *DSM-5*, it's a diagnosis that appears in the 11th edition of the World Health Organization's *International Classification of Diseases* (released in 2018) and has been found to most strongly relate to cumulative interpersonal violence experienced in childhood (Karatzias et al., 2017; World Health Organization, 2018). In the past, many women with complex PTSD have been misdiagnosed and, instead, have received stigmatizing diagnoses (e.g., borderline personality disorder—discussed later in this chapter) that may not have been helpful in their treatment (Courtois & Ford, 2009).

The effects of trauma can also be transmitted intergenerationally. **Historical trauma** is unresolved grief that affects an individual or a group in successive generations of those who have suffered significant trauma (Grayshield, Rutherford, Salazar, Mihecoby, & Luna, 2015). For example, *post-traumatic slave syndrome* describes the idea that the traumatization of slavery and its legacy (i.e., racism, discrimination, and marginalization) continues to manifest in psychological and behavioral concerns among contemporary Black Americans (Leary, 2005; Sotero, 2006). Other research shows that Native American people who descended from generations of those forced into residential schools where abuse and neglect were rampant continue to suffer from psychological distress (Bombay, Matheson, & Anisman, 2014).

Although psychologists' understanding of how trauma can affect people across generations is still in its infancy, research suggests that both biological and psychological mechanisms contribute to transmitting the effects of trauma intergenerationally (Lehrner & Yehuda, 2018; Meloni, 2017). Studies on children and grandchildren of Holocaust survivors showed a higher likelihood of historical trauma if their mother or grandmother had PTSD than if their father did (for a review, see Lehrner & Yehuda, 2018). This finding has led some researchers to explore the potential influence of trauma on pre-natal development; others believe the difference can be explained by the fact that mothers generally play a larger role than fathers in child rearing (Bowers & Yehuda, 2016).

In contrast, other research shows evidence of *post-traumatic growth*, or positive psychological changes as a result of experiencing trauma. For example, contemporary Black Americans may have also inherited legacies of strength, spirituality, perseverance, vitality, dynamism, and resiliency (Hicks, 2015). Another study, which focused on Brazilian Holocaust survivors and their children, showed that the degree to which survivors developed their own stories about

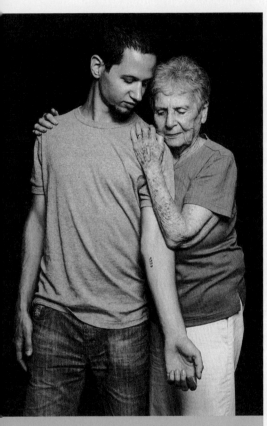

In this photo, Holocaust survivor Livia Ravek is pictured with her grandson, Daniel Philosoph. She was tattooed with the number 4559 while a prisoner in Auschwitz. Her grandson had the same number tattooed on his arm more than 60 years later. This practice has been described as a way to make the intergenerational trauma of the Holocaust visible (Brouwer & Horwitz, 2015).

their experience with trauma influenced resiliency in their children (Braga, Mello & Fiks, 2012). In some cases, children revisited places of historical importance to re-create a trauma narrative and to enhance a collective bond and a renewed engagement in political and social action.

Eating Disorders

What eating disorders are identified in the DSM, and how are they related to gendered messages about women's bodies?

Gender also influences the development of eating disorders. In one study, Austrian adolescents were screened for eating disorders, and 30.9% of the women were considered at risk but only 14.6% of the men were (Zeiler et al., 2016). As we saw in Chapter 6, dominant cultural messages that promote a thin ideal create an environment of risk for young women. Internalizing these messages and believing that one must be thin in order to be beautiful is a main risk factor for eating disorders (Culbert, Racine, & Klump, 2015). However, Black women are less likely than White women to internalize the thin ideal, and research suggests they're also likely to find larger bodies attractive and are more likely to be satisfied with their bodies (Kronenfeld, Reba-Harrelson, Von Holle, Reyes, & Bulik, 2010; Neumark-Sztainer et al., 2002). Black women also report experiencing fewer pressures to be thin, especially from their peers and the media (Ordaz et al., 2018). Overall, research suggests that White women engage in dieting behavior more frequently and have higher rates of eating disorders than women of color; however, women of color do engage in binge eating at rates that approach those of White women (Striegel-Moore et al., 2003; Talleyrand, 2012).

Not all women who are exposed to the thin ideal develop an eating disorder. In addition to cultural factors, other variables make some women more susceptible to internalizing this norm and developing an eating disorder. These include both genetic and environmental risk factors, such as abuse and a history of being bullied or teased about weight (Culbert et al., 2015; Neumark-Sztainer, Falkner, Story, Perry, & Hannan, 2002).

The *DSM-5* identifies several kinds of eating disorders. **Anorexia nervosa** involves restricting one's intake of food to the point that a significant reduction in body weight occurs (American Psychiatric Association, 2013). Fear of gaining weight and disturbance in how one's weight is perceived are also part of this disorder. Less than 1% of the population has anorexia, but it's three times more common in women than in men (Hudson, Hiripi, Pope, & Kessler, 2007).

try it for yourself

Many feminists consider the diagnosis of complex PTSD to be empowering because it's a way to acknowledge how a history of repeated trauma can lead to psychological problems. Think about how diagnoses shape people's lives, in general, as well as how this one may, in particular. When should diagnoses be created and used? When are diagnoses helpful, and when do they do more harm than good? Ask friends and family members the same questions. Do you get consistent responses or a range? Do you notice any patterns to what people share?

The mortality rate for anorexia is higher than for any other eating disorder. A meta-analysis indicated that approximately 5.1% of people with anorexia died per year, and 1 in 5 of those who died had committed suicide (Arcelus, Mitchell, Wales, & Nielsen, 2011). Moreover, researchers have found that women with anorexia are likely to be shy and socially isolated, and they typically experience shame about themselves and their bodies (Treasure, Corefield, & Cardi, 2012). They also tend to compare themselves to others, be perfectionistic, and be more submissive than women without anorexia. Anorexia can be a way of coping with shame and a response to feeling socially excluded—it can also provide a sense of control.

Bulimia nervosa is characterized by binge eating episodes in which a person eats a great deal in a brief period of time and feels out of control while doing so (American Psychiatric Association, 2013). It also involves compensatory behavior such as throwing up, exercising excessively, or using laxatives. Bulimia is more common in the general population than anorexia and affects 1% to 2% of women (Smink, van Hoeken, & Hoek, 2012). It has many of the same risk factors as anorexia, including idealization of the thin ideal, a sense of perfectionism, and a generally negative emotional state (Culbert et al., 2015; Stice, 2002). Having parents and peers who model body dissatisfaction and eating pathology is another risk factor for bulimic symptoms (Stice, 2002). Bulimia is also strongly related to heavy drinking and depression (Keski-Rahkonen et al., 2013).

Women constantly encounter magazines such as these, and they contribute to the message that girls and women should strive to be thinner. Given this context, it is unsurprising that women have such high rates of eating disorders. Do you read magazines like these? Do you know people who do? Do you think they affect the way women view their bodies? How can women navigate our culture without developing an eating disorder?

Binge eating disorder is a diagnosis that was added to the *DSM-5*. This disorder involves recurrent episodes of binge eating in which a person feels distressed and disgusted over each episode (American Psychiatric Association, 2013). About 2.6% of women and 1.1% of men are diagnosed with binge eating disorder over the course of their lifetimes (Kessler et al., 2013). However, data from one study looking at a general sample of people in the community, rather than those seeking treatment for an eating disorder, showed that men engage in overeating, which is related to binge eating, more than women do (Striegel-Moore et al., 2009).

Because there are no compensatory behaviors in binge eating disorder, people with this disorder tend to be higher weight. Given our culture of fat shaming, higher-weight individuals who binge eat may internalize a sense of shame about their weight. In one study, internalizing a bias against being higher weight was related to depression and other poor health outcomes in individuals with binge eating disorder (Pearl, White, & Grilo, 2014). Moreover, higher-weight people are often teased or bullied by others. In fact, research has shown that being teased about one's weight is related to greater incidences of binge eating (Herbozo, Stevens, & Thurston, 2017; Neumark-Sztainer et al., 2002; Vartanian & Porter, 2016). Teasing causes distress and a tendency to compare oneself negatively to others; binge eating can be seen as a way to cope with the negative feelings that this causes.

Although the rates of clinically diagnosable eating disorders are relatively low, the rates of behaviors related to eating disorders are quite high. Table 13.1 shows data from a study of predominantly White women and men, ages 18 to 35, about the percentage of participants who reported either very often or always engaging in certain behaviors (Striegel-Moore et al., 2009). Body checking (e.g., pinching oneself to see the amount of fat; monitoring to see if one's fat jiggles or spreads) and body avoidance (e.g., wearing baggy clothing; avoiding mirrors) were quite common, as was losing control over eating. A study of Austrian adolescents from grades 5 through 11 had similar results; 29% of girls and 14% of

TABLE 13.1 Symptoms of Eating Disorders Experienced by Women and Men

Symptom	Women (%)	Men (%)
Binge eating at least once a week	10.0	8.0
Body avoidance	11.3	4.4
Body checking	22.5	8.9
Fasting	6.3	4.0
Loss of control over eating	29.6	20.0
Over-eating	18.0	26.0
Using laxatives	3.1	3.0
Vomiting	3.7	1.5

Note. Data from Striegel-Moore et al. (2009).

your turn

How does our culture's obsession with thinness affect your relationship with your body and food? How might this be different if you had a different gender identity? How can women avoid developing an eating disorder in this culture?

boys felt like they lost control over their eating, 28% of girls and 11% of boys felt as though they were fat when others said they were thin, and 31% of girls and 23% of boys said that thinking about food dominated their lives (Zeiler et al., 2016).

Overall, given our cultural idealization of the thin female body, many women engage in behaviors that are symptomatic of eating disorders. A good question for future research may not be why some women develop eating disorders but, rather, how most women resist them.

Borderline Personality Disorder

What is borderline personality disorder, and how has it been historically diagnosed in a way that can be considered sexist?

Borderline personality disorder (BPD) is defined in the *DSM-5* as involving a poor sense of self, including self-criticism and feelings of emptiness, and impairments in interpersonal relationships, including impaired empathy and intimacy (American Psychiatric Association, 2013). A classic symptom of BPD is an interpersonal pattern of neediness and alternating between extreme idealization and devaluation. In other words, someone with BPD may absolutely love someone one day and then, in response to a perceived slight or abandonment, absolutely hate that person the next day. Other symptoms include anxiousness, separation anxiety, depression, and impulsivity. Individuals with BPD often engage in impulsive behavior, such as shopping or gambling sprees, and may engage in self-injurious behavior such as cutting.

Traditionally, the understanding of BPD was extremely gendered, and until recently, indications were that around 75% of people diagnosed were women (Shaw & Proctor, 2005). However, that number was generated from studies of individuals who sought treatment and received this diagnosis. Recent epidemiological work investigating rates of BPD among a general sample of people, as opposed to only those who have sought therapy, has shown that women and men have BPD at equal rates—around 6.2% of women and 5.6% of men over the course of their lives (Sansone & Sansone, 2011). Women and men were found to typically display different symptoms. Women were more likely to have depression, anxiety, eating disorders, and symptoms of trauma; men were more likely to have explosive traits such as anger outbursts and to engage in substance abuse. Given the higher rates of substance abuse among men, those men with BPD are more likely to receive substance abuse treatment rather than traditional psychotherapy, which may explain why they might not have been identified in earlier assessments of prevalence.

The traditional practice of over-diagnosing women with this disorder has been an example of gender bias in the field. Feminist scholars have argued that BPD diagnoses were given both to women who rejected feminine norms and acted angry as well as to those who acted in ways consistent with feminine norms but turned their distress inward in the form of self-injury (Chesler, 2005; Shaw & Proctor, 2005). For this reason, BPD was conceptualized in pejorative ways—it was a diagnosis given to patients whom therapists found difficult to deal with (Shaw & Proctor, 2005).

BPD is also strongly linked to experiences of childhood trauma, including emotional and sexual abuse; it's estimated that 40% to 70% of people with BPD have experienced child abuse (Ball & Links, 2009). An interpersonal pattern of idealization and devaluation can make sense in the context of an abuse history in which the person whom the victim loves the most is also the one who's being abusive. Given that childhood trauma is an important factor in BPD, a diagnosis of complex PTSD may be more appropriate for some who are diagnosed with BPD (Ford & Courtois, 2014). This may be an especially useful perspective because the diagnosis of complex PTSD doesn't have the same negative connotations as the diagnosis of BPD. However, other research has suggested that complex PTSD can be distinguished from BPD because participants with BPD were more concerned with abandonment, were more likely to have unstable relationships, and were more impulsive (Cloitre, Garvert, Weiss, Carlson, & Bryant, 2014)

The link between child abuse and BPD is complicated. For example, parents who are impulsive and hostile may genetically pass down impulsive and hostile traits as well as raise their children in an unstable and violent environment (Bornovalova et al., 2013). Furthermore, children who are aggressive or overly anxious may contribute to stress experienced by their parents, which could increase the risk that the parents will mistreat them. Research using twins has

Pre-menstrual Dysphoric Disorder

The diagnostic category **pre-menstrual dysphoric disorder (PMDD)** was added to the *DSM-5* to be applied when women have symptoms of depression that start before the onset of their period and end soon after the period is over. In the previous edition, PMDD was included in an appendix as a diagnosis requiring further study, and there was considerable controversy about moving PMDD into the main part of the *DSM* (Zachar & Kendler, 2014).

On the one hand, many women find a PMDD diagnosis helpful in describing and managing their symptoms. Approximately 3% to 8% of women meet the criteria for PMDD, and 13% to 18% have some symptoms that cause distress or impairment (Halbreich, Borenstein, Pearlstein, & Kahn, 2003). Knowledge of PMDD can help women access treatment that they may not otherwise receive.

On the other hand, many feminists see PMDD as a way of pathologizing women's natural reproductive processes

When women express negative emotions, they're often asked if they're having their period or are "PMSing." This reaction dismisses or minimizes women's real experiences of sadness, frustration, and anger.

and dismissing legitimate emotions that women may feel when they have their periods (Ussher, 2011). For example, women are often dismissed as just "PMSing" when they're appropriately expressing anger, and there's concern that having an official PMDD diagnosis could worsen this misperception. Indeed, it's important to validate emotions that occur pre-menstrually. Research suggests that in couples where there is inadequate expression of emotions and inadequate support, PMS symptoms are more severe (Ussher, 2011). Women who are overburdened all month long may find they can't cope as well as they did before their period, or their period may provide an acceptable reason to express their distress. As a result, women may express anger that they felt all month but otherwise suppressed during the pre-menstrual phase. If a woman receives a PMDD diagnosis, others may be more likely to dismiss negative emotions expressed during her period.

Another concern is that PMDD was added to the *DSM-5* because doing so benefited pharmaceutical companies. Even before PMDD was officially added to the *DSM*, the drug company Eli Lilly re-packaged Prozac as Sarafem to be prescribed to women diagnosed with PMDD. This was a profitable move, considering that the Prozac patent had expired and releasing it under a new name for a different diagnosis let the company extend the patent. In fact, one of the justifications for including PMDD in the *DSM-5* was that a medication had already been developed to treat it (Cosgrove & Wheeler, 2013). Moreover, 75% of the mood disorders task force members working on the *DSM-5* had ties to the pharmaceutical industry (Cosgrove & Wheeler, 2013). Given this background, many psychologists are concerned that including PMDD in the *DSM-5* was a move driven by drug companies that will cause people to minimize the social realities of women's distress and focus only on biological explanations.

Have you or someone you know ever had real anger or frustration dismissed as "PMSing"? Do you think a PMDD diagnosis is empowering or oppressing?

shown that, while there's a link between child abuse and BPD, some of that link involves shared genetic traits (Bornovalova et al., 2013). Other researchers have begun to look outside of the family for contributors to BPD. In one study, peer teasing was related to symptoms of BPD above and beyond the contribution of family factors (Stitt, Francis, Field, & Carr, 2015).

Feminist Therapy

How are feminist therapists similar to and different from traditional therapists?

Feminist therapists, like all other therapists, seek to relieve their clients' distress. In their work they use a variety of research-supported techniques to treat mental illness, including cognitive behavioral approaches. They may also prescribe medications as appropriate or work in coordination with a psychiatrist who prescribes medications. However, feminist therapists conceptualize their clients' problems more broadly than traditional therapists do. Instead of viewing mental illness solely as a disease that manifests within a person, feminist therapists also view it as a response to the relative powerlessness experienced by socially marginalized groups. Therefore, feminist therapists see mental illness in women partially as a response to patriarchy (Israeli & Santor, 2000). In emphasizing that the personal is political, feminist therapists see a woman's depression, anxiety, or other disorders not just as arising from biology or dysfunctional thinking styles, but also as arising from her situation in a sexist society (Worell & Remer, 1992). Therefore, feminist therapy focuses on more than making women feel better. Feminist therapists help women see how their problems reflect broader social issues. Feminist therapists also often work to change aspects of society, such as reducing violence against women or advocating for an adequate minimum wage and increased support for women living in poverty (Kahn, 2000).

Let's imagine, as an example, a Black lesbian experiencing racism, sexism, and homophobia. She may experience depression and have thoughts such as "People hate me and I am worthless" (Brown, 2006, pp. 20–21). A traditional therapist may diagnose major depression and begin cognitive therapy designed to help this woman challenge and change her irrational thinking. A feminist therapist may also use these approaches but would additionally recognize the broader systems of power and discrimination that influence this woman's life. The feminist therapist would be more likely to consider that the woman's thoughts may not be a cognitive distortion but may reflect the disempowerment she experiences as a result of discrimination. The feminist therapist might also work to reduce discrimination and encourage this client to develop stronger social networks to also collectively promote change.

Because of this perspective, a primary goal of feminist therapy is to help clients develop a *feminist consciousness* (Brown, 2004). In other words, feminist therapists help clients distinguish internal and external sources of distress so they don't unnecessarily blame themselves for their mental health concerns. As the clients' feminist consciousness increases, they may experience relief from their distress. In one study of primarily White women who participated in feminist consciousness-raising groups, researchers found a decrease in depressive symptoms and an increase in self-esteem (Weitz, 1982). Although consciousness-raising groups are no longer as popular as they were in the 1970s, feminist therapists continue to work to alleviate women's suffering by helping them to realize the links between their own experiences and wider social structures (Marecek, 2017). Support groups for women still exist, especially for women in abusive relationships (Tutty, Babins-Wagner, & Rothery, 2016). These groups help women understand the dynamics of their relationships, including the influences of gender role socialization. They also help women build skills to develop and maintain healthy and safe relationships. Research suggests that such groups improve women's general mental health and self-esteem (Tutty et al., 2016).

Feminist Therapy = Good Therapy

Many techniques associated with feminist therapy are now considered essential parts of good therapy for everyone and are used by practitioners who may not identify as feminists (Brown, 2006). For example, feminist therapists see the therapeutic relationship as collaborative and egalitarian (Rader & Gilbert, 2005; Worell & Remer, 1992). In this view, the therapist isn't considered an all-powerful expert but, rather, acts as a partner in helping the client. Creating a collaborative therapeutic relationship in which the client feels truly heard and understood has been identified as a key component of successful treatment in all types of therapies (Ackerman & Hilsenroth, 2003).

Also, feminist therapists may be more likely than non-feminist ones to tell clients about their own experiences, a practice known as self-disclosure (Mahalik, Van Ormer, & Simi, 2000; Worell & Remer, 1992). For example, if a client struggles to balance work and family responsibilities, a therapist who faces similar challenges may disclose her own experiences and strategies for coping. Such self-disclosure promotes trust, empathy, and a sense of equality between therapist and client. The American Psychological Association (APA) supports appropriate levels self-disclosure when it can benefit the client but discourages self-disclosure if it would impair the therapist's competence, effectiveness, or objectivity (Behnke, 2015). A meta-analysis examining the effects of counselor self-disclosure in therapy showed that self-disclosure was related to positive outcomes, including more disclosure by the client, positive feelings toward the therapist, and an increased desire to continue therapy (Henretty, Currier, Berman, & Levitt, 2014).

Another component that has been integrated into feminist therapy that has also become a part of any good therapy is a focus on **multicultural competence**. Being able to recognize how multiple, intersecting aspects of clients' social identities influence their lives is an important part of understanding clients and developing good therapeutic relationships. Multicultural therapists are keenly aware of the dangers of stereotypes and assumptions about universality of experience when working with clients of diverse backgrounds (Enns, 2012). In 2003, the APA developed guidelines for therapists to be trained in multicultural competence, and an updated version was approved in 2017 (American Psychological Association, 2003, 2017). Competence involves being aware of how therapists' own cultures influence their worldview, and understanding how their own social and cultural identities—ones often associated with greater power and privilege—assist them in navigating the world.

A multiculturally competent therapist would also consider how cultural socialization informs mental health. For example, it's useful for all therapists to understand that a cultural emphasis on saving face and not exposing personal weakness among some clients with Asian identities may make it difficult for those individuals to seek treatment and openly talk about their problems (Au, 2017). Similarly, some women place great value on their roles as wives and mothers. In one study, a group of South Asian women who were survivors of IPV reported that disclosing their abuse caused others in their community to view them as "mentally weak" and as "inadequate wives and mothers" (Singh & Hays, 2008, p. 98). The group leader noted that therapy was improved when members had time to socialize before group and when the start and stop times of the group were flexible.

Multicultural competency means applying knowledge about the values of a particular group on an individualized basis. In other words, while understanding cultural differences is important, every individual from a given culture is a unique person, so it's also important not to stereotype. For example, not all Asian American clients are concerned about saving face. Knowing when to generalize about a client's cultural heritage and when to consider that person's unique situation has been labeled *dynamic sizing* (Sue, 1998). Clinicians develop flexibility so they can recognize that a client's situation may be a complicated blend of individual and cultural factors.

Psychologists are also beginning to talk about *class competency* and how to modify traditional psychotherapy practice when working with people with lower incomes. This perspective emphasizes the benefits of therapists being aware of their own beliefs about social class and poverty and being willing to discuss the role of poverty in their clients' mental health (Goodman et al., 2013). Psychologists may also have to modify how they conduct their practice. For example, therapists may need to travel to community agencies in order meet clients where it's convenient for them rather than convenient for the therapist (Goodman et al., 2013). Therapists may also help clients to access resources. The client discussed earlier who complained that her previous therapist had reported her to social services for not having food described a different experience with her current therapist: "If I'm low on food, you know, it's okay, 'Come on we'll have a session in the car headed for the food pantry' . . . You know, just providing me with resources that I don't know of" (p. 189).

Not only are many feminist approaches generally considered good therapy, but they draw from a wide variety of therapeutic perspectives. For example, feminist therapists may use cognitive behavioral techniques to help clients change their thinking styles (Brown, 2006). Many feminist therapists who work closely with patients who've experienced trauma use a variety of techniques, including exposure to memories of the trauma and narrative techniques that encourage women to tell their story and re-frame their experience as one of survival rather than victimization (Brosi & Rolling, 2010; Marecek, 2017).

Another approach involves integrating the practice of mindfulness into treatment. Mindfulness, which is based in Buddhist philosophical thought, involves a non-judgmental acceptance of one's sensations and emotions as well as what has happened in one's life. It can be fostered through meditation, attending to breathing, or activities such as yoga or tai chi. Mindfulness is an increasingly popular therapeutic practice and has been consistently related to therapeutic benefits. A meta-analysis of over 200 studies showed that mindfulness-based interventions were effective in alleviating a wide variety of problems, including stress, anxiety, and depression (Khoury et al., 2013).

Mindfulness can be particularly helpful for women who have experienced trauma, which often involves a cycle of attempting to suppress memories of the experience but then experiencing unwanted memories and flashbacks. Facilitating a mindful acceptance of what happened, in the absence of self-judgment or blame, can help stop this negative cycle and reduce intrusive thoughts, avoidance, and shame (Boyd, Lanius, & McKinnon, 2018; Follette, Palm, & Pearson, 2006). When women are distressed due to experiences of abuse or violence, acceptance of what happened is

Dr. Laura Brown, who contributed the nearby Spotlight feature, is a renowned feminist therapist. She has written or edited more than 10 books and has produced over 150 additional professional publications. She identifies the construct of *Tikkun Olam*, the Hebrew term for "healing the world," as central to her work.

often a path to decreasing self-blame and being able to move on (Ussher, 2011). One woman who had been sexually abused said, "I've accepted that it's happened, and I think I've just got to deal with any sort of effect it's having on me now. Which otherwise, I'd just go on living . . . an' letting it take over everything, and it would ruin my life" (p. 187).

Feminist Techniques

Even though there's a great deal of overlap between feminist therapy and good therapeutic practices in general, therapists who self-identify as feminist therapists are more likely to use certain techniques (Moradi, Fischer, Hill, Jome, & Blum, 2000). These include focusing on how the personal is political, encouraging clients to take care of themselves instead of prioritizing or only focusing on the needs of others, and assisting clients with increasing their own assertiveness and autonomy (Moradi et al., 2000). Moreover, feminist therapists can be agents of social change (Singh & Burnes, 2010).

Promoting Consciousness Raising Emphasizing that the personal is political can be considered part of consciousness raising for clients (Israeli & Santor, 2000). For example, feminist therapists can help clients see their personal problems as part of larger structural problems, such as the sexist oppression of women. For such clients, this realization can reduce self-blame and increase empathy and kindness toward the self (Richmond, Geiger, & Reed, 2013).

This was the case for a White, female law student who experienced depression, insomnia, and anxiety that interfered with her academic and social lives (Richmond et al., 2013). She described her father as strict, verbally abusive, and having negative views of women. Her symptoms started in middle school, where she was teased for developing breasts early. They worsened severely in college when her boyfriend's roommate raped her. At this point she experienced guilt and self-blame, thinking it was her fault because she had passed out drunk in the bed and didn't stop the rape when she came to.

spotlight on . . .

Being a Feminist Therapist

Contributed by Laura Brown, PhD

In my culture, we say, "To heal one life is to heal the world," and feminist therapy allows me to heal the world one hour and one life at a time.

Feminist therapy has facilitated the formation of meaningful connections with many of my clients. We've written together about our work, mourned shared losses together, and come to see one another as equal human beings striving toward empowerment. When colleagues complain about burnout, I don't relate because this model keeps me fully engaged with those I work with.

Like other feminist therapists, I understand my clients' distress and behavior in the framework of a larger cultural and political lens. Problematic behaviors are often attempts to overcome danger, violation, or persistent unfairness, which decrease quality of life. If a diagnosis is required, I arrive at it collaboratively with my client.

Feminist therapists also seek to situate their offices so they will be welcoming to diverse people. This might mean being near a bus line and/or in a neighborhood where people of many identities will feel safe and not at risk of harassment. With regard to fees, I balance personal financial security with being available to clients from a range of incomes. Because feminist therapy emphasizes egalitarian relationships, I continually consider how to address the imbalance of power that characterizes a psychotherapy relationship.

Through therapy, this woman began to see how what she considered to be private, personal problems were due to sexism around her (Richmond et al., 2013). Her childhood was dominated by her father being the powerful decision maker and making her feel unimportant. Her teenage years were controlled by feeling shame about her developing body while coping with conflicting media messages that encouraged her to be sexy without being sexual. She realized that her guilt about the rape stemmed from her parents voicing rape myths, such as the ideas that good girls are virgins and that only promiscuous girls get raped. Through therapy, she developed a feminist consciousness and began to see herself as a survivor rather than a victim.

Encouraging Self-Care Feminist therapists encourage clients to engage in self-care. Women who are depressed often sacrifice their own needs in order to meet the needs of others (LaFrance, 2010). Many of these women think that taking time for themselves is selfish rather than an aspect of positive self-care. Several studies have shown that this is particularly the case for many women of color, who face pressures of conforming to gendered cultural expectations of self-sacrifice (Beauboef-Lafontant, 2007; Gratch, Bassett, & Attra, 1995; Mendez-Luck & Anthony, 2015).

For clients like these, making sure that their personal needs are met can be an essential part of treatment. For example, many mothers rarely sit down and eat a meal themselves; instead, they grab leftovers off their children's plates or nibble something here and there as they're making a meal. For these women, a simple act of self-care can be to sit down with a plate of food and eat it. Other acts of self-care include taking time for exercise or reading a book for pleasure. Of course, engaging in self-care can be easier said than done if a woman is struggling to survive and can't carve out time for herself in this way. Nevertheless, increasing self-care can be a path toward alleviating depression. One woman described how exercise was "my only sanity. That was my only one hour to myself" (LaFrance, 2010, p. 131).

Cultivating Assertiveness and Autonomy Another feminist approach involves encouraging women to increase their assertiveness and autonomy. For example, self-defense training teaches what to do in the case of a sexual assault or attack. One study showed that women who'd taken this type of training had increased assertiveness, more self-esteem, and a greater sense of control as well as decreased anxiety, depression, and avoidance behaviors (Brecklin & Ullman, 2005). Teaching women how to appropriately express anger in an assertive way can also alleviate their distress.

Dialectical behavioral therapy (DBT) is a technique developed for individuals diagnosed with BPD that combines training in social skills, mindfulness, emotion regulation, and assertiveness, known as interpersonal effectiveness (Linehan, 1993a). A meta-analysis demonstrated that DBT is an effective treatment and reduces suicidal and self-injurious behavior (Kliem, Kröger, & Kosfelder, 2010). DBT has also been used effectively with individuals who have a variety of disorders, particularly eating disorders (Lenz, Taylor, Fleming, & Serman, 2014).

A goal of the assertiveness training component of DBT is to be able to express anger in a calm and adaptive way that will be more likely to elicit a positive response from others. The skills to help clients do this can be summarized by the acronym DEAR MAN: Describe, Express, Assert, Reinforce, (be) Mindful, Appear confident, and Negotiate (Linehan, 1993b). One study showed that clients who went through DBT were better able to use assertive expressions of anger rather than allowing angry feelings to overwhelm them (Kramer et al., 2016). For example, before treatment, a woman said, "I am so full of rage . . . I feel overwhelmed, I was so pissed off when I was at work, I just had to leave and go do it [self-harming behaviour]" (p. 10). After therapy, a different woman said, "I'm able to stand up for myself now. . . . For example, my boyfriend . . . keeps track of all my appointments in his own agenda, even the ones that don't concern him. There I realized: these are my appointments! [imagines talking to the boyfriend] 'don't write down my appointments in your agenda . . . I'm not ok with that!!' That's what I said to him, I refuse to let things go that way" (p. 10).

Feminist therapists also encourage their clients to do a *sex role analysis*. This involves increasing their awareness of how sex/gender-role stereotypes have negatively impacted their lives. As part of this work, therapists may encourage clients to reject traditional norms of femininity. For example, a woman who's constantly stressed about keeping her house clean could be encouraged to be less hard on herself and let the dirty dishes sit overnight (Ussher, 2011). However, some feminist therapists also encourage clients to value the feminine aspects of themselves, a perspective more consistent with cultural feminism (Marecek & Kravetz, 1998; Worell & Remer, 1992). As an example, a client who has been told her whole life that she's overly emotional could be encouraged to see being in touch with her emotions as a positive aspect of herself.

Advocating for Social Justice Many feminist therapists, as well as others such as multicultural and class-competent therapists, are committed to fighting oppression and inequality and advocating for social justice. Many therapists are trained simply to focus on helping individuals. But training in feminist therapy, multicultural competence, and class competence encourages therapists to look more broadly at social factors that need to be acknowledged and, ultimately, changed in order to help clients thrive (Goodman et al., 2013; Vera & Speight, 2003). For example, psychologists may be involved in advocating for better public schools, a living wage, prison reform, and violence prevention programs. They may be involved in community outreach, self-help support, consulting, and working to change public policy.

Psychologists and counselors may also find themselves in the role of advocate rather than traditional therapist. For example, if a client is about to face eviction and is experiencing depression or insomnia, helping her access resources would be more important than trying to help her re-frame her problems through cognitive therapy or uncovering the unconscious source of her difficulties. Therapists may also involve clients in social justice efforts through working in partnership with community-based organizations (Goodman et al., 2013). In these ways, feminist therapists broaden their focus beyond (but still including) the individual to advocating for social change to help end oppression and the distress that accompanies it.

Conclusion

Women with mental health issues have been called mad throughout the ages, and some aspects of femininity continue to be associated with madness. However, the mental health problems that women frequently experience today partially stem from the oppressive environments in which they live. It's limiting to see these problems as pathologies instead of as reasonable reactions to a bad situation. Psychological treatment and medication can be helpful, but treatment that doesn't account for aspects of women's social environments will have limited effectiveness. When environments change for the better, women's lives can improve.

Chapter Review

SUMMARY

Women and Madness: A Historical Perspective

- Women who have violated gendered expectations or cultural standards have often been labeled as "mad."

- Hysteria was a common diagnosis given to women for centuries. Specific symptoms varied across culture and time periods, but it was generally connected to women's reproductive functions and/or sexuality.

- Treatments for "madness" evolved as beliefs about mental health changed and medical knowledge advanced. For example, rest cures gave way to institutionalization, which subsequently gave way to treatment with drugs such as Valium and Prozac.

- The *DSM* profoundly influences how mental illness is understood and treated, but feminists have criticized the manual for pathologizing femininity and considering variation in gender identity as abnormal.

- Feminist clinicians note that much of the distress that women experience can be considered reasonable reactions to challenging life circumstances.

Mental Health Diagnoses

- Women are diagnosed with depression, anxiety, PTSD, and eating disorders more frequently than are men. Even when diagnosis rates are low, as with eating disorders, rates of behaviors and symptoms associated with disorders can be quite high.

- Biological and cognitive factors may contribute to different rates of diagnoses, such as indirect relationships between hormones and depression and a greater tendency to ruminate in women.

- Socialization and gender roles also contribute to mental illness. For example, depression is related to self-silencing and not expressing negative emotions or anger, and although women are encouraged to "do femininity," doing it too well has been linked to depression.

- Intersecting aspects of social identities can contribute to women's experiences of distress and complicate the way women, especially women of color, understand their distress and engage in help-seeking behaviors. Sexual harassment and discrimination related to marginalized aspects of social identities have been linked to depression and anxiety.

- Therapists have not always been affirming of sexual minority identities; conversion therapy has now been deemed harmful and is illegal in some states.

- Poverty is a significant life stressor that has been linked to mental illness, and women are more likely than men to live in poverty. Poverty can contribute to barriers to receiving adequate treatment.

- Experiencing violence and abuse is related to experiencing depression, PTSD, and BPD, and symptoms, such as those of depression, can be considered a reasonable response to these experiences.

- BPD was believed to be more common among women, but recent research indicates that rates are actually similar for women and men.

Feminist Therapy

- Feminist therapists focus on how structural inequalities contribute to women's difficulties rather than assuming that there is something innately wrong with individual women.

- Feminist therapy is characterized by a focus on egalitarianism within the therapeutic relationship. Feminist therapists have also embraced the need for multicultural and class competence as part of their training and practice.

- Feminist therapists encourage women to engage in self-care, to consider how gender roles influence their mental health, and to act assertively. Many feminist therapists also engage in social justice advocacy work to help alleviate oppressive conditions.

KEY TERMS

hysteria (p. 541)

deinstitutionalization (p. 545)

medical model (p. 547)

dependent personality disorder (DPD) (p. 548)

gender dysphoria (p. 549)

major depression (p. 550)

rumination (p. 552)

self-silencing (p. 553)

marianismo (p. 553)

conversion therapy (p. 557)

agoraphobia (p. 559)

generalized anxiety disorder (p. 560)

panic disorder (p. 560)

specific phobia (p. 560)

post-traumatic stress disorder (PTSD) (p. 560)

complex PTSD (p. 561)

historical trauma (p. 562)

anorexia nervosa (p. 563)

bulimia nervosa (p. 564)

binge eating disorder (p. 565)

borderline personality disorder (BPD) (p. 566)

pre-menstrual dysphoric disorder (PMDD) (p.568)

multicultural competence (p. 571)

dialectical behavioral therapy (DBT) (p. 575)

THINK ABOUT IT

1. How has the history of mental illness influenced the way distress is labeled among different types of women? In what ways do diagnostic labels help women? In what ways do they reveal biased assumptions? Are there better ways to "name the pain"?

2. Imagine you've been asked to develop a psychoeducation program to address gender disparities in rates of depression. Based on the research described in this chapter, design a program that helps to raise awareness about depression risk factors.

3. Go to a bookstore or search the web for self-help guides for dealing with anxiety. What are the main suggestions in these sources? Do they offer recommendations on how to develop a feminist consciousness? If not, why might that be?

4. Go to the Psychology's Feminist Voices website (feministvoices.com) and look up Beverly Greene's profile. Watch her oral history excerpt on African American Feminist Therapy. After listening to her talk, think about the ways in which feminist therapy differs from common perceptions of therapy. In what ways can feminist therapy uniquely promote social change?

ONLINE RESOURCES

- **American Foundation for Suicide Prevention** — resources to raise awareness and aid those affected by suicide: afsp.org

- **Dr. Laura Brown** — a website featuring video links and writings by internationally known feminist therapist Laura Brown. A feminist clinical and forensic psychologist in independent practice in Seattle, Washington, she writes about feminist therapy, cultural competency, and psychological trauma: drlaurabrown.com

- **National Alliance on Mental Illness** — resources from the nation's largest grassroots mental health organization dedicated to building better lives for the millions of Americans affected by mental illness: nami.org

- **National Institute of Mental Health** — information about mental health symptoms and treatment options: nimh.mih.gov

14

Tensions, Action, and Hope for the Future

IN 2013, CALLIOPE WONG, a transgender Chinese American woman, applied to Smith College, a prestigious all-women's school in Massachusetts. However, because financial aid documents listed her sex as M, she received a rejection letter explaining that she couldn't attend Smith because applicants must have a F sex assignment at the time of application (The Editorial Board, 2015). Wong, stung by this rejection, wrote about her experiences on a Tumblr blog called transwomen@Smith and launched a nationwide protest. In 2015, Smith College revised its policy and began to admit transwomen.

Smith is one of many women's colleges that have opened admissions to anyone who identifies as a woman ("Women's Colleges with Trans-Inclusive Policies," n.d.). Women's colleges differ as to whether or not transmen or non-binary individuals can apply or whether they can remain as students if they transition while enrolled (Padawar, 2014). To address the complexity of this issue, several schools have encouraged shifts in practices to reflect inclusivity (e.g., replacing the word *sisterhood* with *siblinghood* in songs, developing gender-inclusive housing, asking students to indicate their pronouns on forms that they complete).

To complicate matters, transmen on campus actually have a lot of social capital—they tend to be popular and are desired dating partners. One lesbian woman at Wellesley who expressed frustration that transmen were competing with her for romantic partners noted: "The trans men are always getting this extra bit of acknowledgment. Even though we're in a women's college, the fact is men and masculinity get more attention and more value in this social dynamic than women do" (Padawar, 2014, para. 49). Although this situation may be viewed positively as reflecting inclusivity, some women on these campuses object to the fact that masculinity has so much power at traditionally women's colleges. For example, transmen have had success in student government elections. Those who are concerned feel that women's colleges should be places only for those who identify as women; they object to diluting ideas of sisterhood to accommodate transmen (Padawar, 2014).

Calliope Wong enrolled in the honors program at the University of Connecticut, majoring in English and as a pre-med student after she was rejected by Smith College. A classically trained pianist, she also won a grant to make a recording of piano music. She hopes to become an endocrinologist and notes, "I am many things besides being trans" (Stiepock, 2016, para.16).

This controversy illustrates the fact that feminists don't always agree. In many arenas, including feminist circles, decisions about who is included and excluded can reflect struggles within power hierarchies. As we saw in Chapter 2, tensions within feminism arise, in part, from the multiple sources of inequality that women face.

Therefore, feminists continually reflect on hidden power dynamics—for example, by asking questions like these: Whose concerns are the most pressing? Who qualifies as a feminist? What goals should we try to achieve? and Which feminist perspective is the most effective in achieving those goals? Considering such questions often exposes power disparities that need careful attention in order to ensure equity and inclusion. In this chapter, we'll explore how questions like these can reveal conflicts and tensions within feminism. We'll then discuss ways in which people can work across these tensions to build coalitions that can address specific social goals. Finally, we'll examine how psychologists, in particular, are using findings from research to promote change at both individual and structural levels.

The Future of Feminism: Challenges and Controversies

In Chapter 1, we highlighted that there are many different kinds of feminism. Given this, it's not surprising that there are many issues on which feminists disagree with one another. We'll start by discussing a few such sources of tension within the feminist movement.

Whose Concerns Are the Most Pressing? The Case of Inclusion

What are the tensions associated with identifying who is considered a woman, and how do they reflect the prioritizing of some people's concerns over others' concerns?

Discussions and disagreements about the admission of transwomen or nonbinary individuals to women's colleges reflect the broader controversy about what it means to be a woman. This isn't a new phenomenon. In 1851, at the Women's Convention in Akron, Ohio, the former slave, abolitionist, and women's rights activist Sojurner Truth famously declared, "Ain't I a woman?" She was responding to the ways in which White womanhood was constructed (e.g., as passive, fragile) as compared to Black womanhood (e.g., as strong, resilient). Truth argued that stereotypes of women being weak and passive were inherently inaccurate since Black women demonstrated strength and resilience. This, she argued, undercut the idea that women couldn't lead because they were weak.

When Truth made her famous statement, many White women feared that her comments would divert attention away from the suffrage movement and toward emancipation (Crenshaw, 1989). They worried that without a singular, focused goal (i.e., suffrage), they would lose political momentum. As a result, they worked to move the conversation away from slavery and the oppression of Black people. This limited focus privileged White women and ignored the harsh realities of slavery, which was the most pressing concern for Truth.

The tension between White feminists and those advocating for racial justice increased after the passage of the 15th Amendment allowing Black men to vote in 1870 (Fields-White, 2011). Some White feminists cast their advocacy for women's suffrage in racist terms, implying that (White) women's votes would be needed to counteract the negative influence of Black men's votes. Black feminists such as Ida Wells explicitly advocated for the end of racial oppression and the lynching of Black people, but she was often in conflict with White feminists (Fields-White, 2011). By focusing on voting rights and ignoring the additional oppression that Black women experienced, White feminists excluded Black women from the movement.

Second and third wave feminists have continued to struggle with inclusion and exclusion, as well as whether it makes sense to talk about women as a singular group at all. In her book *Gender Trouble*, philosopher and gender theorist Judith Butler (1989) argued that a unified category of "woman" does not exist. For example, a wealthy Black lesbian's experience of sexism is different from that of a poor White heterosexual woman; a middle-class immigrant Latinx woman has very different experiences from those of a White transgender woman with a disability. Yet, Butler pointed out, women aren't just simply *different* from one another. As we discussed in Chapter 2, our society deems some identities as *inferior* and others as *superior*. This inevitably creates power inequities among women because some voices and concerns will be more readily heard and taken more seriously than others.

When feminist activist Betty Friedan (1963) wrote *The Feminine Mystique*, she explored the difficulties of a specific group of women: relatively wealthy, mostly White, cisgender American women. Her observations were extremely important for many women who shared these social identity characteristics, and they helped usher in the second wave feminist movement. However, they excluded the experiences of a great many other women in the United States. For example, there was no equivalent second wave feminist movement that rallied resources to end the exploitation of poor, female, domestic workers. Because these women lacked access to the same level of political power as Friedan, their concerns didn't receive mainstream attention (hooks, 1984). Given this context, when Butler claimed there is no universal concept of "woman," she was drawing attention to the way in which that concept has privileged some women over others and has falsely suggested a universal experience that doesn't actually exist.

The Vagina Monologues

The play *The Vagina Monologues* was written and produced by feminist playwright Eve Ensler based on her interviews with over 200 women. Many women view the show as a way to celebrate having vaginas and providing a safe space for women to talk about sex and sexual violence. Performers and viewers alike find the experience empowering. For example, a student directing the show said, "Being on stage and performing is a way to tell a story that may not necessarily be yours, but it could be very close. It is therapeutic in a unique way" (Donahoe, 2012, paras. 3–4). Proceeds from performances are generally donated to organizations that work to prevent sexual violence.

Critics of the play claim it prioritizes the experiences of privileged White women. Most monologues don't indicate a race or ethnicity, but a few are marked to be played by women with specific ethnic accents. In most performances of *The Vagina Monologues*, however, White women perform the unmarked monologues, which are generally positive in tone, and women of color perform the marked ones. Most of the monologues written for women of color involve violence or other negative experiences; the only rape in the show is experienced by a woman of color (Cooper, 2007). According to one critic, this conveys the message that only privileged White women can enjoy their vaginas (Cooper, 2007). In 2006, the University of Michigan attempted to stage a performance of the show casting only women of color so that they would perform both the distressing monologues and the positive ones (Capriccioso, 2006). However, this move was considered exclusionary, and those who give the rights to perform *The Vagina Monologues* considered revoking them in this instance. Ultimately, the University of Michigan production did allow White women to audition and perform.

Other criticisms are that the show reduces women to one body part (their vaginas) and assumes that all women have vaginas and that everyone who has a vagina is a woman (Hall, 2005). In this way, critics claim, it makes intersex and transgender individuals invisible or abnormal. In 2014, Mount Holyoke College cancelled a performance of *The Vagina Monologues* because the play offered what the college identified as "an extremely narrow perspective on what it means to be a woman" (Mulhere, 2015, para. 5). While some students applauded this decision, others found it problematic. Eve Enlser responded that the play was never meant to imply that being a woman means having a vagina, but that "over 51% of the population has vaginas, clitorises, vulvas, and many to this day do not feel comfortable, familiar, free, or endowed with agency over them" (Ensler, 2015, para. 2). However, this controversy raises questions about how to define what it means to be a woman and how to engage in discussions about issues that are important to some women without excluding others.

What do you think? Is *The Vagina Monologues* empowering or oppressing?

Issues of inclusion and exclusion continue to be a source of tension within feminism in the 21st century. For example, in Chapter 2 we mentioned how organizers of the 2017 Women's March in Washington struggled with inclusivity and messaging, and in Chapter 9 we pointed out how pro-life feminists were excluded from the march. In fact, conflict is an inevitable part of organizing. How to determine which issues to place at the forefront and whose voices to elevate is a necessary conversation feminists will continue to have. Doing feminism is an active process—one that involves continual reflection and critical thinking.

Who Can Be a Feminist? The Case of Men

What are the advantages and challenges of including men in the feminist movement?

Some feminists find the participation of men in the feminist movement to be problematic, but others think men can play an important role (Almassi, 2015). Especially because of their relative positions of power within Western society and their access to other men in settings where women are excluded, boys and men may be able to promote change in ways that girls and women cannot. For example, in 2013, an English air force base hired a comedian to entertain the troops who then started telling rape jokes (Kilmartin, 2017). The general in charge of the base was offended and walked out. Although he did not act in the moment, he did use the situation as a teachable moment when he sent an email the next day apologizing to the troops for failing them as a leader. He noted that such jokes were unacceptable and that he should have shut down the show. This public apology promoted an atmosphere where it was clear that sexism was not acceptable. Given that men are more likely than women to be in leadership roles, they're often in positions to promote positive change within organizations. When men work to create an environment in which speaking up against sexism is acceptable, women will be in a better position to self-advocate as well (Drury & Kaiser, 2014).

Furthermore, men are more likely than women to be present when misogynistic talk happens, since it often occurs in all-male environments (e.g., locker rooms, fraternities, boardrooms). Men generally over-estimate the extent to which other men support such talk. Usually, one or a small number of men instigate sexist talk and other men either laugh along or keep silent; these responses are often interpreted as indicating agreement with the ideas being expressed (Flood, 2011). For example, research has shown that perpetrators of sexual assault over-estimate the extent to which their friends are comfortable with

Men who support feminism can and do contribute to the feminist movement. Do you know any feminist-identified men? If so, ask them about the joys and challenges of identifying as a feminist. If not, ask some men why they don't identify as feminists.

sexual aggression (Dardis, Murphy, Bill, & Gidycz, 2016). These misperceptions contribute to pluralistic ignorance, as discussed in Chapter 7. Most men, however, are actually uncomfortable with sexist and sexually aggressive talk, but they're generally not comfortable overtly speaking up or calling out the instigator (Flood, 2011; Kilmartin et al., 2008). Men who do speak up against sexism have a great deal of power to change the dynamics of all-male environments and to create spaces where sexism and gender-based violence are not tolerated (Flood, 2011).

Despite the advantages associated with men engaging with feminism and supporting gender equality, tension remains. For one thing, members of the public generally view men who advocate for feminism in a more positive light than women who do (Drury & Kaiser, 2014). Also, men who act as allies against sexism are less likely than feminist women to be seen as self-advocates, as complainers, as hyper-sensitive, or as "crying prejudice" (Drury & Kaiser, 2014; Eliezer & Major, 2012; Rasinski & Czopp, 2010, p. 9). In general, people who aren't the targets of prejudice can be more effective advocates than the targets themselves. One reason is that people capture the attention of others when they advocate for groups they don't belong to (Gervais & Hillard, 2014). For example, research has shown that White people who confront racism are less likely to be seen as rude and are more likely than Black people who confront racism to be perceived as persuasive (Rasinski & Czopp, 2010). However, this very fact can be seen as unfair. It can be frustrating that someone with dominant status (e.g., a White man) is rewarded for being an advocate while someone with subordinate status (e.g., a Latinx woman) is seen as complaining. This dynamic can exacerbate power disparities and cause tension, even among like-minded feminists.

Men's potential power in some feminist circles also opens up the possibility that men will be seen as leaders and even set feminist agendas. However, this dynamic has the potential to ignore the voices of women and transgender individuals. As a result, feminist men are encouraged to learn to truly hear voices that aren't representative of their own. Law professor Jonathan Crowe (2011) has written about men's role in feminism, and he encourages feminist men to be humble and to realize that their experiences and understanding of the world are limited—something that can be difficult for White, cisgender, middle-class, heterosexual men who are used to seeing the world as reflecting their own experiences. Crowe encourages men to move beyond feeling guilty or resentful of being blamed and, instead, to commit to doing something to support gender equality.

As discussed in prior chapters, men can listen to women and encourage female voices in meetings, do more housework and child care, mentor and sponsor women at work, speak out against sexism or sexist language when with other men, advocate politically for issues that benefit women and members of other marginalized groups, and speak out against issues such as domestic violence and workplace harassment. To emphasize the importance of action, Jonathan Crowe quoted feminist activist singer Kathleen Hanna: "Feminism isn't something that you are, it's something that you do" (Crowe, 2018, para. 16). He then added: "Pro-feminist men should take this to heart. Talk is cheap, but concrete action is what is really needed" (para. 16).

Feminist men also experience tensions from dominant society. After all, boys and men face tremendous pressure to adhere to strict norms about masculinity (Kilmartin & Smiler, 2015). When they violate these norms, there can be significant negative social consequences such as teasing or social exclusion, which cause many men to reluctantly engage in misogynist behaviors (Moss-Racusin, Phelan, & Rudman, 2010). In one study, researchers found that women liked feminist men more than men did, but both groups saw feminist men as less likely to be masculine and more likely to be gay than non-feminist men (Rudman, Mescher, & Moss-Racusin, 2013).

Psychologist Chris Kilmartin (2017) has stated that men won't stop being sexist until such behavior causes them to lose status with other men. A strategy to address this situation involves challenging stereotypes of what it means to be a male feminist. For example, in one study, male undergraduates who were assigned to read a paragraph with a positive portrayal of feminist men were subsequently more supportive of feminism than those who read a paragraph with a negative portrayal (Wiley, Srinivasan, Finke, Firnhaber, & Shilinsky, 2013). Wade Davis, a former NFL player and pro-feminist advocate, tries to ask questions and keep the conversation going with other men. However, he acknowledges that he sometimes receives backlash for speaking out on behalf of women: "I think that when we get attacked by other men, that's the cost that you pay for being an advocate. As an ally, you're supposed to take the bullet so that other women don't have to. If you're not willing to pay that cost, then you are not ready to join the movement" (Fessler, 2017, para. 27).

Which Feminism Is Most Effective?
The Case of Intergenerational Conflict

How has tension between generations been a challenge to feminism, and how does this reflect over-arching tensions among those who hold different feminist perspectives?

As discussed in Chapter 1, tensions within feminism often arise because of contradictions among various perspectives. This is evident in the ways different generations understand and enact feminism. For example, bell hooks, a Black feminist activist in her 60s, has been a vocal critic of Beyoncé, a Black singer in her 30s (Coker, 2014). In objecting to Beyoncé's use of her body, her compliance with dominant standards of beauty, and her self-sexualization, hooks has stated that Beyoncé is "colluding in the construction of herself as a slave"; hooks also sees a "part" of Beyoncé as "a terrorist especially in terms of the impact on young girls" (para. 3). Those who regard Beyoncé as a contemporary feminist icon find these criticisms to be insulting and controversial.

In fact, in response to hooks, other feminists have written in defense of Beyoncé. One Black feminist journalist, Roxane Gay (2014), defended Beyoncé, saying she has agency and choice in the images of herself that she portrays. Janet Mock, a transwoman feminist activist, saw the criticism as reflecting a wider problem of the dismissal of the feminine within feminism—especially among Black feminine feminists—which, she argued, is itself a reflection of patriarchy (Solis, 2016). These disagreements highlight the controversies associated with cultural feminism that we discussed in Chapter 1. They also reflect the tension within feminism around self-sexualization, which we discussed in Chapter 7. Many feminists, especially (but not limited to) older ones, view self-sexualization as oppressive; but other feminists, often (but not only) younger ones, view it as an empowered choice and a way of exploring one's own sexuality (Lerum & Dworkin, 2009).

Generational tensions were also evident during the primaries for the 2016 U.S. presidential election. Gloria Steinem and Madeline Albright, two prominent White second wave feminists, rebuked young women who were supporting Bernie Sanders, the primary (male) challenger to eventual Democratic nominee Hillary Clinton. When introducing Clinton at a rally, Madeline Albright, who had served as the first female U.S. secretary of state, noted, in reference to the fight for women's rights in general, that "there's a special place in hell for women who don't help each other!" (Rappeport, 2016, para. 4). The same weekend, Gloria Steinem, one of the leaders of second wave feminism, commented that women were supporting Sanders in order to meet young men. Steinem said, "When you're young, you're thinking: 'Where are the boys? The boys are with Bernie'" (para. 9). Young feminists were appalled by this statement. One woman wrote on Reddit: "It's such a ridiculous thing to say. A feminist, basically saying that young women are incapable of having thoughts and opinions of their own. Unreal" (Contrera, 2016, para. 4). An online petition demanded that Steinem apologize, and she later did so, saying she was sorry if her remarks were taken to mean that young women weren't serious in their politics (Contrera, 2016).

This debate reflects, among other things, the likelihood that Albright and Steinem viewed Clinton's gender as a key factor in supporting a candidate, while younger feminists may have been more focused on Sanders's broader social justice agenda. In a larger sense, the debate reflected the women's different understandings of what feminism is and how it should be enacted. However, such conflict need not be seen in a negative light. Older and younger feminists alike grapple with how best to address the current status of women, and conflicts within the movement can be a source of strength if people with different perspectives can come together in dialogue (Novak & Richmond, 2016).

Building Bridges: A Call for Allyship

How can people with diverse social identities work together to meet common goals?

If each person has a complex combination of social identity characteristics that have been shaped by societal systems of power and oppression, how can feminists identify and achieve any shared political goals? The key is to form links and have open conversations with people who may not share your experiences. Decades ago, Audre Lorde (1984), a Black lesbian feminist poet, noted that it would be impossible to form a successful movement by assuming everyone is alike. Rather, it's our differences that enable us to learn and grow from our interactions with one another. One strategy to do this is through coalition building across social identity groups. **Allyship** is a lifelong process in which individuals who are privileged develop relationships with individuals who are marginalized as a way to address social injustice.

The process of allyship has been discussed as a series of stages (Edwards, 2007). In the first stage, people act as allies in certain situations because of self-interest. Those in this stage only seek to protect and help members of marginalized groups who are close to them. For example, they may speak up on behalf of a friend or a sister, but they wouldn't see larger patterns of social injustice. In the second stage, people can be considered aspiring allies and are motivated by an altruistic desire to help. Individuals in this stage become aware of social inequities and may feel guilty about their power and privilege. They see members of marginalized groups as victims in need of assistance and see themselves as being in a position to rescue others. Those in this stage want approval from and are very sensitive to criticism from members of the groups they are seeking to help.

The final stage involves becoming an ally for social justice (Edwards, 2007). Instead of seeing members of marginalized groups as victims, people in this stage can see how systems of oppression hurt everyone in different ways. Aboriginal activist Lilla Watson is noted for articulating this perspective: "If you have come here to help me, then you are wasting your time. . . . But if you have come because your liberation is bound up with mine, then let us work together" ("About," n.d., para. 1). Instead of being sensitive to criticism, those in this stage of allyship welcome criticism as a way to help them uncover the places where their privilege affects their worldview. Black queer feminist scholar Omi Osun Joni L. Jones notes that becoming an ally requires an ability to spot all forms of oppressive tendencies, even in oneself (scooby43215, 2010). An ally in this stage works to dismantle systems of oppression such as sexism, racism, and classism in partnership with members of different social groups. This process involves a dedication to relationship building that includes openness, active listening, self-questioning, and an investment of significant time and energy (Almassi, 2015; also see Table 14.1).

TABLE 14.1 Tips for Being an Ally

Practices of Effective Allies	Example
Acknowledging your privilege	Recognizing the areas in which you're privileged, and using that privilege to help dismantle the oppressive systems you benefit from.
Giving credit to others	Explicitly acknowledging those you draw from, and not taking credit for the work of others who are marginalized.
Being a good listener	Listening to an array of people from marginalized groups to deepen your understanding of issues.
Taking action	Realizing that it's not enough to say you're an ally, but that action is essential.
Avoiding self-labeling	Recognizing that you can strive to be an ally but that those who are part of marginalized groups have to decide if you are, and that being an ally to one group member doesn't mean all group members will perceive you in this way.
Continually educating yourself	Continuing to search out information to further your understanding, and realizing that those who are part of marginalized groups are unlikely to take the lead in educating you.
Making an effort not to be isolated	Interacting and engaging with diverse communities.
Playing a supporting role	Recognizing that privilege may give you a louder voice, and using that voice to shift attention away from yourself and toward those who are not heard.
Engaging with those who share your identities	If you're White, talking with other White people about racism; if you're able-bodied, calling out examples of ableism; and so on.
Seeing criticism as an opportunity for growth	Taking responsibility, apologizing, and changing your behavior when you're called out for not recognizing privilege and/or for acting in a hurtful way.
Seeking emotional support from other allies	Not expecting members of marginalized groups to support you as you work through your internalized racism, classism, and other prejudices; recognizing that support should come from other allies.

Note. Ideas adapted from Lawrence (2017) and Utt (2013).

Allyship has benefits that can promote change at both individual and systemic levels. In one study, Black feminist men described that their female feminist friends enabled them to practice new ways of "doing gender" within the context of their friendship (White & Gaines, 2006). This included finding new ways to express emotions, developing non-violent strategies to address anger inside and outside the home, and showing a willingness to accept and respect women's leadership. Also, across generations, allies can learn to "teach the conflicts" (Detloff, 1997, p. 91). In other words, they can come to understand that there are conflicting positions within feminism and that it isn't necessary to agree on everything in order to work together to support social change.

Feminist Activism: Changing Women's Lives

What are some issues that feminist activists have worked on, and what progress has been made?

Allyship can be beneficial in engagement with activism, and activism can take place at many levels. At the individual level, allies can show support and work alongside others by confronting bias when they see it. For example, one study showed that White female allies successfully confronted racism by correcting friends who used outdated terms such as *colored people,* by telling colleagues that their mocking of Asian student names was offensive, and by pointing out situations where they experienced privilege due to being White (Case, 2012). Other research showed that training men to be allies increased the likelihood that they would identify and challenge stereotypes about gender in the workplace (Wagner, Yates, & Walcott, 2012). As these studies demonstrate, allies can challenge the status quo and promote change by personally taking action.

try it for yourself

Think about the issues you've read about and discussed this semester. What do you think are the most pressing issues for women today? Ask your friends and family members what they think. Do you all agree on what the key issues are? Do the responses vary according to other factors, such as age, sexual orientation, social class, or ethnicity of the responder?

Activism also happens at structural levels—most notably, when individuals work together to advocate for legislative and policy change. The following discussion highlights a few contemporary examples of projects that seek to create social change on a large scale.

Minimum Wage

In the United States in 2016, over 16 million women were living in poverty (Patrick, 2017). Advocacy to raise the minimum wage has been undertaken in response to this problem, and it has gained momentum in recent years with many cities and states raising their minimum wage (Jones, 2017). The federal minimum wage of $7.25 an hour hasn't been raised since 2009, and as of January 2018, the District of Columbia and 29 states have raised their minimum wage above federal guidelines. Raising the minimum wage would, in particular, positively impact women who make up two thirds of minimum-wage workers and tipped workers (Vogtman, 2017).

Some economists originally feared that raising the minimum wage would make it more difficult for businesses to afford to pay their workers and would lead to workers being laid off. However, more recent economic data show that minimum wage increases positively affect over 97% of workers and that any resulting job losses are negligible in number and largely temporary (Cooper, Mishel, & Zipperer, 2018). For example, researchers determined that a substantial minimum wage increase, like the one from $9.47 to $13.00 per hour in Seattle, Washington, could increase both productivity and income for low-wage workers and that these positive effects would grow in magnitude over time (Rinz & Voorheis, 2018). In fact, the authors calculated that a substantial minimum wage increase could have greatly decreased the wages lost by low-wage earners during the recession of 2008.

It has been suggested that raising the minimum wage to $15.00 by 2024 would affect 41.5 million workers, 56% of whom are women (Cooper, 2017). This number includes 7.5 million mothers with children. The wage change would benefit 43% of Black and 38% of Latinx working women, significantly enhancing their quality of life. In another study, researchers estimated that, if the minimum wage had been $15.00 an hour during the period 2008–2012, between 2,800 and 5,500 deaths could have been avoided in New York City because of a documented link between poverty and poor health (Tsao et al., 2016).

Workplace Equality

Activism related to workplace equality focuses on many topics, but three common issues are the pay gap, paid leave, and affordable child care. Much of the focus has been on passing legislation at local and national levels to address these ongoing, and long-standing, concerns.

In 2009, passage of the Lilly Ledbetter Fair Pay Act signaled progress toward closing the pay gap. This legislation permits women to sue their employer after noticing wage discrimination in any paycheck—not just the first one, as had previously been required (Ledbetter, 2016). Although the act was a positive step, activists argue that it's insufficient because lawsuits require that the plaintiff know what her colleagues are earning (and in one study, researchers found that almost half of all workers are either discouraged or forbidden from discussing their salaries; Hayes & Hartmann, 2011). This puts the burden on those who are being discriminated against to prove their case rather than on companies to actually end pay discrimination. Some companies, however, are taking the initiative and instituting policies that involve complete transparency in salaries (Dishman, 2015). Companies that have tried these policies report increased dedication to the company and reduced turnover because no one feels they were lied to about salary.

Even if the pay gap were to be closed tomorrow, there would still be inequity in the workplace. As we've discussed throughout this book, women disproportionately take on caretaking responsibilities at home, even when working full-time (e.g., Bianchi, Sayer, Milkie, & Robinson, 2012; Fillo, Simpson, Rholes, & Kohn, 2015; Yavorsky, Kamp Dush, & Schoppe-Sullivan, 2015). For this reason, paid leave and affordable child care are critical issues worthy of activism.

The United States currently has no national legislation mandating paid leave, but individual states are taking the initiative to provide paid leave for their residents. For example, the Rhode Island state legislature passed a law in 2014 offering up to four weeks of paid time off in order to bond with a newborn, an adopted child, or a foster child or to care for a sick family member. Workers are paid a percentage of their salary up to $795 a week, and the program is funded by a small payroll tax. A study of small and medium companies in Rhode Island found that the majority of them favored the policies (Bartel, Rossin-Slater, Rhum, & Waldfogel, 2016). Other paid leave laws have been passed in Washington, D.C., California, New Jersey, New York, and Washington State (effective 2020).

In the absence of legislation, some individual companies have developed generous leave policies to help attract and retain talented women (Adamczyk, 2015; Malacoff, 2017). In many cases, however, these policies allow more leave for mothers (or only allow leave for mothers) or "primary caretakers," under the assumption that one parent (generally, the mother) will do the bulk of the child care. Gender-neutral leave policies, in contrast, make it easier for couples to have truly shared parenting. Some companies (such as Netflix) are offering paid leave to all parents and caregivers, and some (such as Etsy) have a broader view of parenting that includes surrogacy and adoption (see Table 14.2). However, while these

TABLE 14.2 Paid Leave Policies at Selected Companies

Company	Policy
Amazon	4 weeks before a mother gives birth and 10 weeks after giving birth, as well as an additional 6 weeks for any parent
American Express	20 weeks for new parents (both mothers and fathers) for both full- and part-time workers; the company also offers $35,000 for adoption, surrogacy, or infertility treatments
Bill and Melinda Gates Foundation	52 weeks of leave for parents after the birth of a child
Etsy	26 weeks of leave for biological, adoptive, or surrogate parents; employees can take this leave anytime within the first two years after the birth or adoption
Facebook	4 months for any parent
Google	18 weeks for birth mothers, 12 weeks for primary caretakers (including adoptive parents), and 7 weeks for non-primary caretakers
Microsoft	12 weeks for any parent
Netflix	1 year of leave for any parent
Spotify	24 weeks of leave for mothers and fathers, in addition to 1 month that can be used to transition back to work by working from home or part-time
Yahoo	16 weeks for birth mothers and 8 weeks for non-birth parents

Note. Information drawn from Adamczyk (2015) and Malacoff (2017).

your turn

If you are working, what kind of benefits does your company provide? What kind of benefits would you hope to find in a future company? How could you find out if your employer offers child-care leave? How much leave does your school offer its employees?

are positive steps, they largely benefit high-wage, corporate employees. Although low-wage employees within these companies can benefit from them, employers of most low-wage workers rarely have such generous leave policies.

Paid leave implies that parents will return to the workplace, but this depends on access to affordable child care. The possibility for universal child care in the United States may seem remote; however, the nation actually did have universal child care at one point. Between 1943 and 1946, the Lanham Act provided child care to women who were asked to work while men were fighting in World War II (Cohen, 2015). Wartime stimulus funds were provided to local communities, and child-care centers were built and staffed. The quality of the child care was quite high, and the cost was only 50 cents a day (around $7 in today's dollars). Children who utilized these services had better outcomes years later on almost every indicator compared to those who did not (Herbst, 2013).

For example, when they were adults, they were more likely to be employed, likely to be earning more money, less likely to be on public assistance, and more likely to be in good health. Children who lived in states that spent more money on the Lanham Act did better than children from states that spent less.

Although there is currently no national publicly funded pre-school program in the United States, many states do have publicly funded programs. Some of these target low-income children, while others provide access to all children and are considered "universal" child-care programs (Sanchez & Nadworny, 2017). These programs vary in quality and in the percentage of eligible children who are enrolled. Furthermore, there are huge disparities in funding levels from location to location. For example, in 2016, Mississippi spent less than $2,000 per child, but Washington, D.C., spent more than $15,000. Of course, more funding translates into higher-quality programs.

There's a great deal of evidence that high-quality child care benefits children. Some research has shown that the benefits are particularly strong for poor children, especially when those students are placed in universal pre-school programs instead of programs specifically for low-income students (Cascio, 2017). However, other studies have found benefits for programs that target lower-income students. A study of over 1 million children in a public pre-school program for lower-income students in North Carolina showed positive impacts in reading and math scores, as well as a decreased number of children being placed in special education programs and held back in their grade (Dodge, Bai, Ladd, & Muschkin, 2017). There were also benefits for students not enrolled in the pre-school program. The authors hypothesized positive spillover effects in which teachers are able to pay more attention to everyone if more students in the class are well prepared.

Gun Violence

Feminists also work to create communities that are peaceful and secure and where everyone's basic needs can be met. Reducing gun violence is one goal in this effort. The group Mothers of the Movement consists of Black women whose children were killed by police and gun violence (Morrison, 2016). Since losing their children, these mothers have strived to increase transparency and accountability for police who kill in the line of duty and to demand better gun control measures. Also, the grassroots organization Moms Demand Action for Gun Sense in America was founded by Sharon Watts after the Sandy Hook Elementary School shooting in Newtown, Connecticut ("Moms Demand Action," n.d.). It now has a chapter in every state and has been the center of advocacy to reduce gun violence. Mothers aren't the only ones taking on this issue, however. After the shooting of 14 students and 3 staff members at Marjory Stoneman Douglas High School in Parkland, Florida, March for Our Lives, a student group, organized a walkout of schools and a protest in Washington, D.C. (Gomez & Jackson, 2018).

Groups that work to reduce gun violence have had some successes. For example, Moms Demand Action pressured Starbucks to stop allowing customers to carry concealed weapons. It also advocated for Facebook to stop allowing illegal gun sales on its platform. In 2016, the group's #groceriesnotguns campaign sought to stop Kroger supermarkets from allowing customers to openly carry guns in their stores ("Tell Kroger," n.d.).

Leadership in gun policy is also being shaped by female governors (Turcotte, 2018). For example, Kate Brown of Oregon has signed legislation prohibiting those convicted of domestic violence or stalking from buying a firearm. Also, Rhode Island governor Gina Raimondo has signed legislation prohibiting those who have "red flag" indicators of violence, including making threats of violence in person or on social media, from buying guns.

Reproductive Justice

As we saw in Chapter 9, the reproductive justice movement supports the rights of women to either have or not have children and to parent the children they do have in safe and healthy environments (Ross & Solinger, 2017; Silliman, Fried, Ross, & Gutierrez, 2004). Reproductive justice is inherently linked to other movements that advocate for social justice and basic human rights, as Figure 14.1 shows. Basic human rights were first articulated in 1948 in the Universal Declaration of Human Rights (United Nations General Assembly, 1948). These include civil and political rights such as the rights to vote, assemble, and be treated without discrimination. They also include economic and social rights, such as the rights to a living wage and access to food, shelter, education, and safety. Women working in the reproductive justice framework advocate for economic equality, environmental safety, and an end to violence against all women (Ross & Solinger, 2017; Silliman et al., 2004).

There has been substantial grassroots activism in the reproductive justice movement. For example, the Asian Community for Reproductive Justice worked with environmental advocate groups to close a toxic waste plant in Oakland, California in 2001 (Asian Communities for Reproductive Justice, 2005). The group also advocated to decrease the amount of toxins that workers are exposed to as nail salon staff. The Mothers Milk Project has worked with Native American women to reduce environmental toxins that can make their way into breastmilk (Silliman et al., 2004). Another group, Forward Together, sponsored the Strong Families movement, which is dedicated to helping families thrive. Members have worked to document the negative effects of incarceration on families and have started a collection of art projects focusing on the rights of transwomen of color. In 2011, Strong Families started the celebration of Mamas Day in order

FIGURE 14.1 The intersectionality of reproductive justice. The reproductive justice movement advocates for women to be able to freely make decisions about if, when, and with whom to have children. It also focuses on the need to raise children in a safe and healthy environment. In order to achieve these goals, this movement is closely aligned with many other social justice movements.

Note. Adapted from Lerum (2010).

to represent women who aren't traditionally depicted in Mother's Day cards. On mamasday.org, a person can get a free e-card with beautiful images of diverse women and their families. This organization has also worked locally in states such as New Mexico on campaigns that include reducing abortion stigma and advocating for affordable health care and paid sick days for city workers.

Environmentalism

Ecofeminism is a hybrid movement in which both environmental and feminist concerns are seen as connected to patriarchy. Regardless of whether they identify as ecofeminists, feminist activists are often at the forefront of environmental movements. For example, in 2016, Native American women led a movement to stop the Dakota Access Pipeline from running through North Dakota (Walker, 2016). They were concerned that this pipeline would disturb sacred lands, contaminate the Missouri River, and fuel climate change. Protests took place for months during the summer and fall of 2016, and by October 2016 there were thousands of protestors and 140 protesters had been arrested (Yan, 2016). The protests were ultimately unsuccessful, as the pipeline opened in January 2017 under executive order of President Donald Trump, and by June 2017 there had already been an oil spill (Visser, 2017).

Other environmental activists are working on a variety of projects, including cleaning waterways to help salmon migrate, helping undocumented immigrants who have suffered in wildfires in California, and providing support to transgender individuals who have been impacted by natural disasters (Lewis, 2018). Activists also work on legislation. In New York, The Climate Community and Protection Act would move the state toward 100% renewable energy, and resources would be equitably shared with disadvantaged communities. In Seattle, Got Green, an environmental advocacy group, successfully passed a law diverting money from taxes on sugary drinks to programs that reduce food insecurity (gotgreenAdmin, 2017).

try it for yourself

Even though many women are at the center of activist movements, their roles often get erased from the narratives. Find a social activist movement in history that interests you, and research the roles of women in that movement. How hard do you have to work to learn about the women's roles? Have their roles been overlooked or minimized in the common narratives?

Environmental activism takes place across the globe. In India, Suryamani Bhagat is a grassroots environmental activist who founded the Jharkhand Save the Forest Movement to enable Indigenous people to manage their own forests. The techniques of reforestation are influenced by both Indigenous wisdom and scientific knowledge. Women are considered to be especially important in this work as they are seen as healers with particular knowledge of the forest. Through the work of this organization, forests around 45 villages have been slowly re-growing (Global Greengrants Fund, 2015).

At the same time, though, some women at the forefront of global environmental activism have experienced harassment. Bhagat, for example, has been subject to verbal harassments and threats. In Indonesia, a prominent environmental activist named Aleta Baum was forced to flee her home for a year because of death threats (Win, 2014).

Joys and Perils of Activism

What are the advantages and disadvantages of engaging in activism, and why is self-care important?

Activism often starts out of necessity. For example, when a person feels threatened, activism becomes a way to channel anger into action and transform helplessness into empowerment. In one study, researchers found that a sample of mostly White college students with disabilities reported learning self-advocacy as children because of the constant need to deal with discrimination and stigma (Kimball, Moore, Vaccaro, Troiano, & Newman, 2016). These students subsequently drew on their early lessons to engage in college-wide activism about disability rights as well as other issues. Certain popular political movements, such as the Chicano Movement, the Arab Spring, and Black Lives Matter, have been energized by young people affected by systemic racial/ethnic inequalities (Hope, Keels, & Durkee, 2016). In this context, several studies have shown that when Latinx and Black college students have more awareness of political disadvantages and experience incidents of racism, they're more likely to participate in activism as a way to adaptively cope and actively resist (Cronin, Levin, Branscombe, van Laar, & Tropp, 2012; Hope & Jagers, 2014; Szymanski, 2012; Szymanski & Lewis, 2015).

Activism can help people feel empowered by seeing themselves as part of a group, working in solidarity with others, and promoting change (Drury, Cocking, Beale, Hanson, & Rapley, 2005). In one study of largely White college students, those who engaged in activism had higher levels of well-being, including a greater sense of meaning in life and a sense of hope (Klar & Kasser, 2009). However, some types of activism have more positive psychological effects than others. For example, another study investigated the mental health of primarily Asian and White undergraduate women who either did or did not tweet about their experiences of sexism (Foster, 2015). Those who tweeted had increased psychological well-being; the researcher suggested that tweeting may increase well-being because it has the potential to reach a wide audience. Another benefit is that it may be less likely to result in retaliation than, say, directly reporting an incident of sexual harassment.

This poster was designed for the Women's March on Washington, which took place the day after the U.S. presidential inauguration in 2017. Many people consider this march to be a key part of a resurgence in feminist activism.

Tweeting about social issues has been criticized as a sign of being less engaged (referred to as slacktivism) than doing in-person activism. However, activists often use social media as a way of fighting back against sexism experienced both on- and offline, using Tumblr posts, YouTube videos, and personal blogs to document their own experiences of sexual assault, harassment, or being slut-shamed (Rentschler, 2014). Social media can also serve to connect activists with other like-minded individuals. For example, the Me Too movement gained prominence when the #MeToo hashtag was popularized in 2017. This allowed women who had experienced sexual assault or harassment to find solidarity with other women. It also increased awareness of the extremely high frequency of sexual assault while decreasing the stigma associated with discussing it (Jayson,

2017). However, as we discussed in Chapter 10, some people who had experienced sexual trauma found the constant reminders of trauma to be triggering rather than empowering (LaMotte, 2017).

The way discrimination is perceived can play a role in whether acting against it can be beneficial or harmful. In one study, researchers found that predominantly White undergraduate women who saw gender discrimination as a pervasive and ongoing problem had increased well-being if they talked with other people about it or informed the media (Foster, 2014). However, if they saw the discrimination as an isolated event, they reported greater well-being if they didn't report it—probably, the researcher suggested, because reporting was seen as more of a hassle than not reporting. Activism can also elicit negative responses and retaliation. For example, when a group of faculty complained about the removal of contraceptives from their health-care plan at Belmont Abbey College, a Catholic school, their names were mentioned in an email about the case sent to all faculty from the university president (Stripling, 2009). This had negative social repercussions for those faculty members who had complained and was considered retaliation by the U.S. Equal Employment Opportunity Commission.

When people become highly active in social justice causes, including feminism, they run the risk of developing physical or psychological problems associated with overwork and disillusionment. In one study, researchers interviewed social justice activists who had suffered from symptoms of burnout (Chen & Gorski, 2015). These individuals reported physical and psychological health problems such as insomnia due to worrying about what needed to be done, physical health problems linked to exhaustion, and depression and anxiety linked to a sense of hopelessness and despair. One activist noted, "You can start to think that what you're doing makes no difference . . . and you kind of move into despair" (p. 376).

your turn

Do you know anyone who's engaged in activism? Do you engage in any activism yourself? Do you know any activists who have experienced signs of burnout? How have activists you've known tended to their own self-care?

The same study found that burnout was related to infighting among fellow activists (generally about who was getting credit for the work being done), increased sensitivity to injustice, and a lack of personal self-care (Chen & Gorski, 2015). Participants reported a culture of selflessness in which self-care was perceived as a sign of privilege and people felt guilty for engaging in it. In a study of Black queer college-student activists, researchers found that burnout was related to experiencing multiple sources of discrimination, feeling a lack of social support, and not engaging in self-care (Vaccaro & Mena, 2011).

Ideally, activists can make time and locate resources to get adequate sleep, eat well, exercise, and find a supportive community to confide in, whether in person or online (Khan, 2015). Activists can also benefit from anticipating resistance by being prepared for negative comments and backlash (whether online or in person) in order to reduce frustration and disappointment when such resistance occurs (Gorski, 2015). Research has shown that activists can benefit from a practice that incorporates mindfulness, such as meditation or yoga (Gorski, 2015). This practice enables them to stay calm and focused in stressful situations, to slow down and see the big picture, and to engage in self-care without feeling guilty for doing so.

Psychology and Activism

How do psychologists promote social justice?

On April 22, 2017, more than 1 million people in 600 cities participated in a march to defend the role of science in society (marchforscience.com). This march was purposely labeled a celebration, rather than a protest, because of a fear that scientists would be seen as a special interest group rather than as a group of objective professionals (Marcus & Oransky, 2017). In the past, some scientists had expressed concern that their scholarship and careers might be called into question if they appeared to have a political agenda (Benderly, 2015). However, scientists who wish to advocate for public policy may not need to worry about their credibility as much as they might have thought. For example, participants in one experiment were shown one of six different statements made by a fictional climate scientist on a Facebook page and were asked to rate the extent to which they found him credible and trustworthy (Kotcher, Myers, Vraga, Stenhouse, & Maibach, 2017). Some of the statements were policy neutral and simply stated facts; others advocated for a specific policy position. The credibility of this fictional climate scientist wasn't influenced when he advocated for specific policy positions. The authors concluded that scientists who wish to engage in advocacy could do so without negatively impacting their credibility with the public.

Today, many scientists do believe that if they want to effectively communicate important findings to the public and promote policy change, they have to be more

spotlight on . . .

Getting Involved

There are many ways to engage in social activism at individual, local, national, and global levels. If you're interested in doing so, some examples include

1. Talking to friends and family about what you've learned in this class and engaging in debate if necessary.

2. Combating everyday sexism by confronting it when you see it and/or by posting in the everyday sexism project (everydaysexism.com).

3. Getting involved in activism on campus—either by joining an existing feminist group on campus or by starting one yourself.

4. Taking care of yourself. You can't help others if you don't help yourself.

5. Conducting research that addresses individuals who have been historically marginalized within psychology, discussing this research with other people, and sharing your findings with the general public.

6. Voting for government officials who support policies that would benefit the lives of women and members of other oppressed groups. These can be on the local, state, or national level.

7. Campaigning for those officials to raise awareness about policies that would benefit women and members of other marginalized groups.

8. Running for leadership positions on campus and/or in community or professional organizations you're part of—or even running for local, state, or national government positions.

9. Donating time to community organizations that focus on social justice goals.

active and engaged in communities (Hernandez, 2017). They have concluded that science and activism can be complementary. Especially when scientists discover inequities that directly influence people's lives, they may feel compelled to act. For example, it was the scientific knowledge gathered by Virginia Tech professor Marc Edwards, along with the active persistence of concerned mother LeeAnne Walters, that exposed toxic levels of lead in the public water supply of Flint, Michigan (McQuaid, 2016). Despite receiving hundreds of complaints from residents about the poisoned water, it took the power of science combined with activism to actually capture national attention and begin to hold city officials accountable.

As part of the scientific community, some psychologists use research to advance social justice goals. In Chapter 1, we discussed the doll studies of Mamie and Kenneth Clark (Clark & Clark, 1947). Their studies were a key part of the case *Brown v. Board of Education*, the 1954 U.S. Supreme Court ruling that led to the desegregation of public schools in the United States. More recently, psychological science was central to the public debate over marriage equality. During the *Hollingsworth v. Perry* federal court cases on same-sex marriage in California, psychological research played a critical role in convincing jurors to rule in favor of same-sex marriage (Fingerhut & Peplau, 2013). These examples show the power of psychological science to promote change.

Changing Academic and Professional Fields: Increasing Women's Participation in STEM

As we saw in Chapter 2, women are under-represented in STEM fields (Ceci & Williams, 2011). Psychologists have identified numerous factors that may contribute to this and have suggested interventions that may boost women's participation. Many organizations are applying this research to help girls and women in STEM. For example, psychological research suggests that simply understanding that stereotype threat exists can help to reduce it (Johns, Schmader, & Martens, 2005), as can doing self-affirmations of one's strengths and values before taking a test (Martens, Johns, Greenberg, & Schimel, 2006). Further, being exposed to female experts in math, science, and engineering has been shown to increase women's sense of comfort with and participation in STEM fields (Stout, Dasgupta, Hunsinger, & McManus, 2011). This research suggests that role models in STEM fields can provide **stereotype inoculation**— in other words, they can protect people from negative stereotypes about their social group by acting as a "social vaccine" (Dasgupta, 2011, p. 231). Female role models can help girls and women see that they can be successful in math and science even though others may view those fields as masculine domains.

As we saw in Chapter 3, some universities are working to create environments that encourage women to participate in STEM. For example, we mentioned the strides that Harvey Mudd College has made to increase women's participation in STEM. In addition, Carnegie Mellon University has applied the knowledge gained from research to foster a welcoming environment for women and to increase female representation in STEM. By 2016, 48.5% of the school's computer science majors were women ("CMU's Proportion of Undergraduate Women," 2016). The school's philosophy, simply put, is that women need the same things as men to succeed. According to Lenore Blum, a computer science professor at Carnegie Mellon, "Women need the same things that have always been available to men—mentors, networks and role models, as well as friends who are also computer science majors" (Spice, 2014, para. 7).

your turn

What does the composition of students in STEM majors at your school look like? How does this compare to the demographics of the entire student body? What do you think are the best ways to increase women's participation in STEM fields? Is your school doing anything to address this issue?

In fact, research has shown that when women were working on engineering tasks in groups, women had more confidence and enjoyed the work more when the groups had equal numbers of women and men or when women were in the majority (Dasgupta, Scircle, & Hunsinger, 2015). They also talked more when they were in the majority. When women worked in groups where men were in the majority, first-year female students felt more anxious, and many women were less enthusiastic about pursuing engineering as a career.

Changing Public Opinion: Consciousness Raising among Young People

Psychologists are on the front lines in helping young people to develop activist voices. For example, in 2010, an organization called SPARK (Sexualization Protest: Action, Resistance, Knowledge) was founded by Deb Tolman and Lyn Mikel Brown, two psychologists who have extensively studied the sexualization of girls and how girls can act as social change agents. SPARK has initiated a number of actions designed to empower girls and women (see http://www.sparkmovement.org/spark-actions/). One campaign, undertaken in 2012, aimed to get the teen magazine *Seventeen* to include non-edited images of real girls instead of extensively Photoshopped images of models. *Seventeen* subsequently committed to using some non-models in the magazine (Krupnick, 2012). SPARK also advocated for Google to have more gender parity in the representation of those it features in "Google doodles." The organization's success with this campaign led it to partner with Google to add a feature to a Google Maps app that alerts users if they're near a place where a woman made history.

More recently, after conducting research on transgender youth of color, psychologist Anneliese Singh co-founded the Georgia Safe Schools Coalition and Trans Resilience Project. This coalition educates about and advocates for issues affecting LGBTQ students and families. In 2017, the group hosted the annual GSA Youth Summit to develop activism among students. Participants learned how to help Georgia's schools become safe and affirming environments for all students, regardless of sexual orientation or gender identity/ expression. Members of the coalition did this by educating LGBTQ students about their rights, helping them to develop anti-harassment and bullying policies at their schools, working with students to create and grow LGBTQ affinity groups, and advocating with students for trans-affirming language and facilities. Students who attended were also provided with resources to help them advocate for themselves—for example, how to explain to teachers and administrators about the Day of Silence or how to have conversations with parents about prom dates.

Changing Laws and Norms: Beatrice Wright's Legacy

Many scholars acknowledge that social psychologist Beatrice Wright's life's work was the catalyst for widespread social change for individuals with disabilities (Dunn & Elliott, 2005). When her book *Physical Disability: A Psychological Approach* was published in 1960, it was the first theory-driven psychological approach toward understanding the experiences of people with disabilities. In it, she compassionately documented the ways in which social stigma contributed to the decreased well-being and marginalization of people with disabilities. This work was influential in the development of federal legislation, including the Rehabilitation Act of 1973 and the Americans with Disabilities Act of 1990 (Dunn & Elliot, 2005). Because approximately 40 million Americans have a disability (12.8% of the population; Kraus, Lauer, Coleman, & Houtenville, 2018), these laws greatly improve the quality of life for a substantial portion of the population.

Wright's work was also influential in changing the language that psychologists, and others, use. Wright believed that the way psychologists describe people, in either devaluing or empowering ways, matters because language ultimately shapes how we think, feel, and act toward others (Dunn & Elliot, 2005). For example, she encouraged *client* over *patient* because *client* suggests that people are active collaborators, rather than passive recipients. Partly due to her work, it's now also normative to use a "placing the person first" approach— for example, saying "person with a disability" rather than "disabled person" (Wright, 1991).

This has actually led to formal changes within the field of psychology (Dunn & Elliot, 2005). For example, in 2001, the fifth edition of the *APA Publication Manual* clarified that psychologists should use the term *disability* to describe characteristics linked to an individual (e.g., "A person who is blind has a *disability*") and the term *handicap* to describe the consequences of stereotypic beliefs, laws, and the environment (e.g., "Wheelchair access to older buildings is *handicapped* by the absence of ramps"; American Psychological Association, 2001).

Today, Wright's legacy is evident in psychological research on human strengths as well as in sub-disciplines such as positive psychology (Dunn & Elliot, 2005). Psychologists exploring these topics don't solely focus on individuals' perceived deficits. Instead, they also seek to understand a person's strengths and sources of well-being and happiness. This holistic approach affirms human dignity and reduces bias and stigma by ensuring that the focus isn't disproportionately negative (Dunn & Elliot, 2005).

Psychologists Reaching Out

Psychologists also disseminate scientific findings. By doing so, they help legislators develop new laws, assist institutions in implementing socially beneficial policies and programs, and keep the public attentive to important social issues. For example, the American Psychological Association's Committee on Women in Psychology has spearheaded several task forces that have produced reports used by journalists, advocacy organizations, parents, and psychologists to create awareness and ignite change. These full reports, including *The Trafficking of Girls and Women* (2014) and *The Sexualization of Girls* (2007), can be accessed by the general public on the Committee website. Psychologists also write for popular websites, such as *Huffington Post*, and provide editorials for major newspapers, such as *The New York Times*. This allows important psychological findings to reach a widespread public audience.

The American Psychological Association also sponsors a Congressional Fellowship Program that facilitates pairing psychologists with a congressperson or congressional committee for a one-year staff position. In this role, they help draft legislation and assist in congressional hearings. Psychologists also oversee large research projects that inform policies. For example, those who advocate for high-quality, affordable child care can point to the results of a large longitudinal study conducted by psychologists at the National Institute of Child Health and Human Development that followed over 1,000 children from infancy until the ninth grade. One main finding is that the quality of early child care makes a difference in children's development (NICHD Early Child

Care Research Network, 2002). To date, almost 600 research publications have resulted from this one longitudinal study.

Some psychologists also act in collaboration with corporations so that psychological research informs their practices. For example, in Chapter 6 we talked about the Dove Real Beauty campaign. Nancy Etcoff, a clinical psychologist, was one of the researchers who worked with Dove to explore women's views of their bodies (Etcoff, Orbach, Scott, & D'Agostino, 2004). In a similar vein, Tomi-Ann Roberts, a social psychologist and co-originator of objectification theory, served as a consultant for the U by Kotex campaign, bringing her expertise as a researcher of objectification and sexualization as well as her knowledge of personal and cultural attitudes about menstruation (Roberts, 2016). It wasn't always a comfortable partnership, but she believes that "the advocacy work . . . despite its pitfalls, feels true to the feminist promise of our feminist theory [objectification theory]" (p. 292).

Psychologists do activism in less formal ways too. This is often referred to as street activism (Singh & Burnes, 2010)—they attend rallies, participate in community social justice groups, lobby for legislation, and provide self-care workshops for other activists. Psychologist Leonore Tiefer summed it up well when she said, "All you need to start a movement is to get a bunch of people talking together in a room" (Liebert, Leve, & Hui, 2011, p. 697). When psychologists bring their expertise to those conversations, the results can have a powerful, positive impact.

Have you ever "run to the noise," as Michelle Obama called for? What makes you more, or less, likely to do this? How would you explain to others the importance of "running to the noise"?

Conclusion: "Run to the Noise"

In her commencement address at Oberlin College in May 2015, Michelle Obama gave useful advice to college students about how to engage with conflict rather than avoid it. "Today, I want to urge you to actively seek out the most contentious, polarized, gridlocked places you can find . . . because so often, throughout our history, those have been the places where progress really happens—the places where minds are changed, lives transformed, where our great American story unfolds" (Cunningham, 2015, para. 2). Obama noted that students might be tempted to seek out only like-minded individuals, but she encouraged them to also seek out the opinions of those who differ from them: "You need to run to, not away from, the noise" (para. 6).

It can be difficult to engage with people who are different from you and/or who hold beliefs that you disagree with. You may have had difficult discussions in this class throughout the semester. You may also have discussed some of the course material with friends and family outside of class and found that they don't share your perspectives. This may have been hard, yet these tensions reveal opportunities for growth and change. As you finish this semester and consider what you've learned and how your beliefs have or have not been challenged, we encourage you to run to the noise. Talking with others about the issues you've learned about in this class, listening to other perspectives, and struggling with tensions might inspire you to engage in activism that aligns with your values.

We hope this book has helped you to understand the diversity of feminist perspectives and the psychology of women and gender. As you can see, this field encompasses many issues that need addressing. Exactly how to do that is complicated and not always clear-cut. Innovative theories and methods will help, and we are excited that you (yes, you) might be able to build on the ideas in this book.

Chapter Review

SUMMARY

The Future of Feminism: Challenges and Controversies

- There is no one experience of being a woman. Feminism continues to struggle with insufficiently recognizing the needs of women such as transwomen, women of color, and poor women.
- Men can be effective advocates for feminism, but when they advocate for feminism, they're often given more respect and credibility than women.
- Conflict among feminist perspectives continues to cause tension—for example, in intergenerational conflict.

Building Bridges: A Call for Allyship

- Through working as allies, people can come together across social identity groups to create positive social change.
- Becoming an ally is a process with the ultimate goal of joining with other people to advocate for social justice.

Feminist Activism: Changing Women's Lives

- Feminists have worked on a variety of social issues that both directly and indirectly connect to gender. These issues include increasing the minimum wage, achieving equality at work, reducing gun violence, advocating for reproductive justice, and improving the environment.

Joys and Perils of Activism

- Activism is often motivated by oppression. Activists can experience increased well-being, but they can also experience retaliation and burnout.

Psychology and Activism

- Psychologists and psychological researchers have been key in promoting change, both within and outside the discipline.

- Psychologists have advocated to increase women's participation in STEM, have worked with youth to bring awareness to issues such as the negative effects of objectification, and have sought to change laws and norms to create greater equality for those who have disabilities.
- Psychologists also work to disseminate scientific findings in a variety of contexts to improve the lives of all people.

KEY TERMS

allyship (p. 589)

stereotype inoculation (p. 602)

THINK ABOUT IT

1. How can you "run to the noise"? What are the opportunities and challenges associated with engaging in debates about feminism and in exploring some of the tensions discussed in this chapter and the book as a whole? What kinds of debates and conversations about these topics have you had with friends and family?

2. What do you believe are the most pressing social justice concerns? Spend some time exploring local, national, and global groups that address these issues. Are there any legislative priorities? If not, in what other ways is activism addressing these concerns? Look to see if psychological research can contribute to advancing a specific cause in that domain.

3. Reflect on this book. What issue do you think did not get enough coverage? Explore this issue in an academic search engine, and imagine you could add a section to this textbook. What would you say?

4. Imagine a friend asks, "What is psychology of women and gender?" How would you respond? How has this course changed the way you view psychology and society?

5. What are your thoughts about feminism and its role in society? Have your thoughts changed over the course of the semester?

ONLINE RESOURCES

- **Black Lives Matter** — information about the Black Lives Matter network and its efforts to establish dignity, justice, and respect: blacklivesmatter.com
- **Crunk Feminist Collective** — a space for hip-hop-generation feminists of color to discuss and debate ideas and to provide support in the struggle to identify shared feminist goals: crunkfeministcollective.com
- **Girls Globe** — a website aimed at connecting girls and women across the globe in order to educate and inspire people to take action on human rights, social justice, and gender equality: girlsglobe.org
- **Lachrista Greco** — Lachrista Greco is creator of the Guerrilla Feminism digital activist network; her website features links to her writing about activism and offers a digital activist library and information about guerilla feminism: lachristagreco.com
- **National Organization for Women** — highlights the activities of the largest U.S. grassroots feminist organization dedicated to a multi-issue and multi-strategy approach to women's rights: now.org

glossary

abstinence-only sex education: Programs teaching that abstaining until marriage is the only way to avoid pregnancy, STIs, and negative psychological consequences.

abstinence-plus sex education: Programs promoting abstinence as the most effective way to prevent pregnancy and disease but also including information about contraception and strategies for safer sex practices.

active constructive responding: A positive pattern of interacting that involves responding enthusiastically to a conversational partner and asking follow-up questions to prolong the conversation and sense of excitement.

affirmative consent: Mutual, explicit, voluntary, active consent that is given before a sexual act.

age concealment: Beauty work undertaken to hide the signs of aging and to be able to "pass" as younger than one's chronological age.

ageism: Prejudice related to a person's actual or perceived age.

agentic: A characteristic way of being, commonly associated with men, involving assertiveness, dominance, competitiveness, and acting to get things done.

agoraphobia: A type of anxiety related to being outside of the home or being in a public place.

allyship: A lifelong process in which individuals who are privileged develop relationships with individuals who are marginalized as a way to address social injustice.

ambivalent sexism: A form of sexism that includes the two related, but complementary, components of hostility and benevolence.

amplification: A technique that women can use in meetings to support each other: One woman repeats what another woman said and gives credit to the original speaker.

androcentric: Male-centered.

androgen-insensitivity syndrome (AIS): A condition in which testosterone is present but cannot connect with cell receptors. Individuals with AIS have XY chromosomes, no female-typical internal organs, and active testes.

anorexia nervosa: A disorder that involves self-imposed food restriction resulting in significantly reduced body weight, fear of gaining weight, and disturbance in how one's weight is perceived.

aromantic: A term used to describe a person who experiences little to no romantic attraction.

assisted reproductive technologies (ART): Techniques for treating infertility, including intrauterine insemination, in vitro fertilization, and surrogacy.

attachment fertility theory: A theory suggesting that early human survival was enhanced when women and men worked together to ensure the survival of their offspring.

attachment parenting: A style of parenting by which parents focus on meeting the child's needs on her or his schedule.

baby blues: The experience of crying, poor sleep, irritability, and anxiety after the birth of a baby.

backlash effects: The social and economic penalties that may be experienced when individuals violate gender stereotypes.

beauty norms: Shared standards for attractiveness, whether implicitly or explicitly stated, that are held by members of a given social group.

beauty work: Body modifications done to conform to social norms of attractiveness.

behavioral theories: A group of theories that emphasize how aspects of the environment influence behavior.

belief in a just world: The belief that most people get what they deserve.

benevolent sexism: A component of ambivalent sexism that consists of beliefs that girls and women should be treated differently than men because they are special and in need of protection.

bereavement: Grief associated with losing a relative or a close friend through death.

binegativity: A social stigma directed at bisexual people that can come from both heterosexuals and those who identify as lesbian or gay.

binge eating disorder: A disorder involving recurrent episodes of binge eating in which a person feels distressed and disgusted over each episode.

body dissatisfaction: The state of not feeling comfortable or satisfied with one's physical appearance.

body esteem: The degree to which people view their bodies positively.

body image self-consciousness: Body surveillance during sexual activity due to concerns about how one looks to a sexual partner. Also known as body image self-consciousness during physical intimacy.

body shame: An ongoing experience of negative emotions as a result of judging one's body as undesirable.

body surveillance: Viewing one's body from an observer's perspective and evaluating one's physical appearance.

borderline personality disorder (BPD): A disorder involving a poor sense of self including self-criticism, feelings of emptiness, and impairments in interpersonal relationships, including impaired empathy and intimacy.

borderwork: Activities, such as teasing about cooties or playing catch games, that reinforce the borders between girls' spaces and boys' spaces.

bridge work: Work, often part-time, obtained after retirement from one job that provides a transition between employment and full retirement.

bulimia nervosa: A disorder characterized by binge eating episodes, in which a person eats a great deal and feels out of control while doing so, and compensatory behavior, such as throwing up, exercising excessively, or using laxatives.

bystander intervention: Intervening when one witnesses a problematic situation.

castration anxiety: The fear that one's penis will be cut off; according to Freud, this occurs in young boys as part of the Oedipus complex.

casual sex: Sex that occurs outside of the context of a committed relationship.

childhood sexual abuse: Any sexual activity between an adult and a minor.

cisgender identity: Gender identification that matches the sex a person was assigned at birth.

coercive power: A type of power that leads survivors to think they will experience negative consequences if they do not comply with their abusers' demands.

cognitive developmental theories: Theories emphasizing that (a) children's understanding of gender goes through stages that correspond to the development of cognitive skills and (b) children are active participants in their attempt to understand and take on gender roles.

cognitive distraction: In the context of sex, a shift of focus from how a woman feels about what she's experiencing in the sexual encounter to worrying about how her partner perceives her appearance—also known as cognitive distraction during sex; more broadly, a shift to a secondary focus that interferes with one's ability to focus on the primary task, experience, or goal.

colorism: A preference for lighter skin that stems from a history of racism and greater privilege for those with light skin and/or those who are perceived as White.

coming out: A process by which LGBTQ individuals accept, appreciate, and inform themselves and others about their LGBTQ identity.

communal: A characteristic way of being, commonly associated with women, involving warmth, friendliness, concern for others, and emotional expressiveness.

comparable worth: The idea that jobs requiring the same education and skill and giving similar value should pay the same wage.

complex PTSD: A set of trauma responses described by survivors who faced ongoing, prolonged interpersonal violence during childhood and adolescence; symptoms include an inability to foster stable relationships, stress-related physical ailments, and difficulty maintaining boundaries and personal safety.

compliant sex: Sex that occurs when a person agrees to sexual acts that are actually unwanted.

comprehensive sex education: Programs that include communication and interpersonal skills training in addition to information about abstinence and contraception; sex and sexuality are framed as positive and healthy components of life.

compulsory heterosexuality: The idea that sexual preferences are formed through the social ideal of heterosexuality, ultimately leading girls and women to prioritize the sexual desires of men.

congenital adrenal hyperplasia (CAH): An inherited condition that causes the adrenal gland to over-produce androgens, which influences fetal genetic development and can also affect development later on.

consensually non-monogamous (CNM) relationships: Committed romantic relationships among partners who agree that they can have sexual and emotional commitments with other people.

conversion therapy: A form of therapy that seeks to change a client's sexual orientation from LGBQ to heterosexual; this type of therapy has been deemed harmful by the APA and is banned in some states.

co-rumination: Extensive discussing of problems and dwelling on negatives in conversation with another person.

cultivation theory: The idea that greater exposure to the media makes it more likely that the images seen there will seem realistic and believable.

cultural feminism: A type of feminism that focuses on the differences between women and men and views women's inequality as related to the lack of value placed on the unique experiences, perspectives, and qualities of women.

cultural spillover theory: The idea that widespread cultural support for violence leads to increased acceptability for violence in other aspects of life.

custodial role: Full-time, and often permanent, care and guardianship of a grandchild.

cyberbullying: Bullying through electronic communication such as texts, emails, social media posts, and the like.

cycle of abuse: A cycle within ongoing abusive relationships that consists of a tension-building stage, a violent episode, and a loving and contrition phase.

dating scripts: Lessons absorbed from popular culture that describe supposedly "normal" behaviors in the context of dating.

deinstitutionalization: The mass release of people from psychiatric hospitals in the latter half of the 20th century related to an increase in the use of psychiatric medications, concern for patients' rights, and decreased federal funding for inpatient care.

dependent personality disorder (DPD): A disorder characterized by traits such as fear of disagreeing with others and difficulty in making everyday decisions without reassurance.

dialectical behavioral therapy (DBT): A therapeutic technique developed for individuals diagnosed with borderline personality disorder that combines training in social skills, mindfulness, emotion regulation, and assertiveness.

differences perspective: The idea that women and men are more different than similar.

differential parental investment theory: A theory suggesting that women are more invested in their offspring than men because of women's greater contributions to parenting through gestation and breastfeeding.

discrimination: A form of prejudice that involves the unfair treatment of an individual on account of being part of a social group that is less powerful than the dominant group.

disenfranchised grief: Grief that cannot be expressed openly because the loss is not recognized or acknowledged by those around the bereaved individual.

disorders of sex development (DSD): The medical term, replacing *intersex*, that encompasses a variety of conditions in which chromosomal, gonadal, or anatomical features are not sex typical; some clinicians and researchers now define DSD as "differences of sex development" to address stigma concerns.

doing gender: Performing or enacting behaviors associated with a specific gender in day-to-day life.

domestic violence: Any abusive, violent, coercive, forceful, or threatening act by one member of a family or household toward another.

doula: A paid professional whose job is to support a mother during childbirth.

elder abuse: A single or repeated act, occurring within the context of a trusting relationship, that causes harm to a person over the age of 60.

elderspeak: A pattern of speaking aimed at older adults characterized by simplified speech, a high pitch, and an exaggerated tone similar to baby-talk.

Electra complex: A version of the Oedipus complex for girls: Girls love their fathers, resent their mothers, and experience penis envy and can only resolve these conflicts by accepting the inferior status of femininity.

emotion work: Tasks that make others feel loved and cared for.

emotional social support: Support that enables us to feel nurtured and/or cared for by others.

empowerment: The capacity to attain power.

empty-nest syndrome: The experience of depression, loneliness, identity crisis, or emotional distress after children leave the home.

ethic of care: A moral perspective that considers how a given action will affect interpersonal relationships and the well-being of others.

ethic of justice: A moral perspective based on abstract principles of right and wrong.

ethnocentrism: The tendency to judge other groups according to the values of one's own group.

expectancy role value theory: A theory suggesting that people make decisions about the activities they want to pursue based on both the expectation that doing the activity will lead to success and the value they put on the activity.

face-ism: A tendency to have greater facial prominence (i.e., a larger proportion of the image devoted to the face) in depictions of men, while body prominence is more typical in images of women.

family caregiving: Unpaid assistance provided to an older adult or an adult with chronic or disabling conditions.

fat talk: Negative body talk, usually in informal conversations, in which people, typically girls and women, express dissatisfaction with their bodies, especially in terms of weight or body size/shape.

feminism: A movement to end sexism, sexist exploitation, and oppression.

feminist epistemologies: Ways to critique and produce methods of creating knowledge that attempt to address biases against certain groups of people, including girls and women.

feminist psychology: A perspective within the field of psychology in which work is explicitly informed by feminism, in contrast to more general research and theory about girls and women; feminist psychology is an explicitly political perspective because it aims to advance social justice.

5-alpha reductase deficiency: A condition in which individuals have XY chromosomes but lack sufficient quantities of the enzyme 5-alpha reductase, so they're unable to convert testosterone into dihydrotesterone and, therefore, cannot masculinize their external genitalia in utero.

gender constancy: The understanding that even if a change in physical appearance takes place, a girl will still be a girl and a boy will still be a boy.

gender deviance neutralization: The idea that when people act in a way that's gender atypical in one domain, they overcompensate by acting in a gender-stereotypical way in another domain.

gender dysphoria: A disorder diagnosed when individuals express a strong desire to be treated as a gender different from the one they were assigned at birth.

gender essentialism: The idea that men and women are fundamentally different because of deep and unchanging properties that are generally due to biology or genetics.

gender expression: The external manifestation of a person's gender identity, which may or may not conform to the socially defined behaviors and external characteristics that are considered to be masculine or feminine.

gender identity: One's understanding of oneself as gendered, based on a fundamental sense of belonging to a sex/gender category regardless of sex assignment at birth.

gender intensification: The process during puberty in which girls and boys start to more rigidly enact their gender roles.

gender labeling: The ability to say whether someone is female or male.

gender microaggressions: Brief, everyday acts of sexism, whether intentional or unintentional, that demean and insult a person based on that individual's gender.

gender rigidity: A sense of inflexibility in terms of what girls and boys are supposed to do.

gender roles: The behaviors within a culture that are generally considered acceptable or desirable for a person based on that individual's actual or perceived sex.

gender schema theory: A cognitive theory that focuses on how, in developing an understanding of themselves, children integrate their network of assumptions about how people with different genders are supposed to think, feel, and act (i.e., their gender schema).

gender segregation: The tendency for children to segregate on the basis of actual or perceived gender identity.

gender socialization: The internalization of the social expectations and attitudes associated with one's perceived gender.

gender stratification hypothesis: The idea that differences found between women and men (especially on cognitive skills) relate to the level of gender equality in a country.

gender transitioning: For transgender individuals, the process of publicly demonstrating one's gender in both appearance and behavior.

gender-based violence: Violence that is motivated by anger, hatred, or bias because of a person's gender.

gender-fair language: The use of symmetrical linguistic forms and inclusive terms (e.g., *they* instead of *he*; *first-year student* instead of *freshman*) to refer to all people.

generalized anxiety disorder: A disorder that involves chronic debilitating worry about many aspects of life.

glass ceiling: An invisible barrier that keeps many women from rising to the highest levels of leadership.

glass cliff: The tendency for women to be promoted to leadership positions when a company is in a precarious position or at risk for failure.

glass escalator: The tendency for men to be promoted to leadership positions very rapidly when they work in traditionally female-dominated fields.

goal congruity perspective: The idea that people want to engage in activities that meet their goals.

hate crime: A crime that is motivated by bias.

heteronormativity: The idea that people fall into two distinct, or binary, sex categories (M or F), that those categories have aligning gender roles (male or female), and that sexual desires are most naturally linked to the other sex.

heterosexism: A bias that assumes all people are heterosexual (at least until proven otherwise) and that it is more desirable to be heterosexual.

heterosexist harassment: A form of harassment that involves expressing a negative view toward sexual minority identities (gay, lesbian, bisexual) whether or not the target of the harassment identifies as a member of a sexual minority group.

hidden curriculum: The ways in which the school environment indirectly teaches norms, beliefs, and values.

historical trauma: Unresolved grief that affects an individual or a group in successive generations of those who have suffered significant trauma.

hookup: Sexual activity between two people with no expectation of commitment, although there is disagreement as to exactly what activities constitute hooking up.

horizontal occupational gender segregation: The tendency for women and men to cluster in different professions.

hostile sexism: A component of ambivalent sexism that consists of negative and derogatory beliefs about girls and women.

hostile work environment: A form of harassment that occurs when the atmosphere at a workplace is hostile, intimidating, and/or offensive.

hysteria: The first mental illness associated with women and associated with reproduction, sexuality, or traditional femininity at different points in history.

identity-based bullying: Aggression directed toward people who are actual or perceived members of a devalued social group because of that group membership.

imperialism: A practice that extends a country's power through either diplomacy or war, or both.

in vitro fertilization (IVF): A treatment for infertility by which egg production is stimulated, several eggs are extracted, the egg is fertilized with sperm outside of the body, and one or more embryos are implanted after fertilization has taken place.

infertility: An inability to become pregnant after 12 months of regular unprotected sexual intercourse.

informational social support: Support that involves others giving advice or ideas to help us find strategies or resources to better cope with life events.

instrumental social support: Support that involves others providing us tangible assistance in terms of money, goods, or services.

intensive parenting: The idea that parents, especially mothers, are expected to be fully immersed in the parenting experience, seek expert advice on how to parent, engage their children in cognitively stimulating activities in order to ensure optimal brain development, and feel ultimately fulfilled in their role.

intermittent labor: In terms of household labor, tasks that are done only occasionally and for which there's usually some leeway as to when they need to get done.

internalization: The process of taking on the standards and norms of dominant society as one's own and then striving to meet those standards.

internalized biphobia: See *internalized homophobia.*

internalized heterosexism: See *internalized homonegativity.*

internalized homonegativity: The internalization of negativity about one's sexual minority identity. See also *internalized biphobia, internalized heterosexism,* and *internalized homophobia.*

internalized homophobia: Among some individuals who are uncomfortable with their sexual orientation, internalized feelings of negativity toward being LGBQ. Also called *internalized biphobia.* See also *internalized heterosexism* and *internalized homonegativity.*

internalized transphobia: The internalization of negative messages about transgender people by someone who identifies as transgender.

interoceptive awareness: Awareness of one's internal physiological signals.

intersectionality: The ways in which different types of oppression (e.g., racism, classism, homophobia, transphobia, ableism, sexism) are interconnected and, therefore, cannot be examined separately; also the way multiple social identity variables influence any psychological variable being studied.

intersex: A term used to describe a wide variety of conditions in which chromosomal, gonadal, or anatomical features are not sex typical.

intimate partner violence (IPV): A form of domestic violence involving violence by one member of an intimate couple against the other.

intrauterine insemination (IUI): A treatment for infertility by which washed and concentrated sperm are injected directly into the uterus at the time of ovulation.

intuitive eating: Eating in response to physiological cues of hunger and satiation rather than situational or emotional cues; also referred to as mindful eating.

Klinefelter syndrome (KS): A condition in which a person's chromosomal type has more than one X chromosome plus one or two Y chromosomes.

launching phase: The period during which children are in the process of leaving the parental home.

learned hopefulness: The belief that an abuser can change, which can contribute to survivors remaining committed to abusive relationships.

legitimizing myths: Attitudes, values, or beliefs that exist to justify social hierarchies.

leisure innovation: Engaging in new leisure activities as part of retirement.

lesbian feminism: A type of radical feminism that focuses on sexuality and reproduction as a central place of oppression.

LGBTQ: An acronym that identifies people with diverse gender and sexual minority identities; the letters refer to lesbian, gay, bisexual, transgender, and queer.

liberal feminism: A type of feminism that focuses on the similarities between women and men and on using government policies to eliminate barriers that keep women from achieving their potential.

low-control labor: In terms of household labor, tasks in which the person doing them has little control over where and when they're done. See also *routine labor*.

major depression: Feelings of sadness or emptiness, diminished pleasure in activities, negative thought patterns reflecting worthlessness or guilt, and physical symptoms such as fatigue, weight gain or loss, and excessive sleeping or insomnia.

male gaze: Visual attention to women's bodies that may come from a heterosexual man or that may represent internalization of the idea that women are sexual objects to be looked at.

marianismo: A concept that underlies the gender socialization of Latinx girls and women that encourages self-sacrifice and the repression of anger.

masturbation: Stimulation of oneself sexually, usually through touching one's genitals, to result in sexual pleasure.

mate retention behaviors: Controlling behaviors that serve to keep a partner away from potential rivals and ensure the partner's fidelity.

maternal gatekeeping: The process of mothers limiting how involved fathers are allowed to be in caring for children.

maternal wall: Discrimination that mothers experience in pay and promotion.

matrix of domination: The idea that all systems of bias (e.g., racism, homophobia, sexism) stem from the same systems of social stratification.

medical gaze: A process of dehumanization that occurs when medical providers treat a person's body separate from that person's sense of self.

medical model: A model that assumes mental health concerns are the result of physical problems that can be treated through medical intervention.

menarche: The first menstrual period.

menopause: The permanent end of menstrual periods, resulting from decreased hormone production in the ovaries.

mentor: A person with more experience who can help and guide someone with less experience.

militarism: The prioritization and justification of military values within both military and civilian life.

minority stress theory: The idea that having a marginalized identity carries additional social stressors that can worsen mental and physical health outcomes.

miscarriage: The experience of losing a pregnancy before the 20th week of gestation.

misgender: To use a pronoun that doesn't accurately reflect a person's gender identity.

misogyny: Hatred of girls and women.

model minority: The perception that a given minority group is an ideal example of a minority group—for example, the perception that Asian American students are hard-working, smart, and over-achieving.

modern sexism: Gender bias that is communicated in subtle or indirect ways.

monosexual: A term used to describe a person who is sexually attracted to only one sex/gender.

morning sickness: The experience of nausea and vomiting that many women experience during the first 12 weeks of pregnancy.

mother blaming: The idea that mothers should be held responsible for the actions, health, behavior, and well-being of their children.

motherhood mandate: The social pressure on women to become mothers.

motherhood wage penalty: The tendency for mothers to earn less than non-mothers do.

mujerista: An identity label that prioritizes the lives of Latinx women; mujeristas especially act toward the decolonization of all people.

multicultural competence: A therapeutic skill that involves recognizing how multiple, intersecting aspects of clients' social identities influence their lives; multiculturally competent therapists are keenly aware of the dangers of stereotypes and assumptions about universality of experience when working with clients.

myth of meritocracy: The perception that economic mobility is easily attainable through hard work.

name shifting: A strategy by which some individuals (usually women) use their surname in some situations (e.g., professional settings) and their spouse's name in other settings (e.g., familial situations).

networking: A process through which people interact with those in or connected to their social networks in order to make contacts who can help them further their careers.

neurosexism: Reinforcement or justification of gender stereotypes based on the claim that there are biologically based differences between women and men.

normative discontent: The idea that the normal state for women with respect to their bodies is to feel unhappy or dissatisfied.

objectification: The viewing of a person as an object to be looked at rather than as a human being inhabiting a skin.

objectification theory: The theory that women internalize the perspective of an observer as the primary way of viewing their bodies.

observational learning: Learning by watching what others do.

Oedipus complex: A stage at which, according to Freud, boys love their mothers and hate their fathers; the conflict is eventually resolved by learning to identify with the father.

operant conditioning: A process of learning that occurs through associating actions with consequences by receiving reinforcement (or rewards) or punishment.

oppression: The ways in which certain people experience degradation because of political, economic, or social realities (e.g., poverty, homelessness, lack of access to health care).

outercourse: Forms of sexual activity that don't involve penile-vaginal penetration; sometimes considered a means of contraception.

overt sexism: Unequal treatment of women that is identifiable and, therefore, easily documented.

panic disorder: A disorder involving panic attacks that appear unpredictably as well as fear about having panic attacks.

paternalistic chivalry: The idea that women should be protected and cherished—at least, as long as they conform to traditional gender roles.

paternity uncertainty: The notion that men can never be 100% sure that the offspring they raise are their own.

patriarchy: A social system in which men hold positions of authority and power.

penis envy: According to Freud, the envy that young girls experience when they realize that they do not have a penis.

performative bisexuality: A sexual script in which heterosexual women make out and engage in sexual activities with other women for the enjoyment of men who are watching them.

perimenopause: The few years before and the 12 months after a woman's last menstrual cycle.

physical abuse: Acts of physical force intended to cause physical pain.

pinkwashing: The highlighting of a company's or organization's concern for breast cancer by promoting pink or pink ribbon products.

plasticity: The ability of the brain to change to a certain degree in response to aspects of the environment and learning experiences.

pluralistic ignorance: The mistaken belief that one's own attitudes and behaviors are different from those of others.

polyamourous (poly) relationships: Consensual romantic and/or sexual relationships with multiple partners, with all partners having knowledge of the non-monogamous nature of the relationships.

polygamy: The practice of one husband having many wives.

positivism: The idea that science is progressive and cumulative and that it relies on objectivity, neutrality, and rationality.

post-abortion syndrome: A term used by anti-abortion advocates to describe a negative psychological reaction to abortion; research has not supported the existence of this syndrome.

post-colonial/transnational feminism: A type of feminism that connects women's inequality to the legacy of colonization and critiques the belief that women in Western countries are the most liberated in the world.

post-feminism: The idea that the women's movement has achieved its goals and, therefore, feminism is no longer needed.

post-partum anxiety: Feelings after the birth of a child that include worry, a sense of dread, obsessive checking, difficulty sleeping, and other physical symptoms such as dizziness, nausea, and headaches.

post-partum depression: Feelings of sadness, anxiety, exhaustion, guilt and worthlessness, and suicidal ideation lasting at least two weeks that can be experienced after giving birth.

post-traumatic growth: A positive psychological change that can occur following a struggle with highly challenging life circumstances.

post-traumatic stress disorder (PTSD): A disorder that occurs after directly experiencing or witnessing a shocking or frightening event; symptoms include re-experiencing the event through dreams or flashbacks, avoiding stimuli associated with the trauma, having a general sense of numbness, and physiological reactivity such as being easily startled or having insomnia.

postmenopause: The period beginning 12 months after a woman has had her last menstrual period (or has had an oophorectomy) and continuing until the end of the woman's life.

postmodern perspective: The idea that knowledge isn't objective; rather, it is constructed and, therefore, can change as a function of time, place, or culture.

prejudice: A negative attitude toward someone because of that person's actual or perceived membership in a certain social group.

pre-menstrual dysphoric disorder (PMDD): A disorder that is diagnosed when women have symptoms of depression that start before the onset of their period and end soon after the period is over.

principle of least interest: The idea that the person who wants a relationship less has greater power within that relationship.

privilege: The social, economic, and/or political advantages that some people enjoy simply because they're part of a certain group, rather than because of anything they did or failed to do.

psychoanalytic theories: A group of theories based on the underlying idea that gender development (and personality development in general) is controlled by unconscious forces.

psychological abuse: A type of abuse in which perpetrators act in ways that cause fear, shame, isolation, or deprivation; it can involve emotional and/or verbal abuse.

psychology of women: A subfield of psychology that focuses on the lives and experiences of girls and women.

queer feminism: A type of feminism that claims inequality is related to the ways in which the categories of woman and man have been constructed, studied, and used to organize society.

quid pro quo harassment: A form of harassment that occurs when a supervisor requests sexual favors in exchange for workplace benefits, such as a raise or a promotion, or to prevent negative events, such as being fired or demoted.

radical feminism: A type of feminism that views women's unjust treatment as the most fundamental form of oppression and that advocates for separatism.

rape: Penetration, no matter how slight, of the vagina or anus with any body part or object, or oral penetration by a sex organ of another person, without the consent of the victim.

rape myth: A false belief about how and why rape occurs.

reappropriation: The process of a person or group of people from a subordinate group intentionally reclaiming a slur that was previously used by a dominant group to oppress or stigmatize them.

relational aggression: Indirect forms of aggression that involve damaging others' existing or potential relationships and/or social status.

relative resources theory: The idea that the person who brings more resources to the relationship gets to use those resources to avoid doing chores.

reproductive justice movement: A feminist movement centering around four basic rights: (a) to have children, (b) to not have children, (c) to parent one's children in a safe, healthy environment, and (d) to express one's sexual and gender identity free from oppression and fear.

resiliency: The capacity to successfully adapt to trauma or stress.

restorative justice: Rehabilitation modeled on Indigenous peacemaking processes involving facilitated meetings between perpetrators and survivors, with the goal of achieving reconciliation and commitment to peace.

role enhancement theory: The idea that people experience an increase in energy and well-being when they are engaged in multiple roles (e.g., worker, mother, sister, friend) as a result of being so involved and engaged.

role loss hypothesis: The idea that parents, particularly mothers, will experience a decrease in well-being when their role as caregiver is no longer needed.

role strain relief hypothesis: The idea that parents, particularly mothers, will have an increase in well-being after children leave home because of a decrease in daily demands, time constraints, and work–family conflicts.

routine labor: In terms of household labor, tasks that must be done frequently on a regular schedule. See also *low-control labor*.

rumination: A tendency to obsessively mull over one's problems and all of the causes and consequences of the situation.

safe sex: Sex involving birth control, often condoms, in order to minimize the risk of STIs and pregnancy; sometimes referred to as safer sex.

sandwich generation: The group of individuals, primarily women, who are simultaneously caring for their children and their aging parents.

scapegoating: Blaming a person or a group for things that are not their fault.

second shift: The phenomenon of women coming home from their jobs and doing another round of work in the home.

self-fulfilling prophesy: The idea that expectations for how someone is going to behave influence that person's behavior so that the expectations are fulfilled, making the prophesy come true.

self-objectification: The process of turning the objectifying gaze on oneself in order to evaluate the extent to which one conforms to societal standards of beauty.

self-sexualization: Purposely engaging in behaviors or practices that are associated with sexualization (e.g., wearing push up-bras, entering wet T-shirt contests).

self-silencing: Women's inhibiting of self-expression in order to please another person, and their sacrificing of their own needs in order to maintain relationships.

self-socialization: Children's process of looking for clues about how to behave and integrating this information into an understanding of how one actually does behave.

sex positivity: The idea that all sexual expression and behavior is healthy as long as it is practiced with explicit consent from all parties involved.

sex trafficking: Commercial sex induced by force, fraud, or coercion.

sex work: An umbrella term that refers to the exchange of sexual services, performances, or products for compensation.

sex/gender binary: The idea that there are only two sexes, and that a person must be assigned a sex of either female (F) or male (M) that will align with a predictable gender.

sexism: A bias based on the belief that men are superior to women.

sexual agency: A sense of being comfortable with and in control of one's own sexuality.

sexual assault: A general term that refers to different types of sexual abuse, including rape, attempted rape, unwanted sexual touching, and/or sexual harassment.

sexual assertiveness: The ability to ask for what one wants and to refuse what one doesn't want within a sexual encounter.

sexual configurations theory (SCT): The idea that sexuality is multi-faceted, socially situated, and dynamic and can be best understood along a variety of dimensions.

sexual double standard: A perspective in which women are judged more harshly than men for engaging in comparable sexual behaviors.

sexual orientation: An individual's predisposition toward sexual and/or romantic attraction for persons of the same sex/gender (homosexual) and/or the other sex/gender (heterosexual).

sexual scripts: Descriptions of behaviors that constitute "normal" sexual behavior in a given culture.

sexual socialization: The process of learning about sexuality.

sexual strategies theory: A theory suggesting that women and men developed different mating strategies to ensure survival: Men maximized potential offspring through sexual activity with many women, while women were selective with sexual partners in order to find stable mates who would contribute resources to promote their children's survival.

sexualization: The imposition of sexuality on others, the consideration of people as sex objects, and/or the valuing of people merely for their sexual appeal or sexual behavior.

similarities perspective: The idea that women and men are more similar than different.

slut shaming: Criticism of girls and women for their actual or presumed engagement in sexual behaviors.

social comparison: Comparison of oneself to others to assess where one stands in relation to the standards and norms of dominant society.

social construction theories: Theories, based on a postmodern perspective, that focus on (a) how cultural beliefs about gender exist to uphold particular social and economic systems and inequalities, as well as (b) how to enact gender.

social exchange: The idea that economic models of trading goods and services apply to interpersonal relationships (e.g., if one member of a couple makes a lot of money, the other partner may do more housework).

social identity: A person's sense of self based on that individual's affiliations with different social groups.

social learning theories: Theories asserting that learning takes place in a social setting but that children do not need to be directly reinforced or punished in order to learn.

social mothers: Women who take on the motherhood role through social (rather than biological) means, including adopting, fostering, or becoming a stepmother.

social role theory: The idea that differences between women and men arise from the different roles they have traditionally held (e.g., caretaker, provider) rather than from biologically based differences passed down through evolutionary forces. Also known as *social structural theory.*

social stratification: A social structure by which people are ranked in a hierarchy such that some people and groups have more power and status than others.

social structural theory: See *social role theory.*

social support: A feeling of being cared for and having support and assistance from people around us, including family, friends, and romantic partners.

socialist feminism: A type of feminism that links gender oppression with capitalism.

specific phobia: Fear of a specific object or activity (e.g., spiders, hang gliding).

spectatoring: During sex, an "out-of-body" experience in which a woman's focus shifts to things other than the sexual encounter.

sponsor: A person who advocates for another person in order to help that individual get a job or a promotion.

stereotype: A set of beliefs about the characteristics of a particular group that are generalized to all members of that group.

stereotype embodiment theory: The idea that people learn age-related stereotypes at a young age, internalize them as self-stereotypes, and are subsequently influenced by them in thoughts and actions.

stereotype inoculation: The idea that identifying with role models who share one or more aspects of social identity can protect people from negative stereotypes about their social group within a specific context (e.g., in STEM fields).

stereotype threat: The idea that when people think their social group does poorly on a certain task (or think that others believe this is true), their anxiety about confirming that stereotype can actually undermine their performance.

sticky floor: The tendency for women to remain at the bottom of an organizational hierarchy in jobs that provide limited opportunities for advancement.

stigma awareness: For individuals with marginalized identities, a heightened fear of encountering future discrimination because of prior experiences with violence and discrimination.

stillbirth: The death of a fetus after the 20th week of gestation.

stranger harassment: Harassment of women in public places by men who are strangers.

strategic essentialism: The support of gender essentialist beliefs as a strategic choice to help advocate for social causes that uniquely affect large numbers of women.

stratified reproduction: The unequal situation in which those with more resources based on factors such as class, race, ethnicity, or migration status have greater autonomy and choice with regard to their ability to have and raise children.

structural inequalities: Specific laws and policies within organizations, institutions, and governments that give men (and members of other privileged groups) more resources and advantages than women (and members of less privileged groups).

surrogacy: A treatment for infertility in which one woman is contracted to bear a child for another woman.

tend-and-befriend coping strategy: An evolutionary theory of social support according to which women nurture and protect others in times of stress (i.e., tend) and develop social networks that can help facilitate these patterns (i.e., befriend).

tentative speech forms: Patterns of speaking that involve hedges (e.g., *mostly*), hesitations (e.g., *um*), tag questions (e.g., *right?*), and intensifiers (e.g., *very*).

terror management theory: The idea that because humans fear death, anything that reminds us that we are mortal and will die needs to be managed in a way that reduces our anxiety.

"think manager–think male" bias: The idea that the traits many people associate with leadership are agentic ones that are also associated with masculinity.

third world feminism: A type of post-colonial feminism that claims feminism should not focus on commonalities among women but, instead, should address issues from multiple perspectives and not assume a unified position.

time availability: The idea that the person with the most available time should do a larger proportion of housework.

token: A member of a socially marginalized group whose group makes up less than 15% of the workforce in a workplace setting.

token resistance: Saying *no* to sex but really meaning *yes*.

tonic immobility: An involuntary "frozen" body response that occurs in high-fear situations.

transformational leader: A leader who inspires others, stimulates optimism and excitement about the future of the organization, and focuses on mentorship.

transgender: A gender identity (woman, man, or other gendered identity labels) and/or a gender expression (feminine, masculine, or other gendered expressive labels) that doesn't conform to societal expectations for the sex a person was assigned at birth.

tripartite model of social influence: A model of the key factors that influence body image: parents, peers, and the media.

Turner's syndrome (TS): A condition in which a person has only 45 chromosomes and is missing the X sex chromosome; sometimes referred to as a chromosomal pattern of XO.

vertical occupational gender segregation: The tendency for men to hold positions with higher status, authority, and pay than women within any given field.

victim blaming: A type of blame that shifts responsibility away from the perpetrator and onto the survivor.

voluntary childlessness: The choice not to have children.

widowhood effect: The elevated risk of mortality following the death of a spouse.

womanist: An identity label that stems from the experiences of Black women and other women of color; the term encompasses feminism but differs because it doesn't prioritize sexism over other forms of oppression (e.g., racism).

womb envy: According to Karen Horney, men's envy of women's reproductive ability.

women of color feminism: A type of feminism that sees women's inequality as deeply linked to White supremacy, a form of racism in which White people are considered superior to people of color.

work–family conflict: A conflict that occurs when work interferes with family obligations or family life interferes with work.

work–family enrichment: A two-way process in which what happens at work benefits family life and what happens in the family benefits work.

references

Introduction

Artis, A. B. (2008). Improving marketing students' reading comprehension with the SQ3R method. *Journal of Marketing Education*, *30*, 130–137. doi: 10.1177/0273475308318070

Callender, A. A., Franco-Watkins, A. M., & Roberts, A. S. (2016). Improving metacognition in the classroom through instruction, training, and feedback. *Metacognition and Learning*, *11*, 215–235. doi: 10.1007/s11409-015-9142-6

Carlston, D. L. (2011). Benefits of student-generated note packets: A preliminary investigation of SQ3R implementation. *Teaching of Psychology*, *38*, 142–146. doi: 10.1177/0098628311411786

Dunlosky, J., & Rawson, K. A. (2012). Overconfidence produces underachievement: Inaccurate self evaluations undermine students' learning and retention. *Learning and Instruction*, *22*, 271–280. doi: 10.1016/j.learninstruc.2011.08.003

Immordino-Yang, M. H. (2016). *Emotions, learning, and the brain: Exploring the educational implications of affective neuroscience*. New York, NY: Norton.

Kornell, N., & Bjork, R. A. (2008). Learning concepts and categories: Is spacing the "enemy of induction"? *Psychological Science*, *19*, 585–592. doi: 10.1111/j.1467-9280.2008.02127.x

McDaniel, M. A., Howard, D. C., & Einstein, G. O. (2009). The read-recite-review study strategy: Effective and portable. *Psychological Science*, *20*, 516–522. doi: 10.1111/j.1467-9280.2009.02325.x

Robinson, F. P. (1941). *Effective study*. New York, NY: Harper and Brothers.

Symons, C. S., & Johnson, B. T. (1997). The self-reference effect in memory: A meta-analysis. *Psychological Bulletin*, *121*, 371–394. doi: 10.1037/0033-2909.121.3.371

Taraban, R., Rynearson, K., & Kerr, M. (2000). College students' academic performance and self-reports of comprehension strategy use. *Reading Psychology*, *21*, 283–308. doi: 10.1080/027027100750061930

Chapter 1

Adams, R. (2013, September 23). This is why it's more expensive to be a woman. *Huffington Post*. Retrieved from http://www.huffingtonpost.com/2013/09/23/beauty-products_n_3975209.html

Alexander, S., & Ryan, M. (1997). Social constructs of feminism: A study of undergraduates at a women's college. *College Student Journal*, *31*, 555–567.

American Association of University Women. (2017, Spring). *The simple truth about the gender pay gap*. Retrieved from http://www.aauw.org/aauw_check/pdf_download/show_pdf.php?file=The-Simple-Truth

American Psychological Association. (2009). *Publication manual of the American Psychological Association* (6th ed.). Washington, D.C.: Author.

Anderson, K. J. (2015). *Modern misogyny: Anti-feminism in a post-feminist era*. Oxford, United Kingdom: Oxford University Press.

Anderson, K. J., Kanner, M., & Elsayegh, N. (2009). Are feminists man haters? Feminists' and nonfeminists' attitudes toward men. *Psychology of Women Quarterly*, *33*, 216–224. doi: 10.1111/j.1471-6402.2009.01491.x

Anzaldúa, G. (2007). *Borderlands/La frontera: The new mestiza* (3rd ed.). San Francisco, CA: Aunt Lute Books.

Archibald, T., & Wilson, A. L. (2011). *Rethinking empowerment: Theories of power and the potential for emancipatory praxis*. Paper presented at the Adult Education Research Conference, Toronto, ON, Canada. Retrieved from http://newprairiepress.org/cgi/viewcontent.cgi?article=3127&context=aerc

Banks, K. H., Murray, T., Brown, N., & Hammond, W. P. (2014). The impact of feminist attitudes on the relation between racial awareness and racial identity. *Sex Roles*, *70*, 232–239. doi: 10.1007/s11199-014-0350-3

Bargad, A., & Hyde, J. S. (1991). Women's studies. *Psychology of Women Quarterly*, *15*, 181–201. doi:10.1111/j.1471-6402.1991.tb00791.x

Berman, J. (2015, February 2). Why that "Like a Girl" Super Bowl ad was so groundbreaking. *Huffington Post*. Retrieved from http://www.huffingtonpost.com/2015/02/02/always-super-bowl-ad_n_6598328.html

Bianchi, S. M., Sayer, L. C., Milkie, M. A., & Robinson, J. P. (2012). Housework: Who did, does or will do it, and how much does it matter? *Social Forces*, *91*, 55–63. doi: 10.1093/sf/sos120

Bobel, C. (2008). Resisting, but not too much: Interrogating the paradox of natural mothering. In J. Nathanson & L. C. Tuley (Eds.), *Mother knows best: Talking back to the "experts"* (pp. 113–123). Toronto, Canada: Demeter Press.

Boisnier, A. D. (2003). Race and women's identity development: Distinguishing between feminism and womanism among Black and White women. *Sex Roles*, *49*, 211–218. doi: 10.1023/A:1024696022407

Borecka, N. (n.d.). Entitlement and apathy, the case of women against feminism. *Lone Wolf Magazine*. Retrieved from https://lonewolfmag.com/women-against-feminism/

Brown, L. M. (2005). *Girlfighting: Betrayal and rejection among girls*. New York, NY: New York University Press.

Bryant, E. (2008, August 10). European nations offer incentives to have kids. *SFGate*. Retrieved from http://www.sfgate.com/news/article/European-nations-offer-incentives-to-have-kids-3201278.php

Burn, S. M., Aboud, R., & Moyles, C. (2000). The relationship between gender social identity and support for feminism. *Sex Roles, 42,* 1081–1089. doi: 10.1023/A:1007044802798

Butler, J. (1990). *Gender trouble.* New York, NY: Routledge.

Carr, M. D., & Wiemers, E. E. (2016, August). *The decline in lifetime earnings mobility in the U.S.: Evidence from survey-linked administrative data.* Washington, DC: Washington Center for Equitable Growth. Retrieved from http://equitablegrowth.org/working-papers/the-decline-in-lifetime-earnings-mobility-in-the-u-s-evidence-from-survey-linked-administrative-data/

Carroll, E. J. (1994, February). The future of American womanhood. *Esquire, 121*(2), 58–67.

Center for American Women and Politics. (n.d.). *Women in the U.S. Congress 2017.* Retrieved from http://www.cawp.rutgers.edu/women-us-congress-2017

Chatterji, P., & Markowitz, S. (2004). *Does the length of maternity leave affect maternal health?* (NBER Working Paper No. 10206). Retrieved from: http://www.nber.org/papers/w10206.pdf

Chrisler, J. C., de las Fuentes, C., Durvasula, R. S., Esnil, E. M., McHugh, M. C., Miles-Cohen, S. E., Williams, J. L., & Wisdom, J. P. (2013). The American Psychological Association's Committee on Women in Psychology: 40 years of contributions to the transformation of psychology. *Psychology of Women Quarterly, 37,* 444–454. doi: 10.1177/0361684313505442

Chronicle of Higher Education. (2015, August 21). *Almanac 2015–16.* Retrieved from http://www.icuf.org/newdevelopment/wp-content/uploads/2010/06/Chronicle-Almanac-2015-16.pdf

Clark, K. B., & Clark, M. P. (1947). Racial identification and preference in Negro children. In T. M. Newcomb & E. L. Hartley (Eds.), *Readings in social psychology* (pp. 602–611). New York, NY: Henry Holt.

Cohn, D., Livingston, G., & Wang, W. (2014, April 8). *After decades of decline, a rise in stay-at-home mothers.* Washington, DC: Pew Research Center. Retrieved from http://assets.pewresearch.org/wp-content/uploads/sites/3/2014/04/Moms-At-Home_04-08-2014.pdf

Cole, E. R. (2009). Intersectionality and research in psychology. *American Psychologist, 64,* 170–180. doi: 10.1037/a0014564

Cole, E. R., & Zucker, A. N. (2007). Black and White women's perspectives on femininity. *Cultural Diversity and Ethnic Minority Psychology, 13,* 1–9. doi: 10.1037/1099-9809.13.1.1

Collins, G. (2009). *When everything changed: The amazing journey of American women from 1960 to the present.* New York, NY: Little, Brown.

Comas-Diaz, L. (2008). 2007 Carolyn Sherif Award Address: Spirita: Reclaiming womanist sacredness into feminism. *Psychology of Women Quarterly, 32,* 13–21. doi: 10.1111/j.1471-6402.2007.00403.x

Crawford, M., & Kimmel, E. (1999). Promoting methodological diversity in feminist research. *Psychology of Women Quarterly, 23,* 1–6. doi: 10.1111/j.1471-6402.1999.tb00337.x

Crawford, M., & Marecek, J. (1989). Psychology reconstructs the female: 1968–1988. *Psychology of Women Quarterly, 13,* 147–165. doi: 10.1111/j.1471-6402.1989.tb00993.x

Crenshaw, K. (1993). Race, gender, and violence against women. In M. Minow (Ed.), *Family matters: Readings on family and the law* (pp. 230–232). New York, NY: New Press.

Crick, N. R., & Grotpeter, J. K. (1995). Relational aggression, gender, and social-psychological adjustment. *Child Development, 66,* 710–722. doi: 10.1111/j.1467-8624.1995.tb00900.x

Cundiff, J. L. (2012). Is mainstream psychological research "womanless" and "raceless"? An updated analysis. *Sex Roles, 67,* 158–173. doi: 10.1007/s11199-012-0141-7

Denmark, F., Russo, N. F., Frieze, I. H., & Sechzer, J. A. (1988). Guidelines for avoiding sexism in psychological research: A report of the Ad Hoc Committee on Nonsexist Research. *American Psychologist, 43,* 582–585. doi: 10.1037/0003-066X.43.7.582

Donovan, J. (2006). *Feminist theory: The intellectual traditions* (3rd ed.). New York, NY: The Continuum International Publishing Group.

Duesterhaus, M., Grauerholz, L., Weichsel, R., & Guittar, N. A. (2011). The cost of doing femininity: Gendered disparities in pricing of personal care products and services. *Gender Issues, 28,* 175–191. doi: 10.1007/s12147-011-9106-3

Eagly, A. H., Eaton, A., Rose, S., Riger, S., & McHugh, M. (2012). Feminism and psychology: Analysis of a half-century of research on women and gender. *American Psychologist, 67,* 211–230. doi: 10.1037/a0027260

Eagly, A. H., & Riger, S. (2014). Feminism and psychology: Critiques of methods and epistemology. *American Psychologist, 69,* 685–702. doi: 10.1037/a0037372

Eisele, H., & Stake, J. (2008). The differential relationship of feminist attitudes and feminist identity to self-efficacy. *Psychology of Women Quarterly, 32,* 233–244. doi: 10.1111/j.1471-6402.2008.00432.x

Eliezer, D., & Major, B. (2012). It's not your fault: The social costs of claiming discrimination on behalf of someone else. *Group Processes & Intergroup Relations, 15,* 487–502. doi: 10.1177/1368430211432894

Else-Quest, N. M., & Grabe, S. (2012). The political is personal: Measurement and application of nation-level indicators of gender equity in psychological research. *Psychology of Women Quarterly, 36,* 131–144. doi: 10.1177/0361684312441592

Enns, C. Z. (2004). *Feminist theories and feminist psychotherapies: Origins, themes, and diversity* (2nd ed.). New York, NY: Haworth Press.

Enns, C. Z., & Forrest, L. M. (2005). Toward defining and integrating multicultural feminist pedagogies. In C. Z. Enns & A. L. Sinacore (Eds.), *Teaching and social justice: Integrating multicultural and feminist theories in the classroom* (pp. 3–24). Washington, DC: American Psychological Association.

Etcoff, N. L., Stock, S., Haley, L. E., Vickery, S. A., & House, D. A. (2011). Cosmetics as a feature of the extended human phenotype: Modulation of the perception of biologically important facial signals. *PLoS ONE, 6*(10), e25656. doi: 10.1371/journal.pone.0025656

Faludi, S. (1992). *Backlash: The undeclared war against women.* New York, NY: Vintage.

Fillo, J., Simpson, J. A., Rholes, W. S., & Kohn, J. L. (2015). Dads doing diapers: Individual and relational outcomes associated with the division of childcare across the transition to parenthood. *Journal of Personality and Social Psychology, 108,* 298–316. doi: 10.1037/a0038572

Fine, C. (2010). *Delusions of gender: How our minds, society, and neurosexism create difference.* New York, NY: Norton.

Fine, M. (1994). Dis-stance and other stances: Negotiations of power inside feminist research. In A. Gitlin (Ed.), *Power and method: Political activism and educational research* (pp. 13–35). Abingdon, United Kingdom: Routledge.

Fine, M., & Roberts, R. A. (1999). Erika Apfelbaum 1979 revisited. *Feminism & Psychology, 9,* 261–265. doi: 10.1177/0959353599009003002

Fischer, A. R., & Good, G. E. (1994). Gender, self, and others: Perceptions of the campus environment. *Journal of Counseling Psychology, 41,* 343–355. doi: 10.1037/0022-0167.41.3.343

Fitz, C. C., Zucker, A. N., & Bay-Cheng, L. Y. (2012). Not all nonlabelers are created equal: Distinguishing between quasi-feminists and neoliberals. *Psychology of Women Quarterly, 36,* 274–285. doi: 10.1177/0361684312451098

Flood, M. (2011). Men as students and teachers of feminist scholarship. *Men and Masculinities, 14,* 135–154. doi: 10.1177/1097184X11407042

Franke-Ruta, G. (2013, November 22). Why is maternity care such an issue for Obamacare opponents? *The Atlantic*. Retrieved from https://www.theatlantic.com/politics/archive/2013/11/why-is-maternity-care-such-an-issue-for-obamacare-opponents/281396/

Freud, S. (1949a). *An outline of psychoanalysis* (J. Strachey, Trans.). New York, NY: Norton. (Original work published 1940)

Freud, S. (1949b). *Three essays on the theory of sexuality* (J. Strachey, Trans.). London, United Kingdom: Imago. (Original work published 1905)

Fried, C. (2016, July 11). Pink Tax Repeal Act aims to make pricing fair to women. *Consumer Reports*. Retrieved from https://www.consumerreports.org/shopping/pink-tax-repeal-act-aims-to-make-pricing-fair-to-women/

Friedan, B. (1963). *The feminine mystique*. New York, NY: Norton.

Friedman, C. K., & Ayres, M. (2013). Predictors of feminist activism among sexual-minority and heterosexual college women. *Journal of Homosexuality, 60*, 1726–1744. doi: 10.1080/00918369.2013.824335

Garza, A. (2014, October 7). A herstory of the #BlackLivesMatter movement. *The Feminist Wire*. Retrieved from http://www.thefeministwire.com/2014/10/blacklivesmatter-2/

Geiger, A., & Kent, L. (2017, March 8). Number of women leaders around the world has grown, but they're still a small group. *Pew Research Center*. Retrieved from http://www.pewresearch.org/fact-tank/2017/03/08/women-leaders-around-the-world/

Gibson, M. (2011, August 12). The "bra burning" Miss America protest. *Time*. Retrieved from http://content.time.com/time/specials/packages/article/0,28804,2088114_2087975_2087965,00.html

Gilligan, C. (1982). *In a different voice*. Cambridge, MA: Harvard University Press.

Golden, C. (2004). The intersex and the transgendered: Rethinking sex/gender. In J. C. Chrisler, P. D. Rozee, & C. Golden (Eds.), *Lectures in the psychology of women*. (3rd ed., pp. 94–109). New York, NY: McGraw Hill.

Grant, A., & Sandberg, S. (2015). Madam C.E.O., get me a coffee. *The New York Times*. Retrieved from http://www.nytimes.com/2015/02/08/opinion/sunday/sheryl-sandberg-and-adam-grant-on-women-doing-office-housework.html?_r=0

Gupta, P. (2014, October 7). Aziz Ansari: "I'm a feminist." *Salon*. Retrieved from http://www.salon.com/2014/10/07/aziz_ansari_im_a_feminist/

Haaken, J., & Yragui, N. (2003). Going underground: Conflicting perspectives on domestic violence shelter practices. *Feminism & Psychology, 13*, 49–71. doi: 10.1177/0959353503013001008

Hall, E. J., & Rodriguez, M. S. (2003). The myth of post-feminism. *Gender & Society, 17*, 878–902. doi: 10.1177/0891243203257639

Harcourt, W. (2012). Crossborder feminisms: Wendy Harcourt in conversation with Srilantha Batliwala, Sunila Abeysekera and Rawwida Baksh. *Development, 55*, 190–197. doi: 10.1057/dev.2012.12

Hare-Mustin, R. T. (2017). Those were the best of times, and then . . . *Women & Therapy, 40*, 346–357. doi: 10.1080/02703149.2017.1241574

Hare-Mustin, R. T., & Marecek, J. (1990). *Making a difference: Psychology and the construction of gender*. New Haven, CT: Yale University Press.

Henley, N. M. (2005, January 29). *Psychology's Feminist Voices oral history project interview with Nancy Henley/Interviewers: A. Rutherford & W. Pickren*. Retrieved from http://www.feministvoices.com/assets/Feminist-Presence/Henley/NancyHenleyTranxcript.pdf

Henley, N. M., Meng, K., O'Brien, D., McCarthy, W. J., & Sockloskie, R. J. (1998). Developing a scale to measure the diversity of feminist attitudes. *Psychology of Women Quarterly, 22*, 317–348. doi: 10.1111/j.1471-6402.1998.tb00158.x

Henrich, J., Heine, S. J., & Norenzayan, A. (2010). The weirdest people in the world? *The Behavioral and Brain Sciences, 33*, 61–83. doi: 10.1017/S0140525X0999152X

Herr, R. S. (2013). Third world, transnational, and global feminisms. In A. Doolin (Ed.), *Encyclopedia of race and racism* (2nd ed., pp. 190–195). New York, NY: Macmillan Reference USA.

Hochschild, A., & Machung, A. (1989). *The second shift: Working parents and the revolution at home*. New York, NY: Viking.

Holiday, J. M. (2010). The word, the body, and the kinfolk: The intersection of transpersonal thought with womanist approaches to psychology. *International Journal of Transpersonal Studies, 29*(2), 103–120. Retrieved from http://digitalcommons.ciis.edu/ijts-transpersonalstudies/vol29/iss2/10

hooks, b. (1994). *Teaching to transgress: Education as the practice of freedom*. New York, NY: Routledge.

hooks, b. (2000). *Feminism is for everybody: Passionate politics*. London, United Kingdom: Pluto Press.

Hudson, J. I., Hiripi, E., Pope, H. G., & Kessler, R. C. (2007). The prevalence and correlates of eating disorders in the National Comorbidity Survey Replication. *Biological Psychiatry, 61*, 348–358. doi: 10.1016/j.biopsych.2006.03.040

Hurt, M. M., Nelson, J. A., Turner, D. L., Haines, M. E., Ramsey, L. R., Erchull, M. J., & Liss, M. (2007). Feminism: What is it good for? Feminine norms and objectification as the link between feminist identity and clinically relevant outcomes. *Sex Roles, 57*, 355–363. doi: 10.1007/s11199-007-9272-7

Hyers, L. L. (2007). Resisting prejudice every day: Exploring women's assertive responses to anti-Black racism, anti-Semitism, heterosexism, and sexism. *Sex Roles, 56*, 1–12. doi: 10.1007/s11199-006-9142-8

I need feminism because. . . . (2013, February 17). *Lippy*. Retrieved from http://www.lippymag.co.uk/i-need-feminism-because/

I don't need feminism because I am not a disgusting hypocritical man-hater (n.d.). *Me.Me*. Retrieved from https://me.me/i/i-dont-need-feminism-because-i-am-not-a-dis-5371881

Isasi-Diaz, A. M. (1992). Mujerista theology's method: A liberative praxis, a way of life. *Listening, 27*, 41–54.

Isasi-Diaz, A. M. (1996). *Mujerista theology: A theology for the twenty-first century*. Maryknoll, NY: Orbis.

Keller, E. F. (1987). The gender/science system: Or, is sex to gender as nature is to science? *Hypatia, 2*(3), 37–49.

Kilmartin, C., & Smiler, A. P. (2015). *The masculine self* (5th ed.). Cornwall-on-Hudson, NY: Sloan.

Kohlberg, L. (1969). Stage and sequence: The cognitive-developmental approach to socialization. In D. A. Goslin (Ed.), *Handbook of socialization theory and research* (pp. 347–380). Chicago, IL: Rand McNally.

LaMantia, K., Wagner, H., & Bohecker, L. (2015). Ally development through feminist pedagogy: A systemic focus on intersectionality. *Journal of LGBT Issues in Counseling, 9*, 136–153. doi: 10.1080/15538605.2015.1029205

Leaper, C., & Arias, D. M. (2011). College women's feminist identity: A multidimensional analysis with implications for coping with sexism. *Sex Roles, 64*, 475–490. doi: 10.1007/s11199-011-9936-1

Léonie. (n.d.). I need feminism not because I hate men but because people think that's what being a feminist means [Pinterest post]. Retrieved from https://www.pinterest.com/pin/431853051746893158/

Levant, R. F. (2014). At 15 years, we've come a long way, baby. *Psychology of Men & Masculinity, 15*, 1–3. doi: 10.1037/a0035319

Liss, M., Crawford, M., & Popp, D. (2004). Predictors and correlates of collective action. *Sex Roles, 50,* 771–779. doi: 10.1023/B:SERS.0000029096.90835.3f

Liss, M., & Erchull, M. J. (2010) Everyone feels empowered: Understanding feminist self-labeling. *Psychology of Women Quarterly, 34,* 85–96. doi: 10.1111/j.1471-6402.2009.01544.x

Liss, M., Hoffner, C., & Crawford, M. (2000). What do feminists believe? *Psychology of Women Quarterly, 24,* 279–284. doi: 10.1111/j.1471-6402.2000.tb00210.x

Liss, M., O'Connor, C., Morosky, E., & Crawford, M. (2001). What makes a feminist? Predictors and correlates of feminist social identity in college women. *Psychology of Women Quarterly, 25,* 124–133. doi: 10.1111/1471-6402.00014

Lottes, I. L., & Kuriloff, P. J. (1994). Sexual socialization differences by gender, Greek membership, ethnicity, and religious background. *Psychology of Women Quarterly, 18,* 203–219. doi: 10.1111/j.1471-6402.1994.tb00451.x

Maine, M. (2000). *Body wars: Making peace with women's bodies.* Carlsbad, CA: Gürze Books.

Marcotte, A. (2015, February 23). Patricia Arquette's feminism: Only for White women. *Slate.* Retrieved from http://www.slate.com/blogs/xx_factor/2015/02/23/patricia_arquette_on_pay_equality_insulting_to_feminism.html

McCarter-Spaulding, D. (2008). Is breastfeeding fair? Tensions in feminist perspectives on breastfeeding and the family. *Journal of Human Lactation, 24,* 206–212. doi: 10.1177/0890334408316076

Mednick, M. T., & Urbanski, L. L. (1991). The origins and activities of APA's division of the psychology of women. *Psychology of Women Quarterly, 15,* 651–663. doi: 10.1111/j.1471-6402.1991.tb00437.x

Miller, D. T., Taylor, B., & Buck, M. L. (1991). Gender gaps: Who needs to be explained? *Journal of Personality and Social Psychology, 61,* 5–12. doi: 10.1037/0022-3514.61.1.5

Mohanty, C. T. (2003). *Feminism without borders: Decolonizing theory, practicing solidarity.* Durham, NC: Duke University Press.

Napikoski, L. (2017, September 30). Combahee River Collective. *ThoughtCo.* Retrieved from https://www.thoughtco.com/combahee-river-collective-information-3530569

National Women's Law Center. (2017, September). *The wage gap: The who, how, why, and what to do* (fact sheet). Retrieved from https://nwlc.org/wp-content/uploads/2016/09/The-Wage-Gap-The-Who-How-Why-and-What-to-Do-2017-2.pdf

Nelson, J. A., Liss, M., Erchull, M. J., Hurt, M. M., Ramsey, L. R., Turner, D. L., & Haines, M. E. (2008). Identity in action: Predictors of feminist self-identification and collective action. *Sex Roles, 58,* 721–728. doi: 10.1007/s11199-007-9384-0

Nicholson, L. (2010). Feminism in "waves": Useful metaphor or not? In C. McCann & S. Kim (Eds.), *Feminist theory reader: Local and global perspectives* (pp. 49–95). New York, NY: Routledge.

Norsworthy, K. L., & Khuankaew, O. (2013). Feminist border crossings: Our transnational partnership in peace and justice work. In J. A. Kottler, M. Englar-Carlson, & J. Carlson (Eds.), *Helping beyond the 50-minute hour: Therapists involved in meaningful social action* (pp. 222–233). New York, NY: Routledge/Taylor & Francis.

O'Connor, C., & Joffe, H. (2014). Gender on the brain: A case study of science communication in the new media environment. *PLoS ONE, 9,* e110830. doi: 10.1371/journal.pone.0110830

Orenstein, P. (2000). *Flux: Women on sex, work, love, kids, and life in a half-changed world.* New York, NY: Anchor Books.

Ossana, S. M., Helms, J. E., & Leonard, M. M. (1992). Do "womanist" identity attitudes influence college women's self-esteem and perceptions of environmental bias? *Journal of Counseling and Development, 70,* 402–408. doi: 10.1002/j.1556-6676.1992.tb01624.x

Parlee, M. B. (1975). Psychology. *Signs, 1,* 119–138. doi: 10.1086/493210

Phillips, L. (2006). Womanism: On its own. In L. Phillips (Ed.), *The womanist reader* (pp. xix–lv). New York, NY: Taylor & Francis.

Poindexter-Cameron, J. M., & Robinson, T. L. (1997). Relationships among racial identity attitudes, womanist identity attitudes, and self-esteem in African American college women. *Journal of College Student Development, 38,* 288–296.

Pope, K. S. (1993). Licensing disciplinary actions for psychologists who have been sexually involved with a client: Some information about offenders. *Professional Psychology: Research and Practice, 24,* 374–377. doi: 10.1037/0735-7028.24.3.374

Rampton, M. (2015, October 25). *Four waves of feminism.* Retrieved from http://www.pacificu.edu/about-us/news-events/three-waves-feminism

Rasinski, H. M., & Czopp, A. M. (2010). The effect of target status on witnesses' reactions to confrontations of bias. *Basic and Applied Social Psychology, 32,* 8–16. doi: 10.1080/01973530903539754

Reeves, R. V. (2017). *Dream hoarders: How the American upper middle class is leaving everyone else in the dust, why that is a problem, and what to do about it.* Washington, DC: Brookings Institution Press.

Reid, A., & Purcell, N. (2004). Pathways to feminist identification. *Sex Roles, 50,* 759–769. doi: 10.1023/B:SERS.0000029095.40767.3c

Reid, P. T. (1993). Poor women in psychological research. *Psychology of Women Quarterly, 17,* 133–150. doi: 10.1111/j.1471-6402.1993.tb00440.x

Riger, S. (1992). Epistemological debates, feminist voices: Science, social values, and the study of women. *American Psychologist, 47,* 730–740. doi: 10.1037/0003-066X.47.6.730

Ring, T. (2015, April 21). This year's Michigan Womyn's Music Festival will be the last. *The Advocate.* Retrieved from https://www.advocate.com/michfest/2015/04/21/years-michigan-womyns-music-festival-will-be-last

Rosenthal, E. (2013, June 30). American way of birth, costliest in the world. *The New York Times.* Retrieved from http://www.nytimes.com/2013/07/01/health/american-way-of-birth-costliest-in-the-world.html?_r=0

Rosette, A. S., & Tost, L. P. (2013). Perceiving social inequity: When subordinate-group positioning on one dimension of social hierarchy enhances privilege recognition on another. *Psychological Science, 24,* 1420–1427. doi: 10.1177/0956797612473608

Roy, R. E., Weibust, K. S., & Miller, C. T. (2007). Effects of stereotypes about feminists on feminist self-identification. *Psychology of Women Quarterly, 31,* 146–156. doi: 10.1111/j.1471-6402.2007.00348.x

Rudman, L. A., & Fairchild, K. (2007). The F word: Is feminism incompatible with beauty and romance? *Psychology of Women Quarterly, 31,* 125–136. doi: 10.1111/j.1471-6402.2007.00346.x

Rudman, L. A., & Phelan, J. E. (2007). The interpersonal power of feminism: Is feminism good for relationships? *Sex Roles, 57,* 787–799. doi: 10.1007/s11199-007-9319-9

RuPaul. (1995). *Lettin it all hang out: An autobiography.* New York, NY: Hyperion.

Russo, J. (2015, January 31). *Game on: How consumers plan on getting their kicks for Super Bowl XLIX.* Retrieved from http://www.nielsen.com/us/en/insights/news/2015/game-on-how-consumers-plan-on-getting-their-kicks-for-super-bowl-xlix.html

Rutherford, A., & Granek, L. (2010). Emergence and development of the psychology of women. In J. C. Chrisler & D. R. McCreary (Eds.), *Handbook of gender research in psychology* (Vol. 1, pp. 19–41). New York, NY: Springer.

Saris, R., & Johnston-Robledo, I. (2000). Poor women are still shut out of mainstream psychology. *Psychology of Women Quarterly, 24,* 233–235. doi: 10.1111/j.1471-6402.2000.tb00204.x

Saunders, K. J., & Kashubeck-West, S. (2006). The relations among feminist identity development, gender-role orientation, and psychological well-being in women. *Psychology of Women Quarterly, 30,* 199–211. doi: 10.1111/j.1471-6402.2006.00282.x

Schick, V. R., Zucker, A. N., & Bay-Cheng, L. Y. (2008). Safer, better sex through feminism: The role of feminist ideology in women's sexual well-being. *Psychology of Women Quarterly, 32,* 225–232. doi: 10.1111/j.1471-6402.2008.00431.x

Schwab, N. (2014, April 18). Ginsburg: Make ERA part of the constitution. *U.S. News & World Report.* Retrieved from http://www.usnews.com/news/blogs/washington-whispers/2014/04/18/justice-ginsburg-make-equal-rights-amendment-part-of-the-constitution

Sherif, C. W. (1979). Social values, attitudes, and involvement of the self and somatic changes during the menstrual cycle. *Nebraska Symposium on Motivation, 27,* 1–64.

Shields, S. A. (1975). Functionalism, Darwinism, and the psychology of women. *American Psychologist, 30,* 739–754. doi: 10.1037/h0076948

Shields, S. A. (2007). Passionate men, emotional women: Psychology constructs gender difference in the late 19th century. *History of Psychology, 10,* 92–110. doi: 10.1037/1093-4510.10.2.92

Smith, C. A., Johnston-Robledo, I., McHugh, M. C., & Chrisler, J. C. (2010). Words matter: The language of gender. In J. C. Chrisler & D. R. McCreary (Eds.), *Handbook of gender research in psychology* (Vol. 1, pp. 361–378). New York, NY: Springer.

Stern, M. (2014, August 14). Joseph Gordon-Levitt on "Sin City" and why he considers himself a male feminist. *Daily Beast.* Retrieved from https://www.thedailybeast.com/joseph-gordon-levitt-on-sin-city-and-why-he-considers-himself-a-male-feminist

Stewart, A. J., & Dottolo, A. L. (2006). Feminist psychology. *Signs, 31,* 493–509. doi: 10.1086/491683

Sullivan, N. (2003). *A critical introduction to queer theory.* New York, NY: New York University Press.

Swavola, E., Riley, K., & Subramanian, R. (2016). *Overlooked: Women and jails in an era of reform.* New York, NY: Vera Institute of Justice. Retrieved from http://www.safetyandjusticechallenge.org/wp-content/uploads/2016/08/overlooked-women-in-jails-report-web.pdf

Swim, J. K., Hyers, L. L., Cohen, L. L., & Ferguson, M. J. (2001). Everyday sexism: Evidence for its incidence, nature, and psychological impact from three daily diary studies. *Journal of Social Issues, 57,* 31–54. doi: 10.1111/0022-4537.00200

Swim, J. K., Mallett, R. K., & Stangor, C. (2004). Understanding subtle sexism: Detection and use of sexist language. *Sex Roles, 51,* 117–128. doi: 10.1023/B:SERS.0000037757.73192.06

Taylor, V., & Whittier, N. (1992). Collective identity in social movement communities: Lesbian feminist mobilization. In A. D. Morris & C. M. Mueller (Eds.), *Frontiers in social movement theory* (pp. 104–129). New Haven, CT: Yale University Press.

Teo, T. (2015). Critical psychology: A geography of intellectual engagement and resistance. *American Psychologist, 70,* 243–254. doi: 10.1037/a0038727

Twenge, J. M., & Zucker, A. N. (1999). What is a feminist? Evaluations and stereotypes in closed- and open-ended responses. *Psychology of Women Quarterly, 23,* 591–605. doi: 10.1111/j.1471-6402.1999.tb00383.x

Unger, R. K. (1979). Toward a redefinition of sex and gender. *American Psychologist, 34,* 1085–1094. doi: 10.1037/0003-066X.34.11.1085

Unger, R. K. (1983). Through the looking glass: No Wonderland yet! (The reciprocal relationship between methodology and models of reality). *Psychology of Women Quarterly, 8,* 9–32. doi: 10.1111/j.1471-6402.1983.tb00614.x

Unger, R. K. (2010). Leave no text behind: Teaching the psychology of women during the emergence of second wave feminism. *Sex Roles, 62,* 153–158. doi: 10.1007/s11199-009-9740-3

UNICEF. (2013, March 7). *Child marriages: 39,000 every day* [Press Release]. *UNICEF.* Retrieved from http://www.unicef.org/media/media_68114.html

Vagianos, A. (2015, February 3). The reaction to #LikeAGirl is exactly why it's so important. *Huffington Post.* Retrieved from http://www.huffingtonpost.com/2015/02/03/why-like-a-girl-is-so-important_n_6598970.html

Valenzuela, A. (1993). Liberal gender role attitudes and academic achievement among Mexican-origin adolescents in two Houston inner-city Catholic schools. *Hispanic Journal of Behavioral Sciences, 15,* 310–323. doi: 10.1177/07399863930153002

Vandiver, P. (2010). *Feminism: A male anarchist's perspective.* Retrieved from http://theanarchistlibrary.org/library/pendleton-vandiver-feminism-a-male-anarchist-s-perspective

Walker, A. (1983). *In search of our mothers' gardens: Womanist prose.* San Diego, CA: Harcourt Brace Jovanovich.

Waters, E. (2017). *Lesbian, gay, bisexual, transgender, queer, and HIV-affected hate violence in 2016: A 20th anniversary report from the National Coalition of Anti-Violence Programs.* New York, NY: New York City Anti-Violence Project. Retrieved from http://avp.org/wp-content/uploads/2017/06/NCAVP_2016HateViolence_REPORT.pdf

Weaver, M. (2017, March 14). Burqa bans, headscarves and veils: A timeline of legislation in the west. *The Guardian.* Retrieved from https://www.theguardian.com/world/2017/mar/14/headscarves-and-muslim-veil-ban-debate-timeline

Weeks, J. (2015, May 18). Women-owned firms springing up all over. *American Express Open Forum.* Retrieved from: https://www.americanexpress.com/us/small-business/openforum/articles/women-owned-firms-springing/

Wehbi, S. (2010). Lebanese women disability rights activists: War-time experiences. *Women's Studies International Forum, 33,* 455–463. doi: 10.1016/j.wsif.2010.05.001

Weisstein, N. (1992). Psychology constructs the female, or the fantasy life of the male psychologist (with some attention to the fantasies of his friends the male biologist and the male anthropologist). In J. S. Bohan (Ed.), *Seldom seen, rarely heard: Women's place in psychology* (pp. 61–78). Boulder, CO: Westview Press. (Originally published in 1968).

Westkott, M. (1986). *The feminist legacy of Karen Horney.* New Haven, CT: Yale University Press.

whoneedsfeminism. (2014, August 27). I need feminism because I refuse to be victimized by social, cultural, or political misogyny [Tumblr post]. Retrieved from http://whoneedsfeminism.tumblr.com/post/95944131484/i-need-feminism-because-i-refuse-to-be-victimized

Williams, M. E. (2015, February 2). The Super Bowl was a win for feminism. *Salon.* Retrieved from http://www.salon.com/2015/02/02/the_super_bowl_was_a_win_for_feminism/

Women Against Feminism. (2014, January 18). I don't need feminism because I believe in equality not entitlements & supremacy [Facebook group post]. Retrieved from http://womenagainstfeminism.tumblr.com/post/87344820850

Yakushko, O. (2007). Do feminist women feel better about their lives? Examining patterns of feminist identity development and women's subjective well-being. *Sex Roles, 57,* 223–234. doi: 10.1007/s11199-007-9249-6

Yoder, J. D., Tobias, A., & Snell, A. F. (2011). When declaring "I am a feminist" matters: Labeling is linked to activism. *Sex Roles, 64*, 9–18. doi: 10.1007/s11199-010-9890-3

Yost, M. R., & Chmielewski, J. F. (2013). Blurring the line between researcher and researched in interview studies: A feminist practice? *Psychology of Women Quarterly, 37*, 242–250. doi: 10.1177/0361684312464698

Zeisler, A. (2014). Worst sales pitch ever: The ad industry's shameless history of using feminism to sell products. *Salon.* Retrieved from http://www.salon.com/2014/07/21/worst_sales_pitch_ever _the_ad_industrys_shameless_history_of_using_feminism_to_sell _products/

Zucker, A. N. (2004). Disavowing social identities: What it means when women say, "I'm not a feminist, but . . ." *Psychology of Women Quarterly, 28*, 423–435. doi: 10.1111/j.1471-6402 .2004.00159.x

Chapter 2

Abele, A. E., & Wojciszke, B. (2014). Communal and agentic content in social cognition: A dual perspective model. In J. M. Olson & M. P. Zanna (Eds.), *Advances in experimental social psychology* (Vol. 50, pp. 195–255). Waltham, MA: Academic Press.

Abrams, J. A., Maxwell, M., Pope, M., & Belgrave, F. Z. (2014). Carrying the world with the grace of a lady and the grit of a warrior: Deepening our understanding of the "strong Black woman" schema. *Psychology of Women Quarterly, 38*, 503–518. doi: 10.1177/0361684314541418

Addady, M. (2015, October 15). How women would articulate historic quotes by famous men. *Fortune.* Retrieved from http://fortune.com/2015/10/15/jennifer-lawrence-woman -in-a-meeting/

Afro-Europe. (2012, May 13). Black French flight attendant forced to hide dreadlocks under a wig [Blog post]. Retrieved from http://afroeurope.blogspot.com/2012/05/black-french -flight-attendant-pressured.html

Alsultany, E. (2002). Los intersticios: Recasting moving selves. In G. E. Anzaldua & A. Keating (Eds.), *This bridge we call home* (pp. 106–109). New York, NY: Routledge.

Anderson, K. J., & Leaper, C. (1998). Meta-analyses of gender effects on conversational interruption: Who, what, when, where, and how. *Sex Roles, 39*, 225–252. doi: 10.1023/A:1018802521676

Andreoletti, C., Leszczynski, J. P., & Disch, W. B. (2015). Gender, race, and age: The content of compound stereotypes across the life span. *The International Journal of Aging & Human Development, 81*, 27–53. doi: 10.1177/0091415015616395

Ashley, W. (2014). The angry Black woman: The impact of pejorative stereotypes on psychotherapy with Black women. *Social Work in Public Health, 29*, 27–34. doi: 10.1080/19371918 .2011.619449

Bakan, D. (1966). *The duality of human existence.* Chicago, IL: Rand McNally.

Barreto, M., & Ellemers, N. (2005). The burden of benevolent sexism: How it contributes to the maintenance of gender inequalities. *European Journal of Social Psychology, 35*, 633–642. doi: 10.1002/ejsp.270

Basow, S. (2004). The hidden curriculum: Gender in the classroom. In M. A. Paludi & M. A. Paludi (Eds.), *Praeger guide to the psychology of gender* (pp. 117–131). Westport, CT: Praeger/ Greenwood.

Battle, M. (2017, May 16). Times Black girls were suspended for their hairstyles. *Elite Daily.* Retrieved from https://www .elitedaily.com/life/culture/black-girls-natural-hair-racism -schools/1953497

Becker, J. C., & Swim, J. K. (2012). Reducing endorsement of benevolent and modern sexist beliefs: Differential effects of addressing harm versus pervasiveness of benevolent sexism. *Social Psychology, 43*, 127–137. doi: 10.1027/1864-9335 /a000091

Begun, S., & Walls, E. N. (2015). Pedestal or gutter: Exploring ambivalent sexism's relationship with abortion attitudes. *Affilia: Journal of Women & Social Work, 30*, 200–215. doi: 10.1177/0886109914555216

Bennett, S. (2012, July 31). On Twitter, men are retweeted far more than women (and you're probably sexist, too). *Adweek.* Retrieved from http://www.adweek.com/socialtimes/twee-q -sexist-twitter/467654

Berry, C. (2014, November 1). They call me Doctor Berry. *The New York Times.* Retrieved from http://www.nytimes.com/2014 /11/02/opinion/sunday/they-call-me-doctor-berry.html

Biernat, M., & Sesko, A. K. (2013). Evaluating the contributions of members of mixed-sex work teams: Race and gender matter. *Journal of Experimental Social Psychology, 49*, 471–476. doi: 10.1016/j.jesp.2013.01.008

Bird, S. E. (1999). Gendered construction of the American Indian in popular media. *Journal of Communication, 49*, 61–83. doi: 10.1111/j.1460-2466.1999.tb02803.x

Blay, Z. (2017, January 21). Watch 6-year-old Sophie Cruz give one of the best speeches of The Women's March. *Huffington Post.* Retrieved from http://www.huffingtonpost.com/entry /sophie-cruz_us_58839698e4b096b4a23201f6

Bosak, J., Sczesny, S., & Eagly, A. H. (2008). Communion and agency judgments of women and men as a function of role information and response format. *European Journal of Social Psychology, 38*, 1148–1155. doi: 10.1002/ejsp.538

Bowleg, L. (2013). "Once you've blended the cake, you can't take the parts back to the main ingredients": Black gay and bisexual men's descriptions and experiences of intersectionality. *Sex Roles, 68*, 754–767. doi: 10.1007/s11199-012-0152-4

Braun, V., & Kitzinger, C. (2001). Telling it straight? Dictionary definitions of women's genitals. *Journal of Sociolinguistics, 5*, 214–232. doi: 10.1111/1467-9481.00148

Brescoll, V. L. (2011). Who takes the floor and why: Gender, power, and volubility in organizations. *Administrative Science Quarterly, 56*, 622–641. doi: 10.1177/0001839212439994

Bridges, J. (2017). Gendering metapragmatics in online discourse: "Mansplaining man gonna mansplain . . ." *Discourse, Context & Media, 20*, 94–102. doi: 10.1016/j.dcm.2017.09.010

Brown, D. L., White-Johnson, R. L., & Griffin-Fennell, F. D. (2013). Breaking the chains: Examining the endorsement of modern Jezebel images and racial-ethnic esteem among African American women. *Culture, Health & Sexuality, 15*, 525–539. doi: 10.1080/13691058.2013.772240

Brunson, R. K. (2007). "Police don't like black people": African-American young men's accumulated police experiences. *Criminology & Public Policy, 6*, 71–101. doi: 10.1111/j.1745-9133 .2007.00423.x

Bucholtz, M. (2001). The Whiteness of nerds: Superstandard English and racial markedness. *Journal of Linguistic Anthropology, 11*, 84–100. doi: 10.1525/jlin.2001.11.1.84

Butler, O. E. (1993). *Parable of the sower.* New York, NY: Warner Books.

Cadinu, M., Maass, A., Rosabianca, A., & Kiesner, J. (2005). Why do women underperform under stereotype threat? Evidence for the role of negative thinking. *Psychological Science, 16*, 572–578. doi: 10.1111/j.0956-7976.2005.01577.x

Cameron, D. (2015, July 15). Just don't do it. *Language: A feminist guide.* Retrieved from https://debuk.wordpress.com /2015/07/05/just-dont-do-it/

Capogna, K. (2015, December 4). How I feel when men tell me to smile. *Huffington Post*. Retrieved from http://www.huffingtonpost.com/kyle-capogna/how-i-feel-when-men-tell-me-to-smile_b_8687410.html

Carli, L .L. (2001). Gender and social influence. *Journal of Social Issues, 57*, 725–741. doi: 10.1111/0022-4537.00238

Case, K. A. (2013). Beyond diversity and Whiteness: Developing a transformative and intersectional model of privilege studies pedagogy. In K. A. Case (Ed.), *Deconstructing privilege: Teaching and learning as allies in the classroom* (pp. 1–14). New York, NY: Routledge.

Cashdan, E. (1998). Smiles, speech, and body posture: How women and men display sociometric status and power. *Journal of Nonverbal Behavior, 22*, 209–228. doi: 10.1023/A:1022967721884

Cauterucci, C. (2015, December 29). New Chrome app helps women stop saying "just" and "sorry" in emails. *Slate*. Retrieved from http://www.slate.com/blogs/xx_factor/2015/12/29/new_chrome_app_helps_women_stop_saying_just_and_sorry_in_emails.html

Chapleau, K. M., Oswald, D. L., & Russell, B. L. (2007). How ambivalent sexism toward women and men supports rape myth acceptance. *Sex Roles, 57*, 131–136. doi: 10.1007/s11199-007-9196-2

Chapman, R., & Ciment, J. (2015). *Culture wars: An encyclopedia of issues, viewpoints and voices*. New York, NY: Routledge.

Chen, E. S., & Tyler, T. R. (2001). Cloaking power: Legitimizing myths and the psychology of the advantaged. In A. Y. Lee-Chai & J. A. Bargh (Eds.), *The use and abuse of power: Multiple perspectives on the causes of corruption* (pp. 241–261). New York, NY: Psychology Press.

Chenoweth, E., & Pressman, J. (2017, January 7). This is what we learned by counting the women's marches. *The Washington Post*. Retrieved from https://www.washingtonpost.com/news/monkey-cage/wp/2017/02/07/this-is-what-we-learned-by-counting-the-womens-marches/?utm_term=.66c92e7ad5c2

Chira, S. (2017, June 14). The universal phenomenon of men interrupting women. *The New York Times*. Retrieved from https://www.nytimes.com/2017/06/14/business/women-sexism-work-huffington-kamala-harris.html

Choma, R. (2016, February 2). Ted Cruz slams idea of women in combat. *Mother Jones*. Retrieved from http://www.motherjones.com/politics/2016/02/ted-cruz-slams-idea-women-combat

Christie, A. M. (2017, January 23). The so called "Women's March" made me embarrassed to be a female. *We Need to Talk about Islam*. Retrieved from https://www.weneedtotalkaboutislam.com/single-post/2017/01/24/The-so-called-Womens-March-made-me-feel-embarrassed-to-be-a-female

Chun, J. J., Lipsitz, G., & Shin, Y. (2013). Intersectionality as a social movement strategy: Asian immigrant women advocates. *Signs, 38*, 917–940. doi: 10.1086/669575

Cichy, K. E., Li, J., McMahon, B. T., & Rumrill, P. D. (2015). The workplace discrimination experiences of older workers with disabilities: Results from the National EEOC ADA Research Project. *Journal of Vocational Rehabilitation, 43*, 137–148. doi: 10.3233/JVR-150763

Clarke, V., Burns, M., & Burgoyne, C. (2008). "Who would take whose name?" Accounts of naming practices in same-sex relationships. *Journal of Community & Applied Social Psychology, 18*, 420–439. doi: 10.1002/casp.936

Cohen, G. L., & Garcia J. (2005). "I am us": Negative stereotypes as collective threats. *Journal of Personality and Social Psychology, 89*, 566–582. doi: 10.1037/0022-3514.89.4.566

Cole, E. R. (2009). Intersectionality and research in psychology. *American Psychologist, 64*, 170–180. doi: 10.1037/a0014564

Collins, P. H. (1990). *Black feminist thought: Knowledge, consciousness, and the politics of empowerment*. New York, NY: Routledge.

Collins, P. H. (2004). *Black sexual politics: African Americans, gender, and the new racism*. New York, NY: Routledge.

Conway, M., & Vartanian, L. R. (2000). A status account of gender stereotypes: Beyond communality and agency. *Sex Roles, 43*, 181–199. doi: 10.1023/A:1007076813819

Cortina, L. M. (2008). Unseen injustice: Incivility as modern discrimination in organizations. *The Academy of Management Review, 33*, 55-75. doi: 10.2307/20159376

Cortina, L. M., Kabat-Farr, D., Magley, V. J., & Nelson, K. (2017). Researching rudeness: The past, present, and future of the science of incivility. *Journal of Occupational Health Psychology, 22*, 299–313. doi: 10.1037/ocp0000089

Cozzarelli, C., Tagler, M. J., & Wilkinson, A. V. (2002). Do middle-class students perceive poor women and poor men differently? *Sex Roles, 47*, 519–529. doi: 10.1023/A:1022038200071

Crenshaw, K. W. (1993). Beyond racism and misogyny: Black feminism and 2 Live Crew. In D. T. Meyers (Ed.), *Feminist social thought: A reader* (pp. 245–263). New York, NY: Routledge.

Croom, A. M. (2013). How to do things with slurs: Studies in the way of derogatory words. *Language & Communication, 33*, 177–204. doi: 10.1016/j.langcom.2013.03.008

Crosby, F. J., Iyer, A., Clayton, S., & Downing, R. A. (2003). Affirmative action: Psychological data and the policy debates. *American Psychologist, 58*, 93–115. doi: 10.1037/0003-066X.58.2.93

Cukan, A. (2001, June 29). FedEx sued for dreadlocks discrimination. *United Press International*. Retrieved from https://www.upi.com/Archives/2001/06/29/FedEx-sued-for-dreadlocks-discrimination/6832993787200/

Dalmia, S. (2017, January 2). Why the Women's March on Washington has already failed. *The Week*. Retrieved from http://theweek.com/articles/667163/why-womens-march-washington-already-failed

Dardenne, B., Dumont, M., Sarlet, M., Phillips, C., Balteau, E., Degueldre, C., . . . Collette, F. (2013). Benevolent sexism alters executive brain responses. *NeuroReport, 24*, 572–577. doi: 10.1097/WNR.0b013e3283625b5b

Davenport, L. D. (2016). The role of gender, class, and religion in biracial Americans' racial labeling decisions. *American Sociological Review, 81*, 57–84. doi: 10.1177/0003122415623286

Deaux, K., & Lewis, L. L. (1984). Structure of gender stereotypes: Interrelationships among components and gender label. *Journal of Personality and Social Psychology, 46*, 991–1004. doi: 10.1037/0022-3514.46.5.991

Desmond-Harris, J. (2017, January 21). To understand the Women's March on Washington, you need to understand intersectional feminism. *Vox*. Retrieved from https://www.vox.com/identities/2017/1/17/14267766/womens-march-on-washington-inauguration-trump-feminism-intersectionaltiy-race-class

Donovan, R. A., & West, L. M. (2015). Stress and mental health: Moderating role of the strong Black woman stereotype. *Journal of Black Psychology, 41*, 384–396. doi: 10.1177/0095798414543014

Dossou, M. (2013, July 3). Natural hair vs. corporate America: Why are we still fighting this battle? *Ebony*. Retrieved from http://www.ebony.com/style/fighting-for-our-hair-in-corporate-america-032/2#axzz455ljbIc4

Dusenbery, M., & Lee, J. (2012, June 22). Charts: The state of women's athletics, 40 years after Title IX. *MotherJones*. Retrieved from http://www.motherjones.com/politics/2012/06/charts-womens-athletics-title-nine-ncaa

Eagly, A., & Sczesny, S. (2009). Stereotypes about women, men, and leaders: Have times changed? In M. Barreto, M. K. Ryan, & M. T. Schmitt (Eds.), *The glass ceiling in the 21st century: Understanding barriers to gender equality* (pp. 21–47). Washington, DC: American Psychological Association.

Eagly, A., & Carli, L. (2007). *Through the labyrinth: The truth about how women become leaders.* Boston, MA: Harvard Business Review Press.

Eagly, A. H., & Carli, L. L. (2003). The female leadership advantage: An evaluation of the evidence. *The Leadership Quarterly, 14,* 807–834. doi: 10.1016/j.leaqua.2003.09.004

Ebert, I., Steffens, M. C., & Kroth, A. (2014). Warm, but maybe not so competent? Contemporary implicit stereotypes of women and men in Germany. *Sex Roles, 70,* 359–375. doi: 10.1007/s11199-014-0369-5

Ellemers, N., & Barreto, M. (2009). Collective action in modern times: How modern expressions of prejudice prevent collective action. *Journal of Social Issues, 65,* 749–768. doi: 10.1111/j.1540-4560.2009.01621.x

Etaugh, C. E., Bridges, J. S., Cummings-Hill, M., & Cohen, J. (1999). "Names can never hurt me?" The effects of surname use on perceptions of married women. *Psychology of Women Quarterly, 23,* 819–823. doi: 10.1111/j.1471-6402.1999.tb00400.x

Fair, B. (2011). Constructing masculinity through penetration discourse: The intersection of misogyny and homophobia in high school wrestling. *Men and Masculinities, 14,* 491–504. doi: 10.1177/1097184X10375936

Falcón, S. M. (2008). Mestiza double consciousness: The voices of Afro-Peruvian women on gendered racism. *Gender & Society, 22,* 660–680. doi: 10.1177/0891243208321274

Ferber, A. L., & O'Reilly Herrera, A. (2013). Teaching privilege through an intersectional lens. In K. A. Case (Ed.), *Deconstructing privilege: Teaching and learning as allies in the classroom* (pp. 115–131). New York, NY: Routledge.

Fiedler, K., Messner, C., & Bluemke, M. (2006). Unresolved problems with the "I," the "A," and the "T": A logical and psychometric critique of the Implicit Association Test (IAT). *European Review of Social Psychology, 17,* 74–147. doi: 10.1080/10463280600681248

Fischer, A. R. (2006). Women's benevolent sexism as reaction to hostility. *Psychology of Women Quarterly, 30,* 410–416. doi: 10.1111/j.1471-6402.2006.00316.x

Fiske, S. T. (1998). Stereotyping, prejudice, and discrimination. In D. T. Gilbert, S. T. Fiske, & G. Lindzey (Eds.), *The handbook of social psychology* (4th ed., Vol. 2, pp. 357–411). New York: McGraw-Hill.

Fiske, S. T (2010a). Interpersonal stratification: Status, power, and subordination. In S. T. Fiske, D. T. Gilbert, & G. Lindzey (Eds.), *Handbook of social psychology* (5th ed., pp. 941–982). Hoboken, NJ: Wiley.

Fiske, S. T. (2010b). *Social beings: Core motives in social psychology.* New York, NY: Wiley.

Fiske, S. T., Cuddy, A. J. C., Glick, P., & Xu, J. (2002). A model of (often mixed) stereotype content: Competence and warmth respectively follow from status and competition. *Journal of Personality and Social Psychology, 82,* 878–902. doi: 10.1037/0022-3514.82.6.878

Fitzsimmons, E. (2014, December 20). A scourge is spreading. M.T.A.'s cure? Dude, close your legs. *The New York Times.* Retrieved from http://www.nytimes.com/2014/12/21/nyregion/MTA-targets-manspreading-on-new-york-city-subways.html?_r=0

Foster, R. A., & Keating, J. P. (1992). Measuring androcentrism in the Western God-concept. *Journal for the Scientific Study of Religion, 31,* 366–375.

Freedman, E. (2013). *No turning back: The history of feminism and the future of women.* New York, NY: Ballantine Books.

Galinsky, A. D., Wang, C. S., Whitson, J. A., Anicich, E. M., Hugenberg, K., & Bodenhausen, G. V. (2013). The reappropriation of stigmatizing labels the reciprocal relationship between power and self-labeling. *Psychological Science, 24,* 2020–2029. doi: 10.1177/0956797613482943

Gandy, I. (2017, April 17). Black hair discrimination is real – but is it against the law? *Rewire.* Retrieved from https://rewire.news/ablc/2017/04/17/black-hair-discrimination-real-but-is-it-against-law/

Gaucher, D., Hunt, B., & Sinclair, L. (2015). Can pejorative terms ever lead to positive social consequences? The case of SlutWalk. *Language Sciences, 52,* 121–130. doi: 10.1016/j.langsci.2015.03.005

Gazzola, S. B., & Morrison, M. A. (2014). Cultural and personally endorsed stereotypes of transgender men and transgender women: Notable correspondence or disjunction? *International Journal of Transgenderism, 15*(2), 76–99. doi: 10.1080/15532739.2014.937041

Gearty, R. (2001, June 29). Suit upbraids FedEx on bias: Dreadlock ban targeted. *New York Daily News.* Retrieved from http://www.nydailynews.com/archives/news/suit-upbraids-fedex-bias-dreadlock-ban-targeted-article-1.900948

Ghavami, N., & Peplau, L. A. (2013). An intersectional analysis of gender and ethnic stereotypes: Testing three hypotheses. *Psychology of Women Quarterly, 37,* 113–127. doi: 10.1177/0361684312464203

Givens, S. B., & Monahan, J. L. (2005). Priming mammies, jezebels, and other controlling images: An examination of the influence of mediated stereotypes on perceptions of an African American woman. *Media Psychology, 7,* 87–106. doi: 10.1207/S1532785XMEP0701_5

Glaser, N. (2014, October 1). A comedian nails the scary reason why women smile when strange men tell them to. *Upworthy.* Retrieved from http://www.upworthy.com/a-comedian-nails-the-scary-reason-why-women-smile-when-strange-men-tell-them-to

Glick, P., & Fiske, S. T. (1997). Hostile and benevolent sexism: Measuring ambivalent sexist attitudes toward women. *Psychology of Women Quarterly, 21,* 119–135. doi: 10.1111/j.1471-6402.1997.tb00104.x

Glick, P., & Fiske, S. T. (2001). An ambivalent alliance: Hostile and benevolent sexism as complementary justifications for gender inequality. *American Psychologist, 56,* 109–118. doi: 10.1037/0003-066X.56.2.109

Glick, P., Fiske, S. Tr, Mladinic, A., Saiz, J. L., Abrams, D., Masser, B., . . . López, W. L. (2000). Beyond prejudice as simple antipathy: Hostile and benevolent sexism across cultures. *Journal of Personality and Social Psychology, 79,* 763–775. doi: 10.1037/0022-3514.79.5.763

Goins-Phillips, T. (2017, January 24). Trans community: Women's March protesters' focus on female genitalia was "oppressive." *The Blaze.* Retrieved from http://www.theblaze.com/news/2017/01/24/trans-community-womens-march-protesters-focus-on-female-genitalia-was-oppressive/

Goldin, C., & Shim, M. (2004). Making a name: Women's surnames at marriage and beyond. *The Journal of Economic Perspectives, 18,* 143–160. doi: 10.1257/0895330041371268

Gooding, G. E., & Kreider, R. M. (2010). Women's marital naming choices in a nationally representative sample. *Journal of Family Issues, 31,* 681–701. doi: 10.1177/0192513X09344688

Goodman, D. J. (2011). *Promoting diversity and social justice: Educating people from privileged groups* (2nd ed.). New York, NY: Routledge.

Gordon, E. (Host). (2006, June 22). Banned hairstyles at Six Flags theme park [Radio broadcast episode]. Retrieved from http://www.npr.org/templates/story/story.php?storyId=5503209

Greenwood, D., & Isbell, L. M. (2002). Ambivalent sexism and the dumb blonde: Men's and women's reactions to sexist jokes. *Psychology of Women Quarterly, 26,* 341–350. doi: 10.1111/1471-6402.t01-2-00073

Grossman, A. L., & Tucker, J. S. (1997). Gender differences and sexism in the knowledge and use of slang. *Sex Roles, 37*, 101–110. doi: 10.1023/A:1025644921272

Gunnarsson, L. (2017). Why we keep separating the "inseparable": Dialecticizing intersectionality. *European Journal of Women's Studies, 24*, 114–127. doi: 10.1177/1350506815577114

Haddock, G., Zanna, M. P., & Esses, V. M. (1993). Assessing the structure of prejudicial attitudes: The case of attitudes toward homosexuals. *Journal of Personality and Social Psychology, 65*, 1105–1118. doi: 10.1037/0022-3514.65.6.1105

Hahm, H. C., Ozonoff, A., Gaumond, J., & Sue, S. (2010). Perceived discrimination and health outcomes: A gender comparison among Asian-Americans nationwide. *Women's Health Issues, 20*, 350–358. doi: 10.1016/j.whi.2010.05.002

Haines, H. L., Deaux, K., & LoFaro, N. (2016). The times they are a-changing . . . or are they not? A comparison of gender stereotypes, 1983–2014. *Psychology of Women Quarterly, 40*, 353–363. doi: 10.1177/0361684316634081

Hall, J. A. (2006). Nonverbal behavior, status, and gender: How do we understand their relations? *Psychology of Women Quarterly, 30*, 384–391. doi: 10.1111/j.1471-6402.2006.00313.x

Hall, J. A., Carter, J. D., & Horgan, T. G. (2000). Gender differences in nonverbal communication of emotion. In A. H. Fischer (Ed.), *Gender and emotion: Social psychological perspectives* (pp. 97–117). New York, NY: Cambridge University Press.

Hall, J. A., Coats, E. J., & LeBeau, L. S. (2005). Nonverbal behavior and the vertical dimension of social relations: A meta-analysis. *Psychological Bulletin, 131*, 898–924. doi: 10.1037/0033-2909.131.6.898

Hamilton, M. C. (1991). Masculine bias in the attribution of personhood: People = male, male = people. *Psychology of Women Quarterly, 15*, 393–402. doi: 10.1111/j.1471-6402.1991.tb00415.x

Hancock, A. B., & Rubin, B. A. (2015). Influence of communication partner's gender on language. *Journal of Language and Social Psychology, 34*, 46–64. doi: 10.1177/0261927X14533197

Hare, K. (2016, December 13). Now hair this! *Chicago Defender*. Retrieved from https://chicagodefender.com/2016/12/13/now-hair-this/

Harnois, C. E. (2015). Race, ethnicity, sexuality, and women's political consciousness of gender. *Social Psychology Quarterly, 78*, 365–386. doi: 10.1177/0190272515607844

Harrington, E. F., Crowther, J. H., & Shipherd, J. C. (2010). Trauma, binge eating, and the "strong Black woman." *Journal of Consulting and Clinical Psychology, 78*, 469–479. doi: 10.1037/a0019174

Hayes, E., & Swim, J. K. (2013). African, Asian, Latina/o, and European Americans' responses to popular measures of sexist beliefs: Some cautionary notes. *Psychology of Women Quarterly, 37*, 155–166. doi: 10.1177/0361684313480044

Hayes, P. A. (2001). *Addressing cultural complexities in practice: A framework for clinicians and counselors*. Washington, DC: American Psychological Association.

Hegarty, P., Watson, N., Fletcher, L., & McQueen, G. (2011). When gentlemen are first and ladies are last: Effects of gender stereotypes on the order of romantic partners' names. *British Journal of Social Psychology, 50*, 21–35. doi: 10.1348/014466610X486347

Heilman, M. E., Wallen, A. S., Fuchs, D., & Tamkins, M. M. (2004). Penalties for success: Reactions to women who succeed at male gender-typed tasks. *Journal of Applied Psychology, 89*, 416–427. doi: 10.1037/0021-9010.89.3.416

Henley, N. M. (1977). *Body politics: Power, sex and nonverbal communication*. Englewood Cliffs, NJ: Prentice-Hall.

Hess, A. (2014, May 29). "If I can't have them, no one will": How misogyny kills men. *Slate*. Retrieved from http://www.slate.com/blogs/xx_factor/2014/05/29/elliot_rodger_hated_men_because_he_hated_women.html

Hines, C. (1999). Rebaking the pie: The woman as dessert metaphor. In M. Bucholtz, A. C. Liang, & A. Laurel (Eds.), *Reinventing identities: The gender self in discourse* (pp. 145–162). Bethesda, MD: Oxford University Press.

Hodge. J. (2012, July 25). Gender focus panel: On reclaiming negative words. *Gender Focus*. Retrieved from http://www.gender-focus.com/2012/07/25/gender-focus-panel-on-reclaiming-negative-words/

Hoffnung, M. (2006). What's in a name? Marital name choice revisited. *Sex Roles, 55*, 817–825. doi: 10.1007/s11199-006-9133-9

Hom, C. (2008). The semantics of racial epithets. *The Journal of Philosophy, 105*, 416–440.

Honey, M. (2017, February 24). Black women speak about natural hair bias in the workplace. *Teen Vogue*. Retrieved from https://www.teenvogue.com/story/black-women-natural-hair-bias-discrimination

hooks, b. (1989). *Talking back: Thinking feminist, thinking black*. Cambridge, MA: South End Press.

Hornsby, J. (2001). Meaning and uselessness: How to think about derogatory words. *Midwest Studies in Philosophy, 25*, 128–141. doi: 10.1111/1475-4975.00042

Jacobi, T., & Schweers, D. (2017). *Justice, interrupted: The effect of gender, ideology and seniority at Supreme Court oral arguments* (Northwestern Law & Econ Research Paper No. 17-03). Retrieved from https://papers.ssrn.com/sol3/papers.cfm?abstract_id=2933016

Johnson, A. G. (2006). *Privilege, power, and difference*. Boston, MA: McGraw-Hill.

Johnson, A. M., Godsil, R. D., MacFarlane, J., Tropp, L. R., & Goff, P. A. (2017, February). *The "good hair" study: Explicit and implicit attitudes toward Black women's hair*. Retrieved from the Perception Institute website: https://perception.org/wp-content/uploads/2017/01/TheGood-HairStudyFindingsReport.pdf

Johnson, D. R., & Scheuble, L. K. (1995). Women's marital naming in two generations: A national study. *Journal of Marriage and Family, 57*, 724–732. doi: 10.2307/353926

Johnson, D. R., & Scheuble, L. K. (2002). What should we call our kids? Choosing children's surnames when parents' last names differ. *The Social Science Journal, 39*, 419–429. doi: 10.1016/S0362-3319(02)00203-3

Juan, M. D., Syed, M., & Azmitia, M. (2016). Intersectionality of race/ethnicity and gender among women of color and White women. *Identity: An International Journal of Theory and Research, 16*, 225–238. doi: 10.1080/15283488.2016.1229606

Judd, C. M., & Park, B. (1993). Definition and assessment of accuracy in social stereotypes. *Psychological Review, 100*, 109–128. doi: 10.1037/0033-295X.100.1.109

Kahn, A. (2015, January 18). 6 ways to respond to sexist microaggressions in everyday conversation. *Everyday Feminism*. Retrieved from http://everydayfeminism.com/2015/01/responses-to-sexist-microaggressions/

Karpowitz, C. F., & Mendelberg, T. (2014). *The silent sex: Gender, deliberation, and institutions*. Princeton, NJ: Princeton University Press.

Keller, R. M., & Galgay, C. E. (2010). Microaggressive experiences of people with disabilities. In D. W. Sue (Ed.), *Microaggressions and marginality: Manifestation, dynamics, and impact* (pp. 241–267). Hoboken, NJ: Wiley.

Kelly, D. H. (2015, February 6). On mansplaining. *The f word*. Retrieved from https://www.thefword.org.uk/2015/02/mansplaining/

Ken, I. (2010). *Digesting race, class, and gender: Sugar as a metaphor.* New York, NY: Palgrave Macmillian.

Kite, L. (2012, November 24). Beauty whitewashed: How White ideals exclude women of color. *Everyday Feminism.* Retrieved from http://everydayfeminism.com/2012/11/beauty-whitewashed/

Koenig, A. M., Eagly, A. E., Mitchell, A. A., & Ristikari, T. (2011). Are leader stereotypes masculine? A meta-analysis of three research paradigms. *Psychological Bulletin, 137,* 616–642. doi: 10.1037/a0023557

Koeser, S., Kuhn, E. A., & Sczesny, S. (2015). Just reading? How gender-fair language triggers readers' use of gender-fair forms. *Journal of Language and Social Psychology 34,* 343–357. doi: 10.1177/0261927X14561119

Koeser, S., & Sczesny, S. (2014). Promoting gender-fair language: The impact of arguments on language use, attitudes, and cognitions. *Journal of Language and Social Psychology, 33,* 548–560. doi: 10.1177/0261927X14541280

Kraus, M. W., & Keltner, D. (2009). Signs of socioeconomic status: A thin-slicing approach. *Psychological Science, 20,* 99–106. doi: 10.1111/j.1467-9280.2008.02251.x

Lack, C. (2015, April 30). The impact of stereotypes on African-American females. *Skeptic Ink.* Retrieved from http://www.skepticink.com/gps/2015/04/30/the-impact-of-stereotypes-on-african-american-females/

LaFrance, M. (2001). Gender and social interaction. In R. Unger (Ed.), *Handbook on the psychology of women and gender* (pp. 245–255). Hoboken, NJ: Wiley.

Lakoff, R. (1975). *Language and women's place.* New York, NY: Harper and Row.

Lambdin, J. R., Greer, K. M., Jibotian, K. S., Wood, K. R., & Hamilton, M. C. (2003). The animal = male hypothesis: Children's and adult's beliefs about the sex of non-sex-specific stuffed animals. *Sex Roles, 48,* 471–482. doi: 10.1023/A:1023567010708

Latu, I. M., Stewart, T. L., Myers, A. G., Lisco, C. G., Estes, S. B., & Donahue, D. K. (2011). What we "say" and what we "think" about female managers: Explicit versus implicit associations of women with success. *Psychology of Women Quarterly, 35,* 252–266. doi: 10.1177/0361684310383811

Leaper, C., & Robnett, R.D. (2011). Women are more likely than men to use tentative language, aren't they? A meta-analysis testing for gender differences and moderators. *Psychology of Women Quarterly, 35,* 129–142. doi: 10.1177/0361684310392728

Lee, J. J., & Rice, C. (2007). Welcome to America? International student perceptions of discrimination. *Higher Education, 53,* 381–409. doi 10.1007/s10734-005-4508-3

Lei, X. (2006). Sexism in language. *Journal of Language and Linguistics, 5,* 87–94.

Levant, R. F., & Richmond, K. (2016). The gender role strain paradigm and masculinity ideologies. In Y. J. Wong & S. R. Wester (Eds.), *APA handbook of men and masculinities* (pp. 23–49). Washington, DC: American Psychological Association.

Lewis, J. A., Mendenhall, R., Harwood, S. A., & Browne Huntt, M. (2016). "Ain't I a woman?" Perceived gendered racial microaggressions experienced by Black women. *The Counseling Psychologist, 44,* 758–780. doi: 10.1177/0011000016641193

Liberman, M. (2007, February 27). The social psychology of linguistic naming and shaming. *The Language Log.* Retrieved from http://itre.cis.upenn.edu/~myl/languagelog/archives/004244.html

Lilienfeld, S. O. (2017). Microaggressions: Strong claims, inadequate evidence. *Perspectives on Psychological Science, 12,* 138–169. doi: 10.1177/1745691616659391

Linneman, T. J. (2013). Gender in jeopardy! Intonation variation on a television game show. *Gender & Society, 27,* 82–105. doi: 10.1177/0891243212464905

Liss, M., & Erchull, M. J. (2013). Differences in beliefs and behaviors between feminist actual and anticipated mothers. *Psychology of Women Quarterly, 37,* 381–391. doi: 10.1177/0361684312468334

Litosseliti, L. (2013). *Gender and language theory and practice.* New York, NY: Routledge.

Litsky, F. (2001, August 28). Diana Golden Brosnihan, skier, dies at 38. *The New York Times.* Retrieved from http://www.nytimes.com/2001/08/28/sports/diana-golden-brosnihan-skier-dies-at-38.html

Lorber, J., & Moore, L. J. (2007). *Gendered bodies: Feminist perspectives.* New York, NY: Roxbury.

Lorde, A. (2007). Learning from the 60s. In A. Lorde & C. Clarke (Eds.), *Sister outsider: Essays & speeches by Audre Lorde* (pp. 134–144). Berkeley, CA: Crossing Press.

Love Ramirez, T., & Blay, Z. (2016, July 5). Why people are using the term "Latinx." *Huffington Post.* Retrieved from http://www.huffingtonpost.com/entry/why-people-are-using-the-term-latinx_us_57753328e4b0cc0fa136a159

MacKinnon, C. (1989). *Toward a feminist theory of the state.* Cambridge, MA: Harvard University Press.

Magnoli, G. (2015, February 19). Timeline of Isla Vista massacre reconstructs a murderous sequence. *Noozhawk.* Retrieved from http://www.noozhawk.com/article/timeline_of_isla_vista_massacre_investigation_report

Marcotte, A. (2015, July 24). The war on female voices is just another way of telling women to shut up. *The Daily Dot.* Retrieved from http://www.dailydot.com/opinion/vocal-fry-99-percent-invisible-womens-voices/

Mascret, N., & Cury, F. (2015). "I'm not scientifically gifted, I'm a girl": Implicit measures of gender-science stereotypes—Preliminary evidence. *Educational Studies, 41,* 462–465. doi: 10.1080/03055698.2015.1043979

Masser, B. M., & Abrams, D. (2004). Reinforcing the glass ceiling: The consequences of hostile sexism for female managerial candidates. *Sex Roles, 51,* 609–615. doi: 10.1007/s11199-004-5470-8

Mast, M. S., & Sczesny, S. (2010). Gender, power, and nonverbal behavior. In J. C. Chrisler & D. R. McCreary (Eds.), *Handbook of gender research in psychology* (Vol. 1, pp. 411–425). New York, NY: Springer.

Mattis, J. S., Grayman, N. A., Cowie, S., Winston, C., Watson, C., & Jackson, D. (2008). Intersectional identities and the politics of altruistic care in a low-income, urban community. *Sex Roles, 59,* 418–428. doi: 10.1007/s11199-008-9426-2

May, N. (2017, March 8). A day without whiny women in America. *LifeZette.* Retrieved from http://www.lifezette.com/momzette/day-without-whiny-women-america/

McCurdy, C. (2013, October 8). Are gender-neutral pronouns actually doomed? *Pacific Standard.* Retrieved from https://psmag.com/are-gender-neutral-pronouns-actually-doomed-94802108005a#.bp99v8fnt

McHugh, M. C., & Hambaugh, J. (2010). She said, he said: Gender, language, and power. In J. C. Chrisler & D. R. McCreary (Eds.), *Handbook of gender research in psychology* (Vol. 1, pp. 379–410). New York, NY: Springer.

McIntosh, P. (1989, July/August). White privilege: Unpacking the invisible knapsack. *Peace and Freedom Magazine,* 10–12. Retrieved from https://nationalseedproject.org/images/documents/Knapsack_plus_Notes-Peggy_McIntosh.pdf

McMahon, J. M., & Kahn, K. B. (2016). Benevolent racism? The impact of target race on ambivalent sexism. *Group Processes & Intergroup Relations, 19,* 169–183. doi: 10.1177/1368430215583153

Mehl, M. R., Vazire, S., Ramírez-Esparza, N., Slatcher, R. B., & Pennebaker, J. W. (2007). Are women really more talkative than men? *Science, 317*(5834), 82. doi: 10.1126/science.1139940

Merritt, R. D., & Harrison, T. W. (2006). Gender and ethnicity attributions to a gender- and ethnicity-unspecified individual: Is there a people = White male bias? *Sex Roles, 54*, 787–797. doi: 10.1007/s11199-006-9046-7

Merskin, D. (2010). The S-word: Discourse, stereotypes, and the American Indian woman. *The Howard Journal of Communications, 21*, 345–366. doi: 10.1080/10646175.2010.519616

Mitchell, G., & Tetlock, P. E. (2017). Popularity as a poor proxy for utility: The case of implicit prejudice. In S. O. Lilienfeld & I. D. Waldman (Eds.), *Psychological science under scrutiny: Recent challenges and proposed solutions* (pp. 164–195). Malden, MA: Wiley Blackwell.

Moely, B. E., & Kreicker, K. (1984). Ladies and gentlemen, women and men: A study of the connotations of words indicating gender. *Psychology of Women Quarterly, 8*, 348–353. doi: 10.1111/j.1471-6402.1984.tb00642.x

Mok, T. A. (1998). Getting the message: Media images and stereotypes and their effect on Asian Americans. *Cultural Diversity and Mental Health, 4*, 185–202. doi: 10.1037/1099-9809.4.3.185

Mosthof, M. (2017, January 30). If you're not talking about the criticism surrounding the Women's March, then you're part of the problem. *Bustle.* Retrieved from https://www.bustle.com/p/if-youre-not-talking-about-the-criticism-surrounding-the-womens-march-then-youre-part-of-the-problem-33491

Moyer, R. S. (1997). Covering gender on memory's front page: Men's prominence and women's prospects. *Sex Roles, 37*, 595–618. doi: 10.1023/A:1025615220731

Myers, K. (2010). Ladies first: Race, class, and the contradictions of a powerful femininity. *Sociological Spectrum, 24*, 11–41. doi: 10.1080/02732170490254374

Nadal, K. L. (2013). *That's so gay! Microaggressions and the lesbian, gay, bisexual, and transgender community.* Washington, DC: American Psychological Association.

Nadal, K. L., Davidoff, K. C., Davis, L. S., Wong, Y., Marshall, D., & McKenzie, V. (2015). A qualitative approach to intersectional microaggressions: Understanding influences of race, ethnicity, gender, sexuality, and religion. *Qualitative Psychology, 2*, 147–163. doi: 10.1037/qup0000026

Nadal, K. L., Mazzula, S. L., Rivera, D. P., & Fujii-Doe, W. (2014). Microaggressions and Latina/o Americans: An analysis of nativity, gender, and ethnicity. *Journal of Latina/o Psychology, 2*, 67–78. doi: 10.1037/lat0000013

Newport, F. (2001, February 21). Americans see women as emotional and affectionate, men as more aggressive. *Gallup.* Retrieved from http://www.gallup.com/poll/1978/Americans-See-Women-EmotionalAffectionate-Men-More-Aggressive.aspx

Niedlich, C., & Steffens, M. C. (2015). On the interplay of (positive) stereotypes and prejudice: Impressions of lesbian and gay applicants for leadership positions. *Sensoria: A Journal of Mind, Brain & Culture, 11*, 70–80. doi: 10.7790/sa.v11i1.408

Nilsen, A. P. (1996). Of ladybugs and billy goats: What animal species names tell about human perceptions of gender. *Metaphor & Symbolic Activity, 11*, 257–271. doi: 10.1207/s15327868ms1104_2

Nielsen, L. B. (2000). Situating legal consciousness: Experiences and attitudes of ordinary citizens about law and street harassment. *Law and Society Review, 34*, 1055–1090.

Norton, L. (2010, September 29). What's the strongest muscle in the human body? *LiveScience.* Retrieved from http://www.livescience.com/32823-strongest-human-muscles.html

"Our mission." (n.d.). *Women's March.* Retrieved from https://www.womensmarch.com/mission1/

Perlmutter, D. (2017, January 26). "Pussy" symbolism and the masked hatred of the Women's March. *Frontpage Mag.* Retrieved from http://www.frontpagemag.com/fpm/265582/pussy-symbolism-and-masked-hatred-womens-march-dawn-perlmutter

Phillips, B. S. (1990). Nicknames and sex role stereotypes. *Sex Roles, 23*, 281–289. doi: 10.1007/BF00290049

Poon, L. (2015, September 28). "Ze" or "they"? A guide to using gender-neutral pronouns. *CityLab.* Retrieved from http://www.citylab.com/navigator/2015/09/ze-or-they-a-guide-to-using-gender-neutral-pronouns/407167/

Prewitt-Freilino, J. L., Caswell, T. A., & Laakso, E. K. (2012). The gendering of language: A comparison of gender equality in countries with gendered, natural gender, and genderless languages. *Sex Roles, 66*, 268–281. doi: 10.1007/s11199-011-0083-5

Purdie-Vaughns, V., & Eibach, R. P. (2008). Intersectional invisibility: The distinctive advantages and disadvantages of multiple subordinate-group identities. *Sex Roles, 59*, 377–391. doi: 10.1007/s11199-008-9424-4

Ramanathan, L. (2017, January 24). Was the Women's March just another display of white privilege? Some think so. *The Washington Post.* Retrieved from https://www.washingtonpost.com/lifestyle/style/was-the-womens-march-just-another-display-of-white-privilege-some-think-so/2017/01/24/00bbdcca-e1a0-11e6-a547-5fb9411d332c_story.html?utm_term=.d6ddcea41717

Reid, S. A., Keerie, N., & Palomares, N. A. (2003). Language, gender salience and social influence. *Journal of Language and Social Psychology, 22*, 210–233. doi: 10.1177/0261927X03022002004

Renninger, L. A., Wade, T. J., & Grammer, K. (2004). Getting that female glance: Patterns and consequences of male nonverbal behavior in courtship contexts. *Evolution and Human Behavior, 25*, 416–431. doi: 10.1016/j.evolhumbehav.2004.08.006

Rezaei, A. R. (2011). Validity and reliability of the IAT: Measuring gender and ethnic stereotypes. *Computers in Human Behavior, 27*, 1937–1941. doi: 10.1016/j.chb.2011.04.018

Rios, D., & Stewart, A. (2016). Recognizing privilege by reducing invisibility: The Global Feminisms Project as a pedagogical tool. In K. A. Case (Ed.), *Deconstructing privilege: Teaching and learning as allies in the classroom* (pp. 115–131). New York, NY: Routledge.

Rogers, K. (2016, November 18). Amid division, a march in Washington seeks to bring women together. *The New York Times.* Retrieved from https://www.nytimes.com/2016/11/19/us/womens-march-on-washington.html

Romero, R. E. (2000). The icon of the strong Black woman: The paradox of strength. In L. C. Jackson & B. Greene (Eds.), *Psychotherapy with African American women: Innovations in psychodynamic perspective and practice* (pp. 235–238). New York, NY: Guilford Press.

Rudman, L. A. (1998). Self-promotion as a risk factor for women: The costs and benefits of counterstereotypical impression management. *Journal of Personality and Social Psychology, 74*, 629–645. doi: 10.1037/0022-3514.74.3.629

Rudman, L. A., & Fairchild, K. (2004). Reactions to counterstereotypic behavior: The role of backlash in cultural stereotype maintenance. *Journal of Personality and Social Psychology, 87*, 157–176. doi: 10.1037/0022-3514.87.2.157

Ruggiero, K. M., & Taylor, D. M. (1997). Why minority group members perceive or do not perceive the discrimination that confronts them: The role of self-esteem and perceived control. *Journal of Personality and Social Psychology, 72*, 373–389. doi: 10.1037/0022-3514.72.2.373

Ryan, M. K., Haslam, A. S., & Postmes, T. (2007). Reactions to the glass cliff: Gender differences in the explanations for the precariousness of women's leadership positions. *Journal of Organizational Change Management, 20*, 182–197. doi: 10.1108/09534810710724748

Sadker, M., & Sadker, D. (1994). *Failing at fairness: How our schools cheat girls.* New York, NY: Touchstone.

Salomon, K., Burgess, K. D., & Bosson, J. K. (2015). Flash fire and slow burn: Women's cardiovascular reactivity and recovery following hostile and benevolent sexism. *Journal of Experimental Psychology, 144*, 469–479. doi: 10.1037/xge0000061

Salvatore, J., & Shelton, J. N. (2007). Cognitive costs of exposure to racial prejudice. *Psychological Science, 18*, 810–815. doi: 10.1111/j.1467-9280.2007.01984.x

Saucier, D. A., Till, D. F., Miller, S. S., O'Dea, C. J., & Andres, E. (2015). Slurs against masculinity: Masculine honor beliefs and men's reactions to slurs. *Language Sciences, 52*, 108–120. doi: 10.1016/j.langsci.2014.09.006

Saxena, J. (2015, July 22). Examples of male vocal fry. *The Toast.* Retrieved from http://the-toast.net/2015/07/22/examples-of-male-vocal-fry/

Scheuble, L. K., & Johnson, D. R. (2005). Married women's situational use of last names: An empirical study. *Sex Roles, 53*, 143–151. doi: 10.1007/s11199-005-4288-3

Schlehofer, M. M., Casad, B. J., Bligh, M. C., & Grotto, A. R. (2011). Navigating public prejudices: The impact of media and attitudes on high-profile female political leaders. *Sex Roles, 65*, 69–82. doi: 10.1007/s11199-011-9965-9

Schug, J., Alt, N. P., Lu, P. S., Gosin, M., & Fay, J. L. (2017). Gendered race in mass media: Invisibility of Asian men and Black women in popular magazines. *Psychology of Popular Media Culture, 6*, 222–236. doi: 10.1037/ppm0000096

Sellers, R. M., Rowley, S. A., Chavous, T. M., Shelton, J. N., & Smith, M. A. (1997). The Multidimensional Inventory of Black Identity: A preliminary investigation of reliability and construct validity. *Journal of Personality and Social Psychology, 73*, 805–815. doi: 10.1037/0022-3514.73.4.805

Sesko, A. K., & Biernat, M. (2010). Prototypes of race and gender: The invisibility of Black women. *Journal of Experimental Social Psychology, 46*, 356–360. doi: 10.1016/j.jesp.2009.10.016

Settles, I. H. (2006). Use of an intersectional framework to understand Black women's racial and gender identities. *Sex Roles, 54*, 589–601. doi: 10.1007/s11199-006-9029-8

Shepherd, M., Erchull, M. J., Rosner, A., Taubenberger, L., Forsyth Queen, E., & McKee, J. (2011). "I'll get that for you": The relationship between benevolent sexism and body self-perceptions. *Sex Roles, 64*, 1–8. doi: 10.1007/s11199-010-9859-2

Shields, S. A. (2008). Gender: An intersectionality perspective. *Sex Roles, 59*, 301–311. doi: 10.1007/s11199-008-9501-8

Simon, S., & O'Brien, L. T. (2015). Confronting sexism: The effect of moral credentialing on interpersonal costs of target confrontations. *Sex Roles, 73*, 245–257. doi: 10.1007/s11199-015-0513-x

Slade, M. (2015). Who wears the pants? The difficulties men face when trying to take their spouse's surname after marriage. *Family Court Review, 53*, 336–351. doi: 10.1111/fcre.12149

Solnit, R. (2015). *Men explain things to me.* Chicago, IL: Haymarket Books.

Spelman, E. (1990). *Inessential woman.* Boston, MA: Beacon Press.

Stephens, D. P., & Phillips, L. D. (2003). Freaks, gold diggers, divas, and dykes: The sociohistorical development of adolescent African American women's sexual script. *Sexuality & Culture, 7*, 3–49. doi: 10.1007/BF03159848

Stockman, F. (2017, January 9). Women's march on Washington opens contentious dialogues about race. *The New York Times.* Retrieved from https://www.nytimes.com/2017/01/09/us/womens-march-on-washington-opens-contentious-dialogues-about-race.html

Stroessner, S. J. (1996). Social categorization by race or sex: Effects of perceived non-normalcy on response times. *Social Cognition, 14*, 247–276. doi: 10.1521/soco.1996.14.3.247

Suarez, E. (1996). Woman's freedom to choose her surname: Is it really a matter of choice? *Women's Rights Law Reporter, 18*, 233–242.

Sue, D. W. (2010). *Microaggressions in everyday life: Race, gender, and sexual orientation.* Hoboken, NJ: Wiley.

Sue, D. W., & Capodilupo, C. M. (2008). Racial, gender, and sexual orientation microaggressions: Implications for counseling and psychotherapy. In D.W. Sue & D. Sue (Eds.), *Counseling the culturally diverse: Theory and practice* (pp. 105–131). Hoboken, NJ: Wiley.

Swann, J. (1992). *Girls, boys, and language.* Oxford, UK: Blackwell.

Swim, J. K., Aikin, K. J., Hall, W. S., & Hunter, B. A. (1995). Sexism and racism: Old-fashioned and modern prejudices. *Journal of Personality and Social Psychology, 68*, 199–214. doi: 10.1037/0022-3514.68.2.199

Swim, J. K., & Campbell, B. (2001). Sexism: Attitudes, beliefs, and behaviors. In R. Brown & S. L. Gaertner (Eds.), *Blackwell handbook of social psychology: Intergroup processes* (pp. 218–238). Malden, MA: Blackwell.

Swim, J. K., & Cohen, L. L. (1997). Overt, covert, and subtle sexism: A comparison between the Attitude toward Women and Modern Sexism Scales. *Psychology of Women Quarterly, 21*, 103–118. doi: 10.1111/j.1471-6402.1997.tb00103.x

Swim, J. K., Mallett, R., & Stangor, C. (2004). Understanding subtle sexism: Detection and use of sexist language. *Sex Roles, 51*, 117–128. doi: 10.1023/B:SERS.0000037757.73192.06

Tajfel, H., & Turner, J. C. (1979). An integrative theory of intergroup conflict. In W. G. Austin & S. Worchel (Eds.), *The social psychology of intergroup relations* (pp. 33–47). Monterey, CA: Brooks/Cole.

Takiff, H. A., Sanchez, D. T., & Stewart, T. L. (2001). What's in a name? The status implications of students' terms of address for male and female professors. *Psychology of Women Quarterly, 25*, 134–144. doi: 10.1111/1471-6402.00015

Tannen, D. (1995). The power of talk: Who gets heard and why. *Harvard Business Review, 73*, 138–148.

Tanzer, D. (1985). Real men don't eat strong women: The virgin-madonna-whore complex updated. *The Journal of Psychohistory, 12*, 487–495.

Tariq, M., & Syed, J. (2017). Intersectionality at work: South Asian Muslim women's experiences of employment and leadership in the United Kingdom. *Sex Roles, 77*, 510–522. doi: 10.1007/s11199-017-0741-3

Tavris, C., & Wade, C. (1984). *The longest war: Sex differences in perspective* (2nd ed.). San Diego, CA: Harcourt.

Teeman, T. (2017, March 23). Sexism, race and the mess of "Miss Saigon" on Broadway. *The Daily Beast.* Retrieved from https://www.thedailybeast.com/sexism-race-and-the-mess-of-miss-saigon-on-broadway

Thomas, A. J., & King, C. T. (2007). Gendered racial socialization of African American mothers and daughters. *Family Journal, 15*, 137–142. doi: 10.1177/1066480706297853

Tiedens, L. Z., & Fragale, A. R. (2003). Power moves: Complementarity in dominant and submissive nonverbal behavior. *Journal of Personality and Social Psychology, 84*, 558–568. doi: 10.1037/0022-3514.84.3.558

Tolentino, J. (2017, January 18). The somehow controversial Women's March on Washington. *The New Yorker.* Retrieved from http://www.newyorker.com/culture/jia-tolentino/the-somehow-controversial-womens-march-on-washington

Twenge, J. M. (1997). Changes in masculine and feminine traits over time: A meta-analysis. *Sex Roles, 36*, 305–325. doi: 10.1007/BF02766650

Twenge, J. M. (2001). Changes in women's assertiveness in response to status and roles: A cross-temporal meta-analysis, 1931–1993. *Journal of Personality and Social Psychology, 81*, 133–145. doi: 10.1037/0022-3514.81.1.133

Twenge, J. M., Campbell, W. K., & Gentile, B. (2012). Generational increases in agentic self-evaluations among American college students, 1966–2009. *Self and Identity, 11*, 409–427. doi: 10.1080/15298868.2011.576820

Urken, R. K. (2012, November 15). Changing your name: Do it right or pay the price. *Aol.* Retrieved from https://www.aol.com/2012/11/15/changing-your-name-do-it-right-or-pay-the-price/

Van Laar, J. (2017, January 25). Back-and-forth responses to Women's March all miss the point. *Red State.* Retrieved from http://www.redstate.com/jenvanlaar/2017/01/25/responses-responses-womens-march-miss-point/

Wallace, M. (1990). *Black macho and the myth of the superwoman.* New York, NY: The Dial Press.

Wasserman, B. D., & Weseley, A. J. (2009). ¿Qué? Quoi? Do languages with grammatical gender promote sexist attitudes? *Sex Roles, 61*, 634–643. doi: 10.1007/s11199-009-9696-3

Watson, N. N., & Hunter, C. D. (2015). Anxiety and depression among African American women: The costs of strength and negative attitudes toward psychological help-seeking. *Cultural Diversity and Ethnic Minority Psychology, 21*, 604–612. doi: 10.1037/cdp0000015

Wells, V. (2016, March 23). #Naturalisprofessional: Campaign challenges notion that natural hair is not for the workplace. *Madame Noire.* Retrieved from http://madamenoire.com/621514/naturalisprofessional-campaign-challenges-notion-that-natural-hair-is-not-for-the-workplace/

West, C., & Zimmerman, D. H. (1987). Doing gender. *Gender & Society, 1*, 125–151. doi: 10.1177/0891243287001002002

Wildman, S. M. (1996). *Privilege revealed: How invisible preference undermines America.* New York, NY: New York University Press.

Winfrey Harris, T. (2014, November 6). The truth behind the "strong Black woman" stereotype. *Alternet.* Retrieved from http://www.alternet.org/truth-behind-strong-black-woman-stereotype

Wise, T., & Case, K. A. (2013). Pedagogy for the privileged: Addressing inequality and injustice without shame or blame. In K. A. Case (Ed.), *Deconstructing privilege: Teaching and learning as allies in the classroom* (pp. 115–131). New York, NY: Routledge.

Wong, A. (2015, January 30). The activity gap. *The Atlantic.* Retrieved from https://www.theatlantic.com/education/archive/2015/01/the-activity-gap/384961/

Wood, W., & Eagly, A. H. (2010). Gender. In S. T. Fiske, D. T. Gilbert, & G. Lindzey (Eds.), *Handbook of social psychology* (5th ed., Vol. 1, pp. 629–667). New York, NY: Wiley.

Woodford, M. R., Howell, M. L., Kulick, A., & Silverschanz, P. (2013). "That's so gay": Heterosexual male undergraduates and the perpetuation of sexual orientation microaggressions on campus. *Journal of Interpersonal Violence, 28*, 416–435. doi: 10.1177/0886260512454719

Wright, S., & Hay, J. (2002). Fred and Wilma: A phonological conspiracy. In S. Benor, M. Rose, D. Sharma, J. Sweetland, & Q. Zhang (Eds.), *Gendered practices in language* (pp. 175–191). Stanford, CA: CSLI Publications.

Wright, S. C. (2001). Strategic collective action: Social psychology and social change. In R. Brown & S. L. Gaertner (Eds.), *Blackwell handbook of social psychology: Intergroup processes* (pp. 409–430). Malden, MA: Blackwell.

Yaeger, T. (n.d.). Who narrates the world? The OpEd Project by-line report. *The OpEd Project.* Retrieved from http://www.theopedproject.org/index.php?option=com_content&view=article&id=817&Itemid=149

Yamawaki, N. (2007). Rape perception and the function of ambivalent sexism and gender-role traditionality. *Journal of Interpersonal Violence, 22*, 406–423. doi: 10.1177/0886260506297210

Zhou, Y. (2000). The fall of "the other half of the sky"? Chinese immigrant women in the New York area. *Women's Studies International Forum, 23*, 445–459. doi: 10.1016/S0277-5395(00)00106-0

Zimman, L. (2015). Facebook, the gender binary, and third-person pronouns. In A. Northover (Ed.), *The OUPblog Tenth Anniversary Book: Ten years of academic insights for the thinking world* (pp. 137–142). New York, NY: Oxford University Press.

Chapter 3

Alexander, M. G., & Fisher, T. D. (2003). Truth and consequences: Using the bogus pipeline to examine sex differences in self-reported sexuality. *Journal of Sex Research, 40*, 27–35. doi: 10.1080/00224490309552164

American Association for the Advancement of Science. (2010, September 8). *Barriers for women scientists survey report: Conducted exclusively for L'Oréal by Cell Associates.* Retrieved from https://www.aaas.org/sites/default/files/migrate/uploads/0928loreal_survey_report.pdf

Archer, J. (2004). Sex differences in aggression in real-world settings: A meta-analytic review. *Review of General Psychology, 8*, 291–322. doi: 10.1037/1089-2680.8.4.291

Archer, L., Dewitt, J., & Osborne, J. (2015). Is science for us? Black students' and parents' views of science and science careers. *Science Education, 99*, 199–237. doi: 10.1002/sce.21146

Aron, L., & Loprest, P. (2012). Disability and the education system. *The Future of Children, 22*, 97–122. doi: 10.1353/foc.2012.0007

Aschbacher, P. R., Li, E., & Roth, E. J. (2010). Is science me? High school students' identities, participation and aspirations in science, engineering, and medicine. *Journal of Research in Science Teaching, 47*, 564–582. doi: 10.1002/tea.20353

Baumeister, R. F., Campbell, J. D., Krueger, J. I., & Vohs, K. D. (2003). Does high self-esteem cause better performance, interpersonal success, happiness, or healthier lifestyles? *Psychological Science in the Public Interest, 4*, 1–44. doi: 10.1111/1529-1006.01431

Bergen, M., & Huet, E. (2017, August 7). Google fires author of divisive memo on gender differences. *Bloomberg Technology.* Retrieved from https://www.bloomberg.com/news/articles/2017-08-08/google-fires-employee-behind-controversial-diversity-memo

Bishop, K. M., & Wahlsten, D. (1997). Sex differences in the human corpus callosum: Myth or reality? *Neuroscience & Biobehavioral Reviews, 21*, 581–601. doi: 10.1016/S0149-7634(96)00049-8

Bjorklund, D. F., & Shackelford, T. K. (1999). Differences in parental investment contribute to important differences between men and women. *Current Directions in Psychological Science, 8*, 86–89. doi: 10.1111/1467-8721.00020

Brescoll, V. L., & Uhlmann, E. L. (2008). Can an angry woman get ahead? Status conferral, gender, and expression of emotion in the workplace. *Psychological Science, 19*, 268–275. doi: 10.1111/j.1467-9280.2008.02079.x

Brown, C., Dashjian, L. T., Acosta, T. J., Mueller, C. T., Kizer, B. E., & Trangsrud, H. B. (2012). The career experiences of male-to-female transsexuals. *The Counseling Psychologist, 40*, 868–894. doi: 10.1177/0011000011430098

Buss, D. M. (1995). Psychological sex differences: Origins through sexual selection. *American Psychologist, 50*, 164–168. doi: 10.1037/0003-066X.50.3.164

Buss, D. M., & Schmitt, D. P. (1993). Sexual strategies theory: An evolutionary perspective on human mating. *Psychological Review, 100*, 204–232. doi: 10.1037/0033-295X.100.2.204

Buss, D. M., & Schmitt, D. P. (2011). Evolutionary psychology and feminism. *Sex Roles, 64*, 768–787. doi: 10.1007/s11199-011-9987-3

Camarata, S., & Woodcock, R. (2006). Sex differences in processing speed: Developmental effects in males and females. *Intelligence, 34*, 231–252. doi: 10.1016/j.intell.2005.12.001

Carothers, B. J., & Reis, H. T. (2013). Men and women are from Earth: Examining the latent structure of gender. *Journal of Personality and Social Psychology, 104*, 385–407. doi: 10.1037/a0030437

Ceci, S. J., Williams, W. M., & Barnett, S. M. (2009). Women's underrepresentation in science: Sociocultural and biological considerations. *Psychological Bulletin, 135*, 218–261. doi: 10.1037/a0014412

Chaplin, T. M., & Aldao, A. (2013). Gender differences in emotion expression in children: A meta-analytic review. *Psychological Bulletin, 139*, 735–765. doi: 10.1037/a0030737

Cherney, I. D., & Ryalls, B. O. (1999). Gender-linked differences in the incidental memory of children and adults. *Journal of Experimental Child Psychology, 72*, 305–328. doi: https://doi.org/10.1006/jecp.1999.2492

Clayton, J. A., & Collins, F. S. (2014). NIH to balance sex in cell and animal studies. *Nature, 509*, 282–283. Retrieved from https://www.nature.com/polopoly_fs/1.15195!/menu/main/topColumns/topLeftColumn/pdf/509282a.pdf

Cohen, J. (1988). *Statistical power analysis for the behavioral sciences* (2nd ed.). Hillsdale, NJ: Erlbaum.

Costa P., Jr., Terracciano, A., & McCrae, R. R. (2001). Gender differences in personality traits across cultures: Robust and surprising findings. *Journal of Personality and Social Psychology, 81*, 322–331. doi: 10.1037/0022-3514.81.2.322

Croft, A., Schmader, T., & Block, K. (2015). An underexamined inequality: Cultural and psychological barriers to men's engagement with communal roles. *Personality and Social Psychology Review, 19*, 343–370. doi: 1088868314564789

Danaher, K., & Crandall, C. S. (2008). Stereotype threat in applied settings re-examined. *Journal of Applied Social Psychology, 38*, 1639–1655. doi: 10.1111/j.1559-1816.2008.00362.x

de Vries, G. J. (2004). Minireview: Sex differences in adult and developing brains: Compensation, compensation, compensation. *Endocrinology, 145*, 1063–1068. doi: 10.1210/en.2003-1504

de Vries, G. J., & Södersten, P. (2009). Sex differences in the brain: The relation between structure and function. *Hormones and Behavior, 55*, 589–596. doi: 10.1016/j.yhbeh.2009.03.012

Diekman, A. B., Clark, E. K., Johnston, A. M., Brown, E. R., & Steinberg, M. (2011). Malleability in communal goals and beliefs influences attraction to STEM careers: Evidence for a goal congruity perspective. *Journal of Personality and Social Psychology, 101*, 902–918. doi: 10.1037/a0025199

Dreary, I. J., Thorpe, G., Wilson, V., Starr, J. M., & Whalley, L. J. (2003). Population sex differences in IQ at age 11: The Scottish mental survey 1932. *Intelligence, 31*, 533–542. doi: 10.1016/S0160-2896(03)00053-9

Dupre, J. (2016). A post genomic perspective on sex and gender. In D. L. Smith (Ed.), *How biology shapes philosophy: New foundations for naturalism* (pp. 227–247). Cambridge, MA: Cambridge University Press.

Eagly, A. H. (1995). The science and politics of comparing women and men. *American Psychologist, 50*, 145–158. doi: 10.1037/0003-066X.50.3.145

Eagly, A. H. (2009). The his and hers of prosocial behavior: An examination of the social psychology of gender. *American Psychologist, 64*, 644–658. doi: 10.1037/0003-066X.64.8.644

Eagly, A. H., & Crowley, M. (1986). Gender and helping behavior: A meta-analytic review of the social psychological literature. *Psychological Bulletin, 100*, 283–308. doi: 10.1037/0033-2909.100.3.283

Eagly, A. H., & Mladinic, A. (1994). Are people prejudiced against women? Some answers from research on attitudes, gender stereotypes, and judgments of competence. *European Review of Social Psychology, 5*, 1–35. doi: 10.1080/14792779543000002

Eagly, A. H., & Wood, W. (1999). The origins of sex differences in human behavior: Evolved dispositions versus social roles. *American Psychologist, 54*, 408–423. doi: 10.1037/0003-066X.54.6.408.

Eagly, A. H., & Wood, W. (2011). Feminism and the evolution of sex differences and similarities. *Sex Roles, 64*, 758–767. doi: 10.1007/s11199-011-9949-9

Eccles, J. S. (1994). Understanding women's educational and occupational choices. *Psychology of Women Quarterly, 18*, 585–609. doi: 10.1111/j.1471-6402.1994.tb01049.x

Else-Quest, N. M., Higgins, A., Allison, C., & Morton, L. C. (2012). Gender differences in self-conscious emotional experience: A meta-analysis. *Psychological Bulletin, 138*, 947–981. doi: 10.1037/a0027930

Else-Quest, N. M., Hyde, J. S., & Linn, M. C. (2010). Cross-national patterns of gender differences in mathematics: A meta-analysis. *Psychological Bulletin, 136*, 103–127. doi: 10.1037/a001805

Espinosa, L. (2011). Pipelines and pathways: Women of color in undergraduate STEM majors and the college experiences that contribute to persistence. *Harvard Educational Review, 81*, 209–241.

Farrel, B., & Farrel, P. (2007). *Men are like waffles, women are like spaghetti*. Irvine, CA: Harvest House.

Faulkner, V. N., Crossland, C. L., & Stiff, L. V. (2013). Predicting eighth-grade algebra placement for students with individualized education programs. *Exceptional Children, 79*, 329–345.

Feingold, A. (1994). Gender differences in personality: A meta-analysis. *Psychological Bulletin, 116*, 429–456. doi: 10.1037/0033-2909.116.3.429

Ferri, B. (2010). A dialogue we've yet to have: Race and disability studies. In C. Dudley-Marling & A. Gurn (Eds.), *The myth of the normal curve* (pp. 139–150). New York, NY: Peter Lang.

Fine, C. (2010). *Delusions of gender: How our minds, society, and neurosexism create difference*. New York, NY: Norton.

Fine, C., Jordan-Young, R., Kaiser, A., & Rippon, G. (2013). Plasticity, plasticity, plasticity . . . and the rigid problem of sex. *Trends in Cognitive Sciences, 17*, 550–551. doi: 10.1016/j.tics.2013.08.010

Fisher, T. D. (2013). Gender roles and pressure to be truthful: The bogus pipeline modifies gender differences in sexual but not non-sexual behavior. *Sex Roles, 68*, 401–414. doi: 10.1007/s11199-013-0266-3

Foschi, M. (2000). Double standards for competence: Theory and research. *Annual Review of Sociology, 26*, 21–28. doi: 10.1146/annurev.soc.26.1.21

Gentile, B., Grabe, S., Dolan-Pascoe, B., Twenge, J. M., Wells, B. E., & Maitino, A. (2009). Gender differences in domain-specific self-esteem: A meta-analysis. *Review of General Psychology, 13*, 34–45. doi: 10.1037/a0013689

Gettler, L. T., McDade, T. W., Feranil, A. B., & Kuzawa, C. W. (2011). Longitudinal evidence that fatherhood decreases testosterone in human males. *Proceedings of the National Academy of Sciences, 108*, 16194–16199. doi: 10.1073/pnas.1105403108

Gillen, A., & Tanenbaum, C. (2014, September). *Exploring gender imbalance among STEM doctoral degree recipients* (Issue Brief). Washington DC: American Institutes of Research. Retrieved from http://www.air.org/sites/default/files/downloads/report/STEM%20PhDs%20Gender%20Imbalance%20Sept%202014c.pdf

Gilligan, C. (1982). *In a different voice*. Cambridge, MA: Harvard University Press.

Goetz, A. T., & Shackelford, T. K. (2009). Sexual conflict in humans: Evolutionary consequences of asymmetric parental investment and paternity uncertainty. *Animal Biology*, 59, 449–456. doi: 10.1163/157075509X12499949744342

Goetz, A. T., Shackelford, T. K., Romero, G. A., Kaighobadi, F., & Miner, E. J. (2008). Punishment, proprietariness, and paternity: Men's violence against women from an evolutionary perspective. *Aggression and Violent Behavior*, 13, 481–489. doi: 10.1016/j.avb.2008.07.004

Gray, J. (1992). *Men are from Mars, women are from Venus: The classic guide to understanding the opposite sex* (20th anniversary ed.). New York, NY: Harper.

Grunspan, D. Z., Eddy, S. L., Brownell, S. E., Wiggins, B. L., Crowe, A. J., & Goodreau, S. M. (2016). Males under-estimate academic performance of their female peers in undergraduate biology classrooms. *PloS One, 11*(2), e0148405. doi: 10.1371/journal.pone.0148405

Guiso, L., Monte, F., Sapienza, P., & Zingales, L. (2008). Culture, gender, and math. *Science, 320*, 1164–1165. doi: 10.1126/science.1154094

Gunderson, E. A., Ramirez, G., Levine, S. C., & Beilock, S. L. (2012). The role of parents and teachers in the development of gender-related math attitudes. *Sex Roles, 66*, 153–166. doi: 10.1007/s11199-011-9996-2

Haier, R. J., Jung, R. E., Yeo, R. A., Head, K., & Alkire, M. T. (2005). The neuroanatomy of general intelligence: Sex matters. *NeuroImage, 25*, 320–327. doi: 10.1016/j.neuroimage.2004.11.019

Halpern, D. F. (2006). Assessing gender gaps in learning and academic achievement. In P. A. Alexander & P. H. Winne (Eds.), *Handbook of educational psychology* (pp. 635–653). Mahwah, NJ: Lawrence Erlbaum.

Halpern, D. F., Eliot, L., Bigler, R. S., Fabes, R. A., Hanish, L. D., Hyde, J., . . . Martin, C. L. (2011). The pseudoscience of single-sex schooling. *Science, 333*, 1706–1707. doi: 10.1126/science.1205031

Halpern, D. F., & LaMay, M. L. (2000). The smarter sex: A critical review of sex differences in intelligence. *Educational Psychology Review, 12*, 229–246. doi: 1040-726X/00/0600-0229

Hammrich, P. L., Price, L., & Nourse, S. (2002). *Daughters with disabilities: Reframing science, math, and technology for girls with disabilities*. Retrieved from ERIC database (ED466868): http://files.eric.ed.gov/fulltext/ED466868.pdf

Hare-Mustin, R. T, & Marecek, J. (1988). The meaning of difference: Gender theory, postmodernism, and psychology. *American Psychologist, 43*, 455–464. doi: 10.1037/0003-066X.43.6.455

Harley, W. F. (2011). *His needs, her needs: Building an affair proof marriage*. Ada, MI: Revell.

Harris, J., Hirsh-Pasek, K., & Newcombe, N. S. (2013). Understanding spatial transformations: Similarities and differences between mental rotation and mental folding. *Cognitive Processing, 14*, 105–115. doi: 10.1007/s10339-013-0544-6

Harvey, S. (2011). *Act like a lady, think like a man: What men really think about love, relationships, intimacy and commitment*. New York, NY: Amistad.

Hawley, C. E., Cardoso, E., & McMahon, B. T. (2013). Adolescence to adulthood in STEM education and career development: The experience of students at the intersection of underrepresented minority status and disability. *Journal of Vocational Rehabilitation, 39*, 193–204. doi: 10.3233/JVR-130655

Hess, C., Gault, B., & Yi, Y. (2013). *Accelerating change for women of color faculty in STEM: Policy, action, and collaboration*. Washington, DC: Institute for Women's Policy Research. Retrieved from https://iwpr.org/wp-content/uploads/wpallimport/files/iwpr-export/publications/C409-FINAL.pdf

Hillard, A. L., Schneider, T. R., Jackson, S. M., & LaHuis, D. (2014). Critical mass or incremental change? The effects of faculty gender composition in STEM. In V. Demos, C. W. Berheide, & M. T. Segal (Eds.), *Gender transformation in the academy* (pp. 355–374). Bingley, United Kingdom: Emerald Group.

Hollenshead, C., & Thomas, G. (2001). Resisting from the margins: The coping strategies of Black women and other women of color faculty members at a research university. *Journal of Negro Education, 70*, 166–175.

Hollingsworth, L. S. (1914). Variability as related to sex differences in achievement: A critique. *American Journal of Sociology, 19*, 510–530. doi: 10.1086/212287

Houtte, M. V. (2004). Why boys achieve less at school than girls: The difference between boys' and girls' academic culture. *Educational Studies, 30*, 159–173. doi: 10.1080/0305569032000159804

Huguet, P., & Régner, I. (2009). Counter-stereotypic beliefs in math do not protect school girls from stereotype threat. *Journal of Experimental Social Psychology, 45*, 1024–1027. doi: 1016/j.jesp.2009.04.029

Hyde, J. S. (2005). The gender similarities hypothesis. *American Psychologist, 60*, 581–592. doi: 10.1037/0003-066X.60.6.581

Hyde, J. S. (2014). Gender similarities and differences. *Annual Review of Psychology, 65*, 373–398. doi: 10.1146/annurev-psych-010213115057

Hyde, J. S., Fennema, E., & Lamon, S. J. (1990). Gender differences in mathematics performance: A meta-analysis. *Psychological Bulletin, 107*, 139–155. doi: 10.1037/0033-2909.107.2.139

Hyde, J. S., Lindberg, S. M., Linn, M. C., Ellis, A. B., & Williams, C. C. (2008). Gender similarities characterize math performance. *Science, 321*, 494–495. doi: 10.1126/science.1160364

Hyde, J. S., & Linn, M. C. (1988). Gender differences in verbal ability: A meta-analysis. *Psychological Bulletin, 104*, 53–69. doi: 10.1037/0033-2909.104.1.53

Hyde, J. S., & Mertz, J. E. (2009). Gender, culture, and mathematics performance. *Proceedings of the National Academy of Sciences, 106*, 8801–8807. doi: 10.1073/pnas.0901265106

Ingalhalikar, M., Smith, A., Parker, D., Satterthwaite, T. D., Elliott, M. A., Ruparel, K., . . . Verma, R. (2014). Sex differences in the structural connectome of the human brain. *Proceedings of the National Academy of Sciences, 111*, 823–828. doi: 10.1073/pnas.1316909110

Jacobs, J. E. (1991). Influence of gender stereotypes on parent and child mathematics attitudes. *Journal of Educational Psychology, 83*, 518–527. doi: 10.1037/0022-0663.83.4.518

Jaffee, S., & Hyde, J. S. (2000). Gender differences in moral orientation: A meta-analysis. *Psychological Bulletin, 126*, 703–726. doi.org/10.1037/0033-2909.126.5.703

Jäncke, L., Gaab, N., Wüstenberg, T., Scheich, H., & Heinze, H. J. (2001). Short-term functional plasticity in the human auditory cortex: An fMRI study. *Cognitive Brain Research, 12*, 479–485. doi: 10.1016/S0926-6410(01)00092-1

Joel, D., Berman, Z., Tavor, I., Wexler, N., Gaber, O., Stein, Y., . . . Liem, F. (2015). Sex beyond the genitalia: The human brain mosaic. *Proceedings of the National Academy of Sciences, 112*, 15468–15473. doi: 10.1073/pnas.1509654112

Joel, D., & McCarthy, M. M. (2017). Incorporating sex as a biological variable in neuropsychiatric research: Where are we now and where should we be? *Neuropsychopharmacology. 42*, 379–385. doi: 10.1038/npp.2016.79

Johnson, W., Carothers, A., & Deary, I. J. (2008). Sex differences in variability in general intelligence: A new look at the old question. *Perspectives on Psychological Science, 3*, 518–531. doi: 10.1111/j.1745-6924.2008.00096.x

Kachchaf, R., Ko, L., Hodari, A., & Ong, M. (2015). Career-life balance for women of color: Experiences in science and engineering academia. *Journal of Diversity in Higher Education*, 8, 175–191. doi: 10.1037/a0039068

Kaiser, A., Haller, S., Schmitz, S., & Nitsch, C. (2009). On sex/gender related similarities and differences in fMRI language research. *Brain Research Reviews*, 61, 49–59. doi: 10.1016/j.brainresrev.2009.03.005

Kanter, R. M. (1977). Some effects of proportions on group life: Skewed sex ratios and responses to token women. *American Journal of Sociology*, 82, 965–990. doi: 10.1086/226425

Ketelaar, T., & Ellis, B. J. (2000). Are evolutionary explanations unfalsifiable? Evolutionary psychology and the Lakatosian philosophy of science. *Psychological Inquiry*, 11, 1–21. doi: 10.1207/S15327965PLI1101_01

King, E. B., Hebl, M. R., George, J. M., & Matusik, S. F. (2010). Understanding tokenism: Antecedents and consequences of a psychological climate of gender inequity. *Journal of Management*, 36, 482–510. doi: 10.1177/0149206308328508

Kitzinger, C. (1994). Should psychologists study sex differences? *Feminism & Psychology*, 4, 501–506. doi: 10.1177/0959353594044003

Kling, K. C., Hyde, J. S., Showers, C. J., & Buswell, B. N. (1999). Gender differences in self-esteem: A meta-analysis. *Psychological Bulletin*, 125, 470–500. doi: 10.1037/0033-2909.125.4.470

Levine, S. C., Vasilyeva, M., Lourenco, S. F., Newcombe, N. S., & Huttenlocher, J. (2005). Socioeconomic status modifies the sex difference in spatial skill. *Psychological Science*, 16, 841–845. doi: 10.1111/j.1467-9280.2005.01623.x

Lunsford, S. K., & Bargerhuff, M. E. (2006). A project to make the laboratory more accessible to students with disabilities. *Journal of Chemical Education*, 83, 407–409. doi: 10.1021/ed083p407

Machin, S., & Pekkinarin, T. (2008). Global sex differences in test score variability. *Science*, 322, 1331–1332. doi: 10.1126/science.1162573

Maeda, Y., & Yoon, S. (2013). A meta-analysis on gender differences in mental rotation ability measured by the Purdue Spatial Visualization Tests: Visualization of rotations (PSVT:R). *Educational Psychology Review*, 25, 69–94. doi: 10.1007/s10648-012-9215-x

Maguire, E. A., Gadian, D. G., Johnsrude, I. S., Good, C. D., Ashburner, J., Frackowiak, R. S., & Frith, C. D. (2000). Navigation-related structural change in the hippocampi of taxi drivers. *Proceedings of the National Academy of Sciences*, 97, 4398–4403. doi: 10.1073/pnas.070039597

Marks, G. (2008). Accounting for the gender gaps in student performance in reading and mathematics: Evidence from 31 countries. *Oxford Review of Education*, 34, 89–109. doi: 10.1080/03054980701565279

Mayo Clinic. (n.d.). Test ID: TTFB. Testosterone, Total, Bioavailable, and Free, Serum. Retrieved from http://www.mayomedical laboratories.com/test-catalog/Clinical+and+Interpretive/83686

McCormick, K. T., MacArthur, H. J., Shields, S. A., & Dicicco, E. C. (2016). New perspectives on gender and emotion. In T.-A. Roberts, N. Curtin, L. E. Duncan, & L. M. Cortina (Eds.), *Feminist perspectives on building a better psychological science of gender* (pp. 213–230). New York, NY: Springer.

Merton, R. K. (1948). The self-fulfilling prophecy. *Antioch Review*, 8, 193–210.

Miller, A. (2013, March). A champion of change. *Monitor on Psychology*, 44(3). Retrieved from http://www.apa.org/monitor/2013/03/champion.aspx

Miller, D. I., & Halpern, D. F. (2014). The new science of cognitive sex differences. *Trends in Cognitive Sciences*, 18, 37–45. doi: 10.1016/j.tics.2013.10.011

Miller, L. C., & Fishkin, S. A. (1997). On the dynamics of human bonding and reproductive success: Seeking a window on the adapted-for-human-environmental interface. In J. Simpson & D. Kenrick (Eds.), *Evolutionary social psychology* (pp. 197–235). Mahwah, NJ: Erlbaum.

Moon, N. W., Todd, R. L., Morton, D. L., & Ivey, E. (2012). *Accommodating students with disabilities in science, technology, engineering, and mathematics (STEM): Findings from research and practice for middle grades through university education*. Atlanta, GA: Center for Assistive Technology and Environmental Access, Georgia Institute of Technology. Retrieved from http://advance.cc.lehigh.edu/sites/advance.cc.lehigh.edu/files/accommodating.pdf

Moss-Racusin, C. A., Dovidio, J. F., Brescoll, V. L., Graham, M. J., & Handelsman, J. (2012). Science faculty's subtle gender biases favor male students. *Proceedings of the National Academy of Sciences*, 109, 16474–16479. doi: 10.1073/pnas.1211286109

Muller, M. N., Marlowe, F. W., Bugumba, R., & Ellison, P. T. (2009). Testosterone and paternal care in East African foragers and pastoralists. *Proceedings of the Royal Society of London B: Biological Sciences*, 276, 347–354. doi: 10.1098/rspb.2008.1028

National Science Board. (2014). *Science and engineering indicators* (NSB 14-01). Arlington VA: National Science Foundation. Retrieved from https://www.nsf.gov/statistics/seind14/content/etc/nsb1401.pdf

Nelson, J. A. (2015). Are women really more risk-averse than men? A re-analysis of the literature using expanded methods. *Journal of Economic Surveys*, 29, 566–585. doi: 10.1111/joes.12069

Nettle, D. (2002). Height and reproductive success in a cohort of British men. *Human Nature*, 13, 473–491. doi: 10.1007/s12110-002-1004-7

O'Connor, C., & Joffe, H. (2014). Gender on the brain: A case study of science communication in the new media environment. *PLoS ONE*, 9(10), e110830. doi: 10.1371/journal.pone.0110830

Pahlke, E., Hyde, J. S., & Allison, C. M. (2014). The effects of single-sex compared with coeducational schooling on students' performance and attitudes: A meta-analysis. *Psychological Bulletin*, 140, 1042–1072. doi: 10.1037/a0035740

Penn Medicine. (2013, December 2). *Brain connectivity study reveals striking differences between men and women* [Press Release]. Retrieved from http://www.uphs.upenn.edu/news/News_Releases/2013/12/verma/

Pennington, C. R., Kaye, L. K., Qureshi, A. W., & Heim, D. (2018). Controlling for prior attainment reduces the positive influence that single-gender classroom initiatives exert on high school students' scholastic achievements. *Sex Roles*, 78, 385–393. doi: 10.1007/s11199-017-0799-y

Peters, J., Shackelford, T. K., & Buss, D. M. (2002). Understanding domestic violence against women: Using evolutionary psychology to extend the feminist functional analysis. *Violence and Victims*, 17, 255–264. doi: 10.1891/vivi.17.2.255.33644

Petersen, J. L., & Hyde, J. S. (2010). A meta-analytic review of research on gender differences in sexuality, 1993–2007. *Psychological Bulletin*, 136, 21–38. doi: 10.1037/a0017504

Pipher, M. (2005). *Reviving Ophelia*. New York, NY: Penguin.

Prentice, D. A., & Miller, D. T. (2006). Essentializing differences between women and men. *Psychological Science*, 17, 129–135. doi: 10.1111/j.1467-9280.2006.01675.x

Priess, H. A., & Hyde, J. S. (2010). Gender and academic abilities and preferences. In J. C. Chrisler & D. R. McCreary (Eds.), *Handbook of gender research in psychology* (Vol. 1, pp. 297–316). New York, NY: Springer.

Rankel, L., Amorosi, C., & Graybill, C. M. (2008). Low-cost laboratory adaptations for precollege students who are blind or visually impaired. *Journal of Chemical Education*, 85, 243–247. doi: 10.1021/ed085p243

Reilly, D. (2012). Gender, culture, and sex-typed cognitive abilities. *PLoS ONE, 7*(7), e39904. doi: 10.1371/journal.pone.0039904

Robinson, M. D., & Johnson, J. T. (1997). Is it emotion or is it stress? Gender stereotypes and the perception of subjective experience. *Sex Roles, 36,* 235–258. doi: 10.1007/BF02766270

Rose, H. (2000). Introduction. In H. Rose & S. Rose (Eds.), *Alas, poor Darwin: Arguments against evolutionary psychology* (pp. 1–16). New York, NY: Harmony Books.

Rosenthal, R. (1979). The file drawer problem and tolerance for null results. *Psychological Bulletin, 86,* 638–641. doi: 10.1037/0033-2909.86.3.638

Rothbart, M. K., Hanley, D., & Albert, M. (1986). Gender differences in moral reasoning. *Sex Roles, 15,* 645–653. doi: 10.1007/BF00288220

Rutherford, A., & Granek, L. (2010). Emergence and development of the psychology of women. In J. C. Chrisler, & D. R. McCreary (Eds.), *Handbook of gender research in psychology* (Vol. 1, pp. 19–41). New York, NY: Springer.

Salerno, J. M., & Peter-Hagene, L. C. (2015). One angry woman: Anger expression increases influence for men, but decreases influence for women, during group deliberation. *Law and Human Behavior, 39,* 581–592. doi: 10.1037/lhb0000147

Sax, L. (2007). *Why gender matters: What parents and teachers need to know about the emerging science of sex differences.* Easton, PA: Harmony Press.

Schmader, T., Johns, M., & Forbes, C. (2008). An integrated process model of stereotype threat effects on performance. *Psychological Review, 115,* 336–356, doi: 10.1037/0033-295X.115.2.336.

Settles, I. H., Cortina, L. M., Stewart, A. J., & Malley, J. (2007). Voice matters: Buffering the impact of a negative climate for women in science. *Psychology of Women Quarterly, 31,* 270–281. doi: 10.1111/j.1471-6402.2007.00370.x

Shapiro, J. R., & Williams, A. M. (2012). The role of stereotype threats in undermining girls' and women's performance and interest in STEM fields. *Sex Roles, 66,* 175–183. doi: 10.1007/s11199-011-0051-0

Sharp, M. J., & Getz, J. G. (1996). Substance use as impression management. *Personality and Social Psychology Bulletin, 22,* 60–67. doi: 10.1177/0146167296221006

Shen, H. (2013). Mind the gender gap. *Nature, 495,* 22–24. Retrieved from https://www.nature.com/polopoly_fs/1.12550!/menu/main/topColumns/topLeftColumn/pdf/495022a.pdf

Shetterly, M. L. (2016). *Hidden figures: The American dream and the untold story of the Black women mathematicians who helped win the space race.* New York, NY: William Morrow.

Shields, S. (1975). Functionalism, Darwinism, and the psychology of women. *American Psychologist, 30,* 739–754. doi: 10.1037/h0076948

Shields, S. A. (2007). Passionate men, emotional women: Psychology constructs gender difference in the late 19th century. *History of Psychology, 10,* 92–110. doi: 10.1037/1093-4510.10.2.92

Shields, S. A. (2013). Gender and emotion: What we think we know, what we need to know, and why it matters. *Psychology of Women Quarterly, 37,* 423–435. doi: 10.1177/0361684313502312

Shih, M., Pittinsky, T. L., & Ambady, N. (1999). Stereotype susceptibility: Identity salience and shifts in quantitative performance. *Psychological Science, 10,* 80–83. doi: 10.1111/1467-9280.00111

Shors, T. J., Chua, C., & Falduto, J. (2001). Sex differences and opposite effects of stress on dendritic spine density in the male versus female hippocampus. *The Journal of Neuroscience, 21,* 6292–6297.

Smith, C. A., & Konik, J. (2011). Feminism and evolutionary psychology: Allies, adversaries, or both? An introduction to a special issue. *Sex Roles, 64,* 595–602. doi: 10.1007/s11199-011-9985-5

Smith, J. L., Cech, E., Metz, A., Huntoon, M., & Moyer, C. (2014). Giving back or giving up: Native American student experiences in science and engineering. *Cultural Diversity and Ethnic Minority Psychology, 20,* 413–429. doi: 10.1037/a0036945

Spencer, S. J., Steele, C. M., & Quinn, D. M. (1999). Stereotype threat and women's math performance. *Journal of Experimental Social Psychology, 35,* 4–28. doi: 10.1006/jesp.1998.1373

Spivak, G. C. (1990). Criticism, feminism, and the institution: Elizabeth Grosz interviews Gayatri Chakravorty Spivak. In G. C. Spivak, *The post-colonial critic: Interviews, strategies, dialogues* (S. Harasym, Ed., pp. 1–16). New York, NY: Routledge.

Stake, J. E., & Eisele, H. (2010). Gender and personality. In J. C. Chrisler & D. R. McCreary (Eds.), *Handbook of gender research in psychology* (Vol. 2, pp. 19–40). New York, NY: Springer.

Staley, O. (2016, August 22). Harvey Mudd College took on gender bias and now more than half its computer-science majors are women. *Quartz Magazine.* Retrieved from https://qz.com/730290/harvey-mudd-college-took-on-gender-bias-and-now-more-than-half-its-computer-science-majors-are-women/

Steele, C. M., & Aronson, J. (1995). Stereotype threat and the intellectual test performance of African Americans. *Journal of Personality and Social Psychology, 69,* 797–811. doi: 10.1037/0022-3514.69.5.797

Stoet, G., & Geary, D. C. (2012). Can stereotype threat explain the gender gap in mathematics performance and achievement? *Review of General Psychology, 16,* 93–102. doi: 10.1037/a0026617

Strang, E., & Peterson, Z. D. (2016). Use of a bogus pipeline to detect men's underreporting of sexually aggressive behavior. *Journal of Interpersonal Violence.* Advance online publication. doi: 10.1177/0886260516681157

Stricker, L. J., & Ward, W. C. (2004). Stereotype threat, inquiring about test takers' ethnicity and gender, and standardized test performance. *Journal of Applied Social Psychology, 34,* 665–693. doi: 10.1111/j.1559-1816.2004.tb02564.x

Su, R., Rounds, J., & Armstrong, P. I. (2009). Men and things, women and people: A meta-analysis of sex differences in interests. *Psychological Bulletin, 135,* 859–884. doi: 10.1037/a0017364

Sullivan, A. L., & Artiles, A. J. (2011). Theorizing racial inequity in special education: Applying structural inequity theory to disproportionality. *Urban Education, 46,* 1526–1552. doi: 10.1177/0042085911416014

Summers, L. (2005, January 14). Remarks at NBER Conference on Diversifying the Science & Engineering Workforce. Harvard University, Office of the President. Retrieved from http://www.harvard.edu/president/speeches/summers_2005/nber.php

Suzuki, B. H. (2002). Revisiting the model minority stereotype: Implications for student affairs practice and higher education. *New Directions for Student Services, 2002*(97), 21–32. doi: 10.1002/ss.36

Tarampi, M. R., Heydari, N., & Hegarty, M. (2016). A tale of two types of perspective taking: Sex differences in spatial ability. *Psychological Science, 27,* 1507–1516. doi: 10.1177/0956797616667459

Terman, L. M., & Merrill, M. A. (1937). *Measuring intelligence.* Boston, MA: Houghton Mifflin.

Thompson, H. B. (1903). The mental traits of sex: An empirical investigation of the normal mind in men and women. *Classics in the History of Psychology.* Retrieved from http://psychclassics.yorku.ca/Thompson/

Thompson, T. L., Kiang, L., & Witkow, M. R. (2016). "You're Asian; You're supposed to be smart": Adolescents' experiences with the model minority stereotype and longitudinal links with identity. *Asian American Journal of Psychology, 7,* 108–119. doi: 10.1037/aap0000038

Thornhill, R., & Palmer, C. T. (2000). *A natural history of rape*. Cambridge, MA: The MIT Press.

Unger, R. K. (1979). Toward a redefinition of sex and gender. *American Psychologist, 34*, 1085–1094. doi: 10.1037/0003-066X.34.11.1085

Unger, R. K., & Crawford, M. (1993). Sex and gender: The troubled relationship between terms and concepts. *Psychological Science, 4*, 122–124. doi: 10.1111/j.1467-9280.1993.tb00473.x

van Anders, S. M. (2013). Beyond masculinity: Testosterone, gender/sex, and human social behavior in a comparative context. *Frontiers in Neuroendocrinology, 34*, 198–210. doi: 10.1016/j.yfrne.2013.07.001

van Anders, S. M. (2015). Beyond sexual orientation: Integrating gender/sex and diverse sexualities via sexual configurations theory. *Archives of Sexual Behavior, 44*, 1177–1213. doi: 10.1007/s10508-015-0490-8

van Anders, S. M., Steiger, J., & Goldey, K. L. (2015). Effects of gendered behavior on testosterone in women and men. *Proceedings of the National Academy of Sciences, 112*, 13805–13810. doi: 10.1073/pnas.1509591112

van Anders, S. M., Tolman, R. M., & Volling, B. L. (2012). Baby cries and nurturance affect testosterone in men. *Hormones and Behavior, 61*, 31–36. doi: 10.1016/j.yhbeh.2011.09.012

van Hemert, D. A., van de Vijver, F. J., & Vingerhoets, A. J. (2011). Culture and crying: Prevalences and gender differences. *Cross-Cultural Research, 45*, 399–431. doi: 10.1177/1069397111404519

Voyer, D. (2011). Time limits and gender differences on paper-and-pencil tests of mental rotation: A meta-analysis. *Psychonomic Bulletin & Review, 18*, 267–277. doi: 10.3758/s13423-010-0042-0

Voyer, D., Postma, A., Brake, B., & Imperato-McGinley, J. (2007). Gender differences in object location memory: A meta-analysis. *Psychonomic Bulletin & Review, 14*, 23–38. doi: 10.3758/BF03194024

Voyer, D., & Voyer, S. D. (2014). Gender differences in scholastic achievement: A meta-analysis. *Psychological Bulletin, 140*, 1174–1204. doi: 10.1037/a0036620

Wallentin, M. (2009). Putative sex differences in verbal abilities and language cortex: A critical review. *Brain and Language, 108*, 175–183. doi: 10.1016/j.bandl.2008.07.001

Wang, M. T. (2012). Educational and career interests in math: A longitudinal examination of the links between classroom environment, motivational beliefs, and interests. *Developmental Psychology, 48*, 1643–1657. doi: 10.1037/a0027247

Wang, M. T., Eccles, J. S., & Kenny, S. (2013). Not lack of ability but more choice: Individual and gender differences in choice of careers in science, technology, engineering, and mathematics. *Psychological Science, 24*, 770–775. doi: 10.1177/0956797612458937

Williams, J. C., Phillips, K. W., & Hall, E. V. (2014). *Double jeopardy? Gender bias against women of color in science*. Retrieved from http://www.uchastings.edu/news/articles/2015/01/double-jeopardy-report.pdf

Yoder, J. B., & Mattheis, A. (2016). Queer in STEM: Workplace experiences reported in a national survey of LGBTQA individuals in science, technology, engineering, and mathematics careers. *Journal of Homosexuality, 63*, 1–27. doi: 10.1080/00918369.2015.1078632

Yoder, J. D. (1994). Looking beyond numbers: The effects of gender status, job prestige, and occupational gender-typing on tokenism processes. *Social Psychology Quarterly, 57*, 150–159.

Zell, E., Krizan, Z., & Teeter, S. R. (2015). Evaluating gender similarities and differences using metasynthesis. *American Psychologist, 70*, 10–20. doi: 10.1037/a0038208

Zell, E., Strickhouser, J. E., Lane, T. N., & Teeter, S. R. (2016). Mars, Venus, or Earth? Sexism and the exaggeration of psychological gender differences. *Sex Roles, 75*, 287–300. doi: 10.1007/s11199-016-0622-1

Zusman, M., Knox, D., & Lieberman, M. (2005). Gender differences in reactions to college course requirements or "why females are better students." *College Student Journal, 39*, 621–626.

Chapter 4

Aguayo-Romero, R. A., Reisen, C. A., Zea, M. C., Bianchi, F. T., & Poppen, P. J. (2015). Gender affirmation and body modification among transgender persons in Bogotá, Colombia. *International Journal of Transgenderism, 16*, 103–115. doi: 10.1080/15532739.2015.1075930

Alarie, M., & Gaudet, S. (2013). "I don't know if she is bisexual or if she just wants to get attention": Analyzing the various mechanisms through which emerging adults invisibilize bisexuality. *Journal of Bisexuality, 13*, 191–214. doi: 10.1080/15299716.2013.780004

Alderson, J., Madill, A., & Balen, A. (2004). Fear of devaluation: Understanding the experience of intersexed women with androgen insensitivity syndrome. *British Journal of Health Psychology, 9*, 81–100. doi: 10.1348/135910704322778740

Alimahomed, S. (2010). Thinking outside the rainbow: Women of color redefining queer politics and identity. *Social Identities: Journal for the Study of Race, Nation and Culture, 16*, 151–168. doi: 10.1080/13504631003688849

American Psychiatric Association. (2013). *Diagnostic and statistical manual of mental disorders* (5th ed.). Arlington, VA: American Psychiatric Publishing.

Ansara, Y. G., & Hegarty, P. (2014). Methodologies of misgendering: Recommendations for reducing cisgenderism in psychological research. *Feminism & Psychology, 24*, 259–270. doi: 10.1177/0959353514526217

Aranda, F., Matthews, A. K., Hughes, T. L., Muramatsu, N., Wilsnack, S. C., Johnson, T. P., & Riley, B. B. (2015). Coming out in color: Racial/ethnic differences in the relationship between level of sexual identity disclosure and depression among lesbians. *Cultural Diversity and Ethnic Minority Psychology, 21*, 247–257. doi: 10.1037/a0037644

Bailey, J. M., Pillard, R. C., Dawood, K., Miller, M. B., Farrer, L. A., Trivedi, S., & Murphy, R. L. (1999). A family history study of male sexual orientation. *Behavior and Genetics, 29*, 79–86. doi: 10.1023/A:1021652204405

Balthazart, J. (2012). Brain development and sexual orientation. *Colloquium Series on the Developing Brain, 3*(2), 1–134. doi: 10.4199/C00064ED1V01Y201208DBR008

Baroncini, M., Jissendi, P., Catteau-Jonard, S., Dewailly, D., Pruvo, J. P., Francke, J. P., & Prevot, V. (2010). Sex steroid hormones-related structural plasticity in the human hypothalamus. *Neuroimage, 50*, 428–433. doi: 10.1016/j.neuroimage.2009.11.074

Barr, S. M., Budge, S. L., & Adelson, J. L. (2016). Transgender belongingness as a mediator between strength of transgender identity and well-being. *Journal of Counseling Psychology, 63*, 87–97. doi: 10.1037/cou0000127

Beauchamp, T., & D'Harlingue, B. (2012). Beyond additions and exceptions: The category of transgender and new pedagogical approaches for women's studies. *Feminist Formations, 24*(2), 25–51. doi: 10.1353/ff.2012.0020

Begun, S., & Kattari, S. K. (2016). Conforming for survival: Associations between transgender visual conformity/passing and homelessness experiences. *Journal of Gay and Lesbian Social Services, 18*, 54–66. doi: 10.1080/10538720/2016/1125821.

Bell, M. (2016, November 5). Why be LGBT when you can be LGBTIQCAPGNGFNBA? The story of an escalating acronym. *The Spectator*. Retrieved from https://www.spectator.co.uk/2016/11/why-be-lgbt-when-you-can-be-lgbtiqcapgngfnba/

Benson, K. E. (2013). Seeking support: Transgender client experiences with mental health services. *Journal of Feminist Family Therapy, 25*, 17–40. doi: 10.1080/08952833.2013.755081

Berenbaum, S. A. (1999). Effects of early androgens on sex-typed activities and interests in adolescents with congenital adrenal hyperplasia. *Hormones and Behavior, 35*, 102–110. doi: 10.1006/hbeh.1998.1503

Birkett, M., Koenig, B., & Espelage, D. L. (2009). LGB and questioning students in schools: The moderating effects of homophobic bullying and school climate on negative outcomes. *Journal of Youth and Adolescence, 38*, 989–1000. doi: 10.1007/s10964-008-9389-1

Birnkrant, J. M., & Przeworski, A. (2017). Communication, advocacy, and acceptance among support-seeking parents of transgender youth. *Journal of Gay & Lesbian Mental Health, 21*, 132–153. doi: 10.1080/19359705.2016.1277173

Bockting, W., Robinson, B., Benner, A., & Scheltema, K. (2004). Patient satisfaction with transgender health services. *Journal of Sex & Marital Therapy, 30*, 277–294. doi: 10.1080/00926230490422467

Bockting, W. O., Miner, M. H., Swinburne Romine, R. E., Hamilton, A., & Coleman, E. (2013). Stigma, mental health, and resilience in an online sample of the US transgender population. *American Journal of Public Health, 103*, 943–951. doi: 10.2105/AJPH.2013.301241

Bogaert, A. F. (2006). Toward a conceptual understanding of asexuality. *Review of General Psychology, 10*, 241–250. doi: 10.1037/1089-2680.10.3.241

"Born this way: Stories of young transgender children." (2014, June 8). *CBS News*. Retrieved from http://www.cbsnews.com/news/born-this-way-stories-of-young-transgender-children/

Bosson, J. K., Weaver, J. R., & Prewitt-Freilino, J. L. (2012). Concealing to belong, revealing to be known: Classification expectations and self-threats among persons with concealable stigmas. *Self and Identity, 11*, 114–135. doi: 10.1080/15298868.2010.513508

Bourke, E., Snow, P., Herlihy, A., Amor, D., & Metcalfe, S. (2014). A qualitative exploration of mothers' and fathers' experiences of having a child with Klinefelter syndrome and the process of reaching this diagnosis. *European Journal of Human Genetics, 22*, 18–24. doi: 10.1038/ejhg.2013.102

Bowcott, O. (2009, September 11). Caster Semenya has one of the 46 types of "intersex" conditions. *The Guardian*. Retrieved from http://www.guardian.co.uk/sport/2009/sep/11/caster-semenya-runner-intersex.

Bowleg, L., Huang, J., Brooks, K., Black, A., & Burkholder, G. (2003). Triple jeopardy and beyond: Multiple minority stress and resilience among Black lesbians. *Journal of Lesbian Studies, 7*(4), 87–108. doi: 10.1300/J155v07n04_06

Bregman, H. R., Malik, N. M., Page, M. J., Makynen, E., & Lindahl, K. M. (2013). Identity profiles in lesbian, gay, and bisexual youth: The role of family influences. *Journal of Youth and Adolescence, 42*, 417–430. doi: 10.1007/s10964-012-9798-z

Breslow, A., Brewster, M., Velez, B., Wong, S., Geiger, E., & Soderstrom, B. (2015). Resilience and collective action: Exploring buffers against minority stress for transgender individuals. *Psychology of Sexual Orientation and Gender Diversity, 2*, 253–265. doi: 10.1037/sgd0000117

Brewster, M. E., & Moradi, B. (2010). Perceived experiences of anti-bisexual prejudice: Instrument development and evaluation. *Journal of Counseling Psychology, 57*, 451–468. doi: 10.1037/a0021116

Budge, S. L., Adelson, J. L., & Howard, K. A. (2013). Anxiety and depression in transgender individuals: The roles of transition status, loss, social support, and coping. *Journal of Consulting and Clinical Psychology, 81*, 545–557. doi: 10.1037/a0031774

Budge, S. L., Orovecz, J. J., & Thai, J. L. (2015). Trans men's positive emotions: The interaction of gender identity and emotion labels. *The Counseling Psychologist, 43*, 404–434. doi: 10.1177/0011000014565715

Bueno, A. (2015, October 6). Kris Jenner admits she was "angry" over Caitlyn Jenner's infamous "Vanity Fair" interview. *ET Online*. Retrieved from http://www.etonline.com/news/173406_kris_jenner_admits_she_was_angry_over_caitlyn_jenner_infamous_vanity_fair_interview/

Burri, A., Cherkas, L., Spector, T., & Rahman, Q. (2011). Genetic and environmental influences on female sexual orientation, childhood gender typicality and adult gender identity. *PloS One, 6*(7), e21982. doi: 10.1371/journal.pone.0021982

Butler, J. (1990). *Gender trouble: Feminism and the subversion of identity*. New York, NY: Routledge.

Callahan, G. (2009). *Between XX and XY: Intersexuality and the myth of two sexes*. Chicago, IL: Chicago Review Press.

Carroll, L., Gilroy, P. J., & Ryan, J. (2002). Counseling transgendered, transsexual, and gender-variant clients. *Journal of Counseling and Development, 80*, 131–139. doi: 10.1002/j.1556-6678.2002.tb00175.x

Catinari, S., Vass, A., & Heresco-Levy, U. (2006). Psychiatric manifestations in Turner syndrome: A brief survey. *Israel Journal of Psychiatry and Related Sciences, 43*, 293–295.

Cederlöf, M., Ohlsson Gotby, A., Larsson, H., Serlachius, E., Boman, M., Långström, N., . . . Lichtenstein, P. (2014). Klinefelter syndrome and risk of psychosis, autism and ADHD. *Journal of Psychiatric Research, 48*, 128–130. doi: 10.1016/j.jpsychires.2013.10.001

Charania, G. R. (2005). Regulated narratives in anti-homophobia education: Complications in coming out stories. *Canadian Woman Studies, 24*(2–3), 31–37.

Christopoulos, P., Deligeoroglou, E., Laggari, V., Christogiorgos, S., & Creatsas, G. (2008). Psychological and behavioural aspects of patients with Turner syndrome from childhood to adulthood: A review of the clinical literature. *Journal of Psychosomatic Obstetrics & Gynecology, 29*, 45–51. doi: 10.1080/01674820701577078

Cohen, K. M., & Savin-Williams, R. C. (1996). Developmental perspectives on coming out to self and others. In R. C. Savin-Williams & K. M. Cohen (Eds.), *The lives of lesbians, gays, and bisexuals: Children to adults* (pp. 113–151). Belmont, CA: Brooks/Cole Cengage Learning.

Cohen-Kettenis, P. T., & Pfafflin, F. (2003). *Transgenderism and intersexuality in childhood and adolescence: Making choices*. Thousand Oaks, CA: Sage.

Colapinto, J. (2000). *As nature made him: The boy who was raised as a girl*. New York, NY: Harper Collins.

Connell, R. (2009). Accountable conduct: "Doing gender" in transsexual and political retrospect. *Gender & Society, 23*, 104–111. doi: 10.1177/0891243208327175

Creighton, S. M., & Liao, L. M. (2004). Changing attitudes to sex assignment in intersex. *BJU International, 93*, 659–664. doi: 10.1111/j.1464-410X.2003.04694.x

Creighton, S. M., & Minto, C. L. (2001). Sexual function in adult women with complete androgen insensitivity syndrome. *Journal of Pediatric and Adolescent Gynecology, 14*, 144–145. doi: 10.1016/S1083-3188(01)00117-6

Creighton, S. M., Minto, C. L., & Steele, S. J. (2001). Objective cosmetic and anatomical outcomes at adolescence of feminising surgery for ambiguous genitalia done in childhood. *The Lancet, 358*(9276), 124–125. doi: 10.1016/S0140-6736(01)05343-0

Creighton, S. M., Minto, C. L., & Woodhouse, C. (2001). Long term sexual functioning in intersex conditions with ambiguous genitalia. *Journal of Pediatric and Adolescent Gynecology, 14*, 141–142. doi: 10.1016/S1083-3188(01)00111-5

Cull, M. (2002). Treatment of intersex needs open discussion. *British Medical Journal, 324*(7342), 919. doi: 10.1136/bmj.324.7342.919

Davis, G. (2015). *Contesting intersex: The dubious diagnosis.* New York, NY: New York University Press.

Dean, M. L., & Tate, C. C. (2017). Extending the legacy of Sandra Bem: Psychological androgyny as a touchstone conceptual advance for the study of gender in psychological science. *Sex Roles, 76*, 643–654. doi: 10.1007/s11199-016-0713-z

DeBlaere, C., Brewster, M. E., Bertsch, K. N., DeCarlo, A. L., Kegel, K. A., & Presseau, C. D. (2014). The protective power of collective action for sexual minority women of color: An investigation of multiple discrimination experiences and psychological distress. *Psychology of Women Quarterly, 38*, 20–32. doi: 10.1177/ 0361684313493252

de María Arana, M. (2005, April 28). *A human rights investigation into the medical "normalization" of intersex people: A report of a public hearing by the Human Rights Commission of the city and county of San Francisco.* Retrieved from https://oii.org.au/wp-content/uploads/2009/03/sfhrc_intersex_report.pdf

Dessens, A. B., Slijper, F. M., & Drop, S. L. (2005). Gender dysphoria and gender change in chromosomal females with congenital adrenal hyperplasia. *Archives of Sexual Behavior, 34*, 389–397. doi: 10.1007/s10508-005-4338-5

Devor, A. H. (2004). Witnessing and mirroring: A fourteen stage model of transsexual identity formation. *Journal of Gay & Lesbian Psychotherapy, 8*, 41–67.

de Vries, A. L., McGuire, J. K., Steensma, T. D., Wagenaar, E. C., Doreleijers, T. A., & Cohen-Kettenis, P. T. (2014). Young adult psychological outcome after puberty suppression and gender reassignment. *Pediatrics, 134*, 696–704. doi: 10.1542/peds.2013-2958

Diamond, L. M. (2007). A dynamical systems approach to the development and expression of female same-sex sexuality. *Perspectives on Psychological Science, 2*, 142–161. doi: 10.1111/j.1745-6916.2007.00034.x

Diamond, L. M. (2008a). Female bisexuality from adolescence to adulthood: Results from a 10-year longitudinal study. *Developmental Psychology, 44*, 5–14. doi: 10.1037/0012-1649.44.1.5

Diamond, L. M. (2008b). *Sexual fluidity: Understanding women's love and desire.* Cambridge, MA: Harvard University Press.

Diamond, M., & Watson, L. A. (2004). Androgen insensitivity syndrome and Klinefelter's syndrome: Sex and gender considerations. *Child and Adolescent Psychiatric Clinics of North America, 13*, 623–640. doi: 10.1016/j.chc.2004.02.015

Diaz, T., & Bui, N. H. (2016). Subjective well-being in Mexican and Mexican American women: The role of acculturation, ethnic identity, gender roles, and perceived social support. *Journal of Happiness Studies, 18*, 607–624. doi: 10.1007/s10902-016-9741-1

dickey, l. m., Budge, S. L., Katz-Wise, S. L., & Garza, M. V. (2016). Health disparities in the transgender community: Exploring differences in insurance coverage. *Psychology of Sexual Orientation and Gender Diversity, 3*, 275–282. doi: 10.1037/sgd0000169

Douglas, D. D. (2012). Venus, Serena, and the inconspicuous consumption of blackness: A commentary on surveillance, race talk, and new racism(s). *Journal of Black Studies, 43*, 127–145. doi:10.1177/0021934711410880

Dreger, A., Feder, E. K., & Tamar-Mattis, A. (2012). Prenatal dexamethasone for congenital adrenal hyperplasia. *Journal of Bioethical Inquiry, 9*, 277–294. doi: 10.1007/s11673-012-9384-9

Drescher, J., Cohen-Kettenis, P., & Winter, S. (2012). Minding the body: Situating gender identity diagnoses in the ICD-11. *International Review of Psychiatry, 24*, 568–577. doi: 10.3109/09540261.2012.741575

Duberman, M. (2013). *Stonewall.* New York, NY: Open Road Media.

Dworkin, S. L., Swarr, A. L., & Cooky, C. (2013). (In)justice in sport: The treatment of South African track star Caster Semenya. *Feminist Studies, 39*, 40–69.

Dyar, C., Feinstein, B. A., & London, B. (2015). Mediators of differences between lesbians and bisexual women in sexual identity and minority stress. *Psychology of Sexual Orientation and Gender Diversity, 2*, 43–51. doi: 10.1037/sgd0000090

Dyar, C., Feinstein, B. A., Schick, V., & Davila, J. (2017). Minority stress, sexual identity uncertainty, and partner gender decision making among nonmonosexual individuals. *Psychology of Sexual Orientation and Gender Diversity, 4*, 87–104. doi: 10.1037/sgd0000213

Dyar, C., Lytle, A., London, B., & Levy, S. R. (2015). Application of bisexuality research to the development of a set of guidelines for intervention efforts to reduce binegativity. *Translational Issues in Psychological Science, 1*, 352–362. doi: 10.1037/tps0000045

Egan, S. K., & Perry, D. G. (2001). Gender identity: A multidimensional analysis with implications for psychosocial adjustment. *Developmental Psychology, 37*, 451–463. doi: 10.1037/0012-1649.37.4.451

Ehrensaft, D. (2014). Found in transition: Our littlest transgender people. *Contemporary Psychoanalysis, 50*, 571–592. doi: 10.1080/00107530.2014.942591

El Abd, S., Turk, J., & Hill, P. (1995). Psychological characteristics of Turner syndrome. *Child Psychology & Psychiatry & Allied Disciplines, 36*, 1109–1125. doi: 10.1111/j.1469-7610.1995.tb01360.x

Elder, A. B. (2016). Experiences of older transgender and gender nonconforming adults in psychotherapy: A qualitative study. *Psychology of Sexual Orientation and Gender Diversity, 3*, 180–186. doi: 10.1037/sgd0000154

Elders, M. J., Satcher, D., & Carmona, R. (2017, June). *Re-thinking genital surgeries on intersex infants.* Retrieved from http://www.palmcenter.org/wp-content/uploads/2017/06/Re-Thinking-Genital-Surgeries-1.pdf

Elsas, L. J., Ljungqvist, A., Ferguson-Smith, M. A., Simpson, J. L., Genel, M., Carlson, A. S., & Ehrhardt, A. A. (2000). Gender verification of female athletes. *Genetics in Medicine, 2*, 249–254. doi: 10.1097/00125817-200007000-00008

Endendijk, J. J., Beltz, A. M., McHale, S. M., Bryk, K., & Berenbaum, S. A. (2016). Linking prenatal androgens to gender-related attitudes, identity, and activities: Evidence from girls with congenital adrenal hyperplasia. *Archives of Sexual Behavior, 45*, 1807–1815. doi: 10.1007/s10508-016-0693-7

Engberg, H., Butwicka, A., Nordenström, A., Hirschberg, A. L., Falhammar, H., Lichtenstein, P., & Landén, M. (2015). Congenital adrenal hyperplasia and risk for psychiatric disorders in girls and women born between 1915 and 2010: A total population study. *Psychoneuroendocrinology, 60*, 195–205. doi: 10.1016/j.psyneuen.2015.06.017

Fassinger, R. E., & Arseneau, J. R. (2007). "I'd rather get wet than be under that umbrella": Differentiating the experiences and identities of lesbian, gay, bisexual, and transgender people. In K. J. Bieschke, R. M. Perez, & K. A. DeBord (Eds.), *Handbook of counseling and psychotherapy with lesbian, gay, bisexual, and transgender clients* (2nd ed., pp. 19–49). Washington, DC: American Psychological Association.

Fausto-Sterling, A. (2000). *Sexing the body: Gender politics and the construction of sexuality.* New York, NY: Basic Books.

Fein, L. A., Salgado, C. J., Alvarez, C. V., & Estes, C. M. (2017). Transitioning transgender: Investigating the important aspects of the transition: A brief report. *International Journal of Sexual Health, 29*, 80–88. doi: 10.1080/19317611.2016.1227013

Fincke, D. (2014, July 16). Why do we need labels like "gay," "bi," "trans," and "cis"? *Patheos*. Retrieved from http://www.patheos.com/blogs/camelswithhammers/2014/07/why-do-we-need-labels-like-gay-bi-trans-and-cis/

"5-alpha reductase deficiency." (2017, April). *Genetics Home Reference*. Retrieved from http://ghr.nlm.nih.gov/condition/5-alpha-reductase-deficiency#statistics

Fliegner, M., Krupp, K., Brunner, F., Rall, K., Brucker, S. Y., Briken, P., & Richter-Appelt, H. (2014). Sexual life and sexual wellness in individuals with complete androgen insensitivity syndrome (CAIS) and Mayer-Rokitansky-Küster-Hauser syndrome (MRKHS). *The Journal of Sexual Medicine, 11*, 729–742. doi: 10.1111/jsm.12321

Flores, A. R., Herman, J. L., Gates, G. J., & Brown, T. N. T. (2016, June). *How many adults identify as transgender in the United States?* Los Angeles, CA: The Williams Institute. Retrieved from http://williamsinstitute.law.ucla.edu/wp-content/uploads/How-Many-Adults-Identify-as-Transgender-in-the-United-States.pdf

Foucault, M. (1973). *The birth of the clinic: An archaeology of medical perception*. New York, NY: Vintage Books.

Friedman, E. J. (2014). *Cisgenderism in gender attributions: The ways in which social, cognitive, and individual factors predict misgendering* (Unpublished doctoral dissertation). City University of New York, New York, NY.

Gagné, P., Tewksbury, R., & McGaughey, D. (1997). Coming out and crossing over: Identity formation and proclamation in a transgender community. *Gender & Society, 11*, 478–508. doi: 10.1177/089124397011004006

Galupo, M. P., Davis, K. S., Grynkiewicz, A. L., & Mitchell, R. C. (2014). Conceptualization of sexual orientation identity among sexual minorities: Patterns across sexual and gender identity. *Journal of Bisexuality, 14*, 433–456. doi: 10.1080/15299716.2014.933466

Galupo, M. P., Henise, S. B., & Mercer, N. L. (2016). "The labels don't work very well": Transgender individuals' conceptualizations of sexual orientation and sexual identity. *International Journal of Transgenderism, 17*, 93–104. doi: 10.1080/15532739.2016.1189373

Garofalo, R., Deleon, J., Osmer, E., Doll, M., & Harper, G. W. (2006). Overlooked, misunderstood and at-risk: Exploring the lives and HIV risk of ethnic minority male-to-female transgender youth. *Journal of Adolescent Health, 38*, 230–236. doi: 10.1016/j.jadohealth.2005.03.023

Gatta, M., Pertile, R., & Battistella, P. A. (2011). A case study of young patients affected by Turner syndrome: Competency and psychopathology. *Giornale Italiano Di Psicopatologia / Italian Journal of Psychopathology, 17*, 435–444.

Gazzola, S. B., & Morrison, M. A. (2014). Cultural and personally endorsed stereotypes of transgender men and transgender women: Notable correspondence or disjunction? *International Journal of Transgenderism, 15*, 76–99. doi: 10.1080/15532739.2014.937041

Girardin, C. M., & Van Vliet, G. (2011). Counselling of a couple faced with a prenatal diagnosis of Klinefelter syndrome. *Acta Paediatrica, 100*, 917–922. doi: 10.1111/j.1651-2227.2011.02156.x

"Glossary of terms—transgender." (n.d.). *GLAAD*. Retrieved from https://www.glaad.org/reference/transgender

Gooren, L. (2006). The biology of human psychosexual differentiation. *Hormones and Behavior, 50*, 589–601. doi: 10.1016/j.yhbeh.2006.06.011

Gough, B., Weyman, N., Alderson, J., Butler, G., & Stoner, M. (2008). "They did not have a word": The parental quest to locate a "true sex" for their intersex children. *Psychology & Health, 23*, 493–507. doi: 10.1080/14768320601176170

Grant, J. M., Mottet, L., Tanis, J. E., Harrison, J., Herman, J., & Keisling, M. (2011). *Injustice at every turn: A report of the national transgender discrimination survey*. Washington, DC: National Center for Transgender Equality and National Gay and Lesbian Task Force. Retrieved from http://www.thetaskforce.org/static_html/downloads/reports/reports/ntds_full.pdf

Greene, B. (2000). African American lesbian and bisexual women. *Journal of Social Issues, 56*, 239–249. doi: 10.1111/0022-4537.00163

Gregor, C., Davidson, S., & Hingley-Jones, H. (2016). The experience of gender dysphoria for pre-pubescent children and their families: A review of the literature. *Child & Family Social Work, 21*, 339–346. doi: 10.1111/cfs.12150

Grossman, A., D'Augelli, A., Jarrett Howell, T., & Hubbard, S. (2005). Parents' reactions to transgender youths' gender nonconforming expression and identity. *Journal of Gay and Lesbian Social Services, 18*, 3–16. doi: 10.1300/J041v18n01_02

Grov, C., Bimbi, D. S., Nanín, J. E., & Parsons, J. T. (2006). Race, ethnicity, gender, and generational factors associated with the coming-out process among gay, lesbian, and bisexual individuals. *Journal of Sex Research, 43*, 115–121. doi: 10.1080/00224490609552306

Grumbach, M. M., Hughes, I., & Conte, F. A. (2003). Disorders of sex differentiation. In P. R. Larsen, H. M. Kronenberg, S. Melmed, & K. S. Polonsky (Eds.), *Williams textbook of endocrinology* (10th ed., pp. 842–1002). Philadelphia, PA: W. B. Saunders.

Ha, N. Q., Dworkin, S. L., Martínez-Patiño, M. J., Rogol, A. D., Rosario, V., Sánchez, F. J., . . . Vilain, E. (2014). Hurdling over sex? Sport, science, and equity. *Archives of Sexual Behavior, 43*, 1035–1042. doi: 10.1007/s10508-014-0332-0

Hall, A., Bostanci, A., & Wright, C. F. (2010). Non-invasive prenatal diagnosis using cell-free fetal DNA technology: Applications and implications. *Public Health Genomics, 13*, 246–255. doi: 10.1159/000279626

Hendricks, M. L., & Testa, R. J. (2012). A conceptual framework for clinical work with transgender and gender nonconforming clients: An adaptation of the minority stress model. *Professional Psychology: Research and Practice, 43*, 460–467. doi: 10.1037/a0029597

Henne, K. (2014). The "science" of fair play in sport: Gender and the politics of testing. *Signs, 39*, 787–812. doi: 10.1086/674208

Herek, G. M., & Gonzalez-Rivera, M. (2006). Attitudes toward homosexuality among U.S. residents of Mexican descent. *Journal of Sex Research, 43*, 122–135. doi: 10.1080/00224490609552307

Herlihy, A. S., Gillam, L., Halliday, J. L., & McLachlan, R. I. (2011). Postnatal screening for Klinefelter syndrome: Is there a rationale? *Acta Paediatrica, 100*, 923–933. doi: 10.1111/j.1651-2227.2011.02151.x

Herman, J. L. (2013). Gendered restrooms and minority stress: The public regulation of gender and its impact on transgender people's lives. *Journal of Public Management & Social Policy, 19*, 65–80.

Higa, D., Hoppe, M. J., Lindhorst, T., Mincer, S., Beadnell, B., Morrison, D. M., . . . Mountz, S. (2014). Negative and positive factors associated with the well-being of lesbian, gay, bisexual, transgender, queer, and questioning (LGBTQ) youth. *Youth & Society, 46*, 663–687. doi: 10.1177/0044118X12449630

Holmes, M. M. (2008). Mind the gaps: Intersex and (re-productive) spaces in disability studies and bioethics. *Journal of Bioethical Inquiry, 5,* 169–181. doi: 10.1007/s11673-007-9073-2

Hughes, I. A. (2010). The quiet revolution: Disorders of sex development. *Best Practice & Research Clinical Endocrinology & Metabolism, 24,* 159–162. doi: 10.1016/j.beem.2010.03.005

Human Rights Watch. (2017, July). *"I want to be like nature made me": Medically unnecessary surgeries on intersex children in the US.* Retrieved from https://www.hrw.org/sites/default/files/report_pdf/lgbtintersex0717_web_0.pdf

Hunt, J., & Moodie-Mills, A. (2012, June 29). *The unfair criminalization of gay and transgender youth: An overview of the experiences of LGBT youth in the juvenile justice system.* Washington, DC: Center for American Progress. Retrieved from https://cdn.americanprogress.org/wp-content/uploads/issues/2012/06/pdf/juvenile_justice.pdf

Hunter, S. (2005). *Midlife and older LGBT adults: Knowledge and affirmative practice for the social services.* Binghamton, NY: Haworth Press.

Hunter, S. (2007). *Coming out and disclosures: LGBT persons across the life span.* Binghamton, NY: Haworth Press.

"Is a person who is intersex a hermaphrodite?" (n.d.). *Intersex Society of North America.* Retrieved from http://www.isna.org/faq/hermaphrodite

Jackson, A. (2015, July 31). The high cost of being transgender. *CNN.* Retrieved from http://www.cnn.com/2015/07/31/health/transgender-costs-irpt/index.html

Kacere, L. (2013, September 23). 5 ways using correct gender pronouns will make you a better trans* ally. *Everyday Feminism.* Retrieved from http://everydayfeminism.com/2013/09/correct-gender-pronouns-to-be-trans-ally/

Karkazis, K. (2008). *Fixing sex: Intersex, medical authority, and lived experience.* Durham, NC: Duke University Press.

Karkazis, K., & Fishman, J. R. (2017). Tracking U.S. professional athletes: The ethics of biometric technologies. *The American Journal of Bioethics, 17,* 45–60. doi: 10.1080/15265161.2016.1251633

Katz-Wise, S. L. (2014). Sexual fluidity in young adult women and men: Associations with sexual orientation and sexual identity development. *Psychology & Sexuality, 6,* 189–208. doi: 10.1080/19419899.2013.876445

Katz-Wise, S. L., & Budge, S. L. (2015). Cognitive and interpersonal identity processes related to mid-life gender transitioning in transgender women. *Counselling Psychology Quarterly, 28,* 150–174. doi: 10.1080/09515070.2014.993305

Katz-Wise, S. L., Reisner, S. L., White Hughto, J., & Keo-Meier, C. L. (2015). Differences in sexual orientation diversity and sexual fluidity in attractions among gender minority adults in Massachusetts. *Journal of Sex Research, 53,* 74–84. doi: 10.1080/00224499.2014.1003028

Kenagy, G. P. (2005). Transgender health: Findings from two needs assessment studies in Philadelphia. *Health & Social Work, 30,* 19–26. doi: 10.1093/hsw/30.1.19

Kessler, S. J. (2002). *Lessons from the intersexed.* New Brunswick, NJ: Rutgers University Press.

Kessler, S. J., & McKenna, W. (2000). Gender construction in everyday life: Transsexualism (abridged). *Feminism & Psychology, 10,* 11–29. doi: 10.1177/0959353500010001003

Killermann, S. (2015, March 16). The Genderbread Person v3. *It's Pronounced Metrosexual.* Retrieved from http://itspronouncedmetrosexual.com/2015/03/the-genderbread-person-v3/

Kinsey, A. C., Pomeroy, W. B., & Martin, C. E. (1948). *Sexual behavior in the human male.* Oxford, United Kingdom: W. B. Saunders.

Kitzinger, C. (1995). Social constructionism: Implications for lesbian and gay psychology. In A. R. D'Augelli & C. J. Patterson (Eds.), *Lesbian, gay and bisexual identities over the lifespan: Psychological perspectives.* Oxford, United Kingdom: Oxford University Press.

Kitzinger, C., & Wilkinson, S. (1995). Transitions from heterosexuality to lesbianism: The discursive construction of lesbian identities. *Developmental Psychology, 31,* 95–104. doi: 10.1037/0012-1649.31.1.95

Klein, C., & Gorzalka, B. B. (2009). Sexual functioning in transsexuals following hormone therapy and genital surgery: A review. *Journal of Sexual Medicine, 6,* 2922–2939. doi: 10.1111/j.1743-6109.2009.01370.x

Koken, J. A., Bimbi, D. S., & Parsons, J. T. (2009). Experiences of familial acceptance: Rejection among transwomen of color. *Journal of Family Psychology, 23,* 853–860. doi: 10.1037/a0017198

Kosciw, J. G., Palmer, N. A., & Kull, R. M. (2015). Reflecting resiliency: Openness about sexual orientation and/or gender identity and its relationship to well-being and educational outcomes for LGBT students. *American Journal of Community Psychology, 55,* 167–178. doi: 10.1007/s10464-014-9642-6

Kuiper, A. J., & Cohen-Kettenis, P. T. (1998). Gender role reversal among postoperative transsexuals. *International Journal of Transgenderism, 2,* 1–16.

La Jeunesse, M. (2015, October 15). These emoji celebrate your unique penis. *Mashable.* Retrieved from http://mashable.com/2015/10/15/penis-emoji/#0IdsZrcl2mqd

Lajic, S., Nordenström, A., & Hirvikoski, T. (2011). Long-term outcome of prenatal dexamethasone treatment of 21-hydroxylase deficiency. *Pediatric Adrenal Diseases, 20,* 96–105. doi: 10.1159/000321228

Lauerma, H. (2001). Klinefelter's syndrome and sexual homicide. *Journal of Forensic Psychiatry, 12,* 151–157. doi: 10.1080/09585180010027888

Lawrence, A. A. (2005). Sexuality before and after male-to-female sex reassignment surgery. *Archives of Sexual Behavior, 34,* 147–166. doi: 10.1007/s10508-005-1793-y

Lee, P. A., Houk, C. P., Ahmed, S. F., & Hughes, I. A. (2006). Consensus statement on management of intersex disorders. *Pediatrics, 118,* e488–e500. doi: 10.1542/peds.2006-0738

Leidolf, E. M., Curran, M., Scout, & Bradford, J. (2008). Intersex mental health and social support options in pediatric endocrinology training programs. *Journal of Homosexuality, 54,* 233–242. doi: 10.1080/00918360801982074

Lenning, E., & Buist, C. L. (2013). Social, psychological and economic challenges faced by transgender individuals and their significant others: Gaining insight through personal narratives. *Culture, Health & Sexuality, 15,* 44–57. doi: 10.1080/13691058.2012.738431

Lev, A. I. (2004). *Transgender emergence: Therapeutic guidelines for working with gender variant people and their families.* New York, NY: Hawthorn.

LeVay, S. (1991). A difference in hypothalamic structure between heterosexual and homosexual men. *Science, 253*(5023), 1034–1037.

Levy, A. (2009, November 30). Either/or: Sports, sex, and the case of Caster Semenya. *The New Yorker.* Retrieved from https://www.newyorker.com/magazine/2009/11/30/eitheror

Lombardi, E. L., Wilchins, R. A., Priesing, D., & Malouf, D. (2001). Gender violence: Transgender experiences with violence and discrimination. *Journal of Homosexuality, 42,* 89–101. doi: 10.1300/J082v42n01_05

Macarow, A. (2015, February 9). These eleven countries are way ahead of the U.S. on trans issues. *attn:.* Retrieved from https://www.attn.com/stories/868/transgender-passport-status

Majd, K., Marksamer, J., & Reyes, C. (2009, Fall). *Hidden injustice: Lesbian, gay, bisexual, and transgender youth in juvenile courts*. Retrieved from http://www.nclrights.org/wp-content /uploads/2014/06/hidden_injustice.pdf

Mallon, G. P., & De Crescenzo, T. (2009). Social work practice with transgender and gender variant children and youth. In G. P. Mallon (Ed.), *Social work practice with transgender and gender variant youth* (2nd ed., pp. 65–86). New York, NY: Routledge.

McCartney, J. (n.d.). About. *The Great Wall of Vagina*. Retrieved from http://www.greatwallofvagina.co.uk/about

McKenna, W., & Kessler, S. J. (2000). Retrospective response. *Feminism & Psychology, 10*, 66–72. doi: 10.1177/09593535 00010001010

McLemore, K. A. (2015). Experiences with misgendering: Identity misclassification of transgender spectrum individuals. *Self and Identity, 14*, 51–74. doi: 10.1080/15298868.2014.950691

Meier, S. C., Pardo, S. T., Labuski, C., & Babcock, J. (2013). Measures of clinical health among female-to-male transgender persons as a function of sexual orientation. *Archives of Sexual Behavior, 42*, 463–474. doi: 10.1007/s10508-012-0052-2

Messner, M. A. (2002). *Taking the field: Women, men & sports*. Minneapolis, MN: University of Minnesota Press.

Meyer, I. H. (2003). Prejudice, social stress, and mental health in lesbian, gay and bisexual populations: Conceptual issues and research evidence. *Psychological Bulletin, 129*, 674–697. doi: 10.1037/0033-2909.129.5.674

Meyer, W., III, Bockting, W., Cohen-Kettenis, P., Coleman, E., DiCeglie, D., Devor, H., . . . Wheeler, C. C. (2001). The Harry Benjamin International Gender Dysphoria Association's standards of care for gender identity disorders, sixth version. *International Journal of Transgenderism, 5*, 1–30. doi: 10.1300/J056v13n01_01

Minter, S. P. (2006). Do transsexuals dream of gay rights? Getting real about transgender inclusion. In P. Currah, R. M. Juang, & S. P. Minter (Eds.), *Transgender rights* (pp.141–170). Minneapolis, MN: University of Minnesota Press.

Mitra, P. (2014). Male/female or other: The untold stories of female athletes with intersex variations in India. In J. Hargreaves & E. Anderson (Eds.), *Routledge handbook of sport, gender and sexuality* (pp. 384–394). New York, NY: Routledge.

Mizock, L., & Fleming, M. Z. (2011). Transgender and gender variant populations with mental illness: Implications for clinical care. *Professional Psychology: Research and Practice, 42*, 208–213. doi: 10.1037/a0022522

Mizock, L., & Hopwood, R. (2016). Conflation and interdependence in the intersection of gender and sexuality among transgender individuals. *Psychology of Sexual Orientation and Gender Diversity, 3*, 93–103. doi: 10.1037/sgd0000157

Mizock, L., & Lewis, T. K. (2008). Trauma in transgender populations: Risk, resilience, and clinical care. *Journal of Emotional Abuse, 8*, 335–354.

Mohr, J. J., Jackson, S. D., & Sheets, R. L. (2016). Sexual orientation self-presentation among bisexual-identified women and men: Patterns and predictors. *Archives of Sexual Behavior, 46*, 1465–1479. doi: 10.1007/s10508-016-0808-1

Mohr, J. J., & Kendra, M. S. (2011). Revision and extension of a multidimensional measure of sexual minority identity: The Lesbian, Gay, and Bisexual Identity Scale. *Journal of Counseling Psychology, 58*, 234–245. doi: 10.1037/a0022858

Money, J., Hampson, J. G., & Hampson, J. L. (1955). Hermaphroditism: Recommendations concerning assignment of sex, change of sex and psychologic management. *Bulletin of the Johns Hopkins Hospital, 97*(4), 284–300.

Moradi, B., DeBlaere, C., & Huang, Y. P. (2010). Centralizing the experiences of LGB people of color in counseling psychology. *The Counseling Psychologist, 38*, 322–330. doi: 10.1177 /0011000008330832

Morgan, E. M., & Thompson, E. M. (2006). Young women's sexual experiences within same-sex friendships: Discovering and defining bisexual and bi-curious identity. *Journal of Bisexuality, 6*, 7–34. doi: 10.1300/J159v06n03_02

Nadal, K. L., & Corpus, M. J. (2013). "Tomboys" and "baklas": Experiences of lesbian and gay Filipino Americans. *Asian American Journal of Psychology, 4*, 166–175. doi: 10.1037/a0030168

Nadal, K. L., Skolnik, A., & Wong, Y. (2012). Interpersonal and systemic microaggressions: Psychological impacts on transgender individuals and communities. *Journal of LGBT Issues in Counseling, 6*, 55–82. doi: 10.1080/15538605.2012.648583

Nanda, S. (2014). *Gender diversity: Cross cultural variations*. Long Grove, IL: Waveland Press.

Newcomb, M. E., & Mustanski, B. (2010). The importance of measuring internalized homophobia/homonegativity: Reply to Ross, Rosser, and Smolenski. *Archives of Sexual Behavior, 39*, 1209–1211. doi: 10.1007/s10508-010-9655-7.

Nussbaum, E. (2000). A question of gender. *Discover, 21*(1), 92–99.

Olson, K. R., Key, A. C., & Eaton, N. R. (2015). Gender cognition in transgender children. *Psychological Science, 26*, 467–474. doi: 10.1177/0956797614568156

Parks, C. A., Hughes, T. L., & Matthews, A. K. (2004). Race/ethnicity and sexual orientation: Intersecting identities. *Cultural Diversity and Ethnic Minority Psychology, 10*, 241–254. doi: 10.1037/1099 -9809.10.3.241

Pasterski, V., Geffner, M., Brain, C., Hindmarsh, P., Brook, C., & Hines, M. (2011). Prenatal hormones and childhood sex segregation: Playmate and play style preferences in girls with congenital adrenal hyperplasia. *Hormones and Behavior, 59*, 549–555. doi: 10.1016/j.yhbeh.2011.02.007

Pinto, N., & Moleiro, C. (2015). Gender trajectories: Transsexual people coming to terms with their gender identities. *Professional Psychology: Research and Practice, 46*, 12–20. doi: 10.1037 /a0036487

Pinto, S. A. (2014). ASEXUally: On being an ally to the asexual community. *Journal of LGBT Issues in Counseling, 8*, 331–343. doi: 10.1080/15538605.2014.960130

Prause, N., & Graham, C. A. (2007). Asexuality: Classification and characterization. *Archives of Sexual Behavior, 36*, 341–356. doi: 10.1007/s10508-006-9142-3

Reisner, S. L., Perkovich, B., & Mimiaga, M. J. (2010). A mixed methods study of the sexual health needs of New England transmen who have sex with nontransgender men. *AIDS Patient Care and STDs, 24*, 501–513. doi: 10.1089/apc.2010.0059

Richmond, K., Carroll, K., & Demboske, K. (2010). Gender identity disorder: Concerns and controversies. In J. C. Chrisler & D. R. McCreary (Eds.), *Handbook of gender research in psychology* (Vol. 2, pp. 111–131). New York, NY: Springer.

Riggle, E. D. B., & Mohr, J. J. (2015). A proposed multifactor measure of positive identity for transgender identified individuals. *Psychology of Sexual Orientation and Gender Diversity, 2*, 78–85. doi: 10.1037/sgd0000082

Riley, B. H. (2010). GLB adolescent's "coming out." *Journal of Child and Adolescent Psychiatric Nursing, 23*, 3–10. doi: 10.1111/j.1744-6171.2009.00210.x

Roen, K. (2008). "But we have to do something": Surgical "correction" of atypical genitalia. *Body & Society, 14*, 47–66. doi: 10.1177/1357034X07087530

Rolle, L., Ceruti, C., Timpano, M., Falcone, M., & Frea, B. (2015). Quality of life after sexual reassignment surgery. In C. Trombetta, G. Liguori, & M. Bertolotto (Eds.), *Management of gender dysphoria: A multidisciplinary approach* (pp. 193–203). New York, NY: Springer.

Rosario, M., Schrimshaw, E. W., & Hunter, J. (2004). Ethnic/ racial differences in the coming-out process of lesbian, gay, and bisexual youths: A comparison of sexual identity development over time. *Cultural Diversity and Ethnic Minority Psychology, 10*, 215–228. doi: 10.1037/1099-9809.10.3.215

Rosario, M., Schrimshaw, E. W., Hunter, J., & Levy-Warren, A. (2009). The coming-out process of young lesbian and bisexual women: Are there butch/femme differences in sexual identity development? *Archives of Sexual Behavior, 38*, 34–49. doi: 10.1007/s10508-007-9221-0

Rosenberg, M. (2002). Children with gender identity issues and their parents in individual and group treatment. *American Academy of Child and Adolescent Psychiatry, 41*, 619–621. doi: 10.1097/00004583-200205000-00020

Ross, L. E., Dobinson, C., & Eady, A. (2010). Perceived determinants of mental health for bisexual people: A qualitative examination. *American Journal of Public Health, 100*, 496–502. doi: 10.2105/AJPH.2008.156307

Ryan, C. (2003). Lesbian, gay, bisexual, and transgender youth: Health concerns, services, and care. *Clinical Research and Regulatory Affairs, 20*, 137–158. doi: 10.1081/CRP-120021078

Ryan, C., Huebner, D., Diaz, R. M., & Sanchez, J. (2009). Family rejection as a predictor of negative health outcomes in White and Latino lesbian, gay, bisexual young adults. *Pediatrics, 123*, 346–352. doi: 10.1542/peds.2007-3524

Ryan, C., Russell, S. T., Huebner, D., Diaz, R., & Sanchez, J. (2010). Family acceptance in adolescence and the health of LGBT young adults. *Journal of Child and Adolescent Psychiatric Nursing, 23*, 205–213. doi: 10.1111/j.1744-6171.2010.00246.x

Saffin, L. A. (2011). Identities under siege: Violence against transpersons of color. In E. A. Stanley & N. Smith (Eds.), *Captive genders: Trans embodiment and the prison industrial complex* (pp. 141–162). Oakland, CA: AK Press.

Sanchez, N. F., Sanchez, J. P., & Danoff, A. (2009). Health care utilization, barriers to care, and hormone usage among male-to-female transgender persons in New York City. *American Journal of Public Health, 99*, 713–719. doi: 10.2105/AJPH.2007.132035

Saucier, D. M., & Ehresman, C. (2010). The physiology of sex differences. In J. C. Chrisler & D. R. McCreary (Eds.), *Handbook of gender research in psychology* (Vol. 1, pp. 215–233). New York, NY: Springer.

Savin-Williams, R. C. (2005). *The new gay teenager*. Cambridge, MA: Harvard University Press.

Scales Rostosky, S., Riggle, E. D., Pascale-Hague, D., & McCants, L. E. (2010). The positive aspects of a bisexual self-identification. *Psychology & Sexuality, 1*, 131–144. doi: 10.1080/19419899.2010.484595

Scarlette-Callis, A. (2014). Bisexual, pansexual, queer: Non-binary identities and the sexual borderlands. *Sexualities, 17*, 63–80. doi: 10.1177/1363460713511094

Schagen, S. E., Cohen-Kettenis, P. T., Delemarre-van de Waal, H. A., & Hannema, S. E. (2016). Efficacy and safety of gonadotropin-releasing hormone agonist treatment to suppress puberty in gender dysphoric adolescents. *Journal of Sexual Medicine, 13*, 1125–1132. doi: 10.1016/j.jsxm.2016.05.004

Scherrer, K. S. (2008). Coming to an asexual identity: Negotiating identity, negotiating desire. *Sexualities, 11*, 621–641. doi: 10.1177/1363460708094269

Schultz, J. (2005). Reading the catsuit: Serena Williams and the production of Blackness at the 2002 U.S. Open. *Journal of Sport and Social Issues, 29*, 338–357. doi: 10.1177/0193723505276230

Scout, N. (2016). Transgender health and well-being: Gains and opportunities in policy and law. *American Journal of Orthopsychiatry, 86*, 378–383. doi: 10.1037/ort0000192

Segal, C. (2017, January 5). Nation's first known "intersex" birth certificate issued in New York City. *PBS*. Retrieved from http://www.pbs.org/newshour/rundown/new-york-city-issues-nations-first-birth-certificate-marked-intersex/

Serano, J. (2007). *Whipping girl: A transsexual woman on sexism and the scapegoating of femininity*. Emeryville, CA: Seal.

Shield, S. (2007). The doctor won't see you now: Rights of transgender adolescents to sex reassignment treatment. *New York University Review of Law & Social Change, 31*, 361–433.

Sieczkowski, C. (2014, March 7). Why transgender athlete Chloie Jonsson is suing CrossFit over discrimination. *Huffington Post*. Retrieved from http://www.huffingtonpost.com/entry/transgender-chloie-jonsson-sues-crossfit_n_4921038

Simpson, J. L., Ljungqvist, A., Ferguson-Smith, M. A., de la Chapelle, A., Elsas, L. J., II, Ehrhardt, A. A., . . . Carlson, A. (2000). Gender verification in the Olympics. *Journal of the American Medical Association, 284*, 1568–1569. doi: 10.1001/jama.284.12.1568

Singh, A. A. (2013). Transgender youth of color and resilience: Negotiating oppression and finding support. *Sex Roles, 68*, 690–702. doi: 10.1007/s11199-012-0149-z

Singh, A. A., Hays, D. G., & Watson, L. S. (2011). Strength in the face of adversity: Resilience strategies of transgender individuals. *Journal of Counseling and Development, 89*, 20–27. doi: 10.1002/j.1556-6678.2011.tb00057.x

Singh, A. A., & McKleroy, V. S. (2011). "Just getting out of bed is a revolutionary act": The resilience of transgender people of color who have survived traumatic life events. *Traumatology, 17*, 34–44. doi: 10.1177/1534765610369261

Smith, D. (2009, August 22). Caster Semenya row: "Who are White people to question the makeup of an African girl? It is racism." *The Guardian*. Retrieved from https://www.theguardian.com/sport/2009/aug/23/caster-semenya-athletics-gender

Smith, J. L. (2015). Counseling for empowerment: Working with girls, parents, and women dealing with Turner's syndrome. *Social Work & Christianity, 42*, 488–496.

Sobel, V., & Imperato-McGinley, J. (2004). Gender identity in XY intersexuality. *Child and Adolescent Psychiatric Clinics of North America, 13*, 609–622. doi: 10.1016/j.chc.2004.02.014

Spector, T. (2014, February 18). Why does the search for a gay gene freak everyone out? *Slate*. Retrieved from http://www.slate.com/blogs/outward/2014/02/18/gay_gene_research_why_does_it_make_people_freak_out.html

Springer, K. W., Mager Stellman, J., & Jordan-Young, R. M. (2012). Beyond a catalogue of differences: A theoretical frame and good practice guidelines for researching sex/gender in human health. *Social Science & Medicine, 74*, 1817–1824. doi: 10.1016/j.socscimed.2011.05.033

Stets, J. E., & Burke, P. J. (2005). Identity verification, control, and aggression in marriage. *Social Psychology Quarterly, 68*, 160–178. doi: 10.1177/019027250506800204.

Stone, A. L. (2009). More than adding a T: American lesbian and gay activists' attitudes towards transgender inclusion. *Sexualities, 12*, 334–354. doi: 10.1177/1363460709103894

Stotzer, R. L. (2008). Gender identity and hate crimes: Violence against transgender people in Los Angeles County. *Sexuality Research & Social Policy, 5*, 43–52. doi: 10.1525/srsp.2008.5.1.43

Stryker, S. (2008). *Transgender history*. Berkeley, CA: Seal Press.

Tate, C. C., & Pearson, M. D. (2016). Toward an inclusive model of lesbian identity development: Outlining a common and nuanced model for cis and trans women. *Journal of Lesbian Studies, 20*, 97–115. doi: 10.1080/10894160.2015.1076237

Tate, C. C., Youssef, C. P., & Bettergarcia, J. N. (2014). Integrating the study of transgender spectrum and cisgender experiences of self-categorization from a personality perspective. *Review of General Psychology, 18*, 302–312. doi: 10.1037/gpr0000019

Teh, Y. K. (2001). Mak nyahs (male transsexuals) in Malaysia: The influence of culture and religion on their identity. *International Journal of Transgenderism, 5*, 97–103.

Thompson, E. M., & Morgan, E. M. (2008). "Mostly straight" young women: Variations in sexual behavior and identity development. *Developmental Psychology*, 44, 15–21. doi: 10.1037/0012-1649.44.1.15

Toft, D. J., & Rehan, K. M. (2014, June 20). Fertility treatments for Turner syndrome: Options for motherhood when you have TS. *Endocrineweb*. Retrieved from http://www.endocrineweb.com/conditions/turner-syndrome/fertility-treatments-turner-syndrome

Topp, S. S. (2012). Against the quiet revolution: The rhetorical construction of intersex individuals as disordered. *Sexualities*, 16, 180–194. doi: 10.1177/1363460712471113

United Nations. (2015, September). *Ending violence and discrimination against lesbian, gay, bisexual, transgender and intersex people*. Retrieved from http://www.who.int/hiv/pub/msm/Joint_LGBTI_Statement_ENG.pdf?ua=1

van Anders, S. M. (2015). Beyond sexual orientation: Integrating gender/sex and diverse sexualities via sexual configurations theory. *Archives of Sexual Behavior*, 44, 1177–1213. doi: 10.1007/s10508-015-0490-8

van der Sluis, W. B., Bouman, M., de Boer, N. K., Buncamper, M. E., van Bodegraven, A. A., Neefjes-Borst, E. A., . . . Mullender, M. G. (2016). Long-term follow-up of transgender women after secondary intestinal vaginoplasty. *Journal of Sexual Medicine*, 13, 702–710. doi: 10.1016/j.jsxm.2016.01.008

Van Houdenhove, E., Gijs, L., T'Sjoen, G., & Enzlin, P. (2015). Stories about asexuality: A qualitative study on asexual women. *Journal of Sex & Marital Therapy*, 41, 262–281. doi: 10.1080/0092623X.2014.889053

Veldorale-Griffin, A., & Darling, C. A. (2016). Adaptation to parental gender transition: Stress and resilience among transgender parents. *Archives of Sexual Behavior*, 45, 607–617. doi: 10.1007/s10508-015-0657-3

Vos, A. A., & Bruinse, H. W. (2010). Congenital adrenal hyperplasia: Do the benefits of prenatal treatment defeat the risks? *Obstetrical & Gynecological Survey*, 65, 196–205. doi: 10.1097/OGX.0b013e3181d61046

Walls, N. E., Kane, S. B., & Wisneski, H. (2010). Gay-straight alliances and school experiences of sexual minority youth. *Youth and Society*, 41, 307–332. doi: 10.1177/0044118X09334957

Warne, G., Grover, S., Hutson, J., Sinclair, A., Metcalfe, S., Northam, E., . . . Murdoch Children's Research Institute Sex Study Group. (2005). A long-term outcome study of intersex conditions. *Journal of Pediatric Endocrinology and Metabolism*, 18, 555–568. doi: 10.1515/JPEM.2005.18.6.555

Whitam, F. L., Diamond, M., & Martin, J. (1993). Homosexual orientation in twins: A report on 61 pairs and three triplet sets. *Archives of Sexual Behavior*, 22, 187–206. doi: 10.1007/BF01541765

Wiesemann, C. (2011). Is there a right not to know one's sex? The ethics of "gender verification" in women's sports competition. *Journal of Medical Ethics*, 37, 216–220. doi: 10.1136/jme.2010.039081

Wilson, E. C., Garofalo, R., Harris, R. D., Herrick, A., Martinez, M., Martinez, J., & Belzer, M. (2009). Transgender female youth and sex work: HIV risk and a comparison of life factors related to engagement in sex work. *AIDS and Behavior*, 13, 902–913. doi: 10.1007/s10461-008-9508-8

Witchel, A. (2012, January 12). Cynthia Nixon's life after "Sex." *The New York Times Magazine*. Retrieved from http://www.nytimes.com/2012/01/22/magazine/cynthia-nixon-wit.html

Withycombe, J. L. (2011). Intersecting selves: African American female athletes' experiences of sport. *Sociology of Sport Journal*, 28, 478–493. doi: 10.1123/ssj.28.4.478

Wong, W. I., Pasterski, V., Hindmarsh, P. C., Geffner, M. E., & Hines, M. (2013). Are there parental socialization effects on the sex-typed behavior of individuals with congenital adrenal hyperplasia? *Archives of Sexual Behavior*, 42, 381–391. doi: 10.1007/s10508-012-9997-4

Xavier, J., Bradford, J., Hendricks, M., Safford, L., McKee, R., Martin, E., & Honnold, J. A. (2013). Transgender health care access in Virginia: A qualitative study. *International Journal of Transgenderism*, 14, 3–17. doi: 10.1080/15532739.2013.689513

Xavier, J. M., & Simmons, R. (2000). *The Washington Transgender Needs Assessment Survey: Executive summary*. Retrieved from http://www.glaa.org/archive/2000/tgneedsassessment1112.shtml

Yost, M. R., & Thomas, G. D. (2012). Gender and binegativity: Men's and women's attitudes toward male and female bisexuals. *Archives of Sexual Behavior*, 41, 691–702. doi: 10.1007/s10508-011-9767-8

Zamboni, B. D. (2006). Therapeutic considerations in working with the family, friends, and partners of transgendered individuals. *The Family Journal*, 14, 174–179. doi: 10.1177/1066480705285251

Zeiler, K., & Wickström, A. (2009). Why do "we" perform surgery on newborn intersexed children? The phenomenology of the parental experience of having a child with intersex anatomies. *Feminist Theory*, 10, 359–377. doi: 10.1177/1464700109343258

Zimman, L. (2016). Transsexuality. In N. Naples, R. C. Hoogland, M. Wickramasinghe, & W. C. A. Wong (Eds.), *The Wiley Blackwell encyclopedia of gender and sexuality studies* (Vol. X, pp. 115–143). Hoboken, NJ: Wiley-Blackwell.

Zulch, M. (2015, December 15). 7 queer issues "Transparent" season 2 totally gets right. *Bustle*. Retrieved from https://www.bustle.com/articles/129770-7-queer-issues-transparent-season-2-totally-gets-right

Chapter 5

Abad, C., & Pruden, S. (2013). Do storybooks really break children's gender stereotypes? *Frontiers in Psychology*, 4, 1–4. doi: 10.3389/fpsyg.2013.00986

Ahlqvist, S., Halim, M., Greulich, F., Lurye, L., & Ruble, D. (2013). The potential benefits and risks of identifying as a tomboy: A social identity perspective. *Self and Identity*, 12, 563–581. doi: 10.1080/15298868.2012.717709

Anderson, D., & Hamilton, M. (2005). Gender role stereotyping of parents in children's picture books: The invisible father. *Sex Roles*, 52, 145–151. doi: 10.1007/s11199-005-1290-8

Anderson, M. (2016, February 26). Where's the color in kids' lit? Ask the girl with 1,000 books (and counting). *National Public Radio*. Retrieved from http://www.npr.org/sections/ed/2016/02/26/467969663/wheres-the-color-in-kids-lit-ask-the-girl-with-1-000-books-and-counting

Anne, K. (2015, December 21). JK Rowling, we all know you didn't write Hermione as Black in the Harry Potter books—but it doesn't matter. *Independent*. Retrieved from http://www.independent.co.uk/voices/j-k-rowling-we-all-know-you-didnt-write-hermione-as-black-in-the-harry-potter-books-but-it-doesnt-a6781681.html

Anyon, J. (2006). Social class and the hidden curriculum of work. In G. Handel (Ed.), *Childhood socialization* (2nd ed., pp. 369–394). New Brunswick, NJ: Aldine Transaction.

Ashmore, R., Deaux, K., & McLaughlin-Volpe, T. (2004). An organizing framework for collective identity: Articulation and significance of multidimensionality. *Psychological Bulletin*, 130, 80–114. doi: 10.1037/0033-2909.130.1.80

Aubrey, J. S., & Harrison, K. (2004). The gender-role content of children's favorite television programs and its links to their gender-related perceptions. *Media Psychology, 6,* 111–146. doi: 10.1207/s1532785xmep0602_1

Auster, C. J., & Mansbach, C. S. (2012). The gender marketing of toys: An analysis of color and type of toy on the Disney Store website. *Sex Roles, 67,* 375–388. doi: 10.1007/s11199-012-0177-8

Baker, K., & Raney, A. (2007). Equally super? Gender-role stereotyping of superheroes in children's animated programs. *Mass Communication & Society, 10,* 25–41. doi: 10.1080/15205430709337003

Bandura, A. (1971). *Social learning theory.* Morristown, NJ: General Learning Press.

Barry, E. (2018, March 24). In Sweden's preschools, boys learn to dance and girls learn to yell. *The New York Times.* Retrieved from https://www.nytimes.com/2018/03/24/world/europe/sweden-gender-neutral-preschools.html

Bates, L. (2015, May 22). How school dress codes shame girls and perpetuate rape culture. *Time.* Retrieved from http://time.com/3892965/everydaysexism-school-dress-codes-rape-culture/

Beall, A. E. (1993). A social constructionist view of gender. In A. E. Beall & R. J. Sternberg (Eds.), *The psychology of gender* (pp. 127–147). New York, NY: Guilford.

Beardsworth, S. (2004). *Julia Kristeva: Psychoanalysis and modernity.* Albany, NY: State University of New York Press.

Beasley, B., & Standley, C. T. (2002). Shirts vs. skins: Clothing as an indicator of gender role stereotyping in video games. *Mass Communication & Society, 5,* 279–293. doi: 10.1207/S15327825MCS0503_3

Bègue, L., Sarda, E., Gentile, D. A., Bry, C., & Roché, S. (2017). Video games exposure and sexism in a representative sample of adolescents. *Frontiers in Psychology, 8,* Article 466. doi: 10.3389/fpsyg.2017.00466

Bell, L. M. (2014, November 20). How "The Hunger Games" is challenging gender stereotypes—by empowering boys. *Huffington Post.* Retrieved from http://www.huffingtonpost.co.uk/laura-m-bell/hunger-games-gender-stereotypes_b_6185320.html

Bem, S. L. (1983). Gender schema theory and its implications for child development: Raising gender-aschematic children in a gender-schematic society. *Signs, 8,* 598–616.

Bennett, R. (2014, August 31). *Feminist movie review: Divergent.* Retrieved from http://www.gender-focus.com/2014/08/31/feminist-movie-review-divergent/

Berlan, E. D., Corliss, H. L., Field, A. E., Goodman, E., & Austin, S. B. (2010). Sexual orientation and bullying among adolescents in the Growing Up Today study. *The Journal of Adolescent Health, 46,* 366–371. doi: 10.1016/j.jadohealth.2009.10.015

Bettie, J. (2002). Exceptions to the rule: Upwardly mobile White and Mexican American high school girls. *Gender & Society, 16,* 403–422. doi: 10.1177/0891243202016003008

Biddle, S., Whitehead, S., O'Donovan, T., & Nevill, M. (2005). Correlates of participation in physical activity for adolescent girls: A systematic review of recent literature. *Journal of Physical Activity & Health, 2,* 423–434. doi: 10.1123/jpah.2.4.423

Bigler, R., Arthur, A., Hughes, J., & Patterson, M. (2008). The politics of race and gender: Children's perceptions of discrimination and the US presidency. *Analyses of Social Issues and Public Policy, 8,* 83–112. doi: 10.1111/j.1530-2415.2008.00161.x

Blake, J. J., Butler, B. R., Lewis, C. W., & Darensbourg, A. (2011). Unmasking the inequitable discipline experiences of urban Black girls: Implications for urban educational stakeholders. *The Urban Review, 43,* 90–106. doi: 10.1007/s11256-009-0148-8

Blakemore, J., Berenbaum, S., & Liben, L. (2009). *Gender development.* New York, NY: Taylor and Francis Group.

Blakemore, J., & Centers, R. (2005). Characteristics of boys' and girls' toys. *Sex Roles, 53,* 619–633. doi: 10.1007/s11199-005-7729-0

Bos, H. H., & Sandfort, T. (2015). Gender nonconformity, sexual orientation, and Dutch adolescents' relationship with peers. *Archives of Sexual Behavior, 44,* 1269–1279. doi: 10.1007/s10508-014-0461-5

Braun, S. S., & Davidson, A. J. (2017). Gender (non)conformity in middle childhood: A mixed methods approach to understanding gender-typed behavior, friendship, and peer preference. *Sex Roles, 77,* 16–29. doi: 10.1007/s11199-016-0693-z

Bridges, J. (1993). Pink or blue: Gender-stereotypic perceptions of infants as conveyed by birth congratulations cards. *Psychology of Women Quarterly, 17,* 193–205. doi: 10.1111/j.1471-6402.1993.tb00444.x

Brown, G., Craig, A., & Halberstadt, A. (2015). Parent gender differences in emotion socialization behaviors vary by ethnicity and child gender. *Parenting, 15,* 135–157. doi: 10.1080/15295192.2015.1053312

Browne, B. (1998). Gender stereotypes in advertising on children's television in the 1990s: A cross-national analysis. *Journal of Advertising, 27,* 83–96. doi: 10.1080/00913367.1998.10673544

Bulcroft, R., Carmody, D., & Bulcroft, K. (1996). Patterns of parental independence giving to adolescents: Variations by race, age, and gender of children. *Journal of Marriage and Family, 58,* 866–883. doi: 10.2307/353976

bumpreveal. (2017, April 6). Best gender reveal ideas of 2017 [Blog post]. Retrieved from https://bumpreveal.com/content/best-gender-reveal-ideas-2017/

Burn, S., O'Neil, A., & Nederend, S. (1996). Childhood tomboyism and adult androgyny. *Sex Roles, 34,* 419–428. doi: 10.1007/BF01547810

Bussey, K., & Bandura, A. (1999). Social cognitive theory of gender development and differentiation. *Psychological Review, 106,* 676–713. doi: 10.1037/0033-295X.106.4.676

Carr, C. (1998). Tomboy resistance and conformity: Agency in social psychological gender theory. *Gender & Society, 12,* 528–553. doi: 10.1177/089124398012005003

Carr, C. (2007). Where have all the tomboys gone? Women's accounts of gender in adolescence. *Sex Roles, 56,* 439–448. doi: 10.1007/s11199-007-9183-7

Carroll, J. (2007, July 20). Do Americans want to be surprised by the sex of their baby? *Gallup.* Retrieved from http://www.gallup.com/poll/28180/Americans-Want-Surprised-Sex-Their-Baby.aspx

Cassell, J., Huffaker, D., Tversky, D., & Ferriman, K. (2006). The language of online leadership: Gender and youth engagement on the Internet. *Developmental Psychology, 42,* 436–449. doi: 10.1037/0012-1649.42.3.436

Causer, C. (2013). Ribbons and wheels and engineers? That's what girls are made of. *IEEE Potentials, 32*(5), 15–17. doi: 10.1109/MPOT.2013.2267018

Chaplin, T., Cole, P., & Zahn-Waxler, C. (2005). Parental socialization of emotion expression: Gender differences and relations to child adjustment. *Emotion, 5,* 80–88. doi: 10.1037/1528-3542.5.1.80

Chan, C. S. (2008). Asian American women and adolescent girls: Sexuality and sexual expression. In J. C. Chrisler, C. Golden, & P. D. Rozee (Eds.), *Lectures on the psychology of women* (4th ed., pp. 221–231). New York, NY: McGraw-Hill.

Cherney, I. D., & London, K. (2006). Gender-linked differences in the toys, television shows, computer games, and outdoor activities of 5- to 13-year-old children. *Sex Roles, 54,* 717–726. doi: 10.1007/s11199-006-9037-8.

Chesley, N. (2011). Stay-at-home fathers and breadwinning mothers: Gender, couple dynamics, and social change. *Gender & Society, 25,* 642–664. doi: 10.1177/0891243211417433

Chodorow, N. (1978). *The reproduction of mothering: Psychoanalysis and the sociology of gender.* Berkeley, CA: University of California Press.

Cicero, E. C., & Wesp, L. M. (2017). Supporting the health and well-being of transgender students. *The Journal of School Nursing, 33,* 95–108. doi: 10.1177/1059840516689705

Clemans, K., DeRose, L. M., Graber, J., & Brooks-Gunn, J. (2010). Gender in adolescence: Applying a person-in-context approach to gender identity and roles. In D. R. McCreary & J. C. Chrisler (Eds.), *Handbook of gender research in psychology* (Vol.1, pp. 527–557). New York, NY: Springer.

Coltrane, S. (2000). Research on household labor: Modeling and measuring the social embeddedness of routine family work. *Journal of Marriage and Family, 62,* 1208–1233. doi: 10.1111/j.1741-3737.2000.01208.x

Common Sense. (2017). The common sense census: Media use by tweens and teens. *Common Sense.* Retrieved from https://www.commonsensemedia.org/sites/default/files/uploads/research/0-8_executivesummary_release_final_1.pdf

Consortium on the Management of Disorders of Sex Development. (2006). *Clinical guidelines for the management of disorders of sex development in childhood.* Whitehouse Station, NJ: Intersex Society of North America. Retrieved from http://www.accordalliance.org/wp-content/uploads/2013/07/clinical.pdf

Corvin, A., & Fitzgerald, M. (2000). Evidence-based medicine, psychoanalysis and psychotherapy. *Psychoanalytic Psychotherapy, 14,* 143–151. doi: 10.1080/02668730000700141

Coyne, S. M., Linder, J. R., Rasmussen, E. E., Nelson, D. A., & Collier, K. M. (2014). It's a bird! It's a plane! It's a gender stereotype! Longitudinal associations between superhero viewing and gender stereotyped play. *Sex Roles, 70,* 416–430. doi: 10.1007/s11199-014-0374-8

Coyne, S. M., Linder, J. R., Rasmussen, E. E., Nelson, D. A., & Birkbeck, V. (2016). Pretty as a princess: Longitudinal effects of engagement with Disney princesses on gender stereotypes, body esteem, and prosocial behavior in children. *Child Development, 87,* 1909–1925. doi: 10.1111/cdev.12569

Coyne, S. M., Stockdale, L., Linder, J. R., Nelson, D. A., Collier, K. M., & Essig, L. W. (2017). Pow! Boom! Kablam! Effects of viewing superhero programs on aggressive, prosocial, and defending behaviors in preschool children. *Journal of Abnormal Child Psychology, 45,* 1523–1535. doi: 10.1007/s10802-016-0253-6

Crouter, A., Head, M., Bumpus, M., & McHale, S. (2001). Household chores: Under what conditions do mothers lean on daughters? *New Directions for Child and Adolescent Development, 94,* 23–42. doi: 10.1002/cd.29

Craig, S. L., McInroy, L. B., McCready, L. T., & Alaggia, R. (2015). Media: A catalyst for resilience in lesbian, gay, bisexual, transgender, and queer youth. *Journal of LGBT Youth, 12,* 254–275. doi: 10.1080/19361653.2015.1040193

Craig, S. L., McInroy, L. B., McCready, L. T., Di Cesare, D. M., & Pettaway, L. D. (2015). Connecting without fear: Clinical implications of the consumption of information and communication technologies by sexual minority youth and young adults. *Clinical Social Work Journal, 43,* 159–168. doi: 10.1007/s10615-014-0505-2

Crenshaw, K. W., Ocen, P., & Nanda, J. (2015). *Black girls matter: Pushed out, overpoliced, and underprotected.* New York, NY: Center for Intersectionality and Social Policy Studies. Retrieved from https://static1.squarespace.com/static/53f20d90e4b0b80451158d8c/t/54d2d37ce4b024b41443b0ba/1423102844010/BlackGirlsMatter_Report.pdf

dbarry1917. [Screen name]. (2011, May 6). *Riley on marketing* [Video file]. Retrieved from https://www.youtube.com/watch?v=-CU040Hqbas

Davison, K., Werder, J., Trost, S., Baker, B., & Birch, L. (2007). Why are early maturing girls less active? Links between pubertal development, psychological well-being, and physical activity among girls at ages 11 and 13. *Social Science & Medicine, 64,* 2391–2404. doi: 10.1016/j.socscimed.2007.02.033

DeLeón, B. (1996). Career development of Hispanic adolescent girls. In B. J. R. Leadbeater & N. Way (Eds.), *Urban girls: Resisting stereotypes, creating identities* (pp. 380–398). New York, NY: New York University Press.

DeLoach, C. (n.d.). How to host a gender-reveal party. *Parents.* Retrieved from http://www.parents.com/pregnancy/my-baby/gender-prediction/how-to-host-a-gender-reveal-party/

Denner, J., & Dunbar, N. (2004). Negotiating femininity: Power and strategies of Mexican American girls. *Sex Roles, 50,* 301–314. doi: 10.1023/B:SERS.0000018887.04206.d0

Devor, A. H. (2004). Witnessing and mirroring: A fourteen stage model of transsexual identity formation. *Journal of Gay and Lesbian Psychotherapy, 8,* 41–67. doi: 10.1300/J236v08n01_05

Diekman, A., & Murnen, S. (2004). Learning to be little women and little men: The inequitable gender equality of nonsexist children's literature. *Sex Roles, 50,* 373–385. doi: 10.1023/B:SERS.0000018892.26527.ea

Dill, K. E., & Thill, K. P. (2007). Video game characters and the socialization of gender roles: Young people's perceptions mirror sexist media depictions. *Sex Roles, 57,* 851–864. doi: 10.1007/s11199-007-9278-1

Dimen, M. (2005). Sexuality and suffering, or the eew! factor. *Studies in Gender and Sexuality, 6,* 1–18. doi: 10.1080/15240650609349262

Dishman, R., Hales, D., Pfeiffer, K., Felton, G., Saunders, R., Ward, D., Dowda, M., & Pate, R. (2006). Physical self-concept and self-esteem mediate cross-sectional relations of physical activity and sport participation with depression symptoms among adolescent girls. *Health Psychology, 25,* 396–407. doi: 10.1037/0278-6133.25.3.396

Dockterman, E. (2014, February 2). The war on pink: GoldieBlox toys ignite debate over what's good for girls. *Time.* Retrieved from http://time.com/3281/goldie-blox-pink-aisle-debate/

Ehrensaft, D. (2011). Boys will be girls, girls will be boys: Children affect parents as parents affect children in gender nonconformity. *Psychoanalytic Psychology, 28,* 528–548. doi: 10.1037/a0023828

Ehrensaft, D. (2014a). Child, family, and community transformations: Findings from interviews with mothers of transgender girls. *Journal of GLBT Family Studies, 10,* 354–379. doi: 10.1080/1550428X.2013.834529

Ehrensaft, D. (2014b). Found in transition: Our littlest transgender people. *Contemporary Psychoanalysis, 50,* 571–592. doi: 10.1080/00107530.2014.942591

Eichstedt, J., Serbin, L., Poulin-Dubois, D., & Sen, M. (2002). Of bears and men: Infants' knowledge of conventional and metaphorical gender stereotypes. *Infant Behavior & Development, 25,* 296–310. doi: 10.1016/S0163-6383(02)00081-4

Ellithorpe, M. E., & Bleakley, A. (2016). Wanting to see people like me? Racial and gender diversity in popular adolescent television. *Journal of Youth and Adolescence, 45,* 1426–1437. doi: 10.1007/s10964-016-0415-4

Endendijk, J. J., Groeneveld, M. G., van Berkel, S. R., Hallers-Haalboom, E. T., Mesman, J., & Bakermans-Kranenburg, M. J. (2013). Gender stereotypes in the family context: Mothers, fathers, and siblings. *Sex Roles, 68,* 577–590. doi: 10.1007/s11199-013-0265-4

England, D., Descartes, L., & Collier-Meek, M. (2011). Gender role portrayal and the Disney Princesses. *Sex Roles, 64,* 555–567. doi: 10.1007/s11199-011-9930-7

Epstein, B. J. (2014). "The case of the missing bisexuals": Bisexuality in books for young readers. *Journal of Bisexuality, 14,* 110–125. doi: 10.1080/15299716.2014.872483

Epstein, R., Blake, J. J., & González, T. (2017). *Girlhood interrupted: The erasure of Black girls' childhood.* Washington, DC: Center on Poverty and Inequality at the Georgetown University Law Center. Retrieved from http://www.law.georgetown.edu/academics/centers-institutes/poverty-inequality/upload/girlhood-interrupted.pdf

Fabes, R., Martin, C., & Hanish, L. (2003). Young children's play qualities in same-, other-, and mixed-sex peer groups. *Child Development, 74,* 921–932. doi: 10.1111/1467-8624.00576

Fagot, B., Leinbach, M., & Hagan, R. (1986). Gender labeling and the adoption of sex-typed behaviors. *Developmental Psychology, 22,* 440–443. doi: 10.1037/0012-1649.22.4.440

Fausto-Sterling, A., Coll, C., & Lamarre, M. (2012). Sexing the baby: Part 2—Applying dynamic systems theory to the emergences of sex-related differences in infants and toddlers. *Social Science & Medicine, 74,* 1693–1702. doi: 10.1016/j.socscimed.2011.06.027

Fine, C. (2010). *Delusions of gender: How our minds, society, and neurosexism create difference.* New York, NY: Norton.

Fitzpatrick, M., & McPherson, B. (2010). Coloring within the lines: Gender stereotypes in contemporary coloring books. *Sex Roles, 62,* 127–137. doi:10.1007/s11199-009-9703-8

Fonagy, P. (2003). Psychoanalysis today. *World Psychiatry, 2,* 73–80.

Frawley, T. (2008). Gender schema and prejudicial recall: How children misremember, fabricate, and distort gendered picture book information. *Journal of Research in Childhood Education, 22,* 291–303. doi: 10.1080/02568540809594628

Freeman, N. (2007). Preschoolers' perceptions of gender appropriate toys and their parents' beliefs about genderized behaviors: Miscommunication, mixed messages, or hidden truths? *Early Childhood Education Journal, 34,* 357–366. doi:10.1007/s10643-006-0123-x

Freud, S. (1999). *The interpretation of dreams* (J. Crick, Trans.). Oxford, United Kingdom: Oxford University Press. (Original work published 1900)

Freud, S. (1961a). The dissolution of the Oedipus complex. In J. Strachey (Ed. and Trans.), *The standard edition of the complete psychological works of Sigmund Freud* (Vol. XIX, pp. 171–180). London, United Kingdom: Hogarth Press. (Original work published 1924)

Freud, S. (1961b). Some psychical consequences of the anatomical distinction between the sexes. In J. Strachey (Ed. and Trans.), *The standard edition of the complete psychological works of Sigmund Freud* (Vol. XIX, pp. 241–258). London, United Kingdom: Hogarth Press. (Original work published 1925)

Fromberg, D. P. (1999). The role of higher education in professional preparation for early childhood education. *Child and Youth Care Forum, 28,* 33–42. doi: 10.1023/A:1021950618712

Fulcher, M., Sutfin, E., & Patterson, C. (2008). Individual differences in gender development: Associations with parental sexual orientation, attitudes, and division of labor. *Sex Roles, 58,* 330–341. doi: 10.1007/s11199-007-9348-4

Galambos, N., Almeida, D., & Petersen, A. (1990). Masculinity, femininity, and sex role attitudes in early adolescence: Exploring gender intensification. *Child Development, 61,* 1905–1914. doi: 10.1111/j.1467-8624.1990.tb03574.x

Garber, M. (2015, August 25). Call it the Bechdel-Wallace test. *The Atlantic.* Retrieved from https://www.theatlantic.com/entertainment/archive/2015/08/call-it-the-bechdel-wallace-test/402259/

Garrahy, D. A. (2001). Three third-grade teachers' gender-related beliefs and behavior. *The Elementary School Journal, 102,* 81–94. doi: 10.1086/499694

George, D. S. (2016, December 2). Ten-year-olds tackle 'The Lie' of demeaning stereotypes in video. *The Washington Post.* Retrieved from: https://www.washingtonpost.com/local/education/ten-year-olds-tackle-the-lie-of-demeaning-stereotypes-in-powerful-video/2016/12/02/69b7e162-b02a-11e6-8616-52b15787add0_story.html?utm_term=.b92e4aca0e3b

Gerding, A., & Signorielli, N. (2014). Gender roles in tween television programming: A content analysis of two genres. *Sex Roles, 70,* 43–56. doi: 10.1007/s11199-013-0330-z

Gergen, K. J. (2001). *Social construction in context.* London, United Kingdom: Sage.

Gil, R. M., & Vazquez, C. I. (1996). *The Maria paradox: How Latinas can merge Old World traditions with New World self-esteem.* New York, NY: Putnam.

Goldberg, A. (2007). (How) does it make a difference? Perspectives of adults with lesbian, gay, and bisexual parents. *American Journal of Orthopsychiatry, 77,* 550–562. doi: 10.1037/0002-9432.77.4.550

Goldberg, A., Kashy, D., & Smith, J. (2012). Gender-typed play behavior in early childhood: Adopted children with lesbian, gay, and heterosexual parents. *Sex Roles, 67,* 503–515. doi: 10.1007/s11199-012-0198-3

Goodyear, S. (2016, January 12). Seat of unrest. *Daily News.* Retrieved from http://interactive.nydailynews.com/2016/01/transgender-students-war-over-public-school-bathrooms/

Green, M., Bobrowicz, A., & Ang, C. S. (2015). The lesbian, gay, bisexual and transgender community online: Discussions of bullying and self-disclosure in YouTube videos. *Behaviour & Information Technology, 34,* 704–712. doi: 10.1080/0144929X.2015.1012649

Green, V., Bigler, R., & Catherwood, D. (2004). The variability and flexibility of gender-typed toy play: A close look at children's behavioral responses to counterstereotypic models. *Sex Roles, 51,* 371–386. doi: 10.1023/B:SERS.0000049227.05170.aa

Greytak, E. A., Kosciw, J. G., & Boesen, M. J. (2013). Putting the "T" in "resource": The benefits of LGBT-related school resources for transgender youth. *Journal of LGBT Youth, 10,* 45–63. doi: 10.1080/19361653.2012.718522

Grossman, A., D'Augelli, A., Howell, T., & Hubbard, S. (2005). Parents' reactions to transgender youths' gender nonconforming expression and identity. *Journal of Gay & Lesbian Social Services, 18,* 3–16. doi: 10.1300/J041v18n01_02

Grossman, A. H., & D'Augelli, A. R. (2006). Transgender youth: Invisible and vulnerable. *Journal of Homosexuality, 51,* 111–128. doi: 10.1300/J082v51n01_06

Grossman, A. H., Haney, A. P., Edwards, P., Alessi, E. J., Ardon, M., & Howell, T. J. (2009). Lesbian, gay, bisexual and transgender youth talk about experiencing and coping with school violence: A qualitative study. *Journal of LGBT Youth, 6,* 24–46. doi: 10.1080/19361650802379748

Guo, J. (2016, January 25). Researchers have found a major problem with "The Little Mermaid" and other Disney movies. *The Washington Post.* Retrieved from https://www.washingtonpost.com/news/wonk/wp/2016/01/25/researchers-have-discovered-a-major-problem-with-the-little-mermaid-and-other-disney-movies/

Hagan, L. K., & Kuebli, J. (2007). Mothers' and fathers' socialization of preschoolers' physical risk taking. *Journal of Applied Developmental Psychology, 28,* 2–14. doi: 10.1016/j.appdev.2006.10.007

Halim, M., & Ruble, D. (2010). Gender identity and stereotyping in early and middle childhood. In J. C. Chrisler & D. R. McCreary (Eds.), *Handbook of gender research in psychology* (Vol. 1, pp. 495–525). New York, NY: Springer.

Halim, M., Ruble, D., & Amodio, D. (2011). From pink frilly dresses to "one of the boys": A social-cognitive analysis of gender identity development and gender bias. *Social and Personality Psychology Compass, 5*, 933–949. doi: 10.1111/j.1751-9004.2011.00399.x

Halim, M. L., Ruble, D. N., & Tamis-LeMonda, C. S. (2013). Four-year-olds' beliefs about how others regard males and females. *British Journal of Developmental Psychology, 31*, 128–135. doi: 10.1111/j.2044-835X.2012.02084.x

Halim, M., Ruble, D., Tamis-LeMonda, C., & Shrout, P. (2013). Rigidity in gender-typed behaviors in early childhood: A longitudinal study of ethnic minority children. *Child Development, 84*, 1269–1284. doi: 10.1111/cdev.12057

Halim, M. L. D., Ruble, D. N., Tamis-LeMonda, C. S., Shrout, P. E., & Amodio, D. M. (2017). Gender attitudes in early childhood: Behavioral consequences and cognitive antecedents. *Child Development, 88*, 882–899. doi: 10.1111/cdev.12642

Hamilton, M., Anderson, D., Broaddus, M., & Young, K. (2006). Gender stereotyping and under-representation of female characters in 200 popular children's picture books: A twenty-first century update. *Sex Roles, 55*, 757–765. doi: 10.1007/s11199-006-9128-6

Hannon, L., DeFina, R., & Bruch, S. (2013). The relationship between skin tone and school suspension for African Americans. *Race and Social Problems, 5*, 281–295. doi: 10.1007/s12552-013-9104-z

Harris, A. (2005). *Gender as soft assembly.* New York, NY: Routledge.

Hayward, C., Killen, J., Wilson, D., & Hammer, L. (1997). Psychiatric risk associated with early puberty in adolescent girls. *Journal of the American Academy of Child & Adolescent Psychiatry, 36*, 255–262.

Hemmings, A. (2000). The "hidden" corridor curriculum. *The High School Journal, 83*(2), 1–10.

Hill, S. (2002). Teaching and doing gender in African American families. *Sex Roles, 47*, 493–506. doi: 10.1023/A:1022026303937

Hill, J. P., & Lynch, M. E. (1983). The intensification of gender-related role expectations during early adolescence. In J. Brooks-Gunn & A. C. Petersen (Eds.), *Girls at puberty* (pp. 201–228). New York, NY: Springer.

Horn, S. (2007). Adolescents' acceptance of same-sex peers based on sexual orientation and gender expression. *Journal of Youth and Adolescence, 36*, 363–371. doi: 10.1007/s10964-006-9111-0

Horney, K. (1932). The dread of women. *International Journal of Psychoanalysis, 13*, 348–360.

Hvistendahl, M. (2012). *Unnatural selection: Choosing boys over girls, and the consequences of a world without men.* New York, NY: PublicAffairs.

Jung, C. G. (1915). The theory of psychoanalysis. *Psychoanalytic Review, 2*, 29–51.

Kane, E. (2006). "No way my boys are going to be like that!" Parents' responses to children's gender nonconformity. *Gender and Society, 20*, 149–176. doi: 10.1177/0891243205284276

Kane, E. (2009). "I wanted a soul mate": Gendered anticipation and frameworks of accountability in parents' preferences for sons and daughters. *Symbolic Interaction, 32*, 372–389. doi: 10.1525/si.2009.32.4.372

Karraker, K., Vogel, D., & Lake, M. (1995). Parents' gender-stereotyped perceptions of newborns: The eye of the beholder revisited. *Sex Roles, 33*, 687–701. doi: 10.1007/BF01547725

Kleman, J. (2015, September 12). Transgender children: This is who he is—I have to respect that. *The Guardian.* Retrieved from http://www.theguardian.com/society/2015/sep/12/transgender-children-have-to-respect-who-he-is

Kok, J. L., & Findlay, B. (2006). An exploration of sex-role stereotyping in Australian award-winning children's picture books. *The Australian Library Journal, 55*, 248–261. doi: 10.1080/00049670.2006.10721857

Kortenhaus, C., & Demarest, J. (1993). Gender role stereotyping in children's literature: An update. *Sex Roles, 28*, 219–232. doi: 10.1007/BF00299282

Kosciw, J. G., Greytak, E. A., Palmer, N. A., & Boesen, M. J. (2014). *The 2013 National School Climate Survey: The experiences of lesbian, gay, bisexual and transgender youth in our nation's schools.* New York, NY: Gay Lesbian & Straight Education Network. Retrieved from https://www.glsen.org/sites/default/files/2013%20National%20School%20Climate%20Survey%20Full%20Report_0.pdf

Koss, M. (2015). Diversity in contemporary picture books: A content analysis. *Journal of Children's Literature, 41*, 32–42.

Lacroix, C. (2004). Images of animated others: The orientalization of Disney's cartoon heroines from The Little Mermaid to The Hunchback of Notre Dame. *Popular Communication, 2*, 213–229. doi: 10.1207/s15405710pc0204_2

Langhout, R. D., & Mitchell, C. A. (2008). Engaging contexts: Drawing the link between student and teacher experiences of the hidden curriculum. *Journal of Community & Applied Social Psychology, 18*, 593–614. doi:10.1002/casp.974

Lease, A., Kennedy, C., & Axelrod, J. (2002). Children's social constructions of popularity. *Social Development, 11*, 87–109. doi: 10.1111/1467-9507.00188

Leedy, M., LaLonde, D., & Runk, K. (2003). Gender equity in mathematics: Beliefs of students, parents, and teachers. *School Science and Mathematics, 103*, 285–292. doi: 10.1111/j.1949-8594.2003.tb18151.x

Leichsenring, F., Rabung, S., & Leibing, E. (2004) The efficacy of short-term psychodynamic psychotherapy in specific psychiatric disorders: A meta-analysis. *Archives of General Psychiatry, 61*, 1208–1216. doi: 10.1001/archpsyc.61.12.1208

Lenhart, A., Purcell, K., Smith, A., & Zickuhr, K. (2010, February 3). *Social media and young adults.* Washington, DC: Pew Research Center. Retrieved from http://www.pewinternet.org/2010/02/03/social-media-and-young-adults/

Lester, J. (2014). Homonormativity in children's literature: An intersectional analysis of queer-themed picture books. *Journal of LGBT Youth, 11*, 244–275. doi: 10.1080/19361653.2013.879465

Levant, R. F., & Richmond, K. (2015). Teaching the psychology of men and masculinity to undergraduates. In D. S. Dunn (Ed.), *The Oxford handbook of undergraduate psychology education* (pp. 659–670). Oxford, United Kingdom: Oxford University Press.

Lever, J. (1976). Sex differences in children's play. *Social Problems, 23*, 478–487. doi: 10.2307/799857

Levy, G., & Haaf, R. (1994). Detection of gender-related categories by 10-month-old infants. *Infant Behavior and Development, 17*, 457–459. doi: 10.1016/0163-6383(94)90037-X

Lytton, H., & Romney, D. (1991). Parents' differential socialization of boys and girls: A meta-analysis. *Psychological Bulletin, 109*, 267–296. doi: 10.1037/0033-2909.109.2.267

Maccoby, E. (1998). *The two sexes: Growing up apart, coming together.* Cambridge, MA: Harvard University Press.

Mahr, K. (2016, September 3). Protests over black girls' hair rekindle debate about racism in South Africa. *CNN.* Retrieved from https://www.washingtonpost.com/world/africa/protests-over-black-girls-hair-rekindle-debate-about-racism-in-south-africa/2016/09/02/27f445da-6ef4-11e6-993f-73c693a89820_story.html?utm_term=.6812a08a542e

Matthes, J., Prieler, M., & Adam, K. (2016). Gender-role portrayals in television advertising across the globe. *Sex Roles, 75*, 314–327. doi: 10.1007/s11199-016-0617-y

Martin, C., & Dinella, L. (2012). Congruence between gender stereotypes and activity preference in self-identified tomboys and non-tomboys. *Archives of Sexual Behavior, 41*, 599–610. doi: 10.1007/s10508-011-9786-5

Martin, C. L., Eisenbud, L., & Rose, H. (1995). Children's gender-based reasoning about toys. *Child Development, 66,* 1453–1471. doi: 10.1111/j.1467-8624.1995.tb00945.x

Martin, C., & Fabes, R. (2001). The stability and consequences of young children's same-sex peer interactions. *Developmental Psychology, 37,* 431–446. doi: 10.1037/0012-1649.37.3.431

Martin, C., Kornienko, O., Schaefer, D., Hanish, L., Fabes, R., & Goble, P. (2013). The role of sex of peers and gender-typed activities in young children's peer affiliative networks: A longitudinal analysis of selection and influence. *Child Development, 84,* 921–937. doi: 10.1111/cdev.12032

Martin, C. L., & Ruble, D. (2004). Children's search for gender cues. Cognitive perspectives on gender development. *Current Directions in Psychological Science, 13,* 67–70. doi: 10.1111/j.0963-7214.2004.00276.x

Martin, C., Ruble, D., & Szkrybalo, J. (2002). Cognitive theories of early gender development. *Psychological Bulletin, 128,* 903–933. doi: 10.1037/0033-2909.128.6.903

Mayes-Elma, R. (2006). *Females and Harry Potter: Not all that empowering.* Lanham, MD: Rowman & Littlefield.

McCabe, J., Fairchild, E., Grauerholz, L., Pescosolido, B. A., & Tope, D. (2011). Gender in twentieth-century children's books: Patterns of disparity in titles and central characters. *Gender & Society, 25,* 197–226. doi: 10.1177/0891243211398358

McGuffey, C. S., & Rich, B. L. (1999). Playing in the gender transgression zone: Race, class, and hegemonic masculinity in middle childhood. *Gender & Society, 13,* 608–627. doi: 10.1177/089124399013005003

McGuire, J. K., Anderson, C. R., Toomey, R. B., & Russell, S. T. (2010). School climate for transgender youth: A mixed method investigation of student experiences and school responses. *Journal of Youth & Adolescence, 39,* 1175–1188. doi:10.1007/s10964-010-9540-7

Meltzer, M. (2015, October 15). Where have all the tomboys gone? *The New York Times.* Retrieved from http://www.nytimes.com/2015/10/15/fashion/where-have-all-the-tomboys-gone.html?_r=0

Miller, C., Lurye, L., Zosuls, K., & Ruble, D. (2009). Accessibility of gender stereotype domains: Developmental and gender differences in children. *Sex Roles, 60,* 870–881. doi: 10.1007/s11199-009-9584-x

Miller, L. M., Schweingruber, H., & Brandenburg, C. L. (2001). Middle school students' technology practices and preferences: Re-examining gender differences. *Journal of Educational Multimedia and Hypermedia, 10,* 125–140.

Milmo, D. (August 31, 2012). Lego's "sexist" friends range for girls spurs 35% profit rise. *The Guardian.* Retrieved from http://www.theguardian.com/lifeandstyle/2012/aug/31/lego-friends-profit-rise

Mitchell, J. (1974). *Psychoanalysis and feminism.* New York, NY: Allen Lane.

Mondschein, E. R., Adolph, K. E., & Tamis-LeMonda, C. S. (2000). Gender bias in mothers' expectations about infant crawling. *Journal of Experimental Child Psychology, 77,* 304–316. doi: 10.1006/jecp.2000.2597

Morgan, B. L. (1998). A three generational study of tomboy behavior. *Sex Roles, 39,* 787–800. doi: 10.1023/A:1018816319376

Murnen, S. K., Greenfield, C., Younger, A., & Boyd, H. (2016). Boys act and girls appear: A content analysis of gender stereotypes associated with characters in children's popular culture. *Sex Roles, 74,* 78–91. doi: 10.1007/s11199-015-0558-x

Negy, C., & Woods, D. J. (1992). The importance of acculturation in understanding research with Hispanic-Americans. *Hispanic Journal of Behavioral Sciences, 14,* 224–247.

Nesi, J., & Prinstein, M. J. (2015). Using social media for social comparison and feedback-seeking: Gender and popularity moderate associations with depressive symptoms. *Journal of Abnormal Child Psychology, 43,* 1427–1438. doi: 10.1007/s10802-015-0020-0

Ochman, J. M. (1996). The effects of nongender-role stereotyped, same-sex role models in storybooks on the self-esteem of children in grade three. *Sex Roles, 35,* 711–735. doi: 10.1007/BF01544088

O'Neil, J. M., & Luján, M. L. (2009). Preventing boys' problems in schools through psychoeducational programming: A call to action. *Psychology in the Schools, 46,* 257–266. doi: 10.1002/pits.20371

Olson, K., Key, A., & Eaton, N. (2015). Gender cognition in transgender children. *Psychological Science, 26,* 467–474. doi: 10.1177/0956797614568156

Parks, C. (2016, January 20). Oregon schools risk law suits over transgender kids and bathrooms, lawyers warn. *The Oregonian.* Retrieved from http://www.oregonlive.com/pacific-northwest-news/index.ssf/2016/01/laws_on_transgender_students_i.html

Pate, R., Dowda, M., O'Neill, J., & Ward, D. (2007). Change in physical activity participation among adolescent girls from 8th to 12th grade. *Journal of Physical Activity and Health, 4,* 3–16. doi: 10.1123/jpah.4.1.3

Payne, E., & Smith, M. (2014). The big freak out: Educator fear in response to the presence of transgender elementary school students. *Journal of Homosexuality, 61,* 399–418. doi: 10.1080/00918369.2013.842430

Person, E. S., & Ovesey, L. (1983). Psychoanalytic theories of gender identity. *Journal of the American Academy of Psychoanalysis, 11,* 203–226.

Phoenix, A., Frosh, S., & Pattman, R. (2003). Producing contradictory masculine subject positions: Narratives of threat, homophobia and bullying in 11–14 year old boys. *Journal of Social Issues, 59,* 179–195. doi: 10.1111/1540-4560.t01-1-00011

Picket, K. (2015, July 4). California family discusses 4-year-old transgender child. *The Daily Caller.* Retrieved from http://dailycaller.com/2015/07/04/california-family-discusses-4-year-old-transgender-child/

Pipher, M. (1994). *Reviving Ophelia: Saving the selves of adolescent girls.* New York, NY: Penguin.

Plummer, D. C. (2001). The quest for modern manhood: Masculine stereotypes, peer culture and the social significance of homophobia. *Journal of Adolescence, 24,* 15–23. doi: 10.1006/jado.2000.0370

Politt, K. (1991, April 7). Hers: The Smurfette principle. *The New York Times.* Retrieved from http://www.nytimes.com/1991/04/07/magazine/hers-the-smurfette-principle.html

Powlishta, K., Sen, M., Serbin, L., Poulin-Dubois, D., & Eichstedt, J. (2001). From infancy through middle childhood: The role of cognitive and social factors in becoming gendered. In R. Unger (Ed.), *Handbook of the psychology of women and gender* (pp. 116–132). New York, NY: Wiley.

Priess, H., Lindberg, S., & Hyde, J. (2009). Adolescent gender role identity and mental health: Gender intensification revisited. *Child Development, 80,* 1531–1544. doi: 10.1111/j.1467-8624.2009.01349.x

Publishing statistics on children's books about people of color and first/native nations and by people of color and first/native nations authors and illustrators. (n.d.). Retrieved from the Cooperative Children's Book Center website: https://ccbc.education.wisc.edu/books/pcstats.asp

Quinn, P., Yahr, J., Kuhn, A., Slater, A., & Pascalis, O. (2002). Representation of the gender of human faces by infants: A preference for female. *Perception, 31,* 1109–1122. doi: 10.1068/p3331

Radic, M. (2018, March 3). Do this year's Best Picture Oscar nominees pass the Bechdel test? *The New Yorker.* Retrieved from https://www.newyorker.com/culture/culture-desk/do-this-years-best-picture-oscar-nominees-pass-the-bechdel-test

Rahilly, E. P. (2015). The gender binary meets the gender-variant child: Parents' negotiations with childhood gender variance. *Gender & Society, 29,* 338–361. doi: 10.1177/0891243214563069

Raley, S., & Bianchi, S. (2006). Sons, daughters, and family processes: Does gender of children matter? *Annual Review of Sociology, 32,* 401–421. doi: 10.1146/annurev.soc.32.061604.12310

Reay, D. (2001). "Spice girls," "nice girls," "girlies," and "tomboys": Gender discourses, girls' cultures and femininities in the primary classroom. *Gender and Education, 13,* 153–166. doi: 10.1080/09540250120051178

Reisner, S. L., Vetters, R., Leclerc, M., Zaslow, S., Wolfrum, S., Shumer, D., & Mimiaga, M. J. (2015). Mental health of transgender youth in care at an adolescent urban community health center: A matched retrospective cohort study. *The Journal of Adolescent Health, 56,* 274–279. doi: 10.1016/j.jadohealth.2014.10.264

Richman, E., & Shaffer, D. (2000). If you let me play sports: How might sport participation influence the self-esteem of adolescent females? *Psychology of Women Quarterly, 24,* 189–199. doi: 10.1111/j.1471-6402.2000.tb00200.x

Rubin, J., Provenzano, F., & Luria, Z. (1974). The eye of the beholder: Parents' views on sex of newborns. *American Journal of Orthopsychiatry, 44,* 512–519. doi: 10.1111/j.1939-0025.1974.tb00905.x

Ruble, D., & Martin, C. (1998). Gender development. In W. Damon (Ed.), *Handbook of child psychology* (pp. 933–1016). New York, NY: Wiley.

Ruble, D. N., Martin, C., & Berenbaum, S. (2006). Gender development. In N. Eisenberg (Ed.), *Handbook of child psychology* (6th ed., Vol. 3, pp. 858–933). New York, NY: Wiley.

Ruble, D., Taylor, L., Cyphers, L., Greulich, F., Lurye, L., & Shrout, P. (2007). The role of gender constancy in early gender development. *Child Development, 78,* 1121–1136. doi: 10.1111/j.1467-8624.2007.01056.x

Ryan, C. L., Patraw, J. M., & Bednar, M. (2013). Discussing princess boys and pregnant men: Teaching about gender diversity and transgender experiences within an elementary school curriculum. *Journal of LGBT Youth, 10,* 83–105. doi: 10.1080/19361653.2012.718540

Sanchez, D., Vandewater, E. A., & Hamilton, E. R. (2017). Examining marianismo gender role attitudes, ethnic identity, mental health, and substance use in Mexican American early adolescent girls. *Journal of Ethnicity in Substance Abuse.* Advance online publication. doi: 10.1080/15332640.2017.1356785

Schaub, M. (2015, December 21). Black actress cast as Hermione: J. K. Rowling enthusiastically approves. *L.A. Times.* Retrieved from http://www.latimes.com/books/jacketcopy/la-et-jc-black-hermione-jk-rowling-approves-20151221-htmlstory.html

Scott, A. O., & Dargis, M. (2012, April 4). A radical female hero from dystopia. *The New York Times.* Retrieved from http://www.nytimes.com/2012/04/08/movies/katniss-everdeen-a-new-type-of-woman-warrior.html?pagewanted=1&_r=1&hp

Seavey, C., Katz, P., & Zalk, S. (1975). Baby X. *Sex Roles, 1,* 103–109. doi: 10.1007/BF00288004

Sengupta, R. (2006). Reading representations of Black, East Asian, and White women in magazines for adolescent girls. *Sex Roles, 54,* 799–808. doi: 10.1007/s11199-006-9047-6

Shipp, T. D., Shipp, D. Z., Bromley, B., Sheahan, R., Cohen, A., Lieberman, E., & Benacerraf, B. (2004). What factors are associated with parents' desire to know the sex of their unborn child? *Birth, 31,* 272–279. doi: 10.1111/j.0730-7659.2004.00319.x

Shutts, K., Kenward, B., Falk, H., Ivegran, A., & Fawcett, C. (2017). Early preschool environments and gender: Effects of gender pedagogy in Sweden. *Journal of Experimental Child Psychology, 162,* 1–17. doi: 10.1016/j.jecp.2017.04.014

Sidorowicz, L., & Lunney, G. (1980). Baby X revisited. *Sex Roles, 6,* 67–73. doi: 10.1007/BF00288362

Silver, A. (2010). Twilight is not good for maidens: Gender, sexuality, and the family in Stephenie Meyers' Twilight Series. *Studies in the Novel, 42,* 121–138. doi: 10.1353/sdn.2010.0009

Singh, A. A. (2013). Transgender youth of color and resilience: Negotiating oppression and finding support. *Sex Roles, 68,* 690–702. doi: 10.1007/s11199-012-0149-z

Sinno, S., & Killen, M. (2009). Moms at work and dads at home: Children's evaluations of parental roles. *Applied Developmental Science, 13,* 16–29. doi: 10.1080/10888690802606735

Sinno, S., & Killen, M. (2011). Social reasoning about second-shift parenting. *British Journal of Developmental Psychology, 29,* 313–329. doi: 10.1111/j.2044-835X.2010.02021.x

Skelton, C. (2006). Boys and girls in the elementary school. In C. Skelton, B. Francis, & L. Smulyan (Eds.), *The SAGE handbook of gender and education* (pp. 139–151). Thousand Oaks, CA: Sage.

Skelton, C., Carrington, B., Hutchings, M., Read, B., & Hall, I. (2009). Gender "matters" in the primary classroom: Pupils' and teachers' perspectives. *British Education Research Journal, 35,* 187–204. doi: 10.1080/01411920802041905

Skiba, R. J., Michael, R. S., Nardo, A. C., & Peterson, R. L. (2002). The color of discipline: Sources of racial and gender disproportionality in school punishment. *The Urban Review, 34,* 317–342. doi: 10.1023/A:1021320817372

Skoog, T., & Stattin, H. (2014). Why and under what contextual conditions do early-maturing girls develop problem behaviors? *Child Development Perspectives, 8,* 158–162. doi: 10.1111/cdep.12076

Smith, D. S., & Juvonen, J. (2017). Do I fit in? Psychosocial ramifications of low gender typicality in early adolescence. *Journal of Adolescence, 60,* 161–170. doi: 10.1016/j.adolescence.2017.07.014

Solis, J. (1995). The status of Latino children and youth: Challenges and prospects. In R. E. Zambrana (Ed.), *Understanding Latino families: Scholarship, policy, and practice* (pp. 62–81). Newbury Park, CA: Sage.

Stermer, S. P., & Burkley, M. (2015). SeX-Box: Exposure to sexist video games predicts benevolent sexism. *Psychology of Popular Media Culture, 4,* 47–55. doi: 10.1037/a0028397

Stevens, D. (2014, February 18). The sexy "Frozen" moment no one is talking about. *Huffington Post.* Retrieved from http://www.huffingtonpost.com/2014/02/18/sexy-frozen-moment_n_4802792.html?

Tagliabue, J. (2012, November, 14). Swedish school's big lesson begins with dropping personal pronouns. *The New York Times.* Retrieved from http://www.nytimes.com/2012/11/14/world/europe/swedish-school-de-emphasizes-gender-lines.html?_r=0

Thomas, W. (1997). Navajo cultural constructions of gender and sexuality. In S. E. Jacobs (Ed.), *Two-spirit people: Native American gender identity, sexuality, and spirituality* (pp. 156–173). Urbana, IL: University of Illinois Press.

Thompson, T., & Zerbinos, E. (1995). Gender roles in animated cartoons: Has the picture changed in 20 years? *Sex Roles, 32,* 651–673. doi: 10.1007/BF01544217

Thorne, B. (1993). *Gender play: Girls and boys in school.* New Brunswick, NJ: Rutgers University Press.

Thorne, B., & Luria, Z. (1986). Sexuality and gender in children's daily lives. *Social Problems, 33,* 176–190. doi: 10.2307/800703

Trautner, H., Ruble, D., Cyphers, L., Kirsten, B., Behrendt, R., & Hartmann, P. (2005). Rigidity and flexibility of gender stereotypes in childhood: Developmental or differential? *Infant and Child Development, 14*, 365–381. doi: 10.1002/icd.39

Tsao, Y. (2008). Gender issues in young children's literature. *Reading Improvement, 45*, 108–114.

Tukachinsky, R., Mastro, D., & Yarchi, M. (2015). Documenting portrayals of race/ethnicity on primetime television over a 20-year span and their association with national-level racial/ethnic attitudes. *Journal of Social Issues, 71*, 17–38. doi: 10.1111/josi.12094

Turner-Bowker, D. (1996). Gender stereotyped descriptors in children's picture books: Does "curious Jane" exist in the literature? *Sex Roles, 35*, 461–488. doi: 10.1007/BF01544132

Untitled Productions [Screen name]. (2016, September 8). *The Lie* [Video file]. Retrieved from https://vimeo.com/182020903

van Beusekom, G., Baams, L., Bos, H. M., Overbeek, G., & Sandfort, T. G. (2016). Gender nonconformity, homophobic peer victimization, and mental health: How same-sex attraction and biological sex matter. *The Journal of Sex Research, 53*, 98–108. doi: 10.1080/00224499.2014.993462

Vilakazi, T. (2016, September 1). South African students protest against school's alleged racist hair policy. *CNN*. Retrieved from http://www.cnn.com/2016/08/31/africa/south-africa-school-racism/

Voyer, D., & Voyer, S. (2014). Gender differences in scholastic achievement: A meta-analysis. *Psychological Bulletin, 140*, 1174–1204. doi: 10.1037/a0036620

Wagner, L. (2017). Factors influencing parents' preferences and parents' perceptions of child preferences of picturebooks. *Frontiers in Psychology, 8*, Article 1448. doi: 10.3389/fpsyg.2017.01448

Weinraub, M., Clemens, L., Sockloff, A., Ethridge, T., Gracely, E., & Myers, B. (1984). The development of sex role stereotypes in the third year: Relationships to gender labeling, gender identity, sex-typed toy preference, and family characteristics. *Child Development, 55*, 1493–1503. doi: 10.2307/1130019

Weitzman, L., Eifler, D., Hokada, E., & Ross, C. (1972). Sex-role socialization in picture books for preschool children. *American Journal of Sociology, 77*, 1125–1150. doi: 10.1086/225261

West, C., & Zimmerman, D. H. (1987). Doing gender. *Gender & Society, 1*, 125–151. doi: 10.1177/0891243287001002002

Westen, D. (1999). The scientific status of unconscious processes: Is Freud really dead? *Journal of the American Psychoanalytic Association, 47*, 1061–1106. doi: 10.1177/000306519904700404

Westen, D., & Gabbard, G. O. (2002). Developments in cognitive neuroscience II: Implications for theories of transference. *Journal of the American Psychoanalytic Association, 50*, 99–134. doi: 10.1177/00030651020500011601

Whitmar, L. (2016, January 25). 2016 Oscar best picture nominations and the Bechdel Test. Retrieved from https://www.theodysseyonline.com/2016-oscar-best-picture-nominations-bechdel-test

Willer, L. (2001). Warning: Welcome to your world baby, gender message enclosed. An analysis of gender messages in birth congratulation cards. *Women and Language, 24*, 16–23.

Williams, J. M., & Currie, C. (2000). Self-esteem and physical development in early adolescence: Pubertal timing and body image. *The Journal of Early Adolescence, 20*, 129–149. doi: 10.1177/0272431600020002002

Women's Media Center. (2015). *The status of women in the U.S. media 2015.* Retrieved from http://wmc.3cdn.net/83bf6082a319460eb1_hsrm680x2.pdf

Wong, W., & Hines, M. (2015). Effects of gender color-coding on toddlers' gender-typical toy play. *Archives of Sexual Behavior, 44*, 1233–1242. doi: 10.1007/s10508-014-0400-5

Woodburn, D., & Kopić, K. (2016, July). *The Ruderman white paper on employment of actors with disabilities in television.* Retrieved from http://www.rudermanfoundation.org/wp-content/uploads/2016/07/TV-White-Paper_final.final_.pdf

Zosuls, K., Ruble, D., Tamis-LeMonda, C., Shrout, P., Bornstein, M., & Greulich, F. (2009). The acquisition of gender labels in infancy: Implications for sex-typed play. *Developmental Psychology, 45*, 688–701. doi: 10.1037/a0014053

Zosuls, K. M., Ruble, D. N., & Tamis-LeMonda, C. S. (2014). Self-socialization of gender in African American, Dominican immigrant, and Mexican immigrant toddlers. *Child Development, 85*, 2202–2217. doi: 10.1111/cdev.12261

Chapter 6

Afshar, H. (2000). Gendering the millennium: Globalising women. *Development in Practice, 10*, 527–534. doi:10.1080/09614520050116686

Ainley, V., & Tsakiris, M. (2013). Body conscious? Interoceptive awareness, measured by heartbeat perception, is negatively correlated with self-objectification. *PLoS One, 8*(2), e55568. doi: 10.1371/journal.pone.0055568

Ali, S. (2005). Why here, why now? Young Muslim women wearing hijab. *The Muslim World, 95*, 515–530. doi: 10.1111/j.1478-1913.2005.00109.x

Als, H. (2003, October 27). Ghosts in the house: How Toni Morrison fostered a generation of Black writers. *The New Yorker, 79*(32), 64–72.

American Society for Aesthetic Plastic Surgery. (2014). *Cosmetic surgery national data bank statistics.* Retrieved from http://www.surgery.org/sites/default/files/2014-Stats.pdf

American Society for Aesthetic Plastic Surgery. (2016). *Cosmetic surgery national data bank statistics.* Retrieved from https://www.surgery.org/sites/default/files/ASAPS-Stats2016.pdf

Andrew, R., Tiggemann, M., & Clark, L. (2015). Predictors of intuitive eating in adolescent girls. *Journal of Adolescent Health, 56*, 209–214. doi: 10.1016/j.jadohealth.2014.09.005

Archer, D., Iritani, B., Kimes, D. D., & Barrios, M. (1983). Face-ism: Five studies of sex differences in facial prominence. *Journal of Personality and Social Psychology, 45*, 725–735. doi: 10.1037/0022-3514.45.4.725

Aubeeluck, A., & Maguire, M. (2002). The Menstrual Joy Questionnaire items alone can positively prime reporting of menstrual attitudes and symptoms. *Psychology of Women Quarterly, 26*, 160–162. doi: 10.1111/1471-6402.00054

Augustus-Horvath, C. L., & Tylka, T. L. (2009). A test and extension of objectification theory as it predicts disordered eating: Does women's age matter? *Journal of Counseling Psychology, 56*, 253–265. doi: 10.1037/a0014637

Avalos, L. C., & Tylka, T. L. (2006). Exploring a model of intuitive eating with college women. *Journal of Counseling Psychology, 53*, 486–497. doi: 10.1037/0022-0167.53.4.486

Awad, G. H., Norwood, C., Taylor, D. S., Martinez, M., McClain, S., Jones, B., . . . & Chapman-Hilliard, C. (2015). Beauty and body image concerns among African American college women. *Journal of Black Psychology, 41*, 540–564. doi: 10.1177/0095798414550864

Bacon, L. (2008). *Health at every size: The surprising truth about your weight.* Dallas, TX: Benbella Books.

Bacon, L., & Aphramor, L. (2011). Weight science: Evaluating the evidence for a paradigm shift. *Nutrition Journal, 10*(9). doi: 10.1186/1475-2891-10-9

Bailey, S. D., & Ricciardelli, L. A. (2010). Social comparisons, appearance related comments, contingent self-esteem and their relationships with body dissatisfaction and eating disturbance among women. *Eating Behaviors, 11*, 107–112. doi: 10.1016/j.eatbeh.2009.12.001

Baker, K. (2012, June 7). The decline of the Jewish girl nose job. *Jezebel*. Retrieved from http://jezebel.com/5916532/the-decline-of-the-jewish-girl-nose-job

Bakr, S. W. A. (2014). A hijab proper: The veil through feminist narrative inquiry. *Visual Culture & Gender, 9*, 5–17.

Bartky, S. L. (1990). *Femininity and domination: Studies in the phenomenology of oppression*. New York, NY: Routledge.

Barwick, A., Bazzini, D., Martz, D., Rocheleau, C., & Curtin, L. (2012). Testing the norm to fat talk for women of varying size: What's weight got to do with it? *Body Image, 9*, 176–179. doi: 10.1016/j.bodyim.2011.08.003

Basow, S. (1991). The hairless ideal: Women and their body hair. *Psychology of Women Quarterly, 15*, 83–96. doi: 10.1111/j.1471-6402.1991.tb00479.x

Basow, S. A., & Braman, A. C. (1998). Women and body hair: Social perceptions and attitudes. *Psychology of Women Quarterly, 22*, 637–645. doi: 10.1111/j.1471-6402.1998.tb00182.x

Bazzini, D. G., Pepper, A., Swofford, R., & Cochran, K. (2015). How healthy are health magazines? A comparative content analysis of cover captions and images of Women's and Men's Health magazine. *Sex Roles, 72*, 198–210. doi: 10.1007/s11199-015-0456-2

Bearman, S. K., Presnell, K., Martinez, E., & Stice, E. (2006). The skinny on body dissatisfaction: A longitudinal study of adolescent girls and boys. *Journal of Youth and Adolescence, 35*, 217–229. doi: 10.1007/s10964-005-9010-9

Beauboeuf-Lafontant, T. (2003). Strong and large Black women? Exploring relationships between deviant womanhood and weight. *Gender & Society, 17*, 111–121. doi: 10.1177/0891243202238981

Beausang, C. C., & Razor, A. G. (2000). Young Western women's experiences of menarche and menstruation. *Health Care for Women International, 21*, 517–528. doi: 10.1080/07399330050130304

Becker, A. E. (2004). Television, disordered eating, and young women in Fiji: Negotiating body image and identity during rapid social change. *Culture, Medicine and Psychiatry, 28*, 533–559. doi: 10.1007/s11013-004-1067-5

Becker, A. E., Burwell, R. A., Herzog, D. B., Hamburg, P., & Gilman, S. E. (2002). Eating behaviours and attitudes following prolonged exposure to television among ethnic Fijian adolescent girls. *British Journal of Psychiatry, 180*, 509–514. doi: 10.1192/bjp.180.6.509

Becker, C. B., Wilson, C., Williams, A., Kelly, M., McDaniel, L., & Elmquist, J. (2010). Peer-facilitated cognitive dissonance versus healthy weight eating disorders prevention: A randomized comparison. *Body Image, 7*, 280–288. doi: 10.1016/j.bodyim.2010.06.004

Befort, C., Robinson Kurpius, S. E., Hull-Blanks, E., Nicpon, M. F., Huser, L., & Sollenberger, S. (2001). Body image, self-esteem, and weight-related criticism from romantic partners. *Journal of College Student Development, 42*, 407–419. doi: 10.1353/csd.2005.0062

Bellinger, W. (2007). Why African American women try to obtain "good hair." *Sociological Viewpoints, 23*, 63–72.

Ben-Tovim, D. I., & Walker, M. K. (1995). Body image, disfigurement and disability. *Journal of Psychosomatic Research, 39*, 283–291. doi: 10.1016/0022-3999(94)00143-S

Bennett, C., & Harden, J. (2014). An exploration of mothers' attitudes towards their daughters' menarche. *Sex Education, 14*, 457–470. doi: 10.1080/14681811.2014.922862

Beren, S. E., Hayden, H. A., Wilfley, D. E., & Striegel-Moore, R. H. (1997). Body dissatisfaction among lesbian college students: The conflict of straddling mainstream and lesbian cultures. *Psychology of Women Quarterly, 21*, 431–445. doi: 10.1111/j.1471-6402.1997.tb00123.x

Berg, D. H., & Coutts, L. B. (1993). Virginity and tampons: The beginner myth as a case of alteration. *Health Care for Women International, 14*, 27–38. doi: 10.1080/07399339309516024

Berg, D. H., & Coutts, L. B. (1994). The extended curse: Being a woman every day. *Health Care for Women International, 15*, 11–22. doi: 10.1080/07399339409516090

Berger, J. (1972). *Ways of seeing*. London, United Kingdom: Penguin.

Bergeron, S. M., & Senn, C. Y. (1998). Body image and sociocultural norms: A comparison of heterosexual and lesbian women. *Psychology of Women Quarterly, 22*, 385–401. doi: 10.1111/j.1471-6402.1998.tb00164.x

Bessenoff, G. R. (2006). Can the media affect us? Social comparison, self-discrepancy, and the thin ideal. *Psychology of Women Quarterly, 30*, 239–251. doi: 10.1111/j.1471-6402.2006.00292.x

Blagg, K., Whitemore-Schanzenbach, D., Gunderson, C., & Ziliak, J. (2017, August). *Assessing food insecurity on campus: A national look at food insecurity among America's college students*. Washington, DC: Urban Institute. Retrieved from https://www.urban.org/sites/default/files/publication/92331/assessing_food_insecurity_on_campus_3.pdf

Bombak, A. (2014). Obesity, health at every size, and public health policy. *American Journal of Public Health, 104*, 60–67. doi: 10.2105/AJPH.2013.301486

Brady, J. L., Kaya, A., Iwamoto, D., Park, A., Fox, L., & Moorhead, M. (2017). Asian American women's body image experiences: A qualitative intersectionality study. *Psychology of Women Quarterly, 41*, 479–496. doi: 10.1177/0361684317725311

Braun, V., Tricklebank, G., & Clarke, V. (2013). "It shouldn't stick out from your bikini at the beach": Meaning, gender, and the hairy/hairless body. *Psychology of Women Quarterly, 37*, 478–493. doi: 10.1177/0361684313492950

Brewster, M. E., Velez, B. L., Esposito, J., Wong, S., Geiger, E., & Keum, B. T. (2014). Moving beyond the binary with disordered eating research: A test and extension of objectification theory with bisexual women. *Journal of Counseling Psychology, 61*, 50–62. doi: 10.1037/a0034748

Britton, L. E., Martz, D. M., Bazzini, D. G., Curtin, L. A., & LeaShomb, A. (2006). Fat talk and self-presentation of body image: Is there a social norm for women to self-degrade? *Body Image, 3*, 247–254. doi: 10.1016/j.bodyim.2006.05.006

Brooks-Gunn, J., & Ruble, D. N. (1986). Men's and women's attitudes and beliefs about the menstrual cycle. *Sex Roles, 14*, 287–299. doi: 10.1007/BF00287580

Brown, L. S. (1987). Lesbians, weight, and eating: New analyses and perspectives. In Lesbian Psychologies Collective (Ed.), *Lesbian psychologies: Explorations and challenges* (pp. 294–309). Urbana, IL: University of Illinois Press.

Buchanan, T. S., Fischer, A. R., Tokar, D. M., & Yoder, J. D. (2008). Testing a culture-specific extension of objectification theory regarding African American women's body image. *The Counseling Psychologist, 36*, 697–718. doi: 10.1177/0011000008316322

Burgard, D. (2009). What is health at every size? In E. D. Rothblum & S. Solovay (Eds.), *The fat studies reader* (pp. 42–53). New York, NY: New York University Press.

Burmeister, J. M., & Carels, R. A. (2014). Weight-related humor in the media: Appreciation, distaste, and anti-fat attitudes. *Psychology of Popular Media Cultures, 3*, 223–238. doi: 10.1037/ppm0000029

Burmeister, J. M., Kiefner, A. E., Carels, R. A., & Musher-Eizenman, D. R. (2013). Weight bias in graduate school admissions. *Obesity, 21*, 918–920. doi: 10.1002/oby.20171

Calfas, J. (2017, May 8). People are confused about Dove's new body wash bottles. *Fortune*. Retrieved from http://fortune.com/2017/05/08/dove-body-wash-bottles/

Calogero, R. (2004). A test of objectification theory: The effect of the male gaze on appearance concerns in college women. *Psychology of Women Quarterly, 28*, 16–21. doi: 10.1111/j.1471-6402.2004.00118.x

Calogero, R. M., Boroughs, M., & Thompson, J. K. (2007). The impact of Western beauty ideals on the lives of women and men: A sociocultural perspective. In V. Swami & A. Furnham (Eds.), *Body beautiful: Evolutionary and sociocultural perspectives* (pp. 259–298). New York, NY: Palgrave Macmillan.

Calogero, R. M., Davis, W. N., & Thompson, J. K. (2005). The role of self-objectification in the experience of women with eating disorders. *Sex Roles, 52*, 43–50. doi: 10.1007/s11199-005-1192-9

Calogero, R. M., & Thompson, J. K. (2009). Sexual self-esteem in American and British college women: Relations with self-objectification and eating problems. *Sex Roles, 60*, 160–173. doi: 10.1007/s11199-008-9517-0

Calogero, R. M., & Thompson, J. K. (2010). Gender and body image. In J. C. Chrisler & D. R. McCreary (Eds.), *Handbook of gender research in psychology* (Vol. 2, pp. 153–184). New York, NY: Springer.

Campos, P. (2004). *The obesity myth: Why America's obsession with weight is hazardous to your health.* New York, NY: Gotham Press.

Capodilupo, C. M. (2015). One size does not fit all: Using variables other than the thin ideal to understand Black women's body image. *Cultural Diversity and Ethnic Minority Psychology, 21*, 268–278. doi: 10.1037/a0037649

Carr, D., & Friedman, M. A. (2005). Is obesity stigmatizing? Body weight, perceived discrimination, and psychological well-being in the United States. *Journal of Health and Social Behavior, 46*, 244–259. doi: 10.1177/002214650504600303

Cash, T. F., & Henry, P. E. (1995). Women's body images: The results of a national survey in the USA. *Sex Roles, 33*, 19–28. doi: 10.1007/BF01547933

Cash, T. F., Novy, P. L., & Grant, J. R. (1994). Why do women exercise? Factor analysis and further validation of the reasons for exercise inventory. *Perceptual and Motor Skills, 78*, 539–544. doi: 10.2466/pms.1994.78.2.539

Chang, Y. T., Hayter, M., & Wu, S. C. (2010). A systematic review and meta-ethnography of the qualitative literature: Experiences of the menarche. *Journal of Clinical Nursing, 19*, 447–460. doi: 10.1111/j.1365-2702.2009.03019.x

Chen, E. Y., & Brown, M. (2005). Obesity stigma in sexual relationships. *Obesity Research, 13*, 1393–1397. doi: 10.1038/oby.2005.168

Chen, H.-Y., Yarnal, C., Chick, G., & Jablonski, N. (2018). Egg white or sun-kissed: A cross-cultural exploration of skin color and women's leisure behavior. *Sex Roles, 78*, 255–271. doi: 10.1007/s11199-017-0785-4

Choma, B. L., Visser, B. A., Pozzebon, J. A., Bogaert, A. F., Busseri, M. A., & Sadava, S. W. (2010). Self-objectification, self-esteem, and gender: Testing a moderated mediation model. *Sex Roles, 63*, 645–656. doi: 10.1007/s11199-010-9829-8

Chrisler, J. C. (2008). PMS as a culture-bound syndrome. In J. C. Chrisler, C. Golden, & P. D. Rozee (Eds.), *Lectures on the psychology of women* (4th ed., pp. 154–171). New York, NY: McGraw Hill.

Chrisler, J. C. (2012). "Why can't you control yourself?" Fat *should be* a feminist issue. *Sex Roles, 66*, 608–616. doi: 10.1007/s11199-011-0095-1

Chrisler, J. C., Gorman, J. A., Manion, J., Murgo, M., Barney, A., Adams-Clark, A., . . . & McGrath, M. (2016). Queer periods: Attitudes toward and experiences with menstruation in the masculine of centre and transgender community. *Culture, Health & Sexuality, 18*, 1238–1250. doi: 10.1080/13691058.2016.1182645

Chrisler, J. C., Johnston, I. K., Champagne, N. M., & Preston, K. E. (1994). Menstrual joy: The construct and its consequences. *Psychology of Women Quarterly, 18*, 375–387. doi: 10.1111/j.1471-6402.1994.tb00461.x

Christel, D. A., & Dunn, S. C. (2016). Average American women's clothing size: Comparing National Health and Nutritional Examination Surveys (1988–2010) to ASTM International Misses & Women's Plus Size clothing. *International Journal of Fashion Design, Technology and Education, 10*, 129–136. doi: 10.1080/17543266.2016.1214291

Chua, T. H. H., & Chang, L. (2016). Follow me and like my beautiful selfies: Singapore teenage girls' engagement in self-presentation and peer comparison on social media. *Computers in Human Behavior, 55*, 190–197. doi: 10.1016/j.chb.2015.09.011

Ciao, A. C., Latner, J. D., Brown, K. E., Ebneter, D. S., & Becker, C. B. (2015). Effectiveness of a peer-delivered dissonance-based program in reducing eating disorder risk factors in high school girls. *International Journal of Eating Disorders, 48*, 779–784. doi: 10.1002/eat.22418

Cohen, R., Newton-John, T., & Slater, A. (2018). 'Selfie'-objectification: The role of selfies in self-objectification and disordered eating in young women. *Computers in Human Behavior, 79*, 68–74. doi: 10.1016/j.chb.2017.10.027

Coleman, L., & Coleman, J. (2002). The measurement of puberty: A review. *Journal of Adolescence, 25*, 535–550. doi: 10.1006/jado.2002.0494

Collins, P. H. (1990). *Black feminist thought.* Boston, MA: Unwin Hyman.

Coltrane, S., & Messineo, M. (2000). The perpetuation of subtle prejudice: Race and gender imagery in 1990s television advertising. *Sex Roles, 42*, 363–389. doi: 10.1023/A:1007046204478

Conley, T. D., & Ramsey, L. R. (2011). Killing us softly? Investigating portrayals of women and men in contemporary magazine advertisements. *Psychology of Women Quarterly, 35*, 469–478. doi: 10.1177/0361684311413383

Connell, K. M., Coates, R., Doherty-Poirier, M., & Wood, F. M. (2013). A literature review to determine the impact of sexuality and body image changes following burn injuries. *Sexuality and Disability, 31*, 403–412. doi: 10.1007/s11195-013-9321-9

Cooper, S. C., & Koch, P. B. (2007). "Nobody told me nothin": Communication about menstruation among low-income African American women. *Women & Health, 46*, 57–78. doi: 10.1300/J013v46n01_05

Copeland, G. A. (1989). Face-ism and primetime television. *Journal of Broadcasting & Electronic Media, 33*, 209–214. doi: 10.1080/08838158909364075

Corning, A. F., Bucchianeri, M. M., & Pick, C. M. (2014). Thin or overweight women's fat talk: Which is worse for other women's body satisfaction? *Eating Disorders, 22*, 121–135. doi: 10.1080/10640266.2013.860850

Costos, D., Ackerman, R., & Paradis, L. (2002). Recollections of menarche: Communication between mothers and daughters regarding menstruation. *Sex Roles, 46*, 49–59. doi: 10.1023/A:1016037618567

Covert, J. J., & Dixon, T. L. (2008). A changing view: Representation and effects of the portrayal of women of color in mainstream women's magazines. *Communication Research, 35*, 232–256. doi: 10.1177/0093650207313166

Cox, R. (2015). *Transgender men: Objectification and body image* [Prezi Slides]. Retrieved from https://prezi.com/uzy_ohw_ozól/transgender-men-the-psychological-impact-of-objectification/

Cromer, B. A., Enrile, B., McCoy, K., Gerhardstein, M. J., Fitzpatrick, M., & Judis, J. (1990). Knowledge, attitudes and behavior related to sexuality in adolescents with chronic disability. *Developmental Medicine & Child Neurology, 32*, 602–610. doi: 10.1111/j.1469-8749.1990.tb08544.x

Currah, P., & Minter, S. (2000). *Transgender equality: A handbook for activists and policymakers*. Retrieved from http://www.thetaskforce.org/static_html/downloads/reports/reports/TransgenderEquality.pdf

Darden, J. (2010, October 19). Sesame Street writer pens "I Love My Hair" song to empower daughter. *Huffington Post*. Retrieved from http://www.huffingtonpost.com/jenee-darden/sesame-street-writer-pens_b_767353.html

Darke, P. A. (2004). The changing face of representations of disability in the media. In J. Swain, S. French, C. Barnes, & C. Thomas (Eds.), *Disabling barriers—Enabling environments* (2nd ed., pp. 100–105). Thousand Oaks, CA: Sage.

de Bruin, A. P., Woertman, L., Bakker, F. C., & Oudejans, R. R. D. (2009). Weight-related sport motives and girls' body image, weight control behaviors, and self-esteem. *Sex Roles, 60*, 628–641. doi: 10.1007/s11199-008-9562-8

Delaney, J., Lupton, M. J., & Toth, E. (1988). *The curse: A cultural history of menstruation* (Rev. ed.). Urbana, IL: University of Illinois Press.

DeMaria, A. L., & Berenson, A. B. (2013). Prevalence and correlates of pubic hair grooming among low-income Hispanic, Black, and White women. *Body Image, 10*, 226–231. doi: 10.1016/j.bodyim.2013.01.002

Dion, K. E., Berscheid, E., & Walster, E. (1972). What is beautiful is good. *Journal of Personality and Social Psychology, 24*, 285–290. doi: 10.1037/h0033731

Dittmar, H., Halliwell, E., & Stirling, E. (2009). Understanding the impact of thin media models on women's body-focused affect: The roles of thin-ideal internalization and weight-related self-discrepancy activation in experimental exposure effects. *Journal of Social and Clinical Psychology, 28*, 43–72. doi: 10.1521/jscp.2009.28.1.43

Dodd, D. K., Harcar, V., Foerch, B. J., & Anderson, H. T. (1989). Face-ism and facial expressions of women in magazine photos. *The Psychological Record, 39*, 325–331.

Dohnt, H. K., & Tiggemann, M. (2005). Peer influences on body dissatisfaction and dieting awareness in young girls. *British Journal of Developmental Psychology, 23*, 103–116. doi: 10.1348/026151004X20658

Drewnowski, A., & Specter, S. E. (2004). Poverty and obesity: The role of energy density and energy costs. *The American Journal of Clinical Nutrition, 79*, 6–16.

Droogsma, R. A. (2007). Redefining hijab: American Muslim women's standpoints on veiling. *Journal of Applied Communication Research, 35*, 294–319. doi: 10.1080/00909880701434299

Dubick, J., Mathews, B., & Cady, C. (2016, October). *Hunger on campus: The challenge of food insecurity for college students*. Retrieved from https://studentsagainsthunger.org/wp-content/uploads/2016/10/Hunger_On_Campus.pdf

Dunkel, T. M., Davidson, D., & Qurashi, S. (2010). Body satisfaction and pressure to be thin in younger and older Muslim and non-Muslim women: The role of Western and non-Western dress preferences. *Body Image, 7*, 56–65. doi: 10.1016/j.bodyim.2009.10.003

Easter, M. (2017, August 10). Money flowing into the natural hair industry is a blessing and curse for those who built it up. *L.A. Times*. Retrieved from http://www.latimes.com/business/la-fi-natural-hair-industry-20170809-htmlstory.html

Eisenberg, M. E., Berge, J. M., & Neumark-Sztainer, D. (2013). Dieting and encouragement to diet by significant others: Associations with disordered eating in young adults. *Health Promotion, 27*, 370–377. doi: 10.4278/ajhp.120120-QUAN-57

Eneli, I. U., Crum, P. A., & Tylka, T. L. (2008). The trust model: A different feeding paradigm for managing childhood obesity. *Obesity, 16*, 2197–2204. doi: 10.1038/oby.2008.378

Engeln, R. (2017). *Beauty sick: How the cultural obsession with appearance hurts girls and women*. New York, NY: Harper Collins.

Engeln-Maddox, R. (2006). Buying a beauty standard or dreaming of a new life? Expectations associated with media ideals. *Psychology of Women Quarterly, 30*, 258–266. doi: 10.1111/j.1471-6402.2006.00294.x

Engeln-Maddox, R., Salk, R. H., & Miller, S. A. (2012). Assessing women's negative commentary on their own bodies: A psychometric investigation of the negative body talk scale. *Psychology of Women Quarterly, 36*, 162–178. doi: 10.1177/0361684312441593

Erchull, M. J. (2013). Distancing through objectification? Depictions of women's bodies in menstrual product advertisements. *Sex Roles, 68*, 32–40. doi: 10.1007/s11199-011-0004-7

Erchull, M. J., & Richmond, K. (2015). "It's normal . . . Mom will be home in an hour": The role of fathers in menstrual education. *Women's Reproductive Health, 2*, 93–110. doi: 10.1080/23293691.2015.1089149

Ernsberger, P. (2009). Does social class explain the connection between weight and health? In E. D. Rothblum & S. Solovoy (Eds.), *The fat studies reader* (pp. 25–36). New York, NY: New York University Press.

Etcoff, N., Orbach, S., Scott, J., & D'Agostino, H. (2004). *"The real truth about beauty: A global report": Findings of the global study on women, beauty and well-being*. Retrieved from http://www.clubofamsterdam.com/contentarticles/52%20Beauty/dove_white_paper_final.pdf

Evans, P. C., & McConnel, A. R. (2003). Do racial minorities respond in the same way to mainstream beauty standards? Social comparison processes in Asian, Black, and White women. *Self and Identity, 2*, 153–167. doi: 10.1080/15298860390129908

Fabian, L. J., & Thompson, J. K. (1989). Body image and eating disturbance in young females. *International Journal of Eating Disorders, 8*, 63–74. doi: 10.1002/1098-108X(198901)8:1<63::AID-EAT2260080107>3.0.CO;2-9

Falconer, J. W., & Neville, H. A. (2000). African American college women's body image: An examination of body mass, African self-consciousness, and skin color satisfaction. *Psychology of Women Quarterly, 24*, 236–243. doi: 10.1111/j.1471-6402.2000.tb00205.x

Fardouly, J., & Vartanian, L. R. (2015). Negative comparisons about one's appearance mediate the relationship between Facebook usage and body image concerns. *Body Image, 12*, 82–88. doi: 10.1016/j.bodyim.2014.10.004

Feeding America. (2017, September). *Poverty and hunger fact sheet*. Retrieved from http://www.feedingamerica.org/assets/pdfs/fact-sheets/poverty-and-hunger-fact-sheet.pdf

Feltman, C. E., & Szymanski, D. M. (2017). Instagram use and self-objectification: The roles of internalization, comparison, appearance commentary, and feminism. *Sex Roles, 78*, 311–324. doi: 10.1007/s11199-017-0796-1

Ferguson, C. J. (2013). In the eye of the beholder: Thin-ideal media affects some, but not most, viewers in a meta-analytic review of body dissatisfaction in women and men. *Psychology of Popular Media Culture, 2*, 20–37. doi: 10.1037/a0030766

Festinger, L. (1954). A theory of social comparison processes. *Human Relations, 7*, 117–140. doi: 10.1177/001872675400700202

Fingerson, L. (2005). Agency and the body in adolescent menstrual talk. *Childhood, 12*, 91–110. doi: 10.1177/0907568205049894

Fingerson, L. (2006). *Girls in power: Gender, body, and menstruation in adolescence*. Albany, NY: State University of New York Press.

Fink, B., Neave, N., Manning, J. T., & Grammer, K. (2006). Facial symmetry and judgements of attractiveness, health and personality. *Personality and Individual Differences, 41*, 491–499. doi: 10.1016/j.paid.2006.01.017

Fiske, S. T., Bersoff, D. N., Borgida, E., Deaux, K., & Heilman, M. E. (1991). Social science research on trial: Use of sex stereotyping research in Price Waterhouse v. Hopkins. *American Psychologist, 46*, 1049–1060. doi: 10.1037/0003-066X.46.10.1049

Forbes, G. B., Adams-Curtis, L. E., White, K. B., & Holmgren, K. M. (2003). The role of hostile and benevolent sexism in women's and men's perceptions of the menstruating woman. *Psychology of Women Quarterly*, *27*, 58–63. doi: 10.1111/1471-6402.t01-2-00007

Franzoi, S. L. (1995). The body-as-object versus the body-as-process: Gender differences and gender considerations. *Sex Roles*, *33*, 417–437. doi: 10.1007/BF01954577

Frederick, D. A., Forbes, G. B., Grigorian, K. E., & Jarcho, J. M. (2007). The UCLA body project I: Gender and ethnic differences in self-objectification and body satisfaction among 2,206 undergraduates. *Sex Roles*, *57*, 317–327. doi: 10.1007/s11199-007-9251-z

Fredrickson, B. L., & Roberts, T-A. (1997). Objectification theory: Toward understanding women's lived experiences and mental health risks. *Psychology of Women Quarterly*, *21*, 173–206. doi: 10.1111/j.1471-6402.1997.tb00108.x

Fredrickson, B. L., Roberts, T-A., Noll, S. M., Quinn, D. M., & Twenge, J. M. (1998). That swimsuit becomes you: Sex differences in self-objectification, restrained eating, and math performance. *Journal of Personality and Social Psychology*, *75*, 269–284. doi: 10.1037/0022-3514.75.1.269

Ganahl, D. J., Prinsen, T. J., & Netzley, S. B. (2003). A content analysis of prime time commercials: A contextual framework of gender representation. *Sex Roles*, *49*, 545–551. doi: 10.1023/A:1025893025658

Gapinski, K. D., Brownell, K. D., & LaFrance, M. (2003). Body objectification and "fat talk": Effects on emotion, motivation, and cognitive performance. *Sex Roles*, *48*, 377–388. doi: 10.1023/A:1023516209973

Garnett, B. R., Buelow, R., Franko, D. L., Becker, C., Rodgers, R. F., & Austin, S. B. (2014). The importance of campaign saliency as a predictor of attitude and behavior change: A pilot evaluation of social marketing campaign fat talk free week. *Health Communication*, *29*, 984–995. doi: 10.1080/10410236.2013.827613

Gerbner, G., Gross, L., Morgan, M., & Signorielli, N. (1994). Growing up with television: The cultivation perspective. In J. Bryant & D. Zillman (Eds.), *Media effects: Advances in theory and research* (pp. 17–42). Hillsdale, NJ: Erlbaum.

Gervais, S. J., Holland, A. M., & Dodd, M. D. (2013). My eyes are up here: The nature of the objectifying gaze toward women. *Sex Roles*, *69*, 557–570. doi: 10.1007/s11199-013-0316-x

Gleason, J. H., Alexander, A. M., & Somers, C. L. (2000). Later adolescents' reactions to three types of childhood teasing: Relations with self-esteem and body image. *Social Behavior and Personality*, *28*, 471–479. doi: 10.2224/sbp.2000.28.5.471

Goffman, E. (1979). *Gender advertisements*. Cambridge, MA: Harvard University Press.

Goldenberg, J. L., Pyszczynski, T., Greenberg, J., & Solomon, S. (2000). Fleeing the body: A terror management perspective on the problem of human corporeality. *Personality and Social Psychology Review*, *4*, 200–218. doi: 10.1207/S15327957PSPR0403_1

Goldenberg, J. L., & Roberts, T.-A. (2004). The beast within the beauty: An existential perspective on the objectification and condemnation of women. In J. Greenberg, S. L. Koole, & T. Pyszczynski (Eds.), *Handbook of experimental existential psychology* (pp. 71–85). New York, NY: Guilford Press.

Gonçalves, S. F., & Gomes, A. R. (2012). Exercising for weight and shape reasons vs. health control reasons: The impact on eating disturbance and psychological functioning. *Eating Behaviors*, *13*, 127–130. doi: 10.1016/j.eatbeh.2011.11.011

Grabe, S., & Hyde, J. S. (2006). Ethnicity and body dissatisfaction among women in the United States: A meta-analysis. *Psychological Bulletin*, *132*, 622–640. doi: 10.1037/0033-2909.132.4.622

Grabe, S., Hyde, J. S., & Lindberg, S. M. (2007). Body objectification and depression in adolescents: The role of gender, shame, and rumination. *Psychology of Women Quarterly*, *31*, 164–175. doi: 10.1111/j.1471-6402.2007.00350.x

Grabe, S., Routledge, C., Cook, A., Andersen, C., & Arndt, J. (2005). In defense of the body: The effect of mortality salience on female body objectification. *Psychology of Women Quarterly*, *29*, 33–37. doi: 10.1111/j.1471-6402.2005.00165.x

Grabe, S., Ward, L. M., & Hyde, J. S. (2008). The role of the media in body image concerns among women: A meta-analysis of experimental and correlational studies. *Psychological Bulletin*, *134*, 460–476. doi: 10.1037/0033-2909.134.3.460

Grammer, K., Fink, B., Møller, A. P., & Thornhill, R. (2003). Darwinian aesthetics: Sexual selection and the biology of beauty. *Biological Reviews*, *78*, 385–407. doi: 10.1017/S1464793102006085

Grammer, K., & Thornhill, R. (1994). Human (Homo Sapiens) facial attractiveness and sexual selection: The role of symmetry and averageness. *Journal of Comparative Psychology*, *108*, 233–242. doi: 10.1037/0735-7036.108.3.233

Gray, E. (2015, March 27). The removal of Rupi Kaur's Instagram photos shows how terrified we are of periods. *Huffington Post*. Retrieved from http://www.huffingtonpost.com/2015/03/27/rupi-kaur-period-instagram_n_6954898.html

Greenberg, B. S., & Worrell, T. R. (2007). New faces on television: A 12-season replication. *The Howard Journal of Communications*, *18*, 277–290. doi: 10.1080/10646170701653651

Grose, R. G., & Grabe, S. (2014). Sociocultural attitudes surrounding menstruation and alternative menstrual products: The explanatory role of self-objectification *Health Care for Women International*, *35*, 677–694. doi: 10.1080/07399332.2014.888721

Haines, M. E., Erchull, M. J., Liss, M., Turner, D. L., Nelson, J. A., Ramsey, L. R., & Hurt, M. M. (2008). Predictors and effects of self-objectification in lesbians. *Psychology of Women Quarterly*, *32*, 181–187. doi: 10.1111/j.1471-6402.2008.00422.x

Hall, C. C. I. (1995a). Asian eyes: Body image and eating disorders of Asian and Asian American women. *Eating Disorders*, *3*, 8–19. doi: 10.1080/10640269508249141

Hall, C. C. I. (1995b). Beauty is in the soul of the beholder: Psychological implications of beauty and African American women. *Cultural Diversity and Mental Health*, *1*, 125–137. doi: 10.1037/1099-9809.1.2.125

Han, E., Norton, E. C., & Stearns, S. C. (2009). Weight and wages: Fat versus lean paychecks. *Health Economics*, *18*, 535–548. doi: 10.1002/hec.1386

Hardit, S. K., & Hannum, J. W. (2012). Attachment, the tripartite influence model, and the development of body dissatisfaction. *Body Image*, *9*, 469–475. doi: 10.1016/j.bodyim.2012.06.003

Harrison, K. (2003). Television viewers' ideal body proportions: The case of the curvaceously thin woman. *Sex Roles*, *48*, 255–264. doi: 10.1023/A:1022825421647

Harrison, K., & Fredrickson, B. L. (2003). Women's sports media, self-objectification, and mental health in black and white adolescent females. *Journal of Communication*, *53*, 216–232. doi: 10.1111/j.1460-2466.2003.tb02587.x

Harrison, K., Taylor, L. D., & Marske, A. L. (2006). Women's and men's eating behavior following exposure to ideal-body images and text. *Communication Research*, *33*, 507–529. doi: 10.1177/0093650206293247

Hatem, M. (1988). Egypt's middle class in crisis: The sexual division of labor. *The Middle East Journal*, *42*, 407–422.

Hausenblas, H. A., & Fallon, E. A. (2006). Exercise and body image: A meta-analysis. *Psychology and Health*, *21*, 33–47. doi: 10.1080/14768320500105270

Havens, B., & Swenson, I. (1988). Imagery associated with menstruation in advertising targeted to adolescent women. *Adolescence*, *23*, 89–97.

Heard, K. V., Chrisler, J. C., Kimes, L. A., & Siegel, H. N. (1999). Psychometric evaluation of the Menstrual Joy Questionnaire. *Psychological Reports*, *84*, 135–136. doi: 10.2466/PR0.84.1.135-136

Hebl, M. R., King, E. B., & Lin, J. (2004). The swimsuit becomes us all: Ethnicity, gender, and vulnerability to self-objectification. *Personality and Social Psychology Bulletin*, *30*, 1322–1331. doi: 10.1177/0146167204264052

Heilman, M. E., & Stopeck, M. H. (1985). Being attractive, advantage or disadvantage? Performance-based evaluations and recommended personnel actions as a function of appearance, sex, and job type. *Organizational Behavior and Human Decision Processes*, *35*, 202–215. doi: 10.1016/0749-5978(85)90035-4

Herbenick, D., Schick, V., Reece, M., Sanders, S., & Fortenberry, J. D. (2010). Pubic hair removal among women in the United States: Prevalence, methods, and characteristics. *The Journal of Sexual Medicine*, *7*, 3322–3330. doi: 10.1111/j.1743-6109.2010.01935.x

Hesse-Biber, S. N., Howling, S. A., Leavy, P., & Lovejoy, M. (2004). Racial identity and the development of body image issues among African American adolescent girls. *The Qualitative Report*, *9*, 49–79.

Heuer, C. A., McClure, K. J., & Puhl, R. M. (2011). Obesity stigma in online news: A visual content analysis. *Journal of Health Communication*, *16*, 976–987. doi: 10.1080/10810730.2011.561915

Hope, C. (1982). Caucasian female body hair and American culture. *Journal of American Culture*, *5*, 93–99. doi: 10.1111/j.1542-734X.1982.0501_93.x

Hurt, M. M., Nelson, J. A., Turner, D. T., Haines, M. E., Ramsey, L. R., Erchull, M. J., & Liss, M. (2007). Feminism: What is it good for? Feminine norms and objectification as the link between feminist identity and clinically relevant outcomes. *Sex Roles*, *57*, 355–363. doi: 10.1007/s11199-007-9272-7

Jackson, T. E., & Falmagne, R. J. (2013). Women wearing white: Discourses of menstruation and the experience of menarche. *Feminism & Psychology*, *23*, 379–398. doi: 10.1177/0959353512473812

Jeffers, M. (2005, September 12). Behind Dove's "real beauty." *Adweek*. Retrieved from http://www.adweek.com/news/advertising/behind-doves-real-beauty-81469

Johnson, S. M., Edwards, K. M., & Gidycz, C. A. (2015). Interpersonal weight-related pressure and disordered eating in college women: A test of an expanded tripartite influence model. *Sex Roles*, *72*, 15–24. doi: 10.1007/s11199-014-0442-0

Johnston, J., & Taylor, J. (2008). Feminist consumerism and fat activists: A comparative study of grassroots activism and the Dove real beauty campaign. *Signs*, *33*, 941–966. doi: 10.1086/528849

Johnston-Robledo, I., Sheffield, K., Voigt, J., & Wilcox-Constantine, J. (2007). Reproductive shame: Self-objectification and young women's attitudes toward their reproductive functioning. *Women & Health*, *46*, 25–39. doi: 10.1300/J013v46n01_03

Jones, B. C., DeBruine, L. M., & Little, A. C. (2007). The role of symmetry in attraction to average faces. *Perception & Psychophysics*, *69*, 1273–1277. doi: 10.3758/BF03192944

Jones, D. C. (2001). Social comparison and body image: Attractiveness comparisons to models and peers among adolescent girls and boys. *Sex Roles*, *45*, 645–664. doi: 10.1023/A:1014815725852

Jones, D. C., Vigfusdottir, T. H., & Lee, Y. (2004). Body image and the appearance culture among adolescent girls and boys: An examination of friend conversations, peer criticism, appearance magazines, and the internalization of appearance ideals. *Journal of Adolescent Research*, *19*, 323–339. doi: 10.1177/0743558403258847

Jones, M. D., Crowther, J. H., & Ciesla, J. A. (2014). A naturalistic study of fat talk and its behavioral and affective consequences. *Body Image*, *11*, 337–345. doi: 10.1016/j.bodyim.2014.05.007

Jones, T. (2013). The significance of skin color in Asian and Asian-American communities: Initial reflections. *UC Irvine Law Review*, *3*, 1105–1123.

Kalman, M. B. (2003). Taking a different path: Menstrual preparation for adolescent girls living apart from their mothers. *Health Care for Women International*, *24*, 868–879. doi: 10.1080/07399330390244275

Karnani, A. (2007). Doing well by doing good—Case study: "Fair & Lovely" whitening cream. *Strategic Management Journal*, *28*, 1351–1357. doi: 10.1002/smj.645

Kasardo, A. E., & McHugh, M. C. (2015). From fat shaming to size acceptance: Challenging the medical management of fat women. In M. C. McHugh & J. C. Chrisler (Eds.), *The wrong prescription for women: How medicine and media create a "need" for treatments, drugs, and surgery* (pp. 179–201). Santa Barbara, CA: Praeger.

Katrevich, A. V., Register, J. D., & Aruguete, M. S. (2014). The effects of negative body talk in an ethnically diverse sample of college students. *North American Journal of Psychology*, *16*, 43–52.

Kawamura, K., & Rice, T. (2009). Body image among Asian Americans. In N. Tewari & A. Alvarez (Eds.), *Asian American psychology: Current perspectives* (pp. 537–557). New York, NY: Taylor & Francis.

Keery, H., van den Berg, P., & Thompson, J. K. (2004). An evaluation of the tripartite influence model of body dissatisfaction and eating disturbance with adolescent girls. *Body Image*, *1*, 237–251. doi: 10.1016/j.bodyim.2004.03.001

Kelly, A. M., Wall, M., Eisenberg, M. E., Story, M., & Neumark-Sztainer, D. (2005). Adolescent girls with high body satisfaction: Who are they and what can they teach us? *Journal of Adolescent Health*, *37*, 391–396. doi: 10.1016/j.jadohealth.2004.08.008

Kerr, A. E. (2005). The paper bag principle: Of the myth and the motion of colorism. *Journal of American Folklore*, *118*, 271–289. doi: 10.1353/jaf.2005.0031

Kerr, A. E. (2006). *The paper bag principle: Class, colorism, and rumor and the case of Black Washington, DC*. Knoxville, TN: University of Tennessee Press.

Kessler, E., Rakoczy, K., & Staudinger, U. M. (2004). The portrayal of older people in prime time television series: The match with gerontological evidence. *Ageing and Society*, *24*, 531–552. doi: 10.1017/S0144686X04002338

Kieren, D. K., & Morse, J. M. (1992). Preparation factors and menstrual attitudes of pre-and postmenarcheal girls. *Journal of Sex Education and Therapy*, *18*, 155–174. doi: 10.1080/01614576.1992.11074050

Kilbourne, J. (1999). *Can't buy my love: How advertising changes the way we think and feel*. New York, NY: Simon & Schuster.

Kimmel, M. (2013, July 2013). Fired for being beautiful. *The New York Times*. Retrieved from http://www.nytimes.com/2013/07/17/opinion/fired-for-being-beautiful.html?_r=3

King, M., & Ussher, J. M. (2013). It's not all bad: Women's construction and lived experience of positive premenstrual change. *Feminism & Psychology*, *23*, 399–417. doi: 10.1177/0959353512440351

Kissling, E. A. (1996). "That's just a basic teen-age rule": Girls' linguistic strategies for managing the menstrual communication taboo. *Journal of Applied Communication Research*, *24*, 292–309. doi: 10.1080/00909889609365458

Koff, E., & Rierdan, J. (1995a). Early adolescent girls' understanding of menstruation. *Women & Health*, *22*, 1–19. doi: 10.1300/J013v22n04_01

Koff, E., & Rierdan, J. (1995b). Preparing girls for menstruation: Recommendations from adolescent girls. *Adolescence, 30*, 795–811.

Koff, E., Rierdan, J., & Stubbs, M. L. (1990). Conceptions and misconceptions of the menstrual cycle. *Women & Health, 16*, 119–136. doi: 10.1300/J013v16n03_07

Konrath, S. H., & Schwarz, N. (2007). Do male politicians have big heads? Face-ism in online self-representations of politicians. *Media Psychology, 10*, 436–448. doi: 10.1080/15213260701533219

Konrath, S., Au, J., & Ramsey, L. R. (2012). Cultural differences in face-ism: Male politicians have bigger heads in more gender-equal cultures. *Psychology of Women Quarterly, 36*, 476–487. doi: 10.1177/0361684312455317

Kozee, H. B., Tylka, T. L., & Bauerband, L. A. (2012). Measuring transgender individuals' comfort with gender identity and appearance: Development and validation of the Transgender Congruence Scale. *Psychology of Women Quarterly, 36*, 179–196. doi: 10.1177/0361684312442161

Kronenfeld, L. W., Reba-Harrelson, L., Von Holle, A., Reyes, M. L., & Bulik, C. M. (2010). Ethnic and racial differences in body size perception and satisfaction. *Body Image, 7*, 131–136. doi: 10.1016/j.bodyim.2009.11.002

Langlois, J. H., Kalakanis, L., Rubenstein, A. J., Larson, A., Hallam, M., & Smoot, M. (2000). Maxims or myths of beauty? A meta-analytic and theoretical review. *Psychological Bulletin, 126*, 390–423. doi: 10.1037/0033-2909.126.3.390

Laus, M. F., Braga Costa, T. M. B., & Almeida, S. S. (2013). Body image dissatisfaction and aesthetic exercise in adolescents: Are they related? *Estudos de Psicologia, 18*, 163–171. doi: 10.1590/S1413-294X2013000200001

Lauzen, M. M., & Dozier, D. M. (2005a). Maintaining the double standard: Portrayals of age and gender in popular films. *Sex Roles, 52*, 437–446. doi: 10.1007/s11199-005-3710-1

Lauzen, M. M., & Dozier, D. M. (2005b). Recognition and respect revisited: Portrayals of age and gender in prime-time television. *Mass Communication & Society, 8*, 241–256. doi: 10.1207/s15327825mcs0803_4

Lee, H. E., Taniguchi, E., Modica, A., & Park, H. (2013). Effects of witnessing fat talk on body satisfaction and psychological well-being: A cross-cultural comparison of Korea and the United States. *Social Behavior and Personality, 41*, 1279–1295. doi: 10.2224/sbp.2013.41.8.1279

Lee, J. (2008). "A Kotex and a smile": Mothers and daughters at menarche. *Journal of Family Issues, 29*, 1325–1347. doi: 10.1177/0192513X08316117

Lei, I., Knight, C., Llewellyn-Jones, D., & Abraham, S. (1987). Menstruation and the menstrual cycle: Knowledge and attitudes of mothers and daughters. *Australian Journal of Sex, Marriage and Family, 8*, 33–42. doi: 10.1080/01591487.1987.11004369

Levine, M. P., & Harrison, K. (2004). Media's role in the perpetuation and prevention of negative body image and disordered eating. In J. K. Thompson (Ed.), *Handbook of eating disorders and obesity* (pp. 695–717). New York, NY: Wiley.

Levine, M. P., Smolak, L., & Hayden, H. (1994). The relation of sociocultural factors to eating attitudes and behaviors among middle school girls. *The Journal of Early Adolescence, 14*, 471–490. doi: 10.1177/0272431694014004004

Lieberman, M., Gauvin, L., Bukowski, W. M., & White, D. R. (2001). Interpersonal influence and disordered eating behaviors in adolescent girls: The role of peer modeling, social reinforcement, and body-related teasing. *Eating Behaviors, 2*, 215–236. doi: 10.1016/S1471-0153(01)00030-7

Lindberg, S. M., Grabe, S., & Hyde, J. S. (2007). Gender, pubertal development, and peer sexual harassment predict objectified body consciousness in early adolescence. *Journal of Research on Adolescence, 17*, 723–742. doi: 10.1111/j.1532-7795.2007.00544.x

Lopez, E., Blix, G. G., & Blix, A. G. (1995). Body image of Latinas compared to body image of non-Latina White women. *Health Values, 19*, 3–10.

Lowes, J., & Tiggemann, M. (2003). Body dissatisfaction, dieting awareness, and the impact of parental influence in young children. *British Journal of Health Psychology, 8*, 135–147. doi: 10.1348/135910703321649123

Mangweth-Matzek, B., Rupp, C. I., Hausmann, A., Assmayr, K., Mariacher, E., Kemmler, G., Whitworth, A. B., & Biebl, W. (2006). Never too old for eating disorders or body dissatisfaction: A community study of elderly women. *International Journal of Eating Disorders, 39*, 583–586. doi: 10.1002/eat.20327

Marván, M. L., Ramírez-Esparza, D., Cortés-Iniestra, S., & Chrisler, J. C. (2006). Development of a new scale to measure beliefs about and attitudes toward menstruation (BATM): Data from Mexico and the United States. *Health Care for Women International, 27*, 453–473. doi: 10.1080/07399330600629658

Mastro, D. E., & Stern, S. R. (2003). Representations of race in television commercials: A content analysis of prime-time advertising. *Journal of Broadcasting & Electronic Media, 47*, 638–647. doi: 10.1207/s15506878jobem4704_9

Mathias, Z., & Harcourt, D. (2014). Dating and intimate relationships of women with below-knee amputation: An exploratory study. *Disability and Rehabilitation, 36*, 395–402. doi: 10.3109/09638288.2013.797509

McClure, K. J., Puhl, R. M., & Heuer, C. A. (2011). Obesity in the news: Do photographic images of obese persons influence anti-fat attitudes? *Journal of Health Communication, 16*, 359–371. doi: 10.1080/10810730.2010.535108

McCreary, D. R., & Sadava, S. W. (1999). Television viewing and self-perceived health, weight, and physical fitness: Evidence for the cultivation hypothesis. *Journal of Applied Social Psychology, 29*, 2342–2361. doi: 10.1111/j.1559-1816.1999.tb00114.x

McDonald, K., & Thompson, J. K. (1992). Eating disturbance, body image dissatisfaction, and reasons for exercising: Gender differences and correlational findings. *International Journal of Eating Disorders, 11*, 289–292. doi: 10.1002/1098-108X(199204)11:3<289::AID-EAT2260110314>3.0.CO;2-F

McDougall, L. J. (2013) Towards a clean slit: How medicine and notions of normality are shaping female genital aesthetics. *Culture, Health, and Sexuality, 15*, 774–787. doi: 10.1080/13691058.2013.780639

McFarlane, J., Martin, C. L., & Williams, T. M. (1988). Mood fluctuations: Women versus men and menstrual versus other cycles. *Psychology of Women Quarterly, 12*, 201–223. doi: 10.1111/j.1471-6402.1988.tb00937.x

McKinley, N. M. (1999). Women and objectified body consciousness: Mothers' and daughters' body experience in cultural, developmental, and familial context. *Developmental Psychology, 35*, 760–769. doi: 10.1037/0012-1649.35.3.760

McKinley, N. M., & Hyde, J. S. (1996). The Objectified Body Consciousness Scale: Development and validation. *Psychology of Women Quarterly, 20*, 181–215. doi: 10.1111/j.1471-6402.1996.tb00467.x

McLaren, L., Kuh, D., Hardy, R., & Gauvin, L. (2004). Positive and negative body-related comments and their relationship with body dissatisfaction in middle-aged women. *Psychology & Health, 19*, 261–272. doi: 10.1080/0887044031000148246

McLean, S. A., Paxton, S. J., Wertheim, E. H., & Masters, J. (2015). Photoshopping the selfie: Self photo editing and photo investment are associated with body dissatisfaction in adolescent girls. *International Journal of Eating Disorders, 48*, 1132–1140. doi: 10.1002/eat.22449

McPherson, M. E., & Korfine, L. (2004). Menstruation across time: Menarche, menstrual attitudes, experiences, and behaviors. *Women's Health Issues, 14*, 193–200. doi: 10.1016/j.whi.2004.08.006

Mears, A. (2011). *Pricing beauty: The making of a fashion model.* Berkeley, CA: University of California Press.

Meekosha, H., & Dowse, L. (1997). Distorting images, invisible images: Gender, disability and the media. *Media International Australia, 84,* 91–101. doi: 10.1177/1329878X9708400114

Menzel, J. E., Schaefer, L. M., Burke, N. L., Mayhew, L. L., Brannick, M. T., & Thompson, J. K. (2010). Appearance-related teasing, body dissatisfaction, and disordered eating: A meta-analysis. *Body Image, 7,* 261–270. doi: 10.1016/j.bodyim.2010.05.004

Mercurio, A. E., & Landry, L. J. (2008). Self-objectification and well-being: The impact of self-objectification on women's overall sense of self-worth and life satisfaction. *Sex Roles, 58,* 458–466. doi: 10.1007/s11199-007-9357-3

Mernissi, F. (1987). *Beyond the veil: Male-female dynamics in modern Muslim society* (Rev. ed.). Indianapolis, IN: Indiana University Press.

Mintz, L. B., & Kashubeck, S. (1999). Body image and disordered eating among Asian American and Caucasian college students: An examination of race and gender differences. *Psychology of Women Quarterly, 23,* 781–796. doi: 10.1111/j.1471-6402.1999.tb00397.x

Mitchell, M. K., Ramsey, L. R., & Nelson, S. (2018). The body image of women at a homeless service center: An analysis of an underrepresented, diverse group. *Gender Issues, 35,* 38–51. doi: 10.1007/s12147-017-9192-y

Moin, V., Duvdevany, I., & Mazor, D. (2009). Sexual identity, body image and life satisfaction among women with and without physical disability. *Sexuality and Disability, 27,* 83–95. doi: 10.1007/s11195-009-9112-5

Mond, J. M., Hay, P. J., Rodgers, B., & Owen, C. (2006). An update on the definition of "excessive exercise" in eating disorders research. *International Journal of Eating Disorders, 39,* 147–153. doi: 10.1002/eat.20214

Moos, R. H. (1968). The development of a menstrual distress questionnaire. *Psychosomatic Medicine, 30,* 853–867.

Moradi, B., & Huang, Y. P. (2008). Objectification theory and psychology of women: A decade of advances and future directions. *Psychology of Women Quarterly, 32,* 377–398. doi: 10.1111/j.1471-6402.2008.00452.x

Moradi, B., & Rottenstein, A. (2007). Objectification theory and deaf cultural identity attitudes: Roles in deaf women's eating disorder symptomatology. *Journal of Counseling Psychology, 54,* 178–188. doi: 10.1037/0022-0167.54.2.178

Morris, K. L., Goldenberg, J. L., & Heflick, N. A. (2014). Trio of terror (pregnancy, menstruation, and breastfeeding): An existential function of literal self-objectification among women. *Journal of Personality and Social Psychology, 107,* 181–198. doi: 10.1037/a0036493

Morrison, M. A., Morrison, T. G., & Sager, C. L. (2004). Does body satisfaction differ between gay men and lesbian women and heterosexual men and women? A meta-analytic review. *Body Image, 1,* 127–138. doi: 10.1016/j.bodyim.2004.01.002

Mulvey, L. (1975). Visual pleasure and narrative cinema. *Screen, 16,* 6–18.

Murray, C. D., & Fox, J. (2002). Body image and prosthesis satisfaction in the lower limb amputee. *Disability & Rehabilitation, 24,* 925–931. doi: 10.1080/09638280210150014

Murray, S. H., Touyz, S. W., & Beumont, P. J. (1995). The influence of personal relationships on women's eating behavior and body satisfaction. *Eating Disorders, 3,* 243–252. doi: 10.1080/10640269508249168

Mussap, A. J. (2009). Strength of faith and body image in Muslim and non-Muslim women. *Mental Health, Religion and Culture, 12,* 121–127. doi: 10.1080/13674670802358190

Myers, T. A., & Crowther, J. H. (2008). Is self-objectification related to interoceptive awareness? An examination of potential mediating pathways to disordered eating attitudes. *Psychology of Women Quarterly, 32,* 172–180. doi: 10.1111/j.1471-6402.2008.00421.x

Neal, A. M., & Wilson, M. L. (1989). The role of skin color and features in the Black community: Implications for Black women and therapy. *Clinical Psychology Review, 9,* 323–333. doi: 10.1016/0272-7358(89)90060-3

Neumark-Sztainer, D., Bauer, K. W., Friend, S., Hannan, P. J., Story, M., & Berge, J. M. (2010). Family weight talk and dieting: How much do they matter for body dissatisfaction and disordered eating behaviors in adolescent girls? *Journal of Adolescent Health, 47,* 270–276. doi: 10.1016/j.jadohealth.2010.02.001

Noll, S. M., & Fredrickson, B. L. (1998). A mediational model linking self-objectification, body shame, and disordered eating. *Psychology of Women Quarterly, 22,* 623–636. doi: 10.1111/j.1471-6402.1998.tb00181.x

Noor, N. M. (2009). "Liberating" the hijab. In M. Montero & C. C. Sonn (Eds.), *Psychology of liberation: Theory and applications* (pp. 193–204). New York, NY: Springer.

Okazawa-Rey, M., Robinson, T., & Ward, J. V. (1987). Black women and the politics of skin color and hair. *Women & Therapy, 6,* 89–102. doi: 10.1300/J015V06N01_07

Ousley, L., Cordero, E. D., & White, S. (2007). Fat talk among college students: How undergraduates communicate regarding food and body weight, shape & appearance. *Eating Disorders, 16,* 73–84. doi: 10.1080/10640260701773546

Pashler, H. (1994). Dual-task interference in simple tasks: Data and theory. *Psychological Bulletin, 116,* 220–244. doi: 10.1037/0033-2909.116.2.220

Paxton, S. J., Schutz, H. K., Wertheim, E. H., & Muir, S. L. (1999). Friendship clique and peer influences on body image concerns, dietary restraint, extreme weight-loss behaviors, and binge eating in adolescent girls. *Journal of Abnormal Psychology, 108,* 255–266. doi: 10.1037/0021-843X.108.2.255

Pearl, R. L., Puhl, R. M., & Brownell, K. D. (2012). Positive media portrayals of obese persons: Impact on attitudes and image preferences. *Health Psychology, 31,* 821–829. doi: 10.1037/a0027189

Peat, C. M., & Muehlenkamp, J. J. (2011). Self-objectification, disordered eating, and depression: A test of mediational pathways. *Psychology of Women Quarterly, 35,* 441–450. doi: 10.1177/0361684311400389

Phares, V., Steinberg, A. R., & Thompson, J. K. (2004). Gender differences in peer and parental influences: Body image disturbance, self-worth, and psychological functioning in preadolescent children. *Journal of Youth and Adolescence, 33,* 421–429. doi: 10.1023/B:JOYO.0000037634.18749.20

Polak, M. (2006). From the curse to the rag: Online gURLs rewrite the menstruation narrative. In Y. Jiwani, C. Steenbergen, & C. Mitchell (Eds.), *Girlhood: Redefining the limits* (pp. 191–207). New York, NY: Black Rose Books.

Polivy, J., Garner, D. M., & Garfinkel, P. E. (1986). Causes and consequences of the current preference for thin female physiques. In C. P. Herman, M. P. Zanna, & E. T., Higgins (Eds.), *Physical appearance, stigma, and social behavior* (pp. 89–112). Hillsdale, NJ: Lawrence Erlbaum.

Puhl, R. M., Luedicke, J., & Heuer, C. A. (2013). The stigmatizing effect of visual media portrayals of obese persons on public attitudes: Does race or gender matter? *Journal of Health Communication, 18,* 805–826. doi: 10.1080/10810730.2012.757393

Quinn, D. M., Kallen, R. W., & Cathey, C. (2006). Body on my mind: The lingering effect of state self-objectification. *Sex Roles, 55,* 869–874. doi: 10.1007/s11199-006-9140-x

Raftos, M., Jackson, D., & Mannix, J. (1998). Idealised versus tainted femininity: Discourses of the menstrual experience in Australian magazines that target young women. *Nursing Inquiry, 5*, 174–186. doi: 10.1046/j.1440-1800.1998.530174.x

Rembeck, G., & Gunnarsson, R. (2004). Improving pre- and postmenarcheal 12-year-old girls' attitudes toward menstruation. *Health Care for Women International, 25*, 680–698. doi: 10.1080/07399330490458033

Rhodes, G. (2006). The evolutionary psychology of facial beauty. *Annual Review of Psychology, 57*, 199–226. doi: 10.1146/annurev.psych.57.102904.190208

Riddell, L., Varto, H., & Hodgson, Z. G. (2010). Smooth talking: The phenomenon of pubic hair removal in women. *The Canadian Journal of Human Sexuality, 19*, 121–130.

Ridgway, J. L., & Clayton, R. B. (2016). Instagram unfiltered: Exploring associations of body image satisfaction, Instagram #selfie posting, and negative romantic relationship outcomes. *Cyberpsychology, Behavior, and Social Networking, 19*, 2–7. doi: 10.1089/cyber.2015.0433

Rierdan, J., & Koff, E. (1990). Premenarcheal predictors of the experience of menarche: A prospective study. *Journal of Adolescent Health Care, 11*, 404–407. doi: 10.1016/0197-0070(90)90086-H

Riley, C. A., II. (2005). *Disability and the media: Prescriptions for change.* Hanover, NH: University Press of New England.

Roberts, T.-A. (2004). Female trouble: The menstrual self-evaluation scale and women's self-objectification. *Psychology of Women Quarterly, 28*, 22–26 doi: 10.1111/j.1471-6402.2004.00119.x

Roberts, T. A., & Gettman, J. Y. (2004). Mere exposure: Gender differences in the negative effects of priming a state of self-objectification. *Sex Roles, 51*, 17–27. doi: 10.1023/B:SERS.0000032306.20462.22

Roberts, T.-A., Goldenberg, J. L., Power, C., & Pyszczynski, T. (2002). "Feminine protection": The effects of menstruation on attitudes towards women. *Psychology of Women Quarterly, 26*, 131–139. doi: 10.1111/1471-6402.00051

Robinson, C. L. (2011). Hair as race: Why "good hair" may be bad for black females. *Howard Journal of Communications, 22*, 358–376. doi: 10.1080/10646175.2011.617212

Rodin, J., Silberstein, L. R., & Striegel-Moore, R. H. (1984). Women and weight: A normative discontent. In T. B. Sonderegger (Ed.), *Nebraska symposium on motivation: Psychology and gender* (pp. 267–307). Lincoln, NE: University of Nebraska Press.

Roeper, R. (2005, July 19). How come women can't get the message: Listen! *Chicago Sun-Times*, p. 11.

Root, M. P. (1990). Disordered eating in women of color. *Sex Roles, 22*, 525–536. doi: 10.1007/BF00288168

Rose, J. G., Chrisler, J. C., & Couture, S. (2008). Young women's attitudes toward continuous use of oral contraceptives: The effect of priming positive attitudes toward menstruation on women's willingness to suppress menstruation. *Health Care for Women International, 29*, 688–701. doi: 10.1080/07399330802188925

Ross, C. C. (n.d.). *Why do women hate their bodies?* Retrieved from http://psychcentral.com/blog/archives/2012/06/02/why-do-women-hate-their-bodies/

Rothblum, E. D. (2011). Fat studies. In J. Cawley (Ed.), *The Oxford handbook of the social science of obesity* (pp. 173–183). New York, NY: Oxford University Press.

Rothman, A. J., Baldwin, A. S., Hertel, A. W., & Fuglestad, P. T. (2011). Self-regulation and behavior change: Disentangling behavioral initiation and behavioral maintenance. In K. D. Vohs & R. F. Baumeister (Eds.), *Handbook of self-regulation: Research, theory, and applications* (pp. 106–122). New York, NY: Guilford Press.

Rubin, L. R., Nemeroff, C. J., & Russo, N. F. (2004). Exploring feminist women's body consciousness. *Psychology of Women Quarterly, 28*, 27–37. doi: 10.1111/j.1471-6402.2004.00120.x

Ruby, T. F. (2006). Listening to the voices of hijab. *Women's Studies International Forum, 29*, 54–66. doi: 10.1016/j.wsif.2005.10.006

Salk, R. H., & Engeln-Maddox, R. (2011). "If you're fat, then I'm humongous!" Frequency, content, and impact of fat talk among college women. *Psychology of Women Quarterly, 35*, 18–28. doi: 10.1177/0361684310384107

Salk, R. H., & Engeln-Maddox, R. (2012). Fat talk among college women is both contagious and harmful. *Sex Roles, 66*, 636–645. doi: 10.1007/s11199-011-0050-1

Sanchez-Hucles, J., Hudgins, P. S., & Gamble, K. (2005). Reflection and distortion: Women of color in magazine advertisements. In E. Cole & J. H. Daniel (Eds.) *Featuring females: Feminist analyses of media* (pp. 185–198). Washington, DC: American Psychological Association.

Schwarz, N., & Kurz, E. (1989). What's in a picture? The impact of face-ism on trait attribution. *European Journal of Social Psychology, 19*, 311–316. doi: 10.1002/ejsp.2420190405

Segar, M., Spruijt-Metz, D., & Nolen-Hoeksema, S. (2006). Go figure? Body-shape motives are associated with decreased physical activity participation among midlife women. *Sex Roles, 54*, 175–187. doi: 10.1007/s11199-006-9336-5

Sheldon, P. (2013). Testing parental and peer communication influence on young adults' body satisfaction. *Southern Communication Journal, 78*, 215–232. doi: 10.1080/1041794X.2013.776097

Shomaker, L. B., & Furman, W. (2009). Interpersonal influences on late adolescent girls' and boys' disordered eating. *Eating Behaviors, 10*, 97–106. doi: 10.1016/j.eatbeh.2009.02.003

Shroff, H., & Thompson, J. K. (2006). The tripartite influence model of body image and eating disturbance: A replication with adolescent girls. *Body Image, 3*, 17–23. doi: 10.1016/j.bodyim.2005.10.004

Simes, M. R., & Berg, D. H. (2001). Surreptitious learning: Menarche and menstrual product advertisements. *Health Care for Women International, 22*, 455–469. doi: 10.1080/073993301317094281

Slater, A., & Tiggemann, M. (2002). A test of objectification theory in adolescent girls. *Sex Roles, 46*, 343–349. doi: 10.1023/A:1020232714705

Smolak, L. (2012). Appearance in childhood and adolescence. In N. Rumsey & D. Harcourt (Eds.), *Oxford handbook of the psychology of appearance* (pp. 123–141). London, United Kingdom: Oxford University Press.

Smolak, L., Levine, M. P., & Schermer, F. (1999). Parental input and weight concerns among elementary school children. *International Journal of Eating Disorders, 25*, 263–271. doi: 10.1002/(SICI)1098-108X(199904)25:3<263::AID-EAT3>3.0.CO;2-V

Sparks, G. G., & Fehlner, C. L. (1986). Faces in the news: Gender comparisons of magazine photographs. *Journal of Communication, 36*, 70–79. doi: 10.1111/j.1460-2466.1986.tb01451.x

Strelan, P., & Hargreaves, D. (2005). Women who objectify other women: The vicious circle of objectification? *Sex Roles, 52*, 707–712. doi: 10.1007/s11199-005-3737-3

Strelan, P., Mehaffey, S. J., & Tiggemann, M. (2003). Self-objectification and esteem in young women: The mediating role of reasons for exercise. *Sex Roles, 48*, 89–95. doi: 10.1023/A:1022300930307

Striegel-Moore, R. H., & Franco, D. (2002). Body image issues among girls and women. In T. F. Cash & T. Pruzinsky (Eds.), *Body image: A handbook of theory, research, and practice* (pp. 183–191). New York, NY: Gilford Press.

Striegel-Moore, R. H., & Smolak, L. (2000). The influence of ethnicity on eating disorders in women. In R. M. Eisler & M. Hersen (Eds.), *Handbook of gender, culture, and health*, (pp. 227–253). Mahwah, NJ: Lawrence Erlbaum.

Stubbs, M. L. (2008). Cultural perceptions and practices around menarche and adolescent menstruation in the United States. *Annals of the New York Academy of Sciences, 1135*, 58–66. doi: 10.1196/annals.1429.008

Swami, V., Miah, J., Noorani, N., & Taylor, D. (2014). Is the hijab protective? An investigation of body image and related constructs among British Muslim women. *British Journal of Psychology, 105*, 352–363. doi: 10.1111/bjop.12045

Swami, V., Tran, U. S., Stieger, S., Voracek, M., & the YouBeauty.com Team. (2015). Associations between women's body image and happiness: Results of the YouBeauty.com Body Image Survey (YBIS). *Journal of Happiness Studies, 16*, 705–718. doi: 10.1007/s10902-014-9530-7

Szymanski, D. M., & Henning, S. L. (2007). The role of self-objectification in women's depression: A test of objectification theory. *Sex Roles, 56*, 45–53. doi: 10.1007/s11199-006-9147-3

Taleporos, G., & McCabe, M. P. (2001). The impact of physical disability on body esteem. *Sexuality and Disability, 19*, 293–308. doi: 10.1023/A:1017909526508

Talusan, M. (2015, June 2). Do you applaud Caitlyn Jenner because she is brave, or because she's pretty? *The Guardian.* Retrieved from http://www.theguardian.com/commentisfree/2015/jun/02/applaud-caitlyn-jenner-brave-or-pretty

Taniguchi, E., & Aune, R. K. (2013). Communication with parents and body satisfaction in college students. *Journal of American College Health, 61*, 387–396. doi: 10.1080/07448481.2013.820189

Tantleff-Dunn, S., Barnes, R. D., & Larose, J. G. (2011). It's not just a "woman thing": The current state of normative discontent. *Eating Disorders, 19*, 392–402. doi: 10.1080/10640266.2011.609088

Teitelman, A. M. (2004). Adolescent girls' perspectives of family interactions related to menarche and sexual health. *Qualitative Health Research, 14*, 1292–1308. doi: 10.1177/1049732304268794

Thelen, M. H., & Cormier, J. F. (1995). Desire to be thinner and weight control among children and their parents. *Behavior Therapy, 26*, 85–99. doi: 10.1016/S0005-7894(05)80084-X

Thompson, J. K., Cattarin, J., Fowler, B., & Fisher, E. (1995). The Perception of Teasing Scale (POTS): A revision and extension of the Physical Appearance Related Teasing Scale (PARTS). *Journal of Personality Assessment, 65*, 146–157. doi: 10.1207/s15327752jpa6501_11

Thompson, J. K., Heinberg, L. J., Altabe, M., & Tantleff-Dunn, S. (1999). *Exacting beauty: Theory, assessment, and treatment of body image disturbance.* Washington, DC: American Psychological Association.

Thompson, J. K, & Stice, E. (2001). Thin-ideal internalization: Mounting evidence for a new risk factor for body-image disturbance and eating pathology. *Current Directions in Psychological Science, 10*, 181–183. doi: 10.1111/1467-8721.00144

Thompson, J. K., & Tantleff, S. (1992). Female and male ratings of upper torso: Actual, ideal, and stereotypical conceptions. *Journal of Social Behavior & Personality, 7*, 345–354.

Thompson, M. J. (2000). Gender in magazine advertising: Skin sells best. *Clothing and Textiles Research Journal, 18*, 178–181. doi: 10.1177/0887302X0001800306

Thompson, M. S., & Keith, V. M. (2001). The blacker the berry: Gender, skin tone, self-esteem, and self-efficacy. *Gender & Society, 15*, 336–357. doi: 10.1177/089124301015003002

Tiggemann, M. (2011). Mental health risks of self-objectification: A review of the empirical evidence for disordered eating, depressed mood, and sexual dysfunction. In R. M. Calogero, S. Tantleff-Dunn, & J. K. Thompson (Eds.), *Self-objectification in women: Causes, consequences, and counteractions* (pp. 139–159). Washington, DC: American Psychological Association.

Tiggemann, M., & Hodgson, S. (2008). The hairless norm extended: Reasons for and predictors of women's body hair removal at different body sites. *Sex Roles, 59*, 889–897. doi: 10.1007/s11199-008-9494-3

Tiggemann, M., & Kenyon, S. J. (1998). The hairlessness norm: The removal of body hair in women. *Sex Roles, 39*, 873–885. doi: 10.1023/A:1018828722102

Tiggemann, M., & Kuring, J. K. (2004). The role of body objectification in disordered eating and depressed mood. *British Journal of Clinical Psychology, 43*, 299–311. doi: 10.1348/0144665031752925

Tiggemann, M., & Lynch, J. E. (2001). Body image across the life span in adult women: The role of self-objectification. *Developmental Psychology, 37*, 243–253. doi: 10.1037/0012-1649.37.2.243

Tiggemann, M., & Williamson, S. (2000). The effect of exercise on body satisfaction and self-esteem as a function of gender and age. *Sex Roles, 43*, 119–127. doi: 10.1023/A:1007095830095

Toerien, M., Wilkinson, S., & Choi. P. Y. L. (2005). Body hair removal: The "mundane" production of normative femininity. *Sex Roles, 52*, 399–406. doi: 10.1007/s11199-005-2682-5

Tolaymat, L. D., & Moradi, B. (2011). U.S. Muslim women and body image: Links among objectification theory constructs and the hijab. *Journal of Counseling Psychology, 58*, 383–392. doi: 10.1037/a0023461

Townsend, M. S., Grant, J. A., Monsivais, P., Keim, N., & Drewnowski, A. (2009). Less energy dense diets of low income women in California are associated with higher energy adjusted diet costs. *American Journal of Clinical Nutrition, 89*, 1220–1226. doi: 10.3945/ajcn.2008.26916

Tylka, T. L. (2006). Development and psychometric evaluation of a measure of intuitive eating. *Journal of Counseling Psychology, 53*, 226–240. doi: 10.1037/0022-0167.53.2.226

Tylka, T. L., & Hill, M. S. (2004). Objectification theory as it relates to disordered eating among college women. *Sex Roles, 51*, 719–730. doi: 10.1007/s11199-004-0721-2

Uskul, A. K. (2004). Women's menarche stories from a multicultural sample. *Social Science & Medicine, 59*, 667–679. doi: 10.1016/j.socscimed.2003.11.031

Ussher, J. M. (2006). *Managing the monstrous feminine: Regulating the reproductive body.* New York, NY: Routledge.

Ussher, J. M., & Perz, J. (2013). PMS as a process of negotiation: Women's experience and management of premenstrual distress. *Psychology & Health, 28*, 909–927. doi: 10.1080/08870446.2013.765004

Vaillancourt, T., & Sharma, A. (2011). Intolerance of sexy peers: Intrasexual competition among women. *Aggressive Behavior, 37*, 569–577. doi: 10.1002/ab.20413

Vinkers, C. D., Evers, C., Adriaanse, M. A., & de Ridder, D. T. (2012). Body esteem and eating disorder symptomatology: The mediating role of appearance-motivated exercise in a nonclinical adult female sample. *Eating Behaviors, 13*, 214–218. doi: 10.1016/j.eatbeh.2012.02.006

White, L. R. (2013). The function of ethnicity, income level, and menstrual taboos in postmenarcheal adolescents' understanding of menarche and menstruation. *Sex Roles, 68*, 65–76. doi: 10.1007/s11199-012-0166-y

Wilksch, S. M., Tiggemann, M., & Wade, T. D. (2006). Impact of interactive school-based media literacy lessons for reducing internalization of media ideals in young adolescent girls and boys. *International Journal of Eating Disorders, 39*, 385–393. doi: 10.1002/eat.20237

Wilksch, S. M., & Wade, T. D. (2009). Reduction of shape and weight concern in young adolescents: A 30-month controlled evaluation of a media literacy program. *Journal of the American Academy of Child & Adolescent Psychiatry*, *48*, 652–661. doi: 10.1097/CHI.0b013e3181a1f559

Willis, L. E., & Knobloch-Westerwick, S. (2014). Weighing women down: Messages on weight loss and body shaping in editorial content in popular women's health and fitness magazines. *Health Communication*, *29*, 323–331. doi: 10.1080/10410236.2012.755602

Wolf, N. (1991). *The beauty myth: How images of beauty are used against women*. New York, NY: Random House.

Wolman, C., Resnick, M. D., Harris, L. J., & Blum, R. W. (1994). Emotional well-being among adolescents with and without chronic conditions. *Journal of Adolescent Health*, *15*, 199–204. doi: 10.1016/1054-139X(94)90504-5

Wood, J. M., Koch, P. B., & Mansfield, P. K. (2007). Is my period normal? How college-aged women determine the normality or abnormality of their menstrual cycles. *Women & Health*, *46*, 41–56. doi: 10.1300/J013v46n01_0

Yamamiya, Y., Cash, T. F., Melnyk, S. E., Posavac, H. D., & Posavac, S. S. (2005). Women's exposure to thin-and-beautiful media images: Body image effects of media-ideal internalization and impact-reduction interventions. *Body Image*, *2*, 74–80. doi 10.1016/j.bodyim.2004.11.001

Yaqoob, S. (2004, October 16). *Hijab: A woman's right to choose.* Retrieved from http://www.whatnextjournal.org.uk/Pages/Back/WNext29/Hijab.pdf

Zones, J. S. (2000). Beauty myths and realities and their impacts on women's health. In M. B. Zinn, P. Hondagneu-Sotelo, & M. Messner (Eds.), *Gender through the prism of difference* (2nd ed., pp. 87–103). Boston, MA: Allyn & Bacon.

Zuckerman, M. (1986). On the meaning and implications of facial prominence. *Journal of Nonverbal Behavior*, *10*, 215–229. doi: 10.1007/BF00987481

Zuckerman, M., & Kieffer, S. C. (1994). Race differences in face-ism: Does facial prominence imply dominance? *Journal of Personality and Social Psychology*, *66*, 86–92. doi: 10.1037/0022-3514.66.1.86

Chapter 7

Abel, G., Fitzgerald, L., Healy, C., & Taylor, A. (Eds.). (2010). *Taking the crime out of sex work: New Zealand sex workers' fight for decriminalisation*. Bristol, United Kingdom: Policy Press.

Abma, J. C., & Martinez, G. M. (2017, June 22). Sexual activity and contraceptive use among teenagers in the United States, 2011–2015. *National Health Statistics Reports*, No. 104. Retrieved from https://www.cdc.gov/nchs/data/nhsr/nhsr104.pdf

Addams, C. (2009, August 31). Transsexual clichés and stereotypes in film, television, and print media. Retrieved from http://www.calpernia.com/2009/08/transsexual-cliches-and-stereotypes-in-media/

Al Romaih, W. R., Srinivas, A., Shahtahmasebi, S., & Omar, H. A. (2011). No significant change in sexual behavior in association with Human Papilloma Virus vaccination in young girls. *International Journal of Child and Adolescent Health*, *4*, 351–355.

Alexander, M., & Rosen, R. C. (2008). Spinal cord injuries and orgasm: A review. *Journal of Sex & Marital Therapy*, *34*, 308–324. doi: 10.1080/00926230802096341

Allen, L. (2007). Doing "it" differently: Relinquishing the disease and pregnancy prevention focus in sexuality education. *British Journal of Sociology of Education*, *28*, 575–588. doi: 10.1080/01425690701505367

American Psychiatric Association. (2013). *Diagnostic and statistical manual of mental disorders: DSM-5*. Washington, DC: American Psychiatric Association.

American Psychological Association Task Force on the Sexualization of Girls. (2007). *Report of the APA Task Force on the Sexualization of Girls*. Washington, DC: Author. Retrieved from http://www.apa.org/pi/wpo/sexualization.html

Armstrong, E. A., England, P., & Fogarty, A. C. (2012). Accounting for women's orgasm and sexual enjoyment in college hookups and relationships. *American Sociological Review*, *77*, 435–462. doi: 10.1177/0003122412445802

Armstrong, E. A., Hamilton, L. T., Armstrong, E. M., & Seeley, J. L. (2014). "Good girls": Gender, social class, and slut discourse on campus. *Social Psychology Quarterly*, *77*, 100–122. doi: 10.1177/0190272514521220

Attwood, F. (2007). Sluts and riot grrrls; Female identity and sexual agency. *Journal of Gender Studies*, *16*, 233–247. doi: 10.1080/09589230701562921

Attwood, F., Smith, C., & Barker, M. (2018). "I'm just curious and still exploring myself": Young people and pornography. *New Media & Society*, *20*, 3738–3759. doi: 10.1177/1461444818759271

Averett, P., Moore, A., & Price, L. (2014). Virginity definitions and meaning among the LGBT community. *Journal of Gay & Lesbian Social Services*, *26*, 259–278. doi: 10.1080/10538720.2014.924802

Bamberg, M. (2004). Form and functions of "slut bashing" in male identity constructions in 15-year-olds. *Human Development*, *47*, 331–353. doi: 10.1159/000081036

Basson, R. (2000). The female sexual response: A different model. *Journal of Sex &Marital Therapy*, *26*, 51–65. doi: 10.1080/009262300278641

Basson, R., Leiblum, S., Brotto, L., Derogatis, L., Fourcroy, J., Fugl-Meyer, K., . . . & Schover, L. (2004). Revised definitions of women's sexual dysfunction. *The Journal of Sexual Medicine*, *1*, 40–48. doi: 10.1111/j.1743-6109.2004.10107.x

Bay-Cheng, L. Y. (2003). The trouble of teen sex: The construction of adolescent sexuality through school-based sexuality education. *Sex Education: Sexuality, Society and Learning*, *3*, 61–74. doi: 10.1080/1468181032000052162

Bay-Cheng, L. Y. (2015). The agency line: A neoliberal metric for appraising young women's sexuality. *Sex Roles*, *73*, 279–291. doi: 10.1007/s11199-015-0452-6

Bearman, S. K., Presnell, K., Martinez, E., & Stice, E. (2006). The skinny on body dissatisfaction: A longitudinal study of adolescent girls and boys. *Journal of Youth and Adolescence*, *35*, 217–229. doi: 10.1007/s10964-005-9010-9

Berglas, N. F., Angulo-Olaiz, F., Jerman, P., Desai, M., & Constantine, N. A. (2014). Engaging youth perspectives on sexual rights and gender equality in intimate relationships as a foundation for rights-based sexuality education. *Sexuality Research and Social Policy*, *11*, 288–298. doi: 10.1007/s13178-014-0148-7

Berlatsky, N. (2014, October 1). Black women profiled as prostitutes in NYC. *Reason.com*. Retrieved from http://reason.com/archives/2014/10/01/nypd-profiles-sex-workers-too

Berman, J. R. (2005). Physiology of female sexual function and dysfunction. *International Journal of Impotence Research*, *17*, S44–S51. doi: 10.1038/sj.ijir.3901428

Bersamin, M. M., Walker, S., Waiters, E. D., Fisher, D. A., & Grube, J. W. (2005). Promising to wait: Virginity pledges and adolescent sexual behavior. *Journal of Adolescent Health*, *36*, 428–436. doi: 10.1016/j.jadohealth.2004.09.016

Bleakley, A., Hennessy, M., & Fishbein, M. (2006). Public opinion on sex education in U.S. schools. *Archives of Pediatrics & Adolescent Medicine*, *160*, 1151–1156. doi: 10.1001/archpedi.160.11.1151

Bleakley, A., Hennessy, M., Fishbein, M., & Jordan, A. (2009). How sources of sexual information relate to adolescents' beliefs about sex. *American Journal of Health Behavior, 33*, 37–48. doi: 10.5993/AJHB.33.1.4

Bogle, K. A. (2008). *Hooking up: Sex, dating, and relationships on campus.* New York, NY: New York University Press.

Bounds Littlefield, M. (2008). The media as a system of racialization: Exploring images of African American women and the new racism. *American Behavioral Scientist, 51*, 675–685. doi: 10.1177/0002764207307747

Braun, V. (2009). "The women are doing it for themselves": The rhetoric of choice and agency around female genital "cosmetic surgery." *Australian Feminist Studies, 24*, 233–249. doi: 10.1080/08164640902852449

Braun, V. (2010). Female genital cosmetic surgery: A critical review of current knowledge and contemporary debates. *Journal of Women's Health, 19*, 1393–1407. doi: 10.1089=jwh.2009.1728

Braun, V., & Kitzinger, C. (2001). The perfectible vagina: Size matters. *Culture, Health & Sexuality, 3*, 263–277. doi: 10.1080/13691050152484704

Braun, V., Tricklebank, G., & Clarke, V. (2013). "It shouldn't stick out from your bikini at the beach": Meaning, gender, and the hairy/hairless body. *Psychology of Women Quarterly, 37*, 478–493. doi: 10.1177/0361684313492950

Breines, J. G., Crocker, J., & Garcia, J. A. (2008). Self-objectification and well-being in women's daily lives. *Personality and Social Psychology Bulletin, 34*, 583–598. doi: 10.1177/0146167207313727

Brewster, K. L., & Tillman, K. H. (2008). Who's doing it? Patterns and predictors of youths' oral sexual experiences. *Journal of Adolescent Health, 42*, 73–80. doi: 10.1016/j.jadohealth.2007.08.010

Brooks, S. (2010). Hypersexualization and the dark body: Race and inequality among Black and Latina women in the exotic dance industry. *Sexuality Research & Social Policy, 7*, 70–80. doi: 10.1007/s13178-010-0010-5

Brotto, L. A., & Yule, M. (2017). Asexuality: Sexual orientation, paraphilia, sexual dysfunction, or none of the above? *Archives of Sexual Behavior, 46*, 619–627. doi: 10.1007/s10508-016-0802-7

Brown, J. D., Halpern, C. T., & L'Engle, K. L. (2005). Mass media as a sexual super peer for early maturing girls. *Journal of Adolescent Health, 36*, 420–427. doi: 10.1016/j.jadohealth.2004.06.003

Bushman, B. J. (2005). Violence and sex in television programs do not sell products in advertisements. *Psychological Science, 16*, 702–708. doi: 10.1111/j.1467-9280.2005.01599.x

Bushman, B. J. (2007). That was a great commercial, but what were they selling? Effects of violence and sex on memory for products in television commercials. *Journal of Applied Social Psychology, 37*, 1784–1796. doi: 10.1111/j.1559-1816.2007.00237.x

Bushman, B. J., & Bonacci, A. M. (2002). Violence and sex impair memory for television ads. *Journal of Applied Psychology, 87*, 557–564. doi: 10.1037/0021-9010.87.3.557

Byers, E. S., Sears, H. A., Voyer, S. D., Thurlow, J. L., Cohen, J. N., & Weaver, A. D. (2003). An adolescent perspective on sexual health education at school and at home: I. High school students. *Canadian Journal of Human Sexuality, 12*, 1–17.

Carpenter, L. M. (2001). The ambiguity of "having sex": The subjective experience of virginity loss in the United States. *Journal of Sex Research, 38*, 127–139. doi: 10.1080/00224490109552080

Carpenter, L. M. (2002). Gender and the meaning and experience of virginity loss in the contemporary United States. *Gender & Society, 16*, 345–365. doi: 10.1177/0891243202016003005

Carpenter, L. M. (2009). Virginity loss in reel/real life: Using popular movies to navigate sexual initiation. *Sociological Forum, 24*, 804–827. doi: 10.1111/j.1573-7861.2009.01137.x

Centers for Disease Control and Prevention. (2015, November). *Sexually transmitted disease surveillance 2014.* Atlanta, GA: Author. Retrieved from http://www.cdc.gov/std/stats14/surv-2014-print.pdf

Centers for Disease Control and Prevention. (2016, December 2). *HIV in the United States: At a glance.* Retrieved from http://www.cdc.gov/hiv/statistics/overview/ataglance.html

Chan, Z. C. Y., Chan, T. S., Ng, K. K., & Wong, M. L. (2012). A systematic review of literature about women's knowledge and attitudes toward Human Papillomavirus (HPV) vaccination. *Public Health Nursing, 29*, 481–489. doi: 10.1111/j.1525-1446.2012.01022.x

Claudat, K., & Warren, C. S. (2014). Self-objectification, body self-consciousness during sexual activities, and sexual satisfaction in college women. *Body Image, 11*, 509–515. doi: 10.1016/j.bodyim.2014.07.006

Coleman, E. (2002). Masturbation as a means of achieving sexual health. *Journal of Psychology & Human Sexuality, 14*(2–3), 5–16. doi: 10.1300/J056v14n02_02

Conley, T. D., Ziegler, A., & Moors, A. C. (2013). Backlash from the bedroom: Stigma mediates gender differences in acceptance of casual sex offers. *Psychology of Women Quarterly, 37*, 392–407. doi: 10.1177/0361684312467169

Constantine, N. A., Jerman, P., & Huang, A. X. (2007). California parents' preferences and beliefs regarding school-based sex education policy. *Perspectives on Sexual and Reproductive Health, 39*, 167–175. doi: 10.1363/3916707

Crawford, M., & Popp, D. (2003). Sexual double standards: A review and methodological critique of two decades of research. *Journal of Sex Research, 40*, 13–26. doi: 10.1080/00224490309552163

Currier, D. M. (2013). Strategic ambiguity: Protecting emphasized femininity and hegemonic masculinity in the hookup culture. *Gender & Society, 27*, 704–727. doi: 10.1177/0891243213493960

Cuskelly, M., & Bryde, R. (2004). Attitudes towards the sexuality of adults with an intellectual disability: Parents, support staff, and a community sample. *Journal of Intellectual and Developmental Disability, 29*, 255–264. doi: 10.1080/13668250412331285136

Daniels, K., Daugherty, J., & Jones, J. (2014, December). Current contraceptive status among women aged 15–44: United States, 2011–2013. *National Center for Health Statistics Data Brief*, No. 173. Retrieved from https://www.cdc.gov/nchs/data/databriefs/db173.pdf

Dank, M., Khan, B., Downey, P. M., Kotonias, C., Mayer, D., Owens, C., ... & Yu, L. (2014, March). *Estimating the size and structure of the underground commercial sex economy in eight major U.S. cities.* Retrieved from The Urban Institute website: http://www.frank-cs.org/cms/pdfs/USA/UI/UI_Study_UCSE_12.3.14.pdf

Darling, C. A., & Davdon, J. K., Sr. (1986). Enhancing relationships: Understanding the feminine mystique of pretending orgasm. *Journal of Sex & Marital Therapy, 12*, 182–196. doi: 10.1080/00926238608415405

Delgado-Infante, M. L., & Ofreneo, M. A. P. (2014). Maintaining a "good girl" position: Young Filipina women constructing sexual agency in first sex within Catholicism. *Feminism & Psychology, 24*, 390–407. doi: 10.1177/0959353514530715

Denner, J., & Coyle, K. (2007). Condom use among sexually active Latina girls in alternative high schools. In B. R. Leadbeater, & N. Way (Eds.), *Urban girls revisited: Building strengths* (pp. 281–300). New York, NY: New York University Press.

Diekema, D. S. (2003). Involuntary sterilization of persons with mental retardation: An ethical analysis. *Mental Retardation and Developmental Disabilities Research Reviews*, *9*, 21–26. doi: 10.1002/mrdd.10053

DiIorio, C., Pluhar, E., & Belcher, L. (2003). Parent-child communication about sexuality: A review of the literature from 1980–2002. *Journal of HIV/AIDS Prevention & Education for Adolescents & Children*, *5*, 7–32. doi: 10.1300/J129v05n03_02

Dove, N. L., & Wiederman, M. W. (2000). Cognitive distraction and women's sexual functioning. *Journal of Sex and Marital Therapy*, *26*, 67–78. doi: 10.1080/009262300278650

Dyson, S. (2016). Families and sexuality education. In J. J. Ponzetti Jr. (Ed.), *Evidence-based approaches to sexuality education: A global perspective* (pp. 131–145). New York, NY: Routledge.

Eaton, A. A., Rose, S. M., Interligi, C., Fernandez, K., & McHugh, M. (2016). Gender and ethnicity in dating, hanging out, and hooking up: Sexual scripts among Hispanic and White young adults. *Journal of Sex Research*, *53*, 788–804. doi: 10.1080/00224499.2015.1065954

Eisenberg, M. E., Bernat, D. H., Bearinger, L. H., & Resnick, M. D. (2009). Condom provision and education in Minnesota public schools: A telephone survey of parents. *Journal of School Health*, *79*, 416–424. doi: 10.1111/j.1746-1561.2009.00429.x

Erchull, M. J., & Liss, M. (2013a). Exploring the concept of perceived female sexual empowerment: Development and validation of the Sex is Power Scale. *Gender Issues*, *30*, 39–53. doi: 10.1007/s12147-013-9114-6

Erchull, M. J., & Liss, M. (2013b). Feminists who flaunt it: Exploring the enjoyment of sexualization among young feminist women. *Journal of Applied Social Psychology*, *43*, 2341–2349. doi: 10.1111/jasp.12183

Erchull, M. J., & Liss, M. (2014). The object of one's desire: How perceived sexual empowerment through objectification is related to sexual outcomes. *Sexuality & Culture*, *18*, 773–788. doi: 10.1007/s12119-013-9216-z

Eva Herzigova: Wonderbra ad and empowered women. (2014, November 21). *Evening Standard.* Retrieved from https://www.standard.co.uk/news/world/eva-herzigova-wonderbra-ad-empowered-women-9875267.html

Fahs, B. (2009). Compulsory bisexuality? The challenges of modern sexual fluidity. *Journal of Bisexuality*, *9*, 431–449. doi: 10.1080/15299710903316661

Fahs, B. (2011). *Performing sex: The making and unmaking of women's erotic lives.* Albany, NY: State University of New York Press.

Fahs, B. (2014a). Coming to power: Women's fake orgasms and best orgasm experiences illuminate the failures of (hetero)sex and the pleasures of connection. *Culture, Health & Sexuality*, *16*, 974–988. doi: 10.1080/13691058.2014.924557

Fahs, B. (2014b). Genital panics: Constructing the vagina in women's qualitative narratives about pubic hair, menstrual sex, and vaginal self-image. *Body Image*, *11*, 210–218. doi: 10.1016/j.bodyim.2014.03.002

Fasoli, F., Durante, F., Mari, S., Zogmaister, C., & Volpato, C. (2018). Shades of sexualization: When sexualization becomes sexual objectification. *Sex Roles*, *78*, 338–351. doi: 10.1007/s11199-017-0808-1

Faulkner, S. L. (2003). Good girl or flirt girl: Latinas' definitions of sex and sexual relationships. *Hispanic Journal of Behavioral Sciences*, *25*, 174–200. doi: 10.1177/0739986303025002003

Fennell, J. L. (2011). Men bring condoms, women take pills: Men's and women's roles in contraceptive decision making. *Gender & Society*, *25*, 496–521. doi: 10.1177/0891243211416113

Fielder, R. L., & Carey, M. P. (2010). Predictors and consequences of sexual "hookups" among college students: A short-term

prospective study. *Archives of Sexual Behavior*, *39*, 1105–1119. doi: 10.1007/s10508-008-9448-4

Fielder, R. L., Walsh, J. L., Carey, K. B., & Carey, M. P. (2013). Predictors of sexual hookups: A theory-based, prospective study of first-year college women. *Archives of Sexual Behavior*, *42*, 1425–1441. doi: 10.1007/s10508-013-0106-0

Fielder, R. L., Walsh, J. L., Carey, K. B., & Carey, M. P. (2014). Sexual hookups and adverse health outcomes: A longitudinal study of first-year college women. *The Journal of Sex Research*, *51*, 131–144. doi: 10.1080/00224499.2013.848255

Fine, M. (1988). Sexuality, schooling, and adolescent females: The missing discourse of desire. *Harvard Educational Review*, *58*, 29–53. doi: 10.17763/haer.58.1.u0468k1v2n2n8242

Fine, M., & McClelland, S. (2006). Sexuality education and desire: Still missing after all these years. *Harvard Educational Review*, *76*, 297–338. doi: 10.17763/haer.76.3.w5042g23122n6703

Frankham, J. (2006). Sexual antimonies and parent/child sex education: Learning from foreclosure. *Sexualities*, *9*, 236–254. doi: 10.1177/1363460706063120

Frederick, A., St. John, H. K., Garcia, J. R., & Lloyd, E. A. (2018). Differences in orgasm frequency among gay, lesbian, bisexual, and heterosexual men and women in a U.S. national sample. *Archives of Sexual Behavior*, *47*, 273–288. doi: 10.1007/s10508-017-0939-z

Fugl-Meyer, K. S., Öberg, K., Lundberg, P. O., Lewin, B., & Fugl-Meyer, A. (2006). On orgasm, sexual techniques, and erotic perceptions in 18- to 74-year-old Swedish women. *The Journal of Sexual Medicine*, *3*, 56–68. doi: 10.1111/j.1743-6109.2005.00170.x

Gagnon, J. H., & Simon, W. (1973). *Sexual conduct: The social sources of human sexuality.* Chicago, IL: Aldine Books.

Galea, J., Butler, J., Iacono, T., & Leighton, D. (2004). The assessment of sexual knowledge in people with intellectual disability. *Journal of Intellectual and Developmental Disability*, *29*, 350–365. doi: 10.1080/13668250400014517

Garcia, J. R., Lloyd, E. A., Wallen, K., & Fisher, H. E. (2014). Variation in orgasm occurrence by sexual orientation in a sample of U.S. singles. *Journal of Sexual Medicine*, *11*, 2645–2652. doi: 10.1111/jsm.12669

Garcia, J. R., Reiber, C., Massey, S. G., & Merriwether, A. M. (2012). Sexual hookup culture: A review. *Review of General Psychology*, *16*, 161–176. doi: 10.1037/a0027911

Gartrell, N., & Mosbacher, D. (1984). Sex differences in the naming of children's genitalia. *Sex Roles*, *10*, 869–876. doi: 10.1007/BF00288510

Geasler, M. J., Dannison, L. L., & Edlund, C. J. (1995). Sexuality education of young children: Parental concerns. *Family Relations*, *44*, 184–188. doi: 10.2307/584807

George, A. E., Abatemarco, D. J., Terry, M. A., Yonas, M., Butler, J., & Akers, A. Y. (2013). A qualitative exploration of the role of social networks in educating urban African American adolescents about sex. *Ethnicity & Health*, *18*, 168–189. doi: 10.1080/13557858.2012.708915

Gerassi, L. (2015). From exploitation to industry: Definitions, risks, and consequences of domestic sexual exploitation and sex work among women and girls. *Journal of Human Behavior in the Social Environment*, *25*, 591–605. doi: 10.1080/10911359.2014.991055

Gil, R. M., & Vazquez, C. I. (1996). *The Maria paradox: How Latinas can merge old world traditions with new world self esteem.* New York, NY: G. P. Putnam's Sons.

Gill, R. (2003). From sexual objectification to sexual subjectification: The resexualisation of women's bodies in the media. *Feminist Media Studies*, *3*, 100–106.

Gill, R. (2008). Empowerment/sexism: Figuring female sexual agency in contemporary advertising. *Feminism & Psychology*, *18*, 35–60. doi: 10.1177/0959353507084950

Gill, R. (2009). "Beyond the sexualization of culture" thesis: An intersectional analysis of "sixpacks," "midriffs," and "hot lesbians" in advertising. *Sexualities*, *12*, 137–160. doi: 10.1177/1363460708100916

Gill, R. (2012). Media, empowerment and the "sexualization of culture" debates. *Sex Roles*, *66*, 736–745. doi: 10.1007/s11199-011-0107-1

Glick, P., Larsen, S., Johnson, C., & Branstiter, H. (2005). Evaluations of sexy women in low- and high-status jobs. *Psychology of Women Quarterly*, *29*, 389–395. doi: 10.1111/j.1471-6402.2005.00238.x

Goldschmidt, D. (2015, August 18). "Female Viagra" gets FDA approval. *CNN*. Retrieved from http://www.cnn.com/2015/08/18/health/female-viagra-fda-approval/

Goodin, S. M., Van Denburg, A., Murnen, S. K., & Smolak, L. (2011). "Putting on" sexiness: A content analysis of the presence of sexualizing characteristics in girls' clothing. *Sex Roles*, *65*, 1–12. doi: 10.1007/s11199-011-9966-8

Godwin, J. (2012, October). *Sex work and the law in Asia and the Pacific*. Bangkok, Thailand: United Nations Development Programme. Retrieved from http://www.undp.org/content/dam/undp/library/hivaids/English/HIV-2012-SexWorkAndLaw.pdf

Gorney, C. (2018, January 20). *How to talk to your child about sex, ages 6 to 12*. Retrieved from https://consumer.healthday.com/encyclopedia/children-s-health-10/child-development-news-124/how-to-talk-to-your-child-about-sex-ages-6-to-12-645918.html

Graff, K. A., Murnen, S. K., & Krause, A. K. (2013). Low-cut shirts and high-heeled shoes: Increased sexualization across time in magazine depictions of girls. *Sex Roles*, *69*, 571–582. doi: 10.1007/s11199-013-0321-0

Grover, L. (2014, July 29). This is what sex-positive parenting really looks like. *Huffington Post*. Retrieved from http://www.huffingtonpost.com/lea-grover/this-is-what-sex-positive-parenting-really-looks-like_b_5516707.html

Guttmacher Institute. (2016, March). *Unintended pregnancy in the United States* [Fact sheet]. Retrieved from https://www.guttmacher.org/pubs/FB-Unintended-Pregnancy-US.html?gclid=CI7ypZaH4coCFRBbhgodwocKBw

Hakim, C. (2011). *Erotic capital*. New York, NY: Basic Books.

Hald, G. M., Seaman, C., & Linz, D. (2014). Sexuality and pornography. In D. L. Tolman & L. M. Diamond (Eds.), *APA handbook of sexuality and psychology* (Vol. 2, pp. 3–35). Washington, DC: American Psychological Association.

Halpern, C. T., & Haydon, A. A. (2012). Sexual timetables for oral-genital, vaginal, and anal intercourse: Sociodemographic comparisons in a nationally representative sample of adolescents. *American Journal of Public Health*, *102*, 1221–1228. doi: 10.2105/AJPH.2011.300394

Hamkins, S., & Schultz, R. (2007). *The mother-daughter project*. New York, NY: Hudson Street Press.

Harris, S., Monahan, J. L., & Hovick, S. R. (2014). Communicating new sexual desires and the factors that influence message directness. *Sexual and Relationship Therapy*, *29*, 405–423. doi: 10.1080/14681994.2014.954992

Hayes, R. D., Bennett, C. M., Fairley, C. K., & Dennerstein, L. (2006). Epidemiology: What can prevalence studies tell us about female sexual difficulty and dysfunction? *The Journal of Sexual Medicine*, *3*, 589–595. doi: 10.1111/j.1743-6109.2006.00241.x

Heisler, J. M. (2005). Family communication about sex: Parents and college-aged offspring recall discussion topics, satisfaction, and parental involvement. *The Journal of Family Communication*, *5*, 295–312. doi: 10.1207/s15327698jfc0504_4

Helminiak, D. A. (1989). Self-esteem, sexual self-acceptance, and spirituality. *Journal of Sex Education & Therapy*, *15*, 200–210. doi: 10.1080/01614576.1989.11074961

Herbenick, D., Reece, M., Schick, V., Sanders, S. A., Dodge, B., & Fortenberry, J. D. (2010a). An event-level analysis of the sexual characteristics and composition among adults ages 18 to 59: Results from a national probability sample in the United States. *The Journal of Sexual Medicine*, *7*, 346–361. doi: 10.1111/j.1743-6109.2010.02020.x

Herbenick, D., Reece, M., Schick, V., Sanders, S. A., Dodge, B., & Fortenberry, J. D. (2010b). Sexual behavior in the United States: Results from a national probability sample of men and women ages 14–94. *The Journal of Sexual Medicine*, *7*, 255–265. doi: 10.1111/j.1743-6109.2010.02012.x

Higgins, J. A., Trussell, J., Moore, N. B., & Davidson, J. K. (2010). Virginity lost, satisfaction gained? Physiological and psychological sexual satisfaction at heterosexual debut. *Journal of Sex Research*, *47*, 384–394. doi: 10.1080/00224491003774792

Hite, S. (2004). *The Hite report: A nationwide study of female sexuality*. New York, NY: Seven Stories Press.

Hoffman, B. R. (2014). The interaction of drug use, sex work, and HIV among transgender women. *Substance Use & Misuse*, *49*, 1049–1053. doi:10.3109/10826084.2013.855787

Holland, J., Ramazanoglu, C., Sharpe, S., & Thomson, R. (2010). Deconstructing virginity: Young people's accounts of first sex. *Sexual and Relationship Therapy*, *25*, 351–362. doi: 10.1080/14681994.2010.496970

Holman, A., & Sillars, A. (2012). Talk about "hooking up": The influence of college student social networks on nonrelationship sex. *Health Communication*, *27*, 205–216. doi: 10.1080/10410236.2011.575540

Horowitz, A. D., & Spicer, L. (2013). "Having sex" as a graded and hierarchical construct: A comparison of sexual definitions among heterosexual and lesbian emerging adults in the UK. *Journal of Sex Research*, *50*, 139–150. doi: 10.1080/00224499.2011.635322

Hovell, M., Sipan, C., Blumberg, E., Atkins, C., Hofstetter, C. R., & Kreitner, S. (1994). Family influences on Latino and Anglo adolescents' sexual behavior. *Journal of Marriage and the Family*, *56*, 973–986. doi: 10.2307/353607

Hurlbert, D. F. (1991). The role of assertiveness in female sexuality: A comparative study between sexually assertive and sexually nonassertive women. *Journal of Sex & Marital Therapy*, *17*, 183–190. doi: 10.1080/00926239108404342

Hutchinson, M. K., Jemmott, J. B., III, Jemmott, L. S., Braverman, P., & Fong, G. T. (2003). The role of mother-daughter sexual risk communication in reducing sexual risk behaviors among urban adolescent females: A prospective study. *Journal of Adolescent Health*, *33*, 98–107. doi: 10.1016/S1054-139X(03)00183-6

Ito, K. E., Gizlice, Z., Owen-O'Dowd, J., Foust, E., Leone, P. A., & Miller, W. C. (2006). Parent opinion of sexuality education in a state with mandated abstinence education: Does policy match parental preference? *Journal of Adolescent Health*, *39*, 634–641. doi: 10.1016/j.jadohealth.2006.04.022

Jaccard, J., Dittus, P. J., & Gordon, V. V. (2000). Parent-teen communication about premarital sex factors associated with the extent of communication. *Journal of Adolescent Research*, *15*, 187–208. doi: 10.1177/0743558400152001

Jordan, T. R., Price, J. H., & Fitzgerald, S. (2000). Rural parents' communication with their teenagers about sexual issues. *Journal of School Health*, *70*, 338–344. doi: 10.1111/j.1746-1561.2000.tb07269.x

Kelly, M. (2010). Virginity loss narratives in "teen drama" television programs. *Journal of Sex Research, 47,* 479–489. doi: 10.1080/00224490903132044

Kester, L. M., Zimet, G. D., Fortenberry, J. D., Kahn, J. A., & Shew, M. L. (2013). A national study of HPV vaccination of adolescent girls: Rates, predictors, and reasons for non-vaccination. *Maternal and Child Health Journal, 17,* 879–885. doi: 10.1007/s10995-012-1066-z

Kettl, P., Zarefoss, S., Jacoby, K., Garman, C., Hulse, C., Rowley, F., . . . & Tyson, K. (1991). Female sexuality after spinal cord injury. *Sexuality and Disability, 9,* 287–295. doi: 10.1007/BF01102017

Kim, E. (2011). Asexuality in disability narratives. *Sexualities, 14,* 479–493. doi: 10.1177/1363460711406463

Kim, J. L., Sorsoli, C. L., Collins, K., Zylbergold, B. A., Schooler, D., & Tolman, D. L. (2007). From sex to sexuality: Exposing the heterosexual script on primetime network television. *Journal of Sex Research, 44,* 145–157. doi: 10.1080/00224490701263660

Kim, J. L., & Ward, L. M. (2007). Silence speaks volumes: Parental sexual communication among Asian American emerging adults. *Journal of Adolescent Research, 22,* 3–31. doi: 10.1177/0743558406294916

Kirby, D. (2007, November). *Emerging answers 2007: Research findings on programs to reduce teen pregnancy and sexually transmitted diseases.* Washington, DC: National Campaign to Prevent Teen and Unplanned Pregnancy. Retrieved from https://thenationalcampaign.org/sites/def/files/resource-primary-download/EA2007_full_0.pdf

Kodjak, A. (2018, February 15). Trump administration sued over ending funding of teen pregnancy programs. *National Public Radio.* Retrieved from https://www.npr.org/sections/health-shots/2018/02/15/585879601/trump-administration-sued-for-ending-funding-of-teen-pregnancy-programs

Komisaruk, B. R., & Whipple, B. (2011). Non-genital orgasms. *Sexual and Relationship Therapy, 26,* 356–372. doi: 10.1080/14681994.2011.649252

Kosova, E. (2017, November 17). How much do different kinds of birth control cost without insurance? *National Women's Health Network.* Retrieved from https://www.nwhn.org/much-different-kinds-birth-control-cost-without-insurance/

Kreager, D. A., & Staff, J. (2009). The sexual double standard and adolescent peer acceptance. *Social Psychology Quarterly, 72,* 143–164. doi: 10.1177/019027250907200205

Lamb, S. (2010a). Feminist ideals for a healthy female adolescent sexuality: A critique. *Sex Roles, 62,* 294–306. doi: 10.1007/s11199-009-9698-1

Lamb, S. (2010b). Toward a sexual ethics curriculum: Bringing philosophy and society to bear on individual development. *Harvard Educational Review, 80,* 81–105. doi: 10.17763/haer.80.1.c104834k00552457

Lamb, S., Lustig, K., & Graling, K. (2013). The use and misuse of pleasure in sex education curricula. *Sex Education, 13,* 305–318. doi: 10.1080/14681811.2012.738604

Lambert, T. A., Kahn, A. S., & Apple, K. J. (2003). Pluralistic ignorance and hooking up. *Journal of Sex Research, 40,* 129–133. doi: 10.1080/00224490309552174

Landsburg, S. E. (2004, March). The economics of faking orgasm. *Slate.* Retrieved from http://primary.slate.com/articles/arts/everyday_economics/2004/03/the_economics_of_faking_orgasm.html

Laumann, E. O., Paik, A., & Rosen, R. C. (1999). Sexual dysfunction in the United States: Prevalence and predictors. *Journal of the American Medical Association, 281,* 537–544. doi: 10.1001/jama.281.6.537

Lerum, K., & Dworkin, S. L. (2015). Sexual agency is not a problem of neoliberalism: Feminism, sexual justice, & the carceral turn. *Sex Roles, 73,* 319–331. doi: 10.1007/s11199-015-0525-6

Levy, A. (2005). *Female chauvinist pigs: Women and the rise of raunch culture.* New York, NY: Free Press.

Liddon, N. C., Leichliter, J. S., & Markowitz, L. E. (2012). Human Papillomavirus vaccine and sexual behavior among adolescent and young women. *American Journal of Preventive Medicine, 42,* 44–52. doi: 10.1016/j.amepre.2011.09.024

Liss, M., Erchull, M. J., & Ramsey, L. R. (2011). Empowering or oppressing? Development and exploration of the Enjoyment of Sexualization Scale. *Personality and Social Psychology Bulletin, 37,* 55–68. doi: 10.1177/014616721038611

Manlove, J., Ryan, S., & Franzetta, K. (2007). Contraceptive use patterns across teens' sexual relationships: The role of relationships, partners, and sexual histories. *Demography, 44,* 603–621. doi: 10.1353/dem.2007.0031

Martin, K., Baker, L. V., Torres, J., & Luke, K. (2011). Privates, pee-pees, and coochies: Gender and genital labeling for/with young children. *Feminism & Psychology, 21,* 420–430. doi: 0.1177/0959353510384832

Martin, K. A., & Luke, K. (2010). Gender differences in the ABC's of the birds and the bees: What mothers teach young children about sexuality and reproduction. *Sex Roles, 62,* 278–291. doi: 10.1007/s11199-009-9731-4

Matthews, A. K., Hughes, T. L., & Tartaro, J. (2006). Sexual behavior and sexual dysfunction in a community sample of lesbian and heterosexual women. In A. M. Omoto & H. S. Kurtzman (Eds.), *Contemporary perspectives on lesbian, gay, and bisexual psychology* (pp. 185–205). Washington, DC: American Psychological Association.

Mayhew, A., Mullins, T. L. K., Ding, L., Rosenthal, S. L., Zimet, G. D., Morrow, C., & Kahn, J. A. (2014). Risk perceptions and subsequent sexual behaviors after HPV vaccination in adolescents. *Pediatrics, 133,* 404–411. doi: 10.1542/peds.2013-2822

McCabe, M. P. (1999). Sexual knowledge, experience and feelings among people with disability. *Sexuality and Disability, 17,* 157–170. doi: 10.1023/A:1021476418440

McCormick, N. B. (1994). *Sexual salvation: Affirming women's sexual rights and pleasures.* Westport, CT: Praeger.

McDonough, K. (2014, January 7). Laverne Cox flawlessly shuts down Katie Couric's invasive questions about transgender people. *Salon.* Retrieved from http://www.salon.com/2014/01/07/laverne_cox_artfully_shuts_down_katie_courics_invasive_questions_about_transgender_people/

McDougall, L. J. (2013). Towards a clean slit: How medicine and notions of normality are shaping female genital aesthetics. *Culture, Health & Sexuality, 15,* 774–787. doi: 10.1080/13691058.2013.780639

McKay, A., Byers, E. S., Voyer, S. D., Humphreys, T. P., & Markham, C. (2014). Ontario parents' opinions and attitudes towards sexual health education in the schools. *The Canadian Journal of Human Sexuality, 23,* 159–166. doi: 10.3138/cjhs.23.3-A1

McKee, M. D., & Karasz, A. (2006). "You have to give her that confidence": Conversations about sex in Hispanic mother-daughter dyads. *Journal of Adolescent Research, 21,* 158–184. doi: 10.1177/0743558405285493

Meana, M., & Nunnink, S. E. (2006). Gender differences in the content of cognitive distraction during sex. *Journal of Sex Research, 43,* 59–67. doi: 10.1080/00224490609552299

Ménard, A. D., & Offman, A. (2009). The interrelationships between sexual self-esteem, sexual assertiveness and sexual satisfaction. *The Canadian Journal of Human Sexuality, 18,* 35–45.

Milhausen, R. R., & Herold, E. S. (1999). Does the sexual double standard still exist? Perceptions of university women. *Journal of Sex Research, 36*, 361–368. doi: 10.1080/00224499909552008

Milligan, M. S., & Neufeldt, A. H. (2001). The myth of asexuality: A survey of social and empirical evidence. *Sexuality and Disability, 19*, 91–109. doi: 10.1023/A:1010621705591

Millner, V., Mulekar, M., & Turrens, J. (2015). Parents' beliefs regarding sex education for their children in southern Alabama public schools. *Sexuality Research and Social Policy, 12*, 101–109. doi: 10.1007/s13178-015-0180-2

Mock, J. (2014). *Redefining realness: My path to womanhood, identity, love and so much more.* New York, NY: Atria Press.

Montemurro, B., Bloom, C., & Madell, K. (2003). Ladies night out: A typology of women patrons of a male strip club. *Deviant Behavior, 24*, 333–352. doi: 10.1080/01639620390195213

Montemurro, B., & Siefken, J. M. (2014). Cougars on the prowl? New perceptions of older women's sexuality. *Journal of Aging Studies, 28*, 35–43. doi: 10.1016/j.jaging.2013.11.004

Moore, E., Berkley-Patton, J., Bohn, A., Hawes, S., & Bowe-Thompson, C. (2015). Beliefs about sex and parent–child–church sex communication among church-based African American youth. *Journal of Religion and Health, 54*, 1810–1825. doi: 10.1007/s10943-014-9950-z

Morris, C. (2015, January 20). Things are looking up in America's porn industry. *NBC News.* Retrieved from http://www.nbcnews.com/business/business-news/things-are-looking-americas-porn-industry-n289431

Muehlenhard, C. L., & Shippee, S. K. (2010). Men's and women's reports of pretending orgasm. *Journal of Sex Research, 47*, 552–567. doi: 10.1080/00224490903171794

Murnen, S. K., & Smolak, L. (2012). Social considerations related to adolescent girls' sexual empowerment: A response to Lamb and Peterson. *Sex Roles, 66*, 725–735. doi: 10.1007/s11199-011-0079-1

Nadal, K. L., Davidoff, K. C., & Fujii-Doe, W. (2014). Transgender women and the sex work industry: Roots in systemic, institutional, and interpersonal discrimination. *Journal of Trauma & Dissociation, 15*, 169–183. doi: 10.1080/15299732.2014.867572

New View Campaign. (2014, October). *What's sexually "normal"?* [Fact sheet]. Retrieved from http://newviewcampaign.org/userfiles/file/4%20FACT%20SHEET%20-%20Sexually%20Normal.pdf

Nowatzki, J., & Morry, M. M. (2009). Women's intentions regarding, and acceptance of, self-sexualizing behavior. *Psychology of Women Quarterly, 33*, 95–107. doi:10.1111/j.1471-6402.2008.01477.x

Oliver, M. B., & Hyde, J. S. (1993). Gender differences in sexuality: A meta-analysis. *Psychological Bulletin, 114*, 29–51. doi: 10.1037/0033-2909.114.1.29

Orgocka, A. (2004). Perceptions of communication and education about sexuality among Muslim immigrant girls in the U.S. *Sex Education, 4*, 255–271. doi: 0.1080/146818042000243349

O'Sullivan, L. F., & Meyer-Bahlberg, H. L. (2003). African American and Latina inner-city girls' reports of romantic and sexual development. *Journal of Social and Personal Relationships, 20*, 221–238. doi: 10.1177/0265407503020002006

O'Sullivan, L. F., Meyer-Bahlburg, H. L., & Watkins, B. X. (2001). Mother-daughter communication about sex among urban African American and Latino families. *Journal of Adolescent Research, 16*, 269–292. doi: 10.1177/0743558401163002

Papp, L. J., Hagerman, C., Gnoleba, M. A., Erchull, M. J., Liss, M., Miles-McLean, H., & Robertson, C. M. (2015). Exploring perceptions of slut-shaming on Facebook: Evidence for a reverse sexual double standard. *Gender Issues, 32*, 57–76. doi: 10.1007/s12147-014-9133-y

Paul, E. L., McManus, B., & Hayes, A. (2000). "Hookups": Characteristics and correlates of college students' spontaneous and anonymous sexual experiences. *Journal of Sex Research, 37*, 76–88. doi: 10.1080/00224490009552023

Peluchette, J. V., & Karl, K. (2013). Clothing makes the man (or woman): The impact of workplace attire on self and others' perceptions. In M. A. Paludi (Ed.), *Human resource development quarterly* (pp. 75–86). Santa Barbara, CA: Praeger/ABC-CLIO.

Petersen, J. L., & Hyde, J. S. (2010). A meta-analytic review of research on gender differences in sexuality, 1993–2007. *Psychological Bulletin, 136*, 21–38. doi: 10.1037/a0017504

Petersen, J. L., & Hyde, J. S. (2011). Gender differences in sexual attitudes and behaviors: A review of meta-analytic results and large datasets. *Journal of Sex Research, 48*, 149–165. doi: 10.1080/00224499.2011.551851

Peterson, Z. D. (2010). What is sexual empowerment? A multidimensional and process-oriented approach to adolescent girls' sexual empowerment. *Sex Roles, 62*, 307–313. doi: 10.1007/s11199-009-9725-2

Planned Parenthood. (2012, March). *Sex education in the United States* [Issue brief]. Retrieved from https://www.plannedparenthood.org/files/3713/9611/7930/Sex_Ed_in_the_US.pdf

Porter, J., & Bonilla, L. (2000). Drug use, HIV, and the ecology of street prostitution. In R. Weitzer (Ed.), *Sex for sale: Prostitution, pornography, and the sex industry* (pp. 103–121). New York, NY: Routledge.

Power, J., McNair, R., & Carr, S. (2009). Absent sexual scripts: Lesbian and bisexual women's knowledge, attitudes and action regarding safer sex and sexual health information. *Culture, Health & Sexuality, 11*, 67–81. doi: 10.1080/13691050802541674

Raffaelli, M., Bogenschneider, K., & Flood, M. F. (1998). Parent-teen communication about sexual topics. *Journal of Family Issues, 19*, 315–333. doi: 10.1177/019251398019003005

Ramsey, L., Marotta, J. A., & Hoyt, T. (2017). Sexualized, objectified, but not satisfied: Enjoying sexualization relates to lower relationship satisfaction through perceived partner-objectification. *Journal of Social and Personal, 34*, 258–278. doi: 10.1177/0265407516631157

Ramsey, L. R., & Hoyt, T. (2015). The object of desire: How being objectified creates sexual pressure for women in heterosexual relationships. *Psychology of Women Quarterly, 39*, 151–170. doi: 10.1177/0361684314544679

Raphael, J., & Shapiro, D. L. (2004). Violence in indoor and outdoor prostitution venues. *Violence Against Women, 10*, 126–139. doi: 10.1177/1077801203260529

Rich, A. C. (1980). *Compulsory heterosexuality and lesbian existence.* Denver, CO: Antelope Publications.

Richmond, E. (2018, February 18). Does Trump's education budget even matter? *The Atlantic.* Retrieved from https://www.theatlantic.com/education/archive/2018/02/does-trumps-education-budget-even-matter/553271/

Richters, J., de Visser, R., Rissel, C., & Smith, A. (2006). Sexual practices at last heterosexual encounter and occurrence of orgasm in a national survey. *Journal of Sex Research, 43*, 217–226. doi: 10.1080/00224490609552320

Ringrose, J., Harvey, L., Gill, R., & Livingstone, S. (2013). Teen girls, sexual double standards and "sexting": Gendered value in digital image exchange. *Feminist Theory, 14*, 305–323. doi: 10.1177/1464700113499853

Robbins, C. L., Schick, V., Reece, M., Herbenick, D., Sanders, S. A., Dodge, B., & Fortenberry, J. D. (2011). Prevalence, frequency, and associations of masturbation with partnered sexual behaviors among U.S. adolescents. *Archives of Pediatrics & Adolescent Medicine, 165*, 1087–1093. doi: 10.1001/archpediatrics.2011.142

Roberts, D. (1997). *Killing the black body: Race, reproduction, and the meaning of liberty.* New York, NY: Vintage.

Rogers, A. A., Ha, T., Stormshak, E. A., & Dishion, T. J. (2015). Quality of parent–adolescent conversations about sex and adolescent sexual behavior: An observational study. *Journal of Adolescent Health, 57,* 174–178. doi: 10.1016/j.jadohealth.2015.04.010

Rupp, L. J., Taylor, V., Regev-Messalem, S., Fogarty, A. C., & England, P. (2014). Queer women in the hookup scene: Beyond the closet? *Gender & Society, 28,* 212–235. doi: 10.1177/0891243213510782

Sabina, C., Wolak, J., & Finkelhor, D. (2008). The nature and dynamics of Internet pornography exposure for youth. *CyberPsychology and Behavior, 11,* 691–693. doi: 10.1089/cpb.2007.0179

Sagebin Bordini, G., & Sperb, T. M. (2013). Sexual double standard: A review of the literature between 2001 and 2010. *Sexuality & Culture, 17,* 686–704. doi: 10.1007/s12119-012-9163-0

Sakaluk, J. K., & Milhausen, R. R. (2012). Factors influencing university students' explicit and implicit sexual double standards. *Journal of Sex Research, 49,* 464–476. doi: 10.1080/00224499.2011.569976

Sammons, D. (2010). *Body beautiful: The impact of body image on sexual pleasure in a transgender population* (Unpublished doctoral dissertation). Alliant International University, San Francisco, CA. Retrieved from http://search.proquest.com/docview/748248275?

Sanchez, D. T., & Kiefer, A. K. (2007). Body concerns in and out of the bedroom: Implications for sexual pleasure and problems. *Archives of Sexual Behavior, 36,* 808–820. doi: 10.1007/s10508-007-9205-0

Sandercock, T. (2015). Transing the small screen: Loving and hating transgender youth in Glee and Degrassi. *Journal of Gender Studies, 24,* 436–452. doi: 10.1080/09589236.2015.1021307

Sausa, L. A., Keatley, J., & Operario, D. (2007). Perceived risks and benefits of sex work among transgender women of color in San Francisco. *Archives of Sexual Behavior, 36,* 768–777. doi: 10.1007/s10508-007-9210-3

Sexual intercourse. (2017, November 28). *Encyclopedia Britannica.* Retrieved from https://www.britannica.com/science/sexual-intercourse

Shifren, J. L., Monz, B. U., Russo, P. A., Segreti, A., & Johannes, C. B. (2008). Sexual problems and distress in United States women: Prevalence and correlates. *Obstetrics & Gynecology, 112,* 970–978. doi: 10.1097/AOG.0b013e3181898cdb

Shimizu, C. P. (2007). *The hypersexuality of race: Performing Asian/American women on screen and scene.* Durham, NC: Duke University Press.

Simon, W., & Gagnon, J. H. (1986). Sexual scripts: Permanence and change. *Archives of Sexual Behavior, 15,* 97–120. doi: 10.1007/BF01542219

Simon, W., & Gagnon, J. H. (2003). Sexual scripts: Origins, influences and changes. *Qualitative Sociology, 26,* 491–497. doi: 10.1023/B:QUAS.0000005053.99846.e5

Sinacore, A. L., Jaghori, B., & Rezazadeh, S. M. (2015). Female university students working in the sex trade: A narrative analysis. *Canadian Journal of Counselling & Psychotherapy, 48*(4), 40–56.

Smith, J. K., Liss, M., Erchull, M. J., Kelly, C. M., Adragna, K., & Baines, K. (2018). The relationship between sexualized appearance and perceptions of women's competence and electability. *Sex Roles.* Advance online publication. doi: 10.1007/s11199-018-0898-4

Smolak, L. (2012). Appearance in childhood and adolescence. In N. Rumsey & D. Harcourt (Eds.), *Oxford handbook of the psychology of appearance* (pp. 123–141). London, United Kingdom: Oxford University Press.

Smolak, L., Murnen, S. K., & Myers, T. A. (2014). Sexualizing the self: What college women and men think about and do to be "sexy." *Psychology of Women Quarterly, 38,* 379–397. doi: 10.1177/0361684314524168

Sprecher, S., Harris, G., & Meyers, A. (2008). Perceptions of sources of sex education and targets of sex communication: Sociodemographic and cohort effects. *Journal of Sex Research, 45,* 17–26. doi: 10.1080/00224490701629522

Sprecher, S., Treger, S., & Sakaluk, J. K. (2013). Premarital sexual standards and sociosexuality: Gender, ethnicity, and cohort differences. *Archives of Sexual Behavior, 42,* 1395–1405. doi: 10.1007/s10508-013-0145-6

Stanley, N., Barter, C., Wood, M., Aghtaie, N., Larkins, C., Lanau, A., & Överlien, C. (2018). Pornography, sexual coercion and abuse and sexting in young people's intimate relationships: A European study. *Journal of Interpersonal Violence, 33,* 2919–2944. doi: 10.1177/0886260516633204

Steer, A., & Tiggemann, M. (2008). The role of self-objectification in women's sexual functioning. *Journal of Social and Clinical Psychology, 27,* 205–225. doi: 10.1521/jscp.2008.27.3.205

Stern, A. M. (2005a). *Eugenic nation: Faults and frontiers of better breeding in modern America.* Berkeley, CA: University of California Press.

Stern, A. M. (2005b). Sterilized in the name of public health: Race, immigration, and reproductive control in modern California. *American Journal of Public Health, 95,* 1128–1138. doi: 10.2105/AJPH.2004.041608

Stone, N., Ingham, R., & Gibbins, K. (2013). "Where do babies come from?" Barriers to early sexuality communication between parents and young children. *Sex Education, 13,* 228–240. doi: 10.1080/14681811.2012.737776

Sun, C., Bridges, A., Johnson, J. A., & Ezzell, M. B. (2016). Pornography and the male sexual script: An analysis of consumption and sexual relations. *Archives of Sexual Behavior, 45,* 983–994. doi: 10.1007/s10508-014-0391-2

Tantleff-Dunn, S., Barnes, R. D., & Larose, J. G. (2011). It's not just a "woman thing": The current state of normative discontent. *Eating Disorders, 19,* 392–402. doi: 10.1080/10640266.2011.609088

Tepper, M. S., Whipple, B., Richards, E., & Komisaruk, B. R. (2001). Women with complete spinal cord injury: A phenomenological study of sexual experiences. *Journal of Sex & Marital Therapy, 27,* 615–623. doi: 10.1080/713846817

Thackeray, A. D., & Readdick, C. A. (2003). Preschoolers' anatomical knowledge of salient and non-salient sexual and non-sexual body parts. *Journal of Research in Childhood Education, 18,* 141–148. doi: 10.1080/02568540409595029

Thompson, A. E., & Byers, E. S. (2017). Heterosexual young adults' interest, attitudes, and experiences related to mixed-gender, multi-person sex. *Archives of Sexual Behavior, 46,* 813–822. doi: 10.1007/s10508-016-0699-1

Tiggemann, M., & Hodgson, S. (2008). The hairlessness norm extended: Reasons for and predictors of women's body hair removal at different body sites. *Sex Roles, 59,* 889–897. doi: 10.1007/s11199-008-9494-3

Tolman, D. L. (2004). *Dilemmas of desire: Teenage girls talk about sexuality.* Cambridge, MA: Harvard University Press.

Tolman, D. L. (2006). In a different position: Conceptualizing female adolescent sexuality development within compulsory heterosexuality. In L. M. Diamond (Ed.), *Rethinking positive adolescent female sexual development* (pp. 71–89). San Francisco, CA: Jossey-Bass.

Tolman, D. L. (2012). Female adolescents, sexual empowerment and desire: A missing discourse of gender inequity. *Sex Roles, 66,* 746–757. doi: 10.1007/s11199-012-0122-x

Tolman, D. L., Anderson, S. M., & Belmonte, K. (2015). Mobilizing metaphor: Considering complexities, contradictions, and contexts in adolescent girls' and young women's sexual agency. *Sex Roles, 73*, 298–310. doi: 10.1007/s11199-015-0510-0

Travers, J., Tincani, M., Whitby, P. S., & Boutot, E. A. (2014). Alignment of sexuality education with self determination for people with significant disabilities: A review of research and future directions. *Education and Training in Autism and Developmental Disabilities, 49*, 232–247.

Trotter, E. C., & Alderson, K. G. (2007). University students' definitions of having sex, sexual partner, and virginity loss: The influence of participant gender, sexual experience, and contextual factors. *The Canadian Journal of Human Sexuality, 16*, 11–29.

Trussell, J. (2011). Contraceptive failure in the United States. *Contraception, 83*, 397–404. doi: 10.1016/j.contraception.2011.01.021

Twenge, J. M., Sherman, R. A., & Wells, B. E. (2016). Changes in American adults' reported same-sex sexual experiences and attitudes, 1973–2014. *Archives of Sexual Behavior, 45*, 1713–1730. doi: 10.1007/s10508-016-0769-4

U.S. Food and Drug Administration. (2015, August 18). *FDA approved first treatment for sexual desire disorder* [News release]. Retrieved from http://www.fda.gov/NewsEvents/Newsroom/PressAnnouncements/ucm458734.htm

Van Houdenhove, E., Gijs, L., T'Sjoen, G., & Enzlin, P. (2014). Asexuality: Few facts, many questions. *Journal of Sex & Marital Therapy, 40*, 175–192. doi: 10.1080/0092623X.2012.751073

Vrangalova, Z. (2015). Does casual sex harm college students' well-being? A longitudinal investigation of the role of motivation. *Archives of Sexual Behavior, 44*, 945–959. doi: 10.1007/s10508-013-0255-1

Walker, J. L. (2001). A qualitative study of parents' experiences of providing sex education for their children: The implications for health education. *Health Education Journal, 60*, 132–146. doi: 10.1177/001789690106000205

Walker, T. Y., Elam-Evans, L. D., Singleton, J. A., Yankey, D., Markowitz, L. E., Fredua, B., Williams, C. L., Meyer, S. A., & Stokley, S. (2017, August 25). National, regional, state, and selected local area vaccination coverage among adolescents aged 13–17 years: United States, 2016. *Morbidity and Mortality Weekly Report, 66*(33), 874–882. Retrieved from https://www.cdc.gov/mmwr/volumes/66/wr/pdfs/mm6633a2.pdf

Walsh, K. E., & Berman, J. R. (2004). Sexual dysfunction in the older woman: An overview of the current understanding and management. *Drugs & Aging, 21*, 655–675. doi: 10.2165/00002512-200421100-00004

Ward, L. M. (2003). Understanding the role of entertainment media in the sexual socialization of American youth: A review of empirical research. *Developmental Review, 23*, 347–388. doi: 10.1016/S0273-2297(03)00013-3

Ward, L. M., Seabrook, R. C., Grower, P., Giaccardi, S., & Lippman, J. R. (2018). Sexual object or sexual subject? Media use, self-sexualization, and sexual agency among undergraduate women. *Psychology of Women Quarterly, 42*, 29–43. doi: 10.1177/0361684317737940

Ward, L. M., Seabrook, R. C., Manago, A., & Reed, L. (2016). Contributions of diverse media to self-sexualization among undergraduate women and men. *Sex Roles, 74*, 12–23. doi: 10.1007/s11199-015-0548-z

Warren, C. (1995). Parent-child communication about sex. In T. J. Socha & G. H. Stamp (Eds.), *Parents, children, and communication: Frontiers of theory and research* (pp. 173–201). Hillsdale, NJ: Lawrence Erlbaum.

Watson, L. B., Robinson, D., Dispenza, F., & Nazari, N. (2012). African American women's sexual objectification experiences: A qualitative study. *Psychology of Women Quarterly, 36*, 458–475. doi: 10.1177/0361684312454724

Watson, R. J., Snapp, S., & Wang, S. (2017). What we know and where we go from here: A review of lesbian, gay, and bisexual youth hookup literature. *Sex Roles, 77*, 801–811. doi: 10.1007/s11199-017-0831-2

Weeks, L. (1998, April 26). Drug sparks questions of sexual politics. *The Washington Post.* Retrieved from http://www.washingtonpost.com/wp-srv/national/longterm/viagra/stories/viagra26.htm

Weitz, R. (2010). Changing the scripts: Midlife women's sexuality in contemporary U.S. film. *Sexuality & Culture, 14*, 17–32. doi: 10.1007/s12119-009-9057-y

Weitzer, R. (2007). The social construction of sex trafficking: Ideology and institutionalization of a moral crusade. *Politics & Society, 35*, 447–475. doi: 10.1177/0032329207304319

Weitzer, R. (2009). Sociology of sex work. *Annual Review of Sociology, 35*, 213–234. doi: 10.1146/annurev-soc-070308-120025

Weitzer, R. (2010). Sex work: Paradigms and policies. In R. Weitzer (Ed.), *Sex for sale: Prostitution, pornography, and the sex industry* (2nd ed., pp. 1–43). New York, NY: Routledge.

Wiederman, M. W. (2000). Women's body image self-consciousness during physical intimacy with a partner. *The Journal of Sex Research, 37*, 60–68. doi: 10.1080/00224490009552021

Wiederman, M. W. (2001). "Don't look now": The role of self-focus in sexual dysfunction. *The Family Journal, 9*, 210–214. doi: 10.1177/1066480701092020

Willoughby, B. J., & Vitas, J. (2012). Sexual desire discrepancy: The effect of individual differences in desired and actual sexual frequency on dating couples. *Archives of Sexual Behavior, 41*, 477–486. doi: 10.1007/s10508-011-9766-9

Wilson, E. K., Dalberth, B. T., Koo, H. P., & Gard, J. C. (2010). Parents' perspectives on talking to preteenage children about sex. *Perspectives on Sexual and Reproductive Health, 42*, 56–63. doi: 10.1363/4205610

Wisnieski, D., Sieving, R., & Garwick, A. (2015). Parent and family influences on young women's romantic and sexual decisions. *Sex Education, 15*, 144–157. doi: 10.1080/14681811.2014.986798

Wookey, M. L., Graves, N. A., & Butler, J. C. (2009). Effects of a sexy appearance on perceived competence of women. *The Journal of Social Psychology, 149*, 116–118. doi: 10.3200/SOCP.149.1.116-118

World Bank. (n.d.) *Adolescent fertility rate (births per 1,000 women ages 15–19).* Retrieved from http://data.worldbank.org/indicator/SP.ADO.TFRT

Wosick-Correa, K. R., & Joseph, L. J. (2008). Sexy ladies sexing ladies: Women as consumers in strip clubs. *Journal of Sex Research, 45*, 201–216. doi: 10.1080/00224490801987432

Yarber, W. L., Milhausen, R. R., Crosby, R. A., & Torabi, M. R. (2005). Public opinion about condoms for HIV and STD prevention: A Midwestern state telephone survey. *Perspectives on Sexual and Reproductive Health, 37*, 148–154. doi: 10.1363/3714805

Zelin, A. I., Erchull, M. J., & Houston, J. R. (2015). Is everybody doing it? Perceptions and misperceptions of sexual behavior in the college freshman population. *Gender Issues, 32*, 139–163. doi: 10.1007/s12147-015-9134-5

Zurbriggen, E. L., Ramsey, L. R., & Jaworski, B. K. (2011). Self- and partner-objectification in romantic relationships: Associations with media consumption and relationship satisfaction. *Sex Roles, 64*, 449–462. doi: 10.1007/s11199-011-9933-4

Chapter 8

Aassve, A., Fuochi, G., & Mencarini, L. (2014). Desperate housework: Relative resources, time availability, economic dependency, and gender ideology across Europe. *Journal of Family Issues, 35*, 1000–1022. doi: 10.1177/0192513X14522248

Abell, L., Brewer, G., Qualter, P., & Austin, E. (2016). Machiavellianism, emotional manipulation, and friendship functions in women's friendships. *Personality and Individual Differences*, *88*, 108–113. doi: 10.1016/j.paid.2015.09.001

Adler, P. A., & Adler, P. (1998). *Peer power: Preadolescent culture and identity*. New Brunswick, NJ: Rutgers University Press.

Afifi, W. A., & Faulkner, S. L. (2000). On being "just friends": The frequency and impact of sexual activity in cross-sex friendships. *Journal of Social and Personal Relationships*, *17*, 205–222. doi: 10.1177/0265407500172003

Ajrouch, K. J., Antonucci, T. C., & Janevic, M. R. (2001). Social networks among Blacks and Whites: The interaction between race and age. *The Journals of Gerontology Series B: Psychological Sciences and Social Sciences*, *56*, S112–S118. doi: 10.1093/geronb/56.2.S112

Alberts, J. K., Tracy, S. J., & Trethewey, A. (2011). An integrative theory of the division of domestic labor: Threshold level, social organizing and sensemaking. *Journal of Family Communication*, *11*, 21–38. doi: 10.1080/15267431.2011.534334

Amato, P. R., Booth, A., Johnson, D. R., & Rogers, S. J. (2007). *Alone together: How marriage in America is changing*. Cambridge, MA: Harvard University Press.

Amato, P. R., & Previti, D. (2003). People's reasons for divorcing: Gender, social class, the life course, and adjustment. *Journal of Family Issues*, *24*, 602–626. doi: 10.1177/0192513X03254507

Anapol, D. M. (1997). *Polyamory: The new love without limits*. San Rafael, CA: IntiNet Resource Center.

Archer, J. (2004). Sex differences in aggression in real-world settings: A meta-analytic review. *Review of General Psychology*, *8*, 291–322. doi: 10.1037/1089-2680.8.4.291

Armstrong, E. A., Hamilton, L. T., Armstrong, E. M., & Seeley, J. L. (2014). "Good girls": Gender, social class, and slut discourse on campus. *Social Psychology Quarterly*, *77*, 100–122. doi: 10.1177/0190272514521220

Askari, S. F., Liss, M., Erchull, M. J., Staebell, S. E., & Axelson, S. J. (2010). Men want equality, but women don't expect it: Young adults' expectations for participation in household and child care chores. *Psychology of Women Quarterly*, *34*, 243–252. doi: 10.1111/j.1471-6402.2010.01565.x

Atkinson, M. P., & Boles, J. (1984). WASP (wives as senior partners). *Journal of Marriage and the Family*, *46*, 861–870.

Auchmuty, R. (2012). Law and the power of feminism: How marriage lost its power to oppress women. *Feminist Legal Studies*, *20*, 71–87. doi: 10.1007/s10691-012-9197-6

Babcock, L., & Laschever, S. (2003). *Women don't ask: Negotiation and the gender divide*. Princeton, NJ: Princeton University Press.

Bachen, C. M., & Illouz, E. (1996). Imagining romance: Young people's cultural models of romance and love. *Critical Studies in Media Communication*, *13*, 279–308. doi: 10.1080/15295039609366983

Badahdah, A. M., & Tiemann, K. A. (2005). Mate selection criteria among Muslims living in America. *Evolution and Human Behavior*, *26*, 432–440. doi: 10.1016/j.evolhumbehav.2004.12.005

Baker, M., & Elizabeth, V. (2014). A "brave thing to do" or a normative practice? Marriage after long-term cohabitation. *Journal of Sociology*, *50*, 393–407. doi: 10.1177/1440783312462165

Barker, M. (2005). This is my partner, and this is my . . . partner's partner: Constructing a polyamorous identity in a monogamous world. *Journal of Constructivist Psychology*, *18*, 75–88. doi: 10.1080/10720530590523107

Barrantes, R. J., Eaton, A. A., Veldhuis, C. B., & Hughes, T. L. (2017). The role of minority stressors in lesbian relationship commitment and persistence over time. *Psychology of Sexual Orientation and Gender Diversity*, *4*, 205–217. doi: 10.1037/sgd0000221

Beals, K. P., Impett, E. A., & Peplau, L. A. (2002). Lesbians in love: Why some relationships endure and others end. *Journal of Lesbian Studies*, *6*, 53–63. doi: 10.1300/J155v06n01_06

Bermúdez, J. M., Sharp, E. A., & Taniguchi, N. (2015). Tapping into the complexity: Ambivalent sexism, dating, and familial beliefs among young Hispanics. *Journal of Family Issues*, *36*, 1274–1295. doi: 10.1177/0192513X13506706

Bernard, J. (1972). *The future of marriage*. New York, NY: World Publishing Times Mirror.

Bertrand, M., Kamenica, E., & Pan, J. (2015). Gender identity and relative income within households. *The Quarterly Journal of Economics*, *130*, 571–614. doi: 10.1093/qje/qjv001

Bevvino, D. L., & Sharkin, B. S. (2003). Divorce adjustment as a function of finding meaning and gender differences. *Journal of Divorce & Remarriage*, *39*, 81–97. doi: 10.1300/J087v39n03_04

Bianchi, S. M., Milkie, M. A., Sayer, L. C., & Robinson, J. (2000). Is anyone doing the housework? Trends in the gender division of household labor. *Social Forces*, *79*, 191–228. doi: 10.1093/sf/79.1.191

Bianchi, S. M., Sayer, L. C., Milkie, M. A., & Robinson, J. P. (2012). Housework: Who did, does or will do it, and how much does it matter? *Social Forces*, *91*, 55–63. doi: 10.1093/sf/sos120

Bittman, M., England, P., Sayer, L., Folbre, N., & Matheson, G. (2003). When does gender trump money? Bargaining and time in household work. *American Journal of Sociology*, *109*, 186–214. doi: 10.2307/3598347

Bogle, K. A. (2008). *Hooking up: Sex, dating, and relationships on campus*. New York, NY: New York University Press.

Bonomi, A. E., Altenburger, L. E., & Walton, N. L. (2013). "Double crap!" Abuse and harmed identity in Fifty Shades of Grey. *Journal of Women's Health*, *22*, 733–744. doi: 10.1089/jwh.2013.4344.

Boulton, M. J. (2013). Associations between adults' recalled childhood bullying victimization, current social anxiety, coping, and self-blame: Evidence for moderation and indirect effects. *Anxiety, Stress & Coping*, *26*, 270–292. doi: 10.1080/10615806.2012.662499

Bradshaw, C., Kahn, A. S., & Saville, B. K. (2010). To hook up or date: Which gender benefits? *Sex Roles*, *62*, 661–669. doi: 10.1007/s11199-010-9765-7

Brainerd, E. G., Hunter, P. A., Moore, D., & Thompson, T. R. (1996). Jealousy induction as a predictor of power and the use of other control methods in heterosexual relationships. *Psychological Reports*, *79*, 1319–1325. doi: 10.2466/pr0.1996.79.3f.1319

Brashier, E., Hughes, J. L., & Cook, R. E. (2013). A comparison of women in lesbian and heterosexual dual-income couples: Communication and conflict. *Psi Chi Journal of Psychological Research*, *18*, 170–175.

Brines, J. (1994). Economic dependency, gender, and the division of labor at home. *American Journal of Sociology*, *100*, 652–688.

Brinkman, B. G. (2015). *Detection and prevention of identity-based bullying: Social justice perspectives*. New York, NY: Routledge.

Brown, L. M. (2003). *Girlfighting: Betrayal and rejection among girls*. New York, NY: New York University Press.

Budnick, J. (2016). "Straight girls kissing"? Understanding same-gender sexuality beyond the elite college campus. *Gender & Society*, *30*, 745–768. doi: 10.1177/0891243216657511

Buss, D. M., & Schmitt, D. P. (1993). Sexual strategies theory: An evolutionary perspective on human mating. *Psychological Review*, *100*, 204–232. doi: 10.1037/0033-295X.100.2.204

Buss, D. M., Shackelford, T. K., & McKibbin, W. F. (2008). The mate retention inventory—short form (MRI-SF). *Personality and Individual Differences*, *44*, 322–334. doi: 10.1016/j.paid.2007.08.013

Butterfield, J., & Padavic, I. (2014). The impact of legal inequality on relational power in planned lesbian families. *Gender & Society, 28,* 752–774. doi: 10.1177/0891243214540794

Byrd-Craven, J., Geary, D. C., Rose, A. J., & Ponzi, D. (2008). Co-ruminating increases stress hormone levels in women. *Hormones and Behavior, 53,* 489–492. doi: 10.1016/j.yhbeh.2007.12.002

Carr, D., & Friedman, M. A. (2005). Is obesity stigmatizing? Body weight, perceived discrimination, and psychological well-being in the United States. *Journal of Health and Social Behavior, 46,* 244–259. doi: 10.1177/002214650504600303

Casad, B. J., Salazar, M. M., & Macina, V. (2014). The real versus the ideal: Predicting relationship satisfaction and well-being from endorsement of marriage myths and benevolent sexism. *Psychology of Women Quarterly, 39,* 119–129. doi: 10.1177/0361684314528304

Castro, F. N., Hattori, W. T., & de Araújo Lopes, F. (2015). Intra-sex variation in human mating strategies: Different people, different tactics. *Archives of Sexual Behavior, 44,* 1729–1736. doi: 10.1007/s10508-015-0533-1

Cénat, J. M., Blais, M., Hébert, M., Lavoie, F., & Guerrier, M. (2015). Correlates of bullying in Quebec high school students: The vulnerability of sexual-minority youth. *Journal of Affective Disorders, 183,* 315–321. doi: 10.1016/j.jad.2015.05.011

Chrisler, J. C. (2012). "Why can't you control yourself?" Fat *should be* a feminist issue. *Sex Roles, 66,* 608–616. doi: 10.1007/s11199-011-0095-1

Chun, H., & Lee, I. (2001). Why do married men earn more: Productivity or marriage selection? *Economic Inquiry, 39,* 307–319. doi: 10.1111/j.1465-7295.2001.tb00068.x

Chung, D. (2005). Violence, control, romance and gender equality: Young women and heterosexual relationships. *Women's Studies International Forum, 28,* 445–455. doi: 10.1016/j.wsif.2005.09.005

Cillessen, A. H., & Mayeux, L. (2004). From censure to reinforcement: Developmental changes in the association between aggression and social status. *Child Development, 75,* 147–163. doi: 10.1111/j.1467-8624.2004.00660.x

Civettini, N. (2016). Housework as non-normative gender display among lesbians and gay men. *Sex Roles, 74,* 206–219. doi: 10.1007/s11199-015-0559-9

Claes, M. E. (1992). Friendship and personal adjustment during adolescence. *Journal of Adolescence, 15,* 39–55. doi: 10.1016/0140-1971(92)90064-C

Claffey, S. T., & Mickelson, K. D. (2009). Division of household labor and distress: The role of perceived fairness for employed mothers. *Sex Roles, 60,* 819–831. doi: 10.1007/s11199-008-9578-0

Clarke-Stewart, A., & Brentano, C. (2006). *Divorce: Causes and consequences.* New Haven, CT: Yale University Press.

Collins, V. E., & Carmody, D. C. (2011). Deadly love images of dating violence in the "Twilight Saga." *Affilia, 26,* 382–394. doi:10.1177/0886109911428425

Coltrane, S. (2000). Research on household labor: Modeling and measuring the social embeddedness of routine family work. *Journal of Marriage and Family, 62,* 1208–1233. doi: 10.1111/j.1741-3737.2000.01208.x

Coltrane, S., Parke, R. D., & Adams, M. (2004). Complexity of father involvement in low-income Mexican American families. *Family Relations, 53,* 179–189. doi: 10.1111/j.0022-2445.2004.00008.x

Conley, T. D., Matsick, J. L., Moors, A. C., & Ziegler, A. (2017). Investigation of consensually nonmonogamous relationships: Theories, methods, and new directions. *Perspectives on Psychological Science, 12,* 205–232. doi: 10.1177/1745691616667925

Conley, T. D., Moors, A. C., Matsick, J. L., & Ziegler, A. (2013). The fewer the merrier? Assessing stigma surrounding consensually non-monogamous romantic relationships. *Analyses of Social Issues and Public Policy, 13,* 1–30. doi: 10.1111/j.1530-2415.2012.01286.x

Copen, C. E., Daniels, K., & Mosher, W. D. (2013, April 4). First premarital cohabitation in the United States: 2006–2010 National Survey of Family Growth. *National Health Statistics Reports,* No. 64. Retrieved from http://bibliobase.sermais.pt:8008/BiblioNET/Upload/PDF3/002491.pdf

Copen, C. E., Daniels, K., Vespa, J., & Mosher, W. D. (2012, March 22). First marriages in the United States: Data from the 2006–2010 National Survey of Family Growth. *National Health Statistics Reports,* No. 49. Retrieved from http://citeseerx.ist.psu.edu/viewdoc/download?doi=10.1.1.221.7460&rep=rep1&type=pdf

Craig, L., & Powell, A. (2018). Shares of housework between mothers, fathers and young people: Routine and non-routine housework, doing housework for oneself and others. *Social Indicators Research, 136,* 269–281. doi: 10.1007/s11205-016-1539-3

Crompton, R., & Lyonette, C. (2005). The new gender essentialism: Domestic and family "choices" and their relation to attitudes. *The British Journal of Sociology, 56,* 601–620. doi: 10.1111/j.1468-4446.2005.00085.x

Crouter, A., Head, M., Bumpus, M., & McHale, S. (2001). Household chores: Under what conditions do mothers lean on daughters? *New Direction for Child and Adolescent Development, 94,* 23–42. doi: 10.1002/cd.29

Cunningham, M. (2007). Influences of women's employment on the gendered division of household labor over the life course: Evidence from a 31-year panel study. *Journal of Family Issues, 28,* 422–444. doi: 10.1177/0192513X06295198

Currie, D. H. (1993). "Here comes the bride": The making of a "modern traditional" wedding in Western culture. *Journal of Comparative Family Studies, 24,* 403–421.

D'Angelo, J. D., & Toma, C. L. (2017). There are plenty of fish in the sea: The effects of choice overload and reversibility on online daters' satisfaction with selected partners. *Media Psychology, 20,* 1–27. doi: 10.1080/15213269.2015.1121827

Davies, K., Tropp, L. R., Aron, A., Pettigrew, T. F., & Wright, S. C. (2011). Cross-group friendships and intergroup attitudes: A meta-analytic review. *Personality and Social Psychology Review, 15,* 332–351. doi: 10.1177/1088868311411103

Delgado, M. Y., Ettekal, A. V., Simpkins, S. D., & Schaefer, D. R. (2016). How do my friends matter? Examining Latino adolescents' friendships, school belonging, and academic achievement. *Journal of Youth and Adolescence, 45,* 1110–1125. doi: 10.1007/s10964-015-0341-x

Dempsey, K., & De Vaus, D. (2004). Who cohabits in 2001? The significance of age, gender and religion. *Journal of Sociology, 40,* 157–178. doi: 10.1177/1440783304044028

DePaulo, B. M., & Morris, W. L. (2005). Singles in society and in science. *Psychological Inquiry, 16,* 57–83. doi: 10.1080/1047840X.2005.9682918

Dew, J., & Wilcox, W. B. (2011). If momma ain't happy: Explaining declines in marital satisfaction among new mothers. *Journal of Marriage and Family, 73,* 1–12. doi: 10.1111/j.1741-3737.2010.00782.x

Diamond, L. M. (2002). "Having a girlfriend without knowing it": The relationships of adolescent lesbian and bisexual women. *Journal of Lesbian Studies, 6,* 5–16. doi: 10.1300/J155v06n01_02

Donovan, C., & Hester, M. (2010). "I hate the word 'victim'": An exploration of recognition of domestic violence in same sex relationships. *Social Policy and Society, 9,* 279–289. doi: 10.1017/S1474746409990406

Dougherty, C. (2006). The marriage earnings premium as a distributed fixed effect. *Journal of Human Resources*, *41*, 433–443. doi: 10.3368/jhr.XLI.2.433

Downing, J. B., & Goldberg, A. E. (2011). Lesbian mothers' constructions of the division of paid and unpaid labor. *Feminism & Psychology*, *21*, 100–120. doi: 10.1177/0959353510375869

Dries, K. (2014, April 22). Oprah and Gayle's relationship is "bizarre, unhealthy" says ex-stepmom. *Jezebel*. Retrieved from http://jezebel.com/oprah-and-gayles-relationship-is-bizarre-unhealthy-say-1566117394

Ducharme, J. K., & Kollar, M. M. (2012). Does the "marriage benefit" extend to same-sex union? Evidence from a sample of married lesbian couples in Massachusetts. *Journal of Homosexuality*, *59*, 580–591. doi: 10.1080/00918369.2012.665689

Duffy, A. L., Penn, S., Nesdale, D., & Zimmer-Gembeck, M. J. (2017). Popularity: Does it magnify associations between popularity prioritization and the bullying and defending behavior of early adolescent boys and girls? *Social Development*, *26*, 263–277. doi: 10.1111/sode.12206

Dumas, T. M., Davis, J. P., & Ellis, W. E. (2017). Is it good to be bad? A longitudinal analysis of adolescent popularity motivations as a predictor of engagement in relational aggression and risk behaviors. *Youth & Society*. Advance online publication. doi: 10.1177/0044118X17700319

Duncan, S., Barlow, A., & James, G. (2005). Why don't they marry? Cohabitation, commitment and DIY marriage. *Child and Family Law Quarterly*, *17*, 383–398.

Eagly, A. H., & Wood, W. (1999). The origins of sex differences in human behavior: Evolved dispositions versus social roles. *American Psychologist*, *54*, 408–423. doi: 10.1037/0003-066X.54.6.408

Eastwick, P. W., Luchies, L. B., Finkel, E. J., & Hunt, L. L. (2014). The predictive validity of ideal partner preferences: A review and meta-analysis. *Psychological Bulletin*, *140*, 623–665. doi: 10.1037/a0032432

Eaton, A. A., & Rose, S. M. (2011). Has dating become more egalitarian? A 35-year review using *Sex Roles*. *Sex Roles*, *64*, 843–862. doi: 10.1007/s11199-011-9957-9

Eaton, A. A., & Rose, S. M. (2012). Scripts for actual first date and hanging-out encounters among young heterosexual Hispanic adults. *Sex Roles*, *67*, 285–299. doi: 10.1007/s11199-012-0190-y

Eaton, A. A., Rose, S. M., Interligi, C., Fernandez, K., & McHugh, M. (2015). Gender and ethnicity in dating, hanging out, and hooking up: Sexual scripts among Hispanic and White young adults. *The Journal of Sex Research*, *53*(7), 1–17. doi: 10.1080/00224499.2015.1065954

Egland, K. L., Spitzberg, B. H., & Zormeier, M. M. (1996). Flirtation and conversational competence in cross-sex platonic and romantic relationships. *Communication Reports*, *9*, 105–117. doi: 10.1080/08934219609367643

Erchull, M. J., Liss, M., Axelson, S. J., Staebell, S. E., & Askari, S. F. (2010). Well . . . she wants it more: Perceptions of social norms about desires for marriage and children and anticipated chore participation. *Psychology of Women Quarterly*, *34*, 253–260. doi: 10.1111/j.1471-6402.2010.01566.x

Erickson, R. J. (2005). Why emotion work matters: Sex, gender, and the division of household labor. *Journal of Marriage and Family*, *67*, 337–351. doi: 10.1111/j.0022 2445.2005.00120.x

Ettekal, I., & Ladd, G. W. (2015). Costs and benefits of children's physical and relational aggression trajectories on peer rejection, acceptance, and friendships: Variations by aggression subtypes, gender, and age. *Developmental Psychology*, *51*, 1756–1770. doi: 10.1037/dev0000057

Fan, P.-L., & Marini, M. M. (2000). Influences on gender-role attitudes during the transition to adulthood. *Social Science Research*, *29*, 258–283. doi: 10.1006/ssre.1999.0669

Felmlee, D. H. (1994). Who's on top? Power in romantic relationships. *Sex Roles*, *31*, 275–295. doi: 10.1007/BF01544589

Felmlee, D. H., Sweet, E., & Sinclair, H. C. (2012). Gender rules: Same- and cross-gender friendships norms. *Sex Roles*, *66*, 518–529. doi: 10.1007/s11199-011-0109-z

Ferguson, S. (2017, April 13). What the wedding industrial complex is—And how it's hurting our ideas of love. *Everyday Feminism*. Retrieved from https://everydayfeminism.com/2017/04/wedding-industrial-complex/

Fillo, J., Simpson, J. A., Rholes, W. S., & Kohn, J. L. (2015). Dads doing diapers: Individual and relational outcomes associated with the division of childcare across the transition to parenthood. *Journal of Personality and Social Psychology*, *108*, 298–316. doi: 10.1037/a0038572

Finkel, E. J., Eastwick, P. W., Karney, B. R., Reis, H. T., & Sprecher, S. (2012). Online dating: A critical analysis from the perspective of psychological science. *Psychological Science in the Public Interest*, *13*, 3–66. doi: 10.1177/1529100612436522

Forste, R., & Heaton, T. B. (2004). The divorce generation: Well-being, family attitudes, and socioeconomic consequences of marital disruption. *Journal of Divorce & Remarriage*, *41*, 95–114. doi: 10.1300/J087v41n01_06

Fowers, B. J. (1991). His and her marriage: A multivariate study of gender and marital satisfaction. *Sex Roles*, *24*, 209–221. doi: 10.1007/BF00288892

Frost, D. M., & Gola, K. A. (2015). Meanings of intimacy: A comparison of members of heterosexual and same-sex couples. *Analyses of Social Issues and Public Policy*, *15*, 382–400. doi: 10.1111/asap.12072

Frost, D. M., Meyer, I. H., & Hammack, P. L. (2014). Health and well-being in emerging adults' same-sex relationships: Critical questions and directions for research in developmental science. *Emerging Adulthood*, *3*, 3–13. doi: 10.1177/2167696814535915

Fuhrman, R. W., Flannagan, D., & Matamoros, M. (2009). Behavior expectations in cross-sex friendships, same-sex friendships, and romantic relationships. *Personal Relationships*, *16*, 575–596. doi: 10.1111/j.1475-6811.2009.01240.x

Fuwa, M. (2004). Macro-level gender inequality and the division of household labor in 22 countries. *American Sociological Review*, *69*, 751–767. doi: 10.1177/000312240406900601

Fuwa, M., & Cohen, P. N. (2007). Housework and social policy. *Social Science Research*, *36*, 512–530. doi: 10.1016/j.ssresearch.2006.04.005

Gable, S. L., Gonzaga, G. C., & Strachman, A. (2006). Will you be there for me when things go right? Supportive responses to positive event disclosures. *Journal of Personality and Social Psychology*, *91*, 904–917. doi: 10.1037/0022-3514.91.5.904

Gadalla, T. M. (2008). Impact of marital dissolution on men's and women's incomes: A longitudinal study. *Journal of Divorce & Remarriage*, *50*, 55–65. doi: 10.1080/10502550802365714

Gager, C. T. (2008). What's fair is fair? Role of justice in family labor allocation decisions. *Marriage & Family Review*, *44*, 511–545. doi: 10.1080/01494920802454116

Galician, M.-L. (2004). *Sex, love, and romance in the mass media: Analysis and criticism of unrealistic portrayals and their influence*. New York, NY: Routledge.

Galupo, M. P. (2007). Friendship patterns of sexual minority individuals in adulthood. *Journal of Social and Personal Relationships*, *24*, 139–151. doi: 10.1177/0265407506070480

Galupo, M. P. (2009). Cross-category friendship patterns: Comparison of heterosexual and sexual minority adults. *Journal of*

Social and Personal Relationships, 26, 811–831. doi: 10.1177 /0265407509345651

Galupo, M. P., & Gonzalez, K. A. (2013). Friendship values and cross-category friendships: Understanding adult friendship patterns across gender, sexual orientation and race. *Sex Roles, 68*, 779–790. doi: 10.1007/s11199-012-0211-x

Gatter, K., & Hodkinson, K. (2016). On the differences between Tinder versus online dating agencies: Questioning a myth. An exploratory study. *Cogent Psychology, 3*(1), 1162414. doi: 10.1080 /23311908.2016.1162414

Gillespie, B. J., Lever, J., Frederick, D., & Royce, T. (2015). Close adult friendships, gender, and the life cycle. *Journal of Social and Personal Relationships, 32*, 709–736. doi: 10.1177 /0265407514546977

Gjerdingen, D. K., & Center, B. A. (2005). First-time parents' postpartum changes in employment, childcare, and housework responsibilities. *Social Science Research, 34*, 103–116. doi: 10.1016/j.ssresearch.2003.11.005

Glenn, N., & Marquardt, E. (2001). *Hooking up, hanging out, and hoping for Mr. Right: College women on dating and mating today.* New York, NY: Institute for American Values.

Goldberg, A. E. (2013). "Doing" and "undoing" gender: The meaning and division of housework in same-sex couples. *Journal of Family Theory & Review, 5*, 85–104. doi: 10.1111/jftr.12009

Goldberg, A. E., & Perry-Jenkins, M. (2007). The division of labor and perceptions of parental roles: Lesbian couples across the transition to parenthood. *Journal of Social and Personal Relationships, 24*, 297–318. doi: 10.1177/0265407507075415

Goldberg, A. E., Smith, J. Z., & Perry-Jenkins, M. (2012). The division of labor in lesbian, gay, and heterosexual new adoptive parents. *Journal of Marriage and Family, 74*, 812–828. doi: 10.1111/j.1741-3737.2012.00992.x

Goldstein, J. R., & Kenney, C. T. (2001). Marriage delayed or marriage forgone? New cohort forecasts of first marriage for U.S. women. *American Sociological Review, 66*, 506–519.

Gonzalez, J. T. (1988). Dilemmas of the high-achieving Chicana: The double-bind factor in male/female relationships. *Sex Roles, 18*, 367–380. doi: 10.1007/BF00288389

Greenstein, T. N. (1996). Gender ideology and perceptions of the fairness of the division of household labor: Effects on marital quality. *Social Forces, 74*, 1029–1042. doi: 10.1093/sf/74.3.1029

Greenstein, T. N. (2000). Economic dependence, gender, and the division of labor in the home: A replication and extension. *Journal of Marriage and Family, 62*, 322–335. doi: 10.1111/j.1741-3737.2000.00322.x

Grøntvedt, T. V., & Kennair, L. E. O. (2013). Age preferences in a gender egalitarian society. *Journal of Social, Evolutionary, and Cultural Psychology, 7*, 239–249. doi: 10.1037/h0099199

Guillen, L. (2016, May 11). *Marriage rights and benefits.* Retrieved from http://www.nolo.com/legal-encyclopedia/marriage-rights -benefits-30190.html

Guner, N., Kulikova, Y., & Llull, J. (2014, November). *Does marriage make you healthier?* CEPR Discussion Paper No. DP10245. Retrieved from https://ssrn.com/abstract=2526358

Gupta, S. (2007). Autonomy, dependence, or display? The relationship between married women's earnings and housework. *Journal of Marriage and Family, 69*, 399–417. doi: 10.1111 /j.1741-3737.2007.00373.x

Guzzo, K. B. (2014). Trends in cohabitation outcomes: Compositional changes and engagement among never-married young adults. *Journal of Marriage and Family, 76*, 826–842. doi: 10.1111/jomf.12123

Haferkamp, C. J. (1999). Beliefs about relationships in relation to television viewing, soap opera viewing, and self-monitoring. *Current Psychology, 18*, 193–204. doi: 10.1007/s12144-999-1028-9

Haritaworn, J., Lin, C. J., & Klesse, C. (2006). Poly/logue: A critical introduction to polyamory. *Sexualities, 9*, 515–529. doi: 10.1177/1363460706069963

Hartup, W. W. (1996). The company they keep: Friendships and their developmental significance. *Child Development, 67*, 1–13. doi: 10.111/j.1467-8624.1996.tb01714.x

Hartwell, L. P., Humphries, T. M., Erchull, M. J., & Liss, M. (2015). Loving the green-eyed monster: Development and exploration of the Jealousy Is Good Scale. *Gender Issues, 32*, 245–265. doi: 10.1007/s12147-015-9141-6

Hayes, S. (2014). *Sex, love and abuse: Discourses on domestic violence and sexual assault.* New York, NY: Palgrave Macmillan.

Hefner, V., & Wilson, B. J. (2013). From love at first sight to soul mate: The influence of romantic ideals in popular films on young people's beliefs about relationship. *Communication Monographs, 80*, 150–175. doi: 10.1080/03637751.2013 .776697

Heino, R. D., Ellison, N. B., & Gibbs, J. L. (2010). Relationshopping: Investigating the market metaphor in online dating. *Journal of Social and Personal Relationships, 27*, 427–447. doi: 10.1177/0265407510361614

Hewitt, B., & De Vaus, D. (2009). Change in the association between premarital cohabitation and separation, Australia 1945–2000. *Journal of Marriage and Family, 71*, 353–361. doi: 10.1111/j.1741-3737.2009.00604.x

Hilton, J. M., & Anderson, T. L. (2009). Characteristics of women with children who divorce in midlife compared to those who remain married. *Journal of Divorce & Remarriage, 50*, 309–329. doi: 10.1080/10502550902766365

Hinkelman, L. (2013). *Girls without limits: Helping girls achieve healthy relationships, academic success, and interpersonal strength.* Thousand Oaks, CA: Corwin Press.

Hochschild, A., & Machung, A. (1989). *The second shift: Working parents and the revolution at home.* New York, NY: Penguin Group.

Howland, C. A., & Rintala, D. H. (2001). Dating behaviors of women with physical disabilities. *Sexuality and Disability, 19*, 41–70. doi: 10.1023/A:1010768804747

Institute for Women's Policy Research. (2017, September). *The gender wage gap: 2016* [Fact sheet]. Retrieved from https://iwpr .org/wp-content/uploads/2017/09/C459_9.11.17_Gender -Wage-Gap-2016-data-update.pdf

Jansen, L., Weber, T., Kraaykamp, G., & Verbakel, E. (2016). Perceived fairness of the division of household labor: A comparative study in 29 countries. *International Journal of Comparative Sociology, 57*, 53–68. doi: 10.1177/0020715216642267

Jeuken, E., Beersma, B., ten Velden, F. S., & Dijkstra, M. (2015). Aggression as a motive for gossip during conflict: The role of power, social value orientation, and counterpart's behavior. *Negotiation and Conflict Management Research, 8*, 137–152. doi: 10.1111/ncmr.12053

Jones, L. M., Mitchell, K. J., & Finkelhor, D. (2013). Online harassment in context: Trends from three youth internet safety surveys (2000, 2005, 2010). *Psychology of Violence, 3*, 53–69. doi: 10.1037/a0030309

Juvonen, J., Espinoza, G., & Knifsend, C. (2012). The role of peer relationships in student academic and extracurricular engagement. In S. L. Christenson, A. L. Reschly, & C. Wylie (Eds.), *Handbook of research on student engagement* (pp. 387–401). New York, NY: Springer.

Kamp Dush, C. M., Yavorsky, J. E., & Schoppe-Sullivan, S. J. (2018). What are men doing while women perform extra unpaid labor? Leisure and specialization at the transitions to parenthood. *Sex Roles, 78*, 715–730. doi: 10.1007/s11199-017 -0841-0

Kaplan, D. L., & Keys, C. B. (1997). Sex and relationship variables as predictors of sexual attraction in cross sex platonic friendships between young heterosexual adults. *Journal of Social and Personal Relationships, 14*, 191–206. doi: 10.1177/0265407597142003

Kaplan, R. M., & Kronick, R. G. (2006). Marital status and longevity in the United States population. *Journal of Epidemiology & Community Health, 60*, 760–765.

Kawamura, S., & Brown, S. L. (2010). Mattering and wives' perceived fairness of the division of household labor. *Social Science Research, 39*, 976–986. doi: 10.1016/j.ssresearch.2010.04.004

Kennedy J. E. (2009). Mitigating marginalization: A grounded theory of social and relational development for inclusive adolescents who are deaf or hard of hearing. *The CAEDHH Magazine, 9*, 17–24.

Kennedy, S., & Bumpass, L. (2008). Cohabitation and children's living arrangements: New estimates from the United States. *Demographic Research, 19*, 1663–1692. doi: 10.4054/DemRes.2008.19.47

Kim, D. A., Benjamin, E. J., Fowler, J. H., & Christakis, N. A. (2016). Social connectedness is associated with fibrinogen level in a human social network. *Proceedings of the Royal Society B, Biological Sciences, 283*, 20160958. doi: 10.1098/rspb.2016.0958

King, A. E., & Allen, T. T. (2009). Personal characteristics of the ideal African American marriage partner: A survey of adult black men and women. *Journal of Black Studies, 39*, 570–588. doi: 10.1177/0021934707299637

Kingery, J. N., Erdley, C. A., & Marshall, K. C. (2011). Peer acceptance and friendship as predictors of early adolescents' adjustment across the middle school transition. *Merrill-Palmer Quarterly, 57*, 215–243. doi: 10.1353/mpq.2011.0012

Klinkenberg, D., & Rose, S. (1994). Dating scripts of gay men and lesbians. *Journal of Homosexuality, 26*, 23–35. doi: 10.1300/J082v26n04_02

Korchmaros, J. D., Ybarra, M. L., & Mitchell, K. J. (2015). Adolescent online romantic relationship initiation: Differences by sexual and gender identification. *Journal of Adolescence, 40*, 54–64. doi: 10.1016/j.adolescence.2015.10.004

Kosciw, J., Greytak, E., Bartkiewicz, M. J., Boesen, M. J., & Palmer, N. A. (2012). *The 2011 National School Climate Survey: The experiences of lesbian, gay, bisexual, and transgender youth in our nation's schools.* New York, NY: Gay, Lesbian & Straight Education Network. Retrieved from http://files.eric.ed.gov/fulltext/ED535177.pdf

Kreager, D. A., & Staff, J. (2009). The sexual double standard and adolescent peer acceptance. *Social Psychology Quarterly, 72*, 143–164. doi: 10.1177/019027250907200205

Kroska, A. (2004). Divisions of domestic work: Revising and expanding the theoretical explanations. *Journal of Marriage and Family, 65*, 456–473. doi: 10.1177/0192513X04267149

Kupersmidt, J. B., DeRosier, M. E., & Patterson, C. P. (1995). Similarity as the basis for children's friendships: The roles of sociometric status, aggressive and withdrawn behavior, academic achievement and demographic characteristics. *Journal of Social and Personal Relationships, 12*, 439–452. doi: 10.1177/0265407595123007

Kurdek, L. A. (1995). Developmental changes in relationship quality in gay and lesbian cohabiting couples. *Developmental Psychology, 31*, 86–94. doi: 10.1037/0012-1649.31.1.86

Kurdek, L. A. (2007). The allocation of household labor by partners in gay and lesbian couples. *Journal of Family Issues, 28*, 132–148. doi: 10.1177/0192513X06292019

Lachance-Grzela, M., & Bouchard, G. (2010). Why do women do the lion's share of housework? A decade of research. *Sex Roles, 63*, 767–780. doi: 10.1007/s11199-010-9797-z

Lambert, T. A., Kahn, A. S., & Apple, K. J. (2003). Pluralistic ignorance and hooking up. *Journal of Sex Research, 40*, 129–133. doi: 10.1080/00224490309552174

Laner, M. R., & Ventrone, N. A. (2000). Dating scripts revisited. *Journal of Family Issues, 21*, 488–500. doi: 10.1177/019251300021004004

Lavelle, B., & Smock, P. J. (2012). Divorce and women's risk of health insurance loss. *Journal of Health and Social Behavior, 53*, 413–431. doi: 10.1177/0022146512465758

Lenton, A. P., & Webber, L. (2006). Cross-sex friendships: Who has more? *Sex Roles, 54*, 809–820. doi: 10.1007/s11199-006-9048-5

Levin, S., van Laar, C., & Sidanius, J. (2003). The effects of ingroup and outgroup friendship on ethnic attitudes in college: A longitudinal study. *Group Processes & Intergroup Relations, 6*, 76–92. doi: 10.1177/1368430203006001013

Lichter, D. T., Qian, Z., & Mellot, L. M. (2006). Marriage or dissolution? Union transitions among poor cohabiting women. *Demography, 43*, 223–240. doi: 10.1353/dem.2006.0016

Liddiard, K. (2018). *The intimate lives of disabled people.* New York, NY: Routledge.

Lippman, J. R., Ward, L. M., & Seabrook, R. C. (2014). Isn't it romantic? Differential associations between romantic screen media genres and romantic beliefs. *Psychology of Popular Media Culture, 3*, 128–140. doi: 10.1037/ppm0000034

Liss, M., & Schiffrin, H. H. (2014). *Balancing the big stuff: Finding happiness in work, family, and life.* Lanham, MD: Rowman & Littlefield.

Low, J. (1996). Negotiating identities, negotiating environments: An interpretation of the experiences of students with disabilities. *Disability & Society, 11*, 235–248. doi: 10.1080/09687599650023254

Luhamann, M., & Hawkey, L. C. (2016). Age differences in loneliness from late adolescence to old age. *Developmental Psychology, 52*, 943–959. doi: 10.1037/dev0000117

Lytle, A., & Levy, S. R. (2015). Reducing heterosexuals' prejudice toward gay men and lesbian women via an induced cross-orientation friendship. *Psychology of Sexual Orientation and Gender Diversity, 2*, 447–455. doi: 10.1037/sgd0000135

Maas, M. K., McDaniel, B. T., Feinberg, M. E., & Jones, D. E. (2018). Division of labor and multiple domains of sexual satisfaction among first-time parents. *Journal of Family Issues, 39*, 104–127. doi: 10.1177/0192513X15604343

Mahalik, J. R., Locke, B. D., Ludlow, L. H., Diemer, M. A., Scott, R. P., Gottfried, M., & Freitas, G. (2003). Development of the Conformity to Masculine Norms Inventory. *Psychology of Men & Masculinity, 4*, 123–131. doi: 10.1037/1524-9220.4.1.3

Mahalik, J. R., Morray, E. B., Coonerty-Femiano, A., Ludlow, L. H., Slattery, S. M., & Smiler, A. (2005). Development of the Conformity to Feminine Norms Inventory. *Sex Roles, 52*, 417–435. doi: 10.1007/s11199-005-3709-7

Manning, W. D., & Cohen, J. A. (2012). Premarital cohabitation and marital dissolution: An examination of recent marriages. *Journal of Marriage and Family, 74*, 377–387. doi: 10.1111/j.1741-3737.2012.00960.x

Mannino, C. A., & Deutsch, F. M. (2007). Changing the division of household labor: A negotiated process between partners. *Sex Roles, 56*, 309–324. doi: 10.1007/s11199-006-9181-1

Manzoli, L., Villari, P., Pirone, G. M., & Boccia, A. (2007). Marital status and mortality in the elderly: A systematic review and meta-analysis. *Social Science & Medicine, 64*, 77–94. doi: 10.1016/j.socscimed.2006.08.031

Marche, S. (2013, December 7). The case for filth. *The New York Times.* Retrieved from http://www.nytimes.com/2013/12/08/opinion/sunday/the-case-for-filth.html?pagewanted=3&_r=0&hp&rref=opinion

Marecek, J., Finn, S. E., & Cardell, M. (1982). Gender roles in the relationships of lesbians and gay men. *Journal of Homosexuality*, 8, 45–49. doi: 10.1300/J082v08n02_06

Marmot, M. G., & Wilkinson, R. G. (2006). *Social determinants of health*. Oxford, United Kingdom: Oxford University Press.

Martin, K. A., & Kazyak, E. (2009). Hetero-romantic love and heterosexiness in children's G-rated films. *Gender & Society*, 23, 315–336. doi: 10.1177/0891243209335635

Mazur, E. (2017). Diverse disabilities and dating online. In M. F. Wright (Ed.), *Identity, sexuality, and relationships among emerging adults in the digital age*. Hershey, PA: IGI Global.

McCullough, D., & Hall, D. S. (2003). Polyamory: What it is and what it isn't. *Electronic Journal of Human Sexuality*, 6. Retrieved from http://mail.ejhs.org/volume6/polyamory.htm

McLoyd, V. C., Cauce, A. M., Takeuchi, D., & Wilson, L. (2000). Marital processes and parental socialization in families of color: A decade review of research. *Journal of Marriage and Family*, 62, 1070–1093. doi: 10.1111/j.1741-3737.2000.01070.x

McPherson, M., Smith-Lovin, L., & Cook, J. M. (2001). Birds of a feather: Homophily in social networks. *Annual Review of Sociology*, 27, 415–444. doi: 10.1146/annurev.soc.27.1.415

Messman, S. J., Canary, D. J., & Hause, K. S. (2000). Motives to remain platonic, equity, and the use of maintenance strategies in opposite-sex friendships. *Journal of Social and Personal Relationships*, 17, 67–94. doi: 10.1177/0265407500171004

Mikula, G., Riederer, B., & Bodi, O. (2012). Perceived justice in the division of domestic labor: Actor and partner effects. *Personal Relationships*, 19, 680–695. doi: 10.1111/j.1475-6811.2011.01385.x

Monsour, M. (2002). *Women and men as friends: Relationships across the life span in the 21st century*. Mahwah, NJ: Erlbaum.

Moors, A. C., Rubin, J. D., Matsick, J. L., Ziegler, A., & Conley, T. D. (2014). It's not just a gay male thing: Sexual minority women and men are equally attracted to consensual non-monogamy. *Journal für Psychologie*, 22(1). Retrieved from https://www.journal-fuer-psychologie.de/index.php/jfp/article/view/325/356

Morgan, E. M., & Thompson, E. M. (2007). Young women's sexual experiences within same-sex friendships: Discovering and defining bisexual and bi-curious identity. *Journal of Bisexuality*, 6(3), 7–34. doi: 10.1300/J159v06n03_02

Murray-Close, D., Ostrov, J. M., & Crick, N. R. (2007). A short-term longitudinal study of growth of relational aggression during middle childhood: Associations with gender, friendship intimacy, and internalizing problems. *Development and Psychopathology*, 19, 187–203. doi: 10.1017/S0954579407070101

Nakamura, M., & Akiyoshi, M. (2015). What determines the perception of fairness regarding household division of labor between spouses? *PloS One*, 10, e0132608. doi: 10.1371/journal.pone.0132608

Niemann, Y. F., Romero, A., & Arbona, C. (2000). Effects of cultural orientation on the perception of conflict between relationship and education goals for Mexican American college students. *Hispanic Journal of Behavioral Sciences*, 22, 46–63. doi: 10.1177/0739986300221002

Noël, M. J. (2006). Progressive polyamory: Considering issues of diversity. *Sexualities*, 9, 602–620. doi: 10.1177/1363460706070003

Nudd, T. (2010, December 8). Oprah Winfrey: "I'm not a lesbian." *People*. Retrieved from http://www.people.com/people/article/0,,20447896,00.html

Ogletree, S. M. (2010). With this ring, I thee wed: Relating gender roles and love styles to attitudes towards engagement rings and weddings. *Gender Issues*, 27, 67–77. doi: 10.1007/s12147-010-9090-z

Online dating—Statistics & facts. (n.d.). Retrieved from https://www.statista.com/topics/2158/online-dating/

Online dating statistics. (2017, May 12). Retrieved from https://www.statisticbrain.com/online-dating-statistics/

Otero, H. (2009, January 22). Resentment: How an equal division of labor almost destroyed my marriage. *Babble*. Retrieved from: http://www.babble.com/mom/working-mom-and-stay-at-home-shared-parenting-marriage-trouble/

Papp, L. J., Liss, M., Erchull, M. J., Godfrey, H., & Waaland Kreutzer, L. (2016). The dark side of heterosexual romance: Endorsement of romantic beliefs relates to intimate partner violence. *Sex Roles*, 76, 99–109. doi: 10.1007/s11199-016-0668-0

Parrott, L., & Parrott, L. (2015). *Saving your marriage before it starts: Seven questions to ask before—and after—you marry*. Grand Rapids, MI: Zondervan.

Patterson, G. E., Ward, D. B., & Brown, T. B. (2013). Relationship scripts: How young women develop and maintain same-sex romantic relationships. *Journal of GLBT Family Studies*, 9, 179–201. doi: 10.1080/1550428X.2013.765263.

Pedersen, D. E. (2017). Quantity and quality: A more nuanced look at the association between family work and marital well-being. *Marriage & Family Review*, 53, 281–306. doi: 10.1080/01494929.2016.1177632

Pedersen, W. C., Putcha-Bhagavatula, A., & Miller, L. C. (2011). Are men and women really that different? Examining some of Sexual Strategies Theory (SST)'s key assumptions about sex-distinct mating mechanisms. *Sex Roles*, 64, 629–643. doi: 10.1007/s11199-010-9811-5

Peplau, L. A., & Fingerhut, A. W. (2007). The close relationships of lesbians and gay men. *Annual Review of Psychology*, 58, 405–424. doi: 10.1146/annurev.psych.58.110405.085701

Peplau, L. A., Padesky, C., & Hamilton, M. (1982). Satisfaction in lesbian relationships. *Journal of Homosexuality*, 8(2), 23–35. doi: 10.1300/J082v08n02_04

Pettigrew, T. F., & Tropp, L. R. (2008). How does intergroup contact reduce prejudice? Meta-analytic tests of three mediators. *European Journal of Social Psychology*, 38, 922–934. doi: 10.1002/ejsp.504

Pila, D. (2015). "I'm not good enough for anyone": Legal status and the dating lives of undocumented young adults. *Sociological Forum*, 31, 138–158. doi: 0.1111/socf.12237

Plummer, D. L., Stone, R. T., Powell, L., & Allison, J. (2016). Patterns of adult cross-racial friendships: A context for understanding contemporary race relations. *Cultural Diversity and Ethnic Minority Psychology*, 22, 479–494. doi: 10.1037/cdp0000079

Poortman, A. R., & Van der Lippe, T. (2009). Attitudes toward housework and child care and the gendered division of labor. *Journal of Marriage and Family*, 71, 526–541. doi: 10.1111/j.1741-3737.2009.00617.x

Popp, A. M., Peguero, A. A., Day, K. R., & Kahle, L. L. (2014). Gender, bullying victimization, and education. *Violence and Victims*, 29, 843–856. doi: 10.1891/0886-6708.VV-D-13-00047

Power, C., Koch, T., Kralik, D., & Jackson, D. (2006). Lovestruck: Women, romantic love and intimate partner violence. *Contemporary Nurse*, 21, 174–185. doi: 10.5172/conu.2006.21.2.174

Prigerson, H. G., Maciejewski, P. K., & Rosenheck, R. A. (1999). The effects of marital dissolution and marital quality on health and health service use among women. *Medical Care*, 37, 858–873.

Prinstein, M. J., Boergers, J., & Vernberg, E. M. (2001). Overt and relational aggression in adolescents: Social-psychological adjustment of aggressors and victims. *Journal of Clinical Child Psychology*, 30, 479–491. doi: 10.1207/S15374424JCCP3004_05

Puente, S., & Cohen, D. (2003). Jealousy and the meaning (or nonmeaning) of violence. *Personality and Social Psychology Bulletin, 29*, 449–460. doi: 10.1177/0146167202250912

Pullen, E., Perry, B., & Oser, C. (2014). African American women's preventative care usage: The role of social support and racial experiences and attitudes. *Sociology of Health & Illness, 36*, 1037–1053. doi: 10.1111/1467-9566.12141

Punyanunt-Carter, N. M. (2006). Love on television: Reality perception differences between men and women. *North American Journal of Psychology, 2*, 269–276.

Ramirez, A. J., & Zhang, S. (2007). When online meets offline: The effect of modality switching on relational communication. *Communication Monographs, 74*, 287–310. doi: 10.1080/03637750701543493

Reeder, H. M. (2000). "I like you . . . as a friend": The role of attraction in cross-sex friendship. *Journal of Social and Personal Relationships, 17*, 329–348. doi: 10.1177/0265407500173002

Regan, P. C., & Anguiano, C. (2010). Romanticism as a function of age, sex, and ethnicity. *Psychological Reports, 107*, 972–976. doi: 10.2466/07.09.21.PR0.107.6.972-976

Regan, P. C., Levin, L., Sprecher, S., Christopher, F. S., & Gate, R. (2000). Partner preferences: What characteristics do men and women desire in their short-term sexual and long-term romantic partners? *Journal of Psychology & Human Sexuality, 12*(3), 1–21. doi: 10.1300/J056v12n03_01

Regan, P. C., Medina, R., & Joshi, A. (2001). Partner preferences among homosexual men and women: What is desirable in a sex partner is not necessarily desirable in a romantic partner. *Social Behavior and Personality, 29*, 625–633. doi: 10.2224/sbp.2001.29.7.625

Reilly, M. E., & Lynch, J. M. (1990). Power-sharing in lesbian partnerships. *Journal of Homosexuality, 19*(3), 1–30. doi: 10.1300/J082v19n03_01

Reinhold, S. (2010). Reassessing the link between premarital cohabitation and marital instability. *Demography, 47*, 719–733. doi: 10.1353/dem.0.0122

Reizer, A., & Hetsroni, A. (2014). Media exposure and romantic relationship quality: A slippery slope? *Psychological Reports, 114*, 231–249. doi: 10.2466/21.07.PR0.114k11w6

Rendall, M. S., Weden, M. M., Favreault, M. M., & Waldron, H. (2011). The protective effect of marriage for survival: A review and update. *Demography, 48*, 481. doi: 10.1007/s13524-011-0032-5

Rich, A. (1980). Compulsory heterosexuality and lesbian existence. *Signs: Journal of Women in Culture and Society, 5*, 631–660. doi: 10.1086/493756

Ridgeway, C. L., & Smith-Lovis, L. (1999). Gender and interaction. In J. S. Chafetz (Ed.), *Handbook of the sociology of gender* (pp. 247–274). New York, NY: Plenum.

Rintala, D. H., Howland, C. A., Nosek, M. A., Bennett, J. L., Young, M. E., Foley, C. C., & . . . Chanpong, G. (1997). Dating issues for women with physical disabilities. *Sexuality and Disability, 15*, 219–242. doi: 10.1023/A:1024717313923

Robles, T. F., Slatcher, R. B., Trombello, J. M., & McGinn, M. M. (2014). Marital quality and health: A meta-analytic review. *Psychological Bulletin, 140*, 140–187. doi: 10.1037/a0031859

Rose, A. J. (2002). Co-rumination in the friendships of girls and boys. *Child Development, 73*, 1830–1843. doi: 10.1111/1467-8624.00509

Rose, C. A., Simpson, C. G., & Moss, A. (2015). The bullying dynamic: Prevalence of involvement among a large-scale sample of middle and high school youth with and without disabilities. *Psychology in the Schools, 52*, 515–531. doi: 10.1002/pits.21840

Rose, S. (1985). Is romance dysfunctional? *International Journal of Women's Studies, 8*, 250–265.

Rose, S., & Zand, D. (2000). Lesbian dating and courtship from young adulthood to midlife. *Journal of Gay & Lesbian Social Services, 11*, 77–104. doi: 10.1300/J041v11n02_04

Rose, S., Zand, D., & Cini, M. (1993). Lesbian courtship scripts. In E. D. Rothblum & K. A. Brehony (Eds.), *Boston marriages: Romantic but asexual relationships among contemporary lesbians* (pp. 70–85). Amherst, MA: University of Massachusetts Press.

Roth, M. E., & Gillis, J. M. (2015). "Convenience with the click of a mouse": A survey of adults with Autism Spectrum Disorder on online dating. *Sexuality and Disability, 33*, 133–150. doi: 10.1007/s11195-014-9392-2

Roy, R., Benenson, J. F., & Lilly, F. (2000). Beyond intimacy: Conceptualizing sex differences in same-sex friendships. *The Journal of Psychology, 134*, 93–101. doi: 10.1080/00223980009600852

Rubin, J. D., Moors, A. C., Matsick, J. L., Ziegler, A., & Conley, T. D. (2014). On the margins: Considering diversity among consensually non-monogamous relationships. *Journal für Psychologie, 22*(1). Retrieved from https://www.journal-fuer-psychologie.de/index.php/jfp/article/view/324/355

Rusbult, C. E. (1983). A longitudinal test of the investment model: The development (and deterioration) of satisfaction and commitment in heterosexual involvements. *Journal of Personality and Social Psychology, 45*, 101–117. doi: 10.1037/0021-9010.68.3.429

Salmon, N. (2013). "We just stick together": How disabled teens negotiate stigma to create lasting friendship. *Journal of Intellectual Disability Research, 57*, 347–358. doi: 10.1111/j.1365-2788.2012.01541.x

Saltes, N. (2013). Disability, identity and disclosure in the online dating environment. *Disability & Society, 28*, 96–109. doi: 10.1080/09687599.2012.695577

Schmidt, S. (2017, May 16). The wedding industry in 2017 and beyond. *Market Research Blog.* Retrieved from https://blog.marketresearch.com/the-wedding-industry-in-2017-and-beyond

Schwahn, L. (2018, February 26). Weddings are expensive: How to avoid falling into debt. *USA Today.* Retrieved from https://www.usatoday.com/story/money/personalfinance/budget-and-spending/2018/02/26/planning-wedding-start-budget/355294002/

Schweizer, G. (2018, February 19). The Knot's wedding survey shows how much people are spending to say "I do." *The Penny Hoarder.* Retrieved from https://www.thepennyhoarder.com/life/average-wedding-cost-2017/

Shackelford, T. K., Schmitt, D. P., & Buss, D. M. (2005). Universal dimensions of human mate preferences. *Personality and Individual Differences, 39*, 447–458. doi: 0.1016/j.paid.2005.01.023

Shapiro, J., & Kroeger, L. (1991). Is life just a romantic novel? The relationship between attitudes about intimate relationships and the popular media. *American Journal of Family Therapy, 19*, 226–236. doi: 10.1080/01926189108250854

Simmons, R. (2009). *The curse of the good girl: Raising authentic girls with courage and confidence.* New York, NY: Penguin.

Smart, C. (1984). *The ties that bind: Law, marriage and the reproduction of patriarchal relations.* London, United Kingdom: Routledge.

Smith, B. (2000). *Home girls: A Black feminist anthology.* New Brunswick, NJ: Rutgers University Press.

Smith, C. A., Konik, J. A., & Tuve, M. V. (2011). In search of looks, status, or something else? Partner preferences among butch and femme lesbians and heterosexual men and women. *Sex Roles, 64*, 658–668. doi: 10.1007/s11199-010-9861 8

Smith, J. A., McPherson, M., & Smith-Lovin, L. (2014). Social distance in the United States: Sex, race, religion, age, and education homophily among confidants, 1985 to 2004. *American Sociological Review, 79*, 432–456. doi: 10.1177/0003122414531776

Smock, P. J., Manning, W. D., & Gupta, S. (1999). The effect of marriage and divorce on women's economic well-being. *American Sociological Review, 64*, 794–812.

Sprecher, S., & Felmlee, D. (1997). The balance of power in romantic heterosexual couples over time from "his" and "her" perspectives. *Sex Roles, 37*, 361–379. doi: 10.1023/A:1025601423031

Sprecher, S., & Metts, S. (1989). Development of the Romantic Beliefs Scale and examination of the effects of gender and gender-role orientation. *Journal of Social and Personal Relationships, 6*, 387–411. doi: 10.1177/0265407589064001

Sprecher, S., Schmeekle, M., & Felmlee, D. (2006). The principle of least interest: Inequality in emotional involvement in romantic relationships. *Journal of Family Issues, 27*, 1255–1280. doi: 10.1177/0192513X06289215

staff writers. (2014, March 14). *Oprah Winfrey has opened up about her relationship with best friend Gayle King.* Retrieved from http://www.news.com.au/entertainment/celebrity-life/oprah-winfrey-has-opened-up-about-her-relationship-with-best-friend-gayle-king/story-fn907478-1226854347464

Stanik, C. E., & Ellsworth, P. C. (2010). Who cares about marrying a rich man? Intelligence and variation in women's mate preferences. *Human Nature, 21*, 203–217. doi: 10.1007/s12110-010-9089-x

Stanley, J. L. (2002). Young sexual minority women's perceptions of cross-generational friendships with older lesbians. *Journal of Lesbian Studies, 6*, 139–148. doi: 10.1300/J155v06n01_13

Steptoe, A., Shankar, A., Demakakos, P., & Wardle, J. (2013). Social isolation, loneliness, and all-cause mortality in older men and women. *Proceedings of the National Academy of Sciences of the United States of America, 110*, 5797–5801. doi: 10.1073/pnas.1219686110

Stevens, N. L., Martina, C. M., & Westerhof, G. J. (2006). Meeting the need to belong: Predicting effects of a friendship enrichment program for older women. *The Gerontologist, 46*, 495–502. doi: 10.1093/geront/46.4.495

Stevens, N. L., & Van Tilburg, T. G. (2011). Cohort differences in having and retaining friends in personal networks in later life. *Journal of Social and Personal Relationships, 28*, 24–43. doi: 0.1177/0265407510386191

Stevenson, B., & Wolfers, J. (2007). *Marriage and divorce: Changes and their driving forces* (NBER Working Paper No. 12944). Retrieved from http://www.nber.org/papers/w12944

Stone, P. (2007). *Opting out? Why women really quit careers and head home.* Los Angeles, CA: University of California Press.

Sullivan, O. (2011). An end to gender display through the performance of housework? A review and reassessment of the quantitative literature using insights from the qualitative literature. *Journal of Family Theory & Review, 3*, 1–13. doi: 10.1111/j.1756-2589.2010.00074.x

Symoens, S., Van de Velde, S., Colman, E., & Bracke, P. (2014). Divorce and the multidimensionality of men and women's mental health: The role of social-relational and socio-economic conditions. *Applied Research Quality Life, 9*, 197–214. doi: 10.1007/s11482-013-9239-5

Tach, L. M., & Eads, A. (2015). Trends in the economic consequences of marital and cohabitation dissolution in the United States. *Demography, 52*, 401–432. doi: 10.1007/s13524-015-0374-5

Taylor, S. E. (2011). Social support: A review. In H. S. Friedman (Ed.), *The Oxford handbook of health psychology* (pp. 189–214). New York, NY: Oxford University Press.

Taylor, S. E., Klein, L. C., Lewis, B. P., Gruenewald, T. L., Gurung, R. A., & Updegraff, J. A. (2000). Biobehavioral responses to stress in females: Tend-and-befriend, not fight-or-flight. *Psychological Review, 107*, 411–429. doi:10.1037//0033-295X.107.3.411

TEDx Talks. (2015, May 19). *Every body: Glamour, datability, sexuality & disability: Dr. Danielle Sheypuk.* Retrieved from https://www.youtube.com/watch?v=7PwvGfs6Pok

Thompson, E. M. (2007). Girl friend or girlfriend? Same-sex friendship and bisexual images as a context for flexible sexual identity among young women. *Journal of Bisexuality, 6*(3), 47–67. doi: 10.1300/J159v06n03_04

Treas, J., & Tai, T. (2016). Gender inequality in housework across 20 European nations: Lessons from gender stratification theories. *Sex Roles, 74*, 495–511. doi: 10.1007/s11199-015-0575-9

Turner, R. N., & Feddes, A. R. (2011). How intergroup friendship works: A longitudinal study of friendship effects on outgroup attitudes. *European Journal of Social Psychology, 41*, 914–923. doi: 10.1002/ejsp.843

Underwood, M. K. (2004). Glares of contempt, eye rolls of disgust and turning away to exclude: Non-verbal forms of social aggression among girls. *Feminism & Psychology, 14*, 371–375. doi: 10.1177/0959-353504044637

United Nations, Department of Economic and Social Affairs, Population Division. (2015). *World marriage data 2015.* Retrieved from http://www.un.org/en/development/desa/population/theme/marriage-unions/WMD2015.shtml

United States Bureau of Labor Statistics. (n.d.). *Average hours per day parents spent caring for and helping household children as their main activity.* Retrieved from https://www.bls.gov/charts/american-time-use/activity-by-parent.htm

United States Bureau of Labor Statistics. (2016, December 20). *Charts by topic: Household activities.* Retrieved from https://www.bls.gov/tus/charts/household.htm

United States Census Bureau. (n.d.) *Historical marital status tables.* Retrieved from https://www.census.gov/data/tables/time-series/demo/families/marital.html

United States Department of Education. (2015, May 12). *New data show a decline in school-based bullying* [Press release]. Retrieved from https://www.ed.gov/news/press-releases/new-data-show-decline-school-based-bullying

Van Bavel, J., Schwartz, C., & Esteve, A. (2018). The reversal of the gender gap in education and its consequences for family life. *Annual Review of Sociology.* Advance online publication.

Vandello, J. A., & Cohen, D. (2008). Culture, gender, and men's intimate partner violence. *Social and Personality Psychology Compass, 2*, 652–667. doi:10.1111/j.1751-9004.2008.00080.x

Vătămănescu, E.-M., Andrei, A. G., & Pînzaru, F. (2018). Investigating the online social network development through the Five Cs Model of Similarity: The Facebook case. *Information Technology & People, 31*, 84–110. doi: 10.1108/ITP-06-2016-0135

Verbrugge, L. M. (1977). The structure of adult friendship choices. *Social Forces, 56*, 576–597. doi: 10.1093/sf/56.2.576

Wada, M., Mortenson, W. B., & Hurd Clarke, L. (2016). Older adults' online dating profiles and successful aging. *Canadian Journal on Aging, 35*, 479–490. doi: 10.1017/S0714980816000507

Waite, L. J. (1995). Does marriage matter? *Demography, 32*, 483–507. doi: 10.2307/2061670

Waite, L. J., & Gallagher, M. (2000). *The case for marriage: Why married people are happier, healthier, and better off financially.* New York, NY: Doubleday.

Walker, K. (1994). Men, women, and friendship: What they say, what they do. *Gender & Society, 8*, 246–265. doi: 10.1177/089124394008002007

Wallace, B., Thomson, K. N., & Sher, L. (2010, December 8). Oprah Winfrey: "I'm not a lesbian." *ABC News.* Retrieved from http://abcnews.go.com/Entertainment/oprah-winfrey-relationship-gayle-king-im-lesbian/story?id=12334032

Waller, W. (1938). *The family: A dynamic interpretation.* New York, NY: Gordon.

Weger, H., Jr., & Emmett, M. C. (2009). Romantic intent, relationship uncertainty, and relationship maintenance in young adults' cross-sex friendships. *Journal of Social and Personal Relationships, 26,* 964–988. doi: 10.1177/0265407509347937

Whitty, M. T., & Carr, A. (2006). *Cyberspace romance: The psychology of online relationships.* New York, NY: Palgrave Macmillan.

Wilson, C. M., & Oswald, A. J. (2005). How does marriage affect physical and psychological health? A survey of the longitudinal evidence. *IZA Discussion Paper,* No. 1619. Retrieved from http://papers.ssrn.com/sol3/Papers.cfm?abstract_id=735205

Wu, P., & Chiou, W. (2009). More options lead to more searching and worse choices in finding partners for romantic relationships online: An experimental study. *CyberPsychology & Behavior, 12,* 315–318. doi:10.1089/cpb.2008.0182

Yalom, I. D. (2013). *Love's executioner.* London, United Kingdom: Penguin.

Yavorsky, J. E., Kamp Dush, C. M., & Schoppe-Sullivan, S. J. (2015). The production of inequality: The gender division of labor across the transition to parenthood. *Journal of Marriage and Family, 77,* 662–679. doi: 10.1111/jomf.12189

Ziegler, A., Matsick, J. L., Moors, A. C., Rubin, J. D., & Conley, T. D. (2014). Does monogamy harm women? Deconstructing monogamy with a feminist lens. *Journal für Psychologie, 22*(1). Retrieved from https://www.journal-fuer-psychologie.de/index.php/jfp/article/view/323/354

Chapter 9

Abajobir, A. A., Kisely, S., & Najman, J. M. (2017). A systematic review of unintended pregnancy in cross-cultural settings. *The Ethiopian Journal of Health Development (EJHD), 31,* 138–154.

Abel, E. (2004). Paternal contribution to fetal alcohol syndrome. *Addiction Biology, 9,* 127–133. doi: 10.1080/13556210410001716980

Acker, M. (2009). Breast is best . . . But not everywhere: Ambivalent sexism and attitudes toward private and public breastfeeding. *Sex Roles, 61,* 476–490. doi: 10.1007/s11199-009-9655-z

Ahumuza, S. E., Matovu, J. K., Ddamulira, J. B., & Muhanguzi, F. K. (2014). Challenges in accessing sexual and reproductive health services by people with physical disabilities in Kampala, Uganda. *Reproductive Health, 11.* doi: 10.1186/1742-4755-11-59

Albertini, M., & Mencarini, L. (2014). Childlessness and support networks in later life: New pressures on familistic welfare states? *Journal of Family Issues, 35,* 331–357. doi: 10.1177/0192513X12462537

Allan, J. (2004). Mother blaming: A covert practice in therapeutic intervention. *Australian Social Work, 57,* 57–70. doi: 10.1111/j.0312-407X.2003.00114.x

Allen, S. M., & Hawkins, A. J. (1999). Maternal gatekeeping: Mothers' beliefs and behaviors that inhibit greater father involvement in family work. *Journal of Marriage and the Family, 61,* 199–212. doi: 10.2307/353894

American College of Obstetricians and Gynecologists (2009, February 20). *ACOG issues new guidelines on managing stillbirths.* Retrieved from http://www.acog.org/About-ACOG/News-Room/News-Releases/2009/ACOG-Issues-New-Guidelines-on-Managing-Stillbirths

American College of Obstetricians and Gynecologists Committee on Gynecologic Practice & The Practice Committee of the American Society for Reproductive Medicine. (2014, March). *Female age-related fertility decline* (Committee Opinion No. 589). Retrieved from https://www.acog.org/-/media/Committee-Opinions/Committee-on-Gynecologic-Practice/co589.pdf?dmc=1&ts=20180219T1557207082

American Psychological Association. (2008). *Report of the APA task force on mental health and abortion.* Washington, DC: Author. Retrieved from http://www.apa.org/pi/women/programs/abortion/mental-health.pdf

An overview of abortion laws. (2018, March 1). *The Guttmacher Institute.* Retrieved from https://www.guttmacher.org/state-policy/explore/overview-abortion-laws

Arendell, T. (2000). Conceiving and investigating motherhood: The decade's scholarship. *Journal of Marriage and Family, 62,* 1192–1207. doi: 10.1111/j.1741-3737.2000.01192.x

Arora, S., McJunkin, C., Wehrer, J., & Kuhn, P. (2000). Major factors influencing breastfeeding rates: Mother's perception of father's attitude and milk supply. *Pediatrics, 106,* 1–5. doi: 10.1542/peds.106.5.e67

Askari, S. F., Liss, M., Erchull, M. J., Staebell, S. E., & Axelson, S. J. (2010). Men want equality, but women don't expect it: Young adults' expectations for participation in household and child care. *Psychology of Women Quarterly, 34,* 243–252. doi: 10.1111/j.1471-6402.2010.01565.x

Associated Press. (2015, July 20). Mom accused of leaving kids at food court for job interview. *CBS News.* Retrieved from http://www.cbsnews.com/news/texas-mom-accused-of-leaving-kids-at-food-court-during-job-interview/

Attanasio, L., McPherson, M., & Kozhimannil, K. (2014). Positive childbirth experiences in U.S. hospitals: A mixed methods analysis. *Maternal and Child Health Journal, 18,* 1280–1290. doi: 10.1007/s10995-013-1363-1

Bahadur, N. (2018, January 8). The cost of infertility: This is how real people pay for IVF. *Self.* Retrieved from https://www.self.com/story/the-cost-of-infertility

Baldwin, K., Culley, L., Hudson, N., & Mitchell, H. (2014). Reproductive technology and the life course: Current debates and research in social egg freezing. *Human Fertility, 17,* 170–179. doi: 10.3109/14647273.2014.939723

Bankole, A., Singh, S., & Haas, T. (1998). Reasons why women have induced abortions: Evidence from 27 countries. *International Family Planning Perspectives, 24,* 117–152. doi: 10.2307/3038208

Bar, S., Milanaik, R., & Adesman, A. (2016). Long-term neurodevelopmental benefits of breastfeeding. *Current Opinion in Pediatrics, 28,* 559–566. doi: 10.1097/MOP.0000000000000389

Barnard, W. M. (2004). Parent involvement in elementary school and educational attainment. *Children and Youth Services Review, 26,* 39–62. doi: 10.1016/j.childyouth.2003.11.002

Bartels, J. S. (2015). Parents' growing pains on social media: Modeling authenticity. *Character and Social Media, 1,* 51–70.

Beaujouan, E., Sobotka, T., Brzozowska, Z., & Zeman, K. (2017). Has childlessness peaked in Europe? *Population and Societies, 540,* 1–4.

Bell, A. (2009). "It's way out of my league": Low-income women's experiences of medicalized infertility. *Gender and Society, 23,* 688–709. doi: 10.1177/089124320934370

Belluck, P. (2016, January 26). Panel calls for depression screenings before and after pregnancy. *The New York Times.* Retrieved from http://www.nytimes.com/2016/01/27/health/post-partum-depression-test-epds-screening-guidelines.html?_r=1

Berger, A. P., Potter, E. M., Shutters, C. M., & Imborek, K. L. (2015). Pregnant transmen and barriers to high quality healthcare. *Proceedings in Obstetrics and Gynecology, 5*(2), Article 3. Retrieved from http://ir.uiowa.edu/pog/vol5/iss2/3

Berna, C. (2014, April 21). 34 embryos: My soul-crushing struggle with fertility. *Everyday Health.* Retrieved from http://www.everydayhealth.com/columns/my-health-story/embryos-my-soul-crushing-struggle-with-infertility/

Biehle, S. N., & Mickelson, K. D. (2012). First-time parents' expectations about the division of childcare and play. *Journal of Family Psychology, 26,* 36–45. doi: 10.1037/a0026608

Biggs, M. A., Upadhyay, U. D., McCulloch, C. E., & Foster, D. G. (2017). Women's mental health and well-being 5 years after receiving or being denied an abortion: A prospective, longitudinal cohort study. *JAMA Psychiatry, 74*, 169–178. doi: 10.1001/jamapsychiatry.2016.3478

Boivin, M., & Hassan, G. (2015). Ethnic identity and psychological adjustment in transracial adoptees: A review of the literature. *Ethnic and Racial Studies, 38*, 1084–1103. doi: 10.1080/01419870.2014.992922

Boustani, M. M., Frazier, S. L., Hartley, C., Meinzer, M., & Hedemann, E. (2015). Perceived benefits and proposed solutions for teen pregnancy: Qualitative interviews with youth care workers. *American Journal of Orthopsychiatry, 85*, 80–92. doi: 10.1037/ort0000040.

Brodzinsky, D. (2006). Family structural openness and communication openness as predictors in the adjustment of adopted children. *Adoption Quarterly, 9*, 1–18. doi: 10.1300/J145v09n04_01

Brodzinsky, D., & Smith, S. L. (2014). Post-placement adjustment and the needs of birthmothers who place an infant for adoption. *Adoption Quarterly, 17*, 165–184. doi: 10.1080/10926755.2014.891551

Burrows, J. (2001). The parturient woman: Can there be room for more than "one person with full and equal rights inside a single human skin"? *Journal of Advances in Nursing, 33*, 689–695. doi: 10.1046/j.1365-2648.2001.01700.x

Cacciatore, J., Schnebly, S., & Froen, J. (2009). The effects of social support on maternal anxiety and depression after stillbirth. *Health & Social Care in the Community, 17*, 167–176. doi: 10.1111/j.1365-2524.2008.00814.x

Campbell-Jackson, L., & Horsch, A. (2014). The psychological impact of stillbirth on women: A systematic review. *Illness, Crisis, & Loss, 22*, 237–256. doi: 10.2190/IL.22.3.d

Caplan, P., & Hall-McCorquodale, I. (1985). Mother-blaming in major clinical journals. *American Journal of Orthopsychiatry, 55*, 345–353. doi: 10.1111/j.1939-0025.1985.tb03449.x

Caughey, A. B., Cahill, A. G., Guise, J. M., & Rouse, D. J. (2014). Safe prevention of the primary cesarean delivery. *American Journal of Obstetrics & Gynecology, 210*, 179–193. doi: 10.1016/j.ajog.2014.01.026

Ceballo, R., Graham, E. T., & Hart, J. (2015). Silent and infertile: An intersectional analysis of the experiences of socioeconomically diverse African American women with infertility. *Psychology of Women Quarterly, 39*, 497–511, doi: 10.1177/0361684315581169

Centers for Disease Control and Prevention. (2016a). *Breastfeeding report card: Progressing toward national breastfeeding goals, United States, 2016.* Atlanta, GA: Author. Retrieved from https://www.cdc.gov/breastfeeding/pdf/2016breastfeedingreportcard.pdf

Centers for Disease Control and Prevention. (2016b, February 2). *More than 3 million U.S. women at risk for alcohol-exposed pregnancy.* Retrieved from http://www.cdc.gov/media/releases/2016/p0202-alcohol-exposed-pregnancy.html

Centers for Disease Control and Prevention. (2017, March 7). *Facts about stillbirth.* Retrieved from http://www.cdc.gov/ncbddd/stillbirth/facts.html

Centers for Disease Control and Prevention. (2018, January 2). *Infant mortality.* Retrieved from https://www.cdc.gov/reproductivehealth/maternalinfanthealth/infantmortality.htm

Chandler, M. A. (2018, January 19). "Badass. Prolife. Feminist." How the "pro-life feminist" movement is straddling the March for Life and Women's March. *The Washington Post.* Retrieved from https://www.washingtonpost.com/news/acts-of-faith/wp/2018/01/19/this-weekend-many-members-of-the-growing-pro-life-feminist-movement-plan-to-attend-both-the-march-for-life-and-the-womens-march/?utm_term=.2c0ef56c545f

Chandra, A., Copen, C., & Stephen, E. (2014). Infertility service use in the United States: Data from the national survey of family growth, 1982–2010. *Natl Health Stat Report, 73*, 1–21.

Child Welfare Information Gateway. (2015a, August). *Adoption options: Where do I start?* Washington, DC: U.S. Department of Health and Human Services, Children's Bureau. Retrieved from https://www.childwelfare.gov/pubPDFs/f_adoptoption.pdf

Child Welfare Information Gateway. (2015b, October). *The adoption home study process.* Washington, DC: U.S. Department of Health and Human Services, Children's Bureau. Retrieved from https://www.childwelfare.gov/pubpdfs/f_homstu.pdf

Childlessness rises for women in their early 30s. (2017, May 3). *Census Blogs: Random Samplings.* Retrieved from https://census.gov/newsroom/blogs/random-samplings/2017/05/childlessness_rises.html

Cockrill, K., & Nack, A. (2013). "I'm not that type of person": Managing the stigma of having an abortion. *Deviant Behavior, 34*, 973–990. doi: 10.1080/01639625.2013.800423

Coley, R. L., & Lombardi, C. M. (2013). Does maternal employment following childbirth support or inhibit low-income children's long-term development? *Child Development, 84*, 178–197. doi: 0.1111/j.1467-8624.2012.01840.x

Colker, R. (2015). Blaming mothers: A disability perspective. *Ohio State Public Law Working Paper, 295*, 1205–1224. doi: 10.2139/ssrn.2604972

Comparing the costs of domestic, international, and foster care adoption. (n.d.). *American Adoptions.* Retrieved from http://www.americanadoptions.com/adopt/the_costs_of_adopting

Courcy, I., & des Rivières, C. (2017). "From cause to cure": A qualitative study on contemporary forms of mother blaming experienced by mothers of young children with autism spectrum disorder. *Journal of Family Social Work, 20*, 233–250. doi: 10.1080/10522158.2017.1292184

Cousineau, T., & Dumar, A. (2007). Psychological impact of infertility. *Best Practice & Research Clinical Obstetrics and Gynaecology, 21*, 293–308. doi: 10.1016/j.bpobgyn.2006.12.003

Creanga, A. A., Berg, C. J., Syverson, C., Seed, K., Bruce, F. C., & Callaghan, W. M. (2015). Pregnancy-related mortality in the United States, 2006–2010. *Obstetrics & Gynecology, 125*, 5–12. doi: 10.1097/AOG.0000000000000564

Cronin, C. (2003). First-time mothers: Identifying their needs, perceptions and experiences. *Journal of Clinical Nursing, 12*, 260–267. doi: 10.1046/j.1365-2702.2003.00684.x

Dadlez, E. M., & Andrews, W. L. (2010). Post-abortion syndrome: Creating an affliction. *Bioethics, 24*, 445–452. doi: 10.1111/j.1467-8519.2009.01739.x

Dahl, B., & Malterud, K. (2015). Neither father nor biological mother. A qualitative study about lesbian co-mothers' maternity care experiences. *Sexual & Reproductive Healthcare, 6*, 169–173. doi: 10.1016/j.srhc.2015.02.002

Davenport, D. (2010, February 16). *Surviving the dreaded adoption home study.* Retrieved from https://creatingafamily.org/adoption-category/surviving-dreaded-homestudy/

David, H. P. (2006). Born unwanted, 35 years later: The Prague study. *Reproductive Health Matters, 14*, 181–190. doi: 10.1016/S0968-8080(06)27219-7

David, R., & Collins, J., Jr. (2007). Disparities in infant mortality: What's genetics got to do with it? *American Journal of Public Health, 97*, 1191–1197. doi: 10.2105/AJPH.2005.068387

de Beauvoir, S. (1949). *The second sex.* New York, NY: Vintage Books.

Debest, C., & Mazuy, M. (2014). Childlessness: A life choice that goes against the norm. *Population & Societies, 508*, 1–4.

Declercq, E., Sakala, C., Corry, M., & Applebaum, S. (2007). Listening to mothers II: Report of the second national U.S. survey of women's childbearing experiences. *The Journal of Perinatal Education, 16*, 9–14. doi: 10.1624/105812407X244769

Deonandan, R., Green, S., & van Beinum, A. (2012). Ethical concerns for maternal surrogacy and reproductive tourism. *Journal of Medical Ethics, 38*, 742–745. doi: 10.1136/medethics-2012-100551

De Roo, C., Tilleman, K., T'Sjoen, G., & De Sutter, P. (2016). Fertility options in transgender people. *International Review of Psychiatry, 28*, 112–119, doi: 10.3109/09540261.2015.1084275

De Sutter, P., Kira, K., Verschoor, A., & Hotimsky, A. (2002). The desire to have children and the preservation of fertility in transsexual women: A survey. *International Journal of Transgenderism, 6*(3). Retrieved from https://www.atria.nl/ezines/web/IJT/97-03/numbers/symposion/ijtvo06no03_02.htm

Dew, J., & Wilcox, W. B. (2011). If momma ain't happy: Explaining declines in marital satisfaction among new mothers. *Journal of Marriage and Family, 73*, 1–12. doi: 10.1111/j.1741-3737.2010.00782.x

Dhillon, J., & Lefebvre, C. (2011, July 29). Fact sheet: Women with disabilities and legal issues concerning reproductive health. *National Health Law Program.* Retrieved from http://www.healthlaw.org/about/staff/jina-dhillon/all-publications/women-with-disabilities-and-legal-reproductive-health-issues#.WrBXoyIpCEc

Dillaway, H., & Pare, E. (2008). Locating mothers: How cultural debates about stay-at-home versus working mothers define women and home. *Journal of Family Issues, 29*, 437–464. doi: 10.1177/0192513X07310309

Dodge, L., Penzias, A., & Hacker, M. (2017). The impact of male partner age on cumulative incidence of live birth following in vitro fertilization. *Human Reproduction, 32*, 80–81.

Dokoupil, T. (2009, April 22). What adopting a White girl taught one Black family. *Newsweek.* Retrieved from http://www.newsweek.com/what-adopting-white-girl-taught-one-black-family-77335

Donnelly, K., Twenge, J. M., Clark, M. A., Shaikh, S. K., Beiler-May, A., & Carter, N. T. (2016). Attitudes toward women's work and family roles in the United States, 1976–2013. *Psychology of Women Quarterly, 40*, 41–54. doi: 10.1177/0361684315590774

Dørheim, S. K., Bondevik, G. T., Eberhard-Gran, M., & Bjorvatn, B. (2009). Sleep and depression in postpartum women: A population-based study. *Sleep, 32*, 847–55. doi: 10.1093/sleep/32.7.847

Dworkin, S., & Wachs, F. (2004). "Getting your body back": Postindustrial fit motherhood in *Shape Fit Pregnancy* magazine. *Gender & Society, 18*, 610–624. doi: 10.1177/0891243204266817

Eidelman, A. I., Schanler, R. J., Johnston, M., Landers, S., Noble, L., Szucs, K., & Viehmann, L. (2012). Breastfeeding and the use of human milk. *Pediatrics, 129*, 827–841. doi: 10.1542/peds.2011-3552

Fairbrother, N., Barr, R. G., Pauwels, J., Brant, R., & Green, J. (2015). Maternal thoughts of harm in response to infant crying: An experimental analysis. *Archives of Women's Mental Health, 18*, 447–455. doi: 10.1007/s00737-014-0471-2

Fairbrother, N., & Woody, S. R. (2008). New mothers' thoughts of harm related to the newborn. *Archives of Women's Mental Health, 11*, 221–229. doi: 10.1007/s00737-008-0016-7

Fairweather-Schmidt, A. K., Leach, L., Butterworth, P., & Anstey, K. J. (2014). Infertility problems and mental health symptoms in a community-based sample: Depressive symptoms among infertile men, but not women. *International Journal of Men's Health, 13*, 75–91. doi: 10.3149/jmh.1302.75

Faludi, S. (1991). *Backlash: The undeclared war against American women.* New York, NY: Crown.

Feder, D. (2006). Feminists to women: Shut up and do as you're told. *Human Events, 62*(9), 15.

Fergusson, D., Horwood, J. L., & Ridder, E. (2006). Abortion in young women and subsequent mental health. *Journal of Child Psychology and Psychiatry, 47*, 16–24. doi: 10.1111/j.1469-7610.2005.01538.x

Finer, L. B., Frohwirth, L. F., Dauphinee, L. A., Singh, S., & Moore, A. M. (2005). Reasons U.S. women have abortions: Quantitative and qualitative perspectives. *Perspectives on Sexual and Reproductive Health, 37*, 110–118. doi: 10.1111/j.1931-2393.2005.tb00045.x

Fingerman, K. L., Cheng, Y. P., Wesselmann, E. D., Zarit, S., Furstenberg, F., & Birditt, K. S. (2012). Helicopter parents and landing pad kids: Intense parental support of grown children. *Journal of Marriage and Family, 74*, 880–896. doi: 10.1111/j.1741-3737.2012.00987.x

Flaxman, S. M., & Sherman, P. W. (2000). Morning sickness: A mechanism for protecting mother and embryo. *The Quarterly Review of Biology, 75*, 113–148.

Foli, K. J., South, S. C., Lim, E., & Jarnecke, A. M. (2016). Post-adoption depression: Parental classes of depressive symptoms across time. *Journal of Affective Disorders, 200*, 293–302. doi: 10.1016/j.jad.2016.01.049

Foster, C. H. (2008). The welfare queen: Race, gender, class, and public opinion. *Race, Gender & Class, 15*, 162–179.

Friedman, S. (2013). *Baby bust: New choices for men and women in work and family.* Philadelphia, PA: Wharton Digital Press.

Fuller-Tyszkiewicz, M., Skouteris, H., Watson, B., & Hill, B. (2012). Body dissatisfaction during pregnancy: A systematic review of cross-sectional and prospective correlates. *Journal of Health Psychology, 18*, 1411–1421. doi: 10.1177/1359105312462437

Garfield, C. F., Duncan, G., Rutsohn, J., McDade, T. W., Adam, E. K., Coley, R. L., & Chase-Lansdale, P. L. (2014). A longitudinal study of paternal mental health during transition to fatherhood as young adults. *Pediatrics, 133*, 836–843. doi: 10.1542/peds.2013-3262

Gaunt, R. (2008). Maternal gatekeeping antecedents and consequences. *Journal of Family Issues, 29*, 373–395. doi: 10.1177/0192513X07307851

Gavin, N. I., Gaynes, B. N., Lohr, K. N., Meltzer-Brody, S., Gartlehner, G., & Swinson, T. (2005). Perinatal depression: A systematic review of prevalence and incidence. *Obstetrics & Gynecology, 106*, 1071–1083. doi: 10.1097/01.AOG.0000183597.31630.db

Ge, X., Natsuaki, M. N., Martin, D., Leve, L., Neiderhiser, J., Shaw, D. S., . . . Reiss, D. (2008). Bridging the divide: Openness in adoption and post-adoption psychosocial adjustment among birth and adoptive parents. *Journal of Family Psychology, 22*, 529–540. doi: 10.1037/a0012817

Geirsson, R. T. (2016). From half to a third: A step towards reducing unnecessary caesarean sections. *BJOG: An International Journal of Obstetrics & Gynaecology, 123*, 1628. doi: 10.1111/1471-0528.1405

Gibbons, L., Belizán, J. M., Lauer, J. A., Betrán, A. P., Merialdi, M., & Althabe, F. (2010). The global numbers and costs of additionally needed and unnecessary caesarean sections performed per year: Overuse as a barrier to universal coverage [World Health Report, Background paper 30]. *World Health Organization.* Retrieved from http://www.who.int/healthsystems/topics/financing/healthreport/30C-sectioncosts.pdf

Gillespie, R. (2003). Childfree and feminine: Understanding the gender identity of voluntarily childless women. *Gender & Society, 17*, 122–136. doi: 10.1177/0891243202238982

Ginsburg, K. (2007). The importance of play in promoting healthy child development and maintaining strong parent–child bonds. *Pediatrics, 119*, 182–191. doi:10.1542/peds.2006-2697

Giscombé, C. L., & Lobel, M. (2005). Explaining disproportionately high rates of adverse birth outcomes among African

Americans: The impact of stress, racism, and related factors in pregnancy. *Psychological Bulletin, 131,* 662–683. doi: 10.1037/0033-2909.131.5.662

Gold, R. (2003, March). Lessons from before Roe: Will past be prologue? *The Guttmacher Report on Public Policy, 6*(1), 8–11. Retrieved from https://www.guttmacher.org/gpr/2003/03/lessons-roe-will-past-be-prologue

Goldberg, A. E. (2010). The transition to adoptive parenthood. In T. W. Miller (Ed.), *Handbook of Stressful Transitions Across the Life Span* (pp. 165–184). New York, NY: Springer.

Goldberg, A. E., Downing, J. B., & Richardson, H. B. (2009). The transition from infertility to adoption: Perceptions of lesbian and heterosexual couples. *Journal of Social and Personal Relationships, 26,* 938–963. doi: 10.1177/0265407509345652

Goldberg, A. E., Kinkler, L. A., Richardson, H. B., & Downing, J. B. (2011). Lesbian, gay, and heterosexual couples in open adoption arrangements: A qualitative study. *Journal of Marriage and Family, 73,* 502–518. doi: 10.1111/j.1741-3737.2010.00821.x

Goldberg, A. E., Moyer, A. M., Kinkler, L. A., & Richardson, H. B. (2012) "When you're sitting on the fence, hope's the hardest part": Experiences and challenges of lesbian, gay, and heterosexual couples adopting through the child welfare system. *Adoption Quarterly, 15,* 1–28. doi: 10.1080/10926755.2012.731032

Goldberg, A. E., & Smith, J. Z. (2011). Stigma, social context, and mental health: Lesbian and gay couples across the transition to adoptive parenthood. *Journal of Counseling Psychology, 58,* 139–150. doi: 10.1037/a0021684

Goldberg, A. E., Smith, J. Z., & Perry-Jenkins, M. (2012). The division of labor in lesbian, gay, and heterosexual new adoptive parents. *Journal of Marriage and Family, 74,* 812–828. doi: 10.1111/j.1741-3737.2012.00992.x

Goldberg, W. A., Prause, J., Lucas-Thompson, R., & Himsel, A. (2008). Maternal employment and children's achievement in context: A meta-analysis of four decades of research. *Psychological Bulletin, 134,* 77–108. doi: 10.1037/0033-2909.134.1.77

Golombok, S., Perry, B., Burston, A., Murray, C., Mooney-Somers, J., Stevens, M., & Golding, J. (2003). Children with lesbian parents: A community study. *Developmental Psychology, 39,* 20–33. doi: 10.1037/0012-1649.39.1.20

Goodwin, A., Astbury, J., & McMeeken, J. (2000). Body image and psychological well-being in pregnancy: A comparison of exercisers and non-exercisers. *Australian and New Zealand Journal of Obstetrics and Gynaecology, 40,* 442–447. doi: 10.1111/j.1479-828X.2000.tb01178.x

Graham, M., & Rich, S. (2014). Representations of childless women in the Australian print media. *Feminist Media Studies, 14,* 500–518. doi: 10.1080/14680777.2012.737346

Grant, A. (2016). "#discrimination": The online response to a case of a breastfeeding mother being ejected from a U.K. retail premises. *Journal of Human Lactation, 32,* 141–151. doi: 10.1177/0890334415592403

Green, J., & Baston, H. (2003). Feeling in control during labor: Concepts, correlates, and consequences. *Birth, 30,* 235–247. doi: 10.1046/j.1523-536X.2003.00253.x

Green, K., & Groves, M. (2008). Attachment parenting: An exploration of demographics and practices. *Early Child Development and Care, 178,* 513–525. doi: 10.1080/03004430600851199

Grall, T. S. (2011, December). *Custodial mothers and fathers and their child support: 2009* (Report No. P60-240). Retrieved from the U.S. Census Bureau website: https://www.census.gov/content/dam/Census/library/publications/2011/demo/p60-240.pdf

Greil, A., & McQuillan, J. (2004). Help-seeking patterns among subfecund women. *Journal of Reproductive and Infant Psychology, 22,* 305–319. doi: 10.1080/02646830412331298332

Greil, A., McQuillan, J., & Slauson-Blevins, K. (2011). The social construction of infertility. *Sociology Compass, 5,* 736–746. doi: 10.1111/j.1751-9020.2011.00397.x

Greil, A. L. (1997). Infertility and psychological distress: A critical review of the literature. *Social Science & Medicine, 45,* 1679–1704. doi: 10.1016/S0277-9536(97)00102-0

The Guardian. (2015, October 28). *India bans foreigners from hiring surrogate mothers.* Retrieved from http://www.theguardian.com/world/2015/oct/28/india-bans-foreigners-from-hiring-surrogate-mothers

Guttmacher Institute. (2016, September). *Induced abortion in the United States* [Fact sheet]. New York, NY: Author. Retrieved from https://www.guttmacher.org/sites/default/files/factsheet/fb_induced_abortion_3.pdf

Haire, A., & McGeorge, C. (2012). Negative perceptions of never-married custodial single mothers and fathers: Applications of a gender analysis for family therapists. *Journal of Feminist Family Therapy, 24,* 24–51. doi: 10.1080/08952833.2012.629130

Hall, W., Tomkinson, J., & Klein, M. (2012). Canadian care providers' and pregnant women's approaches to managing birth: Minimizing risk while maximizing integrity. *Qualitative Health Research, 22,* 575–586. doi: 10.1177/1049732311424292

Hansen, T. (2012). Parenthood and happiness: A review of folk theories versus empirical evidence. *Social Indicators Research, 108,* 29–64. doi: 10.1007/s11205-011-9865-y

Hartwell, L. P., Erchull, M. J., & Liss, M. (2014). Desire for marriage and children: A comparison of feminist and non-feminist women. *Gender Issues, 31,* 102–122. doi: 10.1007/s12147-014-9120-3

Haskins, J. (2015, May 11). Agencies make fertility treatments affordable for low-income women. *Huffington Post.* Retrieved from http://www.huffingtonpost.com/2015/05/11/affordable-fertility-treatments_n_7259418.html

Hayman, B., Wilkes, L., Halcomb, E., & Jackson, D. (2015). Lesbian women choosing motherhood: The journey to conception. *Journal of GLBT Family Studies, 11,* 395–409. doi: 10.1080/1550428X.2014.921801

Hays, S. (1996). *The cultural contradictions of motherhood.* New Haven, CT: Yale University Press.

Healy, S., Humphreys, E., & Kennedy, C. (2016). Midwives' and obstetricians' perceptions of risk and its impact on clinical practice and decision-making in labour: An integrative review. *Women and Birth, 29,* 107–116. doi: 10.1016/j.wombi.2015.08.010

Hebl, M., King, E., Glick, P., Singletary, S., & Kazama, S. (2007). Hostile and benevolent reactions toward pregnant women: Complementary interpersonal punishments and rewards that maintain traditional roles. *Journal of Applied Psychology, 92,* 1499–1511. doi: 10.1037/0021-9010.92.6.1499

Held, L., & Rutherford, A. (2012). Can't a mother sing the blues? Postpartum depression and the construction of motherhood in late 20th-century America. *History of Psychology, 15,* 107–123. doi: 10.1037/a0026219

Hoddinott, P., & Pill, R. (2000). A qualitative study of women's views about how health professionals communicate about infant feeding. *Health Expectations, 3,* 224–233. doi: 10.1111/j.1440-172X.2004.00474.x

Hoffman, K. M., Trawalter, S., Axt, J. R., & Oliver, M. N. (2016). Racial bias in pain assessment and treatment recommendations, and false beliefs about biological differences between blacks and whites. *Proceedings of the National Academy of Sciences, 113,* 4296–4301. doi: 10.1073/pnas.1516047113

Hopper, K., & Aubrey, J. (2016). Bodies after babies: The impact of depictions of recently post-partum celebrities on non-pregnant women's body image. *Sex Roles, 74,* 24–34. doi: 10.1007/s11199-015-0561-2

Hossain, Z., & Roopnarine, J. L. (1993). Division of household labor and child care in dual-earner African-American families with infants. *Sex Roles, 29*, 571–583. doi: 10.1007/BF00289205

Howorth, C. (2017, October 19). Motherhood is hard to get wrong. So why do so many moms feel so bad about themselves? *Time.* Retrieved from http://time.com/magazine/us/4989032/october-30th-2017-vol-190-no-18-u-s/

Hsin, A., & Felfe, C. (2014). When does time matter? Maternal employment, children's time with parents, and child development. *Demography, 51*, 1867–1894. doi: 10.1007/s13524-014-0334-5

Hughes, P., & Riches, S. (2003). Psychological aspects of perinatal loss. *Current Opinion in Obstetrics and Gynecology, 15*, 107–111.

Induced abortion in the United States [Fact sheet]. (2018, January). *The Guttmacher Institute.* Retrieved from https://www.guttmacher.org/fact-sheet/induced-abortion-united-states

Jackson, D., & Mannix, J. (2004). Giving voice to the burden of blame: A feminist study of mothers' experiences of mother blaming. *International Journal of Nursing Practice, 10*, 150–158. doi: 10.1111/j.1440-172X.2004.00474.x

Johanson, R., Newburn, M., & Macfarlane, A. (2002). Has the medicalisation of childbirth gone too far? *British Medical Journal, 324*, 892–895. doi: 10.1136/bmj.324.7342.892

Johnson, S., Burrows, A., & Williamson, I. (2004). "Does my bump look big in this?" The meaning of bodily changes for first-time mothers-to-be. *Journal of Health Psychology, 9*, 361–374. doi: 10.1177/1359105304042346

Johnston-Robledo, I., & Fred, V. (2008). Self-objectification and lower income pregnant women's breastfeeding attitudes. *Journal of Applied Social Psychology, 38*, 1–21. doi: 10.1111/j.1559-1816.2008.00293.x

Johnston-Robledo, I., Wares, S., Fricker, J., & Pasek, L. (2007). Indecent exposure: Self-objectification and young women's attitudes toward breastfeeding. *Sex Roles, 56*, 429–437. doi: 10.1007/s11199-007-9194-4

Jones, L., Lu, M., Lucas-Wright, A., Dillon-Brown, N., Broussard, M., Wright, K., & Ferré, C. (2010). One hundred intentional acts of kindness toward a pregnant woman: Building reproductive social capital in Los Angeles. *Ethnicity & Disease, 20* (Supplement 2), S2-41–S2-48.

Jong, E. (2010, November 6). The madness of modern motherhood. *The Wall Street Journal.* Retrieved from http://online.wsj.com/article/ SB10001424052748704462704557559060 3553674296.html.

Kanner, L. (1949). Problems of nosology and psychodynamics of early infantile autism. *American Journal of Orthopsychiatry, 19*, 416–426. doi: 416. 10.1111/j.1939-0025.1949.tb05441.x

Katz-Wise, S. L, Priess, H. A., & Hyde, J. S (2010). Gender-role attitudes and behavior across the transition to parenthood. *Developmental Psychology, 46*, 18–28, doi: 10.1037/a0017820

Kelly, K. (2014). The spread of "post abortion syndrome" as social diagnosis. *Social Science & Medicine, 102*, 18–25. doi: 10.1016/j.socscimed.2013.11.030

Kelly, Y., Sacker, A., Gray, R., Kelly, J., Wolke, D., & Quigley, M. A. (2008). Light drinking in pregnancy: A risk for behavioural problems and cognitive deficits at 3 years of age? *International Journal of Epidemiology, 38*, 129–140. doi: 10.1093/ije/dyn230

Kenney, N. J., & McGowan, M. L. (2010). Looking back: Egg donors' retrospective evaluations of their motivations, expectations, and experiences during their first donation cycle. *Fertility and Sterility, 93*, 455–466. doi: 10.1016/j.fertnstert.2008.09.081

Kidd, S. A., Eskenazi, B., & Wyrobek, A. J. (2001). Effects of male age on semen quality and fertility: A review of the literature. *Fertility and Sterility, 75*, 237–248. doi: 10.1016/S0015-0282(00)01679-4

Kingdon, C., Givens, J. L., O'Donnell, E., & Turner, M. (2015). Seeing and holding baby: Systematic review of clinical management and parental outcomes after stillbirth. *Birth: Issues in Perinatal Care, 42*, 206–218. doi: 10.1111/birt.12176

Klitzman, R. (2016). Buying and selling human eggs: Infertility providers' ethical and other concerns regarding egg donor agencies. *BMC Medical Ethics, 17*(71), 1–10. doi: 10.1186/s12910-016-0151-z

Ko, J., Farr, S., Dietz, P., & Robbins, C. (2012). Depression and treatment among U.S. pregnant and nonpregnant women of reproductive age, 2005–2009. *Journal of Women's Health, 21*, 830–836. doi: 10.1089/jwh.2011.3466

Koropeckyj-Cox, T., & Pendell, G. (2007). Attitudes about childlessness in the United States: Correlates of positive, neutral, and negative responses. *Journal of Family Issues, 28*, 1054–1082. doi: 10.1177/0192513X07301940

Kramer, M. R., & Hogue, C. R. (2009). What causes racial disparities in very preterm birth? A biosocial perspective. *Epidemiologic Reviews, 31*, 84–98. doi: 10.1093/ajerev/mxp003

Kroska, A. (2004). Divisions of domestic work: Revising and expanding the theoretical explanations. *Journal of Family Issues, 25*, 890–922. doi: 10.1177/0192513X04267149

Kumar, A., Hessini, L., & Mitchell, E. M. (2009). Conceptualising abortion stigma. *Culture, Health & Sexuality, 11*, 625–639. doi: 10.1080/13691050902842741

Kumar, R. (2015, December 11). India's surrogacy tourism takes a hit. The ban on foreign clients. *Foreign Affairs.* Retrieved from https://www.foreignaffairs.com/articles/india/2015-12-11/indias-surrogacy-tourism-takes-hit

Labbok, M. H., Hight-Laukaran, V., Peterson, A. E., Fletcher, V., Von Hertzen, H., & Van Look, P. F. (1997). Multicenter study of the Lactational Amenorrhea Method (LAM): I. Efficacy, duration, and implications for clinical application. *Contraception, 55*, 327–336. doi: 10.1016/S0010-7824(97)00040-1

Laney, E., Hall, M., Anderson, T., & Willingham, M. (2015). Becoming a mother: The influence of motherhood on women's identity development. *Identity, 15*, 126–145. doi: 10.1080/15283488.2015.1023440

Lareau, A. (2002). Invisible inequality: Social class and childrearing in Black families and White families. *American Sociological Review, 67*, 747–776. doi: 10.2307/3088916.

Lawler, D., Begley, C., & Lalor, J. (2015). (Re)constructing myself: The process of transition to motherhood for women with a disability. *Journal of Advanced Nursing, 71*, 1672–1683. doi: 10.1111/jan.12635

Leavesley, G., & Porter, J. (1982). Sexuality, fertility, and contraception in disability. *Contraception, 26*, 417–441. doi: 10.1016/0010-7824(82)90106-8

Lee, M. (2003). The transracial adoption paradox: History, research, and counseling implications of cultural socialization. *The Counseling Psychologist, 31*, 711–744. doi: 10.1177/0011000003258087

Letherby, G. (1999). Other than mother and mothers as others: The experience of motherhood and non-motherhood in relation to "infertility" and "involuntary childlessness." *Women's Studies International Forum, 22*, 359–372. doi: 10.1016/S0277-5395(99)00028-X

Levine, H., Jørgensen, N., Martino-Andrade, A., Mendiola, J., Weksler-Derri, D., Mindlis, I., . . . & Swan, S. H. (2017). Temporal trends in sperm count: A systematic review and meta-regression analysis. *Human Reproduction Update, 23*, 646–659. doi: 10.1093/humupd/dmx022

Light, A., Obedin-Maliver, J., Sevelius, J., & Kerns, J. (2014). Transgender men who experienced pregnancy after female-to-male gender transitioning. *Obstetrics & Gynecology, 124*, 1120–1127. doi: 10.1097/AOG.0000000000000540

Lindgren, H., Malm, M. C., & Radestad, I. (2013/2014). You don't leave your baby: Mother's experiences after a stillbirth. *OMEGA*, *68*, 337–346. doi: 10.2190/OM.68.4.c

Lino, M., Kuczynski, K., Rodriquez, N., & Schap, T. (2017). *Expenditures on children by families, 2015* (Miscellaneous Publication No. 1528-2015). Washington, DC: Center for Nutrition Policy and Promotion, U.S. Department of Agriculture. Retrieved from https://www.cnpp.usda.gov/sites/default/files/crc2015_March2017.pdf

Lintsen, A. M. E., Pasker-de Jong, P. C. M., De Boer, E. J., Burger, C. W., Jansen, C. A. M., Braat, D. D. M., & Van Leeuwen, F. E. (2005). Effects of subfertility cause, smoking and body weight on the success rate of IVF. *Human Reproduction*, *20*, 1867–1875. doi: 10.1093/humrep/deh898

Lipson, J., & Rogers, J. (2000). Pregnancy, birth, and disability: Women's health care experiences. *Health Care for Women International*, *21*, 11–26. doi: 10.1080/073993300245375

Liss, M., & Erchull, M. (2012). Feminism and attachment parenting: Attitudes, stereotypes, and misperceptions. *Sex Roles*, *67*, 131–142. doi: 10.1007/s11199-012-0173-z

Liss, M., & Erchull, M. J. (2013). Differences in beliefs and behaviors between feminist actual and anticipated mothers. *Psychology of Women Quarterly*, *37*, 381–391. doi: 10.1177/0361684312468334

Livingston, G. (2018, January 8). They're waiting longer, but U.S. women today more likely to have children than a decade ago. *Pew Research Center: Social and Demographic Trends*. Retrieved from http://www.pewsocialtrends.org/2018/01/18/theyre-waiting-longer-but-u-s-women-today-more-likely-to-have-children-than-a-decade-ago/

Loth, K., Bauer, K., Wall, M., Berge, J., & Neumark-Sztainer, D. (2011). Body satisfaction during pregnancy. *Body Image*, *8*, 297–300. doi: 10.1016/j.bodyim.2011.03.002

Lothian, J. A. (2014). Promoting optimal care in childbirth. *The Journal of Perinatal Education*, *23*, 174–177. doi: 10.1891/1058-1243.23.4.174

Lucas-Thompson, R. G., Goldberg, W. A., & Prause, J. (2010). Maternal work early in the lives of children and its distal associations with achievement and behavior problems: A meta-analysis. *Psychological Bulletin*, *136*, 915–942. doi: 10.1037/a0020875

Luthar, S. S., & Ciciolla, L. (2016). What it feels like to be a mother: Variations by children's developmental stages. *Developmental Psychology*, *52*, 143–154. doi: 10.1037/dev0000051

Mac Dougall, K., Beyene, Y., & Nachtigall, R. D. (2012). Age shock: Misperceptions of the impact of age on fertility before and after IVF in women who conceived after age 40. *Human Reproduction*, *28*, 350–356. doi: 10.1093/humrep/des409

Mack-Canty, C., & Wright, S. (2004). Family values as practiced by feminist parents: Bridging third-wave feminism and family pluralism. *Journal of Family Issues*, *25*, 851–880. doi: 10.1177/0192513X03261337

Major, B., Cozzarelli, C., Cooper, M. L., Zubek, J., Richards, C., Wilhite, M., & Gramzow, R. (2000). Psychological responses of women after first-trimester abortion. *Archives of General Psychiatry*, *57*, 777–784. doi: 10.1001/archpsyc.57.8.777

Martin, J. A., Hamilton, B. E., Osterman, J. K., & Matthews, M. S. (2017, January 5). Births: Final data for 2015. *National Vital Statistics Reports*, *66*(1). Hyattsville, MD: National Center for Health Statistics. Retrieved from https://www.cdc.gov/nchs/data/nvsr/nvsr66/nvsr66_01.pdf

Martinez, R., Johnston-Robledo, I., Ulsh, H., & Chrisler, J. (2001). Singing "the baby blues": A content analysis of popular press articles about postpartum affective disturbances. *Women & Health*, *31*, 37–56. doi: 10.1300/J013v31n02_02

Mathews, M. E., Leerkes, E. M., Lovelady, C. A., & Labban, J. D. (2014). Psychosocial predictors of primiparous breastfeeding initiation and duration. *Journal of Human Lactation*, *30*, 480–487. doi: 10.1177/0890334414537707

Mayo Clinic Staff. (n.d.). *Infertility: Symptoms and causes*. Retrieved from http://www.mayoclinic.org/diseases-conditions/infertility/symptoms-causes/dxc-20228738

McCormack, K. (2005). Stratified reproduction and poor women's resistance. *Gender & Society*, *19*, 660–679. doi: 10.1177/0891243205278010

McGill, A. (2016, July 15). Is violence in America going up or down? *The Atlantic*. Retrieved from https://www.theatlantic.com/politics/archive/2016/07/is-violence-in-america-going-up-or-down/491384/

McLaren, H. J. (2013). (Un)blaming mothers whose partners sexually abuse children: In view of heteronormative myths, pressures and authorities. *Child & Family Social Work*, *18*, 439–448. doi: 10.1111/j.1365-2206.2012.00863.x

McLoyd, V. C., Cauce, A. M., Takeuchi, D., & Wilson, L. (2000). Marital processes and parental socialization in families of color: A decade review of research. *Journal of Marriage and Family*, *62*, 1070–1093. doi: 10.1111/j.1741-3737.2000.01070.x

McMullin, J., & Marshall, V. (1996). Family, friends, stress, and well-being: Does childlessness make a difference? *Canadian Journal on Aging/La Revue Canadienne du Vieillissement*, *15*, 355–373. doi: 10.1017/S0714980800005821

McQuillan, J., Greil, A., Shreffler, K., Wonch-Hill, P., Gentzler, K., & Hathcoat, J. (2012). Does the reason matter? Variations in childlessness concerns among U.S. women. *Journal of Marriage and Family*, *74*, 1166–1181. doi: 10.1111/j.1741-3737.2012.01015.x

McQuillan, J., Greil, A., White, L., & Jacob, M. (2003). Frustrated fertility: Infertility and psychological distress among women. *Journal of Marriage and Family*, *65*, 1007–1018. doi: 10.1111/j.1741-3737.2003.01007.x

Mercer, R. (2004). Becoming a mother versus maternal role attainment. *Journal of Nursing Scholarship*, *36*, 226–232. doi: 10.1111/j.1547-5069.2004.04042.x

Merz, E., & Liefbroer, A. (2012). The attitude toward voluntary childlessness in Europe: Cultural and institutional explanations. *Journal of Marriage and Family*, *74*, 587–600. doi: 10.1111/j.1741-3737.2012.00972.x

Mohanty, J., & Newhill, C. (2006). Adjustment of international adoptees: Implications for practice and a future research agenda. *Children and Youth Services Review*, *28*, 384–395. doi: 10.1016/j.childyouth.2005.04.013

Morinis, J., Carson, C., & Quigley, M. A. (2013). Effect of teenage motherhood on cognitive outcomes in children: A population-based cohort study. *Archives of Disease in Childhood*, *98*, 959–964. doi: 10.1136/archdischild-2012-302525

Mother's Advocate. (2009). *Healthy birth your way: Six steps to a safer birth*. Retrieved from http://www.mothersadvocate.org/pdf/healthybirth_booklet.pdf

Moyer, A. M., & Goldberg, A. E. (2017). "We were not planning on this, but . . .": Adoptive parents' reactions and adaptations to unmet expectations. *Child & Family Social Work*, *22*, 12–21. doi: 10.1111/cfs.12219

Mugweni, E., Pearson, S., & Omar, M. (2012). Traditional gender roles, forced sex and HIV in Zimbabwean marriages. *Culture, Health & Sexuality*, *14*, 577–590. doi: 10.1080/13691058.2012.671962

Murkoff, H., & Mazel, S. (2008). *What to expect when you're expecting* (4th ed.). New York, NY: Workman Publishing.

Nash, E., Gold, R. B., Mohammed., L., Ansari-Thomas, Z., & Cappello, O. (2018, January 2). Policy trends in the United States, 2017. *The Guttmacher Institute*. Retrieved from https://www.guttmacher.org/article/2018/01/policy-trends-states-2017

Nelson, J. A., Liss, M., Erchull, M. J., Hurt, M. M., Ramsey, L. R., Turner, D. L., & Haines, M. E. (2008). Identity in action: Predictors of feminist self-identification and collective action. *Sex Roles*, *58*, 721–728. doi: 10.1007/s11199-007-9384-0

Nelson, S. K., Kushlev, K., English, T., Dunn, E. W., & Lyubomirsky, S. (2013). In defense of parenthood: Children are associated with more joy than misery. *Psychological Science*, *24*, 3–10. doi: 10.1177/0956797612447798

Newport, F., & Wilke, J. (2013, September 25). Desire for children still norm in the U.S. *Gallup*. Retrieved from http://www.gallup.com/poll/164618/desire-children-norm.aspx

Newton, J. (2014, April 29). Angry mothers stage mass breastfeeding protest at Sports Direct store that asked woman to leave because it was against "company policy." *Daily Mail*. Retrieved from http://www.dailymail.co.uk/news/article-2616220/Angry-mothers-stage-mass-breastfeeding-protest-Sports-Direct-store-asked-woman-leave-against-company-policy.html

Nordqvist, P. (2012). Origins and originators: Lesbian couples negotiating parental identities and sperm donor conception. *Culture, Health & Sexuality*, *14*, 297–311. doi: 10.1080/13691058.2011.639392

Oakley, L. L., Renfrew, M. J., Kurinczuk, J. J., & Quigley, M. A. (2013). Factors associated with breastfeeding in England: An analysis by primary care trust. *BMJ Open*, *3*(6). doi: 10.1136/bmjopen-2013-002765

O'Hara, M., & McCabe, J. (2013). Postpartum depression: Current status and future directions. *Annual Review of Clinical Psychology*, *9*, 379–407. doi: 10.1146/annurev-clinpsy-050212-185612

Ondeck, M. (2014). Healthy birth practice #2: Walk, move around, and change positions throughout labor. *The Journal of Perinatal Education*, *23*, 188–193. doi: 10.1891/1058-1243.23.4.188

Ouko, L., Shantikumar, K., Knezovich, J., Haycock, P., Schnugh, D., & Ramsay, M. (2009). Effect of alcohol consumption on CpG methylation in the differentially methylated regions of H19 and IG-DMR in male gametes: Implications for fetal alcohol spectrum disorders. *Alcoholism: Clinical and Experimental Research*, *33*, 1615–1627. doi: 10.1111/j.1530-0277.2009.00993.x

Park, K. (2005). Choosing childlessness: Weber's typology of action and motives of the voluntarily childless. *Sociological Inquiry*, *75*, 372–402. doi: 10.1111/j.1475-682X.2005.00127.x

Park, N., & Hill, P. (2014). Is adoption an option? The role of importance of motherhood and fertility help-seeking in considering adoption. *Journal of Family Issues*, *35*, 601–626. doi: 10.1177/0192513X13493277

Parks, J. A. (2010). Care ethics and the global practice of commercial surrogacy. *Bioethics*, *24*, 333–340. doi:10.1111/j.1467-8519.2010.01831.x

Patra, J., Bakker, R., Irving, H., Jaddoe, V. W., Malini, S., & Rehm, J. (2011). Dose–response relationship between alcohol consumption before and during pregnancy and the risks of low birthweight, preterm birth and small for gestational age (SGA): A systematic review and meta-analyses. *BJOG: An International Journal of Obstetrics & Gynaecology*, *118*, 1411–1421. doi: 10.1111/j.1471-0528.2011.03050.x

Pearson, C. (2014, August 29). The pressure to have a "perfect" birth. *Huffington Post*. Retrieved from http://www.huffingtonpost.com/2014/08/29/perfect-birth_n_5597119.html

Pelka, S. (2009). Sharing motherhood: Maternal jealousy among lesbian co-mothers. *Journal of Homosexuality*, *56*, 195–217. doi: 10.1080/00918360802623164

Pelton, S., & Hertlein, K. (2011). A proposed life cycle for voluntary childfree couples. *Journal of Feminist Family Therapy*, *23*, 39–53. doi: 10.1080/08952833.2011.548703

Perrin, E. C., Siegel, B. S., Pawelski, J. G., Dobbins, M. I., Lavin, A., Mattson, G., . . . & Yogman, M. (2013). Promoting the well-being of children whose parents are gay or lesbian. *Pediatrics*, *131*, 1374–1383. doi: 10.1542/peds.2013-0377

Peterson, H. (2015). Fifty shades of freedom: Voluntary childlessness as women's ultimate liberation. *Women's Studies International Forum*, *53*, 182–191. doi: 10.1016/j.wsif.2014.10.017

Petri, A. (2016, February 3). The CDC's incredibly condescending warning to young women. *The Washington Post*. Retrieved from https://www.washingtonpost.com/blogs/compost/wp/2016/02/03/the-cdcs-incredibly-condescending-warning-to-young-women/

Public opinion on abortion [Fact sheet]. (2017, July 7). *Pew Research Center*. Retrieved from http://www.pewforum.org/fact-sheet/public-opinion-on-abortion/

Radford, E., & Hughes, M. (2015). Women's experiences of early miscarriage: Implications for nursing care. *Journal of Clinical Nursing*, *24*, 1457–1465. doi: 10.1111/jocn.12781

Raque-Bogdan, T., & Hoffman, M. (2015). The relationship among infertility, self-compassion, and well-being for women with primary or secondary infertility. *Psychology of Women Quarterly*, *39*, 484–496. doi: 10.1177/0361684315576208

Reardon, D., Cougle, J., Rue, V., Shuping, M., Coleman, P., & Ney, P. (2003). Psychiatric admissions of low-income women following abortion and childbirth. *Canadian Medical Association Journal*, *168*, 1253–1256.

Reisz, S., Jacobvitz, D., & George, C. (2015). Birth and motherhood: Childbirth experience and mothers' perceptions of themselves and their babies. *Infant Mental Health Journal*, *36*, 167–178. doi: 10.1002/imhj.21500

The rise of childlessness. (2017, July 27). *The Economist*. Retrieved from https://www.economist.com/news/international/21725553-more-adults-are-not-having-children-much-less-worrying-it-appears-rise

Roberts, D. (1997). *Killing the black body: Race, reproduction, and the meaning of liberty*. New York, NY: Vintage.

Robertson, E., Grace, S., Wallington, T., & Stewart, D. E. (2004). Antenatal risk factors for postpartum depression: A synthesis of recent literature. *General Hospital Psychiatry*, *26*, 289–295. doi: 10.1016/j.genhosppsych.2004.02.006

Rocca, C., Kimport, K., Gould, H., & Foster, D. (2013). Women's emotions one week after receiving or being denied an abortion in the United States. *Perspectives on Sexual and Reproductive Health*, *45*, 122–131. doi: 10.1363/4512213

Romagnoli, A., & Wall, G. (2012). "I know I'm a good mom": Young, low-income mothers' experiences with risk perception, intensive parenting ideology and parenting education programmes. *Health, Risk & Society*, *14*, 273–289. doi: 10.1080/13698575.2012.662634

Ronsmans, C., Graham, W. J., & Lancet Maternal Survival Series Steering Group. (2006). Maternal mortality: Who, when, where, and why. *The Lancet*, *368*, 1189–1200. doi: 10.1016/S0140-6736(06)69380-X

Rosenthal, L., & Lobel, M. (2016). Stereotypes of Black American women related to sexuality and motherhood. *Psychology of Women Quarterly*, *40*, 414–427. doi: 10.1177/0361684315627459

Rouchou, B. (2013). Consequences of infertility in developing countries. *Perspectives in Public Health*, *133*, 174–179. doi: 10.1177/1757913912472415

Rowe-Murray, H., & Fisher, J. (2002). Baby friendly hospital practices: Cesarean section is a persistent barrier to early initiation of breastfeeding. *Birth*, *29*, 124–131. doi: 10.1046/j.1523-536X.2002.00172.x

Ruddick, S. (1989). *Maternal thinking: Toward a politics of peace*. Boston, MA: Beacon.

Rupersburg, N. (2015, April 2). Things you should never say to a woman who doesn't want kids. *Marie Claire*. Retrieved from http://www.marieclaire.com/sex-love/news/a13932/things-you-should-never-say-to-a-woman-who-doesnt-want-kids/

Russo, N. F. (1976). The motherhood mandate. *Journal of Social Issues, 32,* 143–153. doi: 10.1111/j.1540-4560.1976.tb02603.x

Russo, N. F. (2014). Abortion, unwanted childbearing, and mental health. *Salud Mental, 37,* 283–291.

Salzillo, L. (2015, July 30). Catholic nun explains pro-life in a way that may stun the masses. *The Daily Kos*. Retrieved from http://www.dailykos.com/story/2015/7/30/1407166/-Catholic-Nun-Explains-Pro-Life-In-A-Way-That-May-Stun-The-Masses

Saxton, M. (2013). Disability rights and selective abortion. In A. L. Ferber, K. Holcomb, & T. Wentling (Eds.), *Sex, gender, and sexuality: The new basics* (2nd ed., pp. 182–191). New York, NY: Oxford University Press.

Scheib, J. E., Riordan, M., & Rubin, S. (2003). Choosing identity-release sperm donors: The parent's perspective 13–18 years later. *Human Reproduction, 18,* 1115–1127. doi: 10.1093/humrep/deg227

Schiffrin, H. H., Liss, M., Miles-McLean, H., Geary, K. A., Erchull, M. J., & Tashner, T. (2014). Helping or hovering? The effects of helicopter parenting on college students' well-being. *Journal of Child and Family Studies, 23,* 548–557. doi: 10.1007/s10826-013-9716-3

Schiller, C. E., Meltzer-Brody, S., & Rubinow, D. R. (2015). The role of reproductive hormones in postpartum depression. *CNS Spectrums, 20,* 48–59. doi: 10.1017/S1092852914000480

Schoendorf, K. C., Hogue, C. J., Kleinman, J. C., & Rowley, D. (1992). Mortality among infants of Black as compared with White college-educated parents. *New England Journal of Medicine, 326,* 1522–1526. doi: 10.1056/NEJM199206043262303

Sears, W., & Sears, M. (2003). *The baby book.* New York, NY: Little, Brown.

Sedgh, G., Ashford, L. S., & Hussain R. (2016, June). *Unmet need for contraception in developing countries: Examining women's reasons for not using a method.* New York, NY: Guttmacher Institute. Retrieved from https://www.guttmacher.org/sites/default/files/report_pdf/unmet-need-for-contraception-in-developing-countries-report.pdf

Sedgh, G., Singh, S., Shah, I., Åhman, E., Henshaw, S., & Bankole, A. (2012). Induced abortion: Incidence and trends worldwide from 1995 to 2008. *The Lancet, 379,* 625–632. doi: 10.1016/S0140-6736(11)61786-8

Segrin, C., Woszidlo, A., Givertz, M., & Montgomery, N. (2013). Parent and child traits associated with overparenting. *Journal of Social and Clinical Psychology, 32,* 569–595. doi: 10.1521/jscp.2013.32.6.569

Shapiro, G. (2014). Voluntary childlessness: A critical review of the literature. *Studies in the Maternal, 6,* 1–15. doi: 10.16995/sim.9

Sharma, E., Saha, K., Ernala, S. K., Ghoshal, S., & De Choudhury, M. (2017). Analyzing ideological discourse on social media: A case study of the abortion debate. *Proceedings of the Annual Computational Social Science Conference of the Computational Social Science Society of the Americas: October 19–22, Santa Fe, NM.* doi: 10.1145/3145574.3145577

Shawe, J., Delbaere, I., Ekstrand, M., Hegaard, H. K., Larsson, M., Mastroiacovo, P., & . . . Tydén, T. (2015). Preconception care policy, guidelines, recommendations and services across six European countries: Belgium (Flanders), Denmark, Italy, the Netherlands, Sweden and the United Kingdom. *The European Journal of Contraception and Reproductive Health Care, 20*(2), 77–87. doi: 10.3109/13625187.2014.990088

Silliman, J., Fried, M. G., Ross, L., & Gutierrez, E. R. (2004). *Undivided rights: Women of color organize for reproductive justice.* Cambridge, MA: South End Press.

Skouteris, H., Carr, R., Wertheim, E., Paxton, S., & Duncombe, D. (2005). A prospective study of factors that lead to body dissatisfaction during pregnancy. *Body Image, 2,* 347–361. doi: 10.1016/j.bodyim.2005.09.002

Slaughter, A. M. (2015). *Unfinished business.* London, United Kingdom: Oneworld Publications.

Smith, J., Hawkinson, K., & Paull, K. (2011). Spoiled milk: An experimental examination of bias against mothers who breastfeed. *Personality and Social Psychology Bulletin, 37,* 867–878. doi: 10.1177/0146167211401629

Smith, L., Frost, J., Levitas, R., Bradley, H., & Garcia, J. (2006). Women's experiences of three early miscarriage management options: A qualitative study. *British Journal of General Practice, 54,* 198–205.

Snitow, A. (1992). Feminism and motherhood: An American reading. *Feminist Review, 40,* 32–51. doi: 10.2307/1395276

Solivan, A. E., Wallace, M. E., Kaplan, K. C., & Harville, E. W. (2015). Use of a resiliency framework to examine pregnancy and birth outcomes among adolescents: A qualitative study. *Families, Systems, & Health, 33,* 349–355. doi: 10.1037/fsh0000141

South, S. C., Foli, K. J., & Lim, E. (2013). Predictors of relationship satisfaction in adoptive mothers. *Journal of Social and Personal Relationships, 30,* 545–563. doi: 10.1177/0265407512462681

Stanik, C. E., & Bryant, C. M. (2012). Marital quality of newlywed African American couples: Implications of egalitarian gender role dynamics. *Sex Roles, 66,* 256–267. doi: 10.1007/BF00289205

Steiger, K. (2013, January 25). Christian radio hosts: Feminists are selfish, narcissistic, family destroying whores. *Raw Story*. Retrieved from http://www.rawstory.com/2013/01/christian-radio-hosts-feminists-are-selfish-narcissistic-family-destroying-whores/

Stein, P. (2017, January 18). Is there a place at the Women's March for women who are politically opposed to abortion? *The Washington Post*. Retrieved from https://www.washingtonpost.com/local/social-issues/is-there-a-place-for-anti-abortion-women-at-the-womens-march-on-washington/2017/01/17/2e6a2da8-dcbd-11e6-acdf-14da832ae861_story.html?utm_term=.956f64f869da

Steinberg, J., McCulloch, C., & Adler, N. (2014). Abortion and mental health: Findings from the national comorbidity survey-replication. *Obstetrics and Gynecology, 123,* 263–270. doi: 10.1097/AOG.0000000000000092

Steinberg, L. (2001). We know some things: Adolescent–parent relationships in retrospect and prospect. *Journal of Research on Adolescence, 11,* 1–20. doi: 10.1111/1532-7795.00001

Steinberg, L., & Silk, J. S. (2002). Parenting adolescents. In M. Bornstein (Ed.), *Handbook of parenting* (Vol. 1, pp. 103–135).

Stevens, D. P., Minnotte, K. L., Mannon, S. E., & Kiger, G. (2006). Family work performance and satisfaction: Gender ideology, relative resources and emotion work. *Marriage and Family Review, 40,* 47–74. doi: 10.1300/J002v40n04_04

Strang, V., & Sullivan, P. (1985). Body image attitudes during pregnancy and the postpartum period. *Journal of Obstetric, Gynecologic, & Neonatal Nursing, 14,* 332–337. doi: 10.1111/j.1552-6909.1985.tb02251.x

Strnadová, I., Bernoldová, J., Adamčíková, Z., & Klusáček, J. (2017). Good enough support? Exploring the attitudes, knowledge and experiences of practitioners in social services and child welfare working with mothers with intellectual disability. *Journal of Applied Research in Intellectual Disabilities, 30,* 563–572. doi: 10.1111/jar.12307

Sugden, J., & Malhotra, A. (2015, November 16). Foreign couples in limbo after India restricts surrogacy services. *The Wall Street Journal*. Retrieved from http://www.wsj.com/articles/foreign-couples-in-limbo-after-india-restricts-surrogacy-services-1447698601

Sutton, R., Douglas, K., & McClellan, L. (2011). Benevolent sexism, perceived health risks, and the inclination to restrict pregnant women's freedoms. *Sex Roles*, 65, 596–605. doi: 10.1007/s11199-010-9869-0

Swanson, K., Connor, S., Jolley, S., Pettinato, M., & Wang, T. (2007). Context and evolution of women's experiences to miscarriage during the first year after loss. *Research in Nursing and Health*, 30, 2–16. doi: 10.1002/nur.20175

Swanson, K., Karmali, Z., Powell, S., & Pulvermakher, F. (2003). Miscarriage effects on couples' interpersonal and sexual relationships during the first year after loss: Women's perceptions. *Psychosomatic Medicine*, 65, 902–910. doi: 10.1097/01.PSY.0000079381.58810.84

Tanaka, K., & Johnson, N. (2014). Childlessness and mental well-being in a global context. *Journal of Family Issues*, 1, 1–19. doi: 10.1177/0192513X14526393

Tanderup, M., Reddy, S., Patel, T., & Nielsen, B. (2015). Reproductive ethics in commercial surrogacy: Decision-making in IVF clinics in New Delhi, India. *Journal of Bioethical Inquiry*, 12, 491–501. doi: 10.1007/s11673-015-9642-8

Task Force on Ethics and Law. (2005). ESHRE task force on ethics and law 10: Surrogacy. *Human Reproduction*, 20, 2705–2707. doi: 10.1093/humrep/dei147

Tiran, D. (2014). Nausea and vomiting in pregnancy: An "alternative" approach to care. *British Journal of Midwifery*, 22, 544–550. doi: 10.12968/bjom.2014.22.8.544

Uffalussy, J. (2014, February 6). The cost of IVF: 4 things I learned while battling infertility. *Forbes*. Retrieved from http://www.forbes.com/sites/learnvest/2014/02/06/the-cost-of-ivf-4-things-i-learned-while-battling-infertility/#56d7a0bc2a79

Umansky, L. (1996). *Motherhood reconceived: Feminism and the legacy of the sixties*. New York, NY: New York University Press

Van Laningham, J. L., Scheuble, L. K., & Johnson, D. R. (2012). Social factors predicting women's consideration of adoption. *Michigan Family Review*, 16, 1–21. doi: 10.3998/mfr.4919087.0016.101

van Niekerk, A., & van Zyl, L. (2016). The ethics of surrogacy: Women's reproductive labour. *Journal of Medical Ethics*, 21, 345–349.

van Scheppingen, M. A., Denissen, J. J., Chung, J. M., Tambs, K., & Bleidorn, W. (2017). Self-esteem and relationship satisfaction during the transition to motherhood. *Journal of Personality and Social Psychology*, 114, 973–991. doi: 10.1037/pspp0000156

Vega, T. (2014, April 25). Infertility viewed through the prism of race. *The New York Times*. Retrieved from http://www.nytimes.com/2014/04/26/us/infertility-endured-through-a-prism-of-race.html?ref=tanzinavega

Vernon, P. (2009, June 13). It takes guts to say: "I don't want children." *The Guardian*. Retrieved from http://www.theguardian.com/commentisfree/2009/jun/14/polly-vernon-childlessness-cameron-diaz-babies

Victora, C. G., Bahl, R., Barros, A. J., França, G. V., Horton, S., Krasevec, J., . . . & Group, T. L. B. S. (2016). Breastfeeding in the 21st century: Epidemiology, mechanisms, and lifelong effect. *The Lancet*, 387, 475–490. doi: 10.1016/S0140-6736(15)01024-7

von Sydow, K. (1999). Sexuality during pregnancy and after childbirth: A metacontent analysis of 59 studies. *Journal of Psychosomatic Research*, 47, 27–49. doi: 10.1016/S0022-3999(98)00106-8

Warner, J. (2006). *Perfect madness: Motherhood in the age of anxiety*. New York, NY: Riverhead Books.

Watson, B., Broadbent, J., Skouteris, H., & Fuller-Tyszkiewicz, M. (2015). A qualitative exploration of body image experiences of women progressing through pregnancy. *Women and Birth*, 462, 1–8. doi: 10.1016/j.wombi.2015.08.007

Waxman, B. F. (1994). Up against eugenics: Disabled women's challenge to receive reproductive health services. *Sexuality and Disability*, 12, 155–171. doi: 10.1007/BF02547889

Weistra, S., & Luke, N. (2017). Adoptive parents' experiences of social support and attitudes towards adoption. *Adoption & Fostering*, 41, 228–241. doi: 10.1177/0308575917708702

Wenzel, A., Haugen, E., Jackson, L., & Robinson, K. (2003). Prevalence of generalized anxiety at eight weeks postpartum. *Archives of Women's Mental Health*, 6, 43–49. doi: 10.1007/s00737-002-0154-2

Weschler, T. (2015). *Taking charge of your fertility, 20th anniversary edition: The definitive guide to natural birth control, pregnancy achievement, and reproductive health*. New York, NY: Random House

Williams, J. F., Smith, V. C., & Committee on Substance Abuse. (2015). Fetal alcohol spectrum disorders. *Pediatrics*, 136, e1395–e1406. doi: 10.1542/peds.2015-3113.

Wilson, H., & Huntington, A. (2006). Deviant (m)others: The construction of teenage motherhood in contemporary discourse. *Journal of Social Policy*, 35, 59–76. doi: 10.1017/S0047279405009335

Winter, M. (2013, November 10). My abortion. *New York Magazine*. Retrieved from http://nymag.com/news/features/abortion-stories-2013-11/

Wischmann, T., Korge, K., Scherg, H., Strowitzki, T., & Verres, R. (2012). A 10-year follow-up study of psychosocial factors affecting couples after infertility treatment. *Human Reproduction*, 27, 3226–3232. doi:10.1093/humrep/des293

World Health Organization. (2018). *WHO recommendations: Intrapartum care for a positive childbirth experience*. Geneva, Switzerland: Author. Retrieved from http://apps.who.int/iris/bitstream/10665/260178/1/9789241550215-eng.pdf?ua=1

Yaniv, O. (2012, December 29). Weed out: More than a dozen city maternity wards regularly test new moms for marijuana and other drugs. *The New York Daily News*. Retrieved from http://www.nydailynews.com/new-york/weed-dozen-city-maternity-wards-regularly-test-new-mothers-marijuana-drugs-article-1.1227292

Ye, J., Betrán, A. P., Guerrero Vela, M., Souza, J. P., & Zhang, J. (2014). Searching for the optimal rate of medically necessary cesarean delivery. *Birth*, 41, 237–244. doi: 10.1111/birt.12104

Yogman, M., Garfield, C. F., & Committee on Psychosocial Aspects of Child and Family Health. (2016). Fathers' roles in the care and development of their children: The role of pediatricians. *Pediatrics*, 138, e1–e17. doi: 10.1542/peds.2016-1128

Zeiler, K., & Malmquist, A. (2014). Lesbian shared biological motherhood: The ethics of IVF with reception of oocytes from partner. *Medicine, Health Care and Philosophy*, 17, 347–355. doi: 10.1007/s11019-013-9538-5

Chapter 10

Adema, W., Clarke, C., & Frey, V. (2015). *Paid parental leave: Lessons from OECD countries and selected U.S. states* (OECD Social, Employment and Migration Working Papers No. 172). Paris, France: OECD Publishing. Retrieved from http://www.oecd-ilibrary.org/social-issues-migration-health/paid-parental-leave_5jrqgvqqb4vb-en

Aitken, Z., Garrett, C. C., Hewitt, B., Keogh, L., Hocking, J. S., & Kavanagh, A. M. (2015). The maternal health outcomes of paid maternity leave: A systematic review. *Social Science & Medicine*, *130*, 32–41. doi: 10.1016/j.socscimed.2015.02.001

Alonso-Villar, O., & Cotal, D. R. (2013). *The occupational segregation of Black women in the United States: A look at its evolution from 1940 to 2010* (ECINEQ Working Paper 2013-304). Retrieved from http://www.ecineq.org/milano/WP/ECINEQ2013-304.pdf

Amato, P., & Rivera, F. (1999). Paternal involvement and children's behavior problems. *Journal of Marriage and the Family*, *61*, 375–384. doi: 10.2307/353755

American Civil Liberties Union. (n.d.). *Know your rights: Transgender people and the law*. Retrieved from https://www.aclu.org/know-your-rights/transgender-people-and-law

Artavia, D. (2013, August 23). LGBT teachers forced back into the closet. *Advocate*. Retrieved from http://www.advocate.com/youth/2013/08/23/lgbt-teachers-forced-back-closet.

Avellar, S., & Smock, P. (2003). Has the price of motherhood declined over time? A cross-cohort comparison of the motherhood wage penalty. *Journal of Marriage and Family*, *65*, 597–607. doi: 10.1111/j.1741-3737.2003.00597.x

Avendano, M., Berkman, L. F., Brugiavini, A., & Pasini, G. (2015). The long-run effect of maternity leave benefits on mental health: Evidence from European countries. *Social Science & Medicine*, *132*, 45–53. doi: 10.1016/j.socscimed.2015.02.037

Aviv, R. (2016). The cost of caring. *The New Yorker*. Retrieved from http://www.newyorker.com/magazine/2016/04/11/the-sacrifices-of-an-immigrant-caregiver

Barron, L. (2003). Ask and you shall receive? Gender differences in negotiators' beliefs about requests for a higher salary. *Human Relations*, *56*, 635–662. doi: 10.1177/00187267030566001

Baumle, A. (2009). The cost of parenthood: Unraveling the effects of sexual orientation and gender on income. *Social Science Quarterly*, *90*, 983–1002. doi: 10.1111/j.1540-6237.2009.00673.x

Belkin, L. (2003, October 26). The opt-out revolution. *New York Times Magazine*. Retrieved from http://www.nytimes.com/2003/10/26/magazine/26WOMEN.html

Berdahl, J. L. (2007). The sexual harassment of uppity women. *Journal of Applied Psychology*, *92*, 425–437. doi: 10.1037/0021-9010.92.2.425

Berdahl, J. L., & Moore, C. (2006). Workplace harassment: Double jeopardy for minority women. *Journal of Applied Psychology*, *91*, 426–436. doi: 10.1037/0021-9010.91.2.426

Berger, L., Hill, J., & Waldfogel, J. (2005). Maternity leave, early maternal employment and child health and development in the U.S. *The Economic Journal*, *115*, F29–F47. doi: 10.1111/j.0013-0133.2005.00971.x

Beyer, D., Weiss, R., & Wilchins, J. (2014). *New Title VII and EEOC rulings protect transgender employees*. Retrieved from http://transgenderlawcenter.org/wp-content/uploads/2014/01/TitleVII-Report-Final012414.pdf

Bhattacharya, T. (2018, April 10). Women are leading the wave of strikes in America. Here's why. *The Guardian*. Retrieved from https://www.theguardian.com/commentisfree/2018/apr/10/women-teachers-strikes-america

Blair-Loy, M. (2003). *Competing devotions*. Cambridge, MA: Harvard University Press.

Blakemore, J., & Centers, R. (2005). Characteristics of boys' and girls' toys. *Sex Roles*, *53*, 619–633. doi: 10.1007/s11199-005-7729-0

Bowles, H., Babcock, L., & Lai, L. (2007). Social incentives for gender differences in the propensity to initiate negotiations: Sometimes it does hurt to ask. *Organizational Behavior and Human Decision Processes*, *103*, 84–103. doi: 10.1016/j.obhdp.2006.09.001

Bowles, H., Babcock, L., & McGinn, K. (2005). Constraints and triggers: Situational mechanics of gender in negotiation. *Journal of Personality and Social Psychology*, *89*, 951–965. doi: 10.1037/0022-3514.89.6.951

Budge, S. L., Tebbe, E. N., & Howard, K. A. (2010). The work experiences of transgender individuals: Negotiating the transition and career decision-making processes. *Journal of Counseling Psychology*, *57*, 377–393. doi: 10.1037/a0020472

Budig, M., & England, P. (2001). The wage penalty for motherhood. *American Sociological Review*, *66*, 204–225.

Budig, M. J., Misra, J., & Boeckmann, I. (2012). The motherhood penalty in cross-national perspective: The importance of work–family policies and cultural attitudes. *Social Politics: International Studies in Gender, State & Society*, *19*, 163–193. doi: 10.1093/sp/jxs006

Cabrera, N., Tamis–LeMonda, C., Bradley, R., Hofferth, S., & Lamb, M. (2000). Fatherhood in the twenty-first century. *Child Development*, *71*, 127–136. doi: 10.1111/1467-8624.00126

Caliper Research and Development Department. (2014). *Women leaders research paper*. Princeton, NJ: Caliper Corporation. Retrieved from http://www.calipermedia.calipercorp.com.s3.amazonaws.com/whitepapers/us/Women-Leaders-2014.pdf

Carlson, D. L., Hanson, S., & Fitzroy, A. (2016). The division of child care, sexual intimacy, and relationship quality in couples. *Gender & Society*, *30*, 442–466. doi: 10.1177/0891243215626709

Carlsson, M., Reshid, A. A., & Rooth, D-O. (2015, November 18). *Explaining the gender wage gap among recent college graduates: Pre-labor market factors of employer discrimination*. Retrieved from http://www.diva-portal.org/smash/get/diva2:911336/FULLTEXT01.pdf

Carter, N., & Silva, C. (2010). *Mentoring: Necessary but insufficient for advancement*. New York, NY: Catalyst. Retrieved from http://www.catalyst.org/system/files/Mentoring_Necessary_But_Insufficient_for_Advancement_Final_120610.pdf

Castro, Y., & Gordon, K. (2012). A review of recent research on multiple roles and women's mental health. In P. Lunberg-Love, K. Nadal, & M. A. Paludi (Eds.), *Women and mental disorders: Vol. 1. Understanding women's unique life experiences* (pp. 37–54). Santa Barbara, CA: Praeger.

Catanzarite, L. (2002). Dynamics of segregation and earnings in brown-collar occupations. *Work and Occupations*, *29*, 300–345. doi: 10.1177/0730888402029003003

Chamberlain, L. J., Crowley, M., Tope, D., & Hodson, R. (2008). Sexual harassment in organizational context. *Work and Occupations*, *35*, 262–295. doi: 10.1177/0730888408322008

Chamberlin, J. (2018, January). 4 questions for Tomi-Ann Roberts. *Monitor on Psychology*. Retrieved from http://www.apa.org/monitor/2018/01/conversation-roberts.aspx

Chatterjee, R. (2018, February 21). A new study finds that 81 percent of women have experienced sexual harassment. *NPR*. Retrieved from https://www.npr.org/sections/thetwo-way/2018/02/21/587671849/a-new-survey-finds-eighty-percent-of-women-have-experienced-sexual-harassment

Chatterji, P., & Markowitz, S. (2012). Family leave after childbirth and the mental health of new mothers. *Journal of Mental Health Policy and Economics*, *15*, 61–76.

Child Care Aware of America (2015). *Parents and the high cost of child care*. Retrieved from http://www.usa.childcareaware.org/advocacy-public-policy/resources/reports-and-research/costofcare/

Child Care Aware of America (2017). *Parents and the high cost of child care*. Retrieved from https://usa.childcareaware.org/wp-content/uploads/2017/12/2017_CCA_High_Cost_Report_FINAL.pdf

Chin, J. L., Desormeaux, L., & Sawyer, K. (2016). Making way for paradigms of diversity leadership. *Consulting Psychology Journal: Practice and Research, 68,* 49–71. doi: 10.1037/cpb0000051

Chung, Y. B. (1995). Career decision making of lesbian, gay, and bisexual individuals. *Career Development Quarterly, 44,* 178–190. doi: 10.1002/j.2161-0045.1995.tb00684.x

Cognard-Black, A. (2012). Riding the glass escalator to the principal's office. *Teorija in Praksa, 49,* 878–900.

Cohen, P., & Huffman, M. (2003). Occupational segregation and the devaluation of women's work across U.S. labor markets. *Social Forces, 81,* 881–908. doi: 10.1353/sof.2003.0027

Cohen, P., Huffman, M., & Knauer, S. (2009). Stalled progress? Gender segregation and wage inequality among managers, 1980–2000. *Work and Occupations, 36,* 318–342. doi: 10.1177/0730888409347582

Coltrane, S. (2010). Gender theory and household labor. *Sex Roles, 63,* 791–800. doi: 10.1007/s11199-010-9863-6

Cook, A., & Glass, C. (2014). Above the glass ceiling: When are women and racial/ethnic minorities promoted to CEO? *Strategic Management Journal, 35,* 1080–1089. doi: 10.1002/smj.2161

Cooper, M. (2000). Being the "go-to guy": Fatherhood, masculinity, and the organization of work in Silicon Valley. *Qualitative Sociology, 23,* 379–405. doi: 10.1023/A:1005522707921

Corbett, C., & Hill, C. (2012). *Graduating to a pay gap: The earnings of women and men one year after college graduation.* Washington, DC: American Association of University Women. Retrieved from https://www.aauw.org/files/2013/02/graduating-to-a-pay-gap-the-earnings-of-women-and-men-one-year-after-college-graduation.pdf

Correll, S., Benard, S., & Paik, I. (2007). Getting a job: Is there a motherhood penalty? *American Journal of Sociology, 112,* 1297–1339. doi: 10.1086/511799

Cortes, P., & Pan, J. (2013). Outsourcing household production: Foreign domestic workers and native labor supply in Hong Kong. *Journal of Labor Economics, 31,* 327–371. doi: 10.1086/668675

Covert, B. (2014a, March). Condolences, you're hired! *Slate.* Retrieved from http://www.slate.com/articles/business/moneybox/2014/03/general_motors_recall_is_mary_barra_the_latest_victim_of_the_glass_cliff.html

Covert, B. (2014b, October). Secret service director Julia Pierson was a victim of the "glass cliff." *New Republic.* Retrieved from https://newrepublic.com/article/119675/julia-pierson-women-leaders-and-perils-glass-cliff

Covert, B. (2018, April 5). Oklahoma teachers strike for a 4th day to protest rock-bottom education funding. *The Nation.* Retrieved from https://www.thenation.com/article/oklahoma-teachers-strike-for-a-fourth-day-to-protest-rock-bottom-education-funding/

Crittenden, A. (2001). *The price of motherhood: Why the most important job in the world is still the least valued.* New York, NY: Henry Holt.

Croft, A., Schmader, T., Block, K., & Baron, A. (2014). The second shift reflected in the second generation: Do parents' gender roles at home predict children's aspirations? *Psychological Science, 1,* 1–11. doi: 10.1177/0956797614533968

Crosby, F. J., Williams, J. C., & Biernat, M. (2004). The maternal wall. *Journal of Social Issues, 60,* 675–682. doi: 10.1111/j.0022-4537.2004.00379.x

Cuddy, A., Fiske, S., & Glick, P. (2004). When professionals become mothers, warmth doesn't cut the ice. *Journal of Social Issues, 60,* 701–718. doi: 10.1111/j.0022-4537.2004.00381.x

Currah, P. (2008). Expecting bodies: The pregnant man and transgender exclusion from the Employment Non-Discrimination Act. *Women's Studies Quarterly, 36,* 330–336. doi: 10.1353/wsq.0.0101

Dastagir, A. E. (2018, April 2). Teacher strikes in Oklahoma, West Virginia, Kentucky show the power of women. *USA Today.* Retrieved from https://www.usatoday.com/story/news/nation/2018/04/02/teacher-strikes-oklahoma-west-virginia-arizona-show-power-women/478517002/

del Río, C., & Alonso-Villar, O. (2015). The evolution of occupational segregation in the United States, 1940–2010: Gains and losses of gender–race/ethnicity groups. *Demography, 52,* 967–988. doi: 10.1007/s13524-015-0390-5

DeLoach, C. P. (1995). Women in rehabilitation. In A. E. Dell Orto & R. P. Marinelli (Eds.), *Encyclopedia of disability and rehabilitation* (pp. 762–776). New York, NY: Macmillan.

Desilver, D. (2017, March 23). Access to paid family leave varies widely across employers, industries. *Pew Research Center.* Retrieved from http://www.pewresearch.org/fact-tank/2017/03/23/access-to-paid-family-leave-varies-widely-across-employers-industries/

Dey, J. G., & Hill, C. (2007). *Behind the pay gap.* Washington, DC: American Association of University Women Educational Foundation. Retrieved from https://www.aauw.org/files/2013/02/Behind-the-Pay-Gap.pdf

Donnelly, K., Twenge, J. M., Clark, M. A., Samia, K. S., Beiler-May, A., & Carter, N. T. (2016). Attitudes toward women's work and family roles in the United States, 1976–2013. *Psychology of Women Quarterly, 40,* 41–54. doi: 10.1177/0361684315590774

Dougherty, C. (2006). The marriage earnings premium as a distributed fixed effect. *Journal of Human Resources, 41,* 433–443. doi: 10.3368/jhr.XLI.2.433

Dufu, T. (2013, May). Refining mentorship: Watch the video. *Levo.* Retrieved from http://www.levo.com/articles/from-the-founders/levo-league-launches-mentors-technology

Eagly, A., & Carli, L. (2007). *Through the labyrinth: The truth about how women become leaders.* Boston, MA: Harvard Business School Publishing Corporation.

Eagly, A. H., Johannesen-Schmidt, M. C., & van Engen, M. L. (2003). Transformational, transactional, and laissez-faire leadership styles: A meta-analysis comparing women and men. *Psychological Bulletin, 129,* 569–591. doi: 10.1037/0033-2909.129.4.569

EEOC. (n.d.). What you should know about EEOC and the enforcement protections for LGBT workers. Retrieved from https://www.eeoc.gov/eeoc/newsroom/wysk/enforcement_protections_lgbt_workers.cfm

Eilperin, J. (2016, September 13). White House women want to be in the room where it happens. *The Washington Post.* Retrieved from https://www.washingtonpost.com/news/powerpost/wp/2016/09/13/white-house-women-are-now-in-the-room-where-it-happens/?noredirect=on&utm_term=.6b1c35410058

Enchautegui, M. E., Johnson, M., & Gelatt, J. (2015). *Who minds the kids when mom works a nonstandard schedule?* Washington, DC: Urban Institute. Retrieved from http://www.urban.org/sites/default/files/publication/64696/2000307-Who-Minds-the-Kids-When-Mom-Works-a-Nonstandard-Schedule.pdf

England, P. (2010). The gender revolution uneven and stalled. *Gender & Society, 24,* 149–166. doi: 10.1177/0891243210361475

England, P. (2017). *Comparable worth: Theories and evidence.* London, United Kingdom: Routledge.

England, P., Allison, P., & Wu, Y. (2007). Does bad pay cause occupations to feminize, does feminization reduce pay, and how can we tell with longitudinal data? *Social Science Research, 36,* 1237–1256. doi: 10.1016/j.ssresearch.2006.08.003

England, P., Bearak, J., Budig, M. J., & Hodges, M. J. (2016). Do highly paid, highly skilled women experience the largest motherhood penalty? *American Sociological Review, 81,* 1161–1189. doi: 10.1177/0003122416673598

England, P., Budig, M., & Folbre, N. (2002). Wages of virtue: The relative pay of care work. *Social Problems*, *49*, 455–473. doi: 10.1525/sp.2002.49.4.455

England, P., & Folbre, N. (1999). The cost of caring. *The Annals of the American Academy of Political and Social Science*, *561*, 39–51. doi: 10.1177/000271629956100103

Farber, M. (2017, March 8). Nearly 30% of men worldwide think women shouldn't work. *Fortune*. Retrieved from http://fortune.com/2017/03/08/study-men-think-women-should-stay-home/

Featherstone, L. (2004). *Selling women short: The landmark battle for workers' rights at Wal-Mart*. New York, NY: Basic Books.

Filipovic, J. (2016, February 20). Why sexism at the office makes women love Hillary Clinton. *The New York Times*. Retrieved from https://www.nytimes.com/2016/02/21/opinion/campaign-stops/why-sexism-at-the-office-makes-women-love-hillary-clinton.html?_r=0

Fine, C. (2010). *Delusions of gender: How our minds, society, and neurosexism create difference*. New York, NY: Norton.

Fischbach, A., Lichtenthaler, P. W., & Horstmann, N. (2015). Leadership and gender stereotyping of emotions: Think manager–think male? *Journal of Personnel Psychology*, *14*, 153–162. doi: 10.1027/1866-5888/a000136

Fleming, S. (2015). Déjà vu? An updated analysis of the gender wage gap in the U.S. hospitality sector. *Cornell Hospitality Quarterly*, *56*, 180–190. doi: 10.1177/1938965514567680

Fletcher, J. (1998). Relational practice: A feminist reconstruction of work. *Journal of Management Inquiry*, *7*, 163–186. doi: 10.1177/105649269872012

Frech, A., & Damaske, S. (2012). The relationships between mothers' work pathways and physical and mental health. *Journal of Health and Social Behavior*, *53*, 396–412. doi: 10.1177/0022146512453929

Furtado, D. (2016). Fertility responses of high-skilled native women to immigrant inflows. *Demography*, *53*, 27–53. doi: 10.1007/s13524-015-0444-8

García-López, G. (2008). "Nunca te toman en cuenta [They never take you into account]." The challenges of inclusion and strategies for success of Chicana attorneys. *Gender and Society*, *22*, 590–612. doi: 10.1177/0891243208321120

Glasmeier, A. K. (2016, June 20). New 2015 living wage data. *The Living Wage Calculator*. Retrieved from http://livingwage.mit.edu/articles/18-new-2015-living-wage-data

Glass, C., & Cook, A. (2016). Leading at the top: Understanding women's challenges above the glass ceiling. *The Leadership Quarterly*, *27*, 51–63. doi: 10.1016/j.leaqua.2015.09.003

Glass, C., & Fodor, E. (2011). Public maternalism goes to market: Recruitment, hiring, and promotion in postsocialist Hungary. *Gender & Society*, *25*, 5–26. doi: 10.1177/0891243210390518

Goldberg, A. E., & Perry-Jenkins, M. (2007). The division of labor and perceptions of parental roles: Lesbian couples across the transition to parenthood. *Journal of Social and Personal Relationships*, *24*, 297–318. doi: 10.1177/0265407507075415

Goldin, C., Kerr, S. P., Olivetti, C., & Barth, E. (2017). The expanding gender earnings gap: Evidence from the LEHD-2000 Census. *American Economic Review*, *107*, 110–114. doi: 10.1257/aer.p20171065

Goldscheider, F., Bernhardt, E., & Lappegård, T. (2015). The gender revolution: A framework for understanding changing family and demographic behavior. *Population and Development Review*, *41*, 207–239. doi: 10.1111/j.1728-4457.2015.00045.x

Grant, A., & Sandberg, S. (2015, February). Madam C.E.O., get me a coffee. *The New York Times*. Retrieved from http://mobile.nytimes.com/2015/02/08/opinion/sunday/sheryl-sandberg-and-adam-grant-on-women-doing-office-housework.html?referrer=

Grant, J. M., Mottet, L. A., Tanis, J., Harrison, J., Herman, J. L., & Keisling, M. (2011). *Injustice at every turn: A report of the National Transgender Discrimination Survey*. Washington, DC: National Center for Transgender Equality and National Gay and Lesbian Task Force. Retrieved from http://www.thetaskforce.org/static_html/downloads/reports/reports/ntds_full.pdf

Greenhaus, J., & Powell, G. (2006). When work and family are allies: A theory of work–family enrichment. *Academy of Management Review*, *31*, 72–92. doi: 10.5465/AMR.2006.19379625

Grimshaw, D., & Rubery, J. (2015). *The motherhood pay gap: Review of the issues, theory and international evidence* [Conditions of Work and Employment Series No. 57]. Geneva, Switzerland: International Labour Office. Retrieved from https://www.escholar.manchester.ac.uk/api/datastream?publicationPid=uk-ac-man-scw:292866&datastreamId=FULL-TEXT.PDF

Gross, D. (2008, October). Starbucks to require employee availability around the clock and cut workforce in major national initiative. *Industrial Workers of the World*. Retrieved from http://www.iww.org/node/4451

Gruber, J. E. (1998). The impact of male work environments and organizational policies on women's experiences of sexual harassment. *Gender & Society*, *12*, 301–320. doi: 10.1177/0891243298012003004

Gupta, V. K., Han, S., Mortal, S. C., Silveri, S. D., & Turban, D. B. (2018). Do women CEOs face greater threat of shareholder activism compared to male CEOs? A role congruity perspective. *Journal of Applied Psychology*, *103*, 228–236. doi: 10.1037/apl0000269

Gupta, V. K., Mortal, S. C., & Turban, D. B. (2018, January 22). Research: Activist investors are more likely to target female CEOs. *Harvard Business Review*. Retrieved from https://hbr.org/2018/01/research-activist-investors-are-more-likely-to-target-female-ceos

Haas, L., & Hwang, C. (2008). The impact of taking parental leave on fathers' participation in childcare and relationships with children: Lessons from Sweden. *Community, Work and Family*, *11*, 85–104. doi: 10.1080/13668800701785346

Hall, L. J., & Donaghue, N. (2013). "Nice girls don't carry knives": Constructions of ambition in media coverage of Australia's first female prime minister. *British Journal of Social Psychology*, *52*, 631–647. doi: 10.1111/j.2044-8309.2012.02114.x

Hardy, C., & Jones-DeWeever, A. (2014). Black women in the economy. In the National Coalition on Black Civic Participation Black Women's Roundtable, *Black Women in the United States, 2014: Progress and Challenges* (pp. 20–24). Retrieved from https://www.washingtonpost.com/r/2010-2019/WashingtonPost/2014/03/27/National-Politics/Stories/2FinalBlackWomenintheUS2014.pdf

Hass, N. (2012, July). Marissa Mayer stares down "glass cliff" at Yahoo. *The Daily Beast*. Retrieved from http://www.thedailybeast.com/articles/2012/07/18/marissa-mayer-stares-down-glass-cliff-at-yahoo.html

Hegewisch, A., & Hartmann, H. (2014). *Occupational segregation and the gender wage gap: A job half done*. Washington, DC: Institute for Women's Policy Research. Retrieved from https://iwpr.org/wp-content/uploads/wpallimport/files/iwpr-export/publications/C419.pdf

Heilman, M., & Chen, J. (2005). Same behavior, different consequences: Reactions to men's and women's altruistic citizenship behavior. *Journal of Applied Psychology*, *90*, 431–441. doi: 10.1037/0021-9010.90.3.431

Herr, J., & Wolfram, C. (2012). Work environment and opt-out rates at motherhood across high-education career paths. *Industrial & Labor Relations Review*, *65*, 928–950. doi: 10.1177/001979391206500407

Hodges, M., & Budig, M. (2010). Who gets the daddy bonus? Organizational hegemonic masculinity and the impact of fatherhood on earnings. *Gender & Society*, *24*, 717–745. doi: 10.1111/j.1741-3737.2003.00597.x

Hogue, M., DuBois, C., & Fox-Cardamone, L. (2010). Gender differences in pay expectations: The roles of job intention and self-view. *Psychology of Women Quarterly*, *34*, 215–227. doi: 10.1111/j.1471-6402.2010.01563.x

hooks, b. (2013, October). Dig deep: Beyond lean in. *The Feminist Wire*. Retrieved from http://www.thefeministwire.com/2013/10/17973/

Hymowicz, C. (2012, January). Behind every great woman: The rise of the CEO mom has created a new kind of trophy husband. *Bloomberg Business*. Retrieved from http://www.bloomberg.com/bw/magazine/behind-every-great-woman-01042012.html

Institute for Women's Policy Research. (2017a, April). *The gender wage gap by occupation 2016 and by race and ethnicity* [Fact sheet]. Retrieved from https://iwpr.org/wp-content/uploads/2017/04/C456.pdf

Institute for Women's Policy Research. (2017b, September). *The gender wage gap: 2016* [Fact sheet]. Retrieved from https://iwpr.org/wp-content/uploads/2017/09/C459_9.11.17_Gender-Wage-Gap-2016-data-update.pdf

International Labour Office. (2010). *Maternity at work: A review of national legislation*. Geneva, Switzerland: Author. Retrieved from http://www.ilo.org/wcmsp5/groups/public/—dgreports/—dcomm/—publ/documents/publication/wcms_124442.pdf

Jahren, A. H. (2016, March 4). She wanted to do research, he wanted to talk about feelings. *The New York Times*. Retrieved from http://www.nytimes.com/2016/03/06/opinion/sunday/she-wanted-to-do-her-research-he-wanted-to-talk-feelings.html?login=email

Jans, L., & Stoddard, S. (1999). *Chartbook on women and disability in the United States*. Berkeley, CA: InfoUse. Retrieved from http://www.infouse.com/disabilitydata/womendisability/womendisability.pdf

Johnson, C. A., & Hawbaker, K. T. (2018, March 28). #MeToo: A timeline of events. *The Chicago Tribune*. Retrieved from http://www.chicagotribune.com/lifestyles/ct-me-too-timeline-20171208-htmlstory.html

Johnson, R., & Lo Sasso, A. (2006). The impact of elder care on women's labor supply. *Inquiry: The Journal of Health Care Organization, Provision, and Financing*, *43*, 195–210. doi: 10.5034/inquiryjrnl_43.3.195

Kalmijn, M. (1999). Father involvement in childrearing and the perceived stability of marriage. *Journal of Marriage and the Family*, *61*, 409–421. doi: 10.2307/353758

Kantor, J. (2014, August). Working anything but 9 to 5. *The New York Times*. Retrieved from http://www.nytimes.com/interactive/2014/08/13/us/starbucks-workers-scheduling-hours.html

Katz-Wise, S. L., Priess, H. A., & Hyde, J. S. (2010). Gender-role attitudes and behavior across the transition to parenthood. *Developmental Psychology*, *46*, 18–28, doi: 10.1037/a0017820

Kay, F. M., & Gorman, E. H. (2012). Developmental practices, organizational culture, and minority representation in organizational leadership: The case of partners in large U.S. law firms. *The ANNALS of the American Academy of Political and Social Science*, *639*, 91–113. doi: 10.1177/0002716211420232

Kelly, G. (2016, January 6). Paternity leave: How Britain compares with the rest of the world. *The Telegraph*. Retrieved from https://www.telegraph.co.uk/men/fatherhood/paternity-leave-how-britain-compares-with-the-rest-of-the-world/

Killewald, A. (2013). A reconsideration of the fatherhood premium: Marriage, coresidence, biology, and fathers' wages. *American Sociological Review*, *78*, 96–116. doi: 10.1177/0003122412469204

Kim, M. (1999). Inertia and discrimination in the California state civil service. *Industrial Relations*, *38*, 46–68. doi: 10.1111/0019-8676.00109

Kim, M., Kang, S. K., Yee, B., Shim, S. Y., & Chung, M. (2016). Paternal involvement and early infant neurodevelopment: The mediation role of maternal parenting stress. *BMC Pediatrics*, *16*, 212–220. doi: 10.1186/s12887-016-0747-y

Kirchmeyer, C. (2006). The different effects of family on objective career success across gender: A test of alternative explanations. *Journal of Vocational Behavior*, *68*, 323–346. doi: 10.1016/j.jvb.2005.05.002

Koenig, A., Eagly, A., Mitchell, A., & Ristikari, T. (2011). Are leader stereotypes masculine? A meta-analysis of three research paradigms. *Psychological Bulletin*, *137*, 616–642. doi: 10.1037/a0023557

Kolb, D. (2009). Too bad for the women or does it have to be? Gender and negotiation research over the past twenty-five years. *Negotiation Journal*, *25*, 515–531. doi: 10.1111/j.1571-9979.2009.00242.x

Konik, J., & Cortina, L. M. (2008). Policing gender at work: Intersections of harassment based on sex and sexuality. *Social Justice Research*, *21*, 313–337. doi: 10.1007/s11211-008-0074-z

Krogstad, J. M. (2014, May 5). More women than men earn the federal minimum wage. *Pew Research Center*. Retrieved from http://www.pewresearch.org/fact-tank/2014/05/05/more-women-than-men-earn-the-federal-minimum-wage/

Kumar, D. (2014). Disrupting the cultural capital of brogrammers. *ACM Inroads*, *5*(3), 28–29. doi: 10.1145/2655759.2655765

Latu, I. M., Stewart, T. L., Myers, A. C., Lisco, C. G., Estes, S. B., & Donahue, D. K. (2011). What we "say" and what we "think" about female managers: Explicit versus implicit associations of women with success. *Psychology of Women Quarterly*, *35*, 252–266. doi: 10.1177/0361684310383811

Levanon, A., England, P., & Allison, P. (2009). Occupational feminization and pay: Assessing causal dynamics using 1950–2000 U.S. census data. *Social Forces*, *88*, 865–891. doi: 10.1353/sof.0.0264

Lieber, R. (2015, August). Bringing paternity leave into the mainstream. *The New York Times*. Retrieved from http://www.nytimes.com/2015/08/08/your-money/bringing-paternity-leave-into-the-mainstream.html

Liss, M., & Schiffrin, H. H. (2014). *Balancing the big stuff: Finding happiness in work, family, and life*. Lanham, MD: Rowman & Littlefield.

Livingston, G. (2016, September 26). Among 41 nations, U.S. is the outlier when it comes to paid parental leave. *Pew Research Center*. Retrieved from http://www.pewresearch.org/fact-tank/2016/09/26/u-s-lacks-mandated-paid-parental-leave/

Maass, A., Cadinu, M., & Galdi, S. (2013). Sexual harassment: Motivations and consequences. In M. Ryan & R. Branscombe (Eds.), *The Sage handbook of gender and psychology* (pp. 341–358). Thousand Oaks, CA: Sage.

Maldonado, M. M. (2006). Racial triangulation of Latino/a workers by agricultural employers. *Human Organization*, *65*, 353–361. doi: 10.17730/humo.65.4.a84b5xykr0dvp911

Mandel, H., & Semyonov, M. (2005). Family policies, wage structures, and gender gaps: Sources of earnings inequality in 20 countries. *American Sociological Review*, *70*, 949–967. doi: 10.1177/000312240507000604

Mandell, B., & Pherwani, S. (2003). Relationship between emotional intelligence and transformational leadership style: A gender comparison. *Journal of Business and Psychology*, *17*, 387–404. doi: 10.1023/A:1022816409059

Marks, M., & Harold, C. (2011). Who asks and who receives in salary negotiation. *Journal of Organizational Behavior*, *32*, 371–394. doi: 10.1002/job.671

Mathews, J. (1985, September 5). Comparable worth rule overturned. *The Washington Post*. Retrieved from https://www.washingtonpost.com/archive/politics/1985/09/05/comparable-worth-rule-overturned/75192da6-d7a3-496c-8058-b1fc78853c8e/?utm_term=.d6ab50f60040

Matos, K., & Galinsky, E. (2014). *2014 National Study of Employers*. Retrieved from http://familiesandwork.org/downloads/2014NationalStudyOfEmployers.pdf

McAlvey, J. (2018, March 12). The West Virginia teacher's strike shows that winning big requires creating a crisis. *The Nation*. Retrieved from https://www.thenation.com/article/the-west-virginia-teachers-strike-shows-that-winning-big-requires-creating-a-crisis

McClean, E., Martin, S. R., Emich, K. J., & Woodruff, T. (2017). The social consequences of voice: An examination of voice type and gender on status and subsequent leader emergence. *Academy of Management Journal*. Advance online publication. doi: 10.5465/amj.2016.0148

Miller, C. (2014, April). Technology's man problem. *The New York Times*. Retrieved from http://www.nytimes.com/2014/04/06/technology/technologys-man-problem.html

Miller, C. (2016, March 18). As women take over a male dominated field, the pay drops. *The New York Times*. Retrieved from http://www.nytimes.com/2016/03/20/upshot/as-women-take-over-a-male-dominated-field-the-pay-drops.html?partner=rss&emc=rss&_r=1

Mintz, B., & Krymkowski, D. H. (2010). The intersection of race/ethnicity and gender in occupational segregation: Changes over time in the contemporary United States. *International Journal of Sociology*, 40, 31–58. doi: 10.2753/IJS0020-7659400402

Moreau, J. (2017, October 5). Federal civil rights law doesn't protect transgender workers, Justice Department says. *NBC News*. Retrieved from https://www.nbcnews.com/feature/nbc-out/federal-civil-rights-law-doesn-t-protect-transgender-workers-justice-n808126

Mulcahy, M., & Linehan, C. (2014). Females and precarious board positions: Further evidence of the glass cliff. *British Journal of Management*, 25, 425–438. doi: 10.1111/1467-8551.12046

Nepomnyaschy, L., & Waldfogel, J. (2007). Paternity leave and fathers' involvement with their young children: Evidence from the American Ecls–B. *Community, Work and Family*, 10, 427–453. doi: 10.1080/13668800701575077

Ng, E. S., Schweitzer, L., & Lyons, S. T. (2012). Anticipated discrimination and a career choice in nonprofit: A study of early career Lesbian, Gay, Bisexual, Transgendered (LGBT) job seekers. *Review of Public Personnel Administration*, 32, 332–352. doi: 10.1177/0734371X12453055

Nordell, J. (2014, August). Why aren't women advancing at work? Ask a transgender person. *New Republic*. Retrieved from https://newrepublic.com/article/119239/transgender-people-can-explain-why-women-dont-advance-work

Organisation for Economic Co-operation and Development. (n.d.-a). Employment: Time spent in paid and unpaid work, by sex. *OECD.Stat*. Retrieved from http://stats.oecd.org/index.aspx?queryid=54757

Organisation for Economic Co-operation and Development (n.d.-b). Work-life balance. *OECD Better Life Index*. Retrieved from http://www.oecdbetterlifeindex.org/topics/work-life-balance/

O'Ryan, L. W., & McFarland, W. P. (2010). A phenomenological exploration of the experiences of dual-career lesbian and gay couples. *Journal of Counseling and Development*, 88, 71–79. doi: 10.1002/j.1556-6678.2010.tb00153.x

Page, T. E., Pina, A., & Giner-Sorolla, R. (2016). "It was only harmless banter!" The development and preliminary validation of the Moral Disengagement in Sexual Harassment Scale. *Aggressive Behavior*, 42, 254–273. doi: 10.1002/ab.21621

Parnell, M. K., Lease, S. H., & Green, M. L. (2012). Perceived career barriers for gay, lesbian, and bisexual individuals. *Journal of Career Development*, 39, 248–268. doi: 10.1177/0894845310386730

Paustian-Underdahl, S. C., Walker, L. S., & Woehr, D. J. (2014). Gender and perceptions of leadership effectiveness: A meta-analysis of contextual moderators. *Journal of Applied Psychology*, 99, 1129–1145. doi: 10.1037/a0036751

Patrick, K. (2017, September). *National snapshot: Poverty among women and families 2016*. Washington, DC: National Women's Law Center. Retrieved from https://nwlc-ciw49tixgw5lbab.stackpathdns.com/wp-content/uploads/2017/09/Poverty-Snapshot-Factsheet-2017.pdf

Ragins, B. R., Ehrhardt, K., Lyness, K. S., Murphey, D. D., & Capman, J. F. (2016). Anchoring relationships at work: High-quality mentors and other supportive work relationships as buffers to ambient racial discrimination. *Personnel Psychology*, 70, 211–256. doi: 10.1111/peps.12144

Reed, O. M., Franks, A. S., & Scherr, K. C. (2015). Are perceptions of transgender individuals affected by mental illness stigma? A moderated mediation analysis of anti-transgender prejudice in hiring recommendations. *Psychology of Sexual Orientation and Gender Diversity*, 2, 463–469. doi: 10.1037/sgd0000138

Reid, E. (2015). Embracing, passing, revealing, and the ideal worker image: How people navigate expected and experienced professional identities. *Organization Science*, 26, 997–1017. doi: 10.1287/orsc.2015.0975

Richardson, A. (2013, August, 8). "Half the mothers I know have been driven from their jobs." *The Guardian*. Retrieved from https://www.theguardian.com/money/2013/aug/08/workplace-discrimination-pregnant-women-mothers-common

Ruderman, M., Ohlott, P., Panzer, K., & King, S. (2002). Benefits of multiple roles for managerial women. *Academy of Management Journal*, 45, 369–386. doi: 10.2307/3069352

Ruffing, K. (2018, March 14). Women and disability insurance: Five facts you should know. *Center on Budget and Policy Priorities*. Retrieved from https://www.cbpp.org/research/social-security/women-and-disability-insurance-five-facts-you-should-know#_ftn10

Rumens, N. (2010). Workplace friendships between men: Gay men's perspectives and experiences. *Human Relations*, 63, 1541–1562. doi: 10.1177/0018726710361987

Ryan, M., & Haslam, S. (2005). The glass cliff: Evidence that women are over-represented in precarious leadership positions. *British Journal of Management*, 16, 81–90. doi: 10.1111/j.1467-8551.2005.00433.x

Ryan, M. K., Haslam, S. A., Hersby, M. D., & Bongiorno, R. (2011). Think crisis–think female: The glass cliff and contextual variation in the think manager–think male stereotype. *Journal of Applied Psychology*, 96, 470–484. doi: 10.1037/a0022133

Saad, L. (2014, August 29). The "40-hour" workweek is actually longer—by seven hours. *Gallup*. Retrieved from http://www.gallup.com/poll/175286/hour-workweek-actually-longer-seven-hours.aspx

Sandberg, S. (2013). *Lean in: Women, work, and the will to lead*. New York, NY: Knopf.

Savani, K., Stephens, N. M., & Markus, H. R. (2011). The unanticipated interpersonal and societal consequences of choice: Victim blaming and reduced support for the public good. *Psychological Science*, 22, 795–802. doi: 10.1177/0956797611407928

Schein, V. (1973). The relationship between sex role stereotypes and requisite management characteristics. *Journal of Applied Psychology, 57,* 95–100. doi: 10.1037/h0037128

Schilt, K. (2010). *Just one of the guys? Transgender men and the persistence of gender inequality.* Chicago, IL: University of Chicago Press.

Schmitt, M. T., Spoor, J. R., Danaher, K., & Branscombe, N. R. (2009). Rose-colored glasses: How tokenism and comparisons with the past reduce the visibility of gender inequality. In M. Barreto, M. K. Ryan, & M. T. Schmitt (Eds.), *The glass ceiling in the 21st century: Understanding barriers to gender equality* (pp. 49–71). Washington, DC: American Psychological Association.

Schneer, J. A., & Reitman, F. (2002). Managerial life without a wife: Family structure and managerial career success. *Journal of Business Ethics, 37,* 25–38. doi: 10.1023/A:1014773917084

Schneider, A. (2002). Shattering negotiation myths: Empirical evidence on the effectiveness of negotiation style. *Harvard Negotiation Law Review, 7,* 143–233.

Sczesny, S. (2003). A closer look beneath the surface: Various facets of the think-manager–think-male stereotype. *Sex Roles, 49,* 353–363. doi: 10.1023/A:102511220

Seales, R. (2018, May 12). What has #MeToo actually changed? *BBC News.* Retrieved from http://www.bbc.com/news/world -44045291

Sears, B., & Mallory, C. (2011). *Documented evidence of employment discrimination & its effects on LGBT people.* Los Angeles, CA: The Williams Institute. Retrieved from https:// williamsinstitute.law.ucla.edu/wp-content/uploads/Sears -Mallory-Discrimination-July-20111.pdf

Siegel, R. (2018). Pregnancy as a normal condition of employment: Comparative and role-based accounts of discrimination. *William and Mary Law Review, 59,* 969–1006. Retrieved from https:// papers.ssrn.com/sol3/papers.cfm?abstract_id=3108210

Slaughter, A.-M. (2012, July). Why women still can't have it all. *The Atlantic.* Retrieved from http://www.theatlantic.com/magazine /archive/2012/07/why-women-still-cant-have-it-all/309020/

Slaughter, A. M. (2015). *Unfinished business: Women men work family.* New York, NY: Random House.

Smith, D. L. (2014). The relationship between employment and veteran status, disability and gender from 2004–2011 Behavioral Risk Factor Surveillance System (BRFSS). *Work, 49,* 325–334. doi: 10.3233/WOR-131648

Smith, R. (2012). Money, benefits, and power. A test of the glass ceiling and glass escalator hypotheses. *The ANNALS of the American Academy of Political and Social Science, 639,* 149–172. doi: 10.1177/0002716211422038

Snyder, K., & Green, A. (2008). Revisiting the glass escalator: The case of gender segregation in a female dominated occupation. *Social Problems, 55,* 271–299. doi: 10.1525/sp.2008.55.2.271

Sojo, V. E., Wood, R. E., & Genat, A. E. (2016). Harmful workplace experiences and women's occupational well-being: A meta-analysis. *Psychology of Women Quarterly, 40,* 10–40. doi: 10.1177/0361684315599346

Spiggle, T. (2015, March 23). Why Young v. UOS is a big win for pregnant workers. *Huffington Post.* Retrieved from https:// www.huffingtonpost.com/tom-spiggle/why-young-v-ups-is-a -big_b_6956498.html

Stephens, N., & Levine, C. (2011). Opting out or denying discrimination? How the framework of free choice in American society influences perceptions of gender inequality. *Psychological Science, 22,* 1231–1236. doi: 10.1177/0956797611417260

Stepler, R. (2017, March 23). Key takeaways on Americans' views of and experiences with family and medical leave. *Pew Research Center.* Retrieved from http://www.pewresearch.org/fact -tank/2017/03/23/key-takeaways-on-americans-views-of -and-experiences-with-family-and-medical-leave/

Stone, P. (2007). *Opting out? Why women really quit careers and head home.* Oakland, CA: University of California Press.

Sullivan, O., Gershuny, J., & Robinson, J. P. (2018). Stalled or uneven Gender Revolution? A long-term processual framework for understanding why change is slow. *Journal of Family Theory & Review, 10,* 263–279. doi:10.1111/jftr.12248

Szalai, J. (2014, January). The complicated origins of "having it all." *The New York Times.* Retrieved from http://www.nytimes .com/2015/01/04/magazine/the-complicated-origins-of -having-it-all.html?_r=0

Tale, S., Goldring, R., & Spiegelman, M. (2017, August). *Characteristics of public elementary and secondary school teachers in the United States: Results from the 2015–16 National Teacher and Principal Survey.* Washington, DC: U.S. Department of Education. Retrieved from https://nces.ed.gov/pubs2017/2017072.pdf

Tanaka, S. (2005). Parental leave and child health across OECD countries. *The Economic Journal, 115,* F7–F28. doi: 10.1111/j.0013-0133.2005.00970.x

Tannen, D. (2016, February). Our impossible expectations of Hillary Clinton and all women in authority. *The Washington Post.* Retrieved from https://www.washingtonpost.com/opinions /our-impossible-expectations-of-hillary-clinton-and-all-women -in-authority/2016/02/19/35e416d0-d5ba-11e5-be55 -2cc3c1e4b76b_story.html

Tilcsik, A. (2011). Pride and prejudice: Employment discrimination against openly gay men in the United States. *American Journal of Sociology, 117,* 586–626. doi: 10.1086/661653

Tinsley, C. H., Cheldelin, S. I., Schneider, A. K., & Amanatullah, E. T. (2009). Women at the bargaining table: Pitfalls and prospects. *Negotiation Journal, 25,* 233–248. doi: 10.1111/j.1571-9979 .2009.00222.x

Trades Union Congress. (2016). *Still just a bit of banter? Sexual harassment in the workplace in 2016.* London, United Kingdom: Author. Retrieved from https://www.tuc.org.uk/sites/default /files/SexualHarassmentreport2016.pdf

Tufekci, Z. (2014, March 18). No Nate, brogrammers may not be macho but that's not all there is to it. *The Medium.* Retrieved from https://medium.com/message/no-nate-brogrammers-may -not-be-macho-but-thats-not-all-there-is-to-it-2f1fe84c5c9b# .22psl8k84

United States Senate. (n.d.). *Women in the Senate.* Retrieved from https://www.senate.gov/artandhistory/history/common /briefing/women_senators.htm#1

U.S. Census Bureau. (2004). *Section 1. Population.* In *Statistical abstract of the United States: 2004–2005.* Retrieved from https://www.census.gov/prod/2004pubs/04statab/pop.pdf

U.S. Department of Labor. (2015 July). *Key characteristics of working women with disabilities.* Retrieved from https://www.dol .gov/wb/resources/women_with_disability_issue_brief.pdf

U.S. Department of Labor. (n.d.). *Women in the labor force.* Retrieved from https://www.dol.gov/wb/stats/NEWSTATS /facts/women_lf.htm#one

Vedantam, S. (2010, May). How the sex bias prevails. *The Sydney Morning Herald.* Retrieved from http://www.smh.com.au /national/how-the-sex-bias-prevails-20100514-v4mv.html

Voyer, D., & Voyer, S. D. (2014). Gender differences in scholastic achievement: A meta-analysis. *Psychological Bulletin, 140,* 1174–1204. doi: 10.1037/a0036620

Walsh, J. (2011). *Failing its families: Lack of paid leave and work–family supports in the U.S.* New York, NY: Human Rights Watch. Retrieved from https://www.hrw.org/sites/default /files/reports/us0211webwcover.pdf

Warner, J. (2015). *The women's leadership gap: Women's leadership by the numbers.* Retrieved from https://www.americanprogress .org/issues/women/reports/2015/08/04/118743/the -womens-leadership-gap/

Warner, J., & Corley, D. (2017, May 21). The women's leadership gap. *Center for American Progress.* Retrieved from https://www.americanprogress.org/issues/women/reports/2017/05/21/432758/womens-leadership-gap/

Weller, C. (2016, Aug. 22). These 10 countries have the best parental leave policies in the world. *Business Insider.* Retrieved from http://www.businessinsider.com/countries-with-best-parental-leave-2016-8

Welsh, S., Carr, J., MacQuarrie, B., & Huntley, A. (2006). "I'm not thinking of it as sexual harassment": Understanding harassment across race and citizenship. *Gender & Society, 20,* 87–107. doi: 10.1177/0891243205282785

Westervelt, A. (2016, February). Having it all kinda sucks. *Huffpost Parents.* Retrieved from http://www.huffingtonpost.com/amy-westervelt/having-it-all-kinda-sucks_b_9237772.html?te=TheMid

Wiener-Bronner, D. (2017, December 18). The ranks of women CEOs got even smaller this year. *CNN: Money.* Retrieved from http://money.cnn.com/2017/12/18/news/women-ceos-2017/index.html

Williams, C. L. (1992). The glass escalator: Hidden advantages for men in the "female" professions. *Social Problems, 39,* 253–267. doi: 10.2307/3096961

Williams, C. L. (2013). The glass escalator, revisited gender inequality in neoliberal times. *Gender & Society, 27,* 609–629. doi: 10.1177/0891243213490232

Williams, J. (2014, April). Sticking women with the office housework. *The Washington Post.* Retrieved from https://www.washingtonpost.com/news/on-leadership/wp/2014/04/16/sticking-women-with-the-office-housework/

Williams, J., & Boushey, H. (2010, January). *The three faces of work–family conflict: The poor, the professionals, and the missing middle.* Retrieved from https://papers.ssrn.com/sol3/papers.cfm?abstract_id=2126314

Williams, J., & Cooper, H. (2004). The public policy of motherhood. *Journal of Social Issues, 60,* 849–865. doi: 10.1111/j.0022-4537.2004.00390.x

Williams, J., Manvell, J., & Bornstein, S. (2006). *"Opt out" or pushed out? How the press covers work/family conflict—The untold story of why women leave the workforce.* San Francisco, CA: The Center for Work Life Law. Retrieved from http://worklifelaw.org/Publications/OptOutorPushedOut.pdf

Williams, N. (2011, October 25). Infographic: Women and mentoring in the U.S. *LinkedIn Official Blog.* Retrieved from http://blog.linkedin.com/2011/10/25/mentoring-women/

Women and Hollywood. (n.d). *2017 statistics.* Retrieved from http://womenandhollywood.com/resources/statistics/2017-statistics/

Woodhams, C., Lupton, B., & Cowling, M. (2015). The presence of ethnic minority and disabled men in feminised work: Intersectionality, vertical segregation and the glass escalator. *Sex Roles, 72,* 277–293. doi: 10.1007/s11199-014-0427-z

Woods, K. C., Buchanan, N. T., & Settles, I. H. (2009). Sexual harassment across the color line: Experiences and outcomes of cross- versus intraracial sexual harassment among Black women. *Cultural Diversity and Ethnic Minority Psychology, 15,* 67–76. doi: 10.1037/a0013541

World Economic Forum. (2017). *The global gender gap report 2017.* Retrieved from http://www3.weforum.org/docs/WEF_GGGR_2017.pdf

Wu, C., & Eamon, M. K. (2011). Patterns and correlates of involuntary unemployment and underemployment in single-mother families. *Children and Youth Services Review, 33,* 820–828. doi:10.1016/j.childyouth.2010.12.003

Yakushko, O. (2009). Xenophobia and prejudice: Understanding attitudes toward recent immigrants. *The Counseling Psychologist, 37,* 36–66.

Yap, M., & Konrad, A. (2009). Gender and racial differentials in promotions: Is there a sticky floor, a mid-level bottleneck, or a glass ceiling? *Industrial Relations, 64,* 593–619.

Yoder, J., & Aniakudo, P. (1996). When pranks become harassment: The case of African American women firefighters. *Sex Roles, 35,* 253–270. doi: 10.1007/BF01664768

Zavodny, M. (2015). Do immigrants work in worse jobs than U.S. Natives? Evidence from California. *Industrial Relations: A Journal of Economy and Society, 54,* 276–293. doi: 10.1111/irel.12087

Chapter 11

AARP Public Policy Institute. (2015, June). *Caregiving in the U.S.: 2015 report.* Retrieved from https://www.aarp.org/content/dam/aarp/ppi/2015/caregiving-in-the-united-states-2015-report-revised.pdf

Adelman, M., Gurevitch, J., Vries, B. D., & Blando, J. A. (2006). Openhouse: Community building and research in the LGBT aging population. In D. Kimmel, T. Rose, & S. David (Eds.), *Lesbian, gay, bisexual, and transgender aging: Research and clinical perspectives* (pp. 247–264). New York, NY: Columbia University Press.

American Society for Aesthetic Plastic Surgery. (2014). *Cosmetic surgery national data bank: Statistics.* Retrieved from http://www.surgery.org/sites/default/files/2014-Stats.pdf

American Society of Plastic Surgeons. (2014). *2014 plastic surgery statistics report.* Retrieved from http://www.plasticsurgery.org/Documents/news-resources/statistics/2014-statistics/plastic-surgery-statsitics-full-report.pdf

Andreoletti, C., Leszczynski, J. P., & Disch, W. B. (2015). Gender, race, and age: The content of compound stereotypes across the life span. *The International Journal of Aging and Human Development, 81,* 27–53. doi: 10.1177/0091415015616395

Antonucci, T. C., Akiyama, H., & Takahashi, K. (2004). Attachment and close relationships across the life span. *Attachment & Human Development, 6,* 353–370. doi: 10.1080/1461673042000303136

Arias, E., Heron, M., & Xu, J. (2016, November 28). United States life tables, 2012. *National Vital Statistics Reports, 65*(8). Hyattsville, MD: National Center for Health Statistics. Retrieved from https://www.cdc.gov/nchs/data/nvsr/nvsr65/nvsr65_08.pdf

Armstrong, M. J. (2003). Is being a grandmother being old? Cross-ethnic perspectives from New Zealand. *Journal of Cross-Cultural Gerontology, 18,* 185–202. doi: 10.1023/B:JCCG.0000003089.53598.73

Ayers, B., Forshaw, M., & Hunter, M. S. (2010). The impact of attitudes towards the menopause on women's symptom experience: A systematic review. *Maturitas, 65,* 28–36. doi: 10.1016/j.maturitas.2009.10.016

Balsis, S., & Carpenter, B. D. (2006). Evaluations of elderspeak in a caregiving context. *Clinical Gerontologist, 29,* 79–96. doi: 10.1300/J018v29n01_07

Barnett, I., van Sluijs, E., Ogilvie, D., & Wareham, N. J. (2014). Changes in household, transport and recreational physical activity and television viewing time across the transition to retirement: Longitudinal evidence from the EPIC-Norfolk cohort. *Journal of Epidemiology and Community Health, 68,* 747–753. doi: 10.1136/jech-2013-203225

Barnett, M. A., Scaramella, L. V., Neppl, T. K., Ontai, L. L., & Conger, R. D. (2010). Grandmother involvement as a protective factor for early childhood social adjustment. *Journal of Family Psychology, 24,* 635–645. doi: 10.1037/a0020829

Beals, K. P., & Peplau, L. A. (2001). Social involvement, disclosure of sexual orientation, and the quality of lesbian relationships. *Psychology of Women Quarterly, 25,* 10–19. doi: 10.1111/1471-6402.00002

Bennett, T., & Gaines, J. (2010). Believing what you hear: The impact of aging stereotypes upon the old. *Educational Gerontology, 36*, 435–445. doi: 10.1080/03601270903212336

Bent, K. N., & Magilvy, J. K. (2006). When a partner dies: Lesbian widows. *Issues in Mental Health Nursing, 27*, 447–459. doi: 10.1080/01612840600599960

Berger, U., Der, G., Mutrie, N., & Hannah, M. K. (2005). The impact of retirement on physical activity. *Ageing & Society, 25*, 181–195. doi: 10.1017/S0144686X04002739

Betancourt, J. R., Green, A. R., Carrillo, J. E., & Ananeh-Firempong, O., II. (2003). Defining cultural competence: A practical framework for addressing racial/ethnic disparities in health and health care. *Public Health Reports, 118*, 293–302. doi: 10.1093/phr/118.4.293

Blau, D. M. (1998). Labor force dynamics of older married couples. *Journal of Labor Economics, 16*, 595–629. doi: 10.1086/209900

Boerner, K., Jopp, D. S., Carr, D., Sosinsky, L., & Kim, S. K. (2014). "His" and "her" marriage? The role of positive and negative marital characteristics in global marital satisfaction among older adults. *The Journals of Gerontology, Series B: Psychological Sciences and Social Sciences, 69*, 579–589. doi: 10.1093/geronb/gbu032

Boisclair, D., Lusardi, A., & Michaud, P. C. (2017). Financial literacy and retirement planning in Canada. *Journal of Pension Economics & Finance, 16*, 277–296. doi: 10.1017/S1474747215000311

Bookwala, J., & Schulz, R. (2000). A comparison of primary stressors, secondary stressors, and depressive symptoms between elderly caregiving husbands and wives: The caregiver health effects study. *Psychology and Aging, 15*, 607–616. doi: 10.1037/0882-7974.15.4.607

Bouchard, G. (2014). How do parents react when their children leave home? An integrative review. *Journal of Adult Development, 21*, 69–79. doi: 10.1007/s10804-013-9180-8

Bradford, J. B., Putney, J. M., Shepard, B. L., Sass, S. E., Rudicel, S., Ladd, H., & Cahill, S. (2016). Healthy aging in community for older lesbians. *LGBT Health, 3*, 109–115. doi: 10.1089/lgbt.2015.0019

Brazil, K., Bédard, M., Willison, K., & Hode, M. (2003). Caregiving and its impact on families of the terminally ill. *Aging & Mental Health, 7*, 376–382. doi: 10.1080/1360786031000150649

Brazil, K., Thabane, L., Foster, G., & Bédard, M. (2009). Gender differences among Canadian spousal caregivers at the end of life. *Health & Social Care in the Community, 17*, 159–166. doi: 10.1111/j.1365-2524.2008.00813.x

Brien, M. J., Dickert-Conlin, S., & Weaver, D. A. (2001, January). *Widows waiting to wed? (Re)marriage and economic incentives in Social Security widow benefits* (ORES Working Paper No. 89). Retrieved from Social Security Administration website: https://www.ssa.gov/policy/docs/workingpapers/wp89.html

Bristowe, K., Hodson, M., Wee, B., Almack, K., Johnson, K., Daveson, B. A., . . . & Harding, R. (2018). Recommendations to reduce inequalities for LGBT people facing advanced illness: ACCESSCare national qualitative interview study. *Palliative Medicine, 32*, 23–35. doi: 10.1177/0269216317705102

Brooks, A. T. (2010). Aesthetic anti-ageing surgery and technology: Women's friend or foe? *Sociology of Health & Illness, 32*, 238–257. doi: 10.1111/j.1467-9566.2009.01224.x

Bulanda, J. R. (2011). Gender, marital power, and marital quality in later life. *Journal of Women & Aging, 23*, 3–22. doi: 10.1080/08952841.2011.540481

Burns, R. A., Browning, C. J., & Kendig, H. L. (2015). Examining the 16-year trajectories of mental health and wellbeing through the transition into widowhood. *International Psychogeriatrics, 27*, 1979–1986. doi: 10.1017/S1041610215000472

Byles, J. E., Tavener, M., Robinson, I., Parkinson, L., Warner-Smith, P., Stevenson, D., . . . & Curryer, C. (2013). Transforming retirement: New definitions of life after work. *Journal of Women & Aging, 25*, 24–44. doi: 10.1080/08952841.2012.717855

Calasanti, T. (2005). Ageism, gravity, and gender: Experiences of aging bodies. *Generation, 29*(3), 8–12.

Calasanti, T. (2007). Bodacious berry, potency wood and the aging monster: Gender and age relations in anti-aging ads. *Social Forces, 86*, 335–355. doi: 10.1353/sof.2007.0091

Calasanti, T. (2016). Combating ageism: How successful is successful aging? *The Gerontologist, 56*, 1093–1101. doi: 10.1093/geront/gnv076

Calasanti, T. M., & Slevin, K. F. (2001). *Gender, social inequalities, and aging.* New York, NY: Altamira.

Carnlöf, C., Iwarzon, M., Jensen-Urstad, M., Gadler, F., & Insulander, P. (2017). Women with PSVT are often misdiagnosed, referred later than men, and have more symptoms after ablation. *Scandinavian Cardiovascular Journal, 51*, 299–307. doi: 10.1080/14017431.2017.1385837

Centers for Disease Control and Prevention. (n.d.). *2014 cancer types grouped by race and ethnicity.* Retrieved from https://nccd.cdc.gov/uscs/cancersbyraceandethnicity.aspx

Cherlin, A., Cumberworth, E., Morgan, S. P., & Wimer, C. (2013). The effects of the great recession on family structure and fertility. *Annals of the American Academy of Political and Social Science, 650*, 214–231. doi: 10.1177/0002716213500643

Cheung, J., & Hocking, P. (2004). The experience of spousal carers of people with multiple sclerosis. *Qualitative Health Research, 14*, 153–166. doi: 10.1177/1049732303258382

Chrisler, J. C. (2007). Body image issues of women over 50. In V. Muhlbauer & J. C. Chrisler (Eds.), *Women over 50* (pp. 6–25). New York, NY: Springer.

Chrisler, J. C. (2011). Leaks, lumps, and lines: Stigma and women's bodies. *Psychology of Women Quarterly, 35*, 202–214. doi: 10.1177/0361684310397698

Chrisler, J. C., Barney, A., & Palatino, B. (2016). Ageism can be hazardous to women's health: Ageism, sexism, and stereotypes of older women in the healthcare system. *Journal of Social Issues, 72*, 86–104. doi: 10.1111/josi.12157

Chrisler, J. C., Gorman, J. A., Serra, K. E., & Chapman, K. R. (2012). Facing up to aging: Mid-life women's attitudes toward cosmetic procedures. *Women & Therapy, 35*, 193–206. doi: 10.1080/02703149.2012.684540

Chrisler, J. C., Rossini, M., & Newton, J. R. (2015). Older women, power, and the body. In V. Muhlbauer, J. C. Chrisler, & F. L. Denmark (Eds.), *Women and aging: An international, intersectional power perspective* (pp. 9–30). New York, NY: Springer.

Chung, S., Domino, M. E., Stearns, S. C., & Popkin, B. M. (2009). Retirement and physical activity: Analyses by occupation and wealth. *American Journal of Preventive Medicine, 36*, 422–428. doi: 10.1016/j.amepre.2009.01.026

Coltrane, S., & Messineo, M. (2000). The perpetuation of subtle prejudice: Race and gender imagery in 1990s television advertising. *Sex Roles, 42*, 363–389. doi: 10.1023/A:1007046204478

Conger, C. (Producer). (2014, October 15). Mastectomy tatoos [Audio podcast]. Retrieved from http://www.stuffmomnevertoldyou.com/podcasts/mastectomy-tatoos.htm

Connidis, I. A. (2014). Age relations and family ties over the life course: Spanning the macro-micro divide. *Research in Human Development, 11*, 291–308. doi: 10.1080/15427609.2014.967050

Connors, S. K., Goodman, M. S., Myckatyn, T., Margenthaler, J., & Gehlert, S. (2016). Breast reconstruction after mastectomy at a comprehensive cancer center. *SpringerPlus, 5*, 955. doi: 10.1186/s40064-016-2375-2

Cornwell, E. Y., & Waite, L. J. (2009). Social disconnectedness, perceived isolation, and health among older adults. *Journal of Health and Social Behavior*, *50*, 31–48. doi: 10.1177/002214650905000103

Cosco, T. D., Prina, A. M., Perales, J., Stephan, B. C., & Brayne, C. (2014). Operational definitions of successful aging: A systematic review. *International Psychogeriatrics*, *26*, 373–381. doi: 10.1017/S1041610213002287

Covert, J. J., & Dixon, T. L. (2008). A changing view: Representation and effects of the portrayal of women of color in mainstream women's magazines. *Communication Research*, *35*, 232–256. doi: 10.1177/0093650207313166

Croghan, C. F., Moone, R. P., & Olson, A. M. (2014). Friends, family, and caregiving among midlife and older lesbian, gay, bisexual, and transgender adults. *Journal of Homosexuality*, *61*, 79–102. doi: 10.1080/00918369.2013.835238

Cunningham, J., & Williams, K. N. (2007). A case study of resistiveness to care and elderspeak. *Research and Theory for Nursing Practice*, *21*, 45–56. doi: 10.1891/rtnpij-v21i1a006

Czaja, S. J., Sabbag, S., Lee, C. C., Schulz, R., Lang, S., Vlahovic, T., . . . & Thurston, C. (2016). Concerns about aging and caregiving among middle-aged and older lesbian and gay adults. *Aging & Mental Health*, *20*, 1107–1118. doi: 10.1080/13607863.2015.1072795

Dare, J. S. (2011). Transitions in midlife women's lives: Contemporary experiences. *Health Care for Women International*, *32*, 111–133. doi: 10.1080/07399332.2010.500753

Deerinwater, J. (2016, September 13). Meet the Native women at the heart of the Dakota Access Pipeline protests. *Wear Your Voice*. Retrieved from https://wearyourvoicemag.com/identities/feminism/meet-women-heart-dakota-access-pipeline-protests

Deevey, S. (2000). Cultural variation in lesbian bereavement experiences in Ohio. *Journal of the Gay & Lesbian Medical Association*, *4*, 9–17. doi: 10.1023/A:1009526210103

Dennerstein, L., Dudley, E., & Guthrie, J. (2002). Empty nest or revolving door? A prospective study of women's quality of life in midlife during the phase of children leaving and re-entering the home. *Psychological Medicine*, *32*, 545–550. doi: 10.1017/S0033291701004810

de Villiers, T. J., Gass, M. L. S., Haines, C. J., Hall, J. E., Lobo, R. A., Pierroz, D. D., & Rees, M. (2013). Global consensus statement on menopausal hormone therapy. *Climacteric*, *16*, 203–204. doi: 10.3109/13697137.2013.771520

de Vries, B. (2014). LG(BT) persons in the second half of life: The intersectional influences of stigma and cohort. *LGBT Health*, *1*, 18–23. doi: 10.1089/lgbt.2013.0005

DiGiacomo, M., Davidson, P. M., Byles, J., & Nolan, M. T. (2013). An integrative and socio-cultural perspective of health, wealth, and adjustment in widowhood. *Health Care for Women International*, *34*, 1067–1083. doi: 10.1080/07399332.2012.712171

Doley, R., Bell, R., Watt, B., & Simpson, H. (2015). Grandparents raising grandchildren: Investigating factors associated with distress among custodial grandparent. *Journal of Family Studies*, *21*, 101–119. doi: 10.1080/13229400.2015.1015215

Drummond, J. D., Brotman, S., Silverman, M., Sussman, T., Orzeck, P., Barylak, L., & Wallach, I. (2013). The impact of caregiving: Older women's experiences of sexuality and intimacy. *Affilia: Journal of Women and Social Work*, *28*, 415–428. doi: 10.1177/0886109913504154

Duberley, J., Carmichael, F., & Szmigin, I. (2014). Exploring women's retirement: Continuity, context and career transition. *Gender, Work, & Organization*, *21*, 71–90. doi: 10.1111/gwao.12013

Duncan, C. (2003). Assessing anti-ageism routes to older worker re-engagement. *Work, Employment and Society*, *17*, 101–120. doi: 10.1177/0950017003017001265

Duncan, C., & Loretto, W. (2004). Never the right age? Gender and age-based discrimination in employment. *Gender, Work, & Organization*, *11*, 95–115. doi: 10.1111/j.1468-0432.2004.002222.x

Elder, M. (2016, February). *Antiaging products and services: The global market*. Retrieved from https://www.bccresearch.com/market-research/healthcare/anti-aging-products-services-report-hlc060C.html

Ellis, R. R., & Simmons, T. (2014, October). *Coresident grandparents and their grandchildren: 2012*. Washington, DC: U.S. Census Bureau. Retrieved from https://www.census.gov/content/dam/Census/library/publications/2014/demo/p20-576.pdf

Emile, M., Chalabaev, A., Stephan, Y., Corrion, K., & d'Arripe-Longueville, F. (2014). Aging stereotypes and active lifestyle: Personal correlates of stereotype internalization and relationships with level of physical activity among older adults. *Psychology of Sport and Exercise*, *15*, 198–204. doi: 10.1016/j.psychsport.2013.11.002

Erickson, J. J., Martinengo, G., & Hill, E. J. (2010). Putting work and family experiences in context: Differences by family life stage. *Human Relations*, *63*, 955–979. doi: 10.1177/0018726709353138

Fallbjörk, U., Salander, P., & Rasmussen, B. H. (2012). From "no big deal" to "losing oneself": Different meanings of mastectomy. *Cancer Nursing*, *35*(5), E41–E48. doi: 10.1097/NCC.0b013e31823528fb

Fileborn, B., Thorpe, R., Hawkes, G., Minichiello, V., Pitts, M., & Dune, T. (2015). Sex, desire and pleasure: Considering the experiences of older Australian women. *Sexual and Relationship Therapy*, *30*, 117–130. doi: 10.1080/14681994.2014.936722

Finnegan, J. R., Meischke, H., Zapka, J. G., Leviton, L., Meshack, A., Benjamin-Garner, R., . . . & Weitzman, E. R. (2000). Patient delay in seeking care for heart attack symptoms: Findings from focus groups conducted in five U.S. regions. *Preventive Medicine*, *31*, 205–213. doi: 10.1006/pmed.2000.0702

Foley, P. F., & Lytle, M. C. (2015). Social cognitive career theory, the theory of work adjustment, and work satisfaction of retirement-age adults. *Journal of Career Development*, *42*, 199–214. doi: 10.1177/0894845314553270

Foster, L., & Walker, A. (2015). Active and successful aging: A European policy perspective. *The Gerontologist*, *55*, 83–90. doi: 10.1093/geront/gnu028

Fredrickson, B. L., Roberts, T.-A., Noll, S. M., Quinn, D. M., & Twenge, J. M. (1998). That swimsuit becomes you: Sex differences in self-objectification, restrained eating, and math performance. *Journal of Personality and Social Psychology*, *75*, 269–284. doi: 10.1037/0022-3514.75.1.269

Fredriksen-Goldsen, K. I., Cook-Daniels, L., Kim, H. J., Erosheva, E. A., Emlet, C. A., Hoy-Ellis, C. P., . . . & Muraco, A. (2014). Physical and mental health of transgender older adults: An at-risk and underserved population. *The Gerontologist*, *54*, 488–500. doi: 10.1093/geront/gnt021

Fuller-Thomson, E., & Minkler, M. (2000). The mental and physical health of grandmothers who are raising their grandchildren. *Journal of Mental Health and Aging*, *6*, 311–323.

Furman, F. K. (1997). *Facing the mirror: Older women and beauty shop culture*. New York, NY: Routledge.

Gander, K. (2014, October 2). Why do some forms of cancer receive more research funding than others? *Independent*. Retrieved from http://www.independent.co.uk/life-style/health-and-families/health-news/why-do-some-forms-of-cancer-receive-more-research-funding-than-others-9771396.html

Gendron, T., Maddux, S., Krinsky, L., White, J., Lockeman, K., Metcalfe, Y., & Aggarwal, S. (2013). Cultural competence training for healthcare professionals working with LGBT older adults. *Educational Gerontology, 39*, 454–463. doi:10.1080/03601277.2012.701114

Gerard, J. M., Landry-Meyer, L., & Roe, J. G. (2006). Grandparents raising grandchildren: The role of social support in coping with caregiving challenges. *The International Journal of Aging & Human Development, 62*, 359–383. doi:10.2190/3796-DMB2-546Q-Y4AQ

Gillen, M., & Kim, H. (2009). Older women and poverty transition: Consequences of income source changes from widowhood. *Journal of Applied Gerontology, 28*, 320–341. doi:10.1177/0733464808326953

Giordano, S. H., Cohen, D. S., Buzdar, A. U., Perkins, G., & Hortobagyi, G. N. (2004). Breast carcinoma in men: A population-base study. *Cancer, 101*, 51–57. doi: 10.1002/cncr.20312

Goldin, C., & Katz, L. F. (2016, September). *Women working longer: Facts and some explanations* (NBER Working Paper No. 22607). Retrieved from National Bureau of Economic Research website: http://www.nber.org/papers/w22607

Gooren, L. J., Wierckx, K., & Giltay, E. J. (2014). Cardiovascular disease in transsexual persons treated with cross-sex hormones: Reversal of the traditional sex difference in cardiovascular disease pattern. *European Journal of Endocrinology, 170*, 809–819. doi: 10.1530/EJE-14-0011

Gorchoff, S. M., John, O. P., & Helson, R. (2008). Contextualizing change in marital satisfaction during middle age: An 18-year longitudinal study. *Psychological Science, 19*, 1194–1200. doi:10.1111/j.1467-9280.2008.02222.x

Gott, M., Hinchliff, S., & Galena, E. (2004). General practitioner attitudes to discussing sexual health issues with older people. *Social Science & Medicine, 58*, 2093–2103. doi: 10.1016/j.socscimed.2003.08.025

Greve, W., & Bjorklund, D. F. (2009). The Nestor effect: Extending evolutionary developmental psychology to a lifespan perspective. *Developmental Review, 29*, 163–179. doi: 10.1016/j.dr.2009.04.001

Grippo, K. P., & Hill, M. S. (2008). Self-objectification, habitual body monitoring, and body dissatisfaction in older European American women: Exploring age and feminism as moderators. *Body Image, 5*, 173–182. doi: 10.1016/j.bodyim.2007.11.003

Grover, N., & Dang, P. (2013). Empty nest syndrome vs empty nest trigger: Psychotherapy formulation based on systemic approach—A descriptive case study. *Psychological Studies, 58*, 285–288. doi: 10.1007/s12646-013-0207-9

Grundy, E. M., Albala, C., Allen, E., Dangour, A. D., Elbourne, D., & Uauy, R. (2012). Grandparenting and psychosocial health among older Chileans: A longitudinal analysis. *Aging & Mental Health, 16*, 1047–1057. doi: 10.1080/13607863.2012.692766

Hagen, J. D., & DeVries, H. M. (2004). Marital satisfaction at the empty-nest phase of the family life cycle: A longitudinal study. *Marriage & Family: A Christian Journal, 7*, 83–98.

Halliwell, E., & Dittmar, H. (2003). A qualitative investigation of women's and men's body image concerns and their attitudes toward aging. *Sex Roles, 49*, 675–684. doi: 10.1023/B:SERS.0000003137.71080.97

Handy, J., & Davy, D. (2007). Gender ageism: Older women's experiences of employment agency practices. *Asia Pacific Journal of Human Resources, 45*, 85–99. doi: 10.1177/1038411107073606

Hardy, M. (2006). Older workers. In R. H. Binstock & L. K. George (Eds.), *Handbook of aging and the social sciences* (pp. 201–218). New York, NY: Academic Press.

Harley, D. A., & Teaster, P. B. (2016). *Handbook of LGBT elders: An interdisciplinary approach to principles, practices, and policies.* New York, NY: Springer.

Harris, M. B. (1994). Growing old gracefully: Age concealment and gender. *Journal of Gerontology, 49*, P149–P158. 10.1093/geronj/49.4.P149

Harris, P. B. (2008). Another wrinkle in the debate about successful aging: The undervalued concept of resilience and the lived experience of dementia. *The International Journal of Aging and Human Development, 67*, 43–61. doi: 10.2190/AG.67.1.c

Hebl, M. R., King, E. B., & Lin, J. (2004). The swimsuit becomes us all: Ethnicity, gender, and vulnerability to self-objectification. *Personality and Social Psychology Bulletin, 30*, 1322–1331. doi: 10.1177/0146167204264052

Heckler, A. (2017, October 6). *Cheapest and most expensive states for assistive living: 2017 update.* Retrieved from https://www.after55.com/blog/assisted-living-costs-cheapest-most-expensive-states/

Henetz, P. (2012, March 21). Utah woman oldest to climb seven continents' highest peaks. *The Salt Lake Tribune.* Retrieved from http://archive.sltrib.com/story.php?ref=/sltrib/news/53763936-78/masheter-lake-salt-carol.html.csp

Herman, R. E., & Williams, K. N. (2009). Elderspeak's influence on resistiveness to care: Focus on behavioral events. *American Journal of Alzheimer's Disease and Other Dementias, 24*, 417–423. doi: 10.1177/1533317509341949

Heron, M. (2016, June 30). Death: Leading causes for 2014. *National Vital Statistics Reports, 65*(5). Hyattsville, MD: National Center for Health Statistics. Retrieved from https://www.cdc.gov/nchs/data/nvsr/nvsr65/nvsr65_05.pdf

Hess, T. M., Auman, C., Colcombe, S. J., & Rahhal, T. A. (2003). The impact of stereotype threat on age differences in memory performance. *The Journals of Gerontology, Series B: Psychological Sciences and Social Sciences, 58*, P3–P11. doi: 10.1093/geronb/58.1.P3

Hoge, W. (2000, January 23). Rylstone journal: The stately "calendar girls" dressed so simply in pearls. *The New York Times.* Retrieved from http://www.nytimes.com/2000/01/23/world/rylstone-journal-the-stately-calendar-girls-dressed-so-simply-in-pearls.html

Hughes, M. (2009). Lesbian and gay people's concerns about ageing and accessing services. *Australian Social Work, 62*, 186–201. doi: 10.1080/03124070902748878

Hurd Clarke, L., & Griffin, M. (2007). The body natural and the body unnatural: Beauty work and aging. *Journal of Aging Studies, 21*, 187–201. doi: 10.1016/j.jaging.2006.11.001

Hurd Clarke, L., & Griffin, M. (2008). Visible and invisible ageing: Beauty work as a response to ageism. *Ageing and Society, 28*, 653–674. doi: 10.1017/S0144686X07007003

Hurd Clarke, L., Griffin, M., & Maliha, K. (2009). Bat wings, bunions, and turkey wattles: Body transgressions and older women's strategic clothing choices. *Ageing and Society, 29*, 709–726. doi: 10.1017/S0144686X08008283

Hutchinson, S. L., & Wexler, B. (2007). Is "raging" good for health? Older women's participation in the Raging Grannies. *Health Care for Women International, 28*, 88–118. doi: 10.1080/07399330601003515

Ingham, C. A., Eccles, F. R., Armitage, J. R., & Murray, C. D. (2017). Same-sex partner bereavement in older women: An interpretative phenomenological analysis. *Aging & Mental Health, 21*, 917–925. doi: 10.1080/13607863.2016.1181712

Jackson, J. B., Miller, R. B., Oka, M., & Henry, R. G. (2014). Gender differences in marital satisfaction: A meta-analysis. *Journal of Marriage and Family, 76*, 105–129. doi: 10.1111/jomf.12077

Jacobs, J. C., Laporte, A., Van Houtven, C. H., & Coyte, P. C. (2014). Caregiving intensity and retirement status in Canada. *Social Science & Medicine, 102*, 74–82. doi: 10.1016/j.socscimed.2013.11.051.

Jacobson, N. C., Lord, K. A., & Newman, M. G. (2017). Perceived emotional social support in bereaved spouses mediates the relationship between anxiety and depression. *Journal of Affective Disorders, 211*, 83–91. doi: 10.1016/j.jad.2017.01.011

Jenkins, C. L., Edmundson, A., Averett, P., & Yoon, I. (2014). Older lesbians and bereavement: Experiencing the loss of a partner. *Journal of Gerontological Social Work, 57*, 273–287. doi: 10.1080/01634372.2013.850583

Jewett, P. I., Gangnon, R. E., Trentham-Dietz, A., & Sprague, B. L. (2014). Trends of postmenopausal estrogen plus progestin prevalence in the United States between 1970 and 2010. *Obstetrics and Gynecology, 124*, 727–733. doi: 10.1097/AOG .0000000000000469

Katz, S., & Calasanti, T. (2015). Critical perspectives on successful aging: Does it "appeal more than it illuminates"? *The Gerontologist, 55*, 26–33. doi: 10.1093/geront/gnu027

Keppel, B. (2006). Affirmative psychotherapy with older bisexual women and men. *Journal of Bisexuality, 6*, 85–104. doi: 10.1300 /J159v06n01_06

Kite, M. E., & Johnson, B. T. (1988). Attitudes toward older and younger adults: A meta-analysis. *Psychology and Aging, 3*, 233–244. doi: 10.1037/0882-7974.3.3.233

Kite, M. E., Stockdale, G. D., Whitley, B. E., & Johnson, B. T. (2005). Attitudes toward younger and older adults: An updated meta-analytic review. *Journal of Social Issues, 61*, 241–266. doi: 10.1111/j.1540-4560.2005.00404.x

Kornadt, A. E., & Rothermund, K. (2012). Internalization of age stereotypes into the self-concept via future self-views: A general model and domain-specific differences. *Psychology and Aging, 27*, 164–172. doi: 10.1037/a0025110

Kornadt, A. E., Voss, P., & Rothermund, K. (2013). Multiple standards of aging: Gender-specific age stereotypes in different life domains. *European Journal of Ageing, 10*, 335–344. doi: 10.1007/s10433-013-0281-9

Kraus, L., Lauer, E., Coleman, R., & Houtenville, A. (2018, January). *2017 disability statistics annual report.* Durham, NH: Institute on Disability, University of New Hampshire. Retrieved from https://disabilitycompendium.org/sites/default/files/user -uploads/AnnualReport_2017_FINAL.pdf

Krekula, C. (2016). Contextualizing older women's body images: Time dimensions, multiple reference groups, and age codings of appearance. *Journal of Women & Aging, 28*, 58–67. doi: 10.1080/08952841.2015.1013829

LaDonna Bravebull Allard urges UN to halt Dakota Access Pipeline. (2016, October 3). *Camp of the Sacred Stones.* Retrieved from http://sacredstonecamp.org/blog/2016/10/3/ladonna -bravebull-allard-urges-un-to-halt-dakota-access-pipeline

Lahey, J. N. (2008). Age, women, and hiring: An experimental study. *The Journal of Human Resources, 43*, 30–56. doi: 10.3368 /jhr.43.1.30

Lauzen, M. M., & Dozier, D. M. (2005a). Maintaining the double standard: Portrayals of age and gender in popular films. *Sex Roles, 52*, 437–446. doi: 10.1007/s11199-005-3710-1

Lauzen, M. M., & Dozier, D. M. (2005b). Recognition and respect revisited: Portrayals of age and gender in prime-time television. *Mass Communication & Society, 8*, 241–256. doi: 10.1207/s15327825mcs0803_4

Laven, J. S., Visser, J. A., Uitterlinden, A. G., Vermeij, W. P., & Hoeijmakers, J. H. (2016). Menopause: Genome stability as new paradigm. *Maturitas, 92*, 15–23. doi: 10.1016/j.maturitas .2016.07.006

Lee, M., & Carr, D. (2007). Does the context of spousal loss affect the physical functioning of older widowed persons? A longitudinal analysis. *Research on Aging, 29*, 457–487. doi: 10.1177/0164027507303171

Leland, J. (2008, October 6). In "sweetie" and "dear," a hurt for the elderly. *The New York Times.* Retrieved from http://www .nytimes.com/2008/10/07/us/07aging.html

Lemish, D., & Muhlbauer, V. (2012). "Can't have it all": Representations of older women in popular culture. *Women & Therapy, 35*, 165–180. doi: 10.1080/02703149.2012.684541

Leopold, T., & Skopek, J. (2015). Convergence or continuity? The gender gap in household labor after retirement. *Journal of Marriage and Family, 77*, 819–832. doi: 10.1111/jomf.12199

Levy, B. (2000). Handwriting as a reflection of aging self-stereotypes. *Journal of Geriatric Psychiatry, 33*, 81–94.

Levy, B. (2009). Stereotype embodiment: A psychosocial approach to aging. *Current Directions in Psychological Science, 18*, 332–336. doi: 10.1111/j.1467-8721.2009.01662.x

Levy, B. R., Ashman, O., & Dror, I. (2000). To be or not to be: The effects of aging stereotypes on the will to live. *OMEGA— Journal of Death and Dying, 40*, 409–420. doi: 10.2190/Y2GE -BVYQ-NF0E-83VR

Levy, B. R., Hausdorff, J. M., Hencke, R., & Wei, J. Y. (2000). Reducing cardiovascular stress with positive self-stereotypes of aging. *The Journals of Gerontology, Series B: Psychological Sciences and Social Sciences, 55*, P205–P213. doi: 10.1093 /geronb/55.4.P205

Levy, B. R., & Myers, L. M. (2004). Preventive health behaviors influenced by self-perceptions of aging. *Preventive Medicine, 39*, 625–629. doi: 10.1016/j.ypmed.2004.02.029

Levy, S. R., & Macdonald, J. L. (2016). Progress on understanding ageism. *Journal of Social Issues, 72*, 5–25. doi: 10.1111/josi .12153

Liang, J., & Luo, B. (2012). Toward a discourse shift in social gerontology: From successful aging to harmonious aging. *Journal of Aging Studies, 26*, 327–334. doi: 10.1016/j.jaging .2012.03.001

Liechty, T., Yarnal, C., & Kerstetter, D. (2012). "I want to do everything!": Leisure innovation among retirement-age women. *Leisure Studies, 31*, 389–408. doi: 10.1080/02614367.2011.573571

Lips, H. M., & Hastings, S. L. (2012). Competing discourses for older women: Agency/leadership vs. disengagement/ retirement. *Women & Therapy, 35*, 145–164. doi: 10.1080 /02703149.2012.684533

Live-in caregiver salary. (n.d.). Retrieved from https://www .payscale.com/research/US/Job=Live-In_Caregiver/Salary

Livingston, G. (2014, November 14). *Four-in-ten couples are saying "I do," again: Growing number of adults have remarried.* Washington, DC: Pew Research Center. Retrieved from http:// www.pewsocialtrends.org/2014/11/14/four-in-ten-couples -are-saying-i-do-again/

Livingston, G., & Parker, K. (2010, September 9). *Since the start of the Great Recession, more children raised by grandparents.* Washington, DC: Pew Research Center. Retrieved from http:// www.pewsocialtrends.org/2010/09/09/since-the-start-of -the-great-recession-more-children-raised-by-grandparents/

Lock, M. (1994). Menopause in cultural context. *Experimental Gerontology, 29*, 307–317. doi: 10.1016/0531-5565(94)90011-6

Lodge, A. C., & Umberson, D. (2016). Sexual intimacy in mid- and late-life couples. In J. Bookwala (Ed.), *Couple relationships in the middle and later years: Their nature, complexity, and role in health and illness* (pp. 115–134). Washington, DC: American Psychological Association.

Looker, A. C., & Frenk, S. M. (2015, August). *Percentage of adults aged 65 and over with osteoporosis or low bone mass at the femur neck or lumbar spine: United States, 2005–2010.* Retrieved from the Centers for Disease Control and Prevention website: https://www.cdc.gov/nchs/data/hestat/osteoporsis /osteoporosis2005_2010.pdf

Loretto, W., & Vickerstaff, S. (2013). The domestic and gendered context for retirement. *Human Relations, 66,* 65–86. doi: 10.1177/0018726712455832

Lubitow, A., & Davis, M. (2011). Pastel injustice: The corporate use of pinkwashing for profit. *Environmental Justice, 4,* 139–144. doi: 10.1089/env.2010.0026

Ludwig, F. M., Hattjar, B., Russell, R. L., & Winston, K. (2007). How caregiving for grandchildren affects grandmothers' meaningful occupations. *Journal of Occupational Science, 14,* 40–51. doi: 10.1080/14427591.2007.9686582

Lusardi, A., & Mitchell, O. S. (2008). Planning and financial literacy: How do women fare? *American Economic Review: Papers & Proceedings, 98,* 413–417. doi: 10.1257/aer.98.2.413

Lusardi, A., & Mitchell, O. S. (2011). Financial literacy and retirement planning in the United States. *Journal of Pension Economics & Finance, 10,* 509–525. doi: 10.1017/S147474721100045X

Lusardi, A., & Mitchell, O. S. (2016, September). *Older women's labor market attachment, retirement planning, and household debt* (NBER Working Paper No. 22606). Retrieved from National Bureau of Economic Research website: http://www.nber.org/papers/w22606

Maas, A. H. E. M., & Appelman, Y. E. A. (2010). Gender differences in coronary heart disease. *Netherlands Heart Journal, 18,* 598–603. doi: 10.1007/s12471-010-0841-y

Mahmood, U., Hanlon, A. L., Koshy, M., Buras, R., Chumsri, S., Tkaczuk, K. H., . . . & Feigenberg, S. J. (2013). Increasing national mastectomy rates for the treatment of early stage breast cancer. *Annals of Surgical Oncology, 20,* 1436–1443. doi: 10.1245/s10434-012-2732-5

Mangweth-Matzek, B., Rupp, C. I., Hausmann, A., Assmayr, K., Mariacher, E., Kemmler, G., Whitworth, A. B., & Biebl, W. (2006). Never too old for eating disorders or body dissatisfaction: A community study of elderly women. *International Journal of Eating Disorders, 39,* 583–586. doi: 10.1002/eat.20327

Manzoli, L., Villari, P., Pironec, G. M., & Boccia, A. (2007). Marital status and mortality in the elderly: A systematic review and meta-analysis. *Social Science & Medicine, 64,* 77–94. doi: 10.1016/j.socscimed.2006.08.031

Marken, D. M., Pierce, D., & Baltisberger, J. A. (2010). Grandmother's use of routines to manage custodial care of young children. *Physical & Occupational Therapy in Geriatrics, 28,* 360–375. doi: 10.3109/02703181.2010.535119

Marques, S., Lima, M. L., Abrams, D., & Swift, H. (2014). Will to live in older people's medical decisions: Immediate and delayed effects of aging stereotypes. *Journal of Applied Social Psychology, 44,* 399–408. doi: 10.1111/jasp.12231

Martinson, M., & Berridge, C. (2015). Successful aging and its discontents: A systematic review of the social gerontology literature. *The Gerontologist, 55,* 58–69. doi: 10.1093/geront/gnu037

Mastro, D. E., & Stern, S. R. (2003). Representations of race in television commercials: A content analysis of prime-time advertising. *Journal of Broadcasting & Electronic Media, 47,* 638–647. doi: 10.1207/s15506878jobem4704_9

Mausbach, B. T., Roepke, S. K., Chattillion, E. A., Harmell, A. L., Moore, R., Romero-Moreno, R., . . . & Grant, I. (2012). Multiple mediators of the relations between caregiving stress and depressive symptoms. *Aging & Mental Health, 16,* 27–38. doi: 10.1080/13607863.2011.615738

Mazure, C. M., & Swendsen, J. (2016). Sex differences in Alzheimer's disease and other dementias. *The Lancet Neurology, 15,* 451–452. doi: 10.1016/S1474-4422(16)00067-3

McHugh, M. C., & Interligi, C. (2015). Sexuality and older women: Desirability and desire. In V. Muhlbauer, J. C. Chrisler, & F. L. Denmark (Eds.), *Women and aging: An international, intersectional power perspective* (pp. 9–30). New York, NY: Springer.

Merlan, A. (2016, December 8). Meet the brave, audacious, astonishing women who built the Standing Rock movement. *Jezebel.* Retrieved from http://jezebel.com/meet-the-brave-audacious-astonishing-women-who-built-1789756669

Metcalfe, K. A., Semple, J., Quan, M. L., Holloway, C., Wright, F., Narod, S., . . . & Zhong, T. (2017). Why some mastectomy patients opt to undergo delayed breast reconstruction: Results of a long-term prospective study. *Plastic and Reconstructive Surgery, 139,* 267–275. doi: 10.1097/PRS.0000000000002943

Metcalfe, K. A., Semple, J., Quan, M. L., Vadaparampil, S. T., Holloway, C., Brown, M., . . . & Narod, S. A. (2012). Changes in psychosocial functioning 1 year after mastectomy alone, delayed breast reconstruction, or immediate breast reconstruction. *Annals of Surgical Oncology, 19,* 233–241. doi: 10.1245/s10434-011-1828-7

Minkler, M., & Roe, K. M. (1993). *Grandmothers as caregivers: Raising children of the crack cocaine epidemic.* Thousand Oaks, CA: Sage.

Mitchell, B. A., & Lovegreen, L. D. (2009). The empty nest syndrome in midlife families: A multimethod exploration of parental gender differences and cultural dynamics. *Journal of Family Issues, 30,* 1651–1670. doi: 10.1177/0192513X09339020

Monge-Naranjo, A., & Faisal, S. (2015). Age and gender differences in long-term unemployment: Before and after the Great Recession. *Economic Synopses.* Retrieved from https://papers.ssrn.com/sol3/papers.cfm?abstract_id=2688941

Montemurro, B., & Siefken, J. M. (2014). Cougars on the prowl? New perceptions of older women's sexuality. *Journal of Aging Studies, 28,* 35–43. doi: 10.1016/j.jaging.2013.11.004

Moore, S. M., & Rosenthal, D. A. (2015). Personal growth, grandmother engagement and satisfaction among non-custodial grandmothers. *Aging & Mental Health, 19,* 136–143. doi: 10.1080/13607863.2014.920302

Moorman, S. M., Booth, A., & Fingerman, K. L. (2006). Women's romantic relationships after widowhood. *Journal of Family Issues, 27,* 1281–1304. doi: 10.1177/0192513X06289096

Moss, M. S., & Moss, S. Z. (2014). Widowhood in old age: Viewed in a family context. *Journal of Aging Studies, 29,* 98–106. doi: 10.1016/j.jaging.2014.02.001

Murphy, D. A., Roberts, K. J., & Herbeck, D. M. (2012). HIV-positive mothers with late adolescent/early adult children: "Empty nest" concerns. *Health Care for Women International, 33,* 387–402. doi: 10.1080/07399332.2012.655395

Musil, C. M., & Ahmad, M. (2002). Health of grandmothers: A comparison by caregiver status. *Journal of Aging and Health, 14,* 96–121. doi: 10.1177/089826430201400106

Nano, M. T., Gill, P. G., Kollias, J., Bochner, M. A., Malycha, P., & Winefield, H. R. (2005). Psychological impact and cosmetic outcome of surgical breast cancer strategies. *ANZ Journal of Surgery, 75,* 940–947. doi: 10.1111/j.1445-2197.2005.03517.x

Narayan, C. (2008). Is there a double standard of aging? Older men and women and ageism. *Educational Gerontology, 34,* 782–787. doi: 10.1080/03601270802042123

Nelson, A. (2002). Unequal treatment: Confronting racial and ethnic disparities in health care. *Journal of the National Medical Association, 94,* 666–668.

Nemmers, T. M. (2005). The influence of ageism and ageist stereotypes on the elderly. *Physical & Occupational Therapy in Geriatrics, 22*(4), 11–20. doi: 10.1080/J148v22n04_02

Nettles, S. M. (2016). Aging women of color: Engagement and place. *Women & Therapy, 39,* 337–353. doi: 10.1080/02703149.2016.1116866

Ncumark, D., Burn I., & Button, P. (2015, October). *Is it harder for older workers to find jobs? New and improved evidence from a field experiment* (NBER Working Paper No. 21669). Retrieved from National Bureau of Economic Research website: http://www.nber.org/papers/w21669

Ng, R., Allore, H. G., Monin, J. K., & Levy, B. R. (2016). Retirement as meaningful: Positive retirement stereotypes associated with longevity. *Journal of Social Issues, 72*, 69–85. doi: 10.1111/josi.12156

Ng, T. W. H., & Feldman, D. C. (2012). Evaluating six common stereotypes about older workers with meta-analytical data. *Personnel Psychology, 65*, 821–858. doi: 10.1111/peps.12003

Noone, J., Alpass, F., & Stephens, C. (2010). Do men and women differ in their retirement planning? Testing a theoretical model of gendered pathways to retirement preparation. *Research on Aging, 32*, 715–738. doi: 10.1177/0164027510383531

North, M. S., & Fiske, S. T. (2016). Resource scarcity and prescriptive attitudes generate subtle, intergenerational older-worker exclusion. *Journal of Social Issues, 72*, 122–145. doi: 10.1111/josi.12159

Obermeyer, C. M. (2000). Menopause across cultures: A review of the evidence. *Menopause, 7*, 184–192.

Obermeyer, C. M., Reher, D., & Saliba, M. (2007). Symptoms, menopause status, and country differences: A comparative analysis from DAMES. *Menopause, 14*, 788–797. doi: 10.1097/gme.0b013e318046eb4a

O'Connor, B. P., & St. Pierre, E. S. (2004). Older persons' perceptions of the frequency and meaning of elderspeak from family, friends, and service workers. *The International Journal of Aging and Human Development, 58*, 197–221. doi: 10.2190/LY83-KPXD-H2F2-JRQ5

Oksanen, T., Vahtera, J., Westerlund, H., Pentti, J., Sjösten, N., Virtanen, M., . . . & Kivimäki, M. (2011). Is retirement beneficial for mental health? Antidepressant use before and after retirement. *Epidemiology, 22*, 553–559. doi: 10.1097/EDE.0b013e31821c41bd

Orth, U., Trzesniewski, K. H., & Robins, R. W. (2010). Self-esteem development from young adulthood to old age: A cohort-sequential longitudinal study. *Journal of Personality and Social Psychology, 98*, 645–658. doi: 10.1037/a0018769

Oseola McCarty. (n.d.). *The Philanthropy Hall of Fame*. Retrieved from http://www.philanthropyroundtable.org/almanac/hall_of_fame/oseola_mccarty

Patrick, K. (2017, September). National snapshot: Poverty among women & families, 2016 [Fact sheet]. *National Women's Law Center*. Retrieved from https://nwlc-ciw49tixgw5lbab.stackpathdns.com/wp-content/uploads/2017/09/Poverty-Snapshot-Factsheet-2017.pdf

Pew Research Center. (2013, March 14). *Modern parenthood: Roles of moms and dads converge as they balance work and family*. Washington, DC: Author. Retrieved from http://www.pewsocialtrends.org/files/2013/03/FINAL_modern_parenthood_03-2013.pdf

Pinquart, M., & Sörensen, S. (2007). Correlates of physical health of informal caregivers: A meta-analysis. *The Journals of Gerontology, Series B: Psychological Sciences and Social Sciences, 62*, P126–P137. doi: 10.1093/geronb/62.2.P126

Price, C. A., & Nesteruk, O. (2015). What to expect when you retire: By women for women. *Marriage & Family Review, 51*, 418–440. doi: 10.1080/01494929.2015.1059784

Pruchno, R. A., & McKenney, D. (2002). Psychological well-being of Black and White grandmothers raising grandchildren: Examination of a two-factor model. *The Journals of Gerontology, Series B: Psychological Sciences and Social Sciences, 57*, P444–P452. doi: 10.1093/geronb/57.5.P444

Quéniart, A., & Charpentier, M. (2012). Older women and their representations of old age: A qualitative analysis. *Ageing and Society, 32*, 983–1007. doi: 10.1017/S0144686X1100078X

Rabin, R. C. (2017, January 29). After mastectomies, an unexpected blow: Numb new breasts. *The New York Times*. Retrieved from https://www.nytimes.com/2017/01/29/well/live/after-mastectomies-an-unexpected-blow-numb-new-breasts.html

Raver, J. L., & Nishii, L. H. (2010). Once, twice, or three times as harmful? Ethnic harassment, gender harassment, and generalized workplace harassment. *Journal of Applied Psychology, 95*, 236–254. doi: 10.1037/a0018377

Reitzes, D. C., Mutran, E. J., & Fernandez, M. E. (1996). Does retirement hurt well-being? Factors influencing self-esteem and depression among retires and workers. *The Gerontologist, 36*, 649–656. doi: 10.1093/geront/36.5.649

Richardson, V. E., Bennett, K. M., Carr, D., Gallagher, S., Kim, J., & Fields, N. (2015). How does bereavement get under the skin? The effects of late-life spousal loss on cortisol levels. *The Journals of Gerontology, Series B: Psychological Sciences and Social Sciences, 70*, 341–347. doi: 10.1093/geronb/gbt116

Rikleen, L. S. (2016, March 10). Older women are being forced out of the workforce. *Harvard Business Review*. Retrieved from https://hbr.org/2016/03/older-women-are-being-forced-out-of-the-workforce

Robinson, T., Callister, M., & Magoffin, D. (2009). Older characters in teen movies from 1980–2006. *Educational Gerontology, 35*, 687–711. doi: 10.1080/03601270802708426

Rose, S. M., & Hospital, M. M. (2015). Lesbians over 60: Newer every day. In V. Muhlbauer, J. C. Chrisler, & F. L. Denmark (Eds.), *Women and aging: An international, intersectional power perspective* (pp. 117–146). New York, NY: Springer.

Rosenwald, M. S. (2012, August 1). Retirement community women bare (almost) all for calendar. *The Washington Post*. Retrieved from https://www.washingtonpost.com/blogs/rosenwald-md/post/retirement-community-women-bare-almost-all-for-calendar/2012/08/01/gJQA8OdIPX_blog.html

Rowe J. W., & Kahn R. L. (1987). Human aging: Usual versus successful. *Science, 237*, 143–149. doi: 10.1126/science.3299702

Rowe, J. W., & Kahn, R. L. (2015). Successful aging 2.0: Conceptual expansions for the 21st century. *The Journals of Gerontology, Series B: Psychological Sciences and Social Sciences, 70*, 593–596. doi: 10.1093/geronb/gbv025

Roy, M., & Payette, H. (2012). The body image construct among Western seniors: A systematic review of the literature. *Archives of Gerontology and Geriatrics, 55*, 505–521. doi: 10.1016/j.archger.2012.04.007

Sandberg-Thoma, S. E., Snyder, A. R., & Jang, B. J. (2015). Exiting and returning to the parental home for boomerang kids. *Journal of Marriage and Family, 77*, 806–818. doi: 10.1111/jomf.12183

Schmidt, P. J., Murphy, J. H., Haq, N., Rubinow, D. R., & Danaceau, M. A. (2004). Stressful life events, personal losses, and perimenopause-related depression. *Archives of Women's Mental Health, 7*, 19–26. doi: 10.1007/s00737-003-0036-2

Schope, R. D. (2005). Who's afraid of growing old? Gay and lesbian perceptions of aging. *Journal of Gerontological Social Work, 45*(4), 23–39. doi: 10.1300/J083v45n04_03

Schubert, C. C., Boustani, M., Callahan, C. M., Perkins, A. J., Hui, S., & Hendrie, H. C. (2008). Acute care utilization by dementia caregivers within urban primary care practices. *Journal of General Internal Medicine, 23*, 1736–1740. doi: 10.1007/s11606-008-0711-0

Schulz, R., & Martire, L. M. (2004). Family caregiving of persons with dementia: Prevalence, health effects, and support strategies. *The American Journal of Geriatric Psychiatry, 12*, 240–249. doi: 10.1176/appi.ajgp.12.3.240

Shadyab, A. H., Macera, C. A., Shaffer, R. A., Jain, S., Gallo, L. C., Gass, M. L., . . . & LaCroix, A. Z. (2017). Ages at menarche and menopause and reproductive lifespan as predictors of exceptional longevity in women: The Women's Health Initiative. *Menopause, 24*, 35–44. doi: 10.1097/GME.0000000000000710

Sheriff, M., & Weatherall, A. (2009). A feminist discourse analysis of popular-press accounts of postmaternity. *Feminism & Psychology, 19*, 89–108. doi: 10.1177/0959353508098621

Shippy, R. A., Cantor, M. H., & Brennan, M. (2004). Social networks of aging gay men. *The Journal of Men's Studies, 13*, 107–120. doi: 10.3149/jms.1301.107

Shiu, C., Muraco, A., & Fredriksen-Goldsen, K. (2016). Invisible care: Friend and partner care among older lesbian, gay, bisexual, and transgender (LGBT) adults. *Journal of the Society for Social Work and Research, 7*, 527–546. doi: 10.1086/687325

Shlomo, S. B., Taubman-Ben-Ari, O., Findler, L., Sivan, E., & Dolizki, M. (2010). Becoming a grandmother: Maternal grandmothers' mental health, perceived costs, and personal growth. *Social Work Research, 34*, 45–57. doi :10.1093/swr/34.1.45

Slevec, J., & Tiggemann, M. (2011). Media exposure, body dissatisfaction, and disordered eating in middle-aged women: A test of the sociocultural model of disordered eating. *Psychology of Women Quarterly, 35*, 617–627. doi: 10.1177/0361684311420249

Smirnova, M. H. (2012). A will to youth: The woman's anti-aging elixir. *Social Science & Medicine, 75*, 1236–1243. doi: 10.1016/j.socscimed.2012.02.061

Smith, D. C., Prentice, R., Thompson, D. J., & Herrmann, W. L. (1975). Association of exogenous estrogen and endometrial carcinoma. *New England Journal of Medicine, 293*, 1164–1167. doi: 10.1056/NEJM197512042932302

Sommer, B., Avis, N., Meyer, P., Ory, M., Madden, T., Kagawa-Singer, M., . . . & Adler, S. (1999). Attitudes toward menopause and aging across ethnic/racial groups. *Psychosomatic Medicine, 61*, 868–875.

Spedale, S., Coupland, C., & Tempest, S. (2014). Gender ageism and organizational routines at work: The case of day-parting in television broadcasting. *Organization Studies, 35*, 1585–1604. doi: 10.1177/0170840614550733

Speelman, C. P., Clark-Murphy, M., & Gerrans, P. (2013). Decision making clusters in retirement savings: Gender differences dominate. *Journal of Family and Economic Issues, 34*, 329–339. doi: 10.1007/s10834-012-9334-z

Spring, L. (2015). Older women and sexuality—Are we still just talking lube? *Sexual and Relationship Therapy, 30*, 4–9. doi: 10.1080/14681994.2014.920617

Srikanth, V. K., Fryer, J. L., Zhai, G., Winzenberg, T. M., Hosmer, D., & Jones, G. (2005). A meta-analysis of sex differences prevalence, incidence and severity of osteoarthritis. *Osteoarthritis and Cartilage, 13*, 769–781. doi: 10.1016/j.joca.2005.04.014

Stahl, S. T., & Schulz, R. (2014). Changes in routine health behaviors following late-life bereavement: A systematic review. *Journal of Behavioral Medicine, 37*, 736–755. doi: 10.1007/s10865-013-9524-7

Standing Rock Sioux historian: Dakota Access Co. attack comes on anniversary of Whitestone Massacre. (2016, September 8). *Democracy Now!* Retrieved from https://www.democracynow.org/2016/9/8/standing_rock_sioux_historian_dakota_access

Standing, T. S., Musil, C. M., & Warner, C. B. (2007). Grandmothers' transitions in caregiving to grandchildren. *Western Journal of Nursing Research, 29*, 613–631. doi: 10.1177/0193945906298607

Strang, V. R., Koop, P. M., & Peden, J. (2002). The experience of respite during home-based family caregiving for persons with advanced cancer. *Journal of Palliative Care, 18*, 97–104.

Stroebe, M., & Schut, H. (2015). Family matters in bereavement: Toward an integrative intra-interpersonal coping model. *Perspectives on Psychological Science, 10*, 873–879. doi: 10.1177/1745691615598517

Stroebe, W., Zech, E., Stroebe, M. S., & Abakoumkin, G. (2005). Does social support help in bereavement? *Journal of Social and Clinical Psychology, 24*, 1030–1050. doi: 10.1521/jscp.2005.24.7.1030

Sullivan, A. R., & Fenelon, A. (2014). Patterns of widowhood mortality. *The Journals of Gerontology, Series B: Psychological Sciences and Social Sciences, 69*, 53–62. doi: 10.1093/geronb/gbt079

Sullivan, L., & Meschede, T. (2016). Race, gender, and senior economic well-being: How financial vulnerability over the life course shapes retirement for older women of color. *Public Policy & Aging Report, 26*, 58–62. doi: 10.1093/ppar/prw001

Sun, Y., Kim, S. W., Heo, C. Y., Kim, D., Hwang, Y., Yom, C. K., & Kang, E. (2014). Comparison of quality of life based on surgical technique in patients with breast cancer. *Japanese Journal of Clinical Oncology, 44*, 22–27. doi: 10.1093/jjco/hyt176

Tavener, M., Vo, K., & Byles, J. E. (2015). Work and other activities in retirement. *Journal of the American Geriatrics Society, 63*, 1476–1477. doi: 10.1111/jgs.13548

Taylor, D. J., Kuchibhatla, M., & Østbye, T. (2008). Trajectories of caregiving time provided by wives to their husbands with dementia. *Alzheimer's Disease and Associated Disorders, 22*, 131–136. doi: 10.1097/WAD.0b013e31815bebba

Tejada-Vera, B. (2013, March). Mortality from Alzheimer's disease in the United States: Data for 2000 and 2010. *NCHS Data Brief* (No. 116). Hyattsville, MD: National Center for Health Statistics. Retrieved from https://www.cdc.gov/nchs/data/databriefs/db116.pdf

Thiele, D. M., & Whelan, T. A. (2008). The relationship between grandparent satisfaction, meaning, and generativity. *The International Journal of Aging & Human Development, 66*, 21–48. doi: 10.2190/AG.66.1.b

Thomas, H. N., Hess, R., & Thurston, R. C. (2015). Correlates of sexual activity and satisfaction in midlife and older women. *The Annals of Family Medicine, 13*, 336–342. doi: 10.1370/afm.1820

Thompson, D., Jr. (2010, February 9). Cancer research: Where the funding goes. *Everyday Health.* Retrieved from http://www.everydayhealth.com/cancer/cancer-research-where-funding-goes.aspx

Tiggemann, M., & Lynch, J. E. (2001). Body image across the life span in adult women: The role of self-objectification. *Developmental Psychology, 37*, 243–253. doi: 10.1037/0012-1649.37.2.243

Umberson, D., & Williams, K. (2005). Marital quality, health, and aging: Gender equity? *The Journals of Gerontology, Series B: Psychological Sciences and Social Sciences, 60*, S109–S113. doi: 10.1093/geronb/60.Special_Issue_2.S109

United States Bone and Joint Initiative. (2014). *The burden of musculoskeletal diseases in the United States* (3rd ed.). Retrieved from http://www.boneandjointburden.org

U.S. Department of Health and Human Services. (2004). *Bone health and osteoporosis: A report of the Surgeon General.* Rockville, MD: U.S. Department of Health and Human Services. Retrieved from https://www.ncbi.nlm.nih.gov/books/NBK45513/pdf/Bookshelf_NBK45513.pdf

U.S. Department of Health and Human Services. (2014). *The health consequences of smoking: 50 years of progress. A report of the Surgeon General.* Atlanta, GA: U.S. Department of Health and Human Services. Retrieved from https://www.surgeongeneral.gov/library/reports/50-years-of-progress/full-report.pdf

U.S. Department of Labor, Bureau of Labor Statistics. (2016, February 25). *Volunteering in the United States—2015* [News release]. Retrieved from https://www.bls.gov/news.release/pdf/volun.pdf

Utz, R. L. (2011). Like mother, (not) like daughter: The social construction of menopause and aging. *Journal of Aging Studies, 25*, 143–154. doi: 10.1016/j.jaging.2010.08.019

van den Bogaard, L., Henkens, K., & Kalmijn, M. (2014). So now what? Effects of retirement on civic engagement. *Ageing and Society, 34*, 1170–1192. doi: 10.1017/S0144686X13000019 van der Heide, I., van Rijn, R. M., Robroek, S. J. W., Burdorf, A., & Proper, K. I. (2013). Is retirement good for your health? A systematic review of longitudinal studies. *BMC Public Health, 13*, 1180. doi: 10.1186/1471-2458-13-1180

Vespa, J., Lewis, J. M., & Kreider, R. M. (2013, August). *America's families and living arrangements: 2012* (Census Bureau Publication No. P20-570). Washington, DC: U.S. Census Bureau. Retrieved from https://www.census.gov/prod/2013pubs/p20-570.pdf

Viña, J., & Lloret, A. (2010). Why women have more Alzheimer's disease than men: Gender and mitochondrial toxicity of amyloid-β peptide. *Journal of Alzheimer's Disease, 20*(S2), 527–533. doi: 10.3233/JAD-2010-100501

Vitaliano, P. P., Young, H. M., & Zhang, J. (2004). Is caregiving a risk factor for illness? *Current Directions in Psychological Science, 13*, 13–16. doi: 10.1111/j.0963-7214.2004.01301004.x

Vo, K., Forder, P. M., Tavener, M., Rodgers, B., Banks, E., Bauman, A., & Byles, J. E. (2015). Retirement, age, gender and mental health: Findings from the 45 and Up Study. *Aging & Mental Health, 19*, 647–657. doi: 10.1080/13607863.2014.962002

von Känel, R., Mausbach, B. T., Patterson, T. L., Dimsdale, J. E., Aschbacher, K., Mills, P. J., & Grant, I. (2008). Increased Framingham coronary heart disease risk score in dementia caregivers relative to non-caregiving controls. *Gerontology, 54*, 131–137. doi: 10.1159/000113649

Weiss, D., & Lang, F. R. (2012). "They" are old but "I" feel younger: Age-group dissociation as a self-protective strategy in old age. *Psychology and Aging, 27*, 153–163. doi: 10.1037/a0024887

White, C. (2017, February 1). World's oldest surgeon, 89, is still performing operations. *Metro*. Retrieved from http://metro.co.uk/2017/02/01/worlds-oldest-surgeon-89-is-still-performing-operations-6420890/

Whitley, D. M., Lamis, D. A., & Kelley, S. J. (2016). Mental health stress, family resources and psychological distress: A longitudinal mediation analysis in African American grandmothers raising grandchildren. *Journal of Clinical Psychology, 72*, 563–579. doi: 10.1002/jclp.22272

Whitman, J. S., Cormier, S., & Boyd, C. J. (2000). Lesbian identity management at various stages of the coming out process: A qualitative study. *International Journal of Sexuality & Gender Studies, 5*, 3–18. doi: 10.1023/A:1010181416984

Wilcox, S., Evenson, K. R., Aragaki, A., Wassertheil-Smoller, S., Mouton, C. P., & Loevinger, B. L. (2003). The effects of widowhood on physical and mental health, health behaviors, and health outcomes: The Women's Health Initiative. *Health Psychology, 22*, 513–522. doi: 10.1037/0278-6133.22.5.513

Wild, K., Wiles, J. L., & Allen, R. E. (2013). Resilience: Thoughts on the value of the concept for critical gerontology. *Ageing & Society, 33*, 137–158.

Williams, B. R., Zhang, Y., Sawyer, P., Mujib, M., Jones, L. G., Feller, M. A., & Ahmed, A. (2011). Intrinsic association of widowhood with mortality in community-dwelling older women and men: Findings from a prospective propensity-matched population study. *The Journals of Gerontology, Series A: Biological Sciences and Medical Sciences, 66*, 1360–1368. doi: 10.1093/gerona/glr144

Williams, K. N., Herman, R., Gajewski, B., & Wilson, K. (2009). Elderspeak communication: Impact on dementia care. *American Journal of Alzheimer's Disease and Other Dementias, 24*, 11–20. doi: 10.1177/1533317508318472

Winblad, B., Amouyel, P., Andrieu, S., Ballard, C., Brayne, C., Brodaty, H., . . . & Fratiglioni, L. (2016). Defeating Alzheimer's disease and other dementias: A priority for European science and society. *The Lancet Neurology, 15*, 455–532. doi: 10.1016/S1474-4422(16)00062-4

Winterich, J. A. (2003). Sex, menopause, and culture: Sexual orientation and the meaning of menopause for women's sex lives. *Gender & Society, 17*, 627–642. doi: 10.1177/0891243203253962

Winterich, J. A. (2007). Aging, femininity, and the body: What appearance changes mean to women with age. *Gender Issues, 24*, 51–69. doi: 10.1007/s12147-007-9045-1

Witten, T. M. (2014). It's not all darkness: Robustness, resilience, and successful transgender aging. *LGBT Health, 1*(1), 24–33. doi: 10.1089/lgbt.2013.0017

Women's Health Initiative Steering Committee. (2004). Effects of conjugated equine estrogen in postmenopausal women with hysterectomy: The Women's Health Initiative randomized controlled trial. *Journal of the American Medical Association, 291*, 1701–1712. doi: 10.1001/jama.291.14.1701

Women's Institute for a Secure Retirement. (2014). *Impact of retirement risk on women: 2013 risks and processes of retirement survey report*. Retrieved from https://www.soa.org/Files/Research/Projects/research-2013-impact-retire-risks-women.pdf

Women's Institute for a Secure Retirement. (n.d.). *Single older African American women and poverty: Happy 50th anniversary of the Civil Rights Act of 1964*. Retrieved from http://www.wiserwomen.org/index.php?id=145&page=single-older-african-american-women-poverty

Woody, I. (2014). Aging out: A qualitative exploration of ageism and heterosexism among aging African American lesbians and gay men. *Journal of Homosexuality, 61*, 145–165. doi: 10.1080/00918369.2013.835603

Wright, S. L., & Canetto, S. S. (2009). Stereotypes of older lesbians and gay men. *Educational Gerontology, 35*, 424–452. doi: 10.1080/03601270802505640

Writing Group for the Women's Health Initiative Investigators. (2002). Risks and benefits of estrogen plus progestin in healthy postmenopausal women: Principal results from the Women's Health Initiative randomized controlled trial. *Journal of the American Medical Association, 288*, 321–333. doi: 10.1001/jama.288.3.321

Wu, J., Gale, C. P., Hall, M., Dondo, T. B., Metcalfe, E., Oliver, G., . . . & West, R. M. (2018). Impact of initial hospital diagnosis on mortality for acute myocardial infarction: A national cohort study. *European Heart Journal: Acute Cardiovascular Care, 7*, 139–148. doi: 10.1177/2048872616661693

Zick, C. D., Mayer, R. N., & Smith, K. R. (2015). Putting it off: Family breast cancer history and women's retirement planning. *Psycho-Oncology, 24*, 1500–1505. doi: 10.1002/pon.3759

Ziel, H. K., & Finkle, W. D. (1975). Increased risk of endometrial carcinoma among users of conjugated estrogens. *New England Journal of Medicine, 293*, 1167–1170. doi: 10.1056/NEJM197512042932303

Zisook, S., Shuchter, S. R., & Mulvihill, M. (1990). Alcohol, cigarette, and medication use during the first year of widowhood. *Psychiatric Annals, 20*, 318–326. doi: 10.3928/0048-5713-19900601-09

Zivin, K., & Christakis, N. A. (2007). The emotional toll of spousal morbidity and mortality. *The American Journal of Geriatric Psychiatry, 15*, 772–779. doi: 10.1097/JGP.0b013e318050c9ae

Chapter 12

Abajian, S. M. (2016). Documenting militarism: Challenges of researching highly contested practices within urban schools. *Anthropology & Education Quarterly, 47*, 25–41. doi: 10.1111/aeq.12133

Abbey, A., Jacques-Tiura, A., & Parkhill, M. R. (2010). Sexual assault among diverse populations of women: Common ground, distinctive features, and unanswered questions. In H. Landrine & N. F. Russo (Eds.), *Handbook of diversity in feminist psychology* (pp. 391–425). New York, NY: Springer.

Abbey, A., Wegner, R., Woerner, J., Pegram, S. E., & Pierce, J. (2014). Review of survey and experimental research that examines the relationship between alcohol consumption and men's sexual aggression perpetration. *Trauma, Violence, & Abuse, 15,* 265–282. doi: 10.1177/1524838014521031

Abu-Ras, W. M., & Suarez, Z. E. (2009). Muslim men and women's perception of discrimination, hate crimes, and PTSD symptoms post 9/11. *Traumatology, 15*(3), 48–63. doi: 10.1177/1534765609342281

Afifi, T. O., Boman, J., Fleisher, W., & Sareen, J. (2009). The relationship between child abuse, parental divorce, and lifetime mental disorders and suicidality in a nationally representative adult sample. *Child Abuse & Neglect, 33,* 139–147. doi: 10.1016/j.chiabu.2008.12.009

Ahrens, C. E., Abeling, S., Ahmad, S., & Hinman, J. (2010). Spirituality and well-being: The relationship between religious coping and recovery from sexual assault. *Journal of Interpersonal Violence, 25,* 1242–1263. doi: 10.1177/0886260509340533

Ahrens, C. E., & Aldana, E. (2012). The ties that bind: Understanding the impact of sexual assault disclosure on survivors' relationships with friends, family, and partners. *Journal of Trauma & Dissociation, 13,* 226–243. doi: 10.1080/15299732.2012.642738

Ahrens, C. E., Campbell, R., Ternier-Thames, N. K., Wasco, S. M., & Sefl, T. (2007). Deciding whom to tell: Expectations and outcomes of rape survivors' first disclosures. *Psychology of Women Quarterly, 31,* 38–49. doi: 10.1111/j.1471-6402.2007.00329.x

Allen, C. (2015). "People hate you because of the way you dress": Understanding the invisible experiences of veiled British Muslim women victims of Islamophobia. *International Review of Victimology, 21,* 287–301. doi: 10.1177/0269758015591677

Allroggen, M., Rau, T., Ohlert, J., & Fegert, J. M. (2017). Lifetime prevalence and incidence of sexual victimization of adolescents in institutional care. *Child Abuse & Neglect, 66,* 23–30. doi: 10.1016/j.chiabu.2017.02.015

American Psychological Association Task Force on the Sexualization of Girls. (2007). *Report of the APA Task Force on the Sexualization of Girls.* Retrieved from http://www.apa.org/pi/wpo/sexualization.html

Amnesty International. (2017). *Key principles on the use and transfer of armed drones.* London, United Kingdom: Author. Retrieved from https://www.amnesty.org/download/Documents/ACT3063882017ENGLISH.PDF

Amnesty International. (n.d.). *Maze of injustice: A summary of Amnesty International's findings.* Retrieved from http://www.amnestyusa.org/our-work/issues/women-s-rights/violence-against-women/maze-of-injustice

Amnesty International reveals alarming impact of online abuse against women. (2017, November 20). *Amnesty International.* Retrieved from https://www.amnesty.org/en/latest/news/2017/11/amnesty-reveals-alarming-impact-of-online-abuse-against-women/

Anderson, C. A., Bushman, B. J., Donnerstein, E., Hummer, T. A., & Warburton, W. (2015). SPSSI research summary on media violence. *Analyses of Social Issues and Public Policy, 15,* 4–19. doi: 10.1111/asap.12093

Anderson, C. A., Suzuki, K., Swing, E. L., Groves, C. L., Gentile, D. A., Prot, S., . . . & Petrescu, P. (2017). Media violence and other aggression risk factors in seven nations. *Personality and Social Psychology Bulletin, 43,* 986–998. doi: 10.1177/0146167217703064

Anderson, K. L. (2013). Why do we fail to ask "why" about gender and intimate partner violence? *Journal of Marriage and Family, 75,* 314–318. doi: 10.1111/jomf.12001

Anderson, L. A., & Whiston, S. C. (2005). Sexual assault education programs: A meta-analytic examination of their effectiveness. *Psychology of Women Quarterly, 29,* 374–388. doi: 10.1111/j.1471-6402.2005.00237.x

Aosved, A. C., & Long, P. J. (2006). Co-occurrence of rape myth acceptance, sexism, racism, homophobia, ageism, classism, and religious intolerance. *Sex Roles, 55,* 481–492. doi: 10.1007/s11199-006-9101-4

Badenes-Ribera, L., Bonilla-Campos, A., Frias-Navarro, D., Pons-Salvador, G., & Monterde-i-Bort, H. (2016). Intimate partner violence in self-identified lesbians: A systematic review of its prevalence and correlates. *Trauma, Violence, & Abuse, 17,* 284–297. doi: 10.1177/1524838015584363

Balsam, K. F., & Szymanski, D. M. (2005). Relationship quality and domestic violence in women's same-sex relationships: The role of minority stress. *Psychology of Women Quarterly, 29,* 258–269. doi: 10.1111/j.1471-6402.2005.00220.x

Barnett, M. D., Hale, T. M., & Sligar, K. B. (2017). Masculinity, femininity, sexual dysfunctional beliefs, and rape myth acceptance among heterosexual college men and women. *Sexuality & Culture, 21,* 741–753. doi: 10.1007/s12119-017-9420-3

Baron, L., Straus, M. A., & Jaffee, D. (1988). Legitimate violence, violent attitudes, and rape: A test of the cultural spillover theory. *Annals of the New York Academy of Sciences, 528,* 79–110. doi: 10.1111/j.1749-6632.1988.tb50853.x

Basow, S. A., & Thompson, J. (2012). Service providers' reactions to intimate partner violence as a function of victim sexual orientation and type of abuse. *Journal of Interpersonal Violence, 27,* 1225–1241. doi: 10.1177/0886260511425241

Bastomski, S., & Smith, P. (2017). Gender, fear, and public places: How negative encounters with strangers harm women. *Sex Roles, 76,* 73–88. doi: 10.1007/s11199-016-0654-6

Beaulaurier, R. L., Seff, L. R., & Newman, F. L. (2008). Barriers to help-seeking for older women who experience intimate partner violence: A descriptive model. *Journal of Women & Aging, 20,* 231–248. doi: 10.1080/08952840801984543

Beck, J. (2018, January 17). When pop culture sells dangerous myths about romance. *The Atlantic.* Retrieved from https://www.theatlantic.com/entertainment/archive/2018/01/when-pop-culture-sells-dangerous-myths-about-romance/549749/

Bedera, N., & Nordmeyer, K. (2015). "Never go out alone": An analysis of college rape prevention tips. *Sexuality & Culture, 19,* 533–542. doi: 10.1007/s12119-015-9274-5

Begany, J. J., & Milburn, M. A. (2002). Psychological predictors of sexual harassment: Authoritarianism, hostile sexism, and rape myths. *Psychology of Men & Masculinity, 3,* 119–126. doi: 10.1037/1524-9220.3.2.119

Berg, K. K. (2014). Cultural factors in the treatment of battered women with privilege: Domestic violence in the lives of white European-American, middle-class, heterosexual women. *Affilia, 29,* 142–152. doi: 10.1177/0886109913516448

Bergman, M. E., Langhout, R. D., Palmeiri, P. A., Cortina, L., & Fitzgerald, L. F. (2002). The (un)reasonableness of reporting: Antecedents and consequences of reporting sexual harassment. *Journal of Applied Psychology, 87,* 230–242. doi: 10.1037/0021-9010.87.2.230

Bergsma, L. J., & Carney, M. E. (2008). Effectiveness of health-promoting media literacy education: A systematic review. *Health Education Research, 23,* 522–542. doi: 10.1093/her/cym084

Berlatsky, N. (2014, July 28). Even if you don't like it, you're supposed to appear that you do. *The Atlantic.* Retrieved from https://www.theatlantic.com/politics/archive/2014/07

/black-women-street-harassment-even-if-you-dont-like-it-youre-supposed-to-appear-that-you-do/375175/

Bhogal, M. S., & Corbett, S. (2016). The influence of aggressiveness on rape-myth acceptance among university students. *Psychiatry, Psychology and Law, 23,* 709–715. doi: 10.1080/13218719.2016.1142931

Black, M. C., Basile, K. C., Breiding, M. J., Smith, S. G., Walters, M. L., Merrick, M. T., Chen, J., & Stevens, M. R. (2011, November). *The National Intimate Partner and Sexual Violence Survey: 2010 summary report—Executive summary.* Atlanta, GA: Centers for Disease Control and Prevention. Retrieved from https://www.cdc.gov/violenceprevention/pdf/nisvs_executive_summary-a.pdf

Blanchard, E. (2011). The technoscience question in feminist international relations: Unmanning the U.S. war on terror. In J. A. Tickner & L. Sjoberg (Eds.), *Feminism and international relations: Conversations about the past, present, and future* (pp. 146–163). New York, NY: Routledge.

Blay, Z. (2016, January 25). "SNL" did a sketch about rape again and it still wasn't funny. *Huffington Post.* Retrieved from http://www.huffingtonpost.com/entry/snl-did-a-sketch-about-rape-again-and-it-still-wasnt-funny_us_56a64641e4b076aadcc736e5

Bliss, S. L., Oh, E. J., & Williams, R. L. (2007). Militarism and sociopolitical perspectives among college students in the U.S. and South Korea. *Peace and Conflict, 13,* 175–199. doi: 10.1080/10781910701271218

Bogar, C. B., & Hulse-Killacky, D. (2006). Resiliency determinants and resiliency processes among female adult survivors of childhood sexual abuse. *Journal of Counseling & Development, 84,* 318–327. doi: 10.1002/j.1556-6678.2006.tb00411.x

Bohner, G. (2001). Writing about rape: Use of the passive voice and other distancing text features as an expression of perceived responsibility of the victim. *British Journal of Social Psychology, 40,* 515–529. doi: 10.1248/01446601164957.

Bonomi, A. E., Altenburger, L. E., & Walton, N. L. (2013). "Double crap!" Abuse and harmed identity in *Fifty Shades of Grey. Journal of Women's Health, 22,* 733–744. doi: 10.1089/jwh.2013.4344

Boots, D. P., Wareham, J., Bartula, A., & Canas, R. (2016). A comparison of the batterer intervention and prevention program with alternative court dispositions on 12-month recidivism. *Violence Against Women, 22,* 1134–1157. doi: 10.1177/1077801215618806

Bouie, J. (2015, June 18). The deadly history of "they're raping our women." *Slate.* Retrieved from http://www.slate.com/articles/news_and_politics/history/2015/06/the_deadly_history_of_they_re_raping_our_women_racists_have_long_defended.html

Bradshaw, C., Kahn, A. S., & Saville, B. K. (2010). To hook up or date: Which gender benefits? *Sex Roles, 62,* 661–669. doi: 10.1007/s11199-010-9765-7

Brem, M. J., Florimbio, A. R., Grigorian, H., Wolford-Clevenger, C., Elmquist, J., Shorey, R. C., . . . & Stuart, G. L. (2017). Cyber abuse among men arrested for domestic violence: Cyber monitoring moderates the relationship between alcohol problems and intimate partner violence. *Psychology of Violence.* Advance online publication. doi: 10.1037/vio0000130

Brennan, C. L., Swartout, K. M., Goodnight, B. L., Cook, S. L., Parrott, D. J., Thompson, M. P., . . . & Leone, R. M. (2018). Evidence for multiple classes of sexually violent college men. *Psychology of Violence.* Advance online publication. doi: 10.1037/vio0000179

Brewin, C. R., Andrews, B., & Valentine, J. D. (2000). Meta-analysis of risk factors for posttraumatic stress disorder in trauma-exposed adults. *Journal of Consulting and Clinical Psychology, 68,* 748–766. doi: 10.1037/0022-006X.68.5.748

Bridges, A. J., Wosnitzer, R., Scharrer, E., Sun, C., & Liberman, R. (2010). Aggression and sexual behavior in best-selling pornography videos: A content analysis update. *Violence Against Women, 16,* 1065–1085. doi: 10.1177/1077801210382866

Briggs, E. C., Thompson, R., Ostrowski, S., & Lekwauwa, R. (2011). Psychological, health, behavioral, and economic impact of child maltreatment. In J. W. White, M. P. Koss, & A. E. Kazdin (Eds.), *Violence against women and children, Vol 1: Mapping the terrain* (pp. 77–97). Washington, DC: American Psychological Association.

Brinkman, B. G., Khan, A., Jedinak, A., & Vetere, L. (2015). College women's reflections on media representations of empowerment. *Psychology of Popular Media Culture, 4,* 2–17. doi: 10.1037/ppm0000043

Brown, A. L., Testa, M., & Messman-Moore, T. L. (2009). Psychological consequences of sexual victimization resulting from force, incapacitation, or verbal coercion. *Violence Against Women, 15,* 898–919. doi: 10.1177/1077801209335491

Brown, M. J., & Groscup, J. (2009). Perceptions of same-sex domestic violence among crisis center staff. *Journal of Family Violence, 24,* 87–93. doi: 10.1007/s10896-008-9212-5

Brownmiller, S. (1975). *Against our will: Men, women and rape.* New York, NY: Bantam Books.

Brownridge, D. A. (2006). Partner violence against women with disabilities: Prevalence, risk, and explanations. *Violence Against Women, 12,* 805–822. doi: 10.1177/1077801206292681

Brownridge, D. A. (2009). Situating research on safety promoting behaviors among disabled and deaf victims of interpersonal violence. *Violence Against Women, 15,* 1075–1079. doi: 10.1177/1077801209340311

Bryant-Davis, T., & Wong, E. C. (2013). Faith to move mountains: Religious coping, spirituality, and interpersonal trauma recovery. *American Psychologist, 68,* 675–684. doi: 10.1037/a0034380

Bushman, B. J. (2018). Teaching students about violent media effects. *Teaching of Psychology, 45,* 200–206. doi: 10.1177/0098628318762936

Bushman, B. J., & Anderson, C. A. (2009). Comfortably numb: Desensitizing effects of violent media on helping others. *Psychological Science, 20,* 273–277. doi: 10.1111/j.1467-9280.2009.02287.x

Bushman, B. J., Jamieson, P. E., Weitz, I., & Romer, D. (2013). Gun violence trends in movies. *Pediatrics, 132,* 1014–1018. doi: 10.1542/peds.2013-1600

Cameron, A. (2006). Stopping the violence: Canadian feminist debates on restorative justice and intimate violence. *Theoretical Criminology, 10,* 49–66. doi: 10.1177/1362480606059982

Cameron, C. A., & Stritzke, W. G. (2003). Alcohol and acquaintance rape in Australia: Testing the presupposition model of attributions about responsibility and blame. *Journal of Applied Social Psychology, 33,* 983–1008. doi: 10.1111/j.1559-1816.2003.tb01935.x

Campbell, J. C. (2002). Safety planning based on lethality assessment for partners of batterers in intervention programs. *Journal of Aggression, Maltreatment & Trauma, 5,* 129–143. doi: 10.1300/J146v05n02_08

Campbell, J. C. (2004). Helping women understand their risk in situations of intimate partner violence. *Journal of Interpersonal Violence, 19,* 1464–1477. doi: 10.1177/0886260504269698

Campbell, J. C., Webster, D., Koziol-McLain, J., Block, C., Campbell, D., Curry, M. A., . . . & Sharps, P. (2003). Risk factors for femicide in abusive relationships: Results from a multisite case control study. *American Journal of Public Health, 93,* 1089–1097. doi: 10.2105/AJPH.93.7.1089

Campbell, R., Wasco, S. M., Ahrens, C. E., Sefl, T., & Barnes, H. E. (2001). Preventing the "second rape": Rape survivors' experiences with community service providers. *Journal of Interpersonal Violence, 16,* 1239–1259. doi: 10.1177/088626001016012002

Capaldi, D. M., Knoble, N. B., Shortt, J. W., & Kim, H. K. (2012). A systematic review of risk factors for intimate partner violence. *Partner Abuse, 3,* 231–280. doi: 10.1891/1946-6560.3.2.e4

Carey, K. B., Durney, S. E., Shepardson, R. L., & Carey, M. P. (2015a). Incapacitated and forcible rape of college women: Prevalence across the first year. *Journal of Adolescent Health, 56,* 678–680. doi: 10.1016/j.jadohealth.2015.02.018

Carey, K. B., Durney, S. E., Shepardson, R. L., & Carey, M. P. (2015b). Precollege predictors of incapacitated rape among female students in their first year of college. *Journal of Studies on Alcohol and Drugs, 76,* 829–837. doi: 10.15288/jsad.2015.76.829

Carmon, I. (2010, September 21). Is rape ever funny? *Jezebel.* Retrieved from http://jezebel.com/5644025/is-rape-ever-funny

Carr, M., Thomas, A. J., Atwood, D., Muhar, A., Jarvis, K., & Wewerka, S. S. (2014). Debunking three rape myths. *Journal of Forensic Nursing, 10,* 217–225. doi: 10.1097/JFN.0000000000000044

Carter, A. (2017, January 5). Department of Defense accomplishments (2009–2016): Taking the long view, investing in the future. Retrieved from https://www.defense.gov/Portals/1/Documents/pubs/FINAL-DOD-Exit-Memo.pdf

Carvalho, A. F., Lewis, R. J., Derlega, V. J., Winstead, B. A., & Viggiano, C. (2011). Internalized sexual minority stressors and same-sex intimate partner violence. *Journal of Family Violence, 26,* 501–509. doi: 10.1007/s10896-011-9384-2

Cashmore, J., & Shackel, R. (2013). *The long-term effects of child sexual abuse* [CFCA Paper No. 11]. Melbourne, Australia: Australian Institute of Family Studies. Retrieved from https://aifs.gov.au/cfca/sites/default/files/cfca/pubs/papers/a143161/cfca11.pdf

Casteel, C., Martin, S. L., Smith, J. B., Gurka, K. K., & Kupper, L. L. (2008). National study of physical and sexual assault among women with disabilities. *Injury Prevention, 14,* 87–90. doi: 10.1136/ip.2007.016451

Centers for Disease Control and Prevention. (2016a, May 3). *Intimate partner violence.* Retrieved from https://www.cdc.gov/violenceprevention/intimatepartnerviolence/

Centers for Disease Control and Prevention. (2016b, July 20). *Intimate partner violence definitions.* Retrieved from https://www.cdc.gov/violenceprevention/intimatepartnerviolence/definitions.html

Chakraborti, N., & Zempi, I. (2012). The veil under attack: Gendered dimensions of Islamophobic victimization. *International Review of Victimology, 18,* 269–284. doi: 10.1177/0269758012446983

Chen, Y., & Ullman, S. E. (2010). Women's reporting of sexual and physical assaults to police in the National Violence Against Women Survey. *Violence Against Women, 16,* 262–279. doi: 10.1177/1077801209360861

Child marriage database. (2018, March). *UNICEF.* Retrieved from http://data.unicef.org/topic/child-protection/child-marriage/

Children's Bureau, Administration for Children & Families, U.S. Department of Health & Human Services. (2016, December 29). *Child abuse & neglect.* Retrieved from https://www.acf.hhs.gov/cb/focus-areas/child-abuse-neglect

Choma, B. L., Foster, M. D., & Radford, E. (2007). Use of objectification theory to examine the effects of a media literacy intervention on women. *Sex Roles, 56,* 581–590. doi: 10.1007/s11199-007-9200-x

Circulating Now. (2015, October 15). Domestic Violence in the 1970s [Blog post]. Retrieved from https://circulatingnow.nlm.nih.gov/2015/10/15/domestic-violence-in-the-1970s

Cities for CEDAW. (n.d.). *UN Women.* Retrieved from https://www.unwomen-usnc.org/gcccedaw

Clark, M. D., & Carroll, M. H. (2008). Acquaintance rape scripts of women and men: Similarities and differences. *Sex Roles, 58,* 616–625. doi: 10.1007/s11199-007-9373-3

Clay-Warner, J., & Burt, C. H. (2005). Rape reporting after reforms: Have times really changed? *Violence Against Women, 11,* 150–176. doi: 10.1177/1077801204271566

Clough, A., Draughon, J. E., Njie-Carr, V., Rollins, C., & Glass, N. (2014). "Having housing made everything else possible": Affordable, safe and stable housing for women survivors of violence. *Qualitative Social Work, 13,* 671–688. doi: 10.1177/1473325013503003

CNN Political Unit. (2013, October 12). Malala to Obama: Drone strikes "fueling terrorism." *CNN.* Retrieved from https://www.cnn.com/2013/10/12/politics/obamas-meet-malalas/index.html

Cockram, J. (2003, November). *Silent voices: Women with disabilities and family and domestic violence.* Nedlands, WA: People with Disabilities (WA) Inc. Retrieved from http://wwda.org.au/wp-content/uploads/2013/12/cockram2.pdf

Cohn, A. M., Zinzow, H. M., Resnick, H. S., & Kilpatrick, D. G. (2013). Correlates of reasons for not reporting rape to police: Results from a national telephone household probability sample of women with forcible or drug-or-alcohol facilitated/incapacitated rape. *Journal of Interpersonal Violence, 28,* 455–473. doi: 10.1177/0886260512455515

Coker, A. L., Fisher, B. S., Bush, H. M., Swan, S. C., Williams, C. M., Clear, E. R., & DeGue, S. (2015). Evaluation of the Green Dot bystander intervention to reduce interpersonal violence among college students across three campuses. *Violence Against Women, 21,* 1507–1527. doi: 10.1177/1077801214545284

Collins, P. H. (2017). On violence, intersectionality and transversal politics. *Ethnic and Racial Studies, 40,* 1460–1473. doi: 10.1080/01419870.2017.1317827

Collins, V. E., & Carmody, D. C. (2011). Deadly love: Images of dating violence in the "Twilight Saga." *Affilia, 26,* 382–394. doi: 10.1177/0886109911428425

Cook, C. L., & Lane, J. (2017). Blaming the victim: Perceptions about incarcerated sexual assault victim culpability among a sample of jail correctional officers. *Victims & Offenders, 12,* 347–380. doi: 10.1080/15564886.2015.1065531

Cook, S. L., Wilson, R. A., & Thomas, E. B. (2018). A history of gender-based violence. In C. B. Travis & J. W. White (Eds.), *APA handbook of the psychology of women* (Vol. 2, pp. 153–173). Washington, DC: American Psychological Association.

Cooley-Quille, M., Boyd, R. C., Frantz, E., & Walsh, J. (2001). Emotional and behavioral impact of exposure to community violence in inner-city adolescents. *Journal of Clinical Child Psychology, 30,* 199–206. doi: 10.1207/S15374424JCCP3002_7

Coolidge, F. L., & Anderson, L. W. (2002). Personality profiles of women in multiple abusive relationships. *Journal of Family Violence, 17,* 117–131. doi: 10.1023/A:1015005400141

Coulter, R. S., Mair, C., Miller, E., Blosnich, J. R., Matthews, D. D., & McCauley, H. L. (2017). Prevalence of past-year sexual assault victimization among undergraduate students: Exploring differences by and intersections of gender identity, sexual identity, and race/ethnicity. *Prevention Science, 18,* 726–736. doi: 10.1007/s11121-017-0762-8

Coxell, A. W., & King, M. B. (2010). Adult male rape and sexual assault: Prevalence, re-victimisation and the tonic immobility response. *Sexual and Relationship Therapy, 25,* 372–379. doi: 10.1080/14681991003747430

Creek, S. J., & Dunn, J. L. (2014). Intersectionality and the study of sex, gender, and crime. In R. Gartner & B. McCarthy (Eds.), *The Oxford handbook of gender, sex, and crime* (pp. 40–58). New York, NY: Oxford University Press.

Crenshaw, K. (1991). Mapping the margins: Intersectionality, identity politics, and violence against women of color. *Stanford Law Review, 43*, 1241–1299.

Crockett, C., Brandl, B., & Dabby, F. C. (2015). Survivors in the margins: The invisibility of violence against older women. *Journal of Elder Abuse & Neglect, 27*, 291–302. doi: 10.1080/08946566.2015.1090361

Cuklanz, L. M. (2000). *Rape on prime time: Television, masculinity, and sexual violence*. Philadelphia, PA: University of Pennsylvania Press.

Cunningham, K. C., & Cromer, L. D. (2016). Attitudes about human trafficking: Individual differences related to belief and victim blame. *Journal of Interpersonal Violence, 31*, 228–244. doi: 10.1177/0886260514555369

Custers, K., & McNallie, J. (2017). The relationship between television sports exposure and rape myth acceptance: The mediating role of sexism and sexual objectification of women. *Violence Against Women, 23*, 813–829. doi: 10.1177/1077801216651340

Custers, K., & Van den Bulck, J. (2013). The cultivation of fear of sexual violence in women: Processes and moderators of the relationship between television and fear. *Communication Research, 40*, 96–124. doi: 10.1177/0093650212440444

Cuthbert, A. (2015). Current and possible future directions in masculinity ideology research. *Psychology of Men & Masculinity, 16*, 134–136. doi: 10.1037/a0038998

Daly, K. (2002). Restorative justice: The real story. *Punishment & Society, 4*, 55–79. doi: 10.1177/14624740222228464

Daly, K., & Stubbs, J. (2006). Feminist engagement with restorative justice. *Theoretical Criminology, 10*, 9–28. doi: 10.1177/1362480606059980

Daniels, E. A., & Zurbriggen, E. L. (2016). The price of sexy: Viewers' perceptions of a sexualized versus nonsexualized Facebook profile photograph. *Psychology of Popular Media Culture, 5*, 2–14. doi: 10.1037/ppm0000048

Dank, M., Khan, B., Downey, P. M., Kotonias, C., Mayer, D., Owens, C., Pacifici, L., & Yu, L. (2014, March). *Estimating the size and structure of the underground commercial sex economy in eight major U.S. cities*. Retrieved from the Urban Institute website: http://www.urban.org/sites/default/files/publication/22376/413047-estimating-the-size-and-structure-of-the-underground-commercial-sex-economy-in-eight-major-us-cities.pdf

Dardis, C. M., Dixon, K. J., Edwards, K. M., & Turchik, J. A. (2015). An examination of the factors related to dating violence perpetration among young men and women and associated theoretical explanations: A review of the literature. *Trauma, Violence, & Abuse, 16*, 136–152. doi: 10.1177/1524838013517559

Davidson, M. M., Butchko, M. S., Robbins, K., Sherd, L. W., & Gervais, S. J. (2016). The mediating role of perceived safety on street harassment and anxiety. *Psychology of Violence, 6*, 553–561. doi: 10.1037/a0039970

Davis, A. Y. (1981). *Women, race, & class*. New York, NY: Random House.

De Antoni, C., & Munhós, A. A. R. (2016). The institutional violence and structural violence experienced by homeless women. *Psicologia em Estudo, 21*, 641–651. doi: 10.4025/psicolestud.v21i4.31840

de Heer, B., & Jones, L. (2017). Measuring sexual violence on campus: Climate surveys and vulnerable groups. *Journal of School Violence, 16*, 207–221. doi: 10.1080/15388220.2017.1284444

Demers, J. M., Ward, S. K., Walsh, W. A., Banyard, V. L., Cohn, E. S., Edwards, K. M., & Moynihan, M. M. (2018). Disclosure on campus: Students' decisions to tell others about unwanted sexual experiences, intimate partner violence, and stalking. *Journal of Aggression, Maltreatment & Trauma, 27*, 54–75. doi: 10.1080/10926771.2017.1382631

Dias, A., Sales, L., Mooren, T., Mota-Cardoso, R., & Kleber, R. (2017). Child maltreatment, revictimization and post-traumatic stress disorder among adults in a community sample. *International Journal of Clinical and Health Psychology, 17*, 97–106. doi: 10.1016/j.ijchp.2017.03.003

Dimond, J. P., Fiesler, C., & Bruckman, A. S. (2011). Domestic violence and information communication technologies. *Interacting with Computers, 23*, 413–421. doi: 10.1016/j.intcom.2011.04.006

Dobash, R. P., & Dobash, R. E. (2012). Who died? The murder of collaterals related to intimate partner conflict. *Violence Against Women, 18*, 662–671. doi: 10.1177/1077801212453984

Donnelly, D. A., Cook, K. J., Van Ausdale, D., & Foley, L. (2005). White privilege, color blindness, and services to battered women. *Violence Against Women, 11*, 6–37. doi: 10.1177/1077801204271431

Donohoe, M. (2013). War, rape, and genocide: Never again? In M. T. Donohoe (Ed.), *Public health and social justice* (pp. 427–434). San Francisco, CA: Jossey-Bass.

Donovan, R. A. (2007). To blame or not to blame: Influences of target race and observer sex on rape blame attribution. *Journal of Interpersonal Violence, 22*, 722–736. doi: 10.1177/0886260507300754

Dorr, L. L. (2004). *White women, rape, and the power of race in Virginia, 1900–1960*. Chapel Hill, NC: University of North Carolina Press.

Duke, A., & Rowlands, T. (2009, June 23). Chris Brown pleads guilty in Rihanna assault case. *CNN*. Retrieved from http://www.cnn.com/2009/SHOWBIZ/Music/06/22/chris.brown.hearing/

Dunlop, B. D., Rothman, M. B., Condon, K. M., Hebert, K. S., & Martinez, I. L. (2001). Elder abuse: Risk factors and use of case data to improve policy and practice. *Journal of Elder Abuse & Neglect, 12*, 95–122. doi: 10.1300/J084v12n03_05

Dutton, D. G. (2006). *The abusive personality: Violence and control in intimate relationships*. New York, NY: Guilford Press.

Dworkin, E. R., Ullman, S. E., Stappenbeck, C., Brill, C. D., & Kaysen, D. (2018). Proximal relationships between social support and PTSD symptom severity: A daily diary study of sexual assault survivors. *Depression and Anxiety, 35*, 43–49. doi: 10.1002/da.22679

Eberstadt, M., & Layden, M. A. (2010). *The social costs of pornography: A statement of findings and recommendations*. Princeton, NJ: The Witherspoon Institute.

Egan, R., & Wilson, J. C. (2012). Rape victims' attitudes to rape myth acceptance. *Psychiatry, Psychology and Law, 19*, 345–357. doi: 10.1080/13218719.2011.585128

Emmers-Sommer, T. M. (2015). An examination of gender of aggressor and target (un)wanted sex and nonconsent on perceptions of sexual (un)wantedness, justifiability and consent. *Sexuality Research and Social Policy, 12*, 280–289. doi: 10.1007/s13178-015-0193-x

Enloe, C. (2016). *Globalization and militarism: Feminists make the link*. Lanham, MD: Rowman & Littlefield.

Estrellado, A. F., & Loh, J. (2016). To stay in or leave an abusive relationship: Losses and gains experienced by battered Filipino women. *Journal of Interpersonal Violence*. Advance online publication. doi: 10.1177/0886260516657912

Fairchild, K. (2010). Context effects on women's perceptions of stranger harassment. *Sexuality & Culture, 14*, 191–216. doi: 10.1007/s12119-010-9070-1

Fairchild, K., & Rudman, L. A. (2008). Everyday stranger harassment and women's objectification. *Social Justice Research, 21*, 338–357. doi: 10.1007/s11211-008-0073-0

Faludi, S. (2007). *The terror dream: Fear and fantasy in post-9/11 America*. New York, NY: Henry Holt.

Farley, M. (2003). Prostitution and the invisibility of harm. *Women & Therapy, 26*, 247–280. doi: 10.1300/J015v26n03_06

Farrell, G., Tilley, N., & Tseloni, A. (2014). Why the crime drop? *Crime and Justice, 43*, 421–490. doi: 10.1086/678081

Farvid, P., Braun, V., & Rowney, C. (2017). "No girl wants to be called a slut!": Women, heterosexual casual sex and the sexual double standard. *Journal of Gender Studies, 26*, 544–560. doi: 10.1080/09589236.2016.1150818

Faver C. A., & Strand E. B. (2003). To leave or to stay? Battered women's concern for vulnerable pets. *Journal of Interpersonal Violence, 18*, 1367–1377. doi: 10.1177/0886260503258028.

Fedina, L., Holmes, J. L., & Backes, B. L. (2018). Campus sexual assault: A systematic review of prevalence research from 2000 to 2015. *Trauma, Violence, & Abuse, 19*, 76–93. doi: 10.1177/1524838016631129

Feigenbaum, A. (2015). From cyborg feminism to drone feminism: Remembering women's anti-nuclear activisms. *Feminist Theory, 16*, 265–288. doi: 10.1177/1464700115604132

Felson, R. B. (2002). Gender differences in power and status. In R. B. Felson (Ed.), *Law and public policy: Violence and gender reexamined* (pp. 50–65). Washington, DC: American Psychological Association.

Ferguson, C. E., & Malouff, J. M. (2016). Assessing police classifications of sexual assault reports: A meta-analysis of false reporting rates. *Archives of Sexual Behavior, 45*, 1185–1193. doi: 10.1007/s10508-015-0666-2

Finch, E., & Munro, V. E. (2005). Juror stereotypes and blame attribution in rape cases involving intoxicants: The findings of a pilot study. *British Journal of Criminology, 45*, 25–38. doi: 10.1093/bjc/azh055

Finkelhor, D., Turner, H., Hamby, S. L., & Ormrod, R. (2011, October). *Polyvictimization: Children's exposure to multiple types of violence, crime, and abuse*. Retrieved from the National Criminal Justice Reference Service website: https://www.ncjrs.gov/pdffiles1/ojjdp/235504.pdf

Firth, M. T. (2014). Childhood abuse and depressive vulnerability in clients with gender dysphoria. *Counselling and Psychotherapy Research, 14*, 297–305. doi: 10.1080/14733145.2013.845236

Fisher, B. S., Cullen, F. T., & Daigle, L. E. (2005). The discovery of acquaintance rape: The salience of methodological innovation and rigor. *Journal of Interpersonal Violence, 20*, 493–500. doi: 10.1177/0886260504267761

Fisher, N. L., & Pina, A. (2013). An overview of the literature on female-perpetrated adult male sexual victimization. *Aggression and Violent Behavior, 18*, 54–61. doi: 10.1016/j.avb.2012.10.001

Flack, W. J., Hansen, B. E., Hopper, A. B., Bryant, L. A., Lang, K. W., Massa, A. A., & Whalen, J. E. (2016). Some types of hookups may be riskier than others for campus sexual assault. *Psychological Trauma: Theory, Research, Practice, and Policy, 8*, 413–420. doi: 10.1037/tra0000090

Flood, M. (2011). Involving men in efforts to end violence against women. *Men and Masculinities, 14*, 358–377. doi: 10.1177/1097184X10363995

Flood, M. (2015). Work with men to end violence against women: A critical stocktake. *Culture, Health & Sexuality, 17*(sup2), 159–176. doi: 10.1080/13691058.2015.1070435

Foley, L. A., Evancic, C., Karnik, K., King, J., & Parks, A. (1995). Date rape: Effects of race of assailant and victim and gender of subjects on perceptions. *Journal of Black Psychology, 21*, 6–18. doi: 10.1177/00957984950211002

Ford, J., & Soto-Marquez, J. G. (2016). Sexual assault victimization among straight, gay/lesbian, and bisexual college students. *Violence and Gender, 3*, 107–115. doi: 10.1089/vio.2015.0030

Ford, J. V. (2017). Sexual assault on college hookups: The role of alcohol and acquaintances. *Sociological Forum, 32*, 381–405. doi: 10.1111/socf.12335

Foubert, J. D., Brosi, M. W., & Bannon, R. S. (2011). Pornography viewing among fraternity men: Effects on bystander intervention, rape myth acceptance and behavioral intent to commit sexual assault. *Sexual Addiction & Compulsivity, 18*, 212–231. doi: 10.1080/10720162.2011.625552

Fowler, S. K., Blackburn, A. G., Marquart, J. W., & Mullings, J. L. (2010). Would they officially report an in-prison sexual assault? An examination of inmate perceptions. *The Prison Journal, 90*, 220–243. doi: 10.1177/0032885510363387

Francia, C. A., Coolidge, F. L., White, L. A., Segal, D. L., Cahill, B. S., & Estey, A. J. (2010). Personality disorder profiles in incarcerated male rapists and child molesters. *American Journal of Forensic Psychology, 28*(3), 55–68.

Franiuk, R., Seefelt, J. L., Cepress, S. L., & Vandello, J. A. (2008). Prevalence and effects of rape myths in print journalism: The Kobe Bryant case. *Violence Against Women, 14*, 287–309. doi: 10.1177/1077801207313971

Franklin, C. A. (2016). Sorority affiliation and sexual assault victimization: Assessing vulnerability using path analysis. *Violence Against Women, 22*, 895–922. doi: 10.1177/1077801215614971

Frazier, P. A., Mortensen, H., & Steward, J. (2005). Coping strategies as mediators of the relations among perceived control and distress in sexual assault survivors. *Journal of Counseling Psychology, 52*, 267–278. doi: 10.1037/0022-0167.52.3.267

Freyd, J. J., DePrince, A. P., & Gleaves, D. H. (2007). The state of betrayal trauma theory: Reply to McNally—Conceptual issues, and future directions. *Memory, 15*, 295–311. doi: 10.1080/09658210701256514

Fuller, J. M. (2009). The science and statistics behind spanking suggest that laws allowing corporal punishment are in the best interests of the child. *Akron Law Review, 42*, 243–317.

Gabrielli, J., Traore, A., Stoolmiller, M., Bergamini, E., & Sargent, J. D. (2016). Industry television ratings for violence, sex, and substance use. *Pediatrics, 138*(3), e20160487. doi: 10.1542/peds.2016-0487

Gallo, E. G., Munhoz, T. N., Loret de Mola, C., & Murray, J. (2018). Gender differences in the effects of childhood maltreatment on adult depression and anxiety: A systematic review and meta-analysis. *Child Abuse & Neglect, 79*, 107–114. doi: 10.1016/j.chiabu.2018.01.003

Garland, T. S., Branch, K. A., & Grimes, M. (2016). Blurring the lines: Reinforcing rape myths in comic books. *Feminist Criminology, 11*, 48–68. doi: 10.1177/1557085115576386

Garrity, S. E. (2011). Sexual assault prevention programs for college-aged men: A critical evaluation. *Journal of Forensic Nursing, 7*, 40–48. doi: 10.1111/j.1939-3938.2010.01094.x

Gershoff, E. T., & Grogan-Kaylor, A. (2016). Spanking and child outcomes: Old controversies and new meta-analyses. *Journal of Family Psychology, 30*, 453–469. doi: 10.1037/fam000191

Gidycz, C. A., & Dardis, C. M. (2014). Feminist self-defense and resistance training for college students: A critical review and recommendations for the future. *Trauma, Violence, & Abuse, 15*, 322–333. doi: 10.1177/1524838014521026

Gidycz, C. A., McNamara, J. R., & Edwards, K. M. (2006). Women's risk perception and sexual victimization: A review of the literature. *Aggression and Violent Behavior, 11*, 441–456. doi: 10.1016/j.avb.2006.01.004

Gidycz, C. A., Orchowski, L. M., & Berkowitz, A. D. (2011). Preventing sexual aggression among college men: An evaluation of a social norms and bystander intervention program. *Violence Against Women*, *17*, 720–742. doi: 10.1177/1077801211409727

Glass N., Eden K. B., Bloom T., & Perrin N. (2010). Computerized aid improves safety decision process for survivors of intimate partner violence. *Journal of Interpersonal Violence*, *25*, 1947–1964. doi: 10.1177/0886260509354508.

Glenn, C., & Goodman, L. (2015). Living with and within the rules of domestic violence shelters: A qualitative exploration of residents' experiences. *Violence Against Women*, *21*, 1481–1506. doi: 10.1177/1077801215596242

Goldberg, H., Stupp, P., Okoroh, E., Besera, G., Goodman, D., & Danel, I. (2016). Female genital mutilation/cutting in the United States: Updated estimates of women and girls at risk, 2012. *Public Health Reports*, *131*, 340–347. doi: 10.1177/003335491613100218

Goldberg, N. G., & Meyer, I. H. (2013). Sexual orientation disparities in history of intimate partner violence: Results from the California Health Interview Survey. *Journal of Interpersonal Violence*, *28*, 1109–1118. doi: 10.1177/0886260512459384

Goldstein, M. (2009, February 12). Chris Brown and Rihanna: The whole story. *Spin*. Retrieved from http://www.spin.com/2009/02/chris-brown-and-rihanna-whole-story/

Goodman, L. A., Banyard, V., Woulfe, J., Ash, S., & Mattern, G. (2016). Bringing a network-oriented approach to domestic violence services: A focus group exploration of promising practices. *Violence Against Women*, *22*, 64–89. doi: 10.1177/1077801215599080

Goodman, L. A., & Epstein, D. (2008). *Listening to battered women: A survivor-centered approach to advocacy, mental health, and justice*. Washington, DC: American Psychological Association.

Gordon, M. T., & Riger, S. (1989). *The female fear: The social cost of rape*. Urbana, IL: University of Illinois Press.

Grabe S. (2016). Transnational feminism in psychology: Moving beyond difference to investigate processes of power at the intersection of the global and local. In T.-A. Roberts, N. Curtin, L. Duncan, & L. Cortina (Eds.), *Feminist perspectives on building a better psychological science of gender* (pp. 295–317). Switzerland: Springer.

Grabe, S., Grose, R. G., & Dutt, A. (2015). Women's land ownership and relationship power: A mixed methods approach to understanding structural inequities and violence against women. *Psychology of Women Quarterly*, *39*, 7–19. doi: 10.1177/0361684314533485

Gross, A. M., Winslett, A., Roberts, M., & Gohm, C. L. (2006). An examination of sexual violence against college women. *Violence Against Women*, *12*, 288–300. doi: 10.1177/1077801205277358

Groth, A. N., & Birnbaum, H. J. (2013). *Men who rape: The psychology of the offender*. New York, NY: Springer.

Grubaugh, A. L., & Resick, P. A. (2007). Posttraumatic growth in treatment-seeking female assault victims. *Psychiatric Quarterly*, *78*, 145–155. doi: 10.1007/s11126-006-9034-7

Gurung, S., Ventuneac, A., Rendina, H. J., Savarese, E., Grov, C., & Parsons, J. T. (2018). Prevalence of military sexual trauma and sexual orientation discrimination among lesbian, gay, bisexual, and transgender military personnel: A descriptive study. *Sexuality Research & Social Policy*, *15*, 74–82. doi: 10.1007/s13178-017-0311-z

Halket, M. M., Gormley, K., Mello, N., Rosenthal, L., & Mirkin, M. P. (2014). Stay with or leave the abuser? The effects of domestic violence victim's decision on attributions made by young adults. *Journal of Family Violence*, *29*, 35–49. doi: 10.1007/s10896-013-9555-4

Hamby, S. (2009). The gender debate about intimate partner violence: Solutions and dead ends. *Psychological Trauma: Theory, Research, Practice, and Policy*, *1*, 24–34. doi: 10.1037/a0015066

Harman, E. A., Gutekunst, D. J., Frykman, P. N., Nindl, B. C., Alemany, J. A., Mello, R. P., & Sharp, M. A. (2008). Effects of two different eight-week training programs on military physical performance. *The Journal of Strength & Conditioning Research*, *22*, 524–534. doi: 10.1519/JSC.0b013e31816347b6

Harrell, E. (2012, December). *Violent victimization committed by strangers, 1993–2010* (NCJ No. 239424). Retrieved from the Bureau of Justice Statistics website: https://www.bjs.gov/content/pub/pdf/vvcs9310.pdf

Harris, K. L. (2018). Yes means yes and no means no, but both these mantras need to go: Communication myths in consent education and anti-rape activism. *Journal of Applied Communication Research*, *46*, 155–178. doi: 10.1080/00909882.2018.1435900

Hartmann, T., Krakowiak, K. M., & Tsay-Vogel, M. (2014). How violent video games communicate violence: A literature review and content analysis of moral disengagement factors. *Communication Monographs*, *81*, 310–332. doi: 10.1080/03637751.2014.922206

Harway, M., & Steel, J. H. (2015). Studying masculinity and sexual assault across organizational culture groups: Understanding perpetrators. *Psychology of Men & Masculinity*, *16*, 374–378. doi: 10.1037/a0039694

Hassouneh, D., & Glass, N. (2008). The influence of gender role stereotyping on women's experiences of female same-sex intimate partner violence. *Violence Against Women*, *14*, 310–325. doi: 10.1177/1077801207313734

Hayes, R. M., Abbott, R. L., & Cook, S. (2016). It's her fault: Student acceptance of rape myths on two college campuses. *Violence Against Women*, *22*, 1540–1555. doi: 10.1177/1077801216630147

Hayes, R. M., Lorenz, K., & Bell, K. A. (2013). Victim blaming others: Rape myth acceptance and the just world belief. *Feminist Criminology*, *8*, 202–220. doi: 10.1177/1557085113484788

Heath, N. M., Lynch, S. M., Fritch, A. M., McArthur, L. N., & Smith, S. L. (2011). Silent survivors: Rape myth acceptance in incarcerated women's narratives of disclosure and reporting of rape. *Psychology of Women Quarterly*, *35*, 596–610. doi: 10.1177/0361684311407870

Henley, N. M., Miller, M., & Beazley, J. A. (1995). Syntax, semantics, and sexual violence: Agency and the passive voice. *Journal of Language and Social Psychology*, *14*, 60–84. doi: 10.1177/0261927X95141004

Herrera, A., Dahlblom, K., Dahlgren, L., & Kullgren, G. (2006). Pathways to suicidal behavior among adolescent girls in Nicaragua. *Social Science & Medicine*, *62*, 805–814. doi: 10.1016/j.socscimed.2005.06.055

Hickman, L. J., Jaycox, L. H., & Aronoff, J. (2004). Dating violence among adolescents: Prevalence, gender distribution, and prevention program effectiveness. *Trauma, Violence, & Abuse*, *5*, 123–142. doi: 10.1177/1524838003262332

Hickman, S., & Muehlenhard, C. (2006). College women's fears and precautionary behaviors relating to acquaintance rape and stranger rape. *Psychology of Women Quarterly*, *21*, 527–547. doi: 10.1111/j.1471-6402.1997.tb00129.x

Higate, P. (2007). Peacekeepers, masculinities, and sexual exploitation. *Men and Masculinities*, *10*, 99–119. doi: 10.1177/1097184X06291896

Hightower, J. (2004). Age, gender and violence: Abuse against older women. *Geriatrics and Aging*, *7*(3), 60–63.

Hightower, J., Smith, M. J., & Hightower, H. C. (2006). Hearing the voices of abused older women. *Journal of Gerontological Social Work*, *46*, 205–227. doi: 10.1300/J083v46n03_12

Hobfoll, S. E., Bansal, A., Schurg, R., Young, S., Pierce, C. A., Hobfoll, I., & Johnson, R. (2002). The impact of perceived child physical and sexual abuse history on Native American women's psychological well-being and AIDS risk. *Journal of Consulting and Clinical Psychology*, 70, 252–257. doi: 10.1037/0022-006X.70.1.252

Hockett, J. M., Smith, S. J., Klausing, C. D., & Saucier, D. A. (2016). Rape myth consistency and gender differences in perceiving rape victims: A meta-analysis. *Violence Against Women*, 22, 139–167. doi: 10.1177/1077801215607539

Hodge, J. P. (2011). *Gendered hate: Exploring gender in hate crime law*. Boston, MA: Northeastern University Press.

Holland, E., & Haslam, N. (2016). Cute little things: The objectification of prepubescent girls. *Psychology of Women Quarterly*, 40, 108–119. doi: 10.1177/0361684315602887

Horner-Johnson, W., & Drum, C. E. (2006). Prevalence of maltreatment of people with intellectual disabilities: A review of recently published research. *Developmental Disabilities Research Reviews*, 12, 57–69. doi: 10.1002/mrdd.20097

Human Rights Campaign. (n.d.). *Violence against the transgender community in 2016*. Retrieved from the Human Rights Campaign website: http://www.hrc.org/resources/violence-against-the-transgender-community-in-2016

Human Rights First. (2016, January 7). *Human trafficking by the numbers*. Retrieved from http://www.humanrightsfirst.org/resource/human-trafficking-numbers

Human Rights Watch. (2015, May). *Embattled: Retaliation against sexual assault survivors in the military*. Retrieved from https://www.hrw.org/sites/default/files/report_pdf/us0515militaryweb.pdf

Humphreys, C. (2007). Domestic violence and child protection: Exploring the role of perpetrator risk assessments. *Child & Family Social Work*, 12, 360–369. doi: 10.1111/j.1365-2206.2006.00464.x

Hyland, P., Shevlin, M., Hansen, M., Vallières, F., Murphy, J., & Elklit, A. (2016). The temporal relations of PTSD symptoms among treatment-seeking victims of sexual assault: A longitudinal study. *Journal of Loss and Trauma*, 21, 492–506. doi: 10.1080/15325024.2015.1117933

Hynes, H. P. (2004). On the battlefield of women's bodies: An overview of the harm of war to women. *Women's Studies International Forum*, 27, 431–445. doi: 10.1016/j.wsif.2004.09.001

Infurna, M. R., Reichl, C., Parzer, P., Schimmenti, A., Bifulco, A., & Kaess, M. (2016). Associations between depression and specific childhood experiences of abuse and neglect: A meta-analysis. *Journal of Affective Disorders*, 190, 47–55. doi: 10.1016/j.jad.2015.09.006

Jacquet, C. (2015, October 15). Domestic violence in the 1970s. *Circulating Now*. Retrieved from https://circulatingnow.nlm.nih.gov/2015/10/15/domestic-violence-in-the-1970s/

Jaffe, P. G., Johnston, J. R., Crooks, C. V., & Bala, N. (2008). Custody disputes involving allegations of domestic violence: Toward a differentiated approach to parenting plans. *Family Court Review*, 46, 500–522. doi: 10.1111/j.1744-1617.2008.00216.x

James, L., Brody, D., & Hamilton, Z. (2013). Risk factors for domestic violence during pregnancy: A meta-analytic review. *Violence and Victims*, 28, 359–380. doi: 10.1891/0886-6708.VV-D-12-00034

James, S. E., Herman, J. L., Rankin, S., Keisling, M., Mottet, L., & Anafi, M. (2016, December). The report of the 2015 U.S. Transgender Survey. Washington, DC: National Center for Transgender Equality. Retrieved from https://www.transequality.org/sites/default/files/docs/USTS-Full-Report-FINAL.PDF

Javaid, A. (2016). Voluntary agencies' responses to, and attitudes toward, male rape: Issues and concerns. *Sexuality & Culture*, 20, 731–748. doi: 10.1007/s12119-016-9348-z

Jensen, R. (2010). Pornography is what the end of the world looks like. In K. Boyle (Ed.), *Everyday pornography* (pp. 105–113). New York, NY: Routledge.

Johnson, M. P. (1995). Patriarchal terrorism and common couple violence: Two forms of violence against women. *Journal of Marriage and Family*, 57, 283–294.

Johnson, M. P. (2009). Differentiating among types of domestic violence: Implications for healthy marriages. In H. E. Peters & C. K. Dush (Eds.), *Marriage and family: Perspectives and complexities* (pp. 281–297). New York, NY: Columbia University Press.

Johnson, M. P. (2011). Gender and types of intimate partner violence: A response to an anti-feminist literature review. *Aggression and Violent Behavior*, 16, 289–296. doi: 10.1016/j.avb.2011.04.006

Johnson, M. P., & Ferraro, K. J. (2000). Research on domestic violence in the 1990s: Making distinctions. *Journal of Marriage and Family*, 62, 948–963. doi: 10.1111/j.1741-3737.2000.00948.x

Joy, M. (2016, January 26). 4 things you need to know about jurisdiction in Indian Country to help end sexual violence. *Everyday Feminism*. Retrieved from http://everydayfeminism.com/2016/01/jurisdiction-indian-country-sexual-violence/

Jozkowski, K. N., Marcantonio, T. L., & Hunt, M. E. (2017). College students' sexual consent communication and perceptions of sexual double standards: A qualitative investigation. *Perspectives on Sexual and Reproductive Health*, 49, 237–244. doi: 10.1363/psrh.12041

Jozkowski, K. N., & Peterson, Z. D. (2013). College students and sexual consent: Unique insights. *Journal of Sex Research*, 50, 517–523. doi: 10.1080/00224499.2012.700739

Jozkowski, K. N., Sanders, S. A., Peterson, Z. D., Dennis, B., & Reece, M. (2014). Consenting to sexual activity: The development and psychometric assessment of dual measures of consent. *Archives of Sexual Behavior*, 43, 437–450. doi: 10.1007/s10508-013-0225-7

Jozkowski, K. N., & Wiersma-Mosley, J. D. (2017). The Greek system: How gender inequality and class privilege perpetuate rape culture. *Family Relations*, 66, 89–103. doi: 10.1111/fare.12229

Jungari, S. B. (2016). Female genital mutilation is a violation of reproductive rights of women: Implications for health workers. *Health & Social Work*, 41, 25–31. doi: 10.1093/hsw/hlv090

Kahlor, L., & Eastin, M. S. (2011). Television's role in the culture of violence toward women: A study of television viewing and the cultivation of rape myth acceptance in the United States. *Journal of Broadcasting & Electronic Media*, 55, 215–231. doi: 10.1080/08838151.2011.566085

Kahn, A. S., Jackson, J., Kully, C., Badger, K., & Halvorsen, J. (2003). Calling it rape: Differences in experiences of women who do or do not label their sexual assault as rape. *Psychology of Women Quarterly*, 27, 233–242. doi: 10.1111/1471-6402.00103

Kanuha, V. K. (2013). "Relationships so loving and so hurtful": The constructed duality of sexual and racial/ethnic intimacy in the context of violence in Asian and Pacific Islander lesbian and queer women's relationships. *Violence Against Women*, 19, 1175–1196. doi: 10.1177/1077801213501897

Karp, D. R., & Frank, O. (2016). Anxiously awaiting the future of restorative justice in the United States. *Victims & Offenders*, 11, 50–70. doi: 10.1080/15564886.2015.1107796

Katz, J., & Schneider, M. E. (2015). (Hetero)sexual compliance with unwanted casual sex: Associations with feelings about first sex and sexual self-perceptions. *Sex Roles*, 72, 451–461. doi: 10.1007/s11199-015-0467-z

Katz-Schiavone, S., Levenson, J. S., & Ackerman, A. R. (2008). Myths and facts about sexual violence: Public perceptions and implications for prevention. *Journal of Criminal Justice and Popular Culture*, 15, 291–311.

Keeling, J., & Fisher, C. (2012). Women's early relational experiences that lead to domestic violence. *Qualitative Health Research, 22,* 1559–1567. doi: 10.1177/1049732312457076

Kelly, J. B., & Johnson, M. P. (2008). Differentiation among types of intimate partner violence: Research update and implications for interventions. *Family Court Review, 46,* 476–499. doi: 10.1111/j.1744-1617.2008.00215.x

Khalid, M. (2011). Gender, orientalism and representations of the "Other" in the War on Terror. *Global Change, Peace & Security, 23,* 15–29. doi: 10.1080/14781158.2011.540092

Khalifeh, H., Howard, L. M., Osborn, D., Moran, P., & Johnson, S. (2013). Violence against people with disability in England and Wales: Findings from a national cross-sectional survey. *PLoS ONE, 8,* e55952. doi: 10.1371/journal.pone.0055952

Kilbane, T., & Spira, M. (2010). Domestic violence or elder abuse? Why it matters for older women. *Families in Society: The Journal of Contemporary Social Services, 91,* 165–170. doi: 10.1606/1044-3894.3979

Kim, H. K., Laurent, H. K., Capaldi, D. M., & Feingold, A. (2008). Men's aggression toward women: A 10-year panel study. *Journal of Marriage and Family, 70,* 1169–1187. doi: 10.1111/j.1741-3737.2008.00558.x

King, D. K. (1988). Multiple jeopardy, multiple consciousness: The context of a Black feminist ideology. *Signs, 14,* 42–72. doi: 10.1086/494491

King's challenge to the nation's social scientists. (1999, January). *Monitor on Psychology, 30*(1). Retrieved from http://www.apa.org/monitor/features/king-challenge.aspx

Kinkartz, S. (2015, June 30). UNICEF 2015 report: Millions of children caught in the middle of conflict. *Deutsche Welle.* Retrieved from http://www.dw.com/en/unicef-2015-report-millions-of-children-caught-in-the-middle-of-conflict/a-18554668

Koyama, E. (2006). Disloyal to feminism: Abuse of survivors within the domestic violence shelter system. In INCITE! Women of Color Against Violence (Ed.), *Color of violence: The INCITE! anthology* (pp. 208–222). Durham, NC: Duke University Press.

Krebs, C. P., Barrick, K., Lindquist, C. H., Crosby, C. M., Boyd, C., & Bogan, Y. (2011). The sexual assault of undergraduate women at historically Black colleges and universities (HBCU). *Journal of Interpersonal Violence, 26,* 3640–3666. doi: 10.1177/0886260511403759

Langenderfer-Magruder, L., Whitfield, D. L., Walls, N. E., Kattari, S. K., & Ramos, D. (2016). Experiences of intimate partner violence and subsequent police reporting among lesbian, gay, bisexual, transgender, and queer adults in Colorado: Comparing rates of cisgender and transgender victimization. *Journal of Interpersonal Violence, 31,* 855–871. doi: 10.1177/0886260514556767

LaPointe, C. A. (2008). Sexual violence: An introduction to the social and legal issues for Native women. In S. Deer, B. Clairmont, C. A. Martell, & M. L. W. Eagle (Eds.), *Sharing our stories of survival: Native women surviving violence* (pp. 31–48). Lanham, MD: AltaMira Press.

Lassri, D., Luyten, P., Fonagy, P., & Shahar, G. (2018). Undetected scars? Self-criticism, attachment, and romantic relationships among otherwise well-functioning childhood sexual abuse survivors. *Psychological Trauma: Theory, Research, Practice, and Policy, 10,* 121–129. doi: 10.1037/tra0000271

Laumann, E. O., Leitsch, S. A., & Waite, L. J. (2008). Elder mistreatment in the United States: Prevalence estimates from a nationally representative study. *The Journals of Gerontology, Series B: Psychological Sciences and Social Sciences, 63,* S248–S254. doi: 10.1093/geronb/63.4.S248

LaViolette, A. B., & Barnett, O. W. (2000). *It could happen to anyone: Why battered women stay* (2nd ed.). Thousand Oaks, CA: Sage.

Leeb, R. T., Paulozzi, L. J., Melanson, C., Simon, T. R., & Arias, I. (2008, January). *Child maltreatment surveillance: Uniform definitions for public health and recommended data elements—version 1.0.* Atlanta, GA: Centers for Disease Control and Prevention. Retrieved from https://www.cdc.gov/violenceprevention/pdf/cm_surveillance-a.pdf

Lehavot, K., Walters, K. L., & Simoni, J. M. (2010). Abuse, mastery, and health among lesbian, bisexual, and two-spirit American Indian and Alaska Native women. *Psychology of Violence, 1,* 53–67. doi: 10.1037/2152-0828.1.S.53

LeMaire, K. L., Oswald, D. L., & Russell, B. L. (2016). Labeling sexual victimization experiences: The role of sexism, rape myth acceptance, and tolerance for sexual harassment. *Violence and Victims, 31,* 332–346. doi: 10.1891/0886-6708.VV-D-13-00148

Lerner, M. J. (1980). *The belief in a just world.* New York, NY: Springer.

Levant, R. F. (2011). Research in the psychology of men and masculinity using the gender role strain paradigm as a framework. *American Psychologist, 66,* 765–776. doi: 10.1037/a0025034

Levant, R. F., & Richmond, K. (2008). A review of research on masculinity ideologies using the Male Role Norms Inventory. *The Journal of Men's Studies, 15,* 130–146. doi: 10.3149/jms.1502.130

Levant, R. F., & Richmond, K. (2016). The gender role strain paradigm and masculinity ideologies. In Y. J. Wong & S. R. Wester, (Eds.), *APA handbook of men and masculinities* (pp. 23–49). Washington, DC: American Psychological Association. doi: 10.1037/14594-002

Lieberman, M., & Freeman, S. M. (2017). Confronting violent bigotry: Hate crime laws and legislation. In E. Dunbar, A. Blanco, D. A. Crèvecoeur-MacPhail, C. Munthe, M. Fingerle, D. Brax, . . . & D. Brax (Eds.), *The psychology of hate crimes as domestic terrorism: U.S. and global issues: Theoretical, legal, and cultural factors* (pp. 43–88). Santa Barbara, CA: Praeger.

Ligiéro, D. P., Fassinger, R., McCauley, M., Moore, J., & Lýytinen, N. (2009). Childhood sexual abuse, culture, and coping: A qualitative study of Latinas. *Psychology of Women Quarterly, 33,* 67–80. doi: 10.1111/j.1471-6402.2008.01475.x

Lisak, D., Gardinier, L., Nicksa, S. C., & Cote, A. M. (2010). False allegations of sexual assault: An analysis of ten years of reported cases. *Violence Against Women, 16,* 1318–1334. doi: 10.1177/1077801210387747

Little, N. J. (2005). From no means no to only yes means yes: The rational results of an affirmative consent standard in rape law. *Vanderbilt Law Review, 58,* 1321–1364.

Littleton, H., & Decker, M. (2017). Predictors of resistance self-efficacy among rape victims and association with revictimization risk: A longitudinal study. *Psychology of Violence, 7,* 583–592. doi: 10.1037/vio0000066

Livio, S. K. (2017, March 14). No child brides in N.J.: Senate approves ban on minors getting married. *NJ.com.* Retrieved from http://www.nj.com/politics/index.ssf/2017/03/nj_senate_votes_to_outlaw_minors_from_getting_marr.html

Logan, T. K., Evans, L., Stevenson, E., & Jordan, C. E. (2005). Barriers to services for rural and urban survivors of rape. *Journal of Interpersonal Violence, 20,* 591–616. doi: 10.1177/0886260504272899

Long, S. M., Ullman, S. E., Long, L. M., Mason, G. E., & Starzynski, L. L. (2007). Women's experiences of male-perpetrated sexual assault by sexual orientation. *Violence and Victims, 22,* 684–701. doi: 10.1891/088667007782793138

Lonsway, K. A., Archambault, J., & Lisak, D. (2009). False reports: Moving beyond the issue to successfully investigate and prosecute non-stranger sexual assault. *Prosecutor, Journal of the National District Attorneys Association, 43*(1), 10–22.

Lonsway, K. A., & Fitzgerald, L. F. (1994). Rape myths: In review. *Psychology of Women Quarterly, 18,* 133–1164. doi: 10.1111/j.1471-6402.1994.tb00448.x

Loveland, J. E., & Raghavan, C. (2017). Coercive control, physical violence, and masculinity. *Violence and Gender, 4,* 5–10. doi: 10.1089/vio.2016.0019

Lowe, M., & Rogers, P. (2017). The scope of male rape: A selective review of research, policy and practice. *Aggression and Violent Behavior, 35,* 38–43. doi: 10.1016/j.avb.2017.06.007

Loya, R. M. (2014). The role of sexual violence in creating and maintaining economic insecurity among asset-poor women of color. *Violence Against Women, 20,* 1299–1320. doi: 10.1177/1077801214552912

Lundy, M., & Grossman, S. F. (2005). Elder abuse: Spouse/intimate partner abuse and family violence among elders. *Journal of Elder Abuse & Neglect, 16,* 85–102. doi: 10.1300/J084v16n01_05

Luthra, R., & Gidycz, C. A. (2006). Dating violence among college men and women: Evaluation of a theoretical model. *Journal of Interpersonal Violence, 21,* 717–731. doi: 10.1177/0886260506287312

Lynch, A. (2012). But what if he doesn't hate all women? Rethinking gender-motivated hate crimes. In A. Browne-Miller (Ed.), *Violence and abuse in society* (Vol. 2, pp. 315–332). Santa Barbara, CA: Praeger.

Macias-Konstantopoulos, W., & Bar-Halpern, M. (2016). Commercially sexually exploited and trafficked minors: Our hidden and forgotten children. In R. Parekh & E. W. Childs (Eds.), *Stigma and prejudice: Touchstones in understanding diversity in healthcare* (pp. 183–202). Totowa, NJ: Humana Press.

Macmillan, R., Nierobisz, A., & Welsh, S. (2000). Experiencing the streets: Harassment and perceptions of safety among women. *Journal of Research in Crime and Delinquency, 37,* 306–322. doi: 10.1177/0022427800037003003

Magley, V. J. (2002). Coping with sexual harassment: Reconceptualizing women's resistance. *Journal of Personality and Social Psychology, 83,* 930–946. doi: 10.1037/0022-3514.83.4.930

Marcantonio, T. L., Jozkowski, K. N., & Lo, W. (2018). Beyond "just saying no": A preliminary evaluation of strategies college students use to refuse sexual activity. *Archives of Sexual Behavior, 47,* 341–351. doi: 10.1007/s10508-017-1130-2

Marx, B. P., Forsyth, J. P., Gallup, G. G., Fusé, T., & Lexington, J. M. (2008). Tonic immobility as an evolved predator defense: Implications for sexual assault survivors. *Clinical Psychology: Science and Practice, 15,* 74–90. doi: 10.1111/j.1468-2850.2008.00112.x

Masten, A. S. (2014). Global perspectives on resilience in children and youth. *Child Development, 85,* 6–20. doi: 10.1111/cdev.12205

Matte, M., & Lafontaine, M. F. (2011). Validation of a measure of psychological aggression in same-sex couples: Descriptive data on perpetration and victimization and their association with physical violence. *Journal of GLBT Family Studies, 7,* 226–244. doi: 10.1080/1550428X.2011.564944

Maurer, T. W. (2016). Perceptions of incapacitated heterosexual sexual assault: Influences of relationship status, perpetrator intoxication, and post-assault sleeping arrangements. *Violence Against Women, 22,* 780–797. doi: 10.1177/1077801215612599

Mayton, D. M., II, Peters, D. J., & Owens, R. W. (1999). Values, militarism, and nonviolent predispositions. *Peace and Conflict: Journal of Peace Psychology, 5,* 69–77. doi: 10.1207/s15327949pac0501_7

McAlinden, A. (2017). Restorative justice and sex offending. In T. Sanders (Ed.), *The Oxford handbook of sex offences and sex offenders* (pp. 437–460). New York, NY: Oxford University Press.

McMahon, S., & Dick, A. (2011). "Being in a room with like-minded men": An exploratory study of men's participation in a bystander intervention program to prevent intimate partner violence. *The Journal of Men's Studies, 19,* 3–18. doi: 10.3149/jms.1901.3

McPhail, B. A. (2002). Gender-bias hate crimes: A review. *Trauma, Violence, & Abuse, 3,* 125–143. doi: 10.1177/15248380020032003

McPhail, B. A., & DiNitto, D. M. (2005). Prosecutorial perspectives on gender-bias hate crimes. *Violence Against Women, 11,* 1162–1185. doi: 10.1177/1077801205277086

Medina, J. (2015, October 14). Sex ed lesson: "Yes means yes," but it's tricky. *The New York Times.* Retrieved from https://www.nytimes.com/2015/10/15/us/california-high-schools-sexual-consent-classes.html?_r=0

Melton, H. C., & Belknap, J. (2003). He hits, she hits: Assessing gender differences and similarities in officially reported intimate partner violence. *Criminal Justice and Behavior, 30,* 328–348. doi: 10.1177/0093854803030003004

Messman-Moore, T., Ward, R. M., Zerubavel, N., Chandley, R. B., & Barton, S. N. (2015). Emotion dysregulation and drinking to cope as predictors and consequences of alcohol-involved sexual assault: Examination of short-term and long-term risk. *Journal of Interpersonal Violence, 30,* 601–621. doi: 10.1177/0886260514535259

Messman-Moore, T. L., Ward, R. M., & Zerubavel, N. (2013). The role of substance use and emotion dysregulation in predicting risk for incapacitated sexual revictimization in women: Results of a prospective investigation. *Psychology of Addictive Behaviors, 27,* 125–132. doi: 10.1037/a0031073

Meyer, S. (2016). Still blaming the victim of intimate partner violence? Women's narratives of victim desistance and redemption when seeking support. *Theoretical Criminology, 2,* 75–90. doi: 10.1177/1362480615585399

Milliken, J., Paul, L. A., Sasson, S., Porter, A., & Hasulube, J. (2016). Sexual assault disclosure recipients' experiences: Emotional distress and changes in the relationship with the victim. *Violence and Victims, 31,* 457–470. doi: 10.1891/0886-6708.VV-D-14-00144

Mitchell, K. J., Finkelhor, D., & Wolak, J. (2013, November). *Sex trafficking cases involving minors.* Retrieved from the Crimes Against Children Research Center at the University of New Hampshire website: http://www.unh.edu/ccrc/pdf/CV313_Final_Sex_Trafficking_Minors_Nov_2013_rev.pdf

Mohanty, C. T., Pratt, M. B., & Riley, R. L. (2008). Introduction: Feminism and U.S. wars—Mapping the ground. In R. L. Riley, C. T. Mohanty, & M. B. Pratt (Eds.), *Feminism and war: Confronting U.S. imperialism* (pp. 1–18). London, United Kingdom: Zed Books.

Mohler-Kuo, M., Dowdall, G. W., Koss, M. P., & Wechsler, H. (2004). Correlates of rape while intoxicated in a national sample of college women. *Journal of Studies on Alcohol, 65,* 37–45. doi: 10.15288/jsa.2004.65.37

Monto, M. A. (2004). Female prostitution, customers, and violence. *Violence Against Women, 10,* 160–188. doi: 10.1177/1077801203260948

Morgan, R. E., & Mason, B. J. (2014, November). *Crimes against the elderly, 2003–2013.* Washington, DC: U.S. Department of Justice. Retrieved from https://www.bjs.gov/content/pub/pdf/cae0313.pdf

Muehlenhard, C. L. (2011). Examining stereotypes about token resistance to sex. *Psychology of Women Quarterly, 35,* 676–683. doi: 10.1177/0361684311426689

Muehlenhard, C. L., Humphreys, T. P., Jozkowski, K. N., & Peterson, Z. D. (2016). The complexities of sexual consent among college students: A conceptual and empirical review. *Journal of Sex Research, 53,* 457–487. doi: 10.1080/00224499.2016.1146651

Muehlenhard, C. L., & Miller, E. N. (1988). Traditional and non-traditional men's responses to women's dating initiation. *Behavior Modification, 12*, 385–403. doi: 10.1177/014544558 80123005

Muehlenhard, C. L., & Rodgers, C. S. (1998). Token resistance to sex: New perspectives on an old stereotype. *Psychology of Women Quarterly, 22*, 443–463. doi: 10.1111/j.1471-6402. 1998 .tb00167.x

Muftić, L. R., Bouffard, J. A., & Bouffard, L. A. (2007). An exploratory study of women arrested for intimate partner violence: Violent women or violent resistance? *Journal of Interpersonal Violence, 22*, 753–774. doi: 10.1177/0886260507300756

Mukherjee, J. S., Barry, D. J., Satti, H., Raymonville, M., Marsh, S., & Smith-Fawzi, M. K. (2011). Structural violence: A barrier to achieving the Millennium Development Goals for women. *Journal of Women's Health, 20*, 593–597. doi: 10.1089 /jwh.2010.2375

Murnen, S. K., Wright, C., & Kaluzny, G. (2002). If "boys will be boys," then girls will be victims? A meta-analytic review of the research that relates masculine ideology to sexual aggression. *Sex Roles, 46*, 359–375. doi: 10.1023/A:1020488928736

Murray, C. E., Horton, G. E., Johnson, C. H., Notestine, L., Garr, B., Pow, A. M., . . . & Doom, E. (2015). Domestic violence service providers' perceptions of safety planning: A focus group study. *Journal of Family Violence, 30*, 381–392. doi: 10.1007 /s10896-015-9674-1

Nasaw, D. (2009, March 16). Survey: Half of Boston teens blame Rihanna for Chris Brown beating. *The Guardian*. Retrieved from https://www.theguardian.com/world/deadlineusa/2009 /mar/16/rihanna-usa

National Task Force to End Sexual and Domestic Violence Against Women. (2016, April 21). *National consensus statement of anti-sexual assault and domestic violence organizations in support of full and equal access for the transgender community.* Retrieved from http://endsexualviolence.org/files/NTFNational ConsensusStmtTransAccessWithSignatories.pdf

Nayak, M. (2006). Orientalism and "saving" U.S. state identity after 9/11. *International Feminist Journal of Politics, 8*, 42–61. doi: 10.1080/14616740500415458

Nerenberg, L. (2002, March). *Preventing elder abuse by family caregivers.* Washington, DC: National Center on Elder Abuse. Retrieved from https://ncea.acl.gov/resources/docs/archive /Preventing-EA-Family-Caregivers-Tech-2002.pdf

Nickerson, A., Steenkamp, M., Aerka, I. M., Salters-Pedneault, K., Carper, T. L., Barnes, J. B., & Litz, B. T. (2013). Prospective investigation of mental health following sexual assault. *Depression and Anxiety, 30*, 444–450. doi: 10.1002/da.22023

Nosek, M. A., Hughes, R. B., Taylor, H. B., & Taylor, P. (2006). Disability, psychosocial, and demographic characteristics of abused women with physical disabilities. *Violence Against Women, 12*, 838–850. doi: 10.1177/1077801206292671

Olson, K. M. (2013). An epideictic dimension of symbolic violence in Disney's Beauty and the Beast: Inter-generational lessons in romanticizing and tolerating intimate partner violence. *Quarterly Journal of Speech, 99*, 448–480. doi: 10.1080 /00335630.2013.835491

Orchowski, L. M., & Gidycz, C. A. (2015). Psychological consequences associated with positive and negative responses to disclosure of sexual assault among college women: A prospective study. *Violence Against Women, 21*, 803–823. doi: 10.1177/1077801215584068

Osman, S. L. (2003). Predicting men's rape perceptions based on the belief that "no" really means "yes." *Journal of Applied Social Psychology, 33*, 683–692. doi: 10.1111/j.1559-1816.2003 .tb01919.x

Papp, L. J., & Erchull, M. J. (2017). Objectification and system justification impact rape avoidance behaviors. *Sex Roles, 76*, 110–120. doi: 10.1007/s11199-016-0660-8

Parratt, K. A., & Pina, A. (2017). From "real rape" to real justice: A systematic review of police officers' rape myth beliefs. *Aggression and Violent Behavior, 34*, 68–83. doi: 10.1016/j.avb .2017.03.005

Paul, B., & Linz, D. G. (2008). The effects of exposure to virtual child pornography on viewer cognitions and attitudes toward deviant sexual behavior. *Communication Research, 35*, 3–38. doi: 10.1177/0093650207309359

Paul, L. A., Walsh, K., McCauley, J. L., Ruggiero, K. J., Resnick, H. S., & Kilpatrick, D. G. (2013). College women's experiences with rape disclosure: A national study. *Violence Against Women, 19*, 486–502. doi: 10.1177/1077801213487746

Pence, E., & Dasgupta, S. D. (2006, June 20). Re-examining "battering": Are all acts of violence against intimate partners the same? Duluth, MN: Praxis International. Retrieved from http://www.ncdsv.org/images/Praxis_ReexaminingBattering _June2006.pdf

Pence, E., & Paymar, M. (1993). *Education groups for men who batter: The Duluth model.* New York, NY: Springer.

Perry, S. W. (2004, December). *A BJS statistical profile, 1992–2002: American Indians and crime* (NCJ No. 203097). Retrieved from http://digitalcommons.unl.edu/cgi/viewcontent.cgi?article =1094&context=publichealthresources

Peter-Hagene, L. C., & Ullman, S. E. (2018). Longitudinal effects of sexual assault victims' drinking and self-blame on post-traumatic stress disorder. *Journal of Interpersonal Violence, 33*, 83–93. doi: 10.1177/0886260516636394

Peterson, C., DeGue, S., Florence, C., & Lokey, C. N. (2017). Lifetime economic burden of rape among U.S. adults. *American Journal of Preventive Medicine, 52*, 691–701. doi: 10.1016/j .amepre.2016.11.014

Peterson, Z. D., & Muehlenhard, C. L. (2004). Was it rape? The function of women's rape myth acceptance and definitions of sex in labeling their own experiences. *Sex Roles, 51*, 129–144. doi: 10.1023/B:SERS.0000037758.95376.00

Peterson, Z. D., & Muehlenhard, C. L. (2007). Conceptualizing the "wantedness" of women's consensual and nonconsensual sexual experiences: Implications for how women label their experiences with rape. *Journal of Sex Research, 44*, 72–88. doi: 10.1080/0022449 0709336794

Picard, P. (2007, January). *Tech abuse in teen relationships.* Retrieved from http://www.loveisrespect.org/wp-content/uploads/2009 /03/liz-claiborne-2007-tech-relationship-abuse.pdf

Plummer, S. B., & Findley, P. A. (2012). Women with disabilities' experience with physical and sexual abuse: Review of the literature and implications for the field. *Trauma, Violence, & Abuse, 13*, 15–29. doi: 10.1177/1524838011426014

Policastro, C., & Finn, M. A. (2017). Coercive control and physical violence in older adults: Analysis using data from the National Elder Mistreatment Study. *Journal of Interpersonal Violence, 32*, 311–330. doi: 10.1177/0886260515585545

Porges, S. W., & Pepe, E. (2015). When not saying NO does not mean yes: Psychophysiological factors involved in date rape. *Biofeedback, 43*, 45–48. doi: 10.5298/1081-5937-43.1.01

Porta, C. M., Mathiason, M. A., Lust, K., & Eisenberg, M. E. (2017). Sexual violence among college students: An examination of individual and institutional level factors associated with perpetration. *Journal of Forensic Nursing, 13*, 109–117. doi: 10.1097/JFN.0000000000000161

Pratt, N. (2013). Weaponising feminism for the "war on terror," versus employing strategic silence. *Critical Studies on Terrorism, 6*, 327–331. doi: 10.1080/17539153.2013.809267

Pryor, D. W., & Hughes, M. R. (2016). Fear of rape among college women: A social psychological analysis. In R. D. Maiuro (Ed.), *Perspectives on college sexual assault: Perpetrator, victim, and bystander* (pp. 59–81). New York, NY: Springer.

Puente, S., & Cohen, D. (2003). Jealousy and the meaning (or nonmeaning) of violence. *Personality and Social Psychology Bulletin, 29*, 449–460. doi: 10.1177/0146167202250912

Qualey, M. L. (2015, May 11). Months after gunman's rampage, some of Chapel Hill's Muslims still live in fear. *Vanity Fair.* Retrieved from http://www.vanityfair.com/news/2015/05 /chapel-hill-shooting-muslims-fear

Raphael, J., & Ashley, J. (2008, May). *Domestic sex trafficking of Chicago women and girls.* Retrieved from http://www.icjia.state .il.us/assets/pdf/ResearchReports/Sex%20Trafficking%20 Report%20May%202008.pdf

Raphael, J., Reichert, J. A., & Powers, M. (2010). Pimp control and violence: Domestic sex trafficking of Chicago women and girls. *Women & Criminal Justice, 20*, 89–104. doi: 10.1080 /08974451003641065

Rehn, E., & Sirleaf, E. J. (2002). *Women, war and peace: The independent experts' assessment on the impact of armed conflict on women and women's role in peace-building.* New York, NY: United Nations Development Fund for Women. Retrievedfromhttps://www.unfpa.org/sites/default/files/pub-pdf /3F71081FF391653DC1256C69003170E9-unicef-Women WarPeace.pdf

Relyea, M., & Ullman, S. E. (2015). Unsupported or turned against: Understanding how two types of negative social reactions to sexual assault relate to postassault outcomes. *Psychology of Women Quarterly, 39*, 37–52. doi: 10.1177/0361684313512610

Rennison, C., & Rand, M. R. (2003). Nonlethal intimate partner violence against women: A comparison of three age cohorts. *Violence Against Women, 9*, 1417–1428. doi: 10.1177 /1077801203259232

Riger, S., & Gordon, M. T. (1981). The fear of rape: A study in social control. *Journal of Social Issues, 37*, 71–92. doi: 10.1111/j .1540-4560.1981.tb01071.x

Rivadeneyra, R., & Ward, L. M. (2005). From Ally McBeal to Sábado Gigante: Contributions of television viewing to the gender role attitudes of Latino adolescents. *Journal of Adolescent Research, 20*, 453–475. doi: 10.1177/0743558405274871

Rivett, M., & Kelly, S. (2006). "From awareness to practice": Children, domestic violence and child welfare. *Child Abuse Review, 15*, 224–242. doi: 10.1002/car.945

Roberto, K. A., Brossoie, N., McPherson, M. C., Pulsifer, M. B., & Brown, P. N. (2013). Violence against rural older women: Promoting community awareness and action. *Australasian Journal on Ageing, 32*, 2–7. doi: 10.1111/j.1741-6612.2012 .00649.x

Roberts, A. L., Austin, S. B., Corliss, H. L., Vandermorris, A. K., & Koenen, K. C. (2010). Pervasive trauma exposure among U.S. sexual orientation minority adults and risk of posttraumatic stress disorder. *American Journal of Public Health, 100*, 2433–2441. doi: 10.2105/AJPH.2009.168971

Robinson, L. (2015, October 6). Rihanna in Cuba: The cover story. *Vanity Fair.* Retrieved from http://www.vanityfair.com /hollywood/2015/10/rihanna-cover-cuba-annie-leibovitz

Robinson, L., & Spilsbury, K. (2008). Systematic review of the perceptions and experiences of accessing health services by adult victims of domestic violence. *Health & Social Care in the Community, 16*, 16–30. doi: 10.1111/j.1365-2524.2007.00721.x

Roe-Sepowitz, D. E., Hickle, K. E., Dahlstedt, J., & Gallagher, J. (2014). Victim or whore: The similarities and differences between victim's experiences of domestic violence and sex trafficking. *Journal of Human Behavior in the Social Environment, 24*, 883–898. doi: 10.1080/10911359.2013.840552

Rosay, A. B., & Mulford, C. F. (2017). Prevalence estimates and correlates of elder abuse in the United States: The National Intimate Partner and Sexual Violence Survey. *Journal of Elder Abuse & Neglect, 29*, 1–14. doi: 10.1080/08946566.2016.1249817

Rosen, L. N. (2007). Rape rates and military personnel in the United States: An exploratory study. *Violence Against Women, 13*, 945–960. doi: 10.1177/1077801207305264

Rothman, E. F., Nagaswaran, A., Johnson, R. M., Adams, K. M., Scrivens, J., & Baughman, A. (2012). U.S. tabloid magazine coverage of a celebrity dating abuse incident: Rihanna and Chris Brown. *Journal of Health Communication, 17*, 733–744. doi: 10.1080/10810730.2011.635778

Rozee, P. D., & Koss, M. P. (2001). Rape: A century of resistance. *Psychology of Women Quarterly, 25*, 295–311. doi: 10.1111 /1471-6402.00030

Rudman, L. A., & Mescher, K. (2012). Of animals and objects: Men's implicit dehumanization of women and likelihood of sexual aggression. *Personality and Social Psychology Bulletin, 38*, 734–746. doi: 10.1177/0146167212436401

Russell, K. J., & Hand, C. J. (2017). Rape myth acceptance, victim blame attribution and just world beliefs: A rapid evidence assessment. *Aggression and Violent Behavior, 37*, 153–160. doi: 10.1016/j.avb.2017.10.008

Russell, T. D., Doan, C. M., & King, A. R. (2017). Sexually violent women: The PID-5, everyday sadism, and adversarial sexual attitudes predict female sexual aggression and coercion against male victims. *Personality and Individual Differences, 111*, 242–249. doi: 10.1016/j.paid.2017.02.019

Sachs-Ericsson, N. J., Sheffler, J. L., Stanley, I. H., Piazza, J. R., & Preacher, K. J. (2017). When emotional pain becomes physical: Adverse childhood experiences, pain, and the role of mood and anxiety disorders. *Journal of Clinical Psychology, 73*, 1403–1428. doi: 10.1002/jclp.22444

Saleem, R., Vaswani, A., Wheeler, E., Maroney, M., Pagan-Ortiz, M., & Brodt, M. (2016). The effects of structural violence on the well-being of marginalized communities in the United States. *Journal of Pedagogy, Pluralism and Practice, 8*(1). Article 10. Retrieved from https://digitalcommons.lesley.edu /jppp/vol8/iss1/10

Sanchez, D. T., Fetterolf, J. C., & Rudman, L. A. (2012). Eroticizing inequality in the United States: The consequences and determinants of traditional gender role adherence in intimate relationships. *Journal of Sex Research, 49*, 168–183. doi: 10.1080/00224499.2011.653699

Saxton, M., Curry, M. A., Powers, L. E., Maley, S., Eckels, K., & Gross, J. (2001). "Bring my scooter so I can leave you": A study of disabled women handling abuse by personal assistance providers. *Violence Against Women, 7*, 393–417. doi: 10.1177/1077801012182523

Scheffer Lindgren, M., & Renck, B. (2008). "It is still so deep-seated, the fear": Psychological stress reactions as consequences of intimate partner violence. *Journal of Psychiatric and Mental Health Nursing, 15*, 219–228. doi: 10.1111/j.1365-2850.2007.01215.x

Seabrook, R. C., Ward, L. M., & Giaccardi, S. (2018). Why is fraternity membership associated with sexual assault? Exploring the roles of conformity to masculine norms, pressure to uphold masculinity, and objectification of women. *Psychology of Men & Masculinity, 19*, 3–13. doi: 10.1037/men0000076

Sell, N. M., Turrisi, R., Scaglione, N. M., Hultgren, B. A., & Mallett, K. A. (2016). Examining the effects of drinking and interpersonal protective behaviors on unwanted sexual experiences in college women. *Addictive Behaviors, 54*, 40–45. doi: 10.1016/j.addbeh.2015.12.003

The Sentencing Project (2013, August). *Report of The Sentencing Project to the United Nations Human Rights Committee: Regarding racial disparities in the United States criminal justice system.*

Washington, DC: Author. Retrieved from http://sentencing project.org/wp-content/uploads/2015/12/Race-and-Justice -Shadow-Report-ICCPR.pdf

Seyler, M. (2012, January 5). Rape in conflict: Battling the impunity that stifles its recognition as a *jus cogens* human right. *Gonzaga Journal of International Law, 15*(1). Retrieved from https://www.law.gonzaga.edu/gjil/2012/01/rape-in-conflict -battling-the-impunity-that-stifles-its-recognition-as-a-jus-cogens -human-right/

Shaw, J., Campbell, R., Cain, D., & Feeney, H. (2017). Beyond surveys and scales: How rape myths manifest in sexual assault police records. *Psychology of Violence, 7*, 602–614. doi: 10.1037/vio0000072

Sherman, L. W., Strang, H., Mayo-Wilson, E., Woods, D. J., & Ariel, B. (2015). Are restorative justice conferences effective in reducing repeat offending? Findings from a Campbell systematic review. *Journal of Quantitative Criminology, 31*, 1–24. doi: 10.1007/s10940-014-9222-9

Sherman, S. G., Footer, K., Illangasekare, S., Clark, E., Pearson, E., & Decker, M. R. (2015). "What makes you think you have special privileges because you are a police officer?" A qualitative exploration of police's role in the risk environment of female sex workers. *AIDS Care, 27*, 473–480. doi: 10.1080/09540121.2014.970504

Simon, A. F., Nolan, S. A., & Ngo, C. T. (2013). Sexual violence as a weapon of war. In J. A. Sigal & F. L. Denmark (Eds.), *Violence against girls and women: International perspectives* (Vol. 2, pp. 75–102). Santa Barbara, CA: Praeger.

Sjoberg, L. (2013). *Gendering global conflict: Toward a feminist theory of war.* New York, NY: Columbia University Press.

Smiler, A. P. (2008). "I wanted to get to know her better": Adolescent boys' dating motives, masculinity ideology, and sexual behavior. *Journal of Adolescence, 31*, 17–32. doi: 10.1016/j. adolescence.2007.03.006

Smith, A. (2013). Rape and war against Native women. In A. L. Ferber, K. Holcomb, & T. Wentling (Eds.), *Sex, gender, and sexuality: The new basics: An anthology* (pp. 323–332). New York, NY: Oxford University Press.

Smith, R. A., & Pick, L. H. (2015). Sexual assault experienced by deaf female undergraduates: Prevalence and characteristics. *Violence and Victims, 30*, 948–959. doi: 10.1891/0886-6708 .VV-D-14-00057

Smith, S. G., Zhang, X., Basile, K. C., Merrick, M. T., Wang, J., Kresnow, M., & Chen, J. (2018, May 9). National Intimate Partner and Sexual Violence Survey: 2015 data brief. *Centers for Disease Control and Prevention.* Retrieved from https://www .cdc.gov/violenceprevention/nisvs/2015NISVSdatabrief.html

Sokoloff, N. J., & Dupont, I. (2005). Domestic violence at the intersections of race, class, and gender: Challenges and contributions to understanding violence against marginalized women in diverse communities. *Violence Against Women, 11*, 38–64. doi: 10.1177/1077801204271476

Soler-Baillo, J. M., Marx, B. P., & Sloan, D. M. (2005). The psychophysiological correlates of risk recognition among victims and non-victims of sexual assault. *Behaviour Research and Therapy, 43*, 169–181. doi: 10.1016/j.brat.2004 .01.004

Southworth, C., Finn, J., Dawson, S., Fraser, C., & Tucker, S. (2007). Intimate partner violence, technology, and stalking. *Violence Against Women, 13*, 842–856. doi: 10.1177 /1077801207302045

Spangaro, J. M., Zwi, A. B., & Poulos, R. G. (2011). "Persist. persist.": A qualitative study of women's decisions to disclose and their perceptions of the impact of routine screening for intimate partner violence. *Psychology of Violence, 1*, 150–162. doi: 10.1037/a0023136

Sprankle, E., Bloomquist, K., Butcher, C., Gleason, N., & Schaefer, Z. (2018). The role of sex work stigma in victim blaming and empathy of sexual assault survivors. *Sexuality Research & Social Policy, 15*, 242–248. doi: 10.1007/s13178-017-0282-0

Springer, K. W., Sheridan, J., Kuo, D., & Carnes, M. (2007). Long-term physical and mental health consequences of childhood physical abuse: Results from a large population-based sample of men and women. *Child Abuse & Neglect, 31*, 517–530. doi: 10.1016/j.chiabu.2007.01.003

Stack, L. (2016, June 6). Light sentence for Brock Turner in Stanford rape case draws outrage. *The New York Times.* Retrieved from https://www.nytimes.com/2016/06/07/us/outrage-in -stanford-rape-case-over-dueling-statements-of-victim-and -attackers-father.html

Stahly, G. B. (2008). Domestic violence and child custody: A critique of recent JCC articles. *Journal of Child Custody, 4*(3–4), 1–18.

Stark, E. (2007). *Coercive control: The entrapment of women in personal life.* Oxford, United Kingdom: Oxford University Press.

Stark, E. (2010). Do violent acts equal abuse? Resolving the gender parity/asymmetry dilemma. *Sex Roles, 62*, 201–211. doi: 10.1007 /s11199-009-9717-2

Starkweather, S. (2007). Gender, perceptions of safety and strategic responses among Ohio university students. *Gender, Place & Culture, 14*, 355–370. doi: 10.1080/09663690701325000

Starzynski, L. L., & Ullman, S. E. (2014). Correlates of perceived helpfulness of mental health professionals following disclosure of sexual assault. *Violence Against Women, 20*, 74–94. doi: 10.1177/1077801213520575

Steel, C. M. (2015). Web-based child pornography: The global impact of deterrence efforts and its consumption on mobile platforms. *Child Abuse & Neglect, 44*, 150–158. doi: 10.1016/j .chiabu.2014.12.009

Steinmetz, K. (2016, May 2). Why LGBT advocates say bathroom "predators" argument is a red herring. *Time.* Retrieved from http://time.com/4314896/transgender-bathroom-bill-male -predators-argument/

Stewart, A. L. (2014). The Men's Project: A sexual assault prevention program targeting college men. *Psychology of Men & Masculinity, 15*, 481–485. doi: 10.1037/a0033947

Stöckl, H., & Penhale, B. (2015). Intimate partner violence and its association with physical and mental health symptoms among older women in Germany. *Journal of Interpersonal Violence, 30*, 3089–3111. doi: 10.1177/0886260514554427

Stoll, L. C., Lilley, T. G., & Pinter, K. (2017). Gender-blind sexism and rape myth acceptance. *Violence Against Women, 23*, 28–45. doi: 10.1177/1077801216636239

Stoner, S. A., Norris, J., George, W. H., Davis, K. C., Masters, N. T., & Hessler, D. M. (2007). Effects of alcohol intoxication and victimization history on women's sexual assault resistance intentions: The role of secondary cognitive appraisals. *Psychology of Women Quarterly, 31*, 344–356. doi: 10.1111/j.1471 -6402.2007.00384.x

Storer, H. L., Casey, E., & Herrenkohl, T. (2016). Efficacy of bystander programs to prevent dating abuse among youth and young adults: A review of the literature. *Trauma, Violence, & Abuse, 17*, 256–269. doi: 10.1177/1524838015584361

Straus, M. A., & Ramirez, I. L. (2004). Criminal history and assault of dating partners: The role of type of prior crime, age of onset, and gender. *Violence and Victims, 19*, 413–434. doi: 10.1891 /vivi.19.4.413.64164

Strouse, J. S., Goodwin, M. P., & Roscoe, B. (1994). Correlates of attitudes toward sexual harassment among early adolescents. *Sex Roles, 31*, 559–577. doi: 10.1007/BF01544280

Sullivan, B. (2007). Rape, prostitution and consent. *Australian & New Zealand Journal of Criminology, 40*, 127–142. doi: 10.1375/acri.40.2.127

Swan, S. C., Gambone, L. J., Caldwell, J. E., Sullivan, T. P., & Snow, D. L. (2008). A review of research on women's use of violence with male intimate partners. *Violence and Victims, 23,* 301–314. doi: 10.1891/0886-6708.23.3.301

Talbot, M. (2015, June 22). The story of a hate crime. *The New Yorker.* Retrieved from http://www.newyorker.com/magazine/2015/06/22/the-story-of-a-hate-crime

Tam, S., & Neysmith, S. (2006). Disrespect and isolation: Elder abuse in Chinese communities. *Canadian Journal on Aging/La Revue canadienne du vieillissement, 25,* 141–151. doi: 10.1353/cja.2006.0043

Teaster, P. B, Dugar, T. A., Mendiondo, M. S., Abner, E. L., Cecil, K. A., & Otto, J. M. (2007, March). *The 2004 survey of state adult protective services: Abuse of vulnerable adults 18 years of age and older.* Retrieved from the National Center for Elder Abuse website: https://ncea.acl.gov/resources/docs/archive/2004-Survey-St-Audit-APS-Abuse-18plus-2007.pdf

TeBockhorst, S. F., O'Halloran, M. S., & Nyline, B. N. (2015). Tonic immobility among survivors of sexual assault. *Psychological Trauma: Theory, Research, Practice, and Policy, 7,* 171–178. doi: 10.1037/a0037953

Tedeschi, R. G., & Calhoun, L. G. (2004). Posttraumatic growth: Conceptual foundations and empirical evidence. *Psychological Inquiry, 15,* 1–18. doi: 10.1207/s15327965pli1501_01

Tennessee, A. M., Bradham, T. S., White, B. M., & Simpson, K. N. (2017). The monetary cost of sexual assault to privately insured U.S. women in 2013. *American Journal of Public Health, 107,* 983–988. doi: 10.2105/AJPH.2017.303742

Testa, M., Hoffman, J. H., & Livingston, J. A. (2010). Alcohol and sexual risk behaviors as mediators of the sexual victimization–revictimization relationship. *Journal of Consulting and Clinical Psychology, 78,* 249–259. doi: 10.1037/a0018914

Thompson, E. J., & Bennett, K. M. (2017). Masculinity ideologies. In R. F. Levant & Y. J. Wong (Eds.), *The psychology of men and masculinities* (pp. 45–74). Washington, DC: American Psychological Association.

Tjaden, P., & Thoennes, N. (2000). Prevalence and consequences of male-to-female and female-to-male intimate partner violence as measured by the National Violence Against Women Survey. *Violence Against Women, 6,* 142–161. doi: 10.1177/10778010022181769

Tjaden, P. G., & Thoennes, N. (2006, January). *Extent, nature, and consequences of rape victimization: Findings from the National Violence Against Women Survey* (NCJ No. 210346). Retrieved from the National Criminal Justice Reference Service website: https://www.ncjrs.gov/pdffiles1/nij/210346.pdf

Tsui, A., Nolan, D., & Amico, C. (2017, July 6). Child marriage in America: By the numbers. *Frontline.* Retrieved from http://apps.frontline.org/child-marriage-by-the-numbers/

Turchik, J. A., Garske, J. P., Probst, D. R., & Irvin, C. R. (2010). Personality, sexuality, and substance use as predictors of sexual risk taking in college students. *Journal of Sex Research, 47,* 411–419. doi: 10.1080/00224490903161621

Turchik, J. A., & Wilson, S. M. (2010). Sexual assault in the U.S. military: A review of the literature and recommendations for the future. *Aggression and Violent Behavior, 15,* 267–277. doi: 10.1016/j.avb.2010.01.005

Turse, N. (2017, June 26). American special ops forces have deployed to 70 percent of the world's countries in 2017. *The Nation.* Retrieved from https://www.thenation.com/article/american-special-ops-forces-have-deployed-to-70-percent-of-the-worlds-countries-in-2017/

Tyson, A. (2017, November 28). Americans are split on the principle of preemptive military force. *Pew Research Center.* Retrieved from http://www.pewresearch.org/fact-tank/2017/11/28/americans-are-split-on-the-principle-of-pre-emptive-military-force/

Ullman, S. E. (2007). A 10-year update on "Review and critique of empirical studies of rape avoidance." *Criminal Justice and Behavior, 34,* 411–429. doi: 10.1177/0093854806297117

Ullman, S. E. (2010). *Talking about sexual assault: Society's response to survivors.* Washington, DC: American Psychological Association.

Ullman, S. E., & Relyea, M. (2016). Social support, coping, and posttraumatic stress symptoms in female sexual assault survivors: A longitudinal analysis. *Journal of Traumatic Stress, 29,* 500–506. doi: 10.1002/jts.22143

Ullman, S. E., Townsend, S. M., Filipas, H. H., & Starzynski, L. L. (2007). Structural models of the relations of assault severity, social support, avoidance coping, self-blame, and PTSD among sexual assault survivors. *Psychology of Women Quarterly, 31,* 23–37. doi: 10.1111/j.1471-6402.2007.00328.x

Ulloa, E., Guzman, M. L., Salazar, M., & Cala, C. (2016). Posttraumatic growth and social violence: A literature review. *Journal of Aggression, Maltreatment & Trauma, 25,* 286–304. doi: 10.1080/10926771.2015.1079286

Ungar, M., Ghazinour, M., & Richter, J. (2013). Annual research review: What is resilience within the social ecology of human development? *Journal of Child Psychology and Psychiatry, 54,* 348–366. doi: 10.1111/jcpp.12025

UNICEF. (2014a, September). *Hidden in plain sight: A statistical analysis of violence against children.* New York, NY: Author. Retrieved from http://files.unicef.org/publications/files/Hidden_in_plain_sight_statistical_analysis_EN_3_Sept_2014.pdf

UNICEF. (2014b, October). *A statistical snapshot of violence against adolescent girls.* New York, NY: Author. Retrieved from https://www.unicef.org/publications/files/A_Statistical_Snapshot_of_Violence_Against_Adolescent_Girls.pdf

UNICEF. (2017, November). *A familiar face: Violence in the lives of children and adolescents.* New York, NY: Author. Retrieved from https://data.unicef.org/wp-content/uploads/2017/10/EVAC-Booklet-FINAL-10_31_17-high-res.pdf

United Nations. (2015, April 15). *Fight against sexual violence in conflict reaches "new juncture,"* Security Council told [Press release]. Retrieved from https://www.un.org/press/en/2015/sc11862.doc.htm

United Nations. (n.d.). *Convention on the Elimination of All Forms of Discrimination against Women.* Retrieved from http://www.un.org/womenwatch/daw/cedaw/

United Nations Statistics Division. (2015). Violence against women. In *The world's women 2015.* Retrieved from https://unstats.un.org/unsd/gender/chapter6/chapter6.html

U.S. Department of Defense. (2016a). *Department of Defense annual report on sexual assault in the military: Fiscal year 2015.* Washington, DC: Author. Retrieved from http://sapr.mil/public/docs/reports/FY15_Annual/FY15_Annual_Report_on_Sexual_Assault_in_the_Military_Full_Report.pdf

U.S. Department of Defense. (2016b, Feb. 9). *Department of Defense (DoD) releases fiscal year 2017 president's budget proposal* [Press release No. NR-046-16]. Retrieved from https://www.defense.gov/News/News-Releases/News-Release-View/Article/652687/department-of-defense-dod-releases-fiscal-year-2017-presidents-budget-proposal

U.S. Department of Justice. (2012, January 06). *An updated definition of rape.* Retrieved from https://www.justice.gov/opa/blog/updated-definition-rape

U.S. Department of Justice, Civil Rights Division. (2016, August 10). *Investigation of the Baltimore City Police Department.* Retrieved from https://www.justice.gov/opa/file/883366/download

Vagi, K. J., Olsen, E. O., Basile, K. C., & Vivolo-Kantor, A. M. (2015). Teen dating violence (physical and sexual) among U.S. high school students: Findings from the 2013 National Youth Risk Behavior Survey. *JAMA Pediatrics*, *169*, 474–482. doi: 10.1001/jamapediatrics.2014.3577

van Wormer, K. (2009). Restorative justice as social justice for victims of gendered violence: A standpoint feminist perspective. *Social Work*, *54*, 107–116. doi: 10.1093/sw/54.2.107

Vanwesenbeeck, I. (2017). Sex work criminalization is barking up the wrong tree. *Archives of Sexual Behavior*, *46*, 1631–1640. doi: 10.1007/s10508-017-1008-3

Victims of Trafficking and Violence Protection Act of 2000. (2000). United States Code. Retrieved from https://www.congress.gov/106/plaws/publ386/PLAW-106publ386.pdf

Violence Policy Center. (2015, September 15). *More than 1,600 women murdered by men in one year, new study finds* [Press release]. Retrieved from http://www.vpc.org/press/more-than-1600-women-murdered-by-men-in-one-year-new-study-finds/

Vissandjée, B., Kantiébo, M., Levine, A., & N'Dejuru, R. (2003). The cultural context of gender identity: Female genital excision and infibulation. *Health Care for Women International*, *24*, 115–124. doi: 10.1080/07399330390170097

Walby, S., Towers, J., & Francis, B. (2015). Is violent crime increasing or decreasing? A new methodology to measure repeat attacks making visible the significance of gender and domestic relations. *British Journal of Criminology*, *56*, 1203–1234. doi: 10.1093/bjc/azv131

Walker, L. E. (2017). *The battered woman syndrome* (4th ed.). New York, NY: Springer.

Walker, S., Spohn, C., & DeLone, M. (2012). *The color of justice: Race, ethnicity, and crime in America* (5th ed.). Belmont, CA: Wadsworth.

Walker, S. J. (1997). When "no" becomes "yes": Why girls and women consent to unwanted sex. *Applied and Preventive Psychology*, *6*, 157–166. doi: 10.1016/S0962-1849(97)80003-0

Walsh, K., Zinzow, H. M., Badour, C. L., Ruggiero, K. J., Kilpatrick, D. G., & Resnick, H. S. (2016). Understanding disparities in service seeking following forcible versus drug- or alcohol-facilitated/incapacitated rape. *Journal of Interpersonal Violence*, *31*, 2475–2491. doi: 10.1177/0886260515576968

Ward, L. M. (2016). Media and sexualization: State of empirical research, 1995–2015. *The Journal of Sex Research*, *53*, 560–577. doi: 10.1080/00224499.2016.1142496

Ward, L. M., Reed, L., Trinh, S. L., & Foust, M. (2014). Sexuality and entertainment media. In D. L. Tolman & L. M. Diamond (Eds.), *APA handbook of sexuality and psychology* (Vol. 2, pp. 373–423). Washington, DC: American Psychological Association.

Ward, L. M., Vandenbosch, L., & Eggermont, S. (2015). The impact of men's magazines on adolescent boys' objectification and courtship beliefs. *Journal of Adolescence*, *39*, 49–58. doi: 10.1016/j.adolescence.2014.12.004

Way, K. (n.d.). I went on a date with Aziz Ansari—It turned into the worst night of my life. *babe*. Retrieved from https://babe.net/2018/01/13/aziz-ansari-28355

Weiss, K. G. (2009). "Boys will be boys" and other gendered accounts: An exploration of victims' excuses and justifications for unwanted sexual contact and coercion. *Violence Against Women*, *15*, 810–834. doi: 10.1177/1077801209333611

Weist, M. D., Kinney, L., Taylor, L. K., Pollitt-Hill, J., Bryant, Y., Anthony, L., & Wilkerson, J. (2014). African American and White women's experience of sexual assault and services for sexual assault. *Journal of Aggression, Maltreatment & Trauma*, *23*, 901–916. doi: 10.1080/10926771.2014.953715

The White House. (2002, September). *The national security strategy of the United States of America*. Retrieved from https://www.state.gov/documents/organization/63562.pdf

Will, J. L., Loper, A. B., & Jackson, S. L. (2016). Second-generation prisoners and the transmission of domestic violence. *Journal of Interpersonal Violence*, *31*, 100–121. doi: 10.1177/0886260514555127

Williams, K. R., & Stansfield, R. (2017). Disentangling the risk assessment and intimate partner violence relation: Estimating mediating and moderating effects. *Law and Human Behavior*, *41*, 344–353. doi: 10.1037/lhb0000249

Williamson, C., & Cluse-Tolar, T. (2002). Pimp-controlled prostitution still an integral part of street life. *Violence Against Women*, *8*, 1074–1092. doi: 10.1177/107780102401101746

Willie, T. C., Khondkaryan, E., Callands, T., & Kershaw, T. (2018). "Think like a man": How sexual cultural scripting and masculinity influence changes in men's use of intimate partner violence. *American Journal of Community Psychology*, *61*, 240–250. doi: 10.1002/ajcp.12224

Wilson, L. C., & Miller, K. E. (2016). Meta-analysis of the prevalence of unacknowledged rape. *Trauma, Violence, & Abuse*, *17*, 149–159. doi: 10.1177/1524838015576391

Wolak, J., Finkelhor, D., & Mitchell, K. J. (2012). How often are teens arrested for sexting? Data from a national sample of police cases. *Pediatrics*, *129*, 4–12. doi: 10.1542/peds.2011-2242

Wolf, M. E., Ly, U., Hobart, M. A., & Kernic, M. A. (2003). Barriers to seeking police help for intimate partner violence. *Journal of Family Violence*, *18*, 121–129. doi: 10.1023/A:1022893231951

Wolff, N., Shi, J., & Siegel, J. A. (2009). Patterns of victimization among male and female inmates: Evidence of an enduring legacy. *Violence and Victims*, *24*, 469–484. doi: 10.1891/0886-6708.24.4.469

Wolitzky-Taylor, K. B., Resnick, H. S., McCauley, J. L., Amstadter, A. B., Kilpatrick, D. G., & Ruggiero, K. J. (2011). Is reporting of rape on the rise? A comparison of women with reported versus unreported rape experiences in the National Women's Study-Replication. *Journal of Interpersonal Violence*, *26*, 807–832. doi: 10.1177/0886260510365869

Wong, J. S., & Balemba, S. (2016). The effect of victim resistance on rape completion: A meta-analysis. *Trauma, Violence, & Abuse*, *19*, 352–365. doi: 10.1177/1524838016663934

World Health Organization. (2016, November). *Violence against women: Intimate partner and sexual violence against women*. Retrieved from http://www.who.int/mediacentre/factsheets/fs239/en/

World Health Organization. (2017, February). *Female genital mutilation*. Retrieved from www.who.int/mediacentre/factsheets/fs241/en/

Wosick, K. R. (2015). Pornography. In J. DeLamater & R. F. Plante (Eds.), *Handbook of the sociology of sexualities* (pp. 413–433). Cham, Switzerland: Springer International.

Yazzie, R., & Zion, J. W. (1996). Navajo restorative justice: The law of equality and justice. In B. Galaway & J. Hudson (Eds.), *Restorative justice: International perspectives* (pp. 157–173). Monsey, NY: Criminal Justice Press.

Yodanis, C. L. (2004). Gender inequality, violence against women, and fear: A cross-national test of the feminist theory of violence against women. *Journal of Interpersonal Violence*, *19*, 655–675. doi: 10.1177/0886260504263868

Zaleski, K. L., Gundersen, K. K., Baes, J., Estupinian, E., & Vergara, A. (2016). Exploring rape culture in social media forums. *Computers in Human Behavior*, *63*, 922–927. doi: 10.1016/j.chb.2016.06.036

Zamir, O., Szepsenwol, O., Englund, M. M., & Simpson, J. A. (2018). The role of dissociation in revictimization across the lifespan: A 32-year prospective study. *Child Abuse & Neglect*, *79*, 144–153. doi: 10.1016/j.chiabu.2018.02.001

Zarit, S., & Toseland,R. (1989). Current and future direction in family caregiving research. *The Gerontologist, 29*, 481–483. doi: 10.1093/geront/29.4.481

Žarkov, D. (2016). Co-option, complicity, co-production: Feminist politics on war rapes. *European Journal of Women's Studies, 23*, 119–123. doi: 10.1177/1350506816637031

Zarling, A., & Berta, M. (2017). An acceptance and commitment therapy approach for partner aggression. *Partner Abuse, 8*, 89–109. doi: 10.1891/1946-6560.8.1.89

Ziering, A. (Producer), Barklow, T. K. (Producer), & Dick, K. (Director). (2012). *The invisible war* [Motion picture]. United States: New Video Group.

Zink, T., & Fisher, B. S. (2006). The prevalence and incidence of intimate partner and interpersonal mistreatment in older women in primary care offices. *Journal of Elder Abuse & Neglect, 18*, 83–105. doi: 10.1300/J084v18n01_04

Zink, T., Fisher, B. S., Regan, S., & Pabst, S. (2005). The prevalence and incidence of intimate partner violence in older women in primary care practices. *Journal of General Internal Medicine, 20*, 884–888. doi: 10.1111/j.1525-1497.2005.0191.x

Zinzow, H. M., & Thompson, M. (2015). Factors associated with use of verbally coercive, incapacitated, and forcible sexual assault tactics in a longitudinal study of college men. *Aggressive Behavior, 41*, 34–43. doi: 10.1002/ab.21567

Zurbriggen, E. L. (2010). Rape, war, and the socialization of masculinity: Why our refusal to give up war ensures that rape cannot be eradicated. *Psychology of Women Quarterly, 34*, 538–549. doi: 10.1111/j.1471-6402.2010.01603.x

Chapter 13

Ackerman, S., & Hilsenroth, M. (2003). A review of therapist characteristics and techniques positively impacting the therapeutic alliance. *Clinical Psychology Review, 23*, 1–33. doi: 10.1016/S0272-7358(02)00146-0

Addis, M., & Mahalik, J. (2003). Men, masculinity, and the contexts of help seeking. *American Psychologist, 58*, 5–14. doi: 10.1037/0003-066X.58.1.5

Alegría, M., Chatterji, P., Wells, K., Cao, Z., Chen, C., Takeuchi, D., . . . & Meng, X.-L. (2008). Disparity in depression treatment among racial and ethnic minority populations in the United States. *Psychiatric Services, 59*, 1264–1272. doi: 10.1176/appi.ps.59.11.1264

Ali, A., Caplan, P. J., & Fagnant, R. (2010). Gender stereotypes in diagnostic criteria. In J. C. Chrisler & D. R. McCreary (Eds.), *Handbook of gender research in psychology* (Vol. 2, pp. 91–109). New York, NY: Springer.

Ali, A., & Toner, B. B. (2001). Symptoms of depression among Caribbean women and Caribbean-Canadian women: An investigation of self-silencing and domains of meaning. *Psychology of Women Quarterly, 25*, 175–180. doi: 10.1111/1471-6402.00019

Amanda Bynes—Serious mental issues. (2012, September 15). *TMZ.* Retrieved from http://www.tmz.com/2012/09/15/amanda-bynes-mental-issues/

American Psychiatric Association. (2013). *Diagnostic and statistical manual of mental disorders* (5th ed.). Arlington, VA: American Psychiatric Publishing.

American Psychological Association. (2003). Guidelines on multicultural education, training, research, practice, and organizational change for psychologists. *American Psychologist, 58*, 377–402. doi: 10.1037/0003-066X.58.5.377

American Psychological Association. (2012). Guidelines for psychological practice with lesbian, gay, and bisexual clients. *American Psychologist, 67*, 10–42. doi: 10.1037/a0024659

American Psychological Association. (2017). *Multicultural guidelines: An ecological approach to context, identity, and intersectionality.* Washington, DC: Author. Retrieved from http://www.apa.org/about/policy/multicultural-guidelines.pdf

Appel, H., Gerlach, A. L., & Crusius, J. (2016). The interplay between Facebook use, social comparison, envy, and depression. *Current Opinion in Psychology, 9*, 44–49. doi: 10.1016/j.copsyc.2015.10.006

Arcelus, J., Mitchell, A., Wales, J., & Nielsen, S. (2011). Mortality rates in patients with anorexia nervosa and other eating disorders: A meta-analysis of 36 studies. *Archives of General Psychiatry, 68*, 724–731 doi: 10.1001/archgenpsychiatry.2011.74

Atwood, N. (2001). Gender bias in families and its clinical implications for women. *Social Work, 46*, 23–36. doi: 10.1093/sw/46.1.23

Au, A. (2017). Low mental health treatment participation and Confucianist familial norms among East Asian immigrants: A critical review. *International Journal of Mental Health, 46*, 1–17. doi: 10.1080/00207411.2016.1264036

Avis, N., & McKinlay, S. (1991). A longitudinal analysis of women's attitudes toward the menopause: Results from the Massachusetts Women's Health Study. *Maturitas, 13*, 65–79. doi: 10.1016/0378-5122(91)90286-Y

Ball, J., & Links, P. (2009). Borderline personality disorder and childhood trauma: Evidence for a causal relationship. *Current Psychiatry Reports, 11*, 63–68. doi: 10.1007/s11920-009-0010-4

Ballou, M. B. (1990). Approaching a feminist-principled paradigm in the construction of personality theory. *Women & Therapy, 9*, 23–40. doi: 10.1300/J015v09n01_02

Bardone-Cone, A., & Cass, K. (2007). What does viewing a pro-anorexia website do? An experimental examination of website exposure and moderating effects. *International Journal of Eating Disorders, 40*, 537–548. doi: 10.1002/eat.20396

Bartlett, A., & Hollins, S. (2018). Challenges and mental health needs of women in prison. *The British Journal of Psychiatry, 212*, 134–136. doi: 10.1192/bjp.2017.42

Bauer, M., Glenn, T., Pilhatsch, M., Pfennig, A., & Whybrow, P. C. (2014). Gender differences in thyroid system function: Relevance to bipolar disorder and its treatment. *Bipolar Disorders, 16*, 58–71. doi: 10.1111/bdi.12150

Baumgarten, M., Battista, R., Infante-Rivard, C., Hanley, J., Becker, R., & Gauthier, S. (1992). The psychological and physical health of family members caring for an elderly person with dementia. *Journal of Clinical Epidemiology, 45*, 61–70. doi: 10.1016/0895-4356(92)90189-T

Beauboeuf-Lafontant, T. (2007). You have to show strength: An exploration of gender, race, and depression. *Gender & Society, 21*, 28–51. doi: 10.1177/0891243206294108

Behnke, S. (2015, March). Ethics, self-disclosure and our everyday multiple identities. *APA Monitor on Psychology, 46*(3), 70. Retrieved from http://www.apa.org/monitor/2015/03/ethics.aspx

Bekker M. H. (1996). Agoraphobia and gender: A review. *Clinical Psychology Review, 16*, 129–146. doi: 10.1016/0272-7358(96)00012-8

Bekker, M. H., & van Mens-Verhulst, J. (2007). Anxiety disorders: Sex differences in prevalence, degree, and background, but gender-neutral treatment. *Gender Medicine, 4*, S178–S193. doi: 10.1016/S1550-8579(07)80057-X

Belle, D., & Doucet, J. (2003). Poverty, inequality, and discrimination as sources of depression among U.S. women. *Psychology of Women Quarterly, 27*, 101–113. doi: 10.1111/1471-6402.00090

Blehar, M. (2006). Women's mental health research: The emergence of a biomedical field. *Annual Reviews of Clinical Psychology, 2*, 135–160. doi: 10.1146/annurev.clinpsy.2.022305.095344

Blum, L., & Stracuzzi, N. (2004). Gender in the Prozac nation: Popular discourse and productive femininity. *Gender & Society*, *18*, 269–286. doi: 10.1177/0891243204263108

Bockting, W., Miner, M., Swinburne-Romine, R., Hamilton, A., & Coleman, E. (2013). Stigma, mental health, and resilience in an online sample of the U.S. transgender population. *American Journal of Public Health*, *103*, 943–951. doi: 10.2105/AJPH.2013.301241

Bolton, J., Cox, B., Clara, I., & Sareen, J. (2006). Use of alcohol and drugs to self-medicate anxiety disorders in a nationally representative sample. *The Journal of Nervous and Mental Disease*, *194*, 818–825. doi: 10.1097/01.nmd.0000244481.63148.98

Bombay, A., Matheson, K., & Anisman, H. (2014). The intergenerational effects of Indian residential schools: Implications for the concept of historical trauma. *Transcultural Psychiatry*, *51*, 320–338. doi: 10.1177/1363461513503380

Bornovalova, M., Huibregtse, B., Hicks, B., Keyes, M., McGue, M., & Iacono, W. (2013). Tests of a direct effect of childhood abuse on adult borderline personality disorder traits: A longitudinal discordant twin design. *Journal of Abnormal Psychology*, *122*, 180–194. doi: 10.1037/a0028328

Bowers, M. E., & Yehuda, R. (2016). Intergenerational transmission of stress in humans. *Neuropsychopharmacology*, *41*, 232–244. doi: 10.1038/npp.2015.247

Boyd, J. E., Lanius, R. A., & McKinnon, M. C. (2018). Mindfulness-based treatments for posttraumatic stress disorder: A review of the treatment literature and neurobiological evidence. *Journal of Psychiatry and Neuroscience*, *43*, 7–25. doi: 10.1503/jpn.170021

Braga, L. L., Mello, M. F., & Fiks, J. P. (2012). Transgenerational transmission of trauma and resilience: A qualitative study with Brazilian offspring of Holocaust survivors. *BMC Psychiatry*, *12*, 134. doi: 10.1186/1471-244X-12-134

Brazelton, E., Greene, K., & Gynther, M. (1996). Femininity, depression and stress in college women. *Social Behavior and Personality*, *24*, 329–334. doi: 10.2224/sbp.1996.24.4.329

Brecklin, L., & Ullman, S. (2005). Self-defense or assertiveness training and women's responses to sexual attacks. *Journal of Interpersonal Violence*, *20*, 738–762. doi: 10.1177/0886260504272894

Brody, D. J., Pratt, L. A., & Hughes, J. P. (2018). *Prevalence of depression among adults aged 20 and over: United States, 2013–2016* (NCHS data brief no. 303). Hyattsville, MD: National Center for Health Statistics. Retrieved from https://www.cdc.gov/nchs/data/databriefs/db303.pdf

Brosi, M. W., & Rolling, E. S. (2010). A narrative journey for intimate partner violence: From victim to survivor. *The American Journal of Family Therapy*, *38*, 237–250. doi: 10.1080/01926180902961761

Brouwer, D. C., & Horwitz, L. D. (2015). The cultural politics of progenic Auschwitz tattoos: 157622, A-15510, 4559, . . . *Quarterly Journal of Speech*, *101*, 534–558. doi: 10.1080/00335630.2015.1056748

Broverman, I. K., Broverman, D. M., Clarkson, F. E., Rosenkrantz, P. S., & Vogel, S. R. (1970). Sex-role stereotypes and clinical judgments of mental health. *Journal of Consulting and Clinical Psychology*, *34*, 1–7. doi: 10.1037/h0028797

Brown, A. (2012, October 30). With poverty comes depression, more than other illnesses. *Gallup*. Retrieved from http://www.gallup.com/poll/158417/poverty-comes-depression-illness.aspx

Brown, L. (2006). Still subversive after all these years: The relevance of feminist therapy in the age of evidence-based practice. *Psychology of Women Quarterly*, *30*, 15–24. doi: 10.1111/j.1471-6402.2006.00258.x

Brown, L. S. (2004). *Subversive dialogues: Theory in feminist therapy*. New York, NY: Basic Books.

Bryant-Davis, T., & Ocampo, C. (2005). The trauma of racism: Implications for counseling, research, and education. *The Counseling Psychologist*, *33*, 574–578. doi: 10.1177/0011000005276581

Buchanan, N. T., & Ormerod, A. J. (2002). Racialized sexual harassment in the lives of African American women. *Women & Therapy*, *25*, 107–124. doi: 10.1300/J015v25n03_08

Burstow, B. (2006). Electroshock as a form of violence against women. *Violence Against Women*, *12*, 372–392. doi: 10.1177/1077801206286404

Bynum, B. (2000). Discarded diagnoses: Drapetomania. *The Lancet*, *356*, 1615. doi: 10.1016/S0140-6736(05)74468-8

Callard, F. (2003). Conceptualisations of agoraphobia: Implications for mental health promotion. *Journal of Public Mental Health*, *2*, 37–45. doi: 10.1108/17465729200300006

Campbell, K. E., Dennerstein, L., Tacey, M., & Szoeke, C. E. (2017). The trajectory of negative mood and depressive symptoms over two decades. *Maturitas*, *95*, 36–41. doi: 10.1016/j.maturitas.2016.10.011

Cantisano, G. T., Domínguez, J. M., & Depolo, M. (2008). Perceived sexual harassment at work: Meta-analysis and structural model of antecedents and consequences. *The Spanish Journal of Psychology*, *11*, 207–218. doi: 10.1017/S113874160000425X

Caplan, P. J. (1995). *They say you're crazy: How the world's most powerful psychiatrists decide who's normal*. Jackson, MI: De Capo.

Centers for Disease Control and Prevention. (2010, October 1). Current depression among adults—United States, 2006 and 2008. *Morbidity and Mortality Weekly Report*, *59*, 1229–1235. Retrieved from https://www.cdc.gov/mmwr/PDF/wk/mm5938.pdf

Céspedes, Y. M., & Huey, S. J. (2008). Depression in Latino adolescents: A cultural discrepancy perspective. *Cultural Diversity and Ethnic Minority Psychology*, *14*, 168–172. doi: 10.1037/1099-9809.14.2.168

Chaplin, T., Cole, P., & Zahn-Waxler, C. (2005). Parental socialization of emotion expression: Gender differences and relations to child adjustment. *Emotion*, *5*, 80–88. doi: 10.1037/1528-3542.5.1.80

Chapman, D. P., Whitfield, C. L., Felitti, V. J., Dube, S. R., Edwards, V. J., & Anda, R. F. (2004). Adverse childhood experiences and the risk of depressive disorders in adulthood. *Journal of Affective Disorders*, *82*, 217–225. doi: 10.1016/j.jad.2003.12.013

Chesler, P. (2005). *Women and madness: Revised and updated*. New York, NY: St. Martin's Griffin.

Chodorow, N. (1978). *The reproduction of mothering*. Berkeley, CA: University of California Press.

Cloitre, M., Garvert, D. W., Weiss, B., Carlson, E. B., & Bryant, R. A. (2014). Distinguishing PTSD, complex PTSD, and borderline personality disorder: A latent class analysis. *European Journal of Psychotraumatology*, *5*, Article No. 25097. doi: 10.3402/ejpt.v5.25097

Cohen, D., & Jacobs, D. H. (2007). Randomized controlled trials of antidepressants: Clinically and scientifically irrelevant. *Debates in Neuroscience*, *1*(1), 44–54. doi: 10.1007/s11559-007-9002-x

Cohen, L., Soares, C., Vitonis, A., Otto, M., & Harlow, B. (2006). Risk for new onset of depression during the menopausal transition: The Harvard study of moods and cycles. *Archives of General Psychiatry*, *63*, 385–390. doi: 10.1001/archpsyc.63.4.385

Coiro, M. (2001). Depressive symptoms among women receiving welfare. *Women & Health*, *32*, 1–23. doi: 10.1300/J013v32n01_01

Cosgrove, L., & Krimsky, S. (2012). A comparison of DSM-IV and DSM-5 panel members' financial associations with industry: A pernicious problem persists. *PLoS Medicine, 9*(3), e1001190. doi: 10.1371/journal.pmed.1001190

Cosgrove, L., & Wheeler, E. (2013). Industry's colonization of psychiatry: Ethical and practical implications of financial conflicts of interest in the DSM-5. *Feminism & Psychology, 23*, 93–106. doi: 10.1177/0959353512467972

Courtois, C. A., & Ford, J. D. (2009). Complex trauma and traumatic stress reactions. In C. A. Courtois & J. D. Ford (Eds.), *Treating complex traumatic stress disorders: An evidence-based guide* (pp. 3–27). New York, NY: Guilford Press.

Culbert, K., Racine, S., & Klump, K. (2015). Research review: What we have learned about the causes of eating disorders—a synthesis of sociocultural, psychological, and biological research. *Journal of Child Psychology and Psychiatry, 56*, 1141–1164. doi: 10.1111/jcpp.12441

Custers, K., & Van den Bulck, J. (2009). Viewership of pro-anorexia websites in seventh, ninth and eleventh graders. *European Eating Disorders Review, 17*, 214–219. doi: 10.1002/erv.910

Cutler, S., & Nolen-Hoeksema, S. (1991). Accounting for sex differences in depression through female victimization: Childhood sexual abuse. *Sex Roles, 24*, 425–438. doi: 10.1007/BF00289332

D'Augelli, A. R. (2002). Mental health problems among lesbian, gay, and bisexual youths ages 14 to 21. *Clinical Child Psychology and Psychiatry, 7*, 433–456. doi: 10.1177/1359104502007003010

Dear, M. J., & Wolch, J. R. (2014). *Landscapes of despair: From deinstitutionalization to homelessness.* Princeton, NJ: Princeton University Press.

DeHart, D. D. (2008). Pathways to prison: Impact of victimization in the lives of incarcerated women. *Violence Against Women, 14*, 1362–1381. doi: 10.1177/1077801208327018

Demartini, B., Ranieri, R., Masu, A., Selle, V., Scarone, S., & Gambini, O. (2014). Depressive symptoms and major depressive disorder in patients affected by subclinical hypothyroidism: A cross-sectional study. *The Journal of Nervous and Mental Disease, 202*, 603–607. doi: 10.1097/NMD.0000000000000168

Dias, K. (2013). The ana sanctuary: Women's pro-anorexia narratives in cyberspace. *Journal of International Women's Studies, 4*(2), 31–45.

Drescher J. (2015) Gender dysphoria. In A. Tasman, J. A. Lieberman, J. Kay, M. B. First, & M. Riba (Eds.), *Psychiatry* (4th ed.). New York, NY: Wiley.

Enns, C. Z. (2012). Feminist approaches to counseling. In E. M. Altmaier & J. C. Hansen (Eds.), *The Oxford handbook of counseling psychology* (pp. 434–459). New York, NY: Oxford University Press.

Epp, C., & Maynard-Moody, S. (2014, January/February). Driving while Black. *Washington Monthly.* Retrieved from http://washingtonmonthly.com/magazine/janfeb-2014/driving-while-black/

Erchull, M. J. (2015). The thin ideal: A "wrong prescription" sold to many and achievable by few. In M. C. McHugh & J. C. Chrisler (Eds.), *The wrong prescription for women: How medicine and media create a "need" for treatments, drugs, and surgery* (pp. 161–178). Santa Barbara, CA: Praeger.

Eriksen, K., & Kress, V. E. (2008). Gender and diagnosis: Struggles and suggestions for counselors. *Journal of Counseling and Development, 86*, 152–163. doi: 10.1002/j.1556-6678.2008.tb00492.x

Feinstein, A., Magalhaes, S., Richard, J. F., Audet, B., & Moore, C. (2014). The link between multiple sclerosis and depression. *Nature Reviews Neurology, 10*, 507–517. doi: 10.1038/nrneurol.2014.139

Fischer, A. R., & Holz, B. K. (2010). Testing a model of women's personal sense of justice, control, well-being, and distress in the context of sexist discrimination. *Psychology of Women Quarterly, 34*, 297–310. doi: 10.1111/j.1471-6402.2010.01576.x

Fivush, R., Brotman, M., Buckner, J., & Goodman, S. (2000). Gender differences in parent-child emotion narratives. *Sex Roles, 42*, 233–253. doi: 10.1023/A:1007091207068

Flentje, A., Heck, N. C., & Cochran, B. N. (2013). Sexual reorientation therapy interventions: Perspectives of ex-ex-gay individuals. *Journal of Gay & Lesbian Mental Health, 17*, 256–277. doi: 10.1080/19359705.2013.773268

Follette, V., Palm, K., & Pearson, A. (2006). Mindfulness and trauma: Implications for treatment. *Journal of Rational-Emotive and Cognitive-Behavior Therapy, 24*, 45–61. doi: 10.1007/s10942-006-0025-2

Ford, J. D., & Courtois, C. A. (2014). Complex PTSD, affect dysregulation, and borderline personality disorder. *Borderline Personality Disorder and Emotion Dysregulation, 1*(1), 1–9. doi: 10.1186/2051-6673-1-9

Foucault, M. (1987). *Mental illness and psychology.* Berkeley, CA: University of California Press. (Original work published 1954)

Fox, J., & Moreland, J. (2015). The dark side of social networking sites: An exploration of the relational and psychological stressors associated with Facebook use and affordances. *Computers in Human Behavior, 45*, 168–176. doi: 10.1016/j.chb.2014.11.083

Fredrickson, B. L., & Roberts, T. A. (1997). Objectification theory. *Psychology of Women Quarterly, 21*, 173–206. doi: 10.1111/j.1471-6402.1997.tb00108.x

Freeman, E., Sammel, M., Lin, H., & Nelson, D. (2006). Associations of hormones and menopausal status with depressed mood in women with no history of depression. *Archives of General Psychiatry, 63*, 375–382. doi: 10.1001/archpsyc.63.4.375.

Freud, S., & Breuer, J. (2004). *Studies of hysteria* (N. Luckhurst, Trans.). New York, NY: Penguin Classics. (Original work published 1896)

Frissa, S., Hatch, S., Gazard, B., Fear, N., & Hotopf, M. (2013). Trauma and current symptoms of PTSD in a South East London community. *Social Psychiatry & Psychiatric Epidemiology, 48*, 1199–1209. doi: 10.1007/s00127-013-0689-8

Geller, J., & Harris, M. (1984). *Women of the asylum: Voices from behind the walls, 1840–1945.* New York, NY: Anchor Books.

Gilman, C. P. (1892/1997). *"The yellow wallpaper" and other stories.* North Chelmsford, MA: Courier Corporation.

Gilman, S. E., Cochran, S. D., Mays, V. M., Hughes, M., Ostrow, D., & Kessler, R. C. (2001). Risk of psychiatric disorders among individuals reporting same-sex sexual partners in the National Comorbidity Survey. *American Journal of Public Health, 91*, 933–939. doi: 10.2105/AJPH.91.6.933

Girgus, J. S., & Yang, K. (2015). Gender and depression. *Current Opinion in Psychology, 4*, 53–60. doi: 10.1016/j.copsyc.2015.01.019

Goldhagen, S., Harbin, V., & Forry, N. (2013, July). *Maryland Child Care Choices Study: Maternal depression among applicants for temporary cash assistance* (Child Trends Publication #2013-30). Washington DC: Child Trends. Retrieved from https://www.childtrends.org/wp-content/uploads/2013/07/2013-30ChildCareChioicesDepression.pdf

Gonzalez, H., Vega, W., Williams, D., Tarraf, W., West, B., & Neighbors, H. (2010). Depression care in the United States: Too little for too few. *JAMA Psychiatry, 67*, 37–46. doi: 10.1001/archgenpsychiatry.2009.168

Goodman, L., Smyth, K., Borges, A., & Singer, R. (2009). When crises collide: How intimate partner violence and poverty intersect to shape women's mental health and coping? *Trauma, Violence, & Abuse, 10*, 306–329. doi: 10.1177/1524838009339754

Goodman, L. A., Pugach, M., Skolnik, A., & Smith, L. (2013). Poverty and mental health practice: Within and beyond the 50-minute hour. *Journal of Clinical Psychology*, *69*, 182–190. doi: 10.1002/jclp.21957

Grant, T. M., Jack, D. C., Fitzpatrick, A. L., & Ernst, C. C. (2011). Carrying the burdens of poverty, parenting, and addiction: Depression symptoms and self-silencing among ethnically diverse women. *Community Mental Health Journal*, *47*, 90–98. doi: 10.1007/s10597-009-9255-y

Gratch, L. V., Bassett, M. E., & Attra, S. L. (1995). The relationship of gender and ethnicity to self-silencing and depression among college students. *Psychology of Women Quarterly*, *19*, 509–515. doi: 10.1111/j.1471-6402.1995.tb00089.x

Grayshield, L., Rutherford, J. J., Salazar, S. B., Mihecoby, A. L., & Luna, L. L. (2015). Understanding and healing historical trauma: The perspectives of Native American elders. *Journal of Mental Health Counseling*, *37*, 295–307. doi: 10.17744/mehc.37.4.02

Green, B. L., Dass-Brailsford, P., Hurtado de Mendoza, A., Mete, M., Lynch, S. M., DeHart, D. D., & Belknap, J. (2016). Trauma experiences and mental health among incarcerated women. *Psychological Trauma: Theory, Research, Practice, and Policy*, *8*, 455–463. doi: 10.1037/tra0000113

Green, B. L., Miranda, J., Daroowalla, A., & Siddique, J. (2005). Trauma exposure, mental health functioning, and program needs of women in jail. *Crime & Delinquency*, *51*, 133–151. doi: 10.1177/0011128704267477

Gross, K. N. (2015). African American women, mass incarceration, and the politics of protection. *Journal of American History*, *102*, 25–33. doi: 10.1093/jahist/jav226

Grote, N. K., Zuckoff, A., Swartz, H., Bledsoe, S. E., & Geibel, S. (2007). Engaging women who are depressed and economically disadvantaged in mental health treatment. *Social Work*, *52*, 295–308. doi: 10.1093/sw/52.4.295

Gutek, B., & Koss, M. (1993). Changed women and changed organizations: Consequences of and coping with sexual harassment. *Journal of Vocational Behavior*, *42*, 28–48. doi: 10.1006/jvbe.1993.1003

Halbreich, U., Borenstein, J., Pearlstein, T., & Kahn, L. S. (2003). The prevalence, impairment, impact, and burden of premenstrual dysphoric disorder (PMS/PMDD). *Psychoneuroendocrinology*, *28*, 1–23. doi: 10.1016/S0306-4530(03)00098-2

Haldeman, D. C. (2002). Gay rights, patient rights: The implications of sexual orientation conversion therapy. *Professional Psychology: Research and Practice*, *33*, 260–264. doi: 10.1037/0735-7028.33.3.260

Hankin, B., & Abramson, L. (2001). Development of gender differences in depression: An elaborated cognitive vulnerability–transactional stress theory. *Psychological Bulletin*, *127*, 773–796. doi: 10.1037/0033-2909.127.6.773

Harshbarger, J., Ahlers-Schmidt, C., Mayans, L., Mayans, D., & Hawkins, J. (2009). Pro-anorexia websites: What a clinician should know. *International Journal of Eating Disorders*, *42*, 367–370. doi: 10.1002/eat.20608

Hauser, C. (2017, February 7). Florida woman whose "stand your ground" defense was rejected is released. *The New York Times*. Retrieved from https://www.nytimes.com/2017/02/07/us/marissa-alexander-released-stand-your-ground.html?_r=1

Helgeson, V. (1994). Relation of agency and communion to well-being: Evidence and potential explanations. *Psychological Bulletin*, *116*, 412–428. doi: 10.1037/0033-2909.116.3.412

Helgeson, V. S., Swanson, J., Ra, O., Randall, H., & Zhao, Y. (2015). Links between unmitigated communion, interpersonal behaviors and well-being: A daily diary approach. *Journal of Research in Personality*, *57*, 53–60. doi: 10.1016/j.jrp.2014.12.007

Henretty, J., Currier, J., Berman, J., & Levitt, H. (2014). The impact of counselor self-disclosure on clients: A meta-analytic review of experimental and quasi-experimental research. *Journal of Counseling Psychology*, *61*, 191–207. doi: 10.1037/a0036189

Herbozo, S., Stevens, S. D., & Thurston, I. B. (2017). The mediating role of appearance comparisons on the relationship between negative appearance commentary and binge eating symptoms. *Eating Behaviors*, *26*, 155–158. doi: 10.1016/j.eatbeh.2017.03.008

Herman-Lewis, J. (1992). *Trauma and recovery: The aftermath of violence: From domestic abuse to political terror*. New York, NY: Basic Books.

Herzberg, D. (2006). "The pill you love can turn on you": Feminism, tranquilizers, and the valium panic of the 1970s. *American Quarterly*, *58*, 79–103. doi: 10.1353/aq.2006.0026

Hicks, S. R. (2015). *A critical analysis of post traumatic slave syndrome: A multigenerational legacy of slavery* (Unpublished doctoral dissertation). California Institute of Integral Studies, San Francisco, CA

Horwitz, A. V. (2010). How an age of anxiety became an age of depression. *The Milbank Quarterly*, *88*(1), 112–138. doi: 10.1111/j.1468-0009.2010.00591.x

Howard, L., Oram, S., Galley, H., Trevillion, K., & Feder, G. (2013). Domestic violence and perinatal mental disorders: A systematic review and meta-analysis. *Plos Med*, *10*(5), e1001452. doi: 10.1371/journal.pmed.1001452

Hudson, J. I., Hiripi, E., Pope, H. G., & Kessler, R. C. (2007). The prevalence and correlates of eating disorders in the National Comorbidity Survey Replication. *Biological Psychiatry*, *61*, 348–358. doi: 10.1016/j.biopsych.2006.03.040

Igartua, K., Gill, K., & Montoro, R. (2009). Internalized homophobia: A factor in depression, anxiety, and suicide in the gay and lesbian population. *Canadian Journal of Community Mental Health*, *22*, 15–30. doi: 10.7870/cjcmh-2003-0011

Infurna, M. R., Reichl, C., Parzer, P., Schimmenti, A., Bifulco, A., & Kaess, M. (2016). Associations between depression and specific childhood experiences of abuse and neglect: A meta-analysis. *Journal of Affective Disorders*, *190*, 47–55. doi: 10.1016/j.jad.2015.09.006

Israeli, A., & Santor, D. (2000). Reviewing effective components of feminist therapy. *Counselling Psychology Quarterly*, *13*, 233–247. doi: 10.1080/095150700300091820

Jack, D., & Dill, D. (1992). The Silencing the Self Scale: Schemas of intimacy associated with depression in women. *Psychology of Women Quarterly*, *16*, 97–106. doi: 10.1111/j.1471-6402.1992.tb00242.x

Jackson, K., Janssen, I., Appelhans, B., Kazlauskaite, R., Karavolos, K., Dugan, S., Avery, E., Shipp-Johnson, K., & Powell, L. (2014). Body image satisfaction and depression in midlife women: The Study of Women's Health Across the Nation (SWAN). *Archives of Women's Mental Health*, *17*, 177–187. doi: 10.1007/s00737-014-0416-9

Jackson, L. (1995). Witches, wives and mothers: Witchcraft persecution and women's confessions in seventeenth-century England. *Women's History Review*, *4*, 63–84. doi: 10.1080/09612029500200075

James, D., & Glaze, L. (2006, September). *Mental health problems of prison and jail inmates* (NCJ 213600). Retrieved from the Bureau of Justice Statistics website: http://www.bjs.gov/content/pub/pdf/mhppji.pdf

Johnson, D., & Whisman, M. (2013). Gender differences in rumination: A meta-analysis. *Personality and Individual Differences*, *55*, 367–374. doi: 10.1016/j.paid.2013.03.019

Kahn, M. (2000, June). Domestic violence against women and girls. *Innocenti Digest* (No. 6). Retrieved from https://www.unicef-irc.org/publications/pdf/digest6e.pdf

Karatzias, T., Cloitre, M., Maercker, A., Kazlauskas, E., Shevlin, M., Hyland, P., . . . & Brewin, C. R. (2017). PTSD and Complex PTSD: ICD-11 updates on concept and measurement in the UK, USA, Germany and Lithuania. *European Journal of Psychotraumatology*, 8, 1–6. doi: 10.1080/20008198.2017.1418103

Kawa, S., & Giordano, J. (2012). A brief historicity of the Diagnostic and Statistical Manual of Mental Disorders: Issues and implications for the future of psychiatric canon and practice. *Philosophy, Ethics, and Humanities in Medicine*, 7, 1–9. doi: 10.1186/1747-5341-7-2

Keski-Rahkonen, A., Raevuori, A., Bulik, C., Hoek, H., Sihvola, E., Kaprio, J., & Rissanen, A. (2013). Depression and drive for thinness are associated with persistent bulimia nervosa in the community. *European Eating Disorders Review*, 21, 121–129. doi: 10.1002/erv.2182

Kessler, R., Berglund, P., Chiu, W., Deitz, A., Hudson, J., Shahly, V., . . . Xavier, M. (2013). The prevalence and correlates of binge eating disorder in the World Health Organization World Mental Health Surveys. *Biological Psychiatry*, 73, 904–914. doi: 10.1016/j.biopsych.2012.11.020

Kessler, R., Petukhova, M., Sampson, N., Zaslavsky, A., & Wittchen, H. (2012). Twelve-month and lifetime prevalence and lifetime morbid risk of anxiety and mood disorders in the United States. *International Journal of Methods in Psychiatric Research*, 21, 169–184. doi: 10.1002/mpr.1359

Khoury, B., Lecomte, T., Fortin, G., Masse, M., Therien, P., Bouchard, V., . . . & Hofmann, S. G. (2013). Mindfulness-based therapy: A comprehensive meta-analysis. *Clinical Psychology Review*, 33, 763–771. doi: 10.1016/j.cpr.2013.05.005

Kim, D. Y. (2016). Psychiatric deinstitutionalization and prison population growth: A critical literature review and its implications. *Criminal Justice Policy Review*, 27, 3–21. doi: 10.1177/0887403414547043

Kliem, S., Kröger, C., & Kosfelder, J. (2010). Dialectical behavior therapy for borderline personality disorder: A meta-analysis using mixed-effects modeling. *Journal of Consulting and Clinical Psychology*, 78, 936–951. doi: 10.1037/a0021015

Kline, A., Ciccone, D., Weiner, M., Interian, A., St. Hill, L., Falca-Dodson, M., Black, C., & Losonczy, M. (2013). Gender differences in the risk and protective factors associated with PTSD: A prospective study of National Guard troops deployed to Iraq. *Psychiatry*, 76, 256–272. doi: 10.1521/psyc.2013.76.3.256

Klonoff, E. A., & Landrine, H. (1996). *Preventing misdiagnosis of women: A guide to physical disorders that have psychiatric symptoms* (Vol. 1). Thousand Oaks, CA: Sage.

Klonoff, E. A., Landrine, H., & Campbell, R. (2000). Sexist discrimination may account for well-known gender differences in psychiatric symptoms. *Psychology of Women Quarterly*, 24, 93–99. doi: 10.1111/j.1471-6402.2000.tb01025.x

Kramer, U., Pascual, L. A., Berthoud, L., De Roten, Y., Marquet, P., Kolly, S., Despland, J., & Page, D. (2016). Assertive anger mediates effects of dialectical behavior informed skills training for borderline personality disorder: A randomized controlled trial. *Clinical Psychology & Psychotherapy*, 23, 189–202. doi: 10.1002/cpp.1956

Krause, E. D., Vélez, C. E., Woo, R., Hoffmann, B., Freres, D. R., Abenavoli, R. M., & Gillham, J. E. (2018). Rumination, depression, and gender in early adolescence: A longitudinal study of a bidirectional model. *The Journal of Early Adolescence*, 38, 923–946. doi: 10.1177/0272431617704956

Kronenfeld, L. W., Reba-Harrelson, L., Von Holle, A., Reyes, M. L., & Bulik, C. M. (2010). Ethnic and racial difference in body size perception and satisfaction. *Body Image*, 7, 131–136. doi: 10.1016/j.bodyim.2009.11.002

Kugelmass, H. (2016). "Sorry, I'm not accepting new patients": An audit study of access to mental health care *Journal of Health and Social Behavior*, 57, 168–183. doi: 10.1177/0022146516647098

LaFrance, M. (2010). *Women and depression: Recovery and resistance*. New York, NY: Routledge.

Lai, R., Park, H., Buchanan, L., & Andrews, W. (2015, July 22). Assessing the legality of Sandra Bland's arrest. *The New York Times*. Retrieved from https://www.nytimes.com/interactive/2015/07/20/us/sandra-bland-arrest-death-videos-maps.html

Lamb, H. R., & Bachrach, L. L. (2001). Some perspectives on deinstitutionalization. *Psychiatric Services*, 52, 1039–1045. doi: 10.1176/appi.ps.52.8.1039

Leary, J. (2005). *Post traumatic slave syndrome*. Milwaukee, WI: Uptone Press.

Lee, W. (2016, September 15). Sandra Bland's family hopes $1.9M settlement results in jail reform nationwide. *Chicago Tribune*. Retrieved from http://www.chicagotribune.com/news/local/breaking/ct-sandra-bland-death-settlement-20160915-story.html

Lehrner, A., & Yehuda, R. (2018). Trauma across generations and paths to adaptation and resilience. *Psychological Trauma: Theory, Research, Practice, and Policy*, 10, 22–29. doi: 10.1037/tra0000302

Lenz, A. S., Taylor, R., Fleming, M., & Serman, N. (2014). Effectiveness of dialectical behavior therapy for treating eating disorders. *Journal of Counseling & Development*, 92, 26–35. doi: 10.1002/j.1556-6676.2014.00127.x

Lev, A. I. (2006). Disordering gender identity: Gender identity disorder in the DSM-IV-TR. *Journal of Psychology & Human Sexuality*, 17, 35–69. doi: 10.1300/J056v17n03_03

Lewis, R., Derlega, V., Griffin, J., & Krowinski, A. (2003). Stressors for gay men and lesbians: Life stress, gay-related stress, stigma consciousness, and depressive symptoms. *Journal of Social and Clinical Psychology*, 22, 716–729. doi: 10.1521/jscp.22.6.716.22932

Liebelson, D., & Wing, N. (2015, July 22). A Texas jail failed Sandra Bland, even if it's telling the truth about her death. *Huffington Post*. Retrieved from http://www.huffingtonpost.com/entry/sandra-bland-jail-death_us_55ae9f12e4b07af29d569875

Liegghio, M., & Caragata, L. (2016). "Why are you talking to me like I'm stupid?" The micro-aggressions committed within the social welfare system against lone mothers. *Affilia*, 31, 7–23. doi: 10.1177/0886109915592667

Lindert, J., von Ehrenstein, O. S., Grashow, R., Gal, G., Braehler, E., & Weisskopf, M. G. (2014). Sexual and physical abuse in childhood is associated with depression and anxiety over the life course: Systematic review and meta-analysis. *International Journal of Public Health*, 59, 359–372. doi: 10.1007/s00038-013-0519-5

Linehan, M. (1993a). *Cognitive-behavioral treatment of borderline personality disorder*. New York, NY: Guilford Press.

Linehan, M. (1993b). *Skills training manual for treating borderline personality disorder*. New York, NY: Guilford Press.

Lynch, S. M., DeHart, D. D., Belknap, J., Green, B. L., Dass-Brailsford, P., Johnson, K. M., & Wong, M. M. (2017). An examination of the associations among victimization, mental health, and offending in women. *Criminal Justice and Behavior*, 44, 796–814. doi: 10.1177/0093854817704452

Mahalik, J. R., Van Ormer, E. A., & Simi, N. L. (2000). Ethical issues in using self-disclosure in feminist therapy. In M. Brabeck (Ed.),

Practicing feminist ethics in psychology (pp. 189–201). Washington, DC: American Psychological Association.

Maines, R. P. (2001). *The technology of orgasm: "Hysteria," the vibrator, and women's sexual satisfaction.* Baltimore, MD: Johns Hopkins University Press.

Makari, G. (1998). Between seduction and libido: Sigmund Freud's masturbation hypothesis and the realignment of his etiological thinking, 1897–1905. *Bulletin of the History of Medicine, 4,* 638–662. doi: 10.1353/bhm.1998.0216

Mallory, C., Brown, T. N. T., & Conron, K. J. (2018, January). Conversion therapy and LGBT youth. *The Williams Institute, UCLA School of Law.* Retrieved from https://williamsinstitute .law.ucla.edu/wp-content/uploads/Conversion-Therapy -LGBT-Youth-Jan-2018.pdf

Marecek, J. (2017). Blowing in the wind: '70s questions for millennial therapists. *Women & Therapy, 40,* 406–417. doi: 10.1080/02703149.2017.1241582

Marecek, J., & Gavey, N. (2013). DSM-5 and beyond: A critical feminist engagement with psychodiagnosis. *Feminism & Psychology, 23,* 3–9. doi: 10.1177/0959353512467962

Marecek, J., & Kravetz, D. (1998). Power and agency in feminist therapy. In I. B. Seu & M. C. Heenan (Eds.), *Feminism and psychotherapy: Reflections on contemporary theories and practices* (pp. 13–29). Thousand Oaks, CA: Sage.

Masson, J. (1984). *The assault on truth: Freudian suppression of the seduction theory.* New York, NY: Farrar Straus & Giroux.

Mauer, M. (2013, February). *The changing racial dynamics of women's incarceration.* Washington, DC: The Sentencing Project. Retrieved from http://sentencingproject.org/wp-content /uploads/2015/12/The-Changing-Racial-Dynamics-of -Womens-Incarceration.pdf

McGeorge, C. R., Carlson, T. S., & Toomey, R. B. (2015). An exploration of family therapists' beliefs about the ethics of conversion therapy: The influence of negative beliefs and clinical competence with lesbian, gay, and bisexual clients. *Journal of Marital and Family Therapy, 41,* 42–56. doi: 10.1111/jmft.12040

McGinley, M., Wolff, J., Rospenda, K., Liu, L., & Richman, J. (2016). Risk factors and outcomes of chronic sexual harassment during the transition to college: Examination of a two-part growth mixture model. *Social Science Research, 60,* 297–310. doi: 10.1016/j.ssresearch.2016.04.002

McHenry, J., Carrier, N., Hull, E., & Kabbaj, M. (2014). Sex differences in anxiety and depression: Role of testosterone. *Frontiers in Neuroendocrinology, 35,* 42–57. doi: 10.1016/j .yfrne.2013.09.001

McLaren, S. (2016). The interrelations between internalized homophobia, depressive symptoms, and suicidal ideation among Australian gay men, lesbians, and bisexual women. *Journal of Homosexuality, 63,* 156–168. doi: 10.1080/00918369 .2015.1083779

McLoughlin, D. M., Kolshus, E., & Jelovac, A. (2017). Systematic review and meta-analysis of randomised controlled trials of bitemporal versus high-dose right unilateral ECT for depression. *Brain Stimulation: Basic, Translational, and Clinical Research in Neuromodulation, 10,* 358. doi: 10.1016/j.brs.2017.01.054

Meloni, M. (2017). Race in an epigenetic time: Thinking biology in the plural. *The British Journal of Sociology, 68,* 389–409. doi: 10.1111/1468-4446.12248

Mendes, E., Saad, L., & McGeeney, K. (2012, May 18). Stay-at-home moms report more depression, sadness, anger. *Gallup.* Retrieved from http://www.gallup.com/poll/154685/stay -home-moms-report-depression-sadness-anger.aspx

Mendez-Luck, C. A., & Anthony, K. P. (2015). Marianismo and caregiving role beliefs among U.S.-born and immigrant Mexican women. *Journals of Gerontology, Series B: Psychological Sciences and Social Sciences, 71,* 926–935. doi: 10.1093 /geronb/gbv083

Meyer, I. H. (2003). Prejudice, social stress, and mental health in lesbian, gay, and bisexual populations: Conceptual issues and research evidence. *Psychological Bulletin, 129,* 674–697. doi: 10.1037/0033-2909.129.5.674

Micale, M. (1993). On the "disappearance" of hysteria: A study in the clinical deconstruction of a diagnosis. *Isis, 84,* 496–526. doi: 10.1086/356549

Moradi, B., Fischer, A., Hill, M., Jome, L., & Blum, S. (2000). Does "feminist" plus "therapist" equal "feminist therapist"? *Psychology of Women Quarterly, 24,* 285–296. doi: 10.1111 /j.1471-6402.2000.tb00211.x

Moradi, B., & Huang, Y. P. (2008). Objectification theory and psychology of women: A decade of advances and future directions. *Psychology of Women Quarterly, 32,* 377–398. doi: 10.1111/j.1471-6402.2008.00452.x

Mouzon, D. M., & McLean, J. S. (2017). Internalized racism and mental health among African-Americans, U.S.-born Caribbean Blacks, and foreign-born Caribbean Blacks. *Ethnicity & Health, 22,* 36–48. doi: 10.1080/13557858.2016.1196652

Muehlenkamp, J. J., & Saris-Baglama, R. N. (2002). Self-objectification and its psychological outcomes for college women. *Psychology of Women Quarterly, 26,* 371–379. doi: 10.1111/1471 -6402.t01-1-00076

Nadal, K. L., Griffin, K. E., Wong, Y., Hamit, S., & Rasmus, M. (2014). The impact of racial microaggressions on mental health: Counseling implications for clients of color. *Journal of Counseling & Development, 92,* 57–66. doi: 10.1002/j.1556 -6676.2014.00130.x

National Alliance on Mental Illness. (2015, April). *A long road ahead: Achieving true parity in mental health and substance use care.* Arlington, VA: Author. Retrieved from https:// www.nami.org/About-NAMI/Publications-Reports/Public -Policy-Reports/A-Long-Road-Ahead/2015-ALongRoad Ahead.pdf

Neumark-Sztainer, D., Croll, J., Story, M., Hannan, P. J., French, S. A., & Perry, C. (2002). Ethnic/racial differences in weight-related concerns and behaviors among adolescent girls and boys: Findings from Project EAT. *Journal of Psychosomatic Research, 53,* 963–974. doi: 10.1016/S0022 -3999(02)00486-5

Neumark-Sztainer, D., Falkner, N., Story, M., Perry, C., & Hannan, P. (2002). Weight-teasing among adolescents: Correlations with weight status and disordered eating behaviors. *International Journal of Obesity & Related Metabolic Disorders, 26,* 123–131. doi: 10.1038/sj.ijo.0801853

Nolen-Hoeksema, S. (2001). Gender differences in depression. *Current Directions in Psychological Science, 10,* 173–176. doi: 10.1111/1467-8721.00142

Nolen-Hoeksema, S. (2012). Emotion regulation and psychopathology: The role of gender. *Annual Review of Clinical Psychology, 8,* 161–187. doi: 10.1146/annurev-clinpsy -032511-143109

Nolen-Hoeksema, S., & Jackson, B. (2001). Mediators of the gender difference in rumination. *Psychology of Women Quarterly, 25,* 37–47. doi: 10.1111/1471-6402.00005

Noonan, M. (2016, December). *Mortality in local jail and state prisons, 2001–2014: Statistical tables* (NCJ 250150). Retrieved from the Bureau of Justice Statistics website: https://www.bjs .gov/content/pub/pdf/msp0114st.pdf

Norris, M., Boydell, K., Pinhas, L., & Katzman, D. (2006). Ana and the Internet: A review of pro-anorexia websites. *International Journal of Eating Disorders, 39,* 443–447. doi: 10.1002 /eat.20305

Ordaz, D. L., Schaefer, L. M., Choquette, E., Schueler, J., Wallace, L., & Thompson, J. K. (2018). Thinness pressures in ethnically diverse college women in the United States. *Body Image, 24*, 1–4. doi: 10.1016/j.bodyim.2017.11.004

Overbeke, G. (2008). Pro-anorexia websites: Content, impact, and explanations of popularity. *Mind Matters: The Wesleyan Journal of Psychology, 3*, 49–62.

Pan, D. (2013, April 29). Timeline: Desensitization and its consequences. *Mother Jones.* Retrieved from http://www.motherjones.com/politics/2013/04/timeline-mental-health-america

Parker, G., & Brotchie, H. (2010). Gender differences in depression. *International Review of Psychiatry, 22*, 429–436. doi: 10.3109/09540261.2010.492391

Patrick, K. (2017, September). *National snapshot: Poverty among women and families 2016.* Washington, DC: National Women's Law Center. Retrieved from https://nwlc-ciw49tixgw5lbab.stackpathdns.com/wp-content/uploads/2017/09/Poverty-Snapshot-Factsheet-2017.pdf

Paxton, S., Neumark-Sztainer, D., Hannan, P., & Eisenberg, M. (2006). Body dissatisfaction prospectively predicts depressive mood and low self-esteem in adolescent girls and boys. *Journal of Clinical Child and Adolescent Psychology, 35*, 539–549. doi: 10.1207/s15374424jccp3504_5

Pearl, R., White, M., & Grilo, C. (2014). Weight bias internalization, depression, and self-reported health among overweight binge eating disorder patients. *Obesity, 22*, E142–E148. doi: 10.1002/oby.20617

Pearlman, L. A., & Courtois, C. A. (2005). Clinical applications of the attachment framework: Relational treatment of complex trauma. *Journal of Traumatic Stress, 18*, 449–459. doi: 10.1002/jts.20052

Peat, C. M., & Muehlenkamp, J. J. (2011). Self-objectification, disordered eating, and depression: A test of mediational pathways. *Psychology of Women Quarterly, 35*, 441–450. doi: 10.1177/0361684311400389

Penning, M. J., & Wu, Z. (2015). Caregiver stress and mental health: Impact of caregiving relationship and gender. *The Gerontologist, 56*, 1102–1113. doi: 10.1093/geront/gnv038

Pillard, R. (2009). From disorder to dystonia: DSM-II and DSM-III. *Journal of Gay & Lesbian Mental Health, 13*, 82–86. doi: 10.1080/19359700802690174

Pratt, L., Brody, D., & Gu, Q. (2017, October). *Antidepressant use in persons aged 12 and over: United States, 2011–2014* (NCHS data brief no. 283). Hyattsville, MD: National Center for Health Statistics. Retrieved from https://www.cdc.gov/nchs/data/databriefs/db283.pdf

Priess, H., Lindberg, S., & Hyde, J. (2009). Adolescent gender-role identity and mental health: Gender intensification revisited. *Child Development, 80*, 1531–1544. doi: 10.1111/j.1467-8624.2009.01349.x

Przybylski, A., Murayama, K., DeHaan, C., & Gladwell, V. (2013). Motivational, emotional, and behavioral correlates of fear of missing out. *Computers in Human Behavior, 29*, 1841–1848. doi: 10.1016/j.chb.2013.02.014

Rader, J., & Gilbert, L. A. (2005). The egalitarian relationship in feminist therapy. *Psychology of Women Quarterly, 29*, 427–435. doi: 10.1111/j.1471-6402.2005.00243.x

Reisner, S. L., White Hughto, J. M., Gamarel, K. E., Keuroghlian, A. S., Mizock, L., & Pachankis, J. E. (2016). Discriminatory experiences associated with posttraumatic stress disorder symptoms among transgender adults. *Journal of Counseling Psychology, 63*, 509–519 doi: 10.1037/cou0000143.

Richmond, K., Geiger, E., & Reed, C. (2013). The personal is political: A feminist and trauma-informed therapeutic approach to working with a survivor of sexual assault. *Clinical Case Studies, 12*, 443–456. doi: 10.1177/1534650113500563

Richmond, K., Levant, R., Smalley, B., & Cook, S. (2015). The Femininity Ideology Scale (FIS): Dimensions and its relationship to anxiety and feminine gender role stress. *Women & Health, 55*, 263–279. doi:10.1080/03630242.2014.996723

Rihanna: Meltdown at the Grammys. (2016, February 17). *TMZ.* Retrieved from http://www.tmz.com/2016/02/17/rihanna-meltdown-grammys-canceled-performance/

Rivera, M. (2002). Linking the psychological and the social: Feminism, poststructuralism, and multiple personality. In M. Dimon & V. Goldner (Eds), *Gender in psychoanalytic space: Between clinic and culture* (pp. 331–351). New York, NY: Other Press.

Sanburn, J. (2015, July 23). Everything we know about the Sandra Bland Case. *Time.* Retrieved from http://time.com/3966220/sandra-bland-video/

Sansone, R. A., & Sansone, L. A. (2011). Gender patterns in borderline personality disorder. *Innovations in Clinical Neuroscience, 8*, 16–20.

Sax, L. (2016, April 21). Why do girls tend to have more anxiety than boys? *The New York Times.* Retrieved from http://well.blogs.nytimes.com/2016/04/21/why-do-girls-have-more-anxiety-than-boys/?_r=0

Seccombe, K., James, D., & Walters, K. (1998). "They think you ain't much of nothing": The social construction of the welfare mother. *Journal of Marriage and the Family, 60*, 849–865. doi: 10.2307/353629

Serovich, J. M., Craft, S. M., Toviessi, P., Gangamma, R., McDowell, T., & Grafsky, E. L. (2008). A systematic review of the research base on sexual reorientation therapies. *Journal of Marital and Family Therapy, 34*, 227–238. doi: 10.1111/j.1752-0606.2008.00065.x

Shaw, C., & Proctor, G. (2005). Women at the margins: A critique of the diagnosis of borderline personality disorder. *Feminism & Psychology, 15*, 483–490. doi: 10.1177/0959-353505057620

Shearer, A., Herres, J., Kodish, T., Squitieri, H., James, K., Russon, J., Atte, T., & Diamond, G. (2016). Differences in mental health symptoms across lesbian, gay, bisexual, and questioning youth in primary settings. *Journal of Adolescent Health, 59*, 38–43. doi: 10.1016/j.jadohealth.2016.02.005

Shidlo, A., & Schroeder, M. (2002). Changing sexual orientation: A consumers' report. *Professional Psychology: Research and Practice, 33*, 249–259 doi: 10.1037//0735-7028.33.3.249

Showalter, E. (1993). Hysteria, feminism, and gender. In S. L. Gilman, H. King, R. Porter, G. S. Rousseau, & E. Showalter (Eds.), *Hysteria beyond Freud* (pp. 286–344). Berkeley, CA: University of California Press.

Showalter, E. (1997). *Hystories: Hysterical epidemics and modern media.* New York, NY: Columbia University Press.

Shriver, M., & Center for American Progress. (2014, January 12). A woman's nation pushes back from the brink: Executive summary. *The Shriver Report.* Retrieved from http://shriverreport.org/a-womans-nation-pushes-back-from-the-brink-executive-summary-maria-shriver/

Siefert, K., Bowman, P., Heflin, C., Danziger, S., & Williams, D. (2000). Social and environmental predictors of maternal depression in current and recent welfare recipients. *American Journal of Orthopsychiatry, 70*, 510–522. doi: 10.1177/1524838009339754

Siegert, R., & Abernethy, D. (2005). Depression in multiple sclerosis: A review. *Journal of Neurology, Neurosurgery & Psychiatry, 76*, 469–475. doi: 10.1136/jnnp.2004.054635

Silverstein, B., Edwards, T., Gamma, A., Ajdacic-Gross, V., Rossler, W., & Angst, J. (2012). The role played by depression associated with somatic symptomatology in accounting for the gender difference in the prevalence of depression. *Social Psychiatry and Psychiatric Epidemiology, 48*, 257–263. doi: 10.1007/s00127-012-0540-7

Simpson, S. S., Yahner, J. L., & Dugan, L. (2008). Understanding women's pathways to jail: Analysing the lives of incarcerated women. *Australian & New Zealand Journal of Criminology, 41*, 84–108. doi: 10.1375/acri.41.1.84

Singh, A. A., & Burnes, T. R. (2010). Feminist therapy and street-level activism: Revisiting our roots and "acting up" in the next decade. *Women & Therapy, 34*(1–2), 129–142. doi: 10.1080/02703149.2011.532457

Singh, A. A., & Hays, D. G. (2008). Feminist group counseling with South Asian women who have survived intimate partner violence. *The Journal for Specialists in Group Work, 33*, 84–102. doi: 10.1080/01933920701798588

Smink, F., van Hoeken, D., & Hoek, H. (2012). Epidemiology of eating disorders: Incidence, prevalence and mortality rates. *Current Psychiatry Reports, 14*, 406–414. doi: 10.1007/s11920-012-0282-y

Smith-Rosenberg, C. (1986). *Disorderly conduct: Visions of gender in Victorian America*. Oxford, United Kingdom: Oxford University Press.

Sotero, M. (2006). A conceptual model of historical trauma: Implications for public health practice and research. *Journal of Health Disparities Research and Practice, 1*, 93–108.

Stice, E. (2002). Risk and maintenance factors for eating pathology: A meta-analytic review. *Psychological Bulletin, 128*, 825–848. doi: 10.1037/0033-2909.128.5.825

Stiles, A. (n.d.). The rest cure, 1873–1925. *BRANCH: Britain, Representation and Nineteenth-Century History*. Retrieved from http://www.branchcollective.org/?ps_articles=anne-stiles-the-rest-cure-1873-1925

Stitt, N., Francis, A., Field, A., & Carr, S. (2015). Positive association between reported childhood peer teasing and adult borderline personality disorder symptoms. *Journal of Child & Adolescent Trauma, 8*, 137–145. doi: 10.1007/s40653-015-0045-0

Striegel-Moore, R., Rosselli, F., Perrin, N., DeBar, L., Wilson, G., May, A., & Kraemer, H. (2009). Gender difference in the prevalence of eating disorder symptoms. *International Journal of Eating Disorders, 42*, 471–474. doi: 10.1002/eat.20625

Striegel-Moore, R. H., Dohm, F. A., Kraemer, H. C., Taylor, C. B., Daniels, S., Crawford, P. B., & Schreiber, G. B. (2003). Eating disorders in White and Black women. *American Journal of Psychiatry, 160*, 1326–1331. doi: 10.1176/appi.ajp.160.7.1326

Sue, S. (1998). In search of cultural competence in psychotherapy and counseling. *American Psychologist, 53*, 440–448. doi: 10.1037/0003-066X.53.4.440

Swim, J., Hyers, L., Cohen, L., & Ferguson, M. (2001). Everyday sexism: Evidence for its incidence, nature, and psychological impact from three daily diary studies. *Journal of Social Issues, 57*, 31–53. doi: 10.1111/0022-4537.00200

Szymanski, D. M., & Henning, S. L. (2007). The role of self-objectification in women's depression: A test of objectification theory. *Sex Roles, 56*, 45–53. doi: 10.1007/s11199-006-9147-3

Talleyrand, R. M. (2012). Disordered eating in women of color: Some counseling considerations. *Journal of Counseling & Development, 90*, 271–280. doi: 10.1002/j.1556-6676.2012.00035.x

Tasca, C., Rapetti, M., Carta, M. G., & Fadda, B. (2012). Women and hysteria in the history of mental health. *Clinical Practice & Epidemiology in Mental Health, 8*, 110–119. doi: 10.2174/1745017901208010110

Tatangelo, G., McCabe, M., Macleod, A., & You, E. (2018). "I just don't focus on my needs." The unmet health needs of partner and offspring caregivers of people with dementia: A qualitative study. *International Journal of Nursing Studies, 77*, 8–14. doi: 10.1016/j.ijnurstu.2017.09.011

Tatangelo, G., McCabe, M., Mellor, D., & Mealey, A. (2016). A systematic review of body dissatisfaction and sociocultural messages related to the body among preschool children. *Body Image, 18*, 86–95. doi: 10.1016/j.bodyim.2016.06.003

Thompson, J., Weiner, R., & Myers, C. (1994). Use of ECT in the United States in 1975, 1980, and 1986. *American Journal of Psychiatry, 151*, 1657–1661. doi: 10.1176/ajp.151.11.1657

Tolin, D., & Foa, E. (2006). Sex differences in trauma and post-traumatic stress disorder: A quantitative review of 25 years of research. *Psychological Bulletin, 132*, 959–992. doi: 10.1037/0033-2909.132.6.959

Tolman, D. L. (2002). Femininity as a barrier to positive sexual health for adolescent girls. In A. E. Hunter & C. Forden (Eds.), *Readings in the psychology of gender: Exploring our differences and commonalities* (pp. 196–206). Needham Heights, MA: Allyn & Bacon.

Tolman, D. L., Impett, E. A., Tracy, A. J., & Michael, A. (2006). Looking good, sounding good: Femininity ideology and adolescent girls' mental health. *Psychology of Women Quarterly, 30*, 85–95. doi: 10.1111/j.1471-6402.2006.00265.x

Tolman, D. L., & Porche, M. V. (2000). The Adolescent Femininity Ideology Scale: Development and validation of a new measure for girls. *Psychology of Women Quarterly, 24*, 365–376. doi: 10.1111/j.1471-6402.2000.tb00219.x

Torres, L., & Taknint, J. T. (2015). Ethnic microaggressions, traumatic stress symptoms, and Latino depression: A moderated mediational model. *Journal of Counseling Psychology, 62*, 393–401. doi: 10.1037/cou0000077

Treasure, J., Corfield, F., & Cardi, V. (2012). A three phase model of the social emotional functioning in eating disorders. *European Eating Disorders Review, 20*, 431–438. doi: 10.1002/erv.2181

Trevillion, K., Oram, S., Feder, G., & Howard, L. (2012). Experiences of domestic violence and mental disorders: A systematic review and meta-analysis. *PloS ONE, 7*(12), e51740. doi: 10.1371/journal.pone.0051740

Tutty, L., Babins-Wagner, R., & Rothery, M. (2016). You're not alone: Mental health outcomes in therapy groups for abused women. *Journal of Family Violence, 31*, 489–497. doi 10.1007/s10896-015-9779-6

Ussher, J. (2010). Are we medicalizing women's misery? A critical review of women's higher rates of reported depression. *Feminism & Psychology, 20*, 9–35. doi: 10.1177/0959353509350213

Ussher, J. (2011). *The madness of women: Myth and experience*. New York, NY: Psychology Press.

Ussher, J. (2013). Diagnosing difficult women and pathologising femininity: Gender bias in psychiatric nosology. *Feminism & Psychology, 23*, 63–69. doi: 10.1177/0959353512467968

Vafaei, A., Ahmed, T., Freire, A. D. N. F., Zunzunegui, M. V., & Guerra, R. O. (2016). Depression, sex and gender roles in older adult populations: The International Mobility in Aging Study (IMIAS). *PloS One, 11*(1), e0146867. doi: 10.1371/journal.pone.0146867

Vance, S. R., Jr., Cohen-Kettenis, P. T., Drescher, J., Meyer-Bahlburg, H. F., Pfäfflin, F., & Zucker, K. J. (2010). Opinions about the DSM gender identity disorder diagnosis: Results from an international survey administered to organizations concerned with the welfare of transgender people. *International Journal of Transgenderism, 12*, 1–14. doi: 10.1080/15532731003749087

Vartanian, L. R., & Porter, A. M. (2016). Weight stigma and eating behavior: A review of the literature. *Appetite, 102*, 3–14. doi: 10.1016/j.appet.2016.01.034

Velez, B. L., Campos, I. D., & Moradi, B. (2015). Relations of sexual objectification and racist discrimination with Latina women's body image and mental health. *The Counseling Psychologist, 43*, 906–935. doi: 10.1177/0011000015591287.

Velez, B. L., Moradi, B., & DeBlaere, C. (2015). Multiple oppressions and the mental health of sexual minority Latina/o individuals. *The Counseling Psychologist, 43*, 1–32. doi: 10.1177/0011000014542836.

Vera, E., & Speight, S. (2003). Multicultural competence, social justice, and counseling psychology: Expanding our roles. *The Counseling Psychologist, 31*, 253–272. doi: 10.1177/0011000003031003001

Wakefield, J. C. (2016). Diagnostic issues and controversies in DSM-5: Return of the false positives problem. *Annual Review of Clinical Psychology, 12*, 105–132. doi: 10.1146/annurev-clinpsy-032814-112800

Warner, J. (2006). *Perfect madness: Motherhood in the age of anxiety.* New York, NY: Penguin.

Watson, N. N., & Hunter, C. D. (2015). Anxiety and depression among African American women: The costs of strength and negative attitudes toward psychological help-seeking. *Cultural Diversity and Ethnic Minority Psychology, 21*, 604–612. doi: 10.1037/cdp0000015

Weitz, R. (1982). Feminist consciousness raising, self-concept, and depression. *Sex Roles, 8*, 231–241. doi: 10.1007/BF00287307

Wells, J. E., & Horwood, L. J. (2004). How accurate is recall of key symptoms of depression? A comparison of recall and longitudinal reports. *Psychological Medicine, 34*, 1001–1011. doi: 10.1017/S0033291703001843

Whitacre, C. C., Reingold, S. C., O'looney, P. A., Blankenhorn, E., Brinley, F., Collier, E., . . . & Lahita, R. (1999). A gender gap in autoimmunity: Task Force on Gender, Multiple Sclerosis and Autoimmunity. *Science, 283*, 1277–1278. doi: 10.1126/science.283.5406.1277

Wilhelm, K., & Parker, G. (1994). Sex differences in lifetime depression rates: Fact or artefact? *Psychological Medicine, 24*, 97–111. doi: 10.1017/S0033291700026878

Williams, D. R., & Williams-Morris, R. (2000). Racism and mental health: The African American experience. *Ethnicity and Health, 5*, 243–268. doi: 10.1080/135578500200009356

Willness, C. R., Steel, P., & Lee, K. (2007). A meta-analysis of the antecedents and consequences of workplace sexual harassment. *Personnel Psychology, 60*, 127–162. doi: 10.1111/j.1744-6570.2007.00067.x

Woods, K. C., Buchanan, N. T., & Settles, I. H. (2009). Sexual harassment across the color line: Experiences and outcomes of cross- versus intraracial sexual harassment among Black women. *Cultural Diversity and Ethnic Minority Psychology, 15*, 67–76. doi: 10.1037/a0013541.

Worell, J., & Remer, P. (1992). *Feminist perspective in therapy: An empowerment model or women.* Hoboken, NJ: Wiley.

World Health Organization. (2017). *Depression and other common mental disorders: Global health estimates.* Geneva, Switzerland: Author. Retrieved from http://apps.who.int/iris/bitstream/handle/10665/254610/WHO-MSD-MER-2017.2-eng.pdf;jsessionid=D071093E2C14771944BADBCE305415EE?sequence=1

World Health Organization. (2018). *International classification of diseases* (11th ed.). Geneva, Switzerland: Author.

Yan, H., Sanchez, R., & Ford, D. (2015, July 23). Sandra Bland's family "infuriated" at video of her arrest. *CNN.* Retrieved from http://www.cnn.com/2015/07/22/us/texas-sandra-bland-arrest/index.html

Yi, Y., Turney, K., & Wildeman, C. (2017). Mental health among jail and prison inmates. *American Journal of Men's Health, 11*, 900–909. doi: 10.1177/1557988316681339

Yohanna, D. (2013). Deinstitutionalization of people with mental illness: Causes and consequences. *Virtual Mentor, 15*, 886–891.

Zachar, P., & Kendler, K. (2014). A diagnostic and statistical manual of mental disorders history of premenstrual dysphoric disorder. *The Journal of Nervous and Mental Disease, 202*, 346–352. doi: 10.1097/NMD.0000000000000128

Zeiler, M., Waldherr, K., Philipp, J., Nitsch, M., Dür, W., Karwautz, A., & Wagner, G. (2016). Prevalence of eating disorder risk and associations with health-related quality of life: Results from a large school-based population screening. *European Eating Disorders Review, 24*, 9–18. doi: 10.1002/erv.2368

Chapter 14

About. (n.d.). *Lilla: International Women's Network.* Retrieved from https://lillanetwork.wordpress.com/about

Adamczyk, A. (2015, November 4). These are the companies with the best parental leave policies. *Time.* Retrieved from http://time.com/money/4098469/paid-parental-leave-google-amazon-apple-facebook/

Almassi, B. (2015). Feminist reclamations of normative masculinity: On democratic manhood, feminist masculinity, and allyship practices. *Feminist Philosophy Quarterly, 1*(2). Article 2. doi: 10.5206/fpq/2015.2.2

American Psychological Association. (2001). *Publication manual of the American Psychological Association* (5th ed.). Washington, DC: Author.

Asian Communities for Reproductive Justice. (2005). *A new vision for advancing our movement for reproductive health, reproductive rights and reproductive justice.* Retrieved from http://strongfamiliesmovement.org/assets/docs/ACRJ-A-New-Vision.pdf

Bartel, A., Rossin-Slater M., Ruhm, C., & Waldfogel, J. (2016, January). *Assessing Rhode Island's Temporary Caregiver Insurance Act: Insights from a survey of employers.* Retrieved from https://www.dol.gov/asp/evaluation/completed-studies/AssessingRhodeIslandTemporaryCaregiverInsuranceAct_InsightsFromSurveyOfEmployers.pdf

Benderly, B. L. (2015, July 30). The value—and risk—of activism. *Science.* Retrieved from http://www.sciencemag.org/careers/2015/07/value-and-risk-activism

Bianchi, S. M., Sayer, L. C., Milkie, M. A., & Robinson, J. P. (2012). Housework: Who did, does or will do it, and how much does it matter? *Social Forces, 91*, 55–63. doi: 10.1093/sf/sos120

Butler, J. (1989). *Gender trouble: Feminism and the subversion of identity.* Abingdon, United Kingdom: Routledge.

Capriccioso, R. (2006, January 17). Rose-colored vision. *Inside Higher Ed.* Retrieved from https://www.insidehighered.com/news/2006/01/17/rose-colored-vision

Cascio, E. U. (2017). Does universal preschool hit the target? Program access and preschool impacts (Discussion Paper #10596). *National Bureau of Economic Research.* Retrieved from https://www.econstor.eu/bitstream/10419/161219/1/dp10596.pdf

Case, K. A. (2012). Discovering the privilege of Whiteness: White women's reflections on anti-racist identity and ally behavior. *Journal of Social Issues, 68*, 78–96. doi: 10.1111/j.1540-4560.2011.01737.x

Ceci, S. J., & Williams, W. M. (2011). Understanding current causes of women's underrepresentation in science. *Proceedings of the National Academy of Sciences, 108*, 3157–3162. doi: 10.1073/pnas.1014871108

Chen, C. W., & Gorski, P. C. (2015, October 10). Burnout in social justice and human rights activists: Symptoms, causes and implications. *Journal of Human Rights Practice, 7*, 366–390. doi: 10.1093/jhuman/huv011

Clark, K. B., & Clark, M. P. (1947). Racial identification and preference in Negro children. In T. M. Newcomb & E. L. Hartley

(Eds.), *Readings in social psychology* (pp. 602–611). New York, NY: Henry Holt.

CMU's proportion of undergraduate women in computer science and engineering soars above national averages: Culture, personal approach makes the difference in attracting more women. (2016, September 12). Retrieved from https://www.cmu.edu/news/stories/archives/2016/september/undergrad-women-engineering-computer-science.html

Cohen, R. (2015, November 18). Who took care of Rosie the Riveter's kids? *The Atlantic.* Retrieved from https://www.theatlantic.com/business/archive/2015/11/daycare-world-war-rosie-riveter/415650/

Coker, H. C. (2014, May 9). What bell hooks really means when she calls Beyoncé a "terrorist." *Jezebel.* Retrieved from http://jezebel.com/what-bell-hooks-really-means-when-she-calls-beyonce-a-t-1573991834

Contrera, J. (2016, February 7). Gloria Steinem is apologizing for insulting female Bernie Sanders supporters. *The Washington Post.* Retrieved from https://www.washingtonpost.com/news/arts-and-entertainment/wp/2016/02/07/gloria-steinem-is-apologizing-for-insulting-female-bernie-sanders-supporters/

Cooper, C. M. (2007). Worrying about vaginas: Feminism and Eve Ensler's *The Vagina Monologues. Signs, 32,* 727–758. doi: 10.1086/499084

Cooper, D. (2017, April 26). Raising the minimum wage to $15 by 2024 would lift wages for 41 million American workers. *Economic Policy Institute.* Retrieved from https://www.epi.org/files/pdf/125047.pdf

Cooper, D., Mishel, L., & Zipperer, B. (2018, April 18). Bold increases in the minimum wage should be evaluated for the benefits of raising low-wage workers' total earnings. *Economic Policy Institute.* Retrieved from https://www.epi.org/files/pdf/143838.pdf

Crenshaw, K. (1989). Demarginalizing the intersection of race and sex: A Black feminist critique of antidiscrimination doctrine, feminist theory and antiracist politics. *The University of Chicago Legal Forum, 140,* 139–167.

Cronin, T. J., Levin, S., Branscombe, N. R., van Laar, C., & Tropp, L. R. (2012). Ethnic identification in response to perceived discrimination protects well-being and promotes activism: A longitudinal study of Latino college students. *Group Processes & Intergroup Relations, 15,* 393–407. doi: 10.1177/1368430211427171

Crowe, J. (2011). Men and feminism: Some challenges and a partial response. *Social Alternatives, 30,* 49–53.

Crowe, J. (2018, January 18). Meet the male (pro)-feminist: Professor Jonathan Crowe. *Broad Agenda Blog.* Retrieved from http://www.broadagenda.com.au/home/meet-the-male-feminist-professor-jonathan-crowe/

Cunningham, P. W. (2015, May 25). Michelle Obama: Run toward controversy. *Washington Examiner.* Retrieved from http://www.washingtonexaminer.com/michelle-obama-run-toward-controversy/article/2565021

Dardis, C. M., Murphy, M. J., Bill, A. C., & Gidycz, C. A. (2016). An investigation of the tenets of social norms theory as they relate to sexually aggressive attitudes and sexual assault perpetration: A comparison of men and their friends. *Psychology of Violence, 6,* 163–171. doi: 10.1037/a0039443

Dasgupta, N. (2011, December 2). Ingroup experts and peers as social vaccines who inoculate the self-concept: The stereotype inoculation model. *Psychological Inquiry, 4,* 231–246. doi: 10.1080/1047840X.2011.607313

Dasgupta, N., Scircle, M. M., & Hunsinger, M. (2015). Female peers in small work groups enhance women's motivation, verbal participation, and career aspirations in engineering. *Proceedings of the National Academy of Sciences, 112,* 4988–4993. doi: 10.1073/pnas.1422822112

Detloff, M. (1997). Mean spirits: The politics of contempt between feminist generations. *Hypatia, 12,* 76–99. doi: 10.1111/j.1527-2001.1997.tb00006.x

Dishman, L. (2015, February 10). A definitive strategy to eliminate the gender pay gap. *Fast Company.* Retrieved from https://www.fastcompany.com/3042067/strong-female-lead/a-definitive-strategy-to-eliminate-the-gender-pay-gap

Dodge, K. A., Bai, Y., Ladd, H. F., & Muschkin, C. G. (2017). Impact of North Carolina's early childhood programs and policies on educational outcomes in elementary school. *Child Development, 88,* 996–1014. doi: 10.1111/cdev.12645

Donahoe, K. (2012, January 20). The value in "The Vagina Monologues." *American Association of University Women.* Retrieved from http://www.aauw.org/2012/01/20/vagina-monologues/

Drury, B. J., & Kaiser, C. R. (2014). Allies against sexism: The role of men in confronting sexism. *Journal of Social Issues, 70,* 637–652. doi: 10.1111/josi.12083

Drury, J., Cocking, C., Beale, J., Hanson, C., & Rapley, F. (2005). The phenomenology of empowerment in collective action. *British Journal of Social Psychology, 44,* 309–328. doi: 10.1348/014466604X18523

Dunn, D. S., & Elliott, T. R. (2005). Revisiting a constructive classic: Wright's *Physical Disability: A Psychosocial Approach. Rehabilitation Psychology, 50,* 183–189. doi: 10.1037/0090-5550.50.2.183

The Editorial Board. (2015, May 5). Transgender students at women's colleges. *The New York Times.* Retrieved from https://www.nytimes.com/2015/05/05/opinion/transgender-students-at-womens-colleges.html

Edwards, K. E. (2007). Aspiring social justice ally identity development: A conceptual model. *NASPA Journal, 43*(4), 39–60. doi: 10.2202/1949-6605.1722

Eliezer, D., & Major, B. (2012). It's not your fault: The social costs of claiming discrimination on behalf of someone else. *Group Processes & Intergroup Relations, 15,* 487–502. doi: 10.1177/1368430211432894

Ensler, E. (2015, January 19). Eve Ensler: I never defined a woman as a person with a vagina. *Time.* Retrieved from: http://time.com/3672912/eve-ensler-vagina-monologues-mount-holyoke-college/

Etcoff, N., Orbach, S., Scott, J., & D'Agostino, H. (2004). *"The real truth about beauty: A global report": Findings of the global study on women, beauty and well-being.* Retrieved from http://www.clubofamsterdam.com/contentarticles/52%20Beauty/dove_white_paper_final.pdf

Fessler, L. (2017, November 16). Men, gather round: This NFL player turned feminist will teach you how to fight sexism. *Quartz.* Retrieved from https://qz.com/1130194/men-gather-round-this-nfl-player-turned-feminist-will-teach-you-how-to-fight-sexism/

Fields-White, M. (2011, March 25). The Root: How racism tainted women's suffrage. *NPR.* Retrieved from https://www.npr.org/2011/03/25/134849480/the-root-how-racism-tainted-womens-suffrage

Fillo, J., Simpson, J. A., Rholes, W. S., & Kohn, J. L. (2015). Dads doing diapers: Individual and relational outcomes associated with the division of childcare across the transition to parenthood. *Journal of Personality and Social Psychology, 108,* 298–316. doi: 10.1037/a0038572

Fingerhut A. W., & Peplau L. A. (2013). Same-sex romantic relationships. In C. Patterson & A. R. D'Augelli (Eds.), *Handbook of psychology and sexual orientation* (pp. 165–178). Oxford, United Kingdom: Oxford University Press.

Flood, M. (2011). Building men's commitment to ending sexual violence against women. *Feminism & Psychology, 21*, 262–267. doi: 10.1177/0959353510397646

Foster, M. D. (2014). The relationship between collective action and well-being and its moderators: Pervasiveness of discrimination and dimensions of action. *Sex Roles, 70*, 165–182. doi: 10.1007/s11199-014-0352-1

Foster, M. D. (2015). Tweeting about sexism: The well-being benefits of a social media collective action. *British Journal of Social Psychology, 54*, 629–647. doi: 10.1111/bjso.12101

Friedan, B. (1963). *The feminine mystique.* New York, NY: Norton.

Gay, R. (2014, May 12). Beyoncé's control of her own image belies the bell hooks "slave" critique. *The Guardian.* Retrieved from https://www.theguardian.com/commentisfree/2014/may/12/beyonce-bell-hooks-slave-terrrorist

Gervais, S. J., & Hillard, A. L. (2014). Confronting sexism as persuasion: Effects of a confrontation's recipient, source, message, and context. *Journal of Social Issues, 70*, 653–667. doi: 10.1111/josi.12084

Global Greengrants Fund. (2015). *Climate justice and women's rights: A guide to supporting grassroots women's action.* Retrieved from https://ffcontentgrantsviz.blob.core.windows.net/media/2538/climate-justice-and-womens-rights2.pdf

Gomez, I., & Jackson, A. (2018, February 18). Women's March organizers are planning a national student walkout to protest gun violence. *CNN.* Retrieved from https://www.cnn.com/2018/02/18/us/national-student-walkout-womens-march-trnd/index.html

Gorski, P. C. (2015). Relieving burnout and the "martyr syndrome" among social justice education activists: The implications and effects of mindfulness. *The Urban Review, 47*, 696–716. doi: 10.1007/s11256-015-0330-0

gotgreenAdmin. (2017, June 5). Our food security victory! *Got Green Seattle.* Retrieved from http://gotgreenseattle.org/media-release-seattle-becomes-first-city-to-devote-sugary-drink-tax-revenue-toward-closing-the-food-gap/

Hall, K. Q. (2005). Queerness, disability, and "The Vagina Monologues." *Hypatia, 20*, 99–119. doi: 10.1111/j.1527-2001.2005.tb00375.x

Hayes, J., & Hartmann, H. (2011). *Women and men living on the edge: Economic insecurity after the Great Recession.* Washington, DC: Institute for Women's Policy Research. Retrieved from https://iwpr.org/publications/women-and-men-living-on-the-edge-economic-insecurity-after-the-great-recession

Herbst, C. M. (2013, December). *Universal child care, maternal employment, and children's long-run outcomes: Evidence from the U.S. Lanham Act of 1940.* Retrieved from https://papers.ssrn.com/sol3/papers.cfm?abstract_id=2374627

Hernandez, D. (2017, April 22). Why some scientists are embracing activism. *The Wall Street Journal.* Retrieved from https://www.wsj.com/articles/why-some-scientists-are-embracing-activism-1492862410

hooks, b. (1984). *Feminist theory: From margin to center.* Brooklyn, NY: South End Press.

Hope, E. C., & Jagers, R. J. (2014). The role of sociopolitical attitudes and civic education in the civic engagement of black youth. *Journal of Research on Adolescence, 24*, 460–470. doi: 10.1111/jora.12117

Hope, E. C., Keels, M., & Durkee, M. I. (2016). Participation in Black Lives Matter and deferred action for childhood arrivals: Modern activism among Black and Latino college students. *Journal of Diversity in Higher Education, 9*, 203–215. doi: 10.1037/dhe0000032

Jayson, S. (2017, November 20). #MeToo isn't just a hashtag, it's destigmatizing—and "that's huge." *USA Today.* Retrieved from https://www.usatoday.com/story/news/nation/2017/11/20/metoo-isnt-just-hashtag-its-actually-destigmatizing-and-thats-huge/882716001/

Johns, M., Schmader, T., & Martens, A. (2005). Knowing is half the battle: Teaching stereotype threat as a means of improving women's math performance. *Psychological Science, 16*, 175–179. doi: 10.1111/j.0956-7976.2005.00799.x

Jones, J. (2017, December 21). 18 states will increase their minimum wages on January 1, benefiting 4.5 million workers. *Economic Policy Institute.* Retrieved from https://www.epi.org/publication/18-states-will-increase-their-minimum-wages-on-january-1-benefitting-4-5-million-workers/

Khan, A. (2015, May 27). Activist burnout is real—and you probably need to read these 4 ways to manage it. *Everyday Feminism.* Retrieved from http://everydayfeminism.com/2015/05/dealing-with-activist-burnout/

Kilmartin, C. (2017). Male allies to women. In J. Schwarz (Ed.), *Counseling women across the lifespan: Empowerment, advocacy, and intervention.* New York, NY: Springer.

Kilmartin, C., & Smiler, A. P. (2015). *The masculine self* (5th ed.). Cornwall-on-Hudson, NY: Sloan.

Kilmartin, C., Smith, T., Green, A., Heinzen, H., Kuchler, M., & Kolar, D. (2008). A real time social norms intervention to reduce male sexism. *Sex Roles, 59*, 264–273. doi: 10.1007/s11199-008-9446-y

Kimball, E. W., Moore, A., Vaccaro, A., Troiano, P. F., & Newman, B. M. (2016). College students with disabilities redefine activism: Self-advocacy, storytelling, and collective action. *Journal of Diversity in Higher Education, 9*, 245–260. doi: 10.1037/dhe0000031

Kitcheyan, A., & Brauer, T. (2018, February 23). Let women in prison have their periods in peace. *Huffington Post.* Retrieved from https://www.huffingtonpost.com/entry/opinion-kitcheyan-brauer-tampons-prison_us_5a8f0b97e4b00804dfe69b71

Klar, M., & Kasser, T. (2009). Some benefits of being an activist: Measuring activism and its role in psychological well-being. *Political Psychology, 30*, 755–777. doi: 10.1111/j.1467-9221.2009.00724.x

Kotcher, J. E., Myers, T. A., Vraga, E. A., Stenhouse, N., & Maibach, E. W. (2017). Does engagement in advocacy hurt the credibility of scientists? Results from a randomized national survey experiment. *Environmental Communication, 11*, 415–429. doi: 10.1080/17524032.2016.1275736

Kraus, L., Lauer, E., Coleman, R., & Houtenville, A. (2018, January). *2017 disability statistics annual report.* Durham, NH: Institute on Disability, University of New Hampshire. Retrieved from https://disabilitycompendium.org/sites/default/files/user-uploads/AnnualReport_2017_FINAL.pdf

Krupnick, E. (2012, July 3). Julia Bluhm protests airbrushing outside *Seventeen* HQ with other teen girls. *Huffington Post.* Retrieved from http://www.huffingtonpost.com/2012/05/02/julia-bluhm-protest-airbrushing-seventeen-magazine_n_1471876.html

LaMotte, S. (2017, October 19). For some, #MeToo sexual assault stories trigger trauma not empowerment. *CNN.* Retrieved from https://www.cnn.com/2017/10/19/health/me-too-sexual-assault-stories-trigger-trauma/index.html

Larimer, S. (2016, January 8). The "tampon tax," explained. *The Washington Post.* Retrieved from https://www.washingtonpost.com/news/wonk/wp/2016/01/08/the-tampon-tax-explained/?noredirect=on&utm_term=.1719a410d0dc

Lawrence, C. (2017, January 3). How to be a better ally in 2017. *Huffington Post.* Retrieved from http://www.huffingtonpost.com/christopher-lawrence/how-to-be-a-better-ally-in-2017_b_13932312.html

Ledbetter, L. (2016, January 28). Lilly Ledbetter: Time to end the wage gap. *USA Today*. Retrieved from http://www.usatoday.com/story/opinion/2016/01/28/lilly-ledbetter-wage-gap-women-obama-column/79319786/

Lerum, K. (2010, January 22). Reflections on reproductive justice on the anniversary of Roe v. Wade. *Sexuality & Society*. Retrieved from https://thesocietypages.org/sexuality/2010/01/22/reflections-on-reproductive-justice-on-the-anniversary-of-roe-v-wade/

Lerum, K., & Dworkin, S. L. (2009). "Bad girls rule": An interdisciplinary feminist commentary on the report of the APA Task Force on the Sexualization of Girls. *The Journal of Sex Research*, 46, 250–263. doi: 10.1080/00224490903079542

Lewis, M. (2018, February 5). 7 amazing environmental justice orgs we NEED to support in 2018. *Everyday Feminism*. Retrieved from https://everydayfeminism.com/2018/02/environmental-justice-orgs/

Liebert, R., Leve, M., & Hui, A. (2011). The politics and possibilities of activism in contemporary feminist psychologies. *Psychology of Women Quarterly*, 35, 697–704. doi: 10.1177/0361684311426691

Lorde, A. (1984). *Sister outside: Essays and speeches*. Berkeley, CA: Crossing Press.

Malacoff, J. (2017, March 10). 12 cool companies with amazing maternity leave policies. *Glassdoor*. Retrieved from https://www.glassdoor.com/blog/12-cool-companies-with-amazing-maternity-leave-policies/

Marcus, A., & Oransky, I. (2017, February 7). Opinion: Should scientists engage in activism? *The Scientist*. Retrieved from http://www.the-scientist.com/?articles.view/articleNo/48344/title/Opinion—Should-Scientists-Engage-in-Activism-/

Martens, A., Johns, M., Greenberg, J., & Schimel, J. (2006). Combating stereotype threat: The effect of self-affirmation on women's intellectual performance. *Journal of Experimental Social Psychology*, 42, 236–243. doi: 10.1016/j.jesp.2005.04.010

McQuaid, J. (2016, December). Without these whistleblowers, we may never have known the full extent of the Flint water crisis. *Smithsonian*. Retrieved from http://www.smithsonianmag.com/innovation/whistleblowers-marc-edwards-and-leeanne-walters-winner-smithsonians-social-progress-ingenuity-award-180961125/

Moms demand action. (n.d.). *Everytown for Gun Safety*. Retrieved from http://everytown.org/moms/

Morrison, A. (2016, July 26). Here's everything you need to know about the mothers of the movement. *Mic*. Retrieved from https://mic.com/articles/149802/here-s-everything-you-need-to-know-about-the-mothers-of-the-movement#.1S0UiXwGB

Moss-Racusin, C. A., Phelan, J. E., & Rudman, L. A. (2010). When men break the gender rules: Status incongruity and backlash against modest men. *Psychology of Men & Masculinity*, 11, 140–151. doi: 10.1037/a0018093

Mulhere, K. (2015, January 21). Inclusive dialogue. *Inside Higher Ed*. Retrieved from https://www.insidehighered.com/news/2015/01/21/womens-college-cancels-play-sayingit-excludes-transgender-experiences

NICHD Early Child Care Research Network (2002). Child-care structure → Process → Outcome: Direct and indirect effects of child-care quality on young children's development. *Psychological Science*, 13, 199–206. doi: 10.1111/1467-9280.00438

Novak, A. N., & Richmond, J. C. (2016). The phrase has been hijacked: Studying generational communication on feminism through social media. In A. Novak & I. J. El-Burki (Eds.), *Defining identity and the changing scope of culture in the digital age* (pp. 156–170). Hershey, PA: Information Science Reference.

Padawar R. (2014, November 19). When women become men at Wellesley. *The New York Times*. Retrieved from https://www.nytimes.com/2014/10/19/magazine/when-women-become-men-at-wellesley-college.html

Patrick, K. (2017, September). *National snapshot: Poverty among women and families 2016*. Washington, DC: National Women's Law Center. Retrieved from https://nwlc-ciw49tixgw5lbab.stackpathdns.com/wp-content/uploads/2017/09/Poverty-Snapshot-Factsheet-2017.pdf

Rappeport, A. (2016, February 7). Gloria Steinem and Madeleine Albright rebuke young women backing Bernie Sanders. *The New York Times*. Retrieved from http://www.nytimes.com/2016/02/08/us/politics/gloria-steinem-madeleine-albright-hillary-clinton-bernie-sanders.html

Rasinski, H. M., & Czopp, A. M. (2010). The effect of target status on witnesses' reactions to confrontations of bias. *Basic and Applied Social Psychology*, 32, 8–16. doi 10.1080/01973530903539754

Rentschler, C. A. (2014). Rape culture and the feminist politics of social media. *Girlhood Studies*, 7, 65–82. doi: 10.3167/ghs.2014.070106

Rinz, K., & Voorheis, J. (2018, March 27). *The distributional effects of minimum wages: Evidence from linked survey and administrative data* (CARRA working paper series 2018-02). Retrieved from https://www.census.gov/content/dam/Census/library/working-papers/2018/adrm/carra-wp-2018-02.pdf

Roberts, T.-A. (2016). Mind the thigh gap? Bringing feminist psychological science to the masses. In T.-A. Roberts, N. Curtin, L. E. Duncan, & L. M. Cortina (Eds.), *Feminist perspectives on building a better psychological science of gender* (pp. 275–293). Cham, Switzerland: Springer International.

Ross, L., & Solinger, R. (2017). *Reproductive justice: An introduction*. Berkeley, CA: University of California Press.

Rudman, L. A., Mescher, K., & Moss-Racusin, C. A. (2013). Reactions to gender egalitarian men: Perceived feminization due to stigma-by-association. *Group Processes & Intergroup Relations*, 16, 572–599. doi: 10.1177/1368430212461160

Sagner, E. (2018, March 25). More states move to end "tampon tax" that's seen as discriminating against women. *NPR*. Retrieved from https://www.npr.org/2018/03/25/564580736/more-states-move-to-end-tampon-tax-that-s-seen-as-discriminating-against-women

Sanchez, C., & Nadworny, E. (2017, May 24). Preschool: A state by state update. *NPR*. Retrieved from https://www.npr.org/sections/ed/2017/05/24/529558627/preschool-a-state-by-state-update

Schenwar, M. (2010, April 12). In prison, toilet paper is the new tampon. *Ms*. Retrieved from http://msmagazine.com/blog/2010/04/12/in-prison-toilet-paper-is-the-new-tampon/

scooby43215. (2010, December 10). *6 rules for allies* [Video file]. Retrieved from https://www.youtube.com/watch?v=SZx6rgs21G0

Silliman, J., Fried, M. G., Ross, L., & Gutierrez, E. R. (2004). *Undivided rights: Women of color organize for reproductive justice*. Boston, MA: South End Press.

Simko-Bednarski, E. (2017, August 29). Federal prisons required to make tampons, pads available. *CNN*. Retrieved from https://www.cnn.com/2017/08/29/health/federal-prisons-free-tampons-pads/index.html

Singh, A. A., & Burnes, T. R. (2010). Feminist therapy and street-level activism: Revisiting our roots and "acting up" in the next decade. *Women & Therapy*, 34, 129–142. doi: 10.1080/02703149.2011.532457

Solis, M. (2016, May 10). In defense of "Lemonade," Janet Mock took a stand for "Black femme feminists" everywhere. *Yahoo News*. Retrieved from https://www.yahoo.com/news/defense-lemonade-janet-mock-took-163800153.html

Spice, N. (2014, June 5). Press release: Women comprise 40 percent of computer science majors among Carnegie Mellon's incoming first-year class. Retrieved from http://www.cmu.edu/news/stories/archives/2014/june/june5_womenincomputerscience.html

Stiepock, L. (2016, March 9). Student Perspective: Calliope Wong. *UConn Today*. Retrieved from https://today.uconn.edu/2016/03/student-perspective-calliope-wong-16/#

Stout, J. G., Dasgupta, N., Hunsinger, M., & McManus, M. A. (2011). STEMing the tide: Using ingroup experts to inoculate women's self-concept in science, technology, engineering, and mathematics (STEM). *Journal of Personality and Social Psychology*, *100*, 255–270. doi: 10.1037/a0021385

Stripling, J. (2009, August 11). Rebuke for religion-driven policy. *Inside Higher Education*. Retrieved from https://www.insidehighered.com/news/2009/08/11/belmont

Szymanski, D. M. (2012). Racist events and individual coping styles as predictors of African American activism. *Journal of Black Psychology*, *38*, 342–367. doi: 10.1177/0095798411424744

Szymanski, D. M., & Lewis, J. A. (2015). Race-related stress and racial identity as predictors of African American activism. *Journal of Black Psychology*, *41*, 170–191. doi: 10.1177/0095798414520707

Tell Kroger we want #groceriesnotguns. (n.d.). *Moms Demand Action for Gun Sense in America*. Retrieved from https://momsdemandaction.org/groceriesnotguns/

Tsao, T. Y., Konty, K. J., Van Wye, G., Barbot, O., Hadler, J. L., Linos, N., & Bassett, M. T. (2016). Estimating potential reductions in premature mortality in New York City from raising the minimum wage to $15. *American Journal of Public Health*, *106*, 1036–1041.

Turcotte, M. (2018, March 22). Women governors are leading the charge to end violence after Parkland. *Ms. Magazine Blog*. Retrieved from http://msmagazine.com/blog/2018/03/02/women-governors-leading-charge-end-gun-violence-parkland/

United Nations General Assembly. (1948). *Universal declaration of human rights* (General Assembly Resolution 217 A). Retrieved from http://www.un.org/en/universal-declaration-human-rights/

Utt, J. (2013, November 8). So you call yourself an ally: 10 things all "allies" need to know. *Everyday Feminism*. Retrieved from http://everydayfeminism.com/2013/11/things-allies-need-to-know/

Vaccaro, A., & Mena, J. A. (2011). It's not burnout, it's more: Queer college activists of color and mental health. *Journal of Gay & Lesbian Mental Health*, *15*, 339–367. doi: 10.1080/19359705.2011.600656

Valenti, J. (2014, August). The case for free tampons. *The Guardian*. Retrieved from http://www.theguardian.com/commentisfree/2014/aug/11/free-tampons-cost-feminine-hygiene-products

Visser, N. (2017, July 1). Thousands fought against the Dakota Access Pipeline. Now it's set to flow oil. *Huffington Post*. Retrieved from https://www.huffingtonpost.com/entry/dakota-access-pipeline-protest-photos_us_592faa01e4b0540ffc847a58

Vogtman, J. (2017, May). *The Raise the Wage Act: Boosting women's paychecks and advancing equal pay* [Fact sheet]. Washington, DC: National Women's Law Center. Retrieved from https://nwlc.org/wp-content/uploads/2017/05/Raise-the-Wage-Act-Boosting-Womens-Pay-Checks.pdf

Wagner, K. C., Yates, D., & Walcott, Q. (2012). Engaging men and women as allies: A workplace curriculum module to challenge gender norms about domestic violence, male bullying and workplace violence and encourage ally behavior. *Work*, *42*(1), 107–113. doi: 10.3233/WOR-2012-1334

Walker, T. (2016, September 6). 3 things you need to know about Indigenous efforts against the Dakota Access Pipeline. *Everyday Feminism*. Retrieved from http://everydayfeminism.com/2016/09/dakota-access-pipeline/

Weiss-Wolf, J. (2015, January 28). Helping women and girls. Period. *The New York Times*. Retrieved from http://kristof.blogs.nytimes.com/2015/01/28/helping-women-and-girls-period/?_r=0

White, A. M., & Gaines, S. J. (2006). "You've got a friend": African American men's cross-sex feminist friendships and their influence on perceptions of masculinity and women. *Journal of Social and Personal Relationships*, *23*, 523–542. doi: 10.1177/0265407506065982

Wiley, S., Srinivasan, R., Finke, E., Firnhaber, J., & Shilinsky, A. (2013). Positive portrayals of feminist men increase men's solidarity with feminists and collective action intentions. *Psychology of Women Quarterly*, *37*, 61–71. doi: 10.1177/0361684312464575

Win, T. L. (2014, August 8). The Indonesian housewife who took on mining companies and won. *Thomson Reuters Foundation News*. Retrieved from http://news.trust.org/item/20140818092642-qdpr9/

Women's colleges with trans-inclusive policies. (n.d.). *Campus Pride*. Retrieved from https://www.campuspride.org/tpc/womens-colleges/

Wright, B. A. (1991). Labeling: The need for greater person-environment individuation. In C. R. Snyder & D. R. Forsyth (Eds.), *Handbook of social and clinical psychology* (pp. 469–487). New York, NY: Pergamon Press.

Yan, H. (2016). Dakota Access Pipeline: What's at stake? *CNN*. Retrieved from http://www.cnn.com/2016/09/07/us/dakota-access-pipeline-visual-guide/

Yavorsky, J. E., Kamp Dush, C. M., & Schoppe-Sullivan, S. J. (2015). The production of inequality: The gender division of labor across the transition to parenthood. *Journal of Marriage and Family*, *77*, 662–679. doi: 10.1111/jomf.12189

credits

Front Matter: Pages ii-iii: Cavan Images/Getty Images; p. vi: (Intro): ONOKY-Photononstop/Alamy Stock Photo; (1): Electra K. Vasileiadou/Getty Images; (2): Ryan McVay/Getty Images; (3): Tony Quinn/Icon Sportswire/Corbis via Getty Images; (8): Anna Larson/Offset/Shutterstock; (9): TerryJ/Getty Images; p. viii: (4): Benedict Evans/Redux; (5): Blend Images/Shutterstock; (6): Robert Daly/The Image Bank/Getty Images; (7):Lula Hyers/Refinery29 for Getty Images; (10):Natalie Fobes/Corbis/Getty Images; (11): Picstudio/Dreamstime.com; (12): James Brey/iStock/Getty Images Plus; (13): James Rich/Shutterstock; (14): John Lund/Sam Diephuis.

Introduction: Page 3: ONOKY - Photononstop/Alamy Stock Photo; p. 4: William Keller; p. Hongqi Zhang/Alamy Stock Photo

Chapter 1: Page 12: Electra K. Vasileiadou/Getty Images; p. 13: The Advertising Archives; p. 15: Rawpixel.com/Shutterstock; p. 20 (1851): Library of Congress; (1920): Library of Congress; (1969): Fred W. McDarrah/Getty Images; (1973): Buddy Mays/Alamy Stock Photo; (2006): David McNew/Getty Images); p. 26 (both): Steph Romeo / W. W. Norton & Company, Inc; p. 28: Christopher Bernard/Getty Images; p. 29: Daniel Leal-Olivas/ AFP/Getty Images; p. 39: Cecil Beaton/Condé Nast via Getty Images; p. 44: Hadot/Dreamstime; p. 51: Ariel Skelley/Getty Images.

Chapter 2: Page 58: Ryan McVay/Getty Images; p. 59: Noam Galai/WireImage/Getty Images; p. 66: Frazer Harrison/Getty Images; p. 72: Harry E. Walker/MCT via Getty Images; p. 80: © The Blade/Jeremy Wadsworth, July 1, 2001; p. 90: Amanda Edwards/FilmMagic/Getty Images; p. 95: AP Photo/Manuel Balce Ceneta; p. 97: Hiroko Masuike/The New York Times/Redux.

Chapter 3: Page 101: Tony Quinn/Icon Sportswire/Corbis via Getty Images; p. 102: Jay Colton/The LIFE Images Collection/Getty Images; p. 111: Tarampi et al. 2016 *A Tale of Two Types of Perspective Taking*, Psychological Science. Copyright © 2016, © SAGE Publications; p. 117: Joel, D., et al. (2015). *Sex beyond the genitalia: The human brain mosaic*. Proceedings of the Natural Academy of Sciences, 112(50), 15468–15473; p. 126: MBI/Alamy Stock Photo; p. 131: Luril Chornysh/Shutterstock; p. 133: jax10289/Shutterstock; p. 140 (left): T.T./Getty Images; (right): Hinterhaus Productions/Getty Images.

Chapter 4: Page 148: Benedict Evans/Redux; p. 149: Karwai Tang/WireImage/Getty Images; p. 156: Diana Mrazikova/VWPics via AP Images; p. 162: Michael Hughes; p. 165: Linze Rice/DNAinfo Chicago; p. 174: Bonnie Jo Mount/The Washington Post via Getty Images; p. 178: www.itspronouncedmetrosexual.com; p. 182: Courtesy Jamie and Sandy Shupe; Kristian Foden-Vencil/OPB News; p. 186: Jeffrey Greenberg/UIG via Getty Images.

Chapter 5: Page 191: Blend Images/Shutterstock; p. 192: Andrea Cipriani Mecchi; p. 194: Frank and Ernest used with the permission of the Thaves and the Cartoonist Group. All rights reserved; p. 198: PeopleImages / Getty Images; p. 209: Valery Sharifulin TASS via Getty Images; p. 210: Driendl Group/Getty Images; p. 211 (both): Photos by Janet McKnight 2012; https://creativecommons.org/licenses/by/2.0/; p. 216: Rod Morata/Getty Images; p. 219: Photo by Janet, 2013; https://creativecommons.org/licenses/by/2.0/; p. 221: Fotosearch; p. 228: Pictorial Press Ltd/Alamy Stock Photo

Chapter 6: Page 232: Robert Daly/The Image Bank/Getty Images; p. 233: Ruby Washington/The New York Times/Redux; p. 235: Cultura Motion/Shutterstock;

p. 242: Tim Robberts/Getty Images; p. 244: Antiquarian Images/Alamy Stock Photo; p. 245 (both): Nickolay Lamm of MyDeals.com/Shutterstock; p. 251: Jon Kopaloff/FilmMagic/Getty Images; p. 251: Albert L. Ortega/Getty Images; p. 252: Pixfly/Getty Images; p. 253: JB Lacroix/WireImage/Getty Images; p. 260: Copyright Malcolm Evans www.evanscartoons.com; p. 266: Chris Clinton/Getty Images.

Chapter 7: Page 274: Lula Hyers/Refinery29 for Getty Images; p. 275: AP Photo/Allen G. Breed; p. 278: Frank Micelotta/Getty Images; p. 282: Hemant Mehta/Getty Images; p. 292: Garo/Phanie/Science Source; p. 296: gawrav/Getty Images; p. 306: Image by Suzanna Scott, 2015; p. 307: The Advertising Archives; p. 309: FX Quadro / Shutterstock.

Chapter 8: Page 317: Anna Larson/Offset/Shutterstock; p. 318: Cooper Neill/Getty Images for The Potter's House; p. 323 (top): Portra/Getty Images; (bottom): James Woodson/Getty Images; p. 326: PeopleImages/Getty Images; p. 330: PHOVOIR/Alamy Stock Photo; p. 338: ahavelaar/Getty Images; p. 341: Revel Pix LLC/Shutterstock; p. 346: Dougal Waters/Getty Images; p. 351: Wise/Aldrich/cartoonstock; p. 353: Elizabethsalleebauer/Getty Images.

Chapter 9: Page 357: TerryJ/Getty Images; p. 358: Daniel Rosenthal/laif/Redux; p. 364 © Tanya Johnson; p. 370: Sebastien Micke/Paris Match/Contour by Getty Images; p. 373: Westend61/Getty Images; p. 376: Mansi Thapliyal/REUTERS/Newscom; p. 384: rubberball/Getty Images; p. 386: Westend61/Getty Images; p. 390: KidStock/Getty Images; p. 396: Annabel Clark/Redux.

Chapter 10: Page 403: Natalie Fobes/Corbis/Getty Images; p. 404: Scott Olson/Getty Images; p. 413: CHASSENET/BSIP/Getty Images; p. 418: Sergey Nivens/Shutterstock; p. 425: Jon Feingersh/agefotostock; p. 428: Monica Schipper/Getty Images for The New York Women's Foundation; p. 432: Zurijeta/Shutterstock; p. 441: Blend Images/Alamy Stock Photo.

Chapter 11: Page 447: Picstudio/Dreamstime; p. 448: Joel Saget/AFP/Getty Images; p. 451: Richard Levine/Alamy Stock Photo; p. 455: Naum Kazhdan/The New York Times/Redux; p. 460: BSIP/UIG via Getty Images; p. 463: Steve Wisbauer/Getty Images; p. 470: Tassii/Getty Images; p. 474: Shestock/Getty Images; p. 477: Thomas Barwick/Getty Images; p. 483: Kaluzny-Thatcher/Getty Images; p. 487: Paul Warner/Getty Images.

Chapter 12: Page 491: James Brey/iStock/Getty Images Plus; p. 492: AP Photo/The News & Observer, Chris Seward; p. 496: AP Photo/Anna Gronewold; p. 504: Lynsey Addario/Getty Images Reportage; p. 513: NPC Collection/Alamy Stock Photo; p. 522: Monkey Business Images/Shutterstock; p. 529: AP Photo/St. Louis Post-Dispatch, J.B. Forbes, File; p. 531: Attila Csaszar/Getty Images.

Chapter 13: Page 537: James Rich/Shutterstock; p. 538: Jonathan Gibby/Getty Images; p. 543: Album/Art Resource, NY; p. 547: H. S. Photos/Science Source; p. 551: stock-eye/Getty Images; p. 553: STOCK4B GmbH/Alamy Stock Photo; p. 562: Uriel Sinai/Getty Images; p. 564: John Birdsall/Alamy Stock Photo; p. 568: JGI/Jaime Grill/Getty Images; p. 572: Laura Brown; p. 575: Monica Almeida/The New York Times/Redux.

Chapter 14: Page 580: John Lund/Sam Diephuis/Getty Images; p. 581: AP Photo/Jessica Hill; p. 586: Sandy Long/Alamy Stock Photo; p. 599: Liza Donovan/Courtesy of The Amplifier Foundation; p. 606: AP Photo/Tony Dejak.

Text

Table 2.4: Glick, P. and Fiske, S. T., Appendix from "The Ambivalent Sexism Inventory: Differentiating Hostile and Benevolent Sexism," Journal of Personality and Social Psychology, 70, no. 3 (1996): 491-512. Copyright © Glick and Fiske. Reprinted with permission from the authors.

Figure 3.3A: Reprinted from Brain and Cognition 28(1), Peters, Laeng, Latham, et al., "A Redrawn Vandenberg and Kuse Mental Rotations Test–Different Versions and Factors That Affect Performance," 39-58, 1995, with permission from Elsevier.

Figure 3.3B: Wai, J., Lubinski, D., & Benbow, P., "Spatial Ability for STEM Domains: Aligning Over 50 Years of Cumulative Psychological Knowledge Solidifies Its Importance," Journal of Educational Psychology, 101, no. 4, 817-835, 2009. Copyright © 2009 American Psychological Association; reprinted with permission.

Figure 3.4: Moss-Racusin, C. A., et al., Figure 1 from "Science Faculty's Subtle Gender Biases Favor Male Students," Proceedings of the National Academy of Sciences, 109, no. 41 (2012): 16474-16479. Reprinted with permission from National Academy of Sciences.

Figure 10.3: Exhibit from "Women in the Workplace 2017," October 2017, McKinsey & Company, www.mckinsey.com. Copyright © 2018 McKinsey & Company. All rights reserved. Reprinted by permission.

Figure 12.1: Figure 1 from "Conceptualizing the 'Wantedness' of Women's Consensual and Nonconsensual Sexual Experiences: Implications for How Women Label Their Experiences with Rape," Zoe D. Peterson and Charlene L. Muehlenhard, The Journal of Sex Research 44(1), 2007, The Society for the Scientific Study of Sexuality. Reprinted by permission of Taylor & Francis Ltd, http://www.tandfonline.com.

Figure 12.2: Gender Neutral Wheel from www.speakoutloud.net, © Clare Murphy PhD 2016. Used by permission of Clare Murphy.

Figure 14.3: Figure 1 from "A New Vision for Advancing Our Movement for Reproductive Health, Reproductive Rights and Reproductive Justice," 2005, Asian Communities for Reproductive Justice. Reprinted by permission of Forward Together.

name index

Page numbers in *italics* refer to illustrations, tables, and figures.

Amanda Bynes—Serious mental issues, 542
Amato, P., 440
Amato, P. R., 323, 342
Ambady, N., 139
American Association for the Advancement of Science, 142
American Association of University Women, 27
American Civil Liberties Union, 430
American College of Obstetricians and Gynecologists, 371
American Psychiatric Association, 162, 302, 303, 304, 549, 550, 560, 563, 564, 565, 566
American Psychological Association, 43, 52, 366, 557, 571, 605
American Psychological Association Task Force on the Sexualization of Girls, 306, 312, 499
American Society for Aesthetic Plastic Surgery, 261, *262,* 457
American Society of Plastic Surgeons, 243, 457
Amico, C., 497
Amnesty International, 505, 511
Amnesty International reveals alarming impact, 505
Amodio, D., 200
Amodio, D. M., 222
Amor, D., 167
Amorosi, C., 141
Ananeh-Firempong, O., II., 467
Anapol, D. M., 344
Andersen, C., 262
Anderson, C. A., 532
Anderson, C. R., 226
Anderson, D., 203
Anderson, H. T., 251
Anderson, K. J., 32, 33, 34, 95
Anderson, K. L., 516
Anderson, L. A., 531
Anderson, L. W., 526
Anderson, M., 192
Anderson, S. M., 313
Anderson, T., 386
Anderson, T. L., 341
Andrei, A. G., 322
Andreoletti, C., 71, 450

Andres, E., 92
Andrew, R., 269
Andrews, B., 512
Andrews, W., 538
Andrews, W. L., 366
Ang, C. S., 210
Anguiano, C., 328
Angulo-Olaiz, F., 289
Aniakudo, P., 428
Anisman, H., 562
Anne, K., 205
Ansara, Y. G., 159
Ansari-Thomas, Z., 364
Anstey, K. J., 371
Anthony, K. P., 574
Antonucci, T. C., 323, 472
Anyon, J., 216
Anzaldúa, G., 35
Aosved, A. C., 509
Aphramor, L., 255
Appel, H., 561
Appelman, Y. E. A., 462
Apple, K. J., 298, 333
Applebaum, S., 383
Aranda, F., 185
Arbona, C., 335
Arcelus, J., 564
Archambault, J., 501
Archer, D., 251
Archer, J., 109, 325
Archer, L., 137
Archibald, T., 17
Arendell, T., 394, 395
Arias, D. M., 34
Arias, E., 465, *465*
Arias, I., 496
Ariel, B., 527
Armitage, J. R., 471
Armstrong, E. A., 280, 298, 302, 327
Armstrong, E. M., 280, 327
Armstrong, M. J., 474
Armstrong, P. I., 134
Arndt, J., 262
Aron, A., 320
Aron, L., 136
Aronoff, J., 516
Aronson, J., 138
Arora, S., 389
Arseneau, J. R., 155, 158
Artavia, D., 409

Arthur, A., 224
Artiles, A. J., 136
Artis, A. B., 6
Aruguete, M. S., 248
Aschbacher, P. R., 137
Ash, S., 523
Ashford, L. S., 363
Ashley, J., 523
Ashley, W., 74
Ashman, O., 452
Ashmore, R., 224
Asian Communities for Reproductive Justice, 596
Askari, S. F., 345, 351, 392
Associated Press, 359
Astbury, J., 380
Atkinson, M. P., 350
Attanasio, L., 385
Attra, S. L., 553, 574
Attwood, F., 279, 285
Atwood, N., 555
Au, A., 571
Au, J., 251
Aubeeluck, A., 267
Aubrey, J., 380
Aubrey, J. S., 207
Auchmuty, R., 337, 343
Audet, B., 551
Augustus-Horvath, C. L., 261
Auman, C., 452
Aune, R. K., 247
Auster, C. J., 211
Austin, E., 326
Austin, S. B., 214, 521
Avalos, L. C., 269
Avellar, S., 415
Avendano, M., 439
Averett, P., 296, 471
Avis, N., 552
Aviv, R., 442
Awad, G. H., 241
Axelrod, J., 215
Axelson, S. J., 345, 351, 392
Axt, J. R., 386
Ayers, B., 458–459
Ayres, M., 34
Azmitia, M., 63
Baams, L., 226
Babcock, J., 165
Babcock, L., 351, 413
Babins-Wagner, R., 570

Bachen, C. M., 328
Bachrach, L. L., 545
Backes, B. L., 510
Bacon, L., 255
Badahdah, A. M., 335
Badenes-Ribera, L., 520
Badger, K., 501
Baes, J., 509
Bahadur, N., 373
Bai, Y., 595
Bailey, J. M., 184
Bailey, S. D., 248
Bakan, D., 70
Baker, B., 228
Baker, K., 207, 243
Baker, L. V., 290
Baker, M., 338, 343
Bakker, F. C., 270
Bakr, S. W. A., 260
Bala, N., 516
Baldwin, A. S., 270
Baldwin, K., 372
Balemba, S., 503
Balen, A., 174
Ball, J., 567
Ballou, M. B., 550
Balsam, K. F., 520
Balsis, S., 468
Balthazart, J., 184
Baltisberger, J. A., 475
Bamberg, M., 280
Bandura, A., 197
Bank, World, 287
Bankole, A., 363
Banks, K. H., 37
Bannon, R. S., 500
Banyard, V., 523
Bar, S., 390
Bardone-Cone, A., 565
Bargad, A., 34
Bargerhuff, M. E., 141
Bar-Halpern, M., 524
Barker, M., 285, 344
Barklow, T. K., 511
Barlow, A., 343
Barnard, W. M., 392
Barnes, H. E., 513
Barnes, R. D., 238, 304
Barnett, I., 482
Barnett, M. A., 474
Barnett, M. D., 506

Barnett, O. W., 519
Barnett, S. M., 135, 142
Barney, A., 467
Baron, A., 435
Baron, L., 511
Baroncini, M., 184
Barr, R. G., 389
Barr, S. M., 157
Barrantes, R. J., 342
Barreto, M., 77
Barrios, M., 251
Barron, L., 412
Barry, E., 223
Bartel, A., 593
Bartels, J. S., 389
Barth, E., 414
Bartkiewicz, M. J., 326
Bartky, S. L., 235
Bartlett, A., 539
Barton, S. N., 510
Bartula, A., 526
Barwick, A., 248
Basile, K. C., 516
Basow, S., 92, 246
Basow, S. A., 239, 523
Bassett, M. E., 553, 574
Basson, R., 301, 302, 303, 304
Bastomski, S., 519
Baston, H., 385
Bates, L., 217
Battistella, P. A., 167
Battle, M., 66
Bauer, K., 380
Bauer, M., 551
Bauerband, L. A., 243
Baumeister, R. F., 132
Baumgarten, M., 554
Baumle, A., 415
Bay-Cheng, L. Y., 33, 37, 288, 313
Bazzini, D., 248
Bazzini, D. G., 248, 270
Beale, J., 599
Beall, A. E., 201
Beals, K. P., 342, 471
Bearak, J., 415
Beardsworth, S., 195
Bearinger, L. H., 286
Bearman, S. K., 238, 304
Beasley, B., 208
Beauboeuf-Lafontant, T., 241, 553, 574

Beauchamp, T., 151
Beaujouan, E., 361
Beaulaurier, R. L., 525
Beausang, C. C., 264, 266
Beazley, J. A., 532
Beck, J., 509
Becker, A. E., 250
Becker, C. B., 256
Becker, J. C., 77
Bédard, M., 469, 470
Bedera, N., 505
Bednar, M., 201
Beersma, B., 325
Befort, C., 249
Begany, J. J., 508
Begley, C., 387
Bègue, L., 208
Begun, S., 80, 160
Behnke, S., 570
Beilock, S. L., 136
Bekker, M. H., 560
Belcher, L., 283
Belgrave, F. Z., 72
Belkin, L., 437
Belknap, J., 518
Bell, A., 374
Bell, K. A., 509
Bell, L. M., 205
Bell, M., 177
Bell, R., 475
Belle, D., 558
Bellinger, W., 242
Belluck, P., 388
Belmonte, K., 313
Beltz, A. M., 157
Bem, S. L., 200
Benard, S., 437
Benderly, B. L., 601
Benenson, J. F., 321
Benjamin, E. J., 319
Benner, A., 162
Bennett, C., 266
Bennett, C. M., 302
Bennett, K. M., 530
Bennett, R., 205
Bennett, S., 93
Bennett, T., 452
Benson, K. E., 162
Bent, K. N., 471
Ben-Tovim, D. I., 243
Berdahl, J. L., 428, 430

Burn, I., 477
Burn, S., 223, 224, 225, 226
Burn, S. M., 34
Burnes, T. R., 573, 606
Burns, M., 89
Burns, R. A., 471
Burri, A., 184
Burrows, A., 380
Burrows, J., 393
Burstow, B., 540, 545
Burt, C. H., 502
Burwell, R. A., 250
Bushman, B. J., 306, 532
Buss, D. M., 114, 115, 334, 336
Bussey, K., 197
Buswell, B. N., 132
Butcher, C., 514
Butchko, M. S., 519
Butler, B. R., 217
Butler, G., 171
Butler, J., 30, 153, 289, 583
Butler, J. C., 311
Butler, O. E., 97
Butterfield, J., 345
Butterworth, P., 371
Button, P., 477
Buzdar, A. U., 462
Byers, E. S., 279, 285
Byles, J., 470
Byles, J. E., 481, 484
Bynum, B., 544
Byrd-Craven, J., 322
Cabrera, N., 440
Cacciatore, J., 377
Cadinu, M., 79, 430
Cady, C., 269
Cahill, A. G., 383
Cain, D., 514
Cala, C., 515
Calasanti, T., 455, 485, 486
Calasanti, T. M., 454, 455
Caldwell, J. E., 521
Calfas, J., 250
Calhoun, L. G., 515
Caliper Research and Development
    Department, 421
Callahan, G., 166, 169, 170, 174
Callands, T., 530
Callard, F., 560
Callender, A. A., 11
Callister, M., 454

Calogero, R., 257
Calogero, R. M., 235, 245,
    258, 259
Camarata, S., 123
Cameron, A., 527
Cameron, C. A., 504
Cameron, D., 94
Campbell, B., 77
Campbell, J. C., 521, 522
Campbell, J. D., 132
Campbell, K. E., 552
Campbell, R., 513, 514, 523, 550
Campbell, W. K., 70
Campbell-Jackson, L., 375
Campos, I. D., 556
Campos, P., 239
Canary, D. J., 325
Canas, R., 526
Canetto, S. S., 451
Cantisano, G. T., 555
Cantor, M. H., 470
Capaldi, D. M., 515
Caplan, P., 393
Caplan, P. J., 547, 548
Capman, J. F., 424
Capodilupo, C. M., 79, 241, 255
Capogna, K., 97
Cappello, O., 364
Capriccioso, R., 584
Caragata, L., 558
Cardell, M., 353
Cardi, V., 564
Cardoso, E., 136
Carels, R. A., 238, 252
Carey, K. B., 299, 504, 510
Carey, M. P., 298, 299, 504, 510
Carli, L., 75, 417, 421, 422
Carli, L. L., 69, 75
Carli, L .L., 82
Carlson, D. L., 440
Carlson, E. B., 567
Carlson, T. S., 557
Carlsson, M., 414
Carlston, D. L., 6
Carmichael, F., 480
Carmody, D., 214
Carmody, D. C., 336, 519
Carmon, I., 506
Carmona, R., 175
Carnes, M., 498
Carney, M. E., 532

Carnlöf, C., 462
Carothers, A., 123
Carothers, B. J., 111, 112,
    113, 120
Carpenter, B. D., 468
Carpenter, L. M., 296
Carr, A., 332
Carr, C., 224, 225
Carr, D., 238, 327, 468, 471
Carr, J., 429
Carr, M., 503
Carr, M. D., 26
Carr, R., 380
Carr, S., 277, 569
Carrier, N., 552
Carrillo, J. E., 467
Carrington, B., 216
Carroll, E. J., 16
Carroll, J., 218
Carroll, K., 162
Carroll, L., 162
Carroll, M. H., 502
Carson, C., 382
Carta, M. G., 541
Carter, A., 528
Carter, J. D., 96
Carter, N., 423
Carvalho, A. F., 520
Casad, B. J., 67, 339
Cascio, E. U., 595
Case, K. A., 65, 68, 591
Casey, E., 531
Cash, T. F., 249, 250, 270
Cashdan, E., 92
Cashmore, J., 498
Cass, K., 565
Cassell, J., 210
Casteel, C., 512
Castro, F. N., 335
Castro, Y., 432
Caswell, T. A., 88
Catanzarite, L., 429
Catherwood, D., 204
Cathey, C., 257
Catinari, S., 168
Cattarin, J., 249
Cauce, A. M., 347, 391
Caughey, A. B., 383
Causer, C., 212
Cauterucci, C., 94
Ceballo, R., 372, 374

Cech, E., 140
Ceci, S. J., 135, 142, 602
Cecil, K. A., 525
Cederlöf, M., 167
Cénat, J. M., 326
Center, B. A., 347
Center for American Progress, 558
Center for American Women and Politics, 17
Centers, R., 211, 410
Centers for Disease Control and Prevention, 287, 288, 375, 381, 385, 390, 462, 494, 515, 551
Cepress, S. L., 509
Ceruti, C., 161
Céspedes, Y. M., 553
Chakraborti, N., 492
Chalabaev, A., 452
Chamberlain, L. J., 430
Chamberlin, J., 429
Champagne, N. M., 267
Chan, C. S., 227
Chan, T. S., 295
Chan, Z. C. Y., 295
Chandler, M. A., 364
Chandley, R. B., 510
Chandra, A., 374
Chang, L., 254
Chang, Y. T., 266
Chapleau, K. M., 82
Chaplin, T., 213, 553, 554
Chaplin, T. M., 120, 130
Chapman, D. P., 559
Chapman, K. R., 457
Chapman, R., 89
Charania, G. R., 181
Charpentier, M., 452
Chatterjee, R., 427
Chatterji, P., 17, 439
Chavous, T. M., 62
Cheldelin, S. I., 413
Chen, C. W., 600
Chen, E. S., 68
Chen, E. Y., 238
Chen, H.-Y., 241
Chen, J., 424
Chen, Y., 501
Chenoweth, E., 59
Cherkas, L., 184
Cherlin, A., 473

Cherney, I. D., 125, 211
Chesler, P., 540, 541, 567
Chesley, N., 197
Cheung, J., 470
Chick, G., 241
Child Care Aware of America, 441, 442
Childlessness rises, 361
Child marriage database, 497
Children's Bureau, 495
Child Welfare Information Gateway, 377, 378
Chin, J. L., 424
Chiou, W., 332
Chira, S., 95
Chmielewski, J. F., 51
Chodorow, N., 196, 553
Choi, P. Y. L., 246
Choma, B. L., 259, 532
Choma, R., 83
Chrisler, J., 389
Chrisler, J. C., 17, 43, 238, 264, 267, 268, 327, 454, 457, 458, 467, 468, 486
Christakis, N. A., 319, 471
Christel, D. A., 234
Christie, A. M., 60, 61
Christogiorgos, S., 168
Christopher, F. S., 334
Christopoulos, P., 168
Chronicle of Higher Education, 16
Chua, C., 110
Chua, T. H. H., 254
Chun, H., 339
Chun, J. J., 63
Chung, D., 336
Chung, J. M., 387
Chung, M., 440
Chung, S., 482
Chung, Y. B., 409
Ciao, A. C., 256
Cicero, E. C., 200
Cichy, K. E., 68
Ciciolla, L., 398
Ciesla, J. A., 248
Cillessen, A. H., 327
Ciment, J., 89
Cini, M., 331
Cities for CEDAW, 533
Civettini, N., 350
Claes, M. E., 323

Claffey, S. T., 352
Clara, I., 560
Clark, E. K., 140
Clark, K. B., 39, 602
Clark, L., 269
Clark, M. D., 502
Clark, M. P., 39, 602
Clarke, C., 439
Clarke, V., 89, 246, 305
Clarke-Stewart, A., 341, 342
Clark-Murphy, M., 481
Clarkson, F. E., 548
Claudat, K., 304, 305
Clayton, J. A., 108
Clayton, R. B., 239
Clayton, S., 77
Clay-Warner, J., 502
Clemans, K., 227
Clinic, Mayo, 117
Cloitre, M., 567
Clough, A., 522
Cluse-Tolar, T., 524
CMU's proportion of undergraduate women, 603
CNN Political Unit, 529
Coates, R., 243
Coats, E. J., 95
Cochran, B. N., 557
Cochran, K., 270
Cocking, C., 599
Cockram, J., 522
Cockrill, K., 367
Cognard-Black, A., 419
Cohen, D., 336, 519, 548
Cohen, D. S., 462
Cohen, G. L., 62
Cohen, J., 91, 120
Cohen, J. A., 343
Cohen, K. M., 185
Cohen, L., 552, 555
Cohen, L. L., 36, 77, 78
Cohen, P., 409
Cohen, P. N., 351
Cohen, R., 239, 594
Cohen-Kettenis, P., 162
Cohen-Kettenis, P. T., 156, 160, 161
Cohn, A. M., 502
Cohn, D., 16
Coiro, M., 558
Coker, A. L., 531

Cunningham, M., 349
Cunningham, P. W., 606
Currah, P., 243, 438
Curran, M., 173
Currie, C., 227
Currie, D. H., 338
Currier, D. M., 298, 299
Currier, J., 571
Curtin, L., 248
Curtin, L. A., 248
Cury, F., 77
Cuskelly, M., 281
Custers, K., 501, 509, 565
Cuthbert, A., 530
Cutler, S., 559
Czaja, S. J., 467, 470, 486
Czopp, A. M., 36, 586
Dabby, F. C., 525
Dadlez, E. M., 366
D'Agostino, H., 237, 606
Dahl, B., 387
Dahlblom, K., 502
Dahlgren, L., 502
Dahlstedt, J., 523
Daigle, L. E., 502
Dalberth, B. T., 283
Dalmia, S., 60
Daly, K., 527
Damaske, S., 432
Danaceau, M. A., 473
Danaher, K., 138–139, 418
Dang, P., 473
D'Angelo, J. D., 332
Daniels, E. A., 499
Daniels, K., 293, 341, 342
Dank, M., 308, 500
Dannison, L. L., 283
Danoff, A., 161
Danziger, S., 558
Darden, J., 242
Dardenne, B., 83
Dardis, C. M., 504, 521, 586
Dare, J. S., 473
Darensbourg, A., 217
Dargis, M., 205
Darke, P. A., 252
Darling, C. A., 158, 303
Daroowalla, A., 539
d'Arripe-Longueville, F., 452
Dasgupta, N., 602, 603
Dasgupta, S. D., 518

Dastagir, A. E., 404
D'Augelli, A., 158, 225
D'Augelli, A. R., 222, 556
Daugherty, J., 293
Dauphinee, L. A., 363
Davdon, J. K., Sr., 303
Davenport, D., 378
Davenport, L. D., 63
David, H. P., 368
David, R., 385
Davidoff, K. C., 308
Davidson, A. J., 224, 226
Davidson, D., 260
Davidson, J. K., 297
Davidson, M. M., 519
Davidson, P. M., 470
Davidson, S., 157
Davies, K., 320
Davila, J., 183
Davis, A. Y., 502
Davis, G., 153, 172, 174, 176
Davis, J. P., 326
Davis, K. S., 180
Davis, M., 465
Davis, W. N., 259
Davison, K., 228
Davy, D., 479
Dawson, S., 520
Day, K. R., 327
dbarry1917, 192
Ddamulira, J. B., 365
Dean, M. L., 153
De Antoni, C., 494
Dear, M. J., 545
de Araújo Lopes, F., 335
Deary, I. J., 123
Deaux, K., 70, 75, 224, 238
de Beauvoir, S., 361
Debest, C., 361
DeBlaere, C., 165, 185, 556
de Bruin, A. P., 270
DeBruine, L. M., 244
De Choudhury, M., 363
Decker, M., 503
Declercq, E., 383, 384
De Crescenzo, T., 157
Deerinwater, J., 448
Deevey, S., 471
DeFina, R., 217
DeGue, S., 513
DeHaan, C., 561

DeHart, D. D., 539
de Heer, B., 511
Delaney, J., 267
Delemarre-van de Waal, H. A., 160
DeLeón, B., 227
Deleon, J., 187
Delgado, M. Y., 320
Delgado-Infante, M. L., 297
Deligeoroglou, E., 168
DeLoach, C., 219
DeLoach, C. P., 407
DeLone, M., 526
del Río, C., 409
Demakakos, P., 321
Demarest, J., 203
DeMaria, A. L., 246
de María Arana, M., 173
Demartini, B., 551
Demboske, K., 162
Demers, J. M., 502
Dempsey, K., 343
Denissen, J. J., 387
Denmark, F., 48
Denner, J., 227, 283
Dennerstein, L., 302, 472, 552
Dennis, B., 507
Deonandan, R., 376
DePaulo, B. M., 343
Depolo, M., 555
DePrince, A. P., 496
Der, G., 482
de Ridder, D. T., 270
Derlega, V., 556
Derlega, V. J., 520
De Roo, C., 370
DeRose, L. M., 227
DeRosier, M. E., 322
Desai, M., 289
Descartes, L., 209
Desilver, D., 439
Desmond-Harris, J., 60, 61
Desormeaux, L., 424
des Rivières, C., 394
Dessens, A. B., 170
De Sutter, P., 370
Detloff, M., 591
Deutsch, F. M., 349, 354
De Vaus, D., 343
de Villiers, T. J., 461
de Visser, R., 303
Devor, A. H., 157, 200

de Vries, A. L., 160
de Vries, B., 470
de Vries, G. J., 115, 116
DeVries, H. M., 473
Dew, J., 352, 391
Dewitt, J., 137
Dey, J. G., 414
D'Harlingue, B., 151
Dhillon, J., 366
Diamond, L. M., 157, 179, 181, 182, 183, 324, 325
Diamond, M., 167, 184
Dias, A., 498
Dias, K., 565
Diaz, R., 187
Diaz, R. M., 185
Diaz, T., 185
Di Cesare, D. M., 210
Dicicco, E. C., 129
Dick, A., 531
Dick, K., 511
Dickert-Conlin, S., 472
dickey, l. m., 161
Diekema, D. S., 293
Diekman, A., 204
Diekman, A. B., 140, 141
Dietz, P., 388
DiGiacomo, M., 470
DiIorio, C., 283, 284, 285
Dijkstra, M., 325
Dill, D., 553
Dill, K. E., 208
Dillaway, H., 395, 397
Dimen, M., 196
Dimond, J. P., 519
Dinella, L., 223, 225
DiNitto, D. M., 493
Dion, K. E., 238
Disch, W. B., 71, 450
Dishion, T. J., 285
Dishman, L., 593
Dishman, R., 228
Dispenza, F., 307
Dittmar, H., 250, 455
Dittus, P. J., 283
Dixon, K. J., 521
Dixon, T. L., 253, 454
Doan, C. M., 506
Dobash, R. E., 521
Dobash, R. P., 521
Dobinson, C., 183

Dockterman, E., 212
Dodd, D. K., 251
Dodd, M. D., 236
Dodge, K. A., 595
Dodge, L., 371
Doherty-Poirier, M., 243
Dohnt, H. K., 238
Dokoupil, T., 379
Doley, R., 475
Dolizki, M., 474
Doll, M., 187
Domínguez, J. M., 555
Domino, M. E., 482
Donaghue, N., 421
Donahoe, K., 584
Donnelly, D. A., 523
Donnelly, K., 397, 405
Donnerstein, E., 532
Donohoe, M., 528
Donovan, C., 336
Donovan, J., 25, 27
Donovan, R. A., 74, 503
Dørheim, S. K., 388
Dorr, L. L., 502
Dossou, M., 66
Dottolo, A. L., 15
Doucet, J., 558
Dougherty, C., 339, 415
Douglas, D. D., 150
Dove, N. L., 305
Dovidio, J. F., 142
Dowda, M., 228
Dowdall, G. W., 510
Downing, J. B., 347, 348, 377, 378
Downing, R. A., 77
Dowse, L., 252
Dozier, D. M., 253, 454
Draughon, J. E., 522
Dreary, I. J., 123
Dreger, A., 173
Drescher, J., 162, 549
Drewnowski, A., 239
Dries, K., 319
Droogsma, R. A., 260
Drop, S. L., 170
Dror, I., 452
Drum, C. E., 512
Drummond, J. D., 469
Drury, B. J., 585, 586
Drury, J., 599

Duberley, J., 480
Duberman, M., 164
Dubick, J., 269
DuBois, C., 412
Ducharme, J. K., 339
Dudley, E., 472
Duesterhaus, M., 26, 27
Duffy, A. L., 326
Dufu, T., 423
Dugan, L., 539
Dugar, T. A., 525
Duke, A., 515
Dumar, A., 371, 372
Dumas, T. M., 326
Dunbar, N., 227
Duncan, C., 477, 479
Duncan, S., 343
Duncombe, D., 380
Dunkel, T. M., 260
Dunlop, B. D., 525
Dunlosky, J., 11
Dunn, D. S., 604, 605
Dunn, E. W., 387
Dunn, J. L., 493
Dunn, S. C., 234
Dupont, I., 513, 523
Dupre, J., 104
Durante, F., 311
Durkee, M. I., 599
Durney, S. E., 504, 510
Dusenbery, M., 65
Dutt, A., 530
Dutton, D. G., 520
Duvdevany, I., 243
Dworkin, E. R., 512
Dworkin, S., 380
Dworkin, S. L., 150, 313, 588
Dyar, C., 183
Dyson, S., 283
Eads, A., 341
Eady, A., 183
Eagly, A., 67, 75, 417, 420, 421, 422
Eagly, A. E., 68
Eagly, A. H., 40, 47, 49, 51, 52, 53, 69, 75, 80, 97, 107, 108, 110, 117, 132, 133, 137, 144, 334, 422
Eamon, M. K., 407
Easter, M., 242
Eastin, M. S., 509

Eastwick, P. W., 332, 334
Eaton, A., 40
Eaton, A. A., 299, 331, 333, 342
Eaton, N., 202
Eaton, N. R., 157
Eberhard-Gran, M., 388
Eberstadt, M., 500
Ebert, I., 77
Ebneter, D. S., 256
Eccles, F. R., 471
Eccles, J. S., 118, 141
Eden, K. B., 522
The Editorial Board, 581
Edlund, C. J., 283
Edmundson, A., 471
Edwards, K. E., 589
Edwards, K. M., 249, 503, 521
EEOC, 430
Egan, R., 502
Egan, S. K., 157
Eggermont, S., 499
Egland, K. L., 324
Ehrensaft, D., 158, 196, 201
Ehresman, C., 169
Ehrhardt, K., 424
Eibach, R. P., 67
Eichstedt, J., 199, 221
Eidelman, A. I., 389
Eifler, D., 202
Eilperin, J., 424
Einstein, G. O., 6
Eisele, H., 37, 132
Eisenberg, M., 554
Eisenberg, M. E., 248, 249,
    286, 510
Eisenbud, L., 214
El Abd, S., 167
Elder, A. B., 161
Elder, M., 455
Elders, M. J., 175
Eliezer, D., 36, 586
Elizabeth, V., 338, 343
Ellemers, N., 77
Elliott, T. R., 604, 605
Ellis, A. B., 109
Ellis, B. J., 115
Ellis, R. R., 475
Ellis, W. E., 326
Ellison, N. B., 332
Ellison, P. T., 116
Ellithorpe, M. E., 206

Ellsworth, P. C., 335
Elsas, L. J., 150
Elsayegh, N., 33
Else-Quest, N. M., 30, 109, 120,
    124, 138
Emich, K. J., 420
Emile, M., 452
Emmers-Sommer, T. M., 507
Emmett, M. C., 324
Enchautegui, M. E., 442
Endendijk, J. J., 157, 197
Eneli, I. U., 269
Engberg, H., 174
Engeln, R., 261
Engeln-Maddox, R., 238, 248, 249
England, D., 209
England, P., 298, 350, 405, 406,
    410, 411, 414, 415
English, T., 387
Englund, M. M., 498
Enloe, C., 528
Enns, C. Z., 15, 23, 24, 25, 26,
    27, 571
Ensler, E., 584
Enzlin, P., 179, 280
Epp, C., 539
Epstein, B. J., 203
Epstein, D., 523, 526
Epstein, R., 218
Erchull, M., 396
Erchull, M. J., 24, 34, 91, 266,
    267, 298, 303, 311, 312,
    336, 345, 351, 392, 395,
    396, 508, 509
Erchull, M.J., 565
Erdley, C. A., 320
Erickson, J. J., 473
Erickson, R. J., 348, 349
Eriksen, K., 550
Ernala, S. K., 363
Ernsberger, P., 239
Ernst, C. C., 553
Eskenazi, B., 371
Espelage, D. L., 187
Espinosa, L., 135
Espinoza, G., 320
Esses, V. M., 85
Estes, C. M., 161
Esteve, A., 350
Estrellado, A. F., 526
Estupinian, E., 509

Etaugh, C. E., 91
Etcoff, N., 237, *237,* 606
Etcoff, N. L., 27
Ettekal, A. V., 320
Ettekal, I., 327
Eva Herzigova: Wonderbra, 312
Evancic, C., 503
Evans, L., 513
Evans, P. C., 255
Evers, C., 270
Ezzell, M. B., 285
Fabes, R., 214, 215
Fabian, L. J., 249
Fadda, B., 541
Fagnant, R., 547
Fagot, B., 199
Fahs, B., 277, 301, 303
Fair, B., 92
Fairbrother, N., 388, 389
Fairchild, E., 203
Fairchild, K., 33, 37, 75, 519
Fairley, C. K., 302
Fairweather-Schmidt, A. K., 371
Faisal, S., 479
Falcón, S. M., 69
Falcone, M., 161
Falconer, J. W., 241
Falduto, J., 110
Falk, H., 223
Falkner, N., 563
Fallbjörk, U., 464
Fallon, E. A., 270
Falmagne, R. J., 267
Faludi, S., 33, 395, 528
Fan, P.-L., 351
Farber, M., 405
Fardouly, J., 254
Farley, M., 524
Farr, S., 388
Farrel, B., 102
Farrel, P., 102
Farrell, G., 495
Farvid, P., 505
Fasoli, F., 311
Fassinger, R., 498
Fassinger, R. E., 155, 158
Faulkner, S. L., 284, 324
Faulkner, V. N., 136
Fausto-Sterling, A., 151, 153, 173,
    174, 220
Faver, C. A., 522

Gould, H., 367
Grabe, S., 30, 241, 250, 255, 261, 262, 268, 529, 530
Graber, J., 227
Grace, S., 388
Graff, K. A., 312
Graham, C. A., 177
Graham, E. T., 372
Graham, M., 361
Graham, M. J., 142
Graham, W. J., 385
Graling, K., 288
Grall, T. S., 361
Grammer, K., 96, 244
Granek, L., 15, 38, 40, 51, 53, 54, 105, 106, 107, 144
Grant, A., 17, 390, 424, 425
Grant, J. A., 239
Grant, J. M., 157, 163, 410, 430
Grant, J. R., 270
Grant, T. M., 553
Gratch, L. V., 553, 574
Grauerholz, L., 26, 203
Graves, N. A., 311
Gray, E., 267
Gray, J., 102
Graybill, C. M., 141
Grayshield, L., 562
Green, A., 419
Green, A. R., 467
Green, B. L., 539, 540
Green, J., 385, 389
Green, K., 396
Green, M., 210
Green, M. L., 423
Green, S., 376
Green, V., 204
Greenberg, B. S., 253
Greenberg, J., 262, 602
Greene, B., 185
Greene, K., 554
Greenfield, C., 212
Greenhaus, J., 432
Greenstein, T. N., 350, 352
Greenwood, D., 82
Greer, K. M., 85
Gregor, C., 157
Greil, A., 371, 372, 374
Greil, A. L., 372
Greulich, F., 225
Greve, W., 474

Greytak, E., 326
Greytak, E. A., 222, 226
Griffin, J., 556
Griffin, K. E., 556
Griffin, M., 454, 455, 456
Griffin-Fennell, F. D., 74
Grigorian, K. E., 259
Grilo, C., 565
Grimes, M., 509
Grimshaw, D., 415
Grippo, K. P., 454
Grogan-Kaylor, A., 495, 496
Grøntvedt, T. V., 334
Groscup, J., 523
Grose, R. G., 268, 530
Gross, A. M., 510
Gross, D., 437
Gross, K. N., 539
Gross, L., 250
Grossman, A., 158, 225
Grossman, A. H., 222
Grossman, A. L., 92
Grossman, S. F., 525, 526
Grote, N. K., 558
Groth, A. N., 506
Grotpeter, J. K., 50
Grotto, A. R., 67
Grov, C., 185
Grover, L., 287
Grover, N., 473
Groves, M., 396
Grower, P., 311
Grubaugh, A. L., 515
Grube, J. W., 296
Gruber, J. E., 430
Gruenewald, T. L., 320
Grumbach, M. M., 167
Grundy, E. M.., 474
Grunspan, D. Z., 141
Grynkiewicz, A. L., 180
Gu, Q., 546
Guardian, The, 376
Guerra, R. O., 555
Guerrero Vela, M., 383
Guerrier, M., 326
Guillen, L., 340
Guise, J. M., 383
Guiso, L., 124
Guittar, N. A., 26
Gundersen, K. K., 509
Gunderson, C., 269

Gunderson, E. A., 136
Guner, N., 339–340
Gunnarsson, L., 64
Gunnarsson, R., 266
Guo, J., 207
Gupta, P., 34
Gupta, S., 341, 350
Gupta, V. K., 427
Gurevitch, J., 470
Gurka, K. K., 512
Gurung, R. A., 320
Gurung, S., 507
Gutek, B., 555
Guthrie, J., 472
Gutierrez, E. R., 360, 596
Guttmacher Institute, 287, 363
Guzman, M. L., 515
Guzzo, K. B., 343
Gynther, M., 554
Ha, N. Q., 149, 150
Ha, T., 285
Haaf, R., 199
Haaken, J., 25
Haas, L., 440
Haas, T., 363
Hacker, M., 371
Haddock, G., 85
Haferkamp, C. J., 329
Hagan, L. K., 213
Hagan, R., 199
Hagen, J. D., 473
Hahm, H. C., 79
Haier, R. J., 116
Haines, H. L., 75
Haines, M. E., 259
Haire, A., 393
Hakim, C., 311
Halberstadt, A., 213
Halbreich, U., 568
Halcomb, E., 369
Hald, G. M., 308
Haldeman, D. C., 557
Hale, T. M., 506
Halim, M., 199, 200, 221, 222, 223, 225
Halim, M. L., 208
Halim, M. L. D., 222
Halket, M. M., 521
Hall, A., 166
Hall, C. C. I., 241, 242
Hall, D. S., 343

Hall, E. J., 33
Hall, E. V., 135
Hall, I., 216
Hall, J. A., 95, 96, 97
Hall, K. Q., 584
Hall, L. J., 421
Hall, M., 386
Hall, W., 384
Hall, W. S., 76
Haller, S., 118
Halliday, J. L., 167
Halliwell, E., 250, 455
Hall-McCorquodale, I., 393
Halpern, C. T., 284, 295
Halpern, D. F., 123, 125, *125*, 126
Halvorsen, J., 501
Hambaugh, J., 85, 87
Hamburg, P., 250
Hamby, S., 516
Hamby, S. L., 495
Hamilton, A., 164, 556
Hamilton, B. E., 382
Hamilton, E. R., 227
Hamilton, L. T., 280, 327
Hamilton, M., 203, 204, 345
Hamilton, M. C., 84, 85
Hamilton, Z., 521
Hamit, S., 556
Hamkins, S., 313
Hammack, P. L., 338
Hammer, L., 227
Hammond, W. P., 37
Hammrich, P. L., 136
Hampson, J. G., 175
Hampson, J. L., 175
Han, E., 238
Han, S., 427
Hancock, A. B., 95
Hand, C. J., 501, 509
Handelsman, J., 142
Handy, J., 479
Hanish, L., 214
Hankin, B., 552
Hanley, D., 134
Hannah, M. K., 482
Hannan, P., 554, 563
Hannema, S. E., 160
Hannon, L., 217
Hannum, J. W., 250
Hansen, T., 362
Hanson, C., 599

Hanson, S., 440
Haq, N., 473
Harcar, V., 251
Harcourt, D., 243
Harcourt, W., 30
Harden, J., 266
Hardit, S. K., 250
Hardy, C., 411
Hardy, M., 478, 479
Hardy, R., 249
Hare, K., 66
Hare-Mustin, R. T., 41, 47, 108
Hargreaves, D., 236
Haritaworn, J., 343
Harley, D. A., 486
Harley, W. F., 102
Harlow, B., 552
Harman, E. A., 511
Harnois, C. E., 63
Harold, C., 412
Harper, G. W., 187
Harrell, E., 502
Harrington, E. F., 74
Harris, A., 196
Harris, G., 284
Harris, J., 125
Harris, K. L., 509
Harris, L. J., 243
Harris, M., 540, 543
Harris, M. B., 455, 456
Harris, P. B., 486
Harris, S., 313
Harrison, K., 207, 250, 259
Harrison, T. W., 84
Harshbarger, J., 565
Hart, J., 372
Hartley, C., 382
Hartmann, H., 408, 409, 411, 592
Hartmann, T., 532
Hartup, W. W., 319
Hartwell, L. P., 336, 395
Harvey, L., 280
Harvey, S., 103
Harville, E. W., 382
Harway, M., 511, 530
Harwood, S. A., 78, 79
Haskins, J., 374
Haslam, A. S., 67
Haslam, N., 499
Haslam, S., 425
Haslam, S. A., 426

Hass, N., 426
Hassan, G., 379
Hassouneh, D., 516
Hastings, S. L., 480
Hasulube, J., 514
Hatch, S., 561
Hatem, M., 260
Hattjar, B., 475
Hattori, W. T., 335
Haugen, E., 388
Hausdorff, J. M., 452
Hause, K. S., 325
Hausenblas, H. A., 270
Hauser, C., 539
Havens, B., 267
Hawbaker, K. T., 429
Hawes, S., 284
Hawkey, L. C., 321
Hawkins, A. J., 392
Hawkins, J., 565
Hawkinson, K., 390
Hawley, C. E., 136
Hay, J., 86
Hay, P. J., 270
Hayden, H., 247
Hayden, H. A., 255
Haydon, A. A., 295
Hayes, A., 298
Hayes, E., 77
Hayes, J., 592
Hayes, P. A., 62, *62*
Hayes, R. D., 302
Hayes, R. M., 508, 509
Hayes, S., 336
Hayman, B., 369
Hays, D. G., 164, 571
Hays, S., 394
Hayter, M., 266
Hayward, C., 227
Head, K., 116
Head, M., 213, 351
Healy, C., 310
Healy, S., 384
Heard, K. V., 267
Heath, N. M., 502
Heaton, T. B., 341
Hebert, K. S., 525
Hébert, M., 326
Hebl, M., 381
Hebl, M. R., 143, 257, 455
Heck, N. C., 557

Heckler, A., 470
Hedemann, E., 382
Heflick, N. A., 263
Heflin, C., 558
Hefner, V., 328, 329
Hegarty, M., 110
Hegarty, P., 86, 159
Hegewisch, A., 408, 409, 411
Heilman, M., 424
Heilman, M. E., 82, 238, 239
Heim, D., 126
Heinberg, L. J., 254
Heine, S. J., 49
Heino, R. D., 332
Heinze, H. J., 116
Heisler, J. M., 284
Held, L., 389
Helgeson, V., 555
Helgeson, V. S., 555
Helminiak, D. A., 311
Helms, J. E., 34
Helson, R., 473
Hemmings, A., 216
Hencke, R., 452
Hendricks, M. L., 163
Henetz, P., 448
Henise, S. B., 155
Henkens, K., 482
Henley, N. M., *31,* 41, 96, 532
Henne, K., 150
Hennessy, M., 284, 285
Henning, S. L., 259, 554
Henretty, J., 571
Henrich, J., 49
Henry, P. E., 249
Henry, R. G., 468
Herbeck, D. M., 473
Herbenick, D., 246, 300, 301
Herbozo, S., 565
Herbst, C. M., 594
Herek, G. M., 185
Heresco-Levy, U., 168
Herlihy, A., 167
Herlihy, A. S., 167
Herman, J. L., 154, 163
Herman, R., 468
Herman, R. E., 468
Herman-Lewis, J., 561
Hernandez, D., 602
Herold, E. S., 280
Heron, M., 461, *461,* 465

Herr, J., 436
Herr, R. S., 31
Herrenkohl, T., 531
Herrera, A., 502
Herrmann, W. L., 460
Hersby, M. D., 426
Hertel, A. W., 270
Hertlein, K., 362
Herzberg, D., 546
Herzog, D. B., 250
Hess, A., 83
Hess, C., 135
Hess, R., 469
Hess, T. M., 452
Hesse-Biber, S. N., 241
Hessini, L., *367,* 368
Hester, M., 336
Hetsroni, A., 329
Heuer, C. A., 252
Hewitt, B., 343
Heydari, N., 110
Hickle, K. E., 523
Hickman, L. J., 516
Hickman, S., 494, 505
Hicks, S. R., 562
Higa, D., 187
Higate, P., 528
Higgins, A., 109
Higgins, J. A., 297
Hightower, H. C., 525
Hightower, J., 525
Hill, B., 380
Hill, C., 414
Hill, E. J., 473
Hill, J., 439–440
Hill, J. P., 225
Hill, M., 573
Hill, M. S., 259, 269, 454
Hill, P., 167, 377
Hill, S., 214
Hillard, A. L., 143, 586
Hilsenroth, M., 570
Hilton, J. M., 341
Himsel, A., 397
Hinchliff, S., 469
Hindmarsh, P. C., 170
Hines, C., 92
Hines, M., 170, 211
Hingley-Jones, H., 157
Hinkelman, L., 325
Hinman, J., 515

Hiripi, E., 16, 563
Hirsh-Pasek, K., 125
Hirvikoski, T., 173
Hite, S., 303
Hobart, M. A., 514
Hobfoll, S. E.., 498
Hochschild, A., 26, 347
Hockett, J. M., 508
Hocking, P., 470
Hodari, A., 140
Hoddinott, P., 391
Hode, M., 470
Hodge, J., 90
Hodge, J. P., 493
Hodges, M., 415
Hodges, M. J., 415
Hodgson, S., 246, 305
Hodgson, Z. G., 246
Hodkinson, K., 333
Hodson, R., 430
Hoeijmakers, J. H., 458
Hoek, H., 564
Hofferth, S., 440
Hoffman, B. R., 309
Hoffman, J. H., 510
Hoffman, K. M., 386
Hoffman, M., 372
Hoffner, C., 33
Hoffnung, M., 89
Hoge, W., 448
Hogue, C. J., 385
Hogue, C. R., 385
Hogue, M., 412
Hokada, E., 202
Holiday, J. M., 35
Holland, A. M., 236
Holland, E., 499
Holland, J., 297
Hollenshead, C., 143
Hollingsworth, L. S., 105
Hollins, S., 539
Holman, A., 299
Holmes, J. L., 510
Holmes, M. M., 173
Holmgren, K. M., 264
Holz, B. K., 550
Hom, C., 90
Honey, M., 66
hooks, b., 15, 32, 67, 419, 583
Hope, C., 246
Hope, E. C., 599

Kattari, S. K., 160, 521
Katz, J., 507
Katz, L. F., 475, 476
Katz, P., 220
Katz, S., 486
Katzman, D., 565
Katz-Schiavone, S., 531
Katz-Wise, S. L., 157, 158, 160,
    161, 179, 180, 391, 436
Kawa, S., 547
Kawamura, K., 243
Kawamura, S., 352
Kay, F. M., 423
Kaye, L. K., 126
Kaysen, D., 512
Kazama, S., 381
Kazyak, E., 328
Keating, J. P., 84
Keatley, J., 309
Keeling, J., 518
Keels, M., 599
Keerie, N., 93
Keery, H., 247
Keim, N., 239
Keith, V. M., 241
Keller, E. F., 42
Keller, R. M., 78
Kelley, S. J., 474
Kelly, A. M., 248
Kelly, D. H., 93
Kelly, G., 440
Kelly, J. B., 521
Kelly, K., 366
Kelly, M., 296
Kelly, S., 521
Kelly, Y., 381
Keltner, D., 96
Ken, I., 63
Kenagy, G. P., 163
Kendig, H. L., 471
Kendler, K., 568
Kendra, M. S., 187
Kennair, L. E. O., 334
Kennedy, C., 215, 384
Kennedy, J. E., 320
Kennedy, S., 342
Kenney, C. T., 337
Kenney, N. J., 372
Kenny, S., 141
Kent, L., 17
Kenward, B., 223

Kenyon, S. J., 246
Keo-Meier, C. L., 180
Keppel, B., 471
Kernic, M. A., 514
Kerns, J., 370
Kerr, A. E., 241
Kerr, M., 6
Kerr, S. P., 414
Kershaw, T., 530
Kerstetter, D., 482
Keski-Rahkonen, A., 564
Kessler, E., 253
Kessler, R., 551, 565
Kessler, R. C., 16, 563
Kessler, S. J., 151, 153, 155, 170,
    171, 172, 173, 174, 175
Kester, L. M., 295
Ketelaar, T., 115
Kettl, P., 301
Key, A., 202
Key, A. C., 157
Keys, C. B., 324
Khalid, M., 503
Khalifeh, H., 512
Khan, A., 532, 600
Khondkaryan, E., 530
Khoury, B., 572
Khuankaew, O., 37
Kiang, L., 137
Kidd, S. A., 371
Kiefer, A. K., 304
Kieffer, S. C., 251
Kiefner, A. E., 238
Kieren, D. K., 266
Kiesner, J., 79
Kiger, G., 397
Kilbane, T., 526
Kilbourne, J., 250
Killen, J., 227
Killen, M., 213
Killermann, S., 178
Killewald, A., 415
Kilmartin, C., 37, 585, 586, 587
Kilpatrick, D. G., 502
Kim, D. A., 319
Kim, D. Y., 545
Kim, E., 281
Kim, H., 482
Kim, H. K., 515
Kim, J. L., 276, 277, 278, 279,
    283, 284

Kim, M., 410, 440
Kim, S. K., 468
Kimball, E. W., 599
Kimes, D. D., 251
Kimes, L. A., 267
Kimmel, E., 15, 53
Kimmel, M., 239
Kimport, K., 367
King, A. E., 335
King, A. R., 506
King, C. T., 72
King, D. K., 493
King, E., 381
King, E. B., 143, 257, 455
King, J., 503
King, M., 268
King, M. B., 506
King, S., 432
Kingdon, C., 375
Kingery, J. N., 320
King's challenge, 499
Kinkartz, S., 527
Kinkler, L. A., 378
Kinsey, A. C., 177
Kira, K., 370
Kirby, D., 287
Kirchmeyer, C., 435
Kisely, S., 368
Kissling, E. A., 267
Kitcheyan, A., 593
Kite, L., 66
Kite, M. E., 450
Kitzinger, C., 92, 144, 181,
    182, 306
Klar, M., 599
Klausing, C. D., 508
Kleber, R., 498
Klein, C., 161
Klein, L. C., 320
Klein, M., 384
Kleinman, J. C., 385
Kleman, J., 222
Klesse, C., 343
Kliem, S., 575
Kline, A., 561
Kling, K. C., 132
Klinkenberg, D., 331
Klitzman, R., 372, 373
Klonoff, E. A., 550, 551, 555
Klump, K., 563
Klusáček, J., 365

Maldonado, M. M., 429
Malhotra, A., 376
Maliha, K., 455
Malik, N. M., 186
Mallett, K. A., 505
Mallett, R., 84
Mallett, R. K., 36, 84
Mălley, J., 143
Mallon, G. P., 157
Mallory, C., 429–430, 557
Malm, M. C., 377
Malmquist, A., 373
Malouf, D., 157
Malouff, J. M., 501
Malterud, K., 387
Manago, A., 311
Mandel, H., 440
Mandell, B., 422
Mangweth-Matzek, B., 238, 454
Manlove, J., 293
Manning, J. T., 244
Manning, W. D., 341, 343
Mannino, C. A., 349, 354
Mannix, J., 267, 393
Mannon, S. E., 397
Mansbach, C. S., 211
Mansfield, P. K., 265
Manvell, J., 433
Manzoli, L., 340, 471
Marcantonio, T. L., 505, 507
Marche, S., *353*
Marcotte, A., 35, 94
Marcus, A., 601
Marecek, J., 40, 47, 108, 353, 547, 570, 576
Margenthaler, J., 464
Mari, S., 311
Marini, M. M., 351
Marken, D. M., 475
Markham, C., 285
Markowitz, L. E., 295
Markowitz, S., 17, 439
Marks, G., 124
Marks, M., 412
Marksamer, J., 187
Markus, H. R., 433
Marlowe, F. W., 116
Marmot, M. G., 319
Marotta, J. A., 305
Marquardt, E., 332–333
Marquart, J. W., 514

Marques, S., 452
Marshall, K. C., 320
Marshall, V., 362
Marske, A. L., 250
Martens, A., 602
Martic, C., 214
Martin, C., 199, 200, 214, 215, 221, 223, 225
Martin, C. E., 177
Martin, C. L., 198, 200, 214, 221, 222, 268
Martin, J., 184
Martin, J. A., 382
Martin, K., 290
Martin, K. A., 282, 328
Martin, S. L., 512
Martin, S. R., 420
Martina, C. M., 321
Martinengo, G., 473
Martinez, E., 238, 304
Martinez, G. M., 295
Martinez, I. L., 525
Martinez, R., 389
Martinson, M., 485, 486
Martire, L. M., 470
Martz, D., 248
Martz, D. M., 248
Marván, M. L., 264
Marx, B. P., 503
Mascret, N., 77
Mason, B. J., 525
Mason, G. E., 506
Masser, B. M., 82
Massey, S. G., 298
Masson, J., 544
Mast, M. S., 96, 97
Masten, A. S., 498
Masters, J., 239
Mastro, D., 206
Mastro, D. E., 253, 454
Matamoros, M., 324
Matheson, G., 350
Matheson, K., 562
Mathews, B., 269
Mathews, J., 411
Mathews, M. E., 389
Mathias, Z., 243
Mathiason, M. A., 510
Matos, K., 440
Matovu, J. K., 365
Matsick, J. L., 343, 344

Matte, M., 520
Mattern, G., 523
Mattheis, A., 137
Matthes, J., 207
Matthews, A. K., 185, 304
Matthews, M. S., 382
Mattis, J. S., 69
Matusik, S. F., 143
Mauer, M., 538
Maurer, T. W., 504
Mausbach, B. T., 470
Maxwell, M., 72
May, N., 60
Mayans, D., 565
Mayans, L., 565
Mayer, R. N., 481
Mayes-Elma, R., 205
Mayeux, L., 327
Mayhew, A., 295
Maynard-Moody, S., 539
Mayo Clinic Staff, 371
Mayo-Wilson, E., 527
Mayton, D. M. II, 528, 529
Mazel, S., 375
Mazor, D., 243
Mazur, E., 332
Mazure, C. M., 465
Mazuy, M., 361
Mazzula, S. L., 78
McAlinden, A., 527
McAlvey, J., 404
McArthur, L. N., 502
McCabe, J., 203, 388
McCabe, M., 554, 555
McCabe, M. P., 243, 289
McCants, L. E., 183
McCarter-Spaulding, D., 28
McCarthy, M. M., 109
McCartney, J., 172
McCarty, Oseola, 448
McCauley, M., 498
McClean, E., 420
McClelland, S., 288
McClure, K. J., 252
McConnel, A. R., 255
McCormack, K., 360
McCormick, K. T., 129, 144
McCormick, N. B., 301
McCready, L. T., 210
McCreary, D. R., 250
McCulloch, C., 366

McCulloch, C. E., 367
McCullough, D., 343
McCurdy, C., 85
McDade, T. W., 116
McDaniel, B. T., 353
McDaniel, M. A., 6
McDonald, K., 269–270
McDonough, K., 308
McDougall, L. J., 246, 306
McFarland, W. P., 423
McFarlane, J., 268
McGaughey, D., 154
McGeeney, K., 554
McGeorge, C., 393
McGeorge, C. R., 557
McGill, A., 395
McGinley, M., 555
McGinn, K., 413
McGinn, M. M., 339
McGowan, M. L., 372
McGuffey, C. S., 215
McGuire, J. K., 226
McHale, S., 213, 351
McHale, S. M., 157
McHenry, J., 552
McHugh, M., 40, 299, 333
McHugh, M. C., 43, 85, 87,
    255, 469
McInroy, L. B., 210
McIntosh, P., 65, 68
McJunkin, C., 389
McKay, A., 285
McKee, M. D., 283
McKenna, W., 151, 155
McKenney, D., 475
McKibbin, W. F., 336
McKinlay, S., 552
McKinley, N. M., 247, 257,
    258, 261
McKinnon, M. C., 572
McKleroy, V. S., 151
McLachlan, R. I., 167
McLaren, H. J., 394
McLaren, L., 249
McLaren, S., 556
McLaughlin-Volpe, T., 224
McLean, J. S., 556
McLean, S. A., 239
McLemore, K. A., 159
McLoughlin, D. M., 545
McLoyd, V. C., 347, 350, 391, 392

McMahon, B. T., 68, 136
McMahon, J. M., 82
McMahon, S., 531
McManus, B., 298
McManus, M. A., 602
McMeeken, J., 380
McMullin, J., 362
McNair, R., 277
McNallie, J., 509
McNamara, J. R., 503
McPhail, B. A., 493
McPherson, B., 204
McPherson, M., 322, 323, 385
McPherson, M. C., 525
McPherson, M. E., 266
McQuaid, J., 602
McQueen, G., 86
McQuillan, J., 371, 372, 374
Mealey, A., 554, 555
Meana, M., 305
Mears, A., 234
Medina, J., 507
Medina, R., 334
Mednick, M. T., 41
Meekosha, H., 252
Mehaffey, S. J., 270
Mehl, M. R., 92
Meier, S. C., 165
Meinzer, M., 382
Melanson, C., 496
Mello, M. F., 563
Mello, N., 521
Mellor, D., 554, 555
Mellot, L. M., 343
Melnyk, S. E., 250
Meloni, M., 562
Melton, H. C., 518
Meltzer, M., 225
Meltzer-Brody, S., 388
Mena, J. A., 600
Ménard, A. D., 313
Mencarini, L., 347, 362
Mendelberg, T., 92
Mendenhall, R., 78, 79
Mendes, E., 554
Mendez-Luck, C. A., 574
Mendiondo, M. S., 525
Menzel, J. E., 249
Mercer, N. L., 155
Mercer, R., 388
Mercurio, A. E., 259

Merlan, A., 448
Mernissi, F., 260
Merrill, M. A., 123
Merritt, R. D., 84
Merriwether, A. M., 298
Merskin, D., 74
Merton, R. K., 136
Mertz, J. E., 124
Merz, E., 362
Meschede, T., 483
Mescher, K., 499, 587
Messineo, M., 253, 454
Messman, S. J., 325
Messman-Moore, T., 510
Messman-Moore, T. L., 504
Messner, C., 77
Messner, M. A., 150
Metcalfe, K. A., 464
Metcalfe, S., 167
Metts, S., 328
Metz, A., 140
Meyer, I. H., 163, 338, 521, 556
Meyer, S., 522
Meyer, W., III, 161
Meyer-Bahlberg, H. L., 283, 284
Meyer-Bahlburg, H. L., 283
Meyers, A., 284
Miah, J., 260
Micale, M., 544, 545
Michael, A., 554
Michael, R. S., 217
Michaud, P. C., 481
Mickelson, K. D., 352, 391
Mihecoby, A. L., 562
Mikula, G., 352
Milanaik, R., 390
Milburn, M. A., 508
Milhausen, R. R., 280, 286
Milkie, M. A., 26, 347, 351, 593
Miller, A., 136
Miller, C., 221, 412, 431
Miller, C. T., 33, 37
Miller, D. I., 125, *125*
Miller, D. T., 52, 103
Miller, E. N., 507
Miller, K. E., 501
Miller, L. C., 114, 334
Miller, L. M., 210
Miller, M., 532
Miller, R. B., 468
Miller, S. A., 248

Watson, N., 86
Watson, N. N., 74, 554
Watson, R. J., 298
Watt, B., 475
Waxman, B. F., 365
Way, K., 509
Weatherall, A., 472, 473
Weaver, D. A., 472
Weaver, J. R., 159
Weaver, M., 30
Webber, L., 324
Weber, T., 352
Wechsler, H., 510
Weden, M. M., 340
Weeks, J., 27
Weeks, L., 275
Weger, H., Jr., 324
Wegner, R., 510
Wehbi, S., 37
Wehrer, J., 389
Wei, J. Y., 452
Weibust, K. S., 33, 37
Weichsel, R., 26
Weiner, R., 545
Weinraub, M., 199
Weiss, B., 567
Weiss, D., 452
Weiss, K. G., 502, 506
Weiss, R., 430
Weisstein, N., 40
Weiss-Wolf, J., 593
Weist, M. D., 513
Weistra, S., 378
Weitz, I., 532
Weitz, R., 281, 570
Weitzer, R., 308, 310
Weitzman, L., 202
Weller, C., 440
Wells, B. E., 279
Wells, J. E., 551
Wells, V., 66
Welsh, S., 429, 519
Wenzel, A., 388
Werder, J., 228
Wertheim, E., 380
Wertheim, E. H., 239, 249
Weschler, T., 369
Weseley, A. J., 88
Wesp, L. M., 200
West, C., 75, 202
West, L. M., 74

Westen, D., 194
Westerhof, G. J., 321
Westervelt, A., 434
Westkott, M., 47
Wexler, B., 487
Weyman, N., 171
Whalley, L. J., 123
Wheeler, E., 547, 568
Whelan, T. A., 474
Whipple, B., 301
Whisman, M., 553
Whiston, S. C., 531
Whitacre, C. C., 551
Whitam, F. L., 184
Whitby, P. S., 289
White, A. M., 591
White, B. M., 513
White, C., 448
White, D. R., 248
White, K. B., 264
White, L., 372
White, L. R., 265, 267
White, M., 565
White, S., 249
Whitehead, S., 228
The White House, 528
White Hughto, J., 180
White-Johnson, R. L., 74
Whitemore-Schanzenbach, D., 269
Whitfield, D. L., 521
Whitley, B. E., 450
Whitley, D. M., 474
Whitman, J. S., 471
Whitmar, L., 206
Whittier, N., 34
Whitty, M. T., 332
whoneedsfeminism, 35
Whybrow, P. C., 551
Wickström, A., 171
Wiederman, M. W., 304, 305
Wiemers, E. E., 26
Wiener-Bronner, D., 406
Wierckx, K., 462
Wiersma-Mosley, J. D., 510
Wiesemann, C., 150
Wilchins, J., 430
Wilchins, R. A., 157
Wilcox, S., 471
Wilcox, W. B., 352, 391
Wilcox-Constantine, J., 268
Wild, K., 486

Wildeman, C., 540
Wildman, S. M., 68
Wiles, J. L., 486
Wiley, S., 587
Wilfley, D. E., 255
Wilhelm, K., 551
Wilke, J., 368
Wilkes, L., 369
Wilkinson, A. V., 71
Wilkinson, R. G., 319
Wilkinson, S., 182, 246
Wilksch, S. M., 256
Will, J. L., 526
Willer, L., 220
Williams, A. M., 138
Williams, B. R., 471
Williams, C. C., 109
Williams, C. L., 419, 420
Williams, D., 558
Williams, D. R., 555, 556
Williams, J., 424, 433, 436, 437, 438, 442
Williams, J. C., 135, 137, 138, 139, 143, 437
Williams, J. F., 381
Williams, J. M., 227
Williams, K., 468
Williams, K. N., 468
Williams, K. R., 526
Williams, M. E., 14
Williams, N., 423
Williams, R. L., 528
Williams, T. M., 268
Williams, W. M., 135, 142, 602
Williams-Morris, R., 555, 556
Williamson, C., 524
Williamson, I., 380
Williamson, S., 270
Willie, T. C., 530
Willingham, M., 386
Willis, L. E., 270
Willison, K., 470
Willness, C. R., 555
Willoughby, B. J., 302
Wilson, A. L., 17
Wilson, B. J., 328, 329
Wilson, C. M., 340
Wilson, D., 227
Wilson, E. C., 158
Wilson, E. K., 283, 284
Wilson, H., 381

subject index

Note: Material in illustrations, figures, or tables is indicated by *italic* page numbers. Footnotes are indicated by n after the page number.

eharmony, 333
Eisenhauer, Karen, 207
elder abuse, 524–526
elder-care, 435
elderspeak, 468
Electra complex, 195
electroconvulsive therapy (ECT), 545
Ellen (TV show), 233
EMCP (engineering, math, computer science, and physics), 134–143
    see also STEM (science, technology, engineering, and mathematics) fields
emotional abuse, 496
emotional intelligence, 422
emotional social support, 321
emotions, gender similarities and differences, 129–130
emotion work, 348–349
employment outside the home, 15–16
empowerment
    advertising and, 14, 233, 312
    consumer-based approach to, 17–18
    defined, 17, 18
empowertising, 14, 233
empty nests, 472–474
empty-nest syndrome, 473
endometriosis, 458
endometrium, 265
Engeln, Renee, 261
Ensler, Eve, 584
environmental activism, 598
epidural anesthesia, 382, *384*
episiotomy, 382, *383,* 384
Equal Pay Act, 410
Equal Rights Amendment (ERA)
    benevolent sexist opposition to, 82–83
    Congressional passage, 21
    liberal feminism and, 23–24
    originally introduced in Congress, 20
    ratification status, 21, 24
estrogen
    bone health and, 465
    decrease after giving birth, 388
    in hormone replacement therapy, 460–461, 462

menopause and, 458, 459, 465
    risks, 161, 460–461, 462
    role in menstrual cycle, 265
    transwomen supplementation, 462
    for Turner's syndrome, 168
Etcoff, Nancy, 606
ethic of care, 133
ethic of justice, 133
ethnocentrism, 29
eugenics movement, 293
#everydaysexism, 78–79
Everyday Sexism Project, 78–79
evolutionary explanations for gender differences, 114–115
exercise, motivations for, 269–270
expectancy role value theory, 118, 135
experimental group, 46
experiments, 46
explicit bias, 76
extraversion, 128

Facebook
    activity of girls and boys, 210
    body image concerns and, 239, 254
    "Like a Girl" campaign and, 14
    on men interrupting women, 95
    non-binary pronouns options, 85
    paid leave policy, *594*
    Women's March and, 59–60
face-ism, 251, *251*
Fahs, Breanne, 246
Fair & Lovely, 234
faked orgasms, 303
fallopian tubes, 265
family caregiving, 469–470
Family Life (magazine), 253
Family Medical Leave Act (FMLA), 439
fathers' role in child care, 440, *441*
fatness and overweight
    discrimination against overweight individuals, 238, 239
    health and, 255
    poverty and, 238–239
    stigmatization in the media, 251–252

fat shaming, 238, 327
fat talk, 248–249, 257
Fauldi, Susan, 33
Fazlalizadeh, Tatyana, 97
fear of missing out (FOMO), 561
Featherstone, Liz, 422
Federer, Roger, 97
female genital mutilation (FGM), 497, 498
female heads of governments, 17
female orgasmic disorder, 303
feminine aesthetics, revival of, 22
feminine behavior
    communal or feminine traits, 70–71, 421
    cultural feminism and, 27, 28, 576
    depression and doing femininity too well, 554–555
    disapproval of deviation from traditional norms, 92, 539, 540–541
    see also gender socialization
Feminine Forever (Wilson), 460
Feminine Mystique, The (Friedan), 40, 583
feminism
    cultural feminism, 27, 28, *31,* 108, 133, 395, 576
    defined, 15
    feminist mothering, 395–397, *396*
    feminist perspectives, 23–32
    first wave, 19, 22–23, 38
    fourth wave, 22
    intergenerational conflict within feminism, 587–589
    issues of inclusion and exclusion, 581–585
    lesbian feminism, 25
    liberal feminism, 23–24, *31,* 396
    misconceptions and negative stereotypes about, 22, 32–33, 35
    post-colonial/transnational feminism, 30–31, *31,* 529
    queer feminism, 29–30, *31*
    radical feminism, 25, *31*
    second wave, 19, 22, 196, 395, 546, 583, 588
    socialist feminism, 25–27, *31*

S

stereotypes *(continued)*
    inferiority of women, 104–105
    internalized stereotypes, 112, 118, 134, 139, 140, 182–183, 452
    Jezebel stereotype of Black women, 74, 78, 307
    microaggressions and, 78
    of Native American women, 74
    of older women, 449–453, 484, 486, 487, *487*
    of older workers, 479
    personality trait similarities and differences, 128–129
    power and, 71
    race/ethnicity and gender association with, 72–75, *73*
    racialized sexist stereotypes, 71–75, 138
    reinforcement of social stratification by, 74
    resistance to change, 75
    self-esteem in women, 132
    self-stereotyping, 75
    in STEM, 137–139
    strong Black woman (SBW) stereotype, 72, 74, 553–554
    in television shows, 206–207
stereotype threat, 137–139, 452, 602
sterilization, 293, *294*
Stern, Howard, 94
sticky floor, 418
stigma awareness, 163
stillbirth, 375, 377
Stonewall Inn, New York, 21, 164
Stop Telling Women to Smile (Fazlalizadeh), 97
Storming of Council, 41
stranger harassment, 519
strategic essentialism, 108
stratified reproduction, 360, 374, 379, 386, 390
Streep, Meryl, 454
street activism, 606
street harassment, 519
"stride of pride," 313
strong Black woman (SBW) stereotype, 72, 74, 553–554
Strong Families movement, 596–597

structural inequalities, 24
structural violence, 494, 498
subordination, *65*, 70
successful aging, 485–487
Summers, Larry, 120
Super Bowl, 13
superheroes and gender stereotypes, 204, 207, 208
surrogacy, 374, 376, *376*
surveys as research method, 44
Susan G. Komen Foundation, 463
swinging, 343
sworn virgins (Balkans), 179
symmetry and beauty norms, 244

gender identity in transgender
children, 156, 158, 201,
202, 222
gender rigidity in transgender
children, 222
human trafficking, 309, 310
intimate partner violence
and, 521
legal issues, 163
LGBTQ community and,
163–164, 165
medical concerns, 159–161
menstruation and, 264
misgendering of, 159
murder and hate crimes against,
16, 243, 494
number identifying as in United
States, 154
passing or recognition, 159–160
perceived as mentally ill, 430
pronouns and new names,
158–159
resiliency of, 164–165
schools and transgender students,
156, 158, 217, 222, 226
sexual displeasure link to body
shame, 304
sexualization in media, 307–308
sexual orientation identity labels,
179–180
sex work and transgender
women, 308–309
stereotypes and transgender
women, 71
stigma awareness, 163, 180
tomboyism in transgender
children, 225
violence against, 160, 243, 326
see also gender transitioning
Transgeneration (documentary), 164
transitioning. *see* gender transitioning
transnational feminists, 30–31,
31, 529
Transparent (web TV series), 165
transracial adoption, 379
Trans Resilience Project, 603–604
transsexual, 160
see also transgender
tripartite model of social influence,
247, 249
Trump, Donald, 286, 421, 598

Truth, Sojurner, 20, 582–583
Tubman, Harriet, 29
Turner's syndrome (TS), 167–168,
264
Twilight book and movie series,
205, 336, 519
Twitter
#blacklivesmatter, 29, *29*
body image concerns and, 239
#everydaysexism, 78–79
girls and women on, 93, 210,
599
Girls Who Code classes, 135
#heforshe campaign, 16
"Like a Girl" campaign and, 14
Michael Hughes and
#wejustneedtopee, *162*
#naturalisprofessional
campaign, 66
#notallmen and #yesallwomen, 83
#sayhername movement, *538*
tweeting about social issues, 599
#yesallwomen, 83
#YouOkSis, 519

ultrasound, 221
Unchained At Last, *496*
Unger, Rhoda, 48, 105–106
Unilever, 234
United States v. Windsor, 21
Universal Declaration of Human
Rights, 596
unmarked language, 86–87, *87*, 88
UPS, 438
uptalk (upspeak), 94
urgency script, 296
U.S. Congress, women in, 17
U.S. Department of Justice, 430
U.S. Equal Employment
Opportunity Commission
(EEOC), 430
using this book, 3–11
Empowering or Oppressing?
boxes, 8
Spotlight On boxes, 5
SQ3R method, 6–10
Try It for Yourself boxes, 5
unique aspects, 4–5
Your Turn boxes, 5

U.S. National Institutes of Health
(NIH), 108
Ussher, Jane, 549
U.S. Supreme Court justices,
female, 95, *95*

vaginal rejuvenation or vaginoplasty,
305
Vagina Monologues, The (Ensler), 584
Valenti, Jessica, 593
Valium ("mother's little helper"),
546
van Anders, Sari, 178
Vanity Fair (magazine), 519
variability (statistics), 120
variables, defined, 44
verbal ability, gender similarities
and differences, 127
verbal abuse, 496
Vernon, Polly, 358
vertical occupational gender segregation, 408, 416, *416*
vestibular bulbs, *291*, 292
Viagra, 275
victim blaming, 501, 506, 509
Victims of Trafficking and Violence
Protection Act, 523
video games and gender
socialization, 208
View, The (TV show), 233
violence against women. *see*
gender-based violence;
intimate partner
violence; rape
Violence Against Women Act,
21, 516
violent resistance, 518, 520
virginity, losing, 295–297
vocal fry, 94
Vogel, Lisa, 25
voluntary childlessness, 360–363
vulvas, 290, *291*, 306, *306*

Walker, Karen, 323–324
"walk of shame," 313
Waller, Willard, 345
Walmart, 422, 437